*Specify if: With Perceptual Disturbances*
Sedative, Hypnotic, or Anxiolytic Intoxication Delirium
Sedative, Hypnotic, or Anxiolytic Withdrawal Delirium
Polysubstance-Related Disorder
Polysubstance Dependence

**Schizophrenia and Other Psychotic Disorders**
Schizophrenia
  Paranoid Type
  Disorganized Type
  Catatonic Type
  Undifferentiated Type
  Residual Type
Schizophreniform Disorder
Schizoaffective Disorder
Brief Psychotic Disorder
Shared Psychotic Disorder
Psychotic Disorder Due to . . . *[indicate the General Medical Condition]*
Substance-Induced Psychotic Disorder
Psychotic Disorder NOS

**Mood Disorders**

**Depressive Disorders**
Major Depressive Disorder
Dysthymic Disorder
Depressive Disorder NOS

**Bipolar Disorders**
Bipolar I Disorder
Bipolar II Disorder
Cyclothymic Disorder
Bipolar Disorder NOS
Mood Disorder Due to . . . *[indicate the General Medical Condition]*
Substance-Induced Mood Disorder
Mood Disorder NOS

**Anxiety Disorders**
Panic Disorder without Agoraphobia
Panic Disorder with Agoraphobia
Agoraphobia without History of Panic Disorder
Specific Phobia
  *Specify type: Animal Type/Natural Environment Type/Blood-Injection-Injury Type/Situational Type/Other Type*
Social Phobia
Obsessive–Compulsive Disorder
Posttraumatic Stress Disorder
Acute Stress Disorder
Generalized Anxiety Disorder
Anxiety Disorder Due to . . . *[indicate the General Medical Condition]*
Substance-Induced Anxiety Disorder *[refer to Substance-Related Disorders for Substance-Specific Codes]*
Anxiety Disorder NOS

**Somatoform Disorders**
Somatization Disorder
Undifferentiated Somatoform Disorder
Conversion Disorder
Pain Disorder
Hypochondriasis
Body Dysmorphic Disorder
Somatoform Disorder NOS

**Factitious Disorders**
Factitious Disorder
Factitious Disorder NOS

**Dissociative Disorders**
Dissociative Amnesia
Dissociative Fugue
Dissociative Identity Disorder
Depersonalization Disorder
Dissociative Disorder NOS

**Sexual and Gender Identity Disorders**

**Sexual Desire Disorders**
Hypoactive Sexual Desire Disorder

**Sexual Aversion Disorder**

**Sexual Arousal Disorders**
Female Sexual Arousal Disorder
Male Erectile Disorder

**Orgasmic Disorders**
Female Orgasmic Disorder
Male Orgasmic Disorder
Premature Ejaculation

**Sexual Pain Disorders**
Dyspareunia
Vaginismus

**Sexual Dysfunction Due to a General Medical Condition**
Sexual Dysfunction NOS

**Paraphilias**
Exhibitionism
Fetishism
Frotteurism
Pedophilia
Sexual Masochism
Sexual Sadism
Transvestic Fetishism
Voyeurism
Paraphilia NOS

**Gender Identity Disorders**
Gender Identity Disorder
Gender Identity Disorder NOS
Sexual Disorder NOS

**Eating Disorders**
Anorexia Nervosa
Bulimia Nervosa
Eating Disorder NOS

**Sleep Disorders**

**Dyssomnias**
Primary Insomnia
Primary Hypersomnia
Narcolepsy
Breathing-Related Sleep Disorder
Circadian Rhythm Sleep Disorder
Dyssomnia NOS

**Parasomnias**
Nightmare Disorder
Sleep Terror Disorder
Sleepw
Parasor.

10689987

**Impulse-Control Disorders Not Elsewhere Classified**
Intermittent Explosive Disorder
Kleptomania
Pyromania
Pathological Gambling
Trichotillomania
Impulse-Control Disorder NOS

**Adjustment Disorders**
Adjustment Disorder

**Personality Disorders**
*Note: These are coded on Axis II.*
Paranoid Personality Disorder
Schizoid Personality Disorder
Schizotypal Personality Disorder
Antisocial Personality Disorder
Borderline Personality Disorder
Histrionic Personality Disorder
Narcissistic Personality Disorder
Avoidant Personality Disorder
Dependent Personality Disorder
Obsessive–Compulsive Personality Disorder
Personality Disorder NOS

**Other Conditions That May Be a Focus of Clinical Intervention**

**Relational Problems**
Relational Problem Related to a Mental Disorder or General Medical Condition
Parent–Child Relational Problem
Partner Relational Problem
Sibling Relational Problem
Relational Problem NOS

**Problems Related to Abuse or Neglect**
Physical Abuse of Child
Sexual Abuse of Child
Neglect of Child
Physical Abuse of Adult
Sexual Abuse of Adult

**Additional Conditions That May Be a Focus of Clinical Attention**
Noncompliance with Treatment
Malingering
Adult Antisocial Behaviour
Borderline Intellectual Functioning
Age-Related Cognitive Decline
Bereavement
Academic Problem
Occupational Problem
Identity Problem
Religious or Spiritual Problem
Acculturation Problem
Phase of Life Problem

FIAT LUX
The University of Lethbridge
School of Health Sciences

# ABNORMAL PSYCHOLOGY

**THOMAS F. OLTMANNS**

*Washington University, St. Louis*

**ROBERT E. EMERY**

*University of Virginia*

**STEVEN TAYLOR**

*University of British Columbia*

PEARSON
Prentice Hall

Toronto

**To Elmer F. Oltmanns 1909–1971** *—T.F.O.*
**To Robert E. Emery 1922–2001** *—R.E.E.*
**To Amy S. Janeck and Alex J. Taylor** *—S.T.*

Library and Archives Canada Cataloguing in Publication

Oltmanns, Thomas F.
Abnormal psychology / Thomas F. Oltmanns, Robert E. Emery, Steven Taylor.—2nd Canadian ed.

Includes bibliographical references and index.
ISBN 0-13-128627-7

1. Psychology, Pathological. 2. Mental illness. I. Emery, Robert E. II. Taylor, Steven, 1960– III. Title.

RC454.O47 2006 616.89 C2004-905754-5

Copyright © 2006, 2002 Pearson Education Canada Inc., Toronto, Ontario.

Original edition published by Pearson Education, Inc., Upper Saddle River, NJ. Copyright © 2004 Pearson Education, Inc.

This edition is authorized for sale only in Canada.

Pearson Prentice Hall. All rights reserved. This publication is protected by copyright and permission should be obtained from the publisher prior to any prohibited reproduction, storage in a retrieval system, or transmission in any form or by any means, electronic, mechanical, photocopying, recording, or likewise. For information regarding permission, write to the Permissions Department.

ISBN 0-13-128627-7

Vice President, Editorial Director: Michael J. Young
Acquisitions Editor: Ky Pruesse
Executive Marketing Manager: Judith Allen
Associate Editor: Paula Drużga
Production Editor: Söğüt Y. Güleç
Copy Editor: Tara Tovell
Proofreader: Gail Copeland
Production Coordinator: Peggy Brown
Manufacturing Coordinator: Susan Johnson
Page Layout: Hermia Chung
Photo Research: Terri Rothman
Art Director: Mary Opper
Cover Design: Michelle Bellemare
Cover Image: Pascal Grandmaison, *Verre* 2, 2004, colour lightjet print, 71" × 71", courtesy of Galerie René Blouin

For permission to reproduce copyrighted material, the publisher gratefully acknowledges the copyright holders listed on page 730, which are considered an extension of this copyright page.

Statistics Canada information is used with the permission of the Minister of Industry, as Minister responsible for Statistics Canada. Information on the availability of the wide range of data from Statistics Canada can be obtained from Statistics Canada's Regional Offices, its World Wide Web site at http://www.statcan.ca, and its toll-free access number 1-800-263-1136.

1 2 3 4 5 10 09 08 07 06

Printed and bound in the USA.

PEARSON
Prentice Hall

# Brief Contents


1 **Examples and Definitions of Abnormal Behaviour** 2

2 **Causes of Abnormal Behaviour: A Systems Approach** 28

3 **Treatment of Psychological Disorders** 66

4 **Classification and Assessment of Abnormal Behaviour** 100

5 **Mood Disorders and Suicide** 138

6 **Anxiety Disorders** 188

7 **Acute and Posttraumatic Stress Disorders, Dissociative Disorders, and Somatoform Disorders** 228

8 **Stress and Physical Health** 268

9 **Personality Disorders** 296

10 **Eating Disorders** 336

11 **Substance Use Disorders** 364

12 **Sexual and Gender Identity Disorders** 404

13 **Schizophrenic Disorders** 442

14 **Dementia, Delirium, and Amnestic Disorders** 480

15 **Mental Retardation and Pervasive Developmental Disorders** 510

16 **Psychological Disorders of Childhood** 546

17 **Adjustment Disorders and Life-Cycle Transitions** 582

18 **Mental Health and the Law** 612

## A Great Way to Learn and Instruct Online

The Pearson Education Canada Companion Website is easy to navigate and is organized to correspond to the chapters in this textbook. Whether you are a student in the classroom or a distance learner you will discover helpful resources for in-depth study and research that empower you in your quest for greater knowledge and maximize your potential for success in the course.

Companion Website

**www.pearsoned.ca/oltmanns**

Enter

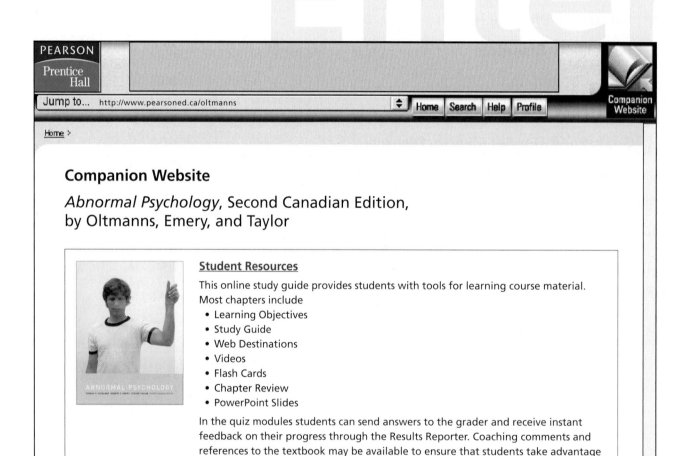

PEARSON Prentice Hall

Jump to... http://www.pearsoned.ca/oltmanns

Home Search Help Profile

Companion Website

Home >

### Companion Website

*Abnormal Psychology*, Second Canadian Edition, by Oltmanns, Emery, and Taylor

**Student Resources**

This online study guide provides students with tools for learning course material. Most chapters include

- Learning Objectives
- Study Guide
- Web Destinations
- Videos
- Flash Cards
- Chapter Review
- PowerPoint Slides

In the quiz modules students can send answers to the grader and receive instant feedback on their progress through the Results Reporter. Coaching comments and references to the textbook may be available to ensure that students take advantage of all available resources to enhance their learning experience.

**Instructor Resources**

A link to this book on the Pearson Education Canada online catalogue (vig.pearsoned.ca) provides instructors with additional teaching tools. Downloadable PowerPoint Presentations and an Instructor's Manual are just some of the materials that may be available. The catalogue is password protected. To get a password, simply contact your Pearson Education Canada Representative or call Faculty Sales and Services at 1-800-850-5813.

# Contents

DSM-IV-TR Tables xiii
Boxes xiv
Preface xvi
About the Authors 1

## 1 Examples and Definitions of Abnormal Behaviour 2

**Overview 3**
Case Study: A Husband's Paranoid Schizophrenia 4
**Recognizing the Presence of Disorder 5**
**Defining Abnormal Behaviour 6**
Harmful Dysfunction 7
Cultural Considerations 9
Further Thoughts: Homosexuality: How Culture Shapes Diagnostic Practice 9
**Who Experiences Abnormal Behaviour? 10**
Case Study: A University Student's Eating Disorder 10
Frequency in and Impact on Community Populations 12
Cross-Cultural Comparisons 13
Research Close-Up: Cross-Cultural Study of Abnormal Behaviour 15
**The Mental Health Professions 15**
**Psychopathology in Historical Context 17**
The Greek Tradition in Medicine 18
The Creation of the Asylum 18
Lessons from the History of Psychopathology 20
**Methods for the Scientific Study of Mental Disorders 20**
Research Methods: The Null Hypothesis and the Burden of Proof 21
The Uses and Limitations of Case Studies 22
Canadian Focus: Dr. Ewen Cameron and the Allan Memorial Institute 23
Clinical Research Methods 24

## 2 Causes of Abnormal Behaviour: A Systems Approach 28

**Overview 29**
Case Study: Meghan's Many Hardships 30
**Brief Historical Perspective: Twentieth-Century Paradigms 31**
General Paresis and the Biological Paradigm 32
Freud and the Psychodynamic Paradigm 32
Psychology, Learning, and the Cognitive Behavioural Paradigm 34
Free Will and the Humanistic Paradigm 35
The Problem with Paradigms 35
**Systems Theory 36**
Holism 36
Causality 37
Research Methods: The Correlational Study 39
Developmental Psychopathology 40
**Biological Factors 40**
The Neuron and Neurotransmitters 41
Neurotransmitters and the Etiology of Psychopathology 41
Neural Networks 42
Further Thoughts: Mind–Body Dualism 42
Major Brain Structures 43
Cerebral Hemispheres 43
Psychophysiology 46
Behaviour Genetics 47
**Psychological Factors 52**
Basic Human Motivations and Temperament 52
Emotions and Emotional Systems 54
Learning and Cognition 55
The Sense of Self 56
Stages of Development 57
**Social Factors 58**
Relationships and Psychopathology 58
Research Close-Up: Marriage and Mental Health 59
Gender and Gender Roles 60
Prejudice and Poverty 60
Societal Values 61
Canadian Focus: Indian Residential Schools: A Failed Experiment in Cultural Assimilation 61

## 3 Treatment of Psychological Disorders 66


**Overview 67**
Frances and the Four Paradigms 68
Case Study: Why Is Frances Depressed? 69
Brief Historical Perspective 71
**Biological Treatments 72**
Electroconvulsive Therapy 72
Psychosurgery 73
Psychopharmacology 73
**Psychodynamic Psychotherapies 75**
Freudian Psychoanalysis 75
Ego Analysis 77
Psychodynamic Psychotherapy 77
**Cognitive Behaviour Therapy 78**
Systematic Desensitization 78
Research Methods: The Experimental Method 79
Other Exposure Therapies 80
Aversion Therapy 80
Contingency Management 81
Social Skills Training 81
Cognitive Techniques 82
Beck's Cognitive Therapy 82
Rational–Emotive Therapy 83
Integration: Empiricism Reigns 83
**Humanistic Therapies 83**
Client-Centred Therapy 84
Gestalt Therapy 84
A Means, Not an End? 85
**Research on Psychotherapy 85**
Does Psychotherapy Work?—Outcome Research 85
Further Thoughts: The Allegiance Effect 88
Psychotherapy Process Research 89
**Changing Social Systems: Couples, Family, and Group Therapy 92**
Couples Therapy 93
Family Therapy 93
Group Therapy 94
Canadian Focus: Treatments for Psychological Disorders: Research and Practice 95
Prevention 96
**Specific Treatments for Specific Disorders 97**
Research Close-Up: Identifying Common Factors and Specific Active Ingredients 97


## 4 Classification and Assessment of Abnormal Behaviour 100


**Overview 101**
Case Study: Obsessions, Compulsions, and Other Unusual Behaviours 102
**Basic Issues in Classification 103**
Categories versus Dimensions 103
From Description to Theory 104
**Classifying Abnormal Behaviour 105**
Brief Historical Perspective 105
Further Thoughts: Labelling Theory 106
The DSM-IV-TR System 107
Research Close-Up: Piblokto q: A Culture-Bound Syndrome 111
**Evaluating Classification Systems 112**
Reliability 112
Validity 112
Research Methods: Diagnostic Reliability 112
Unresolved Questions 114
Problems and Limitations of the DSM-IV-TR System 114
**Basic Issues in Assessment 116**
Assumptions about the Consistency of Behaviour 116
Purposes of Clinical Assessment 116
Evaluating the Usefulness of Assessment Procedures 117
Types of Assessment Procedures 118
**Assessing Psychological Systems 118**
Interviews 119
Observational Procedures 121
Personality Tests and Self-Report Inventories 124
Projective Personality Tests 128
**Assessing Social Systems 130**
**Assessing Biological Systems 130**
Psychophysiological Assessment 131
Brain Imaging Techniques 132
Canadian Focus: Psychological Assessment: Canadian Contributions and Issues 133


## 5 Mood Disorders and Suicide 138


**Overview 139**
Case Study: A TV Reporter's Battle with Depression 141
Brief Case Study: Brian's Manic Episode 142
**Typical Symptoms and Associated Features 142**
Emotional Symptoms 142
Cognitive Symptoms 143

Somatic Symptoms 144
Behavioural Symptoms 144
Other Problems Commonly Associated with Depression 145

**Classification 145**

Brief Historical Perspective 145
Contemporary Diagnostic Systems 146
Course and Outcome 149

**Epidemiology 150**

Incidence and Prevalence 151
Gender Differences 151
Cross-Cultural Differences 151
Risk for Mood Disorders across the Lifespan 152
Comparisons across Generations 154

**Etiological Considerations and Research 154**

Social Factors 155
Research Close-Up: Social Origins of Depression in Women 156
Psychological Factors 158
Canadian Focus: Theoretical Advances in Understanding Depression 161
Biological Factors 163
The Interaction of Social, Psychological, and Biological Factors 169
Research Methods: Analogue Studies of Psychopathology 170

**Treatment 171**

Unipolar Disorders 171
Bipolar Disorders 174
Electroconvulsive Therapy 176
Seasonal Mood Disorders 176

**Suicide 177**

Brief Case Study: Postpartum Suicide 177
Classification of Suicide 178
Epidemiology of Suicide 179
Etiology of Suicide 79
Further Thoughts: Common Elements of Suicide 180
Treatment of Suicidal People 182

## 6 Anxiety Disorders 188

**Overview 189**

Case Study: A Writer's Panic Disorder with Agoraphobia 190

**Typical Symptoms and Associated Features 191**

Anxiety 191
Excessive Worry 192
Panic Attacks 192
Phobias 193
Obsessions and Compulsions 194
Case Study: Ed's Obsessive–Compulsive Disorder 195

**Classification 196**

Brief Historical Perspective 196
Contemporary Diagnostic Systems (DSM-IV-TR) 197
"Lumpers" and "Splitters" 200
Course and Outcome 200

**Epidemiology 201**

Prevalence 201
Comorbidity 201
Further Thoughts: The Relationship between Anxiety and Depression 202
Gender Differences 203
Anxiety across the Lifespan 203
Cross-Cultural Comparisons 204

**Etiological Considerations and Research 205**

Adaptive and Maladaptive Fears 205
Social Factors 205
Psychological Factors 207
Canadian Focus: Anxiety Sensitivity and Panic Attacks 211
Biological Factors 213

**Treatment 218**

Brief Case Study: Ed's Treatment 218
Psychological Interventions 219
Research Methods: Statistical Significance and Clinical Importance 221
Biological Interventions 222

## 7 Acute and Posttraumatic Stress Disorders, Dissociative Disorders, and Somatoform Disorders 228

**Overview 229**

**Acute and Posttraumatic Stress Disorders 230**

Typical Symptoms and Associated Features of ASD and PTSD 230
Case Study: Posttraumatic Stress Disorder in the Canadian Armed Forces 231
Classification of Acute and Posttraumatic Stress Disorders 233
Epidemiology of Trauma, PTSD, and ASD 235
Further Thoughts: PTSD and the Sexual Assault of Women 236
Etiological Considerations and Research on PTSD and ASD 237
Canadian Focus: Does Stress Cause Posttraumatic Stress Disorder? 240
Prevention and Treatment of ASD and PTSD 241

**Dissociative Disorders 243**
Case Study: Dissociative Fugue: Dallae's Journey 244
Hysteria and Unconscious Mental Processes 245
Typical Symptoms of Dissociative Disorders 247
Classification of Dissociative Disorders 247
Further Thoughts: Recovered Memories? 248
Case Study: Dissociative Identity Disorder 250
Epidemiology of Dissociative Disorders 251
Research Close-Up: Implicit Memory in Dissociative Identity Disorder 253
Etiological Considerations and Research on Dissociative Disorders 254
Treatment of Dissociative Disorders 256

**Somatoform Disorders 256**
Typical Symptoms and Associated Features of Somatoform Disorders 256
Classification of Somatoform Disorders 257
Brief Case Study: Body Dysmorphic Disorder 259
Epidemiology of Somatoform Disorders 260
Etiological Considerations and Research on Somatoform Disorders 262
Research Methods: Retrospective Reports 263
Treatment of Somatoform Disorders 264

## 8 Stress and Physical Health 268

**Overview 269**
Case Study: Stress and Bob Carter's Heart Attack 270

**Defining Stress 271**
Stress as a Life Event 271
Stress as Appraisal of Life Events 272

**Typical Symptoms: Responding to Stress 273**
Further Thoughts: Tend and Befriend: The Female's Alternative to Fight or Flight? 273
Psychophysiological Responses to Stress 274
Immune System Responses 274
Illness and Chronic Stress 276
Coping 276
Research Close-Up: Disclosure of Trauma and Immunity 278
Health Behaviour 279

**Classification of Stress and Physical Illness 280**
Brief Historical Perspective 280
Contemporary Approaches 280
Canadian Focus: Endler's Multidimensional Interaction Model of Stress, Anxiety, and Coping 281
Illness as a Cause of Stress 282

**The Role of Psychological Factors in Some Familiar Illnesses 282**
Cancer 282
Pain Management 284
Acquired Immune Deficiency Syndrome (AIDS) 284
Pain Management 284
Sleep Disorders 285

**Cardiovascular Disease 286**
Typical Symptoms and Associated Features of Hypertension and CHD 286
Classification of CVD 287
Epidemiology of CVD 287
Etiological Considerations and Research on CVD 288
Research Methods: Longitudinal Research Designs 291
Prevention and Treatment of Cardiovascular Disease 292

## 9 Personality Disorders 296

**Overview 297**
Case Study: A Car Thief's Antisocial Personality Disorder 299

**Typical Symptoms and Associated Features 300**
Social Motivation 300
Temperament and Personality Traits 301
Context and Personality 303

**Classification 303**
Cluster A: Paranoid, Schizoid, and Schizotypal Personality Disorders 303
Cluster B: Antisocial, Borderline, Histrionic, and Narcissistic Personality Disorders 304
Brief Case Study: Borderline Personality Disorder 305
Cluster C: Avoidant, Dependent, and Obsessive–Compulsive Personality Disorders 306
Personality Disorder Not Otherwise Specified (PD NOS) 307
A Dimensional Perspective on Personality Disorders 307
Brief Case Study: Narcissism from the Perspective of the Five-Factor Model 308
Canadian Focus: Dimensional Assessment of Personality Pathology 309

**Epidemiology 311**
Prevalence in Community and Clinical Samples 311
Gender Differences 312
Stability of Personality Disorders over Time 313
Culture and Personality 313
Research Close-Up: Stability of Personality Disorders in Adolescents 314

**Schizotypal Personality Disorder (SPD) 315**
Brief Case Study: Schizotypal Personality Disorder 315
Research Methods: Cross-Cultural Comparisons 316
Brief Historical Perspective 317
Clinical Features and Comorbidity 317

Etiological Considerations 317
Treatment 318

**Borderline Personality Disorder (BPD) 319**

Brief Case Study: Borderline Personality Disorder 319
Brief Historical Perspective 320
Further Thoughts: Impulse Control Disorders 320
Clinical Features and Comorbidity 321
Etiological Considerations 322
Treatment 323

**Antisocial Personality Disorder (ASPD) 324**

Brief Case Study: Antisocial Personality Disorder 324
Brief Historical Perspective 325
Psychopathy versus Antisocial Personality Disorder 325
Clinical Features and Comorbidity 326
Case Study: Paul Bernardo and Karla Homolka 327
Etiological Considerations 328
Treatment 331

**Dependent Personality Disorder (DPD) 331**

Brief Case Study: Dependent Personality Disorder 331
Brief Historical Perspective 332
Clinical Features and Comorbidity 332
Etiological Considerations 332
Treatment 333

## 10 Eating Disorders 336

**Overview 337**

Case Study: Kate's Anorexia 338

**Typical Symptoms and Associated Features of Anorexia 339**

Further Thoughts: Eating Disorders in Males 339
Refusal to Maintain a Normal Weight 340
Disturbance in Evaluating Weight or Shape 340
Fear of Gaining Weight 340
Cessation of Menstruation 341
Medical Complications 341
Struggle for Control 341
Comorbid Psychological Disorders 342

**Typical Symptoms and Associated Features of Bulimia Nervosa 342**

Binge Eating 343
Case Study: Michelle's Secret 343
Inappropriate Compensatory Behaviour 344
Excessive Emphasis on Weight and Shape 344
Comorbid Psychological Disorders 345
Medical Complications 345

**Classification of Eating Disorders 345**

Brief Historical Perspective 345
Contemporary Classification 346

**Epidemiology of Eating Disorders 347**

Gender Differences and Standards of Beauty 348
Age of Onset 349

**Etiological Considerations and Research 350**

Social Factors 350
Psychological Factors 351
Biological Factors 354
Integration and Alternative Pathways 355

**Treatment of Anorexia Nervosa 356**

Course and Outcome of Anorexia Nervosa 356
Canadian Focus: Treatment at the Montreux Clinic: All You Need Is Love? 357

**Treatment of Bulimia Nervosa 359**

Antidepressant Medications 359
Cognitive Behaviour Therapy 359
Interpersonal Psychotherapy 359
Research Methods: Credible Placebo Control Groups 360
Course and Outcome of Bulimia Nervosa 361

## 11 Substance Use Disorders 364

**Overview 365**

Case Study: Ernest Hemingway's Alcohol Dependence 367

**Typical Symptoms and Associated Features 368**

The Concept of Substance Dependence 368
Alcohol 370
Nicotine 371
Amphetamine and Cocaine 372
Opiates 373
Brief Case Study: Feelings after Injecting Heroin 374
Barbiturates and Benzodiazepines 375
Cannabis 375
Hallucinogens and Related Drugs 376

**Classification 378**

DSM-IV-TR 378
Proposed Subtypes 379
Course and Outcome 380
Other Disorders Commonly Associated with Addictions 380

**Epidemiology 380**

Prevalence of Alcohol Abuse and Dependence 381
Prevalence of Drug and Nicotine Dependence 382

Risk for Addiction across the Lifespan 382
Brief Case Study: Ms. E's Drinking 383

**Etiological Considerations and Research 384**
Social Factors 384
Biological Factors 385
Research Close-Up: The Swedish Adoption Studies 386
Psychological Factors 390
Research Methods: Risk, Risk Factors, and Studies of High-Risk Samples 392
Integrated Systems 393

**Treatment 394**
Detoxification 394
Medications during Remission 395
Self-Help Groups: Alcoholics Anonymous 395
Cognitive Behaviour Therapy 396
Brief Case Study: Relapse to Heroin Use 397
Outcome Results and General Conclusions 398
Canadian Focus: The Controlled Drinking Controversy 400

# 12 Sexual and Gender Identity Disorders 404

**Overview 405**
Case Study: Margaret and Bill's Sexual Communication 406
Brief Historical Perspective 407

**Sexual Dysfunctions 408**
Typical Symptoms and Associated Features 408
Research Close-Up: Sexual Activity in the General Population 409
Classification 410
Brief Case Study: Sexual Aversion Disorder 412
Brief Case Study: Male Erectile Disorder 413
Research Methods: Hypothetical Constructs: The Case of "Sexual Arousal" 415
Brief Case Study: Genital Pain 416
Epidemiology 416
Etiology 418
Treatment 419

**Paraphilias 421**
Typical Symptoms and Associated Features 422
Brief Case Study: Paraphilia 422
Classification 423
Brief Case Study: Masochism 425
Epidemiology 429
Etiology 430
Further Thoughts: The Classification of Rapists 431
Treatment 433

**Gender Identity Disorders 436**
Typical Symptoms and Associated Features 436
Brief Case Study: Transsexualism 437
Epidemiology 437
Etiology 437
Canadian Focus: Nature and Nurture in Gender Identity 438
Treatment 439

# 13 Schizophrenic Disorders 442

**Overview 443**
Case Study: Marilyn's Paranoid Schizophrenia 444
Case Study: Edward's Disorganized Schizophrenia 445

**Typical Symptoms and Associated Features 446**
Positive Symptoms 446
Negative Symptoms 447
Disorganization 448
Case Study: Marsha's Disorganized Speech and Bizarre Behaviour 448

**Classification 450**
Brief Historical Perspective 450
DSM-IV-TR 451
Subtypes 452
Related Psychotic Disorders 453
Course and Outcome 454
Canadian Focus: Long-Term Course of Schizophrenia: Two Examples 455

**Epidemiology 456**
Gender Differences 456
Cross-Cultural Comparisons 457

**Etiological Considerations and Research 458**
Biological Factors 458
Research Close-Up: The Danish High-Risk Project 461
Social Factors 465
Psychological Factors 466
Research Methods: Comparison Groups in Psychopathology Research 468
Integration and Multiple Pathways 469
The Search for Markers of Vulnerability 470

**Treatment 472**
Antipsychotic Medication 472
Psychosocial Treatment 476

## 14 Dementia, Delirium, and Amnestic Disorders 480

**Overview 481**
Case Study: A Physician's Developing Dementia 482
Case Study: Dementia and Delirium—A Niece's Terrible Discoveries 483
**Typical Symptoms and Associated Features 484**
Delirium 485
Dementia 485
Further Thoughts: Memory Changes in Normal Aging 486
Amnestic Disorder 489
Case Study: Alcohol-Induced Persisting Amnestic Disorder—19 Going on 45 490
**Classification 491**
Brief Historical Perspective 491
Specific Disorders Associated with Dementia 492
Research Methods: Genetic Linkage Analysis 495
**Epidemiology of Delirium and Dementia 498**
Prevalence of Dementia 499
Canadian Focus: The Canadian Study of Health and Aging 499
Prevalence by Subtypes of Dementia 500
Cross-Cultural Comparisons 501
**Etiological Considerations and Research 501**
Delirium 501
Dementia 502
**Treatment and Management 505**
Medication 505
Environmental and Behavioural Management 506
Support for Caregivers 507

## 15 Mental Retardation and Pervasive Developmental Disorders 510

**Overview 511**
**Mental Retardation 512**
Typical Symptoms and Associated Features 512
Case Study: A Mother with Mild Mental Retardation 513
Research Methods: Central Tendency, Variability, and Standard Scores 515
Classification 517
Epidemiology 519
Etiological Considerations and Research 520
Treatment: Prevention and Normalization 526
Canadian Focus: Involuntary Sterilization and the Eugenics Movement 526
**Autistic Disorder and Pervasive Developmental Disorders 529**
Typical Symptoms and Associated Features 530
Case Study: A Child with Autistic Disorder 530
Case Study: Temple Grandin: An Anthropologist on Mars 532
Classification 536
Epidemiology 537
Etiological Considerations and Research 538
Treatment 540

## 16 Psychological Disorders of Childhood 546

**Overview 547**
**Externalizing Disorders 548**
Case Study: Bad Boy, Troubled Boy, or All Boy? 548
Typical Symptoms of Externalizing Disorders 549
Classification of Externalizing Disorders 552
Epidemiology of Externalizing Disorders 555
Research Methods: Samples and Sampling 555
Etiology of Externalizing Disorders 556
Brief Case Study: Ms. B's Son 559
Treatment of Externalizing Disorders 562
**Internalizing and Other Disorders 567**
Case Study: Turning the Tables on Tormentors 567
Typical Symptoms of Internalizing and Other Disorders 568
Further Thoughts: Learning Disorders 571
Classification of Internalizing and Other Disorders 572
Epidemiology of Internalizing and Other Disorders 574
Canadian Focus: The Ontario Child Health Study 575
Etiology of Internalizing and Other Disorders 577
Treatment of Internalizing Disorders 579

## 17 Adjustment Disorders and Life-Cycle Transitions 582

**Overview 583**
Case Study: Divorce in Midlife 584
Typical Experiences 585
Classification of Life-Cycle Transitions 585
**The Transition to Adulthood 588**
Typical Experiences of the Adult Transition 588
Classification of Identity Conflicts 589
Epidemiology of Identity Conflicts 590
Etiological Considerations and Research on the Adult Transition 591
Treatment during the Transition to Adult Life 592
Brief Case Study: Samantha's Life Story Is Rewritten 592
**Family Transitions 592**
Typical Experiences of Family Transitions 593
Classification of Troubled Family Relationships 595
Epidemiology of Family Transitions 596
Etiological Considerations and Research on Family Transitions 596
Research Methods: The Concept of Heritability 597
Research Close-Up: The Heritability of Divorce 599
Treatment during Family Transitions 600
Couples Therapy and Family Therapy 601
Brief Case Study: Jan and Bill: Learning to Listen 601
**Aging and the Transition to Later Life 602**
Ageism 603
Typical Experiences of Aging 603
Brief Case Study: Mrs. J's Loss 605
Canadian Focus: Reminiscence among Older Adults 607
Classification of Aging 608
Epidemiology of Aging 608
Etiological Considerations and Research on the Aging Transition 609
Treatment of Psychological Problems in Later Life 609

## 18 Mental Health and the Law 612

**Overview 613**
Case Study: The Tragic Case of Edmond Yu 614
**Mental Health, Criminal Responsibility, and Procedural Rights 615**
Mental Disorder and Criminal Responsibility 615
Canadian Focus: The Mental Disorder Defence: Not Criminally Responsible on Account of a Mental Disorder (NCRMD) 617
Further Thoughts: The Battered Woman Syndrome as a Defence 618
Criminal Proceedings and Fitness to Stand Trial 620
**Mental Health and Civil Law 621**
Libertarianism versus Paternalism in Treating Patients Who Have Mental Disorders 621
Civil Commitment 621
Research Close-Up: The Accuracy of Predictions of Violence 623
Research Methods: Base Rates and Predictions 624
The Rights of Patients with Mental Disorders 627
Deinstitutionalization 628
**Mental Health and Family Law 630**
Children, Parents, and the State 630
Child Custody Disputes 630
Brief Case Study: A Custody Dispute 632
Child Abuse 632
**Professional Responsibilities and the Law 634**
Professional Negligence and Malpractice 634
Confidentiality 636

Glossary 639
References 653
Name Index 698
Subject Index 711
Credits 730

## DSM-IV-TR Tables


Summary of DSM-IV-TR Definition of Mental Disorders 8

DSM-IV-TR Criteria for Obsessive–Compulsive Disorder 108

Major Domains of Information in DSM-IV-TR 109

DSM-IV-TR System for Classifying Mood Disorders 146

Symptoms Listed in DSM-IV-TR for Major Depressive Episodes 147

Symptoms Listed in DSM-IV-TR for Manic Episode 148

Diagnostic Criteria for Panic Attack in DSM-IV-TR 192

Categories Listed as Anxiety Disorders in DSM-IV-TR 197

DSM-IV-TR Diagnostic Criteria for Posttraumatic Stress Disorder (PTSD) 234

DSM-IV-TR Diagnostic Criteria for Acute Stress Disorder (ASD) 235

DSM-IV-TR Diagnostic Criteria for Somatization Disorder 258

DSM-IV-TR Diagnostic Criteria for Psychological Factors Affecting Medical Condition 280

DSM-IV-TR Categories for Psychosocial and Environmental Problems 282

Personality Disorders Listed in DSM-IV-TR 303

DSM-IV-TR Criteria for Schizotypal Personality Disorder 318

DSM-IV-TR Criteria for Borderline Personality Disorder 322

DSM-IV-TR Criteria for Antisocial Personality Disorder 326

DSM-IV-TR Criteria for Dependent Personality Disorder 333

DSM-IV-TR Diagnostic Criteria for Anorexia Nervosa 346

DSM-IV-TR Diagnostic Criteria for Bulimia Nervosa 347

DSM-IV-TR Criteria for Substance Dependence 379

DSM-IV-TR Criteria for Substance Abuse 379

Sexual Dysfunctions Listed in DSM-IV-TR 411

DSM-IV-TR Diagnostic Criteria for Schizophrenia 451

DSM-IV-TR Criteria for Dementia 485

Cognitive Disorders Listed in DSM-IV-TR 492

DSM-IV-TR Criteria for Dementia of the Alzheimer's Type 493

DSM-IV-TR Diagnostic Criteria for Mental Retardation 514

IQ Scores for Patients with Autism and Other Pervasive Developmental Disorders 536

DSM-IV-TR Diagnostic Criteria for Autistic Disorder 537

DSM-IV-TR Diagnostic Criteria for Attention-Deficit/Hyperactivity Disorder 553

DSM-IV-TR Diagnostic Criteria for Oppositional Defiant Disorder 554

DSM-IV-TR Diagnostic Criteria for Conduct Disorder 557

DSM-IV-TR Disorders Usually First Diagnosed in Infancy, Childhood, or Adolescence 573

DSM-IV-TR Diagnostic Criteria for Adjustment Disorder 586

DSM-IV-TR Listing of Other Conditions That May Be a Focus of Clinical Attention 586

# Boxes

## CASE STUDY

A Husband's Paranoid Schizophrenia 4
A University Student's Eating Disorder 10
Meghan's Many Hardships 30
Why Is Frances Depressed? 69
Obsessions, Compulsions, and Other Unusual Behaviours 102
A TV Reporter's Battle with Depression 141
A Writer's Panic Disorder with Agoraphobia 190
Ed's Obsessive–Compulsive Disorder 195
Posttraumatic Stress Disorder in the Canadian Armed Forces 231
Dissociative Fugue: Dallae's Journey 244
Dissociative Identity Disorder 250
Stress and Bob Carter's Heart Attack 270
A Car Thief's Antisocial Personality Disorder 299
Paul Bernardo and Karla Homolka 327
Kate's Anorexia 338
Michelle's Secret 343
Ernest Hemingway's Alcohol Dependence 367
Margaret and Bill's Sexual Communication 406
Marilyn's Paranoid Schizophrenia 444
Edward's Disorganized Schizophrenia 445
Marsha's Disorganized Speech and Bizarre Behaviour 448
A Physician's Developing Dementia 482
Dementia and Delirium—A Niece's Terrible Discoveries 483
Alcohol-Induced Persisting Amnestic Disorder—19 Going on 45 490
A Mother with Mild Mental Retardation 513
A Child with Autistic Disorder 530
Temple Grandin: An Anthropologist on Mars 532
Bad Boy, Troubled Boy, or All Boy? 548
Turning the Tables on Tormentors 567
Divorce in Midlife 584
The Tragic Case of Edmond Yu 614

## BRIEF CASE STUDY

Brian's Manic Episode 142
Postpartum Suicide 177
Ed's Treatment 218
Body Dysmorphic Disorder 259
Borderline Personality Disorder 305
Narcissism from the Perspective of the Five-Factor Model 308
Schizotypal Personality Disorder 315
Borderline Personality Disorder 319
Antisocial Personality Disorder 324
Dependent Personality Disorder 331
Feelings after Injecting Heroin 374
Ms. E's Drinking 383
Relapse to Heroin Use 397
Sexual Aversion Disorder 412
Male Erectile Disorder 413
Genital Pain 416
Paraphilia 422
Masochism 425
Transsexualism 437
Ms. B's Son 559
Samantha's Life Story Is Rewritten 592
Jan and Bill: Learning to Listen 601
Mrs. J's Loss 605
A Custody Dispute 632

## RESEARCH METHODS

The Null Hypothesis and the Burden of Proof 21
The Correlational Study 39
The Experimental Method 79
Diagnostic Reliability 112
Analogue Studies of Psychopathology 170
Statistical Significance and Clinical Importance 221
Retrospective Reports 263
Longitudinal Research Designs 291
Cross-Cultural Comparisons 316
Credible Placebo Control Groups 360
Risk, Risk Factors, and Studies of High-Risk Samples 392
Hypothetical Constructs: The Case of "Sexual Arousal" 415
Comparison Groups in Psychopathology Research 468
Genetic Linkage Analysis 495
Central Tendency, Variability, and Standard Scores 515
Samples and Sampling 555
The Concept of Heritability 597
Base Rates and Predictions 624

## RESEARCH CLOSE-UP

Cross-Cultural Study of Abnormal Behaviour 15
Marriage and Mental Health 59
Identifying Common Factors and Specific Active Ingredients 97
Pibloktoq: A Culture-Bound Syndrome 111
Social Origins of Depression in Women 156
Implicit Memory in Dissociative Identity Disorder 253
Disclosure of Trauma and Immunity 278
Stability of Personality Disorders in Adolescents 314
The Swedish Adoption Studies 386
Sexual Activity in the General Population 409
The Danish High-Risk Project 461
The Heritability of Divorce 599
The Accuracy of Predictions of Violence 623

## FURTHER THOUGHTS

Homosexuality: How Culture Shapes Diagnostic Practice 9
Mind–Body Dualism 42
The Allegiance Effect 88
Labelling Theory 106
Common Elements of Suicide 180
The Relationship between Anxiety and Depression 202
PTSD and the Sexual Assault of Women 236
Recovered Memories? 248
Tend and Befriend: The Female's Alternative to Fight or Flight? 273
Impulse Control Disorders 320
Eating Disorders in Males 339
The Classification of Rapists 431
Memory Changes in Normal Aging 486
Learning Disorders 571
The Battered Woman Syndrome as a Defence 618

## CANADIAN FOCUS

Dr. Ewen Cameron and the Allan Memorial Institute 23
Indian Residential Schools: A Failed Experiment in Cultural Assimilation 61
Treatments for Psychological Disorders: Research and Practice 95
Psychological Assessment: Canadian Contributions and Issues 133
Theoretical Advances in Understanding Depression 161
Anxiety Sensitivity and Panic Attacks 211
Does Stress Cause Posttraumatic Stress Disorder? 240
Endler's Multidimensional Interaction Model of Stress, Anxiety, and Coping 281
Dimensional Assessment of Personality Pathology 309
Treatment at the Montreux Clinic: All You Need Is Love? 357
The Controlled Drinking Controversy 400
Nature and Nurture in Gender Identity 438
Long-Term Course of Schizophrenia: Two Examples 455
The Canadian Study of Health and Aging 499
Involuntary Sterilization and the Eugenics Movement 526
The Ontario Child Health Study 575
Reminiscence among Older Adults 607
The Mental Disorder Defence: Not Criminally Responsible on Account of a Mental Disorder (NCRMD) 617

# Preface

Abnormal psychology is not about "them." Abnormal psychology is about all of us. Emotional suffering touches all of our lives at some point in time. Psychological problems are prevalent and affect many of us directly and all of us indirectly—through our loved ones, friends, and the strangers whose troubled behaviour we cannot ignore.

Abnormal psychology is also about scientific inquiry. We bring both the science and the personal aspects of abnormal psychology to life in this second Canadian edition of our text. We answer pressing intellectual and human questions as accurately, sensitively, and completely as possible, given the pace of new discoveries. Throughout this book, we offer an engaging, yet rigorous treatment of the topics and disorders of abnormal psychology.

## Integrated and Consistent Coverage and DSM-IV-TR

Integration always has been the overriding theme of our textbook. Rather than see abnormal psychology as fractured by competition among paradigms, split between psychology and psychiatry, or divided between scientists and practitioners, we see the most exciting and promising future for abnormal psychology in the integration of theoretical approaches, professional specialties, and science and practice.

We present abnormal psychology as a cohesive field, even with all its variations. Each disorder chapter unfolds in the same way, providing a coherent framework and consistent outline. We open with an Overview followed by one or two Case Studies. We then discuss typical symptoms and associated features, classification, epidemiology, etiological considerations and research, and finally, treatment. Each chapter reflects DSM-IV-TR throughout.

Embedded in this consistent structure are several features designed to help make the human aspects of mental disorders clearer to readers: Our cases, first person accounts, and Canadian Focus features.

## The Latest Science

We do not have simple answers to many pressing personal and intellectual questions. Many of our answers are complicated and equivocal. Others are simply incomplete. Such is the state of abnormal psychology at the beginning of the twenty-first century.

But far worse than offering incomplete answers would be to take the route of those well-intentioned experts, and some unscrupulous ones, who are ready to give "definitive" answers to questions that, in reality, cannot be answered definitively. Sometimes these "experts'" answers are wrong or clearly self-serving. We are candid when the truthful answer is, "Honestly, we do not yet know."

The unanswered questions of abnormal psychology present intriguing and pressing puzzles. These unsolved mysteries challenge all of our intellectual and personal resources as scientific detectives. We include the latest scientific findings throughout this text, including references to hundreds of new scientific studies in this revised Canadian edition. But the measure of a leading edge textbook is not merely the number of new references. It is the number of new studies the authors have reviewed and evaluated before deciding what to include and what to discard. For every new reference in this edition of our text, we have read many additional papers before selecting the one gem to include.

At least as important as including the latest and the best research, we also point to the most promising leads for finding more and better answers in the not-too-distant future. We are seasoned and active investigators, as well as authors. Our research—and this text—are fueled by the suffering of people with emotional conflicts and mental illnesses, and by the intellectual challenges we face in trying to answer some of the very complicated questions posed by abnormal psychology.

## Research Methods: How Psychological Detective Work Is Done

We report on the latest scientific findings, and we also explain in detail how psychological scientists do their detective work. Unlike any other text in this field, however, we do *not* cover research methods in a single chapter. We do this because many of our students have told us that the typical research methods chapter seems dry, difficult, and—to our great disappointment—irrelevant. Students understand the enormous need for new knowledge in this field, but they find the one-shot chapter on research methods to be detached from the substance of abnormal psychology.

Our solution to these problems is to offer brief **Research Methods** inserts in every single chapter. This approach makes the text flexible, and it makes learning research methods more manageable, more focused, and more relevant by connecting them to the chapter content. By the end of the text, this approach also allows us to cover research methods in *more* detail than we could reasonably cover in a single, detached chapter.

## Research Close-Ups

In addition to these discussions of research methods, we also offer **Research Close-Up** sections devoted to a detailed review of a particular study that has proved important in advancing our knowledge in a given area. These sections help make concrete not only the findings of the study, but also its process.

Often, the Research Methods and Research Close-Up features work together. For example, in Chapter 17, the Research Methods discussion is on heritability, while the Research Close-Up focuses on research studies examining the gene–environment correlation and the possible heritability of divorce.

## Further Thoughts

Sometimes a study or problem suggests a departure from current thinking or raises issues that deserve to be examined. Our **Further Thoughts** sections cover these sorts of emerging ideas, such as evidence suggesting that, rather than employing the fight or flight response to threat, females appear to choose a "tend and befriend" approach (Chapter 8), or possible ways of classifying rapists, even though this type of abnormal behaviour is not included in the official diagnostic manual (Chapter 12), or new ways of thinking about the close connection between depression and anxiety (Chapter 6).

## Canadian Perspectives

Our goals in writing this book have been ambitious from the start. We wanted to capture and describe the leading edge of knowledge regarding mental disorders—arising from research throughout the world—while also highlighting Canadian aspects of abnormal psychology. Most texts are for American audiences, and therefore discuss clinical issues, mental health laws, and cultural issues that may not be relevant to Canadian audiences. In this text we introduce readers to Canadian aspects of abnormal psychology. We discuss important aspects of Canada's mental health care system, such as its unique history and structure. Canadian laws as they apply to mental health and mental health practitioners are also described. These laws differ in some important respects from the laws of other countries. Canadian examples of mental disorders are presented, such as prominent cases in which Canada's version of the insanity defence was used.

We also highlight the important work by clinical scientists in Canada, not only in the Canadian Focus boxes, but also throughout the text. Our task has been greatly facilitated by the fact that many of the world's leading researchers in clinical psychology and psychiatry work at Canadian universities. By highlighting Canadian research, we hope our readers will come to appreciate that groundbreaking research does not always come from other countries; chances are that important work on abnormal psychology is being conducted right on your campus.

Throughout this text we have tended to rely on the best available estimates of the prevalence of mental disorders—i.e., the estimates in the latest version of the DSM, DSM-IV-TR (American Psychiatric Association, 2000). These estimates were derived by combining data from many studies, including studies conducted in Canada. However, we also discuss specific Canadian epidemiological studies and results. For example, where good data are available, we consider cross-national differences in the prevalence of mental disorders, and differences between Canada and other regions, such as Europe, Asian countries, and the United States.

To further highlight important Canadian research, in this new Canadian edition we have expanded the Canadian context, for example by increasing the number of **Canadian Focus** boxes. These highlight the findings of many important research programs, such as the Canadian Study of Health and Aging (Chapter 14), the Ontario Child Health Study (Chapter 16), Livesley's cutting-edge work on the genetics of personality disorders conducted at the University of British Columbia (Chapter 9), and Endler's important work on stress, anxiety, and coping, conducted at York University (Chapter 8). Canadian Focus boxes also discuss some important controversies, including the "brainwashing" treatments at the Allan Memorial Institute (Chapter 1), the question of the importance of stressors in posttraumatic stress disorder (Chapter 7), and the feasibility of "controlled drinking" programs for alcoholism (Chapter 11).

We call attention to multicultural issues in abnormal psychology. These are discussed in some of the Canadian Focus boxes, and elsewhere in the text. In Chapter 2, for example, we have included a Canadian Focus on the effects of residential schools, which many First Nations children were once required to attend. The text also contains important discussions of cultural factors in depression, personality disorders, eating disorders, sexual dysfunctions, schizophrenia, and dementia.

### Case Studies

Abnormal psychology is, of course, about real people; people like us. The many case studies we present help readers keep this in mind. Detailed ***Case Studies*** appear near the beginning of every chapter so that the symptoms and etiological issues are presented in the context of real lives and in their genuine complexity. In the extended opening cases, briefer cases, and first-person accounts throughout the chapters, readers see how ordinary lives are disrupted and how treatment proceeds in fits and starts.

Most of the cases are our own. Throughout our careers, we have been active clinicians as well as active researchers. In fact, being a therapist is a lot like being a scientist. As therapists, we develop hypotheses and test them as we work to help individual clients to change. When we gain support for a hypothesis with one client, we wonder if the observation applies to others. Was the cause of this problem unique to this client, or have we discovered a general principle? Did our successful attempt to vary a proven treatment work only for this one client, or are we on to something bigger? Can we prove our clinical hunches to the world in an objective, scientific manner?

The Case Studies help take the reader along on this journey of pain, triumph, frustration, and fresh starts, and are designed to help students think more deeply about psychological disorders, much as our own clinical experience enriches our understanding.

## Paradigms and Systems: The Blind Men and the Elephant

For much of the last century abnormal psychology was dominated by theoretical paradigms, and the belief that someday one single paradigm would triumph and provide all answers to all questions while all other paradigms collapsed into dust.

This circumstance reminds us of the parable of the seven blind men and the elephant. One blind man grasps a tusk and concludes that an elephant is very much like a spear. Another feels a knee and decides an elephant is like a tree, and so on. Our goal from the first edition of *Abnormal Psychology* has been to show the reader the whole elephant. We do this through our unique *integrative systems approach*, in which we focus on what we know rather than what we used to think.

In every chapter, we consider how biological, psychological, and social factors work *together* to produce mental disorders. What causes depression? A chemical imbalance? Cognitive errors? Or racial and gender bias? Our answer is: wrong questions. Depression appears to be caused by a combination of genetic risks, maladaptive patterns of thinking, and dysfunctional social roles (among other influences). Similarly, the appropriate treatment of depression may involve medication, psychotherapy, social action, or all three approaches.

We show how different factors function together in a system of reciprocal influences in producing different psychological disorders. We strive to appreciate the whole elephant even when we know that science has not yet illuminated all of its parts.

## What Else Is New in the Second Canadian Edition?

Every revision involves a fresh look at content and coverage and bringing discussions up-to-date with current research. We have rewritten the openers to the chapters in order to help convey our "us, not them" theme, highlighting the connection between disordered and "normal" behaviour. For example, the opener to the personality disorders chapter (Chapter 9) invites readers to consider the relationship between being skeptical and being paranoid and between self-confidence and grandiosity. There are many changes *within* the chapters of *Abnormal Psychology*, Second Canadian Edition, as well:

**Chapter 1:** Expands on coverage of how culture affects the way we define disorders; also includes updated information on variations in the frequency of disorders across countries. Among the new Canadian material is a discussion of the recommendations of the Canadian committee on empirically supported treatments.

**Chapter 2:** Includes a new section on evolutionary psychology, a streamlined and more accessible presentation of the systems approach, an updated account of psychological factors in mental illness, and an enhanced discussion of behaviour genetics, including two new figures designed to illustrate the differences between, and different implications of, autosomal dominant inheritance and polygenic inheritance. New Canadian material includes an illustration of the diathesis-stress model by drawing on the research on perfectionism by Paul Hewitt (University of British Columbia) and Gordon Flett (York University).

**Chapter 3:** Addresses new research on the benefits of limited therapist self-disclosure; evidence on the controversial increase in prescribing psychotropic medications to children; a controversial new meta-analysis questioning the empirical support for some "empirically supported" therapies. New to the second Canadian edition is a discussion of the recent psychotherapy research by Leslie Greenberg and colleagues at York University.

**Chapter 4:** Updates the debate regarding the use of projective tests; new information on fMRIs and brain imaging. A new Canadian Focus box is added, discussing important assessment research conducted at various Canadian universities.

**Chapter 5:** Expands on coverage of the neurobiology of depression, including the HPA axis as well as neurohormones and brain areas related to depression. Includes new first person accounts of clinical depression. Also includes expanded discussion of evolutionary views of depression and new information on antidepressant medications, especially Selective Serotonin Reuptake Inhibitors (SSRIs). A new Canadian Focus box has been added, featuring depression research by John Abela at McGill University.

**Chapter 6:** Updated information on the neurobiology of panic; expanded coverage of developmental issues and anxiety. New information regarding the comorbidity of anxiety and depression and the use of SSRIs in treating anxiety disorders. Includes recent research on the effectiveness of cognitive behavioural therapy for obsessive–compulsive disorder and generalized anxiety disorder. New Canadian material includes a discussion of anxiety sensitivity research from universities across Canada (e.g., Dalhousie, Manitoba, British Columbia). Important research by other Canadian investigators is also discussed, including work by Adam Radomsky (Concordia University), Henny Westra (University of Western Ontario), Christine Purdon (Waterloo University), and David A. Clark (University of New Brunswick).

**Chapter 7:** Expanded and updated section on posttraumatic stress disorder (PTSD) including biological factors and the impact of September 11. Over 50 new references, including current research on acute stress disorder (ASD) and subclinical ASD as a predictor of future PTSD; the benefits of antidepressants in treating PTSD; the psychological effects of torture; and cognitive behavioural treatments for somatoform disorders. Added emphasis on emotional processing and meaning making in coping with trauma. New Canadian content includes a discussion of the effects of September 11 on Canadians; for example, the work on remote exposure to trauma by Gordon Asmundson at the University of Regina. Lt. General Roméo Dallaire's battle with PTSD is also discussed. Many other Canadian studies discussed in this chapter, including treatment research by Sandra Paivio (Windsor University), and research on recovered memories by Steven Porter (Dalhousie University) and Stephen Lindsay (University of Victoria).

**Chapter 8:** Updated discussion of stress and its consequences, including new statistics on causes of death. New Further Thoughts feature on possible evolutionary influences and gender differences in responses to stress. New research on the cognitive behavioural treatment of sleep disorders, the health benefits of forgiveness, and health and intimate relationships. Among the new Canadian material are discussions of the recent work on stress and coping by Anita DeLongis (University of British Columbia), and research by Ron Martin and Nick Kuiper (University of Western Ontario). The latter psychologists have done important work on the relationships among stress, coping, and sense of humour.

**Chapter 9:** Expanded discussion of evolutionary views of personality disorders; new coverage of the role a distorted self image and misperceptions of others' motives can play the development of personality disorders (PDs.) Updated discussion of dimensional approaches to classifying PDs; new information regarding the prevalence of PDs in community samples; increased coverage of dialectical behaviour therapy. New Canadian content includes a review of recent research by Joel Paris (McGill University) and Paul Links (University of Toronto). New material has been added on Paul Bernardo and Karla Homolka, drawing on recently published new information. The Bernardo/Homolka case raises many important issues about the nature of PDs, particularly antisocial PD.

**Chapter 10:** New research on the longitudinal course of eating disorders following treatment and coverage of eating disorders in men. Expanded discussion of the contribution of genetic factors to eating disorders. A new Canadian Focus box has been added to discuss the controversial treatment for anorexia at Victoria's Montreux Clinic. A great deal of the world's most important eating disorders research comes from Toronto (i.e., University of Toronto, York University, Toronto General Hospital). The work of these researchers is described, including important new studies by Paul Garfinkel, David Garner, Blake Woodside, Caroline Davis, Janet Polivy, Peter Herman, and Allan Kaplan. Important recent research by Howard Steiger (McGill University) and Kristin von Ranson (University of Calgary) is also discussed.

**Chapter 11:** New discussion of the neurobiology of addiction, including mechanisms promoting psychoactive substance tolerance and treatment of drug dependence. New coverage of MDMA (Ecstasy); new first person brief case study on effects of heroin. Updated discussion of developmental influences on drug use. Among the new Canadian content includes findings on conditioning and drug tolerance from McMaster University, and a discussion of research by Konstantine Kazkanis (University of Toronto) on the neuropsychological effects of Ecstasy. Recent research by Sherry Stewart (Dalhousie University) and Robert Pihl (McGill University) is also discussed.

**Chapter 12:** New brief cases on erectile dysfunction; new first person accounts on vaginismus (Kaysen) and sexual masochism (Merkin); new Consensus Conference information on classifying female sexual dysfunctions, led by Rosemary Basson (University of British Columbia) is discussed. Recent research on premature ejaculation research by Sandra Byers (University of New Brunswick) is included, along with new findings from many other Canadian investigators, such as Vernon Quinsey (Queen's University) and Yitzchak Binik (McGill University). A new Canadian Focus box has been added to discuss the tragic case of a Winnipeg boy who, after a botched circumcision, was raised as a girl. This important case raises many important issues about the roles of nature and nurture in the formation of gender identity.

**Chapter 13:** New information on schizophrenia and social class and other environmental risk factors; updated information on brain imaging studies; expanded coverage of second generation or "atypical" antipsychotic drugs. Updated coverage of expressed emotion and relapse. New Canadian content includes a case study of schizophrenia, written by award-winning Toronto journalist Scott Simmie. Findings from University of Toronto researcher Anne Bassett are discussed, concerning the genetics of schizophrenia. Important research by other Canadian investigators is also discussed, including Jim Neufeld (University of Western Ontario), R. Walter Heinrichs (York University), and Debbie Dobson (University of Calgary).

**Chapter 14:** New information on classification of dementias, including frontotemporal dementia and dementia with Lewy bodies; updated information on the neuropathology and genetics of Alzheimer's disease. Expanded and updated discussion of the prevalence of vascular dementia and Alzheimer's disease in men and women. Recent findings from Michael Hayden (University of British Columbia) are discussed, along with results of the Canadian Study of Health and Aging, and the University of Victoria longitudinal study.

**Chapter 15:** Includes new evidence on unusual brain growth patterns in autistic disorder. New research on specific genes involved in some cases of autistic disorder and Rett's disorder; new evidence regarding the validity of the Asperger's disorder diagnostic criteria.

Amongst the new Canadian content includes a discussion of autism research by Susan Bryson (Dalhousie University) and Mary Konstantareas (University of Guelph). Readers are introduced to the Canadian Aboriginal Head Start program, and the is an expanded discussion of Canadian historical perspectives on mental retardation and developmental disorders.

**Chapter 16:** New research on the treatment of children's anxiety disorders; new findings from research to identify youth with psychopathic tendencies. Expanded and updated discussion of gender differences in the development of depression; new information on the treatment of attention deficit-hyperactivity disorder (ADHD) based on the Multi-Modal Treatment (MTA) study and the prevention of children's behaviour problems through parent education, school, and peer interventions. A good deal of recent, important research comes from Canadian researchers, including Charlotte Johnston, Eric Mash, Virginia Douglas, Gabrielle Weiss and Lilly Hechtman, Russell J. Schachar, Richard Tremblay, David Offord, Otfried Spreen, Marlene Moretti, and Jane Garland. Recent Health Canada warnings about the use of SSRIs in children and adolescents is also discussed.

**Chapter 17:** Expanded discussion of development in later life. Expanded discussion of identity development particularly among youth without a university education. New research findings on marriage and emotional well-being. The chapter includes new Canadian epidemiological information relevant to development throughout the lifespan, such as information on the epidemiology of family transitions such as divorce. The Canadian Focus box describes research on reminiscence among older adults done at Trent University.

**Chapter 18:** This chapter on mental health and the law includes a new Canadian Focus box describing the case of Edmond Yu, as documented by Canadian journalist Scott Simmie. This case raises many important questions, such as the issue of involuntary treatment. Along with a discussion of Canadian laws regarding mental health issues, there is a discussion of important new findings by Canadian investigators, including research by Stephen Porter (Dalhousie University). New material is also included on the role of psychologists in divorce mediation.

## Supplements

### For Students

***Speaking Out* on CD-ROM**—It's one thing to read about people who have been diagnosed with various disorders, and quite another actually to hear and see them. This CD-ROM includes video clips showing skilled clinicians interviewing real patients (not actors), and gives students a chance to hear real people talking about their experiences with schizophrenia, anorexia, and other disorders. This CD-ROM can be packaged free with new copies of the second Canadian edition by ordering with the package ISBN 0-13-200349-X or it may be purchased stand-alone by using ISBN 0-13-193333-7.

**Companion Website** (www.pearsoned.ca/oltmanns)—John Conklin of Camosun College has carefully created and selected all of the resources on the Oltmanns, Emery, and Taylor Companion Website to reinforce students' understanding of the concepts in the text. Students can take online quizzes and get immediate scoring and feedback; link to related websites; review key terms with the interactive flashcards; and view clips.

**Study Guide** (ISBN 0-13-197115-8)—The *Study Guide* includes chapter outlines, numerous review and study questions, and other learning aids to help reinforce students' understanding of the concepts covered in the text.

### For Instructors

The Second Canadian Edition of *Abnormal Psychology* comes with a high-tech support package for faculty, all contained on one CD.

**Instructor's Resource CD-ROM** (ISBN 0-13-197114-X)—Includes the *Instructor's Resource Manual*, a *Test Item File* (in Word), a computerized test item file (in TestGen), and *PowerPoint Presentations*.

**Instructor's Resource Manual** (also available through our online catalogue at vig.pearsoned.ca)—John Conklin of Camosun College has created this supplement, which contains lecture and discussion suggestions, student activities, classroom demonstration ideas, and suggestions on how to integrate the Videos in Abnormal Psychology CD-ROM into your course.

**Test Item File** (available in Word and TestGen formats, the TestGen version is also available through our online catalogue at vig.pearsoned.ca)—This comprehensive *Test Item File* by John Conklin has been updated to include new questions on revised text material. It contains multiple-choice, true/false, short answer, and essay questions. The TestGen is designed to allow the creation of personalized exams.

**PowerPoint Presentations** (also available through our online catalogue at vig.pearsoned.ca)—Stephen Porter of Dalhousie University has created *PowerPoint Presentations* that highlight key points and include important tables, figures, and graphics from the text, to give you greater flexibility in your lectures.

**Media and Online Resources** *Speaking Out: Interviews with People Who Struggle with Psychological Disorders:* This new set of 16 video segments allows students to see firsthand accounts of patients with various disorders. The interviews were conducted by licensed clinicians and range in length from 8–25 minutes. Disorders include major depressive disorder, obsessive–compulsive disorder, anorexia nervosa, PTSD, alcoholism, schizophrenia, autism, ADHD, bipolar disorder, social phobia, hypochondriasis, borderline personality disorder, and adjustment to physical illness. These video segments are available on CD-ROM (ISBN 0-13-193333-7), VHS cassettes (ISBN 0-13-193702-2), or DVD (ISBN 0-13-193332-9).

## Acknowledgments

Writing and revising this textbook is a never-ending task that fortunately is also a labour of love. This second Canadian edition is the culmination of years of effort, and is the product of many people's efforts. The first people we wish to thank for their important contributions to making this the text of the future, not of the past, are the following expert Canadian reviewers who have unselfishly offered us a great many helpful suggestions, both in this and in the previous Canadian edition:

E. Michael Coles, Simon Fraser University; N. Edguer, Brandon University; David R. Evans, University of Western Ontario; Amy Janeck, University of British Columbia; Konstantine K. Kakzanis, University of Toronto; Jennifer Mather, University of Lethbridge; Stephen Porter, Dalhousie University; Sherry H. Stewart, Dalhousie University; Scott B. McCabe, University of Waterloo; John Conklin, Camosun College; Danielle Paris, Algonquin College; Tom Harrigan, University of Manitoba & Red River College; Barry Ledwidge, Simon Fraser University; Christine Purdon, University of Waterloo; Marilyn Hadad, Ryerson University.

We have been fortunate to work in a stimulating academic environment that has fostered our interests in studying abnormal psychology and in teaching undergraduate students. We are particularly grateful to our colleagues at the University of Virginia: Eric Turkheimer, Irving Gottesman, Mavis Hetherington, John Monahan, Joseph Allen, Dan Wegner (now at Harvard), David Hill, Cedric Williams, and Peter Brunjes for extended and ongoing discussions of the issues that are considered in this book. Close friends and colleagues at Indiana University have also served in this role, especially Richard McFall and Alexander Buchwald. Many undergraduate and graduate students who have taken our course also have helped to shape the viewpoints that are expressed here. They are too numerous to identify individually, but we are grateful for the intellectual challenges and excitement that they have provided over the past several years.

Many other people have contributed to the text in important ways. Once again, Kimberly Carpenter Emery did extensive legal research for Chapter 18. Carol Manning provided consultation on case study materials. Tara Peris, LaKeesha Woods, Maggie Emery, Maria Whitmore, and Sheri Towe helped with library research and manuscript preparation.

In preparing the second Canadian edition, Steven Taylor is particularly grateful to his University of British Columbia colleagues for their encouragement, advice, and intellectual stimulation: Amy Janeck, Kerry Jang, Dana Thordarson, and Jaye Wald.

We also would like to express our deep appreciation to the Pearson team who share our pride and excitement about this text, and who have worked long and hard to make it the very best text.

Finally, we want to express our gratitude to our families for their patience and support throughout our obsession with this text: Gail and Josh Oltmanns, Sara (Oltmanns) Baber and Billy Baber, and Kimberly, Maggie, Julia, Bobby, Lucy, and John Emery, and Amy Janeck and Alex Janeck Taylor. You remain our loving sources of motivation and inspiration.

*—Tom Oltmanns*
*—Bob Emery*
*—Steve Taylor*

# About the Authors

Thomas F. Oltmanns is Professor of Psychology and Psychiatry at the University of Washington in St. Louis, where he is also Director of Clinical Training in Psychology. He received his B.A. from the University of Wisconsin and his Ph.D. from the State University of New York at Stony Brook. He was a member of the faculty in the Department of Psychology at Indiana University from 1976 to 1986 before moving to the University of Virginia, and later to the University of Washington. He served as Associate Editor of the *Journal of Abnormal Psychology* and as a member of several research review committees for the National Institutes of Health. He was elected president of the Society for a Science of Clinical Psychology in 1993 and has received the "Outstanding Professor Award" from the undergraduate psychology majors at UVa (in 1997 and 2002). He has written extensively about the role of cognitive and emotional factors in mental disorders such as schizophrenia and obsessive–compulsive disorder. His current research on the assessment of personality disorders is funded by the National Institute of Mental Health (NIMH). His previous books include *Schizophrenia* (1980), written with John Neale; *Delusional Beliefs* (1988), edited with Brendan Maher; and *Case Studies in Abnormal Psychology* (sixth edition, 2004), written with John Neale and Gerald Davison.

Robert E. Emery is Professor of Psychology and former Director of Clinical Training at the University of Virginia. He also is Director of the Centre for Children, Families, and the Law and an associate faculty member of the Institute of Law, Psychiatry, and Public Policy at the university. He received a B.A. from Brown University in 1974 and a Ph.D. from SUNY at Stony Brook in 1982. He is on the editorial boards of eight journals and is a member of the Population and Social Sciences study section of NIH. His research focuses on family conflict, children's mental health, and associated legal issues. His 1982 *Psychological Bulletin* paper was designated a "Citation Classic" by the Institute for Scientific Information, and a later *Child Development* paper received the Outstanding Research Publication Award from the American Association for Marriage and Family Therapy in 1989. In 2002, he received The Distinguished Research Award from the Association of Family and Conciliation Courts. He is the author of over 75 to 100 scientific articles and book chapters and two monographs: *Marriage, Divorce, and Children's Adjustment* (1988; 2nd ed., 1998, Sage Publications) and *Renegotiating Family Relationships: Divorce, Child Custody, and Mediation* (1994, Guilford Press).

Steven Taylor is a Professor in the Department of Psychiatry at the University of British Columbia. He received his Ph.D. in clinical psychology at the University of British Columbia in 1991. For 10 years he was Associate Editor of *Behaviour Research and Therapy*, and now is Associate Editor of the *Journal of Cognitive Psychotherapy*. He has served as a member of several research review committees for the National Institutes of Health, and for the Canadian Institutes for Health Research. His research focuses on cognitive and behavioural mechanisms of anxiety disorders, particularly panic disorder, posttraumatic stress disorder, and obsessive–compulsive disorder. He has published over 110 journal articles, over 35 book chapters, and 9 books on anxiety disorders and related topics. His most recent books are on the nature and treatment of panic disorder, posttraumatic stress disorder, and hypochondriasis. He served as a consultant on the text revision of the Diagnostic and Statistical Manual of Mental Disorders (DSM-IV-TR), and is a member of the scientific advisory board of the Anxiety Disorders Association of Canada. He has received early career awards from the Canadian Psychological Association, the Association for Advancement of Behavior Therapy, and the Anxiety Disorders Association of America. He is also a Fellow of the Canadian Psychological Association and a Fellow of the Association of Cognitive Therapy.

# 1 Examples and Definitions of Abnormal Behaviour


Overview
Recognizing the Presence of Disorder
Defining Abnormal Behaviour
Who Experiences Abnormal Behaviour?
The Mental Health Professions
Psychopathology in Historical Context
Methods for the Scientific Study of Mental Disorders

**What is the difference between normal and abnormal behaviour?**

**How do we know whether someone has a mental disorder?**

**How many people suffer from mental disorders?**

**What impact do mental disorders have on people's lives?**

Mental disorders touch every realm of human experience; they are part of the human experience. They can disrupt the way we think, the way we feel, and the way we behave. They also affect relationships with other people. These problems often have a devastating impact on people's lives. Large community surveys indicate that one out of every five Canadians experiences a mental disorder at some point in their life (e.g., Offord et al., 1996). In developed countries like Canada, mental disorders are the second leading cause of disease burden, ranking slightly behind cardiovascular conditions and slightly ahead of cancer (Lopez & Murray, 1998). The purpose of this book is to help you become familiar with the nature of these disorders and the various ways in which psychologists and other mental health professionals are advancing knowledge of their causes and treatment.

Many of us grow up thinking that mental disorders happen to a few unfortunate people. We don't expect them to happen to us or to those we love. In fact, mental disorders are very common. At least one out of every three people will experience a serious form of abnormal behaviour, such as depression, alcoholism, or schizophrenia, at some point during his or her lifetime. When you add up the numbers of people who experience these problems first-hand as well as through relatives and close friends, you realize that, like other health problems, mental disorders affect all of us. That is why, throughout this book, we will try to help you understand not only the kind of disturbed behaviours and thinking that characterize particular disorders but the people to whom they occur and the circumstances that can foster them.

Most importantly, this book is about all of us, not "them"—anonymous people with whom we empathize but do not identify. Just as each of us will be affected by medical problems at some point during our lives, it is also likely that we, or someone we love, will have to cope with that aspect of the human experience known as a disorder of the mind.

## Overview

The symptoms and signs of mental disorders, including such phenomena as depressed mood, panic attacks, and bizarre beliefs, are known as **psychopathology**. Literally translated, this term means "pathology of the mind." **Abnormal psychology** is the application of psychological science to the study of mental disorders.

In the first four chapters of this book, we will look at the field of abnormal psychology in general. We will look at the ways in which abnormal behaviours are broken down into categories of mental disorders that can be more clearly defined for diagnostic purposes, and how those behaviours are assessed. We will also discuss current ideas about the causes of these disorders and ways in which they can be treated.

This chapter will help you begin to understand the qualities that define behaviours and experiences as being abnormal. At what point does the diet that a girl follows in order to perform at her peak as a ballerina or gymnast become an eating disorder? When does grief following the end of a relationship become major depression? The line dividing normal from abnormal is not always clear. You will find that the issue is often one of degree rather than the exact form or content of behaviour.

The case studies in this chapter describe the experiences of two people whose behaviour would be considered abnormal by mental health professionals. Our first case will introduce you to a person who suffered from one of the most obvious and disabling forms of mental disorder, known as schizophrenia. Kevin's life had been relatively unremarkable for many years. He had done well in school, was married, and held a good job. Unfortunately, over a period of several months, the fabric of his normal life began to fall apart. The transition wasn't obvious to either Kevin or his family,

## CASE STUDY **A Husband's Paranoid Schizophrenia**

Kevin and Joyce Warner (not their real names*) had been married for eight years when they sought help from a psychologist for their marital problems. Joyce was 34 years old, worked full-time as a pediatric nurse, and was six months pregnant with her first child. Kevin, who was 35 years old, was working as a librarian at a local university. Joyce was extremely worried about what would happen if Kevin lost his job, especially in light of the baby's imminent arrival.

Although the Warners had come for couples therapy, the psychologist soon became concerned about certain eccentric aspects of Kevin's behaviour. In the first session, Joyce described one recent event that had precipitated a major argument. One day, after eating lunch at work, Kevin had experienced sharp pains in his chest and had difficulty breathing. Fearful, he rushed to the emergency room at the hospital where Joyce worked. The physician who saw Kevin found nothing wrong with him, even after extensive testing. She gave Kevin a few tranquilizers and sent him home to rest. When Joyce arrived home that evening, Kevin told her that he suspected that he had been poisoned at work by his supervisor. He still held this belief.

Kevin's belief about the alleged poisoning raised serious concern in the psychologist's mind about Kevin's mental health. He decided to interview Joyce alone so that he could ask more extensive questions about Kevin's behaviour. Joyce realized that the poisoning idea was "crazy." She was not willing, however, to see it as evidence that Kevin had a mental disorder. Joyce had known Kevin for 15 years. As far as she knew, he had never held any strange beliefs before this time, and he had never taken hallucinogenic drugs or smoked marijuana. Joyce said that Kevin had always been "a thoughtful and unusually sensitive guy." She did not attach a great deal of significance to Kevin's unusual belief. She was more preoccupied with the couple's present financial concerns and insisted that it was time for Kevin to "face reality."

Kevin's condition deteriorated noticeably over the next few weeks. He became extremely withdrawn, frequently sitting alone in a darkened room after dinner. On several occasions, he told her that he felt as if he had "lost pieces of his thinking." It wasn't that his memory was failing, but rather he felt as though parts of his brain were shut off.

Kevin's problems at work also grew worse. His supervisor informed Kevin that his contract would definitely not be renewed. Joyce exploded when Kevin indifferently told her the bad news. His apparent lack of concern was especially annoying. She called Kevin's supervisor, who confirmed the news. He told her that Kevin was physically present at the library, but he was only completing a few hours of work each day. Kevin sometimes spent long periods of time just sitting at his desk and staring off into space and was sometimes heard mumbling softly to himself.

Kevin's speech was quite odd during the next therapy session. He would sometimes start to speak, drift off into silence, then re-establish eye contact with a bewildered smile and a shrug of his shoulders. He had apparently lost his train of thought completely. His answers to questions were often off the point, and when he did string together several sentences, their meaning was sometimes obscure. For example, at one point during the session, the psychologist asked Kevin if he planned to appeal his supervisor's decision. Kevin said, "I'm feeling pressured, like I'm lost and can't quite get here. But I need more time to explore the deeper side. Like in art. What you see on the surface is much richer when you look closely. I'm like that. An intuitive person. I can't relate in a linear way, and when people expect that from me, I get confused."

Kevin's strange belief about poisoning continued to expand. The Warners received a letter from Kevin's mother, who lived in another city 300 km away. She had become ill after going out for dinner one night and mentioned that she must have eaten something that made her sick. After reading the letter, Kevin became convinced that his supervisor had tried to poison his mother, too.

When questioned about this new incident, Kevin launched into a long, rambling story. He said that his supervisor was an ex-police officer, but he had refused to talk

continued

*cont.*

with Kevin about his years in the force. Kevin suspected that this was because the supervisor had been an undercover officer, and was now working as a secret agent. Kevin suggested that an agent from this organization had been sent by his supervisor to poison his mother. Kevin thought that he and Joyce also were in danger. He was particularly wary around men who were about his supervisor's age, because they, too, might be secret agents. Kevin said that he knew much about "what was really going on," but would not elaborate.

Kevin's bizarre beliefs and his disorganized behaviour convinced the psychologist that he needed to be hospitalized. Joyce reluctantly agreed that this was the most appropriate course of action. She had run out of alternatives. Arrangements were made to have Kevin admitted to a psychiatric facility, where the psychiatrist prescribed olanzapine (Zyprexa), a type of antipsychotic medication. Kevin seemed to respond positively to the drug, because he soon stopped talking about plots and poisoning—but he remained withdrawn and uncommunicative. After three weeks of treatment, Kevin's psychiatrist thought that he had improved significantly. Kevin was discharged from the hospital in time for the birth of his baby girl. Unfortunately, when the couple returned to consult with the psychologist, Kevin's adjustment was still a major concern. He did not talk with Joyce about the poisonings, but she noticed that he remained withdrawn and showed few emotions, even toward the baby.

When the psychologist questioned Kevin in detail, he admitted reluctantly that he still believed that he had been poisoned. Slowly, he revealed more of the plot. Immediately after admission to the hospital, Kevin had decided that his psychiatrist could not be trusted. Kevin was sure that he, too, was a secret agent. Kevin believed that he was being interrogated by this clever psychiatrist, so he had "played dumb." He did not discuss the suspected poisonings or the secret organization that had planned them. Whenever he could get away with it, Kevin simply pretended to take his medication. He thought that it was either poison or truth serum.

Kevin was admitted to a different psychiatric hospital soon after it became apparent that his paranoid beliefs had expanded. This time, he was given intramuscular injections of antipsychotic medication in order to be sure that the medicine was actually taken. Kevin improved considerably after several weeks in the hospital. He acknowledged that he had experienced paranoid thoughts. Although he still felt suspicious from time to time, wondering whether the plot had actually been real, he recognized that it could not really have happened, and he spent less and less time thinking about it. ◆

*Throughout this text we use fictitious names to protect the identities of the people involved.

but it eventually became clear that he was having serious problems.

## Recognizing the Presence of Disorder

Some mental disorders are so severe that the people who suffer from them are not aware of the implausibility of their beliefs. Schizophrenia is a form of **psychosis**, a general term that refers to several types of severe mental disorder in which the person is considered to be out of contact with reality. Kevin exhibited several psychotic symptoms. For example, Kevin's firm belief that he was being poisoned by his supervisor had no basis in reality. Other disorders, however, are more subtle variations on normal experience. We will shortly consider some of the guidelines that are applied in determining abnormality.

Mental disorders are typically defined by a set of characteristic features; one symptom by itself is seldom sufficient to make a diagnosis. A group of symptoms that appear together and are assumed to represent a specific type of disorder is referred to as a **syndrome**. Kevin's unrealistic and paranoid belief that he was being poisoned, his peculiar and occasionally difficult to understand patterns of speech, and his oddly unemotional responses are all symptoms of schizophrenia (see Chapter 13). Each symptom is taken to be a fallible, or imperfect, indicator of the presence of the disorder. The significance of any specific feature depends on whether the person also exhibits additional behaviours that are characteristic of a particular disorder.

The duration of a person's symptoms is also important. Mental disorders are defined in terms of *persistent* maladaptive behaviours. Many unusual behaviours and inexplicable experiences are short-lived; if we ignore them, they go away. Unfortunately, some forms of problematic behaviour are not transient, and they eventually interfere with the person's social and occupational functioning. In Kevin's case, he had become completely preoccupied with his suspicions about poison. Joyce tried for several weeks to ignore certain aspects of Kevin's behaviour, especially his delusional beliefs. She didn't want to think about the possibility that his behaviour was abnormal, and instead chose to explain his problems in terms

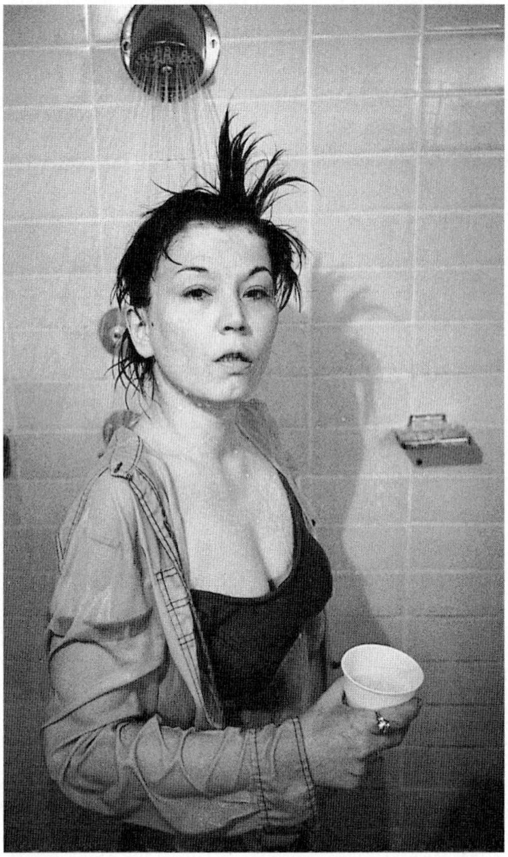

*People with schizophrenia sometimes exhibit disorganized behaviour, like this hospitalized woman.*

of lack of maturity or lack of motivation. But as the problems accumulated, she finally decided to seek professional help. The magnitude of Kevin's problem was measured, in large part, by its persistence.

Impairment in the ability to perform social and occupational roles is another consideration in identifying the presence of a mental disorder. Delusional beliefs and disorganized speech typically lead to a profound disruption of relationships with other people. Like Kevin, people who experience these symptoms will obviously find the world to be a strange, puzzling, and perhaps alarming place. And they often elicit the same reactions in other people. Kevin's odd behaviour and his inability to concentrate on his work had eventually cost him his job. His problems also had a negative impact on his relationship with his wife and his ability to help care for their daughter.

Kevin's situation raises several additional questions about abnormal behaviour. One of the most difficult issues in the field centres on the processes by which mental disorders are identified. Once Kevin's problems came to the attention of a mental health professional, could he have been tested in some way to confirm the presence or absence of a mental disorder?

Psychologists and other mental health professionals do not at present have laboratory tests that can be used to confirm definitively the presence of psychopathology because the processes that are responsible for mental disorders have not yet been discovered. Unlike specialists in other areas of medicine where many specific disease mechanisms have been discovered by advances in the biological sciences, psychologists and psychiatrists cannot test for the presence of a viral infection or a brain lesion or a genetic defect to confirm a diagnosis of mental disorder. Psychologists must still depend on their observations of the person's behaviour and descriptions of personal experience.

Is it possible to move beyond our current dependence on descriptive definitions of psychopathology? Will we someday have valid tests that can be used to establish independently the presence of a mental disorder? If we do, what form might these tests take? The answers to these questions are being sought in many kinds of research studies that will be discussed throughout this book.

## Defining Abnormal Behaviour

Why do we consider Kevin's behaviour to be abnormal? By what criteria do we decide whether a particular set of behaviours or emotional reactions should be viewed as a mental disorder? These are important questions because they determine, in many ways, how other people will respond to the person, as well as who will be responsible for providing help (if help is required). Many attempts have been made to define abnormal behaviour, but none is entirely satisfactory. No one has been able to provide a consistent definition that easily accounts for all situations in which the concept is invoked.

One approach to the definition of abnormal behaviour places principal emphasis on the individual's experience of personal distress. We might say that abnormal behaviour is defined in terms of subjective discomfort that leads the person to seek help from a mental health professional. This definition is fraught with problems, however. Kevin's case illustrates one of the major reasons that this approach does not work. Before his second hospitalization, Kevin was unable or unwilling to appreciate the extent of his problem or the impact his behaviour had on other people. A psychologist would say that he did not have *insight* regarding his disorder. The discomfort was primarily experienced by Joyce, and she had attempted for many weeks to deny the nature of the problem. It would be useless to adopt a definition that considered Kevin's behaviour to be abnormal only after he had been successfully treated.

Another approach is to define abnormal behaviour in terms of statistical norms—how common or rare it is in the general population. By this definition, people with unusually high levels of anxiety or depression would be considered abnormal because their experience deviates from the expected norm. Kevin's paranoid beliefs would be defined as pathological because they are idiosyncratic. Mental disorders are, in fact, defined in terms of experiences not shared by most people.

This approach, however, does not specify *how* unusual the behaviour must be before it is considered abnormal. Some conditions that are typically considered to be forms of psychopathology are extremely rare. For example, gender identity disorder, the belief that one is a member of the opposite sex trapped in the wrong body, affects less than 1 person out of every 30 000. In contrast, other disorders are much more common. In Canada, major depression affects 1 out of every 8 women, and alcohol dependence affects at least 1 out of every 10 men (Ross, 1995; Weissman et al., 1996a). Thus, depression and alcohol problems are far from uncommon.

Another weakness of the statistical approach is that it does not distinguish between deviations that are harmful and those that are not. Many rare behaviours are not pathological. Some "abnormal" characteristics, such as exceptional intellectual, artistic, or athletic ability, may actually confer an advantage on the individual. For these reasons, the simple fact that a behaviour is statistically rare cannot be used to define psychopathology.

## Harmful Dysfunction

One useful approach to the definition of mental disorder has been proposed by Jerome Wakefield (1992b, 1999), who suggests that a condition should be considered a mental disorder if, and only if, it meets two criteria:

1. The condition results from the inability of some internal mechanism (mental or physical) to perform its natural function. In other words, something inside the person is not working properly. Examples of such mechanisms include those that regulate levels of emotion or those that distinguish between real auditory sensations and those that are imagined.
2. The condition causes some harm to the person as judged by the standards of the person's culture. These negative consequences are measured in terms of the person's own subjective distress or difficulty performing expected social or occupational roles.

A mental disorder, therefore, is defined in terms of **harmful dysfunction**. This definition incorporates one element that is based as much as possible on an objective evaluation of performance. The dysfunctions in mental disorders are assumed to be the product of disruptions of thought, feeling, communication, perception, and motivation.

In Kevin's case, the most apparent dysfunctions involved failures of mechanisms that are responsible for perception, thinking, and communication. Disruption of these systems was presumably responsible for his delusional beliefs and his disorganized speech. The natural function of cognitive and perceptual processes is to allow the person to perceive the world in ways that are shared with other people and to engage in rational thought and problem solving. The natural function of linguistic mechanisms is to allow the person to communicate clearly with other people. Therefore, Kevin's abnormal behaviour can be viewed as a pervasive dysfunction cutting across several mental mechanisms.

*Andy Warhol was one of the most influential painters of the twentieth century. His colleague, Jean-Michel Basquiat, was also a promising artist. His dependence on heroin and his ultimately fatal overdose is one extreme example of the destructive and tragic effects of mental disorder.*

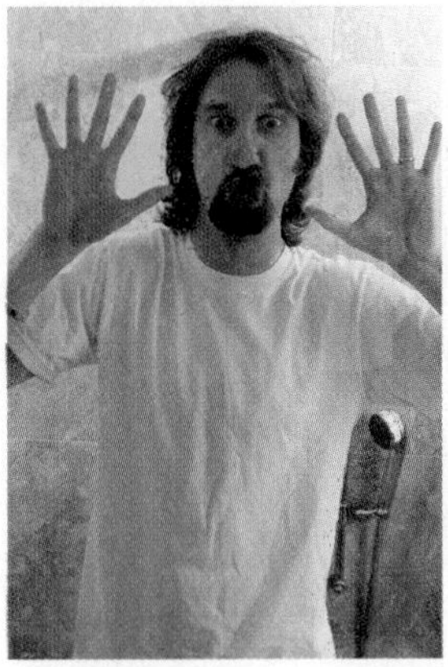

*Entertainers like Ottawa-born Tom Green sometimes do things that seem bizarre or outrageous, but they are voluntary behaviours intended to make money. Unless accompanied by other symptoms, they would not be considered evidence of a mental disorder.*

The harmful dysfunction view of mental disorder recognizes that every type of dysfunction does not lead to a disorder. Only dysfunctions that result in significant harm to the person are considered to be disorders. This is the second element of the definition. There are, for example, many types of physical dysfunction, such as albinism, reversal of heart position, and fused toes, that clearly represent a significant departure from the way that some biological process ordinarily functions. These conditions are not considered to be disorders, however, because they are not necessarily harmful to the person.

Kevin's dysfunctions were, in fact, harmful to his adjustment. They affected both his family relationships—his marriage to Joyce and his ability to function as a parent—and his performance at work. His social and occupational performances were clearly impaired. There are, of course, other types of harm that are also associated with mental disorders. These include subjective distress, such as high levels of anxiety or depression, as well as more tangible outcomes, such as suicide.

The definition of abnormal behaviour in the fourth edition of the *Diagnostic and Statistical Manual of Mental Disorders*, text revision (DSM-IV-TR: APA, 2000), incorporates many of the factors that we have already discussed. The DSM-IV-TR classification system, which is used in Canada and in many other places throughout the world, is discussed in Chapter 4. The definition of abnormal behaviour is summarized in Table 1–1, along with a number of conditions that are specifically excluded from the DSM-IV-TR definition of mental disorders.

The DSM-IV-TR definition places primary emphasis on the consequences of certain behavioural syndromes. Accordingly, mental disorders are defined by clusters of persistent maladaptive behaviours that are associated with personal distress, such as anxiety or depression, or with impairment in social functioning, such as job performance or personal relationships. The official definition, therefore, recognizes the concept of dysfunction, and it spells out ways in which the harmful consequences of the disorder might be identified.

The DSM-IV-TR definition excludes voluntary behaviours, as well as beliefs and actions that are shared by religious, political, or sexual minority groups (e.g., gays and lesbians).

Mental health, like medicine, is an applied rather than a theoretical field. It draws on knowledge from research in the psychological and biological sciences in an effort to help people whose behaviour is disordered. Mental disorders are, in some respects, those problems with which mental health professionals attempt to deal. As their activities and explanatory concepts expand, so does the list of abnormal behaviours. The practical boundaries of abnormal behaviour are defined by the list of disorders that are included in the DSM-IV-TR. The categories in that manual are listed inside the front cover of this book. The DSM-IV-TR provides a simplistic, though practical, answer to our question as to why Kevin's behaviour would be considered abnormal: He would be considered

**TABLE 1–1 Summary of the DSM-IV-TR Definition of Mental Disorders**

**Defining Characteristics**

A behavioural or psychological syndrome (groups of associated features) that is associated with

1. Present distress (painful symptoms), or
2. Disability (impairment in one or more important areas of functioning), or with
3. A significantly increased risk of suffering death, pain, disability, or an important loss of freedom

**Conditions Excluded from Consideration**

This syndrome or pattern must not be merely

1. An expectable and culturally sanctioned response to a particular event (such as the death of a loved one)
2. Deviant behaviour (such as the actions of political, religious, or sexual minorities)
3. Conflicts that are between the individual and society (such as voluntary efforts to express individuality)

to be exhibiting abnormal behaviour because his experiences fit the description of schizophrenia, which is one of the officially recognized forms of mental disorder.

### Cultural Considerations

The process by which the *Diagnostic and Statistical Manual* is constructed and revised is necessarily influenced by cultural considerations. **Culture** is defined in terms of the values, beliefs, and practices that are shared by a specific community or group of people. These values and beliefs have a profound influence on opinions regarding the difference between normal and abnormal behaviour (Lopez & Guarnaccia, 2000).

The impact of particular behaviours and experiences on a person's adjustment depends on the culture in which the person lives. To use Jerome Wakefield's (1992a) terms, "only dysfunctions that are socially-disvalued are disorders" (p. 384). Consider, for example, the DSM-IV-TR concept of female orgasmic disorder, which is defined in terms of the absence of orgasm accompanied by subjective distress or interpersonal difficulties that result from this disturbance (see Chapter 12). A woman who grew up in a society that discouraged female sexuality might not be distressed or impaired by the absence of orgasmic responses. According to DSM-IV-TR, she would not be considered to have a sexual problem. Therefore, this definition of abnormal behaviour is not culturally universal and might lead us to consider a particular pattern of behaviour to be abnormal in one society and not in another.

There have been many instances in which groups representing particular social values have brought pressure to bear on decisions shaping the diagnostic manual (see Further Thoughts). For example, feminist organizations, both within and outside the mental health professions, expressed legitimate concern over the possible inclusion of premenstrual dysphoric disorder in DSM-IV-TR, because they are concerned about the implications of labelling women who have these problems as mentally ill (Caplan, 1995). In a compromise struck in the DSM-IV-TR, premenstrual dysphoric disorder appears in an appendix for disorders recommended for further study. These deliberations are a reflection of the practical nature of the manual and of the health-related professions. Value judgments are an inherent part of any attempt to define "disorder" (Sedgwick, 1981).

## Further Thoughts

### Homosexuality: How Culture Shapes Diagnostic Practice

The influence of cultural changes on psychiatric classification is perhaps nowhere better illustrated than in the case of homosexuality. The psychiatric community had maintained in the first and second editions of the DSM that homosexuality was, by definition, a form of mental disorder. This position was adopted in spite of the attitudes expressed by scientists, who argued that homosexual behaviour was not abnormal (see Chapter 12). Toward the end of the 1960s, as the gay and lesbian rights movement became more forceful and outspoken, some of its leaders challenged the assumption that homosexuality was pathological. They opposed the inclusion of homosexuality in the official diagnostic manual.

Between 1970 and 1974, a dramatic series of events led to important changes in the DSM classification of sexual disorders, especially homosexuality. Gay leaders demanded the removal of homosexuality from the DSM-II. After extended and sometimes heated discussions, the board of trustees responsible for the DSM agreed to comply. This process illustrates quite clearly the ways in which social and political events can influence the classification of mental disorders.

One important consequence of this debate was a shift in the focus on how sexual disorders are classified. The authors of DSM-III came to believe that the classification system should be concerned primarily with people who were upset or disappointed by their sexual lives, whatever their sexual orientation. They were impressed by numerous indications, in both personal appeals as well as the research literature, that homosexuality, per se, was not invariably associated with impaired functioning. They decided that, in order to be considered a form of mental disorder, a condition ought to be associated with subjective distress or seriously impaired social or occupational functioning.

Though political forces were the immediate trigger for the removal of homosexuality from the diagnostic manual, the stage was set for these events by gradual shifts in society's attitudes toward several aspects of sexual behaviour (Minton, 2002). As more and more people came to believe that reproduction was not the main purpose of sexual behaviour, tolerance for greater variety in human sexuality grew. The revision of the DSM's system for describing sexual disorders was, therefore, the product of several forces, cultural as well as political. ◆

Many people think about culture primarily in terms of exotic patterns of behaviour in distant lands. The decisions regarding homosexuality and premenstrual dysphoric disorder remind us that the values of our own culture play an intimate role in our definition of abnormal behaviour. These issues also highlight the importance of cultural change. Culture is a dynamic process; it changes continuously as a result of the actions of individuals. To the extent that our definition of abnormal behaviour is determined by cultural values and beliefs, we should expect that it will continue to evolve over time.

## Who Experiences Abnormal Behaviour?

Having introduced many of the issues that are involved in the definition of abnormal behaviour, we now turn to another clinical example. The woman in our second case study, Mary Childress, suffered from a serious eating disorder known as *bulimia nervosa*. Her problems raise additional questions about the definition of abnormal behaviour.

As you are reading the case, ask yourself about the impact of Mary's eating disorder on her subjective experience and social adjustment. In what ways are these consequences similar to those seen in Kevin Warner's case? How are they different? This case also introduces another important concept associated with the way that we think about abnormal behaviour: How can we identify the boundary between normal and abnormal behaviour? Is there an obvious distinction between eating patterns that are considered to be part of a mental disorder and those that are not? Or is there a gradual progression from one end of a continuum to the other, with each step fading gradually into the next?

Mary's case illustrates many of the characteristic features of bulimia nervosa. As in

### CASE STUDY **A University Student's Eating Disorder**

Mary Childress was, in most respects, a typical 18-year-old undergraduate at a large university. She was popular with other students and a good student, in spite of the fact that she spent little time studying. She and her boyfriend had been dating for about two years. They got along well, cared about each other very much, and planned to get married after they finished their studies. Everything about Mary's life was relatively normal—except for her bingeing and purging.

Mary's eating patterns were wildly erratic. She preferred to skip breakfast entirely, and often missed lunch as well. By the middle of the afternoon, she could no longer ignore the hunger pangs. At that point, on two or three days out of the week, Mary would drive her car to the drive-in window of a fast-food restaurant. Her typical order included three or four double cheeseburgers, several orders of french fries, and a large milkshake (or maybe two). Then she binged, devouring all the food as she drove around town by herself. Later she would go to a private bathroom, where she wouldn't be seen by anyone, and purge the food from her stomach by vomiting. Afterward, she returned to her room, feeling angry, frustrated, and ashamed.

Mary was 165 cm tall and weighed 50 kg. She was neither fat nor thin, but she believed that her body was unattractive, especially her thighs and hips. She was extremely critical of herself and had worried about her weight for many years. Her weight fluctuated quite a bit, from a low of 44 kg when she was in Grade 11 to a high of 57 during her first year of university. Her mother was a "full-figured" woman and bought most of her clothes at a special store. Mary swore to herself at an early age that she would never let herself gain as much weight as her mother had.

Purging had originally seemed like an ideal solution to the problem of weight control. You could eat whatever you wanted and quickly get rid of it so you wouldn't get fat. Unfortunately, the vomiting became a vicious trap. Disgusted by her own behaviour, Mary often promised herself that she would never binge and purge again, but she couldn't stop the cycle.

For the past year Mary had been vomiting at least once almost every day and occasionally as many as three or four times a day. The impulse to purge was very strong. Mary felt bloated after having only a bowl of cereal and a glass of orange juice. If she ate a sandwich and drank a diet soda, she began to ruminate about what she had eaten, thinking "I've got to get rid of that!" Before long, she usually found a bathroom and threw up. Her excessive binges were less frequent than the vomiting. Four or five times a week she experienced an overwhelming urge to eat "forbidden" foods, especially fast food. Her initial reaction was usually a short-lived attempt to resist the impulse. Then she would space out or "go into a zone," becoming only vaguely aware of what she was doing and feeling. In the midst of a serious binge, Mary felt com-

Kevin's case, her behaviour could be considered abnormal not only because it fit the criteria for one of the categories in DSM-IV-TR but also because she suffered from a dysfunction (in this case, of the mechanisms that regulate eating) that was obviously harmful. The impact of the disorder was on both her physical and emotional health. Eating disorders carry with them a high risk of other mental disorders (e.g., depression with suicidal features) and serious physical disorders that can lead to death (Health Canada, 2002). Eating disorders affect many vital organs of the body, including the heart and kidneys. Mary's social functioning and her academic performance were not yet seriously impaired. There are many different ways in which to measure the harmful effects of abnormal behaviour.

Mary's case also illustrates the subjective pain that is associated with many types of abnormal behaviour. In contrast to Kevin, Mary was acutely aware of her disorder. She was frustrated and unhappy. In an attempt to relieve this

*How thin is too thin? This young dancer suffers from an eating disorder. Some experts maintain that the differences between abnormal and normal behaviour are essentially differences in degree; that is, quantitative differences.*

pletely helpless and unable to control herself. When she first started to binge and purge, Mary had to stick her fingers down her throat to make herself vomit. Now, three years after she began experimenting with this pattern of eating, she could vomit without using her fingers.

There weren't any obvious physical signs that would alert someone to Mary's eating problems, but the vomiting had begun to wreak havoc with her body, especially her digestive system. She had suffered severe throat infections and frequent, intense stomach pains. Her dentist had noticed problems beginning to develop with her teeth and gums, undoubtedly a consequence of constant exposure to strong stomach acids.

Mary's attitudes toward nutrition and health were irrational. Although she sometimes ate 10 or 12 double cheeseburgers a day, Mary insisted that she hated junk food, and she considered herself to be a vegetarian. The meat that she ate didn't count, she reasoned, because she seldom kept it down. For someone who could be described as totally preoccupied with food, she gave little thought to its consumption, never planning her meals. Mary was extremely concerned about the health consequences of obesity. She could cite detailed statistics regarding the increased risks for heart disease that are associated with every additional 2 kg that a person gains over her ideal body weight. Of course, the physical consequences of repeated bingeing and purging are infinitely more severe than those associated with modest weight gain, but this irony was lost on Mary.

Her eating problem started to develop when Mary was 15. She had been seriously involved in gymnastics for several years but eventually developed a knee condition that forced her to give up the sport. She gained a few kilograms in the next month or two and decided to lose weight by dieting. Buoyed by unrealistic expectations about the immediate, positive benefits of a diet that she had seen advertised on television, Mary initially adhered rigidly to its recommended regimen. Six months later, after three of these fad diets had failed, she started throwing up as a way to control her intake of food.

Then her father got sick. He was diagnosed with bone cancer when she was in high school (only a couple of months after she had starting purging), and he died the next year. Everyone in the family was devastated. Mary's mother became seriously depressed. Her brother dropped out of high school after his second year and continued living at home. Mary's eating problems multiplied. Her grades suffered, but she managed to maintain an adequate record to graduate and gain admission to university.

Mary looked forward to leaving home and starting over again at university, but her problem followed her. She felt guilty and ashamed about her eating problems. She was much too embarrassed to let anyone know what she was doing and would never eat more than a few mouthfuls of food in a public place like a cafeteria. Mary managed to conceal her bingeing and purging from her roommate Julie, thanks in large part to the fact that Mary was able to bring her own car to campus. The car allowed her to drive off by herself several times a week so that she could binge.

emotional distress, she entered psychological treatment. Unfortunately, painful emotions associated with mental disorders can also interfere with, or delay, the decision to look for professional help. Guilt, shame, and embarrassment often accompany psychological problems and sometimes make it difficult to confide in another person, even though the average therapist has seen such problems many times over.

## Frequency in and Impact on Community Populations

Many important decisions about mental disorders are based on data regarding the frequency with which these disorders occur. At least 4 percent of university women would meet diagnostic criteria for bulimia nervosa (see Chapter 10). These data are a source of considerable concern, especially among those who are responsible for health services on university campuses.

**Epidemiology** is the scientific study of the frequency and distribution of disorders within a population. Epidemiologists are concerned with questions such as whether the frequency of a disorder has increased or decreased during a particular period of time, whether it is more common in one geographic area than in another, and whether certain types of people—based on such factors as gender, race, and socioeconomic status—are at greater risk than other types for the development of the disorder. Health administrators often use such information to make decisions about the allocation of resources for professional training programs, treatment facilities, and research projects.

Two terms are particularly important in epidemiological research. **Incidence** refers to the number of new cases of a disorder that appear in a population during a specific period of time. **Prevalence** refers to the total number of active cases, both old and new, that are present in a population during a specific period of time. The *lifetime prevalence* of a disorder is the total proportion of people in a given population who have been affected by the disorder at some point during their lives. For example, the incidence of depression may rise in a given year, but the prevalence of that disorder in the general population may remain the same.

How common are the disorders listed in DSM-IV? One large investigation, the Cross-National Collaborative Study, was conducted by Myrna M. Weissman and colleagues (1994, 1996a, 1996b, 1997). Approximately 38 000 people living in communities in 10 countries were interviewed. Questions were asked to diagnose several of the major disorders listed in DSM-IV-TR. Table 1–2 shows some of the results. Notice that gender differences are found for many types of mental disorder: Anxiety disorders (obsessive–compulsive disorder, panic disorder, and social phobia) and major depression are more common among women. Bipolar disorder (also known as manic depressive disorder) is equally common among men and women. Other studies show that alcoholism and antisocial personality disorder are more common among men than women (APA, 2000). Notice also in Table 1–2 how the prevalence of disorders varies across countries; the disorders appear to be least prevalent in Taiwan and Korea, compared to Canada, the United States, and West Germany. Patterns like this raise some interesting questions about possible causal mechanisms. What conditions would make women more vulnerable to one kind of disorder and men more vulnerable to another? Why does the prevalence of disorders vary across cultures? There are many possible reasons, including social pressures, patterns of learning, and biological factors.

Research such as the Cross-National Collaborative Study has also compared one-year prevalence rates—the number of people with active symptoms during the 12 months prior to the interview—and lifetime prevalence rates. In most cases, the lifetime rates are much higher. This discrepancy reflects the fact that mental disorders are not always chronic. Most people experience periods of remission, in which their symptoms improve, between active episodes of disorder. Many people recover completely. Therefore, although the relatively high lifetime prevalence rates for disorders such as major depression (Table 1–2) are a source of serious concern, these common disorders are not always enduring.

The data in Table 1–2 indicate that mental disorders are experienced by many people at some point during their lives. Other studies, in Canada and the United States, suggest that 20 to 30 percent of people receive at least one lifetime diagnosis (Health Canada, 2002a; Offord et al., 1996; Robins & Regier, 1991). This information is important, but epidemiologists agree that the figures include people whose

**TABLE 1–2 Lifetime Prevalence Rates (%) for Various Mental Disorders (Cross-National Collaborative Study)**

| | Canada | | United States | | West Germany | | Taiwan | | Korea | |
|---|---|---|---|---|---|---|---|---|---|---|
| | Women | Men | Women | Men | Women | Men | Women | Men | Women | Men |
| Bipolar disorder | 0.5 | 0.7 | 1.0 | 0.8 | 1.0 | 0.0 | 0.3 | 0.3 | 0.2 | 0.6 |
| Major depression | 12.3 | 6.6 | 7.4 | 2.8 | 13.5 | 4.4 | 1.8 | 1.1 | 3.8 | 1.9 |
| Obsessive–compulsive disorder | 2.7 | 2.0 | 2.8 | 1.7 | 1.9 | 2.5 | 0.9 | 0.5 | 2.0 | 1.7 |
| Panic disorder | 1.9 | 0.9 | 2.3 | 1.0 | 3.8 | 1.4 | 0.6 | 0.2 | 2.9 | 0.5 |
| Social phobia | 2.1 | 1.3 | 3.1 | 2.1 | — | — | — | — | 1.0 | 0.1 |

— Not available.

*Source:* Based on M.M. Weissman et al., 1996a, Cross-national epidemiology of major depression and bipolar disorder. *JAMA, 276,* 293–299; M.M. Weissman et al., 1997, The cross-national epidemiology of panic disorder. *Archives of General Psychiatry, 54,* 305–309; M.M. Weissman et al., 1994, The cross-national epidemiology of obsessive–compulsive disorder. *Journal of Clinical Psychiatry, 55 (suppl. 3),* 5–10; M.M. Weissman et al., 1996b, The cross-national epidemiology of social phobia: A preliminary report. *International Clinical Psychopharmacology, 11 (suppl. 3),* 9–14.

problems are not associated with substantial impairment in functioning (Regier et al., 1998).

**Comorbidity and Disease Burden** Data from another epidemiological investigation—the National Cormorbidity Survey (NCS)—indicate that most severe disorders are concentrated in a small segment of the population. Often these are people who simultaneously qualify for more than one disorder, such as major depression and alcoholism. The presence of more than one condition within the same period of time is known as **comorbidity.** Fourteen percent of the people in the NCS sample had three or more lifetime disorders, and 9 out of 10 people with a severe disorder fell into that highly comorbid group (Kessler & Zhao, 1999). These findings have shifted the emphasis of epidemiological studies from counting the absolute number of people who have any kind of mental disorder to measuring the functional impairment associated with these problems.

Mental disorders are highly prevalent, but how do we measure the extent of their impact on people's lives? And how does that impact compare to the effects of other diseases? These are important questions when policymakers must establish priorities for various types of training, research, and health services.

Epidemiologists measure *disease burden* by combining two factors: mortality and disability. The common measure is based on time: lost years of healthy life, which might be caused by premature death (compared to the person's standard life expectancy) or living with a disability (weighted for severity). For purposes of comparison among different forms of disease and injury, the disability produced by major depression is considered to be equivalent to that associated with blindness or paraplegia. A psychotic disorder such as schizophrenia leads to disability that is comparable to that associated with quadriplegia.

The World Health Organization (WHO) sponsored an ambitious study called the Global Burden of Disease Study, which used these measures to evaluate and compare the impact of more than 100 forms of disease and injury throughout the world (Lopez & Murray, 1998; Murray & Lopez, 1997). Although mental disorders are responsible for only 1 percent of all deaths, they produce 47 percent of all disability in economically developed countries, like Canada, and 28 percent of all disability worldwide. The combined index (mortality plus disability) reveals that, as a combined category, mental disorders are the second leading source of disease burden in developed countries (see Figure 1–1). Investigators in the WHO study predict that, relative to other types of health problems, the burden of mental disorders will increase by the year 2020. These surprising results indicate strongly that mental disorders are one of the world's greatest health challenges.

## Cross-Cultural Comparisons

As the evidence regarding the global burden of disease clearly documents, mental disorders affect people all over the world. That does not mean, however, that the symptoms of psychopathology and the expression of emotional

**Impact of Mental Disorders in People's Lives**

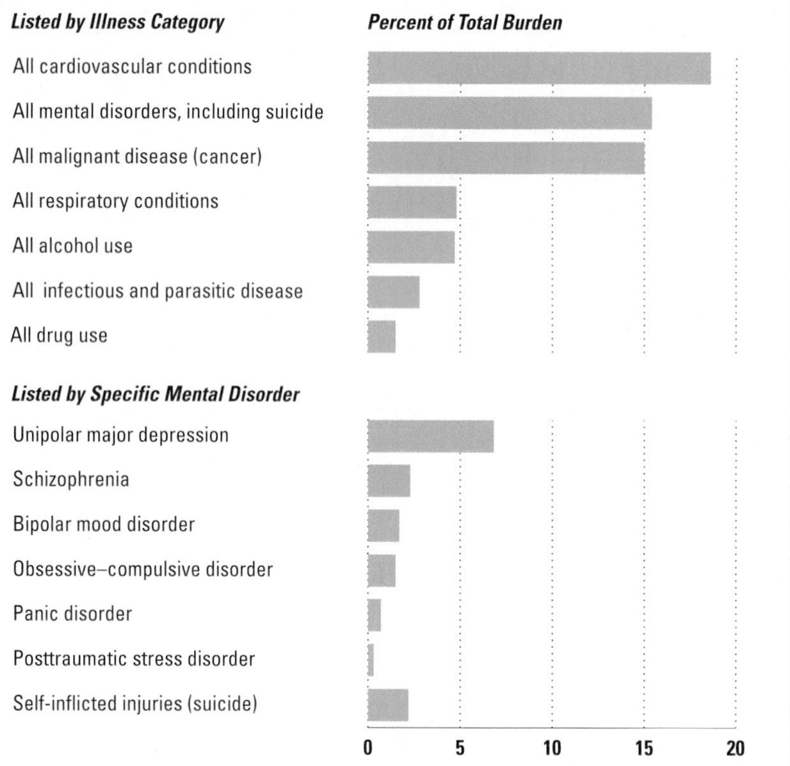


**FIGURE 1–1: Disease burden in economically developed countries measured in disability adjusted life years (DALYs).**

*Source:* C.L. Murray and A.D. Lopez (Eds.), 1996, *The global burden of disease: A comprehensive assessment of mortality and disability from diseases, injuries, and risk factors in 1990 and projected to 2020.* Cambridge, MA: Harvard University Press.

distress take the same form in all cultures. Epidemiological studies comparing the frequency of mental disorders in different cultures suggest that some disorders, like schizophrenia, show important consistencies in cross-cultural comparisons (see Research Close-Up).

Other disorders are more specifically associated with certain cultural and socioeconomic conditions. For example, according to University of Toronto researchers, almost 90 percent of bulimic patients are women (Woodside & Kennedy, 1995). The incidence of bulimia is five times higher among university women than among working women, and it is more common among younger women than among older women. Factors believed to contribute to eating disorders include biological and psychological factors as well as Western society's promotion of the thin body image (Health Canada, 2002a).

The strength and nature of the relationship between culture and psychopathology vary from one disorder to the next. Several general conclusions can be drawn from cross-cultural studies of psychopathology (Draguns, 1994), including the following points:

- All mental disorders are shaped, to some extent, by cultural factors.
- No mental disorders are entirely due to cultural or social factors.
- Psychotic disorders are less influenced by culture than are nonpsychotic disorders.
- The symptoms of certain disorders are more likely to vary across cultures than are the disorders themselves.

We will return to these points as we discuss specific disorders, such as depression,

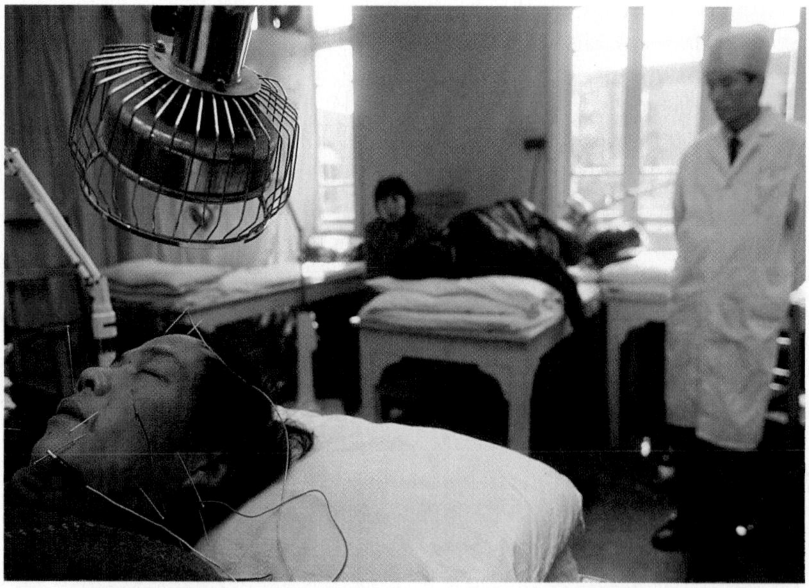

*Mental disorders are found in roughly similar numbers throughout the world, but approaches to treatment vary from one culture to the next. In China, acupuncture is used frequently to treat people who are depressed. Medication and psychotherapy are the most frequently used forms of treatment for depression in Western countries.*

## RESEARCH CLOSE-UP Cross-Cultural Study of Abnormal Behaviour

Some severe forms of psychopathology have been found in virtually every culture that social scientists have studied. One classic paper that supports this conclusion was written by anthropologist Jane Murphy (1976), who studied two groups of non-Western people: the arctic Inuit and the Yoruba of rural, tropical Nigeria in West Africa. Murphy lived with each group for several months, talking with them about their lives and observing their everyday behaviours. She became intimately acquainted with their language and the ways in which they think about problem behaviours.

Murphy discovered that both cultures recognize certain forms of behaviour as "being crazy." These behaviours centre on aberrant beliefs, feelings, and actions: hearing voices when no one is talking; laughing when there is nothing to laugh at; believing things that are so strange that other people cannot imagine them to be true; talking in strange ways that do not make sense to other people; and behaving in erratic or unpredictable ways. These syndromes bear a striking resemblance to the disorder called schizophrenia in DSM-IV-TR. The specific content of hallucinations and delusions varies from one culture to the next, but the underlying processes appear to be the same. Perhaps most important was the observation that the words that the Inuit and Yoruba use to describe "losing one's mind" refer to a set of problematic behaviours rather than to a single problem.

Murphy also noted that members of both groups viewed "crazy behaviour" as being quite different from the behaviours associated with being a shaman or spiritual healer. At certain times, the shaman also behaved in unusual ways, such as responding to voices that other people could not hear or speaking in ways that other people did not understand. This distinction is apparently based primarily on the extent to which these behaviours are controlled (turned on and off voluntarily by the person) and utilized for a socially approved purpose, such as attempting to heal a sick person. One Yoruba villager explained, "When the shaman is healing, he is out of his mind, but he is not crazy." Murphy was able to identify 18 Inuit villagers who had served the group as shaman at some point during their lives. They appeared to be a random sample from the entire group of 500 people. None of them was considered to be mentally disabled by fellow villagers.

The Inuit and Yoruba have their own hypotheses concerning the origins of mental disorders, which often involve magic. They also have developed special treatment procedures, or native healing rituals, that they use to help people with these disorders. These observations indicate that the ways in which societies respond to psychopathology can vary greatly, even if the basic forms of abnormal behaviour with which they are confronted are quite similar.

Murphy's conclusions have been supported by a large-scale epidemiological study of schizophrenia, sponsored by the World Health Organization (WHO) (Jablensky et al., 1992). This study included 1200 patients who were admitted to psychiatric hospitals in nine countries: Colombia, Czechoslovakia, Denmark, India, Nigeria, Taiwan, Russia, England, and the United States. In each setting, the investigators found patients who exhibited symptoms of schizophrenia. The frequency of this disorder was approximately the same in each location, in spite of obvious cultural contrasts between sites in developing (India, Nigeria) and developed (Denmark, England) countries. As in Murphy's report, the WHO study found some cross-cultural variations with regard to the specific subtypes of schizophrenic symptoms and with regard to the outcome of the disorder five years after treatment. Nevertheless, the data support the conclusion that severe forms of mental illness are not limited to Western cultures or developed countries. ◆

phobias, and alcoholism, throughout this book.

## The Mental Health Professions

People receive treatment for psychological problems in many different settings and from various kinds of service providers. Table 1–3, which is based on a survey done in Edmonton, Alberta, shows that specialized mental health professionals, such as psychiatrists, psychologists, and social workers, treat fewer than half (44 percent) of those people who seek help for mental disorders (Bland, Newman, & Orn, 1990). Similar findings were reported in a more recent Ontario study (Goering, Wasylencki, & Durbin, 2000). Another, multiregion survey in the United States also reported a very similar result (40 percent of patients are mainly treated by family doctors: Manderscheid et al., 1999). Table 1–3 shows that most people with mental health problems are treated by family physicians, usually with some form of medication. A smaller proportion of people seek help from other sources, such as social agencies and self-help groups like Alcoholics Anonymous.

Many forms of specialized training prepare people to provide professional assistance to clients suffering from mental disorders. Mental health professionals include clinical psychologists, psychiatrists, social workers,

**TABLE 1–3 Service Utilization for Mental Health Problems**

| Type of Caregiver | Proportion of People with Mental Health Problems Contacting Each Type of Caregiver in the Past Year (%) |
|---|---|
| Family physician | 61 |
| Psychiatrist | 14 |
| Other physician | 14 |
| Clinical psychologist | 16 |
| Social worker | 14 |
| Nurse | 5 |
| Other | 16 |

*Note:* In many cases there was contact with more than one caregiver.

*Source:* R.C. Bland, S.C. Newman, and H. Orn, 1990, Health care utilization for emotional problems: Results from a community survey. *Canadian Journal of Psychiatry, 35,* 397–400.

marriage and family therapists, psychiatric nurses, counsellors, and psychosocial rehabilitation providers. The overall number of professionals providing mental health services continues to grow rapidly, with most of this growth occurring among nonphysicians (Scheffler, Ivey, & Garrett, 1998). Most of these professions require extensive clinical experience in addition to formal academic instruction. In order to provide direct services to clients, psychologists, psychiatrists, social workers, counsellors, nurses, and marriage and family therapists typically need to be licensed in their own specialties by provincial boards of examiners.

**Psychiatry** is the branch of medicine that is concerned with the study and treatment of mental disorders. Psychiatrists complete the normal sequence of coursework and internship training in a medical school (usually four years) before going on to receive specialized residency training (another four years) that is focused on abnormal behaviour. By virtue of their medical training, psychiatrists are licensed to practise medicine and therefore are able to prescribe medication. Most psychiatrists are also trained in the use of psychosocial intervention.

**Clinical psychology** is concerned with the application of psychological science to the assessment and treatment of mental disorders. In Canada, some licensed psychologists hold a master's degree, but most have a Ph.D. (doctor of philosophy). A clinical psychologist usually completes five years of graduate study in a department of psychology, as well as a one-year internship, before receiving a doctoral degree. Clinical psychologists are trained in the use of psychological assessment procedures and in the use of psychotherapy. Within clinical psychology, there are two primary types of clinical training programs. One course of study, which leads to the Ph.D. degree, involves a traditional sequence of graduate training with major emphasis on research methods. The other approach, which culminates in a Psy.D. (doctor of psychology) degree, places greater emphasis on practical skills of assessment and treatment and does not require an independent research project for the dissertation. One can also obtain a Ph.D. degree in *counselling psychology*, a more applied field that focuses on training, assessment, and therapy.

**Social work** is a third profession that is concerned with helping people to achieve an effective level of psychosocial functioning (Peterson et al., 1998). Most practising social workers have a master's degree in social work. In contrast to psychology and psychiatry, social work is based less on a body of scientific knowledge than on a commitment to action. Social work is practised in a wide range of settings, from courts and prisons to schools and hospitals, as well as other social service agencies. The emphasis tends to be on social and cultural factors, such as the effects of poverty on the availability of educational and health services, rather than individual differences in personality or psychopathology. *Psychiatric social workers* receive specialized training in treatment of mental health problems.

Like social workers, *professional counsellors* work in many different settings, ranging from schools and government agencies to mental health centres and private practice. Most are trained at the master's degree level, and the emphasis of their activity is also on providing direct service. *Marriage and family therapy (MFT)* is a multidisciplinary field in which professionals are trained to provide psychotherapy. Most MFTs are trained at the master's level, and many hold a degree in social work, counselling, or psychology as well. Although the theoretical orientation is focused on couples and family issues, approximately half of the people treated by MFTs are seen in individual psychotherapy (Peterson et al., 1998). Psychiatric nursing is a rapidly growing field. Training for this profession typically involves a bachelor's degree in nursing plus specialized training in the treatment of mental health problems.

Another approach to mental health services that is expanding rapidly in size and influence is *psychosocial rehabilitation (PSR)*. Professionals in this area work in crisis, residential, and case management programs for people with severe forms of disorder, such as schizophrenia. PSR workers teach people practical, day-to-day skills that are necessary for living in the community, thereby reducing the need for long-term hospitalization and minimizing the level of disability experienced by their clients. Graduate training is not required for most PSR positions; three out of four people providing PSR services have either a high school education or a bachelor's degree.

It is difficult to say with certainty what the mental health professions will be like in the future. Boundaries between professions change as a function of progress in the development of therapeutic procedures, economic pressures, legislative action, and courtroom decisions. This has been particularly true in the field of mental health, where enormous changes have taken place over the past few decades (Manderscheid et al., 1999; Scheffler, Ivey, & Garrett, 1998). Many psychologists are pursuing the right to prescribe medication (DeLeon, Sammons, & Sexton, 1995). However, in light of the debates among Canadian psychologists (e.g., David Dozois, Keith Dobson, and Louis Pagliaro), and among psychologists in other countries, it is currently unclear whether prescription privileges will enhance the profession of psychology (for example, see Dozois & Dobson, 1995a,b; Pagliaro, 1995).

*Clinical psychologists perform many roles. Some provide direct clinical services. Many are involved in research, teaching, and various administrative activities.*

One thing is certain about the future of the mental health professions: There will always be a demand for people who are trained to help those suffering from abnormal behaviour. Many people experience mental disorders. Unfortunately, most of those who are in need do not get help. In Canada, fewer than half of people with an active mental disorder receive treatment for their condition (Bland, Newman, & Orn, 1997; Lefebvre, Lesage, Cyr, Toupin, & Fournier, 1998). In comparison, in the United States only 20 percent of people with a mental disorder receive treatment (Kessler et al., 1994).

Many factors may account for the failure to receive treatment. Some people who qualify for a diagnosis may not be so impaired as to seek treatment; others, as we shall see, may not recognize their disorder. In some cases, treatment may not be available, the person may not have the time or resources to obtain treatment, or the person may have tried treatments in the past that failed.

## Psychopathology in Historical Context

Throughout history, many other societies have held quite different views of the problems that we consider to be mental disorders. Before leaving this introductory chapter, we must begin to place contemporary approaches to psychopathology in historical perspective.

The search for explanations of the causes of abnormal behaviour dates to ancient times, as do conflicting opinions about the etiology of emotional disorders. References to abnormal behaviour have been found in ancient accounts from Chinese, Hebrew, and Egyptian societies. Many of these records attribute abnormal behaviour to the disfavour of the gods or the mischief of demons. In fact, abnormal behaviour continues to be attributed to demons in some preliterate societies today.

### The Greek Tradition in Medicine

More earthly and less supernatural accounts of the etiology of psychopathology can be traced to the Greek physician Hippocrates (460–377 B.C.), who ridiculed demonological accounts of illness and insanity. Instead, Hippocrates hypothesized that abnormal behaviour, like other forms of disease, had natural causes. Health depended on maintaining a natural balance within the body, specifically a balance of four body fluids (which were also known as the four humours): blood, phlegm, black bile, and yellow bile. Hippocrates argued that various types of disorder, including psychopathology, resulted from either an excess or a deficiency of one of these four fluids. The specifics of Hippocrates' theories obviously have little value today, but his systematic attempt to uncover natural, biological explanations for all types of illness represented an enormously important departure from previous ways of thinking.

The Hippocratic perspective dominated medical thought in Western countries until the middle of the nineteenth century (Golub, 1994). People trained in the Hippocratic tradition viewed "disease" as a unitary concept. In other words, physicians (and others who were given responsibility for healing people who were disturbed or suffering) did not distinguish between mental disorders and other types of illness. All problems were considered to be the result of an imbalance of body fluids, and treatment procedures were designed in an attempt to restore the ideal balance. These were often called "heroic" treatments because they were drastic (and frequently painful) attempts to quickly reverse the course of an illness. They involved bloodletting (intentionally cutting the person to reduce the amount of blood in the body) and purging (the induction of vomiting), as well as the use of heat and cold. These practices continued to be part of standard medical treatments well into the nineteenth century (Starr, 1982).

### The Creation of the Asylum

In Europe during the Middle Ages, "lunatics" and "idiots," as people with mental disorders were commonly called, aroused little interest and were given marginal care. Most people lived in rural settings and made their living through agricultural activities. Disturbed behaviour was considered to be the responsibility of the family rather than the community or the state. Many people were kept at home by their families, and others roamed freely as beggars. People with mental disorders who were violent or appeared dangerous often were imprisoned with criminals. Those who could not subsist on their own were placed in almshouses for the poor.

In the 1600s and 1700s, "insane asylums" were established to house the mentally ill throughout Europe and North America. Mental health services in what was to become Canada were pioneered in Quebec, with the establishment in 1639 of the Hôtel Dieu, founded by the Duchess d'Aiguillon. This was the first asylum to be established in North America. The institution housed not only people with mental disorders but also the poor and people with physical disabilities. Other facilities for the mentally ill were built in Quebec around that time, and during the 1800s were established in other provinces. The mental health institutions in Quebec, unlike those in the rest of Canada, were based on France's colonial administrative practices, whereby the government awarded contracts to religious groups and physicians to develop facilities for treating the mentally ill (Sussman, 1998).

Mental health facilities in Canada were developed on an *ad hoc* basis, with little planning and little coordination among provinces. Often jails or military barracks were converted into asylums (Sussman, 1998). The structure of asylums in the 1800s was different in Canada than in England; in Canada asylums were administered or managed by a superintendent physician, whereas in England asylums were run by government offices and local justices who oversaw the work of the physicians (Bartlett, 2000).

The first privately run asylum in Canada, the Homewood Retreat, was established in 1883 in Guelph. Presaging the private institutions that later developed in the United States and elsewhere, the Homewood Retreat catered to the wealthy, with treatment paid for by patients or their relatives.

Several factors gradually changed the way that society viewed people with mental disorders, and reinforced the relatively new belief that the community as a whole should be responsible for their care (Grob, 1994). Perhaps most important was a change in economic, demographic, and social conditions. In Canada and the United States at the beginning of the nineteenth century there was rapid population growth and the rise of large cities. The increased urbanization of the population was accompanied by a shift from an agricultural to an industrial economy. Lunatic asylums—the original mental hospitals—were created to serve heavily populated cities and to assume responsibilities that had previously been performed by individual families.

Early asylums were little more than human warehouses, but as the nineteenth century began, the moral treatment movement led to improved conditions in at least some mental hospitals. Founded on a basic respect for human dignity and the belief that humanistic care would help to relieve mental illness, moral treatment reform efforts were instituted by leading mental health professionals of the day, such as William Tuke in England, Phillipe Pinel in France, and Benjamin Rush in the United States.

Moral reform efforts were based on the belief that mental disorders were the results of a variety of treatable causes. In line with prevailing beliefs at the time, mental disorders were attributed to a variety of factors, including immoral or excessive behaviour (such as preaching for 16 days and nights, or playing the fife all night), improper living conditions (for example, sleeping in a barn filled with new hay), exposure to unnatural stressors (for example, excessive studying for exams), and physical diseases (for example, measles, small pox) (Hunter, Shannon, & Sambrook, 1986).

Many of the large mental institutions in Canada and elsewhere were built in the nineteenth century as a result of the philosophy of moral treatment. Rather than simply confining mental patients, moral treatment offered support, care, and a degree of freedom. Belief in the importance of reason and the potential benefits of science played an important role in the moral treatment movement. Asylums were constructed in the countryside, segregated from the rest of the community, with the assumption that essential to cure was the removal of the person from the stresses of community and family life, preferably to an institution in the tranquil countryside.

*The first privately run asylum in Canada, the Homewood Retreat, was established in 1883 in Guelph, Ontario.*

In the middle of the 1800s, the mental health advocate Dorothea Dix gave particular impetus to this trend. Dix argued that treating the mentally ill in hospitals was both more humane and more economical than caring for them haphazardly in their communities, and she urged that special facilities be built to house mental patients. Dix and like-minded reformers were successful in their efforts as public mental hospitals gradually spread throughout much of Canada and the United States.

Treatment in the asylums involved a blend of physical and moral procedures. If mental disorders were caused by improper behaviour and difficult life circumstances, presumably they could be cured by moving the person to a more appropriate and therapeutic environment—the asylum. Moral treatment focused on efforts to re-educate the patient, fostering the development of self-control that would allow the person to return to a "healthy" lifestyle. Procedures included occupational therapy, religious exercises, and recreation.

***Dorothea Dix*** *(1802–1887) was an early advocate for the humane treatment of the mentally ill. Many mental institutions were built during the late 1800s due in large part to Dix's efforts.*

Physical treatments included bleeding and purging, which asylum superintendents learned as part of their medical training. Patients who were excited, agitated, or violent were sometimes treated with opium or morphine. Depression was sometimes treated with laxatives. Mechanical restraints were employed only when considered necessary.

Despite the humanitarian goals of the moral reform movement, the nineteenth-century asylums in Canada and elsewhere were typically dirty and overcrowded, housing more patients than the superintendents could realistically treat. Nevertheless, the creation of large institutions for the treatment of mental patients was important because it led to the development of a new profession—psychiatry. By the middle of the 1800s, superintendents of asylums for the insane were almost always physicians who had experience in the care of people with severe mental disorders. The large patient populations within these institutions provided an opportunity for these physicians to observe various types of psychopathology over an extended period of time. They soon began to publish their ideas regarding the causes of these conditions and to experiment with new treatment methods (Grob, 1994).

Superintendents at some asylums claimed very high rates of "cure," often in excess of 90 percent. In fact one superintendent, Dr. Awl, claimed a 100 percent cure rate, earning him the nickname "Dr. Cure-Awl." Such remarkable statistics bore little resemblance to reality and were sometimes based on blatant miscalculations—for example, using only discharge and not admission data, and even counting patients who died as having "recovered" from their mental disorder! (Hunter et al., 1986). Zeal and rivalry among superintendents, and their need to justify the value of their services to the community, served to elevate the reported cure rates.

### Lessons from the History of Psychopathology

The invention and expansion of public mental hospitals set in motion a process of systematic observation and scientific inquiry that led directly to our current system of mental health care. The creation of psychiatry as a professional group, committed to treating and understanding psychopathology, laid the foundation for expanded public concern and financial resources for solving the problems of mental disorders.

There are, of course, many aspects of nineteenth-century psychiatry that, in retrospect, seem to have been naive or misguided. To take only one example, it seems silly to have thought that masturbation would cause mental disorders. In fact, masturbation is now taught and encouraged as part of treatment for certain types of sexual dysfunction (see Chapter 12). The obvious cultural biases that influenced the etiological hypotheses of nineteenth-century physicians seem quite unreasonable today. But, of course, our own values and beliefs influence the ways in which we define, think about, and treat mental disorders. Mental disorders cannot be defined in a cultural vacuum or in a completely objective fashion. The best we can do is to be aware of the problem of bias and include a variety of cultural and social perspectives in thinking about and defining the issues (Manson, 1994).

The other lesson that we can learn from history involves the importance of scientific research. No one today believes "Dr. Cure-Awl's" claim that 100 percent of patients are cured by currently available forms of treatment. During the nineteenth century, physicians were not trained in scientific research methods. Their optimistic statements about treatment outcome were accepted, in large part, on the basis of their professional authority.

Unfortunately, the naive acceptance of idealistic claims has become a regrettable tradition. For the past 150 years, mental health professionals and the public alike have repeatedly embraced new treatment procedures that have been hailed as cures for mental disorders. Perhaps most notorious was a group of somatic (bodily) treatment procedures that was introduced during the 1920s and 1930s (Valenstein, 1986). They included inducing fever, insulin comas, and **lobotomy**, a crude form of brain surgery (see Table 1–4). These dramatic procedures, which have subsequently proved to be ineffective, were accepted with the same enthusiasm that greeted the invention of large public institutions in the nineteenth century. Thousands of patients were subjected to these procedures, which remained widespread until the early 1950s, when more effective pharmacological treatments were discovered. The history of psychopathology teaches us that people who claim that a new form of treatment is effective should be expected to prove it scientifically (see Research Methods).

## Methods for the Scientific Study of Mental Disorders

This book will provide you with an introduction to the scientific study of psychopathology. The application of science to questions regarding abnormal behaviour carries with it the implicit assumption that these problems can be studied systematically and objectively. Such a systematic and objective study is the basis for

**TABLE 1–4 Somatic Treatments Introduced and Widely Employed in the 1920s and 1930s**

| Name | Procedure | Original Rationale |
|---|---|---|
| Fever therapy | Blood from people with malaria was injected into psychiatric patients so that they would develop a fever. | Observation that symptoms sometimes disappeared in patients who became ill with typhoid fever. |
| Insulin coma therapy | Insulin was injected into psychiatric patients to lower the sugar content of the blood and induce a hypoglycemic state and deep coma. | Observed mental changes among some diabetic drug addicts who were treated with insulin. |
| Lobotomy | A sharp knife was inserted through a hole that was bored in the patient's skull, severing nerve fibres connecting the frontal lobes to the rest of the brain. | Observation that the same surgical procedure with chimpanzees led to a reduction in the display of negative emotion during stress. |

*Note:* Lack of critical evaluation of these procedures is reflected in the unusual notoriety bestowed upon their inventors. Julius Wagner-Jauregg, an Austrian psychiatrist, was awarded a Nobel Prize in 1927 for his work in developing fever therapy. Egaz Moniz, a Portuguese psychiatrist, was awarded a Nobel Prize in 1946 for introduction of the lobotomy.

## RESEARCH METHODS

### The Null Hypothesis and the Burden of Proof

Scientists have established a basic and extremely important rule for making and testing any new hypothesis: the scientist who makes a new prediction must prove it to be true. Scientists are not obligated to disprove other researchers' assertions. Until a hypothesis is supported by empirical evidence, the community of scientists assumes that the new prediction is false.

The concepts of the experimental hypothesis and the null hypothesis are central to understanding this essential rule of science. An **experimental hypothesis** is any new prediction made by an investigator. Researchers must adopt and state their experimental hypothesis in both correlational studies and experiments. In all scientific research, the **null hypothesis** is the alternative to the experimental hypothesis. The null hypothesis always predicts that the experimental hypothesis is not true. The rules of science dictate that scientists must assume that the null hypothesis holds until research contradicts it. That is, the burden of proof falls on the scientist who makes a new prediction—who offers an experimental hypothesis.

These rules of science are analogous to rules about the burden of proof that have been adopted in trial courts. In the courtroom, the law assumes that a defendant is innocent until proven guilty. Defendants do not need to prove their innocence; rather, prosecutors need to prove the defendants' guilt. Thus the null hypothesis is analogous to the assumption of innocence, and the burden of proof in science falls on any scientist who challenges the null hypothesis, just as it falls on the prosecutor in a court trial.

These rules in science and in law serve important purposes. Both are conservative principles designed to protect the field from false assertions. Our legal philosophy is that it is better to let a guilty person go free than to punish an innocent person. Scientists adopt a similar philosophy—that false "scientific evidence" is more dangerous than undetected knowledge. Because of these safeguards, we can be reasonably confident when an experimental hypothesis is supported or when a defendant is found guilty.

The value of this conservative approach is obvious when we consider interventions such as institutionalization, medication, and psychotherapy. These are associated with costs, which range from financial considerations, which are certainly important in today's healthcare environment, to the disappointment brought about by false hopes. It is also important to demonstrate that a treatment is not harmful.

The concept of the burden of proof has been extended from scientists developing treatments to practitioners that implement them. The Task Force on Empirically Supported Treatments commissioned by the Canadian Psychological Association recommends that clinicians who provide mental health service should ensure that their treatments are optimally supported by scientific evidence (Hunsley et al., 1999; Hunsley & Johnston, 2000).

There is one more similarity between the rules of science and the rules of the courtroom. Courtroom verdicts do not lead to a judgment that the defendant is "innocent," but only to a decision that she or he is "not guilty." In theory, the possibility remains that a defendant who is found "not guilty" did indeed commit a crime. Similarly, scientific research does not lead to the conclusion that the null hypothesis is true. Scientists never prove the null hypothesis; they only fail to reject it. The reason for this position is that the philosophy of knowledge, epistemology, tells us that it is impossible ever to prove that an experimental hypothesis is false in every circumstance. ◆

finding order in the frequently chaotic and puzzling world of mental disorders. This order will eventually allow us to understand the processes by which abnormal behaviours are created and maintained.

Clinical scientists adopt an attitude of open-minded skepticism, tempered by an appreciation for the research methods that are used to collect empirical data. They formulate specific hypotheses, test them, and then refine them based on the results of these tests. For example, suppose you formulated the hypothesis that people who are depressed will improve if they eat more than a certain amount of chocolate every day. This hypothesis could be tested in a number of ways, using the methods discussed throughout this book. In order to get the most from it, you may have to set aside—at least temporarily—personal beliefs that you have already acquired about mental disorders. Try to adopt an objective, skeptical attitude. We hope to pique your curiosity and share with you the satisfaction, as well as perhaps some of the frustration, of searching for answers to questions about complex behaviour problems.

## The Uses and Limitations of Case Studies

Before we present our first case, we should consider the ways in which case studies can be helpful in the study of psychopathology, as well as some of their limitations. A **case study** presents a description of the problems experienced by one particular person. Detailed case studies can provide an exhaustive catalogue of the symptoms that the person displayed, the manner in which these symptoms emerged, the developmental and family history that preceded the onset of the disorder, and whatever response the person may have shown to treatment efforts. This material often forms the basis for hypotheses about the causes of a person's problems. Descriptions of this sort are especially important for conditions that have not received much attention in the literature and for problems that are relatively unusual. Multiple personality disorder and transsexualism are examples of conditions that are so infrequent that it is difficult to find groups of patients for the purpose of research studies. Much of what we know about these conditions is based on descriptions of individual patients.

Case studies also have several drawbacks. The most obvious limitation of case studies is that they can be viewed from many different perspectives. Any case can be interpreted in several ways, and competing explanations may be equally plausible. Consider, for example, the life of Canadian Glenn Gould, one of the great pianists of the twentieth century. He was famous for his interpretations of classical piano works, including Bach's *Goldberg Variations*, and for his other artistic contributions such as the innovative radio program *The Idea of North*. Yet this eccentric genius suffered from lifelong, and sometimes debilitating, psychological problems. During his childhood and adolescence he displayed unusual behaviours, including marked fears of certain physical objects (for example, red-coloured toys), difficulties empathizing with others, social withdrawal, self-isolation, and ritualized behaviours. These behaviours are suggestive of Asperger's disorder, a variant of autism. As an adult, Gould's musical performances were marked by such eccentricities as humming loudly while playing. He wore layer upon layer of clothing, even during the sweltering summer, for fear of "catching chill." He suffered from bouts of depression, severe anxiety about his health, and psychosomatic symptoms, and was highly anxious about performing in public. These symptoms suggest an anxiety or mood disorder, or possibly a somatoform disorder such as hypochondriasis.

Experts have speculated about the causes of Gould's problems (Ostwald, 1997) and have made conjectures about the influence of biological factors and the effects of his early relationships with his parents. Speculations of this

*Many people lead successful lives and have remarkable achievements in spite of their struggles with mental disorder. Glenn Gould (1932–1982), an acclaimed musical genius, suffered from psychological problems throughout his life, including bouts of severe anxiety, psychosomatic symptoms, and depression.*

## CANADIAN FOCUS Dr. Ewen Cameron and the Allan Memorial Institute

At the height of his career, during the 1950s and 1960s, Dr. D. Ewen Cameron (1901–1967) was one of the most powerful psychiatrists in North America. Cameron spent most of his career directing Montreal's Allan Memorial Psychiatric Institute, which he founded. He became president of several major psychiatric associations, including the Canadian Psychiatric Association, the American Psychiatric Association, and the World Psychiatric Association (Weinstein, 1990).

Cameron was a driven man, working long hours doing research and treating patients. He dreamed of winning the Nobel Prize. He had little patience for conventional therapies of the time, such as psychoanalysis and tranquillizer medications, which he thought were too slow and too weak. Cameron was a man in a hurry. He wanted to speed up the process of therapy and find powerful cures for such mental disorders as schizophrenia (Collins, 1997). But he went terribly wrong, and many patients suffered as a result.

Cameron developed an experimental treatment called *psychic driving,* which he intended as a "brainwashing" method for eradicating all kinds of bad "behaviour patterns" (i.e., psychiatric symptoms) (Gillmor, 1987). The method involved making audiotapes of the patient's psychotherapy sessions, and from these creating short tapes containing the most important things the patient said. These would be played over and over again, piped over headphones in the patient's room. The patient would listen to the tapes for up to 16 hours a day, for months on end. For the first few months, the tapes would consist entirely of negative statements, such as "I am weak and inadequate." Later on, positive statements would be introduced, such as "People like me."

Listening to the tapes was a tormenting experience, and many patients refused to comply. In response, Cameron gave some patients curare, a drug that paralyzes the skeletal muscles, so patients had no choice but to lie in bed and listen to their tapes. Cameron also put some patients into a deep sleep—a coma—by administering insulin or tranquillizers. The tapes were played while the patients slept. To enhance the effects of psychic driving, some patients were given such powerful psychoactive drugs as LSD.

A problem with psychic driving was that it typically had no beneficial effect on the patient's symptoms, and sometimes seemed to make them worse. Part of the problem was that patients sometimes misinterpreted the messages. One patient, Jane, had trouble achieving sexual intimacy with her husband. To treat this problem, Cameron put her into a deep sleep for months while she listened to the message "Jane, you are at ease with your husband." He then awoke her and asked her to repeat back the message in order to check what she had been processing. She said, "Jane, you are a tease with your husband" (Gillmor, 1987).

Faced with the limitations of psychic driving, Cameron added an intervention he called *depatterning,* designed to further eradicate bad behaviour patterns. This method typically involved putting patients into a deep sleep, and then giving them massive doses of electroconvulsive therapy—sometimes 10 shocks per day for months on end (Gillmor, 1987). Long periods of sensory deprivation were also used. Once the depatterning had "prepared" patients, they were then given months of psychic driving.

After they had been "depatterned," patients were like zombies; confused, mute, and robotic, standing in puddles of their own urine. They couldn't recognize friends or relatives, were unable to feed themselves, and couldn't control their bowels or bladder (Collins, 1997). The patients typically recovered to some extent, although many were left with memory problems. Some former patients remained unable to care for themselves for the rest of their lives.

The CIA learned of Cameron's treatments and saw the possibilities for developing brainwashing methods for military purposes (Gillmor, 1987). Accordingly, the CIA funded Cameron's research for a number of years. Funding was stopped once the CIA learned that Cameron's methods were worthless (Weinstein, 1990).

At the time most psychiatrists and psychologists also thought that Cameron's methods were not helpful and possibly dangerous. When Cameron retired from the Allan Memorial Institute, psychic driving and depatterning were discontinued. Several patients later sued the CIA and Cameron's estate for the harm they had suffered as a result of these "treatments." The Canadian government also paid out compensation to over 75 of Cameron's former patients (Collins, 1997).

Cameron was not an evil man; he was an impatient man whose judgment was blinded by his driving ambition for fame and power (Gillmor, 1987; Weinstein, 1990). Nevertheless, much of his work constitutes a dark chapter in the history of Canadian psychiatry.

Fortunately, these days the treatments administered by psychiatrists and clinical psychologists are far different. Electroconvulsive therapy is still used—but carefully applied and only for highly selected psychiatric problems. Psychotherapy and judicious use of medications are the mainstay for treating many mental disorders. Treatments are administered only with the patient's consent, or the consent of his or her caregiver. ◆

sort are intriguing, particularly when they concern someone who played such an important role in the history of music. But we must remember that case studies do not tell us anything conclusive about the causes of psychopathology. In the case of Glenn Gould, psychiatric biographers cannot even agree on the diagnosis. Questions about the causes of mental disorders must be resolved through scientific investigation.

The other main limitation of case studies is that it is risky to draw general conclusions about a disorder from a single example. How can we know that this individual is representative of the disorder as a whole? Are his or her experiences typical for people with this disorder? Again, hypotheses generated on the basis of the single case must be tested in research with larger, more representative samples of patients.

### Clinical Research Methods

The importance of the search for new information about mental disorders has inspired us to build a special feature into this textbook. Each chapter includes a Research Methods feature that explains one particular research issue in some detail. The Research Methods feature in this chapter, for example, is concerned with the null hypothesis, the need to consider not just that your hypothesis may be true, but also that it may be false. A list of the issues addressed in Research Methods throughout this textbook appears in Table 1–5. They are arranged to progress from some of the more basic research methods and issues, such as correlational and experimental designs, toward more complex issues, such as genetic linkage analysis and heritability.

We decided to discuss methodological issues in small sections throughout the book, for two primary reasons. First, the problems raised by research methods are often complex and challenging. Some students find it difficult to digest and comprehend an entire chapter on research methods in one chunk, especially at the beginning of a book. Thus we have broken it down into more manageable bites. Second, and perhaps more important, the methods we discuss generally make more sense and are easier to understand when they are presented in the context of a clinical question they can help answer. Our discussions of research methods are, therefore, introduced while we are explaining contemporary views of particular clinical problems.

Research findings are not the end of the road, either. The fact that someone has managed to collect and present data on a particular topic does not mean that the data are useful. We want you to learn about the problems of designing and interpreting research studies so that you will become a more critical consumer of scientific evidence. If you do not have a background in research design or quantitative methods, the Research Methods features will

**TABLE 1–5 List of Research Methods Featured in This Book**

| Chapter | Topic |
|---|---|
| 1 | The Null Hypothesis and the Burden of Proof |
| 2 | The Correlational Study |
| 3 | The Experiment |
| 4 | Diagnostic Reliability |
| 5 | Analogue Studies of Psychopathology |
| 6 | Statistical Significance and Clinical Importance |
| 7 | Retrospective Reports |
| 8 | Longitudinal Research Designs |
| 9 | Cross-Cultural Comparisons |
| 10 | Credible Placebo Control Groups |
| 11 | Risk, Risk Factors, and Studies of People at Risk |
| 12 | Hypothetical Constructs |
| 13 | Meaningful Comparison Groups |
| 14 | Genetic Linkage Analysis |
| 15 | Central Tendency, Variability, and Standard Scores |
| 16 | Samples and Sampling |
| 17 | The Concept of Heritability |
| 18 | Base Rates and Predictions |

familiarize you with the procedures that psychologists use to test their hypotheses. If you have already had an introductory course in methodology, they will show you how these problems are handled in research on abnormal behaviour.

# Summary

One of our goals in this chapter is to make you more familiar with certain symptoms of **psychopathology**. We have described two relatively common forms of mental disorder: schizophrenia and bulimia nervosa. Schizophrenia is a severe form of mental disorder, a **psychosis**, in which the person is out of touch with reality. Bulimia nervosa is an eating disorder that involves recurrent episodes in which the person cannot control what (or how much) he or she eats. These episodes of binge eating are followed by efforts to prevent weight gain, such as self-induced vomiting. These and many other types of mental disorder are described in greater detail in subsequent chapters of this book.

Mental disorders are defined in terms of typical signs and symptoms rather than identifiable causal factors. A group of symptoms that appear together and are assumed to represent a specific type of disorder is called a **syndrome**. There are no definitive psychological or biological tests that can be used to confirm the presence of psychopathology. At present, the diagnosis of mental disorders depends on observations of the person's behaviour and descriptions of personal experience.

No one has been able to provide a universally accepted definition of abnormal behaviour. Statistical infrequency and subjective distress cannot be used for this purpose because not all infrequent behaviours are pathological and because some people who exhibit abnormal behaviours do not have insight into their conditions. One useful approach defines mental disorders in terms of **harmful dysfunction**. The official classification system, DSM-IV-TR, defines mental disorders as a group of persistent maladaptive behaviours that result in personal distress or impaired functioning.

Various forms of voluntary social deviance and efforts to express individuality are excluded from the DSM-IV-TR definition of mental disorders. Political and religious actions, and the beliefs on which they are based, are not considered to be forms of abnormal behaviour, even when they seem unusual to many other people. We must recognize, however, that the process of defining psychopathology is still influenced by **culture**.

The scientific study of the frequency and distribution of disorders within a population is known as **epidemiology**. Some severe forms of abnormal behaviour, such as schizophrenia, have been observed in virtually every society that has been studied by social scientists. There are also forms of psychopathology—including eating disorders—for which substantial cross-cultural differences have been found. These epidemiological patterns may provide important clues that will help identify factors that influence the causes of mental disorders.

Some of the best information that is currently available on the epidemiology of mental disorders was conducted in epidemiologic studies such as the Cross-National Collaborative Study. These studies suggest that in Canada the lifetime **prevalence** rate for at least one form of mental disorder may be 20 percent or more. Significant gender differences have been found for several types of mental disorder, including anxiety disorders, mood disorders, and alcoholism. Although a very large number of people experience a mental disorder at some time during their lives, most severe disorders are concentrated in a smaller segment of the population (14 percent) that is characterized by a high rate of **comorbidity**. The global burden of mental disorders is very high. They are responsible for 47 percent of all disability in economically developed countries like Canada and 28 percent of all disability worldwide.

Many forms of specialized training prepare people to provide professional help to those who suffer from mental disorders. Psychiatry is a branch of medicine that is concerned with the study and treatment of mental disorders. A **psychiatrist** is licensed to practise medicine and is therefore able to prescribe medication. A **clinical psychologist** has received graduate training in the use of assessment procedures and psychotherapy. Most psychologists also have extensive knowledge regarding research methods, and their training prepares them for the integration of science and practice. Many other professions are also actively involved in the delivery of mental health services. These include social workers, professional counsellors, and psychiatric nurses.

Throughout history, many societies have held different ideas about the problems that we consider to be mental disorders. Asylums were created in Europe, Canada, and the United States during the 1600s and 1700s to house people who were mentally disturbed. Although the earliest asylums were little more than human warehouses, the moral treatment movement led to improved conditions in some mental hospitals. The existence of large institutions for mental patients led to the development of psychiatry as a profession. These physicians, who served as the superintendents of asylums, soon began to develop systems for describing, classifying, and treating people with various types of mental disorder. Their efforts led to the use of scientific methods to test these new ideas.

Scientific methods must be employed in the search for knowledge about mental disorders. A person who proposes a new theory about the causes of a form of psychopathology, or someone who advocates a new treatment procedure, should be expected to prove these claims with scientific evidence. The burden of proof falls on the clinical scientist who offers a new prediction, such as the claim that a particular kind of therapy is effective. In other words, the **null hypothesis** (the alternative to the **experimental hypothesis**) is assumed to be true until it is contradicted by systematic data. Individual **case studies** do not provide conclusive evidence about the causes of, or treatments for, mental disorders.

# Critical Thinking

1. What does it mean for a behaviour to be classified as "abnormal"? Why is it so difficult to produce an abstract definition of abnormal behaviour? Some people argue that psychopathology is nothing more than the list of disorders presented in the *Diagnostic and Statistical Manual*. Do you agree? Can you provide a better definition?
2. Do you think it is possible to eliminate social values from a definition of abnormal behaviour? How would you accomplish this goal? Is there any way of defining mental disorders that would avoid value judgments about which behaviours are adaptive and which are not?
3. The growth of large cities and industrialization led to the creation of large asylums for the mentally disturbed (people who had previously been treated individually by their own families). What kinds of economic and political changes have occurred in our own society over the past few years that might change the way we provide services to people with mental disorders?
4. Case studies provide interesting descriptions of problems, but they don't help us choose among different causal theories. They also don't prove that a particular form of therapy is effective. What kinds of limitations do you see with case studies? Why should we be careful about drawing general conclusions from them?

# Key Terms

**abnormal psychology** 3
**case study** 22
**clinical psychology** 16
**comorbidity** 13
**culture** 9
**epidemiology** 12
**experimental hypothesis** 21
**harmful dysfunction** 7
**incidence** 12
**lobotomy** 20
**null hypothesis** 21
**prevalence** 12
**psychiatry** 16
**psychopathology** 3
**psychosis** 5
**social work** 16
**syndrome** 5

# 2 Causes of Abnormal Behaviour: A Systems Approach

Overview
Brief Historical Perspective: Twentieth-Century Paradigms
Systems Theory
Biological Factors
Psychological Factors
Social Factors

**Why are psychological paradigms outdated?**

**What is the systems approach?**

**How do nature and nurture combine to affect abnormal behaviour?**

**Can difficult life experiences cause psychological problems?**

The search for the causes of different emotional problems is a tale of mystery and suspense, and we are still searching for more clues. Psychologists have developed some good leads, and we follow up on those leads in this chapter. With the exception of a few disorders, however, scientists have not yet solved the case of the cause of abnormal behaviour. We do not yet know how the mystery ends, but we do know one thing: the causes of abnormal behaviour are as complex as the determinants of normal behaviour. With very rare exceptions, abnormal behaviour is not caused by something as simple as a "broken brain." As with normal behaviour, explaining most cases of abnormal behaviour involves unearthing a conspiracy of causes, not a lone culprit.

## Overview

This idea that abnormal behaviour is an enduring puzzle, may surprise you, because the popular media often report on the cause, or *etiology*, of abnormal behaviour under the headline "Case Solved!" Magazine articles explain that depression is caused by a chemical imbalance in the brain. Television advertisements claim that alcoholism is a genetic disease. Books and films portray emotional disturbances as stemming from traumatic childhood experiences. Unfortunately, such media accounts almost always reflect a misleading and oversimplified rush to judgment. They pick one factor out of the lineup of causes, because it makes a good story—and because it is reassuring to think that we have arrested the culprit.

Like the popular media, scientists have offered some oversimplified explanations of the causes of abnormal behaviour. In the twentieth century, psychologists commonly debated the accuracy of four broad theories of abnormal behaviour—the biological, psychodynamic, cognitive behavioural, and humanistic paradigms. A **paradigm** is a set of shared assumptions that includes both the substance of a theory and beliefs about how scientists should collect data and test the theory. Thus, the four paradigms disagreed not only about what causes abnormal behaviour, as we review shortly, but also about how to study it. Fortunately, most psychologists have moved beyond arguing for—or against—a single paradigm, because most forms of psychopathology do not have a single cause.

Contemporary psychologists recognize that abnormal behaviour is determined by *multifactorial causes*, the combination of a variety of biological, psychological, and social factors. In this chapter and throughout the text, we consider multifactorial causes using **systems theory**, an approach that integrates evidence on different biological, psychological, and social influences on abnormal behaviour. Thus, systems theory is often referred to as the *biopsychosocial approach*. Biological contributions to abnormal behaviour range from specific biochemical processes in the brain to broad genetic liabilities passed across generations. Psychological contributions range from automatic cognitive processes to reinforcement for abnormal behaviour. Social and cultural contributions range from conflict in family relationships to gender and racial bias.

Systems theory embraces the task of gathering and integrating evidence on the causes of abnormal behaviour into a coherent whole (Rutter & Rutter, 1993). In so doing, scientists must be honest and admit that we have *not* solved the mystery of what causes most forms of abnormal behaviour. We

*In the fall of 1989, Marc Lépine went on a shooting rampage at the Ecole Polytechnique in Montreal, killing 14 women and injuring 15 others, and then turned the gun on himself. Such horrific events make us desperate to know why, but most abnormal behaviour defies easy explanation.*

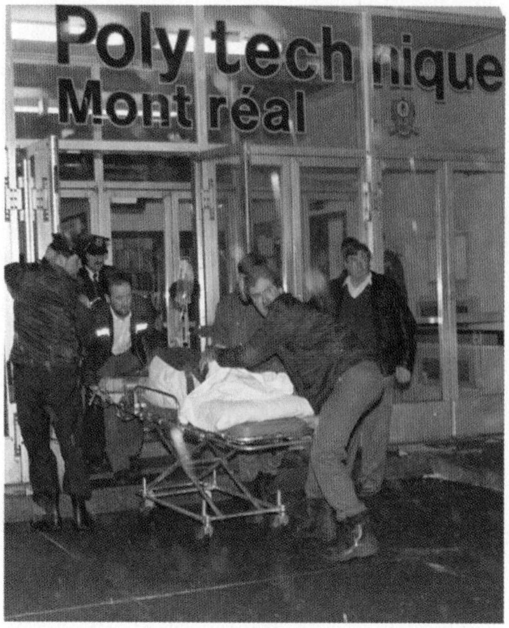


sometimes are frustrated and disappointed that we have not yet solved this case, particularly when accurate answers could help so many people. Still, we are constantly re-energized by the excitement of our detective work—by the process of scientific inquiry and by the need and the potential to find answers that will offer real benefit to so many real people.

In this chapter, we briefly review the four broad paradigms and explain how systems theory has emerged to replace them. We also outline a number of biological, psychological, and social factors that contribute to the development of emotional problems. In later chapters, we return to these concepts when discussing evidence on the causes of specific psychological disorders. Throughout these discussions, we not only share our best clues—the latest research evidence—we also introduce you to the complex, frustrating, and exciting detective work of the psychological scientist. As with every chapter in this text, we begin our investigation with a case study. Most cases, including the following one, come from our own therapy files.

What was causing Meghan's problems? Her case study suggests many plausible alternatives. Some of her troubles seem to be a reaction to a mother whose attentiveness at age 8 seems intrusive at age 14. Maybe Mrs. B.

## CASE STUDY **Meghan's Many Hardships**

At the age of 14, Meghan B. attempted to end her life by taking approximately 20 Tylenol capsules. Meghan took the pills after an explosive fight with her mother over Meghan's grades and over a boy she was dating. Meghan was in her room when she impulsively took the pills, but shortly afterward she told her mother what she had done. Her parents rushed Meghan to the emergency room, where her vital signs were closely monitored. As the crisis was coming to an end, Meghan's parents agreed that she should be hospitalized to make sure that she was safe and to begin to treat her problems.

Meghan talked freely about many of her problems during the 30 days she spent on the adolescent unit of a psychiatric hospital. Most of her complaints focused on her mother. Meghan insisted that her mother was always "in her face," telling her what to do and when and how to do it. Her father was "great," but he was too busy with his job as a chemical engineer to spend much time with her.

Meghan also said she had longstanding problems in school. She barely maintained a C average despite considerable efforts to do better. Meghan said she didn't care about school, and her mother's insistence that she could do much better was a major source of conflict between them. Meghan also complained that she had few friends, either in or outside of school. She was obviously angry as she described her family, school, and friends, but she also showed sadness on a few occasions. She denounced herself as being "stupid" one time, and she cried about being a "reject" when discussing why no friends, including her boyfriend, contacted her while she was in the hospital.

Mrs. B. provided details on the history of Meghan's problems. When Meghan was 2 years old, she had been adopted by Mr. and Mrs. B., who could not have children of their own. According to the adoption agency, Meghan's birth mother was 16 years old when she had the baby. Meghan's biological mother was a drug user, and she haphazardly left the baby in the care of friends and relatives for weeks at a time. Little was known about Meghan's biological father except that he had had some trouble with the law, and Meghan's mother had known him only briefly. When Meghan was 14 months old, her pediatrician reported her mother to a child abuse protection agency after noting bruises on Meghan's thighs and hips.

After a six-month legal investigation, Meghan's mother agreed to give her up for adoption. Meghan came to live with Mr. and Mrs. B. shortly thereafter.

Mrs. and Mr. B. were very loving with Meghan, although Mrs. B., like Meghan, noted that Mr. B. was rarely at home. Everything seemed fine with Meghan until first grade, when teachers began to complain about her. She disrupted the classroom with her restlessness, and she

*continued*

*cont.*

did not complete her schoolwork. In Grade 2, a school psychologist suggested that Meghan was a "hyperactive" child who also had a learning disability, and her pediatrician recommended medication as a treatment. Mrs. B. was horrified by the thought of medication or of sending Meghan to a "resource room" for part of the school day. Instead, she decided to redouble her efforts at parenting.

According to Mrs. B., she and Meghan succeeded in getting Meghan through elementary school in reasonably good shape. Meghan's grades and classroom behaviour remained acceptable as long as Mrs. B. consulted repeatedly with the school. Mrs. B. noted with bitterness, however, that the one problem that she could not solve was Meghan's relationships with other girls. The daughters of Mrs. B.'s friends and neighbours were well behaved and were excellent students. Meghan did not fit in with them. They were polite when they saw her, but Meghan never got invited to play with the other girls.

Mrs. B. had had major conflicts with Meghan ever since Meghan started middle school at the age of 12. Meghan would no longer work regularly with her mother on her homework for the usual two hours each night. In addition, her mother said that Meghan fought with her about everything from picking up her room to her boyfriend, an 18 year old whom Mrs. B. abhorred. Mrs. B. complained that she did not understand what had happened to her daughter. She clearly stated, however, that whatever it was, she would fix it. ◆

became more concerned with her own needs for love than with Meghan's changing needs for parenting. However, Meghan's problems seem bigger than this. We could trace some of her troubles to anger over her failures in school or to rejection by her peers. We also can speculate about the effects of Meghan's early childhood experiences. Surely she was affected adversely by the physical abuse, inconsistent love, and chaotic living arrangements during the first, critical years of her life, but could those distant events account for all of her current problems? Finally, we can wonder about possible biological contributions to Meghan's problems. Did Meghan's mother take drugs during pregnancy that affected the developing baby? Was Meghan a healthy, full-term newborn? Given her biological parents' history of troubled behaviour, could Meghan's problems be caused by genetic factors?

These searching questions defy a ready answer. Abnormal psychology does not have objective tools for pinpointing the specific cause of most types of abnormal behaviour. Still, psychological theory and research do offer some good leads. We introduce current approaches to understanding the causes of psychopathology by first considering them in historical perspective.

## Brief Historical Perspective: Twentieth-Century Paradigms

The search for explanations of the causes of abnormal behaviour dates to ancient times. Unfortunately, many of the traditions begun by Hippocrates died away after the fall of the Roman Empire. Systematic, naturalistic accounts of mental illness were kept alive in Arab cultures (Grob, 1994), but the emphasis on objectivity and careful observation faded in Europe. Fear of witches abounded during the Middle Ages, and witch hunts were conducted with fervour under the formal sanctions of the Roman Catholic Church. However, witchcraft was not the dominant explanation of mental illness. In examining records from British mental incompetency trials dating back to the thirteenth century, Neugebauer (1979) uncovered only one case where officials judged that "lunacy" (a medieval synonym for mental illness) was caused by witches. Explanations that seem reasonable even today were much more frequent—for example, "a blow received on the head," "a long and incurable infirmity," "her husband's death," and "fear of his father" (Neugebauer, 1979).

The rudiments of the scientific method were rediscovered during the Renaissance (approximately 1300–1600), but the scientific method was not applied to the study of abnormal behaviour until much later. In fact, advances in the scientific understanding of abnormal behaviour were not made until the nineteenth and early twentieth centuries, when three major events occurred. One was the discovery of the cause of general paresis, a severe mental disorder that has a deteriorating course and eventually ends in death. The second was the writing of Sigmund Freud, a thinker who has had a profound influence not only on the field of abnormal psychology but also on Western society as a whole. The third was the creation of a new academic discipline called psychology.

## General Paresis and the Biological Paradigm

The **biological paradigm** looks for biological abnormalities that might cause abnormal behaviour. The roots of the biological paradigm can be traced to the study of the condition we now know as *general paresis* (general paralysis). Prior to 1800, general paresis was not recognized as a distinct disorder and therefore attracted no special attention. In 1798, John Haslam distinguished general paresis from other forms of "lunacy" based on its symptoms, which include delusions of grandeur, cognitive impairment (dementia), and progressive paralysis. General paresis also has an unremitting course and ends in death after many years. The diagnosis inspired a search for the cause of the newly recognized disorder. Many different hypotheses were considered and evaluated, and most correctly focused on biological explanations. Still, it took more than 100 years of searching for clues before the mystery was solved.

The breakthrough began with the discovery that people with general paresis had contracted the sexually transmitted disease *syphilis* earlier in their lives. However, even this correct observation was not without missteps. One study conducted by Fournier in 1894, for example, concluded that only 65 percent of paretic patients reported having a history of syphilis. Thus questions were raised about whether syphilis alone caused general paresis. Research conducted in 1897 by Kraft Ebbing demonstrated that Fournier's statistic was wrong. Kraft Ebbing attempted to inoculate paretic patients against syphilis, but none of them became infected when exposed to a mild form of the disease. There could be only one explanation for their body's failure to respond to the inoculation: The patients' reports were wrong, as all of them—not 65 percent of them—had been infected with syphilis previously.

***Sigmund Freud*** *(1856–1939) developed psychoanalytic theory. Freud's approach has been criticized as being unscientific, but the influence of his ideas is unquestionable.*

After the turn of the twentieth century, the spirochete that causes syphilis was discovered. Postmortem examination of the brains of paretic patients proved that the infection had invaded and destroyed parts of the central nervous system. In 1910, Paul Ehrlich, a German microbiologist, developed arsphenamine, an arsenic-containing chemical that destroyed the spirochete and prevented general paresis. Unfortunately, the drug worked only if the patient was treated in the early stages of infection. Later, it was learned that syphilis could be cured by another new discovery, penicillin—the first antibiotic. As a result, general paresis was virtually eliminated when antibiotics became widely available after the end of World War II.

The slow but dramatic discoveries about general paresis gave great impetus to the search for biological causes for other mental disorders. For some problems, the biological approach has been successful in establishing etiology. This is most notable for the cognitive disorders (see Chapter 14) and for many forms of mental retardation (see Chapter 15). Unfortunately, the causes of most forms of mental illness are not as straightforward as for general paresis. Like heart disease and cancer, most mental disorders appear to be "lifestyle diseases" with multifactorial causes, including biological, psychological, and social contributions. These disorders may defy straightforward etiological explanations.

## Freud and the Psychodynamic Paradigm

The **psychodynamic paradigm** asserts that abnormal behaviour is caused by unconscious conflicts stemming from early childhood experiences. This paradigm is solidly rooted in the work and writings of a single individual, Sigmund Freud (1856–1939). Freud was trained as a neurologist and remained interested in biology throughout his life. However, experiences early in his career convinced Freud that abnormal behaviour is caused by mental events that occur outside of conscious awareness, and he spent his lifetime developing an elaborate theory based on this central premise. Many of Freud's contemporaries derided his ideas, but he had an enormous influence on psychology and psychiatry in the twentieth century.

Freud was trained in Paris by Jean Charcot (1825–1893), a neurologist who successfully used hypnosis to treat a disorder that used to be called *hysteria*. Hysteria is characterized by unusual physical symptoms; for example, "hysterical blindness" is the inability to see. The blindness is not caused by an organic impairment, and the afflicted individual may recover sight after resolving an emotional problem.

Freud observed that hysterical patients neither faked their symptoms, nor did they consciously associate them with emotional distress. Thus he suggested that, outside of their conscious awareness, the patients' psychological conflicts somehow were "converted" into physical symptoms. (In fact, such problems are now called *conversion disorder*, as we discuss in Chapter 7). The peculiar problem of hysteria led Freud to believe that many memories, motivations, and protective psychological processes are unconscious, and this basic assumption was the impetus for his elaborate **psychoanalytic theory**. (The term *psychoanalytic theory* refers specifically to Freud's theorizing; the broader term *psychodynamic theory* includes not only Freudian theory but also the revisions of his followers, as we discuss in Chapter 3.)

Psychoanalytic theory divides the mind into three parts: the id, the ego, and the superego. The **id** is present at birth and is the source of basic drives and motivations. The id houses biological drives, such as hunger, as well as two key psychological drives: sex and aggression. (Freud's term *libido* means sexual or life energy.) In Freudian theory, the id operates according to the *pleasure principle*—the impulses of the id seek immediate gratification and create discomfort or unrest until they are satisfied. Thus, in Freud's view, sexual or aggressive urges are akin to biological urges, like hunger.

The **ego** is the part of the personality that must deal with the realities of the world as it attempts to fulfill id impulses as well as perform other functions. Thus the ego operates on the *reality principle*. The ego begins to develop in the first year of life, and it continues to evolve, particularly during the preschool years. Unlike id impulses, which are primarily unconscious, much of the ego resides in conscious awareness.

The third part of the personality is the **superego**, which is roughly equivalent to the conscience. The superego contains societal standards of behaviour, particularly rules that children learn from trying to be like their parents in their later preschool years. In Freud's view, societal rules are attempts to govern id impulses, which means that the three parts of the personality are often in conflict with one another. The ego must constantly mediate between the demands of the id and the prescriptions of the superego. According to Freud, conflict between the superego and the ego produces *moral anxiety*, whereas conflict between the id and the ego produces *neurotic anxiety*.

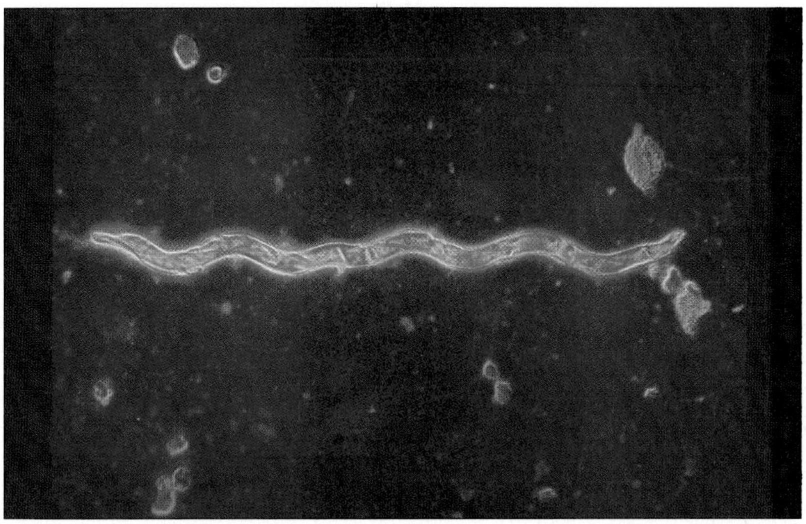

*A microscopic image of the spirochete that causes syphilis and eventually causes general paresis if the syphilis goes untreated.*

Freud suggested that the ego protects itself by utilizing various **defence mechanisms**, unconscious self-deceptions that reduce conscious anxiety by distorting anxiety-producing memories, emotions, and impulses. For example, the defence of *projection* turns the tables psychologically. When you use projection, you project your own feelings onto someone else: "I'm not mad at you. You're mad at me!" A list of some of the more familiar defences can be found in Table 2–1. Freud's profound influence is demonstrated by the fact that many defence mechanisms are a part of everyday language; they also appear in an appendix in DSM-IV-TR on issues requiring further study.

Freud also created a stage theory of development. He suggested that sexual conflicts marked each stage of his theory of *psychosexual development*. The most important psychosexual conflict is the *Oedipal conflict*, which centres around boys' forbidden sexual desires for their mothers. Because these impulses are both overwhelming and impossible to fulfill, boys typically resolve the dilemma by *identifying* with their fathers between the ages of 4 and 6. According to Freud, boys fulfill their desire for their mother by adopting the actions and values of her spouse. In Freud's view, girls face a similar dilemma, which he termed the *Electra complex*. Freud hypothesized that girls, unlike boys, do not desire their opposite gender parent sexually as much as they yearn for something their fathers have and they are "missing"—a penis. This is the Freudian notion of "penis envy."

**TABLE 2-1 Some Freudian Defence Mechanisms**

| | |
|---|---|
| **Denial** | Insistence that an experience, memory, or need did not occur or does not exist. For example, you completely block a painful experience from your memory. |
| **Displacement** | Feelings or actions are transferred from one person or object to another that is less threatening. For example, kicking your dog when you are upset with your boss. |
| **Projection** | Attributing one's own feelings or thoughts to other people. For example, a husband argues that his wife is angry at him when, in fact, he is angry at her. |
| **Rationalization** | Intellectually justifying a feeling or event. For example, after not getting the offer, you decide that a job you applied for was not the one you really wanted. |
| **Reaction Formation** | Converting a painful or unacceptable feeling into its opposite. For example, you "hate" a former lover, but underneath it all you still really love that person. |
| **Repression** | Suppressing threatening material from consciousness but without denial. For example, you "forget" about an embarrassing experience. |
| **Sublimation** | Diverting id impulses into constructive and acceptable outlets. For example, you study hard to get good grades rather than giving in to desires for immediate pleasure. |

It is not difficult to criticize Freud for being overly sexual and blatantly sexist. We also can readily criticize psychoanalytic theory for other reasons, most basically for being vague and untestable. Still, we recognize that Freud offered a host of innovative and penetrating ideas. We view Freud's ideas as broad metaphors that can be valuable in the abstract but not in the specifics. Freud proposed many challenging concepts, and there is substantial research support for some general aspects of his theorizing—for example, that much mental processing occurs outside of conscious awareness (Weston, 1998).

## Psychology, Learning, and the Cognitive Behavioural Paradigm

The **cognitive behavioural paradigm** views abnormal behaviour—and normal behaviour—as the result of different forms of learning. Like the biological and psychodynamic paradigms, the foundations of the cognitive behavioural paradigm can be traced to the nineteenth century, specifically to 1879, when Wilhelm Wundt (1842–1920) began the science of psychology at the University of Leipzig. Wundt's substantive contributions to psychology were limited, in large part because, like Freud, he mistakenly relied on introspection as a scientific tool. Still, Wundt made a profound and lasting contribution by introducing the scientific study of psychological phenomena, including learning.

Learning theorists who followed Wundt had much more success using observations of behaviour rather than introspection as their basic scientific tool. The two most prominent contributors to early learning theory and research were Ivan Pavlov (1849–1936) and B.F. Skinner (1904–1990). These psychological scientists articulated, respectively, the principles of classical conditioning and operant conditioning—concepts that continue to be central to contemporary learning theory.

In his famous experiment, Pavlov (1928) rang a bell every time he fed meat powder to dogs. After repeated trials, the salivation that was produced by the sight of food came to be elicited by the sound of the bell alone. This renowned experiment illustrates Pavlov's theory of **classical conditioning**. Classical conditioning is learning through association, and it involves four key components. There is an *unconditioned stimulus* (the meat powder), a stimulus that automatically produces the *unconditioned response* (salivation). A *conditioned stimulus* (the bell) is a neutral stimulus that, when repeatedly paired with an unconditioned stimulus, comes to produce a *conditioned response* (salivation).[1] Finally, **extinction** occurs once a conditioned stimulus no longer is paired with an unconditioned stimulus. Eventually, the conditioned stimulus no longer elicits the conditioned response.

Skinner's (1953) principle of **operant conditioning** asserts that behaviour is a

[1] Note that the unconditioned response and the conditioned response are very similar (both involve salivation in this example). One difference, though, is that conditioned responses generally are somewhat weaker than unconditioned responses.

function of its consequences. Specifically, behaviour increases if it is rewarded, and it decreases if it is punished. In his numerous studies of rats and pigeons, Skinner identified four different, crucial consequences of behaviour. *Positive reinforcement* occurs when the onset of a stimulus increases the frequency of behaviour (for example, you get paid for your work). *Negative reinforcement* occurs when the cessation of a stimulus increases the frequency of behaviour (when you give in to a nagging friend, thereby stopping the nagging). *Punishment* occurs when the introduction of a stimulus decreases the frequency of behaviour (you spend less money after your parents scold you); and *response cost* is when the removal of a stimulus decreases the frequency of behaviour (you no longer stay out late after your parents take away use of the car).[2] *Extinction* results from ending the contingency or association between a behaviour and its consequences, similar to the concept of extinction in classical conditioning.

The person most responsible for applying learning theory to the study of abnormal behaviour was John B. Watson (1878–1958). Watson called his approach *behaviourism*, arguing that observable behaviour was the only appropriate subject matter for the science of psychology. Watson believed that thoughts and emotions could not be measured objectively; thus he rejected the study of these "internal events." In contrast to Freud, Watson did not offer an elaborate theory of the causes of abnormal behaviour, as he and others who followed him were more concerned with treatment than etiology. However, Watson did make the very important assumption that abnormal behaviour was learned in much the same manner as normal behaviour.

Psychologists after Pavlov, Skinner, and Watson continued to view abnormal behaviour as learned, to emphasize treatment over etiology, and to focus strongly on observable behaviour. However, research increasingly highlighted the importance of cognitive processes in learning; thus "cognitive" is an appropriate modifier for "behavioural" when naming this paradigm.

[2]People frequently use the terms *negative reinforcement* and *punishment* interchangeably, but the two are quite different. With negative reinforcement, behaviour becomes more frequent after an aversive stimulus is removed. With punishment, behaviour becomes less frequent after an aversive stimulus is introduced.

## Free Will and the Humanistic Paradigm

The **humanistic paradigm** argues that the very essence of humanity is *free will*, the belief that human behaviour is a voluntary choice, not a product of internal or external events. The humanistic paradigm is also distinguished by its explicitly positive view of human behaviour. It assumes that human nature is inherently good, and humanistic psychologists blame dysfunctional, abnormal, or aggressive behaviour on society, not on the individual (see Table 2–2). Major advocates of these beliefs included Abraham Maslow (1908–1970), Fritz Perls (1893–1970), and Carl Rogers (1902–1987).

In many respects, the humanistic paradigm was a reaction against *determinism*, the basic assumption that human behaviour is caused by potentially knowable internal and/or external events (an assumption made by the other three paradigms). Because free will, by definition, is not predictably determined, it is impossible to conduct research on the causes of abnormal behaviour within the humanistic paradigm. For this reason, the approach perhaps is best considered an alternative philosophy of human behaviour, not as an alternative psychological theory. (The philosophical debate between free will and determinism also creates conflicts between psychology and law, as we discuss in Chapter 18.) Finally, a note of caution about the appealing term "humanistic": *All* of the paradigms are humanistic in the sense that their ultimate goal is to improve the human condition.

*Psychologist **B.F. Skinner** (1904–1990) outlined the principles of operant conditioning. Skinner's determination to make psychology a science profoundly influenced the discipline in the twentieth century.*

## The Problem with Paradigms

The various paradigms disagree not only about what causes abnormal behaviour but also about how to study it (see Table 2–2). As noted by the influential historian and philosopher Thomas Kuhn (1962), such strong assumptions can both direct and misdirect scientists. Paradigms can tell a researcher or clinician where and how to find answers to questions, but sometimes the apparent guidance can be a hindrance. The idea that a paradigm can be either enlightening or blinding can be illustrated by a brain teaser. Try to solve the following enigma, written by Lord Byron, before looking ahead for the answer:

> I'm not in earth, nor the sun,
> nor the moon.

**TABLE 2-2 Comparison of Biological, Psychodynamic, Cognitive Behavioural, and Humanistic Paradigms**

| Topic | Biological | Psychodynamic | Cognitive Behavioural | Humanistic |
|---|---|---|---|---|
| Inborn human nature | Competitive, but some altruism | Aggressive, sexual | Neutral—a blank slate | Basic goodness |
| Cause of abnormality | Genes, neurochemistry, physical damage | Early childhood experiences | Social learning | Frustrations of society |
| Type of treatment | Medication, other somatic therapies | Psychodynamic therapy | Cognitive behaviour therapy | Nondirective therapy |
| Paradigmatic focus | Bodily functions and structures | Unconscious mind | Observable behaviour | Free will |

You may search all the sky—
I'm not there.
In the morning and evening—
though not at noon,
You may plainly perceive me,
for like a balloon,
I am suspended in air.
Though disease may possess me,
and sickness and pain,
I am never in sorrow nor gloom;
Though in wit and wisdom
I equally reign
I am the heart of all sin and have
long lived in vain;
Yet I ne'er shall be found in the tomb.

What is this poem about? The topic of this rhyme is not the soul or ghosts. It is not life or shadows, or a dozen other possibilities that may have occurred to you. Rather, the topic is the letter *i* (suspended in a<u>i</u>r, the heart of all s<u>i</u>n). Why is the puzzle so difficult to solve? Because most people assume that the solution lies in the content of the poem, not in its form. This illustrates one of Kuhn's central points about paradigms. The assumptions made by a paradigm can act as blinders; they can lead an investigator to overlook what otherwise might be obvious. However, paradigms also can open up new perspectives. For example, now that you have been able to adopt a new "paradigm"—to focus on the form, not the content of words—you can easily solve the following puzzle:

The beginning of eternity, the end of time and space,
The beginning of every end, the end of every place.
It is obvious that the answer is the letter *e*.

Like your initial approach to the brain teaser, the four traditional paradigms make assumptions about the causes of abnormal psychology that can be too narrow. The biological paradigm can overemphasize the *medical model*, the analogy between physical and psychological illnesses, and the approach can locate too many problems "within the skin" of the individual. The psychodynamic paradigm can be unyielding in focusing on the past and the unconscious, even in the face of current life difficulties. The approach also often fails to offer testable hypotheses and relies on case studies instead of systematic research. The cognitive behavioural paradigm can be too literal in focusing on observable events, and it can overlook both biology and the rich social context of human behaviour. Finally, the humanistic approach is antiscientific, for reasons we have already discussed.

In short, each of the paradigms has strengths—and weaknesses. As with the word puzzles, the trick is knowing when to use what strategy. Systems theory has the goal of achieving this flexibility.

## Systems Theory

*Systems theory* integrates evidence on the causes of abnormal behaviour across biological, psychological, and social factors. The roots of this theory lie not only in psychology but also in engineering, computer science, biology, and philosophy.

### Holism

A central principle of systems theory is **holism**, the idea that the whole is more than the sum of its parts. This common statement can be illustrated with numerous familiar examples across many disciplines. A water molecule ($H_2O$) is much more than the sum of two hydrogen atoms and one oxygen atom. A human being is much more than the sum of a nervous system, an organ system, a circulatory system, and so on. Similarly, abnormal psychology is more than the sum of inborn temperament, early childhood experiences, and learning history, or of nature and nurture.

**Reductionism** We can better appreciate the importance of holism when we consider its scientific counterpoint, reductionism. **Reductionism** assumes that the whole is the sum of its parts, and attempts to understand problems by focusing on smaller and smaller units. According to the principle of reductionism, ultimate explanations are found when problems are reduced to their smallest possible components.

The influence of reductionism is pervasive in everyday thinking about the causes of abnormal behaviour. For example, when scientists discover that the depletion of certain chemicals in the brain accompanies depression, the public assumes that brain chemistry is *the* cause of depression. However, it is entirely possible that experiences such as a negative view of the world or living in a prejudiced society cause the changes in brain chemistry that accompany depression. That is, the "chemical imbalance in the brain" may be merely a consequence of adverse life experiences. Unfortunately, the public, and many scientists, seem to overlook this possibility, because reductionism assumes that truth comes in smaller and smaller packages.

**Levels of Analysis** Within and across disciplines, scientists focus on different *levels of analysis* in trying to understand the causes of abnormal behaviour (Hinde, 1992). In fact, the various academic disciplines can be ordered according to whether they focus on a more molar or more molecular level of analysis (Schwartz, 1982; see Table 2–3). Each discipline uses a different "lens" to analyze a subject; one is a microscope, another a magnifying glass, and the third a telescope.

Systems theory asserts that no single academic discipline has a corner on the truth. Rather, systems theory assumes that different academic disciplines—and biological, social, and psychological influences on abnormal behaviour—are explanations at different levels of analysis. Like Russian dolls, accounts at different levels of analysis are nested one inside the other. Each has value for different purposes, and systems theory strives to understand both the parts and the whole.

## Causality

We want you to recognize that the biological, psychological, and social explanations of abnormal behaviour can be compatible ways of conceptualizing etiology that differ only in terms of level of analysis (Cacioppo et al., 2000). It is also true, however, that the cause of any one type of abnormal behaviour might be located primarily within biological, psychological, or social functioning. Scientists hope to identify such specific causes for at least some psychological problems. Our caution, however, is that, at present, we can only rarely attribute differences in functioning to specific abnormalities in biology, psychology, or social systems. For example, we know that the depletion of certain chemicals in the brain is *correlated* with depression, but we do not know whether depression is *caused* by an abnormal chemical imbalance. (See Research Methods for a discussion of correlational studies and the difference between correlation and causation.) It is possible that difficult life experiences actually cause both the depression and the chemical

*Water is more than the sum of two hydrogen atoms and one oxygen atom. According to systems theory, human behaviour—both normal and abnormal—is greater than the sum of genes, emotion, and cognition.*

**TABLE 2–3 Ordering Academic Disciplines by Level of Analysis**

| Level of Analysis | Academic Discipline |
|---|---|
| Beyond Earth | Astronomy |
| Supranational | Ecology, economics |
| National | Government, political science |
| Organizations | Organizational science |
| Groups | Sociology |
| Organisms | Psychology, ethology, zoology |
| Organs | Cardiology, neurology |
| Cells | Cellular biology |
| Biochemicals | Biochemistry |
| Chemicals | Chemistry, physical chemistry |
| Atoms | Physics |
| Subatomic particles | Subatomic physics |
| Abstract systems | Mathematics, philosophy |

*Source:* Based on G.E. Schwartz, 1982, Testing the biopsychosocial model: The ultimate challenge facing behavioral medicine. *Journal of Consulting and Clinical Psychology, 50,* 1040–1053.

imbalance. As another example, we know that parental divorce is correlated with emotional problems among children, but we cannot be certain that divorce causes the problems (Emery, 1999a). It is possible, for example, that genetically determined personality traits influence both marital status and children's well-being (McGue & Lykken, 1992).

**The Diathesis-Stress Model and Multiple Risk Factors** Most emotional problems apparently have multifactorial causes that include biological, psychological, and social factors. One useful way of conceptualizing how multiple events can interact to produce a mental disorder is the *diathesis-stress model*. A **diathesis** is a predisposition toward developing a disorder, for example, an inherited tendency toward depression. A **stress** is a difficult experience, for example, the loss of a loved one through an unexpected death. The diathesis-stress model suggests that mental disorders develop only when a stress is added on top of a predisposition; neither the diathesis nor the stress alone is sufficient to cause the disorder (Zuckerman, 1999).

We commonly think of a diathesis as biological—for example, a genetic predisposition. However, a psychological characteristic can also be a diathesis, such as perfectionism. According to Paul Hewitt (University of British Columbia) and Gordon Flett (York University), there are various forms of perfectionism, which contribute to depression and other forms of psychopathology (see Flett & Hewitt, 2002).

Although it is a useful simplification, one limitation of the diathesis-stress model is the implication that disorders are caused by the combination of only two risk factors, a diathesis and a stress. **Risk factors** are events or circumstances that are correlated with an increased likelihood or risk of a disorder and potentially contribute to causing the disorder. As we have noted, mental disorders appear to be produced by the combination of many different biological, psychological, and social risk factors.

*What caused this accident? A narrow road? A drunk driver? Faulty brakes? A combination of all three factors? Like car accidents and unlike diseases such as general paresis or polio, we will never discover a single cause of mental illnesses, because they have many causes, not one.*

**Equifinality and Multifinality** Another limitation of the diathesis-stress model is that the *same* disorder may have several *different* causes. This is the principle of **equifinality**. There are many routes to the same destination (or disorder), and in fact, we use the term *multiple pathways* as a synonym for equifinality. In some circumstances, many risk factors are involved in the disorder's etiology. In other cases, a single risk factor may be so powerful that it alone produces the disorder.

To help you appreciate the principle of equifinality, let us pose a simple question: What causes automobile accidents? Of course, automobile accidents have many different causes. An accident may be caused by a single defect, such as faulty brakes or a drunk driver. Or it may be caused by a combination of risk factors, such as excessive speed, a wet road, and worn tires. It would be fruitless to search for *the* cause of automobile accidents because they have many causes, not one.

The best evidence indicates that mental illnesses (and many physical illnesses, such as cancer or heart disease) are like car accidents; there are multiple pathways to most mental disorders and multiple risk factors involved in many of these alternative pathways. For example, it appears that depression may be caused primarily by abnormal brain chemistry in some cases, by a pessimistic style of interpretation in other cases, by a serious personal loss in further cases, and by a combination of these and other factors in still other cases.

Equifinality has a mirror concept, the principle of *multifinality*: The *same* event can lead to *different* outcomes. For example, the principle of multifinality indicates that not all childhood experiences (e.g., child abuse) lead to the same adult outcome. Throughout the text, you will repeatedly see examples of this principle, as it seems that the human psyche is indeed a very complex system.

## RESEARCH METHODS

### The Correlational Study

Scientists have developed sophisticated methods for conducting research. The most basic scientific tools are the correlational study and the experiment. In a **correlational study**, the relation between two variables (their co-relation) is studied in a systematic fashion. For example, is there a relationship between parents' substance abuse and substance-use problems in their children? Kristin von Ranson, currently at the University of Calgary, found that parents with substance-use disorders were more likely to have daughters who use and abuse nicotine, alcohol, and illicit drugs (von Ranson, McGue, & Iacono, 2003).

An important statistic for measuring how strongly two variables are related is the **correlation coefficient**. The correlation coefficient is a number that always ranges between −1.00 and +1.00. If all psychology majors got 100 percent correct on a test of research methods and all biology majors got 0 percent correct, the correlation between academic major and research knowledge would be 1.00. If all psychology and biology majors got 50 percent of the items correct, the correlation between major and knowledge would be zero.

Positive correlations (from 0.01 to 1.00) indicate that as one variable goes up, the other variable also goes up. For example, height and weight are positively correlated, as are years of education and employment income. Taller people weigh more; educated people earn more money.

Negative correlations (from −1.00 to −0.01) indicate that as one number gets bigger, the other number gets smaller. For example, research at the University of British Columbia has shown that patients are more likely to prematurely drop out of therapy if they perceive the treatment to be low in credibility (Taylor, 2003). Two variables are more strongly correlated when a correlation coefficient has a higher absolute value, regardless of whether the sign is positive or negative.

A number of variables may be correlated with psychological problems and putatively cause the disorders. The levels of neurotransmitters in the brain are positively correlated with some emotional problems (they are elevated in comparison to normal), and they are negatively correlated with other types of emotional problems (they are depleted in comparison to normal). However, a correlation between two variables must be interpreted cautiously. In particular, you should always remember that correlation does not mean causation.

In interpreting any correlation, there are always two alternative explanations to making a causal conclusion: **reverse causality** and third-variable alternative interpretations. We might want to conclude that X causes Y—that depleted neurotransmitters cause depression. However, the concept of reverse causality indicates that causation could be operating in the opposite direction: Y could be causing X. Depression could be causing the depletion of neurotransmitters.

The **third-variable** possibility offers yet another alternative to causal interpretations. A correlation between any two variables could be explained by their joint relation with some unmeasured factor—a third variable. For example, stress might cause both depression and the depletion of neurotransmitters.

Let us return to the above-mentioned study of psychology and biology majors to illustrate these issues further. Assume that you did find that psychology majors know more about research methods. Based on this correlational finding, could you conclude that studying psychology causes students to learn more about research? No, you could not. A reverse causality interpretation of the correlation might suggest that people who know more about research methods decide to become psychology majors. Knowledge about research causes them to choose this major, not vice versa. A third-variable interpretation of the correlation might suggest that more intelligent people choose to major in psychology, and more intelligent people also know more about the methods of scientific research. According to this interpretation, the correlation between academic major and research knowledge is spurious, an artifact of the relation of both of these variables with the third variable of intelligence.

Another method of research, the experiment, does allow scientists to determine cause and effect relations. However, it often is impractical or unethical to conduct experiments on psychological problems, whereas correlational studies can be conducted with far fewer practical or ethical concerns. Thus the correlational method has the weakness that correlation does not mean causation; but it has the strength that it can be used to conduct research in many real-life circumstances. ◆

**Reciprocal Causality** **Reciprocal causality**, the idea that causality is bidirectional, is one of the most important processes identified by systems theory (von Bertalanffy, 1968). Reciprocal causality is most easily understood when contrasted with *linear causality*, a scientific corollary of reductionism. According to linear assumptions, causation operates in one direction only: Parents cause their children to behave in a certain way, for example. Both formal reviews of the literature and informal observations by millions of parents indicate, however, that children also change their parents' behaviour (Maccoby, 1992). Such mutual influences define reciprocal causality, a process that occurs in all types of natural interaction.

The related concept of **homeostasis**—the tendency to maintain a steady state, is familiar in biology, but it is also widely applicable in psychology. For example, people attempt to maintain a balance between too little stimulation and too much stress or anxiety. Some people are thrill seekers. They find that challenging activities like skydiving provide the right balance between the push of boredom and the pull of excitement. Other people are timid, and they find an equilibrium between the need for novelty and fear of the unknown in a limited and carefully controlled world. The setpoints for optimal levels of stimulation differ like the hotter and cooler settings on a thermostat, but all people engage in the homeostatic process of finding an individualized balance between too little and too much stimulation.

### Developmental Psychopathology

Change is also essential in systems, and *development* is the most basic source of change. Over time, people follow a fairly predictable trajectory of change. Children learn to crawl, walk, and run in an established sequence, and their cognitive skills also unfold in a predictable manner. Development, though, is not limited to children or to the physical and intellectual domains. Development continues throughout adult life, and predictable changes occur in both psychological and social experiences.

Because people develop and change over time, knowledge of normal development is essential to understanding psychopathology. **Developmental psychopathology** is a new approach to abnormal psychology that emphasizes the importance of *developmental norms*—age-graded averages—to determine what constitutes abnormal behaviour (Cicchetti & Cohen, 1995; Rutter & Garmezy, 1983). Developmental norms tell us that a full-blown temper tantrum is normal at 2 years of age, for example, but that kicking and screaming to get one's own way is abnormal at the age of 22. Similarly, we need to understand the developmental progression of a difficult psychological experience like normal grief in order to recognize when mourning should be considered pathological (too intense) or unresolved (too long-lasting).

For these reasons, we frequently consider questions about normal development in this textbook. We also discuss the development of abnormal behaviour itself. Many psychological disorders follow unique developmental patterns. Sometimes there is a characteristic **premorbid history**, a pattern of behaviour that precedes the onset of the disorder. People with schizophrenia, for example, often are withdrawn and awkward before the onset of their psychosis.

A disorder may also have a predictable course, or **prognosis**, for the future. When schizophrenia is untreated, the psychotic symptoms may improve, but day-to-day coping becomes less adequate. By discussing the premorbid adjustment and the course of different psychological disorders, we hope to present abnormal behaviour as a moving picture of development and not just as a diagnostic snapshot.

The remainder of this chapter is divided into sections on biological, psychological, and social factors in the development of psychopathology. In each of these sections we focus most of our discussion on normal development. This material forms a basis for our critical consideration of the causes of abnormal behaviour in subsequent chapters on specific psychological disorders.

## Biological Factors

We begin our discussion of biological factors affecting mental functioning by considering the smallest anatomic unit within the nervous system—the neuron or nerve cell. Next, we present an overview of the major brain structures and current knowledge of their primary behavioural functions. We then turn to a discussion of psychophysiology, the effect of psychological experience on the functioning of various body systems. Finally, we consider the broadest of all biological influences, the effect of genes on behaviour.

In considering biological influences, it is helpful to note the distinction between the study of biological structures and of biological functions. The field of *anatomy* is concerned with the study of biological structures, and the field of *physiology* investigates biological functions. *Neuroanatomy* and *neurophysiology* are subspecialties within these broader fields that focus specifically on brain structures and brain functions. The study of neuroanatomy and neurophysiology is the domain of an exciting, multidisciplinary field of research called *neuroscience*.

## The Neuron and Neurotransmitters

Billions of tiny nerve cells—**neurons**—form the basic building blocks of the brain. Each neuron has four major anatomic components: the soma, or cell body, the dendrites, the axon, and the axon terminal (see Figure 2–1).

The *soma*—the cell body and largest part of the neuron—is where most of the neuron's metabolism and maintenance are controlled and performed. The *dendrites* branch out from the soma; they serve the primary function of receiving messages from other cells. The *axon* is the trunk of the neuron. Messages are transmitted down the axon toward other cells with which a given neuron communicates. Finally, the *axon terminal* is the end of the axon where messages are sent out to other neurons (Barondes, 1993).

Within each neuron, information is transmitted as a change in electrical potential that moves from the dendrites and cell body, along the axon, toward the axon terminal. The axon terminal is separated from other cells by a **synapse**, a small gap filled with fluid. Neurons typically have synapses with thousands of other cells (see Figure 2–2).

Unlike the electrical communication within a neuron, information is transmitted chemically across a synapse to other neurons. The axon terminal contains *vesicles* containing chemical substances called **neurotransmitters**, which are released into the synapse and are received at the **receptors** on the dendrites or soma of another neuron. Dozens of different chemical compounds serve as neurotransmitters in the brain, and the functions of particular neurotransmitters vary. Moreover, different receptor sites are more or less responsive to particular neurotransmitters.

Not all neurotransmitters cross the synapse and reach the receptors on another neuron. The process of **reuptake**, or reabsorption, captures some neurotransmitters in the synapse and returns the chemical substances to the axon terminal. The neurotransmitter then is reused in subsequent neural transmission.

In addition to the neurotransmitters, a second type of chemical affects communication in the brain. *Neuromodulators* are chemicals that may be released from neurons or from endocrine glands (which we discuss shortly). Neuromodulators can influence communication among many neurons by affecting the functioning of neurotransmitters (Ciaranello et al., 1995). Neuromodulators often affect regions of the brain that are quite distant from where they were released.

### The Neuron

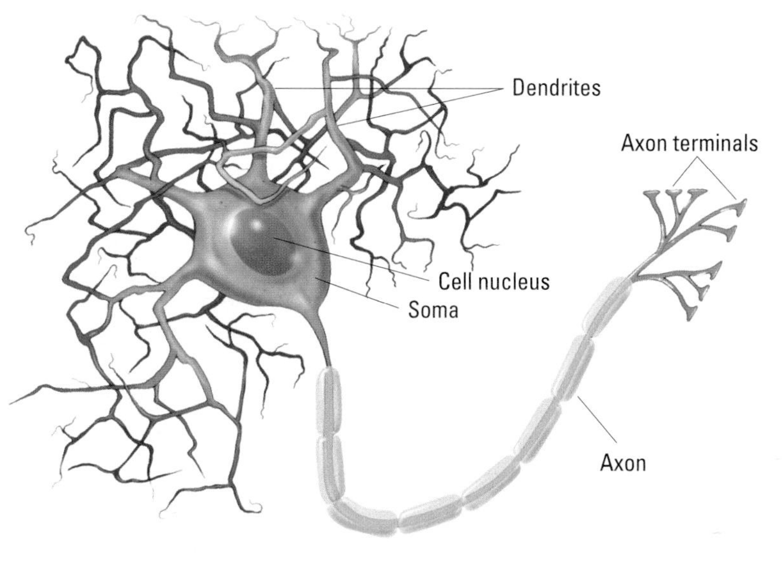


**FIGURE 2–1: The anatomic structure of the neuron, or nerve cell.**

*Source:* Adapted from *Fundamentals of Human Neuropsycology*, 2nd ed., by Brian Kolb and Ian Q. Whislaw. © 1980, 1985, by W.H. Freeman and Company. Reprinted with permission.

## Neurotransmitters and the Etiology of Psychopathology

Scientists have found that disruptions in the functioning of various neurotransmitters are

### Synaptic Transmission

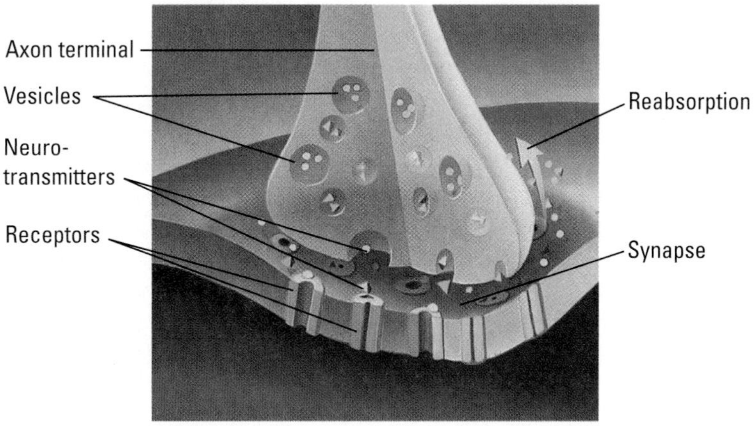


**FIGURE 2–2: When an electrical nerve impulse reaches the end of a neuron, synaptic vesicles release neurotransmitters into the synapse. The chemical transmission between cells is complete when neurotransmitters travel to receptor sites on another neuron.**

*Source:* Keith Kasnot, © National Geographic Image Collection.

present among some people with mental disorders. An oversupply of certain neurotransmitters is found in some mental disorders, an undersupply in other cases, and disturbances in reuptake in other psychological problems. In addition, the density and/or sensitivity of receptors has been implicated as playing a role in some forms of abnormal behaviour.

Much research linking mental disorders with neurotransmitters has investigated how drugs affect the symptoms of a disorder and how they alter brain chemistry. For example, medications that alleviate some of the symptoms of schizophrenia are known to affect the availability of the neurotransmitter *dopamine* in the brains of animals (see Chapter 13). These and related findings suggest that abnormalities in the dopamine system in the brain may be involved in the development of schizophrenia. Other evidence links differences in the availability of various neurotransmitters with depression, hyperactivity, posttraumatic stress disorder, and many other psychological problems, as we discuss throughout the text. As we discuss in Further Thoughts, however, the identification of biochemical differences definitely does *not* mean that these problems are caused by "a chemical imbalance in the brain," even though many people (including many mental health professionals) mistakenly leap to this conclusion.

### Neural Networks

In an effort to better understand brain function, neuroscientists and computer scientists working in the field of artificial intelligence have been developing and testing neural network models of normal and abnormal brain function. These are models in which layers of neurons are connected to one another by axons and dendrites. The connections can be modi-

## Further Thoughts Mind–Body Dualism

Neuroscientists have made exciting findings about brain functioning, and new medications are constantly being developed that have more benefits and fewer side effects in treating certain mental disorders. The technical and practical advances are exciting, but the exciting breakthroughs in neuroscience should not cloud our reasoning about the etiology of psychopathology. In particular, we must not equate a neurophysiological *explanation* of a psychological disorder with the identification of a biological *abnormality.* We have already discussed our concerns about biological reductionism in this regard. Another potential problem stems from **dualism**, the philosophical view that the mind and body are somehow separable.

Dualism dates to the writings of the French philosopher René Descartes (1596–1650), who attempted to balance the dominant religious views of his times with emerging scientific reasoning. Descartes recognized the importance of studying human biology, but he wished to elevate human spirituality beyond that of other animals. In so doing, he argued that many human functions have biological explanations, but some human experiences have no somatic representation. Thus he argued for a distinction—a dualism—between mind and body.

Similar attempts to separate the psyche and the soma have clouded thinking for centuries. One contemporary dualism is that biological explanations may account for psychological abnormalities, but normal psychological experience is somehow independent of biology. Because of this persistent notion of dualism, biological explanations of psychological experience sometimes are erroneously equated with the identification of an abnormality. However, no aspect of the psychological world exists apart from the physical world. Just as a computer software program has an invisible electronic representation in the hardware of microchips, all psychological experience must have an underlying representation in the brain (Turkheimer, 1998; Valenstein, 1998). Even love must have a biochemical explanation, a fact that Calvin ponders in the accompanying cartoon. Love will still be love (we hope) even after scientists identify the "chemical imbalance in the brain" that explains it. The same logic applies to biochemical explanations of psychopathology, which cannot be automatically equated with biochemical abnormalities. ◆

CALVIN AND HOBBES © Watterson. Dist. by UNIVERSAL PRESS SYNDICATE. Reprinted with permission. All Rights Reserved.

fied so that neurons can vary in their excitatory or inhibitory effects on one another. The connections change as a function of experience, according to various rules or algorithms. In other words, the networks can demonstrate learning.

One of the pioneers in this approach was Donald O. Hebb at McGill University. Hebb (1949) realized that human behaviour and mental functioning could not be adequately explained by focusing only on the workings of the brain. Instead, Hebb emphasized a systems approach, whereby environmental events and psychological experiences (e.g., emotions) interact with the nervous system in a way that each modifies the other. So, for example, specific environmental events could produce particular changes in brain function, and in turn changes in brain function could lead the organism to influence the environment in particular ways. In the context of this perspective, Hebb developed models of how networks of neurons can be modified to recognize incoming stimuli ("inputs") and to produce specific responses ("outputs"). Thus, networks of neurons could be modified to perform various tasks. Neural network models have developed considerably since Hebb's early work. Scientists have developed neural network models to simulate many disorders, such as schizophrenia. These models propose that symptoms of mental disorders arise from aberrations in the way the networks process information. These models help guide neuroscientists in their search for the biological correlates of mental disorders.

## Major Brain Structures

Neuroanatomists divide the brain into three subdivisions: the hindbrain, the midbrain, and the forebrain (see Figure 2–3). Basic bodily functions are regulated by the structures of the *hindbrain*, which include the medulla, pons, and cerebellum. The *medulla* controls various bodily functions involved in sustaining life, including heart rate, blood pressure, and respiration. The *pons* serves various functions in regulating stages of sleep. The *cerebellum* serves as a control centre in helping to coordinate physical movements. The cerebellum receives information on body movements and integrates this feedback with directives from higher brain structures about desired actions. Few forms of abnormal behaviour are identified with disturbances in the hindbrain, because the hindbrain's primary role is limited to supervising these basic physical functions (Matthysse & Pope, 1986).

The *midbrain* also is involved in the control of some motor activities, especially those related to fighting and sex. Much of the *reticular activating system* is located in the midbrain, although it extends into the pons and medulla as well. The reticular activating system regulates sleeping and waking. Damage to areas of the midbrain can cause extreme disturbances in sexual behaviour, aggressiveness, and sleep, but such abnormalities typically result from specific and unusual brain traumas or tumours (Matthysse & Pope, 1986).

Most of the human brain consists of the *forebrain*. The forebrain evolved more recently than the hindbrain and midbrain and, therefore, is the site of most sensory, emotional, and cognitive processes. These higher mental processes of the forebrain are linked with the midbrain and hindbrain by the **limbic system**. The limbic system is made up of a variety of different brain structures that are central to the regulation of emotion and basic learning processes. Two of the most important components of the limbic system are the thalamus and the hypothalamus. The *thalamus* is involved in receiving and integrating sensory information from both the sense organs and higher brain structures. The **hypothalamus** also plays a role in sensation, but its more important functions are behavioural ones. The hypothalamus controls basic biological urges, such as eating, drinking, and sexual activity. Much of the functioning of the autonomic nervous system is also directed by the hypothalamus.

## Cerebral Hemispheres

Most of the forebrain is composed of the two **cerebral hemispheres** (see Figure 2–3). Many brain functions are **lateralized**, so that one hemisphere serves a specialized role as the site of specific cognitive and emotional activities. In general, the *left cerebral hemisphere* is involved in language and related functions, and the *right cerebral hemisphere* is involved in spatial organization and analysis. The lateralization and localization of certain brain functions often make it possible to pinpoint brain damage based solely on behavioural difficulties.

The two cerebral hemispheres are connected by the *corpus callosum*, which is involved

*McGill University psychologist **Donald Hebb** (1904–1985) developed one of the first neural network models of the brain.*

**The Healthy Brain**

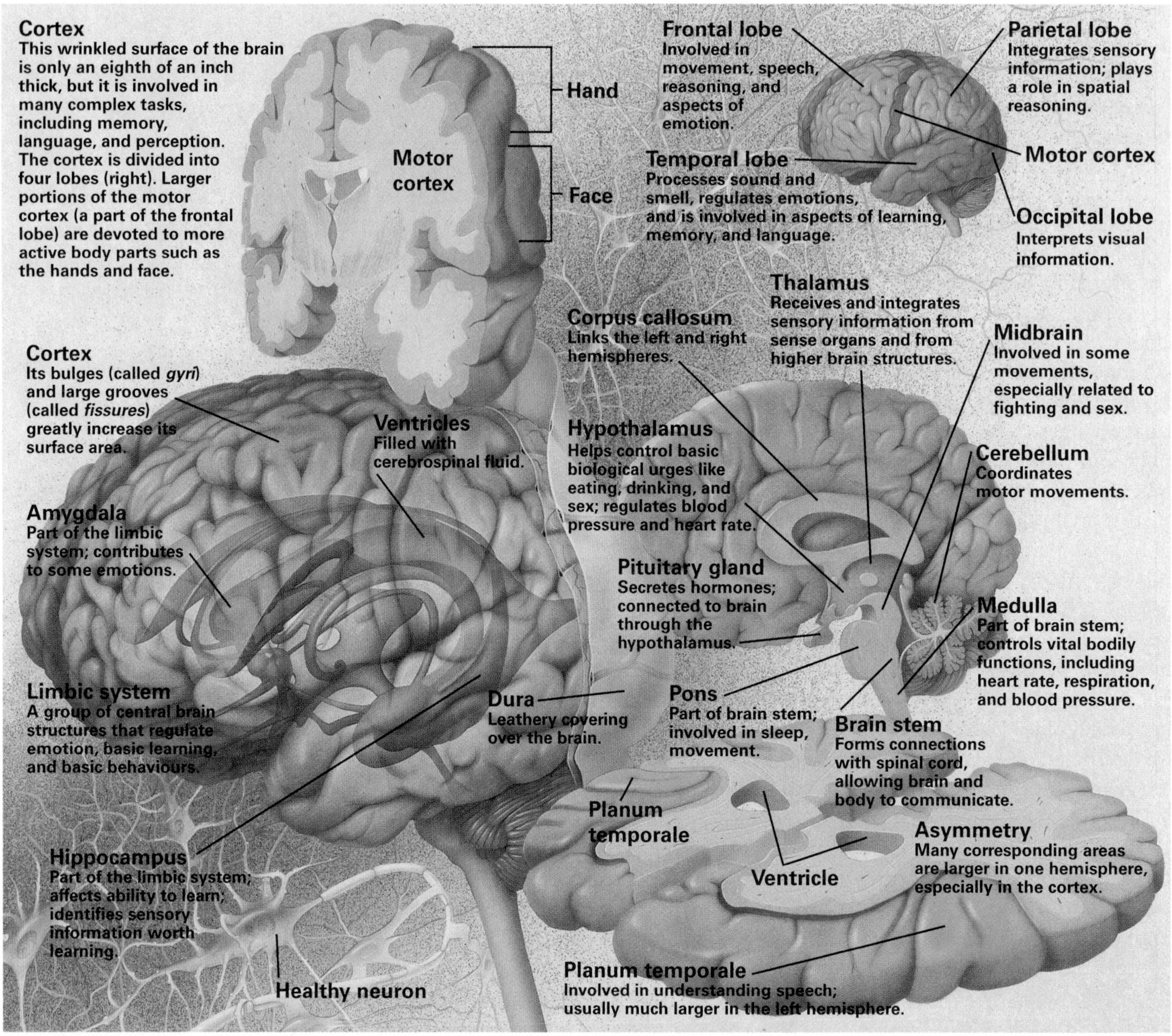
Cortex
This wrinkled surface of the brain is only an eighth of an inch thick, but it is involved in many complex tasks, including memory, language, and perception. The cortex is divided into four lobes (right). Larger portions of the motor cortex (a part of the frontal lobe) are devoted to more active body parts such as the hands and face.
Motor cortex
Hand
Face
Frontal lobe
Involved in movement, speech, reasoning, and aspects of emotion.
Parietal lobe
Integrates sensory information; plays a role in spatial reasoning.
Motor cortex
Temporal lobe
Processes sound and smell, regulates emotions, and is involved in aspects of learning, memory, and language.
Occipital lobe
Interprets visual information.
Thalamus
Receives and integrates sensory information from sense organs and from higher brain structures.
Corpus callosum
Links the left and right hemispheres.
Midbrain
Involved in some movements, especially related to fighting and sex.
Cortex
Its bulges (called *gyri*) and large grooves (called *fissures*) greatly increase its surface area.
Ventricles
Filled with cerebrospinal fluid.
Hypothalamus
Helps control basic biological urges like eating, drinking, and sex; regulates blood pressure and heart rate.
Cerebellum
Coordinates motor movements.
Amygdala
Part of the limbic system; contributes to some emotions.
Pituitary gland
Secretes hormones; connected to brain through the hypothalamus.
Medulla
Part of brain stem; controls vital bodily functions, including heart rate, respiration, and blood pressure.
Limbic system
A group of central brain structures that regulate emotion, basic learning, and basic behaviours.
Dura
Leathery covering over the brain.
Pons
Part of brain stem; involved in sleep, movement.
Brain stem
Forms connections with spinal cord, allowing brain and body to communicate.
Planum temporale
Asymmetry
Many corresponding areas are larger in one hemisphere, especially in the cortex.
Hippocampus
Part of the limbic system; affects ability to learn; identifies sensory information worth learning.
Ventricle
Planum temporale
Involved in understanding speech; usually much larger in the left hemisphere.
Healthy neuron

**FIGURE 2–3:** Scientists are only beginning to discover how the healthy brain performs its complex functions. You should view this complex figure as a rough road map that will be redrawn repeatedly. Like a roadmap, you should not try to memorize the figure, but use it as a guide. You will appreciate more and more detail as you return to examine it repeatedly. Despite the continuing mysteries, increasingly sophisticated tools have allowed researchers to identify more and more of the functions performed by different areas of the brain. For example, the four lobes of the brain's cortex play very different roles in thought, emotion, sensation, and motor movement (see top right of figure). Still, our incomplete knowledge of the healthy brain limits our understanding of brain abnormalities.

in coordinating the different functions that are performed by the left and the right hemispheres of the brain. When we view a cross section of the forebrain, four connected chambers, or **ventricles**, become apparent. The ventricles are filled with cerebrospinal fluid, and they become enlarged in some psychological and neurological disorders.

The **cerebral cortex** is the uneven surface area of the brain that lies just underneath the skull. It is the site of the control and integration of sophisticated memory, sensory, and motor functions. The cerebral cortex is divided into four lobes (see Figure 2–3). The *frontal lobe*, located just behind the forehead, is involved in controlling a number of complex functions,

**The Unhealthy Brain**

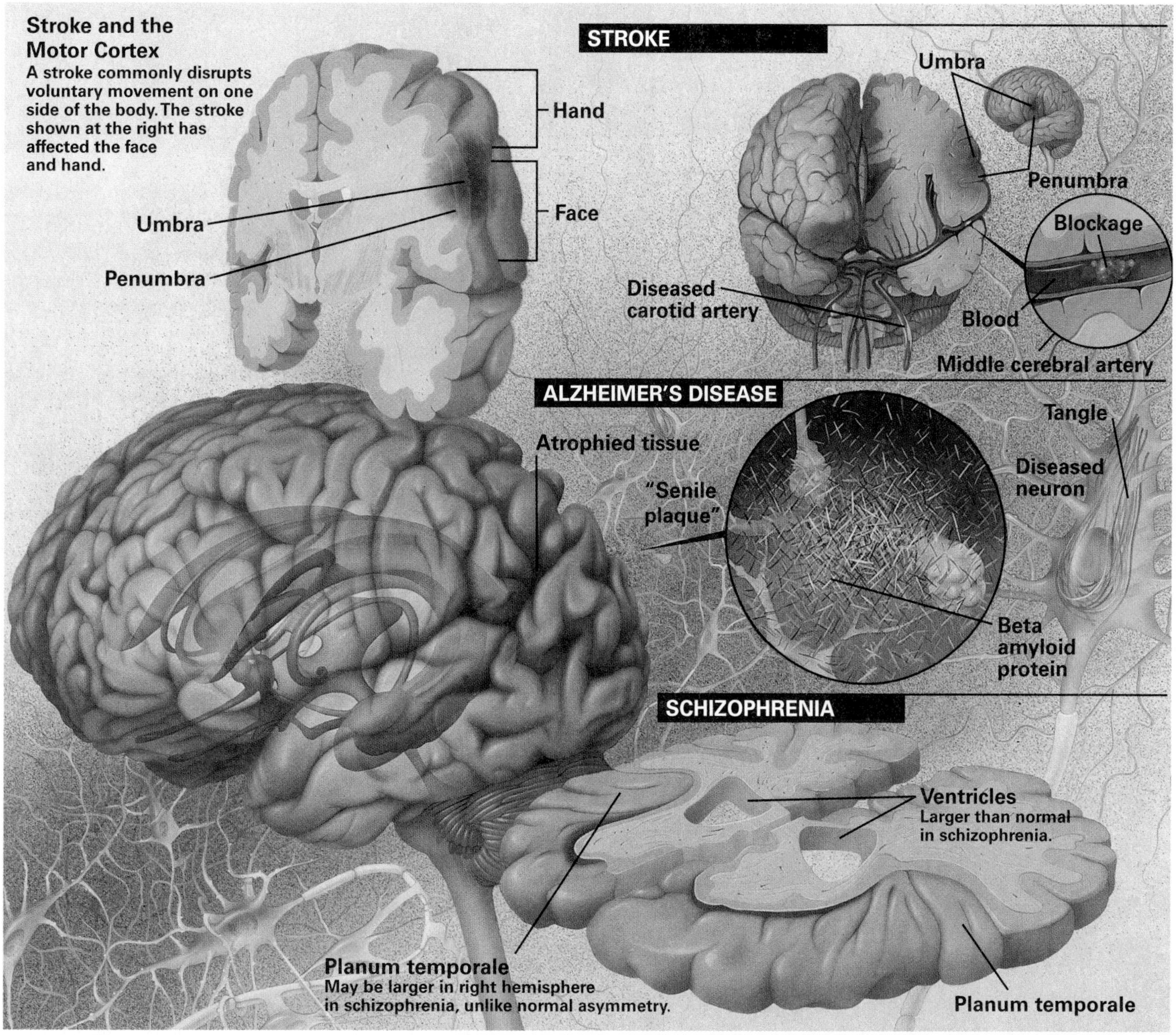


**FIGURE 2–3: Scientists have identified clear brain abnormalities only for some severe mental disorders. A stroke is caused by loss of blood supply to a region of the brain, and it kills off nearby cells (see Chapter 14). Cells die rapidly near the centre of the damaged tissue, the umbra. Cells die less rapidly in the periphery, the penumbra, and may be saved by future medical advances. Alzheimer's disease is a severe cognitive disorder associated with aging (see Chapter 14) that is characterized by atrophied brain tissue, "senile plaques" (caused by clumps of beta amyloid protein), and tangles of diseased or dead neurons. Schizophrenia is a very serious psychotic illness (see Chapter 13) that remains a mystery as a brain disorder, despite some promising leads. For example, among people with schizophrenia the ventricles often are enlarged, and asymmetries in the planum temporale may be reversed.**

*Source:* Keith Kasnot, © National Geographic Image Collection.

including reasoning, planning, emotion, speech, and movement. The *parietal lobe*, located at the top and back of the head, receives and integrates sensory information and also plays a role in spatial reasoning. The *temporal lobe*, located beneath much of the frontal and parietal lobes, processes sound and smell, regulates emotions, and is involved in some aspects of learning, memory, and language. Finally, the *occipital lobe*, located behind the temporal lobe, receives and interprets visual information.

**Major Brain Structures and the Etiology of Psychopathology** The brain is incredibly complex, and scientists are only beginning to understand the relations among various

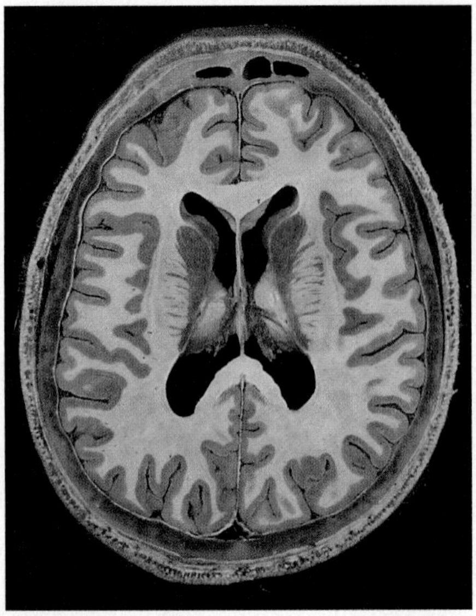

*This cross-sectional image of the brain shows the ventricles, four connected chambers that are filled with cerebrospinal fluid.*

anatomic structures and functions. Because of the rudimentary knowledge we have about the brain, only obvious brain injuries and infections and the most severe mental disorders have clearly been linked with abnormalities in neuroanatomy. In most of these cases, brain damage is extensive. For example, during a *stroke*, blood vessels in the brain rupture, cutting off the supply of oxygen to parts of the brain and thereby killing surrounding brain tissue. This in turn disrupts the functioning of nearby healthy neurons because the brain cannot remove the dead tissue (see Figure 2–3). Tangles of neurons are found in patients with *Alzheimer's disease*, but the damage can be identified only during postmortem autopsies (see Figure 2–3). In patients with schizophrenia, the ventricles of the brain are enlarged, and asymmetries are also found in other brain structures (see Figure 2–3).

At present, the new brain imaging measures are more exciting technically than practically in terms of furthering our understanding of the etiology of psychopathology. Scientific advances frequently follow the development of new measures, however, and there is every reason to hope that advances in brain imaging will lead to improvements in understanding abnormalities in brain structure and function.

## Psychophysiology

**Psychophysiology** is the study of changes in the functioning of the body that result from psychological experiences. Some of these physical reactions to environmental provocations are familiar. A pounding heart, a flushed face, tears, sexual excitement, and numerous other reactions are psychophysiological responses. These and other psychophysiological responses reflect a person's psychological state, particularly the degree and perhaps the type of the individual's emotional arousal.

**Endocrine System** Psychophysiological arousal results from the activity of two different communication systems within the body, the endocrine system and the nervous system. The **endocrine system** is a collection of glands found at various locations throughout the body. Its major components include the ovaries or testes and the pituitary, thyroid, and adrenal glands (see Figure 2–4). Endocrine glands produce psychophysiological responses by releasing **hormones** into the bloodstream—chemical substances that affect the functioning of distant body systems and sometimes act as neuromodulators. The endocrine system regulates some aspects of normal development, particularly physical growth and sexual development. Parts of the endocrine system, particularly the adrenal glands, also are activated by stress and help prepare the body to respond to an emergency (see Chapter 8).

Certain abnormalities in the functioning of the endocrine system are known to cause psychological symptoms. For example, in *hyperthyroidism*, or *Graves' disease*, the thyroid gland secretes too much of the hormone thyroxin, causing restlessness, agitation, and anxiety. Recent research on depression also suggests that endocrine functioning sometimes may be involved in the etiology of this disorder.

**Autonomic Nervous System** The more familiar and basic system of communication within the body is the *nervous system*. The human nervous system is divided into the *central nervous system*, which includes the brain and the spinal cord, and the peripheral nervous system. The *peripheral nervous system* includes all connections that stem from the central nervous system and innervate the body's muscles, sensory systems, and organs.

The peripheral nervous system itself has two subdivisions. The voluntary, *somatic nervous system* governs muscular control, and the involuntary, **autonomic nervous system** regulates the functions of various body organs, such as the heart and stomach. The somatic nervous system controls intentional or voluntary actions like scratching your nose. The autonomic nervous system is responsible for psychophysiological reactions—responses that occur with little or no conscious control.

The autonomic nervous system can be subdivided into two branches, the sympathetic and parasympathetic nervous systems. In general, the *sympathetic nervous system* controls activities associated with increased arousal and energy expenditure, and the *parasympathetic nervous system* controls the slowing of arousal and energy conservation. Thus the two branches work somewhat in opposition to each other as a means of maintaining homeostasis.

**Psychophysiology and the Etiology of Psychopathology** Various theories about the causes of abnormal behaviour have implicated both psychophysiological overarousal and underarousal. For example, overactivity of the autonomic nervous system (a pounding heart or sweaty hands) has been linked with excessive anxiety (see Chapter 6). In contrast, some theories suggest that chronic autonomic underarousal is responsible for the indifference to social rules and the failure to learn from punishment that characterize antisocial personality disorder (see Chapter 9).

Other theories of psychophysiology and abnormal behaviour do not focus on dysfunctions in the autonomic nervous system. Instead, they emphasize psychophysiological assessment as a way of objectively measuring atypical reactions to psychological events. Scientists have developed numerous methods of measuring psychophysiological activity, ranging from assessments of sexual response to indices of muscle tension. We examine some of these psychophysiological measures in Chapter 4.

**The Endocrine System**

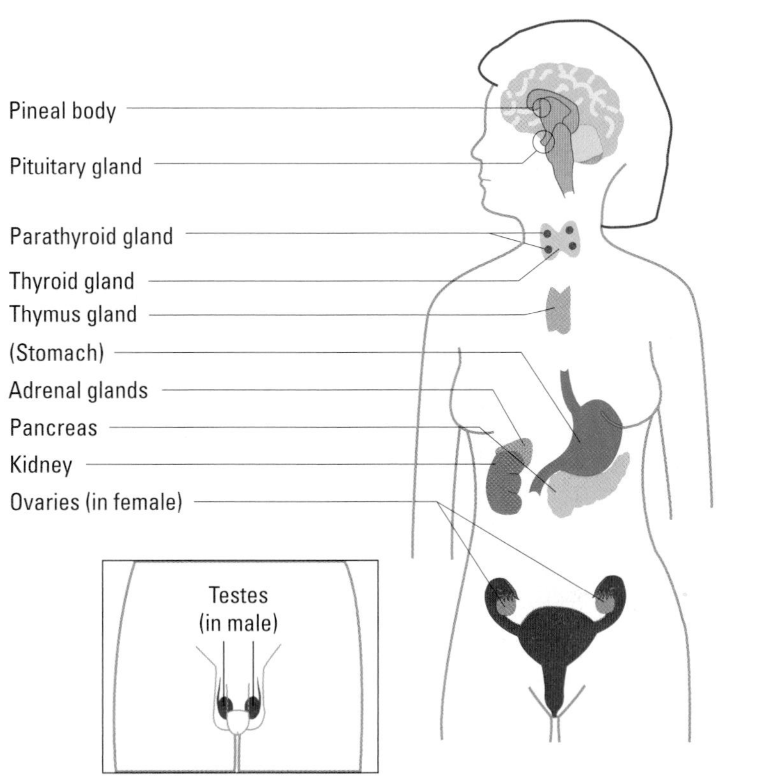


**FIGURE 2–4: The glands that comprise the endocrine system, which affects physical and psychophysiological responses through the release of hormones into the bloodstream.**
*Source:* John G. Seamon and Douglas T. Kenrick, 1994, *Psychology*, 2nd ed., p. 67. Upper Saddle River, NJ: Prentice Hall.

## Behaviour Genetics

Genetic theories simultaneously offer both the most molecular and the most molar explanations of abnormal behaviour. **Genes** are ultramicroscopic units of DNA that carry information about heredity. Genes are located on **chromosomes**, chainlike structures found in the nucleus of cells. Humans normally have 23 pairs of chromosomes. The field of *genetics* identifies specific genes and their hereditary functions, often by literally focusing at the level of molecules. Geneticists typically have training in biochemistry, not psychology.

**Behaviour genetics** is a much broader approach that studies genetic influences on the evolution and development of normal and abnormal behaviour (Plomin, DeFries, & McClearn, 1990; Rutter et al., 2001). Behaviour geneticists study various human characteristics in an attempt to demonstrate that the behaviour has a more or less genetic origin. Behaviour geneticists rarely study individual genes or suggest specific genetic causes of a disorder.

**Some Basic Principles of Genetics** One of the most important principles of genetics is the distinction between genotype and phenotype. A **genotype** is an individual's actual genetic structure. Advances in human genetics—the entire human genome has now been mapped—have allowed scientists to determine more and more aspects of genetic structure. Still, it is impossible to observe much of an individual's genotype directly. Instead, what we observe is the **phenotype**, the expression of a given genotype. There is no one-to-one correspondence between phenotypes and genotypes. Different genotypes can produce similar phenotypes. And phenotypes, but not genotypes, are influenced by environmental experience. This means that it usually is impossible to infer a precise genotype from a given phenotype.

Differences between genotypes and phenotypes are evident in the simple mode of dominant/recessive inheritance that was discovered by the Austrian monk Gregor Mendel (1822–1884) in his famous studies of garden peas. Genes have alternative forms known as *alleles*. Dominant/recessive inheritance occurs when a trait is caused by a single or **autosomal gene** that has only two alleles (for example, A and *a*) and only one *locus*, a specific location on a chromosome. In dominant/recessive inheritance, the phenotypic trait is either present or absent. Figure 2–5 illustrates the patterns of inheritance from parents to children for dominant and recessive disorders. This is the pattern found in Mendel's peas. The gene for colour had only two alleles: A (yellow, dominant) and *a* (green, recessive). Thus, three genotypes are possible: AA, *a*A (or A*a*), and *aa*. Because A is dominant over *a*, however, both AA and *a*A plants will have yellow colour, while *aa* plants will be green. (Figure 2–5 shows the same pattern for the presence or absence of a disorder.) Thus, although three genotypes are possible, only two phenotypes are observed: yellow and green. The top panel in Figure 2–6 illustrates this concept.

Dominant/recessive inheritance causes some rare forms of mental retardation (Plomin, DeFries, & McClearn, 1990), but most mental disorders are not caused by a single gene—if they have genetic causes at all. Instead, they are **polygenic**,—that is, they are caused by more than one gene (Gottesman, 1991). Polygenic inheritance has an important effect on the distribution of traits. In contrast to the categorically different phenotypes (for example, yellow versus green) produced by a single gene, polygenic inheritance produces characteristics that differ only by a matter of degree (for example, height). In fact, the distribution of a phenotype in the population begins to resemble the normal distribution as more genes are involved in determining the trait (see the bottom panel in Figure 2–6). Thus, when someone concludes that a polygenic mental disorder is "genetic," we must be cautious about what this means. It does *not* mean that the disorder is caused by dominant or recessive inheritance, nor does it tell us where to draw the line—the threshold—between normal and abnormal behaviour (see Figure 2–7).

Behaviour geneticists have developed innovative methods for studying broad, genetic contributions to behaviour. The most important behaviour genetic methods are family incidence studies, twin studies, and adoption studies.

**Inheritance of Autosomal Dominant and Autosomal Recessive Disorders**

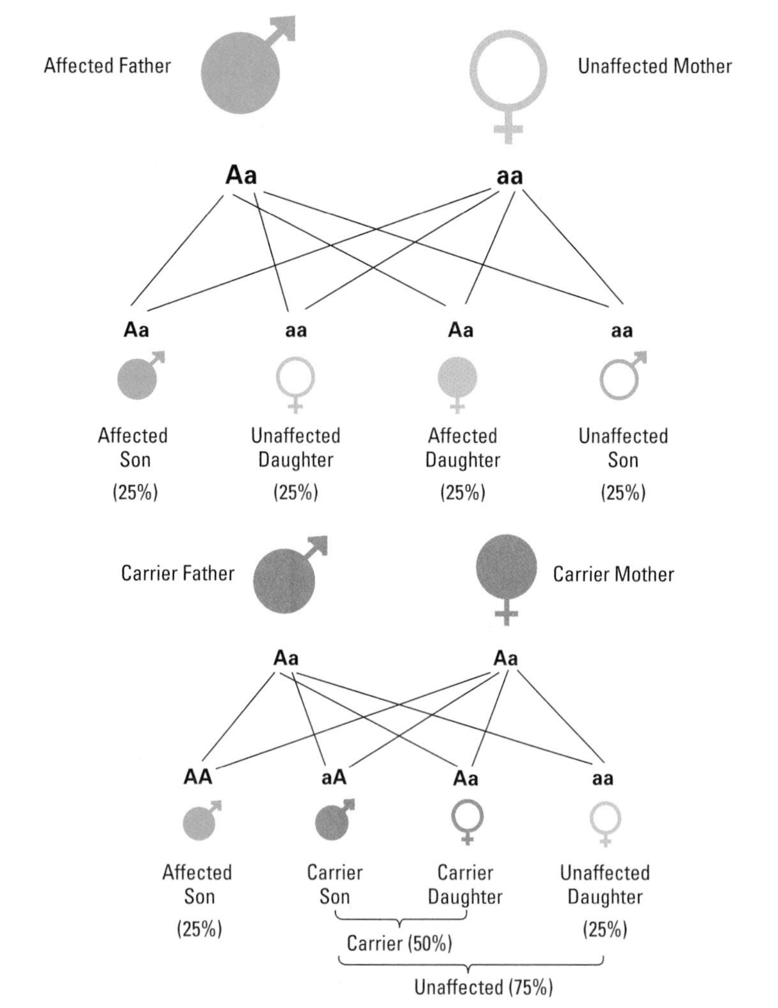


**FIGURE 2–5: Patterns of transmission from parents to children for autosomal dominant (top figure) and autosomal recessive disorders (bottom figure). Note that the disorder is either present or absent for both patterns of inheritance.**

*Source:* Based on S.V. Garaone, M.T. Tsuang, and D.W. Tsuang, 1999, *Genetics of Mental Disorders*. New York: Guilford.

**Family Incidence Studies** Family incidence studies ask whether diseases "run in families." Investigators identify normal and ill **probands**, or index cases, and tabulate the frequency with which other members of their families suffer from the same disorder. If a higher prevalence of illness is found in families where there is an ill proband, this is consistent with genetic causation. The finding also is consistent with environmental causation, however, because families share environments as well as genes. For this reason, no firm conclusions about the relative role of genes or the environment can be reached from family incidence studies alone.

**Twin Studies** Studies of twins, in contrast, can provide strong evidence about genetic and environmental contributions to a disorder. **Monozygotic (MZ) twins** are *identical*. One egg is fertilized by one sperm, and thus MZ twins have identical genotypes. **Dizygotic (DZ) twins** are *fraternal*. These twins are produced from two eggs and two sperm. Thus, like all siblings, DZ twins share an average of 50 percent of their genes, whereas MZ twins share 100 percent of their genes. Of course, most MZ and DZ twin pairs are raised in the same family. Thus MZ and DZ twins differ in their genetic similarity, but they are alike in their environmental experiences.

Comparisons between MZ and DZ twin pairs thus shed light on the genetic and environmental contributions to a disorder. The key comparison involves determining the **concordance rate** of the two sets of twins, specifically whether MZ twins are more alike than DZ twins are alike. A twin pair is concordant when both twins either have the same disorder or are free from the disorder—for example, both suffer from schizophrenia. The twin pair is discordant when one twin has the disorder but the other does not—for example, one twin has schizophrenia but the co-twin does not.

If we assume that the environmental effects on a disorder are the same for DZ twin pairs as they are for MZ twin pairs, then any differences between the concordance rates for MZ and DZ twins must be caused by genetics. If a disorder is purely genetic, for example, scientists should find a concordance rate of 100 percent for MZ twins (who are genetically identical) and 50 percent for DZ twins (who share half of the same genes on average) (see Table 2–4).

In contrast, similar concordance rates for MZ and DZ twins rule out genetic contributions and instead implicate environmental causes of a disorder. Environmental causes are implicated regardless of whether the concordance rates

**Single Gene and Polygenetic Inheritance**

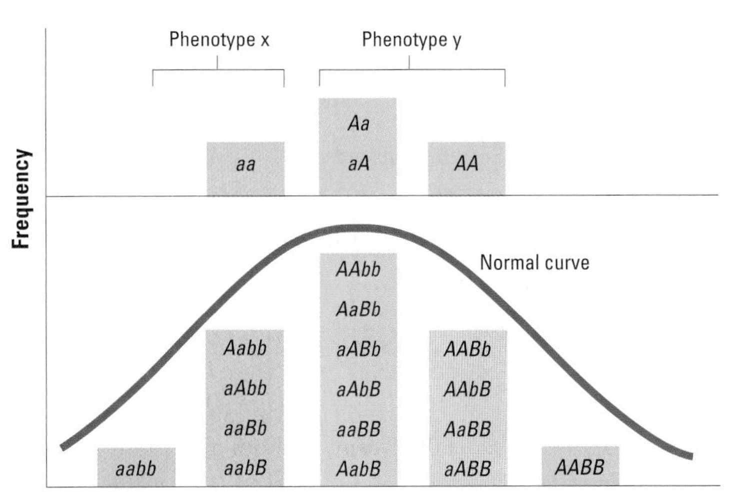


**FIGURE 2–6:** Single genes produce phenotypes that differ qualitatively, as illustrated in the top panel. Multiple genes produce phenotypes that differ quantitatively. As more genes are involved (only two in this illustration), the distribution of traits approximates the normal curve, as illustrated in the bottom panel.

**Inheritance of Polygenic Disorders**

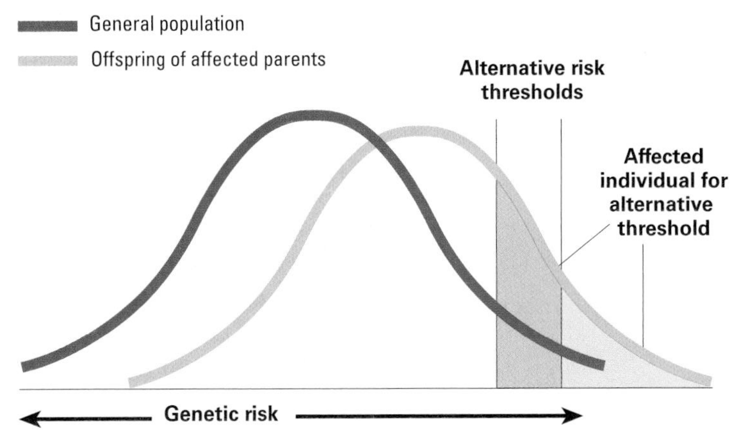


**FIGURE 2–7:** For polygenic disorders, the risk is higher for the offspring of affected (ill) parents, who inherit more of the multiple genes involved in the disorder. Still, the genetic risk varies widely in both the general and the affected population. Because the underlying characteristic is distributed continuously, there is no clear, objective place to mark the threshold of the disorders.

**TABLE 2–4 Twin Studies: Implications of Different Findings**

| Concordance | Supports Influence of | Concordance for Perfect Case[1] |
|---|---|---|
| MZ > DZ | Genes | MZ = 100%; DZ = 50% |
| MZ = DZ; both high | Shared environment | MZ = 100%; DZ = 100% |
| MZ = DZ; both low | Nonshared environment | MZ = 0%; DZ = 0% |

[1] The identified influence explains everything in the perfect case. Actual concordance rates almost always fall between these extremes, thus providing an index of the relative contributions of genes, the shared environment, and/or the nonshared environment.

for MZ and DZ twins are both 0 percent, both 100 percent, or both anywhere in between. However, the level of concordance does provide information about the nature of the environmental contribution. *High* concordance rates for both MZ and DZ twins point to the etiological role of the **shared environment**, the experiences the two twins share in common—for example, growing up in poverty. When both MZ and DZ pairs have similarly high concordance rates, we know that genes do not explain the similarities. Instead, the common cause must be found in the environment shared by the twins. The shared environment would explain *all* of the variance in a trait if the concordance rate was 100 percent for both MZ and DZ twins (see Table 2–4).

Similar but *low* concordance rates for both MZ and DZ pairs point to the influence of the **nonshared environment**, the experiences that are unique to one twin—for example, being the favoured child. In this case, genetic causes are again ruled out, and the importance of unique experiences is indicated by the fact that only one twin has a psychological disorder (Plomin et al., 1994). The nonshared environment would explain *all* of the variance in a trait if the concordance rate was 0 percent for both MZ and DZ twins (see Table 2–4). In real research, of course, nothing is perfect. However, twin studies provide useful estimates of the role played by genes, the shared environment, and the nonshared environment in studying a given disorder.

Evidence from twin studies often indicates that genes have a substantial influence on mental disorders, as we discuss in subsequent chapters. Somewhat surprisingly, behaviour genetic research also indicates that many environmental influences appear to be nonshared. Given this finding, Harris (1995, 1998) argued that peers, who are a part of the nonshared environment, are much more important environmental influences than parents, who are a part of the shared environment. Harris's assertion is interesting, but like other claims about the nonshared environment, it remains only an assertion. Research to date has identified only small effects of the nonshared environment on normal and abnormal behaviour (Turkheimer & Waldron, 2000).

The logic of twin studies depends on the assumption that the environment affects DZ twins in the same way that it influences MZ twins. A number of critics have questioned this assumption. Because of their striking physical resemblance, MZ twins may be treated more similarly than DZ twins. Or if MZ twins have more similar personalities than DZ twins, MZs may seek similar environments and get more similar responses from the environment. If MZ twins experience a more similar environment than DZ twins, then higher concordance rates for MZ twins might result from more similar environmental experiences and not from more similar genetic endowments.

Contemporary behavioural genetics research is a sophisticated enterprise. Responses from questionnaire or interview measures of psychopathology are obtained from hundreds of pairs of MZ and DZ twins. The responses are then used to test complex multivariate statistical models, which examine the effects of genetic and environmental factors, after controlling for potential confounds such as the possibility that MZ twins are treated more similarly than DZ twins. Statistical models are tested and compared to one another to determine which model provides the best fit to the data. The largest behavioural genetic research program in Canada is conducted at the University of British Columbia, by Kerry Jang, John Livesley, and colleagues. These researchers have established a national register of several hundred MZ and DZ twins, who regularly complete measures of personality and psychopathology. As a result of these studies, Jang, Livesley, and colleagues have found, among other things, that normal personality is influenced by a small number of genetic factors, and that the same factors also play a role in personality disorders (Livesley, Jang, & Vernon, 1998).

**Adoption Studies** Adoption studies also provide evidence on the genetic versus environmental contributions to the development of a disorder. In this research design, people who were adopted as infants are compared with their biological versus their adoptive relatives (usually their parents) in terms of concordance for a disorder. If concordance is higher for biological than for adoptive relatives, then genetic factors are involved, because adopted children share their biological relatives' genes but not their environment. On the other hand, if children are more similar to their adoptive than to their biological relatives, then environment must influence the characteristic, because adopted children share their adoptive relatives' environment but not their genes.

The logic of the adoption design might be clearer if we think about the case of the adopted girl, Meghan, from the beginning of this chapter. Genetic influences would be implicated if we found that Meghan (and other adopted children) developed problems similar to those found in their biological, but not among their adoptive, parents. On the other hand, environmental influences must be operating if Meghan and other adopted children developed problems (or strengths!) that were more similar to their adoptive than their biological parents.

Adoption studies have some potential problems—for example, the fact that adoption placement is selective. Still, you can be confident in the findings of behaviour genetic researchers when adoption and twin studies produce similar results (Plomin et al., 1994).

**Misinterpreting Behaviour Genetics Findings** The methods of behaviour genetic research are powerful, and evidence indicates that genes contribute to many psychological disorders. We consider specific findings throughout the text. Unfortunately, people often misinterpret findings from behaviour genetic research.

One serious misinterpretation is that, if it has a genetic component, the emergence of a psychological disorder is inevitable, even predestined. This conclusion is wrong, in part because of polygenic inheritance. The probabilities of alternative outcomes are easily identified for simple dominant/recessive inheritance, but predicting the likelihood of a disorder is far more difficult for polygenic transmission. Moreover, genes alone do not cause the vast majority of emotional disorders. Behaviour genetics studies of mental illnesses typically find concordance rates for MZ twins that are far below 100 percent. Thus genes may predispose someone toward developing a mental disorder, but the problem emerges only when the predisposition is combined with psychological and social stressors. In fact, twin studies provide some of the strongest evidence on the *environmental* contributions to abnormal behaviour (Faraone et al., 1999).

*A festival for twins. Monozygotic (MZ) twins are identical; they develop from a single fertilized egg. Dizygotic (DZ) twins are fraternal; they develop from two different fertilized eggs.*

Behaviour genetic findings also fail to specify what mechanism explains the genetic contribution to a disorder. For example, researchers have found genetic contributions to adult criminality, but there obviously is no "crime gene." What, then, is the mechanism that accounts for the behaviour genetics finding? In the case of criminal behaviour, one of many possibilities is inheritance of an underaroused autonomic nervous system. In psychological terms, this hypothesis suggests that some people are predisposed toward antisocial behaviour, because they are less fearful and less likely to learn from experience. Clearly, this hypothesis involves the essential interplay between a genetic predisposition and the environment, and it allows for prevention or treatment based on environmental changes. The idea, like most hypothesized accounts of genetically mediated abnormal behaviour, is much more rich and complicated than a simple-minded conclusion that "crime is genetic."

It also simply is wrong to think that genetic characteristics cannot be modified or controlled. For example, even in cases where mental retardation has a known genetic cause, certain environmental experiences such as diet or early stimulation have been demonstrated to lead to substantial increases—or decreases—in IQ (Turkheimer, 1991). The conclusion "It's genetic" does not provide an excuse for accepting the status quo. Society remains responsible for helping people to maximize their genetic potential, and individuals remain personally responsible for their actions.

Finally, a word about the long-standing nature–nurture debate. A holistic systems approach clearly views the division between nature and nurture as a false dichotomy, because nature and nurture are inseparable influences. We find much merit, and a little mirth, in the answer that McGill University psychologist Donald Hebb gave over 40 years ago when asked, "What is more important, nature or nurture?" Hebb replied that posing the question was like asking what contributed more to the area of a rectangle, its length or its width (Meaney, 2001).

**Genetics and the Etiology of Psychopathology** Genetic influences are important to recognize, but we are highly skeptical that specific genetic causes will be discovered for many mental disorders. When behaviour genetic researchers find that a disorder is strongly influenced by genes, the public and some scientists seem to feel that we have discovered *the* cause of the problem—and, in fact, hope to discover a specific gene responsible for the disorder (Plomin & Crabbe, 2000). However, remember that (1) most emotional problems, like most normal behaviours, appear to be polygenic; (2) behaviour genetic findings fail to specify the mechanism of genetic influence; and (3) shared or nonshared environmental contributions to a disorder typically are found to be as large as genetic ones.

In short, it is important to recognize pervasive genetic influences on behaviour, but it is essential to think critically and beyond the familiar models of simple dominant and recessive inheritance. For a few, rare forms of mental disorder, scientists have the responsible gene. However, we are unlikely to find a gene for depression, for eating disorders, or for many forms of psychopathology any more than we are likely to find a gene for love.

# Psychological Factors

We have a widely accepted classification of mental disorders, the DSM-IV-TR. However, we do *not* have a widely accepted classification of essential psychological characteristics. Systems theory is a way of organizing and understanding the reciprocal influences of biological, psychological, and social *processes*, but it is silent on the *content* of these three factors. Thus, any listing of the psychological factors involved in mental disorders, including our own, necessarily is incomplete and open to question.

For these reasons, throughout the text we carefully describe the specific psychological factors used in a given line of research or hypothesized to play a role in different psychological disorders. Most of these psychological factors fit into one of the five topics that we consider in the following sections: (1) basic human motivations and temperament; (2) emotion; (3) learning and cognition; (4) the sense of self; and (5) development.

## Basic Human Motivations and Temperament

Any classification of essential psychological characteristics must build its foundation on its view of basic human nature, or what psychologists call species-typical characteristics. What are our basic psychological motivations—motivations that we share with other animals and motivations that are uniquely human? Almost a century ago, Freud proposed an answer to this question. He asserted that sex and aggression are the two basic human drives. Around the same time, Watson and the behaviourists proposed a very different answer: We come into the world as blank slates. Today, psychologists finally are revisiting this essential question in a new, exciting, and often controversial field of study called evolutionary psychology.

**Evolutionary Psychology** **Evolutionary psychology** is the application of the principles of evolution to our understanding of the animal and human mind. Evolutionary psychologists assume that animal and human psychology, like animal and human anatomy, have evolved based on two broad evolutionary principles. *Natural selection* is the process through which successful, genetically determined adaptations to environmental problems become more common over successive generations of offspring. The adaptation is selected by evolution, because it increases *inclusive fitness*, the reproductive success of those who have the adaptation, their offspring, and/or their kin. For example, the large human brain, with its particularly large cerebral cortex, presumably was selected across evolutionary history. The adaptations that a larger brain enabled (e.g., the use of tools for survival and weapons for defence) increased the survival and reproductive success of early humans with larger brains, as well as that of their offspring and kin.

*Sexual selection* is a second way that genetically mediated adaptations can increase inclusive fitness—in this case, by increasing reproductive success through greater access to mates and mating. Mating access can be increased by successful *intrasexual* competition—for example, a dominant male limits the mating opportunities of other males; or by successful *intersexual* selection—for example, a more brightly coloured bird attracts more members of the opposite sex (Gaulin & McBurney, 2001; Larsen & Buss, 2002).

The value of evolutionary psychology comes from the new, empirically testable hypotheses it helps scientists to generate. At different points throughout the text, we raise new ideas based on the principles of evolutionary psychology. Many of these concepts are challenging and exciting, but many of the hypotheses are so new that they barely have been studied. Until more data have been collected, you should view the ideas with both interest and skepticism.

The nature of human nature is one of many areas where evolutionary psychology offers some particularly rich hypotheses. As we have noted, the list of basic human tendencies is far from complete, but two vital qualities that certainly belong on the list are the need to form close relationships and the competition for dominance.

**Attachment Theory** The human need to form close relationships was the focus of detailed theorizing by the influential British psychiatrist John Bowlby (1907–1990). Bowlby was trained in psychoanalysis, but he explicitly rejected Freudian theory by placing the need to form close relationships at the core of his view of development (Bowlby, 1969, 1982). The heart of Bowlby's theory is the observation that infants form **attachments** early in life—special and selective bonds with their caregivers.

Bowlby based his approach, known as *attachment theory*, on findings from *ethology*, the study of animal behaviour. Ethologists have documented that close relationships develop between infants and caregivers in many species of animals. In some species, selective relationships develop in the first hours or days of life, a process called *imprinting*. Human attachments are far more flexible and slow to develop than imprinting, but both patterns can be easily understood in terms of evolutionary psychology. Human infants, like many animal offspring, become distressed when separated from their caregivers. Their displays of distress—long and loud cries—keep them in proximity to their caregivers. Proximity between infants and their caregivers has survival value, because parents protect their offspring from danger. As such, attachment behaviour is hypothesized to result from natural selection.

Unlike many hypotheses based in evolutionary psychology, attachment theory enjoys strong empirical support in studies ranging from observations of animal behaviour to the neuroscience of attachment formation. Still, many questions remain about attachment theory. A basic one is whether all subsequent relationships build on the initial infant–caregiver relationship, or instead, have we evolved to form different kinds of attachments to parents, peers, mates, and children?

Other questions include the role of attachments in the development of psychopathology (Cassidy & Mohr, 2001). As we consider when discussing different disorders, attachment theorists assert that much psychopathology can be traced to the failure to meet a child's basic need to form a secure attachment. Of particular concern are the effects of *insecure* or *anxious attachments*—uncertain or

*A Japanese macaque monkey and her one-month-old baby. Strong bonds between infants and caregivers are found across many species. Disruptions in human attachments may contribute to abnormal behaviour.*

ambivalent parent–child relationships that come from inconsistent and unresponsive parenting during the first year of life (Ainsworth et al., 1978). Anxious attachments are hypothesized to cause children to be mistrustful, dependent, and/or rejecting in subsequent relationships, a pattern that may continue into adult life. Attachment theorists also assert that uncertainties about relationships are created by parental separation and loss during childhood (Bowlby, 1973, 1980). Critics argue that early attachment difficulties are more easily overcome than attachment theory asserts, but they agree that close, supportive relationships promote mental health throughout the lifespan (Rutter & Rutter, 1993).

**Dominance** The development of attachments, or more generally of *affiliation* with other members of the same species, is one of the two broad categories of social behaviours studied by ethologists. The second is **dominance**, the hierarchical ordering of a social group into more and less privileged members (Sloman, Gardner, & Price, 1989). Dominance hierarchies are easily observed in human as well as other animal social groups, and from the perspective of evolutionary psychology, dominance competition is basic to sexual selection. Thus dominance is a good second candidate for our list of species-typical human qualities.

Surprisingly, however, dominance has not been the explicit focus of much research on abnormal behaviour. Still, we see dominance as an implicit focus in many studies. For example, a strong, internal sense of control and effectiveness has been hypothesized to be essential to positive mental health. And it is widely accepted that the best parents are *authoritative* (Maccoby & Martin, 1983)—that is, they are both warmly responsive to children (thereby encouraging a secure attachment) and firm in discipline (thereby maintaining parental authority).

Additional social motivations, as well as cognitive abilities, belong on the list of basic human qualities. Still, we are confident that attachment and dominance will rank high in any final list. It is of interest to note that, in fact, Freud may have agreed with this view. Some contemporary psychodynamic theorists assert that Freud's basic drives of sex and aggression really are metaphors for the broader qualities of affiliation and dominance (Cameron & Rychlak, 1985).

**Temperament** Attachment and dominance are species-typical characteristics, but there are wide *individual differences*—differences between members of the same species—in relating to the social and physical worlds. One of the most important areas of research on individual differences is the study of **temperament**, characteristic styles of relating to the world. Psychologists long debated what elements make up the basic temperamental styles, but recently researchers have reached a consensus (Goldberg, 1993; Zuckerman, 1991). Based on extensive analyses of people's responses to structured questionnaires, researchers have identified five bipolar dimensions of personality, sometimes called "the big five." These are (1) openness to experience—imaginative and curious versus shallow and imperceptive; (2) conscientiousness—organized and reliable versus careless and negligent; (3) extraversion—active and talkative versus passive and reserved; (4) agreeableness—trusting and kind versus hostile and selfish; and (5) neuroticism—nervous and moody versus calm and pleasant. The acronym OCEAN, which uses the first letter of each term, will help you to remember "the big five."

Individual differences in temperament may play a role in a number of psychological disorders, especially personality disorders and child behaviour problems. For example, temperament is viewed as basic to the development of childhood problems ranging from anxiety disorders to hyperactivity. Temperamental contributions to abnormal child behaviour generally are viewed from a systems perspective. In particular, researchers have focused on the *goodness of fit* between a child's biologically based temperament and the psychological and social environments. For example, a "difficult" temperament may increase the risk for child behaviour problems, but parenting determines whether the difficult behaviour grows worse or is controlled (Chess & Thomas, 1984).

## Emotions and Emotional Systems

**Emotions**, internal feeling states, are psychological qualities that are essential to human experience and to our understanding of mental disorders. But we have hundreds of words for different feelings in the English language. What emotions are most essential? Researchers have used statistical analysis to reduce the list to six basic emotions (National Advisory Mental Health Council, 1995):

- Love
- Joy
- Surprise
- Anger
- Sadness
- Fear

This list can be grouped into the even smaller classifications of positive emotion (the left column) and negative emotion (the right column). Of course, negative emotions are most relevant to abnormal psychology, and we have separate chapters that focus primarily on sadness (Chapter 5) and fear (Chapter 6); anger is considered in relation to a number of disorders.

Some evolutionary psychologists are beginning to analyze emotions from a systems perspective. In particular, different *emotional systems* appear to be linked to specific social or psychological motivations (Blanchard, Hebert, & Blanchard, in press; Panksepp, 1988). For example, fear and security are complementary emotions that motivate infants and caretakers to maintain proximity. Other emotional systems likely include rage–fear (associated with fight or flight) and security–anger–sadness (linked with loss). The concept of emotional system is consistent with evolutionary principles and with the biological realities of the brain (Panksepp, 1988).

Emotion also appears to be more "basic" than our next topic, cognition. Emotions often come to us without intention, effort, or desire, whereas we have more control over our thoughts. As we have seen, in fact, emotions are more "basic" in the brain. Emotions are controlled primarily by subcortical brain structures, whereas more abstract cognitive abilities are controlled by the cerebral cortex, a more recent product of evolution. Cognition can shape or modify emotion, but feelings are not wholly controlled by our intellectual interpretations (Panksepp, 1988).

## Learning and Cognition

Emotions, motivations, and temperamental styles can be modified, at least to some degree, by the higher processes of learning and cognition. Earlier, we discussed two critical learning mechanisms: classical and operant conditioning. These modes of learning are essential to normal development, and they also play an important role in the etiology or maintenance of psychological problems. For example, fears can be classically conditioned, and antisocial behaviour often is rewarded.

**Modelling** A third method of learning, known as modelling, was originally identified by researchers in Canada, Albert Bandura and Richard Walters (1963). (Bandura is now at Stanford University.) The concept of **modelling** suggests that people learn much of their behaviour by imitating others, a process that you surely have observed many times. A particular concern for the development of abnormal behaviour is when parents or other important adults model dysfunctional behaviour for children—for example, a parent with alcoholism.

*Canadian-born psychologist **Albert Bandura** (1925– ) extensively studied modelling, the process of learning through imitation.*

**Cognition and Social Cognition** Cognitive psychologists commonly draw analogies between human thinking and computers in describing more complex thought processes. Examples include human information processing, memory systems, and retrieval processes. As we will see in later chapters, evolutionary psychology also has influenced cognitive psychology. The "human computer" may be preprogrammed by natural selection to think in ways that make human decision making more efficient but less objective. Cognitive psychology has had a profound effect on theorizing about mental disorders, particularly among behaviour therapists, who as a result now call themselves cognitive behaviour therapists.

Social psychologists have developed the parallel field of *social cognition*—the study of how humans process information about the social world. The important concept of attribution illustrates the social cognition approach. **Attributions** are perceived causes—people's beliefs about cause–effect relations. If a friend gets mad at you for "ditching" her at a party, for example, you are not likely to examine her motivations scientifically. Instead, you attribute her anger to some reasonable cause, perhaps her tendency to cling to you. Attribution theorists suggest that humans are "intuitive scientists" who routinely draw such conclusions about causality. We use shorthand calculations instead of more detailed methods in attributing causes because the quick assessments are efficient, requiring little cognitive processing. Attributions can be inaccurate, however, in part because they are made intuitively rather than scientifically (Nisbett & Wilson, 1977).

*Vincent van Gogh's self-portraits convey a haunting search for the sense of self.*

Vincent van Gogh (1853–1890). Oil on canvas 65 × 54.5 cm. R.F. 1949-17. Musée d'Orsay, Paris, France. Erich Lessing/Art Resource, NY.

Attribution errors, and other cognitive biases, have been suggested to play a prominent role in the development of abnormal behaviour. Learned helplessness theory, for example, suggests that depression is caused by wrongly attributing negative events to internal, global, and stable causes (Peterson & Seligman, 1984; see Chapter 5). According to this theory, you are at risk for depression if you conclude that the reason for your bad grade on a calculus exam is "I'm stupid." The "stupid" attribution blames the grade on internal, global, and stable causes, a cognition that makes you feel more helpless and ultimately more depressed. Healthier attributions are "The teacher was unfair," "I'm lousy at math," or "I didn't work hard enough," because each attribution is, respectively, external, specific, and unstable in quality.

Another theory suggests that depression is caused by automatic and distorted perceptions of reality, particularly negative cognitive errors (Beck et al., 1979). For example, people prone to depression may draw inaccurate, negative generalizations in processing information about themselves. For instance, they conclude that they are inadequate based on a single unpleasant experience. It is interesting to note that a treatment based on this theory encourages depressed people to be more scientific and less intuitive in evaluating their conclusions (see Chapter 5).

## The Sense of Self

We share emotions and motivations with other animals, and we share some information-processing strategies with computers. Still, our sense of self seems to be a uniquely human quality. The exact definition of our sense of self is elusive. This often is true personally and in various psychological theories.

One important and influential conceptualization is Erik Erikson's (1968) concept of **identity**. Erikson viewed identity as the product of the adolescent's struggle to answer the question "Who am I?" In his view, the conflict caused by this persistent question eventually produces an enduring identity, an integrated sense of individuality, wholeness, and continuity.

Other theorists have countered that we do not have one identity but many "selves." The psychologist George Kelly (1905–1966), for example, emphasized the identities linked with the different roles that people play in life. These include obvious roles like being a daughter, a student, and a friend, as well as less obvious roles, like being a "caretaker," a "jock," or "the quiet one." Kelly argued that people develop many different role identities, various senses of themselves that correspond with actual life roles.

The idea that children and adults must develop **self-control**—internal rules for guiding appropriate behaviour—is an important concept in research on abnormal behaviour. Self-control is learned through the process of *socialization*, wherein parents, teachers, and peers use discipline, praise, and their own example to teach children prosocial behaviour and set limits on their antisocial behaviour. Over time, these standards are *internalized*—that is, the external rules become internal regulations. The result is self-control (Maccoby, 1992).

Self-worth is a related but somewhat different aspect of the sense of self. Various discussions of the importance of high self-esteem have been emphasized by psychodynamic, cognitive behavioural, and humanistic theorists. Sigmund Freud (1940/1969) discussed the importance of a healthy ego, a strong and confident inner reserve. Carl Rogers (1961) highlighted a healthy *self-concept*—feeling worthy and capable—as the core structure of personality in his humanistic approach. Finally, the social learning theorist Albert Bandura (1977) argued for the primacy of **self-efficacy**, the belief that one can achieve desired goals.

Each theorist highlights the importance of the individual's sense of self-worth for mental health. You should consider, however, that low self-esteem could be a result rather than a cause of abnormal behaviour. High self-esteem develops from success and fulfillment, whereas anxiety and depression—and low self-esteem—result from failure, loss, conflict, and rejection. In short, low self-esteem may only be an index of emotional problems, not a cause of them.

## Stages of Development

Developmental change can be relevant to the etiology of psychopathology, particularly periods of very rapid developmental change. These times of *developmental transition* mark the end of one **developmental stage**—a period of continuous and slow change—and the beginning of a new one.

Developmental transitions challenge routine functioning and force us to learn new ways of thinking, feeling, and acting. Normal distress in response to such difficult transitions sometimes can be confused with abnormal behaviour. On the other hand, the stress associated with a developmental transition may precipitate a mental disorder if there is a predisposing diathesis.

Two prominent stage theories are especially relevant to abnormal psychology: Freud's theory of psycho*sexual* development and Erikson's theory of psycho*social* development. As is evident in the name given to his theory, Freud highlighted the child's internal struggles with sexuality as marking the various stages of development. In contrast, Erikson emphasized social tasks and the conflicts involved in meeting the demands of the external world. Importantly, Erikson also suggested that development does not end with adolescence; rather, he proposed that development continues throughout the lifespan.

The key tasks, age ranges, and defining events of these two stage theories are summarized in Table 2–5. In considering differences between the theories, also note that both theorists use similar ages to denote the beginning and end of their developmental stages of childhood. Others also have suggested that key developmental transitions occur around the ages of 1½, 6, and 12. Included among this group is the noted Swiss psychologist Jean Piaget,

**TABLE 2–5 Freud's and Erikson's Stage Theories of Development**

| Age[1] | 0–1½ | 1–3 | 2–6 | 5–12 | 11–20 | 18–30 | 25–70 | 65 on |
|---|---|---|---|---|---|---|---|---|
| Freud | ***Oral*** | ***Anal*** | ***Phallic*** | ***Latency*** | ***Genital*** | | | |
| | Oral gratification through breastfeeding. Meeting one's own needs. | Learning control over environment and inner needs through toilet training. | Sexual rivalry with opposite-gender parent. Oedipal conflicts, penis envy, identification. | Not a stage, as psychosexual development is dormant during these ages. | Mature sexuality and formation of mutual heterosexual relationships. | | | |
| Erikson | ***Basic Trust vs. Basic Mistrust*** | ***Autonomy vs. Shame and Doubt*** | ***Initiative vs. Guilt*** | ***Industry vs. Inferiority*** | ***Identity vs. Role Confusion*** | ***Intimacy vs. Self-absorption*** | ***Generativity vs. Stagnation*** | ***Integrity vs. Despair*** |
| | Developing basic trust in self and others through feeding and caretaking. | Gaining a sense of competence through success in toileting and mastering environment. | Gaining parental approval for initiative rather than guilt over inadequacy. | Curiosity and eagerness to learn leads to a sense of competence or inadequacy. | Identity crisis is a struggle to answer question, "Who am I?" | Aloneness of young adult resolved by forming friendships and a lasting intimate relationship. | Success in work but especially in raising the next generation or failure to be productive. | Satisfaction with the life one lived rather than despair over lost opportunities. |

[1]Ages are approximate as indicated by overlap in age ranges.

who theorized about cognitive development. Irrespective of substantive focus, these ages seem to be key times of transition for children.

The ideas of developmental stages and developmental transitions are basic to many aspects of psychopathology. In fact, Chapter 17 is devoted exclusively to a discussion of difficult developmental transitions throughout the adult lifespan—for example, the transition to adult life, major family transitions, and aging.

# Social Factors

The broadest perspective for understanding the causes of abnormal behaviour is at the level of the social system. There are an almost endless number of potential social influences on behaviour, including many aspects of interpersonal relationships, social institutions, and cultural values. Therefore we must be selective in reviewing social contributions to psychopathology. In this section we begin with a focus on relationships and then move on to a consideration of gender roles, ethnicity, poverty, and broad societal values.

These social perspectives all emphasize that the development of psychopathology is a product of people's *social roles*: styles of behaving according to the expectations of the social situation. Much the way an actor assumes a role in a play, people play roles in their families and in society. In fact, *labelling theory* views emotional disorders themselves in terms of social roles (Rosenhan, 1973). According to labelling theory, abnormal behaviour is created by social expectations; it is only what a given group or society deems to be abnormal. Labelling theory also suggests that people's actions conform to the expectations created by the label, a process termed the *self-fulfilling prophesy* (Rosenthal, 1966). For example, when an elementary school boy is labelled "a troublemaker," both he and his teachers may act in ways that make the label come true.

There is little doubt that expectations affect behaviour. Still, labelling alone cannot somehow cause the severe hallucinations, delusions, and life disruptions that characterize severe disorders like schizophrenia, for example. The roles people play in life—including roles shaped by gender, race, social class, and culture—help to shape who they become, but psychopathology is much more than the expectations a label creates.

## Relationships and Psychopathology

Much evidence links abnormal behaviour with distressed or conflicted relationships. Obvious difficulties like anger and conflict in relationships are tied to a number of emotional disorders ranging from schizophrenia (see Chapter 14) to conduct problems among children (see Chapter 16). Still, it often is impossible to determine if troubled relationships actually cause abnormal behaviour. In many cases, it seems equally or more likely that relationship distress is the effect of individual problems (see Research Close-Up).

**Marital Status and Psychopathology** The relationship between marital status and psychopathology is a good example of the cause–effect dilemma. The demographics of the family have changed greatly over the last few decades. Cohabitation before marriage is frequent, many children are born outside of marriage, and almost half of all marriages end in divorce (Cherlin, 1992). In part because of the uncertainty created by these rapid changes, researchers have frequently examined the psychological consequences of alternative family structures for children and for adults (Emery, 1994, 1999; Gotlib & McCabe, 1990; Whisman et al., 2000).

The findings of this large body of research must be interpreted with caution and care. On the one hand, marital status and psychological problems clearly are *correlated*. Somewhat more emotional problems are found among children and adults from divorced or never-married families than among people living in always-married families (see Chapter 18). On the other hand, despite common assumptions to the contrary, it is not clear that marital status is a direct *cause* of the emotional problems. Alternative explanations include suggestions that common genetic factors cause both emotional disorders and marital disruption (McGue & Lykken, 1992), as well as the likelihood that marital status can be a consequence, not a cause, of some psychological problems among adults (Gotlib & McCabe, 1990). Thus marital status may cause psychopathology, but abnormal behaviour also can create dysfunctional families (see Research Close-Up).

**Social Relationships** In addition to relationships within the family, key relationships outside the family can also affect mental health. For example, research indicates that a good relationship with an adult outside the family can buffer children from the effects of troubled family circumstances (Werner & Smith, 1982). Close relationships also provide protection against the development of psychopathology (Reis, Collins, & Berscheid, 2000).

## RESEARCH CLOSE-UP

### Marriage and Mental Health

Psychologists and social policymakers often raise concerns about a factor that is commonly found to be correlated with psychological well-being: marital status.

Valuable data on the relation between marriage and mental health are available from the Epidemiologic Catchment Area (ECA) study (Robins & Regier, 1991). Thousands of people were interviewed in this study in order to obtain measurements of their mental health. The researchers also examined various life circumstances that were correlated with mental illness, including marital status.

The investigators found consistent correlations between marriage and mental health. As one example, 1.5 percent of people still in their first marriage were diagnosed with depression in the past year. For people who had never married, the one-year prevalence of depression was 2.4 percent. Among those who had been divorced once, 4.1 percent had experienced depression in the past year. Finally, 5.8 percent of the people who had been divorced more than once had experienced an episode of depression in the previous 12 months. Thus, in comparison to people still in their first marriage, the never-married were about one and one-half times as likely to be depressed; people who had been divorced once were almost three times as likely to be depressed; and people divorced more than once were nearly four times as likely to be assigned the diagnosis.

Alcoholism also was found to be correlated with marital status. Among people in their first marriage, 8.9 percent met the diagnostic criteria for alcoholism at some time in their life (not the past year, which was the time frame for depression). For the never-married, the lifetime prevalence was 15 percent. Comparable figures were 16.2 percent for people divorced once and 24.2 percent for people divorced two or more times.

Marital status also was strongly related to a diagnosis of schizophrenia. The lifetime prevalence of schizophrenia was 1.0 percent among the married, 2.1 percent among the never-married, and 2.9 percent among those who had ever separated or divorced. In fact, marital status was related to virtually every psychological disorder that was diagnosed in this study.

How do we interpret the correlation between marriage and mental illness? The usual causal interpretation is that not being married causes emotional problems. According to this reasoning, the absence of a supportive mate makes unmarried people more susceptible to psychological problems, as do divorce and the conflict and loss of support that accompany it. On the other hand, emotional problems may be the cause of marital status. Psychologically disturbed people may have more trouble dating and forming permanent relationships. If they do get married, their emotional struggles may make them or their spouses more unhappy with their marriages and more prone to divorce. Third-variable interpretations offer yet another possibility. Any number of other variables could create a spurious correlation between marital status and abnormal behaviour. We know, for example, that poverty is correlated with an increased risk for remaining single or getting divorced, and we also know that poverty is correlated with an increased risk for developing psychological disorders. Perhaps poverty is a third variable that creates an artificial relation between marriage and mental health.

Alternative explanations of the relation between marriage and mental health hold vastly different implications for the treatment of psychological disorders and for social policy. If marital troubles are the cause of mental illness, our interventions should focus on improving or promoting marriage. If mental illness causes marital troubles, however, psychologists should focus on helping family members to cope with the trying stressor of mental illness. Finally, if the correlation between marital status and psychopathology is caused by a third variable like poverty, our interventions should focus on the third variable.

We have discussed marriage and mental health from a theoretical/methodological perspective, but you may be wondering what psychologists have concluded about the correlation between marriage and mental health. First, the correlation between marriage and mental health may be partly explained by third variables like poverty, but much of it is "real." The correlation is still found even when we exclude the effects of poverty and related "third variables" (Whisman, Sheldon, & Goering, 2000). Second, for severe psychological disorders like schizophrenia, it seems clear that being single or getting divorced is a reaction to, not a cause of, the emotional problem. Severe mental illness causes social difficulties that interfere with getting and staying married (Gotlib & McCabe, 1990). Third, it appears that in some cases being single, getting divorced, or having an unhappy marriage causes some common psychological problems, such as depression, but pre-existing depression also increases the risk for future marital problems (Fincham et al., 1997; Gotlib, Lewinsohn, & Seeley, 1998). It can be depressing to be alone or unhappy, but a depressed partner also makes a marriage difficult.

These differing conclusions remind us of one reason why we follow the systems approach to etiology in this text rather than adopting a paradigms approach. The same life event can play a different role in the etiology of different psychological disorders. Our theory about the relation between marriage and mental illness must be adapted for different psychological disorders. ◆

Research suggests that a few things are critical about **social support**—the emotional and practical assistance received from others. Significantly, one close relationship can provide as much support as being involved in many relationships. The greatest risk comes from having no social support. In addition, it is much worse to be actively rejected than to be neglected (Coie & Kupersmidt, 1983). Especially among children, it is far worse to be "liked least" than not to be "liked most" by your peers.

The association between abnormal behaviour and the lack of supportive peer relationships may have several different causes. In some circumstances, peer rejection may be the cause of emotional difficulties. Being made an outcast surely can cause much distress. In other cases, the lack of a close relationship may be a consequence of psychopathology, as when a disturbed individual is extremely awkward in social relationships. Finally, social support may help people to cope more successfully with emotional problems. The presence or absence of a close relationship might not cause a psychological problem, but once the problem emerges, social support may be the difference between successful and failed coping.

## Gender and Gender Roles

Gender and **gender roles**, expectations regarding the appropriate behaviour of males or females, can dramatically affect social relationships and social interaction. Boys and girls, men and women, are different. One common distinction argues that women are more *relational*, or oriented toward others, whereas men are more *instrumental*, or oriented toward action and achievement (Gilligan, 1982). Whether such differences really exist—and, if they do, what causes them—is open to debate. There is no doubt that some gender differences are determined by genetics and hormones, but there is also little doubt that socially prescribed gender roles exert a strong influence on our behaviour (Maccoby, 1998).

Gender roles may influence the development, expression, or consequences of psychopathology. Some theorists have suggested, for example, that women's traditional roles foster dependency and helplessness, which accounts for the considerably higher rates of depression among women (Nolen-Hoeksema, 1990). Others have suggested that gender roles are not responsible for the etiology of abnormal behaviour, but they do influence how psychopathology is expressed. According to this view, each gender may experience helplessness, but women are allowed to be depressed, whereas men's gender roles dictate that they "carry on" as if nothing were wrong. Instead of becoming depressed, men may express their inner turmoil by becoming physically ill.

Gender and gender roles are controversial and politically charged topics. Throughout this text we will consider differences between men and women in the prevalence of psychological disorders. When appropriate, we interpret this evidence in terms of the roles played by men and women in society.

## Prejudice and Poverty

Prejudice and poverty are broad social influences on psychological well-being. We consider these two factors together because they are so commonly linked in Western countries. According to a large survey of major Canadian cities (Lee, 2000), 30 percent of children 14 years and younger are living below the poverty level. First Nations people in cities, compared to other city-dwellers, are more than twice as likely to live in poverty (56 versus 24 percent). First Nations Canadian children, compared to other Canadian children, experience higher rates of school failure, encounter greater risk of substance abuse and family violence, and are more likely to take their own lives (Gotowiec & Beiser, 1993–1994). As adults, Canadian First Nations people are more likely than other Canadians to suffer from mood, anxiety, and substance-use disorders, and to commit suicide (Health Reports, 2002; Kirmayer, MacDonald, & Brass, 2001; MacMillan et al., 1996).

It is difficult to disentangle the separate effects of prejudice and poverty. Poverty potentially may play several roles in the development of psychopathology. Children from poor city neighbourhoods are witnesses and victims of a good deal of violence in their communities (Richters, 1993). Poverty also increases exposure to chemical toxins, such as to the lead found in old, peeling paint and automotive exhaust fumes. When ingested at toxic levels, lead can damage the central nervous system.

The conditions of poverty are more likely to affect First Nations people because more of them live in poverty. However, the experiences of Canadian First Nations people

*The history of Western society has been marred by blatant racism, such as discrimination against First Nations people. More subtle racism continues to influence social life and mental health today.*

and other Canadians differ in many more ways than socioeconomic status. First Nations people have endured a history of oppression and discrimination, and broad racial prejudices can undermine social opportunities and self-image.

### Societal Values

Broad social values may influence the nature and development of abnormal behaviour. For example, humanistic psychologists have questioned the conflict between the requirements

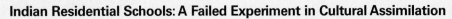

## CANADIAN FOCUS Indian Residential Schools: A Failed Experiment in Cultural Assimilation

European settlers in Canada and the United States clearly realized that their culture differed markedly from the cultures of First Nations people. But what the settlers failed to realize was that First Nations cultures are complex and well developed, with clear guidelines concerning family and societal roles, procedures for educating the young, and religious practices.

By failing to understand the sophistication of First Nations cultures, the settlers assumed that European culture was superior, and that First Nations peoples should therefore adopt European cultural traditions and practices (Haig-Brown, 1988). During the 1800s the Canadian government implemented a series of reforms to encourage, and sometimes coerce, First Nations people to assimilate into European culture. Performance of many First Nations ceremonies and other cultural practices were banned, and it was illegal to publicly wear traditional ceremonial dress unless special permission was obtained from the government (Furniss, 1995).

In the late 1800s the Canadian government set up a system of Indian residential schools—boarding schools where children lived away from their families. The idea was that the best way to make First Nations people assimilate into European culture was to "get them while they were young" by removing them from the influence of their parents (Grant, 1996; Haig-Brown, 1988). A further goal was to teach the children to read and write, and to train them in skills such as farming, cooking, and gardening. At their peak in the 1940s, there were over 70 residential schools across Canada, run by the government and the churches.

First Nations children as young as 4 years old were required to attend these schools for 10 to 11 months a year (Furniss, 1995; Haig-Brown, 1988). School life was harsh. Food was insufficient and the children were often hungry (Haig-Brown, 1988). Corporal punishment was meted out for even minor infractions. Public humiliation was also used as punishment, such as head shaving (Grant, 1996). Children were forbidden to speak their native language, and were brutally punished if they did so:

> My father, who attended the Alberni Indian Residential School for four years in the twenties, was physically tortured by his teachers for speaking Tseshaht: they pushed sewing needles through his tongue, a routine punishment for language offenders. . . . My Dad's attitude became "why teach my children Indian if they are going to be punished for speaking it?", so he would not allow my mother to speak Indian to us in his presence. I never learned to speak my own language. (Haig-Brown, 1988, p. 12)

Children were taught that their traditional ways were "savage" and "evil," and were forced to embrace Christianity (Grant, 1996). Their letters home were censored, and parents had great difficulty visiting their children (Haig-Brown, 1988). When the children did come home on vacation, family and children often felt alienated from one another. The children were afraid to speak their own language at home, and felt ashamed of their families who continued to practise traditional ways (Grant, 1996). Having been raised in an

*continued*

cont.

institution, the children had also lost their sense of family ties.

Some children appeared to benefit from the school system, but most did not (Furniss, 1995). Instead of assimilating First Nations people, the residential school system broke up families and taught First Nations people that they were inferior to others (Haig-Brown, 1988). By the mid-1940s, First Nations leaders across Canada were lobbying the government to end the residential school system in favour of schools on reserves and integration into the public school systems (Furniss, 1995). The last government-administered residential school, the McKay residence in Dauphin, Manitoba, was closed in 1988 (Grant, 1996).

Many children suffered from physical, sexual, and emotional abuse at the hands of school staff. A range of psychological problems has been attributed to the abuse, including substance abuse, depression, suicide, violence, low self-esteem, and symptoms of posttraumatic stress disorder (Furniss, 1995; Grant, 1996). Some of the abusers have been imprisoned, and dozens of cases are currently awaiting trial.

Today, residential schools are a painful memory, and the process of recovery is ongoing (Grant, 1996). Churches have issued apologies for the roles they played, and First Nations peoples are taking steps to rebuild their cultures, to heal the psychologically traumatized, and to regain control of their children's education (Furniss, 1995; Haig-Brown, 1988). At the same time, Euro-Canadians are learning to better understand and respect cultural differences. ◆

for healthy psychological development and societal demands in our frenzied and competitive culture of materialism (Szasz, 1961). From this point of view, personal growth and genuine interpersonal relationships are frustrated by our frenzied pace and focus on "winning." Other people, however, find great value in the material, technological, and scientific gains that accompany industrialization. From this perspective, concerns about society's frustration of personal growth are, in fact, luxuries of the very success that commentators deride.

We do not attempt to address the "mental health" of our culture in this textbook. However, we do recognize the broad influences of society and culture on abnormal behaviour. Our personal lives, our education, and even our science are deeply embedded within contemporary Canadian culture. The broad practices, beliefs, and values of our society play a role in the definition and development of abnormal behaviour and in shaping the scientific enterprise that attempts to uncover the roots of psychopathology.

# Summary

The **biological**, **psychodynamic**, **cognitive behavioural**, and **humanistic** approaches to understanding the causes of abnormal behaviour are alternative **paradigms**, and not just alternative theories. Biological approaches emphasize causes that occur "within the skin." Psychodynamic theory highlights unconscious processes and detailed case histories. Cognitive behavioural viewpoints focus on observable, learned behaviour. Finally, the humanistic paradigm argues that behaviour is not determined but, instead, is a product of free will. In short, these approaches conflict not only in their explanations of abnormal behaviour but also in what they view as acceptable scientific methods.

Although science benefits from competition, the conflict between these broad paradigms has outlived its usefulness, because none of these approaches offers the "right" explanation. Rather, abnormal behaviour is determined by *multifactorial causes*, the combination of different biological, psychological, and social factors. The current challenge for scientists is to integrate evidence on the etiology of different psychological disorders into a coherent whole, a system of contributing factors.

**Systems theory** is a way of integrating biological, psychological, and social contributions to abnormal behaviour. Its central principle is **holism**, the idea that the whole is more than the sum of its parts—a scientific counterpoint to **reductionism**. In systems theory, smaller units are not "ultimate" causes but are subsystems of the larger whole. Other important systems principles include **reciprocal causality**—the idea that causality is circular, and **equifinality**, the idea that there are multiple pathways to the development of any one disorder.

Biological factors relevant to abnormal behaviour begin with the smallest anatomic unit within the nervous system, the **neuron**, or nerve cell. Communication between neurons occurs when the axon terminals release chemical substances called **neurotransmitters** into the **synapse** between nerve cells. Disrupted communication among neurons, particularly disruptions in the functioning of various neurotransmitters, is implicated in the etiology of several types of abnormal behaviour. We must not equate a neurophysiological explanation of a psychological disorder with a biological abnormality, however, since such a conclusion raises concerns about biological reductionism and mind–body dualism.

Neuroanatomists commonly divide the brain into three subdivisions: the hindbrain, the midbrain, and the forebrain. Basic bodily functions are regulated by the structures of the hindbrain, which is rarely implicated in abnormal behaviour. The midbrain controls some motor activities, especially those related to fighting and sex. Damage to the midbrain can cause extreme disturbances, but such abnormalities typically result from specific and unusual brain traumas or tumours.

The forebrain is the location of most sensory, emotional, and cognitive processes. Most of the forebrain is composed of the two cerebral hemispheres, and many brain functions are lateralized, so that each hemisphere is the site of specific cognitive and emotional activities. Finally, the cerebral cortex is the uneven surface area of the brain that lies just underneath the skull. It is the site of the control and integration of sophisticated memory, sensory, and motor functions. Because of the rudimentary state of our knowledge about the brain, only the most severe mental disorders have been clearly linked with abnormalities in neuroanatomy. In most of these cases, brain damage is extensive and obvious.

**Psychophysiology** is the study of changes in the functioning of the body that result from psychological experiences. Psychophysiological arousal is caused by two different communication systems within the body: the **endocrine system** and the nervous system. Endocrine glands release **hormones** into the bloodstream, thus regulating some aspects of normal development as well as some responses to stress. The autonomic nervous system is the part of the central nervous system that is responsible for psychophysiological reactions. It has two branches: the sympathetic and the parasympathetic nervous systems. In general, the sympathetic nervous system controls arousal, and the parasympathetic nervous system controls energy conservation. Both psychophysiological overarousal and underarousal have been implicated in theories of the causes of abnormal behaviour.

**Behaviour genetics** is the study of genetic influences on the development of behaviour. Most forms of abnormal behaviour are **polygenic**; that is, they are caused by more than one **gene**. Polygenic inheritance makes the study of genetic contributions to behaviour difficult but not impossible. Comparisons of **monozygotic (MZ)** and **dizygotic (DZ)** twins can yield information about polygenic contributions, as can adoption studies. It is important to understand that the fact that a psychological disorder has a polygenic component does not mean that the disorder will inevitably appear, and that genetically influenced behaviour is influenced by the environment. Moreover, it is not clear what mechanism may account for behaviour genetic findings. Few single genes directly affect abnormal behaviour; thus genetic effects probably occur at some more basic level—for example, by affecting psychophysiological arousal.

Psychology has not developed a list of its core concepts. Some promise toward this goal is offered by **evolutionary psychology**, the application of the principles of evolution to our understanding of the animal and human mind. Evolutionary psychologists assume that animal and human psychology have evolved based on natural selection and sexual selection. Two basic psychological motivations seen in humans and other animals are the formation of **attachments** and competition for **dominance**. **Emotion** drives these basic motivations, and recent observations suggest that organized systems of emotion may be activated by certain social needs or challenges. **Temperament** is an individual's characteristic style of relating to the world. Researchers recently have agreed in identifying "the big five" dimensions of temperament.

Learning mechanisms include **classical conditioning**, **operant conditioning**, **modelling**, and human cognition. At least some abnormal behaviour is learned, and in the last two decades researchers have highlighted systematic cognitive biases that relate to some psychological disorders.

The sense of self is a uniquely human quality that would seem to play a role in causing emotional problems. It is possible, however, that self-esteem is merely another index of mental health. Finally, the idea of **developmental stages** not only charts the course of normal development, against which abnormal behaviour must be compared, but it also highlights the important issue of developmental transitions.

Social roles influence the definition and development of psychopathology. Evidence links abnormal behaviour with distressed or conflicted family relationships, and **social support** from people other than family members can be an important buffer against stress. **Gender roles** may influence the development, expression, or consequences of psychopathology. Some theorists suggest, for example, that women's traditional roles foster dependency and helplessness. Race and poverty, which are often related, also are broad social influences on psychological well-being in Canada today. Finally, humanistic psychologists have pointed out that there may be conflict between the demands of our competitive society and the requirements for healthy psychological development.

# Critical Thinking

1. What are your beliefs about the causes of abnormal behaviour? Do you adhere to one of the traditional paradigms? Are your reasons for preferring a particular approach personal or scientific? Has the information in this chapter changed your thinking?
2. Think about your social groups—your family, friends, clubs or organizations, or the people you live with. Consider the relationships among people in these groups, and try to understand them better by using concepts from systems theory—for example, reciprocal causality, homeostasis, subsystems.
3. Some people believe that we blame too many social and personal problems on biology. What are your thoughts? Do you think biological abnormalities cause (most) mental disorders? If so, what are the implications for personal responsibility for change? What are our societal responsibilities to people with emotional problems?
4. In what ways do social roles contribute to your behaviour? What roles do you see friends and family members playing—for example, being the "smart one" or the "responsible one" in the family? How do gender and ethnicity shape roles and expectations in our society? Do any of these roles encourage maladaptive or abnormal behaviour?

# Key Terms

attachment 53
attributions 55
autonomic nervous system 46
autosomal gene 48
behaviour genetics 47
biological paradigm 32
cerebral cortex 44
cerebral hemispheres 43
chromosomes 47
classical conditioning 34
cognitive behavioural paradigm 34
concordance rate 49
correlational study 39
correlation coefficient 39
defence mechanism 33
developmental psychopathology 40
developmental stage 57
diathesis 38
dizygotic (DZ) twin 49
dominance 54
dualism 42
ego 33
emotions 54
endocrine system 46
equifinality 38
evolutionary psychology 52
extinction 34
gender roles 59
genes 47
genotype 47
holism 36
homeostasis 39
hormones 46
humanistic paradigm 35
hypothalamus 43
id 33
identity 56
lateralized 43
limbic system 43
modelling 55
monozygotic (MZ) twin 49
neurons 41
neurotransmitters 41
nonshared environment 50
operant conditioning 34
paradigm 29
phenotype 47
polygenic 48
premorbid history 40
probands 49
prognosis 40
psychoanalytic theory 33
psychodynamic paradigm 32
psychophysiology 46
receptors 41
reciprocal causality 39
reductionism 37
reuptake 41
reverse causality 39
risk factors 38
self-control 56
self-efficacy 57
shared environment 50
social support 60
stress 38
superego 33
synapse 41
systems theory 29
temperament 54
third variable 39
ventricles 44

# 3 Treatment of Psychological Disorders

Overview
Biological Treatments
Psychodynamic Psychotherapies
Cognitive Behaviour Therapy
Humanistic Therapies
Research on Psychotherapy
Changing Social Systems: Couples, Family, and Group Therapy
Specific Treatments for Specific Disorders

**How are psychological problems treated?**

**Why do psychological treatments differ so much?**

**Does psychotherapy really "work"?**

**What treatments are most effective for what problems?**

Many people seek psychological help while they are battling bulimia, depression, anxiety, or other mental disorders. According to a recent survey by Statistics Canada, 2.6 million Canadians suffer from mental illness (Richardson, 2003). Other people are free of a specific mental disorder, but they seek help when struggling through major changes in their relationships, or when lost in the search for a happier, more meaningful life. Can psychological treatment help people in any of these circumstances? Once someone makes the difficult decision to seek help, he or she is faced with a whole new set of questions. Does it matter if the therapist is a psychiatrist, clinical psychologist, social worker, or counsellor? Should you look for someone who specializes in the problem needing treatment? Should medication be a part of therapy? What should you expect a therapist to do and say? How can "talking" help? As we will see in this chapter, these are questions that psychological scientists have worked to answer, but the questions also pose pressing personal concerns for a great many people. Psychological problems touch on all of us in one way or another, and we often turn to mental health professionals for help—sometimes in desperation.

## Overview

What can help? Few questions in abnormal psychology are more important than this one. We begin to answer this essential question in this chapter. However, we continue to ask, "What helps?" throughout the text, because one clear answer to "What helps?" is this: Different psychological problems respond better to particular treatments (Antony & Barlow, 2001).

One treatment that can help is **psychotherapy**, the use of psychological techniques and the therapist–client relationship to produce emotional, cognitive, and behaviour change in the client. We can define psychotherapy generally, but it is a challenge to define this elusive process more specifically. One challenge is that, according to one review, there are more than 400 different "schools" of psychotherapy for adults and 200 approaches for children (Kazdin, 1994b)!

This chapter will help you to understand the array of psychological treatments by grouping them according to the four paradigms reviewed in Chapter 2. Advocates of each paradigm have developed very different treatments (Prochaska & Norcross, 1999). In the past, mental health professionals asked one another, "What is your theoretical orientation?" The answer was supposed to be "biological," "psychodynamic," "cognitive behavioural," or "humanistic" (Smith, 1999). Today, the largest group of mental health professionals do *not* identify themselves with a specific paradigm, but instead describe themselves as **eclectic**, which means that they use different treatments for different disorders (Bechtoldt et al., 2001).

The eclectic approach is heartening, as long as different treatments are selected based on scientific evidence indicating that a particular treatment works best for a particular disorder (Chambless & Ollendick, 2000). Selecting treatments that work is the most practical and scientific approach to therapy, and in later chapters we cover specific treatments that have been developed and shown to be effective for specific disorders. In the first section of this chapter, however, we review and contrast biological, psychodynamic, cognitive behavioural, and humanistic approaches to treatment. You need to be familiar with each paradigm's approach, so that you can better understand how and why psychologists have developed specific treatments for various psychological disorders.

In the second section of this chapter, we take a closer look at two broad areas of research on psychotherapy. *Psychotherapy outcome research* addresses the issue of whether and to what extent psychotherapy "works." As you will learn, research shows that, on average, psychotherapy is helpful. Unfortunately, evidence also shows that most people do not get psychological help when they need it, including many people with severe disturbances (see Figure 3–1). The figure shows that the percentage of untreated disorders varies with location and with type of disorder. Another study, conducted by Statistics Canada, revealed that only 40 percent of Canadians with mental disorders receive treatment (Richardson, 2003).

There are various reasons for these results, such as the lack of availability of mental health services. People are more likely to be treated if they have appropriate healthcare coverage (see Canadian Focus on p. 95). Similarly, the person's willingness to seek treatment influences whether or not a disorder is treated. People may be more willing to admit that they need help for some problems (e.g., depression) than for other problems (e.g., alcohol abuse). People who do not meet diagnostic criteria for a mental disorder also may seek psychotherapy for personal growth or to learn better ways of coping with life stressors.

If psychotherapy works, how does it work? This is the question addressed by a second broad area of research, *psychotherapy process research*, which investigates whether and how different aspects of the therapist–client relationship help clients to change. For example, a recent study found that clients improved more in treatment (and liked their therapists better) if the therapists appropriately revealed some information about their own, similar struggles (Barrett & Berman, 2001).

It will help you to keep the biopsychosocial model in mind when considering the various psychological treatments presented in this chapter. Our overview of medication and other medical treatments early in the chapter shows that biological interventions can produce psychological change. Psychotherapy process and outcome research show that psychological interventions also can produce psychological change. Toward the end of the chapter, we discuss a group of treatments that change psychological functioning by altering the social circumstances in which a person operates. These interventions include couples therapy, family therapy, group therapy, and broader attempts to promote mental health by changing societal institutions. In short, as with the causes of abnormal behaviour, treatments can focus on biological, psychological, or social factors.

We introduce our overview of psychological treatments with a case study. As you read the following case, think about what might be wrong with this young woman and what you think might help her. After the case, we discuss how different therapists might treat the same client from a biological, psychodynamic, cognitive behavioural, or humanistic approach.

## Frances and the Four Paradigms

Biological, psychodynamic, cognitive behavioural, and humanistic therapists all would note Frances's depressed mood, her self-blame, and her troubled close relationships. However,

**Untreated Psychological Disorders**

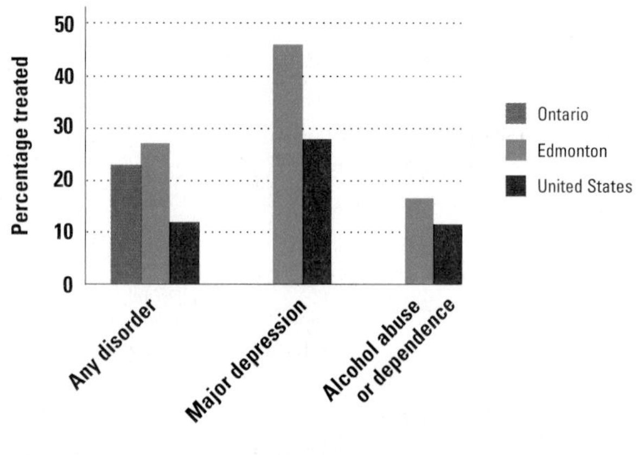


**FIGURE 3–1: Data from epidemiologic surveys conducted in Ontario, Edmonton, and the United States indicate that many diagnosed cases did not receive treatment by a mental health professional in the past year. (Note: Data on major depression and alcohol abuse or dependence were not available from Ontario study.)**

*Source:* Based on R.C. Bland, S.C. Newman, and H. Orn, 1997, Help-seeking for psychiatric disorders. *Canadian Journal of Psychiatry, 42,* 935–942; K.I. Howard, T.A. Cornille, J.S. Lyons, J.T. Vessey, R.J. Lueger, and S.M. Saunders, 1996, Patterns of service utilization. *Archives of General Psychiatry, 53,* 696–703; E. Lin, P. Goering, D.R. Offord, D. Campbell, and M.H. Boyle, 1996, The use of mental health services in Ontario: Epidemiologic findings. *Canadian Journal of Psychiatry, 41,* 572–577.

## CASE STUDY Why Is Frances Depressed?

Frances was a 23-year-old woman who sought psychotherapy for depression. Frances reported having been depressed for almost three years, with periods of relative happiness or deeper despair. When she came into therapy, her depression was severe. She had little appetite and had lost 5 kg over the previous six weeks, and her erratic sleeping patterns were worse than usual. She awoke around 2 or 3 A.M. every night, tossed in bed for several hours, and finally fell asleep again near dawn.

Frances reported feeling profoundly depressed about herself, her new marriage, and life in general. She freely admitted to frequent thoughts of suicide. She once sat in her bathroom holding a razor blade for over an hour, contemplating whether to slash her wrists. But she decided she could never commit the act. Now, she often wished she were dead, but she felt that she "lacked the courage" to take her own life.

Frances also noted that she found herself without motivation. She withdrew from her husband and the few friends she had, and she frequently called in sick at work when she felt blue. Frances's reports of depression were underscored by her careless dress, frequent bouts of crying, and slowed speech and body movements.

Frances reported that she had experienced a happy childhood. She had not known depression until the current episode began in her senior year in college. At first, she convinced herself that she was only suffering from "senior year syndrome." She wasn't sure what to do with her life. Secretly, she longed to move to New York and finally break out and do something exciting. But when she told her parents about her plans, her mother begged Frances to return home. She insisted that the two of them needed to have fun together again after four long years with Frances away at college. After graduation, Frances returned home to live with her parents.

It was shortly after moving home that Frances realized that her difficulties were much more serious than she had thought. She found herself intermittently screaming at her anxious and doting mother and being "super-nice" to her after feeling guilty about losing her temper. Frances described her mother as "a saint." Frances thought that her erratic behaviour toward her mother was all her fault. Her mother apparently agreed. In Frances's mind, she was a failure as a daughter.

Frances described both her mother and her father as loving and giving, but some of her comments about them were far from glowing. She said she was her mother's best friend. When asked if her mother was her best friend, Frances began to cry. She felt like her mother's infant, her parent, or even her husband, but not her friend and certainly not like her grown daughter.

Frances had little to say about her father. She pictured him drinking beer, eating meals, and falling asleep in front of the television.

Throughout the time she lived at home, Frances's depression only seemed to deepen. After a year of living with her parents, she married her high school sweetheart. Frances felt pressured to get married. Both her future husband and her mother insisted that it was time for her to settle down and start a family. At the time, she had hoped that marriage would be the solution to her problems. The excitement of the wedding added to this hope. But after the marriage, Frances said that things were worse—if that were possible. Still, she insisted that her marriage problems were all her fault.

Frances's husband was a young accountant who she said reminded her more and more of her father. He didn't drink, but he spent most of his brief time at home working or reading in his study. She said they had little communication, and she felt no warmth in her marriage. Her husband often was angry and sullen, but Frances said she couldn't blame him for feeling that way. His problem was being married to her. She wanted to love him, but she never had. She was a failure as a wife. She was a failure in life.

The theme of self-blame pervaded Frances's descriptions of her family. She repeatedly noted that, despite their flaws, her parents and her husband were good and loving people. She was the one with the problem. She had everything that she could hope for, yet she was unhappy. One reason she wanted to die was to ease the burden on them. How could they be happy when they had to put up with her foul moods? When she talked about these things, however, Frances's tone of voice often made her sound more angry than depressed. ◆

therapists working within these different paradigms would approach treatment and evaluate Frances in very different ways (see Table 3–1).

Biological therapies approach mental illness by drawing an analogy with physical illness. Thus, a biologically oriented psychiatrist or psychologist would focus first on making a diagnosis of Frances's problems. This would not be difficult in Frances's case, because her symptoms paint a clear picture of depression. The therapist surely would take note of Frances's description of her father, who seems chronically depressed. Perhaps a genetic predisposition toward depression runs in her family.

A biologically oriented therapist would sympathize with Frances's interpersonal problems but would not blame either Frances or her family for their troubles. Rather, the therapist would blame something that neither

**TABLE 3–1 Comparison of Biological, Psychodynamic, Behavioural, and Humanistic Treatments**

| Topic | Biological | Psychodynamic | Behavioural | Humanistic |
|---|---|---|---|---|
| Goal of treatment: | Alter biology to relieve psychological distress | Gain insight into defences/ unconscious motivations | Learn more adaptive behaviours/cognitions | Increase emotional awareness |
| Primary methods: | Diagnosis, medication | Interpretation of defences | Instruction, guided learning, homework | Empathy, support, exploring emotions |
| Role of therapist: | Active, directive, diagnostician | Passive, nondirective, interpreter (may be aloof) | Active, directive, nonjudgmental, teacher | Passive, nondirective, warm, supporter |
| Length of treatment: | Brief, with occasional follow-up visits | Usually long term; some new short-term treatments | Short term, with later "booster" sessions | Varies; length not typically structured |

*"He's in an H.M.O. Get some of the King's horses and a few of the King's men."*

©The New Yorker Collection. 1999 Leo Cullum from cartoonbank.com. All Rights Reserved.

Frances nor her family members could control: depression. It is exhausting to deal with someone who is constantly agitated and depressed. In the end, the therapist might explain that depression can be caused by a chemical imbalance in the brain. Medication would be recommended, and follow-up appointments would be scheduled to monitor the effects of the medication on Frances's mood and on her life.

In contrast, a psychodynamic therapist would take note of Frances's *defence mechanisms*. For example, the therapist would see Frances's justification of her parents' and husband's behaviour as a form of *rationalization*. Perhaps the therapist would also see a pattern of *denial* in Frances's refusal to acknowledge the imperfections of her loved ones and their failure to fulfill her needs. In Frances's seeing herself as a burden on her family, the therapist also might wonder if she was *projecting* onto them her own sense of feeling burdened by her mother's demands and her husband's indifference. Some psychodynamic theorists view depression as "anger turned inward" (see Chapter 5). Thus, getting Frances to express her anger directly toward her family rather than continually admonishing herself might be a goal in overcoming her defences.

A psychodynamic therapist would note Frances's unexpressed anger, but he or she would not challenge Frances's *defences* early in therapy. Instead, the first part of treatment would be more exploratory, focusing largely on Frances's past and her hopes, feelings, and frustrations. The exploration would be directed minimally by the therapist, who would encourage Frances to talk about issues she wanted to discuss. The goal of the unstructured discussions would be to illuminate Frances's unconscious motivations, intrapsychic conflicts, and defences to the therapist and, over time, to Frances herself. To facilitate therapy, the psychodynamic therapist gradually would confront Frances's defences in order to help her gain *insight* into her hidden resentment toward her mother, longing for a relationship with her father, and unfulfilled fantasies about marriage.

A cognitive behaviour therapist would note many of the same issues in Frances's life but would approach therapy quite differently. Rather than focusing on defence mechanisms, a therapist would note Frances's cognitive and behavioural patterns. Frances's self-blame—her pattern of attributing all of her interpersonal difficulties to herself—would be seen as a cognitive error. Her withdrawal from pleasing activities and her apparent unassertiveness also would be seen as contributing to her depression. In comparison to a psychodynamic therapist, a cognitive behaviour therapist would be far more directive in discussing these topics. For example, he or she likely would tell Frances that her thinking was distorted and her cognitive errors were contributing to her depression.

Learning new ways of thinking and acting in the present would be the focus of cognitive behaviour therapy. For example, the therapist probably would encourage Frances to appropriately allocate responsibility to others, not just herself, for her relationship problems, and the therapist might urge her to try out new ways of relating to her mother, father, and husband. The therapist would want Frances to play an active role in this learning process by completing *homework*—activities designed to continue her treatment outside the therapy session. Homework might include careful monitoring of specific conflicts with her family in an attempt to help Frances understand that she is not the cause of all family disputes. A therapist also might teach Frances how to assert herself more with family members. The therapist would expect Frances's depressed mood to begin to lift once she learned to assert her rights and no longer blamed herself for everything that went wrong in her life.

A humanistic therapist would also note Frances's depression, her self-blame, and her unsatisfactory relationships with loved ones. A more prominent focus, however, would be her lack of emotional genuineness—her inability to "be herself" with other people and within herself. Frances's tendencies to bury her true feelings would be explored as they related to the emotions she expressed in the therapy session. The humanistic therapist would want Frances to recognize her inner feelings and would encourage her to make life choices based on her heightened emotional awareness.

In conducting therapy, the humanistic therapist would be nondirective in terms of specific topics for discussion but would continually focus therapy on emotional issues. Initially, the therapist might simply empathize with Frances's feelings of sadness, loneliness, and isolation. Over time, the therapist likely would suggest that Frances had other feelings that she did not express. These might include frustration and guilt over her mother's controlling yet dependent style, and anger at her husband's and her father's self-centredness. The humanistic therapist would tell Frances that her feelings were legitimate and might encourage Frances to "own" her feelings. The humanistic therapist would not directly encourage Frances to act differently, but Frances would be expected to make some changes in her life as a result of her increased emotional awareness.

These approaches to treating Frances are very different, but you may be wondering if a therapist could use the best aspects of each approach. In fact, practitioners and researchers often integrate elements of different approaches when working to find more effective treatments. One straightforward example is when psychotherapy and medication are combined in the hope that the combination will be more effective than either approach alone. Before considering how different approaches can be integrated in practice, however, we first need to elaborate on the differences in theory among the four approaches. The contrasts among them can best be understood by examining the treatments from a historical perspective.

## Brief Historical Perspective

We can trace the roots of psychotherapy to two broad traditions of healing: the spiritual/religious tradition and the naturalistic/scientific tradition (Frank, 1973). The spiritual/religious tradition is an ancient one that attributes both physical and mental ailments to supernatural forces. One of the earliest examples of this tradition is the practice of *trephining*. From skulls unearthed by archaeologists, researchers have concluded that tribal healers performed a primitive form of surgery as a treatment for mental disorders. Trephining involved chipping a hole through the unfortunate sufferer's skull with a crude stone tool. Presumably, the purpose of trephining was to allow evil spirits to escape.

There are numerous other examples throughout history and across cultures in which demons have been viewed as the cause of abnormal behaviour and exorcism has been used as the treatment. Until the seventeenth century, some cases of mental disturbance in Europe and in the North American colonies were attributed to witchcraft (Neugebauer, 1979). Those suspected of being witches were put through painful tests that they often could not pass. One examination was to dunk the

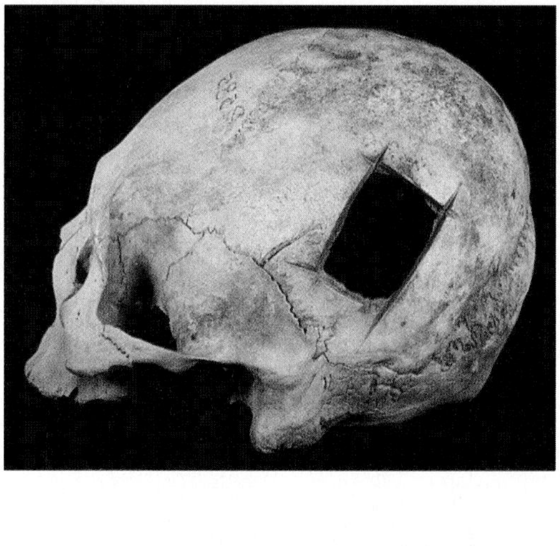

*Trephining was a primitive attempt to treat psychological problems by cracking a hole in the skull of the sufferer. Presumably, evil spirits could escape through the hole, thereby curing the problem.*

suspected witch under water. The only way to pass the test—to be found not a witch—was to drown!

The spiritual/religious tradition certainly has produced bizarre explanations for and treatments of abnormal behaviour. Still, the influence of spiritual beliefs and rituals should not be ignored. Believing is a powerful part of healing. Spiritual beliefs influence how people cope with all sorts of life difficulties. Recognition of the power of shared beliefs also calls attention to the essential role played by ethnicity and culture in influencing treatment preferences and psychotherapy effectiveness. Judging by *New Yorker* cartoons, many of which you will find in this text, the educated elite in North America are accepting of psychotherapy as a cultural institution. Other cultural or ethnic groups may be less accepting, viewing psychotherapy as intrusive or threatening.

Naturalistic/scientific approaches to helping the mentally disturbed also have ancient roots. Hippocrates recommended treatments such as rest, exercise, and a healthy diet (see Chapter 1). In the 1600s, "insane asylums" were developed as a new treatment for the mentally ill. One rationale for these institutions was to remove disturbed individuals from society, but another was the hope that rest and isolation would alleviate their bizarre behaviour. Although the beginnings of scientific approaches can be traced to ancient times, the biological, psychodynamic, cognitive behavioural, and humanistic paradigms did not fully emerge until the nineteenth and early twentieth centuries.

# Biological Treatments

The nineteenth-century detective work involved in discovering the diagnosis, cause, and cure for general paresis is an outstanding example of the fulfillment of the hope of finding successful biological treatments for psychological disorders (see Chapter 2). This remarkable achievement paralleled other medical advances in its course of discovery. First, an increasingly refined and accurate diagnosis is developed. Second, clues about causes are put together like pieces of a puzzle to form a complete picture of the specific etiology of the disease. Third, scientists experiment with various treatments for preventing or curing the disorder until they find an effective treatment. These are far from simple tasks, of course, as shown by the century it took to diagnose general paresis, discover syphilis as its cause, and develop antibiotics as a treatment for the disease.

At present, we cannot tell similar success stories about the development of biological treatments for other mental disorders. One reason for this is that, unlike the single bacterial infection that causes general paresis, most mental disorders appear to be caused by many factors. As a result, scientists have tried to discover biological treatments for various mental disorders without knowing the specific cause of the problem. These treatments focus on *symptom alleviation*, reducing the dysfunctional symptoms of a disorder but not eliminating its root cause (Valenstein, 1998).

Experimentation has produced mixed results in the biological treatment of emotional problems. Early biological treatments designed to alleviate symptoms included bleeding, forced hot baths, the use of various physical restraints, and the surgical removal of sexual organs. Happily, numerous medications, many of which are very effective for symptom alleviation, have been discovered since the 1950s and particularly since the 1980s. Before presenting an overview of these new drugs, we briefly consider two controversial biological treatments: electroconvulsive therapy and psychosurgery.

## Electroconvulsive Therapy

**Electroconvulsive therapy (ECT)** involves the deliberate induction of a seizure by passing electricity through the brain. The technique was developed in 1938 by Ugo Cerletti and Lucio Bini, two Italian physicians who were seeking a treatment for schizophrenia. At the time, schizophrenia was erroneously thought to be rare among people who had epilepsy. This led to speculation that epileptic seizures somehow prevented the disorder. Cerletti and Bini discovered a means of inducing seizures when visiting a slaughterhouse. There they observed electric current being passed through the brains of animals, which produced a convulsion and unconsciousness. Shortly thereafter, the two physicians began to use a modified electroconvulsive technique as an experimental treatment for schizophrenia.

Approximately 100 volts of electric current was passed through the patients' brains in what is now termed *bilateral ECT*. Electrodes are placed on the left and right temples, and the current passes through both brain hemispheres. In *unilateral ECT*, the electric current is passed through only one side of the brain, the nondominant hemisphere. Both procedures induce brief unconsciousness and seizures, but unilateral ECT produces less *retrograde amnesia*—loss of memory of past events, a disturbing side effect of ECT (Lisanby et al., 2000). Unfortunately, unilateral ECT may not be as effective as bilateral ECT. Thus some experts now recommend bilateral ECT if unilateral ECT has not produced improvement after about six sessions (Weiner & Krystal, 1994). Typically, ECT involves a series of 6 to 12 sessions over the course of a few weeks.

ECT failed in its original objective of curing schizophrenia. Moreover, as illustrated in books and in movies like *One Flew over the Cuckoo's Nest*, there is no doubt that ECT was overused in mental hospitals in the middle of the twentieth century, before the development and widespread use of modern medications. ECT is used far more cautiously and far less frequently today. The side effects linked with ECT are rare, but they can be severe. These include long-term memory loss, bone fractures, and death in about 1 to 2 of every 10 000 patients (Weiner & Krystal, 1994). Because of these risks, ECT must be used cautiously. However, evidence indicates that ECT is effective in treating severe depressions that do not respond to other treatments, especially for a patient at high risk for suicide (see Chapter 5).

## Psychosurgery

**Psychosurgery** is a controversial biological treatment, as it involves the surgical destruction of specific regions of the brain. Psychosurgery was introduced in 1935 by Egas Moniz (1874–1953), a Portuguese neurologist. *Prefrontal lobotomy* was the technique refined by Moniz—a procedure in which the frontal lobes of the brain are surgically and irrevocably severed. The technique was widely adopted, and thousands of prefrontal lobotomies were performed throughout the middle of the twentieth century. In fact, Moniz won a Nobel Prize in 1949 for his "discovery" of this "treatment" (Pressman, 1998).

Prefrontal lobotomy was subsequently discredited because of its limited effectiveness and its frequent and severe side effects, which include a significant mortality rate, excessive apathy, and the absence of emotional responsiveness. Ironically, Moniz himself was shot and paralyzed by one of his lobotomized patients, a sad testament to the unpredictable outcome of the procedure (Pressman, 1998).

Although prefrontal lobotomies are no longer performed, some forms of highly circumscribed psychosurgery are used today to treat severe disorders. For example, a form of limited psychosurgery called *cingulotomy* may be effective in treating some very severe cases of obsessive–compulsive disorder when all other treatments have failed (Baer et al., 1995; see Chapter 6). During a cingulotomy, only small, precisely pinpointed regions of the brain are selectively destroyed. Still, the complexity of the brain, our limited knowledge of its functions, and the irreversibility of brain damage combine to make psychosurgery a procedure that is used very rarely today.

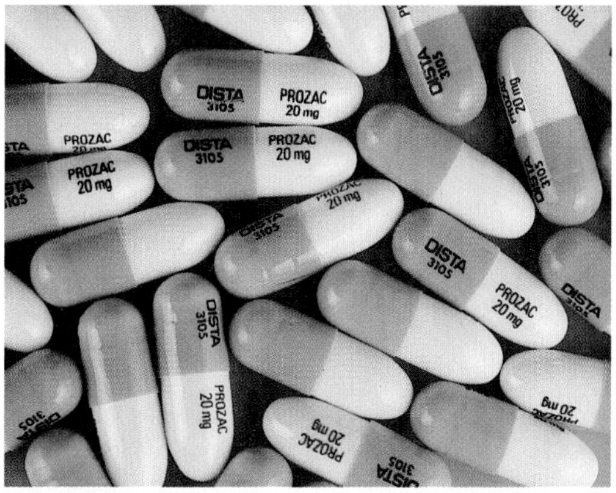


*Prozac is an effective antidepressant that is the best-selling medication for treating psychological problems. More than 40 million people are reported to use Prozac. More than CDN$3.6 billion of Prozac was sold worldwide in 1999.*

## Psychopharmacology

**Psychopharmacology**—the study of the use of medications to treat psychological disturbances—has been the most promising avenue of biological treatment. In recent years, scientists have developed new medications that have increasingly specific effects on emotional states and mental disorders (see Table 3–2).

There are a variety of **psychotropic medications**, chemical substances that affect psychological state. Some psychotropic medications produce rapid changes in thinking, mood, and behaviour. Many antianxiety agents, such as Xanax, have effects that become apparent soon after the medication is taken. Others, such as antidepressant medications, have more subtle influences that build up gradually over time. Still other psychotropic drugs affect people with mental disorders very

**TABLE 3–2 Major Categories of Medications for Treating Psychological Disorders**

| Therapeutic Use | Chemical Structure or Psychopharmacologic Action | Example: *Generic Name* | *Trade Name* |
|---|---|---|---|
| Antipsychotics (also called major tranquilizers or neuroleptics) | Phenothiazines | Chlorpromazine | Thorazine |
| | Thioxanthenes | Thiothixene | Navane |
| | Butyrophenones | Haloperidol | Haldol |
| | Rauwolfia alkaloids | Reserpine | Serpasil |
| | Atypical neuroleptics | Clozapine | Clozaril |
| Antidepressants | Tricyclic antidepressants (TCAs) | Amitriptyline | Elavil |
| | Monoamine oxidase inhibitors (MAOIs) | Phenelzine | Nardil |
| | Selective serotonin reuptake inhibitors (SSRI) | Fluoxetine | Prozac |
| | Atypical antidepressants | Bupropion | Wellbutrin |
| Psychomotor stimulants | Amphetamines | Dextroamphetamine | Dexedrine |
| | Other | Methylphenidate | Ritalin |
| Antimanic | Metallic element | Lithium carbonate | Lithane |
| | Anticonvulsants | Carbamazepine | Tegretol |
| Antianxiety (also called minor tranquilizers) | Benzodiazepines | Diazepam | Valium |
| | Propanediol carbamates | Alprazolam | Xanax |
| | | Meprobamate | Equanil |
| Sedative hypnotic | Barbiturates | Phenobarbital | — |
| | Benzodiazepines | Triazolam | Halcion |
| Antipanic | Benzodiazepines | Alprazolam | Xanax |
| | MAOIs | Phenelzine | Nardil |
| | TCAs | Imipramine | Tofranil |
| Antiobsessional | TCA | Clomipramine | Anafranil |
| | SSRI | Fluoxetine | Prozac |

*Source:* Adapted from Canadian Pharmaceutical Association, 2004, *Compendium of Pharmaceuticals and Specialties*, 39th ed. Ottawa: Author.

differently from the way they affect someone who is functioning normally. Antipsychotic medications help to eliminate delusions and hallucinations among people suffering from schizophrenia, but the same medications would disorient most people and send them into a long, groggy sleep.

The success of psychopharmacology is evident in the expanding development and use of psychotropic medications in recent years. In 1994, 6.5 percent of visits to *all* physicians were for psychotropic medications. Psychiatrists actually prescribe only about a third of these drugs. More often, family and primary care physicians prescribe them (Pincus et al., 1998). Psychostimulants and new antidepressant medications are being used with remarkable frequency. For example, early in the 1990s, the antidepressant medication Prozac outsold *every* prescription medication, including all medications used to treat physical ailments. In 1999, more than CDN$3.6 *billion* of Prozac was sold worldwide (*Worcester Business Journal*, April 24, 2000). As another example, the prescriptions of psychostimulants for preschoolers, which are used to treat inattentive and hyperactive behaviour in children, tripled during the 1990s (Zito et al., 2000).

We review evidence on the effects of antidepressants and other major psychotropic medications in relevant chapters later in the text. For now, there are a few general points that you should note about psychopharmacology. First, evidence indicates that various medications are effective and safe treatments for particular mental disorders. Second, though psychotropic medications typically offer symptom relief, not a cure of an underlying problem, symptom alleviation is extremely important. Still, some commentators worry that psychotropic medication is given too readily to address psychological or social problems (Breggin, 1994). Third, all medications have side effects, some of which are very unpleasant. Partly as a result of unpleasant side effects, many patients do not take their medication as prescribed, and they often experience a relapse as a result. Fourth, many psychotropic drugs must be taken for long periods of time. Because the medications alleviate symptoms but do not produce a cure, it may be necessary to keep taking the drug—for months, years, or sometimes for a lifetime (Klerman et al., 1994).

# Psychodynamic Psychotherapies

Psychodynamic approaches to treatment were first developed during the nineteenth and early twentieth centuries. Joseph Breuer (1842–1925) was one of their earliest advocates. Breuer used hypnosis to induce his troubled patients to talk freely about problems in their lives. Upon awakening from the hypnotic trance, many patients reported relief from their symptoms. Breuer used the principle of *catharsis* to explain the benefits of his hypnotic method. He believed that psychological problems are caused by pent up emotions and that the release of previously unexpressed feelings—catharsis—reduces psychic strain. The sudden release of steam through the whistle of a boiling teapot is an appropriate metaphor for catharsis.

## Freudian Psychoanalysis

Breuer's contemporary and collaborator, Sigmund Freud (1856–1939), adopted the hypnotic method for a time, but he soon concluded that hypnosis was not necessary to encourage open expression. Instead, Freud simply told his patients to speak freely about whatever thoughts crossed their mind. This method, called **free association**, became a cornerstone of Freud's famous treatment, **psychoanalysis**.

Unlike Breuer, Freud did not see catharsis as an end in itself. The true benefit of free association, in Freud's view, was that it revealed aspects of the unconscious mind. Freud found clues to his patients' unconscious desires in their unedited speech. Freud also believed that dreaming (defences presumably are weaker in dreams) and slips of the tongue (now called "Freudian slips"—for example, saying "sin" when you meant to say "sex") provided especially revealing information about the unconscious. Thus, according to Freud, free association, dreams, and slips of the tongue are valuable because they serve as "windows into the unconscious."

**Psychoanalytic Techniques** According to Freud, the psychoanalyst's task is to uncover the unconscious conflicts and motivations that cause psychological difficulties. However, this discovery is only the first step in treatment. In order to overcome their conflicts, patients must come to share the psychoanalyst's understanding of their intrapsychic life. The ultimate goal of psychoanalysis is to bring formerly unconscious material into conscious awareness. This is what Freud called **insight**. Freud asserted that insight is sufficient for curing psychological disorders.

The analyst's main tool for promoting insight is interpretation. In offering an **interpretation**, the analyst suggests hidden meanings to patients' accounts of their past and present life. Typically, interpretations relate to past experiences, especially experiences with loved ones. Recall from Chapter 2, however, that according to Freudian theory, the ego defence mechanisms keep intrapsychic conflicts from conscious awareness. Thus psychoanalysts must overcome defences like reaction formation as patients resist their interpretations. ("Hate my mother? My mother is a *saint!*") Timing is everything in overcoming such *resistance*. The patient must be on the verge of discovering the hidden meaning himself or herself; otherwise, the interpretation will be rejected. For example, return to the case history and consider the dilemma of convincing Frances that deep resentment lies beneath her professed, unwavering love for her mother. Given her long history of subjugating her own needs to those of her mother, Frances would be unlikely to accept such an interpretation if it were made too early in her treatment.

One essential element in probing the unconscious mind and offering interpretations is *therapeutic neutrality*. Psychoanalysts maintain a distant stance toward their patients in order to minimize their influence on free association.

The classical psychoanalyst "sits behind the patient where the patient cannot see him. He tries to create, as far as possible, a controlled laboratory situation in which the individual peculiarities of the analyst shall play as little role as possible in stimulating the patient's reactions" (Alexander & French, 1947, p. 83).

The analyst's distant stance is thought to encourage **transference**, the process whereby patients transfer their feelings about some key figure in their life onto the shadowy figure of the analyst. For psychoanalysis to succeed, the analyst must not respond to transference in a manner that the patient views as critical or threatening. Analysts also must avoid reacting to their patients in the same way as the transference figure had reacted, for example, by responding to Frances's helplessness by becoming overprotective (like her mother). In addition, psychoanalysts must guard against *countertransference*, or letting their own feelings influence their responses to their patients. Instead, the analyst's job is to maintain therapeutic neutrality and offer interpretations that will promote insight about the transference. For example, "You seem frustrated that I won't tell you what to do. I wonder if you have come to expect authority figures to solve your problems for you."

Insight into the transference relationship presumably helps patients understand how and why they are relating to the analyst in the same dysfunctional manner in which they related to a loved one. This awareness creates a new understanding both of past relationships and of unconscious motivations in present relationships. For example, consider a transference that might develop between Frances and a psychoanalyst. Frances might have difficulty accepting a therapeutic relationship in which she was receiving care instead of giving it. She might, therefore, try to get the analyst to reveal personal problems, or perhaps she would bring gifts to her therapist. The therapist's polite refusal of the gifts and of Frances's attempts at caretaking might cause Frances to feel hurt, rejected, and, eventually, angry. As therapy proceeded, these actions could be interpreted as reflecting Frances's style of relating to her mother and her tendency to deny her own needs.

Rather than ridding the patient of defences, one goal of psychoanalysis is to replace them. Defences such as denial and projection are confronted because they distort reality dramatically, whereas "healthier" defences, such as rationalization and sublimation, are left unchallenged. A second goal of psychoanalysis is to help patients become more aware of their basic needs or drives so that they may find socially and psychologically appropriate outlets for them (Maddi, 1980). A goal for Frances, for example, would be to admit that anger is a legitimate and acceptable part of her personality.

**The Decline of Freudian Psychoanalysis** In traditional psychoanalysis, patients meet with their analyst for an hour several times each week. These sessions often go on for years. Because psychoanalysis requires substantial time, expense, and self-exploration, it is accessible only to people who are relatively well functioning, introspective, and financially secure. In many respects, psychoanalysis now is construed more as a process of self-understanding than as a treatment for specific emotional disorders. This view is bolstered by the fact that very little therapy outcome research has been conducted on psychoanalysis. Freud believed that not every patient would benefit from the treatment—a belief shared by many contemporary practitioners. Those suffering from psychotic and personality disorders are thought to be especially unlikely to benefit, whereas people suffering from "neurotic" disorders, especially excessive anxiety, are thought to benefit most.

Although it is still practised, the expense and time involved and the limited evidence for its effectiveness have caused Freudian psychoanalysis to decline greatly. However, variations on Freudian theory have led to various forms of insight-oriented therapy. These revisionist

*"This is getting us nowhere!"*

©The New Yorker Collection. 2000 Gahan Wilson from cartoonbank.com. All Rights Reserved.

approaches are termed **psychodynamic psychotherapy** rather than psychoanalysis. Psychodynamic psychotherapists often are more engaged and directive in therapy, and treatment may be relatively brief in comparison to psychoanalysis.

## Ego Analysis

The development of **ego analysis** was an important innovation in Freudian theory. Ego analysis originated in the work of a number of therapists who were trained in Freudian psychoanalysis but who independently developed somewhat different theories and techniques. Whereas Freud emphasized the paramount role of the id in personality and psychopathology, these new theorists focused much more on the ego. The major function of the ego, according to Freudian theory, is to mediate between the conflicting impulses of the id and the superego (see Chapter 2). Of equal importance to ego analysts, however, is the ego's role in dealing with reality (Hartmann, Kris, & Loewenstein, 1947). Ego analysts, therefore, are concerned with unconscious motivations, but they also consider the patient's dealings with the external world. They also attend to the role of society and culture in producing emotional disturbance, as well as to the effects of current life circumstances and the patient's reactions to them.

Of greatest importance in ego analysis are the patient's past and present interpersonal relationships. The ego analyst Harry Stack Sullivan (1892–1949) was extremely influential in highlighting the role of relationships. He suggested that many characteristics of the personality could be conceptualized in interpersonal rather than intrapsychic terms. Sullivan would be concerned about Frances's relationship with her mother, not just Frances's feelings about her mother. Like many interpersonal theorists, Sullivan saw two basic dimensions of interpersonal relationships. One dimension reflects interpersonal power, ranging from dominance to submission. A second dimension concerns interpersonal closeness, with affiliation on one end of the continuum and hostility at the opposite pole. Sullivan's followers, in fact, have developed a classification of personality based on these two dimensions (Leary, 1957).

Other especially influential ego analysts include Erik Erikson (1902–1994) and Karen Horney (1885–1952). Horney's (1939) most lasting contribution was her suggestion that people have conflicting ego needs to move toward, against, and away from others. Essentially, Horney argued that there are competing human needs for closeness, for dominance, and for autonomy. She viewed people with interpersonal or intrapsychic conflicts as being too rigid in fulfilling only one of these needs. In her view, the key to a healthy personality is finding a balance among the three styles of relating to others. Pause and consider these three needs in relation to Frances. Her characteristic style and conflicting needs should not be too difficult for you to discern.

We introduced Erikson's stage theory of development in Chapter 2. As with other ego analysts, Erikson's critical departure from Freud focused on the interpersonal context. This can be seen in his emphasis on the externally oriented psycho*social* stages of development rather than the internally oriented psycho*sexual* stages. Erikson also introduced the argument that an individual's personality is not fixed by early experience but continues to develop as a result of predictable psychosocial conflicts throughout the lifespan (see Chapter 17). In contrast, Freud viewed personality patterns as being fixed by intrapsychic conflicts that occurred primarily during the first few years of life. He assumed that personality is difficult to change thereafter.

John Bowlby's (1907–1991) *attachment theory* (see Chapter 2) perhaps has had the greatest effect on contemporary psychodynamic thought about interpersonal influences on psychopathology. Freud viewed closeness in relationships as merely a secondary outgrowth of the reduction of primary drives. According to Freud, for example, infants grow close to their mothers, because mothers reduce infants' hunger. In contrast, Bowlby elevated the need for close relationships to a primary human characteristic. From an attachment theory perspective, people are inherently social beings. Our hunger to form close relationships is not so different from our hunger for food, as both reflect a basic human need.

## Psychodynamic Psychotherapy

Many different approaches to psychotherapy have been developed based on the writings of Sullivan, Horney, Erikson, Bowlby, and other theorists influenced by Freud. All these approaches seek to uncover hidden motivations and emphasize the importance of insight. However, psychodynamic psychotherapists are much more actively involved with their patients. They are more ready to direct the patient's recollections, to focus on current life circumstances, and to offer interpretations quickly and directly. Most psychodynamic psychotherapists are also much more "human" in conducting therapy. They may be distant and reflective at times, but they also are willing to offer appropriate emotional support (Garfield, 1989).

*Short-term psychodynamic psychotherapy* is a form of treatment that uses many psychoanalytic techniques. Therapeutic neutrality is typically maintained, and transference remains a central issue, but the short-term psychodynamic therapist actively focuses on a particular emotional issue rather than relying on free association (Garfield, 1989). The short-term approach has gained attention because it typically is limited to 25 sessions or fewer and therefore is less expensive and more amenable to research (Garfield, 1989; Luborsky, Barber, & Beutler, 1993). Current research on psychodynamic psychotherapy generally supports Freud's observation that psychodynamic therapy is ineffective in treating more severe disorders, although it may be effective in treating milder anxiety (Luborsky et al., 1993). There still is a pressing need for further evidence on the technique, however.

# Cognitive Behaviour Therapy

**Cognitive behaviour therapy** focuses on emotional, cognitive, and behaviour change in the present, not insight about the past. The approach includes a diverse array of techniques developed out of psychological research. All cognitive behaviour therapists adhere to the truism, "Actions speak louder than words."

The beginnings of behaviour therapy can be traced to John B. Watson's (1878–1958) writings in the early part of the twentieth century. Watson was the key figure in developing **behaviourism** in North American psychology—the belief that observable behaviours, not unobservable cognitive or emotional states, are the appropriate focus of psychological study. Watson also maintained that abnormal behaviour was learned and could be unlearned, just like normal behaviour. He viewed the behaviour therapist's job as being a teacher. The therapeutic goal is to provide new, more appropriate learning experiences. In developing treatments, behaviour therapists relied heavily on animal learning research, particularly Pavlov's theories of classical conditioning and Skinner's theories of operant conditioning (see Chapter 2). More recently, behaviour therapy has been extensively influenced by the findings of cognitive psychology (Mahoney, 1991). Thus, the term "cognitive behaviour therapy" has largely replaced "behaviour therapy" in describing this set of techniques, but the two terms can be used interchangeably.

Unlike psychoanalysis, behaviour therapy does not offer an elaborate theory about the nature of human personality. Rather, it is a practical approach oriented to changing behaviour rather than trying to alter the dynamics of personality. Perhaps the most important contribution of behaviour therapy is its reliance on empirical evaluation. Cognitive behaviour therapists have asked, "What works?" in hundreds of treatment outcome studies that use the **experimental method** (see Research Methods).

Cognitive behaviour therapists' focus on present behaviour, learning, and cognition can be seen in their diverse treatment techniques. In the following sections we consider some of the most common techniques.

## Systematic Desensitization

A number of behaviour therapy techniques are based on Pavlov's theory of classical conditioning (see Chapter 2). The most influential was developed by Joseph Wolpe (1915–1997), a South African psychiatrist who concentrated his research and therapy on eliminating phobias. Wolpe (1958) assumed that at least some phobias were learned through classical conditioning. He reasoned that if fears could be learned, they could be unlearned. The key was to break the association between stimulus and response.

The technique Wolpe developed is called **systematic desensitization**, and it has three key elements. The first is relaxation training. Wolpe reasoned that, in order to replace anxiety, a new conditioned response—relaxation—must be easily elicited. He focused on the technique of *progressive muscle relaxation*, a method of inducing a calm state through the contraction and subsequent relaxation of all of

# RESEARCH METHODS

## The Experimental Method

The **experiment** is the most powerful of all scientific methods in one very important way: researchers who use experimental methods can determine cause and effect relationships. The experiment has four essential features. It begins with a **hypothesis**—the experimenter's specific prediction about cause and effect. To illustrate, in studies on the treatment of generalized anxiety disorder by Robert Ladouceur (Laval University), Michel Dugas (Concordia University) and their colleagues, it was hypothesized that cognitive behaviour therapy (CBT) would be more effective than no treatment at all (Dugas et al., 2003; Ladouceur et al., 2000).

The second feature of an experiment is the manipulation of an **independent variable**. Independent variables are controlled and deliberately manipulated by the experimenter. In the present example, the independent variable is whether patients receive CBT or no treatment. People who receive an active treatment belong to the **experimental group**. Those who receive no treatment or a placebo belong to the **control group**.

The third feature of the experiment is **random assignment**, ensuring that each subject has a statistically equal chance of receiving different levels of the independent variable. In the present example, picking the number 1 or 2 out of a hat is one of many possible ways of ensuring random assignment to CBT or no treatment. Random assignment is essential, because it ensures that any differences among groups are caused by the independent variable and not by biased selection into groups.

The fourth feature of the experiment is the measurement of the **dependent variable**. The dependent variable is the outcome that is hypothesized to vary according to manipulations in the independent variable. The outcome *depends* on the experimental manipulation—thus the term "dependent variable." In the present example, the symptoms of generalized anxiety disorder would be dependent variables. These symptoms would be expected to change depending on whether the patients received CBT or no treatment at all.

Statistical tests typically are conducted to establish whether the independent variable has changed the dependent variable in a predictable manner, or whether the outcome is a result of chance. According to current conventions, a finding is considered to be **statistically significant** if it would occur by chance in less than 1 out of every 20 experiments. That is, the probability of a chance outcome is less than 5 percent, a specification that is often written as $p < .05$. However, a statistically significant result is not the same as a *clinically significant* finding. A treatment may produce a reliable change in symptoms, for example, but the change may be too small to produce a meaningful difference in the patient's life. The treatment studies by Ladouceur, Dugas, and colleagues evaluated both forms of significance, and found that CBT produced statistically and clinically significant reductions in generalized anxiety symptoms.

We can conclude that an independent variable causes changes in a dependent variable when the experimental method is used correctly and it produces statistically significant results. The ability to establish causation is a powerful strength of the experiment in comparison to the correlational study. The experimental method is limited, however, because many theoretically interesting independent variables cannot be manipulated practically or ethically in real life. We may hypothesize that abusive parenting causes psychological problems, for example, but we obviously cannot randomly assign children to grow up in abusive and nonabusive homes. In fact, practical and ethical limitations make it impossible to use the experiment to test most hypotheses about the causes of abnormal behaviour. Thus, when studying the etiology of abnormal behaviour, we often must rely on correlational studies or analogue studies.

The effectiveness of various psychological treatments often can be studied using an experiment, because researchers can control whether someone receives a particular medication or form of psychotherapy. Still, it is not easy to control completely the independent variable in treatment outcome research. Some people may drop out of treatment, and others may seek additional help. Clinicians might not conduct psychotherapy according to the design of the experiment, or patients might not take their medication as prescribed.

These examples are only a few of the many ways in which the independent variable can be *confounded* with other factors in psychological research. Each of these examples is a threat to the internal validity of the experiment. An experiment has **internal validity** if changes in the dependent variable can be accurately attributed to changes in the independent variable. As we have noted, however, the independent variable can be manipulated poorly, or it can be confounded with other variables. For example, it would be wrong to conclude that a medication was ineffective if the patients failed to take it, or it would be difficult to draw conclusions about psychotherapy if many of the patients dropped out of the study.

In contrast to internal validity, **external validity** refers to whether the findings of an experiment generalize to other circumstances. A number of questions typically can be raised about an experiment's external validity, because some artificiality needs to be introduced to give the experimenter control over the independent variable. In a hypothetical treatment study, for example, perhaps only a very narrow group of patients would be treated. Thus the findings might not generalize to other people with other problems. Or perhaps psychotherapy might last for exactly 10 sessions in the experiment in order to ensure control of the independent variable. Although this would help the study's internal validity, it might compromise the experiment's external validity. The findings might not apply in the real world, where the length of treatment is tailored to the individual patient's needs.

*continued*

*cont.*

There is no finite list of questions that can be raised about the internal and external validity of experiments. A common trade-off, however, is that the experimenter often must sacrifice one for the other. Recognizing this compromise is essential to evaluating science. ◆

***Joseph Wolpe*** *(1915–1997) was a prominent cognitive behaviour therapist. Wolpe developed systematic desensitization, a pioneering technique for eliminating fears.*

the major muscle groups. The second component of systematic desensitization is the construction of a *hierarchy of fears* ranging from very mild to very frightening stimuli. Because anxiety initially is a stronger response to the feared stimulus than is relaxation, Wolpe thought that exposure to fears must be gradual, or the relaxation would be overwhelmed by the anxiety. The third part of systematic desensitization is the *learning process*—namely, the pairing of the feared stimulus with the relaxation response. Wolpe had his clients carry out this pairing in their imagination. Thus systematic desensitization involves imagining increasingly fearful events while simultaneously maintaining a state of relaxation.

Systematic desensitization has been the subject of volumes of research. In fact, the development of the technique can be credited with spurring psychotherapy outcome research in general. Overall, evidence supports the effectiveness of systematic desensitization as a treatment for fears and phobias (O'Leary & Wilson, 1987; Wolpe, 1990). It is not clear, however, that classical conditioning accounts for the change. Alternative interpretations suggest that the true mechanisms for change are the removal of reinforcement for avoidance, the extinction of the fear, increased self-confidence from confronting one's fears, or even the formation of a supportive therapeutic relationship (Kazdin & Wilcoxin, 1976; O'Leary & Wilson, 1987).

## Other Exposure Therapies

Although many factors contribute to effective cognitive behaviour therapy, most investigators agree that *exposure* is the key to fear reduction. This observation has led to the development of variations on desensitization techniques, the most notable of which is in vivo desensitization. **In vivo desensitization** involves gradually being exposed to the feared stimulus in real life while simultaneously maintaining a state of relaxation. Research on in vivo desensitization indicates that the way to overcome fears is to confront them.

Another exposure technique is **flooding**. Unlike desensitization, exposure to the feared stimulus is not gradual in flooding, and there is no attempt to calm initial anxiety. Rather, flooding involves exposure at full intensity. The goal is to eliminate anxiety through extinction by repeatedly presenting the conditioned stimulus until it no longer produces the unconditioned response (see Chapter 2). Someone who was afraid of heights might be brought to the top of the CN Tower in Toronto (the world's tallest freestanding structure). The intense anxiety initially produced by this experience gradually should be extinguished as the individual spends more time at the top of the building. The key to this treatment, and to flooding in general, is to prevent avoidance. Clients must not be allowed to retreat from the stimulus in fear, because the resulting reduction in anxiety would be negatively reinforcing (Wolpe, 1990).

## Aversion Therapy

Unlike systematic desensitization and other exposure techniques, the goal in **aversion therapy** is to create rather than eliminate an unpleasant response. As such, aversion therapy is used primarily in the treatment of substance use disorders such as alcoholism and cigarette smoking. Aversion therapy for these problems involves pairing an unpleasant response with the stimuli that elicit substance use. In working with alcoholism, for example, the typical procedure is to pair the sight, smell, and taste of alcohol with severe nausea produced artificially by a drug.

Aversion therapies have the goal of reducing substance use by associating it with unpleasant consequences. Such treatments are controversial, however, precisely because of their aversive nature. Moreover, data on the effectiveness of aversion therapies are ambiguous (O'Leary & Wilson, 1987). Although these treatments often achieve short-term success, relapse rates are high. Everyday life offers the substance abuser the opportunity, and perhaps the motivation, to desensitize himself or herself to the classically conditioned responses learned in aversion therapy.

### Contingency Management

**Contingency management** is an operant conditioning technique that focuses on directly changing the rewards and punishments for various behaviours. A *contingency* is the relationship between a behaviour and its consequences; thus, contingency management involves changing this relationship. The goal of contingency management is to reward desirable behaviour systematically and to extinguish or punish undesirable behaviour. In order to achieve this goal, the therapist must control relevant rewards and punishments. Thus contingency management is used primarily in circumstances where the therapist has considerable direct or indirect control over the client's environment, such as in institutional settings or when children are brought for treatment by their parents.

The **token economy** is an example of contingency management that has been adopted in many institutional settings. In a token economy, desired and undesired behaviours are clearly identified, contingencies are defined, behaviour is carefully monitored, and rewards or punishments are given according to the rules of the token economy. For example, in a group home for juvenile offenders, a token economy may specify that residents earn tokens for completing schoolwork and household chores, and lose tokens for arguing or fighting. Each resident's behaviour is monitored and recorded, and tokens are "paid" accordingly. The key to the success of the program is that tokens can be exchanged for rewards desired by the residents—for example, going out unescorted on a Saturday night.

Research shows that contingency management successfully changes behaviour for diverse problems such as institutionalized clients with schizophrenia (Paul & Lentz, 1977) and juvenile offenders living in group homes (Phillips et al., 1973). The evidence for success must be interpreted carefully, however. Improvements that occur in the setting where the operant program is in place often do not generalize to real-life situations (Emery & Marholin, 1977). Rewards and punishments in controlled settings often differ from those in the natural environment. A psychologist can set up clear and consistent contingencies for a juvenile living in a group home, but it may be impossible to alter the rewards and punishments the teenager encounters when he or she returns to live with a chaotic family or delinquent peers. In the real world, undesirable behaviour often is rewarded, and punishments for inappropriate behaviour—and rewards for appropriate behaviour—often are inconsistent or delayed. Thus contingency management programs work in controlled environments, but the benefits may not continue after the client leaves for a less carefully regulated environment.

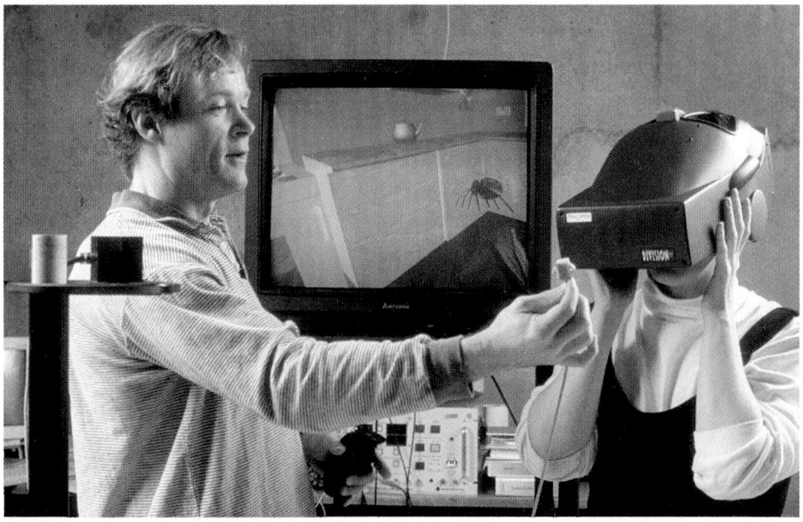

*Some cognitive behaviour therapists are experimenting with using virtual reality for exposure therapy.*

### Social Skills Training

The goal of **social skills training** is to teach clients new ways of behaving that are both desirable and likely to be rewarded in the everyday world (McFall, 1982). Two commonly taught skills are assertiveness (Paterson, 2000) and social problem solving (D'Zurrilla & Goldfried, 1971; Spivack & Shure, 1974).

The goal of *assertiveness training* is to teach clients to be direct about their feelings and wishes. The training may involve a variety of levels of detail in social skills, from learning to make eye contact to asking a boss for a raise. In teaching assertiveness, therapists frequently use **role playing**, an improvisational acting technique that allows clients to rehearse new social skills. Clients try out new ways of acting as the therapist assumes the role of some person in their life. For example, a cognitive behaviour therapist might assume the role of Frances's mother, and ask Frances to try to express some of her frustration to her "mother" during a role play.

Later, the therapist offers feedback and suggests different approaches to the client. In addition to teaching new social skills, assertiveness training seeks to produce cognitive change, such as learning to recognize personal "rights." For example, the cognitive behaviour therapist might tell Frances that she has a right to express her feelings to her mother. She does not have the right to get everything that she wants, however. Thus assertiveness would be defined in terms of expressing her own feelings, not by her success in changing her mother.

*Social problem solving* is a multistep process that has been used to teach children and adults ways to go about solving a variety of life's problems (D'Zurrilla & Goldfried, 1971; Spivack & Shure, 1974). The first step in social problem solving involves assessing and defining the problem in detail. This step is important, as we often see problems as being more manageable when they are defined specifically. For example, a cognitive behaviour therapist would encourage Frances to see her problems in terms of specific difficulties with her family, not as a reflection of her inept personality. "Brainstorming" is the second step in social problem solving. In order to encourage creativity, therapists ask clients to come up with as many alternative solutions as they can imagine—even wild and crazy options—without evaluating these alternatives. The third step in social problem solving involves careful evaluation of each of the options that has been generated. Finally, one alternative is chosen and implemented, and its success in solving the problem is evaluated objectively. If the solution is unsuccessful, the entire process can be repeated until an effective solution is found.

Waterloo University emeritus professor **Donald Meichenbaum** developed an important form of treatment known as self-instruction training. This method has since been used widely throughout the world.

It is difficult to draw general conclusions about the effectiveness of social skills training because the technique has been applied to many specific problems with varying degrees of success. Clients can learn new social skills in therapy, but it is less clear whether these skills are used effectively in real life (O'Leary & Wilson, 1987). We consider the effectiveness of social skills training in treating specific problems in subsequent chapters.

## Cognitive Techniques

Cognitive behaviour therapy often draws on basic research for inspiration in developing therapeutic techniques. All of the cognitive behaviour therapies discussed to this point have foundations in either classical or operant conditioning. Some more recent cognitive techniques are rooted in cognitive psychology.

One example is *attribution retraining*, which is based on the idea that people are "intuitive scientists" who are constantly drawing conclusions about the causes of events in their lives. These perceived causes, which may or may not be objectively accurate, are called *attributions*. Attribution retraining involves trying to change attributions, often by asking clients to abandon intuitive strategies. Instead, clients are instructed in more scientific methods, such as objectively testing hypotheses about themselves and others. For example, first-year university students often attribute their "blues" to their own failings. If they carefully observe the reactions of other first years, however, they may be persuaded into really believing a more accurate causal explanation: the first year of university can be trying, lonely, and stressful, as well as exciting and fun.

*Self-instruction training* is another cognitive technique that is often used with children. In self-instruction training, developed by University of Waterloo psychologist Donald Meichenbaum (1977), the adult first models an appropriate behaviour while saying the self-instruction aloud. Next, the child is asked to repeat the action and also to say the self-instruction aloud. Following this, the child repeats the task while whispering the self-instructions. Finally, the child does the task while repeating the instructions silently. This procedure is designed as a structured way of developing *internalization*, helping children to learn internal controls over their behaviour.

## Beck's Cognitive Therapy

Cognitive behaviour therapy also has been strongly influenced by the clinical work of Aaron Beck (1976). Beck's **cognitive therapy** was developed specifically as a treatment for depression (Beck et al., 1979; see Chapter 5). Beck suggested that depression is caused by errors in thinking. These hypothesized distortions lead depressed people to draw incorrect, negative conclusions about themselves, thus creating and maintaining the depression. Simply put, Beck hypothesized that depressed people see the world through grey-coloured

*Cognitive therapies help people to challenge distorted cognitions and develop more realistic beliefs. Coaches also often have to urge players, fans, and themselves to develop more realistic expectations.*

glasses (as opposed to the rose-coloured variety). According to Beck's analysis, this negative filter makes the world appear much bleaker than it really is.

Beck's cognitive therapy involves challenging these negative distortions by gently confronting clients' cognitive errors in therapy, and asking clients to see how their thinking is distorted based on their own analysis of their life (Beck et al., 1979). For example, a cognitive therapist might ask Frances to keep a record of her various family conflicts, including a brief description of the disputes and of the circumstances that preceded and followed each episode. Together with Frances, the cognitive therapist would use this information to challenge Frances's tendency to blame herself for the troubled relationships, a tendency that presumably results from a cognitive distortion rather than an accurate appraisal of her interactions.

### Rational–Emotive Therapy

Albert Ellis's (1973) **rational–emotive therapy (RET)** is also designed to challenge cognitive distortions. According to Ellis (1962), emotional disorders are caused by *irrational beliefs*. Irrational beliefs are absolute, unrealistic views of the world, such as "Everyone must love me all the time." The rational–emotive therapist searches for a client's irrational beliefs, points out the impossibility of fulfilling them, and uses any and every technique to persuade the client to adopt more realistic beliefs. Rational–emotive therapy shares concepts and techniques in common with Beck's approach, with the similarities outweighing the differences.

### Integration: Empiricism Reigns

Clearly, cognitive behaviour therapy comprises diverse treatments. What unites cognitive behaviour therapists is a commitment to empiricism, not to a particular form of treatment. Cognitive behaviour therapists want treatments that work, and they have been vigorous in conducting psychotherapy outcome research. Research indicates that cognitive behaviour therapies are not the only effective treatments, but this finding does not distress empirically oriented cognitive behaviour therapists. Rather, it challenges them to identify alternative approaches and to incorporate them into the ever-expanding realm of cognitive behaviour therapy. In fact, we envision a blurring of the lines between cognitive behaviour therapy and other approaches, as researchers identify diverse but effective treatments for different disorders.

## Humanistic Therapies

**Humanistic psychotherapy** originally was promoted as a "third force" to counteract what were seen as the overly mechanistic and deterministic views of both the psychodynamic and cognitive behavioural approaches to psychotherapy. Humanists argue that psychodynamic, cognitive behavioural, and biological therapists overlook the most essential of all human qualities: the individual's ability to make choices and freely determine his or her future.

Humanistic therapists believe that emotional distress results from the frustrations of human existence, particularly from alienation from the self and others. They also argue that each individual has the responsibility for finding meaning in her or his own life. Unlike the behaviour therapist, the humanistic therapist does not believe that treatment can solve problems. Rather, treatment is seen only as a way to help individuals make their own life choices and resolve their own dilemmas (Rogers, 1961).

To help clients make choices, humanistic therapists strive to increase *emotional awareness*. They encourage clients to recognize and experience their true feelings. Like psychodynamic approaches, this involves "uncovering" hidden emotions, and some psychologists, therefore, classify the two treatments together as insight therapies. However, humanistic therapists are more concerned with how their clients are feeling than with why they are feeling that way. They focus on experiencing life, not on the structure of the personality. Thus, like behaviour therapy, humanistic therapy is much more oriented to the present than is psychodynamic treatment.

One unique aspect of humanistic psychotherapy is the importance placed on the therapist–client relationship. Humanistic therapists view a genuine and reciprocal relationship between therapist and client as the central means of producing therapeutic change. Therapists from other schools also place importance on the therapist–client relationship, but the relationship is viewed primarily as a means of delivering the treatment. In humanistic therapy, the relationship is the treatment.

## Client-Centred Therapy

Carl Rogers (1902–1987) and his **client-centred therapy** provide the clearest example of the humanistic focus on the therapeutic relationship. Rogers (1951) wrote extensively about the process of fostering a warm and genuine relationship between therapist and client. He particularly noted the importance of **empathy**, or emotional understanding. Empathy involves putting yourself in someone else's shoes as a way of understanding the other person's unique feelings and perspectives. In order to demonstrate empathy, the therapist must communicate this emotional understanding. Empathy is conveyed by reflecting the client's feelings and, at a deeper level, by sharing an understanding of emotions that remain unexpressed.

In forming an empathic relationship, the client-centred therapist does not act as an "expert" who knows more about the client than the client knows about himself or herself. Rather, the humanistic therapist endeavours to share in another human's experience. In fact, Rogers encouraged *self-disclosure* on the part of the therapist. In contrast to the psychoanalyst's distance, client-centred therapists may intentionally reveal aspects of their own feelings and experiences to their clients.

Rogers also felt that client-centred therapists must be able to *demonstrate unconditional positive regard* for their clients. This involves valuing the clients for who they are and refraining from judging them. Because of this basic respect for the client's humanity, client-centred therapists avoid directing the therapeutic process. According to Rogers, if clients are successful in experiencing and accepting themselves, they will achieve their own resolution to their difficulties. Thus client-centred therapy is nondirective.

*Humanistic therapists highlight the importance of empathy in psychotherapy.*

## Gestalt Therapy

Frederich (Fritz) Perls's (1893–1970) **Gestalt therapy** is another variation of the humanistic approach. Perls (1969) shared many of Rogers's therapeutic goals, particularly the goal of helping clients recognize and accept their emotional experiences. Perls especially underscored the importance of experiencing the moment—what he called living in the "here and now." He urged people to be genuine, and he accused many of being phony instead.

Gestalt techniques for increasing emotional awareness differ greatly from client-centred approaches. Rather than being supportive, the Gestalt therapist confronts phoniness, hoping that the client's frustration will provoke genuine emotion. As long as the client is phony, the Gestalt therapist is confrontational. When genuine emotion is expressed, however, the therapist's confrontation switches to support and shared experience. The here and now is critical to this distinction. Talking about emotions is phony. Feeling them is genuine. To a Gestalt therapist, an engaged "I hate you!" is much more genuine than a detached "I'm feeling very angry with you right now."

Gestalt therapists also differ from Rogerians in that they are very directive. In fact, Perls developed a number of specific exercises designed to provoke emotion and thereby heighten awareness. One of the better known strategies is the *empty chair technique*, in which the client has a dialogue with another part of himself or herself who is imagined to be sitting in an empty chair. For example, a Gestalt therapist might tell Frances (from the case history) to imagine that there are two parts to her personality, the "top dog" and the "under dog." The top dog is demanding, critical, and controlling. The under dog feels pushed around, weak, helpless, resentful, and tense. The Gestalt therapist would ask Frances to have her top dog talk to her under dog (the latter being in the empty chair). Then she would switch seats, with the under dog addressing the top dog. This would help Frances better understand these parts of her personality and thereby help her work out the differences between them. Thus, as with other Gestalt techniques, the goal of the empty chair exercise would be to heighten Frances's emotional awareness, including awareness of her conflicting emotions, and thereby increase her genuineness.

### A Means, Not an End?

One problem in evaluating effectiveness is that clients who seek humanistic treatments often are functioning rather well in their lives. They view therapy as a growth experience, not as a treatment for an emotional problem. Another problem is that few investigators have conducted psychotherapy outcome research on humanistic therapy.

We should note, however, that Rogers and his colleagues were strongly committed to psychotherapy *process* research. In fact, process research may be the lasting legacy of humanistic psychotherapy. As we discuss in more detail shortly, research on psychotherapy processes shows that the bond or **therapeutic alliance** between the therapist and client is crucial to the success of therapy—no matter what approach is used (Rogers, 1957; Truax & Carkhuff, 1967). The major task for psychotherapy research is to identify the most effective treatments for specific disorders, but psychologists must not lose sight of the fact that caring, concern, and respect for the individual are essential in treating emotional disorders.

## Research on Psychotherapy

Based on our own evaluation of the extensive research on psychotherapy, we have reached three major conclusions about psychotherapy. First, psychotherapy *does* work—for many people and for many problems. Second, the major approaches to psychotherapy share basic similarities that are often overlooked (e.g., the therapist–client relationship), and these common factors contribute to the success of therapy in important ways. Third, different treatments, including medication, are more or less effective for different disorders. We discuss evidence pertaining to the first conclusion in reviewing psychotherapy *outcome* research. We address the second conclusion when we consider psychotherapy *process* research. We focus on the third conclusion throughout subsequent chapters of the text where we discuss specific biological, psychological, and social interventions that are most effective in preventing or treating specific disorders.

### Does Psychotherapy Work?—Outcome Research

*Psychotherapy outcome research* examines the outcome, or result, of psychotherapy—its effectiveness for relieving symptoms, eliminating disorders, and/or improving life functioning. Hundreds of studies have compared the outcome of psychotherapy with alternative treatments or with no treatment at all. In order to summarize findings across all of these studies, psychologists have invented a new statistical technique called meta-analysis.

**Meta-analysis** is a statistical technique that allows the results from different studies to be combined in a standardized way. The results of a meta-analysis are expressed in standard deviation units, a measure of variation from the mean (see Research Methods in Chapter 15).

In evaluating hundreds of studies of psychotherapy outcome, meta-analysis indicates that the average change produced by psychotherapy is .85 standard deviation units (Smith, Glass, & Miller, 1980). This means that the average client who receives therapy is better off than 80 percent of untreated persons (see Figure 3–2). As another way of evaluating this finding, consider that nine months of reading instruction leads to a .67 standard deviation unit increase in reading achievement among elementary school children (Lambert, Shapiro, & Bergin, 1986). And many well-accepted medical treatments have considerably smaller effect sizes. For example, chemotherapy has about a .10 effect size in reducing mortality following breast cancer (Lipsey & Wilson, 1993).

Meta-analysis is a useful way of summarizing information from a large number of studies, but you may have trouble grasping the meaning of a standard deviation unit. Fortunately, we can convert the figure into a simple improvement rate. A .85 standard deviation change indicates that roughly two-thirds of clients who undergo psychotherapy improve significantly, whereas about one-third of people who receive no treatment improve over time (Rosenthal, 1983). This conclusion suggests that therapy "works," but you should remember one important qualification. Very few researchers have studied whether the benefits of therapy last, and available studies indicate that many benefits diminish in the year or two after treatment ends (Westen & Morrison, 2001).

**Meta-Analysis of Psychotherapy Outcomes**

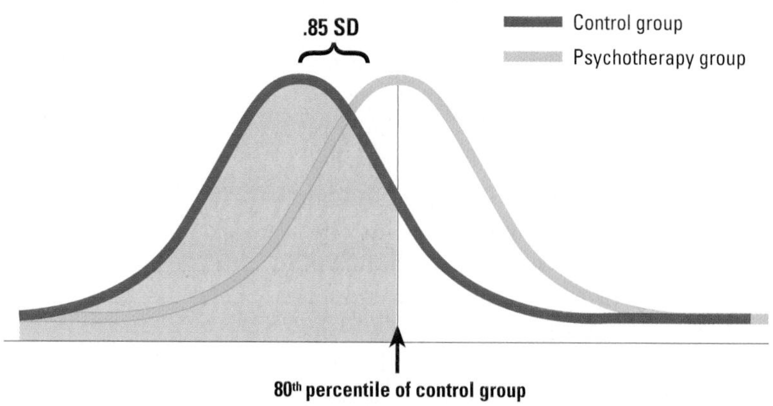


**FIGURE 3–2: The average effect of psychotherapy has been found to be .85 standard deviation units. Thus the average client who receives therapy functions better than 80 percent of untreated controls (shaded area).**

*Adapted from:* M.L. Smith, G.V. Glass, and T.I. Miller, 1980, *The Benefits of Psychotherapy*. Baltimore: Johns Hopkins University Press.

### Do People Improve without Treatment?

Psychologists widely accept that about two-thirds of clients improve in the short-term as a result of psychotherapy. Some skeptics have suggested, however, that far more than one-third of untreated emotional disorders have a *spontaneous remission*. That is, many people with psychological problems may improve without any treatment at all. In fact, the British psychologist Hans Eysenck (1916–1997), who wrote one of the earliest and most famous criticisms of psychotherapy, concluded that psychotherapy was totally ineffective for this very reason. In reviewing early evidence on psychotherapy, Eysenck (1952/1992) agreed that about two out of three people were helped by therapy. However, he asserted that *two-thirds*, not one-third, of people with emotional problems improve without treatment. Thus, he concluded that psychotherapy offered little in the way of extra help.

How many people actually improve without treatment? The standard method for answering this question is to use an experiment (see Research Methods on p. 79). In the basic psychotherapy experiment, people seeking treatment (and who agree to participate in the study) are randomly assigned either to receive psychotherapy or no treatment. People in the *no-treatment control group* typically are assigned to a waiting list, so that they will receive psychotherapy at some time in the future. Many studies have used exactly this method, but the results are difficult to interpret. While waiting for professional therapy, people in no-treatment control groups often seek counselling and advice from family members, friends, or religious leaders. Thus, any improvements in their problems may not be caused by spontaneous remission, but instead the changes may be due to receiving *informal* psychological help.

Informal counselling often is helpful, as you surely know from your own life experiences. In fact, researchers have found that as many as one-half of people seeking psychotherapy improve as a result of simply having unstructured conversations with a professional (Lambert, Shapiro, & Bergin, 1986). Thus, some experts argue that so-called no-treatment controls actually receive some form of treatment. Other experts assert that "just talking" is hardly psychotherapy. Should we consider informal counselling to be part of psychotherapy, or is "just talking" merely a placebo?

**The Placebo Effect** In medicine, *placebos* are pills that are pharmacologically inert; that is, they have no medicinal value. More broadly, placebos are any type of treatment that contains no known active ingredients for treating the condition being evaluated. But the absence of active ingredients does not prevent placebos from healing. The **placebo effect**, the powerful healing produced by apparently inert treatments, has been demonstrated widely and repeatedly in psychotherapy, dentistry, optometry, cardiovascular disease, cancer treatment, and even surgery (Bienenfeld, Frishman, & Glasser, 1996; Shapiro & Morris, 1978). Experts agree that many of the benefits of physical and psychological treatments are produced by placebo effects, which apparently are caused by the recipient's belief in a treatment and expectation of improvement.

Some people view the placebo effect as a nuisance or even as a hoax. This opinion is understandable, because a goal of research is to isolate the active ingredients in a treatment beyond placebo effects. But we can also view placebo effects as treatments—treatments that heal through psychological means. Of course, psychological healing also is the goal of psychotherapy. Thus, for the purposes of understanding and improving psychotherapy, many researchers believe that placebo effects should be embraced and not dismissed (Critelli & Neumann, 1984; Frank & Frank, 1991). Ironically, psychotherapy researchers need to identify the active ingredients in placebos! As we discuss shortly, in fact, research indicates that the client's belief in a treatment and expectation of improvement are essential to the process of successful psychotherapy (Frank & Frank, 1991).

What is the "bottom line" about improvement without treatment? The best estimate seems to be that about one-third of people do improve without treatment. Thus psychotherapy does, indeed, work for many people with many problems.

**Placebo Control Groups** The ultimate goal of treatment research is to identify therapies that produce change above and beyond placebo effects. That is, we want to discover therapies that contain one or more active ingredients for treating a particular disorder. Thus many investigations in medicine and psychotherapy include **placebo control groups**—patients who are given treatments that are intentionally designed to have no active ingredients.

Researchers have long recognized an important complication when using placebo control groups to investigate new medications: The *doctor's* expectations about a medication influence the treatment's effectiveness by subtly increasing the patient's expectations (Rosenthal & Rosnow, 1969). To control for this, scientists invented the **double-blind study** in which neither the physician nor the patient knows whether the prescribed pill is the real medication or a placebo.

Unfortunately, a double-blind study cannot be used in psychotherapy outcome research. You can disguise a placebo pill from a physician, but you cannot disguise a placebo psychotherapy from a therapist. Therapists know—or at least strongly believe—whether or not the treatment they offer is the real thing or a placebo. In fact, recent evidence indicates that the therapist's "allegiance" to one form of therapy or another has a powerful influence on whether the treatment proves to be effective (see Further Thoughts). For this reason, future psychotherapy outcome research will need to study whether clients *and* therapists believe in a treatment and expect it to be effective (Hollon, 1999; Luborsky et al., 1999).

**Contrasting Efficacy and Effectiveness** As you can see, psychotherapy outcome experiments must be carefully controlled. Clients must be randomly assigned to experimental and control conditions, and a no-treatment, placebo, or alternative treatment control group must be selected with care. It also is essential to define clearly the *experimental* treatment. For the purposes of a study, the length of therapy typically is restricted to a set number of sessions, and therapists must follow strict treatment guidelines as detailed in a lengthy *treatment manual*. Investigators also use narrowly defined criteria for selecting clients for the study—for example, limiting treatment to clients who are clinically depressed, have no other disorder, and meet specified background characteristics.

## Further Thoughts The Allegiance Effect

Many psychotherapy outcome studies have compared the effectiveness of two or more alternative treatments instead of using a no-treatment or placebo control group. In many respects, this is a superior method of conducting research on psychotherapy outcome for reasons we have already discussed.

Despite the strengths of the method, researchers have recently recognized an important flaw in most studies that have compared the outcome of two or more treatments. The problem has been termed the allegiance effect. The **allegiance effect** is the tendency for researchers to find that their favourite treatment—the one to which they hold allegiance—is the most effective treatment (Luborsky et al., 1999). In comparing psychodynamic therapy and cognitive behaviour therapy, for example, researchers allied with cognitive behaviour therapy tend to find that treatment to be more effective. In contrast, researchers conducting a similar study, but who are allied with psychodynamic therapy, tend to find the psychodynamic treatment to be more effective. In fact, according to a recent meta-analysis of 29 studies (Luborsky et al., 1999), 69 percent of the variance in the effectiveness of one treatment over another was explained by allegiance effects.

What causes allegiance effects? In discussing the double-blind study, we already suggested one influence: the therapist's expectations about a treatment's effectiveness certainly contributes to whether or not the treatment is, in fact, effective. The allegiance effect also is likely to be caused by other, less subtle influences (Luborsky et al., 1999). When designing a study, researchers probably tend to pick a weak rival alternative treatment. This choice may or may not be intentional, but investigators, of course, want their preferred approach to "win."

Another, not so subtle contribution to the allegiance effect may be the tendency for investigators to publish research papers primarily when their findings are consistent with their initial hypotheses (Luborsky et al., 1999). This is the so-called *file drawer problem* (Rosenthal, 1979). That is, we only know the results of studies that are published, and we can only guess about the results of research still sitting in someone's file drawer. It is likely, for example, that a researcher allied with psychodynamic therapy would quickly publish the findings of a study demonstrating the superiority of psychodynamic therapy. However, the same investigator might not be so eager to publish results showing the superiority of cognitive behaviour therapy! The file drawer problem is not caused primarily by deliberate burying of contradictory findings. Instead, researchers may be genuinely puzzled by, or just not believe, results that contradict their hypotheses.

Finally, let us raise a more positive potential explanation of the allegiance effect. Allegiance may not be a cause of an investigator's research results but an effect of his or her research findings (Luborsky et al., 1999). That is, researchers may adopt an allegiance in favour of the treatment they find to be most effective. We would be delighted if this circumstance fully explained the allegiance effect. Like those conducting research on this topic (Luborsky et al., 1999), however, we doubt that this is so. ◆

Tightly controlled experiments provide important information about the *efficacy* of psychotherapy—that is, whether the treatment *can* work under prescribed circumstances. However, such studies provide little information about the *effectiveness* of the treatment—whether the therapy *does* work in the real world. In the real world, therapies are not assigned at random, therapists vary the type and length of treatment, and clients commonly have multiple problems (Nathan, Stuart, & Dolan, 2000). How does psychotherapy fare under these circumstances?

Studies of the effectiveness of psychotherapy attempt to answer this question. Effectiveness studies use the correlational method and cannot determine cause and effect, but they can provide interesting descriptive information. For example, the magazine *Consumer Reports* (1995, November) surveyed nearly 3000 readers who had seen a mental health professional in the past three years, and the respondents generally rated psychotherapy highly. Among the major findings of the survey were the following (*Consumer Reports*, 1995, November; Seligman, 1995):

- Of the 426 people who were feeling "very poor" at the beginning of treatment, 87 percent reported feeling "very good," "good," or at least "so-so" when they were surveyed.
- Clients of psychologists, psychiatrists, and social workers reported no differences in treatment outcome, but all three professions were rated more effective than marriage counsellors.
- People who received psychotherapy alone reported no more or less improvement than people who received psychotherapy plus medication.

Because the *Consumer Reports* study used the correlational method, we cannot draw conclusions about causation. For example, perhaps people who had good experiences in therapy were more likely to complete the survey than were people who had bad experiences. Still, like other research (Shadish et al., 2000), the *Consumer Reports* study suggests that psychotherapy helps many people in the real world, not just in the laboratory.

*A Consumer Reports study found high levels of satisfaction with psychotherapy. This young woman won her battle with a severe eating disorder and decided to devote her life to helping others.*

**When Does Psychotherapy Work Better?** Psychotherapy works for many but not all people. What factors predict when treatment is more or less likely to be effective? The most important predictor is the nature of a client's problems—the diagnosis. For this reason, we discuss research on specific treatments for specific disorders in every chapter throughout the text. Here, we consider two of the many other predictors of treatment outcome: the length of treatment and the client's background characteristics.

If therapy is going to be effective, it usually will be effective rather quickly. As Figure 3–3 indicates, improvement is greatest in the first several months of treatment. Improvement continues with longer-term therapy but at a notably slower rate (Howard et al., 1986). Although researchers debate whether therapy should work within three months, six months, or one year (Kopta et al., 1994; Seligman, 1995), evidence supports the trend toward providing short-term psychotherapy.

Significantly, clients' background characteristics also predict outcome in psychotherapy. The acronym YAVIS was coined to indicate that clients improve more in psychotherapy when they are "young, attractive, verbal, intelligent, and successful." This finding has caused considerable concern, for it seems to indicate that psychotherapy works best for the most advantaged members of our society (Lorion & Felner, 1986).

## Psychotherapy Process Research

If psychotherapy can be effective, just how does it work? This is the question asked by *psychotherapy process research*, an approach that examines what aspects of the therapist–client relationship predict better outcome.

**Common Factors** One important impetus behind psychotherapy process research comes

**Improvement and the Length of Psychotherapy**

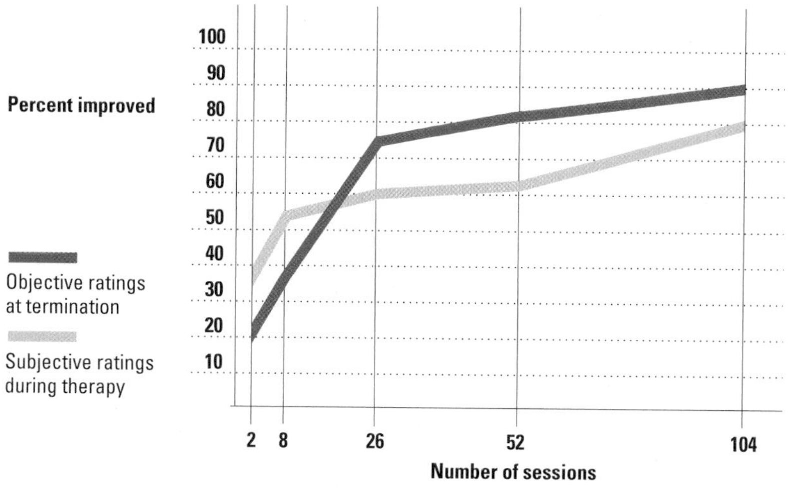


**FIGURE 3–3: Most clients improve relatively early in psychotherapy.**

*Source:* K.J. Howard, S.M. Kopta, M.S. Krause, and D.E. Orlinsky, 1986, The dose-effect relationship in psychotherapy. *American Psychologist, 41*, 159–164.

from studies comparing psychodynamic, cognitive behavioural, and humanistic treatments. Although behaviour therapies are somewhat more effective, especially for anxiety disorders (Shapiro & Shapiro, 1982), meta-analysis generally reveals few sizable differences among approaches (Smith, Glass, & Miller, 1980; Westen & Morrison, 2001). This conclusion suggests that different psychotherapies may share certain *common factors* that make them effective. In fact, a close look at research suggests that the different treatments do share some surprising similarities.

We can illustrate this conclusion with the classic study by Sloane and colleagues (1975). Ninety patients who had moderate difficulties with anxiety, depression, or similar problems were assigned at random to receive either psychodynamic psychotherapy, behaviour therapy, or no treatment. The different therapies were delivered by three psychodynamic and three behaviour therapists, all of whom were highly experienced in their preferred form of treatment. Both treatments lasted for an average of 14 sessions. To ensure that the treatments were offered as planned, the differences between the two therapies were clearly defined (see Table 3–3), and tape recordings of the fifth therapy sessions were made and coded so that the actual treatments could be compared.

All three groups, including the no-treatment group, improved over time, but the treated groups improved significantly more than the untreated group. Behaviour therapy was more effective in a few instances, but on most measures, there were no differences between the two treatment groups.

How can this be? Behaviour therapy and psychodynamic psychotherapy clearly differ. In fact, the investigators found that behaviour therapists talked about as often as their clients talked, gave specific advice, and directed much of the course of therapy. In contrast, psychodynamic therapists talked only one-third as often as their clients, refused to answer specific questions, and followed their clients' lead during the session. Psychodynamic therapists also were more likely to focus on feelings, their underlying causes, and techniques such as free association, whereas behaviour therapists focused on specific behaviours, ways of changing them, and techniques such as systematic desensitization.

What did the very different treatments have in common? Perhaps more than is readily apparent. Surprisingly, behaviour therapists and psychodynamic therapists offered the same number of interpretations. Most importantly, the clients' ratings of therapist warmth, empathy, and genuineness predicted successful outcome in both treatment groups. Clients also rated their personal relationship with their therapists as the single most important aspect of both behaviour therapy and psychodynamic psychotherapy (Sloane et al., 1975).

Psychotherapies *are* more effective when they contain specific factors that are "active ingredients" for treating a particular disorder. This is particularly true when the disorder is more severe (Stevens, Hynan, & Allen, 2000).

**TABLE 3–3 Definitions of Psychotherapy and Behaviour Therapy**

| Technique | Psychotherapy | Behaviour Therapy |
|---|---|---|
| Specific advice | Given infrequently | Given frequently |
| Transference interpretation | May be given | Avoided |
| Resistance interpretation | Used | Not used |
| Dreams | Interested and encouraged | Disinterested |
| Level of anxiety | Maintained when possible | Diminished when possible |
| Relaxation training | Only indirect | Directly undertaken |
| Desensitization | Only indirect | Directly undertaken |
| Assertion training | Indirectly encouraged | Directly encouraged |
| Report of symptoms | Discouraged | Encouraged |
| Childhood memories | Explored | Historical interest only |

*Source:* Differences in technique in behaviour therapy and psychotherapy, as adapted from R.B. Sloane, F.R. Staples, A.H. Cristo, N.J. Yorkston, and K. Whipple, 1975, *Psychotherapy versus Behaviour Therapy*, pp. 237–240. Cambridge, MA: Harvard University Press.

**TABLE 3–4 Common Factors in Effective Brief Psychotherapies**

1. Treatment is offered soon after the problem is identified.
2. Assessment of the problem is rapid and occurs early in treatment.
3. A therapeutic alliance is established quickly, and it is used to encourage change in the client.
4. Therapy is designed to be time-limited, and the therapist uses this to encourage rapid progress.
5. The goals of therapy are limited to a few specified areas.
6. The therapist is directive in managing the treatment sessions.
7. Therapy is focused on a specific theme.
8. The client is encouraged to express strong emotions or troubling experiences.
9. A flexible approach is taken in the choice of treatment techniques.

*Source:* Adapted from M.P. Koss and J.M. Butcher, 1986, Research on brief psychotherapy. In S.L. Garfield and A.E. Bergin (Eds.), *Handbook of Psychotherapy and Behavior Change*, 3rd ed., pp. 627–670. New York: Wiley.

Nevertheless, the importance of common factors has been documented across many different studies (Anderson & Lambert, 1995; Stevens et al., 2000). This has led many experts to conclude that, despite their differences, much of the effectiveness of different forms of psychotherapy is explained by common factors (Goldfried, 1995). You may be able to understand this conclusion best by way of analogy. Consider sports. Hockey and soccer differ greatly, but they also share similarities at a higher level of abstraction. For children, participating in some sport, any sport, may be more important than whether they play basketball or lacrosse. The same may be true for different approaches to psychotherapy that also share important similarities at a higher level of abstraction. In fact, a number of investigators are advocating for *psychotherapy integration*, combining the best elements of different treatments into a unified theory of psychotherapy (Goldfried, 1995).

Many important common factors involve aspects of the therapist–client relationship (Mahoney, 1991; see Table 3–4). Different schools of therapy construe the therapist–client relationship in various ways, but they all recognize its importance (Strupp, 1986). We consider some essential components of this unique relationship—basic issues if diverse approaches to psychotherapy are to be integrated—in the two brief sections that follow.

**Psychotherapy as Social Support** All major schools of psychotherapy emphasize the importance of warmth in the therapist–client relationship. Carl Rogers (1961) argued that warmth, empathy, and genuineness formed the centre, and not the periphery, of the healing process. Freud (1912/1957) also suggested that a client's positive feelings toward the psychoanalyst added to the success of the treatment. Similarly, cognitive behaviour therapists have emphasized warmth in the therapeutic relationship in practice even if it plays a minor role in theory.

Research on psychotherapy process indicates that a therapist's supportiveness is related to positive outcomes across approaches to treatment (Goldfried, 1995). Significantly, objective indicators of a therapist's support are less potent predictors of successful outcome than are a client's rating of the therapist. A supportive relationship is not defined simply by a therapist's behaviour but by a therapist's behaviour in relation to a particular client. Some, perhaps most, people feel that they are understood by a therapist who makes empathic statements, but others may be more comfortable with a therapist who is somewhat detached (Beutler, Crago, & Arizmendi, 1986). Thus clients may perceive different therapeutic stances as supportive, depending on the particular types of relationships with which they are most comfortable.

A supportive therapeutic relationship is important, but therapy is more than this. Rogers (1957) argued that warmth, empathy, and genuineness were *necessary and sufficient* conditions for therapeutic success. However, research indicates that therapist supportiveness is neither necessary nor sufficient for therapeutic success, despite the fact that supportiveness predicts a more successful outcome (Beutler, Crago, & Arizmendi, 1986). Many other factors influence treatment effectiveness.

**Psychotherapy as Social Influence** Psychotherapy is a process of social influence as well as of social support. In fact, Jerome Frank, trained in both psychology and psychiatry, has argued that psychotherapy can be viewed as a process of persuasion—persuading clients to make beneficial changes in their emotional lives (Frank & Frank, 1991). Frank's analysis begins with his very broad definition of psychotherapy as involving

1. A trained, socially sanctioned healer, whose healing powers are accepted by the sufferer and by his social group or an important segment of it.
2. A sufferer who seeks relief from the healer.
3. A circumscribed, more-or-less structured series of contacts between the healer and the sufferer, through which the healer, often with the aid of a group, tries to produce certain changes in the sufferer's emotional state, attitudes, and behaviour. All concerned believe these changes will help him.

Frank (1973) points out that "these three features are common not only to all forms of psychotherapy as the term is generally used, but also to methods of primitive healing" (p. 3).

It is easy to misunderstand Frank's argument. Is he saying that psychotherapy is little more than voodoo? No, his point is just the opposite. Frank argues that psychotherapists need to harness the persuasive power grasped intuitively by traditional healers. "Taboo death" is one dramatic example of this persuasive power. In some cultures, actual deaths have been documented to result from elaborate death curses, even in the absence of physical harm (Frank, 1973).

Frank (1973) calls attention to the persuasive power of therapists, but he highlights a more gentle aspect of persuasion in psychotherapy—instilling hope. People seek professional help when they have been unable to solve their own problems, when they have lost hope. Frank sees therapy as a chance to instill new hope, and in so doing, therapy can help people to make the changes they have been struggling to make (Frank & Frank, 1991).

Psychotherapy process research clearly demonstrates the therapist's social influence. For example, researchers have found that clients tend to adopt beliefs similar to those of their therapists. In fact, treatment is more effective when, over time, clients' beliefs become more similar to those of their therapists (Beutler, Crago, & Arizmendi, 1986; Kelly, 1990). Positive outcomes are more likely when the new beliefs relate directly to psychotherapy—for example, the importance of expressing emotions—than when they reflect broad social and religious values (Beutler, Machado, & Neufeldt, 1994).

In theory, approaches to therapy differ in terms of the degree to which therapists try to influence clients. However, all therapists influence clients in ways that are both obvious and subtle. Even Carl Rogers, the advocate of nondirective therapy, directed his clients. Audiotapes indicate that Rogers was more likely to empathize with certain types of client statements than others (Truax & Carkhuff, 1967). He responded to his clients conditionally, and thereby directed therapy subtly.

Recognition of the therapist's social influence raises questions about values in psychotherapy. Psychotherapy is not value-free. There are values inherent in the nature of therapy itself—for example, the belief that talking is good. Moreover, the values of individual therapists about such topics as love, marriage, work, and family necessarily influence clients. Like the rest of the human race, psychotherapists cannot transcend their own beliefs and values. All we can do is recognize our biases and inform our clients about them.

## Changing Social Systems: Couples, Family, and Group Therapy

Psychotherapy and medication focus on directly changing individual behaviour. However, people's emotional problems also can be changed indirectly by affecting change in their social circumstances. In Frances's case, successfully treating her depression with medication or psychotherapy probably would improve her family relationships. However, successful therapy with her parents and/or husband also might alleviate Frances's depression, and perhaps family therapy would be a more logical or ethical focus of treatment. Even more broadly, some theorists would argue that women like Frances would be less depressed if women were encouraged to assume more independent roles in society. Both these specific and broader concerns are a part of systems approaches to therapy.

Social interventions for psychological disorders include treatments for couples and entire families, group therapy, and even broader efforts at preventing emotional disorders through improving society. As is true of individual psychotherapy, there are different "schools" of couples, family, and group therapy, and the goals of alternative social interventions vary widely. For these reasons, we must be selective in our overview of social approaches to treatment.

### Couples Therapy

**Couples therapy** involves seeing intimate partners together in psychotherapy. This approach is sometimes called *marital therapy* or *marriage counselling*, but the reference to couples captures the range of partners who may seek treatment together. Dating pairs, prospective mates, live-in partners, and gay and lesbian couples also may seek couples therapy.

The goal of couples therapy typically is to improve the relationship, and not to treat the individual. However, couples treatment also may be used to help both partners function more adequately when one member suffers from a psychological problem. In treating relationships, all couples therapists focus on resolving conflicts and promoting mutual satisfaction. Couples therapists do not tell their clients what compromises they should accept or how they should change their relationship. Instead, they typically help partners to improve their *communication* and *negotiation* skills (Gottman, 1999; Jacobson & Christensen, 1996).

The goal of improving communication is best illustrated with an example. A couples therapist might suggest to Frances that she had a problem with "mind reading" in her marriage. Frances may be hoping (or expecting) that her husband would know what she wanted without telling him directly. She might want more attention, for example, but perhaps she never told her husband that lack of attention was a problem. She may expect him to be able to "figure it out for himself." Couples therapists point out that it is impossible to read another person's mind, and they encourage partners in close relationships to communicate their wishes directly (Gottman, 1999). This may sound simple, but learning to be direct can be tricky for many people. Frances may have felt selfish when making requests, for example, or perhaps she wanted to be "surprised" with her husband's attention. She may have thought that his attention would be less meaningful if she asked for it.

Another component of most couples therapies is negotiation or *conflict resolution* (Heitler, 1992). Negotiation is the imprecise art of give and take. Most approaches to negotiation emphasize the importance of clearly defining problems, considering a wide range of solutions, uncovering hidden agendas (unstated issues), and experimenting with alternative solutions. These strategies are similar to the social problem-solving model discussed earlier, and this approach has been effectively applied to work with couples (Emery, 1994). Polite communication also is an essential component of negotiation, and setting ground rules can be essential to encouraging polite communication. Examples of ground rules include not raising your voice, not interrupting the other person, and speaking about your own feelings—that is, not telling your partner how he or she feels (Emery, 1994).

### Family Therapy

**Family therapy** might include two, three, or more family members in the psychotherapy sessions. Family therapy shares many features in common with couples therapy—for example, improving communication and negotiation. Including children in family therapy can add complexity to this treatment approach, however, as does the obvious fact that relationships and treatments get more complicated when more people are involved.

Like couples therapy, family therapy has the general goal of improving satisfaction with relationships. Some forms of family therapy also are designed to resolve specific conflicts, such as disputes between adolescents and their parents (Robin, Koepke, & Nayar, 1986). *Parent management training* is an approach that teaches parents new skills for rearing troubled children (Forehand & McMahon, 1981; Patterson, 1982; see Chapter 16). Moreover, some important forms of family therapy are designed to educate families about how best to cope with the serious psychopathology of one family member (Falloon et al., 1985; see Chapter 13).

As with individual and couples therapy, there are many different theoretical approaches to family therapy (Gurman & Kniskern, 1991). Many approaches to family therapy differ from other treatments, however, in their longstanding emphasis on the application of systems theory. In applying systems theory, family therapists emphasize interdependence among family members and the paramount importance of the family within the larger social system. For example, family systems therapists often call attention to the pattern of *alliances* or strategic loyalties among family members (P. Minuchin, 1985). In well-functioning families, the primary alliance is between the two parents, even when the parents do not live together. In contrast, dysfunctional families often have alliances that cross generations—that is, "teams" that include one parent and some or all of the children opposing the other parent or another child. Like a poorly organized business, families function inadequately when their leaders fail to cooperate. Thus a common goal in systems approaches to family therapy is to strengthen the alliance between the parents, to get parents to work together and not against each other (Emery, 1994; S. Minuchin, 1974).

As demonstrated in the case of Frances, troubled relationships often intensify individual psychopathology, and individual psychological problems commonly strain relationships. It is not surprising, therefore, that family therapy may serve as an effective alternative or adjunct to individual treatment (Alexander, Holtzworth-Munroe, & Jameson, 1994).

*Family therapists attempt to improve mental health by altering family relationships.*

## Group Therapy

Like couples therapy and family therapy, **group therapy** involves the treatment of more than one person at one time. Therapy groups may be as small as 3 or 4 people or as large as 20 or more. Group therapy has numerous variations in terms of paradigmatic approaches and targets for treatment (Yalom, 1985). These variations are far too numerous to discuss here, so we highlight only a few facets of the group approach.

*Psychoeducational groups* are designed to teach group members specific information or skills relevant to psychological well-being. The term *psychoeducational* aptly conveys the goals of this type of group. Teaching is the primary mode of treatment, but the content of the "course" focuses on psychological issues. For example, assertiveness might be taught in a group format. Other psychoeducational groups focus on teaching systematic desensitization or cognitive therapy. In still other circumstances, a common disorder such as an eating disorder, not a common treatment, is the reason for group membership. In fact, psychoeducational groups have been developed for virtually every disorder discussed in this textbook.

There are at least two basic reasons for offering therapy in a psychoeducational group instead of in individual psychotherapy. Less expense is one obvious justification. A second rationale is the support, encouragement, and practice that group members can offer one another. Many people who have psychological problems feel isolated, alone, and sometimes "weird." Thus the simple act of coming to a group can be part of the therapeutic process (Bloch & Crouch, 1987). Learning that you are not alone with your problems can be a powerful experience that is one of the unique "active ingredients" in group therapy.

In contrast to psychoeducational groups, in *experiential group therapy* the relationships among group members form the primary, not a secondary, component of treatment. The experience of interacting with others in a unique setting is the rationale for experiential groups. Group members might be encouraged to look beyond one another's "façades"—to reveal secrets about themselves or otherwise to break down the barriers that we all erect in relationships (Bloch & Crouch, 1987; Yalom, 1985). Group members, in turn, can offer one another feedback and support. In an *encounter group*, for example, group members may question self-disclosure when it is "phony" but support more honest appraisals of oneself.

Experiential group leaders typically adhere to a humanistic approach such as Gestalt therapy, and the members often are well-functioning people who view the group as an opportunity for personal growth. Little research has been conducted on the effectiveness of this type of group.

The *self-help group* has grown tremendously in popularity. Self-help groups bring together people who share a common problem. Self-help group members share information and experiences in an attempt to help themselves and one another. There are thousands of topics that bring people together, and you are no doubt familiar with at least a few self-help groups.

Technically, self-help groups are not therapy groups, and typically are not led by a professional. If there is a leader, it may be someone who already has faced the particular problem, perhaps a former group member. The popularity of self-help groups attests to their perceived benefits. Moreover, available evidence suggests that self-help groups and other treatments can be quite effective even when they are delivered by *paraprofessionals*—people who do have limited professional training but who have personal experience with the problem (Christensen & Jacobson, 1994). However, the lack of research on process and outcome is a notable shortcoming for self-help groups and for group therapy in general (Kaul & Bednar, 1986).

***Zindel Segal*** *is a psychologist at the University of Toronto and the Centre for Addiction and Mental Health. He is a world-renowned authority on the cognitive mechanisms and treatment of depression.*

## CANADIAN FOCUS **Treatments for Psychological Disorders: Research and Practice**

The national healthcare system in Canada has been considered as a possible model for national health care in other countries throughout the world. This system has many advantages, but is far from perfect. An advantage of the Canadian system is that it provides universal access to health care—including treatment for mental health problems—at a substantially lower cost than similar services elsewhere (Evans et al., 1989). Each Canadian province regulates the national insurance system to ensure access to good-quality health care. Within this system, people with mental health problems can obtain services from a variety of providers. They can receive pharmacotherapy and brief counselling from primary care physicians, and pharmacotherapy, psychotherapy, or other treatments from psychiatrists. Clinical psychologists, social workers, and other mental health professionals are also included in this system, provided that their services are delivered in hospitals, schools, or correctional facilities. Many clinical psychologists are also in private practice, where their services are covered not by the government but through private insurance plans or paid for by the patient. Keith Dobson at the University of Calgary has argued that government funding should be provided to private practice psychologists so long as they provide empirically supported services to patients with diagnosable mental health problems (Dobson, 2002).

Despite the strengths of this system, not all people with mental health problems are able to receive adequate care. In some cases the disorders fail to respond to conventional therapies. In other cases, particularly for people living in rural areas, there are no suitably trained healthcare professionals living in the region. To overcome problems such as these, there are several clinical research centres throughout Canada conducting studies to improve the efficacy of drug treatments and psychological therapies. The scientists-practitioners conducting these studies are mostly either psychologists or psychiatrists. Drug studies are often designed by scientists working for pharmaceutical companies, who then invite hospital-based psychiatrists and psychologists to run the studies. A current trend across Canada and the United States is to conduct large, *multi-site studies*. For example, Raymond Lam (University of British Columbia) and colleagues (1995) conducted a placebo-controlled study of fluoxetine (Prozac) for seasonal affective disorder. Patients were recruited from Vancouver, Calgary, Hamilton, Toronto, and Halifax. Similarly, Isaac Marks, Richard Swinson, and colleagues (1993) conducted a placebo-controlled study of the merits of combining Xanax with behaviour therapy in the treatment of panic disorder. Patients were recruited from either London, England, or Toronto. An advantage of multi-site studies, compared to single-site studies, is that a larger number of patients can be recruited. A further advantage is that multi-site studies enable investigators to assess whether the treatments are effective when delivered by therapists from different locations.

Many Canadian research groups have been investigating the efficacy of cognitive behaviour therapy for various disorders, including treatments for pathological gambling, insomnia, major depression, social phobia, panic disorder, obsessive–compulsive disorder, and posttraumatic stress disorder (e.g., Ladouceur et al., 1998; Morin, Colecchi, Stone, Sood, & Brink, 1999; Taylor et al., 2001, 2003a). These

*continued*

*cont.*

studies have examined a number of issues, including the question of whether one treatment is better than another.

A great deal of important research on the treatment of depression comes from the University of Toronto and the affiliated Centre for Addiction and Mental Health. Psychologist Zindel Segal and colleagues, for example, have conducted pioneering research into several aspects of depression treatment, including the cognitive mechanisms of depression (Rector, Segal, & Gemar, 1998), the development of mindfulness meditation techniques for reducing relapse (Segal, Williams, & Teasdale, 2002), and research on the processes and mechanisms of treatment-related change in depression therapies (Segal, Gemar, & Williams, 1999). Some of these researchers' most exciting work concerns the way that drugs and CBT work in treating depression. A recent study by Goldapple, Segal, and colleagues (2004), using PET scans of patients treated with either CBT or Paxil, suggests that CBT treats depression in a "top-down" fashion. That is, CBT appears to change activity in the brain's frontal lobes, which in turn alters activity in the emotional centres of the brain, the limbic system. This finding is consistent with the goal of CBT: to alleviate depression by reducing the patient's tendency to engage in negative thinking. In comparison to CBT, medications like Paxil seem to work in a "bottom-up" manner by altering limbic system activity, which then alters activity in the frontal lobes (Goldapple et al., 2004).

Several investigators have been conducting *dismantling studies,* in which they attempt to identify the most important ingredients of a given treatment (Bouchard et al., 1996; Taylor et al., 1997). Other investigators, such as researchers at the University of Alberta, have been conducting *treatment matching* studies to investigate which interventions work best with which types of patients (Joyce & McCallum, 2004; Piper et al., 1991).

Les Greenberg and colleagues at York University have been investigating the *process* of change during humanistic and experiential psychotherapies (Greenberg et al., 1991; Greenberg & Malcolm, 2002; Greenberg & Watson, 1998). In collaboration with Susan Johnson (University of Ottawa), Greenberg has also developed and investigated emotion-focused couple's therapy, which aims to correct maladaptive negative emotions that are associated with dysfunctional interactions between couples (Greenberg & Johnson, 1988; Johnson, 2000). This form of couples therapy has become one of the most intensely studied and most effective ways of improving distressed relationships (Johnson et al., 1999).

Even though many therapies are effective, an ongoing problem is to find ways to disseminate them to the community. Many people with psychological problems live in rural areas and therefore have difficulty seeing specialists, who are typically based in major metropolitan areas. The major specialty clinics for anxiety disorders, for example, are based in the cities of Hamilton, Vancouver, Toronto, Winnipeg, and Montreal. In an effort to help people in outlying areas, researchers in Toronto and Vancouver have been investigating the merits of administering cognitive behaviour therapy over the telephone. Results suggest that these interventions are effective for panic disorder and for obsessive–compulsive disorder (Swinson et al., 1995; Taylor et al., 2003b). Research is also underway in Hull, Quebec, into the efficacy of therapy delivered by videoconferencing or over the Internet (Bouchard et al., 2000). ◆

*York University psychologist **Les Greenberg** is a leading figure in the development and scientific evaluation of humanistic and experiential psychotherapies.*

## Prevention

Social influences on psychopathology extend far beyond interpersonal relationships. Social institutions such as child-care centres, schools, and work environments are important contributors to mental health, as are such broad societal concerns as poverty, racism, and sexism. Of course, the goal of improving society is hardly the exclusive domain of psychologists. Still, *community psychology* is one approach within clinical psychology that attempts to improve individual well-being by promoting social change.

The concept of prevention is an important consideration in promoting social change. Community psychologists often distinguish among three levels of prevention. **Primary prevention** tries to improve the environment in order to prevent new cases of a mental disorder from developing. The goal of primary prevention is to promote health, not just treat illness. Efforts at primary prevention range from offering prenatal care to impoverished pregnant women to teaching schoolchildren about the dangers of drug abuse.

**Secondary prevention** focuses on the early detection of emotional problems in the hope of preventing them from becoming more serious and difficult to treat. The screening of "at-risk" schoolchildren is one example of an effort at secondary prevention. Crisis centres and hot lines are other examples of efforts to detect and treat problems before they become more serious.

Finally, **tertiary prevention** may involve any of the treatments discussed in this chapter, because the intervention occurs after the illness has been identified. In addition to providing treatment, however, tertiary prevention also attempts to address some of the adverse, indirect consequences of mental illness. Helping the chronically mentally ill to find adequate housing and employment is an example of a tertiary prevention effort.

No one can doubt the importance of prevention, whether directed toward biological, psychological, or social causes of abnormal behaviour. Unfortunately, many prevention efforts face an insurmountable obstacle: We simply do not know the specific cause of most psychological disorders. Prevention efforts directed at broader social change face another obstacle that also seems insurmountable at times. Poverty, racism, and sexism defy easy remedies. We do not wish to blame the victim of social injustice, but blaming the system can be equally problematic. Each individual must take personal responsibility for changing his or her own life, even as we collectively work to shape a world that promotes mental health.

## Specific Treatments for Specific Disorders

The field of psychotherapy began with the development of treatments based solely in theory and case histories. It progressed as researchers documented the superiority of some form of psychotherapy over no treatment at all. Contemporary psychotherapy researchers are advancing knowledge by studying factors common to all therapies and working toward psychotherapy integration (e.g., Greenberg, 2003).

The ultimate goal of treatment research, however, is to identify different therapies that have specific ingredients for treating specific disorders (see Research Close-Up). Consistent with this goal, in subsequent chapters we discuss only treatments that either are promising

### RESEARCH CLOSE-UP **Identifying Common Factors and Specific Active Ingredients**

A study by Thomas Borkovec and Ellen Costello (1993) illustrates how psychotherapy outcome research can account for some common factors across treatments while also isolating specific "active ingredients." These psychologists wanted to identify the effectiveness of different approaches to behaviour therapy in treating generalized anxiety disorder, an emotional problem characterized by excessive anxiety that is experienced in a variety of circumstances (see Chapter 6).

Borkovec and Costello compared two types of behaviour therapy. *Applied relaxation (AR)* involved training clients in the use of relaxation techniques to cope with thoughts, feelings, or situations that provoked anxiety. Most of the 12-session treatments involved discussions of how to anticipate and deal with stressful events, including practice in using relaxation techniques. *Cognitive behaviour therapy (CBT)* began with the same types of discussions and relaxation training as AR did. Most of the sessions, however, involved elements of Beck's cognitive therapy as well as other cognitive techniques designed to alter anxiety-producing thoughts. Finally, a third group of clients received *nondirective therapy (ND)* to test and control for the contributions of common factors to treatment outcome. The 12 sessions of nondirective therapy consisted of offering support and empathy in response to issues the clients chose to explore in therapy.

Borkovec and Costello randomly assigned 55 clients carefully diagnosed as suffering from generalized anxiety disorder (discussed in Chapter 6) to one of the three treatments. All treatments were offered by the same therapists, thus ensuring that differences in outcome would not be due to the therapists' unique skill. This raised a new problem, however. The therapists generally held a cognitive behavioural orientation, and their low expectations for ND—the allegiance effect—might have compromised the success of the treatment. To help control for this possibility, an expert nondirective therapist helped to supervise the ND cases. Finally, audiotapes of a portion of the sessions were coded to ensure that what was supposed to happen during the therapy sessions actually occurred.

A number of measures of the clients' anxiety were administered prior to treatment, immediately after treatment, and six months and one year after treatment. No differences were found among groups prior to treatment, but statistically significant differences were found immediately after treatment. The AR and CBT groups both were functioning significantly better than the ND clients at this time, but they were not significantly different from each other. A year after treatment, differences among groups were clinically significant—and they favoured CBT. Fifty-eight percent of the CBT group was functioning within a normal range, in comparison with 37 percent of the AR clients and 28 percent of ND participants.

These findings indicate that specific "active ingredients" can be identified beyond the influence of common factors. For generalized anxiety disorders, cognitive behaviour therapy has specific benefits both in the short term and in the long run—beyond the general improvement associated with seeking psychotherapy. Still, the study also demonstrated the importance of common factors despite the "active ingredients" in cognitive behaviour therapy. Across all three groups, the best predictor of a successful outcome was the clients' expectations for success, which were measured after the first therapy appointment. ◆

or have proved to be effective for alleviating the symptoms of specific disorders.

We strongly believe that the client's problems, not the therapist's theoretical orientation, should determine the choice of treatment (Smith, 1999). For many emotional problems, sufficient scientific evidence exists to identify the treatment of choice or at least to rule out some less effective forms of therapy (Nathan et al., 1999). In these cases, we feel very strongly that mental health professionals must inform their clients about research evidence and treatment alternatives. If a therapist is not skilled in offering the most effective approach, he or she should offer to refer the client to someone with specialized training.

# Summary

A tremendous number of different treatments have been developed for psychological disorders, but the various forms of **psychotherapy** can be roughly classified into four broad groups. Biological approaches alter the functioning of the body in an attempt to improve psychological well-being, primarily by using **psychopharmacology**, or medication that has psychotropic effects. **Psychodynamic psychotherapies** encourage the exploration of the past in order to obtain **insight** into unconscious motivations. **Cognitive behaviour therapy** focuses on present experience in helping clients overcome maladaptive behaviours and learn adaptive ones. **Humanistic psychotherapy** offers clients warmth, **empathy**, and unconditional positive regard in helping them to heighten emotional awareness and make life choices. More therapists say they are **eclectic**, using different treatments for different disorders and different clients, than say they adhere to any one of these approaches.

Psychotherapy outcome research indicates that therapy "works," but we cannot adequately understand its efficacy without considering how we define therapy and the **placebo effect**. The **allegiance effect** also seems very important to interpreting psychotherapy research, as researchers tend to find that their preferred treatment is most effective.

Still, the major alternative approaches to psychotherapy do not produce dramatically different results. Thus, there is renewed interest in psychotherapy process research and psychotherapy integration. Another area of innovation in psychotherapy is the development of effective treatments that extend into the social system. These interventions include **couples therapy**, **family therapy**, and **group therapy**. They also include efforts to change dysfunctional aspects of the broader society. Thus, consistent with the systems approach, intervention for psychological problems may be directed toward biological, psychological, or social systems.

The future of psychotherapy outcome research involves developing therapies that have effectiveness beyond the common factors found across different approaches to psychotherapy. The task is to identify specific therapies for specific disorders.

# Critical Thinking

1. What are your personal beliefs about the treatment of psychological disorders? Were your beliefs changed by the ideas or evidence presented in this chapter? Why or why not? What research evidence would convince you that treatments for psychological disorders do (or do not) "work"?
2. Do you prefer one of the major paradigms discussed in this chapter? Would you choose a therapist based on her or his "theoretical orientation"? How do you feel about medication in particular? Would it matter if you were treated by a psychiatrist, clinical psychologist, or a social worker?

3. We argue that mental health professionals should offer treatments based on proven effectiveness rather than on theoretical orientation. Do you agree?

4. Some critics have argued that psychotherapy is "the purchase of friendship." What do you think? How are common factors found across different schools of psychotherapy similar to, and different from, friendship?

# Key Terms

**allegiance effect** 88
**aversion therapy** 80
**behaviourism** 78
**client-centred therapy** 84
**cognitive behaviour therapy** 78
**cognitive therapy** 82
**contingency management** 81
**control group** 79
**couples therapy** 93
**dependent variable** 79
**double-blind study** 87
**eclectic** 67
**ego analysis** 77
**electroconvulsive therapy (ECT)** 72
**empathy** 84
**experiment** 79
**experimental group** 79
**experimental method** 78
**external validity** 79
**family therapy** 93
**flooding** 80
**free association** 75
**Gestalt therapy** 84
**group therapy** 94
**humanistic psychotherapy** 83
**hypothesis** 79
**independent variable** 79
**insight** 75
**internal validity** 79
**interpretation** 75
**in vivo desensitization** 80
**meta-analysis** 85
**placebo control groups** 87
**placebo effect** 87
**primary prevention** 96
**psychoanalysis** 75
**psychodynamic psychotherapy** 77
**psychopharmacology** 73
**psychosurgery** 73
**psychotherapy** 67
**psychotropic medications** 73
**random assignment** 79
**rational–emotive therapy (RET)** 83
**role playing** 81
**secondary prevention** 96
**social skills training** 81
**statistically significant** 79
**systematic desensitization** 78
**tertiary prevention** 96
**therapeutic alliance** 85
**token economy** 81
**transference** 76

# 4 Classification and Assessment of Abnormal Behaviour

Overview
Basic Issues in Classification
Classifying Abnormal Behaviour
Evaluating Classification Systems
Basic Issues in Assessment
Assessing Psychological Systems
Assessing Social Systems
Assessing Biological Systems

**Why do we need a system to classify abnormal behaviours?**

**Can the categories in DSM-IV-TR be used reliably?**

**How could the DSM-IV-TR system be improved?**

**What can a psychological test tell you that an interview cannot?**

Imagine that you are a therapist who has begun to interview a new patient. She tells you that she has had trouble falling asleep for the past few weeks. She has become increasingly frustrated and depressed, in part because she is always very tired when she goes to work in the morning. Your job is to figure out how to help this woman. How serious is her problem? What else do you need to know? What questions should you ask and how should you collect the information? The process of gathering this information is called **assessment**. You will want to use data from your assessment to compare her experiences with those of other patients whom you have treated (or read about). Are there any similarities that might help you know what to expect in terms of the likely origins of her problems, how long they will last, and the kinds of treatment that might be most helpful? In order to make those comparisons, you will need a kind of psychological road map to guide your search for additional information. This road map is known as a *classification system*—a list of various types of problems and their associated symptoms. This chapter will describe the classification system that has been developed to describe various forms of abnormal behaviour. It will also summarize the different kinds of assessment tools that psychologists use.

# Overview

One important part of the assessment process is making a diagnostic decision based on the categories in the official classification system that describes mental disorders. **Diagnosis** refers to the identification or recognition of a disorder on the basis of its characteristic symptoms. In the field of mental health, a clinician assigns a diagnosis if the person's behaviour meets the specific criteria for a particular type of disorder, such as schizophrenia or major depressive disorder. This decision is important because it tells the clinician that the person's problems are similar to those that have been experienced by some other people. The diagnosis enables the clinician to refer to the base of knowledge that has accumulated with regard to the disorder. For example, it will provide clues about associated symptoms and treatments that are most likely to be effective. To formulate a comprehensive treatment plan, the clinician utilizes the person's diagnosis plus many other types of information that we will discuss in this chapter.

In some fields, diagnosis refers to causal analysis. If your car doesn't start, you expect that your mechanic's "diagnosis" will explain the origins of the problem. Has the battery lost its charge? Is the fuel line blocked? Is the ignition switch dead? In this situation, the "diagnosis" leads directly to the problem's solution. In the field of psychopathology, assigning a diagnosis does not mean that we understand the etiology of the person's problem (see Chapter 2). Specific etiologies have not been identified for mental disorders. Psychologists can't "look under the hood" in the same way that a mechanic can examine a car. In the case of a mental disorder, assigning a diagnostic label simply identifies the nature of the problem without implying exactly how the problem came into existence.

Our consideration of the assessment enterprise and diagnostic issues will begin with an example from our own clinical experience. In the following pages we will describe Michael, a young man who found himself thinking and acting in ways that he could not seem to control. This case study illustrates the kinds of decisions that psychologists have to make about ways to collect and interpret information, used in diagnosis and assessment.

After learning about Michael's problems, his worries about contamination, his efforts to avoid contamination, and his fear of being with other people, his therapist would be faced

## CASE STUDY Obsessions, Compulsions, and Other Unusual Behaviours

Michael was an only child who lived with his mother and father. He was 16 years old, a little younger than most of the other boys in Grade 11, and he looked even younger. From an academic point of view, Michael was an average student, but he was not a typical teenager in terms of social behaviour. He felt completely alienated from other boys, and he was extremely anxious when he talked to girls. He hated being at school; he despised everything about school. His life at home was not much more pleasant than his experience at school. Michael and his parents argued frequently. His relationship with his father was especially volatile.

One awful incident when he decided to join the track team seemed to sum up Michael's bitter feelings about school. Michael was awkward and somewhat clumsy, hardly an athlete; when he worked out with the other long-distance runners at practice, he soon became the brunt of their jokes. One day, a belligerent teammate forced Michael to take off his clothes and run naked from the bushes to a shelter in the park. When he got there, Michael found an old pair of shorts, which he put on and wore back to the locker room. The experience was humiliating. Later that night, Michael started to worry about those shorts. Who had left them in the park? Were they dirty? Had he been exposed to some horrible disease? Michael quit the track team the next day, but he couldn't put the experience out of his mind.

In the following year, Michael became more and more consumed by anxiety. He was constantly obsessed about "contamination," which he imagined to be spreading from his books and school clothes to the furniture and other objects in his house. When the clothes that he had worn to school rubbed against a chair or a wall at home, he felt as though that spot had become contaminated. He didn't believe this was literally true; it was more like a reminder by association. When he touched something that he had used at school, he was more likely to think of school. That triggered unpleasant thoughts and the negative emotions with which they were associated (anger, fear, sadness).

Michael tried in various ways to minimize the spread of contamination. For example, he took a shower and changed his clothes every evening at 6 o'clock immediately after he finished his homework. After this "cleansing ritual" he was careful to avoid touching his books or dirty clothes as well as anything that they had touched. If he bumped into one of these contaminated objects by accident, he would go into the bathroom and wash his hands. Michael washed his hands 10 or 15 times in a typical evening. He also paced back and forth watching television without sitting down so that he would not touch contaminated furniture.

Whenever he was not in school, Michael preferred to be alone at home, playing games on his computer. He did not enjoy sports, music, or outdoor activities. The only literature that interested him was fantasy and science fiction. Dungeons and Dragons was the only game that held his attention. He read extensively about the magical powers of fantastic characters and spent hours dreaming up new variations on themes described in books about this imaginary realm. When Michael talked about the Dungeons and Dragons characters and their adventures, his speech would sometimes become vague and difficult to follow. Although other students at Michael's school shared his interest in Dungeons and Dragons, he didn't want to play the game with them. Michael said he was different from the other students. He expressed disdain and contempt for other teenagers, as well as for the city in which he lived.

Michael and his parents had been working with a family therapist for more than two years. Although the level of interpersonal conflict in the family had been reduced, Michael's anxiety seemed to be getting worse. He had become even more isolated from other boys his own age, and was actually quite suspicious about their motives. He said that he sometimes felt that they were talking about him, and that they were planning to do something else to him in order to humiliate him again.

His worries about contamination had become almost unbearable to his parents, who were deeply confused and frustrated by his behaviour. They knew that he was socially isolated and extremely unhappy. They believed that he would never be able to resume a more normal pattern of development until he gave up these "silly" ideas. Michael's fears also disrupted his parents' own activities in several ways. They weren't allowed to touch him or his things after being in certain rooms of the house. His peculiar movements and persistent washing were troublesome to them. Michael's father usually worked at home, and he and Michael frequently ended up quarrelling with each other, especially when Michael ran water in the bathroom next to his father's study.

Michael and his mother had always been very close. In fact, he was quite de-

continued

*cont.*

pendent on her, and she was devoted to him. They spent a lot of time together while his father was working. Although they still supported each other, his mother had begun to find it difficult to be close to Michael. He shunned physical contact. When she touched him, he sometimes cringed and withdrew. Once in a while he would shriek, reminding her that she was contaminated by her contact with chairs and other objects like his laundry. Recently, Michael had also become aloof intellectually. His mother felt that he was shutting her out as he seemed to withdraw further into his world of Dungeons and Dragons fantasy and obsessional thoughts about contamination.

Michael's parents eventually decided to seek individual treatment for him. They talked with their family therapist and asked her whether anything could be done to help Michael deal with his fear of contamination. Could he stop his repeated washing? Would he be able to develop normal friendships? ◆

with several important decisions. One involves the level of analysis at which she should think about the problem. Is this primarily Michael's problem, or should she consider this problem in terms of all members of the family? One possibility is that Michael has a psychological disorder that is disrupting the life of his family. It may be the other way around, however. Perhaps the family system as a whole is dysfunctional, and Michael's problems are only one symptom of this dysfunction.

Another set of choices involves the type of data that his therapist will use to describe Michael's behaviour. What kinds of information should be collected? The therapist can consider several sources of data. One is Michael's own report, which can be obtained in an interview or through the use of questionnaires. Another is the report of his parents. The therapist may also decide to employ psychological tests.

In conducting an assessment and arriving at a diagnosis, one question the therapist must ask is whether Michael's abnormal behaviour is similar to problems that have been exhibited by other people. She would want to know if Michael's symptoms fall into a pattern that has been documented by many other mental health professionals. Rather than reinventing the wheel each time a new patient walks into her office, the therapist can use a classification system to streamline the diagnostic process. The classification system serves as a common language among therapists, giving them a form of professional "shorthand" that enables them to discuss issues with colleagues. Because different disorders sometimes respond to different forms of treatment, the distinctions can be very important. In the next section we will review the development and modification of classification systems for abnormal behaviour.

# Basic Issues in Classification

A **classification system** is used to subdivide or organize a set of objects. The objects of classification can be inanimate things, such as CDs, rocks, or books; living organisms, such as plants, insects, or primates; or abstract concepts, such as numbers, religions, or historical periods. Formal classification systems are essential for the collection and communication of knowledge in all sciences and professions.

There are many ways to subdivide any given class of objects. Classification systems can be based on different principles. Some systems are based on descriptive similarities. For example, both a diamond and a ruby may be considered jewels because they are valuable stones. Other systems are based on less obvious characteristics, such as structural similarities. A diamond and a piece of coal, for example, may belong together because they are both made of carbon.

The point is simple: Classification systems can be based on various principles, and their value will depend primarily on the purpose for which they were developed. Different classification systems are not necessarily right or wrong; they are simply more or less useful. In the following section we will consider several fundamental principles that affect all attempts to develop a useful classification or typology of human behaviour.

## Categories versus Dimensions

Classification is often based on "yes or no" decisions (Hempel, 1961). After a category has been defined, an object is either a member of the category or it is not. A **categorical approach to classification** assumes that

*Taxonomy is the science of arranging living organisms into groups. Humans and dolphins belong to the same "class" (mammals) because they share certain characteristics (e.g., are warm-blooded, give birth to live young rather than eggs, and nourish their young).*

distinctions among members of different categories are qualitative. In other words, the differences reflect a difference in kind (quality) rather than a difference in amount (quantity). In the classification of living organisms, for example, we usually consider species to be qualitatively distinct; they are different kinds of living organisms. Human beings are different from other primates; an organism is either human or it is not. Many medical conditions are categorical. Pregnancy is one clear example. A woman is either pregnant or she is not. It doesn't make sense to talk about a woman being "a little bit pregnant."

Although categorically based classification systems are often useful, they are not the only kind of system that can be used to organize information systematically. As an alternative, scientists often employ a **dimensional approach to classification**—that is, one that describes the objects of classification in terms of continuous dimensions. Rather than assuming that an object either has or does not have a particular property, it may be useful to focus on a specific characteristic and determine how much of that characteristic the object exhibits. This kind of system is based on an ordered sequence or on quantitative measurements rather than on qualitative judgments.

*How blue is blue? A dimensional system describes the objects of classification in terms of continuous dimensions, such as the colours of these fabrics.*

For example, in the case of intellectual ability, psychologists have developed sophisticated measurement procedures. Rather than asking whether or not a particular person is intelligent (a "yes or no" judgment), the psychologist sets out to determine how much intelligence the person exhibits on a particular set of tasks. This process offers some advantages over categorical distinctions. For example, it allows scientists to record subtle distinctions that would be lost if they were forced to make all-or-none decisions.

## From Description to Theory

The development of scientific classification systems typically proceeds in an orderly fashion over a period of several years. The initial stages, which focus on simple descriptions or observations, are followed by more advanced theoretical stages. At the latter point, greater emphasis is placed on scientific concepts that explain causal relationships among objects. In the study of many medical disorders, this progression begins with an emphasis on the description of specific symptoms that cluster together and follow a predictable course over time. The systematic collection of more information regarding this syndrome may then lead to the discovery of causal factors.

An example may help to illustrate the progression from descriptive to theoretically based classification. In 1934, a woman in Norway brought her two young sons, who were both mentally retarded, to a physician. The woman reported that the boys often gave off a peculiar, musty odour. Applying ordinary laboratory tests to samples of the children's blood and urine, the physician found high concentrations of phenylalanine—a common amino acid that is present in protein foods. Using the descriptive features of mental retardation and urinary tests for phenylalanine, clinical scientists found other people who had the same condition. They were eventually able to identify the specific nature of the metabolic defect that causes the problem and establish that it can be traced to a recessive gene (Bickel, 1980).

As a direct result of these studies, we now know that this particular form of mental retardation, known as phenylketonuria (PKU), can be produced by an inherited metabolic disorder (see Chapter 15.) People with PKU are missing a liver enzyme that is required to break down phenylalanine (Pollitt, 1987). If a child with PKU is allowed to eat a normal diet, incompletely metabolized products of phenylalanine will accumulate in the blood, cause damage to the developing central nervous system, and eventually lead to mental retardation. Methods of early detection of PKU, using blood tests that are employed soon after birth, were developed in the 1950s. Treatment methods were introduced shortly thereafter. Infants who test positive are placed on a special diet that is very low in phenylalanine, preventing the development of severe mental retardation.

The classification of PKU illustrates the progression from descriptive to theoretical systems. The disorder was originally identified on the basis of observable symptoms—intellectual deficiencies and a peculiar odour. Now PKU is classified in terms of a specifically identified etiological pathway involving a recessive gene and a known metabolic defect.

Clinical scientists hope that similar progress will be made in the field of psychopathology. Mental disorders are currently classified on the basis of their descriptive features or symptoms because specific causal mechanisms have not yet been discovered. While we may eventually develop a more sophisticated, theoretically based understanding of certain disorders, this does not necessarily mean we will ever know the precise causes of disorders. In fact, the most likely explanations for mental disorders involve complex interactions of psychological, biological, and social systems (see Chapter 2).

# Classifying Abnormal Behaviour

We need a classification system for abnormal behaviour for two primary reasons. First, a classification system is useful to clinicians, who must match their clients' problems with the form of intervention that is most likely to be effective. Second, a classification system must be used in the search for new knowledge. The history of medicine is filled with examples of problems that were recognized long before they could be treated successfully. The classification of a specific set of symptoms has often laid the foundation for research that eventually identified a cure or a way of preventing the disorder, as in the case of PKU.

## Brief Historical Perspective

There have been many attempts to classify personality and psychopathology throughout history. The oldest written descriptions can be traced to the Egyptians, Greeks, and Romans, but these bear little resemblance to contemporary perspectives. Progress toward the adoption of a single, internationally accepted system began during the nineteenth century, when cities in Europe and North America established large asylums for people with major mental disorders. The physicians who presided over these institutions had an unprecedented opportunity to observe the behaviour of many patients over an extended period of time. Many different classification systems were introduced during the ensuing years. In some areas, each hospital or university clinic developed and used its own unique system (Kendell, 1975).

Emil Kraepelin (1856–1926), a German psychiatrist, is generally regarded as the father of the categorical classification system that currently prevails in psychopathology. He believed that mental illness could be understood in terms of a finite number of specific disorders. Each disorder was presumed to have an identifiable set of symptoms and a unique course and was the product of a yet to be determined form of cerebral pathology (Berrios & Hauser, 1988). Kraepelin identified two primary forms of psychosis: *dementia praecox* (which we now call schizophrenia) and *manic–depressive psychosis* (which we now call bipolar mood disorder). His views were widely influential, but they did not lead directly to a formal, universally adopted classification system.

Currently, two diagnostic systems for mental disorders are widely recognized. One—the *Diagnostic and Statistical Manual* (DSM)—is published by the American Psychiatric Association. The other—the *International Classification of Diseases* (ICD)—is published by the World Health Organization. Both systems were developed shortly after World War II, and both have been revised several times. Because the DSM is now in its fourth edition, it is called DSM-IV-TR. The "TR" stands for "text revision" and refers to the fact that some of the background material provided in the manual was updated in 2000. The World Health Organization's manual is in its tenth edition and is therefore known as ICD-10.

During the 1950s and 1960s, psychiatric classification systems were widely criticized. One major criticism focused on the lack of consistency in diagnostic decisions (Spitzer & Fleiss, 1974). Independent clinicians frequently disagreed with one another about the use of diagnostic categories as they were listed in the first two editions of the DSM classification system, DSM-I and DSM-II. Objections were also raised from philosophical, sociological, and political points of view. For example, some critics charged that diagnostic categories in psychiatry would be more appropriately viewed as "problems in living" than as medical disorders (Szasz, 1960). Others were concerned about *self-fulfilling prophesies*. In other words, once a psychiatric label had been assigned, the person so labelled might be motivated to continue behaving in ways that were expected from someone who is mentally disturbed (see Further Thoughts). For all of these reasons, many mental health professionals paid less and less attention to the formal process of diagnosis during these years.

## Further Thoughts **Labelling Theory**

What does it mean to be labelled with a psychiatric diagnosis? **Labelling theory** is a perspective on mental disorders that is primarily concerned with the social context in which abnormal behaviour occurs and the ways in which other people respond to this behaviour. It assigns relatively little importance to specific behaviours as symptoms of a disorder that resides within the person. Labelling theory is primarily concerned with the social factors that determine whether a person will be given a psychiatric diagnosis rather than the psychological or biological reasons for the abnormal behaviours (Phelan & Link, 1999). In other words, it is concerned with events that take place after a person has behaved in an unusual way rather than with factors that might explain the original appearance of the behaviour itself.

Sociologist Thomas Scheff believes it is useful to think of mental disorders as maladaptive social roles, with the process of diagnostic labelling being the most important factor in establishing that role for a particular person (1966). Scheff suggests that the symptoms of mental disorders are best viewed as violations of social expectations that are usually taken for granted: showing too much emotion, not showing enough emotion, or talking too much or in strange ways. These behaviours create situations in which a person might be labelled as mentally disturbed.

Scheff maintains that people break these social rules frequently and for many different reasons. For example, consider the crowd at a hotly contested sports event. These behaviours are usually ignored or dismissed as unimportant. Scheff assumes that in such cases the behaviours will be relatively brief. Persistent abnormal behaviours develop only after someone has been brought to the attention of the mental health system and assigned an official diagnostic label. After a diagnosis has been assigned, patients are rewarded for accepting the role—behaving as if they were "crazy"—and punished if they attempt to return to normal social and occupational roles.

According to labelling theory, the probability that a person will receive a diagnosis is determined by several factors. These include the extent of the rule breaking and its visibility, as well as the tolerance level of the community. The most important considerations are the social status of the person who breaks the rules and the social distance between that person and mental health professionals. People from disadvantaged groups, such as racial and sexual minorities and women, are presumably more likely to be labelled than are white males.

The merits and limitations of labelling theory have been hotly debated since the mid-1960s. The theory has inspired research on a number of important questions. Some studies have found that people from lower-status groups, including racial minorities, are indeed more likely to be assigned severe diagnoses (Phelan & Link, 1999). On the other hand, it would also be an exaggeration to say that the social status of the patient is the most important factor influencing the diagnostic process. In fact, clinicians' diagnostic decisions are determined primarily by the form and severity of the patient's symptoms rather than by such factors as gender, race, and social class (Farmer & Griffiths, 1992; Gove, 1990).

Another focus of the debate regarding labelling theory is the issue of stigma and the negative effects of labelling. **Stigma** refers to a stamp or label that sets the person apart from others, connects the person to undesirable features, and leads others to reject the person (Link & Phelan, 1999). Labelling theory claims that negative attitudes toward mental disorders prevent patients from obtaining jobs, finding housing, and forming new relationships. Various kinds of empirical evidence support the conclusion that a psychiatric label can have a harmful impact on a person's life. Negative attitudes are associated with many types of mental disorder, such as alcoholism, schizophrenia, and sexual disorders (Fink & Tasman, 1992). When a person becomes a psychiatric patient, the person expects to be devalued and discriminated against. These expectations cause the person to behave in strained and defensive ways, which may in turn

*continued*

*cont.*

cause others to reject him or her (Link et al., 1997).

Labelling theory has drawn needed attention to several important problems associated with the classification of mental disorders, but it does not provide an adequate explanation for abnormal behaviour. It is clearly an exaggeration to think of mental disorders as nothing more than social roles. Many factors other than the reactions of other people contribute to the development and maintenance of abnormal behaviour. Furthermore, a diagnosis of mental illness can have positive consequences, such as encouraging access to effective treatment. Many patients and their family members are relieved to learn that their problems are similar to those experienced by other people and that help may be available. The effects of diagnostic labelling are not always harmful.

Renewed interest in the value of psychiatric classification grew steadily during the 1970s, culminating in the publication of the third edition of the DSM in 1980. This version of the manual represented a dramatic departure from previous systems. It was clearly a major turning point in the history of psychiatric classification (Jablensky, 1999; Sabshin, 1990). The committee that was responsible for developing DSM-III was chaired by psychiatrist Robert Spitzer. Spitzer and his colleagues made several bold changes in the manual. One broad consideration was their commitment to the production of a classification system that was based on clinical description rather than on theories of psychopathology that had not been empirically validated. This principle led to the elimination of some terms and categories that had been based on psychoanalytic concepts, like neurosis and hysteria (see Chapters 6 and 8). Other major changes included the introduction of a multiaxial system (described below) and the production of specific, detailed criterion sets for each disorder.

All these changes have been retained in both DSM-IV-TR and ICD-10, and are described in the following section. The two manuals are very similar in most respects. Deliberate attempts were made to coordinate the production of DSM-IV-TR and ICD-10. Most of the categories listed in the manuals are identical, and the criteria for specific disorders are usually similar.[1]

## The DSM-IV-TR System

More than 200 specific diagnostic categories are described in DSM-IV-TR. These are arranged under 18 primary headings. A complete list appears on the inside covers of this book. Disorders that present similar kinds of symptoms are grouped together. For example, conditions that include a prominent display of anxiety are listed under "Anxiety Disorders," and conditions that involve a depressed mood are listed under "Mood Disorders."

The manual lists specific criteria for each diagnostic category. We can illustrate the ways in which these criteria are used by examining the diagnostic decisions that would be considered in Michael's case. The criteria for obsessive–compulsive disorder (OCD) are listed in Table 4–1. Michael would meet all of the criteria in "A" for both obsessions and compulsions. His repetitive hand-washing rituals were performed in response to obsessive thoughts regarding contamination. Consistent with criterion "B," Michael admitted that these concerns were irrational. He also meets criterion "C" in that these rituals were time-consuming and interfered with his family's routine. His relationships with friends were severely limited because he refused to invite them to his house, fearing that they would spread contamination.

For various types of disorder, the duration of the problem is considered as well as the clinical picture. Criterion "C" for OCD specifies that the patient's compulsive rituals must take more than one hour each day to perform.

In addition to the *inclusion criteria*, symptoms that must be present, many disorders are also defined in terms of certain *exclusion criteria*. In other words, the diagnosis can be ruled out if certain conditions prevail. For example, in the case of OCD, the diagnosis would not be made if the symptoms occurred only during the course of another disorder, such as a person with alcoholism being preoccupied with thoughts of obtaining another drink (criterion "D").

*Psychiatrist* ***Robert Spitzer*** *chaired the committee that produced DSM-III. Spitzer's vision and forceful leadership helped the committee to accomplish one of the most important changes in psychiatric classification of the twentieth century.*

[1]There are some interesting differences between DSM-IV-TR and ICD-10. There are, for example, differences in the ways in which they subdivide mood disorders and personality disorders. The DSM system also devotes more attention to eating disorders and sexual disorders, which appear to be less prevalent in other cultures (Andrews, Slade, & Peters, 1999; Kendell, 1991).

**TABLE 4–1 DSM-IV-TR Criteria for Obsessive–Compulsive Disorder**

A. **Either obsessions or compulsions: Obsessions** as defined by (1), (2), (3), and (4):

1. Recurrent and persistent thoughts, impulses, or images that are experienced, at some time during the disturbance, as intrusive and inappropriate, and that cause marked anxiety or distress
2. The thoughts, impulses, or images are not simply excessive worries about real-life problems
3. The person attempts to ignore or suppress thoughts, impulses, or images or to neutralize them with some other thought or action
4. The person recognizes that the obsessional thoughts, impulses, or images are a product of his or her own mind (not imposed from without as in thought insertion)

**Compulsions** as defined by (1) and (2):

1. Repetitive behaviours (such as hand-washing, ordering, checking) or mental acts (such as praying, counting, repeating words silently) that the person feels driven to perform in response to an obsession, or according to rules that must be applied rigidly
2. The behaviours or mental acts are aimed at preventing or reducing distress or preventing some dreaded event or situation; however, these behaviours or mental acts either are not connected in a realistic way with what they are designed to neutralize or prevent, or are clearly excessive

B. **At some point during the course of the disorder, the person has recognized that the obsessions or compulsions are excessive or unreasonable.**

C. **The obsessions or compulsions cause marked distress; are time-consuming (take more than one hour a day); or significantly interfere with the person's normal routine, occupational (or academic) functioning, or usual social activities or relationships with others.**

D. **If another Axis I disorder is present, the content of the obsessions or compulsions is not restricted to it (for example, preoccupation with food in the presence of an eating disorder; preoccupation with drugs in the presence of a substance use disorder; or guilty ruminations in the presence of major depressive disorder).**

The DSM-IV-TR employs a *multiaxial classification system*; that is, the person is rated on five separate axes. Each axis is concerned with a different domain of information. Two are concerned with diagnostic categories and the other three provide for the collection of additional relevant data. The rationale for this approach is that to manage individual cases, the clinician must consider several important factors besides specific symptoms. These supplementary factors include the environment in which the patient is living, aspects of the person's health that might affect psychological functions, and fluctuations in the overall level of the patient's adjustment. Table 4–2 lists the five specific axes from DSM-IV-TR.

**Clinical Symptoms and Personality (Axes I and II)** The first two axes are concerned with clinical disorders that are defined largely in terms of symptomatic behaviours. Most diagnoses appear on Axis I, which includes conditions, such as OCD, schizophrenia, and mood disorders, that are the topics of most chapters in this text. Many of the diagnoses that are described on Axis I are characterized by episodic periods of psychological turmoil. Axis II is concerned with more stable, long-standing problems, such as personality disorders and mental retardation. The separation of disorders on Axis I and Axis II is designed to draw attention to long-standing conditions, such as a paranoid or dependent personality style, that might be overlooked in the presence of a more dramatic symptomatic picture, such as the hallucinations and delusions frequently found in schizophrenia. Clinicians are encouraged to list both types of problems when they are present. A person can be assigned more than one diagnosis on either Axis I or Axis II (or on both axes) if he or she meets criteria for more than one disorder.

Michael would receive a diagnosis of obsessive–compulsive disorder on Axis I, and these were, in fact, his most obvious symptoms. On Axis II, Michael would also be coded as meeting criteria for schizotypal personality disorder (see Chapter 9). This judgment depends on a consideration of his long-standing, relatively rigid patterns of interacting with other people and his inability to adjust to the changing requirements of different people and situations. For example, he was suspicious of other people's motives, he did not have any close friends in whom he could confide, and he was very anxious in social situations because he was afraid that other people might take advantage of him. These are important considerations for a therapist who wants to plan a treatment program for Michael, but they are relatively subtle considerations in comparison to the obsessions and compulsions, which were the primary source of conflict with his parents.

**TABLE 4-2 Major Domains of Information in DSM-IV-TR**

| | |
|---|---|
| **Axis I** | **Clinical Disorders and Other Conditions That May Be a Focus of Attention** (includes all mental disorders in the manual except those listed on Axis II). |
| **Axis II** | **Personality Disorders and Mental Retardation** (includes all personality disorders and/or mental retardation. Clinician can also list maladaptive *personality features*, characteristic defence mechanisms, or coping styles). |
| **Axis III** | **General Medical Conditions** (includes medical problems that can cause symptoms of an Axis I or Axis II disorder or act as a psychological stressor). |
| **Axis IV** | **Psychosocial and Environmental Problems** (includes life events from the past year that may have an impact on diagnosis or treatment, such as divorce or unemployment). |
| **Axis V** | **Global Assessment of Functioning** (describes the person's level of psychological, social, and occupational functioning on a single scale from 1 to 100). |

### Medical and Environmental Factors and Overall Functioning (Axes III, IV, and V)

Axis III is concerned with general medical conditions that are outside the realm of psychopathology but may be relevant to either the etiology of the patient's abnormal behaviour or the patient's treatment program. Examples include thyroid conditions, which may lead to symptoms of psychosis, and diabetes in children, which is sometimes associated with conduct disorders. The presence of chronic medical conditions does predict worse outcomes for certain kinds of mental disorders, especially depression (Saavedra et al., 2001). In Michael's case, there were no known physical disorders that were relevant to his psychological problems.

Axis IV is concerned with psychosocial and environmental problems that may affect the diagnosis or treatment of a mental disorder. The clinician is asked to indicate specific factors that are present in the person's life (see Chapter 8 for a more complete discussion of stressful life events and their measurement). The clinician is asked to record those problems that were present during the year prior to the current assessment. Problems that occurred prior to the previous year may be noted if the clinician is convinced that they made a significant contribution to the development of the person's current problems or if they have become a focus of treatment.

Michael's therapist noted the presence of three psychosocial problems: frequent arguments within the family, social isolation, and discord with classmates at school. Stressful circumstances may be the products as well as the causes of mental disorders. In Michael's case, for example, many of the family's arguments were precipitated by his hand-washing rituals. In deciding whether to list social stresses on Axis IV, psychologists need not determine whether the stresses primarily arose from or contributed to the condition. They are all listed if they are relevant to treatment planning, and these were all important considerations in Michael's case.

Finally, Axis V provides for a global rating of adaptive functioning (Goldman, Skodol, & Lave, 1992). This rating is made on a scale of 1 to 100, with higher numbers representing better levels of adjustment. The scale applies to psychological, social, and occupational functioning. Ratings are typically made for the person's current level of functioning. In some circumstances, the clinician might also consider the person's highest level of functioning during the past year. This information is considered useful because it draws attention to recent changes in the patient's condition and because it provides a balanced view of the patient's strengths as well as his or her weaknesses. Michael's psychologist assigned a rating of 50 for his current level of functioning. Michael was performing at an adequate level academically, but his social life was clearly impaired as a consequence of his rituals.

**Culture and Classification** DSM-IV-TR addresses the relation between cultural issues and the diagnosis of psychopathology in two principal ways. First, the manual encourages clinicians to consider the influence of cultural factors in both the expression and recognition of symptoms of mental disorders. People express extreme emotions in ways that are shaped by the traditions of their families and other social groups to which they belong. Intense, public displays of anger or grief might be expected in one culture but considered signs of disturbance in another. Interpretations of emotional distress and other symptoms of disorder are influenced by the explanations that a person's culture assigns to such experiences. Religious beliefs, social roles, and sexual identities all play an important part in constructing meanings that are assigned to these phenomena (Tsai et al., 2001). The accuracy and utility of a clinical diagnosis depend on more than a simple count of the symptoms that appear to be present. They also hinge on the clinician's ability to consider the cultural context in which the problem appeared. This is a particularly challenging task when the clinician and the person with the problem do not share the same cultural background.

The diagnostic manual attempts to sensitize clinicians to cultural issues by including a glossary of **culture-bound syndromes**. These are patterns of erratic or unusual thinking and behaviour that have been identified in diverse societies around the world and do not fit easily into the other diagnostic categories that are listed in the main body of DSM-IV-TR. They are called "culture-bound" because they have sometimes been considered to be unique to particular societies, particularly in non-Western or developing countries. Their appearance is easily recognized and understood to be a form of abnormal behaviour by members of certain cultures, but they do not conform to typical patterns of mental disorder seen in North America or Europe.

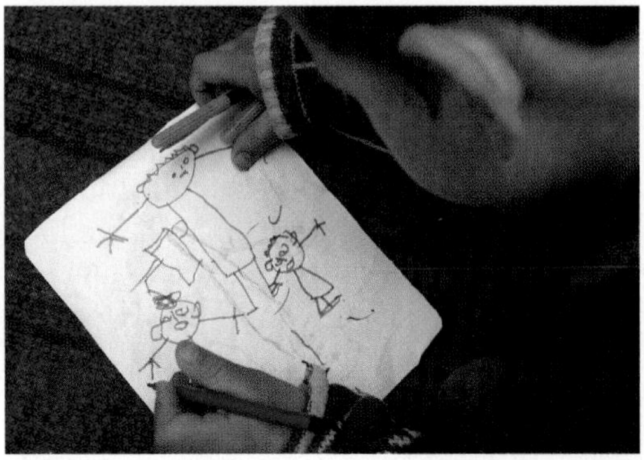

*Axis IV calls for information about life events that may have an impact on diagnosis or treatment. This seven-year-old boy is drawing a picture of his friends who were killed by a bomb in Afghanistan.*

One syndrome of this type, known as *amok*, has been observed among people (primarily men) living in Malaysia and the Philippines. An episode of amok is typically triggered by a perceived slight or insult and is accompanied by paranoid thinking. The man will brood for a period of time and then engage in a violent outburst of aggression directed at the source of the original insult. After the episode, the person may feel exhausted, may be unable to recall various aspects of his behaviour, and typically returns quickly to his premorbid state. The phenomena associated with amok are similar to other problems listed in DSM-IV-TR, such as delusional disorder and brief reactive psychosis (see Chapter 13), but the concepts defined in DSM-IV-TR do not capture the full meaning of amok as it is understood by people in Malaysia.

What is the relation between culture-bound syndromes and the formal categories listed in DSM-IV-TR? The answer is unclear and also varies from one syndrome to the next. Are they similar problems that are simply given different names in other cultures? Probably not, at least not in most instances (Guarnaccia & Rogler, 1999). In some cases, people who exhibit behaviour that would fit the definition of a culture-bound syndrome would also qualify for a DSM-IV-TR diagnosis, if they were diagnosed by a clinician trained in the use of that manual. But everyone who displays the culture-bound syndrome would not meet criteria for a DSM-IV-TR disorder, and of those who do, not all would receive the same DSM-IV-TR diagnosis.

The glossary on culture-bound syndromes has been praised as a significant advance toward integrating cultural considerations into the classification system (Lopez & Guarnaccia, 2000). It has also been criticized for its ambiguity. The most difficult conceptual issue involves the boundary between culture-bound syndromes and categories found elsewhere in the diagnostic manual. Some critics have argued that they should be fully integrated, without trying to establish a distinction (Hughes, 1998). Others have noted that if culturally unique disorders must be listed separately from other, "mainstream" conditions, then certain disorders now listed in the main body of the manual—especially eating disorders, such as bulimia (see the case study in Chapter 1)—should actually be listed as culture-bound syndromes because they are found primarily among people living in

Western or developed cultures. Popular images of women's ideal body shapes clearly play a major role in the etiology and expression of this disorder (see Chapter 10).

Thinking about this issue helps to place the more familiar categories in perspective and shows how our own culture has shaped our views of abnormal behaviour. We must not be misled into thinking that culture only shapes conditions that appear to be exotic in faraway lands; culture shapes various facets of all disorders. Though it is imperfect, the glossary of culture-bound syndromes does serve to make clinicians more aware of the extent to which their own views of what is normal and abnormal have been shaped by the values and experiences of their own culture (Mezzich et al., 2001).

## RESEARCH CLOSE-UP

### Pibloktoq: A Culture-Bound Syndrome

Many of the problems listed in the DSM-IV-TR glossary of culture-bound syndromes are also known as *idioms of distress*. In other words, they represent a manner of expressing negative emotion that is unique to a particular culture and cannot be easily translated or understood in terms of its individual parts. One possible example is the phenomenon called *pibloktoq,* which has long been observed among people living in arctic regions, including Greenland, Canada's Northwest Territories, and Alaska. Medical anthropologists have used a combination of anthropological and clinical research methods to study pibloktoq. These descriptive studies focus on emotional experiences in social and environmental contexts rather than on isolated individuals. Such studies can be used to trace the connection between culture-bound syndromes and the formal diagnostic categories in DSM-IV-TR.

Detailed studies of pibloktoq have been reported by Gussow (1985), Landy (1985), and Dick (1995). Pibloktoq occurs as abrupt dissociative episodes or "attacks," accompanied by confusion and extreme excitement, lasting from 5 to 60 minutes. Attacks are characterized by one or more of the following:

- Tearing off of clothing, sometimes to the point of complete nudity.
- Rapid, incoherent speech. The person may utter meaningless syllables, make barking sounds, utter bird cries, scream, or shout obscenities.
- Fleeing, nude or clothed, from protective shelters across the ice or snow. If indoors, the person may pace back and forth in an agitated manner.
- Rolling in snow, jumping into water, throwing oneself into a snow drift.
- Performing bizarre but harmless acts; e.g., collecting useless objects such as stones.
- Throwing objects about, creating a disordered scene, or breaking furniture. Rarely, if ever, is the sufferer or other people harmed during an attack.
- Coprophagia (feces eating).

During an attack the person becomes extremely strong and is therefore difficult to restrain. The sufferer's desire to escape may not be altogether genuine, but rather seems to represent a dramatic attempt to be pursued, overtaken, and cared for (Gussow, 1985). Attacks may be followed by convulsive seizures. Exhaustion and prolonged sleep are common after-effects. The person may have no recollection of the attack. In between attacks the person appears otherwise normal.

Before an attack, the person may appear withdrawn, tired, depressed, or irritable for a period of hours or days. Pibloktoq may be short-lived, consisting of one or two attacks, or may consist of recurrent attacks.

Many theories have been proposed to explain pibloktoq. One is that it may be a culturally sanctioned way of expressing distress and the desire to be cared for. Consistent with this, pibloktoq attacks are most likely to occur when the person is under some sort of stress (for example, when separated from a loved one) and the attacks typically occur when other people are available to render assistance (Gussow, 1985). Scientists have also speculated that diet-related disorders such as hypocalcemia or hypervitaminosis A (toxic levels of vitamin A) may play a role in pibloktoq (Dick, 1995). Landy (1985), for example, pointed out that Inuit people eat a good deal of liver, kidneys, and fat from arctic fish and mammals, where vitamin A is often stored in poisonous quantities. Landy also observed that the signs and symptoms of pibloktoq are similar to those of vitamin A intoxication. Although this is an interesting hypothesis that merits investigation, at the present time there is no conclusive evidence that pibloktoq arises from dietary factors.

What is the relation between pibloktoq and the diagnostic categories listed in DSM-IV? Pibloktoq resembles the *dissociative disorders,* which are characterized by a disruption in the usually integrated functions of consciousness, memory, identity, or perception. During a pibloktoq attack the person is in a trance-like state, acting completely out of character, and afterwards may have little recollection of the experience. In terms of DSM-IV-TR, pibloktoq could be classified as a *Dissociative Disorder Not Otherwise Specified.*

If pibloktoq is classified as a dissociative disorder, the question may be asked whether it arises from the same psychological mechanisms that are thought to play a role in other dissociative disorders (see Chapter 7). If hypervitaminosis A or hypocalcemia are the primary causes, then pibloktoq would be better regarded as a general medical condition, arising from Inuit dietary habits. Further research is needed to better understand this fascinating culture-bound syndrome, and to learn how it might be related to disorders found in other cultures. ◆

# Evaluating Classification Systems

The *Diagnostic and Statistical Manual* is an evolving document. An enormous effort was devoted to the revision process that resulted in the publication of DSM-IV in 1994. The work extended over more than five years. Final decisions about the manual were made by the task force on DSM-IV, which was composed of 30 distinguished mental health professionals (26 psychiatrists and 4 psychologists). Work groups were appointed to examine each of the major diagnostic categories, such as anxiety disorders, mood disorders, and so on. The work groups made recommendations to the task force on the basis of reviews of the existing literature on the problem, new analyses performed on already-collected sets of data, and large-scale, issue-focused field trials. The text revision, DSM-IV-TR, which provides updated presentations regarding background information on each specific disorder, was published in 2000.

How can we evaluate a system like DSM-IV-TR? Is it a useful classification system? Utility can be measured in terms of two principal criteria: reliability and validity.

## Reliability

**Reliability** refers to the consistency of measurements, including diagnostic decisions. If a diagnostic category is to be useful, it will have to be used consistently. One important form of reliability, known as inter-rater reliability, refers to agreement among clinicians. Suppose, for example, that two psychologists interview the same patient and that each psychologist independently assigns a diagnosis using DSM-IV-TR. If both psychologists decide that the patient fits the criteria for a major depressive disorder, they have used the definition of that category consistently. Of course, one or two cases would not provide a sufficient test of the reliability of a diagnostic category. The real question is whether the clinicians would agree with each other over a large series of patients. The process of collecting and interpreting information regarding the reliability of diagnosing mental disorders is discussed in Research Methods.

## Validity

The ultimate issue in the evaluation of a diagnostic category is whether it is useful. By knowing that a person fits into a particular

## RESEARCH METHODS

### Diagnostic Reliability

As noted by David Dozois at the University of Western Ontario, and colleagues, there are several important domains that need to be covered in order to conduct a comprehensive psychological assessment. Important areas include diagnostic criteria, symptom severity, and measures of theory-specific mechanisms underlying the symptoms or disorders (Dozois & Dobson, 2002; Dozois, Covin, & Brinker, 2003). For diagnoses to be useful, it is important that they must be reliable; different clinicians, for example, should be able to agree on whether or not a patient has a particular disorder.

Several formal procedures have been developed to evaluate diagnostic reliability. Most studies of psychiatric diagnosis in the past 20 years have employed a measure known as **kappa.** Instead of measuring the simple proportion of agreement between clinicians, kappa indicates the proportion of agreement that occurred above and beyond that which would have occurred by chance. Negative values of kappa indicate that the rate of agreement was less than that which would have been expected by chance in this particular sample of people. Thus a kappa of zero indicates chance agreement, and a kappa of 1.0 indicates perfect agreement between raters.

How should we interpret the kappa statistic? There is no easy answer to this question. It would be unrealistic to expect perfect consistency, especially in view of the relatively modest reliability of other diagnostic decisions that are made in medical practice (Cameron & McGoogan, 1981). On the other hand, it isn't very encouraging simply to find that the level of agreement among clinicians is somewhat better than chance. We expect more than that from a diagnostic system, especially when it is used as a basis for treatment decisions. One convention suggests that kappa values of .70 or higher indicate relatively good agreement (Matarazzo, 1983). Values of kappa below .40 are often interpreted as indicating poor agreement.

The reliability of many diagnostic categories has improved since the publication of DSM-III. Increased reliability can be attributed, in part, to the use of more detailed diagnostic criteria for specific disorders. Still, most studies also indicate that there is considerable room for improvement. The reliability of some diagnostic categories remains well below acceptable standards. ◆

group or class, do we learn anything meaningful about that person? For example, if a person fits the diagnostic criteria for schizophrenia, is that person likely to improve when he or she is given antipsychotic medication? Or is that person likely to have a less satisfactory level of social adjustment in five years than a person who meets diagnostic criteria for bipolar mood disorder? Does the diagnosis tell us anything about the factors or circumstances that might have contributed to the onset of this problem? These questions are concerned with the validity of the diagnostic category. The term **validity** refers to the meaning or importance of a measurement—in this case, a diagnostic decision (Hempel, 1961; Kendell, 1989). Importance is not an all-or-none phenomenon; it is a quantitative issue. Diagnostic categories are more or less useful, and their validity (or utility) can be determined in several ways.

Validity is, in a sense, an index of the success that has been achieved in understanding the nature of a disorder. Have important facts been discovered? Systematic studies aimed at establishing the validity of a disorder often proceed in a sequence of phases (Robins & Guze, 1989), which are listed in Table 4–3. After a clinical description has been established, diagnostic categories are refined and validated through this process of scientific exploration.

The types of information generated by the research studies listed in Table 4–3 are associated with specific types of validity. It may be helpful to think of these types of validity in terms of their relationship in time with the appearance of symptoms of the disorder. *Etiological validity* is concerned with factors that contribute to the onset of the disorder. These are things that have happened in the past. Was the disorder regularly triggered by a specific set of events or circumstances? Did it run in families? The ultimate question with regard to etiological validity is whether there are any specific causal factors that are regularly, and perhaps uniquely, associated with this disorder. If we know that a person exhibits the symptoms of the disorder, do we in turn learn anything about the circumstances that originally led to the onset of the problem?

*Concurrent validity* is concerned with the present time and with correlations between the disorder and other symptoms, circumstances, and test procedures. Is the disorder currently associated with any other types of behaviour, such as performance on psychological tests? Do precise measures of biological variables, such as brain structure and function, distinguish reliably between people who have the disorder and those who do not? Clinical studies that are aimed at developing a more precise description of a disorder also fall into this type of validity. For example, the data generated in the various DSM-IV-TR field trials contribute to the concurrent validity of the diagnostic categories with which they were concerned.

*Predictive validity* is concerned with the future and with the stability of the problem over time. Will it be persistent? If it is short-lived, how long will an episode last? Will the disorder have a predictable outcome? Do people with this problem typically improve if they are given a specific type of medication or a particular form of psychotherapy? The overall utility or validity of a diagnostic category depends on the body of evidence that accumulates as scientists seek answers to these questions.

The list of categories included in DSM-IV-TR is based heavily on conventional clinical wisdom. Each time the manual is revised, new categories are added and old categories are dropped, presumably because they are not sufficiently useful. Up to the present time, clinicians have been more willing to include new categories than to drop old ones. It is difficult to know when we would decide that a particular diagnostic category is not valid. At what point in the accumulation of knowledge are clinical scientists willing to conclude that a category is of no use and to recommend that the search for more information should be abandoned? This is a difficult question that the

**TABLE 4–3 Types of Studies Used to Validate Clinical Syndromes**

| |
|---|
| Identification and description of the syndrome, either by clinical intuition or by statistical analyses. |
| Demonstration of boundaries or "points of rarity" between related syndromes. |
| Follow-up studies establishing a distinctive course or outcome. |
| Therapeutic trials establishing a distinctive treatment response. |
| Family studies establishing that the syndrome "breeds true." |
| Demonstration of association with some more fundamental abnormality—psychological, biochemical, or molecular. |

*Source:* Adapted from R.E. Kendell, 1989, Clinical validity. *Psychological Medicine, 19,* 47.

authors of DSM-IV-TR have confronted, and it will become increasingly important in the production of future revisions.

## Unresolved Questions

Several important issues will have to be addressed as more systematic information is collected about the diagnostic categories in DSM-IV-TR. As we saw in Chapter 1, one fundamental question that applies to every disorder involves the boundary between normal and abnormal behaviour. The definitions that are included in the present version of the manual are often vague with regard to this threshold (Widiger & Clark, 2000). Many definitions rely on the requirement that a particular set of symptoms causes "clinically significant distress or impairment in social or occupational functioning." Unfortunately, these concepts are not defined specifically. Clinicians must rely on their own judgment to decide how distressed or how impaired a person must be by his or her symptoms in order to qualify for a diagnosis. These concepts are not defined in the manual, and measurement tools are not provided.

Cutoff points for the number of features that are required for a diagnosis also affect the boundary between normal and abnormal behaviour. The cutoffs listed in DSM-IV-TR were often chosen with little empirical justification. Future research should determine optimal thresholds for each disorder. For example, in the case of schizotypal personality disorder, the present cutoff point is five out of nine features. Perhaps one of the features is unnecessary or redundant with another. In that case, the list could be shortened to eight criteria. Should one or more of the features be given special weight? Are they all equally important? These questions will have to be answered by investigators who explore the validity of each individual diagnostic category.

Specific time periods are also used in the definition of various disorders. The length of time is often based on a relatively arbitrary choice. For example, in the case of schizophrenia, DSM-IV-TR requires that the person exhibit symptoms for at least six months before the diagnosis can be made. An episode of major depression must last at least two weeks. A panic attack must develop abruptly and reach its peak within 10 minutes. The usefulness of these boundaries for the duration of symptoms and disorders is an important topic for future empirical studies.

Finally, we should also mention continuing discussion of the auxiliary axes. The three that have been included in DSM-IV-TR could have been supplemented (or replaced) by other important considerations. In addition to psychosocial problems and a global assessment of functioning, it might be useful to record information regarding factors such as premorbid history, quality of interpersonal relationships, work functioning, family functioning, and/or response to treatment (Hilsenroth et al., 2000). Although each of these factors might provide useful information, classification systems can become too unwieldy and complicated.

## Problems and Limitations of the DSM-IV-TR System

Although DSM-IV-TR is a clear improvement over earlier versions of the DSM classification system, it has been criticized extensively, often with good reason (Follette & Houts, 1996; Houts, 2001). Some clinicians have emphasized conceptual issues. They argue that the syndromes defined in DSM-IV-TR may not represent the most useful ways to think about psychological problems, either in terms of planning current treatments or in terms of designing programs of research. Widespread acceptance of DSM-IV-TR may hinder the consideration of promising alternative classification systems. For example, it might be better to focus on individual symptoms rather than on groups of symptoms.

These critics pose such questions as: Should we design treatments for people who exhibit distorted, negative ways of thinking about themselves, regardless of whether their symptoms happen to involve a mixture of depression, anxiety, or some other pattern of negative emotion or interpersonal conflict? The answer is: We don't know. It would certainly be premature to cut off consideration of these alternatives just because they address problems in a way that deviates from the official diagnostic manual. In our current state of uncertainty, diversity of opinion should be encouraged, particularly if it is grounded in cautious skepticism and supported by rigorous scientific inquiry.

From an empirical point of view, DSM-IV-TR is hampered by a number of problems that suggest that it does not classify clinical problems into syndromes in the simplest and most beneficial way (Widiger & Clark, 2000). One of the thorniest issues involves **comorbidity**, which is defined as the simultaneous appearance of two or more disorders in the same person. Comorbidity rates are very high for mental disorders as they are defined in the DSM system. For example, in the National Comorbidity Survey, among those people who qualified for at least one diagnosis at some point during their lifetime, 56 percent met the criteria for two or more disorders (Kessler, 1995; Kessler et al., 1994). A small subgroup, 14 percent of the sample, actually met the diagnostic criteria for three or more lifetime disorders. That group of people accounted for almost 90 percent of the severe disorders in the study (Figure 4–1).

There are several ways to interpret comorbidity. Some people may independently develop two separate conditions. In other cases, the presence of one disorder may lead to the onset of another. Unsuccessful attempts to struggle with prolonged alcohol dependence, for example, might lead a person to become depressed. Neither of these alternatives creates conceptual problems for DSM-IV-TR. Unfortunately, the very high rate of comorbidity suggests that these explanations account for a small proportion of overlap between categories.

The real problem associated with comorbidity arises when a person with a mixed pattern of symptoms, usually of a severe nature, simultaneously meets the criteria for more than one disorder. Consider, for example, a client who was treated by one of the authors of this text. This man experienced a large number of diffuse problems associated with anxiety, depression, and interpersonal difficulties. According to the DSM-IV-TR system, he would have met the criteria for major depressive disorder, generalized anxiety disorder, and obsessive–compulsive disorder, as well as three types of personality disorder listed on Axis II. It might be said, therefore, that he suffered from at least six types of mental disorder. But is that really helpful? Is it the best way to think about his problems? Would it be more accurate to say that he had a complicated set of interrelated problems that were associated with worrying, rumination, and the regulation of high levels of negative emotion, and that these problems constituted one complex and severe type of disorder?

**Comorbidity of Mental Disorders (NCS Data)**

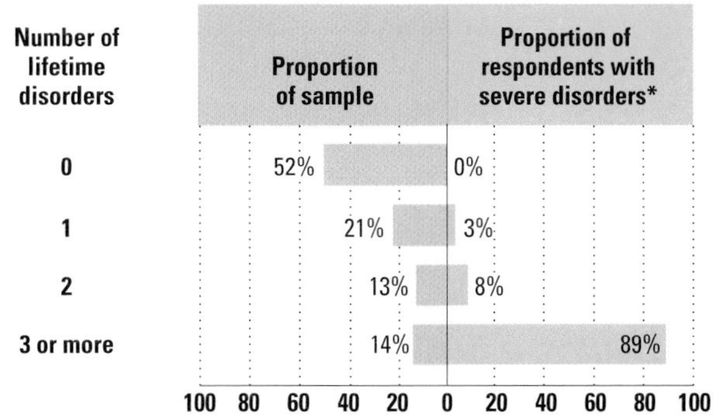


**FIGURE 4–1: Most severe mental disorders are concentrated in a group of people (about one-sixth of the population) who qualify for at least three lifetime disorders.**

*"Severe disorders" were defined to include active mania, nonaffective psychosis, or active disorders of other types that either required hospitalization or created severe role impairment.

*Source:* R.C. Kessler et al., 1994, Lifetime and 12-month prevalence of DSM-IV-TR psychiatric disorders in the United States: Results from the National Comorbidity Survey. *Archives of General Psychiatry, 51,* 13.

The comorbidity issue is related to another limitation of DSM-IV-TR: the failure to make better use of information regarding the course of mental disorders over time. More than 100 years ago, when Emil Kraepelin concluded that schizophrenia and bipolar mood disorder are distinct problems, he relied heavily on observations regarding their long-term course. Unfortunately, most disorders listed in DSM-IV-TR are defined largely in terms of snapshots of symptoms at particular points in time. Diagnostic decisions are seldom based on a comprehensive analysis of the way that a person's problems evolve over time. If someone meets the criteria for more than one disorder, does it matter which one came first? Is there a predictable pattern in which certain disorders follow the onset of others? What is the nature of the connection between childhood disorders and adult problems? Our knowledge of mental disorders would be greatly enriched if greater emphasis were placed on questions regarding lifespan development, a topic that we emphasize throughout this text.

All of these issues must be faced by clinicians when they use the DSM-IV-TR system. Attempts to provide solutions to these problems and limitations will ensure that the classification system will continue to be revised. As before, these changes will be driven by the interaction of clinical experience and empirical evidence.

## Basic Issues in Assessment

Up to this point, we have discussed the development and use of classification systems. But we haven't talked about the way in which a psychologist might collect the information that is necessary to arrive at a diagnostic decision. Furthermore, we have looked at the problem only in relatively general terms. The diagnostic decision is one useful piece of information. It is not, however, a systematic picture of the specific person's situation. It is only a starting point. In the following section we extend our discussion to consider methods of collecting information. In so doing, we discuss a broad range of data that may be useful in understanding psychopathological behaviour.

### Purposes of Clinical Assessment

To appreciate the importance and complexity of assessment procedures, let's go back to the example of Michael. When Michael and his parents initially approached the psychologist, they were clearly upset. But the nature of the problem, in terms of Michael's behaviour and the family as a whole, was not clearly defined. Before he could attempt to help this family, the psychologist had to collect more information. He needed to know more about the range and frequency of Michael's obsessions and compulsions, including when they began, how often he experienced these problems, and the factors that made them better or worse. He also needed to know whether there were other problems, such as depression or delusional beliefs, which might either explain these responses or interfere with their treatment. In addition, he had to learn how Michael got along with classmates, how he was doing in school, and how his parents responded when he behaved strangely. Was his behaviour, at least in part, a response to environmental circumstances? How would the family support (or interfere with) the therapist's attempts to help him change? The psychologist needed to address Michael's current situation in terms of several different facets of his behaviour.

Psychological assessment is the process of collecting and interpreting information that will be used to understand another person. Numerous data-gathering techniques can be used in this process. Several of these procedures are described in the following pages. We must remember, however, not to confuse the process of assessment with this list of techniques. Assessment procedures are tools that can be used in many ways. They cannot be used in an intellectual vacuum. Interviews can be used to collect all sorts of information for all sorts of reasons. Psychological tests can be interpreted in many different ways. The value of assessment procedures can be determined only in the context of a specific purpose.

Three primary goals guide most assessment procedures: making predictions, planning treatments, and evaluating treatments. The practical importance of predictions should be obvious: Many crucial decisions are based on psychologists' attempts to determine the probability of future events. Will a person engage in violent behaviour? Can a person make rational decisions? Is a parent able to care for his or her children? Assessment is also commonly used to evaluate the likelihood that a particular form of treatment will be helpful for a specific patient and to provide guideposts by which the effectiveness of treatment programs can be measured (Hayes, Nelson, & Jarrett, 1987). Different assessment procedures are likely to be employed for different purposes. Those that are useful in one situation may not be helpful in another.

### Assumptions about the Consistency of Behaviour

Assessment involves the collection of specific samples of a person's behaviour. These samples may include things that the person says during an interview, responses that the person makes on a psychological test, or things that the person does while being observed. None of these would be important if we assumed that they were isolated events. They are useful to the extent that they represent examples of the ways in which the person will feel or behave in other situations. Psychologists, therefore, must be concerned about the consistency of behaviour across time and situations. They want to know if they can *generalize*, or draw inferences about the person's behaviour in the natural environment on the basis of the samples of behaviour that are obtained in their assessment. If the client is depressed at this moment, how did she feel one week ago, and how will she feel tomorrow? In other words, is this a persistent phenomenon, or is it a temporary state? If a child is anxious and unable to pay attention in the psychologist's office, will he also exhibit these problems in his classroom? And how will he behave on the playground?

Psychologists typically seek out more than one source of information when conducting a formal assessment. Because we are trying to compose a broad, integrated picture of the person's adjustment, we must collect information from several sources and then attempt to integrate these data. Each piece of information may be considered to be one sample of the person's behaviour. One way of evaluating the possible meaning or importance of this information is to consider the consistency across sources. Do the conclusions drawn on the basis of a diagnostic interview agree with those that are suggested by a psychological test? Do the psychologist's observations of the client's behaviour and the client's self-report agree with observations that are reported by parents or teachers?

**Levels of Analysis** The kind of information that is collected will depend on the way in which the clinician views the problem. Mental disorders are embedded in multiple, interacting systems that involve biological, psychological, and social factors (see Chapter 2). Assessment instruments can be aimed at any of these levels. At one level, the clinician must decide whether to concentrate on the individual client or to focus more broadly on social systems. For example, a depressed married person might be treated as an individual or as part of a couple. In Michael's case, his problem might be viewed in terms of the family system, which also involves his parents. Michael's relatively poor relationships with his peers could also be considered relevant to understanding his problems.

At another level, the clinician has to decide whether to concentrate on psychological variables or biological factors that might also influence the etiology of the problem. In all cases, the clinician's choice of the level of analysis will determine in large part the sorts of assessment instruments that will be employed in the assessment process. Because assessment is a finite process, the decision to use one set of procedures will inevitably lead to the omission of others.

Suppose we decide to focus primarily on psychological variables, as we have done in our description of Michael's case. We must then make decisions regarding where we should focus our attention within the psychological

*Diagnostic interviews provide an opportunity to make detailed inquiries about a person's subjective experience while also observing his or her behaviour.*

system. One relatively broad conceptual scheme involves the consideration of diagnostic categories. Does Michael meet the DSM-IV-TR criteria for obsessive–compulsive disorder? If he does, then the clinician is likely to employ particular forms of intervention. But we also know that not all obsessive–compulsive clients are exactly the same. They worry about different kinds of things—germs, leaving the lights or stove on, having unacceptable thoughts, and the ways in which they attempt to cope with, or neutralize, these fears may also vary tremendously. Response to treatment will also be influenced by additional considerations, such as the person's personality traits, cognitive abilities, social skills, and the presence or absence of comorbid conditions, such as a seriously depressed mood. Therefore, the clinician will require a great deal of additional information in order to formulate a treatment plan.

## Evaluating the Usefulness of Assessment Procedures

The same criteria that are used to evaluate diagnostic categories are used to evaluate the usefulness of assessment procedures: reliability and validity. We have already discussed interrater reliability with regard to diagnostic decisions. In the case of assessment procedures, reliability can refer to various types of consistency. For example, the consistency of measurements over time is known as test–retest reliability. Will a person receive the same score if an assessment procedure is repeated at two different points in time? The internal consistency of items within a test is known as split-half reliability. If a test with many items measures a specific trait or ability, and if the items are divided in half, will the person's scores on the two halves agree with each other? Assessment procedures must be reliable if they are to be useful in either clinical practice or research.

The validity of an assessment procedure refers to its meaning or importance (Foster & Cone, 1995). Is the person's score on this test or procedure actually a reflection of the trait or ability that the test was designed to measure? And does the score tell us anything useful about the person's behaviour in other situations? Knowing that the person has achieved a particular score on this evaluation, can we make meaningful predictions about the person's responses to other tests, or about his or her behaviour in future situations? These are all questions about the validity of an assessment procedure. In general, the more consistent the information provided by different assessment procedures, the more valid each procedure is considered to be.

Cultural differences present an important challenge to the validity of assessment procedures. It is often difficult to understand the thoughts and behaviours of people from a cultural background that is different from our own. Measurement procedures that were constructed for one group may be misleading when they are applied to people from another culture. Language, religion, gender roles, beliefs about health and illness, and attitudes toward the family can all have an important impact on the ways in which psychological problems are experienced and expressed. These factors must be taken into consideration when psychologists collect information about the nature of a specific person's problems. Interviews, observational procedures, and personality tests must be carefully evaluated for cross-cultural validity (Padilla, 2001; Thomas, Turkheimer, & Oltmanns, 2000). Unfortunately, this issue has often been overlooked in treatment planning and in psychopathology research. We should not assume that a questionnaire developed in one culture will necessarily be useful in another. Investigators must demonstrate empirically that it measures the same thing in both groups.

### Types of Assessment Procedures

An enormous array of assessment tools is available to clinicians who are interested in treating or studying abnormal behaviour. Many of these procedures are commonly employed in clinical practice, and they are also used in the process of research. The most useful assessment procedures are likely to vary from one problem to the next. Assessment procedures that are useful in evaluating the effectiveness of a drug treatment program for hospitalized depressed patients may be quite different from those used to predict the need for medication among hyperactive schoolchildren. Our purpose in the rest of this chapter is to outline a range of assessment procedures. This is a selective sampling of measures rather than an exhaustive review of assessment procedures.

We begin our discussion with measures that are typically concerned with psychological variables—characteristic traits and behaviours that are associated with abnormal behaviour. From there, we move to a consideration of the assessment of social systems, such as families and institutional environments (schools and hospitals). The last section of this chapter is concerned with measures used in biological systems—the neurological and biochemical underpinnings of mental disorders. In many cases, the assessment of psychopathology is based on the combined use of measures that cover selective aspects of all of these systems.

At the end of each section is a quick summary of the advantages and limitations of each type of procedure. These summaries are intended only as general guides and not as definitive critiques. Please keep in mind our earlier comment: Each procedure is a tool that can be used for different purposes. The true value of the tool can be determined only in light of the specific purpose for which it is used.

## Assessing Psychological Systems

"Person variables" are typically the first thing that come to mind when we think about the assessment of psychopathology. What did the person do or say? How does the person feel about his or her current situation? What skills and abilities does the person possess, and are there any important cognitive or social deficits that should be taken into consideration? These questions about the individual person can be addressed through a number of procedures, including interviews, observations, and various types of self-report instruments and psychological tests.

## Interviews

Often, the best way to find out about someone is to talk with that person directly. The clinical interview is the most commonly used procedure in psychological assessment. Most of the categories that are defined in DSM-IV-TR are based on information that can be collected in an interview. These data are typically supplemented by information that is obtained from official records (previous hospital admissions, school reports, court files) and interviews with other informants (for example, family members), but the clients' own direct descriptions of their problems are the primary basis for diagnostic decisions. Except for mental retardation, none of the diagnostic categories in DSM-IV-TR is defined in terms of psychological or biological tests.

Interviews provide an opportunity to ask people for their own descriptions of their problems. Many of the symptoms of psychopathology are subjective, and an interview can provide a detailed analysis of these problems. Consider, for example, Michael's problems with anxiety. The unrelenting fear and revulsion that he experienced at school were the central features of his problem. His obsessive thoughts of contamination were private events that could only be known to the psychologist on the basis of Michael's self-report, which was quite compelling. His family could observe Michael's peculiar habits with regard to arranging his schoolbooks, changing his clothes, and washing his hands, but the significance of these behaviours to Michael was not immediately apparent without the knowledge that they were based on an attempt to control or neutralize his anxiety-provoking images of taunting classmates.

Interviews also allow clinicians to observe important features of a person's appearance and nonverbal behaviour. In Michael's case, the psychologist noticed during the initial interview that the skin on Michael's hands and lower arms was red and chafed from excessive scrubbing. He was neatly dressed but seemed especially self-conscious about his hair and glasses, which he adjusted repeatedly. Michael was reluctant to make eye contact, and his speech was soft and hesitant. His obvious discomfort in this social situation was consistent with his own descriptions of the anxiety that he felt during interactions with peers. It was also interesting to note that Michael became visibly agitated when discussing particular subjects, such as the incident with his track team. At these points in the interview, he would fidget restlessly in his seat and clasp his arms closely around his sides. His speech became more rapid, and he began to stutter a bit. On one occasion, he found it impossible to sit still, and he began to pace quickly back and forth across the psychologist's office. These nonverbal aspects of Michael's behaviour provided useful information about the nature of his distress.

The psychologist asked Michael to describe the sequence of events in a typical day. How did he spend his time when he was at school? What were his interests outside of school? How did his rituals and obsessive thoughts interfere with these activities? Taken together, this information provides a broader context in which the specific symptoms can be understood. The relationship that was established between Michael and his psychologist became an essential factor in the subsequent efforts they made toward changing Michael's behaviour.

**Structured Interviews** Assessment interviews vary with regard to the amount of structure that is imposed by the clinician. Some are relatively open-ended, or nondirective. In this type of interview, the clinician follows the train of thought supplied by the client. One goal of nondirective interviews is to help people clarify their subjective feelings and to provide general empathic support for whatever they may decide to do about their problems. In contrast to this open-ended style, some interviews follow a more specific question-and-answer format. Structured interviews, in which the clinician must ask each patient a specific list of detailed questions, are frequently employed for collecting information that will be used to make diagnostic decisions and to rate the extent to which a person is impaired by psychopathology.

Several different structured interviews have been developed for the purpose of making psychiatric diagnoses in large-scale epidemiological and cross-national studies (Segal, 1997). Investigators reasoned that the reliability of their diagnostic decisions would improve if they could ensure that clinicians always made a consistent effort to ask the same questions when they interviewed patients. Other forms of structured diagnostic interviews have been designed for use in the diagnosis of specific types of problems, such as personality disorders, anxiety disorders, dissociative disorders, and the behaviour problems of children.

Structured interviews list a series of specific questions that lead to a detailed description of the person's behaviour and experiences. As an example, consider the Structured Interview for DSM-IV-TR Personality Disorders (SIDP-IV; Pfohl, Blum, & Zimmerman, 1995), which could have been used as part of the assessment process in Michael's situation. The SIDP-IV is a widely adopted semistructured interview that covers all of the DSM-IV-TR personality disorder categories. Selected questions from the SIDP-IV are presented in Table 4–4. We have included in this table several of the questions that are specifically relevant to a diagnosis of schizotypal personality disorder.

Structured interview schedules provide a systematic framework for the collection of important diagnostic information, but they don't eliminate the need for an experienced clinician. If the interviewer is not able to es-

**TABLE 4–4 Sample Items from the Structured Interview for DSM-IV Personality (SIDP-IV)**

Scoring Guidelines:

0 = not present or limited to rare isolated examples.

1 = subthreshold—some evidence of the trait but it is not sufficiently pervasive or severe to consider the criterion present.

2 = present—criterion is clearly present for most of the last five years (i.e., present at least 50 percent of the time during the last five years).

3 = strongly present—criterion is associated with subjective distress or some impairment in social or occupational functioning, or intimate relationships.

**Close Relationships**

This part of the interview asks about your relationships with friends and family. Remember that I'm interested in the way you are when you are your usual self.

1. Neither desires nor enjoys close relationships, including being part of a family — 0 1 2 3

   Do you have close relationships with friends or family?
   (IF YES): What do you enjoy about these relationships?
   (IF NO): Do you wish you had some close relationships?

2. Lacks close friends or confidants other than first-degree relatives — 0 1 2 3

   Not counting your immediate family, do you have close friends you can confide in?

**Perception of Others**

The questions in this section ask about experiences you may have had with other people. Remember that I'm interested in knowing how you feel about these situations when you are your usual self, not during an episode of illness or hospitalization.

1. Suspects, without sufficient basis, that others are exploiting, harming, or deceiving him or her — 0 1 2 3

   Have you had experiences where people who pretended to be your friends took advantage of you?
   (IF YES): What happened?

   How often has this happened?

   Are you good at spotting someone who is trying to deceive or con you?
   (IF YES): Examples?

2. Ideas of reference (excluding delusions of reference) — 0 1 2 3

   Have you ever found that people around you seem to be talking in general, but then you realize their comments are really meant for you?
   (IF YES): How do you know they're talking about you?

   Have you felt like someone in charge changed the rules specifically because of you, but they wouldn't admit it?

   Do you sometimes feel like strangers on the street are looking at you and talking about you?
   (IF YES): Why do you think they notice you in particular?

*Source:* Bruce Pfohl and Nancee Blum, Department of Psychiatry, University of Iowa, Iowa City.

tablish a comfortable rapport with the client, then the interview might not elicit useful information. Furthermore, it is difficult to specify in advance all the questions that should be asked in a diagnostic interview. The client's responses to questions may require clarification. The interviewer must determine when it is necessary to probe further and in what ways to probe. Having lists of specific questions and clear definitions of diagnostic criteria will make the clinician's job easier, but clinical judgment remains an important ingredient in the diagnostic interview.

*Advantages:* The clinical interview is the primary tool employed by clinical psychologists in the assessment of psychopathology. Several features of interviews account for this popularity, including the following issues:

1. The interviewer can control the interaction and can probe further when necessary.
2. By observing the patient's nonverbal behaviour, the interviewer can detect areas of resistance. In that sense, the validity of the information may be enhanced.
3. An interview can provide a lot of information in a short period of time. It can cover past events and many different settings.

*Limitations:* Several limitations in the use of clinical interviews as part of the assessment process must be kept in mind. These include the following considerations:

1. Some patients may be unable or unwilling to provide a rational account of their problems. This may be particularly true of young children, who have not developed verbal skills, as well as some psychotic and demented patients who are unable to speak coherently.
2. People may be reluctant to admit experiences that are embarrassing or frightening. They may feel that they should report to the interviewer only those feelings and behaviours that are socially desirable. Negative stereotypes about people with mental disorders interfere with an open and honest discussion of a person's problems.
3. Subjective factors play an important role in the interpretation of information provided in an interview. The person's responses to questions are not scored objectively, and there is always some variation in the format. The situation is not entirely structured and depends heavily on the training and experience of the interviewer.
4. Information provided by the client is necessarily filtered through the client's eyes. It is a subjective account and may be influenced or distorted by errors in memory and by selective perception.
5. Interviewers can influence their clients' accounts by the ways in which they phrase their questions and respond to the clients' responses.

## Observational Procedures

In addition to the information that we gain from what people are willing to tell us during interviews, we can also learn a lot by watching their behaviour. Observational skills play an important part in most assessment procedures. Sometimes the things that we observe confirm the person's self-report, and at other times the person's overt behaviour appears to be at odds with what he or she says. A juvenile delinquent might express in words his regret at having injured a classmate, but his smile and the twinkle in his eye may raise doubts about the sincerity of his statement. In situations such as this, we must reconcile information that is obtained from different sources. The picture that emerges of another person's adjustment is greatly enriched when data collected from interviews are supplemented by observations of the person's behaviour.

Observational procedures may be either informal or formal. Informal observations are primarily qualitative. The clinician observes the person's behaviour and the environment in which it occurs without attempting to record the frequency or intensity of specific responses. Michael's case illustrates the value of informal observations in the natural environment. When the therapist visited Michael and his parents at their home, he learned that his ritualistic behaviours were more extreme than Michael had originally described. This was useful but not particularly surprising, as patients with OCD are often reluctant to describe in an interview the full extent of their compulsive behaviour. The therapist also learned that the parents themselves were quite concerned with rules and order. Everything in their home was highly polished and in its place. This observation helped the therapist understand the extent to which Michael's parents might contribute to, or reinforce, his rigid adherence to a strict set of rules.

Although observations are often conducted in the natural environment, there are times when it is useful to observe the person's behaviour in a situation that the psychologist can arrange and control. Sometimes it isn't possible to observe the person's behaviour in the natural environment because the behaviour in question occurs infrequently or at times when an observer cannot be present; at other times the environment is inaccessible; and sometimes the behaviour that is of interest is inherently a private act. In these cases, the psychologist may arrange to observe the person's behaviour in a situation that in some ways approximates the real environment. These artificial situations may also allow for more careful measurements of the person's problem than could be accomplished in a more complex situation.

In the case of obsessive–compulsive behaviour, this approach might involve asking the person deliberately to touch an object that would ordinarily trigger ritualistic behaviours. The therapist might collect a set of objects that Michael would not want to touch, such as a schoolbook, a pair of old track shorts, and the knob of a door leading to the laundry room. It would be useful to know specifically which objects he would touch, the degree of discomfort that he experienced when touching them, and the length of time that he was able to wait before washing his hands after touching these objects. This information could also be used as an index of change as treatment progressed.

*Direct observation can provide one of the most useful sources of information about a person's behaviour. In this case, the children and their teacher are being observed from behind a one-way mirror in order to minimize reactivity, the effect that the observer's presence might have on their behaviour.*

**Rating Scales** Various types of procedures can be used to provide quantitative assessments of a person's behaviour that are based on observations. One alternative is to use a **rating scale** in which the observer is asked to make judgments that place the person somewhere along a dimension. For example, a clinician might observe a person's behaviour for an extended period of time and then complete a set of ratings that are concerned with dimensions such as the extent to which the person exhibits compulsive ritualistic behaviours.

Ratings can also be made on the basis of information collected during an interview. The Yale-Brown Obsessive–Compulsive Scale (Y-BOCS; Goodman et al., 1989) is an example of an interview-based rating scale that is used extensively in the evaluation of people with problems like Michael's. Examples of items from the Y-BOCS are presented in Table 4–5. For each topic or set of questions, the interviewer is required to make a rating from 0 to 4, indicating the person's level of distress or impairment. The composite rating—the total across all the items in the scale—can be used as an index of the severity of the disorder.

Rating scales provide abstract descriptions of a person's behaviour rather than a specific record of exactly what the person has done. They require social judgments on the part of the observer, who must compare this person's behaviour with an ideal view of other people (Cairns & Green, 1979). How does this person compare to someone who has never experienced any difficulties in this particular area? How does the person compare to the most severely disturbed patients? Consider the fourth Y-BOCS item in Table 4–5. The interviewer must determine whether the person's attempts to ignore or resist the repetitive thoughts are excessive or unreasonable. In many cases, that is a difficult judgment. The value of these judgments will depend, in large part, on the experience of the person who makes the ratings. They are useful to the extent that the observer is able to synthesize accurately the information that has been collected and then rate the frequency or severity of the problem relative to the behaviour of other people.

**Behavioural Coding Systems** Another approach to quantifying observational data depends on recording the person's actual activities. Rather than making judgments about where the person falls on a particular dimension, **behavioural coding systems**—also known as *formal observation schedules*—focus on the frequency of specific behavioural events (Foster & Cone, 1986). This type of observation, therefore, requires fewer inferences on the part of the observer. Coding systems can be used with observations that are made in the person's natural environment as well as with those that are performed in artificial, or contrived, situations that are specifically designed to elicit the problem behaviour under circumstances in which it can be observed precisely. In some cases, the observations are made directly by a therapist, and at other times the information is provided by people who have a better opportunity to see the person's behaviour in the natural environment, including teachers, parents, spouse, and peers.

Some approaches to systematic observation can be relatively simple. Consider, once again, the case of Michael. After the psychologist had conducted several interviews with Michael and his family, he asked Michael's mother to participate in the assessment process by making detailed observations of his handwashing over a period of several nights. The mother was given a set of forms—one for each day—that could be used to record each incident, the time at which it occurred, and the circumstances that preceded the washing. The day was divided into 30-minute intervals starting at 6:30 A.M., when Michael got out of bed, and ending at 10:30 P.M., when he usually went to sleep. On each line (one for each time interval), his mother indicated whether he had washed his hands, what had been going on just prior to washing, and how anxious (on a scale from 1 to 100) Michael felt at the time that he washed.

Some adult clients are able to complete this kind of record by keeping track of their own behaviour—a procedure known as *self-monitoring*. In this case, Michael's mother was asked to help because she was considered a more accurate observer than Michael and because Michael did not want to touch the form that would be used to record these observations. He believed that it was contaminated because it had touched his school clothes, which he wore to the therapy session.

Two weeks of observations were examined prior to the start of Michael's treatment. They indicated several things, including the times of the day when Michael was most active with his washing rituals (between six and nine

**TABLE 4–5 Sample Items from the Yale-Brown Obsessive–Compulsive Scale**

**Time Occupied by Obsessive Thoughts**

How much of your time is occupied by obsessive thoughts?

0 = None
1 = Mild, less than 1 hour per day
2 = Moderate, 1 to 3 hours per day
3 = Severe, greater than 3 and up to 8 hours per day
4 = Extreme, greater than 8 hours per day

**Interference Due to Obsessive Thoughts**

How much do your obsessive thoughts interfere with your social or work (or role) functioning? Is there anything that you don't do because of them?

0 = None
1 = Mild, slight interference, but overall performance not impaired
2 = Moderate, definite interference, but still manageable
3 = Severe, causes substantial impairment
4 = Extreme, incapacitating

**Distress Associated with Obsessive Thoughts**

How much distress do your obsessive thoughts cause you?

0 = None
1 = Mild, not too disturbing
2 = Moderate, disturbing, but still manageable
3 = Severe, very disturbing
4 = Extreme, near constant and disabling distress

**Resistance against Obsessions**

How much of an effort do you make to resist the obsessive thoughts? How often do you try to disregard or turn your attention away from these thoughts as they enter your mind?

0 = Always
1 = Much resistance
2 = Some resistance
3 = Often yields
4 = Completely yields

**Degree of Control over Obsessive Thoughts**

How much control do you have over your obsessive thoughts? How successful are you in stopping or diverting your obsessive thinking? Can you dismiss them?

0 = Complete control
1 = Much control
2 = Some control
3 = Little control
4 = No control

o'clock at night) and those specific objects and areas in the house that were most likely to trigger a washing incident. This information helped the therapist to plan the treatment procedure, which would depend on approaching Michael's problem at the level that could most easily be handled and moving toward those situations that were the most difficult for him. The observations provided by Michael's mother were also used to mark his progress after treatment began.

*Advantages:* Observational measures, including rating scales and more detailed behavioural coding systems, can provide an extremely useful supplement to information that is typically collected in an interview format. Their advantage lies primarily in the fact that they can provide a more direct source of information than interviews can, because clinicians observe behaviour directly rather than relying on patients' self-reports (Foster & Cone, 1986; Gottman, 1985). Specific types of observational measures have distinct advantages:

1. Rating scales are primarily useful as an overall index of symptom severity or functional impairment.
2. Behavioural coding systems provide detailed information about the person's behaviour in a particular situation.

*Limitations:* Observations are sometimes considered to be similar to photographs: They provide a more direct or realistic view of behaviour than do people's recollections of their actions and feelings. But just as the quality of a photograph is influenced by the quality of the camera, the film, and the process that is used to develop it, the value of observational data depends on the procedures that are used to collect them (Nietzel, Bernstein, & Milich, 1994). Thus, observations have a number of limitations:

1. Observational procedures can be time-consuming and therefore expensive. Raters usually require extensive training before they can use a detailed behavioural coding system.
2. Observers can make errors. Their perception may be biased, just as the inferences of an interviewer may be biased. The reliability of ratings as well as behavioural coding must be monitored.
3. People may alter their behaviour, either intentionally or unintentionally, when they know that they are being observed—a phenomenon known as **reactivity**. For example, a person who is asked to count the number of times that he washes his hands may wash less frequently than he does when he is not keeping track.
4. Observational measures tell us only about the particular situation that was selected to be observed. We don't know if the person will behave in a similar way elsewhere or at a different time, unless we extend the scope of our observations.
5. There are some aspects of psychopathology that cannot be observed by anyone other than the person who has the problem. This is especially true for subjective experiences, such as guilt or low self-esteem.

## Personality Tests and Self-Report Inventories

Personality tests are another important source of information about an individual's adjustment. Tests provide an opportunity to collect samples of a person's behaviour in a standardized situation. These samples of behaviour presumably reflect underlying abilities or personality traits. In any psychological test, the person who is being tested is presented with some kind of standard stimuli. The stimuli may be specific questions that can be answered true or false. They might be problems that require solutions, or they can be completely ambiguous inkblots. Exactly the same stimuli are used every time that the test is given. In that way, the clinician can be sure that differences in performance can be interpreted as differences in abilities or traits rather than differences in the testing situation.

The psychologist observes people's responses in the test situation and draws inferences or makes predictions about how they will behave in other situations. For example, achievement tests present students with a series of mathematical and verbal problems. Performance on these standardized problems is taken as a reflection of the amount the student has learned and is also used to predict how well he or she will do in future academic situations.

**Personality Inventories** Because of their structure, **personality inventories** are sometimes referred to as "objective tests." They consist of a series of straightforward statements;

the person being tested is typically required to indicate whether each statement is true or false in relation to himself or herself. Several types of personality inventories are widely used. Some are designed to identify personality traits in a normal population, and others focus more specifically on psychopathological problems. We have chosen to focus on the most extensively used personality inventory—the Minnesota Multiphasic Personality Inventory (MMPI)—to illustrate the characteristics of these tests as assessment devices.

The original version of the MMPI was developed in the 1940s at the University of Minnesota by Starke Hathaway (1903–1984) and his colleagues. For the past 40 years, it has been the most widely used psychological test. Thousands of research articles have been published on the MMPI (Archer, 1992). The inventory was revised several years ago, and it is currently known as the MMPI-2 (Butcher & Williams, 2000; Greene, 2000).

The MMPI-2 is based on a series of more than 500 statements that cover topics ranging from physical complaints and psychological states to occupational preferences and social attitudes. Examples are statements such as, "I sometimes keep on at a thing until others lose their patience with me"; "My feelings are easily hurt"; and "There are persons who are trying to steal my thoughts and ideas." After reading each statement, the person is instructed to indicate whether it is true or false. Scoring of the MMPI-2 is objective. After the responses to all questions are totalled, the person receives a numerical score on each of 10 clinical scales as well as 4 validity scales.

Before considering the possible clinical significance of a person's MMPI-2 profile, the psychologist will examine a number of validity scales, which reflect the patient's attitude toward the test and the openness and consistency with which the questions were answered. The L (Lie) Scale is sensitive to unsophisticated attempts to avoid answering in a frank and honest manner. For example, one statement on this scale says, "At times I feel like swearing." Although this is perhaps not an admirable trait, virtually all normal subjects indicate that the item is true. Subjects who indicate that the item is false (does not apply to them) receive one point on the L scale. Several responses of this sort would result in an elevated score on the scale and would indicate that the person's overall test results should not be interpreted as a true reflection of his or her feelings. Other validity scales reflect tendencies to exaggerate problems, carelessness in completing the questions, and unusual defensiveness.

If the profile is considered valid, the process of interpretation will be directed toward the 10 clinical scales, which are described in Table 4–6. Some of these scales carry rather obvious meaning, whereas others are associated with a more general or mixed pattern of symptoms. For example, Scale 2 (Depression) is a relatively straightforward index of degree of depression. Scale 7 (Psychasthenia), in contrast, is more complex and is based on items that measure anxiety, insecurity, and excessive doubt. There are many different ways to obtain an elevated score on any of the clinical scales, because each scale is composed of many items. Even the more obvious scales can indicate several different types of problems. Therefore, the pattern of scale scores is more

*Psychologist **Starke Hathaway** created the Minnesota Multiphasic Personality Inventory (MMPI), which has become the most widely employed objective test of personality.*

**TABLE 4–6 Clinical Scales for the MMPI**

| Scale Number | Scale Name | Interpretation of High Scores |
|---|---|---|
| 1 | Hypochondriasis | Excessive bodily concern; somatic symptoms |
| 2 | Depression | Depressed; pessimistic; irritable; demanding |
| 3 | Hysteria | Physical symptoms of functional origin; self-centred; demands attention |
| 4 | Psychopathic Deviate | Asocial or antisocial; rebellious; impulsive, poor judgment |
| 5 | Masculinity–Femininity | Male: aesthetic interests Female: assertive; competitive; self-confident |
| 6 | Paranoia | Suspicious, sensitive; resentful; rigid; may be frankly psychotic |
| 7 | Psychasthenia | Anxious; worried; obsessive; lacks self-confidence; problems in decision making |
| 8 | Schizophrenia | May have thinking disturbance, withdrawn; feels alienated and unaccepted |
| 9 | Hypomania | Excessive activity; lacks direction; low frustration tolerance; friendly |
| 0 | Social-Introversion | Socially introverted; shy; sensitive; overcontrolled; conforming |

important than the elevation of any particular scale.

Rather than depending only on their own experience and clinical judgment, which may be subject to various sorts of bias and inconsistency, many clinicians analyze the results of a specific test on the basis of an explicit set of rules that are derived from empirical research (Greene, 2000). This is known as an **actuarial interpretation**. We can illustrate this process using Michael's profile. The profile is first described in terms of the pattern of scale scores, beginning with the highest and proceeding to the lowest. Those that are elevated above a scale score of 70 are most important, and interpretations are sometimes based on the "high-point pair." Following this procedure, Michael's profile could be coded as a 2–0; that is, his highest scores were on Scales 2 and 0. The clinician then looks up this specific configuration of scores in a kind of MMPI-2 "cookbook" to see what sort of descriptive characteristics apply. One cookbook offers the following statement about adolescents (mostly 14 and 15 years old) who fit the 2–0/0–2 code type:

> Eighty-seven percent of the 2–0/0–2s express feelings of inferiority to their therapists. They say that they are not good-looking, that they are afraid to speak up in class, and that they feel awkward when they meet people or try to make a date (91 percent of high 2–0/0–2s). Their therapists see the 2–0/0–2s as anxious, fearful, timid, withdrawn, and inhibited. They are depressed, and very vulnerable to threat. The 2–0/0–2 adolescents are overcontrolled; they cannot let go, even when it would be appropriate for them to do so. They are afraid of emotional involvement with others and, in fact, seem to have little need for such affiliation. These adolescents are viewed by their psychotherapists as schizoid; they think and associate in unusual ways and spend a good deal of time in personal fantasy and daydreaming. They are serious young people who tend to anticipate problems and difficulties. Indeed, they are prone toward obsessional thinking and are compulsively meticulous. (Marks, Seeman, & Haller, 1974, p. 201)

Several comments must be made about this statement. First, nothing is certain. Actuarial descriptions are probability statements. They indicate that a certain proportion of the people who produce this pattern of scores will be associated with a certain characteristic or behaviour. If 87 percent of the adolescents who produce this code type express feelings of inferiority, 13 percent do not. Many aspects of this description apply to Michael's current adjustment, but they don't all fit. The MMPI-2 must be used in conjunction with other assessment procedures. The accuracy of actuarial statements can be verified through interviews with the person or through direct observations of his or her behaviour.

*Advantages:* The MMPI-2 has several advantages in comparison to interviews and observational procedures. In clinical practice, it is seldom used by itself, but, for the following reasons, it can serve as a useful supplement to other methods of collecting information.

1. The MMPI-2 provides information about the person's test-taking attitude, which alerts the clinician to the possibility that clients are careless, defensive, or exaggerating their problems.
2. The MMPI-2 covers a wide range of problems in a direct and efficient manner. It would take a clinician several hours to go over all of these topics using an interview format.
3. Because the MMPI-2 is scored objectively, the initial description of the person's adjustment is not influenced by the clinician's subjective impression of the client.
4. The MMPI-2 can be interpreted in an actuarial fashion, using extensive banks of information regarding people who respond to items in a particular way.

*Limitations:* The MMPI-2 also has a number of limitations. Some of its problems derive from the fact that it has been used for many years. When the MMPI-2 was developed in the late 1980s, its authors decided to maintain the same clinical scales (see Table 4–6). New standardization data were obtained, and some old-fashioned items were replaced, but the underlying structure of the MMPI-2 is still based on diagnostic concepts and dimensions of psychopathology that were used 40 years ago (Helmes & Reddon, 1993). More specific limitations of the MMPI-2 are listed below.

1. The test is not particularly sensitive to certain forms of psychopathology, espe-

cially those that have been added with the publication of DSM-III and DSM-IV-TR. These include certain types of anxiety disorders, personality disorders, and subtypes of mood disorders.

2. The test depends on the person's ability to read and respond to written statements. Some people cannot complete the rather extensive list of questions. These include many people who are acutely psychotic, intellectually impaired, or poorly educated.
3. Specific data are not always available for a particular profile. Many patients' test results do not meet criteria for a particular code type with which extensive data are associated. Therefore, actuarial interpretation is not really possible for these profiles.
4. Some studies have found that profile types are not stable over time. It is not clear whether this instability should be interpreted as lack of reliability or as sensitivity to change in the person's level of adjustment.

**Other Self-Report Inventories** Sophisticated personality inventories like the MMPI are not the only approach to the measurement of subjective psychological states. Many other questionnaires and checklists have been developed to collect information about adjustment problems, including subjective mood states such as depression and anxiety, patterns of obsessive thinking, and attitudes about drinking alcohol, eating, and sexual behaviour. One example is the Beck Depression Inventory (BDI), which is used extensively in both clinical and research settings as an index of severity of depression. Sample items from the BDI are presented in Table 4–7.

The format of most self-report inventories is similar to that employed with objective personality tests like the MMPI-2. The primary difference is the range of topics covered by the instrument. Tests like the MMPI-2 are designed to measure several dimensions that are related to abnormal behaviour, whereas a self-report inventory is aimed more specifically at a focal topic or at one aspect of the person's adjustment. Self-report inventories usually don't include validity scales, and they may not be standardized on large samples of normal subjects prior to their use in a clinical setting.

Self-report inventories offer many advantages as supplements to information that is collected during clinical interviews. They are an extremely efficient way to gather specific data regarding a wide range of topics. They can also be scored objectively and, therefore, provide a specific index that is frequently useful in measuring change from one period of time to the next—for example, before and after treatment.

Despite their many advantages, self-report inventories can lead to serious problems if they are used carelessly. The BDI, for example, was designed as an index of change. It can help clinicians identify a *change in severity* of a person's depression from one point in time to another. Unfortunately, many investigators and clinicians have erroneously used it for *diagnostic* purposes. It is a serious mistake to assume that anyone who appears to be depressed on the basis of a self-report inventory would necessarily be diagnosed as being depressed after a clinical interview (Myers & Weissman, 1980; Oliver & Simmons, 1984). Self-report scales sometimes fail to identify patients who are considered depressed on the basis of a clinical

**TABLE 4–7 Sample Items from the Beck Depression Inventory**

| | |
|---|---|
| **A. Sadness** | |
| 0 | I do not feel sad |
| 1 | I feel sad |
| 2 | I am sad all the time and I can't snap out of it |
| 3 | I am so sad or unhappy that I can't stand it |
| **B. Pessimism** | |
| 0 | I am not particularly discouraged about the future |
| 1 | I feel discouraged about the future |
| 2 | I feel I have nothing to look forward to |
| 3 | I feel that the future is hopeless and that things cannot improve |
| **C. Sense of Failure** | |
| 0 | I do not feel like a failure |
| 1 | I feel I have failed more than the average person |
| 2 | As I look back on my life, all I can see is a lot of failures |
| 3 | I feel I am a complete failure as a person |
| **D. Dissatisfaction** | |
| 0 | I get as much satisfaction out of things as I used to |
| 1 | I don't enjoy things the way I used to |
| 2 | I don't get real satisfaction out of anything any more |
| 3 | I am dissatisfied or bored with everything |

interview. One reason for this discrepancy is the fact that some depressed patients consider themselves to be less depressed than they appear to a clinician when they are interviewed (Sayer et al., 1993).

## Projective Personality Tests

In **projective tests**, the person is presented with a series of ambiguous stimuli. The best known projective test, introduced in 1921 by Hermann Rorschach (1884–1922), a Swiss psychiatrist, is based on the use of inkblots. The Rorschach test consists of a series of 10 inkblots. Five contain various shades of grey on a white background, and five contain elements of colour. The person is asked to look at each card and indicate what it looks like or what it appears to be. There are, of course, no correct answers. The instructions are intentionally vague in order to avoid influencing the person's responses through subtle suggestions.

**"It's just a simple Rorschach ink-blot test, Mr. Bromwell, so just calm down and tell me what each one suggests to you."**

Projective techniques such as the Rorschach test were originally based on psychodynamic assumptions about the nature of personality and psychopathology. Considerable emphasis was placed on the importance of unconscious motivations—conflicts and impulses of which the person is largely unaware. In other words, people being tested presumably *project* hidden desires and conflicts when they try to describe or explain the cards. In so doing, they may reveal things about themselves of which they are not consciously aware or that they might not be willing to admit if they were asked directly. The cards are not designed or chosen to be realistic or representational; they presumably look like whatever the person wants them to look like.

Michael did not actually complete any projective personality tests. We can illustrate the way in which these tests might have been used in his case, however, by considering a man who had been given a diagnosis of obsessive–compulsive disorder on Axis I, as well as showing evidence of two types of personality disorder: dependent and schizotypal features. This patient was 22 years old, unemployed, and living with his mother. His father had died in an accident four years earlier. Like Michael, this man was bothered by intrusive thoughts of contamination, and he frequently engaged in compulsive washing (Hurt, Reznikoff, & Clarkin, 1991). His responses to the cards on the Rorschach frequently mentioned emotional distress ("a man screaming"), interpersonal conflict ("two women fighting over something"), and war ("two mushrooms of a nuclear bomb cloud"). He did not incorporate colour into any of his responses to the cards.

The original procedures for scoring the Rorschach were largely impressionistic and placed considerable emphasis on the content of the person's response. Responses given in the example above might be taken to suggest a number of important themes. Aggression and violence are obvious possibilities. Perhaps the man was repressing feelings of hostility, as indicated by his frequent references to war and conflict. These themes were coupled with a guarded approach to emotional reactions, which is presumably reflected by his avoidance of colour. The psychologist might have wondered whether the man felt guilty about something, such as his father's death. This kind of interpretation, which depends heavily on symbolism and clinical inference, provides intriguing material for the clinician to puzzle over. Unfortunately, the reliability and validity of this intuitive type of scoring procedure are very low (Wood, Lilienfeld, Garb, & Nezworski, 2000).

When we ponder the utility of these interpretations, we should also keep in mind the relative efficiency of projective testing procedures. Did the test tell us anything that we didn't already know or that we couldn't have learned in a more straightforward manner? The clinician might learn about a client's feelings of anger or guilt by using a clinical interview, which is often a more direct and efficient way of collecting information.

More recent approaches to the use of projective tests view the person's descriptions of the cards as a sample of his or her perceptual and cognitive styles. The psychologist John Exner has developed an objective scoring procedure for the Rorschach that is based primarily on the form rather than the content of the subject's responses (Exner, 1993, 1999). According to Exner's system, interpretation of the test depends on the way in which the descriptions take into account the shapes and colours on the cards. Does the person see movement in the card? Does she focus on tiny details, or does she base her descriptions on global impressions of the entire form of the inkblot? These and many other considerations contribute to the overall interpretation of the Rorschach test. The reliability of this scoring system is better than would be achieved by informal, impressionistic procedures. As noted by several researchers, including John Hunsley at the University of Ottawa, the validity of the scores still remains open to question (Hunsley & Bailey, 2001; Wood et al., 2001).

There are many different types of projective tests. Some employ stimuli that are somewhat less ambiguous than the inkblots in the Rorschach. The Thematic Apperception Test (TAT), for example, consists of a series of drawings that depict human figures in various ambiguous situations. Most of the cards portray more than one person. The figures and their poses tend to elicit stories with themes of sadness and violence. The person is asked to describe the identities of the people in the cards and to make up a story about what is happening. These stories presumably reflect the person's own ways of perceiving reality.

*Advantages:* The advantages of projective tests centre on the fact that the tests are interesting to give and interpret, and they sometimes provide a way to talk to people who are otherwise reluctant or unable to discuss their problems. Projective tests are more appealing to psychologists who adopt a psychodynamic view of personality and psychopathology because such tests are believed to reflect unconscious conflicts and motivations. Some specific advantages are listed below.

1. Some people may feel more comfortable talking in an unstructured situation than they would if they were required to participate in a structured interview or to complete the lengthy MMPI.
2. Projective tests can provide an interesting source of information regarding the person's unique view of the world, and they can be a useful supplement to information obtained with other assessment tools (Weiner, 2000).
3. To whatever extent a person's relationships with other people are governed by unconscious cognitive and emotional events, projective tests may provide information that cannot be obtained through direct interviewing methods or observational procedures (Meyer & Archer, 2001; Stricker & Gold, 1999).

*Limitations:* There are many serious problems with the use of projective tests. The popularity of projective tests has declined considerably since the 1970s, even in clinical settings, primarily because research studies have found little evidence to support their reliability and validity (Wierzbicki, 1993; Wood, Nezworski, & Stejskal, 1996).

1. Lack of standardization in administration and scoring is a serious problem, even though Exner's system for the Rorschach has made some improvements in that regard.
2. Little information is available on which to base comparisons to normal adults or children.
3. Some projective procedures, such as the Rorschach, can be very time-consuming, particularly if the person's responses are scored with a standardized procedure such as Exner's system.

*Projective tests require a person to respond to ambiguous stimuli. Here, a woman is taking the Thematic Apperception Test (TAT), in which she will be asked to make up a story about a series of drawings of people.*

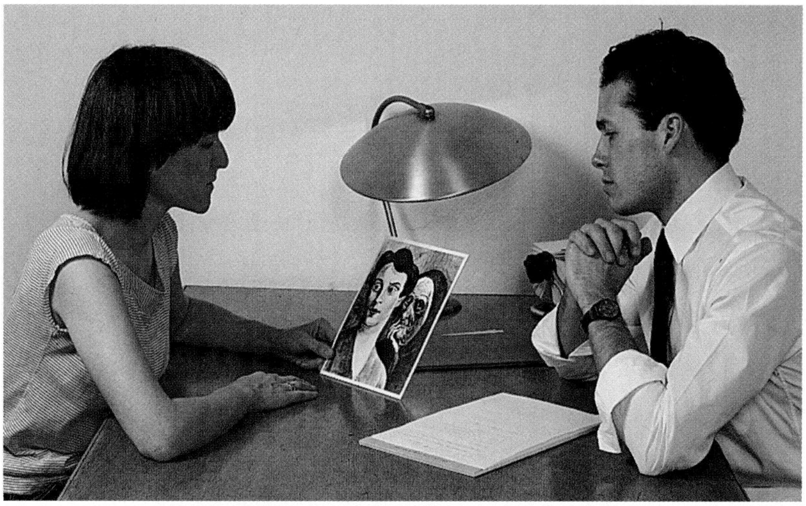

4. The reliability of scoring and interpretation tends to be low.
5. Information regarding the validity of projective tests is primarily negative.

## Assessing Social Systems

The same range of procedures that we have discussed for the assessment of person variables (psychological systems) can also be used to examine situation variables (social systems). For example, clinical interviews can be used to describe the client's family and social environments, both past and present. These are obviously important considerations in planning a treatment program.

In Michael's case, the psychologist was interested in Michael's social relationships with classmates as well as his interactions with his parents. His father indicated that he was quite concerned about Michael's problems and that he was willing to help as they planned a treatment procedure that would allow Michael to learn to cope more effectively with his obsessive thoughts about contamination. Michael's mother also told the psychologist that arguments between Michael and his father often seemed to trigger an increase in the frequency of his compulsive washing rituals. This information convinced the psychologist that Michael's treatment should focus on improving his relationship with his father and not just on his compulsive washing. He made this decision knowing that family conflict and negative family attitudes have a negative impact on the results of treatment for obsessive–compulsive disorder (Leonard et al., 1993; Steketee, 1993).

Many self-report inventories, rating scales, and behavioural coding systems have been designed for the assessment of marital relationships and family systems. One popular self-report inventory is the Family Environment Scale (FES), which is composed of 90 true–false items and was designed to measure the social characteristics of families (Moos, 1990). The scale is composed of 10 subscales that are aimed at three dimensions of the family: *relationships* (cohesion, expressiveness, and conflicts); *personal growth* (independence, achievement orientation, intellectual-cultural orientation, active-recreational orientation, and moral-religious emphasis); and *system maintenance* (organization and control). Extensive testing with large numbers of families has been used to establish norms on the FES for distressed and nondistressed families. The FES has been used widely in clinical settings and in research studies. Unfortunately, evidence regarding test–retest reliability and the validity of the subscales is not impressive (Boyd et al., 1997; L'Abate & Bagarozzi, 1993).

Direct observations can also be used to assess the social climate within a family (Patterson, 1990). The Family Interaction Coding System (FICS) was developed by Gerald Patterson and John Reid, clinical psychologists at the Oregon Research Institute, to observe interactions between parents and children in their homes (Jones, Reid, & Patterson, 1975). A trained observer visits the family's home and collects information for at least 70 minutes just prior to lunch or dinner. Everyone in the family must be present during this time period, and they must stay in a two-room area. For each five-minute block of time, the observer focuses on two members of the family and describes their behaviour, using the coding system. The observer rotates his or her attention from one "target" to the next throughout the observation period.

Trained raters can achieve high levels of reliability with the FICS. In addition, a number of research studies have demonstrated that it is a valid measure of aggressive behaviours in children, as well as a useful way to assess the family context in which these behaviours occur. It can distinguish between the families of children with antisocial behaviour or conduct disorders and nondisturbed families. The FICS is also sensitive to changes that occur during the course of family treatment (Grotevant & Carlson, 1989).

The main problem with the FICS is that it is expensive to train observers to use it, and the process of collecting data is very time-consuming. These problems stem from a focus of detailed elements of interaction. In order to avoid these limitations, some clinicians prefer to use observational systems that concentrate on more global aspects of family interaction (Alexander et al., 1995; Markman et al., 1995).

## Assessing Biological Systems

Clinicians have developed a number of techniques for measuring the effects of biological systems on behaviour. These techniques are seldom used in clinical practice (at least for the diagnosis of psychopathology), but they have been employed extensively in research settings, and it seems possible that they will one day become an important source of information on individual patients.

## Psychophysiological Assessment

Changes in physiological response systems, such as heart rate, respiration rate, and skin conductance, can provide useful information regarding a person's psychological adjustment. The basic components of the human nervous system (reviewed in Chapter 2) include the central nervous system (CNS) and the peripheral nervous system (PNS). The PNS is divided into two parts: the somatic nervous system and the autonomic nervous system. The somatic nervous system is responsible for communication between the brain and external sense receptors, as well as regulation of voluntary muscle movements. The autonomic nervous system is responsible for body processes that occur without conscious awareness, such as heart rate. It maintains equilibrium in the internal environment.

The autonomic nervous system is highly reactive to environmental events and can provide useful information about a person's internal states, such as emotion (Keller, Hicks, & Miller, 2000). Recording procedures have been developed to measure variables such as respiration rate, heart rate, and skin conductance. Table 4–8 summarizes some of the most important psychophysiological responses. As the person becomes aroused, the activity of these systems changes. Psychophysiological measures can, therefore, provide sensitive indices of the person's internal state.

It must be emphasized, however, that all of these measures do not act together. The concept of general arousal was abandoned many years ago (Lacey, 1967). If several physiological responses are measured at the same time, they may not all demonstrate the same strength, or even direction, of response. Moreover, physiological measures frequently disagree with the person's own subjective report. Therefore, as with other assessment procedures, physiological recordings should be used in conjunction with other measures. They represent supplements to, rather than substitutes for, the other types of measures that we have already considered.

Psychophysiological measurements have been used extensively in the assessment of anxiety disorders. Consider Michael's case. He was afraid to touch contaminated objects in his house. If he had been forced to do so, it is likely that his heart rate would have increased dramatically (Haines et al., 1998). Psychophysiological events of this sort can be

**TABLE 4–8 Characteristics of Biological Response Systems and Psychophysiological Measurement Procedures**

| Response System | Psychophysiological Response | Basis of Response |
|---|---|---|
| **Cardiovascular** | Electrocardiogram (EKG) | Action potential of cardiac muscle during contraction |
| | Blood pressure (BP) | Systolic: Force of blood leaving the heart<br>Diastolic: Residual pressure in the vascular system |
| **Electrodermal** | Skin resistance level (SRL) and response (SRR); skin conductance level (SCL) and response (SCR) | Source of signal is uncertain; current theories favour sweat gland activity |
| **Central Nervous System** | Electroencephalogram (EEG)<br>Average evoked response (AER) and event-related potential (ERP) | Electrical activity of cortical neurons<br>Same as EEG in response to specific stimulus |
| | Contingent negative variation (CNV) | Same as EEG, appears during preparatory responses |
| **Specialized Responses** | Sexual (plethysmograph)<br>Respiration rate | Engorgement of genital tissue with blood<br>Inhalation and exhalation of air |
| | Rapid eye movement (REM) sleep latency | Latency to onset of pattern associated with dreaming |
| | Smooth-pursuit eye movement (SPEM) | Visual tracking of an oscillating, pendulum-like stimulus |

*Source:* W.M. Kallman and M.J. Feuerstein, 1986, Psychophysiological procedures. In A.R. Ciminero, K.S. Calhoun, and H.E. Adams (Eds.), *Handbook of behavioral assessment*, 2nd ed., pp. 325–350. New York: Wiley-Interscience.

monitored precisely. To the extent that the clinician might be in need of information that would confirm data from other sources (observation, self-report) or that could be used to measure changes in the person's response to particular stimuli in the environment, physiological measurements may be very useful.

Physiological assessments have also been used in studies of patterns of marital interaction and divorce (see Chapter 17). These measures provide an interesting perspective on the emotional responses of both marital partners. Husbands and wives who are dissatisfied with their marriages experience higher levels of negative emotion. In assessments conducted during interactions that are contrived in the laboratory, husbands often exhibit physiological responses, such as changes in heart rate and skin conductance, that indicate intense arousal, but these feelings are not expressed in their verbal behaviour. Men who show this response are more likely to be dissatisfied with their marriages, and their relationships are more likely to end in divorce (Gottman & Levenson, 1992, 2000). These data suggest that psychophysiological measures represent an important addition to the assessment of marital interactions.

*Advantages:* Physiological procedures are not used frequently in clinical settings, but they are used extensively in research on psychopathology. These tools have several advantages in comparison to other assessment procedures (Drobes, Stritzke, & Coffey, 2000).

1. Psychophysiological recording procedures do not depend on self-report and, therefore, may be less subject to voluntary control. People may be less able to make the assessment show what they want it to show.
2. Some of these measures can be obtained while the subject is sleeping or while the subject is actively engaged in some other activity.

*Limitations:* In addition to the fact that they require relatively sophisticated equipment and a technician who is trained in their use, physiological measures have a number of drawbacks.

1. The recording equipment and electrodes may be frightening or intimidating to some people. These emotional responses can skew results.
2. There are generally low correlations between different autonomic response systems. It is not wise to select arbitrarily one specific physiological measure, such as heart rate, and assume that it is a direct index of arousal.
3. Physiological reactivity and the stability of physiological response systems vary from person to person. The measures may be informative for some people but not for others.
4. Physiological responses can be influenced by many other factors. Some are person variables, such as age and medication, as well as psychological factors, such as being self-conscious or fearing loss of control (Anderson & McNeilly, 1991). Other important considerations are situational variables, such as extraneous noise and electrical activity.

### Brain Imaging Techniques

The past two decades have seen a tremendous explosion of information and technology in the neurosciences. We now understand in considerable detail how neurons in the central nervous system communicate with one another, and scientists have invented sophisticated methods to create images of the living human brain (Gazzaniga et al., 2000). Some of these procedures provide static pictures of various brain structures at rest, just as an X-ray provides a photographic image of a bone or some other organ of the body. Studies of this type are typically concerned with the *size* of various parts of the brain. For example, many studies have compared the average size of the lateral ventricles—large chambers filled with cerebrospinal fluid—in groups of patients with schizophrenia and normal comparison groups. Other methods can be used to create dynamic images of brain functions—reflecting the *rate of activity* in various parts of the brain—while a person is performing different tasks. These functional images allow scientists to examine which parts of the brain are involved in various kinds of events, such as perception, memory, language, and emotional experience. They may also allow us to learn whether specific areas or pathways in the brain are uniquely associated with specific types of mental disorders.

Precise measures of brain structure can be obtained with *magnetic resonance imaging* (*MRI*). In MRI, images are generated using a strong magnetic field rather than X-rays (Posner & DiGirolamo, 2000). A large magnet in the

## CANADIAN FOCUS Psychological Assessment: Canadian Contributions and Issues

Canadian researchers have been at the forefront of many important developments in psychological assessment. Canada contains many of the world's leading neuropsychologists (Hayman-Abello, Hayman-Abello, & Rourke, 2003), and also is a leading country in the development, refinement, and application of many other forms of psychological assessment (Rector, Segal, & Gemar, 1998). In this Canadian Focus box we would like to give you some examples of important Canadian assessment research, and highlight some of the important issues in conducting psychological assessments in Canada.

With regard to assessment research, there are many world-class neuropsychological researchers in Canada. Some are concentrated at the University of Victoria, which is well known for its neuropsychology graduate training program. University of Victoria neuropsychologists include Otfried Spreen, Esther Strauss, and Holly Tuokko. Spreen and Strauss are known, among other things, for their classic compendium of neuropsychological tests, which have proven to be an invaluable resource for neuropsychologists and trainees in that field (Spreen & Strauss, 1998). Tuokko is well known for her development of neuropsychological tests for identifying early signs of dementia, such as the Clock Test (Tuokko & Hadjistavropoulos, 1998; Tuokko et al., 2000; see Chapter 14).

Other important neuropsychological research has been produced by Donald Stuss at the University of Toronto. He is an internationally recognized expert on the nature and assessment of frontal lobe functioning (Stuss, 2002). Other internationally recognized Canadian neuropsychologists include Byron Rourke at the University of Windsor, Konstantine Zakzanis at the University of Toronto, and Tom Tombaugh at Carleton University (Rourke, 2000; Rourke, van der Vlugt, & Rourke, 2002; Tombaugh, 2002; Tombaugh, Grandmaison, & Schmidt, 1995; Zakzanis, 2001; Zakzanis, Young, & Campbell, 2003).

Many Canadian researchers have made important contributions to developing and evaluating instruments for assessing psychopathology. Douglas Jackson at the University of Western Ontario has made many important contributions to the development of methods for assessing normal and abnormal personality (Jackson & Paunonen, 1980; Jackson & Livesley, 1999). Jackson's research is based on the premise that the assessment of personality disorders should be based on the theory and research on normal personality (Jackson & Livesley, 1995). Robert Hare (University of British Columbia) and Stephen Hart (Simon Fraser University) have made important contributions to the assessment of psychopathy (see Chapter 9), just as Eric Mash (University of Calgary) has made highly regarded contributions to the assessment of child psychopathology (Mash & Terdal, 1997). Researchers at Toronto's Addiction Research Foundation, which is now part of the Centre for Addiction and Mental Health, have long been at the forefront of methods for assessing alcohol and drug problems, as well as for examining how the assessment results can be best used to help people overcome those problems (Sobell et al., 1996, 2001; Turner, Annis, & Sklar, 1997). John Hunsley at the University of Ottawa has made many important contributions to the assessment literature, including his work showing that projective tests such as the Rorschach are dubious methods for assessing psychological problems (Hunsley & Bailey, 1999, 2001; Hunsley, Lee, & Wood, 2003). Researchers at McMaster and McGill Universities have made leading contributions to the assessment of family and marital problems (Epstein, Baldwin, & Bishop, 1983). Investigators at the University of Regina have established a productive program of research into the assessment of pain, anxiety about one's health, and related variables (Asmundson et al., 1999; H.D. Hadjistavropoulos, MacLeod, & Asmundson, 1999; T. Hadjistavropoulos & Craig, 2002; T. Hadjistavropoulos, von Baeyer, & Craig, 2001; Wright & Asmundson, 2003).

Canadian researchers have also made many important contributions to developing cognitive methods for assessing anxiety and mood disorders. These methods include tasks developed to assess information processing and memory retrieval in people with emotional disorders, so that the findings can be compared to normal controls. Zindel Segal at the University of Toronto is a leading researcher in this area (Blankstein & Segal, 2001; Gemar et al., 2001; Segal, Gemar, & Williams, 1999).

Numerous Canadian researchers have been at the forefront of efforts to develop and evaluate questionnaire methods of assessing dysfunctional beliefs that may play a role in various forms of psychopathology. Brian Cox (University of Manitoba) and Steven Taylor (University of British Columbia) have developed measures of anxiety sensitivity, which is the fear of anxiety arising from beliefs that anxiety has harmful consequences (Taylor & Cox, 1998a,b). Evidence suggests that anxiety sensitivity plays an important role in panic disorder (Taylor, 1999, 2000; and see Chapter 6). Paul Hewitt at the University of British Columbia has published many influential studies on the nature and assessment of perfectionism, which has been implicated in a variety of psychological disorders (Hewitt et al., 2003; Hewitt et al., 1991).

Other Canadian researchers who have made important contributions to the assessment of cognitive mechanisms include David A. Clark (University of New Brunswick) and Christine Purdon (Waterloo University), whose research has focused on the cognitive assessment of depression and obsessive–compulsive disorder (Clark, 1997; Clark & Purdon, 1995). Researchers at the University of Toronto and Trent University have led the field in their development and evaluation of an instrument to assess alexithymia, which is the inability to put one's emotions into words (Parker, Taylor, & Bagby, 2003; Taylor et al., 1990). Alexithymia has been implicated in many disorders, including stress-related conditions (see Chapter 8). Canadian researchers have made many

continued

cont.

important contributions using psychophysiological methods of assessment, such as the work of Kenneth Prkachin at the University of Northern British Columbia (Prkachin et al., 2001; Prkachin et al., 1999) and Michael Seto at the University of Toronto (Seto & Kuban, 1996).

We will turn now to consider the important issues relevant to psychological assessment in Canada. The most comprehensive statement of these issues comes from the work of Marilyn Bowman at Simon Fraser University (Bowman, 2000). Bowman's extensive review reveals a number of important findings for psychological assessment in Canada. French-speaking Canadians and foreign-born immigrants (e.g., people from China, India, Caribbean nations) represent the largest minority groups in Canada. Bowman highlights the fact that many psychological tests used in Canada have been normed in other countries, such as the United States, rather than Canada. Does this matter? Well, there is evidence that scores on IQ tests differ across countries, and so U.S. norms, for example, may not apply to Canada (Saklofske & Hildebrand, 1999). It is also unclear whether assessment instruments developed for Anglophone Canadians can be applied to Francophones, First Nations Peoples, or Canadian immigrants for whom English is not the first language. Bowman also makes the important point that many psychological tests do not have norms for either Francophone Canadians or immigrant minorities such as Asian Canadians. Bowman concedes that there is little evidence that cognitive abilities, emotional problems, or personality is structured differently in different cultural groups, at least according to international validation studies of the major U.S. instruments. However, she concludes that the need for Canadian tests remains an open empirical question.

Although a number of studies have been published that are relevant to the problems raised by Bowman (Beal et al., 1996; Boyle et al., 1997; Jackson, 1998; Jackson & Livesley, 1999), much more work needs to be done to ensure that tests of psychological problems are reliable and valid in Canadians in general and in the many Canadian ethnic subgroups. Fortunately, in recent years there has been a growing amount of research delineating the properties of the tests (e.g., reliability, validity, and norms) for Francophone Canadians and for other minorities (Blais et al., 1997; Deschesnes, 1998; Lai, 2000; Morin & Maurice, 2001; Weekes et al., 1995). And there are an increasing number of cross-national studies, comparing Canada to other countries in terms of the performance characteristics of psychological tests (Hare et al., 2000; Levav et al., 1998; Watson & Sinha, 1999; Zvolensky et al., 2003). ◆

scanner causes chemical elements in specific brain regions to emit distinctive radio signals. Both CT scanning and MRI can provide a static image of specific brain structures. MRI provides more detailed images than CT scans and is able to identify smaller parts of the brain. For this reason, and because it lends itself more easily to the creation of three-dimensional pictures of the brain, MRI has replaced CT scanning in most research facilities.

In addition to structural MRI, which provides a static view of brain structures, advances in the neurosciences have also produced techniques that create images of brain functions (Raichle, 2001). *Positron emission tomography (PET)* is one scanning technique that can be used to create functional brain images (Callicott, 2001). This procedure is much more expensive than the other imaging techniques because it requires a nuclear cyclotron to produce spe-

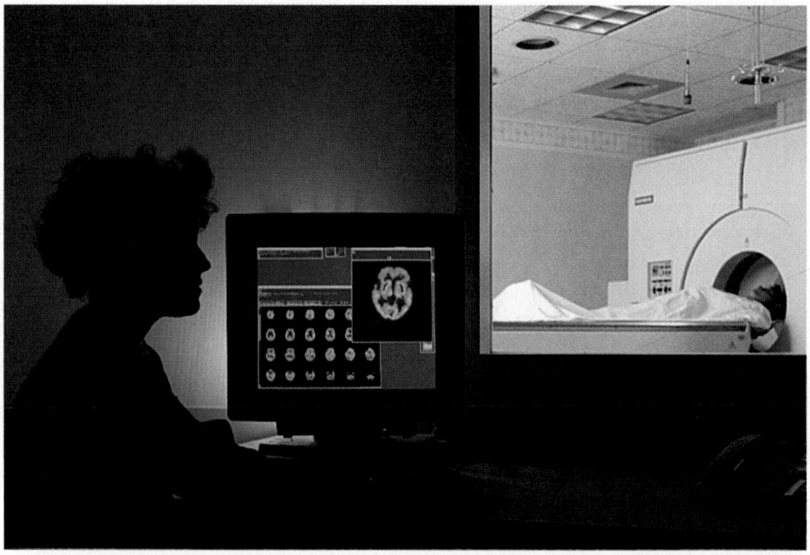

*Positron emission topography (PET scan) can provide useful images of dynamic brain functions. Areas that appear red or yellow indicate areas of the brain that are active (consuming the labelled glucose molecules), whereas those that are blue or green are relatively inactive. Different areas of the brain become active depending on whether the person is at rest or engaged in particular activities when the image is created.*

cial radioactive elements. PET scans are capable of providing relatively detailed images of the brain. In addition, they can reflect changes in brain activity as the person responds to the demands of various tasks.

A second functional imaging procedure is *single photon emission computed tomography*, or *SPECT* (Liddle, 1997). SPECT is more widely available than PET because single-photon-emitting compounds have relatively long physical half-lives. Therefore, they can be manufactured in one location and transported to another, distant location where the imaging procedure is being conducted. On the other hand, the resolution of SPECT images is not as good as that obtained using PET.

The newest and most exciting method of imaging brain functions involves *functional MRI* (*fMRI*). When neurons are activated, their metabolism increases and they require increased blood flow to supply them with oxygen. The magnetic properties of blood change as a function of the level of oxygen that it is carrying. In fMRI, a series of images is acquired in rapid succession. Small differences in signal intensity from one image to the next provide a measure of moment-to-moment changes in the amount of oxygen in blood flowing to specific areas of the brain. While other functional imaging procedures such as PET are only able to measure activities that are sustained over a period of several minutes, fMRI is able to identify changes in brain activity that last less than a second (Cohen & Bookheimer, 2002).

Functional brain imaging procedures have been used extensively to study possible neurological underpinnings of various types of mental disorder (Carter, 1999). For example, in the case of obsessive–compulsive disorder (OCD), studies using PET, SPECT, and fMRI have suggested that symptoms of OCD are associated with multiple brain regions, including the caudate nucleus (one part of the basal ganglia), the orbital prefrontal cortex, and the anterior cingulate cortex (located on the medial surface of the frontal lobe). These pathways are illustrated in Figure 4–2.

They seem to be overly active in people with OCD, especially when the person is confronted with stimuli that provoke his or her obsessions (Adler et al., 2000; Rauch et al., 2001). In the photo on this page, we see functional brain images obtained from a patient with OCD and a person without OCD. Notice that the image from the person with OCD indicates a much higher level of activity in the frontal cortex.

These results are intriguing because they suggest that certain regions and circuits in the brain may somehow be associated with the presence of obsessive–compulsive symptoms. We must emphasize, however, that the results of such imaging procedure are not useful diagnostically with regard to an individual person. In other words, some people with OCD do not exhibit increased metabolism rates in the caudate or the anterior cingulate cortex, and some people who do not have OCD do show increased levels of activity in these brain regions.

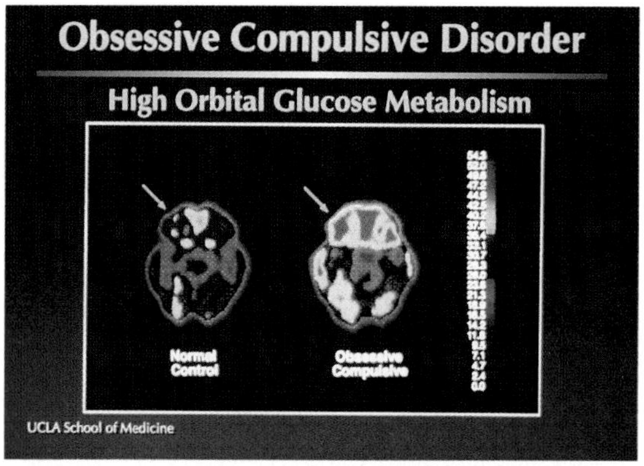


*The PET image on the left shows normal levels of activity in the frontal cortex of a person without OCD. In the image on the right, the brain of a person with OCD shows abnormally high levels of activity in the frontal cortex.*

**Brain Regions Associated with OCD**

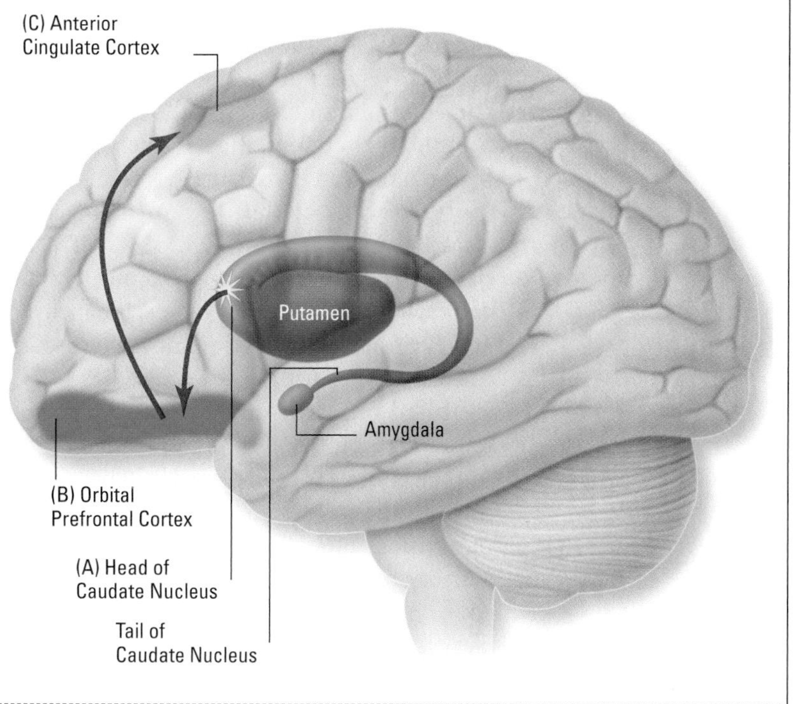


**FIGURE 4–2: When a person with OCD experiences symptoms, an increase in neural activity is seen in the caudate (A), which triggers the urge to "do something," through the orbital prefrontal cortex (B), which gives the feeling that "something is wrong," and back through the anterior cingulate cortex (C), which keeps attention fixed on the feeling of unease.**

*Source:* R. Carter, 1999, *Mapping the mind.* Berkeley, CA: University of California Press.

*Advantages:* Brain imaging techniques provide detailed information regarding the structure of brain areas and activity levels in the brain that are associated with the performance of particular tasks. They have important uses, primarily as research tools:

1. In clinical practice, imaging techniques can be used to rule out various neurological conditions that might explain behavioural or cognitive deficits. These include such conditions as brain tumours and vascular disease.
2. Procedures such as fMRI and PET can help research investigators explore the relation between brain functions and specific mental disorders. This type of information will be considered in several chapters later in this book.

*Limitations:* Brain imaging procedures are used extensively in the study and assessment of neurological disorders. In the field of psychopathology, they are currently research tools and have little clinical importance outside the assessment and treatment of disorders such as Alzheimer's disease (see Chapter 14). Some of the major limitations are listed below.

1. Norms have not been established for any of these measures. It is not possible to use brain imaging procedures for diagnostic purposes.
2. These procedures are relatively expensive—especially PET scans and fMRI—and some procedures must be used cautiously because the patient may be exposed to radioactive substances.
3. We should not assume that all cognitive processes, emotional experiences, or mental disorders are necessarily linked to activity (or the absence of activity) in a specific area of the brain. Scientists are still debating the extent to which these experiences are localized within the brain (Uttal, 2001).

# Summary

Formal **classification systems** for mental disorders have been developed in order to facilitate communication, research, and treatment planning. The current official system published by the American Psychiatric Association is the fourth edition of the *Diagnostic and Statistical Manual of Mental Disorders*, or DSM-IV-TR. It is based on a **categorical approach to classification** and typically employs specific inclusion and exclusion criteria to define each disorder. The categories that are defined in DSM-IV-TR are based primarily on descriptive principles rather than on theoretical knowledge regarding the etiology of the disorders. Five axes are included in this system. Axes I and II are employed for describing mental disorders (personality disorders and mental retardation on Axis II). The remaining three axes are concerned with supplementary information that may also be useful in treatment planning.

Cultural factors play an important role in both the expression and recognition of symptoms of mental disorders. The accuracy and utility of a clinical diagnosis depend on the clinician's ability to consider the cultural context in which the problem appeared. DSM-IV-TR includes a glossary of **culture-bound syndromes**, such as pibloktoq. These patterns of erratic or unusual thinking and behaviour do not fit easily into the other categories that are listed in the main body of the diagnostic manual.

The usefulness of a classification system depends on several criteria, especially **reliability** and **validity**. The reliability of many categories in DSM seems to have improved with the introduction of specific inclusion criteria and exclusion criteria. Nevertheless, serious questions remain about this issue. The reliability of some categories, such as the personality disorders, is still marginal in many studies. Reliability is also likely to be diminished in clinical settings where clinicians are not experts in a particular disorder and reliability is not being monitored. The validity of most categories is still under active investigation.

The general process of collecting and interpreting information is called **assessment**. Many different assessment tools can be used to generate information systematically. Interviews, observations, and tests are among the most frequently used procedures. Assessments can be directed toward biological, psychological, and social systems. In many cases, information is collected and integrated across more than one system, but it is never possible to learn everything about a particular person. Choices have to be made, and some information must be excluded from the analysis.

Psychological systems are typically assessed using interviews, observations, or self-report inventories. Structured diagnostic interviews are used extensively in conjunction with the DSM-IV-TR classification system. They can also form the basis for ratings of the person's adjustment on a number of dimensions. Interviews can be used to collect additional information that is relevant to planning treatment. Their main advantage is their flexibility. Their primary limitation lies in the inability or unwillingness of some clients to provide a rational description of their own problems, as well as the subjective factors that influence the clinician's interpretation of data collected in an interview.

Psychological tests are also used in the assessment of psychological systems. **Personality inventories**, like the MMPI-2, offer several advantages as supplements to interviews and observations. They can be scored objectively, they often contain validity scales that reflect the person's attitude and test-taking set, and they can be interpreted in reference to well-established standards for people with and without specific types of adjustment problems. Some psychologists use **projective personality tests**, like the Rorschach, to acquire information that might not be obtained from direct interviews or observations. Unfortunately, research studies have found little evidence to support the reliability and validity of projective tests. The continued use of these tests is, therefore, controversial.

Social systems, including marital relationships and families, can also be evaluated using interviews, observations, and self-report inventories. Although the instruments that are used for this purpose have not been developed as extensively as those that address psychological systems, they represent an important consideration in thinking about mental disorders and their treatment.

Many different tools are available for assessing biological systems related to mental disorders. These include psychophysiological recording procedures, as well as brain imaging techniques, such as MRI and PET scans. Biological assessment procedures are used extensively in research studies. They do not have diagnostic value in clinical situations, except for the purpose of ruling out certain conditions, such as brain tumours and vascular disease.

# Critical Thinking

1. Do we need a classification system in the field of psychopathology? If so, how should it be evaluated? What are the characteristics of a useful classification system? Should we expect that such a system will be based solely on scientific considerations?
2. What are some of the inherent limitations of a classification system? What are the advantages and disadvantages associated with the process of psychiatric diagnosis? If there are problems, how can they be resolved, or at least minimized?
3. How will your choice of an assessment procedure be influenced by the conceptual frame of reference that you adopt in thinking about a clinical problem? How will it be influenced by the nature of the specific problem that you are trying to address? Why isn't it possible to have a universal assessment battery that could be used consistently for all clinical problems?

# Key Terms

**actuarial interpretation** 126
**assessment** 101
**behavioural coding system** 123
**categorical approach to classification** 103
**classification system** 103
**comorbidity** 115
**culture-bound syndrome** 110
**diagnosis** 101
**dimensional approach to classification** 104
**kappa** 112
**labelling theory** 106
**personality inventories** 124
**projective tests** 128
**rating scale** 122
**reactivity** 124
**reliability** 112
**stigma** 106
**validity** 113

# 5 Mood Disorders and Suicide

Overview
Typical Symptoms and Associated Features
Classification
Epidemiology
Etiological Considerations and Research
Treatment
Suicide

**What is the difference between clinical depression and a low mood?**

**Are there different kinds of depression?**

**Why do some people become depressed after stressful life events while others do not?**

**Why do some people decide to end their own lives?**

Sadness may be the price that we pay for attachments to other people. Losses are inevitable, and we all endure the pain that comes with them. Beyond relatively short-lived feelings of grief and sorrow, prolonged sadness can grow into something much more debilitating. Everyone's life contains the potential for despair. Some people manage to avoid it, but others become overwhelmed by it. When it reaches higher levels of intensity and begins to interfere with a person's ability to function and enjoy life, a low mood is known as clinical depression. In this chapter we will consider emotional disorders that involve prolonged periods of severe depression.

## Overview

If one measures disability in terms of years lived with severe impairments, major depression is the leading cause of disability worldwide. The magnitude of the problem is truly staggering. Depression accounts for more than 10 percent of all disability (see Table 5–1). Experts predict that it will become an even greater problem by the year 2020 (Lopez & Murray, 1998). Younger generations are experiencing higher rates of depression than their predecessors, and those who become depressed are doing so at an earlier age (Burke & Regier, 1996).

Psychopathologists use several terms to describe problems that are associated with emotional response systems. This language can become confusing because most of us already use these words in our everyday vocabulary. Thus we must define these terms as they are used in psychopathology so that our discussion will be clear. **Emotion** refers to a state of arousal that is defined by subjective states of feeling, such as sadness, anger, and disgust. Emotions are often accompanied by physiological changes, such as changes in heart rate and respiration rate. **Affect** refers to the pattern of observable behaviours, such as facial expression, that are associated with these subjective feelings. People also express affect through the pitch of their voices and with their hand and body movements. **Mood** refers to a pervasive and sustained emotional response that, in its extreme form, can colour the person's perception of the world (APA, 2000). The disorders discussed in this chapter are primarily associated with two specific moods: depression and elation.

Depression can refer either to a mood or to a *clinical syndrome*, a combination of emotional, cognitive, and behavioural symptoms. The feelings associated with a **depressed mood** often include disappointment and despair. Although sadness is a universal experience, profound depression is not. No one has been able to identify the exact point at which "feeling down or blue" crosses a line and becomes depression.

People who are in a severely depressed mood describe the feeling as overwhelming, suffocating, or numbing. In the syndrome of depression, which is also called **clinical depression**, a depressed mood is accompanied by several other symptoms, such as fatigue, loss of energy, difficulty in sleeping, and changes in appetite. Clinical depression also involves a variety of changes in thinking and overt behaviour. The person may experience cognitive symptoms, such as extreme guilt, feelings of worthlessness, concentration problems, and thoughts of suicide. Behavioural

**TABLE 5–1 Leading Causes of Disability Worldwide (1990)**

| (As Measured by Years of Life Lived with a Disability, YLD) | Total YLDs | Percent of Total |
|---|---|---|
| ***All Causes*** | ***472.7*** | |
| **1.** Unipolar major depression | 50.8 | 10.7 |
| **2.** Iron-deficiency anemia | 22.0 | 4.7 |
| **3.** Falls | 22.0 | 4.6 |
| **4.** Alcohol use | 15.8 | 3.3 |
| **5.** Chronic obstructive pulmonary disease | 14.7 | 3.1 |
| **6.** Bipolar mood disorder | 14.1 | 3.0 |
| **7.** Congenital anomalies | 13.5 | 2.9 |
| **8.** Osteoarthritis | 13.3 | 2.8 |
| **9.** Schizophrenia | 12.1 | 2.6 |
| **10.** Obsessive–compulsive disorders | 10.2 | 2.2 |

*Source:* A.D. Lopez, and D.J.L. Murray, 1998, The global burden of disease, 1990–2020. *Nature Medicine, 4,* 1241–1243.

symptoms may range from constant pacing and fidgeting to extreme inactivity. Throughout the rest of this chapter, we will use the term **depression** to refer to the clinical syndrome rather than the mood.

**Mania**, the flip side of depression, also involves a disturbance in mood that is accompanied by additional symptoms. **Euphoria**, or elated mood, is the opposite emotional state from a depressed mood. It is characterized by an exaggerated feeling of physical and emotional well-being (APA, 2000). Manic symptoms that frequently accompany an elated mood include inflated self-esteem, decreased need for sleep, distractibility, pressure to keep talking, and the subjective feeling of thoughts racing through the person's head faster than they can be spoken. Mania is, therefore, a syndrome in the same sense that clinical depression is a syndrome.

**Mood disorders** are defined in terms of *episodes*—discrete periods of time in which the person's behaviour is dominated by either a depressed or manic mood. Unfortunately, most people with a mood disorder experience more than one episode. The following case studies illustrate the way that numerous symptoms combine to form syndromes that are used to define mood disorders. They also provide examples of the two primary types of mood disorders: (1) those in which the person experiences only episodes of depression, known as **unipolar mood disorder**; and (2) those in which the person experiences episodes of mania as well as depression, known as **bipolar mood disorder**. Episodes of depression are defined by the same symptoms, regardless of whether the person's disorder is unipolar or bipolar in nature. A small number of patients have only manic episodes with no evidence of depression; they are included in the bipolar category. Years ago, bipolar mood disorder was known as *manic–depressive disorder*. Although this term has been replaced in the official diagnostic manual, some clinicians still prefer to use it because it offers a more direct description of the patient's experience (Jamison, 1995).

What is the difference between normal sadness and clinical depression? Some important considerations regarding this distinction are listed in Table 5–2. The Brief Case Study (on p. 142) illustrates the symptoms of mania, which often appear after a person has already experienced at least one episode of depression. People who experience episodes of both depression and mania are given a diagnosis of bipolar mood disorder. The symptoms of a full-blown manic episode are not subtle. People who are manic typically have terrible judgment and may get into considerable trouble as a result of their disorder. The central feature of mania is a persistently elevated or irritable mood that lasts for at least one week.

## CASE STUDY A TV Reporter's Battle with Depression

Twenty-three-year-old Olivia Cheng is a TV news reporter in Edmonton. The following is her account of her battle with depression:

Looking back, I'd exhibited classic signs of the depression for months but never realized what it all meant. The big tip-off should have been my insomnia. I know now that a drastic change in sleep pattern is a symptom of depression. By day, I became increasingly indecisive and forgetful. I'd lock my keys in my running car, wonder where my wallet was as I held it in my hand, and leave merchandise in stores after paying for it. Reading and writing became difficult as my concentration skills suffered. It became a regular occurrence for me to run into my producer's office long past deadline with poorly written, half-finished stories.

Reporting live on location terrified me because my mind would blank out mid-sentence. I'd stare into the camera and fight the rising panic as I struggled to remember what I'd been trying to say to thousands of viewers. Struggling to keep it together at work, I became convinced that I was unworthy of any professional success I'd achieved. I beat myself up over every little mistake, and was convinced my veteran co-workers wondered what an idiot like me was doing among them.

Socially, I started staying away from my friends. Even though it made no rational sense, I felt isolated and disconnected from people I'd known for years. Plus the slightest thing would trigger uncontrollable crying fits, or worse, frightening rages. My mood swings caused me to withdraw further. I hated myself for not being able to "snap out of it." And I didn't want my friends to see how screwed up and neurotic I was becoming. The one person I didn't hide anything from was my boyfriend who, like me, puzzled over what was happening.

I was finally forced to make a crucial choice: accept the depression and deal with it, or go on fooling myself and never get better. I started taking anti-depressants and was prescribed a two-month medical leave. I also started going to counselling. I hated it. Talking to a stranger about my problems went against every Chinese cultural value I'd ever learned about saving face and staying stoic in the face of hardship. Because my pride still proved to be the greatest obstacle to my recovery, my counsellor, Marie, spent the first few sessions simply reinforcing that depression is a medical illness, not a product of a weak and damaged personality.

When I eventually stopped resisting her, Marie slowly helped me understand that I was no good to anyone if I didn't admit that I needed help. I also learned how people with my anally perfectionist, type-A personality are more prone to depression because of the impossible expectations we set for ourselves.

I started telling my friends in Edmonton about my depression. Their steadfast support was a huge relief. Many of them couldn't believe I'd been too ashamed to tell them sooner. Meanwhile, through the inevitable bad days, my wonderful boyfriend wouldn't let me give up on myself. It meant the world to know he still loved me at my worst.

Many of my workmates guessed I'd been depressed and went out of their way to help me get back on my feet. Left to recover at my own pace, I stayed behind the scenes and filed small stories. It took another two months for me to venture in front of the camera again.

I know how lucky I am. I've survived an illness that evokes shame, stigma and silence in too many of its sufferers. I don't know if I can ever say I'm fully recovered because the fear of relapse always lurks in the shadows of my mind.

The term "mentally ill" probably conjures images in some minds of drooling invalids singing to themselves in the corner. But take a closer look at all the "normal people" around you. At least one of them has battled, or is still battling, mental illness. They just don't like to admit it, and can you blame them? A physical ailment produces stacks of get-well-soon cards. Mental agonies are eclipsed by hushed whispers of "What's wrong with them?" I'm not trying to crack a bitter whip of holier-than-thou proportions here. I'm just trying to sound the alarms of a wake-up call, because the only way to tear down the taboo surrounding depression is to encourage people to talk about it. ◆

*Source:* Cheng, O., 2004, Depression hurts: I know. A TV news reporter talks about her fight with depression. *Vancouver Sun,* May 10, pp. C1 & C5. Material reprinted with the express permission of: "Pacific Newspaper Group," a CanWest Partnership.

**TABLE 5–2 Important Considerations in Distinguishing Clinical Depression from Normal Sadness**

1. The mood change is pervasive across situations and persistent over time. The person's mood does not improve, even temporarily, when he or she engages in activities that are usually experienced as pleasant.
2. The mood change may occur in the absence of any precipitating events, or it may be completely out of proportion to the person's circumstances.
3. The depressed mood is accompanied by impaired ability to function in usual social and occupational roles. Even simple activities become overwhelmingly difficult.
4. The change in mood is accompanied by a cluster of additional signs and symptoms, including cognitive, somatic, and behavioural features.
5. The nature or quality of the mood change may be different from that associated with normal sadness. It may feel "strange," like being engulfed by a black cloud or sunk in a dark hole.

## BRIEF CASE STUDY

### Brian's Manic Episode

The following case provides an account of a manic episode, documented by Toronto psychiatrist Virginia Edward.

Brian, a mechanic who worked in his father's machine shop, was happily married but childless. He began acting quite strangely shortly after his brother had a son. He started to stay up all night, working alone in his garage. He told his wife, Wanda, that he had invented a motor that could run on propane only, and he thought General Motors would buy his invention. He became more and more talkative, with monologues far into the night that Wanda found exhausting. If she protested, he became irate, saying she didn't appreciate him. Then he withdrew all their savings from the bank, for a reason he refused to explain. Uncharacteristically, he berated Wanda for interfering in his life. He was physically much bigger, towering over her and shaking his fist at her. Wanda called her father-in-law, who talked quietly to Brian. Brian then broke into tears, rocking back and forth and lamenting what a failure he was. They took Brian to the local hospital and he agreed to be admitted. After he calmed down, he said he had felt great, as if his ideas were brilliant. He needed little sleep and his thoughts raced. He said that he had never felt so wonderful in his life, but that he also felt he was on a roller coaster that he couldn't get off. ◆

*Source:* Published with permission of Key Porter Books. Copyright © 2002 by Virginia Edwards.

# Typical Symptoms and Associated Features

The most important symptoms and signs of mood disorders can be divided into four general areas: emotional symptoms, cognitive symptoms, somatic symptoms, and behavioural symptoms. Episodes of major depression and mania typically involve all four kinds of symptoms.

## Emotional Symptoms

We all experience negative emotions, such as sadness, fear, and anger. These reactions usually last only a few moments, and they serve a useful purpose in our lives, particularly in our relationships with other people. Emotional reactions serve as signals to other people about our current feelings and needs. They also coordinate our responses to changes in the immediate environment.

Depressed, or **dysphoric** (unpleasant), mood is the most common and obvious symptom of depression. Most people who are depressed describe themselves as feeling utterly gloomy, dejected, or despondent. There is no clear-cut line dividing normal sadness from the depressed mood that is associated with clinical depression. Clinicians use several features to help guide this diagnostic distinction, including the severity, the quality, and the pervasive impact of the depressed mood.

In contrast to the unpleasant feelings associated with clinical depression, manic patients experience periods of inexplicable and unbounded joy known as euphoria. The person may feel extremely optimistic and cheerful—"on top of the world"—even though their inappropriate behaviour can make a shambles of their life circumstances. Bursting with energy, they may exhibit boundless enthusiasm. In bipolar mood disorders, periods of elated mood tend to alternate with phases of depression. The duration of each episode and the frequency of the cycle vary from one patient to the next.

Kay Jamison, professor of psychiatry at Johns Hopkins University School of Medicine, has written an eloquent and moving description of her own experiences with mania and depression. The symptoms of mania are initially quite pleasant. The person may experience periods of increased energy that are accompanied by feelings of enhanced productivity and creativity.

> My manias, at least in their early and mild forms, were absolutely intoxicating states that gave rise to great personal pleasure, an incomparable flow of thoughts, and a ceaseless energy that allowed the translation of new ideas into papers and projects. (1995, pp. 5–6)

Unfortunately, as these feelings become more intense and prolonged, they may become ruinous. It may not be clear when the person's experience crosses the unmarked boundary between being productive and energetic to being out of control and self-destructive. Many depressed and manic patients are irritable. Their anger may be directed either at themselves or at others, and frequently at both. Even when they are cheerful, people in a manic episode are easily provoked to anger. They may become extremely argumentative and abusive, particularly when people challenge their grandiose statements about themselves and their inappropriate judgment.

Anxiety is also common among people with mood disorders, just as depression is a common feature of some anxiety disorders (see Chapter 6). Two out of every three depressed patients also report feeling anxious (Kendall & Watson, 1989). People who are depressed are sometimes apprehensive, fearing that matters will become worse than they already are or that others will discover their inadequacy. They sometimes report that they are chronically tense and unable to relax.

## Cognitive Symptoms

In addition to changes in the way people feel, mood disorders also involve changes in the way people think about themselves and their surroundings. People who are clinically depressed frequently note that their thinking is slowed down, that they have trouble concentrating, and that they are easily distracted. In his book *Holiday of Darkness* (1982, 1990), York University psychologist Norman S. Endler described his personal experiences with bipolar mood disorder. During episodes of depression, he had severe cognitive symptoms:

> My indecisiveness was the worst of all. I couldn't decide what to eat or what to wear. I couldn't decide whether to get out of bed or to stay. I couldn't decide whether to shower or not to shower. I could never decide what I wanted to do because I didn't know myself. I was completely apathetic. . . . Time seemed to move so very slowly for me. . . . In general, I lived in a fog of bewilderment. I was unhappy, confused, lacking in self-confidence and self-esteem, and sure that I was going to be hospitalized. This really scared me. (1982, p. 28)

Guilt and worthlessness are common preoccupations. Researchers David Dozois (University of Western Ontario) and Keith Dobson (University of Calgary) have found that depressed people, compared to control groups, described themselves in terms of more negative and fewer positive adjectives, and are able to recall less positive information about themselves (Dozois & Dobson, 2001). Researchers at Bishop's University have found that depression is associated with low and unstable self-esteem (de Man, Gutierrez, & Sterk, 2001). In other words, depressed people experienced generally low self-esteem, and their levels of self-esteem were prone to fluctuate—perhaps dipping even lower in the face of stressful experiences like failure or rejection.

*The quality of a depressed mood is often different from the sadness that might arise from an event such as the loss of a loved one. Some depressed people say that they feel like they are drowning or suffocating.*

Depressed patients blame themselves for things that have gone wrong, regardless of whether they are in fact responsible. They focus considerable attention on the most negative features of themselves, their environments, and the future—a combination known as the "depressive triad" (Beck, 1967).

In contrast to the cognitive slowness associated with depression, manic patients commonly report that their thoughts are speeded up. Ideas flash through their minds faster than they can articulate their thoughts. Manic patients can also be easily distracted, responding to seemingly random stimuli in a completely uninterpretable and incoherent fashion. Grandiosity and inflated self-esteem are also characteristic features of mania.

Many people experience self-destructive ideas and impulses when they are depressed. Interest in suicide usually develops gradually and may begin with the vague sense that life is not worth living. Such feelings may follow directly from the overwhelming fatigue and loss of pleasure that typically accompany a seriously depressed mood. In addition, feelings of guilt and failure can lead depressed people to consider killing themselves. Over a period of time, depressed people may come to believe that they would be better off dead or that their family would function more successfully and happily without them. Preoccupation with such thoughts then leads to specific plans and may culminate in a suicide attempt.

## Somatic Symptoms

The **somatic symptoms** of mood disorders are related to basic physiological or bodily functions. They include fatigue, aches and pains, and serious changes in appetite and sleep patterns. People who are clinically depressed often report feeling tired all the time. The simplest tasks, which they have previously taken for granted, seem to require an overwhelming effort. Taking a shower, brushing their teeth, and getting dressed in the morning can become virtually impossible.

Sleeping problems are also common, particularly trouble getting to sleep. This disturbance frequently goes hand in hand with cognitive difficulties mentioned earlier. Some people also report having difficulty staying asleep throughout the night, and they awaken two or more hours before the usual time. Early-morning waking is often associated with particularly severe depression. A less common symptom is for a depressed individual to spend more time sleeping than usual.

In the midst of a manic episode, a person is likely to experience a drastic reduction in the need for sleep. Some patients report that reduced sleep is one of the earliest signs of the onset of an episode. Although depressed patients typically feel exhausted when they cannot sleep, a person in a manic episode will probably be bursting with energy in spite of the lack of rest.

Depressed people frequently experience a change in appetite. Although some patients report that they eat more than usual, most reduce the amount that they eat; some may eat next to nothing. Food just doesn't taste good any more. Depressed people can also lose a great deal of weight, even without trying to diet.

People who are severely depressed commonly lose their interest in various types of activities that are otherwise sources of pleasure and fulfillment. One common example is a loss of sexual desire. Depressed people are less likely to initiate sexual activity, and they are less likely to enjoy sex if their partners can persuade them to participate.

Various ill-defined somatic complaints can also accompany mood disorders. Some patients complain of frequent headaches and muscular aches and pains. These concerns may develop into a preoccupation with bodily functions and fear of disease.

## Behavioural Symptoms

The symptoms of mood disorders also include changes in the things that people do and the rate at which they do them. The term **psychomotor retardation** refers to several features of behaviour that may accompany the onset of serious depression. The most obvious behavioural symptom of depression is slowed movement. Patients may walk and talk as if they are in slow motion. Others become completely immobile and may stop speaking altogether. Some depressed patients pause for very extended periods, perhaps several minutes, before answering a question.

In marked contrast to periods when they are depressed, manic patients are typically gregarious and energetic. They may exhibit inappropriate flirtatious or provocative behaviour, and may find it impossible to sit still for more than a moment or two. Manic patients are often easily distracted, flitting from one idea or project to the next. They may be full of plans, which they pursue in a rather indiscriminate fashion.

Jamison's memoir provides vivid descriptions of her own speeded-up behaviour:

> I was a senior in high school when I had my first attack of manic–depressive illness; once the siege began, I lost my mind rather rapidly. At first, everything seemed so easy. I raced about like a crazed weasel, bubbling with plans and enthusiasm, immersed in sports, and staying up all night, night after night, out with friends, reading everything that wasn't nailed down, filling manuscript books with poems and fragments of plays, and making expansive, completely unrealistic, plans for my future. The world was filled with pleasure and promise; I felt great. Not just great, I felt really great. I felt I could do anything, that no task was too difficult. My mind seemed clear, fabulously focused, and able to make intu-

itive mathematical leaps that had up to that point entirely eluded me. Indeed, they elude me still. At the time, however, not only did everything make perfect sense, but it all began to fit into a marvelous kind of cosmic relatedness. My sense of enchantment with the laws of the natural world caused me to fizz over, and I found myself buttonholing my friends to tell them how beautiful it all was. They were less than transfixed by my insights into the webbings and beauties of the universe, although considerably impressed by how exhausting it was to be around my enthusiastic ramblings: You're talking too fast, Kay. Slow down, Kay. You're wearing me out, Kay. Slow down, Kay. And those times when they didn't actually come out and say it, I still could see it in their eyes: For God's sake, Kay, slow down. (pp. 36–37)

### Other Problems Commonly Associated with Depression

Many people with mood disorders suffer from some clinical problems that are not typically considered symptoms of depression. Within the field of psychopathology, the simultaneous manifestation of a mood disorder and other syndromes is referred to as *comorbidity*, suggesting that the person exhibits symptoms of more than one underlying disorder.

Alcoholism and depression are clearly related phenomena. Many people who are depressed also drink heavily, and many people who are dependent on alcohol—approximately 40 percent—have experienced major depression at some point during their lives (Swendsen & Merikangas, 2000). The order of onset for the depression and alcoholism varies from one person to the next. Some people become depressed after they develop a drinking problem; others begin drinking after being depressed. There is also an association between these disorders within families. Alcohol abuse is common among the immediate families of patients with mood disorders. The experience of being in a family in which one or both parents are dependent on alcohol is a risk factor for depression, perhaps because of the increased frequency of stressful life events, as discussed later in this chapter. Eating disorders and anxiety disorders are also more common among first-degree relatives of depressed patients than among people in the general population. The relationships among these disorders are explored in Chapters 6 and 10, respectively.

## Classification

Psychopathologists have proposed hundreds of systems for describing and classifying mood disorders. In the following section we will describe briefly some of the historical figures who played a prominent role in the development of classification systems (Berrios, 1992). This discussion should help place our description of the current diagnostic system, DSM-IV-TR, in perspective.

### Brief Historical Perspective

Although written descriptions of clinical depression can be traced to ancient times, the first widely accepted classification system was proposed by the German physician Emil Kraepelin (1921). Kraepelin divided the major forms of mental disorder into two categories: *dementia praecox*, which we now know as schizophrenia (see Chapter 13), and *manic–depressive psychosis*. He based the distinction on age of onset, clinical symptoms, and the course of the disorder (its progress over time). The manic–depressive category included all depressive syndromes, regardless of whether the patients exhibited manic and depressive episodes or simply depression. In comparison to dementia praecox, manic–depression typically showed an episodic, recurrent course with a relatively good prognosis. Kraepelin observed that most manic–depressive patients returned to a normal level of functioning between episodes of depression or mania.

Despite the widespread acceptance and influence of Kraepelin's diagnostic system, many alternative approaches have been proposed. Two primary issues have been central in the debate regarding definitions of mood disorders. First, should these disorders be defined in a broad or a narrow fashion? A narrow approach to the definition of depression would focus on the most severely disturbed people—those whose depressed mood is entirely pervasive, completely debilitating, and associated with a wide range of additional symptoms. A broader approach to definition would include mild depression, which lies somewhere on the continuum between normal sadness and major depression.

The second issue concerns heterogeneity. All depressed patients do not have exactly the same set of symptoms, the same pattern of onset, or the same course over time. Some patients have manic episodes, whereas others experience only depression. Some exhibit psychotic symptoms, such as delusions and hallucinations, in addition to their symptoms of mood disorder; others do not. In some cases, the person's depression is apparently a reaction to specific life events, whereas in others the mood disorder seems to come out of nowhere. Are these qualitatively distinct forms of mood disorder, or are they different expressions of the same underlying problem? Is the distinction among the different types simply one of severity?

## Contemporary Diagnostic Systems

The DSM-IV-TR approach to classifying mood disorders recognizes several subtypes of depression, placing special emphasis on the distinction between unipolar and bipolar disorders. The overall scheme, outlined in Table 5–3, includes two types of unipolar mood disorder and three types of bipolar mood disorder.

**TABLE 5-3 DSM-IV-TR System for Classifying Mood Disorders**

**UNIPOLAR DISORDERS**

***Major Depressive Disorder***

- One or more major depressive episodes
- No manic or unequivocal hypomanic episodes

***Dysthymic Disorder***

- Depressed mood for at least two years
- Never without these symptoms for more than two months during this period
- No major depressive episode during first two years

**BIPOLAR DISORDERS**

***Bipolar I Disorder***

- One or more manic episodes

***Bipolar II Disorder***

- One or more major depressive episodes
- At least one hypomanic episode
- No manic episodes

***Cyclothymic Disorder***

- Numerous periods with hypomanic symptoms and numerous periods with depressed mood for at least two years
- Never without these symptoms for more than two months during two-year period
- No major depressive episodes
- No manic episode during first two years

**Unipolar Disorders** The unipolar disorders include two specific types: major depressive disorder and dysthymia. In order to meet the criteria for major depressive disorder, a person must experience at least one major depressive episode in the absence of any history of manic episodes. Table 5–4 lists the DSM-IV-TR criteria for a major depressive episode. Although some people experience a single, isolated episode of major depression followed by complete recovery, most cases of unipolar depression follow an intermittent course with repeated episodes.

**Dysthymia** differs from major depression in terms of both severity and duration. Dysthymia represents a chronic mild depressive condition that has been present for many years. In order to fulfill DSM-IV-TR criteria for this disorder, the person must, over a period of at least two years, exhibit a depressed mood for most of the day on more days than not. Two or more of the following symptoms must also be present:

1. Poor appetite or overeating
2. Insomnia or hypersomnia
3. Low energy or fatigue
4. Low self-esteem
5. Poor concentration or difficulty making decisions
6. Feelings of hopelessness

These symptoms must not be absent for more than two months at a time during the two-year period. If at any time during the initial two years the person met criteria for a major depressive episode, the diagnosis would be major depression rather than dysthymia. As in the case of major depressive disorder, the presence of a manic episode would rule out a diagnosis of dysthymia.

The distinction between major depressive disorder and dysthymia is somewhat artificial because both sets of symptoms are frequently seen in the same person. In such cases, rather than thinking of them as separate disorders, it is more appropriate to consider them as two aspects of the same disorder, which waxes and wanes over time. Some experts refer to this combination of major depression and dysthymia as *double depression*, which

**TABLE 5–4 Symptoms Listed in DSM-IV-TR for Major Depressive Episode**

**A. Five or more of the following symptoms have been present during the same two-week period and represent a change from previous functioning; at least one of the symptoms is either (1) depressed mood, or (2) loss of interest or pleasure.**

1. Depressed mood most of the day, nearly every day, as indicated either by subjective report (for example, feels sad or empty) or observation made by others (for example, appears tearful). Note: in children and adolescents, can be irritable mood.
2. Markedly diminished interest or pleasure in all, or almost all, activities most of the day, nearly every day.
3. Significant weight loss when not dieting or weight gain (for example, a change of more than 5 percent of body weight in a month), or decrease or increase in appetite nearly every day. Note: in children, consider failure to make expected weight gains.
4. Insomnia or hypersomnia nearly every day.
5. Psychomotor agitation or retardation nearly every day (observable by others).
6. Fatigue or loss of energy nearly every day.
7. Feelings of worthlessness or excessive or inappropriate guilt nearly every day (not merely self-reproach or guilt about being sick).
8. Diminished ability to think or concentrate, or indecisiveness, nearly every day.
9. Recurrent thoughts of death (not just fear of dying), recurrent suicidal ideation without a specific plan, or a suicide attempt or a specific plan for committing suicide.

may represent a distinct subtype of unipolar depression (Keller, Hirschfeld, & Hanks, 1997).

**Bipolar Disorders** All three types of bipolar disorders involve manic or hypomanic episodes. Table 5–5 lists the DSM-IV criteria for a manic episode. The mood disturbance must be severe enough to interfere with occupational or social functioning. A person who has experienced at least one manic episode would be assigned a diagnosis of bipolar I disorder. The vast majority of patients with this disorder have episodes of major depression in addition to manic episodes.

Some patients experience episodes of increased energy that are not sufficiently severe to qualify as full-blown mania. These episodes are called **hypomania**. A person who has experienced at least one major depressive episode, at least one hypomanic episode, and no full-blown manic episodes would be assigned a diagnosis of *bipolar II disorder*. The symptoms used in DSM-IV-TR to identify a hypomanic episode are the same as those used for manic episode (at least three of the seven symptoms listed in Table 5–5). The differences between manic and hypomanic episodes involve duration and severity. The symptoms need to be present for a minimum of only four days to meet the threshold for a hypomanic episode (as opposed to one week for a manic episode). The mood change in a hypomanic episode must be noticeable to others, but the disturbance must not be severe enough to impair social or occupational functioning or to require hospitalization.

**Cyclothymia** is considered by DSM-IV-TR to be a chronic but less severe form of bipolar disorder. It is, therefore, the bipolar

*Bereavement is part of normal human experience. A clinical diagnosis would not be made following the loss of a loved one unless symptoms persist for more than two months or include marked functional impairment.*

**TABLE 5-5 Symptoms Listed in DSM-IV-TR for Manic Episode**

**A. A distinct period of abnormally and persistently elevated, expansive, or irritable mood, lasting at least one week (or any duration if hospitalization is necessary).**

**B. During the period of mood disturbance, three or more of the following symptoms have persisted (four if the mood is only irritable) and have been present to a significant degree:**

1. Inflated self-esteem or grandiosity.
2. Decreased need for sleep—for example, feels rested after only three hours of sleep.
3. More talkative than usual, or pressure to keep talking.
4. Flight of ideas or subjective experience that thoughts are racing.
5. Distractibility—that is, attention too easily drawn to unimportant or irrelevant external stimuli.
6. Increase in goal-directed activity (either socially, at work or school, or sexually) or psychomotor agitation.
7. Excessive involvement in pleasurable activities that have a high potential for painful consequences—for example, the person engages in unrestrained buying sprees, sexual indiscretions, or foolish business investments.

equivalent of dysthymia. In order to meet criteria for cyclothymia, the person must experience numerous hypomanic episodes and numerous periods of depression (or loss of interest or pleasure) during a period of two years. There must be no history of major depressive episodes and no clear evidence of a manic episode during the first two years of the disturbance.

**Further Descriptions and Subtypes** DSM-IV-TR includes several additional ways of describing subtypes of the mood disorders. These are based on two considerations: (1) more specific descriptions of symptoms that were present during the most recent episode of depression (known as *episode specifiers*) and (2) more extensive descriptions of the pattern that the disorder follows over time (known as *course specifiers*). These distinctions may provide a useful way to subdivide depressed patients, who certainly present a heterogeneous set of problems. On the other hand, the validity of these subtypes is open to question, especially those based on episode specifiers. Long-term follow-up studies suggest that a patient's subtype diagnosis is likely to change over repeated episodes (Angst, Sellaro, & Merikangas, 2000).

One episode specifier allows the clinician to describe a major depressive episode as having melancholic features. **Melancholia** is a term that is used to describe a particularly severe type of depression. Some experts believe that melancholia represents a subtype of depression that is caused by different factors than those that are responsible for other forms of depression (Parker et al., 1995). The presence of melancholic features may also indicate that the person is likely to have a good response to biological forms of treatment, such as antidepressant medication and electroconvulsive therapy (Schatzberg, 1999).

In order to meet the DSM-IV-TR criteria for melancholic features, a depressed patient must either (1) lose the feeling of pleasure associated with all, or almost all, activities or (2) lose the capacity to feel better—even temporarily— when something good happens. The person must also exhibit at least three of the following: (1) the depressed mood feels distinctly different from the depression a person would feel after the death of a loved one; (2) the depression is most often worst in the morning; (3) the person awakens early, at least two hours before usual; (4) marked psychomotor retardation or agitation; (5) significant loss of appetite or weight loss; and (6) excessive or inappropriate guilt.

Another episode specifier allows the clinician to indicate the presence of *psychotic features*—hallucinations or delusions—during the most recent episode of depression or mania. The psychotic features can be either consistent or inconsistent with the patient's mood. For example, if a depressed man reports hearing voices that tell him he is a worthless human being who deserves to suffer for his sins, the hallucinations would be considered "mood congruent psychotic features." Depressed patients who exhibit psychotic features are more likely to require hospitalization and treatment with a combination of antidepressant and antipsychotic medication (Parker et al., 1997).

Another episode specifier applies to women who become depressed or manic following pregnancy. A major depressive or manic episode can be specified as having a *postpartum onset* if it begins within four weeks after childbirth. Because the woman must meet the full criteria for an episode of major depression or mania, this category does not include minor periods of postpartum "blues," which are relatively common.

The DSM-IV-TR course specifiers for mood disorders allow clinicians to describe further the pattern and sequence of episodes, as well as the person's adjustment between episodes. For example, the course of a bipolar disorder can be specified as *rapid cycling* if the person experiences at least four episodes of major depression, mania, or hypomania within a 12-month period. Patients whose disorder follows this problematic course are likely to show a poor response to treatment and are at greater risk than other types of bipolar patients to attempt suicide (Kilzieh & Akiskal, 1999).

A mood disorder (either unipolar or bipolar) is described as following a seasonal pattern if, over a period of time, there is a regular relationship between the onset of a person's episodes and particular times of the year. The most typical seasonal pattern is one in which the person becomes depressed in the fall or winter, followed by a full recovery in the following spring or summer.

Researchers refer to a mood disorder in which the onset of episodes is regularly associated with changes in seasons as **seasonal affective disorder**.[1] The episodes most commonly occur in winter, presumably in response to fewer hours of sunlight. Seasonal depression is usually characterized by somatic symptoms, such as overeating, carbohydrate craving, weight gain, fatigue, and sleeping more than usual. One study found that among outpatients who had a history of at least three major depressive episodes, 16 percent met criteria for the seasonal pattern (Thase, 1989). Most patients with seasonal affective disorder have a unipolar disorder, but many would meet criteria for bipolar II disorder. The latter group typically become depressed in the winter followed by a mood reversal to hypomania in the spring. Relatively few have bipolar I disorder (Oren & Rosenthal, 1992).

[1] "Affect" and "mood" are sometimes used interchangeably in psychiatric terminology. Depression and mania were called "affective disorders" in DSM-III.

## Course and Outcome

To describe the typical course and outcome of mood disorders, it is useful to consider unipolar and bipolar disorders separately. Most studies point to clear-cut differences between these two conditions in terms of age of onset and prognosis (Perris, 1992).

**Unipolar Disorders** Data regarding the onset and course of unipolar mood disorders must be viewed with some caution because virtually all studies have focused exclusively on the people who have sought treatment for their depression. Very little is known about untreated depressions. We do not know whether they become persistent problems; some may improve spontaneously in a short period of time.

People with unipolar mood disorders typically have their first episode in middle age; the average age of onset is in the mid-forties. The length of episodes varies widely. DSM-IV-TR sets the minimum duration at two weeks, but they can last much longer. In one large-scale follow-up study, 10 percent of the patients had depressive episodes that lasted more than two years (Thornicroft & Sartorius, 1993). At least 50 percent of unipolar patients will have more than one depressive episode (Health Canada, 2002a). The mean number of lifetime episodes is five or six.

The results of long-term follow-up studies of treated patients indicate that major depressive disorder is frequently a chronic and recurrent condition in which episodes of severe symptoms may alternate with periods of full or partial recovery (Boland & Keller, 1996; Nierenberg, 2001). When a person's symptoms are diminished or improved, the disorder is considered to be in **remission**, or a period of recovery. **Relapse** is a return of active symptoms in a person who has recovered from a previous episode. These phases of the disorder are represented schematically in Figure 5–1.

Approximately half of all unipolar patients recover within six months of the beginning of an episode. The probability that a patient will recover from an episode decreases

**The Course of an Episode of Major Depression**

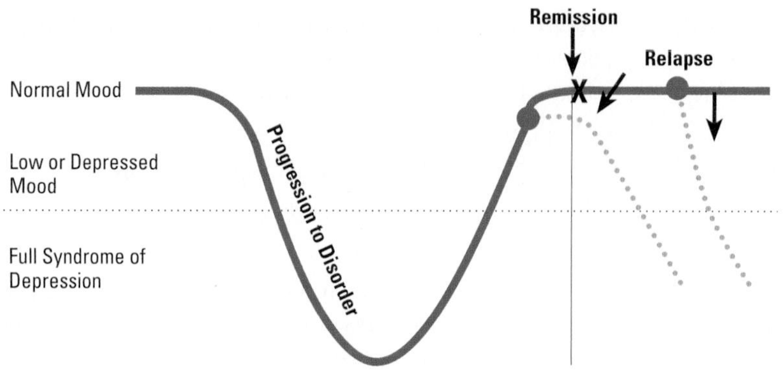


**FIGURE 5-1: The phases leading into (and out of) an episode of depression.**

*Source:* E. Frank, H.A. Swartz, and D.J. Kupfer, 2000, Interpersonal and social rhythm therapy: Managing the chaos of bipolar disorder. *Biological Psychiatry, 48,* 593–604.

after six months, and 10 to 20 percent do not recover after five years. Among those who recover, 50 percent relapse within three years (Hart, Craighead, & Craighead, 2001). The risk of relapse goes down as the period of remission increases. In other words, the longer the person remains free of depression, the better his or her chance of avoiding relapse.

**Bipolar Disorders** Onset of bipolar mood disorders usually occurs between the ages of 28 and 33 years, which is younger than the average age of onset for unipolar disorders. The first episode is just as likely to be manic as depressive (Coryell & Winokur, 1992). The average duration of a manic episode runs between two and three months. Bipolar II patients tend to have shorter and less severe episodes (Coryell et al., 1985; Keller, 1987).

Onset is often gradual and the person may not always be aware that he or she is becoming manic or hypomanic. Norman Endler, for example, became hypomanic without realizing it. It was only later, when friends began to comment on the change in his behaviour, that he realized there was something wrong.

> Most of the time I was busy, busy, busy; taping records, playing tennis, skiing, writing manuscripts, talking to Ann, reading, going to movies, staying up late at night, waking up early in the morning, always on the go—busy, busy, busy. Furthermore, I was boasting about all the energy I had that enabled me to keep up this fast pace. . . . During this period a number of friends told me I could never sit still long enough for them to have a conversation with me. Obviously I was unaware of it. (1982, pp. 4–5)

The long-term course of bipolar disorders is most often episodic, and the prognosis is mixed (Angst, Sellaro, & Angst, 1998). Most patients have more than one episode, and bipolar patients tend to have more episodes than unipolar patients. The length of intervals between episodes is difficult to predict. The long-term prognosis is mixed for patients with bipolar mood disorder. Although some patients recover and function very well, others experience continued impairment. Several studies that have followed bipolar patients over periods of up to 10 years have found that 40 to 50 percent of patients are able to achieve a sustained recovery from the disorder. Many patients, however, remain chronically disabled. Rapid cycling patients are less likely to recover from an episode and are more likely to relapse after they do recover (Coryell et al., 1998; Turvey et al., 1999).

## Epidemiology

Several studies provide detailed information regarding the frequency of mood disorders in various countries around the world (Ayuso-Mateos et al., 2001; Bland, 1997; Sartorius, 2001). Some are based on information collected from nonclinical samples of men and women by investigators using structured diagnostic interviews. In other words, the people who participated in these studies did not have to be in treatment at a hospital or clinic in order to be identified as being depressed. These studies are particularly important because large numbers of people experience serious depression without wanting or being able to seek professional help. Data based exclusively on treatment records would underestimate the magnitude of the problem.

## Incidence and Prevalence

Short periods of sad or depressed mood are quite common. One survey of a nearly 5000 high school students in Ontario, for example, found that 16 percent had often felt sad in the past seven days, and 12 percent had felt depressed during this period (Adlaf & Paglia, 2001). Unfortunately, more severe forms of depression are also common. In fact, unipolar depression is one of the most common forms of psychopathology (Kessler et al., 1994; Robins & Regier, 1991). At some point in their lives, at least 8 percent of Canadians will develop major depressive disorder (Health Canada, 2002a), and about 5 percent of people have experienced the disorder in the past 12 months (Weissman et al., 1996a). According to the results of the Cross-National Collaborative Study, the prevalence of major depression in Canada is similar to the rates found in Europe and the United States, but higher than rates in Taiwan and Korea (Weissman et al., 1996a). Unipolar disorders have been found to be much more common than bipolar disorders. The ratio of unipolar to bipolar disorders is at least 5:1 (Smith & Weissman, 1992).

About 3 to 6 percent of Canadian adults develop dysthymia at some point in their lives (Health Canada, 2002a), which is similar to rates in other Western countries (APA, 2000). Seasonal affective disorder is more prevalent the further one goes from the equator, because there are greater seasonal variations in daylight hours (Lam & Levitt, 1999). According to a community survey in Toronto, 11 percent of people with major depression had the seasonal subtype (Levitt et al., 2000). Bipolar disorder is relatively uncommon, with reported lifetime prevalence rates from community surveys of 0.4 percent to 1.6 percent for bipolar I disorder and 0.5 percent for bipolar II disorder (APA, 2000; Health Canada, 2002a).

Research in Canada and the United States suggests that many depressed people do not receive treatment for their mood disturbance (Parikh, Lesage, Kennedy, & Goering, 1999; Robins & Regier, 1991; see also Figure 3-1 on p. 68). Finding ways to help these people represents an important challenge for psychologists and psychiatrists who treat mood disorders (Davidson & Meltzer-Brody, 1999).

**Roger Bland**, *a professor of psychiatry at the University of Alberta, is a leading researcher in the epidemiology of depression and other mental disorders.*

## Gender Differences

Women, compared to men, are two or three times more vulnerable to depression (Kessler, 2000). This pattern has been reported in study after study, using samples of treated patients as well as community surveys, and regardless of the assessment procedures employed. The increased prevalence of depression among women is apparently limited to unipolar disorders. For the Canadian sample in the Cross-National Collaborative Study, for example, the lifetime prevalence rates for major depression were 12 percent in women but only 7 percent in men. The lifetime prevalence for bipolar I disorder was 0.5 percent for women and 0.7 percent for men (Weissman et al., 1996a). The same pattern of results has been found in other countries.

Some observers have suggested that the high rates for unipolar mood disorders in women reflect shortcomings in the data collection process. Women simply might be more likely than men to seek treatment or to be labelled as being depressed. Another argument holds that culturally determined sanctions make it more difficult for men to admit to subjective feelings of distress such as hopelessness and despair. None of these alternatives has been substantiated by empirical evidence. Research studies clearly indicate that the higher prevalence of depression among women is genuine. Possible explanations for this gender difference have focused on a variety of factors, including sex hormones, stressful life events, and childhood adversity as well as response styles that are associated with gender roles (Hankin & Abramson, 2001; Kessler, 2000). These issues are discussed later in this chapter.

## Cross-Cultural Differences

Questions about the relation between culture and mood disorders were raised early in the twentieth century, when Kraepelin (1921) visited the island of Java (now part of Indonesia). His impression, based on visits to psychiatric hospitals in that country, was that the disorder that he called "manic–depressive insanity" was just as common in Java as it was in Europe. He also noted, however, that patients in Java suffered "almost exclusively states of excitement and often confusion" (Leff, 1992). Manic episodes apparently were much more common in this culture than were episodes of major depression.

Comparisons of emotional expression and emotional disorder across cultural boundaries encounter a number of methodological problems (see Research Close-Up in Chapter 4, and Research Methods in Chapter 9). One problem involves vocabulary. Each culture has its own ways of interpreting reality, including different styles of expressing or communicating symptoms of physical and emotional disorder. Words and concepts that are used to describe illness behaviours in one culture might not exist in other cultures. For example, some African cultures have only one word for both anger and sadness. Interesting adaptations are, therefore, required to translate questions that are supposed to tap experiences such as anxiety and depression. One investigation, which employed a British interview schedule that had been translated into Yoruba—a language spoken in Nigeria—used the phrase "the heart goes weak" to represent depression (Leff, 1988).

We must remember that our own diagnostic categories have been developed within a specific cultural setting; they are not culture-free and are not necessarily any more reasonable than the ways in which other cultures describe and categorize their own behavioural and emotional disorders (Manson & Kleinman, 1998). One illustration of this principle comes from the study of *neurasthenia*, which is relatively common in China but is rarely diagnosed in Western societies. Although the diagnostic term was not introduced to Chinese physicians until the twentieth century, the concept fits closely with ancient traditions in Chinese folk medicine. Neurasthenic patients present many different complaints that focus primarily on physical or somatic symptoms: headaches, insomnia, dizziness, pain, weakness, loss of energy, poor appetite, tingling in the head, and so on. Related psychological symptoms include memory problems, anxiety, disturbing dreams, and poor concentration. Most patients who would be given a diagnosis of neurasthenia in China would qualify for a diagnosis of major depressive disorder if the DSM-IV-TR diagnostic system was applied.

Cross-cultural differences have been confirmed by a number of research projects that have examined cultural variations in symptomatology among depressed patients in different countries. These studies report comparable overall frequencies of mood disorders in various parts of the world, but the specific type of symptom expressed by the patients varies from one culture to the next. In Chinese patients, depression is more likely to be described in terms of somatic symptoms, such as sleeping problems, headaches, and loss of energy (Parker, Cheah, & Roy, 2001). Depressed patients in Europe and North America are more likely to express feelings of guilt and suicidal ideas (Kirmayer, 2001).

Aboriginal Canadians (i.e., First Nations, Inuit, and Métis), compared to non-Aboriginal groups, have higher rates of depression and suicide, although there is some variation from one Aboriginal community to another (Health Canada, 2002a; Kirmayer et al., 2000). According to a 2002 Health Canada report, there are several contributory factors for the higher rates of depression and suicide among Aboriginal Canadians. Because of conflicting messages about the value of their own culture, many Aboriginal people do not have a strong sense of self. Also, cultural instability has led to sexual abuse, family violence, and substance abuse, which are associated with a high risk of depression and suicide. Childhood separation, poverty, and access to firearms are also contributing factors.

Cross-cultural comparisons suggest that, at its most basic level, clinical depression is a universal phenomenon that is not limited to Western or urban societies. They also indicate that a person's cultural experiences, including linguistic, educational, and social factors, may play an important role in shaping the manner in which he or she expresses and copes with the anguish of depression. Cross-cultural variations should also be kept in mind when clinicians attempt to identify central or defining features of depression. We will return to this point later in the chapter when we discuss the rationale behind studies that rely on animal models of depression.

## Risk for Mood Disorders across the Lifespan

Age is an important consideration in the epidemiology of mood disorders. Some readers might expect that the prevalence of depression would be higher among older people than among younger people. This was, in fact, what many clinicians expected prior to large-scale epidemiological investigations, such as the cross-national study. This belief may stem from the casual observation that many older people experience brief episodic states of acute unhappiness, often precipitated by changes in status (for example, retirement, relocation) and loss of significant others (for example, children moving away, deaths of friends and relatives). But brief episodes of sadness and grief are not the same thing as clinical depression.

Although many people mistakenly identify depression with the elderly, data from both Canada and the United States suggest that mood disorders actually are most frequent among young and middle-aged adults (Fogarty et al., 1994; Spaner, Bland, & Newman 1994; Weissman et al., 1991). Prevalence rates for major depressive episodes are significantly lower for people over the age of 65. The frequency of bipolar disorders is also low in the oldest age groups. These findings are illustrated in Figure 5–2, which shows results from a survey by Roger Bland and colleagues in Edmonton. Similar findings have been reported in other countries (for example, Weissman et al., 1991).

Several explanations have been offered for this pattern. One interpretation is based on the fact that elderly people are more likely to experience memory impairments (see Further Thoughts in Chapter 14). People who are in their seventies and eighties may have more

**Lifetime Prevalence of Mood Disorders (Edmonton Data)**

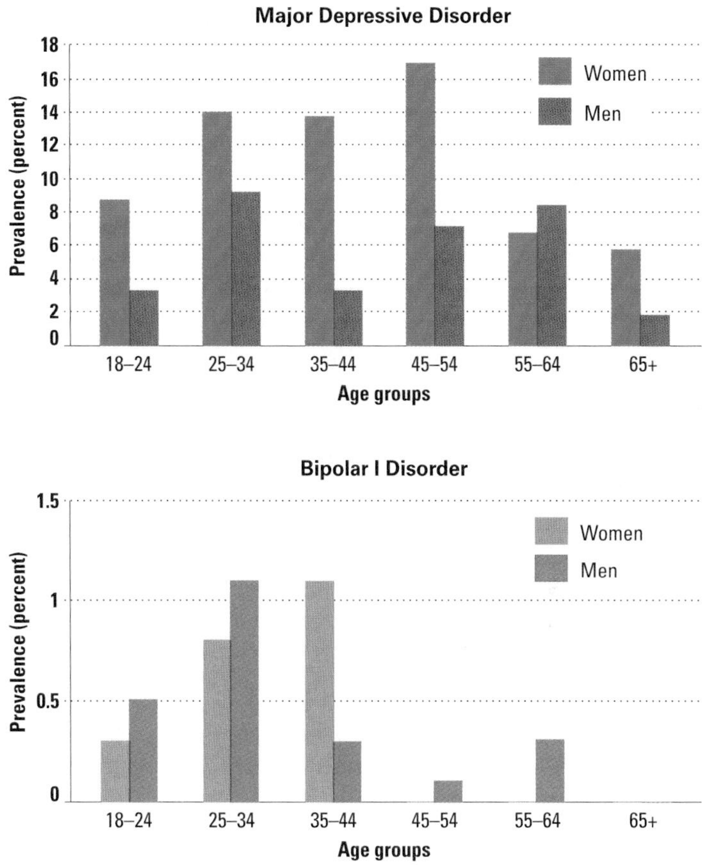


**FIGURE 5–2: Lifetime prevalence of major depressive disorder (top) and bipolar disorder (bottom) by age and gender.**

*Source:* Based on F. Fogarty, J.M. Russell, S.C. Newman, and R.C. Bland, 1994, Mania. *Acta Psychiatrica Scandinavica, 376 (Suppl.)*, 16–23; D. Spaner, R.C. Bland, and S.C. Newman, 1994, Major depressive disorder. *Acta Psychiatrica Scandinavica, 376 (Suppl.)*, 7–15.

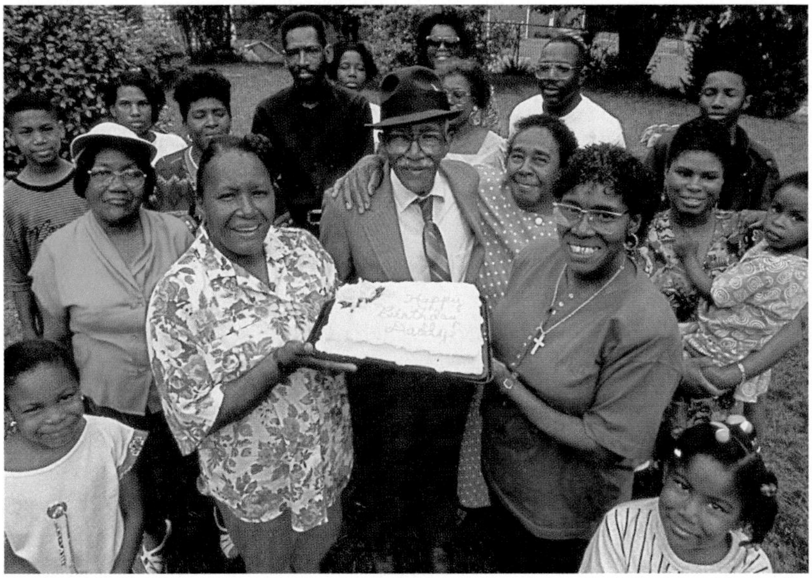

*Contrary to popular views, older people are actually less likely to be depressed than are younger people. Some subgroups of elderly people, however, are at high risk for depression.*

trouble remembering, and therefore may fail to report, episodes of depression that occurred several months before the research interview is conducted. Also, because mood disorders are associated with increased mortality (for example, suicide), many severely depressed people might not have survived into old age. These are both plausible hypotheses that may have influenced the results of epidemiological studies. Nevertheless, most investigators now believe that the effect is genuine: Clinical depression is less common among elderly people than it is among younger adults (Lewinsohn et al., 1993; Wittchen, Knauper, & Kessler, 1994).

Finally, it should be noted that the frequency of depression is much higher among certain subgroups of elderly people. For example, the prevalence of depression is particularly high among those who are about to enter residential care facilities. Elderly people in nursing homes are more likely to be depressed in comparison to a random sample of elderly people living in the community (Zarate & Tohen, 1996).

### Comparisons across Generations

Epidemiological findings on age and depression also raise another important question: Has the frequency of depression increased in recent years? The answer is apparently yes. People born after World War II seem to be more likely to develop mood disorders than were people from previous generations. In fact, several studies have reported a consistent trend toward higher lifetime rates of depression in successively younger generations (Lavori et al., 1987; Wittchen, Knauper, & Kessler, 1994). The average age of onset for clinical depression also seems to be younger in people who were born more recently. This kind of pattern is sometimes called a *birth cohort trend*.

## Etiological Considerations and Research

In the next few pages we turn our attention to current speculation and knowledge about causes of mood disorders. Discussions of this topic must keep in mind the relatively high prevalence of these problems. Major depression is a severely disabling condition that affects at least 8 percent of the population, usually appearing during young adulthood when the person would be expected to be most active and productive. Why hasn't this problem been eliminated through the process of natural selection? Evolutionary theorists suggest that it is because, in addition to being painful and disruptive to a person's life, mild to moderate symptoms of depression may serve a useful purpose (Nesse, 1999; Price, 2000). This argument is focused on those situations in which depression represents a temporary response to circumstances in the person's environment. As we will see, many episodes of depression do seem to be triggered by stressful life events and harsh social circumstances. An evolutionary perspective would hold that the symptoms of depression—slowing down, loss of motivation, withdrawal from other people—may represent a response system that helps the person disengage from a situation that is not going well (McGuire & Troisi, 1998b). For example, someone who is involved in an unsuccessful marriage may eventually become depressed, withdraw, and reconsider the long-term benefits of investing further time and resources in a relationship that is likely to remain unrewarding. At low levels and over brief periods of time, depressed mood may help us refocus our motivations and it may help us to conserve and redirect our energy in response to experiences of loss and defeat. In that sense, we all have the capacity to become depressed.

Psychological explanations for mood disorders focus on individual differences, and they are primarily concerned with the most severe and disabling forms of depression. Why do some people develop major depression and others do not? What kinds of events are associated with a relatively drastic failure of the psychological and biological systems that regulate mood? A disorder that is as common as depression must have many causes rather than one. In Chapter 2, we discussed some general principles that are associated with systems theory. The principle of equifinality, which holds that there are many ways to reach the same outcome, clearly applies in the case in mood disorders. As we will see in the following pages, many people become depressed after being exposed to extremely stressful life events; others become depressed in the apparent absence of such experiences. Some depressed people come from families in which several others have suffered from similar disorders, while others have no family history of depression. Antidepressant medication is helpful in many cases, but for others it provides no relief. These differences suggest strongly that there are many different pathways to depression.

Our consideration of etiological factors is organized around different *levels of analysis* (see Chapter 2). We will consider social, psychological, and biological mechanisms that are involved in the onset and maintenance of mood disorders. This organization should help you appreciate the complementary nature of these analyses. After we have considered the impact of stressful life events on mood, we will discuss psychological factors, such as cognitive biases, that shape a person's response to stress. Then we will review what is known about hormones and brain activities that coordinate our responses to environmental stressors. Biological mechanisms should not be viewed as an alternative to psychological or social explanations of depression. Rather, they help us understand at a microscopic level of analysis how our bodies perform important functions such as regulating emotion and responding to stressful events.

We will discuss evidence regarding unipolar and bipolar mood disorders separately, when it is appropriate. Most research on the etiology of bipolar mood disorders has focused on biological factors, especially genetics. There is also some recent evidence regarding the influence of stressful life events and the onset of manic episodes. Our discussion of psychological factors will focus exclusively on the etiology of unipolar depression because this topic has not been explored extensively with regard to bipolar disorders.

## Social Factors

It should not be surprising that much of the literature on depression focuses on interpersonal loss and separation. From birth to death, our lives are intertwined with those of other people. We are fundamentally social organisms, and we feel sad when someone close to us dies. Similar feelings occasionally follow major disappointments, such as failure to win acceptance to the school of our choice or being fired from a job. In these cases, rather than losing other people, some clinicians have suggested that we may be losing "social roles" or ways in which we think about ourselves.

Various theories of depression have been built around a consideration of the impact of stressful life events. Beginning around the turn of the twentieth century, psychodynamic theories emphasized the central role played by interpersonal relationships and loss of significant others in setting the stage for depression as well as in bringing about a depressive episode (Freud, 1917/1961). Freud's theory laid the intellectual foundation for many subsequent studies of psychological and social factors in the development and maintenance of unipolar depression. He focused interest on the possibility that stressful life events, such as the death of a close friend or family member, may precipitate the onset of mood disorders. (We consider contemporary research on this issue in the next section.) Freud was also interested in the observation that some people who become depressed are extremely dependent on other people for the maintenance of their self-esteem. This hypothesis anticipated subsequent studies of social skills in depression and the importance of interpersonal relationships over the course of mood disorders. We will review these considerations in a later section on psychological factors.

**Stressful Life Events and Unipolar Disorders** Several investigations have explored the relationships between stressful life events and the development of unipolar mood disorders. Do people who become clinically depressed actually experience an increased number of stressful life events? The answer is yes. The experience of stressful life events is associated with an increased probability that a person will become depressed. This correlation has been demonstrated many times (Kessler, 1997; Monroe et al., 1999).

Investigators have faced difficult methodological issues in order to interpret the strong relationship between stressful life events and the onset of depression. One particularly troublesome problem involves the direction of the relationship between life events and mood disorders. For example, being fired from a job might lead a person to become depressed. On the other hand, the onset of a depressive episode, with its associated difficulties in energy and concentration, could easily affect the person's job performance and lead to being fired. Therefore, if depressed people experience more stressful events, what is the direction of effect? Does failure lead to depression, or does depression lead to failure?

*George Brown has made important contributions to knowledge regarding the link between stressful life events and the onset of depression.*

The use of prospective research designs, in which subjects are followed over time, has allowed investigators to address the question of cause and effect (see Research Methods in Chapter 8). Prospective studies have found that stressful life events are useful in predicting the subsequent onset of unipolar depression (Brown, 1998; Kendler, Karkowski, & Prescott, 1999). This evidence supports the argument that, in many cases, stressful life events contribute to the onset of mood disorders.

Although many kinds of negative events are associated with depression, a special class of circumstances—those involving major losses of important people or roles—seems to play a crucial role in precipitating unipolar depression. This conclusion is based, in large part, on a series of studies reported by George Brown and his colleagues. Their studies have compared the living circumstances and life experiences of depressed and nondepressed women, regardless of whether they are receiving treatment for their problems. Brown and Harris (1978) found that "severe" events—those that are particularly threatening and have long-term consequences for the woman's adjustment—increase the probability that a woman will become depressed. Only 16 percent of the events that were reported by all of the women in the study were considered severe. The frequency of nonsevere events was roughly equivalent for depressed and nondepressed women. Most cases of depression appeared after a single severe event. (The Research Close-Up provides further details regarding the nature of these events.) Brown's data suggest that depression is not caused by an accumulation of ordinary hassles and difficulties to which most of us are exposed on a daily basis (Monroe & Simons, 1991).

## RESEARCH CLOSE-UP

### Social Origins of Depression in Women

Some of the most influential studies on the link between depression and stressful life events have been conducted by George Brown, a sociologist, and Tirril Harris, a clinical psychologist, both at Guy's, King's, and St. Thomas' School of Medicine (University of London in England). One of their investigations focused on 400 working-class women between the ages of 18 and 50 with children living at home (Brown, Bifulco, & Harris, 1987). This sample was chosen because previous research had demonstrated that women with children living at home are particularly vulnerable to depression.

The study was completed in two phases, separated by approximately one year. During the first phase, the investigators asked each woman an extensive series of questions about her psychological adjustment (including symptoms of mental disorders as well as self-esteem) and her living circumstances (including personal relationships and social support). During the second phase, the investigators collected information regarding life events and difficulties that had occurred during the follow-up year. They also inquired, once again, about symptoms of depression and other mental disorders. They identified cases of depression using specific diagnostic criteria that ensured that the symptoms were comparable to those found among patients being treated for mood disorders.

The investigators made a concerted effort to describe each life event and to consider the circumstances in which it occurred. Each interviewer recorded detailed descriptions that were later provided to a panel of judges. The judges in turn rated how threatening each event would be to an average woman under the same living circumstances. Brown and his colleagues were particularly interested in the meaning that the events held for the woman. Judges were allowed to consider all information except the woman's mental status and the actual manner in which she responded to the event.

Results were reported only for the 303 women who were not depressed at the time of the first assessment and who completed the second phase of assessment. Within this sample, 130 women experienced a severe event during the follow-up year. Of these women, 29 (22 percent) became depressed. Among the 173 women who did not experience a severe event, only 3 (2 percent) became depressed. In other words, 29 out of 32 (90 percent) women who became depressed had experienced a severe event in the six months prior to onset. This pattern is consistent with other reports that indicate a close association between stressful life events and depression.

Severe events increased the probability of depression, but 78 percent of the 130 women who experienced a severe event in the follow-up year did not become depressed. What is the difference between the circumstances of women who become depressed after a severe event and those who do not? The investigators decided to examine the relationship between severe events and several other aspects of each woman's situation. One consideration involved ongoing difficulties that had been identified at the time of the first interview. Some severe events matched prior difficulties. For example, if a woman's pregnancy was rated as a severe event because she lived in poor housing, the event would have been rated as matching, or linked to, the difficulty. Brown and his colleagues believe that feelings of humiliation, entrapment,

*continued*

*cont.*

and defeat may be especially likely to occur after a person has experienced a difficulty-matching severe event.

In order to test this hypothesis, the investigators developed a procedure for describing severe events in terms of four broad themes: (1) devaluation of the self, (2) entrapment, (3) loss, and (4) danger (Brown, 1998). Among women who experienced a severe event involving danger, only 3 percent became depressed. In those situations where the severe event was considered humiliating, almost 40 percent of the women became depressed. An example would be a woman learning unexpectedly of her husband's long-standing infidelity. In contrast, only 10 percent of the women became depressed if their severe event was a form of loss that did not involve humiliation (such as marital separation initiated by the woman). Women who experienced a severe event that led to feelings of entrapment were three times more likely to become depressed (34 percent) than those women whose severe events involved loss without humiliation or entrapment. An example of an event fitting the entrapment theme would be a woman receiving official notification that her application to move out of appalling housing conditions had been denied.

These data are important for two primary reasons. First, the use of a prospective design minimizes questions about the direction of effect. For these women, depression clearly followed their stressful experiences. Second, the data point to a particularly powerful relationship between the onset of depression and certain kinds of stressful life events. The likelihood that a woman will become depressed is especially high if she experiences a severe event that would be expected to lead to a sense of being devalued as a person or trapped with no way toward a brighter future. ◆

Comparisons among different populations can shed further light on the relation between severe life events and the etiology of depression. Brown (1998) has repeated his study with women living in six different populations in Europe and Africa. Some of these are impoverished urban regions, such as a township in Harare, Zimbabwe, and others are rural. In each sample, Brown found that severe life events preceded the onset of most depressive episodes. He also found very large differences among these communities in terms of their overall prevalence of depression. These differences varied directly in proportion to the frequency with which their women experienced severe life events; communities with the highest rates of severe events produced the highest prevalence of major depression (see Figure 5–3). This pattern suggests that variations in the overall prevalence of depression are driven in large part by social factors that influence the frequency of stress in the community.

**Severe Life Events and Prevalence of Depression**

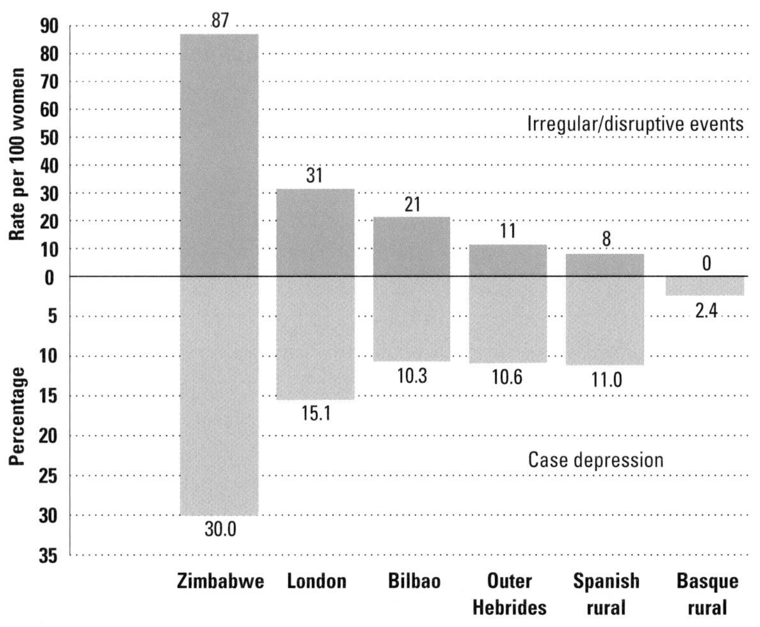


**FIGURE 5–3: Yearly rate of irregular or disruptive severe events per 100 women in six populations and prevalence of cases of depression in the same year.**

**Social Factors and Bipolar Disorders** Most investigations of stressful life events have been concerned with unipolar depression. Less attention has been paid to bipolar mood disorders, but some have found that the weeks preceding the onset of a manic episode are marked by an increased frequency of stressful life events (Hlastala et al., 2000; Johnson & Roberts, 1995). The kinds of events that precede the onset of mania tend to be different from those that lead to depression. While the latter include primarily negative experiences involving loss and low self-esteem, the former include schedule-disrupting events (such as loss of sleep) as well as goal-attainment events. Some patients experience an increase in manic symptoms after they have achieved a significant goal toward which they had been working (Johnson et al., 2000). Examples of this kind of goal attainment event would be a major job promotion, being accepted to a competitive professional school program, or the

*A series of studies comparing the life experiences of women in six communities—including Harare, Zimbabwe—found that the greater the frequency of severe events, the higher the prevalence of depression.*

blossoming of a new romantic relationship. These exhilarating experiences, coupled with the person's ongoing problems with emotion regulation, may contribute to a spiral of positive emotion and excess activity that culminates in a full-blown manic episode.

Aversive patterns of emotional expression and communication within the family can also have a negative impact on the adjustment of people with bipolar mood disorders. Longitudinal studies of bipolar patients have focused on the relation between frequency of relapse and the emotional climate within their families. Patients living with family members who are hostile toward or critical of the patient are more likely to relapse shortly after being discharged from the hospital (Miklowitz, Goldstein, & Neuchterlein, 1995; Miklowitz et al., 1988). Furthermore, bipolar patients who have less social support recover from episodes of depression more slowly than patients with higher levels of social support (Johnson et al., 1999). Stressful life events can also delay recovery from an episode of depression in bipolar patients (Johnson & Miller, 1997). This evidence indicates that the course of bipolar mood disorder can be influenced by the social environment in which the person is living.

## Psychological Factors

Severe events are clearly related to the onset of depression, but they do not provide a complete account of who will become depressed. Many people who do not become depressed also experience severe events. In one study reported by Brown and Harris (1978), only one out of every five women who reported a severe event in the preceding year became depressed. Presumably those who become depressed are somehow more vulnerable to the effects of stress. Several psychological factors may contribute to a person's vulnerability to stressful life events. In the following pages, we will consider two principal areas that have received attention in the research literature: cognitive factors and social skills. These studies have focused almost exclusively on unipolar mood disorders, so we will not discuss bipolar disorders in this section.

**Cognitive Vulnerability** Cognitive theories concerning the origins of unipolar depression are based on the recognition that humans are not only social organisms; they are also thinking organisms, and the ways in which people think about and perceive their world have an important influence on the way that they feel. Two people may react very differently to the same event, in large part because they may interpret the event differently. Cognitive theories about vulnerability to depression have typically focused on the ways in which people respond to negative experiences involving loss, failure, and disappointment (Ingram, Miranda, & Segal, 1998).

*Theoretical Proposals* Psychiatrist Aaron Beck has been the most influential proponent of a cognitive view of depression (see Beck, 1974; Clark, Beck, & Alford, 1999). Beck began with a primary interest in the things that depressed people say, particularly their self-critical thoughts ("I am a completely useless person") and their extremely pessimistic views of their environment ("This city is the worst possible place in which anyone could live"). He has defined the *depressive triad*—negative, demeaning views of the self, the world, and the future—as being central to our understanding of mood disorders. According to this perspective, the negative things that depressed people say represent direct manifestations of fundamental cognitive distortions or erroneous ways of thinking about themselves. These pervasive and persistent negative thoughts presumably play a central role in the onset of depression when they are activated by the experience of a negative life event.

Various types of distortions, errors, and biases are characteristic of the thinking of depressed people. One is the tendency to assign global, personal meaning to experiences of failure. An example might be a person who has been turned down after he tried out for a competitive sports team and says to himself, "This proves that I am a failure" rather than acknowledging that many talented people were being considered, that only a few people could be retained, and difficult decisions had to be made by the coach. Another cognitive distortion associated with depression is the tendency to overgeneralize conclusions about the self based on negative experiences. Following the example raised above, the person might also say to himself, "The fact that I was cut from the team shows that I am also going to fail at everything else." A third type of cognitive error involves drawing arbitrary inferences about the self in the absence of supporting evidence (often in spite of contradictory evidence). In this regard, consider a player who is a member of an athletic team. If they lose a game and the coach is upset, the player might arbitrarily decide that the loss was his fault and the coach doesn't like him, even though nothing about his performance was particularly instrumental with regard to the team's performance in the game. The final types of cognitive bias related to depression are tendencies to recall selectively events with negative consequences and to exaggerate the importance of negative events while simultaneously discounting the significance of positive events. For example, suppose that an athlete is looking back over her experiences during the course of an entire season. She would be more likely to feel depressed about her performance if she tends to dwell on the mistakes that she made and the games that her team lost rather than emphasizing the positive contributions that she made and the successes that she shared with her teammates.

How do these self-defeating biases lead to the onset of depression? According to Beck's theory, cognitive distortions combine to form a general pattern or cognitive **schema** that guides the ways in which people perceive and interpret events in their environment. Schemas are described as enduring and highly organized representations of prior experience. Although schemas may be latent—that is, not prominently represented in the person's conscious awareness at any given point in time—they are presumably reactivated when the person experiences a similar event. Depressive schemas increase the probability that the person will overreact to similar stressful events in the future.

A similar view of cognitive vulnerability to depression has been described in terms of **hopelessness** (Abramson, Metalsky, & Alloy, 1989; Alloy et al., 1999). Hopelessness refers to the person's negative expectations about future events and the associated belief that these events cannot be controlled. According to this view, depression is associated with the expectation that desirable events probably will not occur or that aversive events probably will occur regardless of what the person does. Following a negative life event, the probability that the person will become depressed is a function of the explanations and importance that the person ascribes to these events. These explanations are known as *causal attributions*.

Some people tend to explain negative events in terms of internal, stable, global factors. This pattern has been called a depressogenic attributional style. For example, after failing an important exam, someone who uses this cognitive style would probably think that her poor performance was the result of her own inadequacies (internal), which she has recognized for a long time and which will persist into the future (stable), and which also are responsible for her failure in many other important tasks, both academic and otherwise (global). As in Beck's description of negative schemas, attributional style is not considered to be a sufficient cause of depression. It does represent an important predisposition to depression, however, to the extent that people with a generalized depressogenic attributional style are more likely to develop hopelessness if they experience a negative life event.

*Research Evidence* Several studies have demonstrated that cognitive distortions are indeed more common among depressed people than among people who are not depressed. Furthermore, attributional style is useful in predicting people's responses to negative events (Alloy et al., 1999; Metalsky et al., 1993). This type of evidence indicates that cognitive factors can play an important role in the etiology of mood disorders.

Prospective studies also provide an important perspective on the relevance of cognitive factors. Negative patterns of thinking are present during episodes of depression, but do they predict future emotional problems among

*Separation from a spouse during a war can be extremely stressful. Whether or not the person becomes depressed is influenced by cognitive events as well as interpersonal skills that are used to cope with this difficult situation.*

people who have not yet experienced an episode of depression? A study of university students found that those who displayed negative cognitive styles at the beginning of their first year were much more likely than a comparison group subsequently to develop a major depressive disorder (Alloy, Abramson, & Francis, 1999). Furthermore, laboratory tasks have been used to demonstrate persistent biases toward memory for negative information among those people who later become depressed (Gotlib & Neubauer, 2000). Thus, there is empirical support for the role of cognitive factors as a form of vulnerability to depression.

**Interpersonal Factors and Social Behaviour** What other considerations might be important in explaining the relation between stressful life events and the onset of depression? Several investigators have suggested that in addition to how we think about negative or stressful experiences, the ways in which we actually respond to these events may also influence the probability that we will become depressed. In other words, it's not just how you think about an event or circumstance but the things that you actually do that will determine its eventual outcome. How does the depressed person cope with stressful events and respond to other people? What types of responses does the patient elicit from others? What are the extent and form of social resources that are available to help support the person during a crisis?

Some depressed people create difficult circumstances that increase the level of stress in their lives. In other words, the relationship between stressful life events and depression runs in both directions. Most of the research in this area has been done with female participants because women are more likely to be depressed than men. For example, research by Kate Harkness (currently at Queen's University) and others has shown that in comparison to women who are not depressed and women with other medical disorders, unipolar depressed women generate higher levels of stress, especially in the context of interpersonal relationships (Coyne et al., 2002; Hammen, 2002; Harkness et al., 1999). Maladaptive tactics for coping with marital distress are important factors in this process. For example, when involved in a serious disagreement with a spouse, a depressed person might express escalating complaints and hostile, provocative comments rather than trying to work toward a solution to the conflict. This dynamic process leads to an escalation of stress.

A further example of interpersonal processes in depression comes from research by Myriam Mongrain and colleagues at York University, indicating that people who are self-critical tend to be perceived by others as hostile and to elicit criticism and rejection from others (Mongrain, Lubbers, & Struthers, 2004; Mongrain, Vettess, Shusterm & Kendal, 1998; Vettese & Mongrain, 2000). Thus, self-criticism elicits aversive social interactions, which in turn can worsen a person's mood.

Negative life events, which are not caused by the person's own behaviour, may contribute to the onset of depression. An example might be an economic recession that leads to the loss of a job, increased financial pressures within a family, and marital distress. One of the partners becomes depressed, and then that person may exacerbate the difficulty by behaving in a way that leads to even higher levels of stress and perhaps a further deterioration in his or her mood.

*Social Relationships* The assumptions behind the interpersonal perspective on depression are very different from those incorporated in more cognitively oriented theories. For example, the cognitive perspective might argue that faulty processing of information leads those who are depressed to believe (erroneously) that their relationships with other people are inadequate. Interpersonal theorists suggest that depressed people may actually behave in ways that have a genuinely negative effect on other people, thus alienating themselves from friends and

## CANADIAN FOCUS Theoretical Advances in Understanding Depression

There are many leading Canadian researchers doing important depression research. In this Canadian Focus box we will feature the work of one of these investigators, John Abela at McGill University, whose work has focused on vulnerability factors in depression. There are several noteworthy and innovative aspects of his work. First, he has focused largely on depression in children and adolescents. This is important because depression is a widespread problem in younger Canadians, and because it is unclear whether current models of depression, which have been based on adults, can be applied to youths. Second, Abela has done important research to refine and integrate current models of depression. As we have seen in this chapter, depression is a complex, multifaceted phenomenon (or group of phenomena), and there are many different theories of depression. It is possible that some theories can explain only certain aspects of depression, and it may be necessary to integrate existing models in order to attain a comprehensive model of depression. The ultimate goal of Abela's research is to develop an empirically validated comprehensive theory, which integrates current cognitive, behavioural, interpersonal, psychodynamic, and biological models.

Recent examples of Abela's work include his studies of the weakest link hypothesis, and his research on the integration of the hopelessness and self-esteem models of depression. The weakest link hypothesis is a theoretical refinement of the hopelessness model of depression (Abramson et al., 1989), which we briefly discussed earlier in this chapter. The hopelessness model distinguishes between two types of depression. Hopelessness depression is characterized by low motivation and sadness. Secondary features include lack of energy, sleep disturbance, and increased dependency on others. Nonhopelessless depression is characterized by anhedonia, irritability, appetite disturbance, and somatic symptoms such as aches and pains (Abela & Payne, 2003). According to the hopelessness theory, there are three attributional styles (thinking patterns) that represent vulnerability factors for hopelessness depression. The attributional styles lead the person to feel hopeless when a negative event is experienced (e.g., failing an important exam), which then leads to depression. The three attributional styles are: (a) the tendency to attribute negative events to global and stable causes (e.g., "Bad things always happen to me"); (b) the tendency to perceive negative events as having many disastrous consequences (e.g., "I'll never graduate because I've failed this exam"); and (c) the tendency to view the self as flawed or deficient following negative events (e.g., "Failing this exam proves that I'm a loser").

Research in children has provided mixed support for the hopelessness theory. Some studies have provided full or partial support, while other studies have found no support at all (e.g., Abela, 2001; Abela & Sarin, 2002). The weakest link hypothesis (Abela & Sarin, 2002) is a modification of the hopelessness theory that attempts to reconcile the inconsistent findings. The hypothesis states that a person's vulnerability to depression is determined by his or her most depressogenic attributional style. For example, one person might be vulnerable to depression only because he tends to attribute negative events to global and stable causes (e.g., "Bad luck follows me everywhere, like a black cloud over my head"). Another person might be vulnerable to depression only because she tends to perceive negative events as having disastrous consequences (e.g., "Bad things, no matter how small, can quickly escalate into disasters").

Research by Abela and colleagues provides support for the weakest link hypothesis (Abela & Payne, 2003; Abela & Sarin, 2002), and thereby advances our understanding of the causes of depression. For example, Abela and Sarin (2002) asked Grade 7 students to complete measures of depressive symptoms and depressogenic inferential styles. Ten weeks later the children completed the measures of depressive symptoms and rated the occurrence of negative events. In line with the weakest link hypothesis, the children's "weakest links" interacted with negative events to predict increases in hopelessness depression symptoms.

Abela has also extended the work by Metalsky et al. (1993) on integrated models of depression. This research has examined the merits of integrating two models; the hopelessness (weakest link) model, and the Brown and Harris (1978) self-esteem model. The latter proposes that low self-esteem is a vulnerability factor to depression that interacts with negative events to lead to the development of hopelessness, which then leads to depression. The self-esteem and hopelessness models can be integrated by proposing that depressogenic inferential styles interact with negative events to predict increases in depression in people with low but not high self-esteem. High self-esteem is thought to serve as a buffer against depression following negative events. Research generally offers support for this hypothesis in adults and children, although there have been some inconsistent findings, which could be spurious (chance) results (Abela, 2002; Abela & Payne, 2003; Metalsky et al., 1993).

To illustrate, Abela and Payne (2003) conducted a prospective study of children in Grades 3 and 7. Initially, the children completed measures of depressive symptoms, self-esteem, and depressogenic inferential styles. Six weeks later they completed measures of depressive symptoms and reported the occurrence of negative events. In line with the integrated theory of depression, depressogenic inferential styles interacted with negative events to predict increases in hopelessness depression in boys with low but not high self-esteem. But contrary to the integrative theory, depressogenic inferential styles interacted with negative events to predict increases in hopelessness depression symptoms in girls with high but not low self-esteem. Given that the latter finding was both unexpected and inconsistent with previous research, the authors suggested that this was probably a spurious result. ◆

*Peter Lewinsohn's model of depression inspired much of the research on interpersonal factors in depression. His longitudinal studies have contributed important information regarding the role of cognitive factors and social skills in the development of depression.*

family members (Coyne, 1999; Joiner, Coyne, & Blalock, 1999).

The interpersonal perspective has produced some interesting findings regarding factors that contribute to depression. Several research studies have demonstrated that depressed people do indeed have a negative impact on other people's moods and on their nonverbal behaviour (Joiner & Metalsky, 1995; Segrin & Abramson, 1994). In addition, depressed people have smaller and less supportive social networks than do people who are not depressed. They know fewer people, interact with them less often, and consider them to be less supportive. Family interactions are generally more negative and argumentative. Perhaps most importantly, these maladaptive patterns of interpersonal relationships are ongoing characteristics of the individual's behaviour that persist into periods of symptomatic remission. They are not evident only during active episodes of major depression.

*Response Styles and Gender* Another perspective on the development of depression has emphasized response styles, which represent a slightly different aspect of coping behaviour. This approach has been developed in an effort to explain gender differences in the frequency of depression. The manner in which a person responds to the onset of a depressed mood seems to influence the duration and the severity of the mood (Nolen-Hoeksema, 1994, 2000). Two different response styles have been emphasized in this work. Some people respond to feelings of depression by turning their attention inward, contemplating the causes and implications of their sadness. This is called a *ruminative style*. Writing in a diary or talking extensively with a friend about how one feels are indications of a ruminative style. Other people employ a *distracting style* to divert themselves from their unpleasant mood. They work on hobbies, play sports, or otherwise become involved in activities that draw their attention away from symptoms of depression.

The first hypothesis of the response styles model is that people who engage in ruminative responses have longer and more severe episodes of depression than do people who engage in distracting responses. The second hypothesis is that women are more likely to employ a ruminative style in response to depression, whereas men are more likely to employ a distracting style. Because the ruminative style leads to episodes of greater duration and intensity, women are more susceptible to depression than men are.

Research evidence provides support for both of the response style hypotheses. A ruminative response style is relatively stable over time and tends to be associated with longer and more severely depressed moods. Furthermore, women are more likely than men to exhibit a ruminative coping style in response to the onset of a depressed mood. Prospective data indicate that people with a ruminative response style are more likely to experience the onset of a depressive episode than are people who employ a distracting style. Rumination also predicts the severity of the depressive episode (Just & Alloy, 1997; Nolen-Hoeksema, 2000).

**Integration of Cognitive and Interpersonal Factors** The factors that we have considered in the preceding pages almost certainly work in combination rather than individually. We do not need to decide whether cognitive vulnerabilities are somehow more or less important than interpersonal behaviours because they are undoubtedly different sides of the same coin. The development of depression must be understood in terms of several stages: vulnerability, onset, and maintenance. Cognitive factors and interpersonal skills play an important role within each stage (Gotlib & Hammen, 1992; Hankin & Abramson, 2001; Ingram, Miranda, & Segal, 1998).

Vulnerability to depression is influenced by experiences during childhood, including events such as being repeatedly neglected or harshly criticized by parents. Negative ways of thinking about the world and dysfunctional interpersonal skills are presumably learned early in life (Ingram & Ritter, 2000). As the child grows up, the combination of biased cognitive schemas and deficits in interpersonal skills then affects his or her social environment in several ways: It increases the likelihood that the person will enter problematic relationships; it diminishes the person's ability to resolve conflict after it occurs; and it minimizes the person's ability to solicit support and assistance from other people (Hammen & Garber, 2001).

The onset of depression is most often triggered by life events and circumstances. The stressful life events that precipitate an episode frequently grow out of difficult personal and family relationships. Gender differences in empathy may be another factor that helps to explain why women are more likely than men to develop depression (Zahn-Waxler et al., 1991). Women are more likely to respond empathically to life events that happen to friends and family members. Men, in contrast, are affected primarily by things that happen directly to them. The impact of these experiences depends on the meanings that people assign to them. People become depressed when they interpret events in a way that diminishes their sense of self-worth.

Persistent interpersonal and cognitive problems also serve to maintain a depressed mood over an extended period of time and help it escalate to clinical proportions. Depressed people behave in ways that elicit negative reactions and rejection from others. For example, their low mood and lack of enthusiasm may mean that others are less likely to seek them out socially. They are also more likely to be acutely aware of criticism and rejection. Their negative cognitive schemas remain activated, accentuating the impact of stressful circumstances.

### Biological Factors

We have considered a number of social and psychological factors that contribute to the etiology of mood disorders. Biological factors are also influential in the regulation of mood. Various studies, including research by Kerry Jang and colleagues at the University of British Columbia suggest that genetic factors are somehow involved in unipolar and bipolar disorders (Jang et al., 2004). Evidence also suggests that hormonal abnormalities are regularly associated with depression, and that depression is associated with abnormalities in the activation of specific regions of the brain (Goldapple et al., 2004).

**Genetics** In Kraepelin's early writings on manic–depressive psychoses, he noted the presence of a "hereditary taint" in the majority of cases. This inference was based on his observation that many of the patients' relatives exhibited symptoms of the same disorder. Subsequent studies have confirmed his impression that genetic factors are involved in the transmission of mood disorders (Sullivan, Neale, & Kendler, 2000). They have also provided useful insights regarding the utility of the unipolar/bipolar distinction because bipolar disorders appear to be much more heritable than unipolar disorders.

***Family Studies*** If the development of mood disorders is influenced by genetic factors, these disorders should be more common among the biological relatives of people who are depressed than they are among the general population. First-degree relatives (siblings, parents, and children) of patients with mood disorders should be more vulnerable to the disorder because they share 50 percent of their genes with an affected individual. Several carefully controlled studies have confirmed this hypothesis. Family studies begin with the identification of an individual who has been diagnosed as having a mood disorder—the *proband*. Researchers obtain as much information as possible about the proband's relatives, through personal interviews, family informants, or mental health records. They use this information to decide whether each relative fits criteria for mood disorders. They can then compare the lifetime morbid risk among the patient's relatives with those figures already established for the general population.

Family studies indicate that unipolar and bipolar disorders run in families (Katz & McGuffin, 1993). This is illustrated in Figure 5–4, which summarizes data from several family studies of mood disorder. When these studies were conducted, the lifetime risk for major depressive disorder in the general population was estimated to be 5 percent (i.e., somewhat lower that today's 8 percent), whereas the lifetime risk for bipolar disorder was approximately 1 percent. With these figures in mind, consider the frequency of disorder among the relatives of unipolar probands in Figure 5–4. The risk for bipolar disorder among their relatives is close to that seen in the general population, but the risk for unipolar disorder is almost double. Among the relatives of bipolar probands, the risk for both bipolar and unipolar disorder is much higher than that seen in the general population. The combined risk for both types of mood disorder is about 19 percent, almost double the combined risk of 10 percent found among the relatives of unipolar probands. Both types of mood disorder are, therefore, markedly familial. Note that these findings support the conclusion that bipolar mood disorders should be considered a separate type of mood disorder because the risk for

**Family History for Mood Disorder**

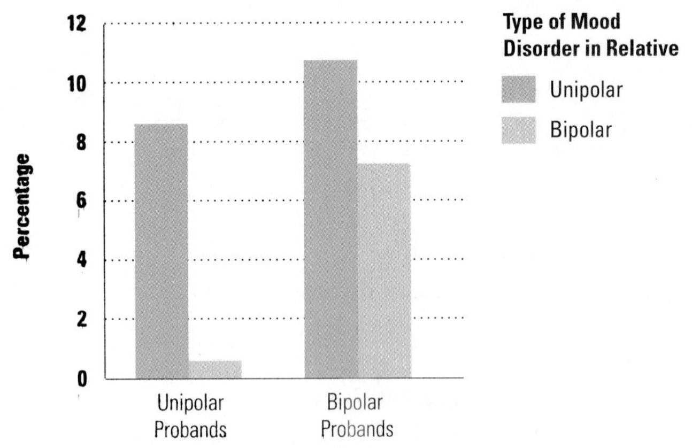


**FIGURE 5–4: Average morbid risk for mood disorders in first-degree relatives of unipolar and bipolar patients. (Based on 7 studies of relatives of unipolar probands and 12 studies of relatives of bipolar probands.)**

*Source:* R. Katz and P. McGuffin, 1993, The genetics of affective disorders. In D. Fowles (Ed.), *Progress in experimental personality and psychotherapy research.* New York: Springer.

bipolar disorder is elevated only among the families of probands who have bipolar disorders themselves (Winokur et al., 1995).

*Twin Studies* The comparison of monozygotic (MZ) and dizygotic (DZ) twin pairs provides a more stringent test of the possible influence of genetic factors (see Chapter 2). Several twin studies of mood disorders have reported higher concordance rates among MZ than among DZ twins (Bierut et al., 1999; Jang et al., 2004; Kendler & Prescott, 1999).

One classic study used national twin and psychiatric registers in Denmark to identify 110 pairs of same-sex twins in which at least one member was diagnosed as having a mood disorder (Bertelson et al., 1977). The concordance rates for bipolar disorders in MZ and DZ twins were .69 and .19, respectively. For unipolar disorders, concordance rates for MZ and DZ twins were .54 and .24, respectively. The fact that the concordance rates were significantly higher for MZ than for DZ twins indicates that genetic factors are involved in the transmission of both bipolar and unipolar mood disorders. The fact that the difference between the MZ and DZ rate was somewhat higher for bipolar than for unipolar disorders may suggest that genes play a more important role in bipolar disorders than in unipolar disorders. Similar patterns of MZ and DZ concordance rates have been reported subsequently from twin studies of mood disorders conducted in Sweden (Torgersen, 1986) and in England (McGuffin, Katz, Watkins, & Rutherford, 1996).

Twin studies also tell us that environmental factors influence the expression of a genetically determined vulnerability to depression. The best evidence for the influence of nongenetic factors is the concordance rates in MZ twins, which consistently fall short of 100 percent. If genes told the whole story, MZ twins would always be concordant. Mathematical analyses have been used to estimate the relative contributions of genetic and environmental events to the etiology of mood disorders. The results of these analyses are expressed in terms of **heritability**, which can range from 0 percent (meaning that genetic factors are not involved) to 100 percent (meaning that genetic factors alone are responsible for the development of the trait in question) (see Research Methods in Chapter 17). These analyses indicate that genetic factors are particularly influential in bipolar mood disorders, for which the heritability estimate is 80 percent. Genes and environment contribute about equally to the etiology of major depressive disorder, in which the heritability estimate is 52 percent. The genetic contribution may be relatively minor for dysthymia or neurotic depression, where the heritability estimate is only 10 percent (Katz & McGuffin, 1993).

*Genetic Risk and Sensitivity to Stress* How do genetic factors and stressful life events interact to bring about depression? The combined effects of genetic and environmental factors can be evaluated by incorporating the investigation of stressful life events into the traditional twin design. One important study that followed this procedure employed a large sample of female same-sex twins in a study of unipolar mood disorder (Kendler et al., 1995).

The sample was divided into four groups, based on levels of genetic risk:

- Highest genetic risk: women with a depressed MZ co-twin
- High genetic risk: women with a depressed DZ co-twin
- Low genetic risk: women with a nondepressed DZ co-twin
- Lowest genetic risk: women with a nondepressed MZ co-twin

These groups were further subdivided into those who had experienced a severe life event (death of a close relative, assault, serious marital problems, divorce/breakup) during the follow-up period and those who had not. The data from these comparisons are illustrated in Figure 5–5.

Two primary conclusions can be drawn from these results. First, severe life events increase the probability that a person will become depressed, even among those who presumably have a relatively low genetic risk for the disorder. Second, the magnitude of the environmental effect is much larger for people who are genetically predisposed to the development of unipolar depression. Therefore the effects of the environment and genetic factors are not independent. Genetic factors apparently control the person's sensitivity to environmental events.

**Factors Affecting Risk for Depression**

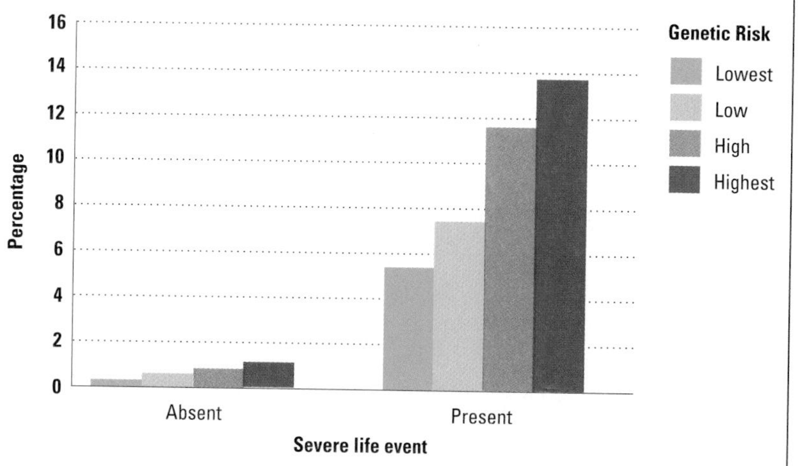


**FIGURE 5–5: Risk of onset of major depression as a function of genetic liability and the presence or absence of a severe life event.**

*Source:* Kendler et al., 1995, Stressful life events, genetic liability, and onset of an episode of major depression in women. *American Journal of Psychiatry, 152,* 833–842.

### *Mode of Transmission and Linkage Studies*

The family and twin studies indicate that genetic factors play an important role in the development of mood disorders. They have not, however, established the operation of a particular mode of inheritance. Most investigators view mood disorders as being polygenic—that is, they are influenced by several different genes.

In contrast, some investigators favour the single-locus model of inheritance, which holds that one gene at a particular location, or locus, on a particular chromosome is responsible for mood disorders. To support their arguments they have searched for evidence of chromosomal linkage between the locus of a known gene and the locus for a gene that is responsible for mood disorders. Two loci are said to be linked when they occupy positions that are close together on the same chromosome. Linkage is usually detected by examining the degree of association between two or more traits within specific families (see Research Methods in Chapter 14).

Linkage studies of mood disorders have focused on bipolar patients because genetic factors appear to be more influential in bipolar than in unipolar disorders, and because transmission within some specific families follows the pattern expected in a simple Mendelian dominant trait. With the introduction of new gene-mapping techniques, our knowledge in this area is expanding dramatically. Thus far, the results are mixed. Preliminary reports of linkage to regions on various chromosomes have turned out to be erroneous. And findings from one laboratory often fail to replicate when they are tested by other investigators. The most consistent results across different studies focus on chromosome 18. Genetic markers located in several different locations on chromosome 18 appear to be linked to the presence of bipolar mood disorder in certain families (McMahon et al., 2001; Souery et al., 2001).

The possibility of detecting linkage to known traits is very exciting. This knowledge might eventually enable mental health professionals to identify those individuals who are vulnerable to a disorder before the onset of overt symptoms. At the same time, however, two important cautions should be kept in mind with regard to genetic linkage studies. One problem involves genetic heterogeneity. Within the general population, there may be more than one locus that is capable of producing the trait in question. Mood disorders may be linked to one marker within a certain extended family and to an entirely different marker in another family. Second, it will not be possible to establish linkage unless a single gene of main effect is responsible for the development of a particular disorder. In the case of mood disorders, as we have seen, several genes might be responsible (Hyman & Moldin, 2001).

**The Neuroendocrine System** Various kinds of central nervous system events are associated with the connection between stressful life events and major depression. In the following sections, we will consider evidence regarding hormones and specific regions of the brain. These are the biological underpinnings of the social and psychological factors that we have described thus far. They are part of the process by which the brain communicates with the rest of the body and mobilizes activities in response to changes in the external environment.

The endocrine system plays an important role in regulating a person's response to stress. Endocrine glands, such as the pituitary, thyroid, and adrenal glands, are located at various sites throughout the body (see Figure 2–4). In response to signals from the brain, these glands secrete hormones into the bloodstream. One important pathway in the endocrine system that may be closely related to the etiology of mood disorders is called the *hypothalamic–pituitary–adrenal (HPA) axis*. When the person detects a threat in the environment, the hypothalamus signals the pituitary gland to secrete a hormone called ACTH, which in turn modulates secretion of hormones, such as cortisol, from the adrenal glands into the bloodstream. Increased levels of cortisol help the person to prepare to respond to the threat by increasing alertness and delivering more fuel to muscles while also decreasing interest in other activities that might interfere with self-protection (such as sleeping and eating). This system is illustrated in Figure 5–6.

Interest in the relation between mood disorders and the endocrine system was stimulated in part by descriptions of Cushing's syndrome, a disease associated with the adrenal glands that results in abnormally high concentrations of the hormone cortisol in the bloodstream (Sonino & Fava, 2001). Approximately half of all patients with Cushing's syndrome are also clinically depressed. After Cushing's syndrome is corrected, most patients also recover from their depression. This pattern suggests that abnormally

**Hormonal System Known as the HPA Axis**

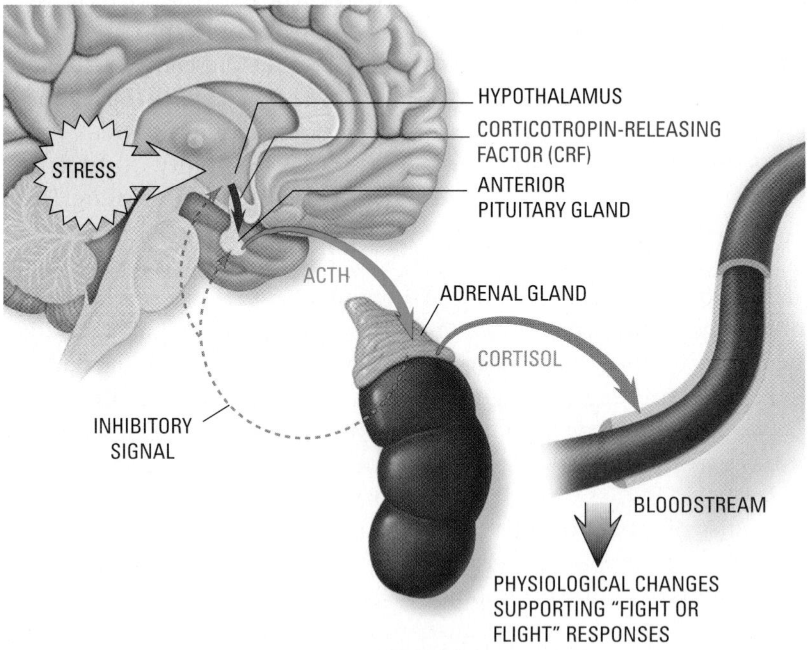


**Effects of CRF Application to Brain in Animals**

| DECREASED | INCREASED |
|---|---|
| Eating | Restless activity in familiar environments |
| Sleeping | Withdrawal in unfamiliar environments |
| Reproductive activity | |

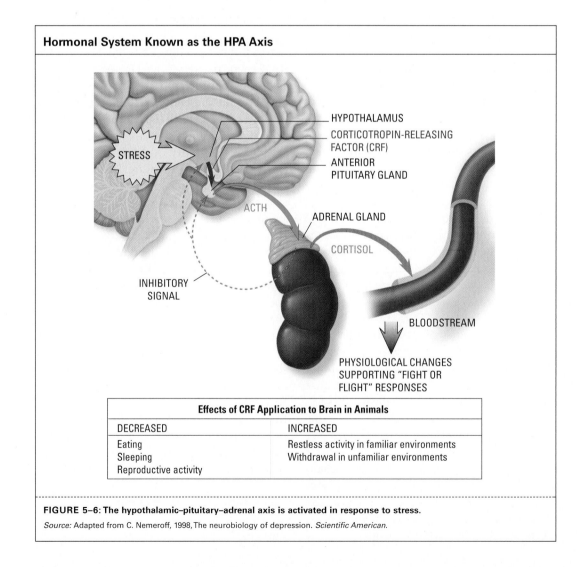

**FIGURE 5–6: The hypothalamic–pituitary–adrenal axis is activated in response to stress.**

*Source:* Adapted from C. Nemeroff, 1998, The neurobiology of depression. *Scientific American.*

high levels of cortisol may lead to the onset of depression (Plotsky et al., 1998).

An association between the HPA axis and depression is also indicated by evidence regarding the *dexamethasone suppression test (DST)*, which has been used extensively to study endocrine dysfunction in patients with mood disorders (Nemeroff, 1998). Dexamethasone is a potent synthetic hormone. People who have taken a test dose of dexamethasone normally show a suppression of cortisol secretion because the hypothalamus is fooled into thinking that there is already enough cortisol circulating in the system. Some depressed people show a different response: approximately half of depressed patients show a failure of suppression in response to the DST. After their symptoms have improved, most of these patients exhibit a normal response on the DST. This pattern is consistent with the hypothesis that a dysfunction of the HPA axis may be involved in the development or maintenance of clinical depression, at least for some people (Whybrow, 1997).

In what ways might endocrine problems be related to other etiological factors? Several possibilities exist. In terms of the specific link between the endocrine system and the central nervous system, overproduction of cortisol may lead to changes in brain structure and function. At a more general level, hormone regulation may provide a process through which stressful life events interact with a genetically determined predisposition to mood disorder. Stress causes the release of adrenal steroids, such as cortisol, and steroid hormones play an active role in regulating the expression of genes (Haskett, 1993).

**Brain Imaging Studies** The newest tools in the search for biological underpinnings of mood disorders are those that allow scientists to create detailed images of brain structures and to monitor ongoing brain functions in living patients (see Chapter 4 for a description of these procedures). The brain circuits that are involved in the experience and control of emotion are complex, centreing primarily on the limbic system and its connections to the prefrontal cortex and the anterior cingulate cortex. Brain imaging studies indicate that severe depression is often associated with abnormal patterns of activity as well as structural changes in various brain regions (Davidson et al., 2002). Some of these areas of the brain are illustrated in Figure 5–7. See Figure 2–3 for illustrations of the amygdala, hippocampus, and other structures involved in the limbic system.

Abnormal patterns of activation in regions of the prefrontal cortex (PFC) are often found in association with depression. This evidence has been collected using functional brain imaging procedures, such as PET and fMRI. Some areas show *decreased activity*, especially the dorsolateral prefrontal cortex on the left side of the brain. This area of the PFC is involved in planning that is guided by the anticipation of emotion. A person who has a deficit of this type might have motivational problems, such as an inability to work toward a pleasurable goal. Other areas of the PFC have been found to show *abnormally elevated* levels of activity in depressed people. These include the orbital PFC and the ventromedial PFC, areas of the brain that are important for determining a person's responses to reward and punishment. More specifically, the orbital PFC inhibits inappropriate behaviours and helps the person ignore immediate rewards while working toward long-term goals. The ventromedial PFC is involved in the experience of emotion and the process of assigning meaning to perceptions. Overactivity in these regions of the brain might be associated with the prolonged experience of negative emotion.

The anterior cingulate cortex (ACC) provides a connection between the functions of attention and emotion. It allows us to focus on subjective feelings and to consider the relation between our emotions and our behaviour. For example, the ACC is activated when a person has been frustrated in the pursuit of a goal, or when he or she experiences an emotion, such as sadness, in a situation where it was not expected. People suffering from major depressive disorder typically show decreased activation of the ACC (Davidson et al., 2002). A reduction in ACC activity might be reflected in a failure to appreciate the maladaptive nature of prolonged negative emotions and a reduced ability to engage in more adaptive behaviours that might help to resolve the person's problems.

The amygdala (see Figure 5–7), almond-sized nuclei near the tip of the hippocampus on each side of the brain, appear to be an important part of the neural circuit involved in emotion (Whybrow, 1997). They are extensively connected to the hypothalamus. This system is responsible for monitoring the emotional significance of information that is

**Areas of the Brain Involved in Depression**

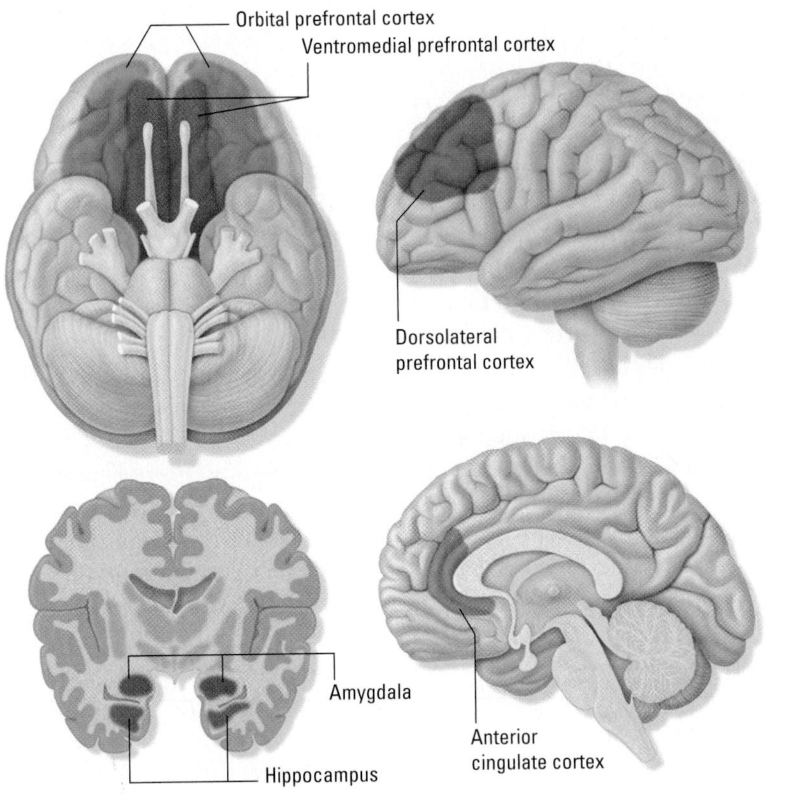


**FIGURE 5–7: Brain regions involved in emotion and mood disorders.**

*Source:* After R.J. Davidson et al., 2002, Depression: Perspectives from affective neuroscience. *Annual Review of Psychology, 53,* p. 575.

processed by the brain and regulating social interactions. Functional imaging studies have identified elevated levels of resting blood flow and glucose metabolism in the amygdala among patients with major depressive disorder and bipolar mood disorder (Drevets, 1999). Higher metabolism rates are associated with more severe levels of depression. Patients who respond positively to treatment show a normalization of amygdala metabolism (Goldapple et al., 2004; and see Chapter 3).

It is tempting to infer from this pattern that the increased activity reflected in images of the amygdala represents, at the neurochemical level of analysis, a reflection of the distorted cognitive functions that have been described by clinical psychologists in association with depression (Drevets & Raichle, 1998). Of course, this kind of speculation will need to be tested using more detailed research strategies in which specific cognitive processes are measured while brain activities are recorded in depressed and nondepressed people.

**Neurotransmitters** Communication and coordination of information within and between areas of the brain depend on neurotransmitters, chemicals that bridge the gaps between individual neurons (see Chapter 2). Over the past several decades, scientists have gathered a great deal of information concerning the neurochemical underpinnings of depression and mania (Healy, 1997; Whybrow, 1997). Our knowledge in this area began with the accidental discovery, during the 1950s, of several drugs that have the ability to alter people's moods. The development of antidepressant drugs stimulated research on several specific neurotransmitters that have been shown to be responsible for their effects. Most notable among these are serotonin, norepinephrine, and dopamine. Each neurotransmitter works in a broad set of pathways connecting fairly specific brain locations.

Serotonin is the chemical messenger that is enhanced by medications such as Prozac. It has a profound effect on a person's mood, with higher levels being associated with feelings of serenity and optimism. Serotonin also plays an important role in areas of the brain that regulate sleep and appetite. Figure 5–8 illustrates serotonin pathways, which include connections involving the amygdala, the hypothalamus, and areas of the cortex. The beneficial effects of drugs like Prozac (see the section on treatment of depression) provide the most convincing evidence for the argument that some type of malfunction in serotonin pathways is involved in the etiology of depression.

We know that the relationship between neurotransmitters and depression is complex, and the specific mechanisms are not well understood (Healy, 1997; Nestler, 1998). There may be more than 100 different neurotransmitters in the central nervous system, and each neurotransmitter is associated with several types of postsynaptic receptors. It seems unlikely that a heterogeneous disorder like depression, which involves a dysregulation of many cognitive and emotional functions, will be linked to only one type of chemical messenger or only one loop in the brain's circuitry. Current theories tend to emphasize the interactive effects of several neurotransmitter systems, including serotonin, norepinephrine, dopamine, and neuropeptides (short chains of amino acids that exist in the brain and appear to modulate the activity of the classic neurotransmitters) (Nemeroff, 1998; Whybrow, 1997).

### The Interaction of Social, Psychological, and Biological Factors

We have considered a variety of social, psychological, and biological factors that appear to be related to the etiology of mood disorders. How can these factors be combined or integrated? Do we need to choose among them, advocating either a radical biological or psychological perspective? Some clinicians have, in fact, argued that some mood disorders are

**Serotonin Pathways**

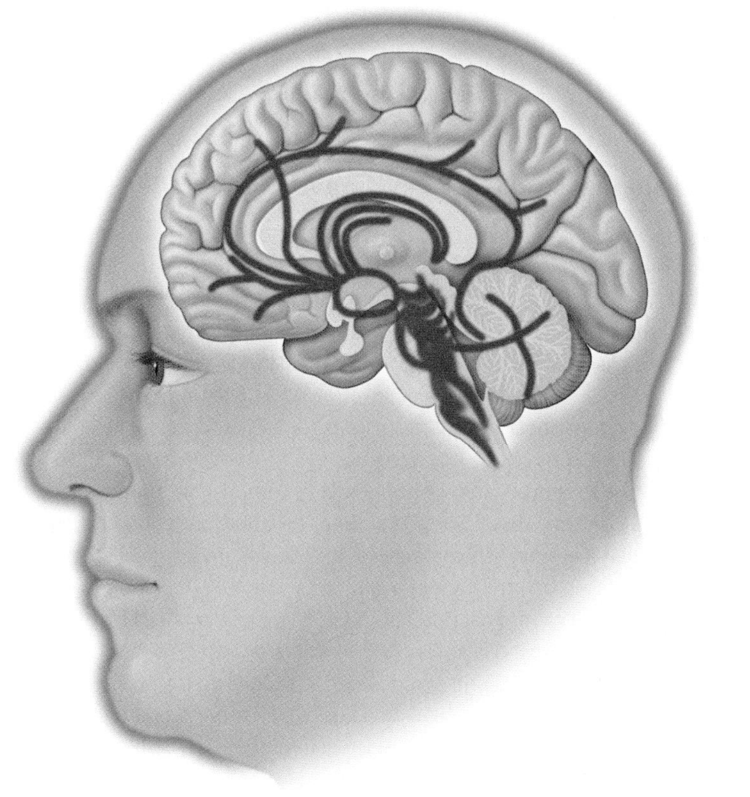

**FIGURE 5–8: Areas of the brain connected by paths involving the neurotransmitter serotonin.**

*Source:* After R. Carter, 1998, *Mapping the mind,* p. 29. Berkeley, CA: University of California Press.

*Rats wearing "water wings" in a forced swim test. One (left) shows vigorous motor activity while the other (right) shows passive behaviour (floating without limb movement) that is considered an analogue for depression.*

caused by biological factors and others are caused by psychological factors (that is, different causes for different people). We favour the systems view, which holds that mood disorders are typically produced by a combination of interacting systems, with each representing a different level of analysis.

One type of research that illustrates this point has employed an animal model of depression (see Research Methods). When laboratory animals are exposed to uncontrollable stress (such as a 15-minute forced swim in cold water from which they cannot escape), they frequently exhibit behavioural symptoms that are similar to (yet obviously not the same as) those seen in depressed humans. The animals develop deficits in motor activity, sleep, and eating behaviours. This type of stress-induced depression in laboratory rats produces various temporary effects on neurotransmitters, including changes in the concentration of norepinephrine, serotonin, and dopamine in the specific regions of the limbic system and the frontal cortex. Rats that show these neurochemical consequences following exposure to stress exhibit signs of depression. If the neurotransmitters are not depleted, the rats do not appear to be depressed. Furthermore, administering antidepressant drugs to these animals has been shown to reverse or prevent the behavioural effects of uncontrollable stress. Selective breeding experiments have been able to produce subtypes of rats that differ in their response to behavioural challenges (such as the forced swim test), as well as in their response to antidepressant medication (Connor, Kelly, & Leonard, 1997; Weiss, Cierpial, & West, 1998).

# RESEARCH METHODS

## Analogue Studies of Psychopathology

Many questions about the etiology of psychopathology cannot be addressed using highly controlled laboratory studies with human subjects. For example, does prolonged exposure to uncontrollable stress cause anxiety disorders? This kind of issue has been addressed using *correlational studies* with people who have the disorders in question, but experiments on these issues cannot be done with human subjects. For important ethical reasons, investigators cannot randomly assign people to endure conditions that are hypothesized to produce full-blown disorders like major depression. The best alternative is often to study a condition that is similar, or analogous, to the clinical disorder in question. Investigations of this type are called **analogue studies** because they focus on behaviours that resemble mental disorders~~or~~ isolated features of mental disorders~~th~~at appear in the natural environment.

Many analogue studies depend on the use of *animal models* of psychopathology, which have provided important insights regarding the etiology of conditions such as anxiety, depression, and schizophrenia (Mineka & Zinbarg, 1991). Some clinicians have argued that mental disorders like depression cannot be modelled in a laboratory setting using animals as subjects. Cognitive symptoms~~su~~ch as Beck's depressive triad~~ca~~nnot be measured with animals. Do monkeys feel guilty? Can rats experience hopelessness or suicidal ideas? But these symptoms are not necessarily the most central features of the disorder. Particular somatic and behavioural symptoms are characteristic of depression. Many of these aspects of mood disorder are seen in animals. The value of any analogue study hinges, in large part, on the extent to which the analogue condition is similar to the actual clinical disorder. Some models are more compelling than others.

Another type of analogue study is concerned with human behaviours that resemble psychopathology. For example, many investigators have studied university students who produce high scores on paper-and-pencil measures of depression or anxiety. The rationale for these studies hinges on the notion that these people experience problems that are similar to mood or anxiety disorders. According to York University psychologist Gordon Flett, there is a good deal of evidence that there is a continuum of severity of depression, from mild to severe (Flett et al., 1997).

*continued*

*cont.*

Similarly, there appears to be a continuum of severity between mild to severe anxiety. Therefore analogue studies may be useful because they enable us to investigate the mild-to-moderate end of the continuum.

An example of analogue research is Adam Radomsky's experiments on compulsive checking and memory confidence, conducted at Concordia University. People with obsessiveeompulsive disorder (OCD) often engage in compulsive checking; they might check and re-check switches on electrical appliances or stove knobs, to ensure that it has been properly turned off. People with OCD often distrust their memories, and this apparently causes them to repeatedly check. Using an analogue sample of university students, Radomsky tested the hypothesis that repeated checking actually causes memory distrust. Students were asked to repeatedly check either that a stove had been switched off or that a sink tap had been turned off (by repeatedly turning the item on and off). Then all students were asked to check that a stove was off. Students who had repeatedly checked the stove, compared to the comparison (sink) group, had lower confidence in their memory of leaving the stove off (Radomsky et al., 2003).

Analogue studies have an important advantage over other types of research design in psychopathology: They can employ an experimental procedure. Therefore the investigator can draw strong inferences about cause and effect. The main concern with analogue studies is whether the results of a particular investigation can be generalized to situations outside the laboratory. If a particular set of circumstances produced a set of maladaptive behaviours in the laboratory, is it reasonable to assume that similar mechanisms produce the actual clinical disorder in the natural environment?

In actual practice, questions about the etiology of disorders like OCD or depression will probably depend on converging evidence generated from the use of many different research designs. Theories should be tested using studies of clinical patients as well as investigations based on analogue conditions. The combination of results from these complementary research methods has provided important information regarding several disorders that are discussed in this book. ◆

This animal model illustrates the need to consider the interaction between biological and psychological phenomena. The data on stress-induced depression in rats suggest that neurochemical processes may be reactions to environmental events, such as uncontrollable stress in rats or severe life events in people. Psychological and biological explanations of depression are complementary views of the same process, differing primarily in terms of their level of analysis.

## Treatment

Several procedures, both psychosocial and biological, have proved to be useful in the treatment of mood disorders. We have already mentioned that antidepressant medications are effective with many depressed patients. Current psychological interventions emphasize helping the depressed person become more aware of maladaptive cognitive patterns and teaching interpersonal skills. In the following pages we will examine some of the more prominent contemporary approaches to the treatment of unipolar and bipolar mood disorders, as well as the research evidence on their usefulness.

### Unipolar Disorders

Most psychological approaches to the treatment of depression owe some debt to psychodynamic procedures and Freud's emphasis on the importance of interpersonal relationships. According to Freud's view, the primary goal of therapy should be to help the patient understand and express the hostility and frustration that are being directed against the self. These negative emotions are presumably rooted in dysfunctional relationships with other people. Freud also placed considerable emphasis on the apparently irrational beliefs that depressed people hold about themselves and their world. These cognitive factors are also emphasized by cognitive therapists.

**Cognitive Therapy** Cognitive therapy has been developed and promoted by Aaron Beck and his colleagues (e.g., Beck et al., 1979; Clark, Beck, & Alford, 1999). His model assumes that emotional dysfunction is influenced by the negative ways in which people interpret events in their environments and the things that they say to themselves about those experiences. Based on the assumption that depression will be relieved if these maladaptive schemas are changed, cognitive therapists focus on helping their patients replace self-defeating thoughts with more rational self-statements.

A specific example may help illustrate this process. Consider the case of Cathy, a depressed lawyer. Cathy focused a great deal of attention on relatively minor negative events

***Aaron Beck** has developed an influential cognitive theory of depression, emphasizing the importance of distorted ways of thinking about the self. He has pioneered the use of cognitive therapy for the treatment of depression.*

at work, blaming herself for anything other than a perfect performance. Her therapist helped her to recognize that she was engaging in a pattern of cognitive distortion that Beck has labelled "selective abstraction." Taking a detail out of context, she would invariably ignore those aspects of her performance that refuted the conclusion that she was professionally incompetent. Her therapist helped her overcome these tendencies by teaching her to question her conclusions and to develop more objective ways of evaluating her experiences.

Cathy also tended to think about herself in absolute and unvarying terms. During the course of therapy, she learned to recognize this pattern and to substitute more flexible self-statements. Instead of saying to herself, "I am a hopeless introvert and will never be able to change," she learned to substitute, "I am less comfortable in social situations than some other people, but I can learn to be more confident."

Although Beck's approach to treatment emphasizes the importance of cognitive events, it shares many features with behavioural approaches to intervention. Cognitive therapists are active and directive in their interactions with clients, and they focus most of their attention on their clients' current experience. They also assume that people have conscious access to cognitive events: Our thinking may not always be rational, but we can discuss private thoughts and feelings. Another important aspect of Beck's approach to treatment, and a characteristic that it shares with the behavioural perspective, is a serious commitment to the

*"I think the dosage needs adjusting. I'm not nearly as happy as the people in the ads."*

©The New Yorker Collection. Barbara Smaller from cartoonbank.com. Used with permission. All Rights Reserved.

empirical evaluation of the efficacy of treatment programs. Several studies have found that cognitive therapy is effective in the treatment of nonpsychotic, unipolar depression (Sanderson & McGinn, 2001; Strunk & DeRubeis, 2001). Two direct comparisons of cognitive therapy and behavioural therapy in the treatment of major depressive disorder have found that both types of treatment are effective, with neither being superior to the other (Hollon et al., 1993).

**Interpersonal Therapy** Interpersonal therapy is another contemporary approach to the psychological treatment of depression (Klerman et al., 1984; Weissman, Markowitz, & Klerman, 2000). It is focused primarily on current relationships, especially those involving family members. The therapist helps the patient develop a better understanding of the interpersonal problems that presumably give rise to depression and attempts to improve the patient's relationships with other people by building communication and problem-solving skills. Therapy sessions often include nondirective discussions of social difficulties and unexpressed or unacknowledged negative emotions, as well as role playing to practise specific social skills.

**Antidepressant Medications** The types of medication that are used most frequently in the treatment of unipolar mood disorders fall into four general categories: selective serotonin reuptake inhibitors (SSRIs), tricyclics (TCAs), monoamine oxidase inhibitors (MAOIs), and "other," more recently developed drugs. Among patients who respond positively to antidepressant medication, improvement is typically evident within 4 to 6 weeks, and the current episode is often resolved within 12 weeks (DePaulo & Horvitz, 2002; Schulberg et al., 1999). Medication is usually continued for at least 6 to 12 months after the patient has entered remission in order to reduce the chance of relapse.

*Selective Serotonin Reuptake Inhibitors* The **selective serotonin reuptake inhibitors (SSRIs)** were developed in the early 1980s and are now the most frequently used form of antidepressant medication, accounting for more than 80 percent of all prescriptions written for that purpose (Hirschfeld, 2001). Unlike the original forms of antidepressant medication,

**TABLE 5–6 Medications for Unipolar Mood Disorders**

| Drug Class | Generic Name (Trade Name) | Mode of Action |
|---|---|---|
| Selective serotonin reuptake inhibitors (SSRI) | Fluoxetine (Prozac)<br>Paroxetine (Paxil)<br>Sertraline (Zoloft)<br>Citalopram (Celexa)<br>Fluvoxamine (Luvox) | Block 5-HT reuptake |
| Tricyclic antidepressants (TCA) | Amitriptyline (Elavil)<br>Clomipramine (Anafranil)<br>Imipramine (Tofranil) | Block reuptake of 5-HT and norepinephrine |
| Monoamine oxidase inhibitors (MAOI) | Phenelzine (Nardil) | Deactivate enzyme that breaks down monoamines |
| Other antidepressants | Trazodone (Desyrel) | Block 5-HT reuptake and block 5-HT receptors |
| | Buproprion (Wellbutrin) | Block norepinephrine and dopamine reuptake |
| | Venlafaxine (Effexor) | Block reuptake of 5-HT and norepinephrine |

*Note:* 5-HT is serotonin.

which were discovered by accident, SSRIs were synthesized in the laboratories of pharmaceutical companies on the basis of theoretical speculation regarding the role of serotonin in the etiology of mood disorders. There are many specific types of SSRIs (see Table 5–6). Controlled outcome studies indicate that Prozac and other SSRIs are about as effective as traditional forms of antidepressant medication (Kroenke et al., 2001; Masand & Gupta, 1999).

The SSRIs inhibit the reuptake of serotonin into the presynaptic nerve ending and thus promote neurotransmission in serotonin pathways by increasing the amount of serotonin in the synaptic cleft. They are called "selective" because they seem to have little if any effect on the uptake of norepinephrine and dopamine. Nevertheless, the SSRIs are not entirely selective, in the sense that some of them do block reuptake of other neurotransmitters. They also vary in the potency with which they block serotonin reuptake. Their effectiveness in treating depression does not seem to be directly related to either the extent to which a particular SSRI is selective with regard to serotonin or its potency in blocking serotonin reuptake (Healy, 1997).

The SSRIs are typically considered to be easier to use than TCAs or MAOIs. They also have fewer side effects (such as constipation and drowsiness), and they are less dangerous in the event of an overdose. This does not mean, of course, that they are completely without side effects. Some patients experience nausea, headaches, and sleep disturbances, but these symptoms are usually mild and short term. The most troublesome side effects associated with SSRIs are sexual dysfunction and weight gain (Sussman & Ginsberg, 1998). The rate of decreased sexual desire and orgasmic dysfunction may be as high as 50 percent among both men and women taking SSRIs. Weight changes in response to SSRIs vary in relation to length of treatment. Many patients experience an initial weight loss, but most regain this weight after six months. Those who continue to take the medication may gain an average of 9 kg.

A further concern is Health Canada (and similar agencies in other countries) had a warning in 2004 about the safety and efficacy of SSRIs for children and adolescents. As noted in a recent report by University of British Columbia psychiatrist Jane Garland (2004), there is evidence suggesting that these medications may not be effective in children and adolescents, and may be associated with an increased risk of suicide. Health Canada advises that patients (or their caregivers) should consult the treating physician to confirm that the benefits of the drug still outweigh its potential risks.

*Tricyclics* The **tricyclics (TCAs)**, such as imipramine (Tofranil) and amitriptyline (Elavil), have been in relatively widespread use since the 1950s, but their use has declined since the introduction of the SSRIs because they have more side effects. Common reactions include blurred vision, constipation, drowsiness, and a drop in blood pressure. The TCAs affect brain functions by blocking the uptake of neurotransmitters (especially norepinephrine) from the synapse. Several controlled double-blind studies indicate that TCAs benefit many depressed patients, although improvements might not be evident until two or three weeks after the beginning of treatment (Friedman & Kocsis, 1996; Schatzberg, 1999). The several different kinds of tricyclic medication vary in potency and side effects, but they are generally equal in terms of effectiveness. Comparisons of TCAs and SSRIs indicate that they are approximately equal in terms of success rates, with positive responses being shown by 50 to 60 percent of depressed patients (Schulberg et al., 1999).

*Monoamine Oxidase Inhibitors* The antidepressant effects of **monoamine oxidase inhibitors (MAOIs)**, such as phenelzine (Nardil), were discovered at about the same time as those of the tricyclic drugs. These drugs have not been used as extensively as tricyclics, however, primarily for two reasons. First, patients who use MAOIs and also consume foods containing large amounts of the compound tyramine, such as cheese and chocolate, often develop high blood pressure. Second, some early empirical evaluations of antidepressant medications suggest that MAOIs are not as effective as tricyclics.

More recent studies have shown that MAOIs are indeed useful in the treatment of depressed patients (Friedman & Kocsis, 1996). They can be used safely when the patient avoids foods such as cheese, beer, and red wine. In addition, MAOIs are now widely used in the treatment of certain anxiety disorders, especially agoraphobia and panic attacks (see Chapter 6).

**The Efficacy of Psychotherapy and Medication** Considerable time and energy have been devoted to the evaluation of psychological and pharmacological treatments for depression. The bottom line in this lengthy debate—based on extensive reviews of the research literature—is that cognitive therapy and antidepressant medication are both effective forms of treatment for people who suffer from unipolar depression (DeRubeis et al., 1999). This is true for people with major depressive disorder as well as dysthymia. Interpersonal psychotherapy is also effective. Moreover, research by Kate Harkness (Queen's University) and colleagues has shown that interpersonal psychotherapy can prevent the relapse of depression, apparently by decreasing the potency of stressful life events (Harkness et al., 2002). Cognitive therapy also reduces the risk of depression relapse (Dozois & Dobson, 2002).

In practice, many experts recommend treatment with a combination of psychotherapy and medication (Boland & Keller, 2001; Kupfer & Frank, 2001). Recent efforts to evaluate and compare the effects of medication and psychotherapy have focused on the treatment of depression in primary care settings (Schulberg et al., 1999). Investigators have focused on patients in primary care because most depressed people who receive treatment are seen by their family physician rather than a mental health specialist. Special efforts are being made to increase family physicians' ability to recognize and treat mood disorders. Randomized trials indicate that medication and psychotherapy are approximately equivalent in primary care settings. For example, following 11 weeks of treatment, one study found that 64 percent of patients had recovered from an episode of depression, and the recovery rate was the same regardless of whether the patients had been assigned to receive an SSRI or problem-solving therapy (Barrett et al., 2001). Both groups showed more improvement than patients who received a placebo treatment. Thus, either form of treatment is a reasonable choice for the initial treatment of unipolar depression.

## Bipolar Disorders

Treatment of bipolar mood disorders has also focused on the combined use of medication and psychotherapy. A variety of mood stabilizing drugs are employed with bipolar patients. They are used to help people recover from episodes of mania and depression and also on a long-term maintenance basis to reduce the frequency of future episodes (Mitchell & Malhi, 2002). Antidepressant medications are sometimes used, usually in combination with a mood stabilizer, for the treatment of bipolar patients (Kupfer et al., 2001). Clinicians must be cautious, however, because antidepressants can sometimes trigger a switch from depression into a hypomanic or manic episode. We do not have extensive evidence regarding the effectiveness and safety of long-term antidepressant medication for bipolar disorders (Ghaemi et al., 2001).

*Lithium* In 1949, the Australian psychiatrist John Cade discovered that the salt *lithium carbonate* was effective in treating bipolar mood disorders. An extensive literature indicates that lithium carbonate is an effective form of treatment in the alleviation of manic episodes, and it remains the first choice for treating bipolar disorders. It is also useful in the treatment of bipolar patients who are experiencing a depressive episode. Perhaps most importantly, bipolar patients who continue to take lithium between episodes are significantly less likely to experience a relapse (Kleindienst & Greil, 2000; Tondo et al., 2001).

Unfortunately, there are also some limitations associated with the use of lithium. Many bipolar patients, perhaps 40 percent, do not improve when they take lithium (Mendlewicz, Souery, & Rivelli, 1999). Nonresponse is particularly common among rapid cycling patients, those who exhibit a mixture of manic and depressed symptoms, and those with comorbid alcohol abuse. Compliance with medication is also a frequent problem; at least half the people for whom lithium is prescribed either fail to take it regularly or stop taking it against their psychiatrist's advice. The main reasons that patients give for discontinuing lithium involve its negative side effects, including nausea, memory problems, weight gain, and impaired coordination.

*Anticonvulsant Medications* Often, bipolar patients who do not respond to lithium are prescribed anticonvulsant drugs, particularly carbamazepine (Tegretol) or valproic acid (Depakene) (Walden et al., 1998). Outcome data suggest that slightly more than 50 percent of bipolar patients respond positively to these drugs. Like lithium, carbamazepine and valproic acid can be useful in reducing the frequency and severity of relapse, and they can be used to treat acute manic episodes. Valproic acid may be more effective than lithium for the treatment of rapid cycling bipolar patients and those with mixed symptoms of mania and depression in a single episode (Gadde & Krishnan, 1997). Common side effects include gastrointestinal distress (nausea, vomiting, and diarrhea) and sedation.

*Psychotherapy* Although medication is the most important method of treatment for bipolar disorders, psychotherapy can be an effective supplement to biological intervention. Both cognitive therapy and interpersonal therapy have been adapted for use with bipolar disorders. Cognitive therapy can address the patient's reactions to stressful life events as well as his or her reservations about taking medication (Craighead & Miklowitz, 2000).

A variation on interpersonal therapy, known as "interpersonal and social rhythm therapy" has been developed for use with bipolar patients (Frank, Swartz, & Kupfer, 2000). It is based on the recognition that a repeated episode of either mania or depression is often precipitated by one of the following factors: stressful life events, disruptions in social rhythms (the times of day in which the person works, sleeps, and so on), and failure to take medication. Special emphasis is placed on monitoring the interaction between symptoms (especially the onset of hypomanic or manic episodes) and social interactions. Therapists help patients learn to lead more orderly lives, especially with regard to sleep–wake cycles, and to resolve interpersonal problems effectively. Regulation of sleep and work patterns is also important. This therapy program is employed in combination with the long-term use of mood stabilizing medication.

Support for the use of psychological treatments for bipolar mood disorders hinges, in part, on clinical intuition and compelling testimonials from grateful patients. Consider, for example, the following personal statement from Kay Jamison (1995), whose descriptions of her own experience with bipolar disorder were cited earlier in this chapter:

> At this point in my existence, I cannot imagine leading a normal life without both taking lithium and having had the benefits of psychotherapy. Lithium

> prevents my seductive but disastrous highs, diminishes my depressions . . . and makes psychotherapy possible. But, ineffably, psychotherapy heals. It makes some sense of the confusion, reins in the terrifying thoughts and feelings, returns some control and hope and possibility of learning from it all. (pp. 88–89)

Unfortunately, enthusiastic endorsements based on personal experience do not constitute strong evidence in favour of a treatment procedure (see Research Methods in Chapter 1). Some preliminary evidence does suggest that the combination of psychotherapy and medication may be more beneficial than medication alone, but the data are not conclusive (Callahan & Bauer, 1999; Frank et al., 1999; Solomon et al., 1995). Recent research by Patelis-Siotis and colleagues (2001) at Hamilton Psychiatric Hospital, suggests that cognitive-behavioural therapy is a useful adjunct to medication treatment of bipolar disorder. There is an obvious need for more extensive research on the effectiveness of various types of psychosocial treatment for bipolar mood disorders.

*Electroconvulsive therapy is an effective form of treatment for severely depressed patients. It should be considered for people who do not improve with psychotherapy or antidepressant medication.*

Although mood disorders are very common and respond well to treatment, they often go unrecognized. Most depressed people do not receive adequate treatment.

### Electroconvulsive Therapy

The procedure known as electroconvulsive therapy (or ECT) has proved beneficial for many patients suffering from unipolar or bipolar mood disorders (see Chapter 3 for a review of the background of ECT). Electroconvulsive therapy is typically administered in an inpatient setting and consists of a series of treatments given three times a week for two to seven weeks (Abrams, 1997; Fink, 2001). Many patients show a dramatic improvement after six to eight sessions, but some require more. In current clinical practice, muscle relaxants are always administered before a patient receives ECT. This procedure has eliminated bone fractures and dislocations that were unfortunate side effects of techniques used many years ago. The electrodes can be placed either bilaterally (on both sides of the head) or unilaterally (at the front and back of the skull on one side of the patient's head). Unilateral placement on the nondominant hemisphere (the right side of the head for right-handed people) may minimize the amount of postseizure memory impairment, but it may also be less effective (Kellner, 1997).

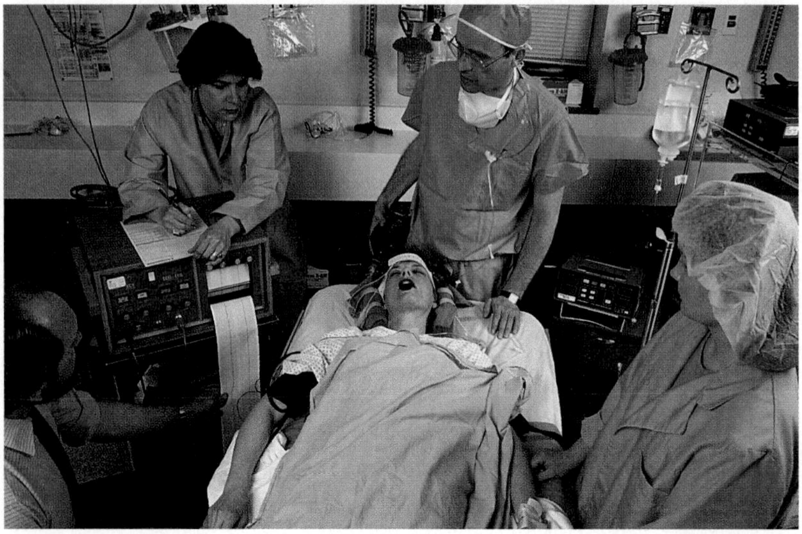

Although how ECT works remains largely a mystery (Nobler & Sackeim, 1998), empirical studies have demonstrated that it is an effective form of treatment for severely depressed patients (for example, Gagne et al., 2000). Reservations regarding the use of ECT centre around widely publicized, although infrequent, cases of pervasive and persistent memory loss. Reviews of the research evidence indicate that ECT-induced changes in memory and other cognitive functions are almost always short-lived, and ECT does not induce loss of neurons or other changes in brain structure (Calev et al., 1995).

No one denies that ECT is an invasive procedure that should usually be reserved for patients who have been resistant to other forms of intervention, such as medication and cognitive therapy. Nevertheless, it remains a viable and legitimate alternative for some severely depressed patients, especially those who are so suicidal that they require constant supervision to prevent them from harming themselves. Rapid cycling bipolar patients and depressed patients with psychotic symptoms may also be more responsive to ECT than to medication (Fink, 2001). As always, the risks of treatment must be carefully weighed against those associated with allowing the disorder to follow its natural course.

### Seasonal Mood Disorders

The observation that changes in seasons can help bring on episodes of mood disorder leads to the relatively obvious implication that some patients might respond to manipulations of the natural environment. For centuries, physicians have prescribed changes in climate for their depressed clients (Wehr, 1989). The prominent French psychiatrist Jean Esquirol (1772–1840) reportedly advised a patient whose depression appeared when the days grew shorter to move from Belgium to Italy during the winter.

Modern light therapy was introduced in the 1980s (Rosenthal, 1998). Typical treatment involves exposure to bright (2500 lux), broad-spectrum light for one to two hours every day. The time of day during which the person is exposed to the light may not matter, but some patients respond best to early morning treatments. Some patients also respond positively to shorter periods (30 minutes) of high-intensity (10 000 lux) light (Hill, 1992). This high-intensity light is roughly equivalent to the amount of light that would be generated by a 750-watt spotlight focused on a surface 1 square metre in area. The light source—most often a rectangular box containing fluorescent ceiling fixtures—must be placed close (90 cm) to the patient at eye level. Improvement in the person's mood is often seen within two to five days.

Outcome studies have found that light therapy is an effective form of treatment for seasonal affective disorder (Neuhaus & Rosenthal, 1997; Wesson & Levitt, 1998). The most difficult issue in evaluating this type of treatment has been to control for placebo effects. It is not possible to conduct a true double-blind study because patients know that they are being exposed to light, and they often believe that light will be helpful. One study used a comparison between treatment with a bright white light (supposedly the treatment that would be most effective) and treatment with a dimmer red light (the placebo condition) (Wileman et al., 2001). Improvement rates were approximately equivalent in both groups, suggesting that light therapy might not be as effective as some clinicians have suggested. Nevertheless, the overall state of the research evidence is mixed, and many patients with seasonal affective disorders do respond well to light therapy. It is still considered by many clinicians to be a useful approach to this disorder. It is not exactly clear why or how light therapy works, but the process may help the body to normalize circadian rhythms, which regulate processes such as hormone secretion (Whybrow, 1997).

## Suicide

To the outside observer, Dr. Killinger-Johnson seemed to have it all. She was considered to be elegant and attractive, had a successful professional career, and had a prosperous husband, a baby she loved, and no debts or other obvious stressors. Why would such a successful person choose to end her own life? Suicide is an extremely personal, private, and complicated act. We may never know exactly why Dr. Killinger-Johnson killed herself and her baby. Perplexing cases such as this illustrate the challenges faced by clinicians, who must try to understand suicide so that they can more effectively prevent it.

Friends, neighbours, and professional colleagues were stunned by Dr. Killinger-Johnson's suicide. None had noticed that she

### BRIEF CASE STUDY

**Postpartum Suicide**

Dr. Suzanne Killinger-Johnson, a successful psychotherapist and well-to-do daughter of two distinguished Toronto doctors, killed herself and her six-month-old baby Cuyler by jumping in front of an oncoming subway train. The night before, Suzanne was clutching her baby in a Toronto subway station. She had been standing by the platform for quite some time. Transit officials became concerned, so they called the police. Officers spoke with Suzanne and she left. About 90 minutes later a similar thing happened at another subway station. This time the police drove her home, leaving her in the care of her husband and relatives. During rush hour the next morning Suzanne slipped out of the house with her baby and drove her silver Mercedes sport utility vehicle to yet another subway station. Commuters watched in horror as Suzanne dived in front of an oncoming train, clutching her baby to her chest. The infant was killed instantly. Suzanne died several days later. (*Sources:* CBC News, August 12, 2000; Myers, 2000; Robertson & Cairns, 2000). ◆

was depressed. Nor were there any indications of substance abuse or other mental disorders. In this respect, her situation was unusual, although it is possible that signs of depression or other mental disorders might have been identified if she had been assessed by a mental health professional. Although many people who commit suicide do not appear to be depressed, and psychopathology doesn't explain all suicidal behaviour, there is undoubtedly a strong relationship between depression and self-destructive acts. The available evidence suggests that at least 50 percent of all suicides occur as a result of, or in the context of, a primary mood disorder (Jamison, 1999). Moreover, the risk of completed suicide is much higher among people who are clinically depressed than it is among people in the general population. Follow-up studies consistently indicate that 15 to 20 percent of all patients with mood disorders will eventually kill themselves (Clark & Goebel-Fabbri, 1999). Thus it seems reasonable to conclude that there is a relatively close link between depression and suicide.

### Classification of Suicide

Common sense tells us that suicide takes many forms. DSM-IV-TR does not address this issue; rather, it lists *suicidal ideation* (thoughts of suicide) only as a symptom of mood disorders. Clinicians and social scientists have proposed a number of systems for classifying subtypes of suicide, based on speculation regarding different motives for ending one's own life. Therefore, in contrast to the principles that were followed in creating DSM-IV-TR, classification systems for suicide are based on *etiological* theories rather than descriptive factors.

The most influential system for classifying suicide was originally proposed in 1897 by Emile Durkheim (1858–1917), a French sociologist who is one of the most important figures in the history of sociology (Coser, 1977). In order to appreciate the nature of this system, you must understand Durkheim's approach to studying social problems. Durkheim was interested in "social facts," such as religious groups and political parties, rather than the psychological or biological features of particular individuals. His scientific studies were aimed at clarifying the social context in which human problems appear, and they were based on the assumption that human passions and ambition are controlled by the moral and social structures of society. One of his most important scientific endeavours was a comparison of suicide rates among various religious and occupational groups.

In his book *Suicide*, Durkheim (1897/1951) argued that the rate of suicide within a group or a society would increase if levels of social integration and regulation are either excessively low or excessively high. He identified four different types of suicide, which are distinguished by the social circumstances in which the person is living:

- *Egoistic suicide* (diminished integration) occurs when people become relatively detached from society and when they feel that their existence is meaningless. Egoistic suicide is presumably more common among groups such as people who have been divorced and people who are suffering from mental disorders. The predominant emotions associated with egoistic suicide are depression and apathy.
- *Altruistic suicide* (excessive integration) occurs when the rules of the social group dictate that the person must sacrifice his or her own life for the sake of others. One example is the former practice in some First Nations tribes of elderly persons voluntarily going off by themselves to die after they felt they had become a burden to others.
- *Anomic suicide* (diminished regulation) occurs following a sudden breakdown in social order or a disruption of the norms that govern people's behaviour. Anomic suicide explains increased suicide rates that occur following an economic or political crisis or among people who are adjusting to the unexpected loss of a social or occupational role. The typical feelings associated with anomie (a term coined by Durkheim, which literally means "without a name") are anger, disappointment, and exasperation.
- *Fatalistic suicide* (excessive regulation) occurs when the circumstances under which a person lives become unbearable. A slave, for example, might choose to commit suicide in order to escape from the horrible nature of his or her existence. This type of suicide was mentioned only briefly by Durkheim, who thought that it was extremely uncommon.

Durkheim believed that egoistic and anomic suicide were the most common types of suicide in Western industrial societies. Although he distinguished between these two dominant forms, he recognized that they were interconnected and could operate together. Some people may become victims of both diminished integration and ineffective regulation.

Durkheim's system for classifying types of suicide has remained influential. It does have some limitations, however. For example, it does not explain why one person commits suicide while other members of the same group do not. All the people in the group are subject to the same social structures. Another problem with Durkheim's system is that the different types of suicide overlap and may, in some cases, be difficult to distinguish. If the system is used to describe individual cases of suicide, such as that of Dr. Killinger-Johnson, would clinicians be likely to agree on these subtypes? We are not aware of any attempts to evaluate the reliability of such judgments, but it might be quite low.

## Epidemiology of Suicide

Suicide is one of the leading causes of death in both Canadian men and women from adolescence to middle age. In 1998, for example, nearly 4000 Canadians took their lives (Health Canada, 2002a). Disturbingly, suicide rates among Canadian adolescents have doubled over the past 30 years (Stewart et al., 2000). Suicide accounts for 24 percent of all deaths among 15- to 24-year-olds, and 16 percent among 25- to 44-year-olds (Health Canada, 2002a). Suicide rates vary as a function of many factors, including age, gender, and socioeconomic status (see, for example, Figure 5–9).

Suicide attempts are much more common than are completed suicides. The ratio of attempts to completed suicides in the general population is approximately 10 to 1; among adolescents, the ratio is closer to 100 to 1 (Hendin, 1995). There are important gender differences in rates of attempted suicide versus rates of completed suicide. Although more women than men, by a ratio of 1.5 to 1, attempt suicide, men are four times more likely to actually kill themselves (Health Canada, 2002a). This is partly because men tend to choose quicker acting and more lethal means, such as firearms or hanging, whereas women are more likely to overdose on pills (Health Canada, 2002a).

## Etiology of Suicide

Many factors contribute to suicidal behaviour. In the following discussion, we consider some of the variables that operate at the level of the individual person—psychological and biological considerations—and are associated with suicidal behaviour. We also summarize some contemporary research on social factors that are related to suicide.

**Psychological Factors** Many experts have argued that psychological events lie at the core of suicidal behaviour (Schneidman, 1996). Social factors may set the stage for self-destructive acts, but events taking place within the person's mind are most immediately responsible for determining whether a particular individual will attempt to end his or her own life. Prominent among these events are intense emotional distress and hopelessness. An outline of several psychological variables that are commonly associated with suicide is presented in Further Thoughts.

Schneidman (1996) views suicide as an escape from unbearable psychological pain. According to his perspective, psychological pain is produced by prolonged frustration of psychological needs. Personality theorists have identified a number of fundamental human

**Suicide in Canada**

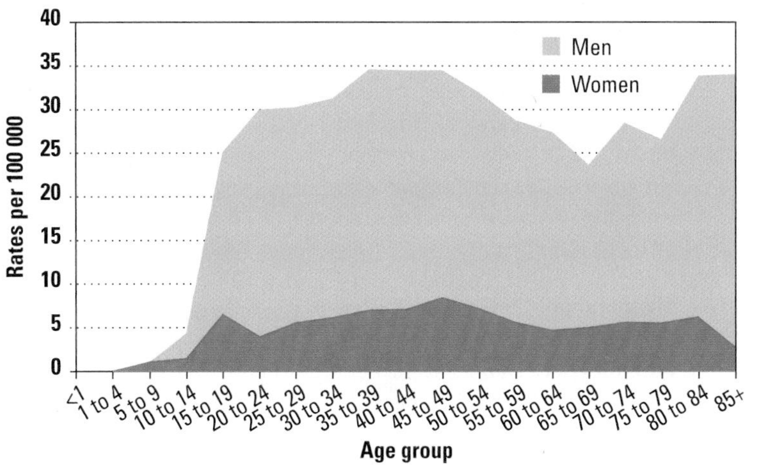


**FIGURE 5–9: Suicide rates according to age and gender.**

*Source:* Health Canada, 2002a, *A report on mental illness in Canada.* Ottawa: Author. © Reproduced with the permission of the Minister of Public Works and Government Services of Canada, 2004.

## Further Thoughts Common Elements of Suicide

Most people who kill themselves are suffering from some form of mental disorder, such as depression, substance dependence, or schizophrenia (Jamison, 1999). No single explanation can account for all self-destructive behaviour. Edwin Schneidman (1996), a clinical psychologist who is a leading authority on suicide, described 10 characteristics commonly associated with completed suicide. Schneidman's list includes features that occur most frequently and may help us understand many cases of suicide:

1. **The common purpose of suicide is to seek a solution**. Suicide is not a pointless or random act. To people who think about ending their own lives, suicide represents an answer to an otherwise insoluble problem or a way out of some unbearable dilemma. It is a choice that is somehow preferable to another set of dreaded circumstances, emotional distress, or disability, which the person fears more than death.

   Attraction to suicide as a potential solution may be increased by a family history of similar behaviour. If someone else whom the person admired or cared for has committed suicide, then the person is more likely to do so.

2. **The common goal of suicide is cessation of consciousness**. People who commit suicide seek the end of conscious experience, which to them has become an endless stream of distressing thoughts with which they are preoccupied. Suicide offers oblivion.

3. **The common stimulus (or information input) in suicide is unbearable psychological pain**. Excruciating negative emotions—including shame, guilt, anger, fear, and sadness—frequently serve as the foundation for self-destructive behaviour. These emotions may arise from any number of sources.

4. **The common stressor in suicide is frustrated psychological needs**. People with high standards and expectations are especially vulnerable to ideas of suicide when progress toward these goals is suddenly frustrated. People who attribute failure or disappointment to their own shortcomings may come to view themselves as worthless, incompetent, or unlovable. Family turmoil is an especially important source of frustration to adolescents. Occupational and interpersonal difficulties frequently precipitate suicide among adults. For example, rates of suicide increase during periods of high unemployment (Yang, Stack, & Lester, 1992).

5. **The common emotion in suicide is hopelessness–helplessness**. A pervasive sense of hopelessness, defined in terms of pessimistic expectations about the future, is even more important than other forms of negative emotion, such as anger and depression, in predicting suicidal behaviour (Weishaar & Beck, 1992). The suicidal person is convinced that absolutely nothing can be done to improve his or her situation; no one can help.

6. **The common cognitive state in suicide is ambivalence**. Most people who contemplate suicide, including those who eventually kill themselves, have ambivalent feelings about this decision. They are sincere in their desire to die, but they simultaneously wish that they could find another way out of their dilemma.

7. **The common perceptual state in suicide is constriction**. Suicidal thoughts and plans are frequently associated with a rigid and narrow pattern of cognitive activity that is analogous to tunnel vision. The suicidal person is temporarily unable or unwilling to engage in effective problem-solving behaviours and may see his or her options in extreme, all-or-nothing terms. As Schneidman points out, slogans such as "death before dishonour" may have a certain emotional appeal, but they do not provide a sensible basis for making decisions about how to lead one's life.

8. **The common action in suicide is escape**. Suicide provides a definitive way to escape from intolerable circumstances, which include painful self-awareness (Baumeister, 1990).

9. **The common interpersonal act in suicide is communication of intention**. One of the most harmful myths about suicide is the notion that people who really want to kill themselves don't talk about it. Most people who commit suicide have told other people about their plans. Many have made previous suicidal gestures. Schneidman estimates that in at least 80 percent of committed suicides, the people provide verbal or behavioural clues that indicate clearly their lethal intentions.

10. **The common pattern in suicide is consistency of lifelong styles**. During crises that precipitate suicidal thoughts, people generally employ the same coping responses that they have used throughout their lives. For example, people who have refused to ask for help in the past are likely to persist in that pattern, increasing their sense of isolation. ◆

needs or motives (Maslow, 1970)—needs for achievement, esteem, belongingness, and safety. Frustration in meeting these needs can lead to prolonged and intense negative emotional states, such as shame, guilt, anger, and grief. Most people who experience these emotions do not attempt suicide. But for some people, suicide appears to offer a solution or a way to end their intolerable distress.

**Biological Factors** Studies of the connection between neurotransmitters and suicide have focused primarily on reduced levels of serotonin, which might be related to poor impulse control as well as increased levels of violent and aggressive behaviour (Asberg, 1994; Lopez et al., 1997). Analogue studies with animals have found that lesions resulting in serotonin dysfunction lead to increases in aggression and failure to inhibit responses that were previously punished. Dysregulation of serotonin systems has been found among people who attempted suicide, and it has also been found among people who have shown other types of violent and aggressive behaviour, such as criminals convicted of murder (Garza-Trevino, 1994).

Serotonin dysfunction has also been linked to depressive disorders. It seems reasonable to wonder whether that connection might explain the findings regarding serotonin and suicide. People who attempt suicide may exhibit abnormal serotonin levels because they are depressed. That might be a reasonable interpretation for some of the data, but the results of other studies indicate that the link to suicide is more direct. Consider, for example, a follow-up study of 92 people who were hospitalized following a suicide attempt (Nordstrom et al., 1994). All of the participants met the criteria for a major depressive disorder. The investigators measured levels of a particular serotonin by-product, 5-HIAA (5-hydroxyindoleacetic acid), in each patient's cerebrospinal fluid (CSF) shortly after admission to the hospital. The patients were divided into two groups on the basis of these measurements: those below the median for CSF 5-HIAA and those above the median. In the first year after their attempted suicide, 11 of the 92 patients committed suicide, and 8 of the 11 who died were from the low CSF 5-HIAA group. This result suggests that biochemical measures might be useful for predicting risk for suicide within groups of depressed patients.

Twin studies and adoption studies have found that genetic factors are involved in the transmission of major mood disorders. Do genes contribute to the risk for suicide indirectly by increasing the risk for mental disorders, such as depression, schizophrenia, and substance abuse? Is there a more direct contribution of genetic factors to self-destructive behaviour? The answer appears to be yes (Roy, Rylander, & Sarchiapone, 1997). One important investigation examined cases of depression and suicide in a group of large Amish families over a period of 100 years (Egeland & Sussex, 1985). Each family included at least one person who suffered from a mood disorder. Within this sample, there were 26 documented instances of suicide. The vast majority of the suicides (92 percent) occurred in people who had been diagnosed as having a mood disorder. Furthermore, most of the suicides occurred in a small subset of four families. The investigators suggested that this pattern might be best explained by the existence of a genetic factor that is associated with suicidal behaviour, independent of risk for major depression. This factor might be associated with impulsive personality characteristics. Suicide appears to be an especially likely outcome when a person inherits a predisposition to both psychopathology and impulsive or violent behaviour.

**Social Factors** Durkheim (1897/1951) believed that suicide rates had increased during the nineteenth century because of an erosion of the influence of traditional sources of social integration and regulation, such as the church and the family. Durkheim's own data and subsequent research by other investigators have provided support for the notion that social structures do represent one important consideration with regard to suicide. For example, Pescosolido and Georgianna (1989) found that religious affiliation is significantly related to suicide rates; lowest rates were found among Catholics and Evangelical Baptists, whereas higher rates were found among mainstream Protestant denominations, such as Episcopalians, Presbyterians, and Lutherans. This pattern can be explained in terms of social networks. People who belong to Catholic and conservative Protestant groups are more likely to participate

*Actress Margaux Hemingway killed herself in 1996 at the age of 41 by taking an overdose of a sedative. She was the fifth person in her family to commit suicide. Her grandfather, Ernest Hemingway, had committed suicide 35 years earlier.*

in the various rituals and activities of the church community. These networks become an important source of emotional support during difficult times, protecting the person from the potential influence of self-destructive impulses.

Social policies regulating access to firearms, especially handguns, also have an effect on suicide rates. Guns are a particularly lethal method of suicide, but are less likely to be used as a method of suicide in regions with highly restrictive gun laws (Loftin et al., 1991; Miller & Hemenway, 1999). Of course, people who have definitely decided to end their own lives inevitably find a way to accomplish that goal, but many people who attempt suicide are ambivalent in their intent. Many attempts are made impulsively. Ready access to guns increases the chance that a person who does engage in an impulsive suicide attempt will die, because gunshot wounds are very likely to be fatal.

Prominent television and newspaper coverage of suicidal deaths, especially those of well-known celebrities, can have disastrous consequences by unintentionally encouraging other people to kill themselves (Martin, 1998). Young people are especially vulnerable to this effect, which is sometimes called *contagious suicide* or a suicide cluster. There was, for example, an increase in rates of suicide in the months immediately after Marilyn Monroe committed suicide. Imitation of this sort may represent a misdirected attempt to lend meaning to a person's life through association with the death of a celebrity. It might also be inspired by the attention that results with increased media coverage that invariably follows in the wake of multiple or sequential suicides. Descriptions of someone else's death may simply reduce some people's resistance to impulsive action.

## Treatment of Suicidal People

Efforts to avoid the tragic consequences of suicidal behaviour can be organized at several levels. One approach would focus on social structures that affect an entire society. Durkheim's theory of suicide, for example, indicates that the social structure of a society influences suicide rates. The social factors that we have just considered suggest some changes that could be made in contemporary Western societies in an effort to reduce the frequency of suicide. For example, more restrictive gun control laws might minimize access to the most lethal method of self-destruction. More cautious reporting by the media of suicidal deaths might reduce the probability of cluster suicides. These are, of course, controversial decisions, in which many other considerations play an important role. The media, for example, are motivated to report stories in a way that will maximize their popularity with the public. And many people oppose gun control legislation for reasons that have nothing to do with suicide rates. Therefore it may be unrealistic to hope that these measures, aimed broadly at the level of an entire population, would be implemented widely. Most treatment programs that are concerned with suicidal behaviour have been directed toward individual persons and their families.

**Crisis Centres and Hot Lines** Many communities have established crisis centres and telephone hot lines to provide support for people who are distraught and contemplating suicide. The purpose of these programs is typically viewed in terms of suicide prevention. Sponsored by various agencies, including community mental health centres, hospitals, and religious groups, these services are often staffed by nonprofessionals, frequently volunteers. They offer 24-hour-a-day access to people who have been trained to provide verbal support for those who are in the midst of a crisis and who may have nowhere else to turn. Rather than provide ongoing treatment, most crisis centres and hot lines help the person through the immediate crisis and then refer him or her to mental health professionals.

Public and professional enthusiasm for suicide prevention centres peaked during the 1960s and 1970s. Unfortunately, data that were reported in the 1970s and 1980s did not support optimistic claims that these centres were "saving lives." Empirical studies showed that suicide rates do not differ in comparisons of similar communities that either have or do not have suicide prevention programs. Availability of crisis centres and hot lines does not seem to reduce suicide rates in communities (Frankish, 1994; Hendin, 1995; Lester, 1997).

Why don't hot lines reduce suicide rates? The challenges faced by these programs are enormous. Think about the characteristics of people who are driven to contemplate suicide. They are often socially isolated, feeling hopeless, and unable to consider alternative solutions. Many people with the most lethal suicidal ideation will not call a hot line or visit a drop-in crisis centre. In fact, most clients of suicide prevention centres are young women; most suicides are committed by elderly men. The primary problem faced by suicide prevention programs is this: The people who they are trying to serve are, by definition, very difficult to reach.

It might be hard to justify the continued existence of crisis centres and hot lines if they are viewed solely in terms of suicide prevention. Only a small proportion of people who call hot lines are seriously suicidal. Most are people who are experiencing serious difficulties and who need to talk to someone about those problems. The value of contact with these individuals should not be underestimated. Crisis centres and hot lines provide support and assistance to very large numbers of people in distress. These services are undoubtedly valuable in their own right, even if serious questions remain about their impact on suicide rates.

### Psychotherapy with Suicidal Clients

Psychological interventions with people who are suicidal can take many forms. These include all the standard approaches to psychotherapy, such as cognitive, behavioural, psychoanalytic,

*Elizabeth Shin was a 19-year-old student at MIT when she committed suicide. Her parents filed a lawsuit against the university, claiming that school officials could have prevented her death. This case involves several very difficult issues, including confidentiality (whether therapists can tell parents about such problems).*

and family therapy. These methods address underlying problems that have set the stage for the person's current problems. Additional treatment guidelines are also dictated by the threat of suicide. The following recommendations cover special considerations that are particularly important when clients have expressed a serious intent to harm themselves (adapted from Berman & Jobes, 1994):

1. *Reduce lethality.* The most important task is to reduce the person's experience of psychological pain (see Further Thoughts on p. 180), from which the person is seeking escape. At a more concrete level, this also involves reducing access to means that could be used to commit suicide, such as guns and pills.
2. *Negotiate agreements.* Therapists frequently ask clients who have threatened to kill themselves to sign a contract, in which the client agrees to postpone self-destructive behaviour for at least a short period of time. This kind of written agreement typically includes the client's consent to contact the therapist directly before engaging in any lethal actions. Of course, these agreements can be broken, but they may provide brakes to inhibit impulsive actions. The process of negotiating the agreement can also help the

clinician to determine the severity of the client's suicidal intentions.

3. *Provide support.* It is often useful to make concrete arrangements for social support during a suicidal crisis. Friends and family members are alerted and asked to be available so that the person is not alone. The presence of others allows the person to discuss his or her problems (if he or she chooses to do so) and also provides supervision that may inhibit dangerous behaviours.
4. *Replace tunnel vision with a broader perspective.* People who are seriously contemplating suicide are typically unable to consider alternative solutions to their problems (see Further Thoughts on p. 180). Death may strike others as an irrational choice, but to people contemplating suicide, in the midst of the crisis, it seems perfectly logical. The therapist must help potential suicide victims develop or recover a more flexible and adaptive pattern of problem solving.

**Medication** Treatment of mental disorders, especially depression and schizophrenia, is usually the most important element of intervention with suicidal clients. The use of various types of medication is often an important part of these treatment efforts. Antidepressant drugs are frequently given to patients who are clinically depressed, and antipsychotic medication is useful with those who meet the diagnostic criteria for schizophrenia (see Chapter 13).

Considerable attention has been devoted recently to the use of selective serotonin reuptake inhibitors (SSRIs), such as fluvoxamine (Luvox) and fluoxetine (Prozac), because of the link between suicide and serotonin dysregulation. Extensive clinical reports suggest that the use of SSRIs in treating depression actually lowers suicide rates (Banki, 1995; Wagner, Zaborny, & Grey, 1994). It should also be noted, however, that placebo-controlled outcome studies have not addressed this specific question. Furthermore, cases have been reported in which treatment with SSRIs has been followed by the development of new suicidal ideation (King, Segman, & Anderson, 1994). This pattern suggests that the relation between serotonin and suicide is neither direct nor simple and that caution is warranted in the use of SSRIs in treating suicidal clients.

**Involuntary Hospitalization** People who appear to be on the brink of committing suicide are often hospitalized, either with their permission or involuntarily (see Chapter 18 for a discussion of the legal issues involved in this process). The primary consideration in such cases is safety. In many cases, commitment to a hospital may be the best way to prevent people from harming themselves. The person's behaviour can be monitored continuously, access to methods of harming oneself can be minimized (though perhaps not entirely eliminated), and various types of treatment can be provided by the hospital's professional staff.

# Summary

**Mood disorders** are defined in terms of emotional, cognitive, behavioural, and **somatic symptoms**. In addition to a feeling of pervasive despair or gloom, people experiencing an episode of major **depression** are likely to show a variety of symptoms, such as diminished interest in their normal activities, changes in appetite and sleep, fatigue, and problems in concentration. In contrast, a person in a manic episode feels elated and energetic. Manic patients also exhibit related symptoms, such as inflated self-esteem, rapid speech, and poor judgment.

DSM-IV-TR lists two major categories of mood disorders. People with **unipolar mood disorders** experience only episodes of depression. People with **bipolar mood disorders** experience episodes of **mania**, which are most often interspersed with episodes of depression. There are two specific types of unipolar mood disorder in DSM-IV-TR. Major depressive disorder is diagnosed if the person has experienced at least one episode of major depression without any periods of mania. **Dysthymia** is a less severe, chronic form of depression in which the person has been depressed for at least two years without a major depressive episode.

A person who has experienced at least one manic episode would receive a diagnosis of bipolar I disorder, regardless of whether he or she has ever had an episode of depression. One episode of major depression combined with evidence of at least one period of **hypomania** would qualify for a diagnosis of bipolar II disorder. **Cyclothymia** is a less severe, chronic form of bipolar mood disorder in which the person has experienced numerous periods of hypomania interspersed with periods of depressed mood.

The validity of the distinction between unipolar and bipolar mood disorders is supported by several types of evidence. Bipolar disorders tend to have an earlier age of onset and a worse prognosis than unipolar disorders.

Mood disorders are among the most common forms of psychopathology. Epidemiological studies have found that the lifetime risk for major depressive disorder is approximately 5 percent and the lifetime risk for dysthymic disorder is approximately 3 percent. Rates for both of these disorders are two or three times higher among women than among men. The lifetime risk for bipolar I disorder is close to 1 percent. Women and men are equally likely to develop bipolar mood disorder. The prevalence of depression appears to be increasing, with people born after World War II being more likely to become clinically depressed than people born in earlier generations.

The etiology of mood disorders can be traced to the combined effects of social, psychological, and biological factors. Social factors include primarily the influence of stressful life events, especially severe losses that are associated with significant people or significant roles. Some studies show that people who are clinically depressed help to create some of the stressful events that they experience, especially those involving interpersonal relationships.

Two types of psychological factors play an important role in the development of mood disorders: cognitive responses to disappointment and failure and interpersonal skills. Cognitive theories are primarily concerned with the way in which depressed people experience a severe event. Beck's **schema** model places principal emphasis on cognitive distortions or the erroneous ways in which some people think about themselves and their environments. The **hopelessness** model holds that depression is associated with the expectation that desirable events will not occur or aversive events will occur regardless of what the person does. Furthermore, people will be more likely to become depressed if they attribute negative events to internal, stable, global factors.

Interpersonal theories focus on the ways in which individuals respond to people and events in their environments. Depressed people behave in ways that have a negative impact on other people. In this way they contribute to the stressful nature of their social environment. Coping behaviours may help to explain gender differences in the prevalence of unipolar depression. A ruminative style, in which the person's attention is turned inward, may be associated with longer and more severe episodes of depression. Women may be more likely than men to employ a ruminative style of response to the onset of a depressed mood.

Family and twin studies indicate that genetic factors play an important role in the etiology of both unipolar and bipolar mood disorders. They also indicate that genetic factors may play a stronger role in the development of bipolar than unipolar disorders. Genes may contribute to the development of depression directly through an effect on the central nervous system and indirectly by influencing the person's sensitivity to environmental events, such as severe stress. The mode of genetic transmission in mood disorders has not been identified. Linkage studies may help to find these pathways and could allow clinical scientists to identify individuals who are genetically predisposed to depression.

Neurochemical messengers in the brain also play a role in the regulation of mood and the etiology of mood disorders. Current thinking is focused on serotonin, norepinephrine, and dopamine, although many other neurotransmitter substances may also be involved in depression. Evidence regarding the long-term effects of antidepressant medications points to the importance of sensitivity and density of postsynaptic receptors as well as the interactive effects of multiple neurotransmitter systems.

Several types of psychological and biological treatment have been shown to be effective for mood disorders. Two types of psychotherapy, cognitive therapy and interpersonal therapy, are beneficial for unipolar and dysthymic patients. Three types of antidepressant medication are also useful in the treatment of major depressive disorder: **selective serotonin reuptake inhibitors**, **tricyclic antidepressants**, and **monoamine oxidase inhibitors**. Medication and psychotherapy are frequently used together. Outcome studies do not consistently favour either psychological or psychopharmacologic treatment.

Three other types of biological treatment are beneficial for specific types of mood disorder. Lithium carbonate and certain anticonvulsant drugs are useful for patients with bipolar mood disorders. Electroconvulsive therapy has been shown to be effective in the treatment of certain depressed patients, and it may be especially useful for patients who are severely suicidal or have failed to respond to other types of treatment. Light therapy seems to be effective for managing seasonal affective disorders.

People commit suicide for many different reasons. Most people who kill themselves are suffering some form of mental disorder, such as depression, substance abuse, or schizophrenia. For some people, suicide represents an escape from unbearable negative emotions or painful self-awareness, which are often the result of frustrated psychological needs. Suicidal ideas are often accompanied by narrow patterns of perception and cognitive activity that make suicide seem like a reasonable solution to an otherwise unbearable dilemma. Serotonin dysfunction and genetic factors seem to contribute to the etiology of suicidal behaviour. Social factors that have been studied in relation to suicide include religious affiliation, gun control laws, and media coverage of suicidal deaths. Efforts to prevent suicide include the use of hot lines and crisis centres, as well as the provision of psychotherapy and medication for people who are willing or able to seek professional treatment.

# Critical Thinking

1. Women are more likely to become depressed at some point during their lives than men are. Can you think of any explanations for this difference? Some data from epidemiological studies suggest that depression is more prevalent among young adults than among elderly persons. Can you explain this fact?
2. Imagine that you're talking to a psychiatrist. She tells you that depression is nothing more than a biochemical imbalance in the brain because certain medications are effective with depressed people. Is she right? What else do we know about the etiology of depression? Suppose a drug changes a neurotransmitter. Does taking that drug eliminate the cause of depression? How do biological factors (neurotransmitters and neurohormones) interact with stress to cause depression? What is the connection?
3. Contemporary psychological views of depression focus on cognitive factors and interpersonal behaviours. What role do each of these variables play in different stages of the disorder (that is, in creating vulnerability to the original onset of depression and in maintaining the symptoms of depression after the disorder has appeared)?
4. What are the relative risks and benefits of (a) medication and (b) cognitive therapy in the treatment of depression? If you were going to be treated, which would seem more useful to you? Imagine that somebody close to you is severely depressed and is threatening suicide. Medication doesn't work. The psychiatrist recommends electroconvulsive therapy but wants your consent. What would you decide? Why?

# Key Terms

**affect** 139
**analogue study** 170
**bipolar mood disorder** 140
**clinical depression** 139
**cyclothymia** 147
**depressed mood** 139
**depression** 140
**dysphoric** 142
**dysthymia** 146
**emotion** 139
**euphoria** 140
**hopelessness** 159
**hypomania** 147
**mania** 140
**melancholia** 148
**monoamine oxidase inhibitors (MAOIs)** 174
**mood** 139
**mood disorders** 140
**psychomotor retardation** 144
**relapse** 149
**remission** 149
**schema** 159
**seasonal affective disorder** 149
**selective serotonin reuptake inhibitors (SSRIs)** 172
**somatic symptoms** 144
**tricyclics (TCAs)** 174
**unipolar mood disorder** 140

# 6 Anxiety Disorders

Overview

Typical Symptoms and Associated Features

Classification

Epidemiology

Etiological Considerations and Research

Treatment

**Why is a panic attack sometimes called a "false alarm"?**

**What is the expected long-term outcome for people with anxiety disorders?**

**Is there a unique causal pathway for each type of anxiety disorder?**

**Do psychological treatments have any advantages over medication for treatment of anxiety?**

Fear and anxiety play important roles in all of our lives. Fear helps us avoid danger in our immediate environment. Have you ever jumped out of the street to avoid a car that was unexpectedly rushing toward you? Or run away from an animal with a menacing growl? The sudden burst of fear that you experienced allowed you to react immediately. Anxiety helps us anticipate and prepare for important events in the future. Remember when you called someone for the first time, performed at a musical recital, or spoke up in class? If you felt anxious in the time leading up to this event, you may have also noticed that your heart was pounding, your mouth was dry, and you were breathing faster. These are some of the physical signs of anxiety. Anxiety may be unpleasant, but it is often adaptive; we would have trouble organizing our lives if it was eliminated completely. Unfortunately, anxiety can also disrupt our lives. There are many ways in which anxiety can become maladaptive. It is often a question of degree rather than kind. We can worry too much, feel anxious too often, or be afraid at inappropriate times. In this chapter we will explore many of the important distinctions that psychologists make among phenomena such as fear, anxiety, worry, and panic. We will discuss the ways in which these experiences can become maladaptive and the ways in which the problems can be treated. In the next chapter, we will consider one other specific form of anxiety, known as posttraumatic stress disorder.

## Overview

Taken together, the various forms of anxiety disorders—including phobias, obsessions, compulsions, and extreme worry—represent the most common type of abnormal behaviour. Studies in Canada and the United States indicate that 12 to 17 percent of adults have at least one type of anxiety disorder in any given year (Kessler et al., 1994; Offord et al., 1996). Anxiety disorders are among the most common psychiatric disorders (APA, 2000), and are associated with significant social and occupational impairment. These disorders are costly not only in terms of personal suffering, but also in terms of lost productivity and health-care costs (e.g., Greenberg et al., 1999; Taylor, 2000). Anxiety disorders lead to significant social and occupational impairment.

Anxiety disorders share several important similarities with mood disorders. From a descriptive point of view, both categories are defined in terms of negative emotional responses. Feelings such as guilt, worry, and anger frequently accompany anxiety and depression. There is also considerable overlap between anxiety disorders and major mood disorders such as depression. Many patients who are anxious are also depressed, and, similarly, many patients who are depressed are also anxious.

The close relationship between symptoms of anxiety and those for depression suggests that these disorders may share common etiological features. In fact, clinicians and researchers have focused on similar considerations when investigating these disorders.

Stressful life events seem to play a role in the onset of both depression and anxiety. Cognitive factors are also important in both types of problems. From a biological point of view, certain brain regions and a number of neurotransmitters are involved in the etiology of anxiety disorders as well as mood disorders.

The following case study illustrates the kinds of symptoms that are included under the heading of anxiety disorders. You will probably notice the overlap among different features of anxiety disorders, including panic, worry, avoidance, and a variety of alarming physical sensations. This narrative was written by Johanna Schneller (1988), a freelance writer who has been treated for panic disorder. *Agoraphobia* refers to an exaggerated fear of being in situations from which escape might be difficult, such as being caught in a traffic jam on a bridge or in a tunnel.

Johanna's description of her problems raises a number of important questions, to which we will return later in the chapter. Was it just a coincidence that her first attack occurred shortly after the difficult experience of moving to a new city, starting a new job, and finding a new apartment? Could the stress of those experiences have contributed to the onset of her disorder? Was there a pattern to her attacks? Why did she feel safe in some situations and not in others? She mentions feeling out of control, as if she were responsible for her attacks. Could she really bring on another attack by remembering one from the past?

## CASE STUDY **A Writer's Panic Disorder with Agoraphobia**

Three years have passed since my first panic attack struck, but even now I can close my eyes and see the small supermarket where it happened. I can feel the shoppers in their heavy coats jostling me with their plastic baskets, and once again my stomach starts to drop away.

It was November. I had just moved cities and completed a long search for a job and an apartment. The air felt close in that checkout line, and black fuzz crept into the corners of my vision. Afraid of fainting, I began to count the number of shoppers ahead of me, then the number of purchases they had. The overhead lights seemed to grow brighter. The cash register made pinging sounds that hurt my ears. Even the edges of the checkout counter looked cold and sharp. Suddenly I became nauseated, dizzy. My vertigo intensified, separating me from everyone else in the store, as if I were looking up from underwater. And then I got hot, the kind of hot you feel when the blood seems to rush to your cheeks and drain from your head at the same time.

My heart was really pounding now, and I felt short of breath, as if wheels were rolling across my chest. I was terrified of what was happening to me. Would I be able to get home? I tried to talk myself down, to convince myself that if I could just stay in line and act as if nothing was happening, these symptoms would go away. Then I decided I wasn't going to faint—I was going to start screaming. The distance to the door looked vast and the seconds were crawling by, but somehow I managed to stay in the checkout line, pay for my bag of groceries and get outside, where I sat on a bench, gulping air. The whole episode had taken ten minutes. I was exhausted.

At home, I tried to analyze what had happened to me. The experience had been terrifying, but because I felt safe in my kitchen, I tried to laugh the whole thing off—really, it seemed ridiculous, freaking out in a supermarket. I decided it was an isolated incident; I was all right, and I was going to forget it ever happened.

Two weeks later, as I sat in a movie theatre, the uncomfortable buzz began to envelop me again. But the symptoms set in faster this time. I mumbled something to my friends about feeling sick as I clambered over them. It was minutes before I caught my breath, hours before I calmed down completely.

A month full of scattered attacks passed before they started rolling in like Sunday evenings, at least once a week. I tried to find a pattern: They always hit in crowded places, places difficult to escape. My whole body felt threatened, primed to run during an attack. Ironically, my attacks were invisible to anyone near me unless they knew what to look for—clenched neck muscles, restless eyes, a shifting from foot to foot—and I was afraid to talk to anyone about them, to perhaps hear something I wouldn't want to hear. What if I had a brain tumour? And I was embarrassed, as if it were my fault that I felt out of control. But then one night I had an attack alone in my bed—the only place I had felt safe. I gave in and called a doctor.

As the weeks passed and the attacks wore on, I began to think maybe I was crazy. I was having attacks in public so often I became afraid to leave my house. I had one on the subway while travelling to work almost every morning but, luckily, never panicked on the job. Instead, I usually lost control in situations where I most wanted to relax: on weekend trips, or while visiting friends. I felt responsible for ruining other people's good time. One attack occurred while I was in a tiny boat deep sea fishing with my family; another hit when I was on a weekend canoe trip with my boyfriend. I also suffered a terrifying attack while on my way to see friends, stuck in traffic, merging into a tun-

*continued*

*cont.*

nel with no exit ramp or emergency lane in sight.

I began declining offers I wanted to accept: all I could think was, "What if I panic in the middle of nowhere?" The times I did force myself to go out, I sat near the doors of restaurants, in aisle seats at movie theatres, near the bathroom at parties. For some reason, I always felt safe in bathrooms, as if whatever happened to me there would at least be easy to clean up.

On days when I didn't have an actual attack, I could feel one looming like a shadow over my shoulder; this impending panic was almost worse than the real thing. By remembering old episodes, I brought on new ones, and each seemed to pull me closer to a vision I had of my mind snapping cleanly in half, like a stalk of celery. ◆

# Typical Symptoms and Associated Features

People with anxiety disorders share a preoccupation with, or persistent avoidance of, thoughts or situations that provoke fear or anxiety. Anxiety disorders frequently have a negative impact on various aspects of a person's life. Johanna found that anxiety and its associated problems constrained both her ability to work and her social relationships. In spite of these problems, most people who knew Johanna probably did not know that she suffered from a mental disorder. In spite of the private terrors that she endured, she was able to carry on most aspects of her life.

In addition to these general considerations, the diagnosis of anxiety disorders depends on several specific types of symptoms, which we discuss in the following sections. We begin with the nature of anxiety, which should be distinguished from more discrete emotional responses, like fear and panic.

## Anxiety

Like depression, the term *anxiety* can refer to either a mood or a syndrome. Here, we use the term to refer to a mood. Specific syndromes associated with anxiety disorders are discussed later in the chapter.

Anxious mood is often defined in contrast to the specific emotion of fear, which is more easily understood. **Fear** is experienced in the face of real, immediate danger. It usually builds quickly in intensity and helps organize the person's behavioural responses to threats from the environment (escaping or fighting back). In contrast to fear, **anxiety** involves a more general or diffuse emotional reaction—beyond simple fear—that is out of proportion to threats from the environment. Rather than being directed toward the person's present circumstances, anxiety is associated with the anticipation of future problems.

Anxiety can be adaptive at low levels, because it serves as a signal that the person must prepare for an upcoming event. When you think about final exams, for example, you may become somewhat anxious. That emotional response may help to initiate and sustain your efforts to study. In contrast, high levels of anxiety become incapacitating by disrupting concentration and performance.

A pervasively anxious mood is often associated with pessimistic thoughts and feelings ("If something bad happens, I probably won't be able to control it"). The person's attention turns inward, focusing on negative emotions and self-evaluation ("Now I'm so upset that I'll never be able to concentrate during the exam!") rather than on the organization or rehearsal of adaptive responses that might be useful in coping with negative events. Taken together, these factors can be used to define maladaptive anxiety, or what Barlow (2001) calls, *anxious apprehension*, which consists of (1) high levels of diffuse negative emotion, (2) a sense of uncontrollability, and (3) a shift in attention to a primary self-focus or a state of self-preoccupation.

*People react with strong negative emotions as they look toward the World Trade Center on September 11, 2001. Negative affect is a blend of several emotions, including fear, anger, sadness, and disgust.*

## Excessive Worry

Worrying is a cognitive activity that is associated with anxiety. In recent years psychologists have studied this phenomenon carefully because they consider it to be critical in the subclassification of anxiety disorders (DSM-IV-TR). **Worry** can be defined as a relatively uncontrollable sequence of negative, emotional thoughts that are concerned with possible future threats or danger. This sequence of worrisome thoughts is usually self-initiated or provoked by a specific experience or ongoing difficulties in the person's daily life. When excessive worriers are asked to describe their thoughts, they emphasize the predominance of verbal, linguistic material rather than images (Borkovec, Ray, & Stoeber, 1998). In other words, worriers are preoccupied with "self-talk" rather than unpleasant visual images.

Because everyone worries at least a little, you might wonder whether it is possible to distinguish between pathological and normal worry. The answer is yes, but there is not a clear line that divides the two kinds of experience. The distinction hinges on quantity—how often the person worries and how many different topics the person worries about. It also depends on the quality of worrisome thought. Excessive worriers are more likely than other people to report that the content of their thoughts is negative, that they have less control over the content and direction of their thoughts, and that in comparison to other adults, their worries are less realistic (Zebb & Beck, 1998). This evidence suggests that the crucial features of pathological worrying may be lack of control and negative affect rather than simply the anticipation of future events.

**TABLE 6–1 Diagnostic Criteria for Panic Attack in DSM-IV-TR**

**A discrete period of intense fear or discomfort, in which four (or more) of the following symptoms developed abruptly and reached a peak within 10 minutes:**

1. Palpitations, pounding heart, or accelerated heart rate
2. Sweating
3. Trembling or shaking
4. Sensations of shortness of breath or smothering
5. Feeling of choking
6. Chest pain or discomfort
7. Nausea or abdominal distress
8. Feeling dizzy, unsteady, lightheaded, or faint
9. Derealization (feelings of unreality) or depersonalization (being detached from oneself)
10. Fear of losing control or going crazy
11. Fear of dying
12. Paresthesias (numbness or tingling sensations)
13. Chills or hot flushes

## Panic Attacks

A **panic attack** is a sudden, overwhelming experience of terror or fright, like the attack that was experienced by Johanna as she waited in the checkout line. Whereas anxiety involves a blend of several negative emotions, panic is more focused. Some clinicians think of panic as a normal fear response that is triggered at an inappropriate time (Barlow, Brown, & Craske, 1994). In that sense, panic is a "false alarm." Descriptively, panic can be distinguished from anxiety in two other respects: It is more intense, and it has a sudden onset.

Panic attacks are defined largely in terms of a list of somatic or physical sensations, ranging from heart palpitations, sweating, and trembling to nausea, dizziness, and chills. Table 6–1 lists the DSM-IV-TR criteria for a panic attack. A person must experience at least 4 of these 13 symptoms in order for the experience to qualify as a full-blown panic attack. The symptoms must develop suddenly and reach a peak intensity within 10 minutes. The actual numbers and combinations of panic symptoms vary from one person to the next, and they may also change over time within the same person.

People undergoing a panic attack also report a number of cognitive symptoms. They may feel as though they are about to die, lose control, or go crazy. Some clinicians believe that the misinterpretation of bodily sensations lies at the core of panic disorder. Patients may interpret heart palpitations as evidence of an impending heart attack, or racing thoughts as evidence that they are about to lose their minds.

Panic attacks are further described in terms of the situations in which they occur, as well as the person's expectations about their occurrence. An attack is said to be expected, or *cued*, if it occurs only in the presence of a particular stimulus. For example, someone who is afraid of public speaking might have a cued panic attack if forced to give a speech in front of a large group of people. Unexpected panic attacks, like Johanna's experience in the grocery checkout line, appear without warning or expectation, as if "out of the blue." The symptoms and timing of panic attacks can vary widely from one person to the next.

Although panic attacks are the hallmark of panic disorder, they also occur in other anxiety disorders. Also, occasional panic attacks are not uncommon in people without anxiety disorders. Ron Norton and colleagues at the University of Winnipeg were the first to discover that panic attacks are not uncommon among university students and other nonclinical samples. Norton's research and later studies by others showed that these panics tend to be milder than those experienced by people with diagnosable panic disorder (Norton et al., 1992).

The Far Side® by Gary Larson © 1990 FarWorks, Inc. All Rights Reserved. Used with permission.

Math phobic's nightmare

## Phobias

**Phobias** are persistent, excessive, narrowly defined fears that are associated with a specific object or situation. Avoidance is an important component of the definition of phobias. A fear is not considered phobic unless the person avoids contact with the source of the fear or experiences intense anxiety in the presence of the stimulus. Phobias are also irrational or unreasonable. Avoiding only snakes that are poisonous or only guns that are loaded would not be considered phobic.

The most straightforward type of phobia involves fear of specific objects or situations. Different types of specific phobias have traditionally been named according to the Greek words for these objects. Examples of typical specific phobias include fear of heights (acrophobia), fear of enclosed spaces (claustrophobia), fear of small animals (zoophobia), fear of blood or injury, and fear of travelling on airplanes.

Some people experience marked fear when they are forced to engage in certain activities, such as public speaking, initiating a conversation, eating in restaurants, or using public washrooms, which might involve being observed or evaluated by other people. Attempts to avoid these feared situations cause serious impairment in the person's social and occupational activities. For example, one young man who was treated by one of the authors of this text was afraid of urinating in public washrooms. He planned his daily schedule with great care so that he would always be near a washroom with a locking door. Consequently, he was unable to attend movies or eat in restaurants unless they happened to have single-person washrooms that he could lock from the inside.

The most complex and incapacitating form of phobic disorder is **agoraphobia**, which literally means "fear of the marketplace (or places of assembly)" and is usually described as fear of public spaces. The case of Johanna provides a brief description of the types of problems experienced by a person suffering from agoraphobia. The fear usually becomes more intense as the distance between the person and his or her familiar surroundings increases, or as avenues of escape are closed off. In that sense, agoraphobia is somewhat different from the other phobias because it is not so much a fear of being close to one specific object or situation (for example, animals, public speaking) as it is of being separated from signals associated with safety.

Typical situations that cause problems include crowded streets and shops, enclosed places like theatres and churches, travelling on public transportation, and driving an automobile on bridges, in tunnels, or on crowded expressways. In any of these situations, the presence of a trusted friend may help the person with agoraphobia feel more comfortable.

*People with agoraphobia are afraid of crowded places from which they might not be able to escape. They also frequently experience panic attacks that are not cued by particular environmental circumstances.*

In the most extreme form of the disorder, agoraphobic patients are unable to venture away from their own homes. Some people with agoraphobia are able to visit public places (for example, shopping malls, theatres), but may remain near exits or aisles so that their escape cannot be easily blocked.

The uncomfortable sensations experienced by people with agoraphobia are similar to those that have already been described for other anxiety disorders. They range from vague feelings of apprehension to specific physical sensations and full-blown panic attacks. People with agoraphobia are frequently afraid that they will experience an "attack" of these symptoms that will be either incapacitating or embarrassing, and that help will not be available to them.

## Obsessions and Compulsions

**Obsessions** are repetitive, unwanted, intrusive cognitive events that may take the form of thoughts or images or impulses. They intrude suddenly into consciousness and lead to an increase in anxiety. Obsessive thinking can be distinguished from worry in two primary ways: (1) Obsessions are usually experienced as coming from "out of the blue," whereas worries are often triggered by problems in everyday living; and (2) the content of obsessions most often involves themes that are perceived as being socially unacceptable or horrific, such as sex, violence, and disease/contamination, whereas the content of worries tends to centre around more acceptable, commonplace concerns, such as money and work (APA, 2000).

**Compulsions** are repetitive behaviours or mental acts that are used to reduce anxiety. Examples include checking many times to be sure that a door is locked or repeating a silent prayer over and over again. These actions are considered by the person who performs them to be senseless or irrational. The person attempts to resist performing the compulsion but cannot. The following case study illustrates many of the most common features of obsessions and compulsions.

Ed's thoughts about violence and death illustrate the anxiety-provoking nature of obsessions. It is not just the intrusive quality of the thought but also the unwanted nature of the thought that makes it an obsession. Some scientists and artists, for example, have reported experiencing intrusive thoughts or inspirational ideas that appear in an unexpected, involuntary way, but these thoughts are not unwanted. Obsessions are unwelcome, anxiety-provoking thoughts. They are also nonsensical; they may seem silly or "crazy." In spite of the recognition that these thoughts do not make sense, the person with full-blown obsessions is unable to ignore or dismiss them.

Examples of typical obsessive thoughts include the following: "Did I kill the old lady?" "Christ was a bastard!" "Am I a sexual pervert?" Examples of obsessive impulses include "I might expose my genitals in public," "I am about to shout obscenities in public," "I feel I might strangle a child." Obsessional images might include mutilated corpses, decomposing fetuses, or a family member being involved in a serious car accident. Although obsessive impulses are accompanied by a compelling sense of reality, obsessive people seldom act upon these impulses.

Most normal people experience obsessions in one form or another. Between 80 and 90 percent of normal subjects report having had intrusive, unacceptable thoughts or impulses that are similar in many ways to those experienced by patients being treated for obsessive–compulsive disorder (Clark, 2004). These include impulses to hurt other people, impulses to do something dangerous, and thoughts of accidents or disease. In contrast to the obsessions described by people who are not in treatment, those experienced by clinical patients occur more frequently, last longer, and are associated with higher levels of discomfort

## CASE STUDY Ed's Obsessive–Compulsive Disorder

Ed, a 38-year-old lawyer, lived with his wife, Phyllis. Most aspects of Ed's life were going well, except for the anxiety-provoking thoughts that lurked beneath his relatively easygoing exterior. One focus of Ed's anxiety was handwriting. He became so tense that his eyes hurt whenever he was forced to write. Feeling exhausted and overwhelmed, Ed avoided writing whenever possible. The problem seemed utterly ridiculous to him, but he couldn't rid himself of his obsessive thoughts.

Sinister meanings had somehow become linked in Ed's imagination to the way in which letters and numbers were formed. The worst letters were P and T (the first letters in "Phyllis" and in "Tim," his younger brother's name). "Improperly" formed letters reminded Ed of violent acts, especially decapitation and strangulation. If the parts of a letter, such as the two lines in the letter T, were not connected, an image of a head that was not attached to its body might pop into his mind.

Closed loops reminded him of suffocation, like a person whose throat had been clamped shut. These images were associated with people whose names began with the malformed letter. As a result of these concerns, Ed's handwriting had become extremely awkward and difficult to read.

These writing problems made it very difficult for Ed to complete his work, especially when he was under time pressure. In one particularly upsetting incident, Ed was responsible for completing an important official form that had to be mailed that day. He came to a section in which he needed to write a capital P and became concerned that he hadn't done it properly. The loop seemed to be closed, which meant that Phyllis might be strangled! He tore up the first copy and filled it out again. When it was finally done to his satisfaction, Ed sealed the form in an envelope and put it in the box for outgoing mail. After returning to his desk, he was suddenly overwhelmed by the feeling that he had indeed made a mistake with that P. If he allowed the form to be mailed, the evil image would be associated forever with his wife. Consumed by fear, Ed rushed back to the mailbox, tore up the envelope, and started a new form. Twenty minutes later, he had the form filled out and back in the mailbox. Then the cycle repeated itself. Each time, Ed became more distraught and frustrated, until he eventually felt that he was going to lose his mind.

In addition to his problems with writing, Ed was also afraid of axes. He would not touch an axe, or even get close to one. Any situation in which he could possibly encounter an axe made him extremely uncomfortable. He refused to shop in hardware stores because they sell axes, and he would not visit museums because their exhibits often contain artifacts such as medieval armour. His fear of axes was quite specific. Ed wasn't afraid of knives, guns, or swords.

One frightening experience seemed to trigger the pervasive anxiety that had plagued Ed for 20 years. When he was 17 years old, some friends persuaded Ed to try smoking marijuana. They told him that it would make him feel high—relaxed, sociable, and perhaps a bit giddy. Unfortunately, Ed didn't react to the drug in the same way that the others had. The physical effects seemed to be the same, but his psychological reaction was entirely different. After sharing two joints with his friends, Ed began to feel lightheaded. Then things around him began to seem unreal, as though he were watching himself and his friends in a movie. The intensity of these feelings escalated rapidly, and panic took over. Frightening thoughts raced through his head. Was he losing his mind? When would it stop? This experience lasted about two hours.

The marijuana incident had an immediate and lasting impact. Ed became preoccupied with a fear of accidentally ingesting any kind of mind-altering drug, especially LSD. Every spot on his skin or clothing seemed as though it might be a microscopic quantity of this hallucinogen. He felt compelled to clean his hands and clothes repeatedly to avoid contamination. Intellectually, Ed knew that these concerns were silly. How could a tiny spot on his hand be LSD? It didn't make any sense, but he couldn't keep the thought out of his mind.

The most horrifying aspect of the drug experience was the sensation of being totally out of control of his actions and emotions. The fear of returning to that state haunted Ed. He struggled to resist impulses that he had never noticed before, such as the temptation to shout obscenities aloud in church. He also began to worry that he might hurt his younger brother. He resisted the impulses with all his might. He never acted on them, but they pervaded his consciousness and absorbed his mental energy.

The thoughts were so persistent and unshakable that Ed began to wonder if he might, in fact, be a pathological killer. Ed spent many hours reading articles about mass murderers. The number 8 came to have special meaning to him because of the number of victims of one particular serial killer. Over time, Ed's fears and worries became focused on numbers and letters. The violent images and impulses became a less prominent part of his everyday life, but the writing difficulties escalated proportionately. ◆

than normal obsessions. Clinical obsessions are also resisted more strongly, and patients report more difficulty dismissing their unwanted thoughts and impulses. Research by David A. Clark (University of New Brunswick), Christine Purdon (University of Waterloo), and others suggests that obsessions are relatively common, and that clinical obsessions differ from normal obsessions in degree rather than in nature (Clark, 2004; Purdon & Clark, 1993). Similarities and continuities have also been observed between clinical compulsions and rituals that are commonly performed by people who do not qualify for a diagnosis of obsessive–compulsive disorder (Muris, Merckelbach, & Clavan, 1997).

Ed's constricted style of forming letters and his habitual pattern of going back to check and correct his writing illustrate the way in which compulsions are used to reduce anxiety. If he did not engage in these ritualistic behaviours, he would become extremely uncomfortable. His concern about someone being strangled or decapitated if the letters were not properly formed was not delusional, because he readily acknowledged that this was a "silly" idea. Nevertheless, he couldn't shake the obsessive idea that some dreadful event would occur if he was not excruciatingly careful about his writing. He felt as though he had to act, even though he knew that his obsessive thought was irrational.

Compulsions reduce anxiety, but they do not produce pleasure. Thus some behaviours, such as gambling and drug use, that people describe as being "compulsive" are not considered true compulsions according to this definition.

Although some clinicians have argued that compulsive rituals are associated with a complete loss of voluntary control, it is more accurate to view the problem in terms of *diminished control*. For example, Ed could occasionally manage to resist the urge to write in his compulsive style; the behaviour was not totally automatic. But whenever he did not engage in this ritualistic behaviour, his subjective level of distress increased dramatically, and within a short period of time he returned to the compulsive writing style.

The two most common forms of compulsive behaviour are cleaning and checking. Compulsive cleaning is often associated with an excessive fear of contamination, or feelings of personal responsibility if something bad was to occur because of the person's negligence (e.g., fear that he or she would leave the stove on, resulting in a serious fire; Clark, 2004). There are passive as well as active features of compulsive cleaning. Compulsive cleaners go out of their way to avoid contact with dirt, germs, and other sources of contamination. Then, when they believe that they have come into contact with a source of contamination, they engage in ritualistic cleaning behaviour, such as washing their hands, taking showers, cleaning kitchen counters, and so on. These rituals typically involve a large number of repetitions. Some people may wash their hands 50 times a day, taking several minutes to scrub their hands up to the elbow with industrial-strength cleanser. Others take showers that last two or three hours in which they wash each part of their body in a fixed order, needing to repeat the scrubbing motion an exact number of times.

Compulsive checking frequently represents an attempt to ensure the person's safety or the safety and health of a friend or family member. The person checks things, such as the stove or the lock on a door, over and over in an attempt to prevent the occurrence of an imagined unpleasant or disastrous event (for example, an accident, a burglary, or an assault).

# Classification

To understand the way in which anxiety disorders are currently classified, we must briefly consider the ways in which they have been described in previous classification systems. This general set of emotional problems was the topic of considerable diagnostic controversy throughout the twentieth century and continues into the twenty-first.

## Brief Historical Perspective

Anxiety and abnormal fears did not play a prominent role in the psychiatric classification systems that began to emerge in Europe during the second half of the nineteenth century (see Chapter 4). Anxiety disorders were probably left out of these descriptions because the authors were primarily superintendents of large asylums. Their patients were people who were psychotic (see Chapter 1) or so out of touch with reality that they could no longer reside in the larger community (Jablensky, 1985; Klerman, 1990a). People with anxiety problems seldom came to the attention of psychiatrists during the nineteenth century because very few cases of anxiety disorder require institutionalization.

Freud and his followers were responsible for some of the first extensive clinical descriptions of pathological anxiety states. Working primarily with patients who were not hospitalized, Freud had an opportunity to treat and study a variety of anxiety-related problems. He described cases of phobia, generalized anxiety, and obsessive–compulsive behaviour. The form of specific symptoms (a phobia as compared to a compulsion) was considered to be less important than the underlying causes, which were presumably similar.

Freud's psychological explanations for the origins of anxiety disorders were extremely influential throughout the twentieth century (Frances et al., 1993; Josephs, 1994). Freud focused primarily on the importance of mental conflicts and innate biological impulses (primarily sexual and aggressive instincts) in the etiology of anxiety (see Chapter 2). This perspective played a central role in the way that anxiety disorders were classified in early versions of the DSM. They were grouped with several other types of problems under the general heading of **neurosis**, a term used to describe persistent emotional disturbances, such as anxiety and depression, in which the person is aware of the nature of the problem. Neurotic disorders are distinguished from psychotic disorders, in which the person is often out of touch with reality and unaware of the nature of his or her problems (see Chapter 1).

The basic outline of Freud's theory of anxiety hinges on the notion that the person's ego can experience a small amount of anxiety as a signal indicating that an instinctual impulse that has previously been associated with punishment and disapproval is about to be acted on. This usually means that the person is going to do something aggressive or sexual that is considered inappropriate. Signal anxiety triggers the use of ego defences—primarily repression—that prevent conscious recognition of the forbidden impulse, inhibit its expression, and thereby reduce the person's anxiety. When the system works as it should, anxiety is adaptive, and the person's behaviour is regulated to conform with social expectations.

Unfortunately, people can still experience pathological levels of anxiety if the system is overwhelmed. Traumatic events or circumstances can lead to extreme levels of free-floating anxiety. The ego is then forced to resort to additional defensive manoeuvres that can produce symptoms such as phobias and compulsions. The specific form of overt symptoms is determined by the defence mechanisms that are employed by the ego, but the underlying process is presumably the same across all of the anxiety neuroses.

Freud's conceptual model for the anxiety neuroses incorporated several important features, including the importance of biologically based impulses, learning experiences based on interactions with other people, and cognitive (or intrapsychic) events that play an important role in mediating between current and past experience. It was firmly grounded in Freud's observations of his own patients' experiences and the process of their treatment with psychoanalysis. Although it served as a useful stimulus to future clinicians and identified many important factors in the etiology of anxiety disorders, his model suffered from a number of weaknesses. Perhaps the major problem was that of measurement. Because Freud's ideas were based on unconscious mental processes that could not be measured directly, his theory of anxiety could not be tested empirically.

## Contemporary Diagnostic Systems (DSM-IV-TR)

The DSM-IV-TR (APA, 2000) approach to classifying anxiety disorders is based primarily on descriptive features, rather than etiological hypotheses, and recognizes several specific subtypes. The overall scheme is outlined in Table 6–2. It includes panic disorder, three types of phobic disorders, obsessive–compulsive disorder, and generalized anxiety disorder, as well as posttraumatic stress disorder (PTSD) and acute stress disorder. We discuss PTSD and acute stress disorder in Chapter 7. The manual also describes problems with anxiety that appear in children, specifically separation anxiety disorder and school refusal. These problems are discussed in Chapter 16.

**Panic Disorder** To meet the diagnostic criteria for **panic disorder**, a person must

**TABLE 6–2 Categories Listed as Anxiety Disorders in DSM-IV-TR**

| | |
|---|---|
| Panic Disorder<br>Without Agoraphobia<br>With Agoraphobia | Obsessive–Compulsive Disorder |
| Agoraphobia (without History of Panic Disorder) | Generalized Anxiety Disorder |
| Specific Phobia | Posttraumatic Stress Disorder |
| Social Phobia | Acute Stress Disorder |

experience recurrent, unexpected panic attacks. At least one of the attacks must have been followed by a period of one month or more in which the person has either persistent concern about having additional attacks, worry about the implications of the attack or its consequences, or a significant change in behaviour related to the attacks. Panic disorder is divided into two subtypes, depending on the presence or absence of agoraphobia.

**Agoraphobia** DSM-IV-TR defines agoraphobia in terms of anxiety about being in situations from which escape might be either difficult or embarrassing. This approach is based on the view that agoraphobia is typically a complication that follows upon the experience of panic attacks (Frances, First, & Pincus, 1995). Avoidance and distress are important elements of the definition. In order to meet the DSM-IV-TR criteria, the person must either avoid agoraphobic situations, such as travelling away from his or her own home; endure the experience with great distress; or insist on being accompanied by another person who can provide some comfort or security. In most cases, the person avoids a wide variety of situations rather than just one specific type of situation. People who fit this description of agoraphobia without meeting the criteria for panic disorder would be assigned a diagnosis of agoraphobia without history of panic disorder.

*Specific phobias are excessive fears associated with specific situations that the person avoids. Acrophobia is the name given to fear of heights.*

**Specific Phobia** A *specific phobia* is defined in DSM-IV-TR as a marked and persistent fear that is excessive or unreasonable, cued by the presence or anticipation of a specific object or situation. Frequently observed types of specific phobia include fear of heights, small animals (such as spiders, bugs, mice, snakes, or bats), tunnels or bridges, storms, illness and injury (including blood), being in a closed place (such as a very small room), and being on certain kinds of public transportation (such as airplanes, buses, or elevators). Exposure to the phobic stimulus must be followed by an immediate fear response. Furthermore, the person must appreciate the fact that the fear is excessive or unreasonable, and the person must avoid the phobic situation. DSM-IV-TR also provides a severity threshold: The avoidance or distress associated with the phobia must interfere significantly with the person's normal activities or relationships with others.

**Social Phobia** A person with a **social phobia** is afraid of (and avoids) social situations. These situations fall into two broad headings: doing something in front of unfamiliar people (performance anxiety) and interpersonal interactions (such as dating and parties).

The central feature of social phobia is an excessive fear of negative evaluations from others. As noted by Lynn Alden (University of British Columbia), who is an internationally recognized expert on social phobia, people with social phobia often worry about their social presentation ("Do I look foolish?") and are frightened of doing or saying something humiliating or embarrassing (Crozier & Alden, 2001; Mellings & Alden, 2000). Research by investigators such as Sheila Woody (also at the University of British Columbia), has revealed that people with social phobia tend to be severely critical of their social skills and become absorbed in evaluating their own performance when interacting with others (Woody, 1996).

A survey by Stein et al. (2000) of nearly 2000 people from Winnipeg and regions of Alberta revealed that the most common socially feared situations were as follows:

- Giving a speech in front of others (fear reported by 15 percent of those surveyed)
- Walking into a room when people are already seated (13 percent)
- Dealing with authority figures (10 percent)
- Making eye contact (10 percent)

- Using a public washroom when others are present (9 percent)
- Going to a party or other social gathering (9 percent)
- Writing in public (7 percent)

Some people have a circumscribed form of social phobia that is focused on one particular type of situation. In other cases, the fear is more generalized, and the person is intensely anxious in almost any situation that involves social interaction. This type of person might be described as being extremely shy. The extensive overlap between generalized social phobia and avoidant personality disorder (see Chapter 9) has created some confusion and has been the topic of numerous research studies (Crozier & Alden, 2001).

**Comorbidity Rates for Anxiety Disorders and Major Depression**

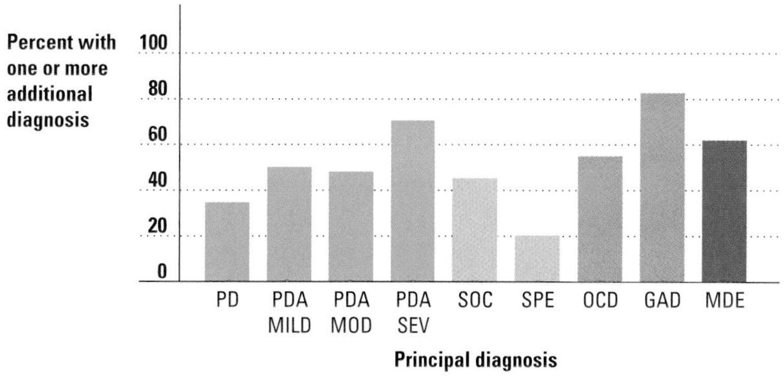


PD, panic disorder; PDA, panic disorder with agoraphobia; SOC, social phobia; SPE, specific phobia; OCD, obsessive–compulsive disorder; GAD, generalized anxiety disorder; MDE, major depression

MILD, MOD (moderate), SEV (severe)

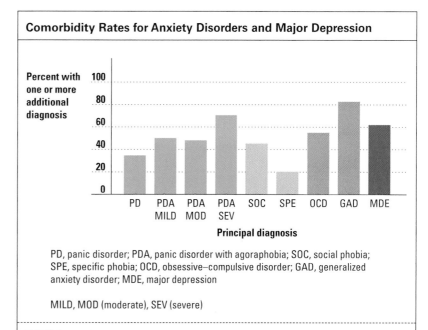

**FIGURE 6–1: Comorbidity rates for anxiety disorders and major depression (percentage of people who met diagnostic criteria for one anxiety or mood disorder who also qualified for at least one additional diagnosis).**

*Source:* T.A. Brown, 1996, Validity of the DSM-III-R and DSM-IV classification systems for anxiety disorders. In Ronald M. Rapee (Ed.), *Current controversies in the anxiety disorders*, p. 27. New York: Guilford Press.

**Generalized Anxiety Disorder** As noted by psychologists Robert Ladouceur (Laval University) and Michel Dugas (Concordia University), people with **generalized anxiety disorder** (GAD) are chronic worriers. Excessive, uncontrollable worry is considered the key feature of the disorder (Ladouceur & Dugas, 2002), which leads to significant distress or impairment in occupational or social functioning. The worry must occur more days than not for a period of at least six months, and it must be about a number of different events or activities. In order to distinguish GAD from other forms of anxiety disorder, DSM-IV-TR notes that the person's worries should not be focused on having a panic attack (as in panic disorder), being embarrassed in public (as in social phobia), or being contaminated (as in obsessive–compulsive disorder). Finally, the person's worries and free-floating anxiety must be accompanied by at least three of the following symptoms: (1) restlessness or feeling keyed up or on edge, (2) being easily fatigued, (3) difficulty concentrating or mind going blank, (4) irritability, (5) muscle tension, and (6) sleep disturbance.

Generalized anxiety disorder remains one of the most controversial anxiety disorders, for several reasons. The diagnostic reliability of GAD is often lower than that for other types of anxiety disorder (Chorpita, Brown, & Barlow, 1998). As noted in Figure 6–1, GAD has the highest degree of overlap with the other anxiety disorders. The validity of GAD as a separate diagnostic category is, therefore, open to question. However, some research suggests that GAD is an important, independent type of anxiety disorder (Kessler, Keller, & Wittchen, 2001).

**Obsessive–Compulsive Disorder** DSM-IV-TR defines obsessive–compulsive disorder (OCD) in terms of the presence of either obsessions or compulsions. Most people who meet the criteria for this disorder actually exhibit both of these symptoms. The person must recognize that the obsessions or compulsions are excessive or unreasonable. The diagnostic manual specifies further that these thoughts must not be simply excessive worries about real problems. Intrusive thoughts about overdue bills, for example, would not qualify as obsessions. The DSM-IV-TR definition also requires that the person must attempt to ignore, suppress, or neutralize the unwanted thoughts or impulses.

The line of demarcation between compulsive rituals and normal behaviour is often difficult to define. How many times should a person wash her hands in a day? How long should a shower last? Is it reasonable to check more than one time to be sure that the door is locked or the alarm clock is set? DSM-IV-TR has established an arbitrary threshold which holds that rituals become compulsive if they cause marked distress, take more than an hour per day to perform, or interfere with normal occupational and social functioning.

### "Lumpers" and "Splitters"

Experts who classify mental disorders can be described informally as belonging to one of two groups, "lumpers" and "splitters" (Mack et al., 1994; Wittchen et al., 2001). Lumpers argue that anxiety is a generalized condition or set of symptoms without any special subdivisions. Splitters distinguish among a number of conditions, each of which is presumed to have its own etiology. During the first half of the twentieth century, psychiatrists tended to adopt a generalized position with regard to anxiety disorders (Jablensky, 1985). In other words, they lumped together the various anxiety disorders. The DSM-IV-TR system splits them into many separate disorders.

Although it is currently not a popular position, a reasonable argument can still be made in favour of a more unified approach to the classification of anxiety disorders (Andrews, 1996; Nesse, 1999). Consider, for example, the cases of Ed in this chapter and Michael in Chapter 4, who had cleaning-related obsessions and compulsions. Both exhibited a relatively wide range of anxiety symptoms. The high rate of comorbidity among anxiety disorders suggests that these cases are not unusual. Should Ed be considered to have both a phobic disorder (fear of axes) and an obsessive–compulsive disorder? Or are these diverse symptoms best viewed as manifestations of the same anxiety disorder? These are questions about the validity of diagnostic categories (see Chapter 4). Decisions regarding the breadth or specificity of anxiety disorders will ultimately depend on evidence from many areas. Do phobias and OCD show distinct, separate patterns in family studies? Do they respond to different types of treatment? Can we distinguish between them in terms of typical patterns of onset and course? Future research efforts are needed to address these issues.

### Course and Outcome

Anxiety disorders are often chronic. Long-term follow-up studies focused on clinical populations indicate that many people continue to experience symptoms of anxiety and associated social and occupational impairment many years after their problems are initially recognized. On the other hand, some people do recover completely. The most general conclusion, therefore, is that the long-term outcome for anxiety disorders is mixed and somewhat unpredictable (Emmanuel, Simmonds, & Tyrer, 1998; Wittchen & Hoyer, 2001; Taylor, 2000; Yonkers et al., 2001).

Consider, for example, the case of panic disorder. The largest and longest follow-up study examined more than 400 patients over a period of four years after they were treated with medication. The investigators found that 45 percent of these patients did not improve and continued to show persistent symptoms of panic disorder through the follow-up period. On the other hand, 31 percent of the group improved quickly and remained in a stable pattern of remission. The others followed an episodic pattern of periodic remission followed by relapse (Katschnig & Amering, 1998). Contrary to expectations, the frequency with which a person experienced panic attacks upon entry to the study—which is often viewed as an indication of the severity of panic disorder—did not predict the course of the disorder or how well the person was able to function at follow-up. Onset of symptoms at a relatively young age and the presence of agoraphobia upon entry to the study did predict a greater level of disability and worse outcome. This suggests that the level of phobic avoidance is a particularly important feature of the disorder in terms of predicting future social impairment and slower recovery (Eaton et al., 1998).

A 15-year longitudinal study of social phobia has also reported that people who have an earlier age of onset often experience a more severe form of the disorder (Merikangas et al., 2002). In most cases, the person's symptoms were first evident during adolescence, and they remained quite stable over time. The participants in this study were young adults in a community sample rather than patients at a clinic; most did not receive treatment for their condition. The results indicate that the natural course of social phobia is often chronic in nature.

The long-term course of obsessive–compulsive disorder also follows a pattern of improvement mixed with some persistent symptoms. One remarkable study has reported outcome information for a sample of 144 patients with severe OCD who were assessed at two follow-up intervals: first about 5 years after they were initially treated at a psychiatric hospital and then again more than 40 years later (Skoog & Skoog, 1999). The data are interesting both because of the very long follow-up interval and because the patients were initially treated between 1947 and 1953, well before the introduction of modern pharmacological and psychological treatments for the disorder. The results are summarized in Figure 6–2. Slightly less than 30 percent of the patients were rated as being recovered at the first follow-up interval. By the time of the 40-year follow-up, almost 50 percent of the patients were considered to show either full recovery or recovery with subclinical symptoms. More than 80 percent of the patients showed improved levels of functioning if we also count people who continued to exhibit some clinical symptoms. Nevertheless, half of the patients in this sample exhibited symptoms of OCD for more than 30 years. This study shows that although many patients do improve, OCD is a chronic disorder for many people.

**Long-Term Outcome of Obsessive–Compulsive Disorder**

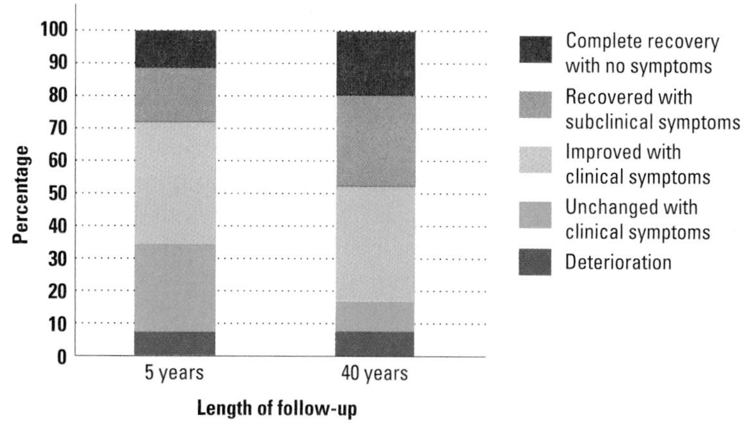


**FIGURE 6–2: Changes in clinical severity for 144 patients with OCD measured 5 years and 40 years after hospitalization.**

*Source:* G. Skoog and I. Skoog, 1999, A 40-year follow-up of patients with obsessive–compulsive disorder. *Archives of General Psychiatry, 56,* 121–127.

# Epidemiology

## Prevalence

Epidemiological surveys in Canada and elsewhere indicate that anxiety disorders are more common than many other mental disorders, including mood disorders and psychotic disorders (Kessler et al., 1994; Offord et al., 1996). Lifetime prevalence of the major anxiety disorders, according to the most recent estimates (DSM-IV-TR), are presented in Table 6–3. Prevalence of acute stress disorder and posttraumatic stress disorder are discussed in the following chapter.

## Comorbidity

The symptoms of various anxiety disorders overlap considerably. Many people who experience panic attacks develop phobic avoidance, and many people with obsessive thoughts would also be considered chronic worriers. One study found that 50 percent of people who met the criteria for one anxiety disorder also met the criteria for at least one other form of anxiety disorder or mood disorder (Brown & Barlow, 1992). This pattern, broken down by specific types of anxiety disorder, is illustrated in Figure 6–1. The highest rates of comorbidity were found for generalized anxiety disorder (82 percent) and severe cases of panic disorder with agoraphobia (72 percent). The lowest rate was found for cases of specific phobia; only 20 percent of the people with this diagnosis met the criteria for an additional type of anxiety disorder. When a secondary diagnosis was made, what was it? The most common secondary diagnosis was generalized anxiety disorder (23 percent of the cases).

Both anxiety and depression are based on emotion, so it is not surprising that considerable overlap also exists between anxiety

**TABLE 6–3 Lifetime Prevalence of the Major Anxiety Disorders (Percentage of Population)**

| | % | Gender Ratio (Female: Male) |
|---|---|---|
| Panic disorder | 1 to 2 | 2:1 to 3:1 |
| Agoraphobia | 1 to 2 | 3:1 |
| Specific phobia | 7 to 11 | approx. 2:1 |
| Social phobia (also called social anxiety disorder) | 3 to 13 | more common in women (exact ratio unknown) |
| Obsessive–compulsive disorder | 2.5 | 1:1 |
| Generalized anxiety disorder | 5 | 2:1 |

*Note:* Prevalence of acute stress disorder and posttraumatic stress disorder is discussed in Chapter 7.

*Source:* Based on American Psychiatric Association, 2000, *Diagnostic and statistical manual of mental disorders,* 4th ed., text revision. Washington, DC: Author.

disorders and mood disorders (Kessler et al., 1998; Regier et al., 1998). Notice in Figure 6–1 that 61 percent of the people who received a primary diagnosis of major depression also qualified for a secondary diagnosis of some type of anxiety disorder. This extensive overlap raises interesting questions about the relation between these general diagnostic categories (see Further Thoughts). Do people who meet the criteria for both depression and an anxiety disorder really suffer from two distinct syndromes? Or should we think about the existence of three types of disorder: "pure" anxiety disorders, "pure" mood disorders, and a third type of disorder that represents a mixture of anxiety and depression? Reasonable arguments have been made on both sides of this debate, which remains unresolved (Barlow & Campbell, 2000; Tyrer, 2001).

Substance dependence is another problem that is frequently associated with anxiety disorders. People who have an anxiety disorder are about three times more likely to have an alcohol use disorder than are people without

## Further Thoughts The Relationship between Anxiety and Depression

Anxiety and depression are closely related concepts. Both are defined primarily in terms of negative emotional responses. In actual clinical practice, they often appear together. People who are anxious are also likely to be depressed, and people who are depressed are frequently anxious. What does this overlapping pattern mean? Some clinicians have argued that anxiety and depression are different manifestations of the same underlying problem. Others hold that they are distinctly different disorders, while recognizing that they can appear together. The relationship between the symptoms of anxiety and those of depression has been the focus of many interesting debates.

Clark and Watson (1991) proposed a model of anxiety and depression that helps to explain the distinction between these conditions. Their proposal is based, in part, on the distinction between two dimensions of mood: positive and negative affect[1] (Tellegen, 1985). A person who is experiencing a high level of **negative affect** would be described as being upset, whereas someone whose level of negative affect is low would be considered calm or relaxed. Adjectives that describe negative affect include angry, guilty, afraid, sad, scornful, disgusted, and worried. A person who is experiencing high levels of **positive affect** would be described as energetic or having a zest for life, whereas someone whose level of positive affect is low would be considered tired or sluggish. Adjectives that describe positive affect include active, delighted, interested, enthusiastic, and proud. These dimensions are largely independent. In other words, a person who is high on one is not necessarily low on the other. Some people are high on both dimensions.

Using this concept of emotional responses as a guide, Clark and Watson examined evidence from several studies that tried to distinguish between anxiety and depression in psychiatric patients as well as in nonclinical subjects. They concluded that the data are best explained in terms of three separate elements: (1) *general distress* (high negative affect), which is common to both anxiety and depression; (2) *physiological hyperarousal*, which is specific to anxiety; and (3) *absence of positive affect*, which is specific to depression. All three elements must be considered in order to describe completely the symptoms of anxiety and depression.

General distress is a diffuse combination of several negative emotional responses, including guilt, anger, fear, sadness, and disgust. These responses may be accompanied by related symptoms, such as mild disturbances of sleep and appetite, distractibility, and vague somatic complaints. According to Clark and Watson's model, elevated levels of general distress indicate that the person may be suffering from a mood disorder, an anxiety disorder, or both. To make a diagnosis, the clinician must take into account the other two elements in their model.

Physiological hyperarousal is presumably associated with anxiety rather than depression. This element of the model is defined in terms of such symptoms as heart palpitations, shortness of breath, excessive sweating, muscular tension and restlessness, shakiness or trembling, and abdominal distress. People with anxiety disorders would presumably exhibit symptoms of somatic hyperarousal as well as high levels of general distress or negative affect.

Absence of positive affect is presumably associated with depression rather than with anxiety. This element of the model is defined in terms of symptoms such as loss of interest in usual activities, inability to experience pleasure (anhedonia), fatigue, and feelings of hopelessness. A patient with a major depressive disorder would be expected to show high levels of negative affect (general distress) in combination with low levels of positive affect.

Anxiety disorders and depression overlap frequently because both conditions are characterized by high levels of general distress. A person who experiences a prolonged period of high negative affect (distress) as well as low levels of positive affect and high levels of somatic symptoms would be likely to report feeling both depressed and anxious.

This model clarifies the phenomenology of anxiety and also explains epidemiological evidence regarding the frequent comorbidity of anxiety and mood disorders. The same three groupings of symptoms (general distress, low positive affect, and somatic arousal) have been found in

*continued*

*cont.*

several different samples of people, ranging from college students to psychiatric patients (Brown, Chorpita, & Barlow, 1998; Watson, Clark, et al., 1995). The fundamental structure of Clark and Watson's model is, therefore, reliable. The model's validity has also received additional empirical support, because the somatic arousal and positive affect scales have repeatedly been able to distinguish between samples of people who are depressed and people who are anxious (Cox et al., 2001; Mineka, Watson, & Clark, 1998). ◆

[1]Clark and Watson use the term *affect* to refer generally to "emotionality," rather than specifically to the observable behaviours associated with emotional responses (see our definition in Chapter 5). Their self-report measure of positive and negative affect, the Positive and Negative Affect Schedule Expanded Form, includes items tapping subjective feelings as well as interests and behaviours (Watson & Clark, 1990).

an anxiety disorder (Kushner, Sher, & Beitman, 1990; Merikangas et al., 1998a). In situations such as these, questions of cause and effect are not clear. Did the person use alcohol in an attempt to reduce heightened anxiety, or did he or she become anxious after drinking excessively? Prospective studies conclude that it works both ways. One study found that among first-year university students, the presence of an anxiety disorder increased by four times the risk for later onset of heavy drinking problems. Conversely, the presence of alcohol dependence among first-year university students caused a similar increase in the probability that the person would later develop a new anxiety disorder (Kushner, Sher, & Erickson, 1999).

*Heavy drinkers are more likely than other people to develop anxiety disorders, and people who are highly anxious are more likely to start to drink heavily.*

### Gender Differences

There are significant gender differences in several types of anxiety disorders. Pertinent data from one large survey are summarized in Table 6–3 (p. 201). The gender difference is particularly large for specific phobias, where women are about twice as likely as men to experience the disorder. Women are two to three times as likely as men to experience panic disorder, agoraphobia (without panic disorder), and generalized anxiety disorder. Social phobia is also more common among women than among men, but the difference is not as striking as it is for other types of phobia. The only type of anxiety disorder for which there does not appear to be a significant gender difference is OCD (Karno & Golding, 1991).

The significant gender differences in the prevalence of anxiety disorders must be interpreted in the light of etiological theories, which are considered in the next section. Several explanations remain plausible (Gater et al., 1998; Lewinsohn et al., 1998). Psychological speculation has focused on such factors as gender differences in child-rearing practices or differences in the way in which men and women respond to stressful life events. Gender differences in hormone functions or neurotransmitter activities in the brain may also be responsible (Leibenluft, 1999; Pigott, 1999; Yonkers & Gurguis, 1995).

### Anxiety across the Lifespan

The prevalence of anxiety disorders tends to be lower among elderly men and women than it is among people in other age groups (Blazer, 1997; Offord et al., 1996). This result is perhaps surprising, in light of the fact that many elderly people face problems associated with loneliness, increased dependency, declining physical and cognitive capacities, and changes in social and economic conditions. To explain this result, University of Toronto psychiatrist Alastair J. Flint suggests that something about the aging process, such as changes in the brain structures that mediate anxiety, may reduce the probability that stressful or threatening life events will lead to the onset of an anxiety disorder (Flint, 1994).

Most elderly people with an anxiety disorder have had the symptoms for many years.

It is relatively unusual for a person to develop a new case of panic disorder, specific phobia, social phobia, or obsessive–compulsive disorder at an advanced age. The only type of anxiety disorder that begins with any noticeable frequency in late life is agoraphobia (Antony & Barlow, 2002; Taylor, 2000).

The diagnosis of anxiety disorders among elderly people is complicated by the need to consider factors such as medical illnesses and other physical impairments and limitations (Carmin, Pollard, & Gillock, 1999). Respiratory and cardiovascular problems may resemble the physiological symptoms of a panic attack. Hearing losses may lead to anxiety in interpersonal interactions. Subsequent avoidance might be inappropriately attributed to the onset of a social phobia. A frail elderly person who falls down on the street may become afraid to leave home alone, but this may be a reasonable concern rather than a symptom of agoraphobia. For reasons such as these, the diagnosis of anxiety disorders must be done with extra caution in elderly men and women.

### Cross-Cultural Comparisons

The focus of typical anxiety complaints can vary dramatically across cultural boundaries. People in Western societies often experience anxiety in relation to their work performance, whereas in other societies people may be more concerned with family issues or religious experiences. In the Yoruba culture of Nigeria, for example, anxiety is frequently associated with fertility and the health of family members (Good & Kleinman, 1985).

Anxiety disorders have been observed in preliterate as well as Westernized cultures. Of course, the same descriptive and diagnostic terms are not used in every culture, but the basic psychological phenomena appear to be similar. Cultural anthropologists have recognized many different culture-bound syndromes that, in some cases, bear striking resemblance to anxiety disorders listed in DSM-IV-TR (Guarnaccia, 1997). The following example of "kayak angst" in an Inuit (Eskimo) hunter illustrates a similar point. The problem sounds a lot like panic disorder.

> Isak H., aged 34, [was a] hunter fisherman of mixed race from Nugatsiak. He had been quite well before. In 1939 he saw a kayak man drowned [sic] and was very much upset. In the summer of 1946, when he was paddling along in his kayak on a calm day with a soft backwash and bright sunshine he suddenly became terrified when looking down to the bottom of the sea. He seemed to feel the kayak filling with water, the point of the kayak being very distant and dim. His head felt queer and he took off his cap. His heart started beating rapidly and he trembled so violently that the kayak shook. Perspiration ran down his face, his heart seemed to turn over and his arms were heavy and numb. He made an effort to reach shore, he vomited, his bowels were loose and he had a strong desire to pass water. Next time he set out in his kayak the same symptoms occurred. He felt more and more terrified of crouching down in his kayak, and he finally gave up all attempts and stopped fishing by kayak. (Katschnig & Amering, 1990, pp. 77–78)

Only a handful of epidemiological studies have attempted to collect cross-cultural data using standardized interviews and specific diagnostic criteria. The largest of these studies is being conducted by the Cross-National Collaborative Group, headed by Myna Weissman of Columbia University, with co-investigators including Roger Bland at the University of Alberta. These researchers have surveyed over 40 000 people living in 10 countries (Canada, United States, Puerto Rico, France, Germany, Italy, Lebanon, Taiwan, Korea, and New Zealand).

So far, the cross-national group has examined the prevalence of three anxiety disorders: panic disorder, obsessive–compulsive disorder, and social phobia (Weissman et al., 1994, 1996b, 1997). These disorders were found in all the countries that were surveyed (not all disorders were assessed in all 10 countries). Results suggest that lifetime prevalence of the three disorders are similar across countries, with the exception that they tend to be less commonly reported in Taiwan.

Another large study, the Cross-National Collaborative Panic Study (1992), assessed more than 1000 panic disordered patients in 14 different countries, including countries in North America, Latin America, and Europe. Panic disorder occurred in all the countries that were included in the study. Nevertheless, some important differences were found among panic patients from different regions. Choking or smothering and fear of dying were more common among patients from southern countries. Phobic avoidance was much more common among panic patients seen at clinics in Canada and the United States compared to patients seen at clinics in Latin American countries.

# Etiological Considerations and Research

Now that we have discussed the various symptoms associated with anxiety disorders and their distribution within the population, we can consider the origins of these disorders. How do these problems develop? Going back to the cases that were presented at the beginning of the chapter, what might account for the onset of Johanna's panic attacks? Why would Ed find himself plagued by violent images and compelled to form letters in a meticulous fashion?

## Adaptive and Maladaptive Fears

Current theories regarding the etiology of anxiety disorders often focus on the evolutionary significance of anxiety and fear. These emotional response systems are clearly adaptive in many situations. They mobilize responses that help the person survive in the face of both immediate dangers and long-range threats. An evolutionary perspective helps to explain why human beings are vulnerable to anxiety disorders, which can be viewed as problems that arise in the regulation of these necessary response systems (Nesse, 1999). The important question is not why we experience anxiety, but why it occasionally becomes maladaptive. When anxiety becomes excessive, or when intense fear is triggered at an inappropriate time or place, these response systems can become more harmful than helpful. In order to understand the etiology of anxiety disorders, we must consider a variety of psychological and biological systems that have evolved for the purpose of triggering and controlling these alarm responses.

Should we expect to find unique etiological pathways associated with each of the types of anxiety disorder listed in DSM-IV-TR? This seems unlikely, particularly in light of the extensive overlap among the various subtypes. Should we expect that all the different types of anxiety disorders are produced by the same causes? This also seems unlikely.

Marks and Nesse (1994) proposed a broad evolutionary perspective for the etiology of anxiety disorders that suggests a middle ground between these two extremes. They suggest that generalized forms of anxiety probably evolved to help the person prepare for threats that could not be identified clearly. More specific forms of anxiety and fear probably evolved to provide more effective responses to certain types of danger. For example, fear of heights is associated with a freezing of muscles rather than running away, which could lead to a fall. Social threats are more likely to provoke responses such as shyness and embarrassment that may increase acceptance by other people by making the individual seem less threatening. Each type of anxiety disorder can be viewed as the dysregulation of a mechanism that evolved to deal with a particular kind of danger. This model leads us to expect that the etiological pathways leading to various forms of anxiety disorders may be partially distinct but not completely independent.

## Social Factors

Stressful life events, particularly those involving danger and interpersonal conflict, can trigger the onset of certain kinds of anxiety disorders. Various aspects of parent–child relationships may leave some people more vulnerable to the development of anxiety disorders when they become adults. Taken together, the evidence bearing on these issues helps explain the relationship between, and the overlap among, anxiety disorders and mood disorders.

**Stressful Life Events** Common sense might suggest that people who experience high stress levels are likely to develop negative emotional reactions, which can range from feeling "on edge" to the onset of full-blown panic attacks. In Chapter 5 we reviewed the literature concerning stressful life events and depression. As we have seen, the measurement of stressful events is a complex matter, and it is difficult to establish causal relations between stress and psychological disorders. Nevertheless, several investigations suggest that stressful life events can influence the onset of anxiety disorders as well as depression. Patients with anxiety disorders are more likely than control subjects to report having experienced a negative event in the months preceding the initial development of their symptoms (de Beurs et al., 2001; Faravelli, Paterniti, & Servi, 1997).

Why do some negative life events lead to depression while others lead to anxiety? The nature of the event may be an important factor in determining the type of mental disorder that appears (Updegraff & Taylor, 2000). This possibility was initially reported by Finlay-Jones and Brown (1981), who interviewed women attending a general medical clinic. This group included women who were depressed, women with anxiety disorders, and women who qualified for a dual diagnosis of anxiety and depression. For the one-year period immediately preceding the onset of their symptoms, 82 percent of the depressed women, 85 percent of the anxious women, and 93 percent of the anxious/depressed women reported at least one severe event. Only 34 percent of the control group reported a similar event.

The investigators then examined the specific nature of the severe events. The women with anxiety symptoms were much more likely to have experienced an event involving danger (lack of security), whereas the women who were depressed were more likely to have experienced a severe loss (lack of hope). Mixed cases frequently reported both types of events. This pattern of results has also been found in more recent investigations (G.W. Brown, 1993; Rueter et al., 1999). These studies suggest that different types of environmental stress may lead to different types of emotional symptoms. Those associated with insecurity, including severe disagreements with other people, and danger seem to be mostly closely associated with anxiety disorders.

Further insights regarding the nature of stressful events and the onset of anxiety disorders have focused more specifically on agoraphobia. Serious interpersonal conflicts seem to be especially common prior to the onset of agoraphobia. Consider, for example, the following list of life events, which were all reported with greater frequency by patients being treated for agoraphobia when they were compared to people visiting a general practice physician (Franklin & Andrews, 1989):

- Increase in serious arguments with partner or parents
- Serious problems with a close friend, neighbour, or relative
- Breakup of a steady relationship

Each of these events was at least four times more common in the agoraphobic group. The relatively high frequency of stressful life events was accompanied by a rather remarkable lack of insight on the part of the agoraphobic patients. When they were asked about their understanding of the development of their disorder, 90 percent said that they found the onset of agoraphobic symptoms "totally baffling and incomprehensible." Thus, although patients with anxiety disorders are usually very much aware of their own subjective discomfort, they may be lacking in self-awareness when it comes to the potential causes of this emotional distress.

**Childhood Adversity** If recent dangers and conflicts can precipitate the full blown symptoms of an anxiety disorder, do past experiences—those that took place years ago—set the stage for this experience? Further research by George Brown and his colleagues indicates that they can (Brown & Harris, 1993). Their studies of these phenomena focus on measures of childhood adversity. This concept included women's recollections of parental indifference (being physically or emotionally neglected by their parents for a period of at least 12 months prior to age 17) and physical abuse (being physically beaten or threatened with violence, usually in an attempt to control or punish the child).

Within a community sample of approximately 400 working-class women, Brown and Harris (1993) found that 25 percent met diagnostic criteria for at least one type of anxiety disorder. The relationship between childhood adversity and the presence of these anxiety disorders is illustrated in Figure 6–3. Women who were suffering from most types of anxiety disorder were more likely than women with no disorder to report having been exposed to parental indifference and physical abuse during childhood or adolescence. This pattern was particularly striking for the women with panic disorder. In contrast, women with specific phobias or only mild symptoms of agoraphobia could not be distinguished from the control group on the basis of childhood adversity. This result is consistent with the notion that somewhat different etiological pathways may be associated with specific phobias than with other, frequently more severe forms of anxiety disorder.

The evidence regarding childhood adversity and the later development of adult psychopathology points, once again, to similarities between depression and certain kinds of anxiety disorders. People who report parental neglect, abuse, and violence are more vulnerable to the development of both mood disorders and anxiety disorders (Kessler et al., 1997; Lara & Klein, 1999). Causal pathways are complex. There does not seem to be a direct connection between particular forms of adverse environmental events and specific types of mental disorder.

**Childhood Adversity and Anxiety Disorders**

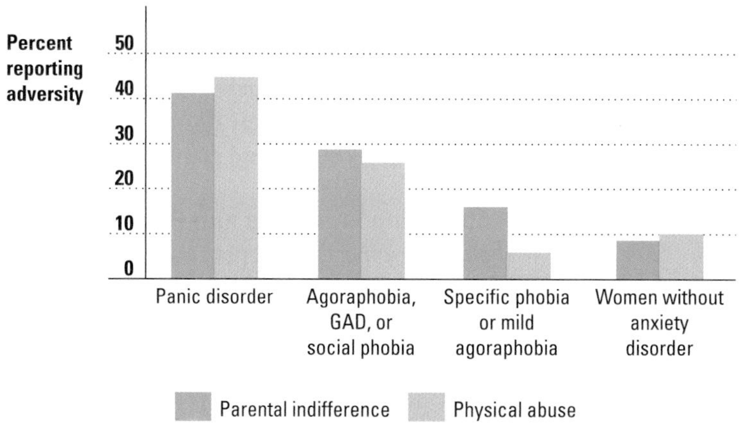


**FIGURE 6–3: Parental indifference and physical abuse are frequently reported by women who later develop panic disorder. They do not seem to be related to specific phobias.**

*Source:* G.W. Brown and T.O. Harris, 1993, Aetiology of anxiety and depressive disorders in an inner-city population. 1. Early adversity. *Psychological Medicine, 23,* 143–154.

**Attachment Relationships and Separation Anxiety** The evidence regarding childhood adversity is similar to another perspective on the etiology of anxiety disorders that has been concerned with the infant's attachment relationship with caretakers. Attachment theory (see Chapter 2) integrates the psychodynamic perspective with field observations of primate behaviour and with laboratory research with human infants. According to the British psychiatrist John Bowlby (1973, 1980), anxiety is an innate response to separation, or the threat of separation, from the caretaker. Those infants who are insecurely attached to their parents are presumably more likely to develop anxiety disorders, especially agoraphobia, when they become adults.

Several studies have found that people with panic disorder and agoraphobia are more likely to report that they had problems associated with insecure attachment as children (Manicavasagar, Silove, & Hadzi-Pavlovic, 1998; Shear, 1996). Anxious attachment as infants may make these individuals more vulnerable, once they are adults, to the threats that are contained in interpersonal conflict, for example, loss of a loved one if a marriage dissolves. This hypothesis fits nicely with the observation (noted previously) that interpersonal conflict is a relatively frequent triggering event for the onset of agoraphobic symptoms. There is also an interesting connection between attachment styles and childhood adversity. People who report childhood adversities involving interpersonal trauma (assault, abuse, neglect) are more likely to be insecurely attached, and they are also more vulnerable to depression and anxiety (Mickelson, Kessler, & Shaver, 1997). This issue will be discussed again in the next chapter, when we discuss posttraumatic stress disorder.

Attachment difficulties are not restricted to agoraphobia. Studies indicate that they also set the stage for other types of anxiety in adults, including generalized anxiety disorder (Cassidy, 1995; Cassidy & Mohr, 2001), social phobia (Eng et al., 2001), and the anxious forms of personality disorder (see Chapter 9; Paris, 1998). Of course, many anxiously attached children do not develop anxiety disorders when they grow up. The suggestion of a causal relationship between childhood attachments and adult anxiety disorders is intriguing, but the evidence supporting it will not be convincing until scientists conduct longitudinal studies to test this hypothesis. The same criticism obviously applies to Brown's research on childhood adversity. To test these hypotheses further, psychologists must conduct studies based on direct observations of parent–child relationships rather than on retrospective accounts of childhood behaviours, which are highly subjective and not always accurate or reliable.

## Psychological Factors

Research suggests that stressful life events and childhood adversity contribute to the development of anxiety disorders. But what are the specific mechanisms that link these experiences to emotional difficulties, such as intense fears, panic attacks, and excessive worry? This question brings our discussion of etiology to a different level of analysis. A number of psychological mechanisms undoubtedly play important roles in helping to shape the development and maintenance of anxiety disorders. They include learning processes and cognitive events.

**Learning Processes and Phobias** Since the 1920s, experimental psychologists working in laboratory settings have been interested in the possibility that specific fears might be learned through classical (or Pavlovian) conditioning (Ayres, 1998). The central mechanism in the classical conditioning process is the association between an unconditioned stimulus (US) and a conditioned stimulus (CS). The US is able to elicit a strong unconditioned emotional response (UR), such as fear. Examples of potential USs are painfully loud and unexpected noises, the sight of dangerous animals, and sudden, intense pain. According to psychologists' original views of the classical conditioning process, the CS could be any neutral stimulus that happened to be present when an intense fear reaction was provoked. Through the process of association, the CS would subsequently elicit a conditioned response (CR), which was similar in quality to the original UR (see Chapter 2). This explanation for the development of specific phobias fits easily with common sense as well as with clinical experience. Many intense, persistent, excessive fears seem to develop after the person has experienced a traumatic event (Antony & Barlow, 2002; Cox & Taylor, 1999).

*Preparedness* Current views on the process by which fears are learned suggest that the process is guided by a *module*, or specialized circuit in the brain, that has been shaped by evolutionary pressures (Öhman & Mineka, 2001). Some psychologists have argued that the mind includes a very large number of prepared modules (specialized neural circuits) that serve particular adaptive functions, such as the recognition of faces and the perception of language (Pinker, 1997). These modules are designed to operate at maximal speed, are activated automatically, and perform without conscious awareness. They are also highly selective, in the sense that the module is particularly responsive to a narrow range of stimuli. Human beings seem to be prepared to develop intense, persistent fears only to a select set of objects or situations. Fear of these stimuli may have conferred a selective advantage upon those people—hundreds of thousands of years ago—who were able to develop fears and consequently avoid certain kinds of dangerous stimuli, such as heights, snakes, and storms. This is not to say that the fears are innate or present at birth but rather that they can be learned and maintained very easily.

Many investigations have been conducted to test various facets of this **preparedness model** (Mineka & Öhman, 2002; Öhman & Mineka, 2001). The results of these studies support many features of the theory. For example, conditioned responses to fear-relevant stimuli (such as spiders and snakes) are more resistant to extinction than are those to fear-irrelevant stimuli (such as flowers). Furthermore, it is possible to develop conditioned fear responses after only one trial of learning.

The process of prepared conditioning may play an important role in the etiology of both social phobias and specific phobias. In specific phobias, the prepared stimuli are things like snakes, heights, storms, and small enclosed places. The prepared stimulus in social phobias might involve other people's faces. We are prepared to fear faces that appear angry, critical, or rejecting if they are directed toward us (Öhman, 1996). This process is presumably an evolutionary remnant of factors involved in establishing dominance hierarchies, which maintain social order among primates. Animals that are defeated in a dominance conflict are often allowed to remain as part of the group if they behave submissively. The responses of people with social phobias may be somewhat analogous, in the sense that they are afraid of directly facing, or being evaluated by, other people. When a performer makes eye contact with his or her audience, an association may develop very quickly between fear and angry or critical facial expressions.

*Observational Learning* We all learn many behaviours through imitation. Albert Bandura's early work on modelling, for example, demonstrated that children who observe a model hitting a doll are more likely to behave aggressively themselves when given the opportunity (see Chapter 2). Similar processes may also affect the etiology of intense fear, because some phobias develop in the absence of any direct experience with the feared object. People apparently learn to avoid certain stimuli if they observe other people showing a strong fear response to those stimuli (Poulton & Menzies, 2002). In other words, the traumatic event does not have to happen to you; it may be enough for you to witness a traumatic event happening to someone else or to watch someone else behave fearfully.

One series of intriguing experiments has combined observational learning with the preparedness formulation (e.g., Mineka & Cook, 1993). These studies focused on an animal model (see Research Methods in Chapter 5) of phobias: fear reactions among rhesus monkeys. Rhesus monkeys raised in their natural environment are markedly afraid of certain kinds of stimuli, such as snakes. Most monkeys reared in the laboratory do not initially react fearfully when they are presented with a toy snake. They quickly acquire this fear, however, after watching a monkey reared in the wild exhibit intense fear in the presence of snakes. The greater the fear exhibited by the wild monkey, the more intense the fears developed by the observer monkey. Further, live observation is not necessary. Monkeys can learn to fear snakes by watching videotapes of other monkeys exhibiting fear reactions.

Fear of snakes is clearly adaptive, because snakes represent a threat to rhesus monkeys in their natural environment. This could be seen as a prepared association. Will monkeys also learn to avoid nonthreatening and presumably unprepared stimuli if they observe a model reacting with intense fear? Is the association between fear and particular stimuli random, or is it selective? The data from these studies indicate that the relationship is, in fact, selective: Monkeys are prepared to learn to avoid fear-relevant stimuli (such as snakes and crocodiles) but are not prepared to learn to avoid fear-irrelevant stimuli (such as rabbits or kittens) (Cook & Mineka, 1991).

Learning experiences are clearly important in the etiology of phobias, but their impact often depends on the existence of prepared associations between stimuli. Furthermore, vicarious learning is often as important as direct experience.

*Vicarious learning can influence the development of strong fear responses. Children who observe adults demonstrating strong emotional responses—like these children in the aftermath of the 1998 tornado that touched down in Norwich, Ontario, destroying their great grandmother's house—may be likelier to develop phobias.*

**Cognitive Factors** Up to this point, we have talked about the importance of life events and specific learning experiences—variables that can be measured outside the organism. But cognitive events also play an important role as mediators between experience and response. Perceptions, memory, and attention all influence the ways that we react to events in our environments. It is now widely accepted that these cognitive factors play a crucial role in the etiology and maintenance of various types of anxiety disorders. We will focus on four aspects of this literature: perception of controllability and predictability, catastrophic misinterpretation (panic attacks), attentional biases and shifts in the focus of attention, and thought suppression.

*Perception of Control* There is an important relationship between anxiety and the perception of control. People who believe that they are able to control events in their environment are less likely to show symptoms of anxiety than are people who believe that they are helpless. This is, of course, part of the reason that the events of September 11, 2001, were so terrifying. The attack on the World Trade Center in New York City was beyond the control of its victims, who were going about their everyday activities.

The importance of this factor can be seen in laboratory studies that have focused on animal models of anxious behaviour, sometimes known as "experimental neurosis." Beginning with Pavlov's research on classical conditioning with dogs in the 1920s (see Chapter 2), experimental psychologists have shown that procedures such as extremely difficult discrimination-learning tasks (in which an animal is required to make choices between two almost identical stimuli, such as a circle and an ellipse) can produce neurotic behaviours that resemble disorders seen in adult humans. Examples include generalized anxiety and agitation, increased startle responses, and the disruption of purposeful behaviours (such as feeding and harm avoidance). The common feature running through all of these procedures involves repeated exposure to uncontrollable or unpredictable environmental events (Chorpita & Barlow, 1998; Mineka & Kihlstrom, 1978).

An extensive body of evidence supports the conclusion that people who believe that they are less able to control events in their environment are more likely to develop global forms of anxiety (Andrews, 1996), as well as various specific types of anxiety disorder (Mineka & Zinbarg, 1998). Laboratory research indicates that feelings of lack of control contribute to the onset of panic attacks among patients with panic disorder (Sanderson, Rapee, & Barlow, 1989). The perception of uncontrollability has also been linked to the submissive behaviour frequently seen among people with social phobias as well as the chronic worries of people with generalized anxiety disorder.

*Catastrophic Misinterpretation* A somewhat different type of cognitive dysfunction has been described by David M. Clark, a psychologist at the University of London, England. According to this view, panic disorder may be caused by the *catastrophic misinterpretation* of bodily sensations or perceived threat (Clark, 1986, 1999). Although panic attacks can be precipitated by external stimuli, they are usually triggered by internal stimuli, such as bodily sensations, thoughts, or images. On the basis of past experience, these stimuli initiate an anxious mood, which leads to a variety of physiological sensations that typically accompany negative emotional reactions (changes in heart rate, respiration rate, dizziness, and so on). Anxious mood is accompanied by a narrowing of the person's attentional focus and an increased awareness of bodily sensations.

The crucial stage comes next, when the person misinterprets the bodily sensation as a catastrophic event. For example, a person who believes that there is something wrong with his heart might misinterpret a slight acceleration in heart rate as being a sign that he is about to have a heart attack. He might say to himself, "My heart will stop and I'll die!" This reaction ensures the continued operation of this feedback loop, with the misinterpretation enhancing the person's sense of threat, and so on, until the process spirals out of control. Thus both cognitive misinterpretation and biological reactions associated with the perception of threat are necessary for a panic attack to occur.

The person's automatic, negative thoughts may also lead him or her to engage in behaviours that are expected to increase his safety, when in fact they are counterproductive. For example, some people believe that they should take deep breaths or monitor their heart rate if they become aroused. This is actually incorrect information, and the alleged safety behaviours can further exaggerate the person's fear response.

Many studies have found that the subjective experience of body sensations is, in fact, closely associated with maladaptive self-statements among patients with panic disorder (McNally, 1994). For example, Westling and Öst (1993) asked people with panic disorder to keep a daily diary in which they would write down a description of each panic attack they experienced during a two-week period. Each record was made during the attack or, if that wasn't possible, immediately after it ended. Most of the panic attack descriptions contained catastrophic misinterpretations of bodily sensations (such as "I'm going to suffocate" or "I'm having a heart attack").

This pattern supports the hypothesis that cognitive factors play a central role in many panic attacks. It also indicates, however, that catastrophic misinterpretations may not account for all instances of panic attacks, unless one assumes that catastrophic misinterpretations are sometimes so rapid that they occur outside of conscious awareness (Clark, 1986). Patients with panic disorder sometimes experience panic attacks in their sleep (Craske & Rowe, 1997). How could that happen if the escalation to panic requires catastrophic misinterpretation of physical sensations? Clark points out that people monitor their bodily sensations while they sleep. For example, bladder distention is detected and awakens the person when there is a need to urinate. Similarly, people who have panic attacks may be able to detect feared bodily sensations while they sleep, and respond to these sensations with alarm. Research provides some support for this hypothesis (Craske & Freed, 1995).

How do episodes of panic naturally come to an end? Adam Radomsky (Concordia University) and colleagues have investigated the intriguing question. Their research indicates that panic attacks come to end for a variety of reasons, including escape or avoidance behaviours, such as taking fast-acting tranquilizers (e.g., Ativan), distracting oneself, performing a soothing breathing exercise, or fleeing a feared situation (Radomsky et al., 1998, 2002).

*Attention to Threat and Biased Information Processing* Earlier in this chapter we discussed how worry involves negative thoughts and images that anticipate some possible future danger. In recent years, several lines of research

## CANADIAN FOCUS Anxiety Sensitivity and Panic Attacks

What makes people vulnerable to experience panic attacks? As David M. Clark (1986) observed, people with panic disorder have an enduring tendency to catastrophically misinterpret harmless bodily sensations such as palpitations, breathlessness, or dizziness. This enduring tendency is known as elevated *anxiety sensitivity;* the tendency to be frightened of bodily sensations, which arises from beliefs that the sensations are harmful (Reiss & McNally, 1985; Taylor, 1999). People with high anxiety sensitivity, for example, are frightened of palpitations because they believe this sensation leads to cardiac arrest. People with low anxiety sensitivity regard palpitations as a harmless sensation.

A good deal of research on anxiety sensitivity has come from Canada. For example, Brian Cox at the University of Manitoba spearheaded the development of measures that capture the full range of features that characterize anxiety sensitivity (Taylor & Cox, 1998a,b). One of these measures was recently used in a large, cross-national study that included participants from Canada, the United States, Mexico, Spain, France, and the Netherlands (Zvolensky et al., 2003). That study found evidence that the basic components of anxiety sensitivity could be identified in various cultures: (1) fear of bodily sensations (e.g., fear of palpitations, arising from the belief they will lead to heart attacks), and (2) a combined factor, consisting of fear of cognitive dyscontrol (e.g., fear of concentration difficulties, arising from the belief that they will lead to insanity) and fear of publicly observable anxiety reactions (e.g., fear of blushing or trembling, arising from the belief that these will attract rejection or ridicule from other people).

Investigations by Sherry Stewart (Dalhousie University) and Randi McCabe (McMaster University) show that people with high anxiety sensitivity, compared to those with low anxiety sensitivity, are more likely to focus their attention on anxiety-related stimuli (Stewart et al., 1998), and are more likely to recall anxiety-related information (McCabe, 1999), perhaps because they focus greater attention on these stimuli. These results reflect a form of biased information processing, where highly anxiety-sensitive people are hypervigilant for threat-related stimuli.

Research from the University of British Columbia showed that anxiety sensitivity is most elevated in panic disorder, compared with other anxiety disorders (Taylor et al., 1992). This is consistent with the view that elevated anxiety plays an especially important role in panic attacks and panic disorder.

Other studies have shown that elevated anxiety sensitivity is a risk factor for the development of panic attacks. For example, research has shown that the severity of a person's anxiety sensitivity is one of the best predictors of whether the person will later experience panic attacks when he or she encounters stressful events (Schmidt, 1999). Research conducted at the University of British Columbia and elsewhere has shown that anxiety sensitivity arises from a combination of genetic factors and environmental (learning) factors (Jang, Stein, Taylor, & Livesley, 1999; Stewart et al., 2001).

Studies by Nova Scotian researchers Sherry Stewart (Dalhousie University) and Margo Watt (St. Francis Xavier University) have sought to pinpoint the specific sorts of learning experiences that are important in producing elevated anxiety sensitivity. These retrospective studies suggest that particular sorts of parent–child interactions are associated with later elevated anxiety sensitivity, which in turn is associated with an increased risk for panic attacks (e.g., Stewart et al., 2001; Watt & Stewart, 2003). Important childhood learning experiences include (1) observing one's parents "losing control" by becoming very angry or drunk, (2) observing one's parents becoming alarmed about their own anxiety-related sensations (e.g., seeing one's father become frightened and become bedridden when he experiences palpitations), (3) having parents repeatedly warn the child about the dangers of bodily sensations (e.g., being told, as a child, that you shouldn't go out and play if you are feeling hot and "feverish"), and (4) receiving reinforcements when one experiences anxiety-related sensations (e.g., staying home from school and receiving treats when you have a stomachache).

Researchers at McMaster University, the University of British Columbia, and elsewhere have also investigated how interoceptive exposure exercises can reduce anxiety sensitivity, both in panic disorder and in other anxiety disorders (Antony & Swinson, 2000; Taylor, 2000, 2004). The Canadian studies, along with research in other parts of the world, have furthered our understanding of panic attacks and their treatment. ◆

Concordia University psychologist **Michel Dugas** is a leading expert on generalized anxiety disorder. His cognitive model of this disorder has led to a promising new treatment.

have converged to clarify the basic cognitive mechanisms involved in worry. Experts now believe that attention plays a crucial role in the onset of this process. People who are prone to excessive worrying are unusually sensitive to cues that signal the existence of future threats (MacLeod et al., 2002; Mathews & Mackintosh, 2000). They attend vigilantly to even fleeting signs of danger, especially when they are under stress. At such times, the recognition of danger cues triggers a maladaptive, self-perpetuating cycle of cognitive processes that can quickly spin out of control.

The threatening information that is generated in this process is presumably encoded in memory in the form of elaborate schemas (see Chapter 5), which are easily reactivated. In comparison with the depressed person, who is convinced that failure will definitely occur, the anxious person is afraid of failure that may occur as a future event, the outcome of which remains uncertain (Beck & Emery, 1985). The threat schemas of anxious people contain a high proportion of "what-if" questions, such as "What am I going to do if I don't do well in school this semester?" (Vasey & Borkovec, 1992).

**Anxious Apprehension and Social Phobia**

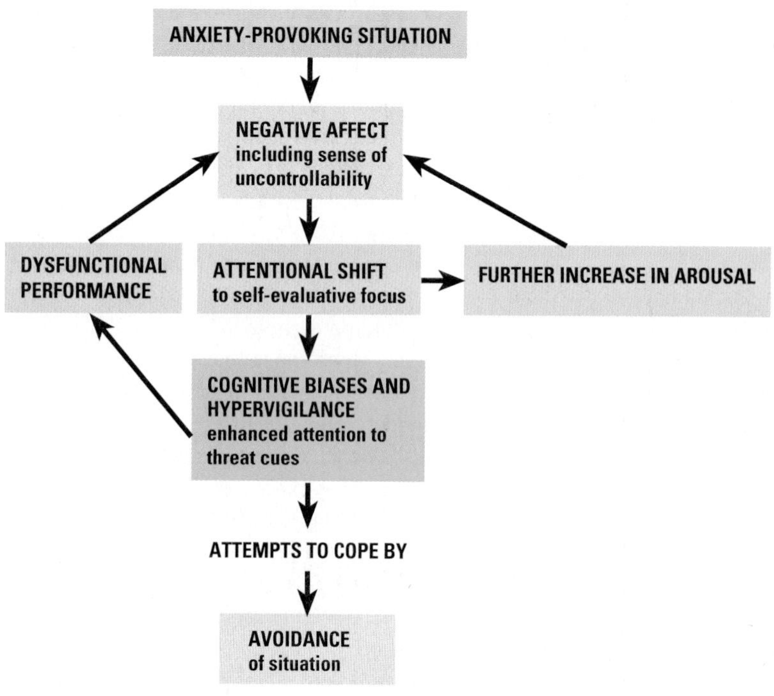


**FIGURE 6–4: Processes involved in the generation of social anxiety.**

*Source:* Adapted from D.H. Barlow, 2001, *Anxiety and its disorders*, 2nd ed., p. 65. New York: Guilford.

Once attention has been drawn to threatening cues, the performance of adaptive, problem-solving behaviours is disrupted, and the worrying cycle launches into a repetitive sequence in which the person rehearses anticipated events and searches for ways to avoid them. The readily accessed network of threat-related schemas then activates an additional series of "what-if" questions that quickly leads to a dramatic increase in negative affect.

According to Michel Dugas (Concordia University) and Robert Ladouceur (Laval University), one factor that perpetuates worry concerns the person's attitudes about uncertainty. People with GAD may tend to worry excessively because they have a low tolerance for accepting uncertainty in their lives. They may worry in an effort to prepare themselves for dealing with potential threat (Dugas et al., 1998; Ladouceur et al., 2000). This **intolerance of uncertainty** is a special sort of sensitivity to threat, which arises from the belief that it is unacceptable that threatening things occur. People who are intolerant of uncertainty become upset by the possibility of threatening events, even when the probability of these events is very small. Considering that daily life is fraught with uncertainties, people who have difficulty dealing with uncertainty are likely to frequently worry and become anxious about threats. Intolerance of uncertainty may lead the person to focus attention on ambiguities or uncertainties in life, in an effort to identify and pre-empt danger (Dugas & Koerner, in press). This model has led to a promising new treatment for GAD (Dugas et al., 2003).

Attentional mechanisms also seem to be involved in the etiology and maintenance of social phobias. People who are capable of performing a particular task when they are alone (in practice) cannot perform it in front of an audience. Barlow (2001) has argued that this deterioration in skill is caused by anxious apprehension, which is similar to Borkovec's description of the process of worrying. The cycle is illustrated in Figure 6–4. An increase in negative affect presumably triggers a shift toward self-focused attention ("Oh, no, I'm getting really upset") and activates cognitive biases and threat schemas ("What if I make a mistake?"). The person becomes distracted by these thoughts, and performance deteriorates. In a sense, the person's fearful expectations become a self-fulfilling prophesy.

*Thought Suppression: Obsessive–Compulsive Disorder* The cognitive model of worry or anxious apprehension places primary emphasis on the role of attentional processes. Worrying is unproductive and self-defeating in large part because it is associated with a focus on self-evaluation (fear of failure) and negative emotional responses rather than on external aspects of the problem and active coping behaviours. We may be consciously aware of these processes and simultaneously be unable to inhibit them. The struggle to control our thoughts often leads to a process known as *thought suppression*, an active attempt to stop thinking about something.

It seems simple to say, "Stop worrying," but it is virtually impossible for some people to do so. In fact, evidence suggests that trying to rid one's mind of a distressing or unwanted thought can have the unintended effect of making the thought more intrusive (Wegner, 1994). Thought suppression might actually increase, rather than decrease, the strong emotions associated with those thoughts. As noted by University of Waterloo psychologist Christine Purdon (1999), there is some evidence for this paradoxical effect of thought suppression in anxiety disorders. However, evidence for its role in OCD is inconsistent. In fact, a recent experiment by Purdon and colleagues (in press) found no evidence of the paradoxical effect of thought suppression in OCD. Nevertheless, people with OCD may become particularly upset about their failures to control (suppress) their obsessions, and this may make the person anxious and depressed and thereby worsen their OCD (Purdon, in press; Purdon, Rowa, & Antony, in press). Similarly, research by Amy Janeck (University of British Columbia) and colleagues reveals that people are excessively preoccupied with their thoughts; they are highly aware of, and monitor their thoughts and engage in "too much thinking about thinking" (Janeck et al., 2003). This may be because people with OCD regard their obsessions as unacceptable and repugnant.

## Biological Factors

Several pieces of evidence indicate that biological events play an important role in the development and maintenance of anxiety disorders. In the following pages we review the role of genetic factors and the use of chemicals to induce symptoms of panic. These factors undoubtedly interact with the social and psychological variables that we have considered in the preceding sections.

**Genetic Factors** Some of the most useful information about the validity of anxiety disorders comes from studies aimed at identifying the influence of genetic factors. These data address the overlap, as well as the distinctions, among various types of anxiety disorder. They also shed additional light on the relationship between anxiety and depression.

*Family Studies* Family studies of panic disorder raise interesting questions about subdivisions under the general heading of anxiety disorders (van den Heuvel et al., 2000). They indicate that the relatives of people with panic disorder show an elevated risk of panic disorder themselves but not an elevated risk of generalized anxiety disorder (see Figure 6–5). The same pattern holds for the relatives of people with generalized anxiety disorder: The relatives exhibit a high rate of GAD but not a high rate of panic disorder (Noyes et al., 1987). Similar results have been reported in other studies (Skre et al., 1994). This evidence is consistent with the proposition that panic disorder and GAD are, indeed, etiologically separate disorders.

A family study of social phobia has demonstrated that the *generalized* form of this disorder (where the person is fearful in most

**Family Data Regarding the Distinction between Panic Disorder and GAD**

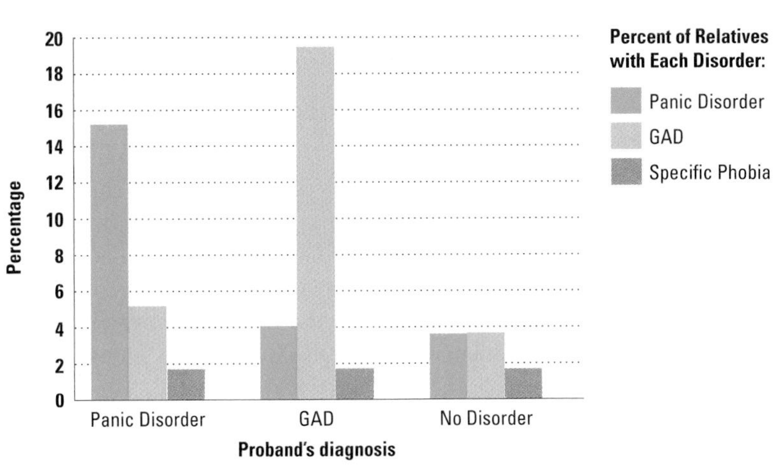


**FIGURE 6–5: Frequency of anxiety disorders in first-degree relatives of three types of people.**

types of social situations) is also familial in nature and etiologically distinct from other types of anxiety disorder. The investigators studied first-degree relatives of people who met the criteria for social phobia and had never had any other type of anxiety disorder (Fyer et al., 1993; Mannuzza et al., 1995). The probands (or "index cases") in the control group were people who had never had a mental disorder. The results indicated that the rate of social phobia was particularly high (16 percent) in the relatives of probands whose social phobia was generalized. In contrast, only 5 percent of the relatives in the control group met the diagnostic criteria for social phobia. Moreover, only 6 percent of the relatives of probands with nongeneralized social phobia (in which the person's fear is limited to one particular type of social situation, such as public speaking) had social phobia themselves. This pattern of results suggest that the nongeneralized form of social phobia is not influenced by genetic factors.

Data regarding obsessive–compulsive disorder suggest that a more general vulnerability to anxiety disorders is genetically transmitted through the family (Wolff et al., 2000). The predisposition can apparently be expressed in different ways, with OCD being only one of them. One study compared the frequency of mental disorders among relatives of patients with OCD to prevalence rates in relatives of people without a mental disorder (Black et al., 1992). The lifetime prevalence of OCD was roughly 2 percent in both groups, no higher than would be expected in the general population. There were significant differences between groups, however, with regard to other types of anxiety disorder. Thirty percent of the patients' relatives met the diagnostic criteria for at least one anxiety disorder, most often GAD. In comparison, only 17 percent of the relatives of the control subjects qualified for a diagnosis of some type of anxiety disorder. The relatives of the OCD probands apparently did not inherit a specific predisposition to this disorder, but they did inherit a more global tendency toward anxiety disorders. The expression of that tendency is presumably influenced by subsequent experience.

The results of the family studies all point toward the potential influence of genetic factors in anxiety disorders. Most of the evidence also supports the validity of the DSM-IV-TR subtypes. Comparisons of panic and GAD support the movement toward separating these disorders in the diagnostic manual. The generalized form of social phobia also seems to be at least somewhat distinct from the other anxiety disorders. On the other hand, data regarding relatives of OCD probands are more consistent with the traditional preference in psychiatric classification for lumping anxiety disorders together.

*Twin Studies* Family studies do not prove the involvement of genes, because family members also share environmental factors (diet, culture, and so on). Twin studies provide a more stringent test of the genetic hypothesis (see Chapter 2). Several studies have found evidence for genetic contributions to anxiety disorder. For example, research at the University of British Columbia indicates that social anxiety arises from a mix of genetic and environmental factors (Stein, Jang, & Livesley, 2002).

The largest and most sophisticated twin studies have been conducted by Kendler and colleagues (e.g., Kendler et al., 2001; Kendler et al., 1992a). The people who participated in this study were not psychiatric patients; they were living in the community and were identified through a statewide registry of twins. Diagnoses were assigned following structured diagnostic interviews conducted by the research team.

Table 6–4 summarizes the results of Kendler's study with regard to several types of anxiety disorder. For each type, concordance rates were significantly higher for MZ twins than for DZ twins. Nevertheless, the MZ concordance rates were also relatively low (in comparison to MZ concordance rates for bipolar mood disorders, for example). Anxiety disorders appear to be modestly heritable, with genetic factors accounting for between 20 and 30 percent of the variance in the transmission of GAD. (See Research Methods in Chapter 17 for a discussion of heritability.)

Kendler and his colleagues have examined the influence of both genetic and environmental factors on the etiology of several types of panic disorder, phobia, GAD, and major depression in these samples of twins (Hettema, Prescott, & Kendler, 2001; Kendler et al., 2001; Kendler et al., 1995). Their analyses have led them to several important conclusions:

1. Genetic risk factors for these disorders are neither highly specific (a different set of genes being associated with each dis-

order) nor highly nonspecific (one common set of genes causing vulnerability for all disorders).

2. Two genetic factors have been identified: one associated with GAD and major depression, and the other with panic disorder and phobias.
3. Environmental risk factors that would be unique to individuals also play an important role in the etiology of all anxiety disorders. Environmental factors that would be shared by all members of a family do not appear to be influential.

**TABLE 6–4 Twin Concordance Rates for Specific Anxiety Disorders**

| Disorder | MZ | DZ |
|---|---|---|
| Panic disorder | .24 | .11 |
| Agoraphobia | .23 | .15 |
| Social phobia | .24 | .15 |
| Animal phobia | .26 | .11 |
| Generalized anxiety disorder | .28 | .17 |

*Source:* Data from the Virginia Twin Registry (K.S. Kendler, M.C. Neale, R.C. Kessler, A.C. Heath, and L.J. Eaves, 1992a, Generalized anxiety disorder in women: A population-based twin study. *Archives of General Psychiatry, 49,* 267–272; and K.S. Kendler, M.C. Neale, R.C. Kessler, A.C. Heath, and L.J. Eaves, 1992b, The genetic epidemiology of phobias in women: The interrelationship of agoraphobia, social phobia, situational phobia, and simple phobia. *Archives of General Psychiatry, 49,* 273–281).

**Neuroanatomy** Laboratory studies of fear conditioning in animals have identified specific pathways in the brain that are responsible for detecting and organizing a response to danger (LeDoux, 2000). The amygdala plays a central role in these circuits, which represent the biological underpinnings of the *evolved fear module* that we discussed earlier in connection with classical conditioning of phobias (see p. 208). Scientists have discovered these pathways by monitoring and manipulating brain activities in animals that are participating in studies using classical conditioning to pair an originally neutral stimulus (the CS) with an aversive stimulus (the US). The results of these studies tell us *where* emotional responses, such as fear and panic, are located in terms of brain regions. They also begin to explain *how* they are produced. That knowledge, coupled with data regarding social and psychological factors, will help us understand *why* people experience problems such as excessive fears and panic attacks.

The brain circuits involved in fear conditioning are illustrated in Figure 6–6. This drawing uses the example of a person who has seen a dangerous snake (Carter, 1998). Sensory information is projected to the thalamus, and from there it is directed to other brain areas for processing. Emotional stimuli follow two primary pathways, both of which lead to the amygdalae. The first pathway (the red arrows) might be called a "short cut," and represents the evolved fear module for conditioned fear. The message follows a direct connection between the thalamus and the amygdalae, which is connected to the hypothalamus. Behavioural responses (such as the "fight or flight" response) are then activated and coordinated through projections from the hypothalamus to endocrine glands and the autonomic nervous system (see Chapter 2, as well as the discussion of the HPA axis in Chapter 5). Notice that this first pathway does not involve connections to cortical areas of the brain that might involve higher-level cognitive functions such as conscious memory or decision making. The amygdalae does store unconscious, emotional memories—the kind that are generated through prepared learning.

A second, complementary path from the thalamus (the purple arrows) leads to the cortex and provides for a detailed, and comparatively slower, analysis of the information that has been detected. Using the example in Figure 6–6, information about the snake would be sent to the visual cortex. Once the pattern is recognized as a snake, the data would be integrated with additional information from memory about its emotional significance ("potentially dangerous"). This message would then be sent to the amygdalae, which could, in turn, trigger an organized response to threat. This second pathway is longer and more complex than the first, and it will take longer to generate a response. The first pathway has presumably evolved because it is adaptive; it provides the organism with an alarm system that can be used to avoid immediate dangers in the environment. The fact that information can follow either path is consistent with the idea that some fear responses are "hard-wired" (easily learned, difficult to extinguish, and mediated by unconscious processes) while others are dependent on higher-level analyses that involved thinking and reasoning.

A word of caution must be added when we consider the functions of these specific neural pathways. The fact that they are involved in processing fearful reactions does not mean

**Two Pathways in the Brain that Detect Danger and Trigger Fear Responses**

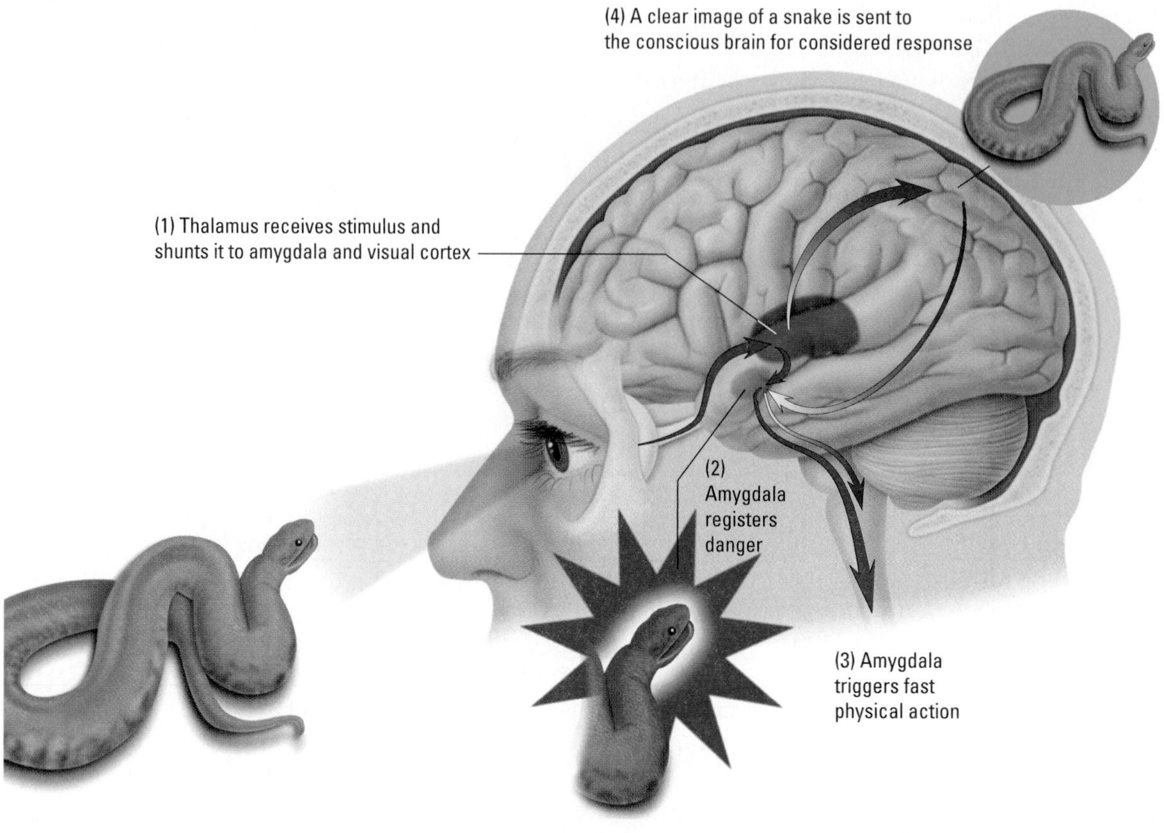
(4) A clear image of a snake is sent to the conscious brain for considered response
(1) Thalamus receives stimulus and shunts it to amygdala and visual cortex
(2) Amygdala registers danger
(3) Amygdala triggers fast physical action

**FIGURE 6–6: (1) Evolved fear module, and (2) slower, indirect route through cortical processing areas.**

*Source:* R. Carter, 1998, *Mapping the mind*, p. 96. Berkeley, CA: University of California Press.

that the amygdalae and associated structures are exclusively dedicated to this particular purpose. Studies with animals have shown that artificial stimulation of the amygdalae can produce different effects, depending in large part on the environmental context in which the animal is stimulated (Kagan, 1998). Anger, disgust, and sexual arousal are all emotional states that are associated with activity in pathways connecting the thalamus, the amygdalae, and their projections to other brain areas. Fear responses are, therefore, only one of the many kinds of behaviour associated with these circuits.

The brain regions that have been identified in studies of fear conditioning seem to play an important role in both phobic disorders (Öhman & Mineka, 2001) and panic disorder (Gorman et al., 2000). In the case of panic disorder, the fear module may be triggered at an inappropriate time. The sensitivity of this pathway is not the same in all people, and it is presumably influenced by genetic factors as well as hormone levels. Social and psychological factors that affect the threshold of the fear module include stressful life events and the development of separation anxiety during childhood (which increases the rate of panic disorder when these children become adults). The subcortical pathway between the thalamus and the amygdalae may be responsible for the misinterpretation of sensory information, which then triggers the hypothalamus and activates a variety of autonomic processes (dramatic increases in respiration rate, heart rate, and so on). Some investigators have also speculated that this brain circuit may be associated with the biased attention to threat cues that has been demonstrated in patients with generalized anxiety disorder (McNally, 1998).

Several other areas of the brain are also associated with anxiety and the symptoms of anxiety disorders. For example, the locus ceruleus, a small area located in the brain stem, has also been the focus of considerable emphasis in research on panic disorder. This area contains a large percentage of the brain's norepinephrine. Neural projections from the locus ceruleus extend to the cerebral cortex as well as various structures in the temporal lobes. Research with monkeys has demonstrated that the firing rate of neurons in the locus ceruleus increases dramatically when a monkey is frightened. Furthermore, electrical stimulation of the locus ceruleus triggers a strong fear response that resembles a panic attack (Goddard & Charney, 1997).

Finally, we should also mention the neurological foundations of OCD. The results of studies using brain imaging procedures with OCD patients do not overlap a great deal with findings for other types of anxiety disorder (Stein, 2000). As we discussed in Chapter 4, obsessions and compulsions are associated with multiple brain regions, including the caudate nucleus, the orbital prefrontal cortex, and the anterior cingulate cortex (see Figure 4–2 on p. 135). These circuits are overly active in people with OCD, especially when the person is confronted with stimuli that provoke his or her obsessions (Adler et al., 2000; Rauch et al., 2001).

**Neurochemistry** *Pharmacological challenge procedures* have played an important role in exploring the neurochemistry of panic disorder. The logic behind this method is simple: If a particular brain mechanism is "challenged," or stressed, by the artificial administration of chemicals, and if that procedure leads to the onset of a panic attack, then the neurochemical process that mediates that effect may also be responsible for panic attacks that take place outside the laboratory. Pharmacological challenge procedures were inspired by a few clinical studies, reported in the 1940s and 1950s, which noted that patients with "anxiety neurosis" sometimes experienced an increase in anxiety following vigorous physical exercise. This change in subjective symptoms appeared to be associated with an extremely rapid and excessive increase in lactic acid in the blood.[2]

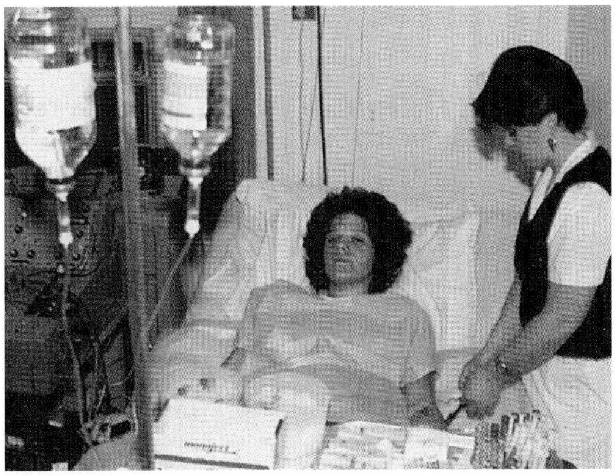

*Clinical scientists have studied factors that influence the onset of panic attacks by using lactate infusion, which can elicit a full-blown panic attack among people who have panic disorder.*

To examine this phenomenon more closely, two psychiatrists decided to infuse lactate directly into anxiety disorder patients and a control group of people who did not have a psychological disorder (Pitts & McClure, 1967). Shortly after the lactate infusion began, 13 out of 14 of the anxiety patients experienced an anxiety attack, which they described as being similar to their typical symptoms. In contrast, only 2 of the 10 normal subjects reported an anxiety attack during lactate infusion.

Since this experiment was reported, a large number of studies have demonstrated that lactate infusions can provoke panic attacks in anywhere from 50 to 90 percent of patients with anxiety or panic disorders, as compared to only 0 to 25 percent of normal control subjects (Barlow, 2001). Unfortunately, the biological process through which this effect is produced is still unknown. Part of the problem is the lack of specificity of the provocative agents. Many other procedures have been found to induce panic in the laboratory. These include the infusion of different chemicals, such as caffeine, as well as the inhalation of air enriched with carbon dioxide. Various pharmacological challenge studies have suggested the influence of serotonin, norepinephrine, GABA, and dopamine in the production of panic attacks (Bourin et al., 1998). The general finding appears to be that *several* neurotransmitter systems are involved in the etiology of panic disorder. This conclusion also applies to other forms of anxiety disorder, such as GAD and social phobia (Ninan, 1999; Nutt, 2001; Pollack, 2001).

Recently, a number of laboratory studies have examined the effects of the peptide cholecystokinin-4 (CCK-4). Research led by Ottawa University psychiatrist Jacques Bradwejn has shown that infusions of this substance trigger panic attacks, particularly in people with

---

[2]Lactic acid is formed during anaerobic respiration, the cellular respiration that occurs in the absence of oxygen. The respiratory and circulatory systems are usually able to support aerobic respiration when a person is resting. These systems become overloaded when skeletal muscles are used strenuously. Muscle fibres then need to depend on anaerobic respiration to generate energy (Hole, 1984). This process converts glucose to pyruvic acid. As the oxygen supply becomes depleted, pyruvic acid is converted to lactic acid, which accumulates in the bloodstream and is later converted back to glucose by the liver.

panic disorder (Bradwejn & Koszycki, 1995). CCK-4 is found in high concentrations in the amygdalae. It is possible that panic attacks sometimes arise when the amygdalae or related brain structures are hypersensitive to CCK-4.

Panic induction procedures should also allow investigators to monitor brain activities that occur during a panic attack. Unfortunately, this is a difficult task for a number of reasons. The brain areas that appear to be most important in panic disorder, such as the amygdalae and the locus ceruleus, are quite small and difficult to distinguish from adjacent structures. Distinguishing them requires imaging equipment that can produce very detailed pictures. Another problem involves the way in which patients may react to the brain imaging procedures, which can be anxiety-provoking because the person must be placed in a small constricted space and his or her movement restrained. People with panic disorder are more likely than others to hyperventilate in these circumstances, and hyperventilation can affect the resulting image. In spite of these problems, it seems likely that techniques such as PET and fMRI will be able to identify regions of the brain that are associated with the experience of panic attacks as well as other forms of anxiety. Studies using fMRI procedures do suggest that changes in the activity level of several brain areas, including the amygdalae, anterior cingulate, and the orbitofrontal cortex are found in people with panic disorder and other forms of anxiety (Bystritsky et al., 2001; Thomas et al., 2001).

Psychological interventions such as cognitive therapy can block lactate-induced panic attacks, and also block panic attacks triggered by other substances such as carbon dioxide (McNally, 1994; Taylor, 2000). Cognitive interventions appear to exert their panic-blocking effects by preventing the person from catastrophically misinterpreting the sensations induced by the substances. In other words, panics are blocked by helping the person realize that the intense sensations induced by lactate or carbon dioxide are harmless. This raises the question of whether the panic-inducing effects of lactate, carbon dioxide, and CCK-4 are due to some underlying biochemical abnormality, or whether they are mediated by the person's beliefs about bodily sensations. People who tend to catastrophically misinterpret bodily sensations (i.e., people with elevated anxiety sensitivity) may tend to panic whenever they are administered any substance that induces strong bodily sensations such as palpitations, dizziness, or breathlessness (Taylor, 1999). Our understanding of panic disorder may be furthered by investigating the biological processes associated with the tendency to catastrophically misinterpret bodily sensations.

## Treatment

Anxiety disorders are one of the areas of psychopathology in which clinical psychologists and psychiatrists are best prepared to improve the level of their clients' functioning. We begin by describing procedures that were used in an effort to help Ed, the person with obsessive–compulsive disorder whose problems were described at the beginning of this chapter.

### BRIEF CASE STUDY
**Ed's Treatment**

Ed's psychiatrist gave him a prescription for clomipramine (Anafranil), an antidepressant drug that is also used to treat people with severe obsessions. Weekly psychotherapy sessions continued as the dose was gradually increased. The medication had a beneficial impact after four weeks. Ed said that he had begun to feel as though he was trapped at the bottom of a well. After the medication, he no longer felt buried. His situation still wasn't great, but it no longer seemed hopeless or unbearable. He was also less intensely preoccupied by his obsessive violent images. They were still there, but they weren't as pressing. The drug had several annoying, though tolerable, side effects. His mouth felt dry, and he was occasionally a bit dizzy. He also noticed that he became tired more easily. Although Ed was no longer feeling seriously depressed, and the intensity of his obsessions was diminished, they had not disappeared, and he was now avoiding writing altogether.

Because the obsessions were still a problem, Ed's psychiatrist referred him to a psychologist who specialized in behaviour therapy for anxiety disorders. He continued seeing the psychiatrist every other week for checks on his medication, which he continued to take. The new therapist told Ed that his fears of particular letters and numbers would be maintained

*continued*

*cont.*

as long as he avoided writing. Ed agreed to begin writing short essays every day, for a period of at least 30 minutes. The content could vary from day to day—anything that Ed felt like writing about—but he was encouraged to include the names of his wife and brother as often as possible. Furthermore, he was instructed to avoid his compulsive writing style, intentionally allowing the parts of letters to be separated or loops to be closed. At the beginning and end of each essay, Ed was required to record his anxiety level so that the therapist could monitor changes in his subjective discomfort. Over a period of 8 to 10 weeks, Ed's handwriting began to change. It was less of a struggle to get himself to write, and his handwriting became more legible.

The final aspect of behavioural treatment was concerned with his fear of axes. Ed and his therapist drew up a list of objects and situations related to axes, arranging them from those that were the least anxiety-provoking through those that were most frightening. They began with the least frightening. In their first exposure session, Ed agreed to meet with the psychologist while a relatively dull, wood-splitting maul was located in the adjoining room. Ed was initially quite anxious and distracted, but his anxiety diminished considerably before the end of their two-hour meeting. Once that had been accomplished, the therapist helped him to confront progressively more difficult situations. These sessions were challenging and uncomfortable for Ed, but they allowed him to master his fears in an orderly fashion. By the end of the twelfth session of exposure, he was able to hold a sharp axe without fear. ◆

## Psychological Interventions

Psychoanalytic psychotherapy has been used to treat patients with anxiety disorders since Freud published his seminal papers at the turn of the twentieth century. The emphasis in this type of treatment is on fostering insight regarding the unconscious motives that presumably lie at the heart of the patient's symptoms, such as Ed's feelings about his brother. Although many therapists continue to employ this general strategy, it has not been shown to be effective in controlled outcome studies.

**Systematic Desensitization and Interoceptive Exposure** Like psychoanalysis, behaviour therapy was initially developed for the purpose of treating anxiety disorders, especially specific phobias. The first widely adopted procedure was known as systematic desensitization (see Chapter 3). In desensitization, the client is first taught progressive muscle relaxation. Then the therapist constructs a hierarchy of feared stimuli, beginning with those items that provoke only small amounts of fear and progressing through items that are most frightening. Then, while the client is in a relaxed state, he or she imagines the lowest item on the hierarchy. The item is presented repeatedly until the person no longer experiences an increase in anxiety when thinking about the object or situation. This process is repeated several times as the client moves systematically up the hierarchy, sequentially confronting images of stimuli that were originally rated as being more frightening.

In the years since systematic desensitization was originally proposed (Wolpe, 1958), many different variations on this procedure have been employed. The crucial feature of the treatment involves systematic maintained exposure to the feared stimulus (Mineka & Thomas, 1999). Positive outcomes have been reported, regardless of the specific manner in which exposure is accomplished. Some evidence indicates that direct ("in vivo") exposure works better than imaginal exposure. A few prolonged exposures can be as effective as a larger sequence of brief exposures. Another variation on exposure procedures, known as flooding, begins with the most frightening stimuli rather than working up gradually from the bottom of the hierarchy. All of these variations on the basic procedure have been shown to be effective in the treatment of phobic disorders. Several research studies have demonstrated that exposure therapy leads to clinically meaningful improvement when compared to placebo treatments. According to anxiety experts Martin Antony and Richard Swinson at McMaster University, positive results are typically maintained several months after the end of treatment (Antony & Swinson, 2000). Exposure is often accomplished in the presence of the therapist, but the treatment can be just as effective when the client directs his or her own systematic exposure in the natural environment.

Research conducted in Toronto by Richard Swinson and colleagues, as well as studies by other researchers, have shown that

**David A. Clark** at the University of New Brunswick is a leading expert on the nature and cognitive behavioural treatment of obsessive–compulsive disorder.

in vivo exposure therapy can be conducted in a variety of different ways, such as by brief consultations with the therapist over the telephone, without requiring the patient to come into the clinic (Antony & Swinson, 2000; Swinson et al., 1995). Exposure can also be conducted in the form of virtual reality exposure therapy. Research at the University of British Columbia, for example, has shown that this form of treatment is useful for treating driving phobia (Wald & Taylor, 2000, 2003). Here, the patient practises driving in a virtual reality simulator, under increasingly more challenging situations (e.g., on a quiet street, then in heavy traffic, then in the rain).

The treatment of panic disorder often includes two specific forms of exposure. One, *situational exposure*, is used to treat agoraphobic avoidance (Taylor, 2000). In this procedure, the person repeatedly confronts the situations that have previously been avoided. These often include crowded public places, such as shopping malls and theatres, as well as certain forms of transportation, such as buses and trains. *Interoceptive exposure*, the other form of exposure, is aimed at reducing the person's fear of internal, bodily sensations that are frequently associated with the onset of a panic attack, such as increased heart and respiration rate and dizziness. The process is accomplished by having the person engage in standardized exercises that are known to produce such physical sensations. These may include spinning in a swivel chair, running in place, or breathing through a narrow straw, depending on the type of sensation that the person fears and avoids. Outcome studies indicate that interoceptive exposure is one of the most important ingredients in the psychological treatment of panic disorder (Antony & Swinson, 2000; Taylor, 2000).

Exposure treatments can be administered in imagination or in the person's natural environment. This tarantula is not dangerous, and it is used in desensitization for people with spider phobias.

**Exposure and Response Prevention** The most effective form of psychological treatment for obsessive–compulsive disorder combines prolonged exposure to the situation that increases the person's anxiety with prevention of the person's typical compulsive response (Franklin & Foa, 2002). Neither component is effective by itself. The combination of exposure and response prevention is necessary because of the way in which people with obsessive–compulsive disorder use their compulsive rituals to reduce anxiety that is typically stimulated by the sudden appearance of an obsession. If the compulsive behaviour is performed, exposure is effectively cut short. Cognitive therapy can be added to exposure and response prevention. This combined approach holds great promise, although more research is needed to evaluate its efficacy (Clark, 2004).

To illustrate the psychological treatment of OCD, consider the treatment program employed with Ed. His obsessive thoughts and images, which centred around violence, were associated with handwriting. They were likely to pop into his mind when he noticed letters that were poorly formed. In an effort to control these thoughts, Ed wrote very carefully, and he corrected any letter that seemed a bit irregular. By the time he entered behaviour therapy, Ed had avoided writing altogether for several months. The therapist arranged for him to begin writing short essays on a daily basis to be sure that he was exposed, for at least 30 minutes each day, to the situation that was most anxiety-provoking. He encouraged Ed to deliberately write letters that did not conform to his compulsive style. In their sessions, for example, Ed was also required to write long sequences of the letter T in which he deliberately failed to connect the two lines. He was not allowed to go back and correct this "mistake." The combination represents prolonged exposure to an anxiety-provoking stimulus and response prevention.

Controlled outcome studies indicate that this approach is effective with most OCD patients (Antony et al., 1998; Clark, 2004). One review of 16 different outcome studies found that after a few weeks of treatment with exposure and response prevention, the typical patient had shown improvements that were clinically important (see Research Methods). On the other hand, some patients (perhaps as many as 20 percent) do not respond positively to this form of treatment, and many continue to exhibit mild symptoms of the disorder after they have been successfully treated (Abramowitz, 1998).

### Relaxation and Breathing Retraining

Behaviour therapists have used relaxation procedures for many years. Relaxation training usually involves teaching the client alternately to tense and relax specific muscle groups while breathing slowly and deeply (Bernstein & Borkovec, 1973; Lehrer & Carr, 1997). This process is often described to the client as an active coping skill that can be learned through consistent practice and used to control anxiety and worry.

Outcome studies indicate that relaxation is a useful form of treatment for generalized anxiety disorder. Borkovec and colleagues have compared applied relaxation and cognitive behaviour therapy to nondirective psychotherapy for the treatment of patients with generalized anxiety disorder (see Research Close-Up in Chapter 3). Patients who received relaxation training and those who received cognitive therapy were more improved at the end of treatment than those who received only nondirective therapy (Borkovec et al., 2002).

## RESEARCH METHODS

### Statistical Significance and Clinical Importance

Let's say that an outcome study reveals a statistical difference in the effectiveness of one treatment versus another (or no treatment at all). Does this automatically mean that the difference is clinically significant? The answer is no. We can explain this point by using a hypothetical example. Imagine that you want to know whether exposure-based treatment is effective in the treatment of social phobia. You could conduct a study, using an experimental design, in which 50 patients with this disorder are randomly assigned to receive exposure therapy and another 50 patients—the control group—are not. The latter group might receive a placebo pill or nondirective supportive psychotherapy for purposes of comparison. Measures of anxiety and avoidance are collected before and after treatment for patients in both groups. Your hypothesis is that exposure treatment will lead to more improvement than will placebo or nondirective therapy. In contrast, the *null hypothesis* holds that the two forms of treatment are not truly different. To conclude that exposure therapy is effective, you must reject the null hypothesis.

After collecting your data, you can use statistical tests to help you decide whether you can reject the null hypothesis. These tests assign a probability to that result, indicating how often we would find that result if there are not really differences between the two treatments. Psychologists have adopted the .05 level, meaning that if a difference occurs only by chance, you would find this difference less than 5 times out of every 100 times you repeated this experiment. Differences that exceed the .05 level, therefore, are assumed to reflect real differences between the variables rather than mere chance. Such results are said to be *statistically significant.*

Statistical significance should not be equated with clinical importance (Jacobson & Truax, 1991). It is possible for an investigator to find statistically significant differences between groups (and therefore reject the null hypothesis) on the basis of relatively trivial changes in the patients' adjustment. Consider the hypothetical example outlined above and suppose that you measured outcome in terms of a rating scale for anxiety whose scores could range from 0 (no symptoms of anxiety) to 100 (highest ratings on all items). Let's also assume that a rating of 50 or higher is typically considered to indicate the presence of important anxiety problems that are often associated with a disruption of the person's social and occupational functioning. Both groups have a mean rating of 85 on the scale prior to treatment. At the end of treatment, the mean rating for the exposure group has dropped to 65, and the mean for the control group is now 75. If you have included enough subjects, and depending on the amount of variation among scores within each group, this difference might reach statistical significance. But is it clinically important? Probably not. The average patient in the exposure group still has a score above the cutoff for identifying meaningful levels of psychopathology.

Clinical importance is sometimes measured in terms of the proportion of people in the treatment group whose outcome scores fall below a certain threshold of severity or within the range of scores that are produced by people without the disorder in question. In the case of social phobia, people treated with exposure therapy do show levels of change that are considered clinically important as well as statistically significant. This has been demonstrated in research conducted at the University of British Columbia (Taylor et al., 1997) and at other universities and clinics throughout the world (Antony & Swinson, 2000). ◆

*Breathing retraining* is a procedure that involves education about the physiological effects of hyperventilation and practice in slow breathing techniques. It is sometimes used in the treatment of panic disorder (Taylor, 2000). This process is somewhat similar to relaxation in the sense that relaxation exercises also include instructions in breathing control. The person learns to control his or her breathing through repeated practice using the muscles of the diaphragm, rather than the chest, to take slow, deep breaths. Although breathing retraining appears to be a useful element in the treatment of panic disorder, the mechanisms involved are not entirely clear. A simple reduction in the frequency of hyperventilation is apparently not the main effect of breathing retraining. Some clinicians believe that the process works by enhancing relaxation or increasing the person's perception of control (Garssen, de Ruiter, & Van Dyck, 1992).

Breathing retraining has become less frequently used in the treatment of panic disorder. This is because evidence shows that hyperventilation is not as important in panic disorder as previously thought, and because breathing retraining does not correct the panic sufferer's tendency to catastrophically misinterpret bodily sensations. These days, breathing retraining tends to be used only in those cases in which there is clear evidence that hyperventilation contributes to the person's panic attacks (Taylor, 2000).

**Cognitive Therapy** Cognitive therapy is used extensively in the treatment of anxiety disorders. Cognitive treatment procedures for anxiety disorders have been developed by Aaron Beck (Beck, 1995; Beck & Emery, 1985), Albert Ellis (1962, 1999), and University of Waterloo psychologist Donald Meichenbaum (1977). They are similar to those employed in the treatment of depression. Therapists help clients identify cognitions that are relevant to their problem; recognize the relation between these thoughts and maladaptive emotional responses (such as prolonged anxiety); examine the evidence that supports or contradicts these beliefs; and teach clients more useful ways of interpreting events in their environment (Schuyler, 1991).

In the case of anxiety disorders, cognitive therapy is usually accompanied by additional behaviour therapy procedures. One cognitive intervention involves an analysis of errors in the ways in which people think about situations in their lives. Typical examples of faulty logic include jumping to conclusions before considering all of the evidence, overgeneralizing ("That C in biology shows I'll never be a doctor"), all-or-none thinking (assuming that one mistake means total failure), and so on.

Another cognitive intervention for anxious patients is called *decatastrophisizing*. In this procedure, the therapist asks the client to imagine what would happen if his or her worst-case scenario actually happened. The same principles that are used in examining faulty logic are then applied to this situation. The therapist might say, "I don't think that you will fail the exam. But what would happen if you did fail the exam?" The client's initial reaction might be catastrophic ("I would die." "My parents would kill me." "I would flunk out of school."). Upon more careful analysis, however, the client might agree that these negative predictions actually represent gross exaggerations that are based on cognitive errors. Discussions in the therapy session are followed by extensive practice and homework assignments during the week. As one way of evaluating the accuracy of their own hypotheses, clients are encouraged to write down predictions that they make about specific situations and then keep track of the actual outcomes.

Dozens of controlled outcome studies attest to the efficacy of cognitive therapy in the treatment of various types of anxiety disorder, including panic disorder, agoraphobia, social phobia, generalized anxiety disorder, and obsessive–compulsive disorder (Antony & Swinson, 2000; Clark, 2004; Fedoroff & Taylor, 2001; Taylor, 2000).

### Biological Interventions

Medication is the most effective and most commonly used biological approach to the treatment of anxiety disorders. Several types of drugs have been discovered to be useful. They are often used in conjunction with psychological treatment.

**Antianxiety Medications** The most frequently used types of minor tranquilizers are from the class of drugs known as benzodiazepines, which includes diazepam (Valium) and alprazolam (Xanax). These drugs reduce many symptoms of anxiety, especially vigilance and subjective somatic sensations, such as increased muscle tension, palpitations, increased perspiration, and gastrointestinal distress. They have relatively less effect on a person's tendency toward worry and rumination. Benzodiazepines were the most widely prescribed form of psychiatric medication until the 1990s.

Benzodiazepines bind to specific receptor sites in the brain that are ordinarily associated with a neurotransmitter known as gamma-aminobutyric acid (GABA). Benzodiazepines, which inhibit the activity of GABA neurons, are of two types, based on their rate of absorption and elimination from the body. Some, such as alprazolam and lorazepam (Ativan), are absorbed and eliminated quickly, whereas others, such as diazepam, are absorbed and eliminated slowly.

Benzodiazepines have been shown to be effective in the treatment of generalized anxiety disorder and social phobia (Fedoroff & Taylor, 2001; Joffe & Gardner, 2000). Drug effects are most consistently evident early in treatment. The long-term effects of benzodiazepines (beyond six months of treatment) are not well established (Mahe & Balogh, 2000). They are not typically beneficial for patients with specific phobias or obsessive–compulsive disorder. Certain high-potency benzodiazepines such as alprazolam (Xanax) are also useful for treating panic disorder (Joffe & Gardner, 2000). However, panic patients are more likely to be treated with selective serotonin reuptake inhibitors (see below) because the latter are effective and do not have the addictive properties of benzodiazepines (Taylor, 2000).

Several studies have found that many patients with panic disorder and agoraphobia relapse if they discontinue taking medication (Taylor, 2000). As noted by Marks, Swinson, and colleagues (1993), in a large treatment outcome study of patients recruited from London, England, and Toronto, exposure therapy may be a preferable form of treatment for patients with a diagnosis of panic disorder with agoraphobia because of high relapse rates that have been observed after alprazolam is withdrawn.

Common side effects of benzodiazepines include sedation accompanied by mild psychomotor and cognitive impairments. These drugs can, for example, increase the risk of automobile accidents, because they interfere with motor skills. They can also lead to problems in attention and memory, especially among elderly patients.

The most serious adverse effect of benzodiazepines is their potential for addiction. Approximately 40 percent of people who use benzodiazepines for six months or more will exhibit symptoms of withdrawal if the medication is discontinued (Michelini et al., 1996). Withdrawal reactions include the reappearance of anxiety, somatic complaints, concentration problems, and sleep difficulties. They are most severe among patients who abruptly discontinue the use of benzodiazepines that are cleared quickly from the system, such as alprazolam. The risk for becoming dependent on benzodiazepines is greatest among people who have a history of abusing other substances, like alcohol.

Another class of antianxiety medication, known as the azapirones, includes drugs that work on entirely different neural pathways than the benzodiazepines (Cadieux, 1996). Rather than inhibiting the activity of GABA neurons, azapirones seem to act on serotonin transmission. The only azapirone in clinical use is known as buspirone (BuSpar). Placebo-controlled outcome studies indicate that buspirone is effective in the treatment of generalized anxiety disorder (Apter & Allen, 1999; Davidson et al., 1999). Some clinicians believe that buspirone is preferable to the benzodiazepines because it does not cause drowsiness and does not interact with the effects of alcohol. The disadvantage is that patients do not experience relief from severe anxiety symptoms as quickly with buspirone as they do with benzodiazepines.

**Antidepressant Medications** The selective serotonin reuptake inhibitors (SSRIs), discussed in Chapter 5, have become the preferred form of medication for treating almost all forms of anxiety disorder. These include drugs such as fluoxetine (Prozac), fluvoxamine (Luvox), sertaline (Zoloft), and paroxetine (Paxil). Reviews of controlled outcome studies indicate that they are at least as effective as other, more traditional forms of antidepressants in reducing symptoms of various anxiety disorders (Davidson, 2001; Fedoroff & Taylor, 2001; Roy-Byrne & Cowley, 2002; Taylor, 2000). They also have fewer unpleasant side effects, they are safer to use, and withdrawal reactions are less prominent when they are discontinued. Therefore, the SSRIs are now considered the first-line medication for treating

*Psychiatrist **Richard P. Swinson** at McMaster University is a leading expert on both cognitive behavioural therapy and drug treatments for anxiety disorders.*

panic disorder, social phobia, and obsessive–compulsive disorder (Joffe & Gardner, 2000; Zohar et al., 2000).

Imipramine (Tofranil), a tricyclic antidepressant medication, has been used for more than 40 years in the treatment of patients with panic disorder. A large number of double-blind, placebo-controlled studies indicate that it produces beneficial results (Jefferson, 1997; Mavissakalian & Ryan, 1998). Psychiatrists often prefer imipramine to antianxiety drugs for the treatment of panic disorder because patients are less likely to become dependent on the drug than they are to high-potency benzodiazepines like alprazolam.

The tricyclic antidepressants are used less frequently than the SSRIs because they produce several unpleasant side effects, including weight gain, dry mouth, and overstimulation (sometimes referred to as an "amphetamine-like" response). Some of the side effects (like feeling jittery, nervous, lightheaded, and having trouble sleeping) are upsetting to patients because they resemble symptoms of anxiety. Side effects often lead patients to discontinue treatment prematurely. In one study of patients who received long-term treatment with imipramine, 50 percent experienced distressing side effects, including 17 percent who found the effects intolerable (Noyes, Garvey, & Cook, 1989).

Clomipramine (Anafranil), another tricyclic antidepressant, has been used extensively in treating obsessive–compulsive disorder. Several placebo-controlled studies have shown clomipramine to be effective in treating OCD (Clark, 2004). Patients who continue to take the drug maintain the improvement, but relapse is common if medication is discontinued.

Table 6–5 summarizes various types of psychological treatment and specific types of medication that are effective with anxiety disorders. These are not the only types of treatment that are available, but they include those that have been subjected to empirical validation. In actual practice, anxiety disorders are often treated with a combination of psychological and biological procedures. The selection of specific treatment components depends on the specific group of symptoms that the person exhibits. However, combined treatments are not always better than singular treatments. As noted by Henny Westra (University of Western Ontario) and colleagues, benzodiazepines such as Xanax may not enhance, and indeed may interfere with, the effects of cognitive behavioural therapies (Westra et al., 2002; Westra & Stewart, 1998).

**TABLE 6–5 Treatments of Choice for Anxiety Disorders**

| Disorder | Medication | Example | Psychological Treatment |
|---|---|---|---|
| | *Drug Class* | *Generic Name (Trade Name)* | |
| **Panic Disorder** | SSRIs | Fluvoxamine (Luvox) | Cognitive therapy |
| | Benzodiazepines | Clonazepam (Rivotril) | Exposure (interoceptive) |
| | TCAs | Imipramine (Tofranil) | Breathing retraining |
| **Agoraphobia** | Benzodiazepines | Lorazepam (Ativan) | Exposure (situational) |
| | SSRIs | Sertraline (Zoloft) | Cognitive therapy |
| | TCAs | Imipramine (Tofranil) | |
| **Generalized Anxiety Disorder** | Benzodiazepines | Alprazolam (Xanax) | Cognitive therapy |
| | Azapirones | Buspirone (BuSpar) | Applied relaxation |
| **Specific Phobias** | Medication not usually recommended | Exposure in vivo | |
| **Social Phobia** | SSRIs | Paroxetine (Paxil) | Exposure in vivo |
| | Benzodiazepines | Clonazepam (Rivotril) | Cognitive therapy |
| | MAOIs | Phenelzine (Nardil) | Social skills training |
| **Obsessive–Compulsive Disorder** | SSRIs | Fluoxetine (Prozac) | Exposure plus response prevention |
| | TCAs | Clomipramine (Anafranil) | Cognitive therapy |

# Summary

Anxiety disorders are defined in terms of a preoccupation with, or persistent avoidance of, thoughts or situations that provoke **fear** or anxiety. **Anxiety** involves a diffuse emotional reaction that is associated with the anticipation of future problems and is out of proportion to threats from the environment. A pervasive anxious mood is typically associated with pessimistic thoughts and feelings. The person's attention may also turn inward, focusing on negative emotions and self-evaluation rather than on the organization or rehearsal of adaptive responses that might be useful in coping with negative events.

A **panic attack** is a sudden, overwhelming experience of terror or fright. Panic attacks are defined largely in terms of a list of somatic sensations, ranging from heart palpitations, sweating, and trembling to nausea, dizziness, and chills.

**Phobias** are persistent and irrational narrowly defined fears that are associated with avoidance of a specific object or situation. The most complex and incapacitating form of phobic disorder is **agoraphobia**, which is usually described as fear of public spaces. It is not so much a fear of being close to one specific object or situation as it is a fear of being separated from signals associated with safety.

**Obsessions** are repetitive, unwanted, intrusive cognitive events that may take the form of thoughts or images or impulses. They intrude suddenly into consciousness and lead to an increase in anxiety. **Compulsions** are repetitive behaviours, considered by the person to be senseless or irrational, that reduce the anxiety associated with obsessions. The person attempts to resist but cannot. The two most common forms of compulsive behaviour are cleaning and checking.

DSM-IV-TR recognizes several specific subtypes of anxiety disorders: **panic disorders** (with or without agoraphobia), phobic disorders (specific phobia, social phobia, and agoraphobia without panic attacks), obsessive–compulsive disorder, and generalized anxiety disorder, as well as posttraumatic stress disorder and acute stress disorder.

Stressful life events can influence the onset of anxiety disorders. Certain kinds of stresses may be differentially associated with particular types of emotional disorders: Severe events involving danger are most often associated with anxiety symptoms, while severe events involving loss are more often associated with depression. Among those people who have developed an anxiety disorder, interpersonal conflict is more characteristic of people with agoraphobia.

The learning model explained the development of phobic disorders in terms of classical conditioning, or the pairing of fear with originally neutral stimuli that happen to be present during a traumatic experience. A modified learning view, known as the **preparedness model**, is based on the recognition that there are biological constraints on the kinds of associations that members of a particular species are able to make. We may be prepared to develop intense, persistent fears only to a select set of objects or situations. People can apparently learn to avoid certain stimuli if they observe other people showing a strong fear response to those stimuli. Studies with infant monkeys support the preparedness model.

Cognitive theorists have argued that panic disorder is caused by the catastrophic misinterpretation of bodily sensations or perceived threat. This theory has the support of several research studies.

People who are prone to excessive **worrying** are unusually sensitive to cues that signal the existence of future threats. The recognition of danger cues triggers a maladaptive, self-perpetuating cycle of cognitive processes that can quickly spin out of control. The threatening information that is generated in this process is presumably encoded in memory in the form of elaborate schemas that are easily reactivated. In comparison to the depressed person, who is convinced that failure will definitely occur, the anxious person is afraid of failure that may occur as a future event. Some people apparently continue to worry, even though it is not productive, because worrying is reinforced by an immediate (though temporary) reduction in uncomfortable physiological sensations.

Family studies support the separate classification of panic disorder and **generalized anxiety disorder**. An increased prevalence of panic disorder is found among the relatives of patients with panic disorder. Similarly, an increased prevalence of generalized anxiety is found among the relatives of patients with generalized anxiety disorder. In other words, the two disorders "breed true." This does not seem to be the case for obsessive–compulsive disorder, where patients' relatives show an increased risk for several types of anxiety disorder rather than a specific risk for OCD.

Twin studies indicate that genetic factors are involved in the etiology of several types of anxiety disorder, especially panic disorder. The evidence is inconsistent for generalized anxiety disorder. There appears to be a modest genetic influence on the development of phobic disorders. The influence of environmental events seems to be greatest in specific phobias.

Studies of fear conditioning in animals have identified specific pathways in the brain that are responsible for detecting and organizing a response to danger. The amygdalae play a central role in these circuits. Several other areas of the brain are also associated with anxiety and the symptoms of anxiety disorders. One example is the locus ceruleus, a small area located in the brain stem. Electrical stimulation of the locus ceruleus triggers a strong fear response that resembles a panic attack.

Pharmacological challenge studies have demonstrated that infusions of lactate and several other kinds of chemicals can provoke panic attacks, but the specific biological process through which this effect is produced is still unknown. Serotonin, norepinephrine, GABA, and dopamine are some of the neurotransmitters that are involved in the production of panic attacks. Many interacting neurotransmitter systems play a role in the etiology of anxiety disorders.

Several psychological approaches to the treatment of anxiety disorders have been shown to be effective. These include the use of exposure and flooding in the treatment of phobic disorders and prolonged exposure and response prevention in the treatment of obsessive–compulsive disorders. Various types of medication are also effective treatments for anxiety disorders. These include benzodiazepines for generalized anxiety disorder, selective serotonin reuptake inhibitors for obsessive–compulsive disorder and panic disorder.

# Critical Thinking

1. What is the difference between being afraid and being anxious? If low levels of anxiety can enhance a person's performance, why and how do high levels of anxiety interfere with that same person's ability to function? What role does worry play in this process?

2. Anxiety and depression frequently appear together. Someone with a diagnosis of clinical depression is also likely to exhibit symptoms of anxiety disorders, and vice versa. In what ways are these maladaptive emotions alike, and how are they different?

3. Stressful life events are correlated with the appearance of both depression and anxiety disorders. Can you think of any ways in which this relationship is different in anxiety than it is in depression? What determines whether a person will become anxious or depressed in response to a serious negative event?

4. How do social, psychological, and biological factors interact in the production of various types of anxiety disorders? Consider as one example, the role of prepared learning and the *evolved fear module* in the development of phobias.

# Key Terms

**agoraphobia** 193
**anxiety** 191
**compulsions** 194
**fear** 191
**generalized anxiety disorder (GAD)** 199
**negative affect** 202
**neurosis** 197
**obsessions** 194
**panic attack** 192
**panic disorder** 197
**phobias** 193
**positive affect** 202
**preparedness model** 208
**social phobia** 198
**worry** 192

# 7 Acute and Posttraumatic Stress Disorders, Dissociative Disorders, and Somatoform Disorders

Overview
Acute and Posttraumatic Stress Disorders
Dissociative Disorders
Somatoform Disorders

**Why do some trauma victims suffer from PTSD?**

**Can one person really have two different personalities?**

**Are physical symptoms sometimes signs of emotional troubles?**

**How powerful is the unconscious mind?**

Before September 11, 2001, the topics covered in this chapter may have seemed like intriguing curiosities. After September 11, the problems we consider here have become very real, very personal, and uncomfortably close to home, even in Canada. A great many people experienced trauma on September 11. Some people, including many children, expressed their fear and anxiety through somatic symptoms, including stomachaches, heart palpitations, and concerns about their physical health. Other people experienced a pervasive sense of unreality, or could not stop thinking about the terrorist attacks. Jennifer Charron, for example, a Canadian-born graphic artist, had studios in World Trade Center's north tower, on the 91st and 92nd floors. Jennifer slept late on the morning of September 11, planning to go to her studios later in the afternoon. She heard about the first jet on the radio, and rushed to her apartment window just in time to see the unthinkable happen again. "I watched this big plane come across the sky and slam into the south tower," the 30-year-old recalls. "I close my eyes [today] and I can still see it." Jennifer spent the rest of September 11 on the phone trying to account for co-workers, numbed by the thought of how things might have been for her if the terrorists had struck in mid-afternoon. "You couldn't get away from it. You were constantly reminded," recalls Jennifer. Emotionally exhausted, she quit her job and returned to Ontario (Gatehouse, 2002).

## Overview

This chapter is not about September 11, but we do consider some complicated issues relevant to an understanding of our emotional reactions to that terrible day. What are normal and abnormal reactions to trauma? What is the best way to address the incredible fear that we naturally feel following trauma? Why do we feel numb in the aftermath of horror?

This last question brings us to an important psychological topic, one that unites the three categories of emotional disorder that we consider in this chapter. Conflicting theories, far too little research, and frequent and often vehement debates focus on the relation between stress, anxiety, and **dissociation**—the disruption of the normally integrated mental processes involved in memory, consciousness, identity, or perception (APA, 2000). Some theorists, including Sigmund Freud, have viewed dissociation as a normal defence mechanism, a way of distancing ourselves from terrible events; others see dissociation as a pathological response. The connection between dissociation and upsetting events explains why we consider traumatic stress disorders, dissociative disorders, and somatoform disorders after discussing anxiety disorders (Chapter 6) and before discussing stress and physical illness (Chapter 8). Anxiety, dissociation, and stress are linked together, but psychologists do not agree about how or why this is so.

There is general agreement that some experiences of dissociation, typically milder ones such as feeling numb, detached, or unreal, are common reactions to trauma. As you will see, however, psychologists disagree vehemently

*A traumatized woman takes shelter after being covered in dust from the collapsing World Trade Center towers. Over 100 000 people directly witnessed the September 11 attacks on the World Trade Center and the Pentagon.*

about a number of related issues. Is anxiety or dissociation the most important feature of traumatic stress disorders? As we noted in Chapter 6, the DSM-IV-TR classifies traumatic stress disorders as anxiety disorders, but we prefer to consider them separately because of their unique importance and because of their dissociative symptoms.

Extreme examples of dissociation raise even more vexing psychological questions. Are problems like the development of multiple personalities outgrowths of the mind of a child attempting to cope with the horrors of repeated trauma? How can stress and anxiety sometimes get "converted" into dramatic physical symptoms in the absence of physical pathology? (We consider the relation between stress and disease in Chapter 8.) Does the experience of dissociation in the disorders we consider here prove that an important part of the human mind is unconscious? Or, instead, should we question the validity of some of these dramatic disorders rather than of our models of the human mind?

Because of the limited research, we must be cautious in attempting to answer these questions. We must also be skeptical in considering topics that are dramatic and often dramatized. At the same time, we cannot help but be captivated and challenged by unusual case studies of the disorders we consider in this chapter. We begin by considering the less controversial and more adequately researched problems of acute and posttraumatic stress disorders.

# Acute and Posttraumatic Stress Disorders

Stress is an inevitable, and in some cases desirable, fact of everyday life. Some stressors, however, are so catastrophic and horrifying that they can cause serious psychological harm. Such **traumatic stress** is defined in DSM-IV-TR as an event that involves actual or threatened death or serious injury to self or others and creates intense feelings of fear, helplessness, or horror. Examples of traumatic stressors include bombings, airplane crashes, rape, military combat, earthquakes, major fires, and devastating automobile wrecks. Both survivors and witnesses are expected to be greatly distressed as a part of their normal response to traumatic stressors. For some victims, the trauma continues long after the event itself has ended.

**Acute stress disorder (ASD)** occurs within four weeks after exposure to traumatic stress and is characterized by dissociative symptoms, re-experiencing of the event, avoidance of reminders of the trauma, and marked anxiety or arousal. **Posttraumatic stress disorder (PTSD)**, like acute stress disorder, is defined by symptoms of re-experiencing, avoidance, and arousal, but in PTSD the symptoms either are longer lasting or have a delayed onset. The following case study is a dramatic illustration of the horrors and effects of traumatic stress.

## Typical Symptoms and Associated Features of ASD and PTSD

Acute and posttraumatic stress disorder are both characterized by (1) re-experienced trauma; (2) marked avoidance of stimuli associated with the trauma; and (3) persistent arousal or increased anxiety. In addition, ASD is characterized by a fourth cluster of problems, dissociative symptoms. The dissociative symptoms were included in the diagnosis of ASD, but not PTSD, because dissociative symptoms are particularly likely to occur in the immediate aftermath of a trauma (Frances et al., 1995).

## CASE STUDY Posttraumatic Stress Disorder in the Canadian Armed Forces

Although war-related trauma is less prevalent than other types of trauma in the Canadian population (Van Ameringen, 2004), it remains an important mental health concern, particularly because it has been previously neglected by the Canadian Forces. A recent report to the Minister of National Defence concluded that posttraumatic stress disorder (PTSD) is a significant problem faced by members of the Canadian Forces, and that more resources should be devoted to its treatment (Marin, 2001). Canada's military plays a prominent role in UN peacekeeping missions. As noted by researchers at the University of Guelph, there is more to peacekeeping-related stress than exposure to military and civilian casualties; contextual stressors such as the soldier's separation from family and other loved ones can exacerbate the stress of peacekeeping duties (Lamerson & Kelloway, 1996). Research from the University of Regina shows that PTSD in peacekeepers is associated with perceptions of poor overall health (Asmundson et al., 2002).

One of the most prominent advocates for the recognition and treatment of PTSD in the Canadian Forces is retired Lt. General Roméo Dallaire. He suffered PTSD as a result of the traumatic events he experienced when he headed a small UN peacekeeping mission to Rwanda in 1993–1994. During that time there was a civil war between the Hutus, who controlled the country, and the Tutsis. In 100 days of genocide, about 800 000 Tutsis and politically moderate Hutus were massacred by the ruling Hutus. By the time the killing ended, the Hutu-dominated genocidal government had been driven from power, and three-quarters of the Tutsi population were dead.

General Dallaire's peacekeeping mission was unable to halt the slaughter. This was because of a variety of factors, including inadequate troops and supplies, along with instructions from his superiors that his peacekeepers should not actively intervene. Thus, Dallaire and his peacekeepers were caught in a bind; their mandate was to help the Rwandan people, but too often they had to stand by helplessly as the slaughter took place. Dallaire was also fired upon, had death threats issued against him, and several of his peacekeepers were butchered (Dallaire, 2003).

General Dallaire has made many public presentations about his experiences in Rwanda (e.g., Dallaire, 2003; Growe, 2003; Koppel, 2002). He has also publicly discussed the treatment he received for PTSD, including medication and psychotherapy (e.g., Dallaire, 2003; Growe, 2000; Koppel, 2002). His experiences, and those of his soldiers, provide a chilling account of what it is like to experience traumatic events.

In his book, *Shake Hands with the Devil*, General Dallaire recalls that Hutu militia readily butchered Tutsis or people without identity cards. Bodies piled up in ditches and bloated corpses clogged the streams and rivers. Hutu patrols roamed the streets, breaking into houses and killing entire families. Children were hacked to pieces with machetes, often in front of their parents. Girls and women were raped, genitally mutilated, and murdered.

> The [Hutu] Gendarmerie had gone door to door checking identity cards. All Tutsi men, women and children were rounded up and moved to the church . . . Methodically, and with much bravado and laughter, the militia moved from bench to bench, hacking with machetes. Some people died immediately, while others with terrible wounds begged for their lives or the lives of their children. No one was spared. . . . Genitalia were a favourite target, the victim left to bleed to death. There was no mercy, no hesitation, no compassion. . . . Those innocent men, women, and children were simply Tutsi. That was their crime. (Dallaire, 2003, pp. 279–281)

Dallaire and his peacekeepers saw Rwanda's rustic landscape and mist-capped hills turn into a stinking nightmare of rotting corpses; "the putrid smell of decaying bodies in the huts along the route not only entered your nose and mouth but made you feel slimy and greasy" (p. 325). Dallaire, like many of his peacekeepers, vomited at the putrid horrors he witnessed. Tears, horror, disgust, rage, and stunned numbness were among the many immediate reactions of the peacekeepers to what they had witnessed.

> You cannot put these things behind you . . . And the more people say that [you can], the more you get mad because you know these things will not disappear . . . I can't sleep. I can't stand the loudness of silence . . . Time does not help. (Dallaire, quoted in Growe, 2000)

General Dallaire has suffered from daily recollections of the horrors he experienced in Rwanda. The smell of fresh fruit could trigger memories of Rwanda, and bushes or piles of wood can trigger memories of corpses piled on top of one another (Dallaire, 2003; Growe, 2000). He becomes distressed when gathered in crowds or in movie theatres, because they remind him of being surrounded by massive crowds in Rwanda (Dallaire, 2003; Growe, 2000). Other reminders similarly affect him.

> Villages had been burnt to the ground, and bodies formed a carpet of rags in all directions. We took turns walking in front of my vehicle to make sure that we did not run over any of them. Even to this day, if I encounter an article of clothing dropped on the street, I go around it and must control the urge to check if it is a body. (Dallaire, 2003, p. 325)

One of Dallaire's peacekeepers, Corporal Chris Cassavoy, described similar experiences. He could not eat grilled chicken because it reminded him of dead bodies, and even back in Canada the sight of children reminded him of how the Hutu militia liked to murder children (Growe, 2000).

How does a person make sense of traumatic events, especially those that shatter one's spiritual beliefs and assumptions about humanity and the world? Developing an understanding of such horrors can be an important part of recovering from PTSD (Janoff-Bulman, 1992), and therefore an exploration of the meaning of the traumatic experience is part of cognitive-behavioural treatments for this disorder (Taylor, 2004). It took time for

*continued*

*cont.*

General Dallaire to make sense of the horrors he had experienced:

> The odour of death in the hot sun; the flies, maggots, rats, and dogs that swarmed to feast on the dead. At times it seemed the smell had entered the pores of my skin. My Christian beliefs had been the moral framework that had guided me throughout my adult life. Where was God in all this horror? Where was God in the world's response? (Dallaire, 2003, p. 289)
>
> After one of my many presentations following my return from Rwanda, a Canadian Forces padre asked me how, after all I had seen and experienced, I could still believe in God. I answered that I know there is a God because in Rwanda I shook hands with the devil. I have seen him, I have smelled him, and I have touched him. I know the devil exists, and therefore I know there is a God. (p. xviii) ◆

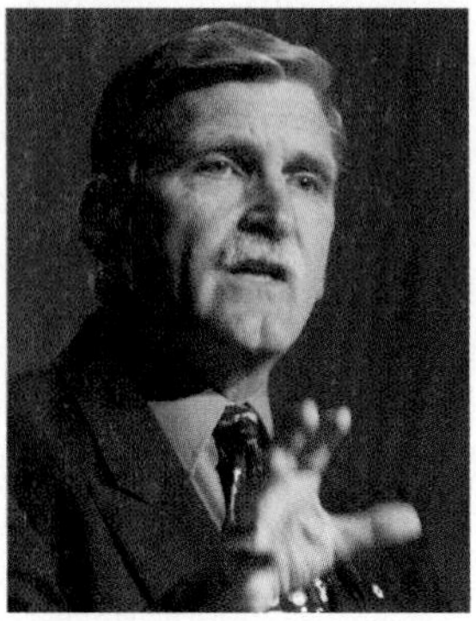

*One of the most prominent advocates for the recognition and treatment of PTSD in the Canadian Forces is retired Lt. General Roméo Dallaire. He suffered PTSD as a result of the traumatic events he experienced when he headed a UN peacekeeping mission to Rwanda in 1993–1994.*

**Re-experiencing** Like General Dallaire, people who have been confronted with a traumatic stressor *re-experience* the event in a number of different ways. Some people experience repeated, distressing images or thoughts of the incident. For example, they visualize the trauma over and over, or they repeatedly question how they might have acted differently. Other people relive the trauma in horrifying dreams. Many people with ASD or PTSD have repeated and intrusive **flashbacks**, sudden memories during which the trauma is replayed in images or thoughts—often at full emotional intensity. In rare cases, re-experiencing occurs as a *dissociative state*, and the person feels and acts as if the trauma actually were recurring in the moment. A combat veteran in a dissociative state might act as if he believes he is back in battle, and he may even take dangerous actions like gathering weapons or barricading himself in his residence. Typically, dissociative states are of short

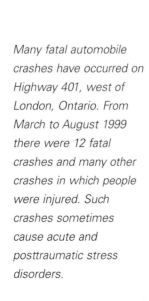

*Many fatal automobile crashes have occurred on Highway 401, west of London, Ontario. From March to August 1999 there were 12 fatal crashes and many other crashes in which people were injured. Such crashes sometimes cause acute and posttraumatic stress disorders.*

duration, but in unusual cases they can last for days.

**Avoidance** Marked or persistent avoidance of stimuli associated with the trauma is another symptom of ASD and PTSD. Trauma victims may attempt to avoid thoughts or feelings related to the event, or they may avoid people, places, or activities that remind them of the trauma. In PTSD, the avoidance also may manifest itself as a general *numbing of responsiveness*. People suffering from PTSD often complain that they suffer from "emotional anesthesia"—their feelings seem dampened or even nonexistent. As a result, they frequently withdraw from others, particularly from close relationships.

**Arousal or Anxiety** Despite their general withdrawal from feelings, people, and painful situations, people with ASD and PTSD also experience symptoms that indicate increased arousal and anxiety in comparison to what they felt before the trauma. Hypervigilance in searching for dangers in their world is a common symptom of PTSD. Many trauma victims also have trouble falling or staying asleep or difficulty maintaining their concentration. Other trauma victims feel restless and agitated, and they may be irritable and subject to angry outbursts. A number of people with PTSD or ASD also have an *exaggerated startle response*, excessive fear reactions to unexpected stimuli, such as loud noises. These various symptoms of anxiety and arousal are the reason why traumatic stress disorders are grouped with the anxiety disorders in DSM-IV-TR.

**Dissociative Symptoms** In addition to re-experiencing, avoidance, and increased arousal, acute stress disorder is characterized by explicit dissociative symptoms. Many people become less aware of their surroundings following a traumatic event. They report feeling dazed, and they may seem "spaced out" to other people. Other people experience *depersonalization*, feeling cut off from themselves or their environment. People with this symptom may report feeling like a robot or as if they were sleepwalking. *Derealization* is characterized by a marked sense of unreality about yourself or the world around you. Immediately after September 11, many people awoke wondering if the terrorist attacks had been only a nightmare—and the sense of unreality continued throughout the day. ASD also may be characterized by features of *dissociative amnesia*, specifically the inability to recall important aspects of the traumatic experience. (We discuss depersonalization, derealization, and dissociative amnesia in more detail when we review the dissociative disorders later in this chapter.) Finally, DSM-IV-TR lists a sense of numbing or detachment from others as dissociative symptoms that characterize acute stress disorder. Note that a very similar symptom is listed as an indicator of avoidance, not dissociation, in the diagnosis of PTSD (see Table 7–1). This discrepancy in diagnostic criteria reflects some of the broader controversy about whether ASD and PTSD should be classified as dissociative or anxiety disorders (van der Kolk & McFarlane, 1996). In fact, research suggests that a subgroup of patients with PTSD dissociate, since they report low anxiety but exhibit high arousal on psychophysiological indicators (Griffin, Resick, & Mechanic, 1997).

## Classification of Acute and Posttraumatic Stress Disorders

**Brief Historical Perspective** Maladaptive reactions to traumatic stress have long been of interest to the military, where "normal" performance is expected in the face of the trauma of combat. Historically, most of the military's concern has focused on battle dropout—that is, men who leave the field of action as a result of what was called "combat neurosis" (Frances et al., 1995). During the Vietnam War, however, battle dropout was less frequent than in earlier wars, but delayed reactions to the trauma of combat were much more frequent (Figley, 1978). This change prompted much interest in posttraumatic stress disorder, a condition first listed in the DSM in 1980 (DSM-III).

The interest in the effects of the Vietnam War was not restricted to veterans from the United States. An estimated 10 000 to 40 000 Canadians served in Vietnam with the U.S. military (Stretch, 1991). An untold number developed posttraumatic stress disorder.

**Contemporary Classification** The basic diagnostic criteria for PTSD—re-experiencing, avoidance, and arousal—have remained more or less the same in revisions of the DSM. However, two significant changes in the classification of traumatic stress disorders were made with the publication of DSM-IV in 1994:

**TABLE 7–1 DSM-IV-TR Diagnostic Criteria for Posttraumatic Stress Disorder (PTSD)**

**A. The person has been exposed to a traumatic event in which both of the following were present:**

1. The person experienced, witnessed, or was confronted with an event or events that involved actual or threatened death or serious injury, or a threat to the physical integrity of self or others.
2. The person's response involved intense fear, helplessness, or horror.

**B. The traumatic event is persistently re-experienced in one (or more) of the following ways:**

1. Recurrent and intrusive distressing recollections of the event including images, thoughts, or perceptions
2. Recurrent distressing dreams of the event
3. Acting or feeling as if the traumatic event were recurring
4. Intense psychological distress at exposure to internal or external cues that symbolize or resemble an aspect of the traumatic event
5. Physiologic reactivity upon exposure to internal or external cues that symbolize or resemble an aspect of the traumatic event

**C. Persistent avoidance of stimuli associated with the trauma and numbing of general responsiveness (not present before the trauma), as indicated by three (or more) of the following:**

1. Efforts to avoid thoughts, feelings, or conversations associated with the trauma
2. Efforts to avoid activities, places, or people that arouse recollections of the trauma
3. Inability to recall an important aspect of the trauma
4. Markedly diminished interest or participation in significant activities
5. Feeling of detachment or estrangement from others
6. Restricted range of affect
7. Sense of a foreshortened future

**D. Persistent symptoms of increased arousal, as indicated by two (or more) of the following:**

1. Difficulty falling or staying asleep
2. Irritability or outbursts of anger
3. Difficulty concentrating
4. Hypervigilance
5. Exaggerated startle response

**E. Duration of the disturbance is more than one month**

*Specify if:*
**Acute**: If duration of symptoms is less than three months
**Chronic**: If duration of symptoms is three months or more

*Specify if:*
**With delayed onset**: If onset of symptoms is at least six months after the stressor

acute stress disorder was included as a separate diagnostic category, and the definition of trauma was altered.

*Acute Stress Disorder* The diagnostic criteria for ASD and PTSD are essentially the same. The two exceptions are that ASD explicitly includes dissociative symptoms and lasts no longer than four weeks (see Table 7–2), whereas PTSD continues for at least one month after a trauma or it has a delayed onset (see Table 7–1). Not surprisingly, many people suffer from ASD after experiencing trauma, and the presence of ASD may predict future PTSD (Harvey & Bryant, 1998, 1999). One hope is that the treatment of ASD will prevent the development of PTSD.

*What Defines Trauma?* Earlier versions of DSM defined trauma as an event "outside the range of usual human experience," but even before September 11, researchers discovered that, unfortunately, many traumatic stressors are a common part of human experience today. The definition of trauma was revised to reflect this fact, and the manual also attempted to define trauma more precisely (Frances et al., 1995).

**TABLE 7-2 DSM-IV-TR Diagnostic Criteria for Acute Stress Disorder (ASD)**

**A. The person has been exposed to a traumatic event in which both of the following were present:**

1. The person experienced, witnessed, or was confronted with an event or events that involved actual or threatened death or serious injury, or a threat to the physical integrity of self or others.
2. The person's response involved intense fear, helplessness, or horror.

**B. Either while experiencing or after experiencing the distressing event, the individual has three (or more) of the following dissociative symptoms:**

1. A subjective sense of numbing, detachment, or absence of emotional responsiveness
2. A reduction in awareness of his or her surroundings (e.g., "being in a daze")
3. Derealization
4. Depersonalization
5. Dissociative amnesia (i.e., the inability to recall an important aspect of the trauma)

**C. The traumatic event is persistently re-experienced in at least one of the following ways: recurrent images, thoughts, dreams, illusions, flashback episodes, or a sense of reliving the experience; or distress on exposure to reminders of the traumatic event.**

**D. Marked avoidance of stimuli that arouse recollections of the trauma (e.g., thoughts, feelings, conversations, activities, places, people).**

**E. Marked symptoms of anxiety or increased arousal (e.g., difficulty sleeping, irritability, poor concentration, hypervigilance, exaggerated startle response, motor restlessness).**

**F. The disturbance causes clinically significant distress or impairment in social, occupational, or other important areas of functioning or impairs the individual's ability to pursue some necessary task, such as obtaining necessary assistance or mobilizing personal resources by telling family members about the traumatic experience.**

**G. The disturbance lasts for a minimum of two days and a maximum of four weeks and occurs within four weeks of the traumatic event.**

Thus DSM-IV-TR has a two-part definition of trauma that includes (1) the experience of an event involving actual or threatened death or serious injury to self or others and (2) a response of intense fear, helplessness, or horror in reaction to the event.

The diagnoses of ASD and PTSD reflect the fact that people often respond in similar ways to trauma, but different traumatic stressors also create unique psychological problems. PTSD following combat exposure was the first focus of research, but valuable efforts have extended research to such traumatic events as rape, child abuse, natural disasters, and torture (Taylor, 2004). Each of these traumas may result in ASD or PTSD.

*Comorbidity and Adjustment Disorder* Many people with PTSD also suffer from another mental disorder. Notably high levels of comorbidity are found for depression, other anxiety disorders, and substance abuse (Breslau et al., 1991; Kessler et al., 1995). Comorbid disorders must be diagnosed and sometimes must be treated separately from PTSD. Other problems associated with PTSD include disturbing physical symptoms like headaches and gastrointestinal problems, and troublesome emotions, particularly anger and grief (see Chapter 17). Another important concern is increased suicide risk. One study found, for example, that 33 percent of rape survivors had thoughts of suicide, and 13 percent actually made a suicide attempt (Kilpatrick et al., 1992).

Differential diagnosis between ASD and PTSD and *adjustment disorder* is based on both the nature of the stressor and the type and severity of symptoms. Adjustment disorders, which we discuss in Chapter 17, are caused by "normal" but painful stressors, such as losing a job, and they involve normal (if distressing) emotional, cognitive, and behavioural reactions to these events. As we have noted, there is controversy about whether ASD and PTSD are anxiety disorders or dissociative disorders, or if they belong in a separate diagnostic category.

## Epidemiology of Trauma, PTSD, and ASD

Recent research has documented that PTSD is prevalent. According to DSM-IV-TR (APA,

## Further Thoughts **PTSD and the Sexual Assault of Women**

Like many other traumatic stressors, sexual assault is not outside the realm of normal human experience. Almost 10 percent of women report having been raped at least once in their lifetime, according to national surveys, and 12 percent report having been sexually molested (Kessler et al., 1995). Other evidence suggests a notably higher prevalence when the data include *acquaintance rapes*, assaults committed by people known to the victim (Goodman, Koss, & Russo, 1993).

Rape can be devastating physically, socially, and emotionally. Thirty-nine percent of rape victims are physically injured on parts of their bodies other than the genitals. A significant proportion of rape victims are infected with a sexually transmitted disease, and about 5 percent of rapes result in pregnancy (Goodman et al., 1993). Socially, sexual assault can undermine women's work, as well as their intimate relationships.

Most victims of sexual assault show the symptoms of PTSD. Victims may reexperience the horrors of the assault; they may feel numbed in reacting to others, particularly sexual partners; they may avoid any potentially threatening situation; and they may maintain both autonomic hyperarousal and hypervigilance against possible victimization. Depression is also common. Sadness, crying, and withdrawal from others often are coupled with sleep and appetite disturbances. Loss of interest in sex, insecurities about sexual identity, sexual dysfunction, and negative feelings toward men also are common (Goodman et al., 1993).

Another frequent psychological problem is that many victims of sexual assault blame themselves, despite the fact that they are the victims. Women may wonder if they unwittingly encouraged their assailant, or they may chastise themselves for not being more cautious in avoiding dangerous circumstances. This irrational self-blame is abetted by cultural myths that women provoke rape or that they actually enjoy it. In fact, *secondary victimization* is a growing concern, as insensitive legal, medical, and even mental health professionals can add to a rape victim's emotional burden rather than alleviating her distress. In fact, victims of acquaintance rape show increased symptoms of PTSD when they receive minimal community assistance and encounter victim-blaming behaviours from professionals who are supposed to help them (Campbell et al., 1999). Such findings may explain why as many as two-thirds of stranger rapes and four-fifths of acquaintance rapes are not reported to authorities. ◆

2000), 8 percent of people experience PTSD at some point in their lives, and 14 to 33 percent of people exposed to a severe trauma will develop ASD. A survey of over 1000 residents of Winnipeg found that 2.7 percent of women and 1.2 percent of men met diagnostic criteria for PTSD in the past month (Stein et al., 1997). A national survey of over 3000 Canadian adults revealed that PTSD had a lifetime prevalence of 11 percent, and a current (past month) prevalence of 3 percent (Van Ameringen, 2004). The most common forms of trauma resulting in PTSD included unexpected death of a loved one, sexual assault, and seeing someone badly injured or killed.

**Trauma and PTSD Are Not Random** Good luck—or bad luck—can play an important role to exposure to events like September 11. In general, however, trauma does not occur completely at random. Because they engage in more risky behaviour, men, young people in their late teens and early 20s, people with a history of conduct disorders, and extroverts all are more likely to experience trauma. People who are anxious or who have a family history of mental illness also experience more trauma, but the reasons for this are less clear. Finally, minorities and people with less education also are exposed to more traumatic stress, because they are more likely to live in dangerous environments.

The development of PTSD following a trauma also is not random. Those who are anxious and easily upset are more likely to develop PTSD after a trauma, as are people with a family or personal history of mental disorder (Breslau et al., 1991, 1995, 1998).

**Course and Outcome** Consistent with the goals in creating the ASD diagnosis, researchers have found that people who suffer from ASD are more likely to develop PTSD subsequently (Bryant & Harvey, 2000). The prediction is far from perfect, however, and two caveats bear special scrutiny in continuing research. First, people with *subclinical* ASD—that is, their symptoms are not severe or pervasive enough to meet diagnostic criteria—nevertheless are at greater risk for PTSD than trauma victims with relatively few psychological symptoms (Harvey & Bryant, 1999). Second, the different symptoms of ASD are not equally good in predicting future PTSD. The presence or absence of three symptoms—numbing, depersonalization, and a sense of reliving the experience—are the best predictors of PTSD in research to date (Bryant & Harvey, 2000). Figure 7–1 lists these and other symptoms of ASD, and shows how strongly their presence or absence predicts PTSD.

Other research documents that the symptoms of PTSD diminish gradually as time passes. For example, the National Comorbidity Survey found that the symptoms of PTSD improved during the first year for many people, although symptoms diminished more gradually over the next several years for the majority of people with PTSD (see Figure 7–2). Symptoms diminished more rapidly among people who received treatment, although this correlational finding does not prove that treatment caused the improvement. Regardless of whether they received treatment, over one-third of people who had suffered from PTSD continued to report symptoms of the disorder 10 years after the traumatic event (Kessler et al., 1995).

Thus, although most people improve over time, PTSD can become a chronic disorder. In fact, one study found continuing symptoms among many World War II prisoners of war—40 *years* after confinement. Only 30 percent of POWs who had suffered from PTSD (as diagnosed by retrospective report) were fully recovered, while 60 percent still had mild to moderate symptoms. Another 10 percent either showed no recovery or had a deteriorating course (Kluznik et al., 1986).

**Predicting PTSD from ASD Symptoms**

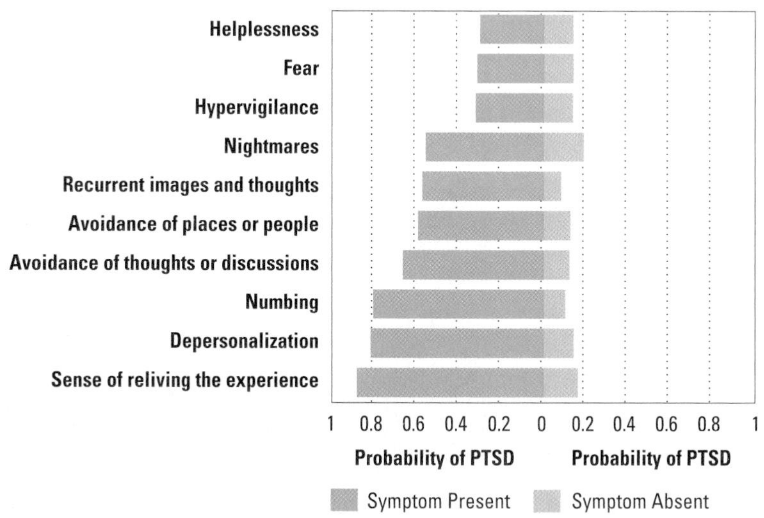


**FIGURE 7–1: Results of a study predicting the probability of developing future PTSD from the presence or absence of ASD symptoms. PTSD was unlikely when any symptom was absent. However, the presence of some symptoms (e.g., hypervigilance) predicted PTSD weakly, while others (e.g., numbing) were strong predictors.**

*Source:* Adapted from R.A. Bryant and A.G. Harvey, 2000, *Acute stress disorder: A handbook of theory, assessment, and treatment*, p. 31. Washington, DC: American Psychological Association.

## Etiological Considerations and Research on PTSD and ASD

By definition, traumatic stressors cause ASD and PTSD. Because not every traumatized person develops ASD or PTSD, however, trauma is a necessary but not a sufficient cause of the disorders. An extremely important task for researchers, therefore, is identifying factors that increase people's risk or resilience in the face of trauma.

**Social Factors in ASD and PTSD** Scientists studying social factors and the risk for PTSD have focused primarily on (1) the nature of the trauma and the individual's level of exposure to it and (2) the availability of social support following the trauma. Victims of trauma are more likely to develop PTSD when the trauma is more intense, life-threatening, and involves greater exposure. For example, victims of attempted rape are more likely to develop PTSD if the rape is completed; if they are physically injured during the assault; and if they perceive the sexual assault as life-threatening (Kilpatrick et al., 1989). Similarly, PTSD is

**The Course of PTSD with and without Treatment**

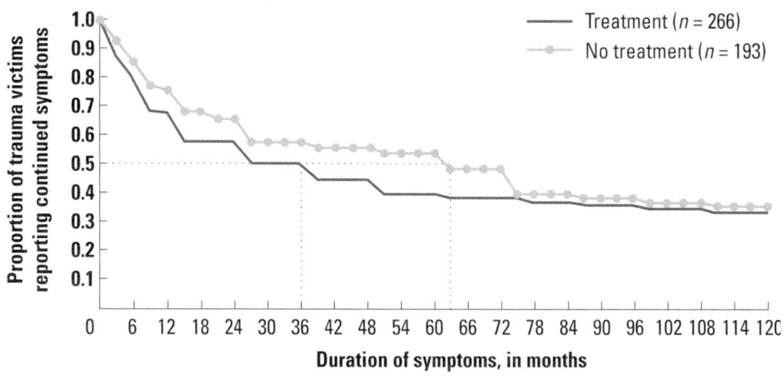


**FIGURE 7–2: The symptoms of PTSD decline over time but persist for 10 years among one-third of people with the disorder. Treatment appears to hasten recovery, but this correlational finding may not mean causation in this study.**

*Source:* R.C. Kessler, A. Sonnega, E. Bromet, M. Hughes, and C.B. Nelson, 1995, Posttraumatic stress disorder in the National Comorbidity Survey. *Archives of General Psychiatry, 52*, 1057.

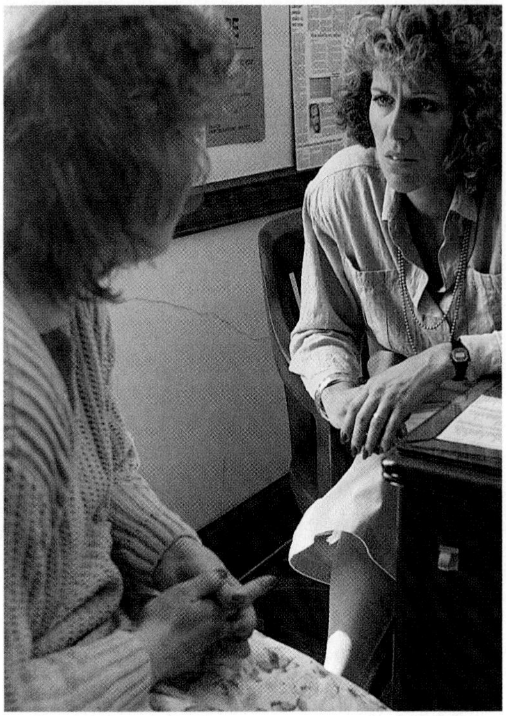

*Rape crisis centres offer women support in dealing with sexual assault.*

more prevalent among soldiers who were wounded, who were involved in the deaths of noncombatants, or who witnessed atrocities (Oei, Lim, & Hennessy, 1990). In the same vein, a study of PTSD following September 11 found a greater prevalence among people who lived south of Canal Street, close to the World Trade Center (Galea et al., 2002).

*Social Support* As with less severe stressors, social support after a trauma can play a crucial role in alleviating long-term psychological damage. A lack of social support is thought to have contributed to the high prevalence of PTSD found among Vietnam veterans (Oei, Lim, & Hennessy, 1990). Following September 11, for example, people who had little social support also were more likely to develop PTSD (Galea et al., 2002).

Evidence on social support provides one rationale for offering immediate assistance to victims of trauma, as we discuss in more detail shortly. For example, many rape victims mistakenly feel guilty and somehow responsible for their attack. Rape crisis centres and rape support groups offer social support that helps women recognize that they are not at fault—they are victims of a heinous crime.

**Biological Factors in ASD and PTSD** Some of the strongest evidence on the importance of biological factors in PTSD comes from twin studies, which show that an interplay of environmental and genetic factors contribute to PTSD. Table 7–3 shows the heritability coefficients for trauma exposure and for PTSD symptoms. Findings from the Canadian civilian sample (Stein et al., 2002) are compared with results from a U.S. Vietnam-era twin registry (Lyons et al., 1993; True et al., 1993). Heritability coefficients range from 0 to 1, with larger numbers indicating that genes make a larger contribution to the variability of the variable in question. The results show that genes make a significant but modest contribution to PTSD symptoms in both civilian and Vietnam-era populations. The findings also indicate that the risk of experiencing a traumatic event is also influenced by genes. For example, the chances of being mugged, beaten up in a bar fight, or being sexually assaulted (i.e., examples of assaultive trauma) are all moderately heritable. Research from the University of British Columbia suggests that the genes that contribute to assaultive trauma are also the same ones that contribute to antisocial personality traits (Jang et al., 2003). In other words, if you have antisocial tendencies (as illustrated, for example, by

**TABLE 7–3 Heritability Coefficients for Trauma Exposure and PTSD Symptoms**

| Variable | Canadian Civilian Twin Sample (UBC Twin Study) | U.S. Vietnam-Era Twin Sample |
|---|---|---|
| Trauma Exposure | | |
| Assaultive trauma | .20 | – |
| Volunteered for SEA service | – | .36 |
| SEA service | – | .35 |
| Combat exposure | – | .47 |
| Received combat decoration | – | .54 |
| PTSD Symptoms | | |
| Re-experiencing | .36 | .25 |
| Avoidance | .28 | .00 |
| Numbing | .36 | .28 |
| Hyperarousal | .29 | .26 |

*Note:* Data synthesized from M.J. Lyons et al. 1993, Do genes influence exposure to trauma? A twin study of combat. *American Journal of Medical Genetics (Neuropsychiatric Genetics), 48,* 22–27; and M.B. Stein, K.L. Jang, S. Taylor, P.A. Vernon, and W.J. Livesley, 2002, Genetic and environmental influences on trauma exposure and posttraumatic stress disorder symptoms: A general population twin study. *American Journal of Psychiatry, 159,* 1675–1681; and W.R. True et al., 1993, A twin study of genetic and environmental contributions to liability for posttraumatic stress symptoms. *Archives of General Psychiatry, 50,* 257–265.

PTSD = posttraumatic stress disorder; SEA = South East Asia. Heritability coefficients range from 0 to 1. The larger the number, the greater the influence of genetic factors on the variability of the variable in question.

a tendency to engage in criminal behaviour or to hang around with criminals in dangerous parts of town), then your risk for being exposed to certain types of traumatic events increases.

*Biological Effects of Exposure to Trauma* People with PTSD show alterations in the functioning of the amygdala, which is a brain structure involved in the processing of emotion (Yehuda, 2002). Other evidence finds that PTSD is associated with increased levels of circulating norepinephrine and general psychophysiological arousal, for example, an increased resting heart rate (Yehuda, 2002). The pattern of biological findings suggests that the sympathetic nervous system is aroused and the fear response is sensitized in PTSD.

The heightened reactivity may be due to the failure of the stress response system to shut down. As we discuss in Chapters 5 and 8, the *hypothalmic–pituitary–adrenal (HPA) axis* is an area of the brain known to be stimulated by normal stress (see Figure 5–6). One of the most important and consistent findings is that normal stress increases the secretion of cortisol from the adrenal cortex. Surprisingly, however, people with PTSD show *lower* levels of cortisol availability. One possible explanation of this paradox is that cortisol serves the homeostatic function of shutting down biological systems that have been aroused by stress. Cortisol levels are high in depression, and this may contribute to the lethargy found among depressed people (see Chapter 5). If so, this suggests that the stress response system is activated but not turned off in PTSD (Yehuda, 2002).

Neuroscience evidence holds the hope of identifying specific processes involved in PTSD that might be altered with new medications. Still, research is in its early stages. Many brain systems are likely to be affected by trauma, and it is not clear whether identified alterations in brain function are abnormalities specific to PTSD, normal biological adaptations to traumatic stress, or possibly indicators of differences that predated the traumatic event (Newport & Nemeroff, 2000; Pitman, 1997).

**Psychological Factors in ASD and PTSD** An early, and still important, perspective on psychological contributions to PTSD focuses on **two-factor theory**, the combination of classical conditioning and operant conditioning (Keane, Zimering, & Caddell, 1985). According to two-factor theory, classical conditioning *creates* fears when the terror inherent in trauma is paired with the cues associated with the traumatic event. Operant conditioning, in turn, *maintains* the fears. Specifically, when fear-producing situations are avoided, the avoidance behaviour is negatively reinforced by the reduction of aversive anxiety.

More recent psychological perspectives focus not only on the general pattern described by two-factor theory but on individual differences in the risk for ASD and PTSD. In addition to pre-existing mental health problems, research indicates that cognitive factors such as expectancies, preparedness, and control influence the risk for PTSD following a trauma. For example, pilots with prior crash training cope more successfully with helicopter crashes than pilots who have received no training, presumably because training increases preparedness and alters their expectations (Shalev, 1996). The importance of preparedness and control also is supported by evidence that, despite greater physical suffering, political activists develop fewer psychological symptoms than non-activists following torture (Basoglu et al., 1997). Such cognitive factors presumably influence how the trauma is encoded in the *fear network*, the cognitive representation of fear that includes both emotional reactions and broader, ongoing beliefs about threats in the environment.

These views may explain fear and avoidance in PTSD, but what about re-experiencing? Some theorists have suggested that re-experiencing results from a breakdown of the balance between anxiety and dissociation. From this perspective, dissociation is an unconscious defence similar to repression that helps victims cope with trauma (Oei, Lim, & Hennessy, 1990). However, research indicates that dissociation is associated with more not less PTSD (Ehlers, Mayou, & Bryant, 1998; Griffin, Resick, & Mechanic, 1997; Harvey, Bryant, & Dang, 1998). Among a sample of Israeli war trauma victims, for example, more dissociation reported within one week following a trauma predicted *more* severe PTSD six months later (Shalev et al., 1996).

Dissociation may not be adaptive, but most theorists agree that victims of trauma must, over time, find a balance between gradually facing their painful emotions while not being overwhelmed by them. Psychologist Edna Foa, a leading PTSD researcher, has highlighted the importance of **emotional processing**, which involves facing fear, diminishing its intensity, and coming to some

**Model of Psychological Factors in PTSD**

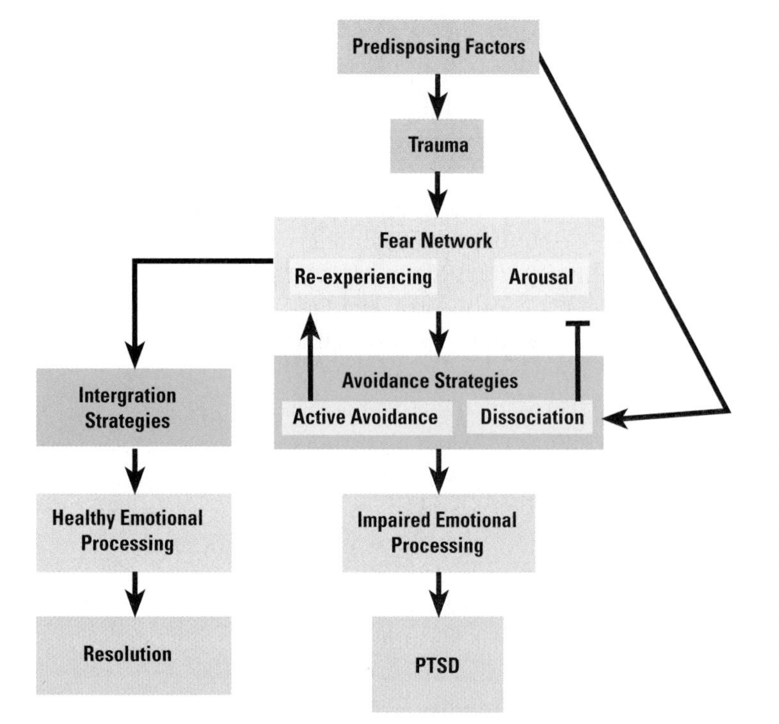


**FIGURE 7–3: Many theorists believe that trauma victims are more likely to develop PTSD if they avoid their fears through excessive dissociation (which may be caused by predisposing personality factors) or active avoidance. In contrast, repeated attempts to integrate the trauma into one's experience—to find meaning in the horror—leads to healthy emotional processing and resolution.**

*Source:* Adapted from: R.A. Bryant and A.G. Harvey, 2000, *Acute stress disorder: A handbook of theory, assessment, and treatment*, p. 38. Washington, DC: American Psychological Association.

new understanding about the trauma and its consequences (Foa & Riggs, 1995; Foa & Street, 2001). According to Foa, three elements are essential for successful emotional processing. First, victims must allow themselves to be emotionally engaged with their traumatic memories. Second, victims need to find a way to articulate and organize their chaotic experience. Third, victims must learn how to develop a balanced view of the world—to come to believe that, despite the trauma, the world is not a terrible place (Foa & Riggs, 1995; Foa & Street, 2001; see Figure 7–3).

The symptoms of PTSD are likely to persist if victims cannot emotionally process their experiences and continue to believe the world is threatening. Victims may feel threatened either because they believe the trauma will recur, they cannot cope with their own emotions, or they have failed to integrate the memory of the trauma into their broader memories and beliefs (Ehlers & Clark, 2000). Integrating the experience of trauma with broader memories and beliefs involves the task of *meaning making*—finding some broader reason or higher value for enduring the trauma.

**Integration and Alternative Pathways** The combined evidence suggests alternative pathways can lead to ASD and PTSD. Anyone might develop ASD or PTSD given a critical level of exposure and a trauma of sufficient intensity. In other cases, a trauma may call attention to or exacerbate a pre-existing psychological disorder. In most cases, however, trauma is a necessary but not sufficient cause of PTSD. The etiology of PTSD involves an interaction of risk factors, including personality factors that predate the trauma, exposure during the trauma, and emotional processing and social support after its occurrence.

## CANADIAN FOCUS **Does Stress Cause Posttraumatic Stress Disorder?**

Clinicians and researchers have long assumed that there is a relationship between the "amount" of stress a person experiences—measured in terms of severity, duration, and proximity to stressful events—and the likelihood of developing posttraumatic stress disorder. Recently Marilyn Bowman, a psychologist at Simon Fraser University, challenged this assumption. Bowman (1997, 1999) reviewed the relevant scientific literature and concluded that stressful events play a minor role in causing posttraumatic stress responses; many people experience traumatic events, yet only a fraction of these people develop PTSD. Bowman claimed that other variables are more important in producing PTSD symptoms, such as personality variables, intelligence, and the person's beliefs or assumptions.

The most important personality variable singled out by Bowman is a dimension known as *negative emotionality* or *neuroticism*. A person's score on this dimension reflects his or her tendency to experience negative emotions such as anxiety, depression, or irritability. A person scoring low on this dimension infrequently experiences these emotions, whereas a person with a high score often experiences these unpleasant feelings (for more on this topic see Further Thoughts in Chapter 6). Bowman's claim about the importance of negative affectivity is based

*continued*

*cont.*

on a small number of studies showing that scores on this dimension are correlated with, or later predict, the severity of PTSD symptoms.

Similarly, scores on IQ tests have been shown to predict the likelihood of developing PTSD symptoms following exposure to traumatic events (for example, Macklin et al., 1998). Presumably, the greater the person's intelligence, the greater the ability to think of ways of coping with traumatic experiences. Various beliefs a person might hold—such as assumptions about stressful events and beliefs about anxiety symptoms—are also correlated with, or predictive of, the severity of posttraumatic stress symptoms. To illustrate, people who have high anxiety sensitivity (see Chapter 6) believe that posttraumatic re-experiencing symptoms are signs that they are going crazy or losing control. When a person holding such a belief subsequently experiences PTSD symptoms, he or she will become very upset and therefore experience more symptoms of arousal (tension, irritability, difficulty sleeping, etc.), and will also increasingly strive to avoid reminders of the traumatic event. Thus, particular beliefs about PTSD symptoms appear to exacerbate or intensify PTSD (Fedoroff et al., 2000).

Is Bowman correct in concluding that the "amount" of traumatic stress plays a relatively minor role in producing posttraumatic stress symptoms? While this assertion is intriguing, it has three main problems. First, researchers have had difficulty coming up with reliable and valid measures of traumatic stress. If one cannot validly measure traumatic stress then it is not possible to draw any firm conclusions about its importance. Some studies have tried to solve this problem by relying on objective, verifiable measures of traumatic stress. Many of these studies have found a relationship between degree of stress and severity of PTSD symptoms. For example, University of Toronto researchers Kuch and Cox (1992) assessed the severity of PTSD symptoms in 124 Holocaust survivors. Sixty-three percent of these people were detained in concentration camps and 46 percent had PTSD. Some survivors were tattooed with Auschwitz identification numbers. This can be regarded as an objective measure of the severity of traumatic stress. Survivors who were tattooed and had been in concentration camps had more severe PTSD symptoms than untattooed survivors who had not been in camps.

Following September 11, people developed PTSD. Most were traumatized because they were in the vicinity of the terrorist attacks, with the likelihood of developing PTSD increasing with proximity to the attack (Galea et al., 2002). A smaller proportion were traumatized by watching the horrific television coverage of the event, such as the televised images of planes smashing into the towers, and pictures of people leaping to their deaths from the burning buildings. The distressing effects of this "remote exposure" have been demonstrated, for example, by Gordon Asmundson and colleagues at the University of Regina (Asmundson et al., in press).

The second problem with Bowman's conclusion is the fact that PTSD does not arise unless the person experiences some sort of stressful experience. There have been no reports of people developing PTSD in the absence of exposure to some sort of stressor. Indeed, it is difficult to see how a person could have, for example, re-experiencing symptoms without having experienced a stressful event. So the stressor is important in that it is essential for PTSD to occur. The third problem is that the vulnerability factors Bowman proposes—negative affectivity, cognitive ability, and various sorts of beliefs—have been implicated in many different kinds of emotional disorders, not just PTSD (Stowe & Taylor, 2001; Taylor, 2000). Why would these factors give rise to PTSD in some people, and to other disorders in other people? It appears that traumatic stressors are needed for these vulnerability factors to give rise to PTSD symptoms. It is possible that two dimensions are important in contributing to PTSD: one defined by the amount of traumatic stress and the other defined in terms of the person's predisposition (diathesis) for developing PTSD, characterized by some combination of vulnerability factors (negative affectivity, intelligence, particular beliefs, etc.). A small amount of stress would be sufficient to cause PTSD in a person with a strong predisposition to develop the disorder. A large amount of stress would be needed to produce PTSD in a person who has only a slight predisposition to develop PTSD. This is an interaction model in which the stressor is an essential component.

Although these problems weaken Bowman's conclusions, her arguments are important in that they highlight the fact that traumatic stressors by themselves are insufficient to cause PTSD symptoms. In order to better understand PTSD, researchers and clinicians need to consider how various predisposing factors interact with stressful events. ◆

## Prevention and Treatment of ASD and PTSD

Trauma is a known cause of ASD and PTSD, and this knowledge makes prevention, as well as treatment, a primary consideration. In considering interventions with trauma victims, it is essential to distinguish among emergency attempts to help trauma victims, treatments for ASD in an effort to prevent PTSD, and specific treatments for PTSD.

### Emergency Treatment of Trauma Victims

**Critical incident stress (CIS)** is a general term referring to *normal* responses to trauma. There is no consensus definition of CIS in the DSM-IV-TR or elsewhere, but the reaction involves (1) cognitive symptoms such as confusion; (2) physical effects like gastrointestinal problems; (3) emotional upset, including fear, anger, and guilt; and (4) behaviour reactions, such as withdrawal, aggression, and substance abuse

(Bryant & Harvey, 2000; Mitchell & Dyregrov, 1993).

The potential for early intervention to ease CIS and prevent PTSD is so important that government agencies in several countries have been formed to deal with natural and man-made disasters. Emergency treatments range from intensive individual counselling sessions with hurricane victims to group discussions with children following an episode of school violence. Intervention approaches differ greatly, but offering immediate social support to trauma victims is a common goal of all early interventions (Raphael et al., 1996).

**PTSD Prevention Programs** People who have just experienced a traumatic event are at risk for developing PTSD (APA, 2000). Accordingly, programs have been developed to prevent PTSD (and other psychopathology) in at-risk populations. Among the most widely used interventions are the various forms of psychological debriefings, such as **critical incident stress debriefing (CISD)** (Mitchell & Everly, 2000). Debriefing is implemented in a single session, 24 to 48 hours post-trauma, either in individual or group formats. The trauma sufferer is presented with information about common reactions to trauma (e.g., PTSD symptoms), and asked to provide the debriefer with a detailed review of the trauma. The debriefer encourages emotional expression and encourages the person to discuss the trauma with others. Avoidance of trauma-related stimuli is discouraged, and the person is encouraged to seek further help if symptoms persist.

Despite the widespread use of psychological debriefing, little evidence about its effects has been available until recently. Research indicates that debriefing, compared to no intervention, is either ineffective or possibly harmful in that it seems to perpetuate PTSD symptoms (Mayou et al., 2000; van Emmerik et al., 2002).

**Treatment of ASD** Few studies of the treatment of ASD have been conducted—a circumstance that is not surprising given that the diagnosis was developed only recently. Nevertheless, some recent research indicates that structured interventions with ASD *can* lead to the prevention of future PTSD. Unlike CISD and other early interventions with trauma victims, these treatments are somewhat longer and targeted at the select group of trauma victims who meet ASD diagnostic criteria. The empirically backed ASD treatments are based on the principles of cognitive behaviour therapy (described shortly), although they are more brief, involving five $1\frac{1}{2}$-hour sessions (Bryant & Harvey, 2000).

**Antidepressants and PTSD** A recent consensus statement on the treatment of PTSD concluded that antidepressant medication and psychotherapy involving therapeutic re-exposure are the two "first-line" therapies for PTSD (Ballenger et al., 2000). The recommendation of using antidepressants as a first-line treatment for PTSD is quite recent (Ledoux & Gorman, 2001). The effectiveness of antidepressants likely is at least partially due to the high comorbidity between PTSD and depression (Newport & Nemeroff, 2000). Notably, traditional antianxiety medications, including the benzodiazepines, are *not* effective in treating PTSD, as shown by research from the University of British Columbia (van Etten & Taylor, 1998).

**Cognitive Behaviour Therapy for PTSD** Psychotherapists who specialize in PTSD have suggested some general principles for the psychological treatment of the disorder. In the order in which they are likely to be addressed in therapy, these include (1) establishing a trusting therapeutic relationship, (2) providing education about the process of coping with trauma, (3) stress-management training, (4) encouraging the re-experience of the trauma, and (5) integrating the traumatic event into the individual's experience (Scurfield, 1985).

Re-exposure to the traumatic event is perhaps the least obvious, but most important, of these strategies (Frueh, Turner, & Beidel, 1995; Rothbaum & Foa, 1996). Therapeutic approaches differ in how re-exposure is encouraged, yet all treatments require the reliving of trauma in some form. Depending on the client, the therapist, and the circumstances of the trauma, *prolonged exposure* might involve confronting feared situations in vivo, confronting fears in one's imagination, or recalling the trauma for extended periods of time. Prolonged exposure therapy typically includes additional cognitive behaviour therapy components—for example, challenging automatic maladaptive thoughts that can result from the experience of trauma such as, "No one cares" or "The world is hopeless."

**Comparative Efficacy of Drugs and Cognitive Behaviour Therapy** A meta-analysis conducted by researchers at the University of British Columbia compared psychological and pharmacological treatments for PTSD (van Etten & Taylor, 1998). Among the most efficacious psychological therapies were behavioural and cognitive behavioural treatments, all of which involve some form of therapeutic re-exposure. These treatments were found to be more effective than hypnosis, psychodynamic psychotherapy, supportive counselling, and placebo controls. The most effective drug treatments were the selective serotonin reuptake inhibitors, such as fluoxetine (Prozac) and sertraline. Behavioural and cognitive behavioural therapies were just as effective as these drugs in reducing PTSD symptoms. Importantly, these psychological therapies had fewer treatment dropouts (15 percent) than drug treatments (32 percent), suggesting that clients find behavioural and cognitive behavioural therapies to be more acceptable and more easily tolerated than drugs.

**Other Treatments** A recent and promising form of psychotherapy for PTSD is known as Emotion Focused Therapy. This treatment bears many similarities to cognitive behavioural treatment. Studies conducted by Sandra Paivio (University of Windsor) and Leslie Greenberg (York University) indicate that Emotion Focused Therapy can be useful in reducing PTSD symptoms and other emotional problems (Paivio & Greenberg, 2000; Paivio & Niewenhuis, 2001).

We should also comment on one more approach to exposure therapy for PTSD: *eye movement desensitization and reprocessing* (EMDR). EMDR has been greeted with considerable clinical enthusiasm—and empirical skepticism. Francine Shapiro (1995) "discovered" that rapid back-and-forth eye movements reduced her own anxiety, and she soon applied the eye movement technique to her clients. She and her proponents have taught EMDR to thousands of practitioners, and case studies and limited research attest to the treatment's effectiveness, particularly in treating PTSD. However, many experts have been skeptical of EMDR due to the lack of a theoretical basis for the treatment (Lohr et al., 1992). In fact, a recent meta-analysis concluded that EMDR can be an effective treatment—to the extent that it incorporates prolonged exposure. Empirical evidence indicates that eye movements add nothing to the treatment's effectiveness (Davidson & Parker, 2001). Another study of EMDR conducted at the University of British Columbia found that EMDR was no more effective than relaxation training, and that both treatments were less effective than behaviour therapy (Taylor et al., 2003).

# Dissociative Disorders

If the dissociative symptoms found in ASD and PTSD are dramatic, the symptoms of **dissociative disorders**—characterized by persistent, maladaptive disruptions in the integration of memory, consciousness, or identity—verge on the unbelievable. The person with a dissociative disorder may be unable to remember many seemingly familiar details about the past; he or she may wander far from home and perhaps assume a new identity; or in extreme cases, two or more personalities may coexist within the same person. These real but apparently rare psychological problems raise probing questions not only about the disorders themselves but about the very nature of the human psyche.

Until recent years, dissociative disorders were of more interest to theorists and novelists than to psychological scientists. You may be familiar with dramatic portrayals of *multiple personality disorder*, as these disorders used to be called, in *Sybil* or the *The Three Faces of Eve*, both of which have been widely read and made into popular motion pictures. Interest in dissociative disorders also has grown among mental health professionals, particularly since the publication of *Sybil* in 1973. However, clinical and theoretical approaches to dissociative disorders are controversial, and as you will soon discover, sound research is sharply limited. We introduce these extraordinary problems in the following case study.

Dallae, discussed on the next page, suffered from **dissociative fugue,** a rare and unusual disorder characterized by sudden, unplanned travel, the inability to remember details about the past, and confusion about identity or the assumption of a new identity. Dissociative fugue typically follows a traumatic event. For example, it is sometimes observed

## CASE STUDY **Dissociative Fugue: Dallae's Journey**

Dallae disappeared mysteriously during final exams during her second year at university. She was reported missing by her roommate, who had last seen Dallae when she was supposed to be studying for her organic chemistry exam. Dallae had been agitated that night. She left her room several times and kept interrupting her roommate, who was cramming for the same exam. Dallae did not take the exam the next day, and she still had not reappeared two days later. When she missed two more final exams, her roommate contacted the authorities.

At first, the police suspected foul play, because it did not seem likely that Dallae had left on her own. None of her personal possessions were missing from her room; even her eyeglasses were still sitting on her desk. However, bank records indicated that Dallae had withdrawn all of her money from her bank account the day before the exam. Investigators also discovered that Dallae had been lying to her parents. She had told them that she had an A average in organic chemistry. In fact, she was failing the course, and she had not attended her laboratory section for almost two months.

After a four-week investigation, the authorities located Dallae in a university town on the East Coast, where she was identified from a missing persons report. She had been brought to a hospital emergency room after she was found wandering on the streets. At the time, she appeared confused and disoriented. She told the emergency room physician that her name was Dawn and that she had been living on the streets and sleeping in dormitory lounges. She said that she had just moved from the West Coast and had come to the town because she hoped eventually to attend the university. She gave a vague and sketchy account about other details of her life. For example, she could not say how she got to the East Coast.

Dallae allowed herself to be voluntarily admitted to the hospital's psychiatric unit. There she talked little and spent most of her time watching television. She told the staff that she was Vietnamese and had been adopted by white parents, but her stories continued to be vague and inconsistent. She said she didn't remember things, but she did not seem greatly distressed by her memory impairment. A CAT scan and neuropsychological tests detected no physical abnormalities or deficits in short-term memory or motor functioning.

A hospital social worker contacted the local police about the disoriented young patient, and the police were able to identify Dallae. The social worker contacted Dallae's parents shortly thereafter, and her mother immediately flew east to see her. When her mother appeared at the hospital a few days after Dallae had been admitted, Dallae did not recognize her. Her mother was greatly distressed by Dallae's indifference, and she noted other puzzling oddities and inconsistencies. For one thing, Dallae was not Vietnamese, and she was not adopted. She had grown up with her married parents, who were Korean immigrants. Her mother also noted that although Dallae was right-handed, she used her left hand to write a note on the ward. Dallae's consistent use of her left hand was confirmed by the staff and by the neuropsychologist who had tested her.

Two nights after her mother arrived, Dallae's memories apparently returned. That night, she attempted suicide by slashing her wrists, but she was discovered by a hospital staff member, who quickly stopped the bleeding. Dallae was intermittently depressed and extremely agitated for the next several days, especially after seeing her mother. Although she would not talk at length, her conversation indicated that much of her memory was now intact, and she began writing with her right hand again.

During the next two weeks, Dallae gradually related details about her life to the psychologist who was treating her. Dallae had been a quiet and obedient girl all through her childhood. Dallae's parents worked very hard, and they had high ambitions for their three children. Dallae's older brother had an MBA and was a very successful young executive. Her older sister currently was editor of the law review at a prestigious law school. Ever since she was a young child, Dallae's parents had planned for her to become a doctor. In fact, all her life her parents had told friends and relatives that Dallae would be a doctor one day.

Dallae worked extremely hard throughout high school and gained admission to a highly regarded university despite her mediocre admission scores. Through continued effort, Dallae had maintained a 3.0 grade point average. Her coursework was becoming overwhelming, however, and her motivation was evaporating. Dallae now admitted, in fact, that she had never been interested in medicine. She also noted that she had wanted to attend the university in the town where she was found. She was drawn there during her episode for reasons she could not explain, and she still did not recall exactly how she had arrived at her destination. Dallae did note, however, that she felt comforted and somewhat relieved after she had made her way east.

Dallae remained sullen and agitated for several weeks after her mother's arrival, and she continued to talk about wanting to die. During discussions with her therapist, Dallae began to talk more freely about her past. She noted that she had been terrified to tell her parents about her grades and her feelings about studying medicine—especially her father. Her father put endless pressure on Dallae to fulfill what she saw as his dream. She cried at length when relating how he had struck her across the face during the previous Thanksgiving break, when she tried to tell him about her lack of interest in studying medicine.

After spending six weeks in the hospital, Dallae was released, and she returned to live with her parents. Her memory was intact at the time of the discharge, except that she continued to have no recollection

*continued*

*cont.*

of her trip across the country or of many of her days living on the streets. She remained uncertain why she thought her name was Dawn, although she did mention being influenced by a television show she had seen about a Vietnamese child who had been adopted. She could not recall the name of the character in the story, but she did remember concluding that she too was Vietnamese and adopted. At the time of Dallae's discharge, her depression had abated somewhat, and she was no longer actively suicidal. She reported being relieved at having told her mother about her feelings about medical school, but she remained very anxious about facing her father's disappointment. ◆

among soldiers following a particularly gruesome battle. For Dallae, perhaps her poor grades could be considered trauma, given her father's intense and constant pressure to succeed.

The travel in dissociative fugue is purposeful, despite the memory impairments. Dallae knew where she was going, and she could provide at least a vague explanation about why she was going there. Purposeful travel is the distinguishing symptom, but the core questions about fugue—and about all dissociative disorders—concern the split between conscious and unconscious psychological experience. How could Dallae be aware of the present but still be unaware of her past? Why didn't all her memories return after she saw her mother? Could she be faking part or all of her "illness"? Several key figures in the history of abnormal psychology have attempted to answer such perplexing questions. In fact, attempts to explain these puzzling disorders resulted in some of the first theories about unconscious psychological processes.

## Hysteria and Unconscious Mental Processes

Dissociative disorders (and somatoform disorders, which we discuss later in the chapter) and the disruptions of consciousness that characterize them once were viewed as expressions of **hysteria**, a term that dates to ancient Greece. In Greek, *hystera* means "uterus," and the term *hysteria* reflects ancient speculation that these disorders were caused by frustrated sexual desires, particularly the desire to have a baby. According to the theory, the uterus becomes detached from its normal location and moves about the body, causing a problem in the location where it eventually lodges. Variants of this somewhat sexist view continued throughout Western history, and as late as the nineteenth century many physicians erroneously believed that hysteria occurred only among women (Showalter, 1997).

**Charcot, Freud, Janet, and the Unconscious Mind** New speculation about the etiology of hysteria emerged toward the end of the nineteenth century. The work of Jean Charcot, who used hypnosis both to treat and to induce hysteria, was particularly important. Charcot greatly influenced the thinking of Freud, who observed Charcot's hypnotic treatments early in his training (see Chapter 2). Charcot also had a strong influence on the work of Freud's contemporary and rival, Pierre Janet (1859–1947). Janet was a French philosophy professor who conducted psychological experiments on dissociation and who later trained as a physician in Charcot's clinic.

Both Janet and Freud were eager to explain and treat hysteria, and the problem led both of them to develop theories about unconscious mental processes. The two competitors differed sharply in their views. Janet saw dissociation as an abnormal process. To him, detachment from conscious awareness occurred only as a part of psychopathology. Thus Janet defined unconscious processes narrowly, consistent with what he observed in dissociative and somatoform disorders. In contrast, Freud considered dissociation as a normal process, a routine means through which the ego defended itself against unacceptable

***Pierre Janet*** *(1859–1947) conducted psychological experiments as a professor in Paris, and he later trained as a physician in Jean Charcot's clinic. Janet's views on dissociation were much more circumscribed than those of his rival, Sigmund Freud.*

*The French neurologist Jean Charcot (1825–1893) demonstrating a case of hysteria at the Salpetiere, a famous hospital in Paris.*

unconscious thoughts. Freud saw dissociation and repression as similar processes, and, in fact, he often used the two terms interchangeably (Erdelyi, 1990; Perry & Laurence, 1984). Thus Freud viewed dissociative and somatoform disorders to be merely two of many expressions of unconscious conflict.

The two theorists criticized each other frequently. Janet thought that Freud greatly overstated the importance of the unconscious; Freud thought that Janet greatly underestimated it. Janet's work became increasingly obscure, however, as Freudian theory dominated the mental health professions throughout much of the twentieth century. As Freudian influences have declined in recent years, scholars have rediscovered Janet's contributions and his more narrow conception of dissociation and unconscious mental processes.

**Unconscious Mental Processes in Cognitive Science** Contemporary psychologists continue to debate dissociation and unconscious processes, but they generally agree about two things. First, unconscious processes do exist, and they play a role in both normal and abnormal emotion and cognition (Epstein, 1994). The challenge of explaining unconscious mental processes is a real one in cognitive science, not merely a remnant of Freudian theory. Second, contemporary cognitive scientists continue to debate the importance of unconscious mental events. For example, one cognitive scientist has said that the unconscious mind is "dumb," not "smart" (Loftus & Klinger, 1992). From this perspective, unconscious mental processes are limited. For example, we are unaware of how we remember. We remember a forgotten event without knowing the strategy we used to access the memory.

*Hypnotized university students reacting to the suggestion that they are on a beach in Hawaii. Performance hypnotists produce such dramatic effects by selecting only highly suggestible subjects for their demonstrations.*

Other contemporary experts suggest a more elaborate model of unconscious mental processes—for example, that we have two systems of information processing: a rational system and an emotionally driven experiential system (Epstein, 1994). The *rational system* involves abstract, logical knowledge that is adaptive for solving complex problems over time. The *experiential system* involves intuitive knowledge based on experience that is adaptive for responding to problems immediately without the delay of thought. The experiential system thus is emotional, powerful, and often illogical (Epstein, 1994). Rationally, we might know that airplanes are safer than automobiles, for example, but emotionally, we are more likely to fear airplanes—especially in the wake of September 11.

Whatever their theory, contemporary cognitive scientists insist that hypotheses about unconscious mental processes must be tested in research. In fact, scientists have created new research techniques to study unconscious processes—for example, the distinction between explicit and implicit memory. *Explicit memory* is the conscious recollection of a past event. **Implicit memory** is indicated by changes in behaviour apparently based on a memory of prior event but with no conscious remembering of the event (Schacter, 1987). To illustrate the distinction, consider the problem of *prosopagnosia*, an impairment of face recognition that sometimes follows specific forms of brain damage. Patients with prosopagnosia have no explicit memory for faces—that is, they are unable to recognize people they know. However, they demonstrate the normal preference for viewing faces that are familiar, even though they claim that the face is not familiar to them (Farah, O'Reilly, & Vecera, 1993). Apparently, patients have an *implicit memory* for familiar faces—that is, recognition occurs at some lower level of perception or consciousness. Such findings indicate a dissociation between conscious and unconscious cognitive processing.

**Hypnosis: Altered State or Social Role?** The nature of **hypnosis**, in which subjects experience loss of control over their actions in response to suggestions from the hypnotist, is a topic of historical importance and contemporary debate about the unconscious mind. All agree that demonstrations of the power of hypnotic suggestion are impressive, and that different people are more or less susceptible to hypnosis. However, some experts assert that hypnosis is the dissociative experience of an altered state of consciousness. Others argue that hypnosis is merely a social role, where the subject voluntarily complies with suggestions due to social expectations and demands (Barnier, 2002; Kihlstrom, 1998b; Kirsch & Lynn, 1995, 1998; Woody & Sadler, 1998). Beware of concluding that hypnosis *must* be real and powerful because you have seen it at work in a group demonstration. The trick that hypnotists use in this circumstance is to select only highly susceptible (or highly compliant!) participants for demonstration purposes.

## Typical Symptoms of Dissociative Disorders

Like many ordinary cognitive processes, the extraordinary symptoms of dissociative disorders apparently involve mental processing that occurs outside of conscious awareness. Extreme cases of dissociation include a split in the functioning of the individual's entire sense of self. In *dissociative identity disorder (DID)*, two or more personalities coexist within a single individual, and one or both of the personalities may be unaware of the existence of the other. Unless we assume that the symptom is feigned, dissociative identity disorder demonstrates that the mind can function on multiple levels of consciousness.

*Depersonalization* is a less dramatic form of dissociation wherein people feel detached from themselves or their social or physical environment. Examples of depersonalization include feeling like a stranger in social interactions and out-of-body experiences—feelings of detachment from one's physical being—for example, the sensation of floating outside yourself and watching your actions as if you were another person.

Another dramatic example of dissociation is *amnesia*—the partial or complete loss of recall for particular events or for a particular period of time. Brain injury or disease can cause amnesia (see Chapter 14), but *psychogenic* (psychologically caused) amnesia results from traumatic stress or other emotional distress. Psychogenic amnesia may occur alone or in conjunction with other dissociative experiences. For example, in dissociative identity disorder one personality may not remember the actions, or even the existence, of another (Spiegel & Cardena, 1991).

**Trauma and the Onset of Dissociative Symptoms** It is widely accepted that fugue and psychogenic amnesia are usually precipitated by trauma, thus providing another link between dissociation and traumatic stress disorders. In these disorders, the trauma is clear and usually sudden, and in most cases, psychological functioning rapidly returns to normal. Much more controversial is the role that trauma might play in dissociative identity disorder (DID). Some researchers and clinicians argue that DID is linked with past, not present, trauma, particularly with chronic child physical or sexual abuse (Gleaves, 1996). Many psychological scientists are skeptical about this assertion, however, because information about childhood trauma is based solely on clients' reports—reports that may be distorted by many factors, including by a therapist's expectations (Lilienfeld et al., 1999). A related issue is the very controversial topic of **recovered memories**, dramatic recollections of long-ago traumatic experiences supposedly blocked from the conscious mind by dissociation (see Further Thoughts).

## Classification of Dissociative Disorders

**Brief Historical Perspective** For centuries, theorists considered dissociative and somatoform disorders as alternative forms of hysteria. However, Freudian proponents, who defined dissociation broadly, classified hysteria as a type of *neurosis*—a diagnostic category that also included anxiety and depressive disorders. The category "neurosis" reflected the Freudian view that unconscious conflict was the common cause of each of these apparently different disorders. Still, the historical link between somatoform and dissociative disorders was preserved in many classification systems. For example, the somatoform and dissociative disorders were listed together as subtypes of "hysterical neurosis" in DSM-II (1968).

The descriptive approach to classification introduced in DSM-III (1980) led to the separation of dissociative and somatoform disorders into discrete diagnostic categories. The distinction is preserved in DSM-IV-TR (2000), because the symptoms of the two disorders differ greatly. Consistent with DSM-IV-TR, we review the two

## Further Thoughts **Recovered Memories?**

Recovered memories are recollections of traumatic experiences that the person has apparently forgotten, often for years or decades, and then recalled. As observed by researchers at the University of Calgary, the topic of recovered memories is highly controversial, both in the field of psychology and in the broader community (Prout & Dobson, 1988). Some documented victims of sexual abuse do not recall the experience many years later (Williams, 1994), but many of these victims were very young when they were abused—and evidence of documented cases of forgetting does not prove that undocumented cases of remembering are accurate! The accuracy of recovered memories is not a minor concern. Some therapists believe that recovering memories is an important part of their therapy with female clients, and they report using some dubious strategies to help their clients "remember" past traumas, particularly physical and sexual abuse (Poole et al., 1995). Many parents faced with accusations of past abuse say that false memories are being created by misguided, overeager therapists. Concern is so great that a new term, *false memory syndrome,* has been coined to account for the implanting of false beliefs (Kihlstrom, 1998a). In the Canadian legal case of *R.* v. *François* (1994), for example, Lorne François was convicted of repeatedly raping a 13-year-old girl in 1985. The only evidence was the girl's testimony. She claimed that she had repressed memories of the sexual assaults. Recollections of the assaults emerged in 1990 when police suggested that if she thought long enough about her past, she might recall something in a "flashback." The girl reported that the flashbacks occurred while trying to recall her past. The conviction was later overturned by the Supreme Court of Canada.

Are recovered memories examples of dissociation or of the power of suggestion? Psychologist Elizabeth Loftus (1993), a memory researcher who has served as an expert witness in many trials, suggests numerous reasons for skepticism. Loftus clearly doubts the validity of any "recovered memory" dating from infancy or toddlerhood, because most experiences prior to school age are forgotten. Few people can report any accurate memories dating back before age three or four (Winograd & Killinger, 1983).

More suspicions emerge from some case histories of recovered memories. Studies indicate that therapists rarely doubt their clients' recovered memories of the past (Loftus, 1993; Loftus & Ketcham, 1994), but the concern embraces much more than a lack of skepticism. Many therapists and popular books encourage people to search for (create?) memories that they do not recall. Symptoms as common as low self-esteem are sometimes interpreted as indications of forgotten trauma. Gaps in memory are also interpreted as a sign of dissociated memories. In the popular book *The Courage to Heal*, the authors state:

> You may think you don't have memories, but often as you begin to talk about what you do remember, there emerges a constellation of feelings, reactions, and recollections that add up to substantial information. To say "I was abused," you don't need the kind of recall that would stand up in a court of law.
>
> Often the knowledge that you were abused starts with a tiny feeling, an intuition. It's important to trust that inner voice and work from there. Assume your feelings are valid. So far, no one we've talked to thought she might have been abused and then later discovered that she hadn't been. (Bass & Davis, 1988, p. 22)

Could such suggestions lead some people to create memories about events that never happened? Determining the truth in any one case is difficult, sometimes impossible. Nevertheless, several studies supply evidence that memories can be inaccurate or even completely false. Dalhousie University psychologist Stephen Porter demonstrated that some people can create false memories for emotional childhood events (Porter & Birt, 2001; Porter et al., 1999, 2000). Participants in the 1999 and 2000 research were university students. The parents of the students were asked to provide information about six emotional events (e.g., serious accidents, medical procedures, animal attacks) that the student may or may not have experienced as a child. The information enabled researchers to construct, for a given student, a fabricated childhood event that could form the basis of a false memory. The experiment consisted of three interviews over two weeks. In the first interview, students were interviewed about a real and a false event, with each introduced to the student as true. In interviews two and three, students were re-interviewed about the false event. Interviewers attempted to elicit a false memory in each student, using methods such as guided imagery (e.g., asking the student to repeatedly imagine the fictitious event) and by encouraging repeated attempts to recover the memory. Porter et al. (1999) found that 26 percent of students created a false memory and 30 percent created a partial false memory (e.g., the student was unsure about whether the false event had occurred). Further results suggested that false memories are most likely to occur for people with dissociative tendencies (i.e., high scores on the Dissociative Experiences Scale) and when the interviewer is engaging, persuasive, and confident (Porter et al., 2000). In a similar study, University of Victoria psychologist Stephen Lindsay and colleagues (2004) demonstrated that two-thirds of research participants accepted a fabricated (experimenter-implanted) grade-school event as having actually happened to them, when the suggestion regarding the event was supplemented by a class photo.

These studies do not prove that all recovered memories of trauma are false. In fact, evidence indicates that memories for emotion-laden events are more accurate than memories for ordinary experiences (Koss, Tromp, & Tharan, 1995). Still, the malleability of memory suggests grounds for great skepticism, particularly when a memory is "recovered" after a therapist encourages a client to search for it. ◆

problems separately. We nevertheless discuss both problems in a single chapter because of their historical relationship and because both apparently involve unconscious processes.

**Contemporary Classification** DSM-IV-TR distinguishes four major subtypes of dissociative disorders: dissociative fugue, dissociative amnesia, depersonalization disorder, and dissociative identity disorder. Dissociative fugue is characterized by sudden and unexpected travel away from home, an inability to recall the past, and confusion about identity or the assumption of a new identity. The case of Dallae is an example of dissociative fugue.

**Dissociative amnesia** involves a sudden inability to recall extensive and important personal information that exceeds normal forgetfulness. The memory loss in dissociative amnesia is not attributable to substance abuse, head trauma, or a cognitive disorder, such as Alzheimer's disease. As with fugue, dissociative amnesia typically is characterized by a sudden onset in response to trauma or extreme stress and by an equally sudden recovery of memory. The most common form of amnesia in dissociative disorders is *selective amnesia*, in which patients do not lose their memory completely but instead are unable to remember only selected personal events and information, often events related to a traumatic experience. (See Chapter 14 for a discussion of other types of amnesia found in cognitive disorders.) In one study of 25 patients in a dissociative disorders clinic, 76 percent had selective amnesia (Coons & Milstein, 1988, cited in Spiegel & Cardena, 1991).

Canada's most famous case of dissociative disorder concerned the Calgary socialite Dorothy Joudrie (1936–2002). She suffered years of violent physical abuse at the hands of her husband, who subsequently left her for another woman. In her guilt and loneliness, Dorothy turned to alcohol. In 1995 when her estranged husband returned to collect some things, Dorothy shot him six times with a .25-calibre Berretta handgun. He survived the attack. Later, he recalled that Dorothy behaved strangely during the shooting; she appeared to be unusually calm and detached. The police officers found her to be distraught and almost disoriented. She had no recollection of the shooting (dissociative amnesia), and reportedly "came to" to discover her husband shot, lying on the garage floor. Dorothy was found

*In 1995 Calgary socialite Dorothy Joudrie (1936–2002) shot her estranged husband six times with a .25-calibre Berretta handgun. She was found not criminally responsible by reason of mental disorder. At the time of the crime she appeared to be suffering from a dissociative disorder.*

not criminally responsible by reason of mental disorder. At the time of the crime she appeared to be suffering from a dissociative disorder (Andrews, 1999).

**Depersonalization disorder** is a less dramatic problem that is characterized by severe and persistent feelings of being detached from oneself. Depersonalization experiences include such sensations as feeling as though you were in a dream or were floating above your body and observing yourself act. Occasional depersonalization experiences are normal and are reported by about half the population. In depersonalization disorder, however, such experiences are persistent or recurrent, and they cause marked personal distress. The onset of the disorder commonly follows a new or disturbing event, such as drug use. All depersonalization experiences are "as-if" feelings, not rigid, delusional beliefs. In fact, some experts question whether depersonalization should be considered a type of dissociative disorder. Unlike other dissociative disorders, depersonalization disorder involves only limited splitting between conscious and unconscious mental processes, and no memory loss occurs (Spiegel & Cardena, 1991).

To many people, the most fascinating subtype of dissociative disorder is **dissociative**

**identity disorder (DID)**, a condition also known as **multiple personality disorder**. This unusual mental disorder is characterized by the existence of two or more distinct personalities in a single individual. At least two of these personalities repeatedly take control of the person's behaviour, and the individual's inability to recall information is too extensive to be explained by ordinary forgetfulness. The original personality especially is likely to have amnesia for subsequent personalities, which may or may not be aware of the "alternates" (Aldridge-Morris, 1989). Recent case histories have identified more and more alternate personalities in DID. The case of "Eve," published in 1957, identified three personalities; "Sybil" was reported to have 16 personalities in a 1973 best-seller (the veracity of which has been questioned; see Rieber, 1999); and some more recent cases have claimed to have a 100, even 1000, alters. Not surprisingly, such claims have generated more controversy about a diagnosis that already was controversial. According to surveys conducted in Canada and the United States, many mental health professionals are skeptical of the validity of the concept of dissociative identity disorder (e.g., Lalonde et al., 2001).

## CASE STUDY Dissociative Identity Disorder

In response to a newspaper inquiry, Nancy came forth to tell her story about her struggles with a dissociative identity disorder. Nancy, who resides in Ontario, gave the following account of her problems, how they arose, and how she has worked to overcome them.

The piano has a place of honour in Nancy's living room. It's a red mahogany Lesage, made in Quebec. But Nancy fears that piano. She will only play it if the doors are locked or if her husband Hugh is around. When she was a girl, she loved to play the classics every day. Sonatina. Rondo. Allegro by Mozart. She concentrated so hard. She shut herself off from her surroundings. "I felt I was inside the music." And while she played, her father molested her. He touched her, he masturbated. From the time she was a toddler, he had abused her. It could happen anywhere in the house. At the piano, she had the music to take her away. But wherever she was, Nancy had grown skilled at using her mind to float away from her father's grasp. She could peel off a piece of herself, so she hardly felt the pain. That ability saved her then. But now it's a problem.

We all dissociate. We all daydream, we cruise along a straight stretch of highway and later we don't really remember the details at all. But for someone like Nancy, those moments of lost time were deeper, more frequent. Her earliest memory of abuse is from when she was about three. Her father comes into her room. He is naked. He picks her up and carries her into his room. He puts her on his bed and gets on top of her. She does not know what he's doing. "Daddy, that hurts my tummy." "No it doesn't, honey." If Daddy says it doesn't, it doesn't. When he is done, Nancy sees something on the sheets. Maybe it's red water.

For another memory, she is about eight. It is a warm day at the house on West Fifth. Nancy is in the living room. Her father is in the sun room, drinking with friends. "Nancy, c'mon out here," he hollers. She doesn't move. He calls her again and she goes. She stands in the middle of the men. She smells the beer. One man pulls her sundress over her head. Another pulls her underpants down. Her father puts his finger inside her. Another man, a relative, puts himself in her mouth. Nancy looks over, sees her mother at the doorway. "Mommy's here. She's going to stop this." But mother turns and leaves. "Oh, I must be bad," the little girl thinks. Another man says, "Pass her over here." After he's done, somebody places her on the couch. Nancy knows where she is, but feels nothing. She is looking at the wall. She sees flowers growing out of it.

By the time she was 11, she couldn't make flowers grow from the wall anymore. But the abuse continued until she was 18, until she got married. Hugh rode into her life and saved her. She told him about some of the past. "You need to talk about this," he told her. Nancy said she was fine. She was married, to the right man. And she was a nurse, which she'd always wanted to be. But that fell apart one night at work. She went to walk into the medication room and walked into the wall instead. She collapsed. She was sick for months. She couldn't drive, couldn't climb stairs. She vomited and had severe headaches. There were many tests. Maybe it was a brain tumour. Or an inner ear problem. Finally, a neurologist said, "Nancy, is it possible you've been under stress?" "It was like a light being turned on," she says. "And I said, 'Yes, I'm 36 and I've been under stress for 33 years.'"

She got therapy and soon even started a self-help group. "I found out it's OK to talk about what happened, to say it out loud. I realized it really wasn't my fault." After a few years she left the group. "I thought I was doing quite well. I'd learned to handle the flashbacks and the memories." But she started getting sick a lot again. There was something that had bothered Nancy for years—the voices inside her. And by this point, they seemed awfully persistent. "There's a saying that it's OK to talk to yourself and as long as you don't answer, you're not crazy." But Nancy noticed she was waking up at night, hearing herself talking and answering. She had said something to her husband years before, "Hughie, I think I'm going crazy. I

*continued*

*cont.*

hear all these voices. They're talking, fighting, arguing." The arguments that rattled through her head could be about something as simple as whether to serve the chicken dinner with baked potatoes or rice. Or whether to go to the mall. "It was like Siamese twins who constantly talk back and forth because they can't do anything without each other." And there was amnesia, confusion, lost time. Nancy was sure she had invited that couple to dinner. They were puzzled why she got angry when they didn't show up.

She was then sent to two psychiatrists. Both made the diagnosis of dissociative identity disorder. There appear to be eight different parts to Nancy's personality. In her mind, each has its own physical appearance. She pictures them with different hair, different glasses. There is Malveen. She's shy, introverted, overwhelmed with guilt. This part of Nancy stopped growing when she was a teenager and met Hugh. There's Dorothy, well organized, able to do 10 things at once. There's another part that's all anger. And there is Just Me, that persistent part she always argued with. Good therapy and the right medication sent that angry personality away. Nancy continues to work on her recovery.

Six years ago, one of the men who abused Nancy in that sunroom on West Fifth was convicted of assault, gross indecency, and sexual intercourse with a female person under 14. The judge called the crimes abhorrent. But because of the way that the judge addressed the jury, the man was granted a new trial. He died before it took place. Nancy's mother and father, both abused as children, are gone now. Mother, a nurse, died 13 years ago on a hospital bed in Nancy's home. Father, a postal worker, then city employee, died seven years ago. Nancy had been looking after him, cleaning his apartment, getting his groceries. She had confronted him and wrung out an apology. He was about to be charged when he died.

Therapy has been hard and slow, but Nancy is not discouraged. "Each of these parts of me was beneficial. They helped me to survive. But it would be good for me now to merge these parts. It would be good to become one healthy person." ◆

*Source*: Adapted from P. Wilson, 2000, Keeping pain at a distance. *Hamilton Spectator*, May 16. Reprinted with permission from the *Hamilton Spectator*.

## Epidemiology of Dissociative Disorders

The prevalence of dissociative disorders is difficult to establish. The conditions generally have been considered to be extremely rare. For example, only about 200 case histories of dissociative identity disorder were reported in the entire world literature prior to 1980 (Greaves, 1980). However, a number of clinicians have diagnosed dissociative identity disorder with much greater frequency in recent years. This increase in diagnosis has occurred in conjunction with growing public concern about child sexual abuse, a traumatic experience that has been hypothesized to play a role in the etiology of many dissociative disorders (Kluft, 1987). Thus, in comparison to the 1980 survey, a 1986 report suggested that approximately 6000 cases of DID had been diagnosed in North America (Coons, 1986).

Obviously, the more recent figures constitute a dramatic increase in the diagnosis of dissociative identity disorder. In fact, a study of a random, nonclinical sample in Winnipeg went even further and suggested an unbelievably high prevalence rate. According to diagnoses obtained through a structured, diagnostic interview, over 10 percent of the adult population was designated as suffering from a dissociative disorder! This figure included 7 percent with dissociative amnesia, 3 percent with dissociative identity disorder, 2 percent with depersonalization disorder, and 0.2 percent with dissociative fugue (Ross, 1991). Another study reported that as many as 40 percent of hospitalized psychiatric patients met DSM-IV-TR criteria for the diagnosis of a dissociative disorder (Ross et al., 2002).

*Chris Sizemore is "Eve," the patient from the book and movie* The Three Faces of Eve. *Sizemore is now cured and is an advocate for the mentally ill.*

Clearly, either some investigators have become overzealous in defining dissociative disorders—a conclusion bolstered by recent research (Waller & Ross, 1997)—or diagnosticians have been highly inaccurate for years. In fact, a small but vocal group of professionals has argued that many patients who are truly suffering from dissociative disorders are misdiagnosed as having schizophrenia, borderline personality disorder, depression, panic disorder, or substance abuse (Gleaves, 1996; Ross, Norton, & Wozney, 1989).

***Nicholas P. Spanos** (1942–1994), a psychologist at Carleton University, was a leading expert on hypnosis, multiple personalities, and false memories. He questioned the reality of multiple personalities, arguing that they are caused by role playing.*

On the other hand, there are many reasons for skepticism: (1) Most cases of dissociative disorders are diagnosed by a handful of ardent advocates. (2) The frequency of the diagnosis of dissociative disorders in general and DID in particular increased rapidly after release of the very popular book and movie, *Sybil*. (3) The number of personalities claimed to exist in cases of DID has grown rapidly, from a handful to 100 or more. (4) Dissociative disorders are diagnosed rarely outside of the United States and Canada; for example, only one unequivocal case of DID has been reported in Great Britain in the last 25 years (Casey, 2001). And (5) the symptoms of dissociation in the most commonly used instruments like the Dissociative Experiences Questionnaire are far less dramatic than those found in dissociative disorders (see Table 7–4).

**Disorder or Role Enactment?** Carleton University psychologist Nicholas Spanos (1942–1994) was a particularly outspoken critic, who argued that multiple personalities are caused by role playing. Spanos (1994) asserted that patients are influenced by their own and their therapists' goals and expectations about DID, and, like an actor who loses all perspective, they come to believe that the role is real.

In support of his sociocognitive model, Spanos and his colleagues conducted analogue experiments on role playing and the "symptoms" of dissociative identity disorder. These studies were inspired by the case of Kenneth Bianchi, the infamous "Hillside Strangler." In 1979, Bianchi was charged with murdering two college women and was implicated in several other rape-murder cases where victims were left naked on the hillsides of Los Angeles. Considerable evidence supported Bianchi's guilt, but he reported frequent episodes of "blanking out," including an inability to remember events from the night that the murders were committed. At the request of his attorney, Bianchi was seen by a mental health expert, who hypnotized Bianchi and suggested to him, "I've talked a bit to Ken, but I think that perhaps there might be another part of Ken that I haven't talked to, another part that maybe feels somewhat differently from the part I've talked to. And I would like to communicate with that other part" (Watkins, 1984). Bianchi responded that he was not Ken but Steve. Steve knew of Ken, and he hated him. Steve also confessed to strangling "all of these girls."

Numerous experts who interviewed Bianchi disagreed about whether his apparent dissociative identity disorder was real or feigned. In fact, the conflicting expert opinion reveals the unreliability of the diagnosis (Aldridge-Morris, 1989). One of the experts was Martin Orne (1927–2000), an internationally recognized authority on hypnosis. Orne tested Bianchi by suggesting new symptoms to him. If Bianchi was faking dissociative identity disorder, he might further the deception by developing the new symptoms. Orne suggested, for example, that if Bianchi really had dissociative identity disorder, he should have a third personality. Sure enough, a third personality, Billy, "emerged" when Bianchi was subsequently hypnotized (Orne, Dingers, & Orne, 1984). While hypnotized, Bianchi also followed Orne's suggestion to hallucinate that his attorney was in the room. Bianchi actually shook hands with the supposed hallucination—a very unusual behaviour because tactile hallucinations are rare for someone under hypnosis. Orne concluded from this and other evidence that Bianchi was indeed faking, and that Bianchi actually suffered from antisocial personality disorder (see Chapter 9). Bianchi's insanity defence failed, and he was found guilty of murder.

In testing his role theory, Spanos simulated procedures from the Bianchi case. In one study, undergraduate students played the role of the accused murderer and were randomly assigned to one of three conditions. In the

**TABLE 7–4 Sample Items from the Dissociative Experiences Questionnaire**

- Some people find that sometimes they are listening to someone talk and they suddenly realize that they did not hear part or all of what was said.
- Some people have the experience of being in a familiar place but finding it strange and unfamiliar.
- Some people have the experience of finding themselves dressed in clothes that they don't remember putting on.
- Some people are told that they sometimes do not recognize friends or family members.
- Some people have the experience of feeling that their body does not seem to belong to them.
- Some people find that in one situation they may act so differently compared with another situation that they feel almost as if they were two different people.

*Source:* E.M. Bernstein and F.W. Putnam, 1986, Development, reliability, and validity of a dissociation scale. *Journal of Nervous & Mental Disease, 174*, 727–735.

"Bianchi" condition, the subjects were hypnotized, and the interviewer asked to communicate with their other part, just as Bianchi's interviewer had asked. Subjects assigned to the second, "hidden part" condition also were hypnotized, but this time it was suggested that hypnosis could get behind the "wall" that hid inner thoughts and feelings from awareness. In the final condition, there was no hypnosis, and subjects simply were told that personality included "walls" between hidden thoughts and feelings.

When subsequently asked, "Who are you?" by the interviewer in the mock murder case, 81 percent of the subjects in the Bianchi condition gave a name different from the one assigned to them in the role play, as did 70 percent of the subjects in the hidden part condition. In contrast, only 31 percent of the subjects in the no-hypnosis condition gave a new name. Increases in amnesia also were found for the two hypnosis conditions in comparison to the control group (Spanos, Weekes, & Bertrand, 1985). These results were replicated in a subsequent study. In this later experiment, hypnotized subjects also provided more "information" on exactly when in the past their alternate personalities had first emerged (Spanos et al., 1986).

These findings certainly raise the caution that the "symptoms" of DID can be induced through role playing and hypnosis (Lilienfeld et al., 1999). However, analogue studies (see Chapter 5) cannot prove that role playing causes real cases of multiple personality, and the multiple identity enactment created in laboratory studies differs from the multiple identities found in DID in numerous ways. For example, amnesia is absent in laboratory studies of multiple identity enactment, but it is widely reported in actual cases of DID (Gleaves, 1996). In fact, the inability to recall important personal information is one diagnostic criterion for the disorder. Moreover, real patients show symptoms even on subtle measures where the "appropriate" answer is not obvious (Scroppo et al., 1998; see Research Close-Up).

## RESEARCH CLOSE-UP

### Implicit Memory in Dissociative Identity Disorder

Controversy abounds today about dissociative identity disorder (DID). Is it a "happening"—a disorder that afflicts the patient? Or is it a "doing"—a role played by the person, perhaps unwittingly, in response to strong social expectations? Implicit memory tasks have the potential to help answer this question, because they assess subtle effects on mental processes that are difficult to feign.

Eric Eich and colleagues (1997) at the University of British Columbia used the implicit memory task of priming to investigate *interpersonality amnesia,* the lack of awareness of the experiences of one personality by an alter, in a group of nine patients with DID. *Priming* involves presenting participants with a set of stimuli and later testing them with a degraded form of the stimuli. Priming effects are demonstrated if the participants identify degraded stimuli more readily if they have been previously exposed to them.

Eich et al. (1997) primed participants with two tasks. In Task 1, participants read and rated a set of words. In Task 2, they reviewed a series of partial but increasingly complete drawings until they were able to identify the depicted object. As tests for each of these priming effects, participants later (1) were presented with a series of three-letter word stems corresponding with words they had rated earlier and asked to name the first word that came to mind with those letters, and (2) repeated the partial drawings task, which now included some items that they had previously identified. The unique aspect of the study was that one personality was primed, while an alter (as well as the primed personality) was tested for implicit memory effects. In all cases, each alter claimed to have no knowledge or memory of the other.

Virtually no words were recounted when the alters were simply asked to identify words that the other personality had rated. More importantly, word stem recall showed notably stronger priming effects when the tests were conducted within the same personality rather than across alters. That is, participants recalled primed words much more often when they were tested as the same personality than when tested as a different personality. In short, their amnesia "passed" the implicit memory test. On the picture completion task, the priming effects were the same within and across the alters. That is, participants were equally likely to identify previously identified pictures between and within alternate personalities.

This research certainly does not resolve the question concerning the nature of DID. It does suggest, however, that amnesia between personalities in DID occurs, but it is not complete. Amnesia is more likely when the implicit memory task permits a wide range of responses (word recall), but less likely when the task is constrained (picture identification) (Eich et al., 1997). Further research with implicit memory tasks may help to pinpoint the memory contents and processes associated with interpersonality amnesia, and in so doing, produce evidence that will be accepted both by skeptics and believers in this fascinating disorder. ◆

Given the current status of research, we reach a cautious conclusion about the epidemiology of dissociative disorders. True dissociative disorders appear to be rare. Although some cases no doubt are misdiagnosed, a much greater problem is the creation of the diagnosis in the minds of clinicians and clients (Merskey, 1992; Piper, 1994; Showalter, 1997). At the same time, we do not doubt the existence of dissociative disorders.

### Etiological Considerations and Research on Dissociative Disorders

Little systematic research has been conducted on the etiology of dissociative disorders; thus, theory and outright speculation dominate. One exception, as we have noted, is the widely held view that the disorders often are precipitated by trauma. Even if trauma contributes to dissociative disorders, it clearly is not a sufficient cause. As we saw in reviewing ASD and PTSD, many people experience trauma without developing a dissociative disorder. Thus, consistent with the systems perspective, other biological, psychological, and social factors must contribute to their development.

**Psychological Factors in Dissociative Disorders** As in Dallae's case, the sudden onset of dissociation in dissociative amnesia and fugue usually can be traced to a specific traumatic experience. Thus, there is little controversy about this etiological link. Much more dispute surrounds the purported association between trauma and DID.

Many case studies suggest that multiple personalities develop in response to trauma, particularly the trauma of child abuse. In fact, some researchers have compiled large numbers of case studies from surveys of practitioners. As Table 7–5 indicates, a history of childhood sexual abuse was noted in 79 percent of 236 cases of DID, according to the results of one survey. Physical abuse was reported in 75 percent of the same cases. Other surveys of clinicians have reported similar results (Gleaves, 1996; Kluft, 1987; Putnam, Curoff, et al., 1986; see Table 7–5), as did a recent study of 21 patients (Scroppo et al., 1998). When interpreting these findings, however, you should note that studies of the long-term consequences of child physical or sexual abuse have found little evidence of dissociation or, indeed, of other consistent forms of psychopathology (Emery & Laumann-Billings, 1998; Rind et al., 1998).

Further, you should be aware that such case studies are based on patients' memories and clinicians' evaluations. They are not objective assessments of the past. Researchers have many concerns about the validity of such *retrospective reports*—evaluations of the past from the vantage point of the present (see Research Methods on p. 263). Memories may be selectively recalled, may be distorted, or may even be created to conform with subsequent experiences. An adequate test of the hypothesized relation between child abuse and dissociative disorders requires *prospective longitudinal research* (see Research Methods in Chapter 8) following trauma victims from childhood into adult life and objective assessments of dissociation throughout development.

Assuming for the moment that the relation is real, how might child abuse lead to the development of multiple personalities? Many young children have an active fantasy life with imaginary friends and dolls or action figures. One theory suggests that the abuse overwhelms children's usual intrapsychic defences, and dissociation is used as a more dramatic alternative. According to this perspective, over time, abused children increasingly use dissociation as a means of coping with distress. If the memory of the abuse is not resolved or if the abuse is repeated, the recurrent use of dissociation can lead to the development of full, alternative personalities during adolescence (Kluft, 1987). In the words of one theorist, "MPD [DID] is a little girl imagining that the abuse is happening to someone else" (Ross, 1997, p. 59).

A related model involves the concept of **state-dependent learning**, a process documented in laboratory research wherein learning that takes place in one state of affect or consciousness is best recalled in the same state of affect or consciousness (Bower, 1990). For example, when you are sad rather than happy, you more easily remember what happened when you were sad in the past. By extension, experiences that occur during a dissociated state may be most easily recalled within the same state of consciousness. It has been hypothesized that through the repeated experience of trauma, dissociation, and state-dependent learning, more complete and autonomous memories develop—ultimately leading to independent personalities (Braun, 1989).

Other speculation has focused on hypnosis as both a cause of, and a treatment for, dissociative disorders. Janet and Freud both were impressed by the similarity in the dissociation experienced during hypnotic states and in hysteria, and one theorist has suggested that multiple personality disorder is caused by self-hypnosis (Bliss, 1986). However, the limited value of hypnosis in treating dissociative disorders raises questions about its etiological or therapeutic significance (Casey, 2001).

**Biological Factors in Dissociative Disorders** Very little evidence and not much more speculation has been offered about the role of biological factors in the etiology of dissociative disorders. One theorist has suggested a developmental disturbance in the orbital-frontal cortex, but this possibility has not been systemically investigated (Forrest, 2001). A preliminary twin study found no genetic contribution to dissociative symptoms, and suggested instead that the shared family environment was an important contributing cause (Waller & Ross, 1997). Another twin study, conducted in collaboration between researchers from McGill University and the University of British Columbia, found that genetic factors played a substantial role, accounting for approximately 50 percent of the variance in dissociative symptoms (Jang et al., 1998). Further research is needed to clarify the role of genes in dissociative disorders.

Still, it is known that dissociative states or permanent dissociation can result from biological causes. Examples include the dramatic personality changes that sometimes accompany substance use or abuse (see Chapter 11) and the amnesia that is found in various cognitive disorders associated with aging (see Chapter 14). In DSM-IV-TR, a diagnosis of dissociative disorders is explicitly excluded if the dissociation occurs in conjunction with substance abuse or organic pathology. However, evidence that biological factors can produce dissociative symptoms is a reason to continue to search for biological contributions to dissociative disorders.

**Social Factors in Dissociative Disorders** A sociological view offers a very different perspective on the etiology of dissociative disorders. At least one theorist has suggested that dissociative disorders are produced by **iatrogenesis**, the manufacture of the dissociative disorders by their treatment. Harold Merskey at the University of Western Ontario suggests that clinicians might be helping to manufacture that which they are seeking, by using the power of suggestion. Merskey (1992) reviewed classic case histories of dissociative identity disorder and concluded that many "cases" were created by the expectations of therapists. Merskey does not doubt the pain experienced by the patients in these cases. He argues, however, that the patients developed multiple personalities in response to leading questions asked by their therapists, not as a result of their own defence mechanisms. Like Spanos (1994), Merskey asserts that DID is little more than a social role. A twist on this reasoning is that perhaps highly hypnotizable people are convinced that they have a dissociative disorder because of their susceptibility to suggestion (Kihlstrom, Glisky, & Angiulo, 1994).

We believe that iatrogensis is a likely explanation for many of the virtual epidemic of DID cases diagnosed in Canada and the United States in recent years. However, evidence that DID can be diagnosed in the general population in Turkey (Akyuz et al., 1999), where there is no public awareness of the disorder, leads us to conclude that DID can develop, albeit rarely, apart from iatrogenesis.

**TABLE 7–5 Correlates of Dissociative Identity Disorder in Two Surveys of Clinicians**

| Item | Ross[1] N = 236 | Putnam[2] N = 100 |
|---|---|---|
| Average age | 30.8 | 35.8 |
| Percentage of females | 87.7% | 92.0% |
| Average years of treatment before diagnosis | 6.7 | 6.8 |
| Average number of personalities | 15.7 | 13.3 |
| Opposite-sex personality present | 62.6% | 53.0% |
| Amnesia between personalities | 94.9% | 98.0% |
| Past suicide attempt | 72.0% | 71.0% |
| History of child physical abuse | 74.9% | 75.0% |
| History of child sexual abuse | 79.2% | 83.9% |

[1]Based on data from C.A. Ross, G.R. Norton, and K. Wozney, 1989, Multiple personality disorder: An analysis of 236 cases. *Canadian Journal of Psychiatry, 34*, 413–418.

[2]Based on data from F.W. Putnam et al., 1986, The clinical phenomenology of multiple personality disorder: Review of 100 recent cases. *Journal of Clinical Psychiatry, 47*, 285–293.

### Treatment of Dissociative Disorders

Dating from the time of Janet and Freud, perhaps the central aspect of the treatment of dissociative disorders has been uncovering and recounting past traumatic events. It is presumed that if the trauma can be expressed and accepted, then the need for dissociation will disappear (Horevitz & Loewenstein, 1994). Many clinicians use hypnosis to help patients explore and relive traumatic events. The painful experience is assumed to be more easily recalled while the patient is under hypnosis. These recollections, in turn, are thought to facilitate the integration of the trauma into conscious experience. Unfortunately, no research is available either on *abreaction*, the emotional reliving of a past traumatic experience, or on hypnosis as a treatment for dissociative disorders (Horevitz & Loewenstein, 1994). In fact, many skeptics are concerned that hypnosis can exacerbate or even create dissociative symptoms—or false memories of past abuse.

The goal of treatment for DID is not to have one personality triumph over the others. Rather, the objective is to reintegrate the different personalities into a whole, and some evidence indicates a better clinical outcome when integration is achieved (Coons & Bowman, 2001; Ellason & Ross, 1997). Integration is not unlike the far less difficult task faced by all of us as we struggle to reconcile the different life roles we play into a coherent sense of self. Dallae, for example, needed to incorporate her parents' expectations for her career success with her own, independent desires, abilities, and acculturation experiences.

Antianxiety, antidepressant, and antipsychotic medications may be used to treat dissociative disorders. The objective in prescribing these medications is to reduce distress, not to cure the disorder. The ultimate goal of reintegrating the dissociated states, memories, or personalities is considered to be more of a psychological than a pharmaceutical task (Horevitz & Loewenstein, 1994).

At this time, no systematic research has been conducted on the effectiveness of any treatment for dissociative disorders, let alone on the comparison of alternative treatments (Maldonado et al., 2001). Advances in therapy await a more accurate description of the disorders and, more generally, a better understanding of the split between conscious and unconscious mental processes. In the meantime, treatments championed for dissociative disorders—and the accuracy of the diagnosis itself—should be viewed with a healthy dose of skepticism.

## Somatoform Disorders

In addition to dissociative disorders, hysteria included what we now know as **somatoform disorders**—problems characterized by unusual physical symptoms that occur in the absence of a known physical illness. There is no demonstrable physical cause for the symptoms of somatoform disorders. They are somatic (physical) in form only—thus their name.[1] We consider somatoform disorders in this chapter together with dissociative disorders, because of their historical connection and because somatoform disorders involve a degree of dissociation. In some cases of somatoform disorder, the dissociation is relatively minor; in other cases, it is dramatic.

### Typical Symptoms and Associated Features of Somatoform Disorders

All somatoform disorders involve complaints about physical symptoms. In contrast to psychosomatic disorders (see Chapter 8), the symptoms of somatoform disorders cannot be explained by an underlying organic impairment. There is nothing physically wrong with the patient. The symptoms are not feigned, however, as the physical problem is very real in the mind, though not the body, of the person with a somatoform disorder.

The physical symptoms can take a number of different forms. In some dramatic cases, the symptom involves substantial impairment of a somatic system, particularly a sensory or muscular system. The patient will be unable to see, for example, or will report a paralysis in one arm. In other types of somatoform disorder, patients experience multiple physical symptoms rather than a single, substantial impairment. In these cases, patients usually have numerous, constantly evolving complaints

[1]The absence of demonstrable physical impairment in somatoform disorders distinguishes them from *psychosomatic illnesses*, stress-related physical disorders that do involve real, organic pathology (Chapter 8). In everyday language, we sometimes say, "His problems are psychosomatic" to indicate that an illness is "all in his head." However, it is somatoform disorders, not psychosomatic disorders, that are purely psychological problems.

about such problems as chronic pain, upset stomach, and dizziness. Finally, some types of somatoform disorder are defined by a preoccupation with a particular part of the body or with fears about a particular illness. The patient may constantly worry that he or she has contracted some deadly disease, for example, and the anxiety persists despite negative medical tests and clear reassurance by a physician.

**Unnecessary Medical Treatment** People with somatoform disorders typically do not bring their problems to the attention of a mental health professional. Instead, they repeatedly consult their physicians about their "physical" problems (Taylor & Asmundson, 2004). This often leads to unnecessary medical treatment. In one epidemiological survey, patients with *somatization disorder* (a type of somatoform disorder) had seen a health care provider more than six times during the previous six months. In addition, 25 percent of people diagnosed with somatization disorder had been hospitalized in the past year, compared with 12 percent of the general population (Swartz et al., 1987). People with body dysmorphic disorder also receive excessive medical care. Three-quarters of patients with the disorder seek medical treatment, primarily dermatologic or surgical, but the medical procedures produce little benefit (Phillips et al., 2001).

Patients with somatoform disorders often complain about realistic physical symptoms that are difficult to evaluate objectively. Thus physicians frequently do not recognize the psychological nature of the patients' problems, and they sometimes perform unnecessary medical procedures. For example, patients with somatoform disorders have surgery twice as often as people in the general population (Zoccolillo & Cloninger, 1986). In fact, some common surgical procedures are performed with startling frequency on patients with somatoform disorders. One research group concluded that, after discounting cancer surgeries, 27 percent of women undergoing a hysterectomy suffered from somatization disorder (Martin, Roberts, & Clayton, 1980).

Such data are distressing not only because of the risk to the patient but also because of the costs of unnecessary medical treatment. Estimates indicate that anywhere from 20 to 84 percent of patients who consult physicians do so for problems for which no organic cause can be found (Swartz et al., 1987). Such visits may account for as much as half of all ambulatory healthcare costs (Kellner, 1985). A variety of emotional problems can motivate people to consult their physicians, including the experience of trauma (Green et al., 1997), but much excessive healthcare utilization is specific to somatoform disorders. For example, patients with somatization disorder are three times more likely to consult physicians than are depressed patients (Morrison & Herbstein, 1988; Zoccolillo & Cloninger, 1986). In fact, healthcare expenditures for patients with somatization disorder are nine times the average annual per capita cost of medical treatment (Smith, Monson, & Ray, 1986).

## Classification of Somatoform Disorders

DSM-IV-TR lists five major subcategories of somatoform disorders: (1) conversion disorder, (2) somatization disorder, (3) hypochondriasis, (4) pain disorder, and (5) body dysmorphic disorder.

**Conversion Disorder** In many respects, the classic type of somatoform disorder is **conversion disorder**. The symptoms of conversion disorder often mimic those found in neurological diseases, and they can be dramatic. "Hysterical" blindness or "hysterical" paralysis are examples of conversion symptoms. Although conversion disorders often resemble neurological impairments, they sometimes can be distinguished from these disorders because they make no anatomic sense. The patient may complain about anesthesia (or pain) in a way that does not correspond with the innervation of the body. In some facial anesthesias, for example, numbness ends at the middle of the face; but the nerves involved in sensation do not divide the face into equal halves (see Figure 7–4).

The term *conversion disorder* accurately conveys the central assumption of the diagnosis—the idea that psychological conflicts are converted into physical symptoms. Conversion disorders were the problems that particularly captivated the attention of Charcot, Freud, and Janet and that led them to develop theories about dissociation and unconscious mental processes.

**The Anatomy of Conversion Disorders**

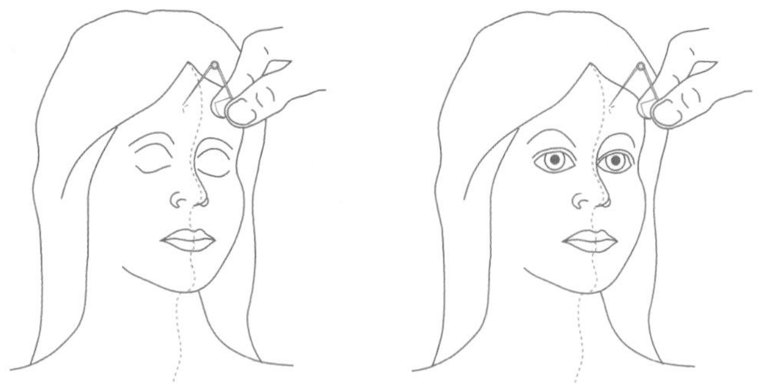

**FIGURE 7–4: Conversion disorder symptoms may make no anatomical sense. As illustrated in this figure, pain insensitivity may be limited to one side of the face, but the nerves involved in pain sensation do not divide the face neatly in half. This symptom thus makes no anatomical sense, suggesting the numbness has a psychogenic origin.**

*Source:* Adapted from D.M. Kaufman, 1985, *Clinical Neurology for Psychiatrists,* 2nd ed., p. 28. Orlando, FL: Grune & Stratton.

**Somatization Disorder** Today, a more common somatoform disorder is **somatization disorder**, characterized by a history of multiple, somatic complaints in the absence of organic impairments. The extent of the health concerns in somatization disorder is apparent from a cursory examination of the DSM-IV-TR diagnostic criteria. In order to be diagnosed with somatization disorder, the patient must complain of at least eight physical symptoms, as listed in Table 7–6. The complaints must involve multiple somatic systems, moreover including symptoms of pain, gastrointestinal symptoms (for example, nausea and diarrhea), sexual symptoms (sexual dysfunction, menstrual difficulties), and pseudoneurologic symptoms. Pseudoneurologic symptoms are complaints that mimic neurological diseases—for example, double vision, numbness, seizures, and amnesia.

Patients with somatization disorders sometimes present their symptoms in a *histrionic* manner—a vague but dramatic, self-centered, and seductive style (see Chapter 9). Patients also may exhibit *la belle indifference* ("beautiful indifference"), a flippant lack of concern about the physical symptoms. For example, a patient may list a long series of somatic complaints in an offhanded and cheerful manner. Although some experts view a histrionic style and la belle indifference as defining characteristics of somatization disorders, research indicates that they are found in only a minority of cases (Lipowski, 1988).

In contrast to some stereotypes, somatization disorder is *not* more common among the aged, who consult health care professionals frequently because of chronic and real physical illnesses (National Institute of Mental Health, 1990). In fact, somatization disorder often begins in adolescence, and according to DSM-IV-TR criteria, it must have an onset prior to the age of 30. The problem is sometimes referred to as *Briquet's syndrome*, in recognition of the French physician Pierre Briquet, who was among the first to call attention to the multiple somatic complaints found in some "hysterias" (National Institute of Mental Health, 1990).

**Hypochondriasis** **Hypochondriasis** is a problem characterized by a fear or belief that

**TABLE 7–6 DSM-IV-TR Diagnostic Criteria for Somatization Disorder**

**A. A history of many physical complaints beginning before age 30 that occur over a period of several years and result in treatment being sought or significant impairment in social, occupational, or other important areas of functioning.**

**B. Each of the following criteria must have been met, with individual symptoms occurring at any time during the course of the disturbance.**

1. Four pain symptoms: A history of pain related to at least four different sites or functions (for example, head, abdomen, back, joints, extremities, chest, rectum, during menstruation, or sexual intercourse, or during urination)
2. Two gastrointestinal symptoms: A history of at least two gastrointestinal symptoms other than pain (for example, nausea, diarrhea, bloating, vomiting other than during pregnancy, or intolerance of several different foods)
3. One sexual symptom: A history of at least one sexual or reproductive symptom other than pain (for example, sexual indifference, erectile or ejaculatory dysfunction, irregular menses, excessive menstrual bleeding, vomiting throughout pregnancy)
4. One pseudoneurologic symptom: A history of at least one symptom or deficit suggesting a neurological disorder not limited to pain (conversion symptoms such as impaired coordination or balance, paralysis or localized weakness, difficulty swallowing or lump in throat, aphonia, urinary retention, hallucinations, loss of touch or pain sensation, double vision, blindness, deafness, seizures; dissociative symptoms such as amnesia; or loss of consciousness other than fainting)

one is suffering from a physical illness. Aspects of this mental disorder surely are familiar to you. The pejorative term *hypochondriac* is a part of everyday language. We all worry about our health, and even unrealistic worries sometimes are normal. Medical students often fear that they have contracted each new disease they encounter in their studies. Many students in abnormal psychology worry that each problem they read about is a perfect description of themselves.

Hypochondriasis is much more serious than these normal and fleeting worries. The preoccupation with fears of disease extends over long periods of time. The worries must last for at least six months according to DSM-IV-TR criteria. In addition, in hypochondriasis, a thorough medical evaluation or examination does not alleviate the fear of the disease. The person still worries that the illness may be emerging or that a test was overlooked. Still, the person with hypochondriasis is not delusional. For example, someone may worry excessively about contracting AIDS and therefore repeatedly go for blood tests. When faced with negative results, however, the person does not delusionally believe that he or she actually has contracted the illness. Nevertheless, the persistent worries that characterize hypochondriasis are severe and preoccupying, and they often lead to substantial impairment in life functioning.

**Pain Disorder** As its name implies, **pain disorder** is characterized by preoccupation with pain. Although there is no objective way to evaluate pain, psychological factors are judged to be significant in creating or intensifying the chronic pain in pain disorder. Complaints seem excessive and apparently are motivated at least in part by psychological factors. For example, some pain disorder patients may seem to relish the attention their illness brings to them. DSM-IV-TR distinguishes between pain disorder that occurs with associated problems in general medical conditions and pain disorder that appears in the absence of such problems. For example, low back pain that begins after a physical injury would be differentiated from back pain that cannot be traced to any physical cause.

As with hypochondriasis and somatization disorder, pain disorder can lead to the repeated, unnecessary use of medical treatments. People who experience chronic pain are at a particular risk for developing a dependence on minor tranquilizers or painkillers. The disorder also frequently disrupts social and occupational functioning.

**Body Dysmorphic Disorder** **Body dysmorphic disorder** is a very different type of somatoform disorder in which the patient is preoccupied with some imagined defect in appearance. The preoccupation typically focuses on some facial feature, such as the nose or mouth, and in some cases may lead to repeated visits to a plastic surgeon. Preoccupation with the body part far exceeds normal worries about physical imperfections. The endless worry causes significant distress, and in extreme cases, it may interfere with work or social relationships.

One controversy is whether the body dysmorphic disorder should be grouped with other somatoform disorders. In Japan and Korea, body dysmorphic disorder is classified as a type of social phobia (Phillips, 1991). The following brief case history illustrates this unusual type of somatoform disorder.

## BRIEF CASE STUDY

### Body Dysmorphic Disorder

A 28-year-old single man became preoccupied at the age of 18 with his minimally thinning hair. Despite reassurance from others that his hair loss was not noticeable, he worried about it for hours a day, becoming "deeply depressed," socially withdrawn, and unable to attend classes or do his schoolwork. Although he could acknowledge the excessiveness of his preoccupation, he was unable to stop it. He saw four dermatologists but was not comforted by their reassurances that his hair loss was minor and that treatment was unnecessary. The patient's preoccupation and subsequent depression have persisted for 10 years and have continued to interfere with his social life and work, to the extent that he avoids most social events and has been able to work only part time as a baker. He only recently sought psychiatric referral, at the insistence of his girlfriend, who said his symptoms were ruining their relationship (Phillips, 1991, pp. 1138–1139). ◆

*Body dysmorphic disorder is characterized by a preoccupation with some imagined defect in appearance.*

**Malingering and Factitious Disorder** Somatoform disorders represent real *psychological* problems, even if the physical symptoms are not real. As such, somatoform disorders must be distinguished from **malingering**, pretending to have a somatoform disorder in order to achieve some external gain, such as a disability payment. Because there is no objective way to test for somatoform disorders, detecting malingering is extremely difficult in the individual case. Besides searching for an obvious reason for feigning an illness, one clue to malingering can be when a patient presents symptoms that are more, not less, dramatic.

A related diagnostic concern is **factitious disorder**, a feigned condition that, unlike malingering, is motivated primarily by a desire to assume the sick role rather than by a desire for external gain. People with factitious disorder pretend to be ill or make themselves appear to be ill, for example, by taking drugs to produce a rapid heart rate. They will undergo extensive and often painful medical procedures in order to garner attention from healthcare professionals. A rare, repetitive pattern of factitious disorder is sometimes calles *Munchausen syndrome*, named after Baron Karl Friedrich Hieronymus von Munchausen, who was renowned for his passion for telling colourful tales.

## Epidemiology of Somatoform Disorders

No one knows how prevalent conversion disorders were during the time of Charcot, Janet, and Freud, but the literature of the period suggests that they were common (Shorter, 1992). Today, conversion disorders are rare, perhaps as infrequent as 50 cases per 100 000 population (Akagi & House, 2001). Ironically, the unusual disorders treated by Freud and Janet appear to have been less enduring than the theories developed to explain them! The decreased prevalence may be a result of improved diagnostic practices, as we suggested in commenting on Janet's case, or, as others have argued, it may reflect Western society's greater acceptance of the expression of inner feelings (Shorter, 1992). A very different—and very controversial—viewpoint is that conversion disorders *are* prevalent today but they take the form of conditions like chronic fatigue syndrome, Gulf War syndrome, and similar puzzling maladies (Showalter, 1997).

Most other somatoform disorders also appear to be relatively rare (APA, 2000). Hypochondriasis also is quite rare, although research from McGill University shows that less severe worrying about physical illness is quite common (Looper & Kirmayer, 2001). Somatization disorder also is rare. According to one North American survey, the lifetime prevalence of somatization disorder is only 0.13 percent (Swartz et al., 1990). However, like hypochondriacal worrying, physical complaints that do not meet all of the diagnostic criteria for somatization disorder are very common (Ladwig et al., 2001). Nearly 12 percent of people suffered from four to six physical symptoms with no identifiable organic cause (fewer than the eight required for the diagnosis of somatization disorder; see Table 7–6) (Swartz et al., 1987). Indeed, a new diagnostic category, *multisomaform disorder*, which requires only three physical symptoms—but chronic ones—has been proposed (Kroenke et al., 1997).

**Gender, SES, and Culture** With the exception of hypochondriasis, all other forms of somatoform disorder are more common among women. This is particularly true of somatization disorder, which may be as much as 10 times more common among women than men (Swartz et al., 1990). Why women? Feminist writers have attributed the dramatically increased risk for hysteria among women living during the time of Freud and Janet to the sexual repression of the Victorian era. In turn, the disproportionate prevalence of somatoform disorders among women in the second half of the twentieth century has been attributed to widespread sexual abuse. Although they are superficially appealing, feminist Elaine Showalter (1977) criticizes both of these views on empirical and feminist grounds. Instead, she argues, "Women still suffer from hysterical symptoms not because we are essentially irrational or because we're all victims of abuse but because, like men, we are human beings who will convert feelings into symptoms when we are unable to speak" (p. 207).

In addition to gender, socioeconomic status, subculture, and culture have long been thought to be related to somatization disorder. However, expected differences between industrialized and nonindustrialized countries were not found in a recent study sponsored by the World Health Organization (see Figure 7–5). McGill University researchers Kirmayer and Young (1998) reported that although somatization is often thought to be a characteristic of specific ethnocultural groups, recent evidence shows that somatization is common in all cultural groups and societies that have been studied. Differences among groups may reflect cultural styles of expressing distress, which are influenced not only by cultural beliefs and practices, but also by familiarity with healthcare systems and pathways to care. For example, the availability of psychiatric services only for the most severely ill—except in a few developed countries—makes people emphasize somatic symptoms in coming to the doctor to ensure that they get appropriate attention (Kirmayer & Young, 1998).

**Somatization across Cultures**

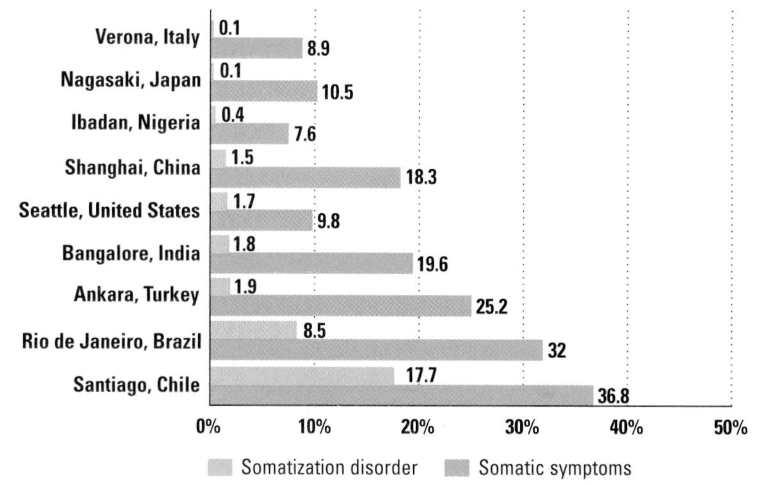


**FIGURE 7–5: Prevalence of somatization disorder and somatic symptoms in different countries. Somatization is not more common in nonindustrialized countries, contrary to common assumptions.**

*Note:* Somatization disorder was based on ICD-10 diagnosis; somatic symptoms included a minimum for four for men and six for women.

*Source:* O. Gureje, G.E. Simon, T.B. Ustun, and D.P. Goldberg, 1997, Somatization in cross-cultural perspective: A World Health Organization study in primary care. *American Journal of Psychiatry, 154,* 989–995.

**Comorbidity** Somatoform disorders typically occur with other psychological problems, particularly depression and anxiety (Guerje et al., 1997; Rogers et al., 1996). The link between depression and somatoform disorders has several possible explanations. Either condition may cause the other, or both could be caused by a third variable, such as life stress. One possibility that primary care physicians must consider carefully is that some patients may express depression indirectly through their somatic complaints (Lipowski, 1988).

As with depression, there are several possible explanations for the comorbidity between somatoform disorders and anxiety, including similarities in the defining symptoms. A particular concern is the accurate, differential diagnosis of panic disorder (see Chapter 6). Some symptoms of panic, such as dizziness, numbness, and fears about dying, may be dismissed by physicians, or they may be misdiagnosed as either hypochondriasis or somatization disorder (Lipowski, 1988).

Finally, somatization disorder has frequently been linked with antisocial personality disorder, a lifelong pattern of irresponsible behaviour that involves habitual violations of social rules (see Chapter 9). The two disorders do not typically co-occur in the same individual, but they often are found in different members of the same family (Lilienfeld, 1992). Because antisocial personality disorder is far more common among men, while somatoform disorders have the opposite pattern, some have speculated that the two problems are flip sides of the same coin. Antisocial personality disorder may be the male expression of high negative emotion and the absence of inhibition, whereas somatization disorder is the female expression of the same characteristics (Lilienfeld, 1992).

## Etiological Considerations and Research on Somatoform Disorders

Despite their historical significance, until very recently little systematic research has been conducted on somatoform disorders. Some sound scientific evidence is finally being gathered, and we can integrate emerging findings with some theoretical considerations within the context of the biopsychosocial model.

**Biological Factors—The Perils of Diagnosis by Exclusion** An obvious—and potentially critical—biological consideration in somatoform disorders is the possibility of misdiagnosis. A patient may be incorrectly diagnosed as suffering from a somatoform disorder when, in fact, he or she actually has a real physical illness that is undetected or is perhaps unknown. The diagnosis of a somatoform disorder requires that *no* organic cause of the symptom can be identified. This is very different from the positive identification of a psychological cause of the symptom.

Because mental health professionals cannot demonstrate psychological causes of physical symptoms objectively and unequivocally, the identification of somatoform disorders involves a process called *diagnosis by exclusion*. The physical complaint is assumed to be a part of a somatoform disorder only when various known physical causes are excluded or ruled out. The possibility always remains, however, that an incipient somatic disease has been overlooked. Some of the problems with diagnosis by exclusion can be appreciated by way of analogy. Consider the difference in certainty between two police lineups, one in which a victim positively identifies a criminal—"That's him!"—versus a second in which an identification is made by ruling out alternatives—"It isn't him or him or him, so it must be that one."

Historically at least, the possibility of misdiagnosis is more than a theoretical concern. Follow-up studies of patients diagnosed as suffering from conversion disorders indicate that somatic illnesses are later detected in some cases (Shalev & Munitz, 1986). Typically, a neurological disease such as epilepsy or multiple sclerosis is the eventual diagnosis. In one classic study, fully a quarter of patients diagnosed as having a conversion symptom later were found to develop a neurological disease (Slater, 1965). Fortunately, recent research has found a much smaller percentage (5 percent or less) of undetected physical illnesses when following up cases of somatoform disorder several years later (Crimlisk et al., 1998; Schuepbach et al., 2002). We attribute the new findings to the improved detection of real physical illnesses, and again wonder how many of the hysteria cases treated by Charcot, Freud, and Janet would be positively diagnosed as physical conditions today.

Although the detection of physical illnesses continues to improve, the problem of diagnosis by exclusion still poses a dilemma. Diagnosticians must weigh the consequences of an incorrect diagnosis of somatoform disorder against the consequences of incorrectly diagnosing a psychological problem as a physical illness.

**Psychological Factors—Imagined or Real Trauma** Both Janet and Freud developed their theories in an attempt to explain the dissociation between emotional conflicts and physical symptoms in somatoform disorders. Initially, both theorists assumed that conversion disorders were caused by a traumatic experience. According to their reasoning, trauma overwhelmed normal coping efforts, and unconscious coping processes were called into action as a result. However, Freud later questioned the accuracy of his patients' *retrospective reports* of traumatic sexual abuse (see Research Methods), and instead he decided that their memories of trauma were fantasized, not real. This conclusion led him to develop his theory of childhood sexuality (Freud, 1924/1962).

Thus, Freud came to believe that dissociation and other intrapsychic defences protected individuals from their unacceptable sexual impulses, not from their intolerable memories (Freud, 1924/1962). In his view, conversion symptoms were expressions of intolerable unconscious psychological conflicts. In Freudian terminology, this is the *primary gain* of the symptom. Ironically, some contemporary theorists have noted that, unfortunately, childhood sexual abuse is all too common, and they have suggested that Freud's initial position may have been the accurate one.

Some contemporary concerns about the nature and prevalence of child sexual abuse may be exaggerated, as we noted earlier in this chapter. Nevertheless, recent evidence *does* suggest that the onset of somatization is triggered by traumatic stress. Increased somatoform pain

## RESEARCH METHODS

### Retrospective Reports

Scientists have long been skeptical about the accuracy of people's reports about the past. In terms of research methods, the concern is the reliability and validity of **retrospective reports**—current recollections of past experiences. When trying to demonstrate a relationship between current problems and childhood experiences, for example, researchers question the accuracy of the patient's reports of past difficulties. Concerns about retrospective reports are one of several reasons why investigators prefer prospective, longitudinal studies over retrospective research designs.

Concerns about retrospective reports focus on three particular issues in abnormal psychology (Brewin, Andrews, & Gotlib, 1993). First, normal memory often is inaccurate, particularly memory for events that occurred long ago and early in life. Second, it is possible that the memories of people with emotional problems are particularly unreliable. Third, abnormal behaviour may systematically bias memory—for example, memory processes may be "mood congruent." Depressed people may tend to remember sad experiences, anxious people may better recall fearful events, and so on.

Brewin et al. (1993) revisited many of these concerns, but they concluded that retrospective memories may be less flawed than some have suggested. A similar conclusion was drawn by University of Windsor psychologist Sandra Paivio (2001). Brewin et al. conceded that retrospective reports are often inaccurate. For example, only moderate correlations are found between children's and parents' reports about their past relationships, and, on average, children report more negative memories about the past. This raises the issue of who is more accurate, but it clearly indicates that either children or parents (or both) are inaccurate. At the same time, the reliability between parents and children increases to an acceptable level for reports of specific, factual aspects of the past. Thus memory for specific, important events in the family may be fairly reliable and valid, but people may "rewrite" their histories with regard to more global and subjective experiences.

Brewin et al. (1993) also questioned the blanket assumption that psychopathology impairs memory. They found many flaws in research that supposedly demonstrated memory impairments for various psychological problems, and concluded that, except for serious mental illness, there is no evidence for memory impairments associated with anxiety or depression. In particular, depressed people do not erroneously recall more than their share of negative events about the past.

For current research methods, Brewin et al. (1993) urge that retrospective reports should not be dismissed out of hand. There are many reasons to prefer prospective, longitudinal research designs over retrospective methods, but longitudinal research is expensive to conduct. Retrospective reports of specific events may be sufficiently reliable and valid to justify using them. Indeed, retrospective research has yielded many important findings in many areas of psychological inquiry. Such studies have paved the way for more intensive, longitudinal designs. For example, retrospective research by Margo Watt and Sherry Stewart (2000) at Dalhousie University has revealed that particular forms of childhood learning experiences may contribute to hypochondriasis (e.g., observing one's parents becoming alarmed about becoming ill). These results are consistent with findings obtained from other research methods (Taylor & Asmundson, 2004). ◆

disorder was found among 418 tortured Bhutanese refugees living in camps in Nepal in comparison to 392 refugees in the same camps who were not tortured (Van Ommeren et al., 2001). Exposure to dead bodies, another gruesome experience, also has been tied to increased somatic symptoms. A study of 358 people who worked in the mortuary during the Gulf War found an increase in somatization from before to after the experience. Somatic symptoms included faintness, pains in the chest, nausea, trouble breathing, hot or cold spells, numbness, and feeling weak. Importantly, somatization increased more among workers with greater exposure to death (McCarroll et al., 2002). Although it is not clear why trauma leads to increased somatization, likely contributors include an increased awareness of one's own body, the somatic consequences of stress, and the expression of psychological distress through complaints about somatic symptoms.

Freud's idea about the primary gain of conversion symptoms is dubious, but he also suggested that hysterical symptoms could produce **secondary gain**, for example, avoiding work or responsibility or to gain attention and sympathy. This view has more support, although cognitive behaviour therapists call this process *reinforcement*, not secondary gain. In addition to positive reinforcement (extra attention) or negative reinforcement (avoidance of work), *learning the sick role* through modelling may be a part of the etiology of somatoform disorders (Lipowski, 1988). Cognitive tendencies also may contribute, especially (1) a tendency to amplify somatic symptoms (Kirmayer, Robbins, & Paris, 1994); (2) *alexithymia*—a deficit in one's capacity to recognize and express the emotions signalled by physiological arousal (Bankier et al., 2001); (3) the misattribution of normal somatic symptoms (Rief, Hiller, & Margraf, 1998); and (4) memory biases (Pauli & Alpers, 2002).

### Social Factors in Somatoform Disorders

Social and cultural theorists have offered a straightforward explanation of the physical symptoms of somatization disorder, hypochondriasis, and pain disorder. Patients with these disorders are experiencing some sort of underlying psychological distress. However, they describe their problems as physical symptoms and, to some extent, experience them that way because of limited insight into their emotional distress and/or the lack of social tolerance of psychological complaints.

Presumably, increased psychological sophistication in the West also explains the decrease in somatoform disorders over the course of the last century (Shorter, 1992). Thus sociocultural theorists assume that people with somatoform disorders really are fearful, sad, or uncertain about their life, but they experience, or at least express, these emotional concerns in terms of physical complaints. A simple analogy for this theorizing is a child who complains about an upset stomach, not about fear of failure, before giving a piano recital.

Historical and sociocultural theory of somatoform disorders has been widely embraced. However, the "beautiful" theory may be slayed by an ugly fact. As noted earlier, somatoform disorders apparently are not more prevalent in nonindustrialized than industrialized countries (see Figure 7–5).

## Treatment of Somatoform Disorders

Charcot, Janet, and Freud encouraged their patients to recall and recount psychologically painful events as a way of treating conversion disorders. In the century or more since their techniques were developed, however, no systematic research was conducted on any "insight" therapies for somatoform disorders. In fact, very little research was conducted on any treatment. Fortunately, this is changing and accumulating evidence indicates that cognitive behaviour therapy is effective in reducing physical symptoms in somatization disorder (Kroenke & Swindle, 2000), hypochondriasis (Taylor & Asmundson, 2004), and body dysmorphic disorder (Rosen, Reiter, & Orosan, 1995).

The most extensive studies of cognitive behavioural treatments focus on pain disorders. Operant approaches to chronic pain attempt to alter contingencies that reward "pain behaviour" and the sick role. The goal is to reward successful coping and life adaptation instead (Fordyce, 1976). Cognitive behaviour therapy also uses cognitive restructuring to address the emotional and cognitive components of pain. Research demonstrates the effectiveness of both variations on behaviour therapy in treating chronic lower back pain (Blanchard, 1994).

Recent evidence also indicates that antidepressants may be helpful in treating somatoform disorders—perhaps, in part, because of their high comorbidity with depression and anxiety. Prozac has been shown to produce more improvement in body dysmorphic disorder in comparison to placebo (Phillips et al., 2002). Antidepressants also have demonstrated benefits beyond placebo effects in the treatment of pain disorder (Fishbain et al., 1998).

One reason for the limited research and interest in the psychological treatment of somatoform disorders is that primary care physicians treat most of these patients (Bass et al., 2001). Patients with somatoform disorders typically consult physicians about their ailments, and they often insist that their problems are physical even after extensive testing has failed to turn up evidence of a physical problem. They are likely to refuse a referral to a mental health professional. Thus primary care physicians often must learn how to manage hypochondriasis, somatization disorder, and related problems in the medical setting.

This can be a difficult task. Primary care physicians may become frustrated by their failure to identify a clear physical problem or may be unsympathetic toward "hypochondriacs" when they have so many patients with "real" problems. Not surprisingly, such reactions can weaken the physician–patient relationship, a consequence that can intensify the problem. In fact, the major recommendation for the medical management of patients with somatization disorder is to establish a strong and consistent physician–patient relationship. Physicians are urged to schedule routine appointments with these patients every month or two and to conduct brief medical exams during this time (National Institute of Mental Health, 1990). This approach not only provides consistent emotional support and medical assurance, but it helps to eliminate the iatrogenic effects of the somatization disorder by reducing unnecessary medical procedures. A physician who is familiar with a patient with somatization disorder is more likely to recognize the psychological origin of the physical complaints and is less likely to order unnecessary medical tests or treatment procedures. In fact, at least one study has documented the effectiveness of this management approach (Smith, Monson, & Ray, 1986). For people with hypochondriasis willing to accept a referral to a mental health practitioner, cognitive behaviour therapy can be highly effective, as demonstrated in studies by University of Manitoba psychologists Patricia Furer and John Walker, and in research by other investigators (Furer, Walker, & Freeston, 2001).

Whatever the approach to treatment, it is essential for the physician to convey a sense of concern about patients' complaints. There is a place for reassurance and optimism about the patient's good health, but the evaluation is likely to be rejected unless it is coupled with some expression of concern. Patients who do not receive this empathy are likely to ignore the physician's advice and simply recruit a new, more understanding physician (National Institute of Mental Health, 1990).

Referrals to a mental health professional must be made with care by primary health care providers. Patients may believe that the recommendation belittles their problems and may reject it out of hand. When a referral is made successfully, the mental health professional might need to coordinate treatment with the referring physician and perhaps offer treatment in a medical setting (Bass et al., 2001).

# Summary

To a greater or lesser extent, all the intriguing disorders we consider in this chapter involve **dissociation**, the disruption of the normally integrated mental processes involved in memory or consciousness. Many of the disorders also are known or hypothesized to be reactions to **traumatic stress**, exposure to some event that involves actual or threatened death or serious injury to self or others and creates intense fear, helplessness, or horror. Sources of traumatic stress include rape, combat, experiencing or witnessing violence, and natural or man-made disasters.

**Acute stress disorder (ASD)** is a short-term reaction to trauma that is characterized by symptoms of dissociation, re-experiencing, avoidance, and increased anxiety or arousal. **Posttraumatic stress disorder (PTSD)** is characterized by very similar symptoms—re-experiencing, numbed responsiveness or avoidance, and increased autonomic arousal—but the symptoms either last for longer than one month or have a delayed onset in PTSD. Trauma may be re-experienced as a **flashback**—a dissociative state in which the person relives the trauma in the moment. The diminished responsiveness has been referred to as emotional anesthesia. The increased arousal in ASD or PTSD may include excessive fear, anxiety, or irritability, as well as general psychophysiological arousal.

Evidence demonstrates that traumatic events are distressingly common. Epidemiological studies also call attention to the particularly devastating consequences of violence, especially rape for women and combat exposure for men. More symptoms of ASD predict later PTSD, and the nature and level of exposure to a traumatic event, as well as social support after the occurrence of the trauma, appear to be crucial to facilitating long-term adjustment. By definition, the experience of trauma is the central cause of PTSD, but other factors appear to be important in its etiology. Genetic factors increase the risk both for experiencing trauma and for experiencing PTSD following trauma. Key psychological contributions include **two-factor theory**, a combination of classical and operant conditioning, and **emotional processing**, which involves facing fear, diminishing its intensity, and coming to some new understanding about the trauma and its consequences.

Early intervention with trauma victims holds the hope of easing pain of **critical incident stress** and helping to prevent the development of PTSD, but data are lacking, including on the effectiveness of **critical incident stress debriefing**. On the other hand, promising evidence suggests that treating acute stress disorder may reduce PTSD. Prolonged exposure is perhaps the least obvious but most important strategy for treatment. Still, PTSD has a chronic course in about one-third of cases.

**Dissociative disorders** are characterized by persistent, maladaptive disruptions in the integration of memory, consciousness, or identity. **Somatoform disorders** are identified by unusual physical symptoms that occur in the absence of a known physical illness. Memories become inaccessible in dissociative disorders; psychological distress is converted into physical symptoms in somatoform disorders. Thus these unusual emotional problems involve unconscious processes by definition, and they challenge psychological theorists to explain those psychological events that occur outside of awareness. In fact, both Freud and Janet developed their influential theories about unconscious processes when attempting to explain these disorders.

Dissociative disorders include **dissociative fugue**, characterized by sudden and unexpected travel away from home, an inability to recall the past, and confusion about identity or the assumption of a new identity; **dissociative amnesia**, a sudden inability to recall extensive and important personal information that exceeds normal forgetfulness; **depersonalization disorder**, a less dramatic problem characterized by severe and persistent feelings of being detached from oneself; and **dissociative identity disorder (DID)**, also known as **multiple personality disorder**, characterized by the existence of two or more distinct personalities in a single individual.

Although some suggest that the conditions are pervasive, dissociative disorders appear to be rare. Some evidence links the conditions with traumatic experiences, particularly with child abuse, but we must be especially cautious in drawing inferences about purported **recovered memories** of past abuse, the sudden remembering of long forgotten traumatic experiences. Evidence is weak or nonexistent on other factors that may contribute to the development of dissociative disorders. Similarly, there is no systematic research on the treatment of dissociative disorders, although clinical tradition emphasizes reliving trauma as a way of reintegrating experience.

The term **conversion disorder** accurately conveys the central assumption of the diagnosis—the idea that psychological conflicts are converted into physical symptoms. **Somatization disorder** is characterized by a history of multiple, somatic complaints in the absence of organic impairments. **Hypochondriasis** is characterized by a fear or belief that the individual is suffering from a physical illness. **Pain disorder** is characterized by preoccupation with pain. Although there is no objective way to evaluate pain, psychological factors are judged to be significant in creating or exacerbating the chronic pain in pain disorder. In **body dysmorphic disorder** the patient is preoccupied with some imagined defect in appearance—a preoccupation that typically focuses on some facial feature, such as the nose or mouth.

True somatoform disorders are rare, although complaints about somatic symptoms that do not have an organic cause are common and represent a significant proportion of medical care. Until recently, the etiology of somatoform disorders has not been the subject of much research. Etiological concerns include the possible misdiagnosis of incipient neurological diseases as somatoform disorders; the experience of trauma; secondary gain or reinforcement for the sick role; cognitive factors, such as a tendency to amplify somatic symptoms; and alexithymia—a deficit in the individual's capacity to recognize and express the emotions signalled by physiological arousal. Cultural influences on somatoform disorders may be less prominent than previously thought.

Treatment research on somatoform disorders is very new and suggests that cognitive behaviour therapy and antidepressant medications are emerging as useful treatments. Investigators also are beginning to identify aspects of effective medical management of somatoform disorders.

# Critical Thinking

1. Do you think that traumatic stress disorders are more similar to anxiety disorders or to dissociative disorders, or do you see ASD and PTSD as being separate from these two diagnostic categories?

2. ASD and PTSD would seem to be purely "psychological" problems, but the disorders are best explained by the systems perspective. What biological, psychological, and social risk factors might combine to cause the disorders? What protective factors would you hypothesize to lower the likelihood of ASD or PTSD following exposure to trauma?

3. There is much controversy about several topics in this chapter, including recovered memories, dissociative identity disorder, hypnosis, and conversion reactions. These topics are difficult to evaluate empirically and require a certain amount of "believing" as opposed to "knowing." Do you "believe" in these phenomena? Why or why not? What evidence would change your beliefs?

4. Do you know people who seem to express their psychological concerns through somatic complaints? How do you explain this? Did you express your feelings in this way as a child, or perhaps do you still do this?

# Key Terms

**acute stress disorder (ASD)** 230
**body dysmorphic disorder** 259
**conversion disorder** 257
**critical incident stress (CIS)** 241
**critical incident stress debriefing (CISD)** 242
**depersonalization disorder** 249
**dissociation** 229
**dissociative amnesia** 249
**dissociative disorders** 243
**dissociative fugue** 243
**dissociative identity disorder (DID)** 249
**emotional processing** 239
**factitious disorder** 260
**flashbacks** 232
**hypnosis** 246
**hypochondriasis** 258
**hysteria** 245
**iatrogenesis** 255
**implicit memory** 246
**malingering** 260
**multiple personality disorder** 250
**pain disorder** 259
**posttraumatic stress disorder (PTSD)** 230
**recovered memories** 247
**retrospective reports** 263
**secondary gain** 263
**somatization disorder** 258
**somatoform disorders** 256
**state-dependent learning** 254
**traumatic stress** 230
**two-factor theory** 239

# 8 Stress and Physical Health


Overview
Defining Stress
Typical Symptoms: Responding to Stress
Classification of Stress and Physical Illness
The Role of Psychological Factors in Some Familiar Illnesses
Cardiovascular Disease

**What exactly is stress?**

**How does stress affect us physically?**

**What is the role of stress in diseases like AIDS, cancer, and heart attacks?**

**Can we prevent disease by coping better with stress?**

How do you feel when you say that you are "stressed out"? You may feel a lot of different feelings—jittery, tired, down, preoccupied, vigilant, defeated, sick, just plain lousy. How do you cope? Do you work hard to solve the problem causing stress? Do you try to calm yourself with meditation or exercise? Distract yourself with parties, alcohol, or drugs? Eat, drink, smoke, take stimulants, sleep little, skip your workouts, do whatever it takes to get through the stress? And what are the consequences of stress and different ways of coping? Can stress *really* make you sick? How?

## Overview

Stress is an unavoidable fact of life, and in this chapter we focus on how adaptive and maladaptive responses to stress are critical to our physical health. Scientists define **stress** as a challenging event that requires physiological, cognitive, or behavioural adaptation. Stress may be produced by minor, daily hassles, like taking an exam, as well as by major events, such as going through a divorce or being caught in a natural disaster such as an icestorm. Research by Anita DeLongis (currently at the University of British Columbia) and colleagues has shown that daily hassles can have a greater impact of psychological distress than the more infrequent, but more severe, major life events (DeLongis et al., 1982). Accordingly, the effects of minor stressors (hassles) are important to consider. As we saw in Chapter 7, *traumatic stress* is caused by exposure to an event that involves actual or threatened death or serious injury to oneself or others and creates intense fear, helplessness, or horror. This chapter is about more normal stress, how we cope with it, and how stress relates to physical well being.

Scientists currently view *every* physical illness—from colds to cancer to AIDS—as a product of the interaction between the mind and body. Thus, there is no longer a limited list of "psychosomatic" (psychologically induced) disorders in the DSM-IV-TR or elsewhere. Evidence also indicates that learning more adaptive ways of **coping**, responses aimed at diminishing the burden of stress, can limit the recurrence or improve the course of many physical illnesses (Lazarus, 2000; O'Brien & DeLongis, 1997). In short, scientists now recognize that the distinction between mind and body is a false dualism (see Chapter 2). Theories of the etiology of physical illnesses have adopted, and in many ways have promoted, the systems approach.

This holistic view of health and disease has brought about major changes in medicine. Of particular note is the rapid development of **behavioural medicine**, a multidisciplinary field that includes both medical and mental health professionals who investigate psychological factors in the symptoms, etiology, and treatment of physical illness and chronic disease. Psychologists who specialize in behavioural medicine often are called **health psychologists**.

Experts in behavioural medicine define disease as "dis-ease," indicating that illness is a departure not only from adaptive biological functioning but also from adaptive social and psychological functioning. Health is successful adaptation to the environment, not merely the absence of somatic illness (Weiner & Fawzy,

1989). In order to promote health, behavioural medicine specialists study and encourage such healthy behaviours as stress management, proper diet, regular exercise, and avoidance of tobacco use. In treating diseases, behavioural medicine includes diverse interventions such as educating parents of chronically ill children, teaching patients strategies for coping with chronic pain, and even running support groups for people with terminal cancer.

In this chapter we discuss a number of innovations in behavioural medicine, and we review evidence on the link between stress and a number of physical illnesses. We also include an extended discussion of a leading killer in Canada and other industrialized countries, cardiovascular disease, in order to illustrate the challenges in studying stress and physical illness. We begin our discussion with a case study.

## CASE STUDY **Stress and Bob Carter's Heart Attack**

One Thursday afternoon, Bob Carter, a salesman for a food wholesaler, was completing his regular route, calling on customers. Throughout the morning, he had felt a familiar discomfort in his chest and left arm. As had been happening on occasion for at least a year, that morning he experienced a few fleeting but sharp pains in the centre and left side of his chest. This was followed by a dull ache in his chest and left shoulder and a feeling of congestion in the same areas. Breathing deeply made the pain worse, but Bob could manage it as long as he took shallow breaths. He continued on his route, alternately vowing to soon see a doctor and cursing his aging body.

After grabbing a hamburger and a beer for lunch, Bob called on a customer who was behind in his payments. At first, Bob shared a cigarette with the customer and chatted with him in a friendly way. He was a salesman after all. Soon it was time to pressure him about the bill. As Bob was raising his voice in anger, a crushing pain returned to his chest and radiated down his left arm. This was much worse than anything he had experienced before. The pain was so intense that Bob was unable to continue speaking. He slumped forward against the table, but with his right arm he waved away any attempts to help him. After sitting still for about 10 minutes, Bob was able to drag himself to his car and drive to his home 50 km away. When his wife saw him shuffle into the house looking haggard and in obvious pain, she called for an ambulance. The Carters soon discovered that Bob had suffered a myocardial infarction (a heart attack).

Bob was 49 years old at the time. He was married and the father of three children. His home life was normal and happy, but it also put a lot of pressures on him. His 24-year-old daughter was living at home while her husband was working overseas. The entire family found this living arrangement stressful because the house seemed so crowded, and they also worried about the welfare of the son-in-law. More stress came from Bob's 21-year-old daughter, who had just graduated from university and was getting married in three weeks. Finally, Bob's 19-year-old son was home from his first year of university, full of rebellion and ideas that challenged Bob's authority. There was no shortage of family stress.

Bob also put plenty of stress on himself. A former high school athlete, he had always been competitive and hard-driving. He wanted to be the best at whatever he did, and right now his goal was to be the best salesman in his company. Bob used his charm, humour, and some not-so-gentle pressure to sell his products, and it worked. But once he had become the best salesman in his wholesaling company, Bob wanted to be the best salesman for the producers whose products he sold. No matter what he accomplished, Bob drove himself hard to meet a new goal.

Bob maintained his drive and competitiveness from his youthful days as a star athlete, but he had not maintained his physical condition. The only exercise he got was playing golf, and he usually rode in a cart instead of walking the course. He was at least 15 kg overweight, smoked a pack and a half of cigarettes a day, ate a lot of fatty red meat, and drank heavily. If he had seen a physician earlier, Bob would have been told that he was a good candidate for a heart attack. As it was, he heard this from a cardiologist only after his heart attack.

Bob recuperated quickly in the hospital. He was tired and in considerable pain for a couple of days, but he was telling jokes before the end of a week. His cardiologist explained what had happened to him and gave Bob a stern lecture about how he needed to change his life style. He wanted Bob to quit smoking, lose weight, cut down on his drinking, and gradually work himself back into shape with a careful program of exercise. He urged Bob to slow down at work and told him to quit worrying about his children—they were old enough to take care of themselves.

To underscore these messages, the cardiologist asked a psychologist from the hospital's behavioural medicine unit to consult with Bob. The psychologist reviewed information on coronary risk with Bob and gave him several pamphlets to read on risk factors. The psychologist also explained that the hospital ran several programs that might interest Bob after discharge. These included workshops on stress management, weight reduction groups, and exercise classes. The psychologist asked Bob if he had other concerns that he wanted to discuss, but Bob said there were none. The psychologist suggested that some issues might come

*continued*

*cont.*

up in the future, and Bob should feel free to raise them with the psychologist or with his cardiologist. The psychologist noted that cardiac patients and their families sometimes had trouble adjusting to the illness and the sudden reminder of the patient's mortality. Bob thanked the psychologist for the information but waved off the professional's offer of assistance much as he had waved off help in the middle of his heart attack.

Bob was discharged from the hospital 10 days after being admitted. Against his doctor's advice, he walked his daughter down the aisle at her wedding the following weekend, and he was back to work within a month. At his six-week check-up, Bob admitted to his cardiologist that he was smoking again. His weight was unchanged, and his exercise and drinking were only a "little better." When the cardiologist chastised Bob for not following medical advice, Bob promised to renew his efforts. He belied his assertion of commitment, however, by commenting that giving up these small pleasures might or might not make him live any longer, but life surely would seem longer without any indulgences. Clearly, one heart attack was not going to get Bob Carter to slow down. ◆

The case of Bob Carter strongly suggests that life stress is a risk factor for the onset of coronary heart disease, an implication supported by a large body of research. The case also raises a number of questions about the link between stress and coronary heart disease. What is the physiological mechanism that transforms psychological stress into coronary risk? Is stress the problem, or is the real culprit the unhealthy behaviours that result from stress—smoking, drinking, and overeating? What is the role of personality in stress? Bob constantly put pressure on himself, whereas another person might have been more likely to "roll with the punches." Can someone like Bob be helped to change his lifestyle, and if so, does this lower the risk for future heart attacks? We consider these and related questions in this chapter. First, though, we need to consider more carefully exactly what we mean by "stress."

# Defining Stress

*Stress* is defined as a challenging event that requires physiological, cognitive, or behavioural adaptation. However, we need to examine this definition closely. Is stress the event itself? Some people would relax after becoming the top salesman, but this achievement only produced another, more difficult challenge for Bob Carter. This suggests that perhaps stress should be defined in terms of the individual's reactions to the event. However, our theories indicate that stress causes adverse reactions. Defining stress in terms of these reactions runs the risk of becoming an exercise in circular logic. In fact, scientists continue to debate whether stress is best defined as a life event or an *appraisal* of life events.

## Stress as a Life Event

Various efforts to quantify stress have attempted to define stress in terms of a life event—a difficult circumstance regardless of the individual's reaction to it. One influential attempt was Holmes and Rahe's (1967) Social Readjustment Rating Scale (SRRS). These investigators assigned stress values to life events based on the judgments of a large group of normal adults. Holmes and Rahe concluded that different stressors cause more or less stress, as indexed by what they called *life change units* (see Table 8–1).

The SRRS and similar instruments have been used frequently in research, and people's ratings of stress have been linked to a wide variety of physical and psychological disorders (Miller, 1989). However, stress checklists have been criticized on several grounds, including that they (1) rely on retrospective reports (see Research Methods in Chapter 7); (2) contain a list of stressors that do not apply to people of different ages and ethnic backgrounds (Contrada et al., 2001) (Is the SRRS a good measure of university student stress?); (3) treat both positive and negative events as stressors (Would you equate getting married with getting fired?); (4) fail to distinguish between short-lived and chronic stressors; and (5) most importantly, treat the same event as causing the same amount of stress for everyone. In regard to this last point, it is obvious, for example, that getting pregnant has a very different meaning for an unwed teenager who failed to use birth control than it has for a married couple in their thirties who were eager to conceive a baby.

A study by Dohrenwend and colleagues (1990) demonstrated empirically how the same stressor often has different meaning for

**TABLE 8–1 The Social Readjustment Rating Scale**

| Life Event | Life Change Units |
|---|---|
| Death of one's spouse | 100 |
| Divorce | 73 |
| Marital separation | 65 |
| Jail term | 63 |
| Death of a close family member | 63 |
| Personal injury or illness | 53 |
| Marriage | 50 |
| Being fired at work | 47 |
| Marital reconciliation | 45 |
| Retirement | 45 |
| Change in the health of a family member | 44 |
| Pregnancy | 40 |
| Sex difficulties | 39 |
| Gain of a new family member | 39 |
| Business readjustment | 39 |
| Change in one's financial state | 38 |
| Death of a close friend | 37 |
| Change to a different line of work | 36 |
| Change in number of arguments with one's spouse | 35 |
| Mortgage over $10 000 | 31 |
| Foreclosure of a mortgage or loan | 30 |
| Change in responsibilities at work | 29 |
| Son or daughter leaving home | 29 |
| Trouble with in-laws | 29 |
| Outstanding personal achievement | 28 |
| Wife beginning or stopping work | 26 |
| Beginning or ending school | 26 |
| Change in living conditions | 25 |
| Revision of personal habits | 24 |
| Trouble with one's boss | 23 |
| Change in work hours or conditions | 20 |
| Change in residence | 20 |
| Change in schools | 20 |
| Change in recreation | 19 |
| Change in church activities | 19 |
| Change in social activities | 18 |
| Mortgage or loan of less than $10 000 | 17 |
| Change in sleeping habits | 16 |
| Change in number of family get-togethers | 15 |
| Change in eating habits | 15 |
| Vacation | 13 |
| Christmas | 12 |
| Minor violations of the law | 11 |

The SRRS rates different stressors as causing more or less life change for people. More difficult stressors have a higher number of "life change units."

*Source:* Reprinted with permission from T.H. Holmes and R.H. Rahe, The Social Readjustment Rating Scale. *Journal of Psychosomatic Research, 11.* © 1967, Pergamon Press.

different people. Table 8–2 lists the percentages of people who reported that a life event produced either a large, moderate, small, or no amount of change in their lives. The same event clearly had very different effects on different participants in the study. For example, the death of a family member (other than a spouse or child) caused a large change for almost 10 percent of the respondents, but it caused no change for over half of them. Because of this variability, many experts argue that stress must be defined in terms of the individual's appraisal of the event.

## Stress as Appraisal of Life Events

Lazarus (1966) offered the leading definition of stress as the appraisal of life events. Lazarus argued that stress arises not from difficult circumstances alone but from the individual's **primary appraisal** or cognitive evaluation of the challenge, threat, or harm posed by a particular event (Lazarus & Folkman, 1984). He asserted that any given life event is a stressor only when it is considered stressful by the individual. For example, an impending exam causes stress when a student feels inadequate in his or her knowledge, but not when he or she feels confident about the subject matter. Lazarus also theorized that **secondary appraisal**, the assessment of one's abilities and resources for coping with a difficult event, is critical to defining stress. Thus, even if a student believes his or her knowledge is inadequate, the stress caused by an impending exam will be minimized if the student has the time and the ability to study adequately.

Lazarus thus defined stress as the combination of a difficult event plus the appraisal of the event as being potentially harmful and exceeding the individual's coping resources. Lazarus's approach addresses many problems, but it runs the risk of being tautological, or circular. What is stress? An event that causes us to feel threatened and overwhelmed. What causes us to feel threatened and overwhelmed? Stress. We agree that stress must be defined in terms of both a life event and the challenge the event causes for the individual. Because of the potential for circularity, however, great caution must be exercised in distinguishing independent variables (stressors) from dependent variables (adverse outcomes) in research on stress.

**TABLE 8–2 Differences in the Amount of Change Caused by the Same Life Event**

| Type of Event | Percentage of Subjects Reporting Each Amount of Change | | | |
|---|---|---|---|---|
| | *Large* | *Moderate* | *Little* | *None* |
| Serious physical illness | 47.2% | 27.8% | 8.3% | 16.7% |
| Relations with mate got worse | 41.2 | 47.1 | 0.0 | 11.8 |
| Relative died (not child/spouse) | 8.3 | 8.3 | 29.2 | 54.2 |
| Close friend died | 5.3 | 15.8 | 29.8 | 49.1 |
| Financial loss (not work related) | 16.3 | 44.2 | 18.6 | 20.9 |
| Assaulted | 18.5 | 22.2 | 40.7 | 18.5 |
| Broke up with a friend | 0.0 | 26.1 | 37.0 | 37.0 |
| Laid off | 13.3 | 63.3 | 13.3 | 10.0 |
| Had trouble with a boss | 17.5 | 35.0 | 32.5 | 15.0 |
| Got involved in a court case | 9.5 | 9.5 | 28.6 | 52.4 |

*Source:* Adapted from B.P. Dohrenwend et al., 1990, Measuring life events: The problem of variability within event categories. *Stress Medicine, 6,* 182.

## Typical Symptoms: Responding to Stress

Stress is a part of life. In fact, stress is an *adaptive* response to many aspects of living. If you had no stress response, you would not be motivated to jump out of the way of a cement truck barrelling down on you, let alone to study for your exams!

The physiologist Walter Cannon (1871–1945), one of the first and foremost stress researchers, conceptualized stress in terms of evolutionary psychology. Cannon (1935) viewed stress as the activation of the **fight or flight response**, the reaction you witness when a cat is surprised by a barking dog (see Further Thoughts). The cat can either flee to safety or turn to scratch at the dog. The fight or flight response has obvious value for survival and

### Further Thoughts — Tend and Befriend: The Female's Alternative to Fight or Flight?

Health psychologist Shelly Taylor and her colleagues (2000) recently hypothesized that fight or flight may be a particularly *male* response to stress and threat. These theorists suggest that females, particularly primate females, are more likely to respond to stress with a pattern that they term **tend and befriend**. *Tending* involves caring for offspring in a way that protects them from harm, and also alters the offspring's neuroendocrine responses in a healthful manner. *Befriending* is responding to threat with social affiliation, thereby reducing the risk of physical danger and encouraging the exchange of resources.

Taylor and her colleagues (2000) conceptualize the origin of the tend and befriend response, like fight or flight, in terms of evolutionary psychology. They hypothesize that the inclusive fitness of a female's genes is increased by caretaking and blending into the environment in response to threat. They argue that social affiliation provides both the safety of numbers and the opportunity to share resources during times of hardship. Attachment is the mechanism hypothesized to modulate tending and befriending, but Taylor's work focuses on the benefits of attachment for the caretaker's rather than the infant's inclusive fitness. That is, it argues that evolution might have selected for caretaking tendencies in adult females.

Taylor and her colleagues (2000) acknowledge that their ideas are speculative, but their novel theorizing suggests many creative directions for new research. Critics might suggest that the biologically based views of female–male differences are sexist, but Taylor is careful to acknowledge cultural influences on gender roles. She and her coworkers also remind us that biology is not destiny. Finally, they speculate that tending and befriending may also be a response in the *male* repertoire, but a less prominent one than fight or flight. ◆

**Walter Cannon** *(1871–1945) was one of the first scientists to conduct systematic research on stress. Cannon focused on the emergency response, the body's physiological preparation for fight or flight.*

inclusive fitness over the course of evolution. Cannon suggested, however, that the evolution of stress in the human environment has outpaced the evolution of our biologically based reactions to a threat. Simply put, Cannon observed that fight or flight is a *maladaptive* reaction to much stress in the modern world such as being reprimanded by one's boss or giving a speech before a large audience.

## Psychophysiological Responses to Stress

You would neither want to run away nor punch your boss when being reprimanded, but your maladaptive physiological reactions are more to the point than the behavioural aspects of fight or flight. Physiologically, the fight or flight response activates your *sympathetic nervous system* (see Figure 8–1): Your heart and respiration rates increase, blood pressure rises, your pupils dilate, blood sugar levels elevate, and your blood flow is redirected in preparation for muscular activity (Baum et al., 1987; Koranyi, 1989). These physiological reactions heighten your attention, provide energy for quick action, and prepare your body for injury (Sapolsky, 1992). Such a physiological reaction is adaptive if a truck *is* headed your way, and presumably it also was an adaptive response to many threats over the course of human evolution. When your boss is yelling, however, the response only leaves your body racing and you feeling nervous and agitated. When repeated over time, your physiological reactions to stress can leave you susceptible to illness.

*Even welcome life events, like graduation or marriage, can be stressful.*

As discussed in Chapter 5, in the brain, the *hypothalmic–pituitary–adrenal (HPA) axis* (see Figure 5–6) is activated by stress, and this eventually leads to the secretion of a variety of hormones. Two hormones are particularly influential. The adrenal medulla secretes *adrenalin* (chemically, the same substance as epinephrine), which acts as a neuromodulator. The hormonal response leads to the release of *norepinephrine* and *epinephrine* into the bloodstream, which activate the sympathetic nervous system throughout the body.

At the same time, the hypothalmus secretes *corticotrophin-releasing factor* (CRF), which causes the pituitary to secrete *adrenocorticotrophic hormone (ACTH)*, and this causes the adrenal cortex to secrete a second hormone, cortisol. **Cortisol** is a corticosteroid that is called the "stress hormone," because its release is so closely linked with stress. Cortisol has a less rapid action than adrenalin, yet it still functions quickly to help the body make repairs in response to injury or infection. One function performed by cortisol is "containment" of pathogens in the body—the same function performed by the exogenous steroids that we take for inflammation and skin irritation. Like externally administered steroids, however, cortisol can promote healing in the short run, but an excess of cortisol can harm the body in a number of ways, including damaging the hippocampus, causing muscular atrophy, and producing hypertension (Sapolsky, 1992; Song & Leonard, 2000; Yehuda, 2002).

## Immune System Responses

Another adverse effect of cortisol is inhibition and potential destruction of various agents in the immune system that ward off infection. Particularly vulnerable are *T cells*, which, along with *B cells*, are the two major types of *lymphocytes*, white blood cells that fight off *antigens*, foreign substances like bacteria that invade the body. Stress impairs immune function through the release of cortisol, but through other mechanisms as well, particularly the action of CRF. The net result is *immunosuppression*, the decreased production of T cells and other immune agents. This, in turn, makes the body more susceptible to infectious diseases during times of stress (Adler, 2001; Song & Leonard, 2000).

Recognition of the adverse effects of stress on immune function has spawned a new and

**Sympathetic and Parasympathetic Divisions of the Autonomic Nervous System**

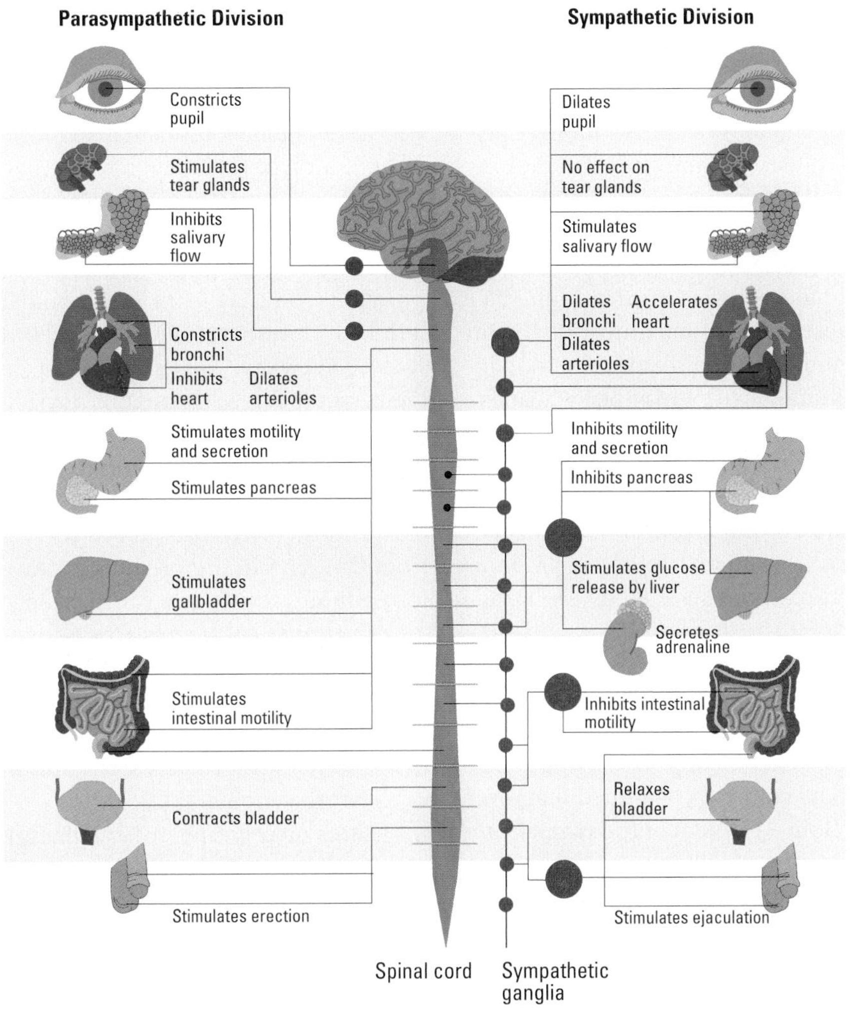


**FIGURE 8–1: The sympathetic nervous system is activated by stress and generally increases arousal. The parasympathetic nervous system typically calms the individual and returns the body to homeostatis.**

*Source:* From *Biology*, 4th ed, by Willis H. Johnson, Louis E. Delanney, Thomas A. Cole, and Austin E. Brooks. Copyright © 1972 by Holt, Rinehart and Winston, Inc.

exciting area of research, called **psychoneuroimmunology (PNI)**, the investigation of the relation between stress and the functioning of the immune system (Adler, 2001; Song & Leonard, 2000). In a variety of real-life contexts, researchers have demonstrated that stress directly affects immune functioning and increases the risk for infectious illness (Kiecolt-Glaser, 1999). In one fascinating study, 90 newly married couples were admitted to a hospital research ward where they engaged in a 30-minute discussion of marital problems. Partners who were more hostile or negative during the interaction showed greater immunosuppression over the next 24 hours in comparison to newlyweds who had more

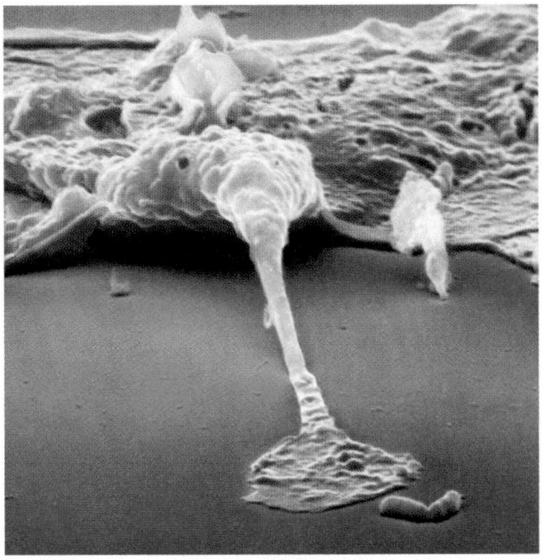

*A white blood cell (microphage) reaches out to capture a bacterium.*

*Hans Selye (1907–1982) was a McGill University physiologist and prolific stress researcher. Selye's concept of the general adaptation syndrome continues to influence contemporary research on the stress response.*

positive conversations (Kiecolt-Glaser et al., 1993). Blood pressure also remained elevated longer following hostile interactions than following friendly interactions.

Why would stress inhibit immune function? As we noted earlier, stress prepares the body for injury, and from an evolutionary perspective, heightened immune functioning would seem to better prepare the body for the infection that may follow injury. Maier, Watkins, and Fleshner (1994) argue, however, that the immune response impairs immediate action, because it creates inflammation, maintains fever, and intensifies pain. Therefore, inhibited immune function may be an adaptive reaction to an immediate physical threat from an evolutionary perspective, even though it is a maladaptive reaction to chronic psychological stress. Once again, it appears that changes in our social environments have outpaced our physiological reactions selected by evolution.

## Illness and Chronic Stress

Cannon (1935) hypothesized that intense or chronic stress overwhelms the body's *homeostasis* (a term he coined). He argued that, over time, the prolonged arousal of the sympathetic nervous system eventually damages the body, because it no longer returns to its normal resting state.

McGill University physiologist Hans Selye (1907–1982), another very influential stress researcher, offered a similar but more specific perspective on the link between illness and chronic stress. Selye (1956) developed the concept of the **general adaptation syndrome (GAS)**, which consists of three stages: alarm, resistance, and exhaustion (see Figure 8–2). The stage of *alarm* occurs first and involves the mobilization of the body in reaction to threat. The stage of *resistance* comes next and is a period of time during which the body is physiologically activated and prepared to respond to the threat. *Exhaustion* is the final stage, and it occurs if the body's resources are depleted by chronic stress. Selye viewed the stage of exhaustion as the key in the development of physical illness from stress. At this stage, the body is damaged by continuous, failed attempts to reactivate the GAS.

Although similar, Selye's theory differs from Cannon's in important ways. An analogy for Cannon's theory is a car in which the engine continues to race instead of idling down after running fast. In contrast, an analogy for Selye's theory is a car that has run out of gas and is damaged because stress keeps turning the key, trying repeatedly and unsuccessfully to restart the engine.

Stress may create physical illness through both mechanisms, but a third explanation may be even more important. Because the stress response uses so much energy, the body may not be able to perform many routine functions, such as storing energy or repairing injuries (Sapolsky, 1992). The result is greater susceptibility to illness. An automotive analogy for the demands of stress in this third model is constantly running a car at high speeds, thus preventing the cooling and lubricant systems from performing their functions well and making breakdown more likely.

## Coping

Stress is challenging, but we are not helpless in the face of ordinary stress. In good ways, and in bad, we have many potential alternatives for coping with stress. In considering different coping strategies, psychological scientists often make a basic distinction between problem-focused and emotion-focused coping (Lazarus & Folkman, 1984). **Problem-focused coping** is externally oriented and involves attempts to change a stressor. If your job is too stressful, you can look for a new one. In contrast, **emotion-focused coping** is an

**Selye's General Adaptation Syndrome (GAS)**

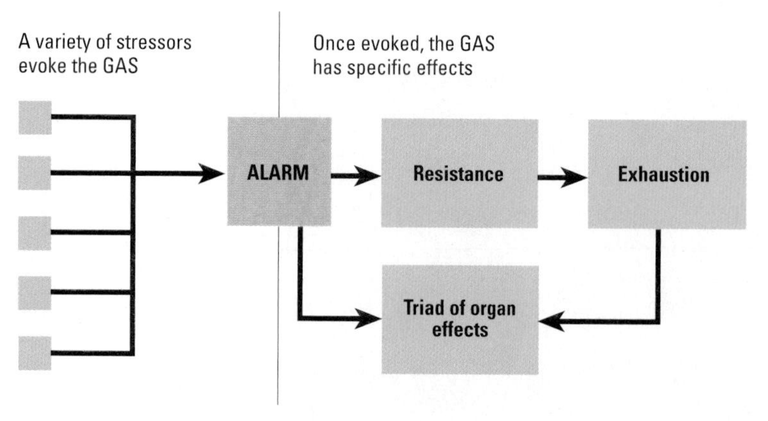
A variety of stressors evoke the GAS
Once evoked, the GAS has specific effects
ALARM
Resistance
Exhaustion
Triad of organ effects

**FIGURE 8–2: Hans Selye assumed that the body was damaged by the immediate alarm in response to stress but more so when the response reached the stage of exhaustion.**

*Source:* Adapted from A. Baum, L.M. Davidson, J.E. Singer, and S.W. Street, 1987, Stress as a psychophysiological response. In A. Baum and J.E. Singer (Eds.), *Handbook of Psychology and Health: Vol. 5. Stress*, p. 4. Hillsdale, NJ: Erlbaum.

attempt to alter internal distress. You can forgive someone for a transgression, and in fact, forgiveness is a response that recently has been shown to have health-promoting effects (Witvliet, Ludwig, & Vander Laan, 2001).

**Outlets for Frustration** Problem-focused coping efforts may have direct physical benefits, as well as the potential to change the stressor. Evidence indicates that responding to stress with physical activity reduces physiological reactions, and in fact, the activity need not be directed at the stressor itself but may include other *outlets for frustration*. For example, rats secrete less cortisol if they can attack another rat or run on a running wheel after the administration of an electric shock (Sapolsky, 1992).

Still, there is a potential problem with responding to stressors directly: It is often unclear if a coping response will be effective, or even whether a stressor can be changed. Consider, for example, if you are stressed out by poor grades in a difficult class. Should you redouble your efforts, drop the course, or accept that this is not your best subject? Problem-focused coping is the appropriate way to conquer many actual stressors, but attempts to change some stressors are doomed to failure. In such cases, efforts at problem-focused coping will increase, not reduce, distress. Thus the only alternative is to accept the stressor for what it is and to use emotion-focused coping to alter your response to it.

**Repression** Emotion-focused coping may involve a deliberate effort to relax or to reevaluate a stressor. Before taking a big exam, you might sit quietly and breathe deeply for several minutes. Other forms of emotion-focused coping involve unconscious or automatic methods for dampening emotional experience. For example, various defence mechanisms, particularly *repression*, have been hypothesized to alter emotional responses to stress—sometimes with maladaptive consequences. A number of experts in behavioural medicine theorize that repression protects people from consciously experiencing unpleasant emotions, but "repressors" thereby place themselves at greater risk for developing stress-related physical illnesses (Somerfield & McCrae, 2000). For example, Bob Carter "swallowed" a lot of his anger, and this allowed him to remain a jovial salesman. However, the repressed anger probably had adverse physiological effects, such as

CALVIN AND HOBBES © Watterson. Dist. by UPS. Reprinted with permission. All rights reserved.

increasing Bob's blood pressure and thereby putting him at greater risk for a heart attack.

The repression hypothesis is difficult to test empirically, because it focuses on unconscious mental processes that are hard to measure. Nevertheless, the hypothesis is supported by evidence from a variety of different types of studies (Cramer, 2000). For example, people who do not acknowledge their experience of anxiety show exaggerated psychophysiological reactions to stress such as increased heart rate and blood pressure (Schwartz, 1989).

Psychophysiological reactions to stress also are greater for "defensive deniers"—people who report positive mental health but whom clinicians judge to have emotional problems (Shedler, Mayman, & Manis, 1993). Other research indicates that when people are encouraged to recount very stressful experiences, they show reductions in various psychophysiological indicators of the stress response (Pennebaker, 1990; Petrie et al., 1995). Whether or not repression causes stress-related illnesses, talking about your feelings clearly is a healthy coping technique (see Research Close-Up).

**Predictability and Control** Findings from animal and human research indicate that certain cognitions, especially predictability and control, also can dramatically affect coping. The importance of *predictability* has been demonstrated repeatedly in laboratory research. For example, rats have smaller physiological responses to shocks that are signalled by the flash of a light than to unsignalled shocks of the same magnitude (Sapolsky, 1992). In one way, predictability is stressful, because the signal elicits a response that is similar to (but weaker than) the response to the actual stressor. However, the signal also decreases negative responding to the actual stressor (Baum et al., 1987). In a sense, predictability allows us to

## RESEARCH CLOSE-UP

### Disclosure of Trauma and Immunity

We all know it's supposed to be good to talk about your feelings, but could disclosure really improve the functioning of the immune system? This was the question asked in a study conducted by Pennebaker, Kiecolt-Glaser, and Glaser (1988). Participants were asked to write about traumatic events in their lives for four consecutive days, especially about things that they had not revealed previously. A control group wrote about trivial topics for the same time period. Twenty-five psychology undergraduates were randomly assigned to the alternative treatments, and all writing took place in the laboratory. Dependent variables included self-reported mood before and after writing; measures of autonomic arousal, including blood pressure and heart rate; and immunological assays of the subject's blood before the study, immediately after writing, and six weeks later.

Evaluations indicated that the students in the disclosure group had indeed written about very upsetting experiences, including difficulties they had coming to university, serious family conflicts, and problems with the other sex. Writing did not produce an immediate benefit, however, as students in the experimental group were more upset immediately after writing than students in the control group. In the long run, however, students who wrote about personal distress had significantly fewer medical visits to the student health centre and better immune responses than did students who wrote about trivia. Further, participants in the personal writing condition improved more on blood pressure and immunological measures when they wrote about previously undisclosed events rather than about events they had discussed with others.

These findings are dramatic, but we do not wish to overinterpret them. Obviously, talking about your feelings will not cure a cold. Still, the study has been replicated by the same research group (Petrie et al., 1995), and, importantly, similar results have been reported by skeptics of the original research. In another recent study, writing about the most traumatic experience in one's life was related to symptom improvement among patients with asthma and rheumatoid arthritis (Smyth et al., 1999). Scientists are still debating exactly why and how disclosure helps. Writing may help people to synthesize and make sense of their experience. Whatever the mechanism, a large body of literature indicates that writing about difficult experiences is helpful both emotionally and physically (Esterling et al., 1999). ◆

begin to cope even before the onset of a stressor. Think of a boy who is bullied. If he knows that every lunch period he will have to face his tormentor, he can begin to prepare for it. This preparation becomes a form of control.

The importance of *control* in coping similarly has been documented in extensive laboratory research with animals and humans. Rats that are able to stop a shock by pressing a bar have a smaller stress response than rats exposed to exactly the same shock but who have no opportunity of stopping it through their own actions (Sapolsky, 1992). Even the illusion of control can help to alleviate stress in humans (Mineka & Kihlstrom, 1978), but the perception of being able to control a stressor is not always a good thing. The perception of control can *increase* stress when people believe they can exercise control but fail to do so, or when they lose control over a formerly controllable stressor (Mineka & Kihlstrom, 1978). Thus control alleviates stress when it can be exercised or even when it is illusory, but failed attempts at control intensify stress.

**Optimism and Humour** Researchers recently have identified a more general style, **optimism**, as another key to effective coping with stress. People with an optimistic coping style have a positive attitude toward dealing with stress, even when it cannot be changed, whereas those with a pessimistic coping style are defeated from the outset (see Table 8–3). Growing evidence indicates that positive thinking is linked with better health habits and less illness for healthy people, as well as for those with heart disease, AIDS, and other serious physical illnesses (Carver & Scheier, 1999; Kubzansky et al., 2001; Shatte et al., 1999). Stress is taxing, but it can be a growth experience if we approach stress optimistically and with positive emotion (Folkman & Moskowitz, 2000).

In a related line of research, psychologists such as Ron Martin and Nicholas Kuiper at the University of Western Ontario have examined whether a sense of humour is an effective buffer against the effects of stress (e.g., Kuiper & Martin, 1993; Martin, 1996, 2001). Early research suggested that stressful life events had less of a distressing effect on people who had a better sense of humour and those who were better able to produce humour under conditions of stress (Martin & Lefcourt, 1983). Later research reveals a more complex relationship. Kuiper and colleagues (2004) found that there are distinct components of sense of humour, which have quite different relationships with psychological well-being, with only some being facilitative and others being detrimental. In other words there are adaptive and maladaptive components of humour (e.g., self-enhancing versus self-defeating). The maladaptive components of humour that are self-focused (e.g., self-demeaning and belaboured humour) are associated with poorer self-esteem, greater depression and anxiety, and poorer judgments of self-competence. Maladaptive forms of sense of humour that focus on others (i.e., aggressive and rude humour) are unrelated to personal well-being. In another study, Kuiper and Nicholl (2004) found evidence to suggest that a greater sense of adaptive humour may sometimes contribute to more positive perceptions of physical health than may actually be warranted. In other words, a sense of humour may influence perceived health rather than actual health. Thus, the use of some forms of humour can protect a person against the emotional effects of stress (i.e., anxiety and depression) but might not protect the person against the physical effects of stress.

### Health Behaviour

A survey of over 9000 Canadians found that job stress was associated with the occurrence of headaches (Wilkins & Beaudet, 1998). A detailed, longitudinal study by Anita DeLongis (currently at the University of British Columbia) and her colleagues showed that daily stress predicts the occurrence of many health problems, including headaches, backaches, flu, and sore throats (DeLongis, Folkman, & Lazarus, 1988). Stress may cause illness directly by altering our physiology, but stress may also cause illness indirectly by disrupting health behaviours (Cohen & Williamson, 1991; see Figure 8–3). **Health behaviour** involves activities that promote good health, and it includes both positive actions like eating, sleeping, and exercising adequately and the avoidance of unhealthy activities such as cigarette smoking, excessive alcohol consumption, and drug use. As we saw in the case of Bob Carter, stress can lead people to engage in less positive and more negative health behaviour, and these poor health habits, and not stress, per se, may be responsible for much of the relation between stress and illness (Cohen & Williamson, 1991). In considering the tremendous importance of health behaviour, you should note that over the last two centuries basic health behaviours—personal hygiene, sanitation, and an adequate diet—are more responsible for our vastly increased health and life expectancy than are scientific advances like the discovery of penicillin (Starr, 1982).

**Following Medical Advice** Stress may also be related to the very important positive health behaviour of following medical advice. In fact, as many as 93 percent of all patients *fail* to adhere fully to medical advice (Taylor, 1990). This is a particular problem for illnesses like

**TABLE 8–3 Coping Tendencies of Optimists and Pessimists**

| Optimists | Pessimists |
|---|---|
| Information seeking | Suppression of thoughts |
| Active coping and planning | Giving up |
| Positive reframing | Self-distraction |
| Seeking benefit | Cognitive avoidance |
| Use of humour | Focus on distress |
| Acceptance | Overt denial |

*Source:* C.S. Carver and M.F. Scheier, 1999, Optimism. In C.R. Snyder (Ed.), *Coping: The Psychology of What Works*, p. 194. New York: Oxford University Press.

**Indirect and Direct Effects of Stress**

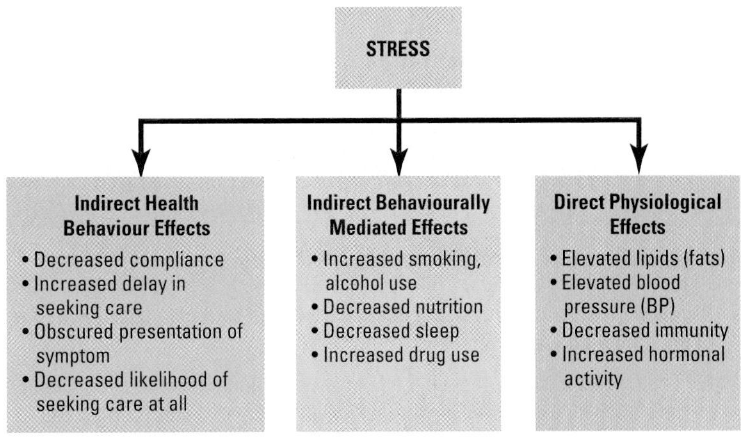


**FIGURE 8–3: Stress can promote illness both directly through adverse physiological effects and indirectly by undermining positive health behaviours and increasing negative health behaviours.**

*Source:* A. Baum, 1994, Behavioral, biological, and environmental interactions in disease processes. In S.J. Blumenthal, K. Matthews, and S. Weiss (Eds.), *New Research Frontiers in Behavioral Medicine: Proceedings of the National Conference*, p. 62. Washington, DC: NIH Publications.

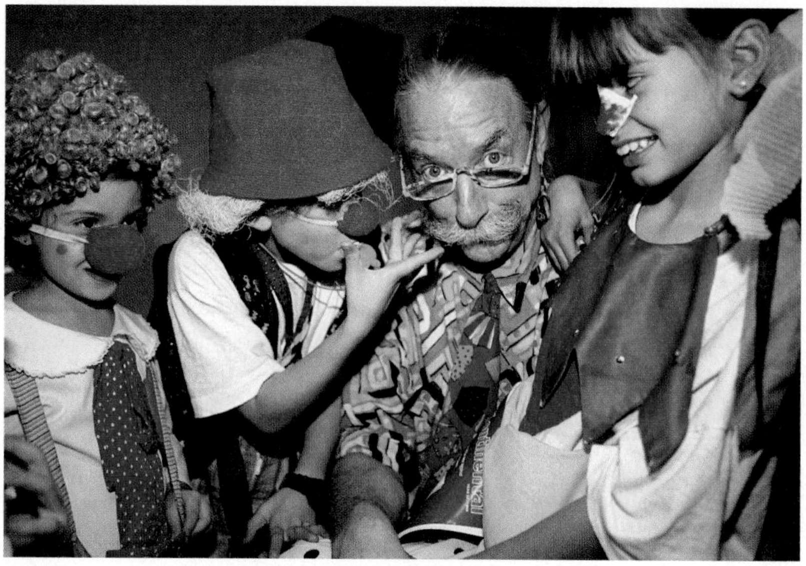

The real-life Patch Adams inspired the film in which Robin Williams played the title role. Adams was a rebellious medical student in the 1960s who wanted to provide holistic care and instill optimism in his patients.

hypertension (high blood pressure) that usually have no obvious symptoms. In such cases patients may discontinue their medication because it produces no noticeable relief, even though it may be controlling a dangerous underlying condition. Stressors such as family conflict also can interfere with adherence to treatments that *do* have clear symptoms. For example, children with insulin dependent diabetes are less likely to adhere to medical recommendations concerning exercise, diet, and testing blood sugars when family conflict is high (Miller-Johnson et al., 1994).

*Illness behaviour*—behaving as if you are sick—also appears to be stress related. Considerable research indicates that increased stress is correlated with such illness behaviours as making more frequent office visits to physicians or allowing chronic pain to interfere with everyday activities (Taylor, 1990). Effective coping with chronic illness involves some ignoring of physical discomfort and living life as normally as possible.

**TABLE 8–4 DSM-IV-TR Diagnostic Criteria for Psychological Factors Affecting Medical Condition**

**A. A general medical condition (coded on Axis III) is present.**

**B. Psychological factors adversely affect the general medical condition in one of the following ways:**

1. The factors have influenced the course of the general medical condition as shown by a close temporal association between the psychological factors and the development or exacerbation, or delayed recovery from, the general medical condition.
2. The factors interfere with the treatment of the general medical condition.
3. The factors constitute additional health risks for the individual.
4. Stress-related physiological responses precipitate or exacerbate symptoms of the general medical condition.

**Social Support** Finally, the fact that many people consult physicians for psychological rather than physical concerns underscores the value of *social support* in coping with stress. Social support not only can encourage positive health behaviour, but research suggests that social support also has direct, physiological benefits. For example, studies have shown that increased social support is associated with adaptive functioning of the immune, cardiovascular, and endocrine systems (Uchino, Cacioppo, & Kiecolt-Glaser, 1996).

## Classification of Stress and Physical Illness

### Brief Historical Perspective

Historically, the only physical illnesses thought to be affected by stress were a few so-called **psychosomatic disorders**, such as ulcers and asthma. The field of psychosomatic medicine was dominated by psychoanalytic psychiatrists who endorsed the *specificity hypothesis*—the idea that specific personality types caused specific psychosomatic diseases. Theorists such as Franz Alexander (1950) attempted to classify psychosomatic illnesses according to the unique personality type that caused it. For example, ulcers were said to arise in passive, dependent people who were not being gratified in their desires to be loved and cared for (Alexander, French, & Pollock, 1968).

### Contemporary Approaches

Research does not support the idea that personality is directly related to psychosomatic symptoms, and contemporary approaches also reject the view that only certain physical illnesses are affected by stress. DSM-IV-TR does not include a list of a limited number of psychosomatic disorders. Instead, virtually any physical illness can be coded on Axis III, *general medical conditions*. When a physical illness is the focus of treatment, the diagnosis of *psychological factors affecting medical condition* is used on Axis I (see Table 8–4). The diagnosis may be used for various psychological factors, including not

## CANADIAN FOCUS

### Endler's Multidimensional Interaction Model of Stress, Anxiety, and Coping

As noted by Carleton University researchers Anisman and Zul (1999), many factors can influence a person's response to stressors, including characteristics of the stressor (e.g., type of stressor, its controllability, predictability, and chronicity) and characteristics of the person (e.g., personality, genetics, and previous experiences dealing with stressors). To understand how these factors play a role in stress, it is important to consider how they might interact with one another. One of the most sophisticated models of stress, anxiety, and coping was developed by the late York University psychologist Norman S. Endler (e.g., Endler, 1997). This model is similar in some ways to the ideas developed by Richard Lazarus (1966), which we discussed earlier. However, Endler's work in many ways refines the way we understand stress by emphasizing the importance of *interactions* among key variables.

Central to Endler's model is the concept of *trait anxiety,* which is defined as one's proneness or predisposition to experiencing *state anxiety.* People with high trait anxiety tend to frequently feel anxious (state anxiety) in response to stressful events. Conversely, people with low trait anxiety less often feel anxious in response to stressors. Endler proposes that there are at least four different kinds of trait anxiety, defined by the sorts of stressors that tend to make a person anxious: *physical danger, social evaluation, daily routine stressors* (minor hassles), and *ambiguous situations.* Endler argues that a person will experience state anxiety only when there is *congruence* between the person's trait anxiety and the type of stressor encountered. Consider, for example, a person who tends to become highly anxious in physically dangerous situations but tends to be calm in most other situations. That person would have a high score on a measure of physical danger trait anxiety, and low scores on measures of other types of trait anxiety. Endler predicts that this person would be most likely to experience state anxiety in physically risky situations (e.g., while rock climbing) and less likely to feel anxious in other situations (e.g., while giving a class presentation).

Many studies have tested Endler's interactional model. Out of 34 tests, most (82 percent) supported the model (Endler, 1997). To illustrate, Endler, Crooks, and Parker (1992) assessed state and trait anxiety in military personnel in a nonthreatening situation and also measured state anxiety just before a parachute jump. Using a questionnaire measure of anxiety, Endler et al. classified the personnel as having either low or high physical danger trait anxiety. When in a nonthreatening situation, the two groups of personnel had equally low levels of state anxiety. But just before the parachute jump the personnel with high physical danger trait anxiety had much higher state anxiety than the personnel with low physical danger trait anxiety. In other words, state anxiety appeared to be the result of an interaction between type of trait anxiety and type of stressor.

In other studies, Endler and colleagues have found similar interaction effects for social evaluation trait anxiety and for ambiguous situations trait anxiety (e.g., Trotter & Endler, 1999; Flett, Endler, & Fairlie, 1999). For example, consider the 1995 referendum concerning Quebec's separation from Canada. The referendum was an ambiguous threat; at the time nobody knew what the outcome would be, or whether the outcome would be harmful to Canadians. As predicted from Endler's model, Flett et al. found that the referendum created much more state anxiety in York University students with high scores on ambiguous situations trait anxiety, compared to York students with lower scores on this form of trait anxiety.

Endler's model proposes that there are various interactions between coping styles and stressors. Three sorts of coping are proposed: *task-oriented* coping, which involves purposeful efforts to solve problems (this is similar to Lazarus's problem-focused coping); *emotion-oriented coping,* which is aimed at reducing one's emotional reaction to stressors (similar to Lazarus's emotion-focused coping); and *avoidance-oriented coping,* which involves using distraction or diversion to avoid dealing with stressful situations. Task-oriented coping tends to be most effective in controllable situations, whereas emotion-oriented coping is most effective in uncontrollable situations. Avoidance-oriented coping can be initially effective as a reaction to stress, but in the long run task-oriented coping is most effective.

A person might have a preferred coping style, such as a tendency to use emotion-oriented coping instead of other forms of coping. However, other aspects of the person (e.g., his or her levels of the various forms of trait anxiety) and of the situation (e.g., whether a physical stressor is present) can influence the person's choice of coping strategy. Thus, there are complex interactions between aspects of the person (coping style, trait anxiety) and aspects of the situation.

Endler's model has important implications for understanding how people cope with physical illnesses. For instance, a woman with high physical danger trait anxiety who detects a breast lump (a physical threat) would experience a high level of state anxiety. How she copes with this situation depends on the interaction between aspects of the stressor and aspects of the person. If the lump is small and she has tended to rely on avoidance-oriented coping in the past, she might decide to avoid medical tests for the time being, in a misguided effort to avoid feeling anxious. It might be only when the lump has become large (and possibly malignant) that she might decide to use problem-oriented coping (i.e., visiting her family doctor). Notice how the choice of coping response can have serious implications for the person's health. ◆

only mental disorders but also psychological symptoms, personality traits, maladaptive health behaviours, or stress-related physiological responses.

DSM-IV-TR also has a separate axis for coding stressors, Axis IV, psychosocial and environmental problems (see Table 8–5). Intuitively, we may understand what stress means, but scientists still are struggling to define and quantify stress objectively. One certainty for the future is that our definitions will need to be refined in DSM-V and other measures.

### Illness as a Cause of Stress

Before discussing the contributions of stress to particular physical illnesses, we should note that, although stress can cause illness, illness also can cause stress. In fact, some diseases lead to major changes in a person's life. For example, consider the effects of the diagnosis of insulin dependent diabetes on a 10-year-old boy and his family. In order to maintain a normal range of blood sugars, the child and his parents must frequently test his blood sugars, adjust to giving and receiving one, two, or three injections of insulin daily, and carefully monitor exercise and diet because of their profound effect on blood sugars. In addition, the child and his family must somehow cope with the stigma of being "different." Finally, they have to learn to cope with the possibility of his suffering profound, long-term side effects from hyperglycemia (high blood sugars), including kidney dysfunction or blindness. As these considerations suggest, helping children, adults, and families cope with chronic illness is another important role of experts in behavioural medicine.

**TABLE 8–5 DSM-IV-TR Categories of Psychosocial and Environmental Problems**

| Category | Examples |
|---|---|
| Problems with primary support group | Death of a family member, family health problems, divorce, sexual abuse, inadequate discipline, family discord, birth of a sibling |
| Problems related to the social environment | Death or loss of a friend, social isolation, discrimination, adjustment to life cycle transition |
| Educational problems | Illiteracy, academic problems, discord with teacher, inadequate school environment |
| Occupational problems | Unemployment, stressful work schedule, job change, discord with boss |
| Housing problems | Homelessness, unsafe neighbourhood, discord with neighbours |
| Economic problems | Extreme poverty, inadequate finances |
| Problems with access to healthcare services | Inadequate healthcare services, inadequate health insurance |
| Problems related to interaction with the legal system/crime | Arrest, litigation, incarceration, victim of crime |
| Other psychosocial problems | Exposure to disasters, war, discord with nonfamily caregivers |

## The Role of Psychological Factors in Some Familiar Illnesses

Thanks to advances in medical science, and especially in public health, far fewer people are dying of infectious diseases at the beginning of the twenty-first century. As you can see in Figure 8–4, infectious disease is no longer at the top of the list of killers. Instead, many of the leading causes of death are *lifestyle diseases* that are affected in many ways by stress and health behaviour.

In the following sections we briefly review evidence on stress and lifestyle factors in the etiology, course, and treatment of cancer, HIV infection, chronic pain, and sleep disorders. Later, we review research in some detail on the relation between stress and today's number one killer, cardiovascular disease. Our goal is to convey a sense of both the breadth and depth of research on stress and illness.

### Cancer

Cancer is a leading cause of mortality in Canada today, accounting for 27 percent of all deaths (Statistics Canada, 2003). The chances of Canadians developing cancer at some point in their lives are 41 percent for men and 38 percent for women (National Cancer Institute of Canada, 2003). The number of new cancer cases and deaths from cancer are generally declining, although the death rate for lung cancer is increasing among Canadian women, possibly because of the growing prevalence of smoking (since the 1950s) among women (Canadian Cancer Society, 2003a, 2003b).

**Leading Causes of Death in Canada in 1995**

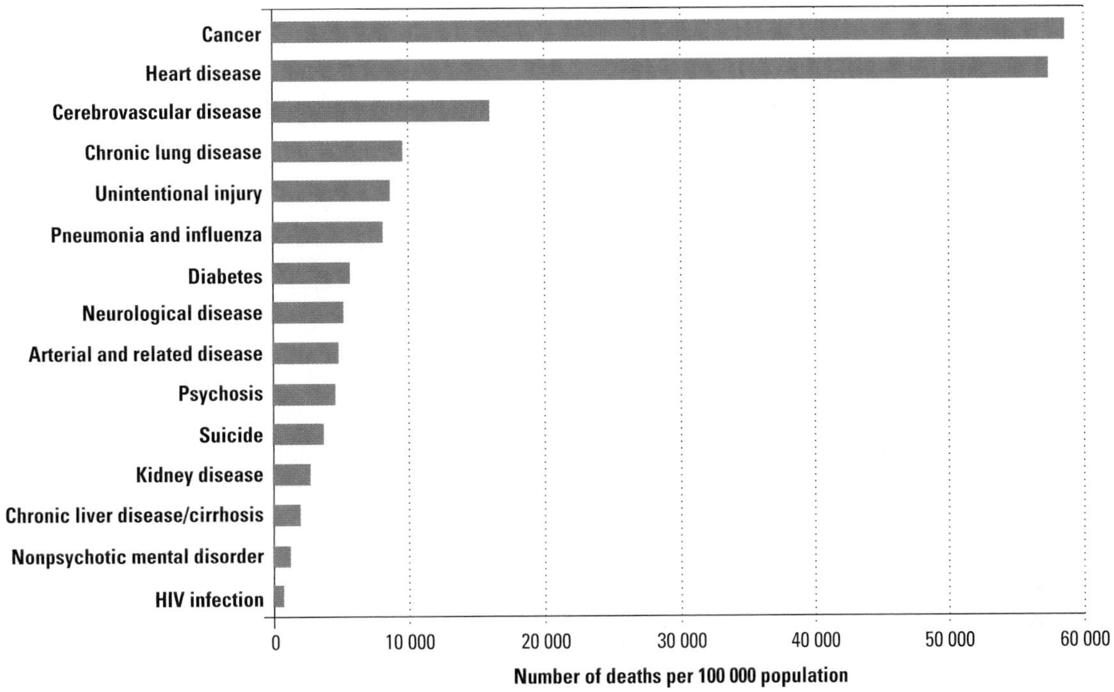


**FIGURE 8–4: Stress and health behaviour play a central role in most of the major causes of death in Canada today.**

*Source:* Statistics Canada, www.statcan.ca/English/Pgdb/People/Health/health35htm. Extracted November 7, 2000.

At first glance, cancer would seem to be the paramount example of a purely biological illness, but the importance of psychological factors becomes apparent upon closer examination. For example, our health behaviour such as cigarette smoking contributes to the extent to which we are exposed to various carcinogens—cancer-causing agents. In Canada, 23 percent of people over the age of 12 are daily smokers, and many more are exposed to second-hand smoke. Thus, many Canadians are exposed to this cancer-causing agent.

Psychological factors also are at least modestly associated with the course of cancer (McKenna et al., 1999). Not surprisingly, cancer patients often are anxious or depressed, and their negative emotions can lead to increases in negative health behaviour such as alcohol consumption and decreases in positive health behaviour such as exercise. The absence of social support also can undermine adherence to unpleasant but vitally important medical treatments for cancer (Anderson, Kiecolt-Glaser, & Glaser, 1994). In facing the spectre of cancer, the encouragement and physical assistance of family and friends can boost patients' resolve to bear treatment side effects such as hair loss and intense nausea.

Some research also indicates that stress may *directly* affect the course of cancer. In animal analogue studies, for example, rats exposed to inescapable shock are less able to reject implanted cancer tumours than rats exposed to escapable shock or no stress at all (Visintainer, Seligman, & Volpicelli, 1982). The adverse effects of stress on the immune system may explain how stress may exacerbate the course of cancer. Evidence indicates that immunity plays an important role in limiting the spread of cancerous tumours, and immunosuppression due to stress may disrupt this protective function (Anderson et al., 1994).

A cause-and-effect relationship between stress and the course of cancer also has been implied by some exciting treatment research. Various psychological treatments have been offered to cancer patients in an attempt to improve their quality of life. The type of intervention varies widely, but treatments often include a structured, self-help group. Many of these interventions are successful in improving the quality of life among cancer patients,

Dr. Peter Jepson-Young—better known simply as Dr. Peter—was a young Vancouver physician who became an active spokesperson for increasing awareness of HIV and AIDS after he tested HIV positive. In his weekly television diaries he personalized the face of AIDS. Before he died, he established the Dr. Peter AIDS Foundation, which provides palliative care for people with HIV/AIDS.

and a few of the psychological interventions appear to have had beneficial *physical* effects (Anderson et al., 1994). For example, one study found that six years after treatment, significantly fewer patients who participated in a support group died (9 percent) in comparison to patients who received no psychosocial treatment (29 percent) (Fawzy et al., 1993).

Any number of factors may explain this striking outcome, including lower stress, increased social support, and improved health behaviour. We must be cautious not to overinterpret the result, however, especially since a recent study of 235 women with breast cancer found that support groups led to decreased reports of pain and psychological symptoms but did *not* affect survival rates (Goodwin et al., 2001). Cancer is a physical illness. We are hardly arguing that psychological factors alone are responsible for causing cancer, nor are we asserting that the disease should be treated psychologically instead of medically. Still, research demonstrates that psychological factors contribute to the course of one of our most dreaded physical illnesses.

### Acquired Immune Deficiency Syndrome (AIDS)

**Acquired immune deficiency syndrome (AIDS)** is caused by the **human immunodeficiency virus (HIV)**, which attacks the immune system and leaves the patient susceptible to infection, neurological complications, and cancers that rarely affect those with normal immune function. People who are HIV positive vary widely in how rapidly they develop AIDS. Some people develop AIDS within months after HIV infection, whereas others remain symptom-free for 10 years or more. HIV and AIDS have reached epidemic proportions throughout the world with a notably high prevalence in Africa. Over 50 000 Canadians are living with HIV/AIDS, and roughly 4200 new cases occur each year (Health Canada, 2003b).

Behavioural factors play a critical role in the transmission of AIDS. Contact with bodily fluids, particularly blood and semen, is very risky, and transmission often occurs during anal sex and also during vaginal intercourse. The use of condoms greatly reduces the risk of the sexual transmission of HIV. Other behaviours that increase the risk for HIV infection include sharing hypodermic needles. Also, an infected mother can transmit the infection to her unborn child (Health Canada, 2000a). Overall, the annual rate of HIV cases has been slowly declining in Canada since 1995, due in part to risk-reducing strategies (e.g., condom use) and the development of new antiretroviral drugs. Early in the epidemic, the people primarily affected were men who had sex with other men (MSM), and people who received blood or blood products. Now, the epidemic affects primarily injection-drug users; MSM; and increasingly, women (Health Canada, 2000a). The proportion of HIV among First Nations people has also been increasing (Health Canada, 2000b).

Scientists and policymakers have launched large-scale media campaigns to educate the public about HIV and AIDS and to change risky behaviour. How effective are these programs? Evidence indicates that although the public has become much more knowledgeable about AIDS, changing behaviour is very difficult. For example, practices such as condom use are now more widely followed, but unprotected sex is still very common even among members of high-risk groups (Taylor, 1995).

Recent evidence has linked increased stress with a more rapid progression of HIV, and the availability of social support is associated with a more gradual onset of symptoms (Evans et al., 1997; Leserman et al., 1999). Research has yet to demonstrate any physical benefits of psychological intervention in HIV, although support groups do report lower distress among treated patients. Broader social support also is extremely important to the AIDS patient's social and psychological well-being. Unfortunately, misunderstanding and fear cause many people, including many health professionals, to distance themselves from AIDS victims rather than offering them understanding, acceptance, and support.

### Pain Management

Pain is associated with a number of acute injuries and illnesses, and it often serves the useful functions of alerting people to a problem and motivating them to seek treatment. Pain is *not* always adaptive, however, and in many cases, pain is not a signal of an underlying condition that can be controlled with treatment. Problematic pain can take the form of recurrent acute pain, or pain can be chronic. Headaches are an example of recurrent acute pain, and lower back problems are a common form of chronic pain.

Chronic pain is not a rare experience. According to a national population survey in 1994–1995, almost 3.9 million Canadians (17 percent of the population) experienced some form of chronic pain (Millar, 1996).

Pain is subjective, and this makes it difficult to evaluate or compare patients' reports about the extent or nature of their pain. Evaluation is especially difficult when pain is not associated with an identifiable injury or illness, as is commonly the case with headaches and lower back pain.

The importance of psychological factors in pain has long been recognized, dating back at least to the pioneering research by Melzack and Wall (1965) at McGill University. Studies by pain investigators such as Gordon J.G. Asmundson at the University of Regina show that depression and anxiety are commonly associated with chronic pain, and that fear of pain may play an important role in perpetuating chronic pain (Asmundson, Norton, & Norton, 1999; Asmundson & Taylor, 1996). Fear of pain appears to contribute to pain chronicity in a number of ways, such as by causing the person to avoid physical exertion, including avoidance of the physical exercises prescribed in pain rehabilitation programs. Pain-related avoidance thereby retards recovery. Avoidance also leads to muscle deconditioning, which increases the chances of re-injury. Fear-related increases in muscle tension can also lead to painful muscle spasms. Understanding the causes of fear of pain has important implications for understanding and treating chronic pain. Recent research by Asmundson and colleagues suggests that anxiety sensitivity (fear of anxiety-related sensations; see Chapter 6) influences the person's fear of pain (Asmundson & Taylor, 1996).

Research from the University of British Columbia also suggests that receiving social support from significant others can reduce pain severity by encouraging the use of pain-coping strategies (Holtzman, Newth, & DeLongis, in press).

Psychologists have tried a number of treatments designed to directly reduce patients' experience of pain. Treatments include hypnosis, biofeedback, relaxation training, and cognitive therapy. Researchers such as Kenneth Craig at the University of British Columbia have reported that pain management programs are successful in treating a wide variety of pain problems stemming from various underlying conditions, including headaches, lower back pain, and facial pain (Grunau & Craig, 1988). Following treatment, patients report less pain, greater satisfaction with their life and relationships, improved employment status, and less reliance on medication. But pain reduction typically is modest at best (Taylor, 1995). As a result, most current efforts focus on the *pain management*, not pain reduction.

## Sleep Disorders

Sleep is very important to good health and psychological well-being, but mental health professionals typically have been concerned with sleep disturbances only as a symptom of some other mental disorder, such as depression or anxiety. This circumstance is changing, however, as more research is being conducted on the nature and treatment of sleep disturbances, such as work by Charles Morin at Laval University (e.g., Morin et al., 1999). Now DSM-IV-TR contains a diagnostic category for primary sleep disorder. **Primary sleep disorder** is a condition where the difficulty in sleeping is the principal complaint, in contrast to sleep disorders due to general medical condition, another mental disorder, or substance use. Two types of primary sleep disorders are listed in DSM-IV-TR. *Dyssomnias* are difficulties in the amount, quality, or timing of sleep. *Parasomnias* are characterized by abnormal events that occur during sleep—for example, nightmares.

The dyssomnias include primary insomnia, primary hypersomnia, narcolepsy, breathing-related sleep disorder, and circadian rhythm sleep disorder. *Primary insomnia* involves difficulties initiating or maintaining sleep, or poor quality of sleeping (e.g., restless sleep), that last for at least a month and significantly impair life functioning. Primary insomnia is a common problem, affecting one in five Canadians (Ruyak, Bilsbury, & Rajda, 2004). It is typically precipitated by stress, although other factors may be involved.

Fortunately, effective treatments have been developed for insomnia that involve stimulus control (only staying in bed during sleep) and resetting circadian rhythms by going to bed and getting up at set times, as well as not napping, regardless of the length of sleep (Bootzin, 2000; Morin et al., 1999). *Primary hypersomnia* is excessive sleepiness characterized by prolonged or daytime sleep, lasting at least a month and significantly interfering with life functioning. Primary hypersomnia is similar to *narcolepsy*, irresistible attacks of refreshing sleep, lasting at least three months. However, narcolepsy also is characterized by the sudden loss of muscle tone for brief periods of time (usually following intense emotion) and/or intrusive periods of dreaming just before awakening. The "sleep-attacks" in narcolepsy are also less resistible than is the general desire to sleep in primary hypersomnia (APA, 2000).

*Breathing-related sleep disorder* involves the disruption in sleep due to breathing problems such as *sleep apnea*, the temporary obstruction of the respiratory airway. People with sleep apnea typically snore loudly due to an airway that is partially obstructed as a result of obesity or other conditions. Sleep apnea patients will stop breathing for 20 to 30 seconds when the obstruction becomes complete, and this is followed by gasping, body movements, or even louder snoring. Not surprisingly, sleep apnea disrupts not only the patients' sleep but also the sleep of others in their vicinity. *Circadian rhythm sleep disorder* is a mismatch between the patients' 24-hour sleeping patterns and their 24-hour life demands that causes significant life distress. The disorder is found more commonly among adolescents and people who work night shifts (APA, 2000).

The parasomnias include nightmare disorder, sleep terror disorder, and sleepwalking disorder. People with *nightmare disorder* are frequently awakened by terrifying dreams. *Sleep terror disorder* also involves abrupt awakening from sleep, typically with a scream, but it differs from nightmare disorder in important respects. People with nightmare disorder recall their dreams and quickly orient to being awake; people with sleep terror disorder recall little of their dreams, show intense autonomic arousal, and are difficult to soothe. Moreover, a person with sleep terror typically returns to sleep fairly quickly and recalls little, if anything, about the episode the following morning.

Finally, *sleepwalking disorder* involves rising from the bed during sleep and walking about in a generally unresponsive state. In extreme cases, the person may use the bathroom, talk (with a minimum of meaningful dialogue), eat, or even run in a frantic attempt to escape some threat. Upon awakening, however, the person cannot remember the episode. Occasional episodes of sleepwalking are fairly common, especially among children. Like all sleep disorders, sleepwalking disorder tends to be diagnosed only if it causes significant distress or impairs the person's ability to function (APA, 2000).

*Nightmares and other sleep disorders are common problems, but scientists only recently have begun to study sleep disorders systematically.*

## Cardiovascular Disease

**Cardiovascular disease (CVD)** is a leading killer in Canada and other industrialized countries (Peters et al., 1998; and see Figure 8–4). Research into this disease provides a good illustration of the importance of stress in understanding health and disease. CVD is a group of disorders that affect the heart and circulatory system. The most important of these illnesses are **hypertension** (high blood pressure) and **coronary heart disease (CHD)**. The most deadly and well-known form of coronary heart disease is **myocardial infarction (MI)**, commonly called a heart attack. Hypertension increases the risk for CHD, as well as for other serious disorders, such as stroke. CHD is the leading cause of premature death in the 35 to 64 age group, and several million Canadians are at elevated risk for CHD (Labronte & Thompson, 1993). In addition to health behaviour, personality styles, behaviour patterns, and forms of emotional expression appear to contribute directly to the development of CVD (Rozanski, Blumenthal, & Kaplan, 1999).

### Typical Symptoms and Associated Features of Hypertension and CHD

Hypertension is often referred to as the "silent killer" because it produces no obvious symptoms. For this reason, high blood pressure often goes undetected, and routine blood pressure monitoring is extremely important. The measurement of blood pressure includes two readings. *Systolic* blood pressure is the highest pressure that the blood exerts against the arteries. This occurs when the heart is pumping blood. *Diastolic* blood pressure is the lowest amount of pressure that the blood creates against the arteries. This occurs between heartbeats. Generally, hypertension is defined by a systolic reading above 140 and/or a diastolic reading above 90 when measured while the patient is in a relaxed state.

The most notable symptom of CHD is chest pain. Typically, the pain is centralized in the middle of the chest, and it often extends through the left shoulder and down the left arm. In less severe forms of the disorder, the pain that accompanies CHD is mild, or it may be sharp but brief. The pain during more severe forms of CHD such as myocardial infarction typically is so intense that it is crippling. In fact, two-thirds of all deaths from CHD occur within 24 hours of a coronary event (Kamarck & Jennings, 1991). In over half of these sudden deaths, the victim received no previous treatment for CHD, an indication that either there were no warning symptoms or the symptoms were mild enough to have been ignored. Research using portable electrocardiogram monitoring and diary recordings indicates that many episodes of inadequate oxygen supply to the heart occur without the patient's being aware (Krantz et al., 1993; Schneiderman, Chesney, & Krantz, 1989).

## Classification of CVD

Myocardial infarction and angina pectoris are the two major forms of coronary heart disease. *Angina pectoris* involves intermittent chest pains that are usually brought on by some form of exertion. Attacks of angina do not damage the heart, but the chest pain can be a sign of underlying pathology that puts the patient at risk for a myocardial infarction. MI (heart attack) does involve damage to the heart, and as noted, it often causes *sudden cardiac death*, which is usually defined as death within 24 hours of a coronary episode.

Hypertension can be primary or secondary. *Secondary hypertension* results from a known problem such as a diagnosed kidney or endocrine disorder. It is called secondary hypertension because the high blood pressure is secondary to—that is, a consequence of—the principal physical disorder. Primary or **essential hypertension** is the major concern of behavioural medicine and health psychology. In the case of essential hypertension, the high blood pressure is the principal disorder. There is no single, identifiable cause of essential hypertension, which accounts for approximately 85 percent of all cases of high blood pressure. Instead, multiple physical and behavioural risk factors are thought to contribute to the primary disorder, elevated blood pressure.

## Epidemiology of CVD

**Risk Factors for CHD** Epidemiological studies have identified several risk indicators for CHD. Men are twice as likely to suffer from CHD as are women, and sex differences are even greater with more severe forms of the disorder. Age is another major risk factor. For men, risk for CHD increases in a linear fashion with increasing age after 40. For women, risk for CHD accelerates more slowly until they reach menopause and increases sharply afterwards. Rates of CHD also are higher among low-income groups. Finally, a positive family history is also linked to an increased risk for CHD, due at least in part to genetic factors (Jenkins, 1988).

**Behaviour and CHD** In addition to these background factors, several health behaviours have been linked to CHD. Hypertension increases the risk for CHD by a factor of two to four. The risk for CHD also is two to three times greater among those who smoke a pack or more of cigarettes a day. Obesity, a fatty diet, elevated serum cholesterol levels, heavy alcohol consumption, and lack of exercise are also related to an increased risk for CHD (Health Canada, 2003a). Specific risk ratios are difficult to identify for each of these factors, however, because weight, diet, cholesterol, alcohol consumption, and exercise all are closely interrelated (Jenkins, 1988).

**Risk Factors for Hypertension** About 20 to 25 percent of Canadians suffer from hypertension (Joffres et al., 1997), and many of the same risk factors that predict CHD also predict high blood pressure, including genetic factors, a high salt diet, health behaviour, and lifestyle factors. Hypertension is more common in

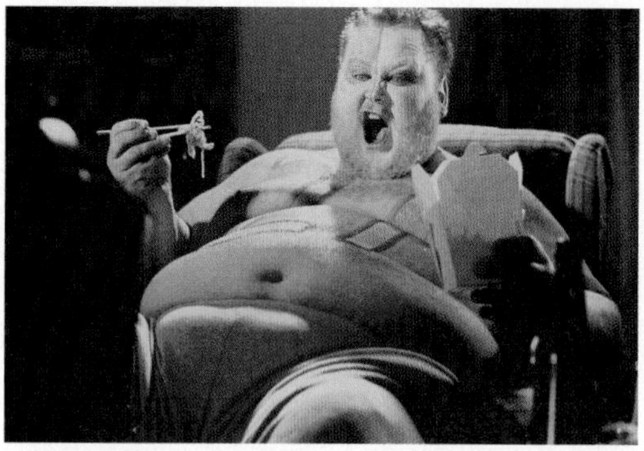

*Heart disease is a lifestyle illness. Obesity, lack of exercise, and a fatty diet all are risk factors for CHD.*

industrialized countries; and is found with greater frequency among low-income groups and people exposed to high levels of chronic life stress (Labronte & Thompson, 1993).

### Etiological Considerations and Research on CVD

**Biological Factors in CVD** The immediate cause of CHD is the deprivation of oxygen to the heart muscle. No permanent damage is caused by the temporary oxygen deprivation (*myocardial ischemia*) that accompanies angina pectoris, but part of the heart muscle dies in cases of myocardial infarction. Oxygen deprivation can be caused by temporarily increased oxygen demands on the heart—for example, as a result of exercise. More problematic is when atherosclerosis causes the gradual deprivation of the flow of blood (and the oxygen it carries) to the heart. *Atherosclerosis* is the thickening of the coronary artery wall that occurs as a result of the accumulation of blood lipids (fats) with age, and which also may be caused by inflammation resulting from stress (Black & Garbutt, 2002). The most dangerous circumstance is when oxygen deprivation is sudden, as occurs in a *coronary occlusion*. Coronary occlusions result either from arteries that are completely blocked by fatty deposits or from blood clots that make their way to the heart muscle.

The immediate biological causes of hypertension are less well understood, as are the more distant biological causes of both hypertension and CHD. As we noted, a positive family history is a risk factor for both hypertension and CHD, and most experts interpret this as a genetic contribution. However, research using animal models of CVD suggests that heritable risk interacts with environmental risk. For example, rats prone to develop hypertension do so only when exposed to salty diets or environmental stress (Schneiderman, Chesney, & Krantz, 1989). Other biological risk factors for CVD, such as obesity and elevated serum cholesterol, involve health behaviours, and therefore we consider them as a part of psychological contributions to the disease.

**Psychological Factors in CVD** The most important of the known psychological contributions to CVD are the wide variety of health behaviours that (1) have a well-documented association with heart disease; (2) decrease the risk for CVD when they are modified; and (3) often are difficult to change. Improved health behaviour—including avoiding or quitting smoking, maintaining a proper weight, following a low-cholesterol diet, exercising frequently, monitoring blood pressure regularly, and taking antihypertensive medication as prescribed—can reduce the risk of heart disease.

Stress also contributes to CVD in two ways. First, stress taxes the cardiovascular system through increased heart rate and blood pressure and can precipitate immediate symptoms or broader episodes of CHD. Second, over the long run, the heart may be damaged by constant stress. In the following sections, we consider four areas of research linking stress to cardiovascular disease: cardiovascular reactivity to stress, actual exposure to life stress, characteristic styles of responding to stress, and depression and anxiety (Krantz et al., 1988; Rozanski et al., 1999).

*Cardiovascular Reactivity to Stress* Increased blood pressure and heart rate are normal reactions to stress, but researchers have long observed that different people exhibit different **cardiovascular reactivity to stress**—greater or lesser increases in blood pressure and heart rate—when they are exposed to stress in the laboratory. Are people who show greater cardiovascular reactivity to stress more likely to develop CVD?

The cardiovascular reactivity hypothesis is increasingly supported by research on patients with CHD (Krantz et al., 1988). Patients with coronary disease show greater cardiovascular reactivity to stress than nonpatients (Corse et al., 1982). In a study of patients with coronary artery disease, patients who reacted to mental stress in the laboratory with greater myocardial ischemia (oxygen deprivation to the heart) had a higher rate of fatal and nonfatal cardiac events over the next five years in comparison to their less reactive counterparts. In fact, mental stress was a better predictor of subsequent cardiac events than was physical stress (exercise testing) (Jiang et al., 1996).

A high-level cardiovascular reactivity will have little effect on an individual if he or she experiences little stress. Because people are exposed to different stressors, real-life stress must also be considered in the equation that predicts CVD.

*Life Stressors and CVD: Job Strain* Considerable evidence indicates that exposure to chronic stress increases risk for cardiovascular disease (Krantz et al., 1988). For example, researchers have linked increased rates of coronary heart disease with high-stress occupations. A stressful job is more than just a demanding job. What appears to be most important is *job strain*, a situation that pairs high psychological demands with a low degree of decisional control (Karasek et al., 1982). A waitress has relatively high demands and low control, for instance, whereas a forest ranger has relatively few demands and a high degree of control. Figure 8–5 portrays a number of occupations and how they vary in terms of psychological demands and decisional control.

Several studies have found a relationship between job strain and CHD (Krantz et al., 1988; Rozanski et al., 1999). For example, among women who participated in the Framingham Heart Study—a major longitudinal study of the development of coronary heart disease—the risk for CHD was one and one-half times higher among those who had high job strain based on objective evaluations of their occupations. The risk was three times higher among women whose self-reports indicated high job strain (LaCroix & Haynes, 1987).

Such strains are not limited to employment, but include work that is performed in other life roles. In an earlier analysis of women in the Framingham study, women who were employed for more than half of their adult lives were no more likely to develop CHD than were homemakers. However, working women with children were more likely to suffer from heart disease. In fact, the risk for CHD increased with the number of children for working women but not for homemakers (Haynes & Feinleib, 1980). This finding echoes the dilemma of contemporary women (and men) who feel strains not only within their occupation but also among their various family roles.

*These stock traders illustrate the Type A behaviour pattern. Type A is a personality style characterized by competitiveness, hostility, urgency, impatience, and achievement striving in response to challenge.*

*Type A Behaviour and Hostility* Characteristic styles of responding to stress may also increase the risk for CVD. In particular, much research has focused on the increased risks associated with the **Type A behaviour pattern**—a competitive, hostile, urgent, impatient, and achievement-striving style of responding to challenge. As originally identified by cardiologists Friedman and Rosenman (1959), the *Type A* individual is a "superachiever" who knows no obstacle to success and who may sacrifice everything for the sake of achievement (Jenkins, 1988). *Type B* individuals, in contrast, are more calm and content. The case of Bob Carter is an example of someone who is Type A; Bob Carter would not allow anything to beat him, including a heart attack.

Friedman and Rosenman developed a structured interview for identifying Type A behaviour. The interviewer not only asks people about their achievement striving, urgency, and hostility but also provokes those very behaviours in the context of a high-stress interview. The classification of Type A based on the interview has predicted CHD in several prospective longitudinal investigations (see Research Methods on p. 291), most notably the Western Collaborative Group Study conducted by Rosenman, Friedman, and colleagues (Booth-Kewley & Friedman, 1987).

Although some studies suggested that Type A was a risk factor for CHD, independent of other risks (e.g., diet), other studies failed to

**Occupational Control and Demand**

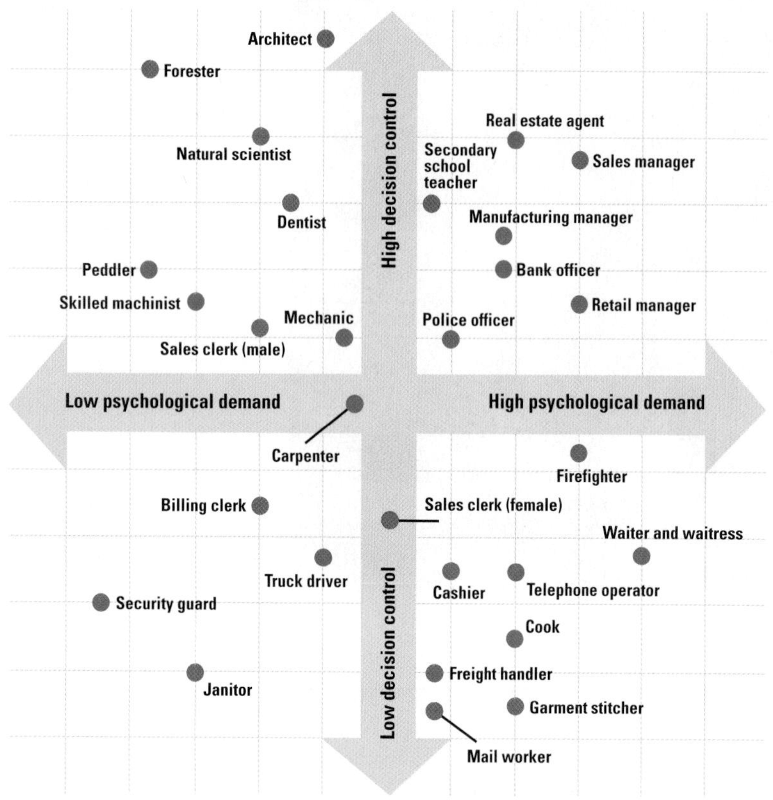


**FIGURE 8–5: Occupations classified according to the degree of demand and control that are associated with them. Jobs with low control and high demands cause more job strain and increased cardiovascular risk.**

*Source:* From R.A. Karasek, 1988. Cited in D.S. Krantz, R.J. Contrada, D.R. Hill, and E. Friedler, Environmental stress and biobehavioral antecedents of coronary heart disease. *Journal of Consulting and Clinical Psychology, 56,* 334.

support this conclusion (Rozanski et al., 1999). One explanation may be that the studies used different research methods, which may have contributed to the conflicting findings. Observation of behaviour is important, as prediction is better when Type A is assessed from a structured interview rather than by self-report questionnaires (Miller et al., 1991). Also, only certain elements of Type A behaviour appear to increase the risk for CHD. In particular, hostility predicts future heart disease better than other aspects of Type A behaviour or the pattern as a whole (Booth-Kewley & Friedman, 1987; Miller et al., 1996; Schneiderman, Chesney, & Krantz, 1989). A Finnish investigation found that three items reliably predicted death among men who had a history of CHD or hypertension: ease with which anger was aroused, argumentativeness, and irritability (Koskenvuo et al., 1988).

Hostility and Type A behaviour interact with both cardiovascular reactivity and exposure to life stress in increasing the risk for heart disease. Evidence indicates that hostile, Type A people exhibit more cardiovascular reactivity to stress than their Type B counterparts (Lyness, 1993). We also can safely assume that hostile, competitive people create and perhaps seek more stress in their lives (Miller et al., 1996).

*Depression and Anxiety* Recent studies have found that depression is three times more common among patients with CHD than in the general population, and longitudinal research indicates that depression predicts future cardiac events (Rozanski et al., 1999). Importantly, the risk for CHD is associated with depressive symptoms, not just clinical depression, but the risk apparently rises with increasing symptoms. Hopelessness is a special problem, and in one study a doubling of the risk of CHD was associated with an affirmative answer to a single question, "Have you felt so sad, discouraged, hopeless or had so many problems that you wondered if anything was worthwhile?" (Anda et al., 1993).

Researchers also have recently tied CHD to anxiety symptoms, although anxiety seems to be associated with only one, crucial aspect of CHD: sudden cardiac death (Rozanski et al., 1999). The link between anxiety, depression, and CHD is just beginning to be studied systematically. Poor health behaviour appears to explain part of the link between CHD and these emotional problems.

**Social Factors in CVD** As you may recognize from your own life, social support from friends and family members, as well as from professionals, can encourage a healthy—or an unhealthy—lifestyle (Pennix et al., 1997). Interpersonal conflict obviously is a source of much of the anger and hostility that can increase the risk for coronary heart disease. In fact, research demonstrates that economic resources, being married, and/or having a close confidant all predict a more positive prognosis among patients with coronary artery disease (R.B. Williams et al., 1992). Finally, cross-cultural differences in the epidemiology of CVD surely are influenced by a range of societal values, such as attitudes about health behaviours like smoking and cultural norms about competition in the workplace.

## RESEARCH METHODS

### Longitudinal Research Designs

The **longitudinal study** is one research design that allows researchers to make stronger inferences about causation from a correlational study. Subjects are studied over time in a longitudinal study, an approach that contrasts with the more common **cross-sectional study** in which subjects are studied only at one point in time. The basic goal of a longitudinal study is to determine whether hypothesized causes come before their assumed effects. We know that causes must precede effects in time. For example, if we can demonstrate that stress comes before heart disease in longitudinal research, it would help scientists to rule out the alternative interpretation (reverse causality), that the illness caused the stress.

A major liability of a longitudinal study is higher cost. It is much less expensive to study both stress and heart disease at one point in time than it is to assess stress now and heart disease as it develops over the next 10 years. One way around this problem is to use the *retrospective study*. In this research design, scientists look backwards in time either by asking subjects to recall past events or by examining records from the past. The retrospective method is inexpensive, but it is of limited value because of distorted memories and limited records.

The **longitudinal design** (sometimes called a **prospective design**) is a more effective and more expensive alternative to the retrospective method. In longitudinal research, supposed causes are assessed in the present, and subjects are then followed to see if the hypothesized effects develop over time. Using the longitudinal method, scientists can assess a range of possible predictors more thoroughly and more objectively than in follow-back studies. Scientists can use standardized tests to measure a wide variety of personality characteristics, such as Type A behaviour or another characteristic called "defensiveness" (socially desirable impression management), to study participants over time. To illustrate, in a three-year longitudinal study, researchers from the University of British Columbia found evidence that defensiveness predicts greater physiological reaction to stress, which in turn leads to higher blood pressure (Rutledge & Linden, 2003).

Researchers use both retrospective and longitudinal methods in studying health and illness and abnormal psychology in general. When you learn that a finding was supported in longitudinal research, you can have greater confidence in the investigator's hypothesis about causality than if the research were cross-sectional. Remember, however, that correlation does not mean causation, even in a longitudinal study. It remains possible that the supposed "cause" and the "effect" both result from some third variable. For example, a researcher might find that Type A behaviour measured at one point in time predicts heart disease several years later. But chronic job stress may cause both the Type A behaviour and the heart disease. Scientists need to use many different types of research methods in order to establish causation. And you need to understand the strengths and weaknesses of research methods, not just the results of a single study, in order to be an informed consumer of scientific information. ◆

Experts recognize the importance of interpersonal and societal influences on CVD and on physical health in general. A multitude of efforts have been directed toward structuring the *social ecology*—the interrelations between the individual and the social world—in such a way as to promote health (Stokols, 1992). As a child, you were exposed to many of these efforts, such as antismoking campaigns or the awards given in school for physical fitness. Health promotion is a common message in the media, and more and more employers also are encouraging health maintenance. Do these broad-scale efforts work? We address this question and other issues in treating CVD, after briefly discussing the integration of risk factors.

**Integration and Alternative Pathways** CVD is an excellent example of the value of the systems approach for understanding both physical and psychological disorders. In considering this integrative perspective, let us return to the analogy between the functioning of the cardiovascular system and an automobile. Some cars are built for high performance, some for economy. Some are defective when they leave the factory. Whatever its original condition, a car's state of repair is affected by how it is driven and how it is maintained. Similarly, CVD is caused by a combination of genetic makeup, an occasional structural defect, maintenance in the form of health behaviour, and how hard the heart is driven by stress, depression, coping, and societal standards.

Much progress has been made in identifying biological, psychological, and social risk factors for CVD. An important goal for future research is to integrate knowledge across risk factors (Kop, 1999). Numerous questions need to be addressed. For example, how do cardiovascular reactivity and the experience of life stress interact in producing risk? How do we distinguish the effects of stress as an immediate, precipitating cause of CHD from its cumulative effects on health over long periods of time? To what extent are the risks associated with stress caused by poor health behaviour and not by stress itself? What are the alternative pathways to the development of CHD? What protects those individuals who do not become ill, even when they are exposed to multiple risk factors?

## Prevention and Treatment of Cardiovascular Disease

Several medications known as *antihypertensives* are effective treatments for reducing high blood pressure. Other drugs, called *beta blockers*, reduce the risk of myocardial infarction or sudden coronary death following a cardiac episode (Johnston, 1989). Still other biomedical interventions reduce the risk factors associated with CVD. For example, serum cholesterol can be lowered with medication.

Because many of the risk factors for CVD are linked with health behaviour, it may be possible to reduce or prevent heart disease with psychological intervention (Rozanski et al., 1999). In the following sections, we consider efforts to alter lifestyle and to lower the risk for heart disease in terms of the three levels of intervention introduced in Chapter 3: primary, secondary, and tertiary prevention.

**Primary Prevention** Numerous public service advertisements attempt to prevent CVD by encouraging people to quit smoking, eat well, exercise, monitor their blood pressure, and otherwise improve their health behaviour. Most of these familiar efforts have not been evaluated systematically, although some evidence suggests that such campaigns can be effective in changing some risk factors, such as improving diet and lowering serum cholesterol (Farquhar et al., 1977).

*A graphic health warning on a pack of cigarettes sold in Canada. In 2000, the Canadian government approved such warnings, the first country in the world to take such an aggressive anti-smoking stance.*

**Secondary Prevention** The treatment of essential hypertension is one of the most important attempts at the secondary prevention of CHD, because hypertension is a significant risk factor for heart disease. Treatments of hypertension fall into two categories. One focuses on improving health behaviour, and the other emphasizes **stress management**—attempts to teach more effective coping skills.

Improvements in health behaviour—including weight reduction, decreased alcohol consumption, and reduced intake of dietary salt—can help lower blood pressure. For many patients these behavioural changes eliminate the need for taking antihypertensive medication (Johnston, 1989). What is less clear is the extent to which psychological intervention brings about improvements in health behaviour. Available evidence suggests that psychological intervention is minimally effective at best, in part because many attempts to change health behaviour are weak or poorly constructed. For example, physicians may simply encourage their patients to lose weight or give them educational pamphlets to read. More intensive treatments appear to be more effective in changing health behaviour, although more research is needed on their effectiveness (Dusseldorp et al., 1999).

The major form of stress management used to treat hypertension is behaviour therapy, particularly relaxation training (see Chapter 3) and biofeedback. **Biofeedback** uses laboratory equipment to monitor physiological processes that generally occur outside conscious awareness and to provide the patient with conscious feedback about these processes. Blood pressure may be displayed on a video screen, for example, so that increases or decreases are readily apparent to the patient.

Biofeedback is based on the theory that people can learn to control the functions of their autonomic nervous system. This is an innovation conceptually and practically, because the functions of the autonomic nervous system traditionally have been viewed as uncontrollable, as conveyed by the term *autonomic*. During biofeedback, the patient can experiment with various coping strategies—for example, imagining lying on a beach—and observe whether the techniques are successful in lowering heart rate or blood pressure.

Both relaxation training and biofeedback produce reliable, short-term reductions in blood pressure. Unfortunately, the reductions are small, often temporary, and considerably less than those produced by antihypertensive medications (Andrews et al., 1984). Although these stress management treatments occasionally may be a useful adjunct to medication, currently they are not an alternative. In particular, the viability of biofeedback has not been supported by empirical evidence, and some well-respected investigators have suggested that this technique should be abandoned altogether as a treatment for hypertension (Johnston, 1989).

The Trials of Hypertension Prevention (TOHP) is an important ongoing study of whether stress management and health behaviour interventions succeed in lowering high blood pressure (TOHP Collaborative Research Group, 1992). In this investigation, more than 2000 women and men with hypertension were randomly assigned to one of seven different treatments. Treatments included three lifestyle interventions—weight reduction, sodium (salt) reduction, and stress management—plus four nutritional supplement conditions. Group meetings were held over several weeks for the three lifestyle interventions. In the nutrition conditions, the patient's ordinary diet was supplemented with dietary agents hypothesized to lower blood pressure: either calcium, magnesium, potassium, or fish oil. Results from Phase I of the study indicated that only the weight reduction and the salt reduction programs were successful in lowering blood pressure over a follow-up period of up to 1½ years. Neither stress management nor any of the dietary supplements produced beneficial effects on blood pressure. Findings from Phase II of the TOHP underscored the importance only of weight loss, as even a modest reduction in weight lowered produced clinically significant reductions in blood pressure (Stevens et al., 2001).

Other attempts at the secondary prevention of CHD have tried to change several health behaviours at once rather than focusing on hypertension alone. The Multiple Risk Factor Intervention Trial (MRFIT) is another important investigation. In this study, over 12 000 men with a high risk for developing CHD were assigned at random to intervention and control groups, and the effectiveness of intervention was evaluated over time. Carefully developed intervention programs, including both education and social support, produced improved health behaviour, including reduced smoking and lower serum cholesterol. However, the men randomly assigned to the treatment groups did not have a lower incidence of heart disease than the men in the control group during the seven years following intervention (MRFIT, 1982). An encouraging interpretation of this discouraging outcome is that the failure to find a treatment effect may have been due to the improved health behaviour of the men in the control group. The control group had a lower disease rate than was expected based on their risk indicators, and the study was conducted during a time when the public's concern with health had increased dramatically.

**Tertiary Prevention** Tertiary prevention of CHD targets patients who have already had a cardiac event, typically an MI. The hope is to reduce the incidence of recurrence of the illness. Exercise programs are probably the most common treatment recommended for MI patients, but evidence of their effectiveness is limited (Johnston, 1989). Some evidence suggests that carefully implemented exercise training programs can reduce the risk for cardiovascular death for up to three years (O'Connor et al., 1989). A recent meta-analysis by psychologist Wolfgang Linden and colleagues at the University of British Columbia suggests that psychosocial interventions—such as cognitive therapy for reducing anxiety or anger, and stress management programs—are useful interventions in cardiac rehabilitation (Linden, Stossel, & Maurice, 1996). These interventions were found to reduce emotional distress, blood pressure, heart rate, and cholesterol level, and were associated with a lower incidence of subsequent MIs. The researchers recommended that psychosocial treatments be routinely used in cardiac rehabilitation programs. Some of the more promising psychosocial interventions are reviewed below.

Treatment programs may dramatically reduce death rates if they are individualized and target multiple health behaviours (Frasure-Smith & Prince, 1985). One patient may benefit from entering a smoking reduction program, a second may be helped by a stress reduction workshop, and a third may be assisted by exercise classes. Together, the findings on successful programs underscore the need to offer behavioural medicine programs that are both highly structured and carefully tailored to the individual. Handing out educational pamphlets or delivering stern lectures in the physician's office does little to alter health behaviour, as we saw in the case of Bob Carter. Some of the most optimistic evidence on the treatment of CHD comes from studies of interventions designed to alter the Type A behaviour pattern (Friedman et al., 1986), a somewhat surprising circumstance given the controversies about the risk research on Type A we discussed earlier. Intervention with Type A individuals following myocardial infarction is multifaceted. For example, it includes **role playing**—improvisational play acting—to teach patients how to respond to stressful interactions with reduced hostility. In role playing, cardiac patients act out their usual responses to such situations as dealing with a bothersome subordinate, and the therapist models alternative, less hostile means of responding to the frustration. In subsequent role plays, the patients try out the new way of coping. Cognitive therapy designed to alter faulty thought patterns also is a part of the intervention with Type A cardiac patients (Thoresen & Powell, 1992). For example, clinicians may use cognitive therapy to challenge patients' beliefs about their self-worth and professional goals (see Chapter 3). At some level, for example, Bob Carter probably believed that he *must* be the best at everything he did in life. One goal of cognitive therapy is to help patients like Bob to develop beliefs and goals that are more realistic—and healthy.

Although evidence is not definitive, studies suggest that Type A behaviour can be modified, and this may reduce the subsequent risk for CHD (Nunes, Frank, & Kornfeld, 1987; Thoresen & Powell, 1992). One study of nearly 600 patients found that stress management training reduced the annual incidence of cardiac events by almost 50 percent in comparison to 300 patients who received standard medical care (Friedman et al., 1986). Importantly, subjects who showed the greatest reduction in Type A behaviour were four times less likely to experience a myocardial infarction during the following two years.

As a final note, we should mention that some valuable treatments focus on the *effects* of heart disease on life stress rather than the other way around. Cardiac patients and their families can be helped to cope more effectively with the social and psychological consequences of having a heart attack, including depression, anxiety, restricted activities, and changes in sexuality, marriage, and family relationships (Johnston, 1985). Since depression is a risk factor for future cardiac illness (Carney et al., 1995), such interventions may, in turn, help to improve the patient's physical health. The link between stress and physical health clearly is a reciprocal one.

# Summary

The DSM-IV-TR no longer contains a list of **psychosomatic disorders**, because every physical illness is a product of the interaction between the psyche and soma, mind and body. This holistic view has influenced both psychology and medicine, as is evidenced by the rapid development of **behavioural medicine**, a multidisciplinary field that investigates psychological factors in physical illness.

**Stress** is a challenging event that requires physiological, cognitive, or behavioural adaptation, but scientists disagree about whether stress is best defined in terms of a life event or the individual's **primary appraisal** of the event and **secondary appraisal** of their coping resources. Despite this controversy, much is known about people's reactions to stress. The **fight or flight response** is a reaction to a threat that is activated by stress and is characterized by intense arousal of the sympathetic nervous system. The **general adaptation syndrome (GAS)** is a more global response to stress that includes the stages of alarm, resistance, and exhaustion. Both responses are mediated by activation of the HPA axis and the secretion of hormones from the adrenal gland, including adrenalin (epinephrine) and **cortisol**. Recent research on **psychoneuroimmunology (PNI)** has identified yet another physiological consequence of stress—less adequate functioning of the immune system.

**Coping** with stress may involve **problem-focused coping**, which is an attempt to change the stressor, or **emotion-focused coping**, which is an attempt to alter distress internally. Predictability and control are other key cognitive evaluations that can greatly facilitate coping, as are having outlets for frustration and **optimism**.

Poor **health behaviour** can be an important consequence of stress, including a decrease in positive actions (e.g., exercise) or an increase in negative actions (e.g., alcohol consumption). Illness behaviour, behaving as if you were sick, also is stress related. Finally, it is clear that illness can cause stress, as well as stress causing illness.

Infectious diseases were the most common causes of death in industrialized countries in 1900, but lifestyle plays a central role in the top causes of death today. Cancer would seem to be a purely biological illness, but behaviour contributes to cancer through exposure to some carcinogens, health behaviour, social support in coping with the illness, and perhaps through effects on immune functioning. **Acquired immune deficiency syndrome (AIDS)** is caused by the **human immunodeficiency virus (HIV)**, which is transmitted through risky behaviours, such as unprotected sex and shared hypodermic needles. Psychologists also work to help people cope with chronic pain, most notably through pain management programs. More attention also is being paid to **primary sleep disorders**

A leading killer in Canada today is **cardiovascular disease (CVD)**, which includes **essential hypertension** (high blood pressure) and **coronary heart disease (CHD)**. CHD includes **myocardial infarction** (MI or heart attack). Several health behaviours have been linked to CVD, and other psychological factors may also contribute to CVD. These include **cardiovascular reactivity**, responses to stressors presented in a laboratory; chronic stressors in real life (e.g., job strain); the hostility component of the Type A behaviour pattern; and depression and anxiety.

Primary prevention of CHD includes attempts to encourage people to improve their health behaviour. The treatment of hypertension through improved **health behaviour**, or **stress management**, is one of the more important attempts at the secondary prevention of CHD. Tertiary prevention of CHD targets patients who have already had a cardiac event—for example, attempting to modify their Type A behaviour. Stress management is also used in tertiary prevention.

# Critical Thinking

1. What are the major sources of stress in your life? How are you affected by this stress? In what ways is stress helpful and in what ways is it harmful?
2. How do you typically cope with stress? Do you ever write about difficult experiences? Do you believe this is helpful? What are your theories about effective and ineffective coping? How would you test your theories in research?
3. Lawyers and politicians question who is responsible for some unhealthy lifestyles. For example, cigarette companies have been sued by people with lung cancer. Is the company responsible, or is the smoker? What is society's responsibility for altering unhealthy lifestyles?
4. How much have you been influenced by public service campaigns or other messages to lead a healthier life? Safe sex campaigns have been targeted particularly toward young people. Have these programs affected your attitudes? Your behaviour?

# Key Terms

**acquired immune deficiency syndrome (AIDS)** 284
**behavioural medicine** 269
**biofeedback** 292
**cardiovascular disease (CVD)** 286
**cardiovascular reactivity to stress** 288
**coping** 269
**coronary heart disease (CHD)** 286
**cortisol** 274
**cross-sectional study** 291
**emotion-focused coping** 276
**essential hypertension** 287
**fight or flight response** 273
**general adaptation syndrome (GAS)** 276
**health behaviour** 279
**health psychologists** 269
**human immunodeficiency virus (HIV)** 284
**hypertension** 286
**longitudinal design** 291
**longitudinal study** 291
**myocardial infarction (MI)** 286
**optimism** 278
**primary appraisal** 272
**primary sleep disorder** 285
**problem-focused coping** 276
**prospective design** 291
**psychoneuroimmunology (PNI)** 275
**psychosomatic disorders** 280
**role playing** 294
**secondary appraisal** 272
**stress** 269
**stress management** 292
**tend and befriend** 273
**Type A behaviour pattern** 289

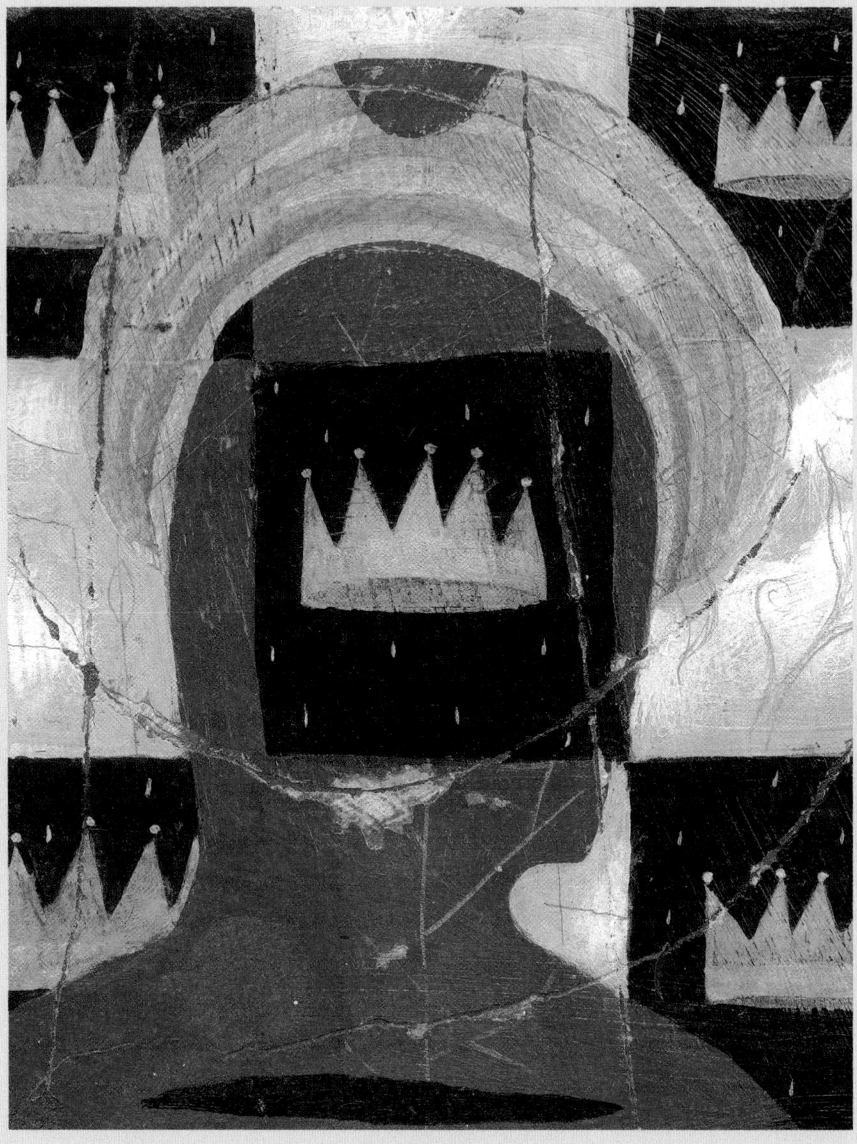

# 9 Personality Disorders

Overview
Typical Symptoms and Associated Features
Classification
Epidemiology
Schizotypal Personality Disorder (SPD)
Borderline Personality Disorder (BPD)
Antisocial Personality Disorder (ASPD)
Dependent Personality Disorder (DPD)

**What is the difference between being eccentric and having a personality disorder?**

**How are normal personality traits related to personality disorders?**

**Do personality disorders set the stage for the later onset of other mental disorders?**

**Why are personality disorders so difficult to treat?**

People are social organisms. Reproduction and survival depend on successful, cooperative interactions with other people. We form social alliances for many purposes, such as raising families, doing our jobs, and living in a community. We also compete with others, and in some cases we have to protect ourselves from others. These relationships are governed by a variety of psychological mechanisms that, taken together, constitute our personalities. **Personality** refers to enduring patterns of thinking and behaviour that define the person and distinguish him or her from other people. Included in these patterns are ways of expressing emotion as well as patterns of thinking about ourselves and other people. For the most part, personality serves as the glue that anchors and facilitates interactions with other people. But it can also go awry. When enduring patterns of behaviour and emotion bring the person into repeated conflict with others, and when they prevent the person from maintaining close relationships with others, an individual's personality may be considered disordered.

The dividing line between eccentricity and personality pathology is difficult to define. We all have our quirks and idiosyncrasies, and there are many different ways to manage relationships with other people. For example, it is often helpful to be skeptical of the things that other people do and say. When does a tendency to be suspicious of other people's motives cross the line into paranoid personality disorder? Self-confidence is another admirable quality, but it can lead to problems if it escalates into full-blown grandiosity. In many ways, the distinctions among healthy traits, eccentricity, and personality pathology depend on the person's ability to adapt to the demands of different situations. Variety and flexibility in interpersonal behaviour are undoubtedly helpful. People with personality disorders can make their own social problems worse (often unwittingly) by persistently responding in ways that do not suit the social challenges that they face.

## Overview

Personality disorders are considered separately from other forms of psychopathology in DSM-IV-TR. Most clinical disorders are listed on Axis I, whereas the personality disorders are listed on Axis II. All of the personality disorders are based on extreme personality traits that are frequently disturbing or annoying to other people.

In order to qualify for a personality disorder diagnosis in DSM-IV-TR, a person must fit the *general definition* of personality disorder (which applies to all 10 subtypes) and must also meet the *specific criteria* for a particular type of personality disorder. The specific criteria consist of a list of traits that characterize the disorder. The general definition of **personality**

**disorder** presented in DSM-IV-TR emphasizes the duration of the pattern and the social impairment associated with the traits in question. The problems must be part of an enduring pattern of inner experience and behaviour that deviates markedly from the expectations of the individual's culture. The pattern must be evident in two or more of the following domains: cognition (such as ways of thinking about the self and other people), emotional responses, interpersonal functioning, or impulse control. This pattern of maladaptive experience and behaviour must also be:

- Inflexible and pervasive across a broad range of personal and social situations
- The source of clinically significant distress or impairment in social, occupational, or other important areas of functioning
- Stable and of long duration, with an onset that can be traced back at least to adolescence or early adulthood

The concept of social dysfunction plays an important role in the definition of personality disorders. It provides a large part of the justification for defining these problems as mental disorders. If the personality characteristics identified in DSM-IV-TR criterion sets typically interfere with the person's ability to get along with other people and perform social roles, they become more than just a collection of eccentric traits or peculiar habits. In fact, most of the clusters of pathological personality traits that are described on Axis II do lead to impaired social functioning or occupational impairment (Oltmanns, Melley, & Turkheimer, 2002).

*Hockey commentator Don Cherry is well-known for his unusual, attention-getting style of dress and for his opinionated, colourful language. Attention seeking is usually not considered abnormal when it is voluntary, especially when it is part of the entertainment industry.*

The personality disorders are among the most controversial categories in the diagnostic system for mental disorders (Clark, Livesley, & Morey, 1997; Kendell, 2002). They are difficult to identify reliably, their etiology is poorly understood, and there is relatively little evidence to indicate that they can be treated successfully. There are some discrepancies between DSM-IV-TR and ICD-10, its European counterpart, in their descriptions of these problems. For example, one type of personality disorder in the DSM system, narcissistic, is not included in ICD-10. For all of these reasons, you should think critically about the validity of these categories.

Although they are difficult to define and measure, personality disorders are also crucial concepts in the field of psychopathology. Several observations support this argument. First, personality disorders are associated with significant social and occupational impairment. They disrupt interpersonal relationships in families and in the workplace. University of British Columbia psychologist Donald Dutton, for example, found that borderline personality traits in men play an important role in many cases of marital violence (Dutton, 1995).

Second, the presence of pathological personality traits during adolescence is associated with an increased risk for the subsequent development of other mental disorders (Johnson et al., 1999; Krueger, 1999). Negative emotionality (high neuroticism) often predicts the later onset of major depression or an anxiety disorder. Impulsivity and antisocial personality increase the person's risk for alcoholism. Third, the presence of a comorbid personality disorder can interfere with the treatment of a disorder such as depression (Mulder, 2002).

The following cases illustrate several of the most important features of personality disorders. Our first case is an example of antisocial personality disorder, which is defined in terms of a pervasive and persistent disregard for, and frequent violation of, the rights of other people. This 21-year-old man was described by Hervey Cleckley (1976) in his classic treatise on this topic. The man had been referred to Cleckley by his parents and his lawyer after his most recent arrest for stealing. The parents hoped that their son might avoid a long prison sentence if Cleckley decided that he was suffering from a mental disorder.

Notice that the fundamental features of Tom's problems were clearly evident by early

## CASE STUDY A Car Thief's Antisocial Personality Disorder

Tom looks and is in robust physical health. His manner and appearance are pleasing. In his face a prospective employer would be likely to see strong indications of character as well as high incentive and ability. He is well informed, alert, and entirely at ease, exhibiting a confidence in himself that the observer is likely to consider amply justified. This does not look like the sort of man who will fail or flounder about in the tasks of life but like someone incompatible with all such thoughts.

In childhood, Tom appeared to be a reliable and manly fellow but could never be counted upon to keep at any task or to give a straight account of any situation. He was frequently truant from school. No advice or persuasion deterred him from his acts, despite his excellent response in all discussions. Though he was generously provided for, he stole some of his father's chickens from time to time, selling them at stores downtown. Pieces of table silver would be missed. These were sometimes recovered from those to whom he had sold them for a pittance or swapped them for odds and ends that seemed to hold no particular interest or value for him. He resented and seemed eager to avoid punishment, but no modification in his behaviour resulted from it. He did not seem wild or particularly impulsive, a victim of high temper or uncontrollable drives. There was nothing to indicate he was subject to unusually strong temptations, lured by definite plans for high adventure and exciting revolt.

He lied so plausibly and with such utter equanimity devised such ingenious alibis or simply denied all responsibility with such convincing appearances of candour that for many years his real career was poorly estimated. Among typical exploits with which he is credited stand these: prankish defecation into the stringed intricacies of the school piano, the removal from his uncle's automobile of a carburetor for which he got 75 cents, and the selling of his father's overcoat to a passing buyer of scrap materials.

At 14 or 15 years of age, having learned to drive, Tom began to steal automobiles with some regularity. Often his intention seemed less that of theft than of heedless misappropriation. A neighbour or friend of the family, going to the garage or to where the car was parked outside an office building, would find it missing. Sometimes the patient would leave the stolen vehicle within a few blocks or miles of the owner, sometimes out on the road where the gasoline had given out. After he had tried to sell a stolen car, his father consulted advisers and, on the theory that he might have some specific craving for automobiles, bought one for him as a therapeutic measure. On one occasion while out driving, he deliberately parked his own car and, leaving it, stole an inferior model that he left slightly damaged on the outskirts of a village some miles away.

Private physicians, scoutmasters, and social workers were consulted. They talked and worked with him, but to no avail. Listing the deeds for which he became ever more notable does not give an adequate picture of the situation. He did not every day or every week bring attention to himself by major acts of mischief or destructiveness. He was usually polite, often considerate in small, appealing ways, and always seemed to have learned his lesson after detection and punishment. He was clever and learned easily. During intervals in which his attendance was regular, he impressed his teachers as outstanding in ability. Some charm and apparent modesty, as well as his very convincing way of seeming sincere and to have taken resolutions that would count, kept not only the parents but all who encountered him clinging to hope. Teachers, scoutmasters, the school principal, and others recognized that in some very important respects he differed from the ordinary bad or wayward youth. They made special efforts to help him and to give him new opportunities to reform or readjust.

When he drove a stolen automobile across a state line, he came in contact with federal authorities. In view of his youth and the wonderful impression he made, he was put on probation. Soon afterward he took another automobile and again left it in the adjoining state. It was a very obvious situation. The consequences could not have been entirely overlooked by a person of his excellent shrewdness. He admitted that the considerable risks of getting caught had occurred to him but felt he had a chance to avoid detection and would take it. No unusual and powerful motive or any special aim could be brought out as an explanation.

Tom was sent to a federal institution in a distant state where a well-organized program of rehabilitation and guidance was available. He soon impressed authorities at this place with his attitude and in the way he discussed his past mistakes and plans for a different future. He seemed to merit parole status precociously and this was awarded him. It was not long before he began stealing again and thereby lost his freedom (Cleckley, 1976, pp. 64–67). ◆

adolescence, and they were exhibited consistently over an extended period of time. The stable, long-standing nature of personality disorders is one of their most characteristic features. In this way, they are distinguished from many other forms of abnormal behaviour that are episodic in nature.

This case is an excellent example of the senseless nature of the illegal and immoral acts committed by people who meet the diagnostic criteria for antisocial personality disorder. Another puzzling feature of this disorder is the person's apparent lack of remorse and the inability to learn from experience that accompany such a history of delinquent behaviour. It is difficult to understand why someone would behave in this manner. Psychopathologists appeal to the notion of personality disorder to help them understand these irrational behaviours.

The case of Tom also illustrates some other important features of personality disorders. Most other forms of mental disorder, such as anxiety disorders and mood disorders, are ego-dystonic; that is, people with these disorders are distressed by their symptoms and uncomfortable with their situations. Personality disorders are usually *ego-syntonic*—the ideas or impulses with which they are associated are acceptable to the person. People with personality disorders frequently do not see themselves as being disturbed. We might also say that they do not have insight into the nature of their own problems. Tom did not believe that his repeated antisocial behaviour represented a problem. The other people for whom he created problems were suffering, but he was not. Many forms of personality disorder are defined primarily in terms of the problems that these people create for others rather than in terms of their own distress.

## Typical Symptoms and Associated Features

The specific symptoms that are used to define personality disorders represent maladaptive variations in several of the building blocks of personality (see Chapter 2). These include motives, perspectives regarding the self and others, temperament and personality traits. We have organized our description of typical symptoms around these issues, which run through the broad mixture of specific symptoms that define the 10 types of personality disorder included in DSM-IV-TR.

### Social Motivation

The concept of *motive* refers to a person's desires and goals (Emmons, 1997). Motives (either conscious or unconscious) describe the way that the person would like things to be, and they help to explain *why* people behave in a particular fashion. For example, a man might have neglected to return a telephone call because he wanted to be alone (rather than because he forgot that someone had called). Two of the most important motives in understanding human personality are *affiliation*—the desire for close relationships with other people—and *power*—the desire for impact, prestige, or dominance (Winter et al., 1998). Individual differences with regard to these motives have an important influence on a person's health and adjustment.

Many of the symptoms of personality disorders can be described in terms of maladaptive variations with regard to needs for affiliation and power. One particularly important issue is the absence of motivation for affiliation. While most people enjoy spending time with other people and want to develop intimate relationships with friends and family members, some people do not. They prefer isolation. Severely diminished or absent motivation for social relationships is one pervasive theme that serves to define certain kinds of personality disorder.

Exaggerated motivation for power (and achievement) also contributes to the picture that describes personality disorders. For example, some people are preoccupied with a need for admiration and the praise of others. They think of themselves as privileged people and insist on special treatment. In some cases, excessive devotion to work and professional accomplishment can lead a person to ignore friends and family members as well as the pursuit of leisure activities. This lack of balance can have a serious disruptive effect on the person's social adjustment.

**Cognitive Perspectives Regarding Self and Others** Our social world also depends on mental processes that determine knowledge of ourselves and other people (Baumeister, 1997). Distortions of these mechanisms are associated with personality disorders. For example, one central issue involves our image of ourselves. When you are able to maintain a realistic and stable image of yourself, you can plan, negotiate, and evaluate your relationships with other people. Knowing (and having confidence in) your own values and opinions is a necessary prerequisite for making independent decisions without the assistance or reassurance of others. Self-image is also intimately connected to mood states. If you vacillate back and forth between unrealistically positive and negative views of yourself, your mood will swing dramatically. You may also need constant reassurance from others and be too dependent on their opinions as a means of maintaining your own self-esteem. We have to be able to evaluate our own importance. Of course, it's useful to think of yourself in positive terms (and many maintain a positive "halo"), but extreme grandiosity can be disruptive. Perhaps even more damaging is a pattern in which people see themselves as socially inept or inferior to other people.

When we misperceive the intentions and motives and abilities of other people, our relationships can be severely disturbed. Paranoid beliefs are one example. Some people believe, without good reason, that other people are exploiting, deceiving, or otherwise trying to harm them. Unreasonable fears of being abandoned, criticized, or rejected are also examples of distorted perception of others' intentions. Working effectively in a group of people also requires realistic appraisal of the talents and abilities of others. In order to cooperate with other people, we must be able to appreciate their competence. People with personality disorders run into problems because they misperceive other people in many different ways (as being either threatening, or uncaring, or incompetent).

Many elements of social interaction also depend on being able to evaluate the nature of our relationships with other people and then to make accurate judgments about appropriate and inappropriate behaviours. A successful relationship with a sexual partner involves knowing when intimacy is expected and when it should be avoided. Some people with personality disorders experience persistent problems in social distance (either becoming too intimate or maintaining too much distance from others). Finally, another important element of interpersonal perception is the ability to empathize with others—to anticipate and decipher their emotional reactions and use that knowledge to guide our own behaviour. Deficits in the ability to understand the emotions of other people represent one of the core features of personality disorders.

## Temperament and Personality Traits

If motivation helps to explain *why* people behave in certain ways, temperament and personality traits describe *how* they behave. *Temperament* refers to a person's most basic, characteristic styles of relating to the world, especially those styles that are evident during the first year of life (Rothbart & Bates, 1997). Definitions of temperament typically include dimensions such as activity level and emotional reactivity. These factors vary considerably in level or degree from one infant to the next and have important implications for later development, such as social and academic adjustment when the child eventually enters school. For example, children who demonstrate a "lack of control" when they are very young are much more likely than their peers to experience problems with hyperactivity, distractibility, and conduct disorder when they are adolescents (Caspi et al., 1995). Young children who are extremely shy are more likely to be anxious and socially inhibited in subsequent years (Eisenberg et al., 1998) (see Chapter 16).

Experts disagree about the basic dimensions of temperament and personality. Some theories are relatively simple, using only three or four dimensions. Others are more complicated and consider as many as 30 or 40 traits. One point of view that has come to be widely accepted is known as the *five-factor model* of personality (Digman, 2002; Trull & McCrae, 2002). The basic traits (also known as *domains*) included in this model have already been summarized in Chapter 2. They are neuroticism, extraversion, openness to experience, agreeableness, and conscientiousness. Each of the five principal domains can be subdivided into six more specific elements or facets (see Table 9–1). Taken as a whole, the five-factor model provides a relatively comprehensive description of any person's behaviour.

Many personality disorders are defined in terms of maladaptive variations on the kinds of traits listed in Table 9–1 (Widiger et al.,

*Is this young Afghan woman more extroverted than the others? Is she a risk-taker? It is impossible to make these personality judgments without more knowledge of the culture in which she lives. She may be unveiled because she is younger than the other women, or because she is not married.*

**TABLE 9–1 Domains and Facets of the Five-Factor Model of Personality**

| **Neuroticism** | ***People with High Scores Are:*** | ***People with Low Scores Are:*** |
|---|---|---|
| Anxiousness | extremely nervous | lack appropriate anxiety |
| Angry–Hostility | hypersensitive; easily angered | unable to express anger |
| Depressiveness | continually depressed | unable to appreciate losses |
| Self-Consciousness | very easily embarrassed | indifferent to opinions of others |
| Impulsiveness | extremely impulsive | restrained or restricted; dull |
| Vulnerability | easily overwhelmed by stress | oblivious to danger |
| **Extraversion** | | |
| Warmth | inappropriately affectionate | can't develop intimate relations |
| Gregariousness | unable to tolerate being alone | socially isolated |
| Assertiveness | domineering, pushy | resigned and ineffective |
| Activity | driven; frantic; distractible | sedentary and passive |
| Excitement Seeking | reckless; careless | dull; monotonous |
| Positive Emotions | giddy; lose control of emotions | solemn; unable to enjoy things |
| **Openness to Experience** | | |
| Fantasy | preoccupied with daydreams | imagination tends to be sterile |
| Aesthetics | obsessed with unusual interests | don't appreciate culture or art |
| Feelings | governed by strong emotionality | seldom have strong feelings |
| Actions | unpredictable | avoid change; stick to routine |
| Ideas | preoccupied with strange ideas | reject new ideas |
| Values | lack guiding belief systems | dogmatic and closed minded |
| **Agreeableness** | | |
| Trust | gullible | paranoid and suspicious |
| Straightforwardness | too self-disclosing | dishonest and manipulative |
| Altruism | often exploited or victimized | no regard for rights of others |
| Compliance | acquiescent; docile; submissive | argumentative; defiant |
| Modesty | meek and self-denigrating | conceited; arrogant; pompous |
| Tendermindedness | overwhelmed by others' pain | callous; coldhearted; ruthless |
| **Conscientiousness** | | |
| Competence | overly perfectionistic | lax; incapable of work |
| Order | preoccupied with rules, order | disorganized; sloppy |
| Dutifulness | places duty above morality | not dependable; unreliable |
| Achievement Striving | workaholic | aimless; no clear goals |
| Self-Discipline | single-minded pursuit of goals | hedonistic; self-indulgent |
| Deliberation | ruminate to excess | makes careless decisions |

*Source:* Adapted from T.A. Widiger, P.T. Costa, Jr., and R.R. McCrae, 2002, A proposal for Axis II: Diagnosing personality disorders using the five-factor model. In P.T. Costa, Jr., and T.A. Widiger (Eds.), *Personality Disorders and the Five-Factor Model of Personality*, 2nd ed., pp. 431–456. Washington, DC: American Psychological Association.

2002a, b). Problems may arise in association with extreme variations in either direction (high or low). Dramatically elevated levels of angry–hostility, impulsiveness, and excitement seeking are particularly important, as are extremely low levels of trust, compliance, and tendermindedness. Although some forms of personality disorder are associated with high levels of anxiousness and vulnerability, people with antisocial personality disorder frequently exhibit unusually low levels of anxiety and concern about danger.

### Context and Personality

Two important qualifications must be made about the development and persistence of individual differences in temperament and personality. First, these differences may not be evident in all situations. Some important personality features may be expressed only under certain challenging circumstances that require or facilitate a particular response. For example, Tom did not always appear to be impulsive and irresponsible. He was usually polite when he was with adults, and he went through intervals in which he followed rules and attended school regularly.

The second qualification involves the consequences of exhibiting particular traits. Social circumstances frequently determine whether a specific pattern of behaviour will be assigned a positive or negative meaning by other people. Difficult temperament, for example, may serve an adaptive function when it is beneficial for an infant to be demanding and highly visible—for example, during a famine or while living in a large institution. On the other hand, in some circumstances, difficult temperament can be associated with an increased risk for certain psychiatric and learning disorders.

Consider the antisocial personality traits that Tom exhibited, especially impulsivity and lack of fear. These characteristics might be maladaptive under normal circumstances, but they could be useful—indeed, admirable—in certain extraordinary settings. War is one extreme example. People in combat situations have to act quickly and decisively, often at great risk to their own physical health. A disregard for personal safety might be adaptive under these circumstances. Tom's ability to lie in a calm and convincing fashion was another interesting trait. Again, this might have been a valuable adaptive skill if Tom had been an espionage agent. The meanings that are assigned to particular traits depend on the environment in which they are observed.

## Classification

The architects of DSM-IV-TR have organized 10 specific forms of personality disorder into 3 clusters on the basis of broadly defined characteristics. The specific disorders in each cluster are listed in Table 9–2. In the following pages we give brief descriptions of these personality disorder subtypes. Later in the chapter we describe in considerably more detail four disorders that are relatively frequent and have been studied extensively: schizotypal, borderline, antisocial, and dependent personality disorders.

### Cluster A: Paranoid, Schizoid, and Schizotypal Personality Disorders

Cluster A includes three disorders: paranoid, schizoid, and schizotypal forms of personality disorder. The behaviour of people who fit the subtypes in this cluster is typically odd, eccentric, or asocial. All three types share similarity with the symptoms of schizophrenia (see Chapter 13). One implicit assumption in the DSM-IV-TR system is that these types of personality disorder may represent behavioural traits or interpersonal styles that precede the onset of full-blown psychosis. Because of their close association with schizophrenia, they are sometimes called *schizophrenia spectrum disorders*.

**Paranoid personality disorder** is characterized by the pervasive tendency to be inappropriately suspicious of other people's motives and behaviours. People who fit the description for this disorder are constantly on

**TABLE 9–2 Personality Disorders Listed in DSM-IV-TR**

| | |
|---|---|
| **Cluster A includes people who often appear odd or eccentric** | |
| Paranoid | Distrust and suspiciousness of others. |
| Schizoid | Detachment from social relationships and restricted range of expression of emotions. |
| Schizotypal | Discomfort with close relationships; cognitive and perceptual distortions; eccentricities of behaviour. |
| **Cluster B includes people who often appear dramatic, emotional, or erratic** | |
| Antisocial | Disregard for and frequent violation of the rights of others. |
| Borderline | Instability of interpersonal relationships, self-image, emotions, and control over impulses. |
| Histrionic | Excessive emotionality and attention seeking. |
| Narcissistic | Grandiosity, need for admiration, and lack of empathy. |
| **Cluster C includes people who often appear anxious or fearful** | |
| Avoidant | Social inhibition, feelings of inadequacy, and hypersensitivity to negative evaluation. |
| Dependent | Excessive need to be taken care of, leading to submissive and clinging behaviour. |
| Obsessive–compulsive | Preoccupation with orderliness and perfectionism at the expense of flexibility. |

guard. They expect that other people are trying to harm them, and they take extraordinary precautions to avoid being exploited or injured. Relationships with friends and family members are difficult to maintain because these people don't trust anyone. They frequently overreact in response to minor or ambiguous events to which they attribute hidden meaning.

When they overreact, people with paranoid personality disorder often behave aggressively or antagonistically. These actions can easily create a self-fulfilling prophesy. In other words, thinking (incorrectly) that he or she is being attacked by others, the paranoid person strikes. The other person is, naturally, surprised, annoyed, and perhaps frightened by this behaviour, and begins to treat the paranoid person with concern and caution. This response serves to confirm the original suspicions of the paranoid individual, who does not comprehend how his or her own behaviour affects others.

Paranoid personality disorder must be distinguished from psychotic disorders, such as schizophrenia and delusional disorder. The pervasive suspicions of people with paranoid personality disorder do not reach delusional proportions. In other words, they are not sufficiently severe to be considered obviously false and clearly preposterous. In actual practice, this distinction is sometimes quite subtle and difficult to make.

**Schizoid personality disorder** is defined in terms of a pervasive pattern of indifference to other people, coupled with a diminished range of emotional experience and expression. These people are loners; they prefer social isolation to interactions with friends or family. Other people see them as being cold and aloof. By their own report, they do not experience strong subjective emotions, such as sadness, anger, or happiness.

**Schizotypal personality disorder** centres around peculiar patterns of behaviour rather than on the emotional restriction and social withdrawal that are associated with schizoid personality disorder. Many of these peculiar behaviours take the form of perceptual and cognitive disturbance. People with this disorder may report bizarre fantasies and unusual perceptual experiences. Their speech may be slightly difficult to follow because they use words in an odd way or because they express themselves in a vague or disjointed manner. Their affective expressions may be constricted in range, as in schizoid personality disorder, or they may be silly and inappropriate.

In spite of their odd or unusual behaviours, people with schizotypal personality disorder are not psychotic or out of touch with reality. Their bizarre fantasies are not delusional, and their unusual perceptual experiences are not sufficiently real or compelling to be considered hallucinations.

## Cluster B: Antisocial, Borderline, Histrionic, and Narcissistic Personality Disorders

Cluster B includes antisocial, borderline, histrionic, and narcissistic personality disorders. According to DSM-IV-TR, these disorders are characterized by dramatic, emotional, or erratic behaviour, and all are associated with marked difficulty in sustaining interpersonal relationships. The rationale for grouping these disorders together is less compelling than that for Cluster A. In particular, antisocial personality disorder clearly involves something more than just a dramatic style or erratic behaviour.

**Antisocial personality disorder** is defined in terms of a persistent pattern of irresponsible and antisocial behaviour that begins during childhood or adolescence and continues into the adult years. The case study of Tom, with which we opened this chapter, illustrates this pattern of behaviour. The DSM-IV-TR definition is based on features that, beginning in childhood, indicate a pervasive pattern of disregard for, and violation of, the rights of others. Once the person has become an adult, these difficulties include persistent failure to perform responsibilities that are associated with occupational and family roles. Conflict with others, including physical fights, is also common. These people are irritable and aggressive with their spouses and children as well as with people outside the home. They are impulsive, reckless, and irresponsible.

We have all read newspaper accounts of famous examples of antisocial personality disorder. These often include people who have committed horrendous acts of violence against other people, including genocidal war crimes and serial murders. You should not be misled, however, into thinking that only serious criminals meet the criteria for this disorder. Many other forms of persistently callous and exploitative behaviour could lead to this diagnosis.

**Borderline personality disorder** centres around a pervasive pattern of instability in mood and interpersonal relationships. People with this disorder find it very difficult to be alone. They form intense, unstable relationships with other people and are often seen by others as being manipulative. Their mood may shift rapidly and inexplicably from depression to anger to anxiety over a pattern of several hours. Intense anger is common and may be accompanied by temper tantrums, physical assault, or suicidal threats and gestures.

Identity disturbance is another feature of borderline personality disorder. People with this disturbance presumably have great difficulty maintaining an integrated image of themselves that simultaneously incorporates their positive and negative features. Therefore, they alternate between thinking of themselves in unrealistically positive terms and then unrealistically negative terms at different moments in time. When they are focused on their own negative features, they have a serious deflated view of themselves and may become seriously depressed. They frequently express uncertainty about such issues as personal values, sexual preferences, and career alternatives. Chronic feelings of emptiness and boredom may also be present.

## BRIEF CASE STUDY

### Borderline Personality Disorder

A single woman of 35 had worked with four therapists over a period of 11 years, before the last of these referred her to me. Since Beatrice had graduated from college at age 22, she had seemed to circulate in a holding pattern. She saw herself as an executive-to-be in the corporate world, but in actuality had held just a few entry-level jobs, and those only briefly. Once or twice she quit in a huff because the job was "not interesting enough" or because "they weren't promoting me fast enough." She had no distinct career goals, nor had she taken any special courses to prepare herself for some particular path. The work problem did not pose a threat to her well-being, since she lived off a large trust fund that her family had set up for her.

On the relational side her situation was not much better. Beatrice had never been "serious" with anyone and had little interest in men apart from their ability to pay compliments to her appearance. Her self-image was contradictory: she alternated between seeing herself as "model pretty" or else ugly. While buying an ice cream, she would feel devastated if the counterman did not make eyes at her; if he did, she would feel "insulted."

She had no hobbies or sustaining interests and found evenings with nothing to do intolerable. On such evenings she would usually engage her mother in long phone conversations (her parents lived in a different city), demanding that her mother come and visit. If this were not possible, she would slam the phone down, only to then call her mother back half an hour later to apologize.

During the time I worked with Beatrice, her most noticeable personality traits were those of anger, argumentativeness, scornfulness, irritability, and vanity. Her intensity and demandingness made her troublesome in her family; her parents and siblings were mostly good-natured and got on well when she was not in their midst (Stone, 1993, pp. 250–251). ◆

**Histrionic personality disorder** is characterized by a pervasive pattern of excessive emotionality and attention-seeking behaviour. People with this disorder thrive on being the centre of attention. They want the spotlight on them at all times. They are self-centred, vain, and demanding, and they constantly seek approval from others. When interacting with other people, their behaviour is often inappropriately sexually seductive or provocative. Their emotions tend to be shallow and may vacillate erratically. They frequently react to situations with inappropriate exaggeration.

The concept of histrionic personality disorder overlaps extensively with other types of personality disorder especially borderline personality disorder. People with both disorders are intensely emotional and manipulative. Unlike people with borderline personality disorder, however, people with histrionic personality disorder have an essentially intact sense of their own identity and a better capacity for stable relationships with other people.

There may be an etiological link between histrionic and antisocial personality disorders. Both may reflect a common, underlying tendency toward lack of inhibition. People with both types of disorder form shallow, manipulative

©The New Yorker Collection 2002. David Sipress from cartoonbank.com. All Rights Reserved.

relationships with others. Family history studies indicate that this predisposition to disinhibition may be expressed as histrionic personality disorder in women and as antisocial personality disorder in men (Cale & Lilienfeld, 2002; Pfohl, 1995).

The essential feature of **narcissistic personality disorder** is a pervasive pattern of grandiosity, need for admiration, and inability to empathize with other people. Narcissistic people have a greatly exaggerated sense of their own importance. They are preoccupied with their own achievements and abilities. Because they consider themselves to be very special, they cannot empathize with the feelings of other people and are often seen as being arrogant or haughty.

There is a considerable amount of overlap between narcissistic personality disorder and borderline personality disorder. Both types of people feel that other people should recognize their needs and do special favours for them. They may also react with anger if they are criticized. The distinction between these disorders hinges on the inflated sense of self importance that is found in narcissistic personality disorder and the deflated or devalued sense of self found in borderline personality disorder (Ronningstam & Gunderson, 1991).

### Cluster C: Avoidant, Dependent, and Obsessive–Compulsive Personality Disorders

Cluster C includes avoidant, dependent, and obsessive–compulsive personality disorders. The common element in all three disorders is presumably anxiety or fearfulness. This description fits most easily with the avoidant and dependent types. In contrast, obsessive–compulsive personality disorder is more accurately described in terms of preoccupation with rules and with lack of emotional warmth than in terms of anxiety.

**Avoidant personality disorder** is characterized by a pervasive pattern of social discomfort, fear of negative evaluation, and timidity. People with this disorder tend to be socially isolated when outside their own family circle because they are afraid of criticism. Unlike people with schizoid personality disorder, they want to be liked by others, but they are extremely shy—easily hurt by even minimal signs of disapproval from other people. Thus they avoid social and occupational activities that require significant contact with other people.

Avoidant personality disorder is often indistinguishable from generalized social phobia (see Chapter 6). In fact, some experts have argued that they are probably two different ways of defining the same condition (Frances, First, & Pincus, 1995). Others have argued that people with avoidant personality disorder have more trouble than people with social phobia in relating to other people (Millon & Martinez, 1995). People with avoidant personality disorder are presumably more socially withdrawn and have very few close relationships because they are so shy. People with social phobia may have a lot of friends, but they are afraid of performing in front of them. This distinction is relatively clear when social phobia is defined narrowly in terms of a particular kind of situation, such as public speaking. It is much more difficult to make if the social phobia is more generalized.

The essential feature of **dependent personality disorder** is a pervasive pattern of submissive and clinging behaviour. People with this disorder are afraid of separating from other people on whom they are dependent for advice and reassurance. Often unable to make everyday decisions on their own, they feel anxious and helpless when they are alone. Like people with avoidant personality disorder, they are easily hurt by criticism, extremely sensitive to disapproval, and lacking in self-confidence. One difference between avoidant and dependent personality disorders involves the point in a relationship at which they experience the most difficulty. People who are avoidant have trouble initiating a relationship (because they are fearful). People who are dependent have trouble being alone or separating from other people with whom they already have a close relationship. For example, a person with dependent personality disorder might be extremely reluctant to leave home in order to attend college.

**Obsessive–compulsive personality disorder (OCPD)** is defined by a pervasive pattern of orderliness, perfectionism, and mental and interpersonal control, at the expense of flexibility, openness, and efficiency. People with this disorder set ambitious standards for their own performance that frequently are so high as to be unattainable. Many would be described as "workaholics." In other words, they are so devoted to work that they ignore friends, family members, and leisure activities. They are so preoccupied with details and rules that they lose sight of the main point of an activity or project. Intellectual endeavours are favoured over feelings and emotional experience. These people are excessively conscientious, moralistic, and judgmental, and they tend to be intolerant of emotional behaviour in other people.

Obsessive–compulsive personality disorder should not be confused with obsessive–compulsive disorder (OCD), which is a type of anxiety disorder (see Chapter 6). A pattern of intrusive, unwanted thoughts accompanied by ritualistic behaviours is used to define OCD. The definition of obsessive–compulsive personality disorder, in contrast, is concerned with personality traits, such as excessively high levels of conscientiousness. Traditional psychodynamic theory has maintained that obsessive–compulsive personality disorder often precedes the onset of OCD. Research generally does not support this position. Most people with OCD do not have obsessive–compulsive personality disorder; people with OCD, like people with other anxiety disorders, are more likely to have avoidant or dependent personalities (Taylor & Livesley, 1995). However, obsessive–compulsive personality disorder may be more closely related to the form of OCD that involves checking rituals than to the form of OCD that involves washing and cleaning rituals (Gibbs & Oltmanns, 1995).

## Personality Disorder Not Otherwise Specified (PD NOS)

In addition to the 10 specific types of personality disorder listed in Table 9–2, DSM-IV-TR allows for a nonspecific diagnosis. This category is used for people who meet the general diagnostic criteria for a personality disorder without meeting the specific criteria for one of the 10 subtypes. For example, a person might exhibit features of more than one PD (while falling below the threshold for any specific diagnosis) and also experience clinically significant distress or impairment in functioning. DSM-IV-TR does not list a specific set of diagnostic criteria for PD NOS, but some investigators have used the category to refer to people would exhibit at least 10 features of specific personality disorders (across all different subtypes) in addition to meeting the general description of personality disorders (Loranger et al., 1994).

The PD NOS diagnosis is important because it may be the most frequently used personality disorders diagnosis. Consider, for example, the results of one study. Approximately 2000 college students participated in an assessment process aimed at the identification of personality disorders. The prevalence rate for at least one type of personality disorder in this sample was 11 percent (Lenzenweger et al., 1997). Half of the people who met diagnostic criteria for a definite personality disorder were assigned a diagnosis of PD NOS; the others fit into at least one of the 10 types of personality disorders listed in the diagnostic manual. This result raises some concern about the categorical approach employed in DSM-IV-TR. The ancillary category called "not otherwise specified" was designed to allow clinicians to assign a diagnosis to occasional patients whose problems fall at the boundaries between official categories. This study suggests that a rather large proportion of people with personality disorders may fit this description.

## A Dimensional Perspective on Personality Disorders

DSM-IV-TR treats personality disorders as discrete categories, and it assumes that there are sharp boundaries between normal and abnormal personalities. The high frequency with which the PD NOS diagnosis is employed is one indication that there are, in fact, a lot of people with serious personality problems who do not fit the official DSM-IV-TR subtypes. Another frequent complaint about the description of personality disorders is the considerable overlap among categories. Many patients meet the criteria for more than one type. It is cumbersome to list multiple diagnoses, especially when the clinician is already asked to list problems on both Axis I and Axis II. In fact, many clinicians are reluctant to make more than one diagnosis on Axis II; consequently, much information is frequently left out.

For these reasons, many experts favour the development of an alternative classification system for personality disorders, one that would be based on a dimensional view of personality pathology (Clark, 1999). A dimensional system might provide a more complete description of each person, and it would be more useful with patients who fall on the boundaries between different types of personality disorder. It could also be easier to use than the DSM-IV-TR approach. One proposal is to use the five-factor model as the basic structure for a comprehensive description of personality problems (Lynam & Widiger, 2001; Widiger, Costa, & McCrae, 2002a). This approach would require the clinician to consider information regarding the 30 personality facets listed in Table 9–1. This system would be economical compared to making a judgment regarding the presence of at least 80 personality disorder features in DSM-IV-TR (approximately 8 features for each of the 10 personality disorder categories). An example of a description based on the five-factor dimensional approach to PDs is provided in the following brief case study.

## BRIEF CASE STUDY

### Narcissism from the Perspective of the Five-Factor Model

Patricia was a 41-year-old married woman who presented at an outpatient mental health clinic complaining of interpersonal difficulties at work and recurring bouts of depression. She reported a long history of banking jobs in which she had experienced interpersonal discord. Shortly before her entrance into treatment, Patricia was demoted from a supervisory capacity at her current job because of her inability to effectively interact with those she was supposed to supervise. She described herself as always feeling out of place with her coworkers and indicated that most of them failed to adequately appreciate her skill or the amount of time she put in at work. She reported that she was beginning to think that perhaps she had something to do with their apparent dislike of her. However, even during the initial treatment sessions, her descriptions of her past and current job situations quickly and inevitably reverted to defensive statements concerning others' mistreatment and lack of appreciation of her. Despite her stated goal of changing her own behaviour to be better liked, it quickly became clear that her actual wish was to cause her coworkers and supervisors to realize her superiority and to treat her accordingly.

. . . Patricia often made condescending remarks about coworkers working under her, indicating that they were inferior to her in intelligence and abilities and thus had little or nothing to offer her. Patricia . . . pretended to have a back injury as an excuse to avoid sales work, thus forcing the other employees to do this less pleasant job while she was given more prestigious loan accounts. She also reported one incident in which a friend had agreed to meet her for dinner but was late because her child was ill. Patricia was highly offended and irritated by what she referred to as her friend's "lack of consideration" in being late. She felt no compassion for her friend or the child. . . .

Patricia's tendency toward suspiciousness . . . was exemplified by her belief that others did not like her and conspired against her to make her job harder (e.g., by "purposely" failing to get necessary paperwork to her on time). Finally, her uncooperativeness was illustrated by her tendency not to follow instructions at work and to refuse to cooperate with her husband at home. . . . For example, although her boss had asked Patricia not to stay at the bank after hours because of security considerations, she often stayed late to work, saying that the boss's request was "stupid and restrictive."

Patricia described herself as both depressed and anxious. . . . She also tended to become enraged when criticized or "treated badly". . . Although Patricia denied feelings of humiliation and insecurity, . . . when criticized she would blush and either defensively make excuses for her behaviour . . . or negate the criticism . . . ("She's just envious of me because I'm smarter than she is").

Other people seldom called or visited with her to talk about their problems; when they did,

*continued*

*cont.*

she responded with intellectual advice usually delivered in a condescending manner, such as, "When you're older, you'll understand better how things are". . . . Her solitary nature in having few friends and keeping to herself at work may in fact have resulted in part from actual rebuffs from others in response to her antagonistic behaviour.

Finally, Patricia perceived herself as accomplished, persistent, and strongly committed to the highest standards of conduct. . . . These impressions may indicate a classic narcissistic inflation of self-image, especially given that she was, even by her own report, having considerable difficulties at work (Corbitt, 2002, pp. 294–297).

This woman's interpersonal difficulties could be succinctly described in terms of a combination of low agreeableness (trust, modesty, altruism, and compliance), low extroversion (warmth and gregariousness), high neuroticism (angry–hostility, anxiousness, and depression), and high conscientiousness (competence, dutifulness, and achievement striving). Based on DSM-IV-TR, she would meet the criteria for narcissistic personality disorder. If the categorical approach were used, however, a complete description of her personality problems would also require that the clinician note the presence of some features of paranoid personality disorder (such as unjustified doubts about the loyalty of coworkers; reacting with rage to perceived attacks on her character or reputation) and obsessive–compulsive personality disorder (excessive devotion to work to the exclusion of leisure activities and friendships), even though she did not exhibit enough features of these other disorders to meet their diagnostic threshold. A dimensional approach like the one illustrated in this case may eventually replace the 10 personality disorder categories on Axis II when the next version of DSM is published.

***W. John Livesley,*** *who is a psychologist and psychiatrist at the University of British Columbia, has played an important role in the development of diagnostic criteria for personality disorders and in the development of dimensional models of these disorders.*

## CANADIAN FOCUS Dimensional Assessment of Personality Pathology

One of the most interesting and important developments in understanding personality disorders comes from the work of W. John Livesley, who is a psychologist and psychiatrist at the University of British Columbia, and an internationally recognized expert on personality disorders. In collaboration with colleagues including UBC psychologist Kerry L. Jang, Livesley sought to identify the basic traits or building blocks of personality disorder, and to investigate the extent to which the traits are influenced by genes and by the environment.

To identify these traits, Livesley surveyed the scientific literature and the opinions of experts in personality disorders. The results were used to develop precise definitions of personality disorder traits (e.g., Livesley, 1986). Statistical techniques such as factor analysis were then used to see whether any of the traits overlapped with one another (e.g., Livesley, Jackson, & Schroeder, 1991). As a result of these investigations, over a dozen distinct traits were identified, including those shown in the lower half of Figure 9–1. The questionnaire Livesley developed to measure these traits is called the *Dimensional Assessment of Personality Pathology (DAPP)*. This measure is one of the most detailed and comprehensive measures of personality disorder traits that has ever been developed.

Most of the traits listed in the figure are self-explanatory, although some require clarification. *Cognitive dysregulation* refers to the tendency to experience depersonalization and to have irrational (unrealistic) thoughts. *Insecure attachment* refers to fear of separation from significant others and intolerance of being alone. *Rejection* is the tendency to be judgmental, hostile, and dominant. *Restricted expression* refers to the tendency to be reluctant to disclose one's feelings and personal information.

These traits cover virtually all the features of the DSM-IV personality disorders. The main difference is that Livesley's traits are explicitly dimensional. To illustrate, a person can have either a high, medium, or low score on submissiveness, depending on the extent that he or she is unassertive, suggestible, and in need of advice.

The next step in the work of Livesley and colleagues was to investigate how these traits grouped together. Livesley, Jang, and Vernon (1998) obtained DAPP scores from three large samples: a group of people with personality disorders, a group of people from the general population, and a group of monozygotic (identical) and dizygotic (fraternal) twins. The results for each group were remarkably similar. As shown in Figure 9–1, the results revealed that the personality disorder traits could be grouped to make up four major dimensions:

1. *Emotional dysregulation:* People with high scores on this dimension tend to experience intense, unstable emotions, interpersonal problems, and dissatisfaction with oneself and one's life.

*continued*

*cont.*

**Four Major Dimensions of Personality Disorder and Their Component Traits**

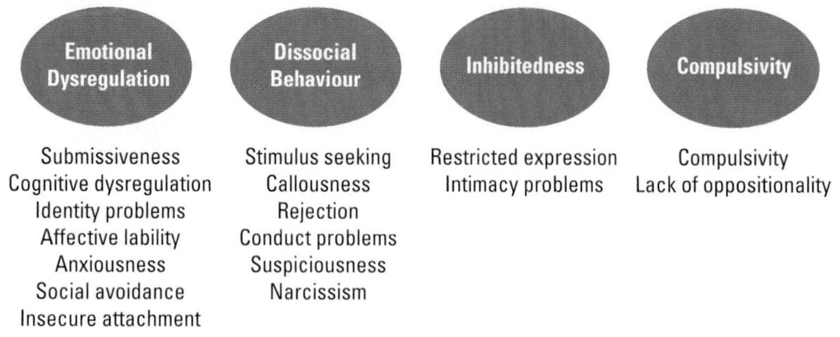


**FIGURE 9–1: These dimensions and their component traits were measured by the Dimensional Assessment of Personality Pathology (DAPP). The dimensions were found in both clinical and general population samples.**

*Source:* Based on W.J. Livesley, K.L. Lang, and P.A. Vernon, 1998, Phenotypic and genetic structure of traits delineating personality disorder. *Archives of General Psychiatry, 55,* 941–948.

2. *Dissocial behaviour:* High scores on this dimension indicate a lack of regard for others, and the tendency to regard people as objects to be exploited.
3. *Inhibitedness:* High scorers tend to be inhibited in expressing themselves and derive little enjoyment from intimate relationships.
4. *Compulsivity:* High scorers tend to be orderly, precise, and conscientious, and tend not to be oppositional in their behaviour toward others.

Notice that these dimensions are similar to four of the five factors in the five-factor model of personality, which we discussed earlier (see Table 9–1). Livesley's emotional dysregulation is similar to neuroticism; dissocial behaviour is similar to agreeableness (reverse-scored; low agreeableness corresponds to high dissocial behaviour); inhibition is similar to extraversion (reverse-scored); and compulsivity is similar to conscientiousness. Livesley and colleagues did not include traits measuring openness to experience, which is possibly why they did not find this fifth factor from the five-factor model of personality.

These results are important because they show that a measure of personality disorder—the DAPP—reveals the same basic dimensions as those identified by measures of normal personality (Table 9–1). This provides further evidence that normal and abnormal personality lie on a continuum, with personality disorder traits representing extremes of normal traits.

Statistical analyses of DAPP scores from Livesley et al.'s (1998) samples of monozygotic and dizygotic twins further enabled the investigators to identify the extent to which the four dimensions (and their component traits) are influenced by genes and by the environment (see Chapter 2). They found that there were genetic and environmental influences specific to each of the four dimensions. The component traits making up each dimension were influenced by genetic and environmental influences specific to each trait as well as by more general genetic and environmental factors, which played a role in shaping all the traits associated with a given dimension.

Livesley's findings have several important implications. First, they are consistent with the idea that personality disorders consist of dimensions, not discrete categories. Each of these dimensions is a product of biological predispositions and environmental experiences, such as learning experiences that take place during the person's early development. Second, the results suggest that there is continuity between normal and abnormal personality. Personality disorders represent extremes of various traits and dimensions; normal or well-adjusted personalities are characterized by less-extreme scores. Third, the results suggest that researchers will need to look for many different types of genetic and environmental influences in order to fully understand the causes of personality disorders. Finally, the findings suggest that the DSM-IV personality disorder categories might be eventually replaced by a dimensional system consisting of four or possibly five main dimensions, similar to those specified in the five-factor model of personality. In the future, personality disorders might be diagnosed by assessing whether a person has extremely high or low scores on scales measuring the major dimensions and on scales measuring the specific traits.

Livesley (2000, 2003) has drawn on these and other findings to develop treatment guidelines for personality disorders. According to Livesley, no single form of treatment can address all the dimensions of a patient's problems. He advocates the use of a wide range of empirically supported treatments, which are implemented in the context of a strong therapeutic relationship. The method is not an eclectic approach to treatment but an integrated framework based on the understanding of the research on the causes of personality disorders. In addition to Livesley's approach, there have been other recent attempts to develop treatment guidelines for personality disorders. Although such guidelines are a step in the right direction, McGill University psychiatrist Joel Paris cautions that more research is needed to evaluate the usefulness of these and other treatment guidelines (Paris, 2002a). ◆

# Epidemiology

Personality disorders are generally considered to be one of the most common forms of psychopathology, but it is difficult to provide empirical support for that claim. With the exception of antisocial personality, these disorders did not receive close scrutiny until after the publication of DSM-III, and they have not been included in large-scale epidemiological studies. Problems and inconsistencies associated with reliance on self-report measures make the problem even more complicated.

## Prevalence in Community and Clinical Samples

How many people in the general population will meet the criteria for at least one personality disorder? In studies that have examined community-based samples of adults, the overall lifetime prevalence for having at least one Axis II disorder (any type) varies between 10 and 14 percent (Ekselius et al., 2001; Torgersen, Kringlen, & Cramer, 2001).

Evidence regarding the prevalence of specific types of personality disorder in community samples is summarized in Figure 9–2. This figure presents summary data that have been averaged across a number of studies (Mattia & Zimmerman, 2001). Among community samples, the highest prevalence rates are found for schizotypal, histrionic, dependent, and obsessive–compulsive personality disorders. Narcissistic personality disorder seems to be the least common form, affecting only 0.2 percent of the population.

Investigators have identified very few cases of narcissistic personality disorder when they have interviewed people in community samples (as opposed to clinic settings). The fact that almost no one endorses narcissistic symptoms does not necessarily mean that the disorder does not occur. Rather, it seems possible that people who experience these features do not recognize the nature of their own problems or are unwilling to admit them. Self-report measures, such as questionnaires and interviews, may not be effective instruments for assessing narcissistic personality disorder. More accurate information might be obtained from other people who know the person well and can report examples of grandiosity, exploitation, or lack of empathy.

One final issue regarding prevalence rates involves comorbidity. There is considerable overlap among categories in the personality disorders. Twenty-five to 50 percent of people who meet the diagnostic criteria for one personality disorder also meet the criteria for another disorder (Maier et al., 1992; Shea, 1995). To some extent, this overlap is due to the fact that similar traits are used to define more than one disorder.

There is also extensive overlap between personality disorders and disorders that are diagnosed on Axis I of DSM-IV-TR. Approximately 75 percent of people who qualify for a diagnosis on Axis II also meet criteria for a syndrome such as major depression, substance dependence, or an anxiety disorder (Dolan-Sewell, Krueger, & Shea, 2001). This overlap may also be viewed from the other direction: Many people who are treated for a mental disorder listed on Axis I, such as depression or alcoholism, would also meet the criteria for a personality disorder (Thomas et al., 1999). Borderline personality disorder appears to be the most common personality disorder among patients treated at mental health facilities (both inpatient and outpatient settings). Averaged across studies, the evidence suggests that this disorder is found among slightly more than 30 percent of all patients who are treated for psychological disorders (Lyons, 1995). Rates are especially high among those who have been hospitalized, but the specific figures vary considerably from one study to the next.

**Prevalence of Personality Disorders in Community Samples**

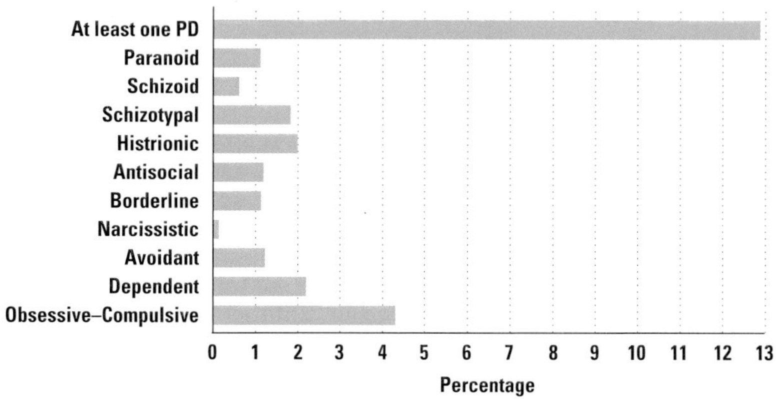


**FIGURE 9–2: Estimates of the prevalence of personality disorders.**

*Source:* J.I. Mattia and M. Zimmerman, 2001, Epidemiology. In W.J. Livesley (Ed.), *Handbook of personality disorders: Theory, research, and treatment.* New York: Guilford.

*Vivien Leigh won Academy Awards for her performances as Scarlett O'Hara in* Gone with the Wind *(1940) and Blanche Du Bois in* A Streetcar Named Desire *(1952). Both characters exhibit blends of histrionic and narcissistic features that fit stereotyped views of female personality traits.*

## Gender Differences

The *overall* prevalence of personality disorders is approximately equal in men and women (Weissman, 1993). There are, however, consistent gender differences with regard to at least one specific disorder: Antisocial personality disorder is unquestionably much more common among men than among women. One epidemiologic study found rates of 4.5 percent for men and 0.8 percent for women (Robins, Tipp, & Przybeck, 1991). Another study reported rates of 5.8 percent for men and 1.2 percent for women (Kessler et al., 1994). Thus antisocial personality disorder is actually an alarmingly common problem among adult males.

Epidemiological evidence regarding gender differences for the other types of personality disorder is much more ambiguous. Very few community-based studies have been done using standardized interviews as a basis for diagnosis. In one community sample of more than 3400 adults, the prevalence of histrionic personality disorder was found to be 2.2 percent in both men and women (Nestadt et al., 1990). Almost nothing is known about the extent of potential gender differences for the other types of personality disorder. Borderline personality disorder and dependent personality disorder may be somewhat more prevalent among women than men (Zimmerman & Coryell, 1989). There has been some speculation that paranoid and obsessive–compulsive personality disorders may be somewhat more common among men than women (Bernstein, Useda, & Siever, 1995).

**Gender Bias and Diagnosis** One of the controversies surrounding the diagnosis of personality disorders involves the issue of gender bias (Widiger, 1998). Critics contend that the definitions of some categories are based on sex role stereotypes and therefore are inherently sexist. The dependent type, for example, might be viewed as a reflection of certain traditionally feminine traits, such as being unassertive or putting the needs of others ahead of one's own. It has been suggested that DSM-IV-TR arbitrarily labels these traits as maladaptive. Traditionally masculine traits, such as being unable to identify and express a wide range of emotions, are presumably not mentioned in the manual. This practice arbitrarily assigns responsibility for interpersonal difficulties to the women themselves. Therefore these definitions may turn traditional sex role behaviours into "disorders" and minimize the extent to which women may simply be trying to cope with unreasonable or oppressive environmental circumstances, including discrimination and sexual abuse (Brown, 1992; Caplan, 1995).

This argument leads to a number of important questions. One is concerned with the presence of bias within the criterion sets themselves. If the criteria for certain categories are based on stereotypes of feminine traits, is it relatively easy for a woman to meet the criteria for that diagnosis even if she is not experiencing significant distress or impairment in other areas of her life? The answer to that question is, tentatively, no (Funtowicz & Widiger, 1999). In other words, the threshold for assigning a diagnosis of personality disorder does not appear to be lower for those types that are based largely on traits that might be considered traditionally feminine (dependent, histrionic, borderline) than for those that are based on traits that might be considered traditionally masculine (antisocial, paranoid, obsessive–compulsive).

A second question is concerned with the possibility of gender bias in the ways that clinicians assign diagnoses to their clients, regardless of whether the criteria themselves are biased. Are clinicians more likely to assign diagnoses such as dependent and borderline personality disorder to a woman than to a man, if both people exhibit the same set of symptoms? The answer to this question is, tentatively, yes. One study, for example, found that both male and female mental health professionals were significantly (though not overwhelmingly) more likely to describe a person as exhibiting symptoms of borderline personality disorder if that person were female rather than male (Becker & Lamb, 1994).

## Stability of Personality Disorders over Time

Temporal stability is one of the most important assumptions about personality disorders. Evidence for the assumption that personality disorders appear during adolescence and persist into adulthood has, until recently, been limited primarily to antisocial personality disorder. A classic follow-up study by Lee Robins (1966) began with a large set of records describing young children treated for adjustment problems at a clinic during the 1920s. Robins was able to locate and interview almost all of these people, who by then were adults. The best predictor of an adult diagnosis of antisocial personality was conduct disorder in childhood. The people who were most likely to be considered antisocial as adults were boys who had been referred to the clinic on the basis of serious theft or aggressive behaviour; who exhibited such behaviours across a variety of situations; and whose antisocial behaviours created conflict with adults outside their own homes. More than half of the boys in Robins's study who exhibited these characteristics were given a diagnosis of antisocial personality disorder as adults.

Another longitudinal study has collected information regarding the prevalence and stability of personality disorders among adolescents (Bernstein et al., 1993). This investigation is particularly important because it did not depend solely on subjects who had been referred for psychological treatment and because it was concerned with the full range of personality disorders. The rate of personality disorders was relatively high in this sample: seventeen percent of the adolescents received a diagnosis of at least one personality disorder. While many of these people continued to exhibit the same problems over time, fewer than half of the adolescents who were originally considered to have a personality disorder qualified for that same diagnosis two years later. This evidence suggests that maladaptive personality traits are frequently transient phenomena among adolescents. Further details regarding the methods and results of this study are presented in the Research Close-Up.

Several other studies have examined the stability of personality disorders among people who have received professional treatment for their problems, especially those who have been hospitalized for schizotypal or borderline disorders. Many patients who have been treated for these problems are still significantly impaired several years later, but the disorders are not uniformly stable. The long-term prognosis is not optimistic for schizotypal and schizoid personality disorders. People with these diagnoses are likely to remain socially isolated and occupationally impaired (McGlashan, 1992). Recovery rates are much better among patients with a diagnosis of borderline personality disorder. To illustrate, long-term (15- to 27-year) studies by Joel Paris and colleagues at McGill University found that people with borderline personality disorder tend to improve over time, to the point that most of them no longer meet full diagnostic criteria for the disorder by the time they reach 40 or 50 years of age (Paris 2002b; Paris, Brown, & Nowlis, 1987; Paris & Zweig-Frank, 2001). In a seven-year follow-up study of patients with borderline personality disorder, University of Toronto psychiatrist Paul Links and colleagues found that patients were more likely to improve over time if they did not have another coexisting personality disorder (Links, Heslegrave, & van Reekum, 1998). Paris (2002b) proposes that mechanisms behind remission could include maturation and learning to better cope with problems.

## Culture and Personality

In DSM-IV-TR, personality disorders are defined in terms of behaviour that "deviates markedly from the expectations of the individual's culture." In setting this guideline, the architects of DSM-IV-TR recognized that judgments regarding appropriate behaviour vary considerably from one society to the next. Some cultures encourage restrained or subtle displays of emotion, whereas others promote visible, public displays of anger, grief, and

## RESEARCH CLOSE-UP

### Stability of Personality Disorders in Adolescents

The first large-scale study of the prevalence and stability of personality disorders among adolescents was conducted by Bernstein et al. (1993). Subjects in this study were identified from a random sample of more than 700 families in upstate New York who had at least one child between the ages of 11 and 21. In families with more than one child in that age range, one child was randomly chosen to become the subject in the study.

Half the adolescents were male, with an average age of 16 years at the time of the first assessment. Sixty-one percent were from intact families, and 76 percent lived in urban areas. They were less representative with regard to race (91 percent were white) and religious background (56 percent were Catholic).

Each adolescent was assessed at two points in time, separated by two years. The investigators collected information about the children's behaviour using both structured interviews (conducted independently with both the adolescents and their mothers) and self-report questionnaires (completed only by the adolescents). These data were combined to identify individuals with various types of personality disorder. These individuals were then further classified as having either a moderate or severe form of the disorder.

A total of 31 percent of the adolescents met the criteria for at least one moderate personality disorder, and 17 percent met the criteria for at least one severe personality disorder. The most prevalent form of moderate disorder was obsessive–compulsive personality disorder, which was found in 13 percent of the adolescents. The most prevalent form of severe disorder was narcissistic personality disorder; 6 percent of the adolescents met these criteria. The least common form of personality disorder in this sample was schizotypal, judging by both the moderate and severe diagnostic thresholds.

Only one significant difference was found between boys and girls: boys were more than twice as likely as girls to qualify for a diagnosis of dependent personality disorder. This result was somewhat surprising in light of the expectation that, in adults, dependent personality disorder is more common among women than among men.

The prevalence of both moderate and severe personality disorders peaked at the age of 12 or 13 years for both boys and girls and then declined. By the time these subjects reached 18 to 21 years of age, the prevalence of severe personality disorder fell to 9 percent for males and 11 percent for females, approximately the same rates found in other epidemiological studies with adult populations.

Less than half the adolescents who received an Axis II diagnosis at the time of the first assessment qualified for a diagnosis at the second assessment. The most persistent forms of personality disorder were the paranoid, narcissistic, obsessive–compulsive, and borderline types. In these categories, 25 to 32 percent of the cases identified at the first assessment continued to meet diagnostic criteria two years later. This pattern indicates that symptoms of personality disorder are frequently unstable during adolescence. They also indicate, however, that a fairly large minority of the adolescents in this study continued to qualify for a diagnosis of personality disorder two years after the problem was originally identified.

The results of this study indicate that personality disorders are relatively common among adolescents in the general population. The conclusions with regard to temporal stability are mixed. On the one hand, symptoms of personality disorder usually are not stable over time. On the other hand, adolescents who exhibit a severe personality disorder at one point in time are much more likely than their peers to have similar problems over the next few years. Some of the subjects followed a stable pattern that is consistent with the image of these disorders presented in DSM-IV-TR. Further studies are needed to determine how many of the adolescents whose problems were stable over this initial two-year period continue to exhibit stable difficulties in subsequent years. ◆

other emotional responses. Behaviour that seems highly dramatic or extraverted (histrionic) in the former cultures might create a very different impression in the latter cultures. Cultures also differ in the extent to which they value individualism (the pursuit of personal goals) as opposed to collectivism (sharing and self-sacrifice for the good of the group) (Triandis, 1994). Someone who seems exceedingly self-centred and egotistical in a collectivist society, such as Japan, might appear to be normal in an individualistic society like Canada or the United States.

The personality disorders may be more closely tied to cultural expectations than any other kind of mental disorder (Alarcon, Foulks, & Vakkur, 1998). Some studies have compared the prevalence and symptoms of personality disorders in different countries, and the data suggest that similar problems do exist in cultures outside North America and Western Europe (Pinto et al., 2000; Yang et al., 2000; Zoccolillo et al., 1999). Nevertheless, much more information is needed before we can be confident that the DSM-IV-TR system for describing personality disorders is valid in other societies. Two questions are particularly important:

1. In other cultures, what are the personality traits that lead to marked interpersonal

difficulties and social or occupational impairment? Are they different from those that have been identified for our own culture?

2. Are the diagnostic criteria that are used to define personality disorder syndromes in DSM-IV-TR (and ICD-10) meaningful in other cultures?

Cross-cultural studies that are designed to address these issues must confront a number of difficult methodological problems (see Research Methods).

Within a particular society, the experiences of people from cultural and ethnic minorities should also be considered carefully before diagnostic decisions are made. Phenomena associated with paranoid personality disorder, including strong feelings of suspicion, alienation, and distrust, illustrate this issue. People who belong to minority groups (and those who are recent immigrants from a different culture) are more likely than members of the majority or dominant culture to hold realistic concerns about potential victimization and exploitation. Clinicians may erroneously diagnose these conditions as paranoid personality disorder if they do not recognize or understand the cultural experiences in which they are formed. In this particular case, it is obviously important for the clinician to consider the person's attitudes and beliefs regarding members of his or her own family or peer group, as well as the person's feelings about the community as a whole.

## Schizotypal Personality Disorder (SPD)

Now that we have reviewed some of the important general issues for the entire set of personality disorders, we consider four specific types of disorder in more detail. We have decided to focus on schizotypal, borderline, and antisocial types because they have been the subject of extended research and debate in the scientific literature. We will also discuss dependent personality disorder to illustrate current thinking about one of the Cluster C disorders, even though this disorder has not been studied as extensively as the other three categories.

We begin each of the four sections with a brief case study. We have chosen cases that are prototypes for each disorder. In other words, these are people who exhibit most, if not all, of the features of the disorder. You should not infer from these descriptions that everyone who meets the criteria for these disorders would represent this type of typical case. Remember, also, that many people simultaneously meet the criteria for more than one personality disorder; these cases are relatively simple examples.

The following case illustrates some of the most important features of schizotypal personality disorder (SPD).

### BRIEF CASE STUDY

**Schizotypal Personality Disorder**

Sandra, when she first came for treatment at the age of 27, presented with marked anxiety in social situations and in getting along with coworkers, eccentric behaviour, and paranoid ideas. She had no close female friends and only one male friend, and though the latter was a sexual relationship, she revealed almost nothing to him about her past. She had many strange beliefs involving astrology, foods, and medicines.

Sandra had only one friend during her adolescence: someone who shared her faddishness about foods and her beliefs in astrology. Girls excluded her from their social groups. She never understood why they rejected her, though it is probable that they considered her "weird" because of her inability to make small talk and her voice pattern: a flat, high-pitched, stilted-sounding monotone that made her come across as mannered and insincere. Added to this peculiarity of speech was her tendency to skip from topic to topic abruptly, giving equal emphasis to each, such that it was difficult to distinguish the trivial from the important. From a therapeutic standpoint, this was particularly bedevilling, since it strained one's intuitive capacities to the uttermost just to figure out what was really bothering her or what was the "main theme" on any particular day.

Her empathic skills were very limited, leading her to comment at times that she found people and their motives completely puzzling: "I can't connect up with them. If they invite me to lunch with them, I can't seem to join in the conversation or else I say the wrong thing, so after a while they don't invite me anymore and

*continued on page 317*

# RESEARCH METHODS

## Cross-Cultural Comparisons

Rules that govern behaviour are not the same in all societies. For many years psychologists studied narrowly defined groups of people. Participants in research studies were usually those who were easily recruited, often undergraduate students. Relatively little information was collected from people living in non-Western societies, and even less attention was paid to ethnic and cultural minorities in Western countries, such as Canada's many different ethnic groups. Over the past 25 years, psychologists have begun to adopt a broader focus in their consideration of human behaviour, including mental disorders.

**Culture** can be defined as the shared way of life of a group or people (Berry et al., 1992). It is a complex system of accumulated knowledge that helps people in a particular society to adapt to their environment and also serves to structure interactions among those people. Social traditions that, in combination, make up a culture include patterns of family organization, sex roles, religious beliefs, health-care practices, and legal systems. A culture's expectations regarding appropriate forms of behaviour are passed down from one generation to the next by a process of social learning.

At the broadest level, culture is a system of meanings that determines the way people think about themselves and their environments. It shapes their most basic view of reality. Consider, for example, the process of bereavement following the death of a close relative. In some First Nations cultures, people learn to expect to hear the spirit of the dead person calling to them from the afterworld (Kleinman, 1988). This is a common experience for people in these cultures. It resembles auditory hallucinations (perceptual experiences in the absence of external stimulation) that are seen in people with psychotic disorders. But among some First Nations peoples, hearing voices from the dead is a normative response; it is not a sign of dysfunction. Perhaps most importantly, this type of experience is not regularly associated with social or occupational impairment. It would be a mistake, therefore, to consider these experiences to be symptoms of a mental disorder.

**Cross-cultural psychology** is the scientific study of ways that human behaviour and mental processes are influenced by social and cultural factors. This field includes the study of *ethnic differences* (among cultural groups living in close proximity within a single nation). Comparison is a fundamental element of any cross-cultural study. Cross-cultural psychologists examine ways in which human behaviours are different, as well as ways in which they are similar, from one culture to the next.

Cross-cultural comparisons are relevant to the study of psychopathology in many ways. One way involves epidemiology—comparisons of the prevalence of disorders across cultures. Investigations aimed at etiological mechanisms, including biological, psychological, and social variables, can also be extremely informative when viewed in cross-cultural perspective. For example, we know that negative patterns of thinking are correlated with depressed mood in middle-class people in Western societies. Is the same relationship found among people living in rural China? Virtually any study of psychopathology would provide useful information if it were replicated in different cultures.

The valuable process of making cross-cultural comparisons can actually be quite difficult. Several complex issues must be faced by investigators who want to study psychopathology in cross-cultural perspective:

1. *Identifying meaningful groups:* The first step in making cross-cultural comparisons is the selection of participants who are representative members of different cultures. This may be a relatively straightforward process if the comparison is to be made between two small, homogeneous groups (perhaps isolated rural villages in two very different countries). The situation becomes much more complex if the investigator's goal is to compare ethnic groups within a large, multicultural society such as Canada. Asian Canadians, for example, include people whose cultural backgrounds can be traced to homelands such as Hong Kong, the People's Republic of China, Japan, and the Philippines. These countries are, to a greater or lesser extent, culturally different from one another. Similarly, diversity can be found among the various First Nations groups. How do we determine which people share a common culture? What is the cultural "unit," and how do we find its boundaries?
2. *Selecting measurement procedures:* Comparison between groups can be valid only if equivalent measurement procedures are used in both cultures (or in all groups). Participants in different cultures often speak different languages (or different dialects). Questionnaires and psychological tests must be cross-validated to ensure that they measure the same concepts in different cultures.
3. *Considering causal explanations:* Suppose that investigators identify a reliable difference between people in two different cultures. They must now decide how to interpret this difference. Is it, in fact, due to cultural variables? Would the differences disappear if other variables, such as poverty, education, and age, were held constant between the two groups?
4. Avoiding culturally biased interpretations: Investigators, who are often middle class and white, must interpret cautiously the results of cross-cultural research. In particular, scientists must not interpret differences between cultures or ethnic groups as being indicative of deficits in minority groups or non-Western cultures. Some cross-cultural psychologists have suggested that it is more important to study developmental processes within cultures or ethnic groups than to compare outcomes between groups. ◆

*cont.*

I eat by myself." If a teaching supervisor wore a dour expression walking down the hall, Sandra assumed the supervisor was dissatisfied with her work, even though it might be a person who was not even assigned to her department.

Though considered a knowledgeable teacher, Sandra had no charm or patience with the children and was eventually given a semi-administrative job where little interaction with others was necessary. With boyfriends, she was comfortable about having sex, but made such fussy and endless-seeming preparations (such as doing her fingernails in the bathroom for half an hour) that the men lost the mood and usually ended the relationship after a few months.

More striking than her empathic difficulties was a curious inability to grasp what one might call the statistics of everyday life. Travel was a great burden, since she felt it necessary to plan for all possible contingencies. She once went to France on an August vacation packing her winter overcoat, because, "There was a cold spell there in the '50s and it could happen again." Furthermore, she sent a packet of clothes on ahead to the hotel because, "What if my baggage got stolen?" She had great difficulty, in other words, aligning her behaviour in harmony with the expectable, in contrast with the remotely possible—all thinkable events being in her mind equally probable (Stone, 1993, pp. 179–180). ◆

## Brief Historical Perspective

The concept of schizotypal personality disorder is closely tied to the history of schizophrenia as a diagnostic entity (Gottesman, 1987). The term was originally coined as an abbreviation for *schizophrenic phenotype*. These maladaptive personality traits are presumably seen among people who possess the genotype that makes them vulnerable to schizophrenia. The symptoms of schizotypal personality disorder represent early manifestations of the predisposition to develop the full-blown disorder. It has been recognized for many years that a fairly large proportion of the family members of schizophrenic patients exhibit strange or unusual behaviours that are similar to, but milder in form than, the disturbance shown by the patient.

## Clinical Features and Comorbidity

The DSM-IV-TR criteria for schizotypal personality disorder are listed in Table 9–3. These criteria represent a blend of those characteristics that have been reported among the relatives of schizophrenic patients and those symptoms that seem to characterize nonpsychotic patients with schizophrenic-like disorders (Siever, Bernstein, & Silverman, 1995). In addition to social detachment, emphasis is placed on eccentricity and cognitive or perceptual distortions.

People who meet the criteria for schizotypal personality disorder frequently meet the criteria for additional Axis II disorders. There is considerable overlap between schizotypal personality disorder and other personality disorders in Cluster A (paranoid and schizoid), as well as with avoidant personality disorder. This finding is not particularly surprising given the conceptual origins of the schizotypal category. There is also quite a bit of overlap between schizotypal personality disorder and borderline personality disorder.

*People with schizotypal PD tend to be loners, and many have social anxiety that can be traced to distrust of other people.*

## Etiological Considerations

Most of the interest in the etiology of schizotypal personality disorder has focused on the importance of genetic factors. Is schizotypal personality disorder genetically related to schizophrenia? Family and adoption studies indicate that the answer is yes (Battaglia & Torgersen, 1996; Kirrane & Siever, 2000). Twin studies have examined genetic contributions to schizotypal personality disorder from a dimensional perspective in which schizotypal personality traits are measured with questionnaires. This evidence also points to a significant genetic contribution (Nigg & Goldsmith, 1994).

The first-degree relatives of schizophrenic patients are considerably more likely than people in the general population to exhibit schizotypal personality disorder. One large study of this type, the Roscommon Family Study, was conducted in a rural county in western Ireland. The investigators interviewed more than 1700 parents and siblings of three groups of probands: 300 schizophrenic patients, 100 patients with major mood disorders, and 150 people with no history of psychiatric disorder (Kendler et al., 1993). Some of the results of this study are summarized in Figure 9–3 (p. 319).

The most striking finding was an increased prevalence of schizotypal personality disorder (6.9 percent) among the relatives of the schizophrenic patients. Prevalence rates for paranoid and avoidant personality disorder were also significantly higher among the relatives of the schizophrenic patients. Kendler and his colleagues did not find increased rates of these personality disorders among the relatives of people with mood disorders. These results suggest that these disorders, especially schizotypal personality disorder, are genetically related to schizophrenia. The diagnostic specificity of this finding remains open to question; some studies have reported that schizotypal personality disorder is found with increased frequency among the children of parents with mood disorders (Erlenmeyer-Kimling et al., 1995).

**TABLE 9–3 DSM-IV-TR Criteria for Schizotypal Personality Disorder**

**A. A pervasive pattern of social and interpersonal deficits marked by acute discomfort with, and reduced capacity for, close relationships as well as by cognitive or perceptual distortions and eccentricities of behaviour, beginning by early adulthood and present in a variety of contexts, as indicated by five (or more) of the following:**

1. Ideas of reference (excluding delusions of reference).
2. Odd beliefs or magical thinking that influences behaviour and is inconsistent with subcultural norms (such as superstitiousness, belief in clairvoyance, or telepathy).
3. Unusual perceptual experiences, including bodily illusions.
4. Odd thinking and speech (vague, circumstantial, metaphorical, overelaborate, or stereotyped).
5. Suspiciousness or paranoid ideation.
6. Inappropriate or constricted affect.*
7. Behaviour or appearance that is odd, eccentric, or peculiar.
8. Lack of close friends or confidants other than first-degree relatives.
9. Excessive social anxiety that does not diminish with familiarity and tends to be associated with paranoid fears rather than with negative judgments about self.

**B. Does not occur exclusively during the course of schizophrenia, a mood disorder with psychotic features, another psychotic disorder, or a pervasive developmental disorder.**

*Inappropriate affect refers to emotional responses that appear to be inconsistent with the social context—for example, uncontrollable giggling at a wake or funeral. Constricted affect refers to the absence of emotional responsiveness, such as lack of facial expressions. See Chapter 13 for a more detailed discussion.

## Treatment

Two important considerations complicate the treatment of people with personality disorders in general and SPD in particular and make it difficult to evaluate the effectiveness of various forms of intervention. One consideration involves the ego-syntonic nature of many personality disorders (discussed earlier). Many people with these disorders do not seek treatment for their problems because they do not see their own behaviour as being the source of distress (Ewing, Falk, & Otto, 1996). A related difficulty involves premature termination: A relatively high proportion of personality disorder patients drop out of treatment before it is completed.

When people with personality disorders appear at hospitals or clinics, it is often because they are also suffering from another type of mental disorder, such as depression or substance abuse. This comorbidity is the second consideration that complicates treatment. "Pure forms" of personality disorder are relatively rare. There is tremendous overlap between specific personality disorder categories and other forms of abnormal behaviour, including disorders that would be listed on both Axis I and Axis II. Treatment is seldom aimed at problem behaviours that are associated with only one type of personality disorder, and the efficacy of treatment is, therefore, difficult to evaluate.

The literature regarding treatment of schizotypal personality disorder, like that dealing with its causes, mirrors efforts aimed at schizophrenia. A few studies have focused on the possible treatment value of antipsychotic drugs, which are effective with many schizophrenic patients. Some studies have found that low doses of antipsychotic medication are beneficial in alleviating cognitive problems and social anxiety in patients who have received a diagnosis of schizotypal personality disorder (Koenigsberg, Woo-Ming, & Siever, 2002; Sanislow & McGlashan, 1998). There is also some indication that patients with schizotypal personality disorder may respond positively to antidepressant medications, including SSRIs. In general, the therapeutic effects of medication are positive, but they tend to be modest.

Clinical experience seems to suggest that these patients do not respond well to insight-oriented psychotherapy, in part because they do not see themselves as having psychological problems and also because they are so uncomfortable with close personal relationships. Some clinicians have suggested that a supportive, educational approach that is focused on fostering basic social skills may be beneficial if the goals of treatment are modest (Crits-Christoph, 1998; Gabbard, 2000). Unfortunately, controlled studies of psychological forms of treatment with schizotypal personality disorder have not been reported.

**Increased Risk for Personality Disorders among Relatives of Patients with Schizophrenia**

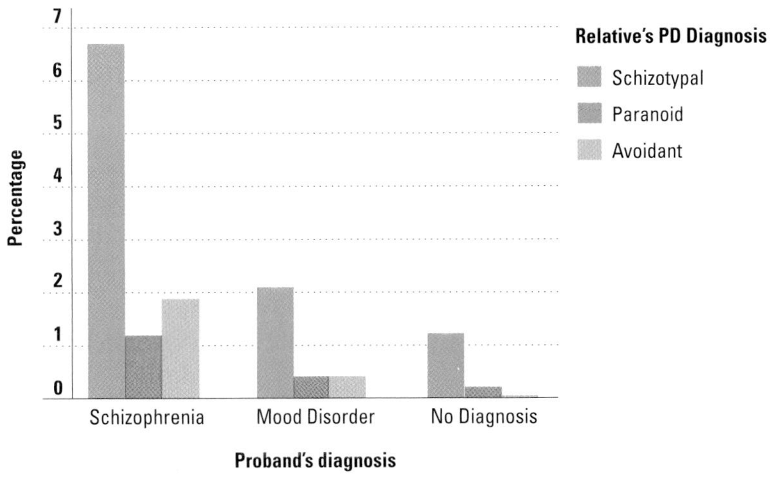


**FIGURE 9–3: Family relationship between schizophrenia and three types of personality disorder.**

*Source:* K.S. Kendler, M. McGuire, A.M. Gruenberg, A. O'Hare, J. Spellman, D. Walsh, 1993, The Roscommon Family Study. III. Schizophrenia-related personality disorders in relatives. *Archives of General Psychiatry, 50,* 781–788.

## Borderline Personality Disorder (BPD)

Borderline personality disorder is one of the most perplexing, most disabling, and most frequently treated forms of personality disorder. Because of the severity of their problems, people with BPD are more likely to come into clinics seeking treatment. Experts on psychiatric classification have discussed the possibility that this diagnostic category might be moved to Axis I when DSM-V is written in the next few years (with a different name, such as "emotion dysregulation disorder"). Of course, no one knows for certain what will happen when the manual is revised. The following case illustrates many of the features associated with this disorder.

### BRIEF CASE STUDY

**Borderline Personality Disorder**

Barbara, a single woman of 24, sought treatment with me shortly after discharge from a hospital, where she had spent three weeks because of depression, panic attacks, and a suicide gesture. This had been her seventh hospitalization—all of them brief, and all for similar symptoms—since age 17. Cheerful and cooperative as a young girl, she underwent a radical change of personality at the time of her menarche. Thereafter, she became irascible, rebellious, moody, and demanding.

For a time she was anorexic; later on, bulimic (maintaining her normal weight by vomiting). Schoolwork deteriorated, and she took up with a wild crowd, abusing marijuana and other drugs and engaging in promiscuous sex. At one point she ran away from home with a boyfriend, and didn't return for three months.

She quit high school with one year to go. Her life became even more chaotic; she scratched her wrists on a number of occasions, and consorted with abusive men who would use her sexually and then beat her up.

By the time I began working with Barbara, she had been abusing alcohol for about a year, and had also become addicted to benzodiazepines. Her proneness to panic-level anxiety now took the form of agoraphobia, necessitating her being accompanied by a parent to her therapy sessions. Premenstrually, her irritability rose to fever pitch: she would strike her parents with her fists, sometimes necessitating help from the police. She would then threaten to kill herself.

Lacking any hobbies or interests, apart from dancing, she was bored to distraction at home, yet afraid to venture out. Nothing gave her any pleasure except glitzy clothes (which her agoraphobia rendered irrelevant).

For a few weeks Barbara dated a man from her neighbourhood, and although she was able to leave the house if she were with him, she used the opportunity in a self-destructive way, going to wild nightclubs and provoking him with demands to the point where he drove her only halfway home, pushing her out of the car, so that she had to hitchhike home at 2 A.M. This precipitated a suicide attempt with a variety of medications (Stone, 1993, pp. 248–249). ◆

### Brief Historical Perspective

The intellectual heritage of borderline personality disorder (BPD) is quite diverse, and it is more difficult to trace than that of schizotypal personality disorder. It is, in fact, rather confusing. Several traditions are important, and in some cases they represent conflicting points of view (Leichtman, 1989).

Psychiatrist Otto Kernberg (1967, 1975) developed an explanation of borderline personality based on psychodynamic theory. According to Kernberg, borderline personality is not a specific syndrome. Rather, it refers to a set of personality features or deficiencies that can be found in individuals with various disorders. In Kernberg's model, the common characteristic of people diagnosed with borderline personality is faulty development of ego structure. Another common feature of people with borderline disorder is *splitting*—the tendency to see people and events alternately as entirely good or entirely bad. Thus a man with borderline personality might perceive his wife as almost perfect at some times and as highly flawed at other times. The tendency toward splitting helps explain the broad mood swings and unstable relationships associated with borderline personalities.

Kernberg's emphasis on a broadly defined level of pathology, rather than on discrete clinical symptoms, resulted in a relatively expansive definition of borderline personality. Viewed from this perspective, borderline disorder can encompass a great many types of abnormal behaviour, including paranoid, schizoid, and cyclothymic personality disorders, impulse control disorders (see Further Thoughts), substance use disorders, and various types of mood disorder.

## Further Thoughts **Impulse Control Disorders**

Failure to control harmful impulses is associated with several of the disorders listed in DSM-IV-TR. People who meet the criteria for borderline personality disorder and antisocial personality disorder engage in various types of impulsive, maladaptive behaviours (most often self-mutilation in the case of BPD and theft and aggression in the case of ASPD). People in the midst of a manic episode frequently become excessively involved in pleasurable activities that can have painful consequences, such as unrestrained buying or sexual indiscretions. These are examples of impulse control problems that appear as part of a more broadly defined syndrome or mental disorder.

DSM-IV-TR includes several additional problems under a heading called **impulse control disorders.** They are coded on Axis I rather than Axis II. Relatively little is known about these problems (Hollander & Rosen, 2000; Hucker, 1997). They are defined in terms of persistent, clinically significant impulsive behaviours that are not better explained by other disorders in DSM-IV-TR. They include the following:

- *Intermittent explosive disorder:* Aggressive behaviours resulting in serious assaultive acts or destruction of property. The level of aggression is grossly out of proportion to any precipitating psychosocial stressors (McElroy, 1999).
- *Kleptomania:* Stealing objects that are not needed for personal use or for their financial value. The theft is not motivated by anger or vengeance (Presta et al., 2002).
- *Pyromania:* Deliberate and purposeful setting of fires, accompanied by fascination with or attraction to fire and things that are associated with it. The behaviour is not motivated by financial considerations (as in arson), social or political ideology, anger, vengeance, or delusional beliefs (Geller, McDermeit, & Brown, 1997).
- *Trichotillomania:* Pulling out one's own hair, resulting in noticeable hair loss as well as significant distress or impairment in social or occupational functioning (O'Sullivan et al., 2000).
- *Pathological gambling:* Repeated maladaptive gambling that is associated with other problems, such as repeated, unsuccessful efforts to stop gambling, restlessness or irritability when trying to stop gambling, lying to family members and friends to conceal the extent of gambling, and committing crimes to finance gambling (Sharpe, 2002).

In most cases, the impulsive behaviour is preceded by increasing tension and followed by a feeling of pleasure, gratification, or relief. The motivation for these impulsive behaviours is, therefore, somewhat different than the motivation for compulsive behaviour (see Chapter 6). Impulsive and compulsive behaviours can be difficult to distinguish, as both are repetitious and difficult to resist. The primary difference is that the original goal for impulsive behaviour is to experience pleasure, and the original goal for compulsive behaviour is to avoid anxiety (Frances, First, & Pincus, 1995).

The most frequent type of impulse control disorder is pathological gambling, which can have devastating effects on the person's finances and personal relationships. According to estimates from Roger Bland at the University of Alberta, and Brian Cox at the University of Manitoba, the lifetime prevalence of pathological gambling in Canada is in the range of 0.4 to 2.6 percent, and seems to be increasing with the spread of legalized gambling (Bland et al., 1993; Cox et al., 2000). About

*continued*

*cont.*

1.2 million Canadians show at least some indication of having problems with gambling, and these people are more likely to be male, and poorer and less educated than people without gambling problems (Marshall & Wynne, 2003). For gamblers who recognize that they have a problem, over half say they have tried to stop in the past year but were unable to do so (Marshall & Wynne, 2003). Their most frequent gambling activity involved the use of video lottery terminals (VLTs) in local bars and restaurant lounges (Wiebe & Cox, 2001). Provinces with tougher regulations on VLTs have fewer cases of pathological gambing (Smith, 2003).

Substance use disorders (see Chapter 11) and personality disorders are commonly associated with pathological gambling (Black & Moyer, 1998). Evidence from twin studies suggests that impulsivity represents a common form of vulnerability to all of three types of disorder, and this predisposition is influenced by genetic factors (Slutske et al., 2000, 2001).

Most gambling is not associated with a mental disorder. Social gambling is a form of recreation that is accepted in most cultures. Professional gambling is an occupation pursued by people whose gambling is highly disciplined. Pathological gambling, in contrast, is out of control, takes over the person's life, and leads to horrendous financial and interpersonal consequences.

The impulse control disorders occupy an interesting and controversial niche in DSM-IV-TR. The implication of impulse control disorders is that people who repeatedly engage in dangerous, illegal, or destructive behaviours must have a mental disorder. If they do not, why do they do these things? Unfortunately, this reasoning quickly becomes circular. Why does he gamble recklessly? Because he has a mental disorder. How do you know he has a mental disorder? Because he gambles recklessly. This logical dilemma is particularly evident in the case of impulse control disorders because these problem behaviours do not appear as part of a broader syndrome in which other symptoms of disorder are also present. In other words, the problem behaviour is the disorder. Until we can step outside this loop, validating the utility of the diagnostic concept by reference to other psychological or biological response systems, we are left with an unsatisfying approach to the definition of these problems. ◆

In an effort to foster research on borderline disorders, these psychodynamic views regarding personality organization were translated into more reliable, descriptive terms by several prominent clinicians. Gunderson (1984, 1994) identified a number of descriptive characteristics that are commonly associated with Kernberg's concept of borderline personality. Gunderson and his colleagues developed a structured interview that would allow clinicians to diagnose the condition reliably and served as the basis for the current definition of BPD in DSM-IV-TR.

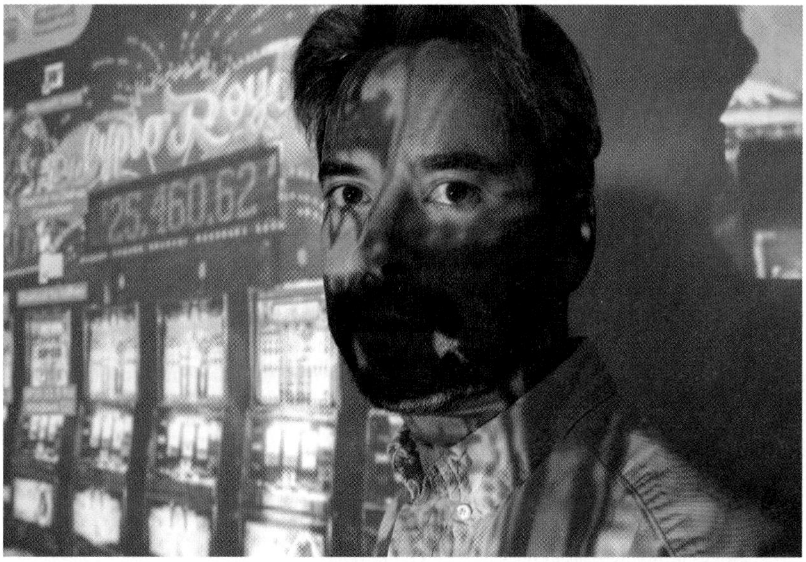


*University of Manitoba psychologist Brian Cox has been studying the effects of gambling since the Manitoba government brought in video-lottery terminals and opened casinos. One goal of his research is to learn why some provinces have a smaller proportion of people with gambling problems than others.*

## Clinical Features and Comorbidity

The DSM-IV-TR criteria for borderline personality disorder are presented in Table 9–4. The overriding characteristic of borderline personality disorder is a pervasive pattern of instability in self-image, in interpersonal relationships, and in mood.

> To be borderline means to lack grounding emotionally and to exist from moment to moment without any sense of continuity, predictability, or meaning. Life is experienced in fragments, more like a series of snapshots than a moving picture. It is a series of discrete points of experience that fail to flow together smoothly or to create an integrated whole. (Moskovitz, 1996, pp. 5–6)

Borderline personality disorder overlaps with several other categories on Axis II, including the histrionic, narcissistic, paranoid, dependent, and avoidant types. There is also a significant amount of overlap between borderline personality disorder and Axis I disorders, especially depression (Trull, 1995; Widiger & Trull, 1993). Many patients with other types of impulse control problems, such as substance dependence and eating disorders, also qualify for a diagnosis of borderline personality disorder.

Follow-up studies suggest many similarities between borderline personality disorder and mood disorders. In many cases, the features of borderline personality disorder are evident before the onset of major depression. For example, one study focused on a group of 100 outpatients with a diagnosis of borderline personality disorder (Akiskal, 1992). During follow-up, 29 percent of the sample developed severe depression. Another longitudinal study of patients who were discharged from a private psychiatric hospital is also interesting in this regard. Of the patients with a pure diagnosis of borderline personality disorder (that is, those who did not receive any other diagnosis on Axis I or II), 23 percent developed major depressive episodes in the course of the 15-year follow-up (McGlashan, 1986).

### Etiological Considerations

Genetic factors do not seem to play a central role in the etiology of borderline personality disorder when it is viewed in terms of the syndrome that is defined in DSM-IV-TR (Torgersen, 1994). It is premature to conclude that genes are irrelevant to the development of this set of problems because neuroticism (one of the personality traits or dimensions that is clearly related to the borderline concept) is influenced by genetic factors (Livesley et al., 1998; Nigg & Goldsmith, 1994). Nevertheless, most of the discussion regarding causes of borderline personality disorder has focused on environmental events.

Some investigators have argued that borderline patients suffer from the negative consequences of parental loss or neglect during childhood (Davis & Akiskal, 1986). This model is supported by studies of the families of borderline patients and by comparisons with the literature on social development in monkeys that examined the effects of separating infants from their mothers. Studies of patients with borderline personality disorder do point toward the influence of widespread problematic relationships with their parents (Guzder et al., 1996). Separation appears to be only one aspect of this complicated picture. Adolescent girls with borderline personality disorder report pervasive lack of supervision, frequent witnessing of domestic violence, and being subjected to inappropriate behaviour by their parents and other adults, including verbal, physical, and sexual abuse (Norden et al., 1995; Weaver & Clum, 1993). The extent and severity of abuse vary widely across individuals. Many patients describe multiple forms of abuse by more than one person.

The association between borderline personality disorder and the patients' recollections of childhood maltreatment raises an important question about the direction of this relationship: Does childhood abuse lead to borderline personality disorder? Or are people with borderline personality disorder simply more likely to remember that they were abused by their parents, due to biased reporting?

Longitudinal data from a study of adolescents provide important evidence on this point (Johnson et al., 1999). People with documented evidence of childhood abuse and neglect were four times more likely than those who had not been mistreated to develop symptoms of personality disorders as young adults. Strongest connections were found for Cluster B disorders (Cohen et al., 1999). Physical abuse was most closely associated with subsequent antisocial personality disorder; sexual abuse with borderline personality disorder; and childhood neglect with antisocial, borderline, narcissistic, and avoidant personality disorder. These data support the argument that maladaptive patterns of parenting and family relationships increase the probability that a person will develop certain types of personality

**TABLE 9–4 DSM-IV-TR Criteria for Borderline Personality Disorder**

**A. A pervasive pattern of instability of interpersonal relationships, self-image, and affects, and marked impulsivity beginning by early adulthood and present in a variety of contexts, as indicated by five (or more) of the following:**

1. Frantic efforts to avoid real or imagined abandonment.
2. A pattern of unstable and intense interpersonal relationships characterized by alternating between extremes of idealization and devaluation.
3. Identity disturbance: markedly and persistently unstable self-image or sense of self.
4. Impulsiveness in at least two areas that are potentially self-damaging (for example, spending, sex, substance abuse, reckless driving, binge eating).
5. Recurrent suicidal behaviour, gestures, or threats, or self-mutilating behaviour.
6. Affective instability due to a marked reactivity of mood (such as intense episodic dysphoria, irritability, or anxiety usually lasting a few hours and only rarely more than a few days).
7. Chronic feelings of emptiness.
8. Inappropriate, intense anger or difficulty controlling anger (for example, frequent displays of temper, constant anger, recurrent physical fights).
9. Transient, stress-related paranoid ideation or severe dissociative symptoms.

disorder. However, further research is needed to establish a causal link between childhood experiences and personality disorder. Many factors are likely to be involved. It is important to recognize that child abuse does not inevitably lead to personality disorders. As observed by McGill University psychiatrist Joel Paris, many people with personality disorders do not have histories of child abuse, and many survivors of child abuse grow up to have normal personalities (Paris, 1998). Research by Paris and colleagues indicates that both environmental risks and neurobiological vulnerability (e.g., neurotransmitter dysregulation) should be taken into account to understand the etiology of borderline personality disorder (Paris et al., 2004; Zelkowitz et al., 2001).

### Treatment

Given that the concept of borderline personality disorder is rooted in psychodynamic theory, it should not be surprising that many clinicians have advocated the use of psychotherapy for the treatment of these conditions. In psychodynamically based treatment, the *transference relationship*, defined as the way in which the patient behaves toward the therapist and which is believed to reflect early primary relationships, is used to increase patients' ability to experience themselves and other people in a more realistic and integrated way (Clarkin et al., 2001; Gabbard, 2000).

As we have said, personality disorders have traditionally been considered to be hard to treat from a psychological perspective, and borderline conditions are among the most difficult. Close personal relationships form the foundation of psychological intervention, and it is specifically in the area of establishing and maintaining such relationships that borderline patients experience their greatest difficulty. Their persistent alternation between overidealization and devaluation leads to frequent rage toward the therapist and can become a significant deterrent to progress in therapy. Not surprisingly, between one-half and two-thirds of all patients with borderline personality disorder discontinue treatment, against their therapists' advice, within the first several weeks of treatment (Kelly et al., 1992).

One promising approach to psychotherapy with borderline patients, called *dialectical behaviour therapy* (DBT), has been developed and evaluated by Linehan (1993; Linehan et al., 2001). This procedure combines the use of broadly based behavioural strategies with the more general principles of supportive psychotherapy. In philosophy, the term *dialectics* refers to a process of reasoning that places opposite or contradictory ideas side by side. In Linehan's approach to treatment, the term refers to strategies that are employed by the therapist in order to help the person appreciate and balance apparently contradictory needs to accept things as they are (such as intense negative emotions) and to work toward changing patterns of thinking and behaviour that contribute to problems in the regulation of emotions. Emphasis is placed on learning to be more comfortable with strong emotions, such as anger, sadness, and fear, and learning to think in a more integrated way that accepts both good and bad features of the self and other people. Traditional behavioural and cognitive techniques, such as skill training, exposure, and problem solving, are also employed to help the patient improve interpersonal relationships, tolerate distress, and regulate emotional responses. Finally, considerable emphasis is placed on the therapist's acceptance of patients, including their frequently demanding, manipulative, and contradictory behaviours. This factor is important, because borderline patients are extremely sensitive to even the most subtle signs of criticism or rejection by other people.

One controlled study of dialectical behaviour therapy produced encouraging results with regard to some aspects of the patients' behaviour (Linehan et al., 1994, 1999). All of the patients in this study were women who met diagnostic criteria for BPD and also had a previous history of suicide attempts or deliberate self-harm. Patients were randomly assigned to receive either DBT or treatment as usual, which was essentially any form of treatment that was available within the community. The

**Joel Paris**, *a psychiatrist at McGill University, has played a leading role in understanding the nature of borderline personality disorder.*

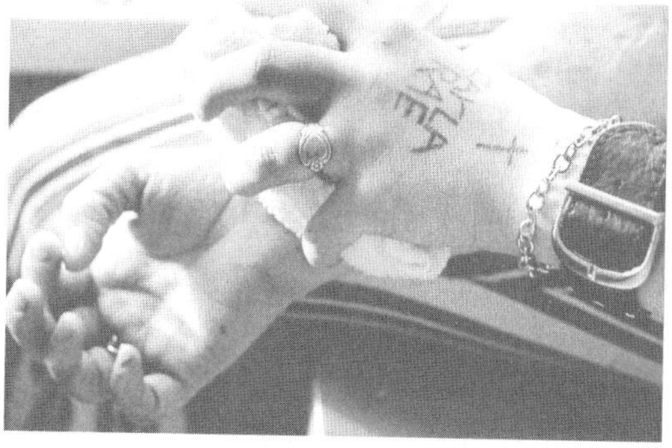

*Some people with borderline personality disorder engage in recurrent suicidal gestures of self-mutilating behaviour.*

adjustment of patients in both groups was measured after one year of treatment and over a one-year period following termination. One of the most important results involved the dropout rate. Almost 60 percent of the patients in the treatment as usual group terminated prematurely, whereas the rate in the DBT group was only 17 percent. The patients who received DBT also showed a significant reduction in the frequency and severity of suicide attempts, spent fewer days in psychiatric hospitals over the course of the study, and rated themselves higher on a measure of social adjustment. The groups did not differ, however, on other important measures, such as level of depression and hopelessness.

Positive results have also been reported in a more recent study in which women with BPD were randomly assigned to either dialectical behaviour therapy or treatment-as-usual. This study did find that the women treated with dialectical behaviour therapy experienced more improvement than the women in the control group with regard to symptoms such as depression and hopelessness (Koons et al., 2001).

In general, these studies suggest that DBT is a promising form of treatment for people with borderline personality disorder. It should be noted, however, that the sample sizes in these studies are quite small. Important methodological questions have been raised about the outcome results, including the possible influence of the allegiance effect (see Research Methods in Chapter 10). DBT has become one of the most popular and rapidly expanding forms of psychological treatment, and it has begun to be used in treating other problems that involve impulsive behaviour, such as substance use disorders and binge eating disorders (Telch, Agras, & Linehan, 2001). Enthusiasm for the therapeutic value of DBT will undoubtedly lead to more rigorous evaluations of its effectiveness in clinical settings.

Psychotropic medication is also used frequently in the treatment of borderline patients. Unfortunately, no disorder-specific drug has been found. Psychiatrists employ the entire spectrum of psychoactive medication with borderline patients, from antipsychotics and antidepressants to lithium and anticonvulsants (Koenigsberg, Woo-Ming, & Siever, 2002; Zanarini & Frankenburg, 2001). Different types of drugs are recommended to treat individual symptoms, such as impulsive aggression, emotional instability, and transient paranoid thinking, but there is no systematic proof that a specific drug is effective for any of the borderline features (Dimeff, McDavid, & Linehan, 1999).

## Antisocial Personality Disorder (ASPD)

Antisocial personality disorder (ASPD) has been studied more thoroughly and for a longer period of time than any of the other personality disorders (Blashfield & McElroy, 1989). Emotional and interpersonal problems also play an important role in the definition of antisocial personality disorder. The following case, written by Robert Hare, an emeritus professor at the University of British Columbia, illustrates the egocentricity that is a central feature of the disorder. It also demonstrates the stunning lack of concern that such people have for the impact of their behaviour on other people, especially those who are close to them.

### BRIEF CASE STUDY

**Antisocial Personality Disorder**

Terry is 21, the second of three boys born into a wealthy and highly respected family. His older brother is a doctor, and his younger brother is a scholarship student in his second year of college. Terry is a first-time offender, serving two years for a series of robberies committed a year ago.

By all accounts, his family life was stable, his parents were warm and loving, and his opportunities for success were enormous. His brothers were honest and hardworking, whereas he simply "floated through life, taking whatever was offered." His parents' hopes and expectations were less important to him than having a good time. Still, they supported him emotionally and financially through an adolescence marked by wildness, testing the limits, and repeated brushes with the law—speeding, reckless driving, drunkenness—but no formal convictions. By age 20 he had fathered two children and was heavily involved in gambling and drugs. When he could no longer obtain money from his family he turned to robbing banks, and he was soon caught and sent to prison. "I wouldn't be here if my parents had come across when I needed them," he said. "What kind of parents would let their son rot in a place like this?" Asked about his children, he replied, "I've

*continued*

*cont.*

never seen them. I think they were given up for adoption. How the hell should I know!" (Hare, 1993, p. 167). ◆

The contrast between Terry's willingness to blame his problems on his parents and his apparent inability to accept responsibility for his own children is striking. It illustrates clearly the callous indifference and shallow emotional experience of the person with antisocial personality disorder.

## Brief Historical Perspective

Current views of antisocial personality disorder have been greatly influenced by two specific books. These books have inspired two different approaches to the definition of the disorder itself. The first book, *The Mask of Sanity*, written by psychiatrist Hervey Cleckley, was originally published in 1941. It includes numerous case examples of impulsive, self-centred, pleasure seeking people who seemed to be completely lacking in certain primary emotions, such as anxiety, shame, and guilt. Cleckley used the term **psychopathy** to describe this disorder. According to Cleckley's definition, the psychopath is a person who is intelligent and superficially charming but is also chronically deceitful, unreliable, and incapable of learning from experience. This diagnostic approach places principal emphasis on emotional deficits and personality traits. Unfortunately, Cleckley's definition was difficult to use reliably because it contained such elusive features as "incapacity for love" and "failure to learn from experience."

The second book that influenced the concept of antisocial personality disorder was a report by Lee Robins of her follow-up study of children who had been treated many years earlier at a child guidance clinic. The book, *Deviant Children Grown Up* (1966), demonstrated that certain forms of conduct disorder that were evident during childhood, especially among boys, were reliable predictors of other forms of antisocial behaviour when these same people became adults. The diagnostic approach inspired by this research study was adopted by DSM-III (APA, 1980). It places principal emphasis on observable behaviours and repeated conflict with authorities, including failure to conform to social norms with respect to lawful behaviour. This approach can be used with greater reliability than psychopathy because it is focused on concrete consequences of the disorder, which are often documented by legal records, rather than subjectively defined emotional deficits, such as lack of empathy.

## Psychopathy versus Antisocial Personality Disorder

Psychopathy and ASPD are two different attempts to define the same disorder. Yet they are sufficiently different that they certainly do not identify the same people, and they are no longer used interchangeably (Arrigo & Shipley, 2001). Critics argued that DSM-III (and DSM-IV-TR) blurs the distinction between antisocial personality and criminality (Hare, Hart, & Harpur, 1991). The DSM emphasizes antisocial behaviours because these can be reliably identified (e.g., by examining the person's criminal record). However, the true meaning of the concept of psychopathy might have been sacrificed in DSM for the sake of improved reliability.

ASPD and psychopathy are similar in that both are characterized by social deviance and behavioural problems (e.g., a history of impulsive and irresponsible behaviour). But ASPD, compared to psychopathy, places a greater emphasis on juvenile delinquency and adult criminal acts. Psychopathy, compared to ASPD, places greater emphasis on particular personality features. The latter include callousness, deceitfulness, egocentricity, failure to form close emotional bonds, low anxiety proneness, superficial charm, lack of remorse, and externalization of blame (Shipley & Arrigo, 2001; Skeem et al., 2003). When a question such as "Tell me what it is like for you to feel guilt" is posed to a psychopath, the typical reaction is irritation, deflection, or a change of subject matter. Psychopaths lack insight into what emotions like guilt and remorse actually feel like (Shipley & Arrigo, 2001).

ASPD and psychopathy also differ in their prevalence. APSD tends to be the rule rather than the exception in correctional settings, with 50 to 80 percent of offenders typically meeting diagnostic criteria. In contrast, only about 15 to 30 percent of correctional offenders in North America typically are classified as psychopaths (Skeem et al., 2003). In forensic settings, almost all psychopaths (about 90 percent) meet diagnostic criteria for ASPD,

Robert Hare, a psychologist at the University of British Columbia, is a leading expert on psychopathy. He developed the Psychopathy Checklist, which has become the standard assessment instrument for this disorder.

but only about 30 percent of people with ASPD are psychopaths (Cunningham & Reidy, 1998; Shipley & Arrigo, 2001). A minority of psychopaths—the so-called corporate or white-collar psychopaths—do not meet criteria for ASPD, usually because they have successfully avoided being caught for their criminal acts. Such psychopaths have avoided establishing a record of criminal acts, and therefore are not diagnosed with ASPD. They may operate on the fringes of legality, using charm, deceit, manipulation, and intimidation to satisfy their selfish desires.

## Clinical Features and Comorbidity

Table 9–5 lists the DSM-IV-TR criteria for antisocial personality disorder. One prominent feature in this definition is the required presence of symptoms of conduct disorder (see Chapter 16) prior to the age of 15, which reflects the impact of Robins's work. The definition also requires the presence of at least three out of seven signs of irresponsible and antisocial behaviour after the age of 15. One of these criteria, "lack of remorse," did not appear in DSM-III but was one of Cleckley's original criteria. Its inclusion in DSM-IV-TR clearly signals an attempt to move the definition back toward the original concept.

Some investigators and clinicians prefer the concept of psychopathy to the DSM-IV-TR definition of antisocial personality. Robert Hare has developed a systematic approach to the assessment of psychopathy, known as the Psychopathy Checklist (PCL), which is based largely on Cleckley's original description of the disorder. The PCL includes two major factors (groups of symptoms): (1) emotional/interpersonal traits and (2) social deviance associated with an unstable or antisocial lifestyle. Key symptoms for both factors are summarized in Table 9–6. The major difference between this definition of psychopathy and the DSM-IV-TR definition of antisocial personality disorder involves the list of emotional and interpersonal traits (although DSM-IV-TR does include being deceitful and failure to experience remorse). Extensive research with the PCL indicates that, contrary to previous experience with Cleckley's criteria, the emotional and interpersonal traits can be used reliably (Hart & Hare, 1997).

The ultimate resolution of this prolonged dispute over the best definition of antisocial personality disorder will depend on systematic comparisons of the two approaches (Lilienfeld, 1994; Skilling et al., 2002). This situation is a classic example of the issues involved in studying the validity of a diagnostic concept (see Chapter 4). How different are these definitions? Which definition is most useful in predicting events such as repeated antisocial behaviour following release from prison? The field trial that was conducted when DSM-IV-TR was being prepared represents one large-scale effort of this type (Widiger et al., 1996). That project did not find any major differences in validity between the DSM-based definition of antisocial personality disorder and a PCL-based definition of psychopathy.

The concept of psychopathy as measured by the Psychopathy Checklist, does, however, appear to have some advantages. Measures on the checklist are among the best predictors of which prison inmates are most likely to commit further criminal offences when they are released from prison (Correctional Services Canada, 2002; Hare et al., 2000). The concept of psychopathy has also been usefully extended for understanding corruption in the corporate world. Psychopaths possess the interpersonal qualities that allow them to charm their way up to the top of the corporate ladder (Babiak, 1995). Screening of corporate leaders for psychopathic traits could prevent some of the massive frauds perpetrated in the business world (Hogben, 2003). Accordingly, Babiak and Hare

**TABLE 9–5 DSM-IV-TR Criteria for Antisocial Personality Disorder**

**A. There is a pervasive pattern of disregard for and violation of the rights of others occurring since age 15, as indicated by three (or more) of the following:**

1. Failure to conform to social norms with respect to lawful behaviour as indicated by repeatedly performing acts that are grounds for arrest.
2. Deceitfulness, as indicated by repeated lying, use of aliases, or conning others for personal profit or pleasure.
3. Impulsivity or failure to plan ahead.
4. Irritability and aggressiveness, as indicated by repeated physical fights or assaults.
5. Reckless disregard for safety of self or others.
6. Consistent irresponsibility, as indicated by repeated failure to sustain consistent work behaviour or honour financial obligations.
7. Lack of remorse, as indicated by being indifferent to or rationalizing having hurt, mistreated, or stolen from another.

**B. The individual is at least 18 years old.**

**C. Evidence of conduct disorder with onset before age 15.**

(2003) developed a checklist for identifying corporate psychopaths. According to their measure, the corporate psychopath exhibits traits such as the following: he or she comes across as smooth, polished, and charming; focuses most conversations on him- or herself; discredits or puts down others to build own image and reputation; lies to coworkers, customers, and business associates; is opportunistic, hates to lose, plays ruthlessly to win; creates a power network in the organization to use for personal gain; shows no regret for making decisions that negatively affect others (e.g., may take great pleasure in firing someone) (Hogben, 2003).

The following case study provides a further illustration of some of the many different manifestations of psychopathy.

**TABLE 9-6 Key Symptoms of Psychopathy**

| Emotional/Interpersonal Traits | Social Deviance (Antisocial Lifestyle) |
|---|---|
| Glib and superficial | Impulsive |
| Egocentric and grandiose | Poor behaviour controls |
| Lack of remorse or guilt | Need for excitement |
| Lack of empathy | Lack of responsibility |
| Deceitful and manipulative | Early behaviour problems |
| Shallow emotions | Adult antisocial behaviour |

*Source:* R.D. Hare, 1993, *Without Conscience: The Disturbing World of the Psychopaths Among Us.* New York: Pocket Books.

## CASE STUDY Paul Bernardo and Karla Homolka

The crimes of Paul Bernardo and Karla Homolka are among the most sadistic and violent in Canadian history. Paul Bernardo was convicted in 1995 of the rape and murder of two 14- and 15-year-old girls whom he and his wife, Karla Homolka, had abducted and used as "sex slaves." The sexual assaults were carefully planned and sadistic. The assaults were recorded by Bernardo on videotape. The jury was shocked and disgusted when the tapes were shown during Bernardo's trial (Pron, 1995; Williams, 1996). Homolka also "gave" her 15-year-old sister, Tammy, to Bernardo as a Christmas present. Tammy was drugged by Homolka and then raped by Bernardo. Tammy died as a result of the drugging. Later, Homolka would pretend for Bernardo that she was her dead sister during their sex play (Williams, 1996).

Bernardo also was the notorious Scarborough rapist, who sexually assaulted as many as 40 women. The rapes were sadistic, involving humiliation and the use of force; during one rape he ripped out a big tuft of the victim's pubic hair, saying, "I want something to remember you by" (Williams, 1996, p. 128). Bernardo's spree of violence lasted about six years, from age 20 to 26. After he was convicted, Bernardo was designated a dangerous offender and is therefore effectively in jail for life. In a plea bargaining agreement, his wife agreed to testify against Bernardo in return for a 12-year prison term. She is due to be released in July 2005 (Williams, 2003).

There has been no debate on Paul Bernardo's psychopathology. According to Robert Hare, an expert on psychopathy from the University of British Columbia, Bernardo is a cold-blooded predator lacking in remorse, and the perfect example of a psychopath (Kaihla, 1996). As we will see, psychopathy is quite similar to antisocial personality disorder. Other writers have reached similar conclusions about Bernardo (Burnside & Cairns, 1995; Williams, 1996). Paul Bernardo was bright, charming, and popular at high school, but was also sly, manipulative, and grandiose. He got good grades and eventually completed a degree in accounting at the University of Toronto (Burnside & Cairns, 1995). Bernardo had a history of petty theft, various scams, and was also involved in cigarette smuggling. He was also violent; he beat his girlfriends and later his wife. After her final beating by Bernardo, Homolka was hospitalized for three days, and finally left him. He showed no remorse or guilt for his crimes, as illustrated by the following examples.

> One day, when they were driving around . . . Paul [Bernardo] pointed out an attractive, young girl who looked to be about fifteen years old. "There's the girl I raped," he said proudly. . . . Karla [Homolka] was happy for him—whatever the king wanted, the king should have—but she was not as confident about his impunity as he was. (Williams, 1996, p. 186)

> Whether he was talking about smuggling cigarettes, or about how the [chain]saw blade jammed up when he was slicing through Mahaffy's shoulder [one of his victims], Bernardo's voice had a breezy tone to it. Cutting up Mahaffy's body was the most disgusting thing he had ever done, he testified. But he was referring more to the grossness of the act than to its morality. (Pron, 1995, p. 523)

Bernardo was a psychopath who enjoyed sado-masochistic sex; "Paul clearly viewed women as something to be used, dominated, manipulated, and controlled" (Burnside & Cairns, 1995, p. 89). His other paraphilias included arousal while watching someone urinate or defecate (Pron, 1995).

Karla Homolka has proved to be a puzzle to psychologists and psychiatrists; indeed, her inscrutability is a central part of why she seems likely to rank as one of the world's most infamous female criminals (Williams, 1996). How could a person partake in abduction and sexual assault and *not* have something psychologically wrong with them? Experts disagree on her diagnosis (Burnside & Cairns, 1995; Pron, 1985; Williams, 1996, 2003). Some

*continued*

cont.

psychologists and psychiatrists regard her as a victim—a battered woman with post-traumatic stress disorder, who was caught in Bernardo's web of charm and coercion. Other experts have pointed out that Homolka was a willing accomplice in Bernardo's sexual assaults; she lied and stole to obtain the drugs to knock the victims unconscious; she clearly appeared to be enjoying herself during some of the videotaped assaults (e.g., when she was performing cunnilingus on an unconscious victim); she showed no remorse over her role in the crimes; she readily testified against Bernardo when it was in her best interests, initiated divorce proceedings, and reported him for cigarette smuggling; and she readily began dating again once she left Bernardo and sent her new lover nude Polaroids of herself. The latter behaviours are not what one would expect from a battered woman with post-traumatic stress disorder. These pieces of evidence suggest that she too may be a psychopath. But on the other hand, her criminal activities appear to have started and ended with her relationship with Bernardo; "when one considers her character at age seventeen, prior to her meeting Paul, Karla does not even register a trickle on either the Antisocial Personality Disorder criteria or the Hare's Psychopathy Checklist" (Burnside & Cairns, 1995, p. 559). "If anything, her happy childhood and uneventful teenage development made her subsequent deviant and murderous behaviour even more mysterious" (Williams, 2003, p. 51).

Homolka apparently enjoyed playing a submissive role in some of their sadomasochistic sex play, and seemingly found Bernardo's exploits to be exciting. Williams (1996, 2003) suggests that she suffers from hybristophilia—a phenomena is which a person is sexually aroused by a partner's violent sexual behaviour. The judge who presided over Homolka's trial stated in his sentencing remarks that she was not a danger to society—unless she met another Paul Bernardo (Williams, 2003).

*Paul Bernardo was convicted in 1995 of rape and murder of women that he and his wife, Karla Homolka, had abducted. The sexual assaults, which were carefully planned and often sadistic, were recorded by Bernardo on videotape. The jury was shocked and disgusted when the tapes were shown during the trial. To people unaware of his crimes, Bernardo was seen as charming, self-assured, and intelligent.*

### Antisocial Behaviour across the Lifespan

Not everyone who engages in antisocial behaviour does so consistently throughout his or her lifetime. Terrie Moffitt, a clinical psychologist at the University of London, has proposed that there are two primary forms of antisocial behaviour: transient and nontransient. Moffitt (1993, 1997) considers adolescence-limited antisocial behaviour to be a common form of social behaviour that is often adaptive and that disappears by the time the person reaches adulthood. This type presumably accounts for most antisocial behaviour, and it is unrelated to antisocial personality disorder.

A small proportion of antisocial individuals, mostly males, engage in antisocial behaviour at all ages. Moffitt calls this type life-course-persistent antisocial behaviour. The specific form of these problems may vary from one age level to the next:

> Biting and hitting at age 4, shoplifting and truancy at age 10, selling drugs and stealing cars at age 16, robbery and rape at age 22, and fraud and child abuse at age 30. The underlying disposition remains the same, but its expression changes form as new social opportunities arise at different points in development. (Moffitt, 1993, p. 679)

Follow-up studies suggest that in some ways psychopaths tend to "burn out" when they reach 40 or 45 years of age. These changes are most evident for the impulsive, socially deviant kinds of behaviour that are represented in the second factor on Hare's Psychopathy Checklist (Harpur & Hare, 1994). Indeed, older psychopaths are less likely to exhibit a pathological "need for excitement" or to engage in impulsive, criminal behaviours. In contrast to this pattern, personality traits associated with the emotional/interpersonal factor on the PCL, such as deceitfulness, callousness, and lack of empathy, do not become less conspicuous over time. These are apparently more stable features of the disorder.

It is not clear whether the age-related decline in social deviance represents a change in personality structure (improved impulse control and diminished sensation seeking). Moffitt's theory suggests that, as psychopaths grow older, they may find new outlets for their aggression, impulsive behaviour, and callous disregard for others. For example, they might resort to fraud or child abuse, for which they are less likely to get caught.

## Etiological Considerations

Psychologists have studied etiological factors associated with psychopathy and antisocial personality disorder more extensively than for any of the other personality disorders. Research studies on this topic fall into three general areas. One is concerned with the biological underpinnings of the disorder, especially the possible influence of genetic factors. The second focus of investigation is social factors. The relationship between familial conflict and the development of antisocial behaviour in children falls under this general heading. The third group of studies has addressed the nature of the psychological factors that might explain the apparent inability of people with antisocial personality disorder to learn from experience.

**Biological Factors** Several investigators have employed adoption methods to evaluate the relative contributions of genetic and environmental factors to the development of antisocial personality disorder and of criminal behaviour more generally (Carey & Gottesman, 1996; McGuffin & Thapar, 1998). This strategy is based on the study of adoptees: people who were separated from their biological parents at an early age and raised by adoptive families (see Chapter 2).

Several adoption studies have found that the development of antisocial behaviour is determined by an interaction between genetic factors and adverse environmental circumstances. In other words, both types of influence are important. The highest rates of conduct disorder and antisocial behaviour are found among the offspring of antisocial biological parents who are raised in an adverse adoptive environment.

Consider, for example, the results of one particularly informative study that was conducted by Cadoret and colleagues (Cadoret et al., 1995; Yates, Cadoret, & Troughton, 1999). The investigators studied men and women who had been separated at birth from biological parents with antisocial personality disorder. This target group was compared to a control group of people who had been separated at birth from biological parents with no history of psychopathology. The offspring and their adoptive parents were interviewed to assess symptoms of conduct disorder, aggression, and antisocial behaviour in the offspring. The adversity of the adoptive home environment was measured in terms of the total number of problems that were present, including severe marital difficulties, drug abuse, or criminal activity.

The results of the study by Cadoret and colleagues indicated that people who were raised in more difficult adoptive homes were more likely to engage in various types of aggressive and antisocial behaviour as children and as adults. Further analyses revealed that the harmful effects of an unfavourable environment were more pronounced in the target group than in the control group. In other words, offspring of antisocial parents were much more likely to exhibit symptoms of conduct disorder (truancy, school expulsion, lying, and stealing) as children and exaggerated aggressive behaviour as adolescents if they were raised in an adverse adoptive home environment. Being raised in an adverse home environment did not significantly increase the probability of conduct disorder, aggression, or antisocial behaviour among offspring in the control group. Thus antisocial behaviour appeared to result from the interaction of genetic and environmental factors.

**Social Factors** Adoption studies indicate that genetic factors interact with environmental events to produce patterns of antisocial and criminal behaviour. The combination of a genetic predisposition toward antisocial behaviour and environmental adversity is particularly harmful. What kinds of events might be involved in this process? Obvious candidates include physical abuse and childhood neglect, as indicated by the longitudinal study of adolescents and their families (Johnson et al., 1999).

How can the interaction between genetic factors and family processes be explained? Moffitt's explanation for the etiology of life-course-persistent antisocial behaviour depends on the influence of multiple, interacting systems. One pathway involves the concept of children's temperament and the effect that their characteristic response styles may have on parental behaviour. Children with a "difficult" temperament—that is, those whose response style is characterized by high levels of negative emotion or excessive activity—may be especially irritating to their parents and caretakers (Bates, Wachs, & Emde, 1994). They may be clumsy, overactive, inattentive, irritable, or impulsive. Their resistance to disciplinary efforts may discourage adults from maintaining persistent strategies in this regard. This type of child may be most likely to evoke maladaptive reactions from parents who are poorly equipped to deal with the challenges presented by this kind of behaviour. Parents may be driven either to use unusually harsh punishments or to abandon any attempt at discipline. This interaction between the child and the social environment fosters the development of poorly controlled behaviour. Antisocial behaviour is perpetuated when the person selects friends who share similar antisocial interests and problems.

*Antisocial behaviour can be perpetuated when the person selects friends who share similar antisocial interests and problems.*

After a pattern of antisocial behaviour has been established during childhood, many factors lock the person into further antisocial activities. Moffitt's theory emphasizes two sources of continuity. The first is a limited range of behavioural skills. The person does not learn social skills that would allow him or her to pursue more appropriate responses than behaviours such as lying, cheating, and stealing. Once the opportunity to develop these skills is lost during childhood, they may never be learned. The second source of continuity involves the results of antisocial behaviour during childhood and adolescence. The person becomes progressively ensnared by the aftermath of earlier choices. Many possible consequences of antisocial behaviour, including being addicted to drugs, becoming a teenaged parent, dropping out of school, and having a criminal record, can narrow the person's options.

**Psychological Factors** Adoption, twin, and family studies provide clues to the types of etiological factors that may cause antisocial personality disorder. Another series of studies, beginning in the 1950s and extending to the present, has been concerned with the psychological mechanisms that may mediate this type of behaviour. These investigations have attempted to explain several characteristic features of psychopathy—such as lack of anxiety, impulsivity, and failure to learn from experience—using various types of laboratory tasks.

Subjects in the laboratory tasks are typically asked to learn a sequence of responses in order either to receive a reward or avoid an aversive consequence, such as electric shock or loss of money. Although the overall accuracy of psychopaths' performance on these tasks is generally equivalent to that of nonpsychopathic subjects, their behaviour sometimes appears to be unaffected by the anticipation of punishment (Lykken, 1957; Newman & Wallace, 1993).

Two primary hypotheses have been advanced to explain the poor performance of psychopaths on these tasks. One point of view is based on Cleckley's argument that psychopaths are emotionally impoverished. Their lack of anxiety and fear is particularly striking. Research support for this hypothesis is based in large part on an examination of physiological responses while subjects are performing laboratory tasks. One particularly compelling line of investigation involves the examination of the eye blink startle reflex. People blink their eyes involuntarily when they are startled by a loud, unexpected burst of noise. For most people, the magnitude of this response is increased if, at the time they are startled, they are engaged in an ongoing task that elicits fear or some other negative emotional state (such as viewing frightening or disgusting stimuli). The magnitude of the startle response is decreased if the person is engaged in a task that elicits positive emotion. Psychopaths' startle responses follow a pattern different from those observed in normal subjects (Herpertz et al., 2001; Patrick & Zempolich, 1998); they do not show the exaggerated startle response that is indicative of fear in the presence of aversive stimuli. This emotional deficit may explain why psychopaths are relatively insensitive to, or able to ignore, the effects of punishment (Hare, 1993).

The other hypothesis holds that psychopaths have difficulty shifting or reallocating their attention to consider the possible negative consequences of their behaviour. Evidence for this explanation is based in large part on the observation that psychopaths respond normally to punishment in some situations but not in others. This is especially evident in mixed-incentive situations, in which the person's behaviour might be either rewarded or punished. Psychopaths are preoccupied with the potential for a successful outcome. They will continue gambling when the stakes are high, even when the odds are badly against them. And they will pursue a potential sexual encounter, even when the other person is trying to discourage their interest. They fail to inhibit inappropriate behaviour because they are less able than other people to stop and consider the meaning of important signals that their behaviour might lead to punishment (Newman, Schmitt, & Voss, 1997; Patterson & Newman, 1993).

Critics of this line of research have noted some problems with existing psychological explanations for the psychopath's behaviour. One limitation is the implicit assumption that most people conform to social regulations and ethical principles because of anxiety or fear of punishment. The heart of this criticism seems to lie in a disagreement regarding the relative importance of Cleckley's criteria for psychopathy. It might be argued that the most crucial features are not low anxiety and failure to learn from experience but lack of shame and pathological egocentricity. According to this perspective, the psychopath is simply a person who has chosen, for whatever reason, to behave in a persistently selfish manner that ignores the feelings and rights of other people. "Rather than moral judgment being driven by anxiety, anxiety is driven by moral judgment" (Levenson, 1992).

### Treatment

People with antisocial personalities seldom seek professional mental health services unless they are forced into treatment by the legal system. When they do seek treatment, the general consensus among clinicians is that it is seldom effective. This widely held impression is based, in part, on the traits that are used to define the disorder; like people with borderline personality disorder, people with antisocial personality disorder are typically unable to establish intimate, trusting relationships, which obviously form the basis for any treatment program.

The research literature regarding the treatment of antisocial personality disorder is sparse (Salekin, 2002). Very few studies have identified cases using official diagnostic criteria for antisocial personality disorder. Most of the programs that have been evaluated have focused on juvenile delinquents, adults who have been imprisoned, or people otherwise referred by the criminal justice system. Outcome is often measured in terms of the frequency of repeated criminal offences rather than in terms of changes in behaviours more directly linked to the personality traits that define the core of antisocial personality. The high rate of alcoholism and other forms of substance dependence in this population is another problem that complicates planning and evaluating treatment programs aimed specifically at the personality disorder itself.

Although no form of intervention has proved to be effective for antisocial personality disorder, psychological interventions that are directed toward specific features of the disorder might be useful. Examples are behavioural procedures that were originally designed for anger management and deviant sexual behaviours (Reid & Gacono, 2000; Sanderlin, 2001). Researchers Marnie E. Rice and Grant T. Harris, at Oak Ridge Mental Health Centre in Ontario, found that behavioural treatments can produce temporary changes in behaviour while the person is closely supervised, but they may not generalize to other settings (Rice & Harris, 1997). Of greater concern are their findings suggesting that while nonpsychopathic offenders tend to benefit from group therapy—in terms of a reduced risk of re-offending—psychopaths tend to become worse after therapy, in terms of an increased likelihood of committing further crimes, particularly violent crimes (Harris, Rice, & Cormier, 1994; Rice, Harris, & Cormier, 1992). According to Hare and colleagues, group therapy and insight-oriented therapy—which teach patients how to develop empathy and improve interpersonal skills—may help psychopaths develop better ways of manipulating, deceiving, and using people, but do little to help them understand themselves (Hare, Cooke, & Hart, 1999).

## Dependent Personality Disorder (DPD)

Dependent personality disorder (DPD) is listed in the third cluster of Axis II in DSM-IV-TR, along with avoidant and obsessive–compulsive personality disorders. Cluster C includes descriptions of various types of people who are anxious or fearful. Those who meet the criteria for DPD assume a submissive role in relationships with other people. They require an extraordinary level of reassurance and support, clinging to others who will take care of them. The following case study illustrates many of the most important features of this disorder.

### BRIEF CASE STUDY

**Dependent Personality Disorder**

The patient, Mrs. S., was 48 years old and married. [She] reported numerous decision-making situations, which provoke anxiety, and attempts to seek reassurance.

*continued*

*cont.*

For example, buying food in the supermarket, deciding what to make for dinner, and buying furniture all provoked anxiety and led Mrs. S. to seek reassurance from her husband. Further, Mrs. S. reported feeling anxious when her husband was not there to reassure her (such as when he was away and Mrs. S. was responsible for trimming the garden bushes and lawn). Finally the patient related numerous anxiety-provoking instances in which decisions she made were initially approved of by an authority figure (such as her husband or physician) and then criticized by an important other (such as after following the instructions of her physician, she was criticized for doing so by a friend).

During school years, Mrs. S. always wanted to be part of the "group," but she felt uncomfortable because no one would assure her explicitly that she "fit in." Moreover, her high school advisor noted on Mrs. S.'s record that she "lacked initiative."

When the patient went to college, she studied nursing because "a lot of people my age went into nursing." When the time came to choose between a university-based or hospital-based program, she relied largely on her mother's advice.

The patient's first job as a nurse went rather smoothly because her supervisors were readily available. Unfortunately, her second position did not work out well. Apparently, Mrs. S. had trouble adjusting because she did not have "supportive" supervisors. She left this position after a short time.

Mrs. S. did not have much of a dating history. Her husband was her first and only lover. She was greatly attracted to him because he was "very forceful" and an "independent decision maker" (Turkat & Carlson, 1984, pp. 156–157). ◆

## Brief Historical Perspective

Dependent personality disorder was introduced as a separate type of mental disorder in DSM-III (APA, 1980). Before then, the concept of dependency was viewed primarily as a personality trait rather than a mental disorder in its own right. It was considered to be a vulnerability factor that increased the person's risk for other types of mental disorder, particularly depression (Bornstein, 1998).

Freud proposed that dependent interpersonal relationships set the stage for later onset of depression (see Chapter 5). Contemporary investigators are still very much interested in that hypothesis. The term *sociotropy* is sometimes used to refer to dependency in that context. According to one version of this theory, people who are dependent, or sociotropic, may be particularly likely to become depressed if they experience a stressful event that is interpersonal in nature. Longitudinal studies suggest that a dependent or sociotropic interpersonal style does predict the later onset of depression (Davila, 2001; Mazure et al., 2000).

## Clinical Features and Comorbidity

The DSM-IV-TR criteria for dependent personality disorder are listed in Table 9–7. These criteria reflect two underlying components: preference for affiliation and fear of criticism and rejection (Bieling, Beck, & Brown, 2000; Livesley, 1995). Preference for affiliation reflects the motivation to remain close to other people who will provide security and comfort. Fear of criticism and rejection reflects a lack of self-confidence and includes actions aimed at eliciting help and approval from others.

Dependent personality disorder overlaps with several other categories listed on Axis II of DSM-IV-TR. The greatest overlap is with borderline personality disorder (Reich, 1996). People with both types of personality disorder are fearful of being abandoned by other people. The reactions that they show are quite different, however. People with BPD become enraged and manipulative when they think they are being abandoned, whereas people with DPD respond with clinging and submissive behaviours (Hirschfeld, Shea, & Weise, 1995).

## Etiological Considerations

Relatively little research has been conducted on the etiology of dependent personality disorder as a separate form of mental disorder. There is, however, a substantial body of evidence concerned with the development of dependency as a personality trait. We must, therefore, use this evidence to draw inferences about pathways leading to dependent personality disorder. The available evidence points toward the importance of social and psychological factors in the development of extreme dependency. Genetic factors seem to play a relatively minor role (Nigg & Goldsmith, 1994).

Overprotective, authoritarian parents are likely to foster the development of dependency in their children (Baker, Capron, & Azorlosa, 1996; Bornstein, 1996). This conclusion is supported by the results of many different types of empirical research. It is also consistent with several different psychological theories that emphasize the importance of parent–child relationships in the formation and maintenance of dependent personality traits. For example, according to attachment theory (Ainsworth, 1989; Bowlby, 1973), children have a basic need to form a secure attachment to adults who will care for them (see Chapter 2). Those who are anxiously or insecurely attached as children are likely to become highly dependent during adolescence and adulthood. The process through which this pattern develops presumably involves the child's expectations about the availability of the parent. Children who have little confidence that attachment figures will be easily accessible and responsive when they need something may attempt to remain unusually close to those people, thus behaving in a clinging and dependent manner.

**TABLE 9–7 DSM-IV-TR Criteria for Dependent Personality Disorder**

**A. A pervasive and excessive need to be taken care of that leads to submissive and clinging behaviour and fears of separation, beginning by early adulthood and present in a variety of contexts, as indicated by five (or more) of the following:**

1. Has difficulty making everyday decisions without an excessive amount of advice and reassurance from others.
2. Needs others to assume responsibility for most major areas of his or her life.
3. Has difficulty expressing disagreement with others because of fear of loss of support or approval (does not include realistic fears of retribution).
4. Has difficulty initiating projects or doing things on his or her own (because of lack of self-confidence in judgment or abilities rather than a lack of motivation or energy).
5. Goes to excessive lengths to obtain nurturance and support from others, to the point of volunteering to do things that are unpleasant.
6. Feels uncomfortable or helpless when alone because of exaggerated fears of being unable to care for himself or herself.
7. Urgently seeks another relationship as a source of care and support when a close relationship ends.
8. Is unrealistically preoccupied with fears of being left to take care of himself or herself.

## Treatment

There is virtually no literature on the outcome of treatment for dependent personality disorder. Therefore we cannot say whether any therapeutic procedures have been shown to be effective with this type of problem. People with this disorder may be less likely to seek treatment than people with other types of mental disorder. When they enter therapy, it is often because they also have other problems, such as depression, an anxiety disorder, or a substance use disorder. Whatever information is available on the treatment of this disorder is based on theoretical speculation and clinical experience (rather than empirical research).

Psychodynamic therapists have written most extensively about the treatment of dependent personality disorder. The primary goal in their approach is to help the person recognize the dependent pattern and the negative impact that it has on his or her relationships. Unfortunately, insight into the self-defeating nature of exceedingly dependent relationships may not be sufficient to allow the person to change his or her behaviour. Behaviour therapists (Goldfried & Davison, 1994) and interpersonal therapists (Benjamin, 1996) emphasize the need to teach skills in assertive communication. The client must learn to communicate feelings (both positive and negative) and desires accurately. The goal is to help the person develop interpersonal skills that will allow him or her to be more independent and self-reliant.

Cognitive therapy may also be beneficial in the treatment of dependent personality disorder. Problem-solving strategies, coupled with regular practice in making decisions, may foster independence and decrease the client's need to depend on other people for reassurance and support in routine situations. Cognitive therapy also addresses irrational or catastrophic self-statements about the potential consequences of behaving more independently or of ending a relationship (Crits-Christoph, 1998).

Psychopharmacology is not typically used as a specific treatment for dependent personality disorder. When medication is employed with such clients, it is usually aimed at the treatment of comorbid Axis I disorders, such as depression, agoraphobia, and panic disorder (Links, Heslegrave, & Villella, 1998).

# Summary

**Personality disorders** are defined in terms of rigid, inflexible, maladaptive ways of perceiving and responding to oneself and one's environment that lead to social or occupational problems or subjective distress. This pattern must be pervasive across a broad range of situations, and it must be stable and of long duration. Among the hallmark features of personality disorders are major problems in interpersonal relationships. Many of the traits and symptoms that are associated with these problems are ego-syntonic. In other words, many people with personality disorders do not see themselves as being disturbed.

Personality disorders are controversial for a number of reasons, including their low diagnostic reliability, the tremendous overlap among specific personality disorder categories, and the relative absence of effective forms of treatment. They are presumably defined in terms of behaviours that deviate markedly from the expectations of the person's culture. Unfortunately, little information is currently available to indicate whether the DSM-IV-TR system for personality disorders will be useful in societies other than Canada, the United States, and Western Europe.

Many systems have been proposed to describe the fundamental dimensions of human personality. One that has become very popular is the five-factor model, which includes the basic traits of neuroticism, extraversion, openness to experience, agreeableness, and conscientiousness. Extreme variations in any of these traits—being either pathologically high or low—can be associated with personality disorders.

DSM-IV-TR lists 10 types of personality disorder, arranged in 3 clusters. There is considerable overlap among and between these types. Cluster A includes **paranoid**, **schizoid**, and **schizotypal personality disorders**. These categories generally refer to people who are seen as being odd or eccentric. Cluster B includes **antisocial**, **borderline**, **histrionic**, and **narcissistic personality disorders**. People who fit into this cluster are generally seen as being dramatic, unpredictable, and overly emotional. Cluster C includes **avoidant**, **dependent**, and **obsessive–compulsive personality disorders**. The common element in these disorders is presumably anxiety or fearfulness.

Dimensional approaches to the description of personality disorder provide an interesting alternative to this categorical system. These procedures rate a person on a number of traits, such as those included in the five-factor model. Dimensional classification systems have the advantage of being better able to account for similarities and differences among people with various combinations of personality traits.

The lifetime prevalence of personality disorders among adults in the general population is between 10 and 14 percent. Borderline personality disorder is the most frequently diagnosed form of personality disorder among people seeking mental health services (both inpatients and outpatients).

The disorders listed in Cluster A, especially schizoid and schizotypal personality disorders, have been viewed as possible antecedents or subclinical forms of schizophrenia. They are defined largely in terms of minor symptoms that resemble the hallucinations and delusions seen in the full-blown disorder, as well as peculiar behaviours that have been observed among the first-degree relatives of schizophrenic patients. Research on the etiology of schizotypal personality disorder has focused primarily on studies of its genetic relationship to schizophrenia.

The most important features of borderline personality disorder revolve around a pervasive pattern of instability in self-image, in interpersonal relationships, and in mood. Some investigators believe that borderline personality disorder is an extremely heterogeneous category that should be further subdivided. Research regarding the etiology of borderline personality disorder has focused on two primary areas. One involves the impact of chaotic and abusive families. The other is concerned with the premature separation of children from their parents. Both sets of factors presumably can lead to problems in emotional regulation.

**Psychopathy** and antisocial personality disorder are two different attempts to define the same disorder. The DSM-IV-TR definition of ASPD places primary emphasis on social deviance in adulthood (repeated lying, physical assaults, reckless and irresponsible behaviour). The concept of psychopathy places greater emphasis on emotional and interpersonal deficits, such as lack of remorse, lack of empathy, and shallow emotions. Adoption studies indicate that the etiology of antisocial behaviour is determined by an interaction between genetic factors and adverse environmental circumstances. Laboratory studies of people who meet the criteria for psychopathy have focused on two hypotheses. One suggests that psychopaths are emotionally impoverished. The other holds that psychopaths have difficulty shifting their attention in order to avoid punishment.

Treatment procedures for people with personality disorders are especially difficult to design and evaluate, for three principal reasons. First, people with these disorders frequently don't have insight into the nature of their problems. Thus they are unlikely to seek treatment, and if they do, they frequently terminate prematurely. Second, pure forms of personality disorder are relatively rare. Most people with a personality disorder who are in treatment also exhibit comorbid forms of personality disorder and/or comorbid Axis I disorders, such as depression or drug addiction. Third, people with personality disorder have difficulty establishing and maintaining meaningful, stable interpersonal relationships of the sort that are required for psychotherapy.

Treatment for schizotypal and borderline personality disorders often involves the use of antipsychotic medication or antidepressant medication. A few controlled studies indicate that these drugs can be beneficial. Long-term outcome tends to be better for patients with borderline than schizotypal personality disorder. Various types of psychological intervention, including psychodynamic procedures as well as dialectical behaviour therapy, have frequently been employed with borderline patients. People with antisocial personality disorder seldom seek treatment voluntarily. When they do, the general consensus among clinicians is that it is seldom effective.

# Critical Thinking

1. DSM-IV-TR lists the personality disorders on a separate axis from the other types of mental disorder. In what ways are these problems different from disorders like depression, schizophrenia, and alcoholism? How are they similar?
2. Imagine that you are a clinical psychologist who is treating a client who is depressed. How would your treatment plan change if you knew that, in addition to a diagnosis of unipolar mood disorder on Axis I, the person also met the DSM-IV-TR criteria for borderline personality disorder? What if the Axis II diagnosis was dependent personality disorder?
3. Think of a typical case of borderline personality disorder, as defined by DSM-IV-TR. How would you describe that person's behaviour in terms of the dimensions of the five-factor model? Can you think of any advantages to considering the person's behaviour in terms of these dimensions rather than using the DSM-IV-TR category?
4. Consider the case of Paul Bernardo, who brutally raped and murdered young women. Do you think he has a DSM-IV personality disorder? What further information would you need to be certain? Is it possible for someone to be a serial rapist and *not* have a mental disorder? What about Karla Homolka—do you think she has a personality disorder?

# Key Terms

**antisocial personality disorder** 304
**avoidant personality disorder** 306
**borderline personality disorder** 305
**cross-cultural psychology** 316
**culture** 316
**dependent personality disorder** 306
**histrionic personality disorder** 305
**impulse control disorders** 320
**narcissistic personality disorder** 306
**obsessive–compulsive personality disorder (OCPD)** 307
**paranoid personality disorder** 303
**personality** 297
**personality disorder** 297
**psychopathy** 325
**schizoid personality disorder** 304
**schizotypal personality disorder** 304

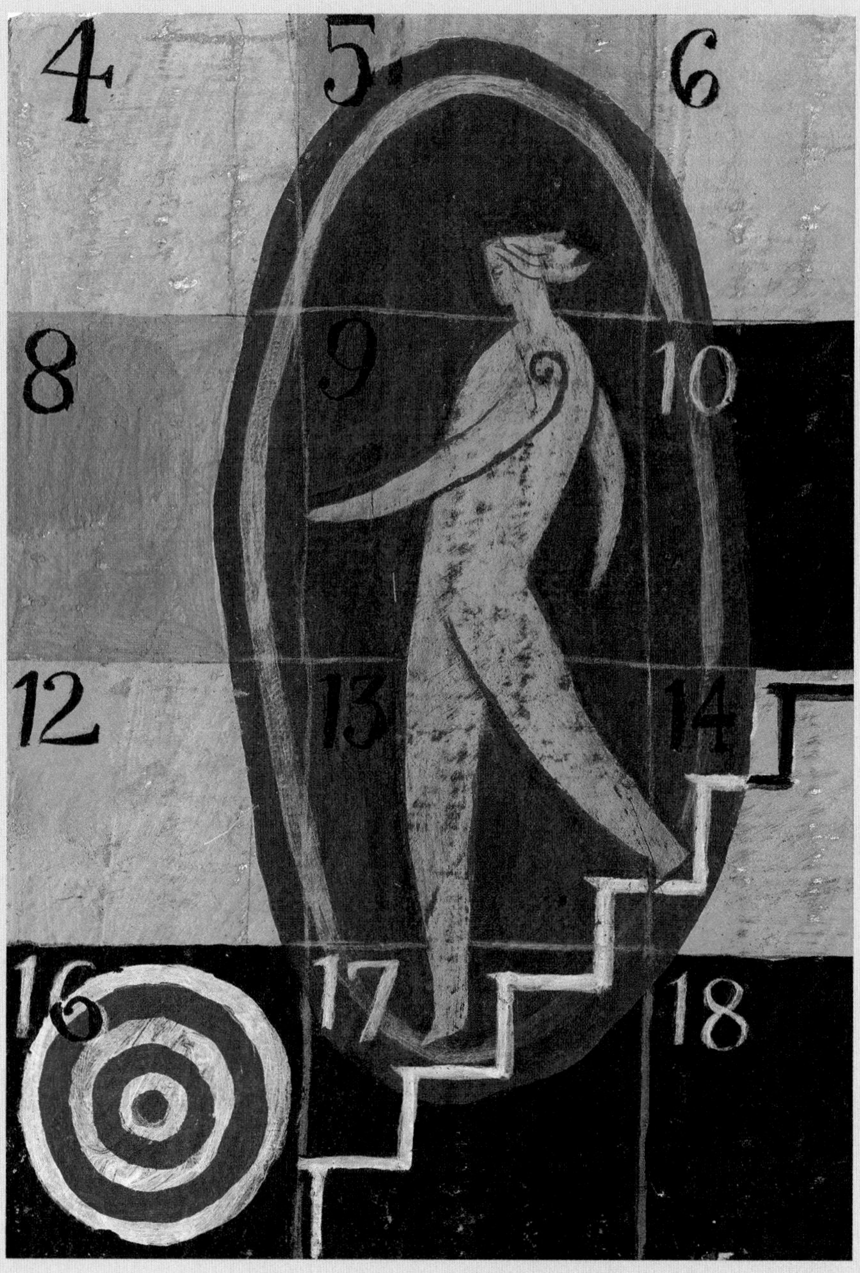


# 10 Eating Disorders

Overview
Typical Symptoms and Associated Features of Anorexia
Typical Symptoms and Associated Features of Bulimia Nervosa
Classification of Eating Disorders
Epidemiology of Eating Disorders
Etiological Considerations and Research
Treatment of Anorexia Nervosa
Treatment of Bulimia Nervosa

**How are anorexia and bulimia alike? How are they different?**

**Do society's standards of beauty contribute to eating disorders?**

**Do people with eating disorders have other psychological problems?**

**How can eating disorders be treated effectively?**

Popular culture in Canada, like many other countries, is obsessed with physical appearance. We are told that "beauty is only skin deep," but the entertainment, cosmetic, fashion, and diet industries are eager to convince young people that "looks are everything." The media often project ideal images of men and women. Perfect men are handsome, strong, athletic, and successful. Perfect women are beautiful and thin—often, extremely thin. In fact, women's thinness is equated with beauty, fitness, success, and ultimately with happiness. Given our culture's obsession with appearance, weight, and diet, it is not surprising that many young people, especially young women, become obsessed with thinness to the point where they develop eating disorders.

## Overview

**Eating disorders** are severe disturbances in eating behaviour that result from the sufferer's obsessive fear of gaining weight. Some experts have suggested that "dieting disorder" is a more accurate term for these behaviours (Beumont, Garner, & Touyz, 1994), because dread of weight gain and obsession with weight loss are central features of eating disorders. DSM-IV-TR lists two major subtypes of eating disorders: anorexia nervosa and bulimia nervosa. The most obvious characteristic of **anorexia nervosa** is extreme emaciation, or more technically, the refusal to maintain a minimally normal body weight. The term *anorexia* literally means "loss of appetite," but this is a misnomer. People with anorexia nervosa *are* hungry, yet they starve themselves nevertheless. Tragically, some actually starve themselves to death.

**Bulimia nervosa** is characterized by repeated episodes of binge eating, followed by inappropriate compensatory behaviours such as self-induced vomiting, misuse of laxatives, or excessive exercise. The literal meaning of the term *bulimia* is "ox appetite," meaning "hungry enough to eat an ox," but people with bulimia nervosa typically have a normal appetite and maintain a normal weight. In fact, most sufferers view their binge eating as a

*The images of women portrayed in advertising and the popular media contribute to the development of eating disorders.*

**Women's Dissatisfaction with Their Appearance**

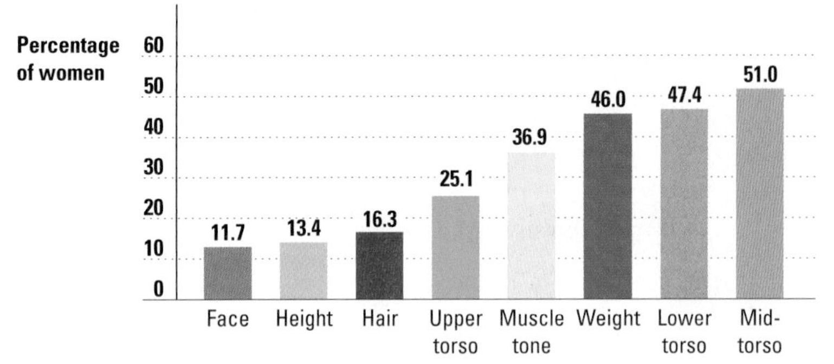


**FIGURE 10–1: Percentage of females reporting that they were "very or mostly dissatisfied" with specific physical attributes in a national sample of women aged 18 to 70 interviewed in 1993.**

*Source:* T.F. Cash and P.E. Henry, 1995, Women's body images: The results of a national survey in the U.S.A., *Sex Roles, 33,* 19–28.

failure of control, not as an indulgence of their excessive appetites or as a relief from the pressures of dieting. Thus people with bulimia nervosa commonly are ashamed and secretive about their binge eating and purging. Princess Diana was one famous woman who publicly admitted to struggling with bulimia.

Both anorexia and bulimia are about 10 times more common among women than men, and they develop most commonly among women in their teens and early twenties. The increased incidence among young people reflects both the intense focus on young women's physical appearance and the difficulties many adolescent girls have in adjusting to the rapid changes in body shape and weight that begin with puberty (Hsu, 1990). Evidence suggests that in Canada and the United States, approximately 40 percent of high school girls are attempting to lose weight compared with 15 percent of boys; in fact, many adolescent boys want to *gain* weight in order to look bigger and stronger (Serdula et al., 1993). Psychologist David M. Garner, who did a good deal of his research at the University of Toronto, surveyed 4000 readers of *Psychology Today*. Of the mostly female sample, 86 percent said they wanted to lose weight. A startling finding was that 24 percent said they were willing to have shorter lives (three or more years) in order to reach their desired weight (Garner, 1997). Other surveys have shown that 50 percent of women have a negative body image, particularly concerning their waist, hips, and thighs (Cash & Henry, 1995; see Figure 10–1). Clearly, cultural attitudes about weight, thinness, and appearance play a central role in causing eating disorders.

Because the symptoms of anorexia nervosa differ considerably from those of bulimia nervosa, we consider the two disorders separately in this chapter. We combine the two disorders when discussing classification, prevalence, and etiology, however, because they share many developmental similarities. For example, many people with anorexia nervosa also binge and purge on occasion; many people with bulimia nervosa have a history of anorexia nervosa. When discussing treatment, we again discuss the two disorders separately, reflecting the important differences in the focus and effectiveness of therapy for each disorder (Keel et al., 2000). We begin our consideration of eating disorders with a case study.

## CASE STUDY Kate's Anorexia

Nineteen-year-old Kate knows first-hand what it's like to struggle with an eating disorder. By the time she was 13, the North Vancouver high school graduate had developed a case of anorexia so serious that she found herself being monitored in a cardiac unit because of a dangerously low heart rate. "I would reward myself at my lowest weight," Kate recalled. "I kept thinking, 'If I made it this far, I can make it even further.' I remember the feeling of my bones protruding. It hurt to lie on the bed because my bones against the flat mat were so uncomfortable."

Kate may look like a typical teen, cellphone in hand, multiple silver earrings, and cherry-red lipstick to match her top, but her level-headedness belies her age. She says a number of factors led up to her anorexia. She wasn't immune to the proliferation of media images of sticklike women. She had lost two grandparents within a short period of time. A relative was dealing with schizophrenia. And she wanted to be in control. She may not have had much say over the world around her, but she *could* control what she ate and how much she weighed. By age 12, she cut out meat. The next year, she became obsessed with exercise.

"Food became an enemy," Kate says. "I remember one morning at home. My mom made me breakfast, and I ran out of the room, yelling and screaming up to my

*continued*

*cont.*

room. I remember thinking about calories. I couldn't drink water because I thought it was bad for me. I thought it had too many calories in it."

Kate spent most of the summer of Grade 8 in B.C.'s Children's Hospital. "I was pissed off," she says. "I didn't want to be there. I didn't think I had a problem. It was a complete refusal. . . . I would storm out of the room and tell people to F off. That was my thing, telling people to fuck off constantly. I couldn't handle it. I was scared.

"I looked like a junkie," she adds. "I looked so sick. I didn't have any nourishment. But that's part of recovery; you have to acknowledge you have anorexia before you're able to do something about it."

Now, Kate is doing whatever she can to maintain healthy eating habits. And she tries not to pay much attention to media images of "perfect" women. "I see these things every day. I'm not, 'I've got to look like that.' Now I think, '*whatever*.'" She has also spoken at one of the parents' support groups at Children's Hospital. "It was neat to hear from their perspective," she says, "They felt they were helpless and wanted to know what they could do to help. One parent started crying, they were so upset their child was going through this. Another said I could give people hope, that this isn't the end." ◆

*Source:* Adapted from "Fear of fat," by Gail Johnson, Associate Editor, *The Georgia Straight*. Issue 1799, June 13–20, 2002, pp. 19–22.

## Typical Symptoms and Associated Features of Anorexia

The classic symptoms that define anorexia nervosa are extreme emaciation, a disturbed perception of one's body, an intense fear of gaining weight, and, in women, the cessation of menstruation. Problems that are commonly associated with anorexia nervosa include obsessive preoccupation with food, purging, a struggle to gain control over persistent hunger mood disturbance, sexual difficulties, lack of impulse control, and medical problems secondary to the weight loss. The core symptoms of anorexia nervosa are generally the same, but the symptoms and associated features can vary from person to person. Eating disorders among men are especially likely to include unique features (see Further Thoughts).

## Further Thoughts **Eating Disorders in Males**

Both anorexia nervosa and bulimia nervosa are about 10 times more common among females than males, but eating disorders *do* occur among males. What do psychologists know about eating disorders among males?

Our culture clearly values extreme thinness far less among males than among females. Adolescent boys often want to be bigger and stronger, not slimmer. Surveys indicate that although the majority of females want to lose weight, males are about equally divided between those who want to lose weight and those who want to gain weight. Another indication of the difference in preferred weights is that women rate themselves as being thin only when they are below 90 percent of their ideal body weight. In contrast, men see themselves as thin even when they weigh as much as 105 percent of their expected weight (Anderson, 2002). In fact, some experts argue that pressures to be big and strong have created a new eating disorder among males. The problem, sometimes called "reverse anorexia nervosa," is characterized by excessive emphasis on extreme muscularity and often accompanied by the abuse of anabolic steroids (Anderson, 2002).

In any case, the more realistic expectations concerning thinness surely contribute to the lower prevalence of anorexia and bulimia among males. However, Toronto researchers have found that men with these eating disorders are less likely to seek treatment than are women, perhaps because they are less likely to recognize the problem or feel more stigmatized because of it (Woodside et al., 2001). Men with anorexia or bulimia deviate far from male norms, and this can lead to rejection and stigmatization by other men, therapists, and even females with eating disorders. The stigma of being a man with an eating disorder can greatly affect one common symptom of anorexia nervosa. Females with anorexia nervosa typically view their appearance positively, perhaps even with a degree of pride. In contrast, anorexia nervosa is much more likely to have a negative effect on the self-esteem of a male, because weight and/or eating struggles are "unmanly"—that is, different from the cultural image of the ideal male (Andersen, 1995).

Anorexia or bulimia are more common among certain subgroups of males than in the general population. Male wrestlers have a particularly high prevalence of eating disorders, a result of the intense pressure to "make weight"—to weigh below the weight cutoffs used to group competitors in a wrestling match. Eating disorders, especially bulimia, also are more

*continued*

*cont.*

common among gay than heterosexual men, an interesting finding since gay men place more emphasis on appearance (Carlat, Camargo, & Herzog, 1997). Finally, men with eating disorders are likelier to have a history of obesity in comparison to women with eating disorders (Andersen, 1995).

*University of Toronto psychiatrist **Paul E. Garfinkel** is a leading authority on eating disorders. His findings regarding the subtypes of anorexia nervosa were incorporated into DSM-IV.*

*Caraline, 28 years old, told a reporter, "I'm not telling you how much I weigh because I'm ashamed I don't weigh less." She later died of complications due to anorexia nervosa.*

### Refusal to Maintain a Normal Weight

The most obvious and most dangerous symptom of anorexia nervosa is a *refusal to maintain a minimally normal body weight*. Many instances of anorexia nervosa begin with a diet designed to lose just a few kilograms. The young woman (or sometimes a man) weighs near or within the normal range of her healthy body weight, and she may decide to lose a little weight, perhaps to fit into some new clothes or to become more fit. In anorexia nervosa, however, the diet goes awry, and losing weight eventually becomes the key focus of the individual's life. Weight falls below the normal range for age, height, and body type, and it often plummets to dangerously low levels.

DSM-IV-TR contains no formal cutoff as to how thin is too thin, but it suggests 85 percent of expected body weight as a rough guideline. The *body mass index*,[1] a calculation derived from weight and height, is another useful way to determine whether or not someone is significantly underweight. Both DSM-IV-TR and the body mass cutoffs represent weights well beyond "thin" and into the realm of "emaciated," but weight loss is far more extreme in many cases of anorexia nervosa: The average victim loses 25 to 30 percent of normal body weight (Hsu, 1990). Some people with anorexia nervosa are not treated until their weight loss becomes life threatening. In fact, experts estimate that over 10 percent of people admitted to hospitals with anorexia nervosa die of starvation, suicide, or medical complications stemming from their extreme weight loss (APA, 2000; Hsu, 1995).

### Disturbance in Evaluating Weight or Shape

A second defining symptom of anorexia nervosa involves a perceptual, cognitive, or affective disturbance in evaluating one's weight and shape. Many individuals with anorexia nervosa steadfastly *deny problems with their weight*. Even when confronted with the possibility of medical complications or with their own withered image in a mirror, some people with anorexia nervosa nevertheless insist that their weight is not a problem.

Other people with the disorder suffer from *a disturbance in the way body weight or shape is experienced*. Sometimes this symptom may stem from a **distorted body image**, an inaccuracy in how people with anorexia nervosa actually perceive their body size and shape. In support of this view, one influential study found that young women with anorexia nervosa overestimated the size of various body parts in comparison to a normal control group (Slade & Russell, 1973).

As observed by psychiatrist Paul E. Garfinkel and colleagues at the University of Toronto, not all people with anorexia nervosa suffer from a distorted body image, and, perhaps more importantly, many people without the disorder inaccurately estimate the size of their body (Garfinkel, Kennedy, & Kaplan, 1995). At a minimum, however, all people with the disorder are *unduly influenced by their body weight or shape in self-evaluation*. Experts agree that, whatever its specific form, a defining characteristic of anorexia nervosa is a disturbance in the way one's body or weight is perceived or evaluated. People with anorexia nervosa do not recognize their emaciation for what it is.

### Fear of Gaining Weight

An *intense fear of becoming fat* is a third central characteristic of anorexia. The fear of gaining weight presents particular problems for treatment. A therapist's encouragement to eat more can terrify someone with anorexia nervosa. They fear that relaxing control, even just a little, will lead to a total loss of control. Ironically, the fear of gaining weight is not soothed by the tremendous weight loss. In fact, the fear may grow more intense as the individual loses more weight (APA, 2000).

[1] You can calculate your own body mass as follows: (1) Multiply your weight in kg by 10 000; (2) divide this number by your height in cm; (3) divide this second number by your height in cm. You can interpret the resulting number according to the body mass index: Under 16 = extremely underweight; 16–18 = significantly underweight; 20–25 = healthy weight; 27–30 = overweight; 30–40 = significantly overweight; over 40 = extremely overweight.

### Cessation of Menstruation

**Amenorrhea**, the absence of at least three consecutive menstrual cycles, is the fourth and final defining symptom of anorexia nervosa in females. Many people with anorexia nervosa also have sexual difficulties, particularly a lack of interest in sex. The amenorrhea and sexual symptoms have led to much speculation, discussed later in the chapter, about the role of sexual appetite and sexual maturation in the etiology of anorexia nervosa. However, evidence indicates that amenorrhea typically is a *reaction* to the physiological changes produced by anorexia nervosa, specifically a low level of estrogen secretion, and not a symptom that precedes the disorder (APA, 1994). Sexual disinterest is also a common reaction to severe weight loss (Keys et al., 1950).

*Olympic-class gymnast Christy Heinrich with her boyfriend in 1993. After a five-year struggle with anorexia nervosa, she died of multiple organ failure in 1994. She weighed less than 23 kg at the time.*

### Medical Complications

Anorexia nervosa can cause a number of medical complications. People with anorexia commonly complain about constipation, abdominal pain, intolerance to cold, and lethargy. Some of these complaints stem from the effects of semistarvation on blood pressure and body temperature, both of which may fall below normal. In addition, the person's skin can become dry and cracked, and some people develop *lanugo*, a fine, downy hair, on their face or trunk of their body. Broader medical difficulties may include anemia, infertility, impaired kidney functioning, cardiovascular difficulties, dental erosion, and osteopenia (bone loss) (Pomeroy, 1996). A particularly dangerous medication complication is an *electrolyte imbalance*, a disturbance in the levels of potassium, sodium, calcium, and other vital elements found in bodily fluids that can lead to cardiac arrest or kidney failure. Anorexia nervosa may begin with the seemingly harmless desire to be a bit thinner or more attractive, but the eating disorder can lead to serious health problems and even death.

### Struggle for Control

Although some people with eating disorders act impulsively, clinical accounts and some research indicate that people suffering from anorexia nervosa are likelier to exhibit excessive conformity and a paramount struggle for control. In one sense, anorexia nervosa is the height of "success" in self-control. The individual with anorexia nervosa has all but conquered one of our most basic biological needs. Consistent with this view, people with anorexia nervosa often take great pride in their self-denial. They feel like masters of control. Even severely malnourished people with anorexia may deny that they have a problem that requires treatment (Kaplan & Garfinkel, 1999). As we discuss in considering the etiology of the disorder, some theorists speculate that the disorder develops out of a desperate pursuit for control. Excessively compliant "good girls" may find that they can be in charge of at least

*Conscientious objectors who became subjects in a study of semistarvation during World War II. Many of the men developed symptoms similar to those found in anorexia nervosa.*

one area of their lives by obsessively regulating their eating behaviours (Bruch, 1982).

### Comorbid Psychological Disorders

Epidemiologic research by Kristin von Ranson, currently at the University of Calgary, reveals that eating disorders are associated with nicotine dependence and drug and alcohol use in women, although this association is not strong (von Ranson et al., 2002). In other words, there is a tendency for eating-disordered women to have substance-use problems, compared to women without eating disorders. However, many eating-disordered women (and men) do not use or abuse alcohol or drugs.

Anorexia nervosa is associated with other psychological problems, particularly obsessive–compulsive disorder (Kasvikis et al., 1986), obsessive–compulsive personality disorder (Gillberg, Rastam, & Gillberg, 1995), and depression (Braun, Sunday, & Halmi, 1994). In many cases, however, these comorbid psychological problems may be reactions to anorexia, not causes or associated features of the disorder.

People with anorexia nervosa *are* obsessed with food and diet, and they often follow compulsive rituals in regard to eating. However, a unique study found that obsessive–compulsive behaviour can result from starvation rather than cause it. In this study, 32 World War II conscientious objectors fulfilled their military obligation by voluntarily undergoing semistarvation for 24 weeks. (The researchers wanted to learn about the effects of starvation on military personnel in the field.) As the men reduced their food intake and lost more and more weight, they developed extensive obsessions about food and compulsive eating rituals. For many of the men, in fact, the obsessions and compulsions continued long after they returned to their normal weight (Keys et al., 1950). Thus some obsessive–compulsive *behaviour* may be a reaction to starvation.

We also need to consider cause and effect carefully when considering the depressive symptoms that commonly accompany anorexia nervosa. Most people with anorexia nervosa show symptoms of mild depression, such as sad mood, irritability, insomnia, social withdrawal, and diminished interest in sex (Braun, Sunday, & Halmi, 1994). Like obsessive–compulsive behaviour, however, depression has been found to be a common secondary reaction to starvation. Although mood disturbances sometimes seem to play a role in the development of anorexia nervosa, depression can also be a reaction to the eating disorder (Cooper, 1995; Hsu, 1990).

Anorexia often co-occurs with the symptoms of bulimia (see Figure 10–2). The core symptoms of bulimia are *binge eating*, in which the individual uncontrollably eats vast amounts of food, and *inappropriate compensatory behaviour*, actions designed to eliminate the consumed food from the body (including self-induced vomiting and the misuse of laxatives, diuretics, enemas, and exercise). In some cases of anorexia nervosa, purging follows episodes of binge eating. However, in other cases purging may be used as a means of further controlling eating that already is dramatically restricted. In still other cases of anorexia, no binge eating or purging is present. People with anorexia nervosa who do *not* binge eat or purge generally are better adjusted on other measures of their mental health—for example, they have lower rates of depression (Braun, Sunday, & Halmi, 1994).

**The Overlap in Eating Disorder Symptoms**

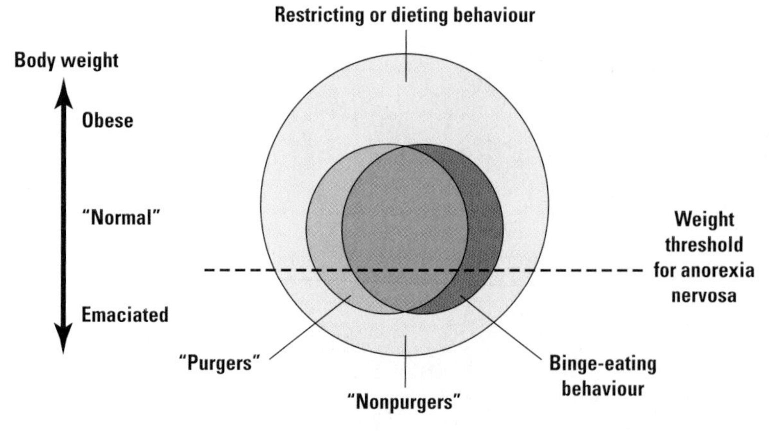


**FIGURE 10–2: Illustration of the relationship between binge eating, purging, and extreme dieting in eating disorders. All three problematic eating behaviours can be found among people with different body weights.**

*Source:* D.M. Garner, M.V. Garner, and L.W. Rosen, 1993, Anorexia nervosa "restrictors" who purge: Implication for subtyping anorexia nervosa. *International Journal of Eating Disorders, 13,* 182.

## Typical Symptoms and Associated Features of Bulimia Nervosa

Bulimia nervosa and anorexia nervosa share many other similarities in addition to the overlap in the symptoms of binge eating and inappropriate compensatory behaviour. One important connection is that many people with bulimia nervosa have a history of anorexia nervosa, as was the circumstance in the following case study.

## Binge Eating

**Binge eating** is defined in DSM-IV-TR as eating an amount of food in a fixed period of time—for example, less than two hours—that is clearly larger than most people would eat under similar circumstances. There have been some attempts to define a binge more objectively, such as eating more than 1000 calories, or subjectively, such as based on the individual's appraisal. Variations in normal eating complicate these alternative definitions, however, as eating a very large number of calories may be normal under certain circumstances and

## CASE STUDY Michelle's Secret

Michelle was a second year university student when she first sought help for a humiliating problem. Several times a week she fell into an episode of uncontrollable binge eating followed by self-induced vomiting. The episodes were particularly likely to occur on "bad days," of which Michelle had many. Michelle had enough control to limit her binge eating to times when her roommate was away. But when Michelle was alone and feeling bad, she typically would buy a 2-litre container of ice cream and perhaps a bag of cookies, and bring the food back to her room, where she secretly gorged herself. The binge brought her some comfort when she first started eating, but when she was finished, she felt physically uncomfortable, sickened by her lack of control, and terrified of gaining weight. To compensate, she would forced herself to vomit by sticking her finger down her throat.

The vomiting brought relief from the physical discomfort and fear of gaining weight, but it did not relieve her shame. Michelle was disgusted by her actions, but she could not stop herself. In fact, the pattern of binge eating and purging had been going on for most of the school year. Michelle decided to seek treatment only when a friend discovered her purging in the bathroom. The friend also had a history of bulimia nervosa, but she had gotten her eating under control. She convinced Michelle to try therapy.

Michelle's eating problems actually began when she was in high school. She had studied ballet since she was eight years old, and with the stern encouragement of her instructor she had struggled to maintain her willowy figure as she became an adolescent. At first she dieted openly, but her parents constantly criticized her inadequate eating. In order to appease them, Michelle occasionally would eat a normal meal but force herself to vomit shortly afterwards. Michelle's parents confronted her and brought her to a psychologist, who treated her for anorexia nervosa. She was 168 cm tall at the time, but she weighed only 43 kg. Michelle was furious at her parents and refused to talk in any depth with the therapist. She allowed herself to gain a few kilograms—to about 48—only to convince her parents that she did not need treatment.

Michelle's weight eventually stabilized between 48 and 50 kg—enough of a gain that her parents had allowed her to stop therapy. Even though she was very thin, Michelle continued to plan her diet with great care. She counted every calorie at every meal every day. Throughout most of her undergraduate years, she starved herself all week so she could eat normally on dates during the weekend. Occasionally, she forced herself to vomit after eating too much, but she did not see this as a big problem. Until the previous summer, she had maintained her weight near her goal of 48 kg. Over the summer, however, Michelle relaxed her diet considerably as she "partied" with old friends. She gained about 7 kg, a healthy weight for her height and body type. But when she returned to university, Michelle became disgusted with her appearance and fearful of gaining even more weight.

Michelle was trying to lose weight when she started her current school year, but she met with little success. She started to purge more frequently in a desperate attempt to lose weight, but she soon found herself binge eating more frequently, too. Michelle was extremely frustrated by her "lack of self-control" and her inability to lose weight. Although she now recognized her past problems with anorexia nervosa, Michelle openly longed for the discipline she had once achieved over her hunger and diet.

By all outward appearances, Michelle was a bright, attractive, successful, and happy young woman. Nevertheless, she admitted to her new therapist that she felt like a failure and a "fake." She longed to have a long-term dating relationship, but although she dated a lot, she had never had a real boyfriend. She also was intensely if privately competitive with her girlfriends. She wanted to be more beautiful and intelligent than other girls, but she inevitably felt inferior to one classmate or another. She was determined at least to be thinner than her girlfriends, but she felt that she had lost all control over this goal. She pretended to be happy and normal, but inside she felt as though she was going to explode. Secretly, she was miserable.

Michelle's frequent struggles with binge eating and purging, her sense of lost control during a binge, and her undue focus on her weight and figure are the core symptoms that define bulimia nervosa. Depression also is commonly associated with the disorder, as it was for Michelle despite her continual struggle to hide her unhappiness from those around her. ◆

*The late Princess Diana publicly acknowledged her battles with bulimia nervosa.*

having two cookies may be considered a "binge" by other people. Thus the present DSM-IV-TR definition relies on a clinician's judgment about normal eating patterns (Garfinkel et al., 1995).

Binges may be planned in advance, or they may begin spontaneously. In either case, binges typically are secret. Most people with bulimia nervosa are ashamed of their eating problems and often go to elaborate efforts to conceal their binge eating. During a binge, the individual typically eats very rapidly and soon feels uncomfortably full. Although the types of foods that are consumed can vary widely, the person often selects ice cream, cookies, or other foods that are high in calories. Foods also may be selected for smooth texture to make vomiting easier, one reason why ice cream is a popular binge food.

Binge eating is commonly triggered by an unhappy mood, which may begin with an interpersonal conflict, self-criticism about weight or appearance, or intense hunger following a period of fasting. The binge initially is comforting and alleviates some of the person's unhappy feelings, but physical discomfort and fear of gaining weight soon override the positive aspects of binge eating (Garfinkel et al., 1995).

A key feature of binge eating is a sense of *lack of control* during a binge. Some individuals experience a binge as a "feeding frenzy," where they lose all control and eat compulsively and rapidly. Others describe the lack of control as a dissociative experience, as if they were watching themselves gorge. It should be noted, however, that the lack of control is not absolute. For example, people with bulimia can stop a binge if they are interrupted unexpectedly. In fact, as the disorder progresses, some people feel more in control of their eating during a binge. Still, they are unable to stop the broader cycle of binge eating and compensatory behaviour.

## Inappropriate Compensatory Behaviour

The inappropriate compensatory behaviours that follow binge eating can take a number of forms. Almost all people with bulimia nervosa engage in **purging**, designed to eliminate the consumed food from the body. The most common form of purging is self-induced vomiting; as many as 90 percent of people with bulimia nervosa engage in this behaviour (APA, 2000). Vomiting brings immediate relief from the physical discomfort caused by a binge, and it reduces morbid fears of gaining weight. Other less common forms of purging include the misuse of laxatives, diuretics (which increase the frequency of urination), and, most rarely, enemas. Purging has only limited effectiveness in reducing caloric intake. Vomiting prevents the absorption of only about half the calories consumed during a binge, and laxatives, diuretics, and enemas have few lasting effects on calories or weight (Kaye et al., 1993).

Compensatory behaviours other than purging include extreme exercise or rigid fasting following a binge. The extent to which these actions actually compensate for binge eating also is questionable, given what we know about the body's biological regulation of weight, a topic we discuss later in this chapter (Brownell & Fairburn, 1995).

## Excessive Emphasis on Weight and Shape

People with bulimia nervosa place *excessive emphasis on body shape and weight* in evaluating themselves, a symptom shared in common with anorexia nervosa (see Table 10–1). Their self-esteem, and much of their daily routine, centre around weight and diet. The individual's sense of self-worth is linked too closely to appearance instead of personality, relationships, or achievements.

### Comorbid Psychological Disorders

Depression is common among individuals with bulimia nervosa, especially those who self-induce vomiting (APA, 2000). Some individuals clearly become depressed prior to developing the eating disorder, and the bulimia may be a reaction to the depression in some of these cases. In many instances, however, depression begins at the same time as or follows the onset of bulimia nervosa (Braun, Sunday, & Halmi, 1994). In such circumstances, the depression may be a reaction to the bulimia rather than a cause of it. In support of this view, evidence indicates that depression often lifts following successful treatment of bulimia nervosa (Mitchell et al., 1990).

Other psychological disorders that may co-occur with bulimia nervosa include anxiety disorders, personality disorders (particularly borderline personality disorder), and substance abuse, such as excessive use of alcohol or stimulants. Although each of these psychological difficulties presents special challenges in treating bulimia, the comorbidity with depression is the most common and most significant clinical concern (Brewerton et al., 1995).

### Medical Complications

A number of medical complications can result from bulimia nervosa. Repeated vomiting can erode dental enamel, particularly on the front teeth, and in severe cases teeth can become chipped and ragged looking. Repeated vomiting can also produce a gag reflex that is triggered too easily and perhaps unintentionally. One consequence of the sensitized gag reflex—one that is just beginning to be reported in the scientific literature—is *rumination:* the regurgitation and rechewing of food (Parry-Jones, 1994). Another possible medical complication is the enlargement of the salivary glands, a consequence that has the ironic effect of making the sufferer's face appear puffy. As in anorexia nervosa, potentially serious medical complications can result from electrolyte imbalances. Rupture of the esophagus or stomach has been reported in rare cases, sometimes leading to death (Pomeroy, 1996).

## Classification of Eating Disorders

### Brief Historical Perspective

Isolated cases of eating disorders have been reported throughout history. In fact, the term *anorexia nervosa* was coined in 1874 by a British physician, Sir William Withey Gull (1816–1890). Still, the history of professional concern with the disorders is very brief. References to eating disorders were rare in the literature prior to 1960, and the disorders have received scientific attention only in recent decades (Fairburn & Brownell, 2002; Striegel-Moore & Smolak, 2001). In fact, the term *bulimia nervosa* was used for the first time only in 1979 (Russell, 1979).

**TABLE 10–1 Anorexia Nervosa and Bulimia Nervosa: Key Differences and Similarities**

| Issue | Anorexia Nervosa | Bulimia Nervosa |
|---|---|---|
| | **Differences** | |
| Eating/weight | Extreme diet; below minimally normal weight | Binge eating/compensatory behaviour; normal weight |
| View of disorder | Denial of anorexia; proud of "diet" | Aware of problem; secretive/ashamed of bulimia |
| Feelings of control | Comforted by rigid self-control | Distressed by lack of control |
| | **Similarities** | |
| Self-evaluation | Unduly influenced by body weight/shape | Unduly influenced by body weight/shape |
| Comorbidity of AN/BN | Some cases of AN also binge and purge | Many cases of BN have history of AN |
| SES*, age, gender | Prevalent among high SES, young, female | Prevalent among high SES, young, female |

*SES = socioeconomic status, which is a measure of a person's standing in the community, usually based on income, occupation, and education. Higher scores on this index correspond to higher incomes, educational levels, and occupations requiring greater levels of training.

The diagnoses of anorexia nervosa and bulimia nervosa first appeared in DSM in 1980 (DSM-III), and although the diagnostic criteria have changed somewhat, the same eating behaviours remain as the central features of these disorders. The only major change in DSM-IV-TR was the creation of a separate diagnostic category for eating disorders. They previously had been listed as a subtype of the Disorders Usually First Diagnosed in Infancy, Childhood, or Adolescence (see Chapter 16), because most eating disorders begin during the teenage years. The new, separate diagnostic grouping reflects the fact that eating disorders sometimes begin during adult life, as well as a more general recognition of the importance of these psychological problems.

## Contemporary Classification

**Anorexia Nervosa** DSM-IV-TR has only two subtypes of eating disorders: anorexia nervosa and bulimia nervosa. Anorexia nervosa is defined by four symptoms: (1) a refusal to maintain weight at or above minimally normal weight for age and height; (2) an intense fear of gaining weight; (3) a disturbance in the way weight or body shape is experienced, undue influence of weight or body shape on self-evaluation, or denial of the seriousness of low body weight; and (4) amenorrhea, the absence of menstruation, in postmenarcheal females (see Table 10–2).

Based on the work of Garfinkel, Moldofsky, and Garner (1980), DSM-IV-TR includes two subtypes of anorexia nervosa. The *restricting type* includes people who rarely engage in binge eating or purging behaviour. In contrast, the *binge-eating/purging type* is defined by regular binge eating and purging during the course of the disorder. People with the binge-eating/purging type make up approximately half of those people with anorexia nervosa, and some evidence indicates that they weigh more before their anorexia, are more impulsive, and have more personality disorders than pure restrictors (Agras, 1987; Garfinkel et al., 1995). However, a recent longitudinal study of 51 women with the restricting type and 85 women with the binge-eating/purging type raises questions about the subtypes. The researchers found no differences between the subtypes in impulsivity, and at an eight-year follow-up 62 percent of the former restrictors met diagnostic criteria for binge-eating/purging, and only 12 percent of the restrictors reported that they had never regularly engaged in binge eating and purging (Eddy et al., 2002).

As we noted earlier, however, many people with anorexia nervosa purge following normal or even restricted eating, not following a binge. Should these people be considered the restricting type or the binge-eating/purging type? Evidence suggests that purging, not binge eating, is the key to distinguishing the subtypes. In a study that compared a sample of 116 pure restricters with both binge/purge (N = 190) and purge only (N = 74) subjects, both of the groups who purged were found to be older, to have had a longer history of anorexia nervosa, to have more obesity in their families, to be more impulsive, and to suffer from more psychopath-ology in comparison to the pure restricters (Garner, Garner, & Rosen, 1993). Thus it is appropriate that DSM-IV-TR defines the binge-eating/purging subtype in terms of *either* binge eating *or* purging (see Table 10–2).

**TABLE 10–2 DSM-IV-TR Diagnostic Criteria for Anorexia Nervosa**

**A. Refusal to maintain body weight at or above a minimally normal weight for age and height (e.g., weight loss leading to maintenance of body weight less than 85 percent of that expected; or failure to make expected weight gain during period of growth, leading to body weight less than 85 percent of that expected).**

**B. Intense fear of gaining weight or becoming fat, even though underweight.**

**C. Disturbance in the way in which one's weight or shape is experienced, undue influence of body weight or shape on self-evaluation, or denial of the seriousness of the current low body weight.**

**D. In postmenarcheal females, amenorrhea—that is, the absence of at least three consecutive menstrual cycles.**

*Specify type:*

**Restricting type:** During the current episode, the person has not regularly engaged in binge eating or purging behaviour.

**Binge-eating/purging type:** During the current episode, the person has regularly engaged in binge eating or purging behaviour.

**Bulimia Nervosa** Bulimia nervosa is defined by five symptoms: (1) recurrent episodes of binge eating over which the individual feels a lack of control; (2) recurrent inappropriate compensatory behaviour; (3) an average frequency of at least two episodes per week over a period of at least three months; (4) undue influence of weight and body shape on self-evaluation; and (5) the disturbance does not occur solely during episodes of anorexia nervosa (see Table 10–3).

Bulimia nervosa also is divided into two subtypes in DSM-IV-TR. The *purging type* is characterized by the regular use of self-induced vomiting or the misuse of laxatives, diuretics, or enemas. The individual with the *nonpurging type* of bulimia nervosa does not regularly purge but instead attempts to compensate for binge eating with fasting or excessive exercise. The purging subtype of bulimia nervosa is more common and is associated with more frequent binge eating, more psychopathology (particularly depression), and more family dysfunction, including parental discord and child sexual abuse (Garfinkel, Lin, & Goering, 1996; McCann et al., 1991).

**TABLE 10–3 DSM-IV-TR Diagnostic Criteria for Bulimia Nervosa**

**A. Recurrent episodes of binge eating. An episode of binge eating is characterized by both of the following:**

1. Eating, in a discrete period of time (e.g., within any two-hour period), an amount of food that is definitely larger than most people would eat during a similar period of time and under similar circumstances.
2. A sense of lack of control over eating during the episode (e.g., a feeling that one cannot stop eating or control what or how much one is eating).

**B. Recurrent inappropriate compensatory behaviour in order to prevent weight gain, such as self-induced vomiting; misuse of laxatives, diuretics, enemas, or other medications; fasting; or excessive exercise.**

**C. The binge eating and inappropriate compensatory behaviours both occur, on average, at least twice a week for three months.**

**D. Self-evaluation is unduly influenced by body shape and weight.**

**E. The disturbance does not occur exclusively during episodes of anorexia nervosa.**

*Specify type:*

**Purging type:** During the current episode, the person has regularly engaged in self-induced vomiting or the misuse of laxatives, diuretics, or enemas.

**Nonpurging type:** During the current episode, the person has used other inappropriate compensatory behaviours, such as fasting or excessive exercise, but has not regularly engaged in self-induced vomiting or the misuse of laxatives, diuretics, or enemas.

**Binge Eating Disorder and Obesity** There has been some debate about whether other eating problems should be included in the DSM-IV-TR list of eating disorders. **Binge eating disorder** is one problem that was given extensive consideration. In fact, provisional diagnostic criteria for binge eating disorder are included in an appendix of DSM-IV-TR for diagnostic categories requiring further study. The proposed disorder involves episodes of binge eating much like those found in bulimia nervosa but without compensatory behaviour.

Research has demonstrated that binge eating is associated with a number of psychological and physical difficulties other than anorexia nervosa and bulimia nervosa (Fairburn & Wilson, 1993). Among these problems is **obesity**, or excess body fat, a circumstance that roughly corresponds with a body weight 20 percent *above* the expected weight. A cutoff of 40 percent above normal is a rough marker of severe overweight (Brownell, 1995). As with binge eating, the DSM-IV-TR committee considered classifying obesity as an eating disorder, but too little information was available to justify this move (Garfinkel et al., 1995). Calling obesity a "mental disorder" is controversial, moreover, especially given the increasing prevalence of overweight individuals in Western societies and throughout the world. In fact, some professionals question our society's constant focus on dieting and our castigation of obese people. Obesity is *not* just a lack of "willpower," as biological factors contribute substantially to body shape and weight (Brownell & Rodin, 1994).

## Epidemiology of Eating Disorders

Estimates of the epidemiology of anorexia and bulimia vary, but it is clear that the prevalence of both disorders has increased dramatically since the 1960s and 1970s (Hoek, 1995; Kendler et al., 1991; Lucas et al., 1999). Figure 10–3 illustrates the surge in the number of new cases of anorexia nervosa based on one investigator's compilation of evidence from a number of different studies (Hoek, 1995). According to this summary, the annual *incidence*, the number of new cases each year, of anorexia nervosa rose from 1 case per million people in 1930–1940 to over 50 cases per million people in 1980–1990. Figure 10–3 also suggests that anorexia nervosa is rare in the general population. It is far more common among certain segments of the population, however, particularly among young women. DSM-IV-TR indicates that lifetime prevalence of anorexia nervosa is 0.5 among females, a figure that is consistent with other estimates (Hoek, 1995). Anorexia nervosa also occurs among males, but it is about 10 times more common among women than men.

Recent decades also seem to have witnessed a torrent of new cases of bulimia nervosa. Changes in the incidence of bulimia nervosa are difficult to document, however, because the

**Incidence of Anorexia Nervosa, 1930–1990**

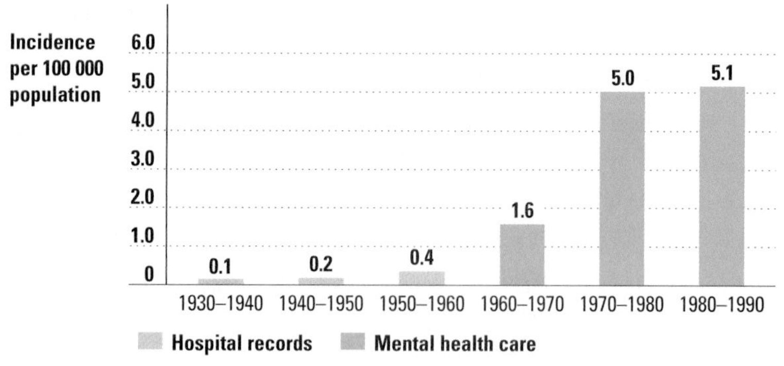


**FIGURE 10–3: Anorexia nervosa has increased dramatically in recent decades. This figure portrays the annual incidence per 100 000 people in the general population based on data pooled from studies of hospital records and outpatient mental health care. Considerably higher rates are found among population subgroups, particularly young women.**

*Source:* H.W. Hoek, 1995, The distribution of eating disorders. In K.D. Brownell and C.G. Fairbanks (Eds.), *Eating Disorders and Obesity: A Comprehensive Handbook*, p. 209. New York: Guilford.

diagnostic term was introduced only in 1979. In an attempt to demonstrate the striking increase in bulimia nervosa over time, investigators, therefore, have examined cohort effects in prevalence rates. A **cohort** is a group that shares some feature in common, particularly time of birth; thus **cohort effects** are differences that distinguish one cohort from another.

Figure 10–4 portrays birth cohort effects in lifetime prevalence rates of bulimia nervosa among a large sample of women who were born either before 1950, between 1950 and 1959, or in 1960 or after. The figure clearly indicates substantial cohort effects in the prevalence of bulimia nervosa. The lifetime prevalence of bulimia nervosa was far greater among the cohort of women born after 1960 than it was for the cohort of women born before 1950. The risk for women born between 1950 and 1959 was intermediate between these two extremes (Kendler et al., 1991). Thus the recent surge of cases of bulimia nervosa is not due to a general increase among all women but instead results from a flood of cases—some say an epidemic—among women born after 1960.

**Bulimia Nervosa among Three Cohorts of Women**

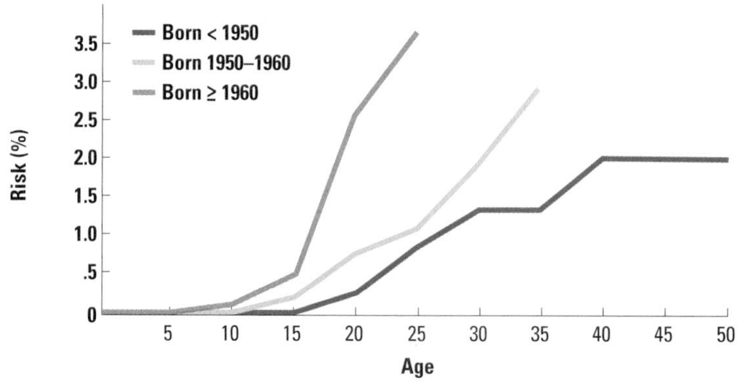


**FIGURE 10–4: The lifetime cumulative risk for developing bulimia nervosa is far greater for women born after 1960 than for women born before 1950. The risk for developing the disorder decreases with age, at least among the earlier birth cohort. Later birth cohorts have not yet moved through the entire age of risk.**

*Source:* K.S. Kendler, C. MacLean, M. Neale, R. Kessler, A. Heath, and L. Evans, 1991, The genetic epidemiology of bulimia nervosa. *American Journal of Psychiatry, 148*, 1631.

Figure 10–4 also shows that new cases of bulimia nervosa develop among women in their twenties and their thirties. Still, the risk of developing the disorder declines with increasing age, at least among older cohorts. The curve flattens at older ages, an indication of the discovery of fewer and fewer new cases among older women. It remains to be seen whether this pattern will be repeated with younger cohorts of women.

Although the frequency of both disorders has increased dramatically since the 1960s and 1970s, experts agree that bulimia nervosa is far more common than anorexia nervosa (Fairburn, Hay, & Welch, 1993; Hoek, 1995).

According to DSM-IV-TR, bulimia nervosa occurs among 1 to 3 percent of women, a rate that is two to six times the number of cases of anorexia nervosa. As we noted earlier, moreover, the prevalence of subclinical bulimia—occasional binge eating and/or purging—is far greater than the number of cases that meet DSM-IV-TR criteria for bulimia nervosa. Finally, we should note again the considerable overlap between anorexia nervosa and bulimia nervosa. About 50 percent of all people with anorexia nervosa engage in episodes of binge eating and purging (Agras, 1987; Garfinkel, Kennedy, & Kaplan, 1995), and perhaps 15 percent of cases of bulimia nervosa have a history of anorexia nervosa (Sullivan, 2002).

## Gender Differences and Standards of Beauty

Both anorexia and bulimia nervosa are approximately 10 times more common among women than among men. Many commentators and scientists propose that this huge difference is explained by gender roles and standards of beauty (Hsu, 1990; Striegel-Moore,

1995). Popular attitudes about women in Canada and other countries often convey the notion that "looks are everything," and thinness is essential to our dominant cultural image of good looks—and happiness. In contrast, young men are valued as much for their achievements as for their appearance, and in any case, the ideal body type for men is considerably larger than for women (Hsu, 1990; Striegel-Moore, 1995). In fact, women are much more likely than men to have a negative body image, and that disparity has been growing over time (Feingold & Mazzella, 1998).

The growing prevalence of eating disorders in recent decades also may be explained by changing standards of beauty. The cultural ideal of beauty changes over time, and increasingly beauty has been equated with thinness. For example, Marilyn Monroe, the movie idol of the 1950s, may seem rather chunky by today's standards. Then there is the ubiquitous Barbie Doll, whose figure translates into 39–18–33 in human equivalents. In fact, researchers have demonstrated the shift toward thinness in the Western view of the "beautiful woman" by examining changes in the dimensions of *Playboy* centrefolds and Miss America Beauty Pageant contestants—cultural icons but dubious role models for young women. Between 1959 and 1988, the ratio of weight to height of these "ideal women" has declined dramatically. In fact, 69 percent of *Playboy* centrefolds and 60 percent of Miss America contestants meet one diagnostic criterion for anorexia nervosa: Their body weight is at least 15 percent below expected weight for their height. The body shapes of these idealized women also have become more androgynous over time. Average bust and hip sizes have decreased, while waist sizes have increased slightly (Garner et al., 1980; Wiseman et al., 1992).

Standards of beauty are relative, not absolute. Today, eating disorders are found almost exclusively in North America, Western Europe, and Japan and other industrialized Asian countries; in other cultures, women who are more rounded are considered to be more beautiful (Hsu, 1990; Striegel-Moore, 1995). This may reflect a relationship between wealth and standards of beauty. In Third World countries, where food is scarce, wealth is positively correlated with body weight. Being larger is a symbol of beauty and success. In industrialized nations, where food is plentiful, wealth is negatively correlated with weight (Hsu, 1989). As the Western saying goes, "You can never be too rich or too thin."

*Model Kate Moss. Contemporary images of women place a premium on slimness and suggest that women should be judged by their appearance. Both of these messages apparently contribute to the etiology of eating disorders.*

## Age of Onset

Both anorexia and bulimia nervosa typically begin in late adolescence or early adulthood. A significant minority of cases of anorexia nervosa begin during early adolescence, particularly as girls approach puberty. The adolescent onset of eating disorders has provoked much speculation about their etiology. Certain characteristics of adolescence have been hypothesized to cause eating disorders; these include hormonal changes (Garfinkel & Garner, 1982), autonomy struggles (Minuchin, Rosman, & Baker, 1978), and problems with sexuality (Coovert, Kinder, & Thompson, 1989). Other theorists have noted that the young adolescent girl is the most idealized cultural image of beauty (Hsu, 1990; Striegel-Moore, 1995). The natural and normal changes in body shape and weight offer a more simple explanation of the adolescent onset. Weight gain is normal during adolescence, but the addition of a few kilograms can trouble a young woman who is focused on the numbers on her scale. Furthermore, breast and hip development not only change body shape, but they also affect self-image, social interaction, and the fit of familiar clothes. As we shall see, each of these explanations may have some value in explaining the age of onset of eating disorders.

# Etiological Considerations and Research

The regulation—and dysregulation—of normal eating and body weight results from a combination of biological, psychological, and social factors.

## Social Factors

The image of the ideal woman as extremely thin and the overriding value placed on young women's appearances are basic starting points in searching for the causes of eating disorders. This statement is supported by the epidemiological evidence we have already reviewed, as well as by related findings:

- Eating disorders are far more common among young women than young men (Hoek, 1995; Hsu, 1990).
- The prevalence of eating disorders in Western societies has risen dramatically in recent decades, as the image of the ideal woman has increasingly emphasized extreme thinness (Garner et al., 1980; Hoek, 1995).
- Garner and Garfinkel (1980) and other researchers (e.g., Byrne, 2002) have shown that eating disorders—particularly anorexia nervosa—are remarkably common among young women working in fields that especially emphasize weight and appearance, such as models, ballet dancers, and gymnasts.
- Young women are particularly likely to develop eating disorders during adolescence and young adult life, an age during which our culture places a particular emphasis on appearance, beauty, and thinness (Hoek, 2002; Hsu, 1990).
- Eating disturbances are more common among young women who report greater exposure to popular media, endorse more gender-role stereotypes, or internalize societal standards about appearance (Heinberg, Thompson, & Stormer, 1995; Stice et al., 1994).
- Eating disorders are considerably more common among the middle- and upper-class, who are especially likely to equate thinness with beauty in women (Hsu, 1990; Thompson, 1996; Wildes, Emery, & Simons, 2001).
- Eating disorders are far more prevalent in industrialized societies, where thinness is the ideal, than in nonindustrialized societies, where a more rounded body type is preferred (Hsu, 1990).
- The prevalence of eating disorders is higher among Arab and Asian women who are living or studying in Western countries than among women living in their native country (Hoek, 2002).

Together, these facts make it clear that adolescent girls and young women are at risk for developing eating disorders, in part because they attempt to shape themselves, quite literally, to fit the image of the ideally proportioned, thin woman. Of course, not every woman in Canada or other countries develops an eating disorder. University of Toronto psychologists Janet Polivy and Peter Herman, who are both internationally recognized experts on eating disorders, observed that culture interacts with a plethora of other factors, such as stressors, to produce eating disorders (Polivy & Herman, 2002).

The person's *internalization* of the ideal of thinness is one basic influence (Thompson & Stice, 2001). Several lines of work support the importance of internalization, including level of exposure to the media. In a recent study, for example, high school girls in Grades 9 and 10 received a free subscription to *Seventeen* magazine at random. One year later, those who received the magazine reported increased negative affect, but only if their body image was more negative and they felt more pressure to be thin than when the study began (Stice, Spangler, & Agras, 2001). Thus, some girls apparently are more vulnerable to the media's message that appearance is all-important, while others are innoculated, at least to some degree.

According to research by York University psychologist Caroline Davis, facial attractiveness (as rated by others) is correlated with eating disorder symptoms, even after controlling for body size. Davis proposed that because attractive women enjoy social advantages, they are especially likely to learn to measure their self-worth by how they look. This leads to dieting, which sometimes leads to eating disorders (Davis et al., 2001).

**Troubled Family Relationships** Troubled family relationships may be another factor that increases vulnerability (Fairburn et al., 1997). Researchers have documented family problems in a number of studies, but the typical patterns differ for anorexia nervosa and bulimia nervosa. Young people with bulimia nervosa report considerable conflict and rejection in their families, difficulties that also may contribute to their depression. In contrast, young people with anorexia generally perceive their families as cohesive and nonconflictual (Fornari et al., 1999; Vandereycken, 2002).

Although the families of young people with anorexia nervosa appear to be well functioning, some theorists see the families as being too close—that is, they are **enmeshed families**, or families whose members are overly involved in one another's lives. Young people with anorexia nervosa are obsessed with controlling their eating, and according to the enmeshment hypothesis, this is because eating is the *only* thing they can control in their intrusive families (Minuchin et al., 1978). A relation between measures of conflictual but controlling parent–child relationships and anorexia nervosa has been found in some research (Humphrey, 1987), but it is not clear whether the extensive and intrusive parental concern is a cause or an effect of the eating disorder. It may be that the parents of an adolescent with anorexia nervosa become "enmeshed" as a worried reaction to their daughter's obviously emaciated appearance, not as a cause of it. In either case, family power struggles over eating often become one focus of the treatment of anorexia nervosa (Polivy & Herman, 2002).

Child sexual abuse is another family difficulty that might contribute to the development of eating disorders. (See Chapter 18 for a discussion of child abuse and child sexual abuse.) A number of clinical observers have noted that a disproportionate number of women with eating disorders report a history of sexual abuse. Although a report of sexual abuse clearly is an essential psychological (and legal) issue in any individual case, recent evidence indicates that sexual abuse does not play a *specific* role in the development of eating disorders. Instead, child sexual abuse apparently increases the risk for a variety of psychological problems during adult life, including, but not limited to, eating disorders. Studies of community samples demonstrate that women with eating disorders are likelier than normal controls to report a history of sexual abuse. However, women with eating disorders are no likelier to report a history of sexual abuse than are women who suffer from other psychological problems (Palmer, 1995; Welch & Fairburn, 1996).

*Rounded bodies once were the Western ideal of beauty for women, as illustrated in* Turkish Bath *painted by Jean Auguste Dominique Ingres in 1859–1863 (Louvre, Paris).*

There are many direct ways in which parents may influence children toward developing eating disorders. Research from York University indicates that young women are especially likely to develop eating disorders if their parents are preoccupied with social appearance and physical attractiveness, especially for young women who are easily made anxious—perhaps because they are more sensitive to, or more likely to internalize, pressures and expectations to conform to family values (Davis et al., 2004).

## Psychological Factors

Researchers have suggested a number of psychological concerns as etiological factors in eating disorders, including dissatisfaction with body image, various problems with control (including having too little and wanting too much), difficulties with sexuality, fear of autonomy, low self-esteem, perfectionism, reactions to dieting, and a number of comorbid psychological disorders, including various mood disorders, anxiety disorders, and personality disorders (e.g., Polivy, Heatherton, & Herman, 1988; Polivy & Herman, 2002). The confusing number of alternative hypotheses reflects two clear facts. First, scientists have not yet identified unequivocal psychological contributors to eating disorders. Second, there will prove to be many alternative pathways to the development of eating disorders, not just one. Here we highlight four of the most promising approaches: control issues, depression/dysphoria, body image dissatisfaction, and reactions to dietary restraint.

#### A Struggle for Perfection and Control

Psychiatrist Hilde Bruch (1904–1984) was one of the first and most prolific clinical observers of eating disorders. Bruch strongly asserted that a *struggle for control* is the central psychological issue in the development of eating disorders (Bruch, 1982). Bruch observed that girls with eating disorders seem to be exceptionally "good"—conforming and eager to please. She further suggested that these exceptionally "good girls" give up too much of the normal adolescent struggle for autonomy and, instead, attempt to please others, particularly their parents. Bruch thus viewed their obsessive efforts to control eating and weight as a way that overly compliant "good girls" control themselves further. At the same time, she also saw their dieting as an attempt to wrest at least a little control from their parents—control over what they eat. In this struggle for control, young people with anorexia nervosa "succeed" and take considerable pride in their extreme self-control. In contrast, people with bulimia nervosa continually strive—and fail—to gain complete control over eating and weight. The success or failure of control, in turn, may explain the denial that characterizes anorexia nervosa and the humiliation that accompanies bulimia nervosa.

Researchers often use the term *perfectionism* to describe the endless pursuit of control described by Bruch and other clinicians. Perfectionists set unrealistically high standards, are self-critical, and demand a performance from themselves that is higher than is required by a given situation. Studies by several investigators, including Paul Hewitt at the University of British Columbia, and researchers at the University of Toronto, have demonstrated that young women with eating disorders are perfectionist both about eating and weight, and about general expectations for themselves (Bastiani et al., 1995; Garner, Olmsted, & Polivy, 1983; Hewitt, Flett, & Ediger, 1995; Sutandar-Pinnock et al., 2003).

Young people with eating disorders may also try to control their own emotions excessively, perhaps as a result of their constant attempt to please others instead of themselves (Bruch, 1982). The result may be a lack of **introceptive awareness**—recognition of internal cues, including various emotional states as well as hunger. Simply put, people with eating disorders may be not tuned in to how they feel—sad, angry, or happy, or even whether they are hungry. In fact, a large study of the development of eating disorders found that a measure of lack of introceptive awareness predicted the development of eating disorders two years in the future (Leon et al., 1993; Leon et al., 1995). Thus excessive external control, perfectionism, and a lack of introceptive awareness appear to be one cluster of psychological contributions to the development of eating disorders.

#### Depression, Low Self-Esteem, and Dysphoria

Depression is another psychological factor that may contribute to eating disorders, particularly to bulimia nervosa. Researchers have found an increased prevalence of depression not only among people with eating disorders but also among the members of their families (Strober, 1995). This has led some experts to speculate that the two problems are etiologically related. In support of this theory, research indicates that antidepressant medications are effective in reducing some symptoms of bulimia nervosa (Mitchell, Raymond, & Specker, 1993).

Other experts suggest, however, that depression may be a reaction to developing bulimia nervosa and especially a reaction to the onset of anorexia nervosa (Hsu, 1990; Polivy & Herman, 2002). In support of this alternative view, research indicates that depression improves markedly following successful group psychotherapy for bulimia (Mitchell et al., 1990). Moreover, in one large study a measure of depression failed to predict either concurrent or future eating disorders (Leon et al., 1995). Another study of anorexia nervosa found considerable depression at the time of the original diagnosis but not at a six-year follow-up (Rastam, Gillberg, & Gillberg, 1995). Thus clinical depression may contribute to the development of eating disorders in a subset of cases, but in most eating disorders, if it is present depression appears to be a secondary problem and not the primary issue (Stice & Agras, 1999).

Despite these conclusions, many researchers and clinicians suggest that depressive *symptoms*, and not necessarily clinical depression, are central factors in various specific aspects of eating disorders. Low self-esteem is a particular concern (Fairburn et al., 1997). More specifically, many observers note that women with eating disorders are preoccupied with their *social self* (Jones, 1985; Striegel-Moore, Silberstein, & Rodin, 1993). The social self includes both how we present ourselves in public and how other people perceive and evaluate us. In eating disorders, preoccupation with the social self may lead to an undue emphasis on physical appearance—a central aspect of young women's self-presentation—as well as considerable anxiety about the social presentation of one's personality. Howard Steiger and colleagues at McGill University found that women with bulimia are more sensitive to negative social interactions; after these interactions they experience greater increases in self-criticism and greater deterioration in mood, and are at increased risk for bingeing (Steiger et al., 1999). In short, women with eating disorders appear to be governed more by external than internal standards.

Depressive symptoms also clearly play a role in maintaining problematic eating behaviours. *Dysphoria* or negative mood states commonly trigger episodes of binge eating in bulimia nervosa and in the binge-eating/purging subtype of anorexia nervosa (Steiger et al., 1999). The dysphoria may be brought on by social criticism or conflict, dissatisfaction with eating and diet, or an ongoing depressive episode. Thus, although most cases of clinical depression appear to be reactions to eating disorders, depression, low self-esteem, and periods of dysphoria can contribute to the onset or maintenance of some eating disorder cases.

**Negative Body Image** A *negative body image*, a highly critical evaluation of one's weight and shape, is another psychological factor that has long been thought to contribute to the development of eating disorders (Polivy & Herman, 2002). Psychologists have used a number of techniques to evaluate a negative body image, including self-report measures, calipers or other devices used to directly estimate the size of various body parts, and schematic figures such as the ones in Figure 10–5 (Thompson, 1996).

**Body Contour Rating Scale**

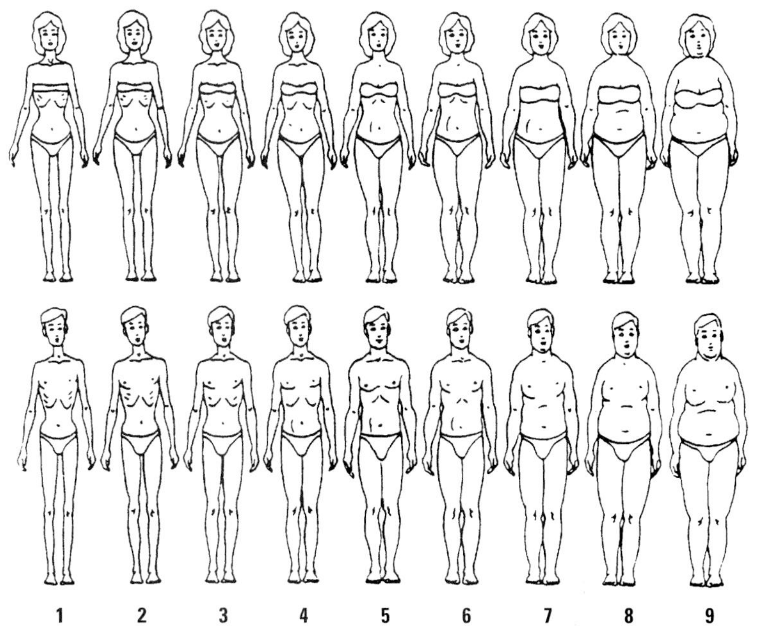


**FIGURE 10–5: These schematic figures are used in research to assess differences between real and ideal body image. People pick two figures, their current and their ideal shape. The discrepancy between the ratings is an index of negative body image.**

*Source:* J.K. Thompson, 1996, Assessing body image disturbance: Measures, methodology, and implementation. In J.K. Thompson (Ed.), *Body Image, Eating Disorders, and Obesity*, p. 79. Washington, DC: American Psychological Association.

Early studies of body image in eating disorders focused on a *distorted body image*, a perceptual inaccuracy in judging one's size, particularly in cases of anorexia nervosa. Current research focuses on *dissatisfaction* with one's body image, a negative evaluation of one's body that includes cognitive and affective elements and not just perceptual distortions. Thus one way to assess a negative body image is to compare people's ratings of their "current" and "ideal" size by asking them to pick from the schematics in Figure 10–5. Body image clearly is an important focus for continued research, as several longitudinal studies have found negative evaluations of weight, shape, and appearance to predict the subsequent development of disordered eating (Attie & Brooks-Gunn, 1989; Cattarin & Thompson, 1994; Striegel-Moore, Silberstein, & Rodin, 1989). A negative body image may be particularly problematic when combined with other risk factors, including perfectionism and low self-esteem (Vohs et al., 1999).

**Dietary Restraint** Research by Peter Herman, Janet Polivy, and their colleagues shows that some symptoms of eating disorders are likely to be effects of *dietary restraint*—that is, direct consequences of restricted eating (Heatherton & Polivy, 1992; Herman & Polivy, 1988). This is ironic, because many of the "out-of-control" symptoms of eating disorders appear to be caused by inappropriate efforts to control eating! These symptoms include binge eating, preoccupation with food, and perhaps out-of-control feelings of hunger.

Inappropriate dieting appears to contribute directly to subsequent binge eating. An overly restrictive diet increases hunger, frustration, and lack of attention to internal cues, all of which make binge eating more likely. People with bulimia typically have a list of "forbidden foods," which are foods they enjoy eating but attempt to avoid when dieting (e.g., cookies, ice cream, and tasty snacks). Notice that these are the foods they typically consume during binges. Exposure to such foods can trigger binges (Polivy & Herman, 1985, 1991).

Because "quick-fix" diets rarely work, dieters are likely to be left with a sense of failure, disappointment, and self-criticism. The negative affect, in turn, makes further binge eating likely and further lowers the self-esteem of people who already have perfectionist standards or a negative body image (Heatherton & Polivy, 1992; Herman & Polivy, 1988). In short, some cases of bulimia nervosa seem to result from the body's rebellion against the individual's attempt to lose an inappropriate amount of weight.

The effects of food deprivation on bingeing may be long-lasting. Polivy, Herman, and colleagues compared World War II combat veterans and former prisoners of war. Binge eating was relatively rare in combat veterans, but was significantly more prevalent in veterans who, as captives in German prisoner-of-war camps, lost significant amounts of weight during their captivity (Polivy et al., 1994).

Dietary restraint also may directly cause some of the symptoms of anorexia nervosa. As we noted earlier, military studies during World War II found that obsessive thoughts about food and compulsive eating rituals were one direct consequence of semistarvation (Keys et al., 1950). The same studies also found that during refeeding, many men felt intense, uncontrollable hunger, even after eating a considerable amount of food. Perhaps a similar reaction explains some of the intense fear of losing control and gaining weight found in anorexia nervosa.

## Biological Factors

Scientists conceptualize normal eating and weight regulation in systems terms, specifically as a result of the interplay among behaviour (e.g., energy expenditure, eating), peripheral physiological activity (e.g., digestion, metabolism), and central physiological activity (e.g., neurotransmitter release). Body–brain–behaviour relationships are regulated in a way to maintain a homeostatic balance among the metabolism of nutrients, the neural regulation of appetite, and the ingestion of food (Blundell, 1995). Evidence also indicates that homeostatic mechanisms govern the regulation of weight. Specifically, the body maintains weight around certain **weight set points**, fixed weights or small ranges of weight. Maintaining weight near a set point is biologically adaptive. Thus, if weight declines, hunger increases, food consumption goes up, and metabolism slows in an attempt to return weight to its set point (Keesey, 1995). The process is very much like the way a thermostat regulates heating and cooling to maintain air temperature at a given setting.

From this systems perspective, it is clear that, even though they can be conceptualized in psychological terms, the effects of dietary restraint also are biological contributors to the development of eating disorders. The hunger and binge eating that follow dietary restraint are a part of the body's attempts to maintain weight at a set point through motivation and behaviour. When deprived of food, the body also attempts to maintain weight at a set point physiologically. In particular, there is a slowing of the *metabolic rate*, the rate at which the body expends energy, and movement toward *hyperlipogenesis*, the storage of abnormally large amounts of fat in fat cells throughout the body (Brownell & Fairburn, 1995). All these reactions have obvious survival value and are likely products of evolutionary psychology. Simply put, the body does not distinguish between intentional attempts to lose weight and potential starvation. Thus some aspects of eating disorders are a result of the individual's struggle against a biological need and binge eating in response to an increasingly urgent biological signal—hunger. (The restricting subtype of anorexia nervosa is an exception.)

Other evidence suggests that biological factors contribute to eating disorders through genetic mechanisms. An extensive twin study of bulimia nervosa found a concordance rate of 23 percent for MZ twins and 9 percent for DZ twins (Kendler et al., 1991). Higher MZ than DZ concordance rates for dysfunctional eating attitudes have also been reported (Klump, McGue, & Iacono, 2000; Rutherford et al., 1993). A recent study compared MZ twins *discordant* for bulimia nervosa, and found that affected twins were more anxious as children. Ill twins currently showed more obsessive–compulsive symptoms and lower feelings of mastery, optimism, and self-esteem in comparison to their identical twin without an eating disorder (Bulik, Wade, & Kendler, 2000). These findings suggest that the symptoms contributed to the development of the eating disorders, but with the exception of childhood anxiety, the differences may have been consequences, not causes, of bulimia nervosa.

It is important to note, however, that MZ–DZ twin differences could be explained by several different heritable mechanisms. It is unlikely that eating disorders are directly inherited, especially given the historically recent surge in prevalence rates. Rather, genetics may influence some personality characteristic that, in turn, increases the risk for bulimia nervosa (Strober and Bulik, 2002). Or a certain body type or weight set point may be inherited, and this may account for the higher concordance rates found among MZ twins. If so, the well-established genetic contributions to determining weight and body type (Bouchard, 2002) contribute to the development of eating disorders only when combined with cultural expectations about thinness—and with individual concerns about living up to these expectations. Genes clearly affect weight set points and body type, but we cannot mindlessly conclude that eating disorders are "genetic" (see Research Methods in Chapter 17).

Several measures of neurophysiology have been found to be linked with eating disorders, including elevations in endogenous opioids, low levels of serotonin, and diminished neuroendocrine functioning (Yates, 1990). Some of these differences in brain functioning, however, appear to be effects of eating disorders and not causes of them. However, according to a recent review from McGill University psychologist Howard Steiger, alterations in brain serotonin appear to contribute to many features of eating disorders, including binge eating, perfectionism, impulsivity, and mood-regulation problems (Steiger, 2003; Steiger et al., 2001). In extremely rare cases, eating disorders have been linked with a specific biological abnormality, such as a hormonal disturbance or a lesion in the *hypothalamus*, the area of the brain that regulates routine biological functions, including appetite (see Chapter 2).

*Many women with eating disorders have a distorted body image, as illustrated by this young woman examining her figure in a mirror that gives the illusion of fatness.*

### Integration and Alternative Pathways

As first emphasized by Garfinkel and Garner (1982), eating disorders are best understood in terms of a systems approach, involving sociocultural, psychological, and biological factors. Social and cultural values that emphasize thinness, beauty, and appearance over personality are the starting point in understanding eating disorders, particularly among young women (Dorian & Garfinkel, 1999). However, cultural factors cannot be a sufficient cause of eating disorders. Although a majority of young women in Western societies today are concerned with weight and shape, only a minority actually develop an eating disorder. Straightforward risk factors include direct familial and social pressures to be thin, a negative body image, dietary restraint, and genetic influences on body weight and shape (Stice, 2001). Less obvious risk factors include preoccupation with external evaluation, lack of introceptive awareness, and preoccupation with conformity and self-control.

Research on the etiology of eating disorders underscores the importance of *equifinality*. There are many pathways to developing an eating disorder. Some women are naturally thin, but their perfectionism drives them to become even thinner. Other women may have a more rounded body type determined by genetics, and as a result of contemporary standards of beauty, they struggle, and repeatedly fail, to mould their body into something it was never meant to be. For some people, an eating disorder is an expression of depression. Others may develop an eating disorder because they focus on outward appearances instead of internal values.

In considering the development of eating disorders, a key issue that remains unresolved is why some women develop anorexia nervosa and others develop bulimia nervosa.

## Treatment of Anorexia Nervosa

The treatments for anorexia nervosa and bulimia nervosa differ in approach and effectiveness; therefore, we consider them separately. The treatment of anorexia nervosa usually focuses on two goals. The first goal is to help the patient gain at least a minimal amount of weight. If weight loss is severe, the patient may be treated in an inpatient setting (Keel et al., 2002), where clinicians may use coercive methods or introduce strict behaviour therapy programs in which rewards such as social activities are made contingent on weight gain. Hospitalization also may be needed to prevent suicide, to address severe depression or medical complications, or to remove the patient temporarily from a dysfunctional social circumstance (Garner & Needleman, 1996).

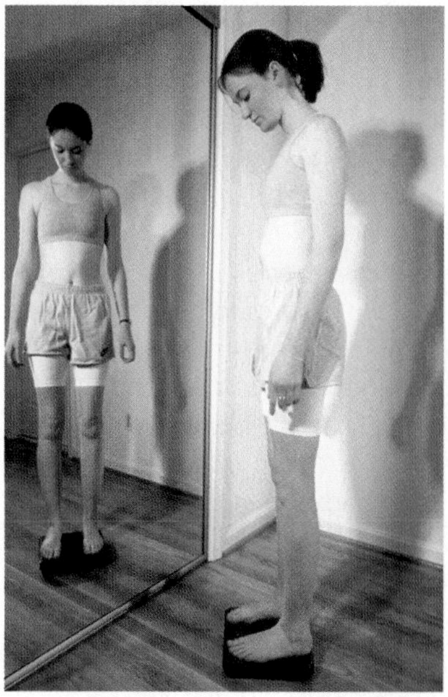

*In treating anorexia nervosa, the first goal is establishing a safer, more normal body weight.*

The second goal in treating anorexia nervosa is more general—to address the broader difficulties that may have caused or are maintaining the disorder. Many different forms of treatment may be used to achieve this goal. The clinical literature commonly advocates family therapy. There are many different forms of family therapy, but perhaps the most common is *structural family therapy,* which views parents' interference with adolescent autonomy—and avoidance of their own disagreements—as the central problems in anorexia nervosa. Structural family therapists attempt to redefine the eating disorder as an interpersonal problem, to get the young person with anorexia nervosa out of the sick role, and to encourage parents to confront their own conflicts directly and not through their children (Minuchin, Rosman, & Baker, 1978). Some evidence indicates that family therapy for anorexia nervosa is more effective than treating the client individually, at least when the client is an adolescent (Robin et al., 1999; Russell et al., 1987).

Clinicians have also tried a number of different individual therapies for anorexia nervosa. Three approaches of note are (1) Bruch's (1982) modified psychodynamic therapy designed to increase introceptive awareness and correct distorted perceptions of self; (2) cognitive behavioural approaches that aim to alter the belief that "weight, shape, or thinness can serve as the sole or predominant referent for inferring personal value or self-worth" (Garner & Bemis, 1982, p. 142); and (3) *feminist therapies,* which encourage young women to pursue their own values rather than blindly adopting prescribed social roles (Fallon, Katzman, & Wooley, 1994). Allan Kaplan (2002), who is head of the eating disorders program at Toronto General Hospital, observed that psychotherapy is still a common treatment for anorexia, but by itself its efficacy remains in question. Similarly, medications such as antidepressants seem to offer little relief for sufferers of anorexia nervosa (Vitousek, 2002).

### Course and Outcome of Anorexia Nervosa

Currently, the most effective approach involves a combination of psychotherapy, nutritional management, and family intervention (Kaplan, 2002). However, evidence on the course and outcome of anorexia nervosa demonstrates that contemporary treatments are only moderately effective. At posttreatment follow-up assessments, 50 to 60 percent of patients have a weight within the normal range, 10 to 20 percent remain significantly below their healthy body weight, and the remainder are intermediate in weight (Hsu, 1990; Steinhausen, 1996). Perhaps as many as 10 percent starve themselves to death or die of related complications, including suicide.

Although important, weight gain is not the only measure of the course of anorexia nervosa. In fact, more than half of women with a history of anorexia nervosa continue to have difficulties with eating, notwithstanding gains in weight. Menstruation returns along with weight gain for most women, but many continue to be preoccupied with diet, weight, and body shape. The following account, written by a young woman after her long and, finally, successful struggle with anorexia nervosa, illustrates some of the continuing problems:

> I do not have a story that ends with a miraculous recovery, and I would be suspicious of anyone who claimed that they had completely gotten over an eating disorder. I continue to struggle with worries about food and my body. I exercise every day without fail. I am prone to stress fractures and will most likely encounter early osteoporosis due to the irreversible effects of starvation on my bones. I am lucky that I will be able to have children someday, though many long-term anorexics are never able to. Despite these lingering effects of the disorder, they pale in comparison to what I consider to be the most detrimental of all. When I look back on those six or so years, it sickens me to realize how much of life I missed. I allowed my obsession with my weight to take over my life. (Zorn, 1998, p. 21)

## CANADIAN FOCUS Treatment at the Montreux Clinic: All You Need Is Love?

One of the world's most famous and controversial clinics for eating disorders was the Montreux residential program, which operated in Victoria, B.C., from 1993 to 2000. The clinic offered round-the-clock care, with patients sometimes staying for many months or longer. Although treatment was expensive, anorexic patients from all over the world were sent to the clinic, often by their wealthy parents. The clinic's founder, Peggy Claude-Pierre, claimed that they were able to "cure" more than 90 percent of people with anorexia. This remarkable success rate was much higher than those of other clinics. Soon the Montreux program attracted a great deal of media publicity, and was featured on TV programs such as *20/20*, *Oprah*, and *The Maury Povich Show*. Claude-Pierre claimed that anorexia could be cured mainly by "unconditional love"—that is, kindness, compassion, empathy, and holding the patients so they felt comforted and safe.

After a series of government investigations and legal battles, in 2000 Claude-Pierre was finally forced to surrender the licence to operate Montreux's residential program. Thus, the residential program was closed down by the government. How could such a thing happen? Part of the answer was simple; more than "unconditional love" is needed to treat anorexia.

Claude-Pierre insisted that her program would save the lives of eating-disorder sufferers that no other program had been able to help. But there was never any outcome study conducted to substantiate her claims. Eating disorder experts who reviewed the program as part of a government investigation later explained there was no evidence to back up claims of any out-of-the-ordinary success rate. Some anorexic patients apparently benefited from the program, but not others. For some of those who did benefit, the gains didn't last; some relapsed and some subsequently died from medical complications or suicide.

The qualifications and treatment practices of Claude-Pierre and her staff were also called into question. Claude-Pierre had no medical training and had not even completed her bachelor's degree in psychology. Her theories about anorexia came entirely from her own experience; the experience of a mother whose two daughters both developed eating disorders. In turn, she trained others at her clinic to be counsellors, some of whom were former or current patients at Montreux. An independent evaluation by eating disorder experts raised concerns that Claude-Pierre and her counsellors were not sufficiently trained or knowledgeable in treating eating disorders.

Most of the patients-turned-counsellors had no training or expertise that would make them competent in caring for fragile and acutely ill anorexics; simply having the disorder does not make one competent as a caregiver. And some of the caregivers still suffered from anorexia. This was very confusing for clients who were trying to normalize their eating and

continued

*cont.*

weight, and would turn to their therapists as role models.

Patients were admitted to the clinic without receiving proper medical or psychological assessment. One three-year-old boy, Dustin, was misdiagnosed by Claude-Pierre as having anorexia and separated from his mother during his 10-month stay at Montreux. A later evaluation by two psychiatrists, as part of the government inquiry, concluded that Dustin did not have anorexia; he had some other disorder such as Asperger's syndrome. They also expressed concerns about the psychological effects of separating the child from his mother for such a long period. No pediatrician or child psychologist or psychiatrist was involved in Dustin's care at Montreux. Another anorexic resident was charged with looking after him. "Unconditional love" was clearly insufficient for helping Dustin; as he refused to eat, feeding soon escalated to yelling and threats to make him eat—or at times he was physically restrained and food was spooned or squirted into his mouth.

There was insufficient medical supervision at the Montreux clinic for the seriously ill patients. Some patients had cardiac arrhythmias as a result of severe weight loss. One patient, Jeannie, weighted only 22 kg when she arrived at Montreux from her home in Scotland. She could barely stand long enough to be weighed, and didn't have the strength to feed herself, even if she'd wanted to. Jeannie was so sick and helpless that she had to be hand-fed like a baby bird. According to an independent evaluation of the Montreux program by Laird Birmingham, head of the St. Paul's Hospital eating disorders program in Vancouver, a number of patients in the program were too ill at the time of admission to be safely cared for in any program that didn't have medical expertise at hand 24 hours a day; "Patients at the same level of severity who were admitted to St. Paul's Hospital were placed on an eating-disorder ward that was staffed at the level of an intensive care ward, because the risk of disastrous—and potentially fatal—complications was so great" (McLintock, 2002, p. 135). An example is a potentially fatal condition called "refeeding syndrome"; when a person begins to take nutrition after a long period of malnourishment, the blood chemistry becomes badly imbalanced, leading to heart problems or even cardiac arrest.

A further concern with Montreux was that the basic rights of the patients were violated. Patients were not permitted to leave the building without permission. Most of the staff interviewed during the government investigation readily admitted that they had sometimes used physical force to prevent patients from leaving. They talked of grabbing patients, of blocking a doorway physically, and of holding them in a bear hug. Most patients, the staff members reported, usually said they wanted to leave when they'd only been in the program a short while. However, the staff said, they knew it was really "the anorexia talking," not the client, and so, normally, either they themselves or a more senior staff member, were able to persuade the patient that they didn't truly want to go.

Patients' incoming and outgoing mail was censored. Incoming mail, the staff members explained, could be "negative" for the client if they were allowed to read it, and outgoing mail could be upsetting to patients or family if it had been written by a patient who was "in a bad head space." Phone calls were also restricted entirely if a patient was "not in a good head space."

Among the media items patients were not normally allowed to watch were any advertisements that might feed into their eating disorder, such as ads for diet programs or low-fat products; "negative talk shows"; or any material, factual or fictional, involving violence or sex. The policy was that no patient was to watch news programs. Similar guidelines applied to books and magazines, CDs, tapes, the radio, and movies. Videos, the policy manual suggested, should be "uplifting in theme and content." Senior staff members had to approve any activity the patient wanted to take up, from music lessons to exercise programs. Something as simple as a 20-minute walk or a trip downtown for coffee had to be approved by Claude-Pierre or a counsellor, even if the patient was going to be within arm's reach of a staff member at all times. Nothing could be done spontaneously.

Health authorities would later call this "imposed therapy," unlawful in British Columbia unless a patient has been legally committed as mentally incompetent by two physicians—not by family members or lay counsellors. None of the patients were legally committed to Montreux, or could be committed to this facility.

Montreux's goal of treating anorexia with unconditional love ultimately proved ineffective in treating their emaciated patients. Staff resorted to force-feeding some patients, as illustrated by the case of Dustin.

Among those experts who independently reviewed the Montreux program, many were concerned by Claude-Pierre's implied promise that she and she alone could offer a cure for every sufferer, still in the absence of any objective evidence to back up her statements. According to Blake Woodside of the Toronto General Hospital's eating disorders program, "Ms. Claude-Pierre [gave] the impression that other available expert treatments are inevitably ineffective. This is both untrue and dangerous" (McLintock, 2002, p. 120). According to Allan Kaplan, head of the eating disorders program at Toronto General Hospital, "The way the clinic worked, with Claude-Pierre having all the decision-making power about how long anyone should stay or when they might work at the clinic as part of their treatment, amounted to autocratic decision making [that] feeds into the 'cult-like' atmosphere that pervades Montreux." (McLintock, 2002, p. 234).

The Montreux clinic continues to operate in Victoria, B.C., although it no longer offers a residential program. ◆

*Sources:* Blatchford (2000); Dineen (2002); McCulloch (2002); McLintock (2002); Meissner (2002); and Stanwick (1999).

# Treatment of Bulimia Nervosa

In recent years, researchers have uncovered promising evidence of the effectiveness of several approaches to treating bulimia nervosa. The most effective forms of treatment include antidepressant medication, cognitive behaviour therapy (delivered both individually and in groups), and interpersonal psychotherapy.

## Antidepressant Medications

All classes of antidepressant medications (see Chapter 5) have been shown to be somewhat effective in treating bulimia nervosa. However, medication alone is *not* the treatment of choice (Garfinkel & Walsh, 1997). Binge eating and compensatory behaviour improve only among a minority of people treated with antidepressants, and relapse is common when medication is stopped (Walsh, 1995). Most importantly, research has shown that, alone or perhaps in combination with medication, psychotherapy is an important component of treatment (Garfinkel & Walsh, 1997; Walsh et al., 1997; Wilson et al., 1999).

## Cognitive Behaviour Therapy

The most thoroughly researched psychotherapy for bulimia nervosa is cognitive behaviour therapy. The cognitive behavioural approach views bulimia as stemming from several maladaptive tendencies, including an excessive emphasis on weight and shape in determining self-esteem; perfectionism; and dichotomous "black or white" thinking (Fairburn, 1996). Fairburn's cognitive behavioural treatment includes three stages. First, the therapist uses education and behavioural strategies to normalize eating patterns. The goal of this stage is to restore a more normal pattern of eating and thereby end the cycle where extreme dietary restraint leads to binge eating and, in turn, to purging. Second, the therapist addresses the client's broader, dysfunctional beliefs about self, appearance, and dieting. Techniques often include a variation of Beck's cognitive therapy (see Chapter 5) to address perfectionism or depression, but individual problems such as poor impulse control or troubled relationships also may be addressed at this stage. Third, the therapist attempts to consolidate gains and prepare the client for expected relapses in the future. Key goals at this final stage of treatment are to develop realistic expectations about eating, weight concerns, and binge eating, as well as clear strategies for coping with relapses in advance (Fairburn, 2002).

Overall, cognitive behaviour therapy leads to a 70 to 80 percent reduction in binge eating and purging across people in treatment. Between one-third and one-half of all clients are able to cease the bulimic pattern completely, and the majority of individuals maintain these gains at six-month to one-year follow-up (Agras et al., 2000; Fairburn et al., 1993). Importantly, cognitive behaviour therapy also has been demonstrated to be effective in group therapy (Mitchell et al., 1990). A recent study conducted by researchers at the Toronto General Hospital suggests that self-help cognitive behavioural programs also can be helpful in treating bulimia (Carter et al., 2003).

## Interpersonal Psychotherapy

Interpersonal psychotherapy, which was originally developed for the treatment of depression (see Chapter 5), also may be an effective treatment for bulimia nervosa. This is surprising because interpersonal therapy does not address eating disorders directly but instead focuses on difficulties in close relationships. Interpersonal therapy for bulimia initially was studied when the treatment was included as a placebo control group in a study of cognitive behaviour therapy (see Research Methods). Fairburn and colleagues (1991, 1993) planned to evaluate whether cognitive behaviour therapy had specific treatment effects above and beyond the nonspecific, general benefits of receiving psychotherapy. The investigators chose interpersonal therapy as a credible placebo treatment because interpersonal problems often are associated with bulimia nervosa. However, they hypothesized that cognitive behaviour therapy would outperform the interpersonal approach. The study also included a third condition, a behaviour therapy alone group, which essentially was cognitive behaviour therapy without the cognitive elements.

When Fairburn and his colleagues (1991) evaluated outcome shortly after treatment, they found that cognitive behaviour therapy was more effective than interpersonal therapy in changing dieting behaviour, self-induced

## RESEARCH METHODS

### Credible Placebo Control Groups

The *placebo* is a treatment that contains no active ingredients for the disorder being treated. A *placebo control group* is a group of patients randomly assigned to receive only a placebo treatment in an outcome study. Scientists must include placebos and placebo control groups in treatment outcome research because the *expectation* of change can produce many psychological (and physical) improvements in psychological and biomedical treatment research. New treatments work, in part, because the patient and the therapist expect them to work.

Placebo treatments are easy to develop when studying medications. Experimenters give patients a pill that looks real but contains no active chemical ingredients—for example, a "sugar pill." Scientists face a much more challenging task in developing placebos for psychological treatments. How can we create a placebo psychological treatment that contains no active ingredients but increases the patient's and the therapist's expectations for change just as much as the real treatment?

As one alternative, experimenters sometimes create a placebo control group by randomly assigning patients to receive an alternative intervention that was not designed as a treatment for the specific disorder being studied. In one study conducted at the University of British Columbia, cognitive therapy was compared to a placebo control called "associative therapy." In the latter intervention, patients were asked to free-associate about their current problems, mentioning whatever thoughts or associations that come to mind, until they traced the associations back to their childhood origins. Although patients found associative therapy to be just as credible as cognitive therapy, associative therapy (unlike cognitive therapy) did not produce any changes in symptoms (Taylor et al., 1997).

In a study of cognitive behaviour therapy for bulimia nervosa, Fairburn et al. (1993) thought interpersonal therapy was a credible placebo. The investigators did not believe that interpersonal therapy contained "specific ingredients" for treating bulimia nervosa. They did expect, however, that patients would view it as a legitimate treatment for their problems.

Offering an alternative treatment does not fully resolve the problem of designing a credible placebo. Researchers typically "believe" in their new treatment—otherwise they would not be studying it, and evidence on the *allegiance effect* demonstrates that such beliefs help make a treatment more successful than the alternatives. The allegiance effect tells us that cognitive behaviour therapy should have been more successful in the Fairburn et al. (1993) study because the investigators were cognitive behaviour therapists. In fact, we are particularly impressed by the positive results for the interpersonal therapy group in this study because interpersonal therapy overcame the allegiance effect. The experimenters did not expect interpersonal therapy to be an effective treatment, but it was effective nevertheless, in this study and in a later replication (Agras et al., 2000).

How can investigators overcome the allegiance effect? This dilemma is resolved in drug treatment research by using a *double-blind study,* where neither the patient nor the therapist knows whether the patient is receiving an active treatment or a placebo. Unfortunately, specific forms of psychotherapy (or placebo therapies) cannot be disguised. Even pill placebo effects are not always easy to interpret. For example, as noted by York University psychologist Leslie Greenberg, evidence indicates that medications, perhaps even placebo medications, are more effective when they produce more side effects (Greenberg et al., 1994). There are at least two possible reasons for this. More disruptive side effects may increase the patient's expectations for change, because the side effects make the drug seem powerful. Or even in a double-blind study, clinicians may be able to determine whether patients are receiving the real medication or a placebo based on the pattern of side effects.

Another way of addressing the allegiance effect in psychotherapy outcome research is to have investigators who hold *opposing* allegiances participate in the same study. Cognitive behaviour therapy could be offered by interpersonal therapists, cognitive behaviour therapists could deliver interpersonal therapy, and so on. This approach overcomes the allegiance effect, but such studies are more difficult and expensive to conduct—and they create a new problem: because the same therapists cannot deliver the two different treatments, we cannot control for outcome effects due to the individual therapists (e.g., therapists' personality). Of course, the alternative also has the problem that *neither* treatment is a placebo, at least in theory.

Scientific findings are greatly enhanced by the use of alternative therapies, pill placebos, and competitions between researchers with opposing allegiance, but there is no perfect placebo control group for psychotherapy outcome research. In the absence of a perfect psychological placebo, two conclusions seem clear. First, we must recognize that the expectations of patients, therapists, and experimenters can influence the findings of therapy outcome research. Second, we are particularly impressed when, contrary to expectations, a treatment that an experimenter views as a placebo proves to be effective. ◆

vomiting, and attitudes about weight and shape. Cognitive behaviour therapy also was more effective than behaviour therapy alone when attitude change was the outcome measure; however, the results of the two behavioural treatments were similar in other respects.

A very different picture emerged at 12-month follow-up (Fairburn et al., 1993) (see Figure 10–6). The improvements brought about by behaviour therapy alone deteriorated over time, and a large number of patients dropped out of this group, perhaps reflecting their dissatisfaction with the treatment. In comparison, the improvements in the cognitive behaviour therapy group remained fairly stable. Most surprising, however, members of the interpersonal therapy group *continued to improve* in the 12 months following the end of treatment. At one-year follow-up, in fact, the improvements for interpersonal therapy equalled the improvements for cognitive behaviour therapy and outdistanced the behaviour therapy alone group.

The continued improvement for the interpersonal therapy group was surprising and impressive, for at least two reasons. First, the interpersonal treatments explicitly excluded direct discussions of eating, diet, and related topics. Second, the investigators had lower expectations for the interpersonal therapy group, and the *allegiance effect* often influences treatment outcome (see Research Methods). Furthermore, a recent, larger study replicated the results of this investigation, although it should be underscored that cognitive behaviour therapy produced more rapid improvement (Agras et al., 2000). Cognitive behaviour therapy clearly is the first-line treatment for bulimia nervosa, but interpersonal therapy and antidepressant medication may be useful supplemental or alternative treatments.

**Effectiveness of Treatments for Bulimia Nervosa over Time**

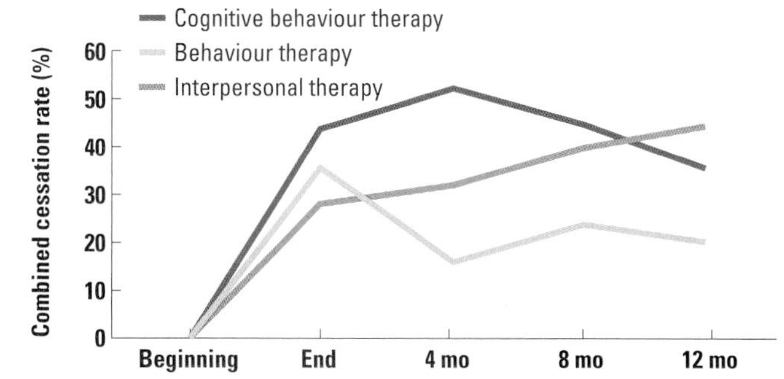


**FIGURE 10–6: Percentage of patients who no longer purged or had episodes of bulimia according to objective or subjective reports. Note the decline for the behaviour therapy group and continued improvement for the interpersonal therapy group over the one-year follow-up interval.**

*Source:* C.G. Fairburn, R. Jones, R.C. Peveler, R.A. Hope, and M. O'Connor, 1993, Psycotherapy and bulimia nervosa: Longer-term effects of interpersonal psychotherapy, behavior therapy, and cognitive behavior therapy. *Archives of General Psychiatry, 50,* 423.

## Course and Outcome of Bulimia Nervosa

Evidence suggests that the outcome for bulimia nervosa is generally more positive than for anorexia nervosa (Herzog et al., 1999; Sullivan, 2002). About half of clients are free of all symptoms of the disorder following treatment, about one in five continue to meet the diagnostic criteria for bulimia nervosa, and the remainder have occasional relapses or subclinical levels of binge eating and compensatory behaviour. Most clients manage to maintain a weight that is generally in the normal range, and—in contrast to anorexia nervosa—mortality is rare (Keel & Mitchell, 1997). Although data are insufficient, it also appears that comorbid psychological disorders tend to improve with improvements in bulimia nervosa (Hsu, 1995; Keel & Mitchell, 1997). One more optimistic finding is that treatment is associated with more rapid recovery, and if effective short-term treatments were involved—cognitive behaviour therapy or antidepressant medication—treatment benefits might be evident even 10 years later (Keel et al., 2002).

# Summary

**Eating disorders** are severe disturbances in eating behaviour that result from the sufferer's obsessive fear of gaining weight. DSM-IV-TR lists two major subtypes of eating disorders: anorexia nervosa and bulimia nervosa. The defining symptoms of **anorexia nervosa** include extreme emaciation, a disturbed perception of one's body, an intense fear of gaining weight, and the cessation of menstruation (in women). People with anorexia nervosa are preoccupied with food, revel in their control over eating, and may have mood disturbances, sexual difficulties, lack of impulse control, and medical problems secondary to the weight loss.

The defining symptoms of **bulimia nervosa** are **binge eating** and compensatory behaviour (**purging** or excessive exercise), a sense of lost control during a binge, and undue focus on weight and shape. Depression is commonly associated with bulimia nervosa; substance abuse and personality disorders are to a much lesser degree.

DSM-IV-TR includes two subtypes of anorexia nervosa. The restricting type includes people who rarely engage in binge eating or purging behaviour, whereas the binge eating/purging type is characterized by regular binge eating and purging. Bulimia nervosa also is divided into two subtypes. The purging type is characterized by the regular use of self-induced vomiting or the misuse of laxatives, diuretics, or enemas. The nonpurging type compensates for binge eating with fasting or excessive exercise. There has been debate about adding to the DSM-IV-TR list of eating disorders. **Binge eating disorder** is included in a special appendix. **Obesity** has been considered for inclusion but rejected.

The prevalence of both anorexia nervosa and bulimia nervosa has increased dramatically in recent years, particularly among young women. Both anorexia and bulimia nervosa are approximately 10 times more common among women than among men, and many scientists blame our society's gender roles and standards of beauty for encouraging eating disorders. Standards of beauty and pubertal changes in body shape and weight also may account for the onset of eating disorders during adolescence and early adulthood.

The regulation of normal eating and weight results from a combination of biological, psychological, and social factors. Each of these levels of analysis helps to explain the etiology of anorexia nervosa and bulimia nervosa. Adolescent girls and young women are at risk, in part, because they attempt to shape themselves to fit the image of the ideal woman. The emphasis on appearances also lessens the value of other roles filled by girls and women. To a lesser extent, family relationships also may influence eating disorders. Four of the most prominent psychological factors in the development of eating disorders are issues of control and perfectionism, dysphoria combined with a lack of **introceptive awareness**, body image dissatisfaction, and reactions to dietary restraint. Biological contributions include the body's attempts to maintain **weight set points**, genetic influences on body weight and shape, and in rare cases a dysfunction of the hypothalamus. Overall, a systems perspective is the best method for conceptualizing eating disorders, and these disorders can develop through several alternative pathways.

Treatments for anorexia nervosa and bulimia nervosa differ in approach and effectiveness. Anorexia nervosa is may require inpatient treatment with the initial goal of gaining weight, even through the use of coercive methods if necessary. Following treatment, 50 to 60 percent of people with anorexia nervosa have a normal weight, and 10 to 20 percent have weights well below normal (the remainder are in between these two groups). About 10 percent of people with the disorder die of starvation, suicide, or medical complications. Changing long-term eating patterns and attitudes in anorexia nervosa is difficult, and no clearly effective psychological treatment or medication has been identified for the disorder.

Treatments for bulimia nervosa are more promising, particularly cognitive behaviour therapy, and to a lesser extent, interpersonal psychotherapy and antidepressant medication. About half of clients with bulimia nervosa are free of all symptoms following treatment, about one in five continues to meet the diagnostic criteria, and the remainder have occasional relapses or subclinical levels of binge eating and compensatory behaviour. Weight is generally in the normal range, and comorbid psychological disorders appear to improve with improvements in bulimia nervosa.

# Critical Thinking

1. Do you agree that the prevalence of eating disorders is influenced by the images of young women portrayed in the popular media? Are these images changing? How would you change them?
2. How do standards of beauty differ across ethnic and cultural groups? How might these differences protect the members of some groups and put others at risk?
3. In their everyday life, many university students, particularly women, face many issues about appearance, food, and eating disorders. How would you criticize or change the focus of research on eating disorders based on your personal experience?
4. If you had an eating disorder, would you want to be treated with cognitive behaviour therapy, interpersonal therapy, or antidepressants? Why? Why might eating disorders be improved for people who receive interpersonal therapy?

# Key Terms

**amenorrhea** 341
**anorexia nervosa** 337
**binge eating** 343
**binge eating disorder** 347
**bulimia nervosa** 337
**cohort** 348
**cohort effects** 348
**distorted body image** 340
**eating disorders** 337
**enmeshed families** 351
**introceptive awareness** 352
**obesity** 347
**purging** 344
**weight set point** 354

# 11 Substance Use Disorders

Overview
Typical Symptoms and Associated Features
Classification
Epidemiology
Etiological Considerations and Research
Treatment

**What evidence is needed to show that a drug is addictive?**

**Where is the boundary between substance abuse and recreational drug use?**

**What are the most important risk factors for alcoholism?**

**How does AA differ from other approaches to treating alcoholism?**

The abuse of alcohol and other drugs is one of the most serious problems facing our society today. Alcohol and drug problems receive a great deal of attention in the popular media, as illustrated by NHL player Ken Daneyko's ongoing battle with alcohol abuse, and by actor Robert Downey, Jr.'s repeated struggles with cocaine addiction. Research efforts, treatment priorities, and national publicity have all helped transform attitudes toward the abuse of chemical substances. The picture of the drug addict as a homeless derelict whose personality defects and lack of motivation are largely responsible for the problem is being replaced by a new view in which substance abuse is seen as a chronic mental disorder that affects people from all walks of life (Leshner, 1997).

*NHL player Ken Daneyko has been battling binge drinking for years. The persistent nature of his problems underscores the chronic nature of many addictions. In 1997 he became one of only a handful of players to openly make use of the NHL's substance-abuse program.*

## Overview

The costs of substance abuse are astronomical. In Canada, the economic costs of alcoholism, based on factors such as health problems associated with alcoholism, days lost from work, and costs from alcohol-related motor vehicle accidents, amount to more than $7.5 billion each year, according to a 1992 estimate (Dingle et al., 2002). Alcohol is also a contributory factor in 27 percent of male suicides and 17 percent of female suicides in Canada (Dingle et al., 2002). In 1995 over 6500 Canadians lost their lives as a result of alcohol consumption, with causes including accidents, diseases caused by alcoholism, and suicide (CCSA/CAMH, 1999). Approximately 30 to 40 percent of homeless people suffer from alcoholism (McCarty et al., 1991). According to the Global Burden of Disease Study, alcohol use was the fourth leading cause of disability worldwide in 1990. Cirrhosis of the liver, which is frequently the result of chronic alcoholism, is a leading cause of death in many countries, including Canada.

Twenty percent of Canadians smoke (Health Canada, 2001). Each year, over 30 000 Canadians die from smoking-related causes, particularly lung cancer, cardiovascular disease, and chronic obstructive lung disease (CCSA/CAMH, 1999). The rate of deaths attributable to the use of tobacco is growing in many places, particularly in developing countries, where 50 percent of adult men are regular smokers. By the year 2020, tobacco is expected to kill between 8 and 9 million people worldwide, more than any single disease, including HIV (Lopez & Murray, 1998; Murray & Lopez, 1997).

DSM-IV-TR uses two terms to describe substance use disorders, and these two terms reflect two different levels of severity. **Substance dependence**, the more severe of the two forms, refers to a pattern of repeated self-administration that often results in tolerance, the need for increased amounts of the drug to achieve intoxication; withdrawal, unpleasant physical and psychological effects that the person experiences when he or she tries to stop taking the drug; and compulsive drug-taking behaviour. **Substance abuse** describes a more broadly conceived, less severe pattern of drug use that is defined in terms of interference with the person's ability to fulfill major role obligations at work or at home, the recurrent use of a drug in dangerous situations, and repeated legal difficulties associated with drug use.

*Addiction* is another, older term that is often used to describe problems such as alcoholism. The term has been replaced in official terminology by the term *substance dependence*, with which it is synonymous, but it is still used informally by many laypeople.

A **drug of abuse**, sometimes called a *psychoactive substance*, is a chemical substance that alters a person's mood, level of perception, or brain functioning (Schuckit, 1999a). All drugs of abuse can be used to increase a person's psychological comfort level (make one feel "high") or to alter levels of consciousness. The list of chemicals on which people can become dependent is long and seems to be growing longer. It includes drugs that are legally available, whether over the counter or by prescription only, as well as many that are illegal (see Table 11–1).

Depressants of the central nervous system (CNS) include alcohol as well as types of medication that are used to help people sleep, called *hypnotics*, and those for relieving anxiety, known as *sedatives* or *anxiolytics*. The CNS stimulants include illegal drugs like amphetamine and cocaine, as well as nicotine and caffeine. The opiates, also called *narcotic analgesics*, can be used clinically to decrease pain. The *cannabinoids*, such as marijuana, produce euphoria and an altered sense of time. At higher doses, they may produce hallucinations. People with a substance use disorder frequently abuse several types of drugs; this condition is known as **polysubstance abuse**.

One basic question we must address is whether we should view each type of addiction as a unique problem. Experts who answer yes to this question point out that each class of abused substance seems to affect the body in distinct ways. For example, when taken orally, some opiates can be used for long periods of time without leading to significant organ damage (Jaffe & Jaffe, 1999). Chronic use of alcohol and tobacco, on the other hand, can have a devastating impact on a person's physical health.

Despite these differences, the various forms of substance abuse share many common elements. All forms of abuse represent an inherent conflict between immediate pleasure and longer-term harmful consequences. The psychological and biochemical effects on the user are often similar, as are the negative consequences for both social and occupational functioning. The reasons for initial experimentation with a drug, the factors that influence the transition to dependence, and the processes that lead to relapse after initial ef-

**TABLE 11–1 Commonly Abused Drugs**

| Class | Examples | Brand Names and Street Names |
|---|---|---|
| CNS Depressants | Alcohol | beer, wine, liquor |
| | Barbiturates | barbs, Amytal, Nembutal, Seconal |
| | Benzodiazepines | *roofies, tanks*, Xanax, Valium, Halcion |
| | Methaqualone | *quaalude, ludes* |
| CNS Stimulants | Amphetamine | *black beauties, crosses, hearts blow* |
| | Cocaine | *coke, crack, flake, rocks, snow crank* |
| | Methamphetamine | *crystal, glass, ice, speed* |
| | Nicotine | cigars, cigarettes, smokeless tobacco |
| | Caffeine | coffee, tea, soft drinks |
| Opiates | Heroin | *horse, smack, H, junk, skag* |
| | Opium | laudanum, paregoric, dover's powder |
| | Morphine | Roxanol, Duramorph |
| | Methadone | Amidone, Dolophine, Methadose |
| | Codeine | Tylenol w/Codeine, Robitussin A-C |
| Cannabinoids | Marijuana | *grass, herb, pot, reefer, smoke, weed* |
| | Hashish | *hash* |
| Hallucinogens | LSD | *acid, microdot* |
| | Mescaline | *buttons, cactus, mesc, peyote* |
| | Psilocybin | *magic mushroom, purple passion* |
| | Phencyclidine | PCP, *angel dust, boat, hog, love boat* |
| | MDMA | *ecstasy, XTC, Adam* |

*Note:* Street names for drugs appear in italics.

forts to change are all similar in many respects. For these reasons, many clinicians and researchers have moved toward a view of substance abuse that emphasizes common causes, behaviours, and consequences (Marlatt et al., 1988). In fact, DSM-IV-TR employs a single set of diagnostic criteria that defines dependence for all types of drugs.

The variety of problems associated with substance use disorders can be illustrated using a case study of alcohol dependence. Ernest Hemingway (1899–1961), a Nobel Prize–winning writer, was severely dependent on alcohol for many years. The following paragraphs, quoted from an article by Johnson (1989), describe the progression of Hemingway's drinking and the problems that it created. They illustrate many typical features of substance dependence, as well as the devastating impact that alcohol can have on various organs of the body. Johnson's description also raises a number of important questions about the etiology of this disorder. Most men and women consume alcoholic beverages at some point during their lives. Why do some people become dependent on alcohol while others do not? What factors influence the transition from social drinking to abuse?

## CASE STUDY **Ernest Hemingway's Alcohol Dependence**

Hemingway began to drink as a teenager, the local blacksmith secretly supplying him with strong cider. His mother noted his habit and always feared he would become an alcoholic. In Italy he progressed to wine, then had his first hard liquor at the officers' club in Milan. His wound [from World War I] and an unhappy love affair provoked heavy drinking: in the hospital, his wardrobe was found to be full of empty cognac bottles, an ominous sign. In Paris in the 1920s, he bought Beaune by the gallon at a wine co-operative, and would and did drink five or six bottles of red at a meal. He taught Scott Fitzgerald to drink wine direct from the bottle, which, he said, was like "a girl going swimming without her swimming suit." In New York he was "cockeyed," he said, for "several days" after signing his contract for *The Sun Also Rises*, probably his first prolonged bout.

It was in Cuba in the 1930s that his drinking first got completely out of hand. One bartender there said he could "drink more martinis than any man I have ever seen." On safari, he was seen sneaking out of his tent at 5 A.M. to get a drink. His brother Leicester said that, by the end of the 1930s, at Key West, he was drinking seventeen Scotch-and-sodas a day, and often taking a bottle of champagne to bed with him at night.

At this period, his liver for the first time began to cause him acute pain. He was told by his doctor to give up alcohol completely, and indeed tried to limit his consumption to three whiskeys before dinner. But that did not last. During World War II his drinking mounted steadily and by the mid-1940s he was reportedly pouring gin into his tea at breakfast. A.E. Hotchner, interviewing him for *Cosmopolitan* in 1948, said he dispatched seven double-size Papa Doubles (the Havana drink named after him, a mixture of rum, grapefruit and maraschino), and when he left for dinner took an eighth with him for the drive. And on top of all, there was constant whiskey: His son Patrick said his father got through a quart of whiskey a day for the last 20 years of his life.

Hemingway's ability to hold his liquor was remarkable. Lillian Ross, who wrote his profile for the *New Yorker*, does not seem to have noticed he was drunk a lot of the time he talked to her. Denis Zaphior said of his last safari: "I suppose he was drunk the whole time but seldom showed it." He also demonstrated an unusual ability to cut down his drinking or even to eliminate it altogether for brief periods, and this, in addition to his strong physique, enabled him to survive.

But despite his physique, his alcoholism had a direct impact on his health beginning with his damaged liver in the late 1930s. By 1959, following his last big drinking bout in Spain, he was experiencing both kidney and liver trouble and possibly hemochromatosis (cirrhosis, bronzed skin, diabetes), edema of the ankles, cramps, chronic insomnia, blood-clotting and high blood uremia, as well as his skin complaints. He was impotent and prematurely aged. Even so, he was still on his feet, still alive; and the thought had become unbearable to him. His father had committed suicide because of his fear of mortal illness. Hemingway feared that his illnesses were not mortal: On July 2, 1961, after various unsuccessful treatments for depression and paranoia, he got hold of his best English double-barrelled shotgun, put two canisters in it, and blew away his entire cranial vault.

Why did Hemingway long for death [and why did he drink]? . . . He felt he was failing his art. Hemingway had many grievous faults, but there was one thing he did not lack: artistic integrity. It shines like a beacon through his whole life. He set himself the task of creating a new way of writing English, and fiction, and he succeeded. It was one of the salient events in the history of our language and is now an inescapable part of it. He devoted to this task immense resources of creative skill, energy, and patience. That in itself was difficult. But far more difficult, as he discovered, was to maintain the high creative standards he had set himself. This became apparent to him in the mid-1930s, and added to his habitual depression. From then on his few successful stories were aberrations in a long downward slide (Johnson, 1989, pp. 58–59).

## Typical Symptoms and Associated Features

Substance dependence is difficult to define. The number of problems that a person encounters seems to provide the most useful distinction between people who are dependent on a substance and those who are not. These problems can be sorted loosely into two general areas: (1) patterns of pathological consumption, including psychological and physiological dependence; and (2) consequences that follow a prolonged pattern of abuse, including social and occupational impairment, legal and financial difficulties, and deteriorating medical condition.

It might seem that the actual amount of a drug of abuse that a person consumes would be the best indication of the existence of a problem. Hemingway, for example, clearly consumed enormous quantities of alcohol over a period of many years. The average person with an alcohol use disorder does drink more frequently and in larger quantities than the average person without an alcohol use disorder (Dawson, 2000). Nevertheless, the amount of a drug that a specific person consumes is not a good way to define substance use disorders, because people vary significantly in the amount of any given drug they can consume. Factors such as age, gender, activity level, and overall physical health influence a person's ability to metabolize various kinds of drugs. For example, some people can drink a lot without developing problems; others drink relatively little and have difficulties.

*"Excuse me, Reverend, but what, exactly, do you have to do to get a drink around here?"*

©The New Yorker Collection, Jack Ziegler from cartoonbank.com. All Rights Reserved.

### The Concept of Substance Dependence

Many psychological features or problems are associated with dependence on chemical substances. One such feature involves *craving*. This word is frequently used to describe a forceful urge to use drugs, but the relationship between craving and drug use is actually very complex (Sayette et al., 2000). People who are dependent on drugs often say that they take the drug to control how they are feeling. They need it to relieve negative mood states or to avoid withdrawal symptoms from previous episodes. They may feel compelled to take the drug as a way to prepare for certain activities, such as public speaking, writing, or sex. Some clinicians refer to this condition as **psychological dependence**.

One useful index of craving is the amount of time that the person spends planning to take the drug. Is access to drugs or alcohol a constant preoccupation? If the person is invited to a party or is planning to eat at a restaurant, does he or she always inquire about the availability of alcoholic drinks? If the person is going to spend a few days at the beach, will he or she worry more about whether liquor stores will be closed on weekends or holidays than about having enough food, clothes, or recreational equipment?

As the problem progresses, it is not unusual for the person who abuses drugs to try to stop. In the case of alcoholism, for example, it is possible for even heavy drinkers to abstain for at least short periods of time. Most clinicians and researchers agree that diminished control over drinking is a crucial feature of the disorder (Walters, 1999). Some experts have described this issue as "freedom of choice." When a person first experiments with the use of alcohol, his or her behaviour is clearly voluntary; the person is not compelled to drink. After drinking heavily for a long period of time, most people with a drinking disorder try to stop. Unfortunately, efforts at self-control are typically short-lived and usually fail.

**Tolerance and Withdrawal** Two particularly important features of substance dependence are the phenomena known as tolerance and withdrawal. These symptoms are usually interpreted as evidence of *physiological dependence*. **Tolerance** refers to the process through which the nervous system becomes less sensitive to the effects of alcohol or any other drug of abuse. For example, a person who has been regularly exposed to alcohol will need to drink increased quantities to achieve the same subjective effect ("buzz," "high," or level of intoxication).

The development of drug tolerance seems to be the result of three separate mechanisms (Julien, 2001). Two are pharmacological and the third is behavioural. *Metabolic tolerance* develops when repeated exposure to a drug causes the person's liver to produce more enzymes that are used to metabolize—that is, break down—the drug. The drug, therefore, is metabolized more quickly and the person has to take increasing larger doses in order to maintain the same level in his or her body. *Pharmacodynamic tolerance* occurs when receptors in the brain (see Figure 2–2) adapt to continued presence of the drug. The neuron may adapt by reducing the number of receptors or by reducing their sensitivity to the drug. This process is known as *down regulation*. As demonstrated by McMaster University researchers, the third process involved in drug tolerance involves *behavioural conditioning mechanisms* (Siegel, 2001; Siegel et al., 2000). Cues that are regularly associated with the administration of a drug begin to function as conditioned stimuli and elicit a conditioned response that is opposite in direction to the natural effect of the drug. As this compensatory response increases in strength, it competes with the drug response so that larger amounts of the drug must be taken to achieve the same effect.

Some drugs are much more likely than others to produce a buildup of tolerance (APA, 2000). The most substantial tolerance effects are found among heavy users of opioids, such as heroin, and CNS stimulants, such as amphetamine and cocaine. Pronounced tolerance is also found among people who use alcohol and nicotine. The evidence is unclear regarding tolerance effects and prolonged use of marijuana and hashish. Most people who use cannabinoids are not aware of tolerance effects, but these effects have been demonstrated in animal studies. Hallucinogens (LSD) and phencyclidine (PCP) may not lead to the development of tolerance.

**Withdrawal** refers to the symptoms experienced when a person stops using a drug. The symptom can go on for several days. For example, alcohol is a CNS depressant, and the heavy drinker's system becomes accustomed to functioning in a chronically depressed state. When the person stops drinking, the system begins to rebound within several hours, producing many unpleasant side effects—hand tremors, sweating, nausea, anxiety, and insomnia. The most serious forms of withdrawal include convulsions and visual, tactile, or auditory hallucinations. Some people develop delirium, a sudden disturbance of consciousness that is accompanied by changes in cognitive processes such as lack of awareness of the environment or inability to sustain attention (see Chapter 14). This syndrome is called *alcohol withdrawal delirium* in DSM-IV-TR (more traditionally known as *delirium tremens*, or *DTs*) if it is induced by withdrawal from alcohol.

The symptoms of withdrawal vary considerably for different kinds of substances. Table 11–2 compares various drugs of abuse in terms of withdrawal and other related characteristics. Unpleasant reactions are most evident during withdrawal from alcohol, opioids, and the general class of sedatives, hypnotics, and anxiolytics (such as Valium and Xanax). Withdrawal symptoms are also associated with stimulants, such as amphetamine, cocaine, and nicotine, though they are sometimes less pronounced than those associated with alcohol and opioids.

Withdrawal symptoms are not often seen after repeated use of cannabis or hallucinogens, and they have not been demonstrated with phencyclidine. Caffeine is the most widely used psychoactive substance in the world. We all know people who crave coffee, especially in the morning. And some heavy coffee users experience severe headaches when they stop drinking caffeine (Hughes et al., 1998; Nehlig, 1999). You may be surprised to see in Table 11–2 that, according to DSM-IV-TR, the use of caffeine is not considered to lead to dependence or withdrawal symptoms. The authors of DSM-IV-TR acknowledged these symptoms, but they decided that the symptoms did not cause clinically significant distress and impairment and, therefore, should not be included in the manual as a type of mental disorder.

All these problems serve to emphasize the fact that symptoms of substance use disorders fall along a continuum. It is convenient to consider these problems in terms of qualitative distinctions: people who can control their drinking and those who cannot; people

**TABLE 11-2 Comparison of Various Psychoactive Substances**

| Substance | Can Produce Dependence | Can Produce Intoxication | Associated Withdrawal | Can Produce Dementia |
|---|---|---|---|---|
| Alcohol | yes | yes | yes | yes |
| Amphetamines | yes | yes | yes | no |
| Caffeine | no | yes | no | no |
| Marijuana/hashish | yes | yes | no | no |
| Cocaine | yes | yes | yes | no |
| Hallucinogens | yes | yes | no | no |
| Inhalants | yes | yes | no | yes |
| Nicotine | yes | no | yes | no |
| Opiates | yes | yes | yes | no |
| Phencyclidine (PCP) | yes | yes | no | no |
| Sedatives, hypnotics, and anxiolytics | yes | yes | yes | yes |

*Source:* Based on data from the DSM-IV-TR.

who crave alcohol and those who do not; people who have developed a tolerance to the drug and those who have not; and so on. In fact, there are no clear dividing lines on any of these dimensions. Drug use disorders lie on a continuum of severity (Bucholz et al., 1996). For this reason it is extremely difficult to define the nature of substance dependence disorders.

People can become dependent on many different kinds of drugs. Although patterns of dependence are similar in some ways for all drugs, each type of drug also has some unique features. In the next few pages we briefly review some of the most important classes of drugs. For each group, we will describe short-term effects on physiology and behaviour, as well as the consequences of long-term abuse. Unless otherwise specified, these descriptions are based on information from McKim's (2000) textbook on drugs and behaviour.

## Alcohol

Alcohol affects virtually every organ and system in the body (Tabakoff & Hoffman, 1999). After alcohol is ingested, it is absorbed through membranes in the stomach, small intestine, and colon. The rate at which it is absorbed is influenced by many variables, including the concentration of alcohol in the beverage (for example, distilled spirits are absorbed more rapidly than beer or wine), the volume and rate of consumption, and the presence of food in the digestive system. After it is absorbed, alcohol is distributed to all the body's organ systems. Almost all the alcohol that a person consumes is eventually broken down or metabolized in the liver. The rate at which alcohol is metabolized varies from person to person, but the average person can metabolize about 30 mL of 90-proof liquor or 360 mL of beer per hour (Nathan, 1993). If the person's consumption rate exceeds this metabolic limit, then blood alcohol levels will rise.

Blood alcohol levels are measured in terms of the amount of alcohol per unit of blood. A "drink" is considered to be 360 mL of beer, 120 mL of wine, or 30 mL of 86-proof whiskey. The average 70 kg person who consumes 5 drinks in 1 hour will have a blood alcohol level of approximately 100 mg per 100 mL of blood, or 100 mg percent (Kowalski, 1998). Alcohol negatively affects cognitive performance (Pihl et al., 2003). In fact, there is a strong correlation between blood alcohol levels and CNS intoxicating effects. According to DSM-IV-TR, the symptoms of alcohol intoxication include slurred speech, lack of coordination, an unsteady gait, nystagmus (involuntary to-and-fro movement of the eyeballs induced when the person looks upward or to the side), impaired attention or memory, and stupor or coma.

**Short-Term Effects** In most provinces the legal limit of alcohol concentration for driving is 100 mg percent. Some legislatures have lowered this limit to 80 mg percent, because slowed reaction times and interference with other driving skills may occur at lower blood alcohol levels (Mejeur, 1999). People with levels of 150 to 300 mg percent will almost always act intoxicated. Neurological and respiration complications begin to appear at higher levels. There is an extreme risk of coma leading to toxic death when blood alcohol levels go above 400 mg percent.

**Consequences of Prolonged Use and Abuse** The long-term abuse of alcohol can have a devastating impact on many areas of a person's life. The disruption of relationships with family and friends can be especially painful. Many people who abuse alcohol experience blackouts. In some cases, abusers may continue to function without passing out, but they will be unable to remember their behaviour. An example is the person who drives home drunk from a party and in the morning finds a dent in the car bumper but can't remember how it got there. Sometimes problem drinkers will be told by a friend about how they behaved at the previous night's party, but they cannot remember what they did.

Regular heavy use of alcohol is also likely to interfere with job performance. Coworkers and supervisors may complain. Attendance at work may become sporadic. Eventually the heavy drinker may be suspended or fired. Related to job performance is the problem of financial difficulties. Losing one's job is clearly detrimental to one's financial stability, as are the costs of divorce, health care, liquor, and so on. Many heavy drinkers encounter problems with legal authorities. These problems may include arrests for drunken driving and public intoxication, as well as charges of spousal and child abuse.

On a biological level, prolonged exposure to high levels of alcohol can disrupt the functions of several important organ systems, especially the liver, pancreas, gastrointestinal system, cardiovascular system, and endocrine system. The symptoms of alcoholism include many secondary health problems, such as cirrhosis of the liver, heart problems (in part, the result of being overweight), and various forms of cancer, as well as severe and persistent forms of dementia and memory impairment or amnestic disorders, such as Korsakoff's syndrome (see Chapter 14). Alcoholism is also associated with nutritional disturbances of many types, because chronic abusers often drink instead of eating balanced meals. In fact, over an extended period of time, alcohol dependence has more negative health consequences than does abuse of any other drug, with the exception of nicotine.

The misuse of alcohol leads to an enormous number of severe injuries and premature deaths in every region of the world (Murray & Lopez, 1997). The specific impact of alcohol varies among geographic regions, in part because of differences in the age structure of different populations. Deaths that result from alcohol-related injuries are much more common among young men, while deaths from alcohol-related diseases are responsible for more deaths among older men (see Figure 11–1).

**Male Deaths Caused by Alcohol Use in Established Market Economies**

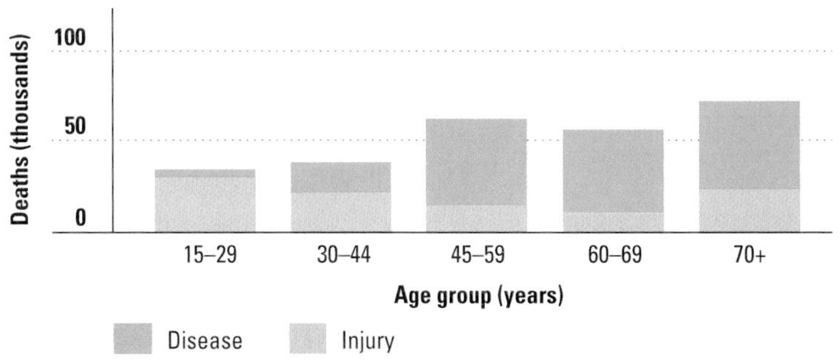


**FIGURE 11–1: Young men are more likely to be killed by alcohol-related injuries, while older men often die as a result of alcohol-related disease.**

*Source:* C.J.L. Murray and A.D. Lopez, 1997, Global mortality, disability, and the contribution of risk factors: Global Burden of Disease Study. *Lancet, 349*, 1436–1442.

## Nicotine

Nicotine is the active ingredient in tobacco, which is its only natural source. Nicotine is almost never taken in its pure form because it can be toxic. Very high doses have extremely unpleasant effects. Controlled doses are easier to achieve by smoking or chewing tobacco, which provides a diluted concentration of nicotine. When tobacco smoke is inhaled, nicotine is absorbed into the blood through the mucous membranes of the lungs, where it enters the bloodstream and is carried to the brain.

**Short-Term Effects** The effects of nicotine on the peripheral nervous system (see Chapter 2) include increases in heart rate and blood pressure. In the central nervous system, nicotine has pervasive effects on a number of neurotransmitter systems (Houezec, 1998). It stimulates the release of norepinephrine from several sites, producing CNS arousal. Nicotine also causes the release of dopamine and norepinephrine in the mesolimbic dopamine pathway, also known as the reward system of the brain. The serotonin system, which also mediates the effects of antidepressant medication, is influenced by nicotine. In fact, some people have suggested that nicotine mimics the effects of antidepressant drugs.

Nicotine has a complex influence on subjective mood states. Many people say that they smoke because it makes them feel more relaxed. Some believe that it helps them control their subjective response to stress. This phenomenon is somewhat paradoxical in light of the fact that nicotine leads to increased

*Heavy smokers consume cigarettes in a manner that serves to maintain a relatively constant level of nicotine in their system.*

arousal of the sympathetic nervous system. Various explanations may account for this apparent inconsistency. One involves differences in dosage levels; low doses of nicotine may lead to increased arousal while higher doses lead to relaxation. Another alternative involves withdrawal. Regular smokers may feel relaxed when they smoke a cigarette because it relieves unpleasant symptoms of withdrawal.

**Consequences of Prolonged Use and Abuse** Nicotine is one of the most harmful addicting drugs. Considerable evidence points to the development of both tolerance and withdrawal symptoms among people who regularly smoke or chew tobacco. The physiological symptoms of withdrawal from nicotine include drowsiness, lightheadedness, headache, muscle tremors, and nausea. People who are attempting to quit smoking typically experience sleeping problems, weight gain, concentration difficulties, and mood swings ranging from anxiety to anger and depression (Piasecki, Fiore, & Baker, 1998). From a psychological point of view, withdrawal from nicotine is just as difficult as withdrawal from heroin. Many people report that these symptoms disappear after a few months, but some have serious cravings for several years after they quit.

People who smoke tobacco increase their risk of developing many fatal diseases, including heart disease, lung disease (bronchitis and emphysema), and various types of cancer (Lopez & Murray, 1998). Large numbers of people are also killed or injured in fires caused by careless smoking. Women who smoke are also more likely to experience fertility problems. Babies born to mothers who smoked during pregnancy are also likely to weigh less than those born to mothers who do not smoke, and they may be more vulnerable to certain types of birth defects.

### Amphetamine and Cocaine

Members of the class of drugs known as **psychomotor stimulants** produce their effects by simulating the actions of certain neurotransmitters, specifically epinephrine, norepinephrine, dopamine, and serotonin. Cocaine is a naturally occurring stimulant drug that is extracted from the leaf of a small tree that grows at high elevations, as in the Andes Mountains. The amphetamines (such as dexedrine and methamphetamine) are produced synthetically.

The stimulants can be taken orally, injected, or inhaled. It is easier to maintain a constant blood level when the drugs are taken orally. They are absorbed more slowly through the digestive system, and their effects are less potent. More dramatic effects are achieved by injecting the drug or sniffing it. Cocaine can also be smoked, using various procedures that have been popularized in the past several years. Some people employ a particularly dangerous procedure called "freebasing," in which the drug is heated and its vapours are inhaled. Many people have been seriously burned when these highly combustible chemicals are accidentally ignited.

**Short-Term Effects** Cocaine and amphetamines are called stimulants because they activate the sympathetic nervous system (Fischman & Haney, 1999). They increase heart rate and blood pressure and dilate the blood vessels and the air passages of the lungs. Stimulants also suppress the appetite and prevent sleep. These effects have been among the reasons for the popularity and frequent abuse of stimulants. They have been used, for example, by truck drivers who want to stay awake on long trips and by students who want to stay awake to study for exams. Unfortunately, in addition to their addicting properties, large doses of amphetamines can also lead to dizziness, confusion, and panic states, which clearly interfere with activities such as driving and studying.

When injected, amphetamines and cocaine produce very similar subjective effects, but the effects of cocaine do not last as long. Low doses of amphetamines make people feel more confident, friendly, and energetic. At higher doses, the person is likely to experience a brief, intense feeling of euphoria. Although many people believe that cocaine enhances sexual arousal and pleasure, most of the evidence suggests that prolonged use leads to sexual dysfunction (Jaffe, 1995). Tolerance develops quickly to the euphoric effects of stimulant drugs. The feelings of exhilaration and well-being are typically followed, several hours later, by the onset of lethargy and a mildly depressed or irritable mood.

Acute overdoses of stimulant drugs can result in irregular heartbeat, convulsions, coma, and death. The intense cardiovascular effects of cocaine can be fatal, even among people who are otherwise strong and healthy.

**Consequences of Prolonged Use and Abuse** High doses of amphetamines and cocaine can induce psychosis. The risk of a psychotic reaction seems to increase with repeated exposure to the drug (Bolla, Cadet, & London, 1998). This syndrome can appear in people who have no prior history of mental disorder, and it usually disappears a few days after the drug has been cleared. Stimulants can also increase the severity of symptoms among people who had already developed some type of psychotic condition. The symptoms of amphetamine psychosis include auditory and visual hallucinations, as well as delusions of persecution and grandeur.

As with other forms of addiction, the most devastating effects of stimulant drugs frequently involve the disruption of occupational and social roles. The compulsion to continue taking cocaine can lead to physical exhaustion and financial ruin. People who are dependent on cocaine must spend enormous amounts of money to support their habit. They may have to sell important assets, such as their homes and cars, in order to finance extended binges. Some people become involved in a variety of criminal activities in order to raise enough money to purchase drugs.

Prolonged use of amphetamines has also been linked to an increase in violent behaviour, but it is not clear whether this phenomenon is due to the drug itself or to the lifestyles with which it is frequently associated. Some violence might be related to a drug-induced increase in paranoia and hostility. Statistics concerning drugs and violent crime are very difficult to interpret. The direct effects of the drug on human behaviour are confounded with various economic and social factors that are associated with buying, selling, and using an expensive, illegal drug like cocaine.

People who discontinue taking stimulant drugs do not typically experience severe withdrawal symptoms. The most common reaction is depression. Long-term exposure to high doses of amphetamine can lead to a profound state of clinical depression, which is often accompanied by ideas of suicide.

## Opiates

The **opiates** (sometimes called *opioids*) are drugs that have properties similar to those of opium. The natural source of opium is a poppy with a white flower. The main active ingredients in opium are morphine and codeine, both of which are widely used in medicine, particularly to relieve pain. They are available legally only by prescription in the United States. In Canada, small quantities of codeine are available without a prescription in over-the-counter painkillers and cough medicines. Heroin is a synthetic opiate that is made by modifying the morphine molecule. It was originally marketed as an alternative to morphine when physicians believed, erroneously, that heroin was not addictive.

The opiates can be taken orally, injected, or inhaled. Opium is sometimes eaten or smoked. When morphine is used as a painkiller, it is taken orally so that it is absorbed slowly through the digestive system. People who use morphine for subjective effects most often inject the drug because it leads more quickly to high concentrations in brain tissue. Heroin can be injected, inhaled through the nose in the form of snuff, or smoked and inhaled through a pipe or tube.

**Short-Term Effects** The opiates can induce a state of dreamlike euphoria, which may be accompanied by increased sensitivity in hearing and vision. People who inject morphine or heroin also experience a rush—a brief, intense feeling of pleasure throughout the entire body. These positive, emotional effects of opiates do not last. They are soon replaced by long-term negative changes in mood and emotion. These unpleasant experiences are relieved for 30 to 60 minutes after each new injection of the drug, but they eventually colour most of the rest of the person's waking experience.

The opiates can induce nausea and vomiting among novice users, constrict the pupils of the eye, and disrupt the coordination of the digestive system. Continued use of opiates decreases the level of sex hormones in both women and men, resulting in reduced sex drive and impaired fertility. High doses of opiates can lead to a comatose state, severely depressed breathing, convulsions, and sometimes death.

Some people mix cocaine and opiates into a mixture known as a *speedball* to enhance the euphoric effects. The following brief case describes the preparation of this combination of drugs and one heroin addict's immediate reaction to the injection of a speedball.

## BRIEF CASE STUDY

### Feelings after Injecting Heroin

He pushes the plunger on the syringe, squirting water into the heroin powder, then strikes a match and waves it just under the metal lid. The liquid bubbles and the heroin quickly dissolves with very little heat required. *That's good,* he thinks. Sometimes the dope is so good it needs hardly any fire to dissolve it. Next, he shakes in a couple of small rocks of cocaine from the foil wrapper and is impressed that they vanish immediately in the solution. He swirls the liquid around, rips open the filter from one of his Marlboros, and uses the white fibres as a strainer through which to draw the liquid speedball into the syringe. He carefully places the loaded syringe between his teeth. He rolls up his sleeve, removes his belt with one hand, and takes a seat on the edge of the toilet. He wraps the belt tight around his right arm and hopes he can get a clean hit on one of the veins he watches come up. *There, I'll go there.*

The needle point feels sharp going in, which is good; it means he's got an unused needle. When he pulls back on the plunger a little stream of blood slithers up into the syringe, discolouring the slightly yellow liquid. He loosens the belt, careful not to dislodge the needle from the vein, takes a breath, and slowly pushes the liquid into his arm. He pulls the needle out and dabs with his finger at the drop of blood left behind on his arm. As he does this he feels the freeze in his arm from the cocaine. His arm feels numb. Then it reaches his stomach and mouth. His heart races. He tastes the medicinal flavour just as the first wave of rushes is reaching his brain. His stomach heaves. His scalp tingles and he gets a little scared at first—the wave of sensation is stronger than usual. He fights the urge to vomit, the heroin kicks in and the nausea retreats as the warm, heroin heat replaces the heart-thumping freeze caused by the cocaine. His heart starts to slow down, or so it seems. A quiet, hollow siren rages in his head. The familiar beads of perspiration crowd each other on his forehead, and one drops onto his arm when he bends over to begin cleaning everything up. He puts away his paraphernalia, threads his belt into his pants, and sits down again. *Good stuff, very good,* he thinks as he nods for a second.

Back on the street now, he decides to have a cup of espresso in a little coffee shop he comes upon. Sitting back at a table with a view of the street, he savours the thick hot coffee, lights a cigarette, and blows the smoke to the ceiling. *Nothing hurts,* he thinks. The lousy job that he needs to hold onto, the flak he catches from his wife, the fact that he is turning forty and doesn't have anything to show for his life—none of it fazes him, but he still thinks about it. A spotty work history, no college, and rent that is three weeks late don't matter right now. He feels warm, loose, and sexy. Was the waitress's smile a flirt or was she smiling because she caught him nodding? *Doesn't matter.* He smiles back and thinks maybe he can buy his wife a gold-plated necklace instead of the real one. It will look just like the one she pointed out anyway.

And that was what he did (Fernandez, 1998, pp. 72–73). ◆

#### Consequences of Prolonged Use and Abuse

The effects of opiates on occupational performance and health depend in large part on the amount of drug that is taken. At high doses, people who are addicted to opiates become chronically lethargic and lose their motivation to remain productive. At low doses, some people who use opiates for an extended period of time can remain healthy and work productively in spite of their addiction. This functioning is, of course, dependent on the person having easy and relatively inexpensive access to opiates. One possibility is being maintained by a physician on methadone, a synthetic opiate that is sometimes used therapeutically as an alternative to heroin.

People who are addicted to opiates become preoccupied with finding and using the drug, in order to experience the rush and to avoid withdrawal symptoms. Tolerance develops rather quickly, and the person's daily dose increases regularly until it eventually levels off and remains steady. Many of the severe health consequences of opiate use are the result of the lifestyle of the addict rather than the drug itself. The enormous expenses and difficulties associated with obtaining illegal opiates almost invariably consume all the person's resources. The person typically neglects housing, nutrition, and health care in the search for another fix. Heroin addicts are much more likely than other people in the general population to die from HIV, violence, and suicide.

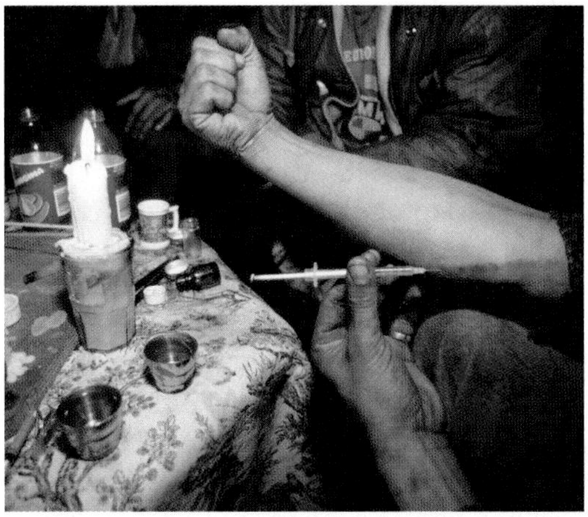

*The positive, emotional effects of opiates do not last. They are soon replaced by long-term negative changes in mood.*

## Barbiturates and Benzodiazepines

The families of drugs known as barbiturates and benzodiazepines are also known informally as tranquilizers, hypnotics, and sedatives. *Tranquilizers* are used to decrease anxiety or agitation. *Hypnotics* are used to help people sleep. *Sedative* is a more general term that describes drugs that calm people or reduce excitement (other than the relief of anxiety). The **barbiturates**, such as phenobarbital (Nembutal) and amobarbital (Amytal), were used for a variety of purposes, including the treatment of chronic anxiety. The **benzodiazepines**, which include diazepam (Valium) and alprazolam (Xanax), have replaced the barbiturates in the treatment of anxiety disorders, in large part because of their lower potential for producing a lethal overdose.

**Short-Term Effects** Sedatives and hypnotics can lead to a state of intoxication that is identical to that associated with alcohol. It is characterized by impaired judgment, slowness of speech, lack of coordination, a narrowed range of attention, and disinhibition of sexual and aggressive impulses. Intravenous use of barbiturates can lead quickly to a pleasant, warm, drowsy feeling that is similar to the experience achieved when taking opiates. The benzodiazepines can sometimes lead to an increase in hostile and aggressive behaviour. Some clinicians call this a "rage reaction" or aggressive dyscontrol.

**Consequences of Prolonged Use and Abuse** People who abruptly stop taking high doses of benzodiazepines may experience symptoms that are sometimes called a *discontinuance syndrome*. These symptoms can include a return—and, in some cases, a worsening—of the original anxiety symptoms, if the medication was being used to treat an anxiety disorder. The person may also develop new symptoms that are directly associated with drug withdrawal. These include irritability, paranoia, sleep disturbance, agitation, muscle tension, restlessness, and perceptual disturbances. Withdrawal symptoms are less likely to occur if the medication is discontinued gradually rather than abruptly.

## Cannabis

Marijuana and hashish are derived from the hemp plant, *Cannabis sativa*. The most common active ingredient in cannabis is a compound called delta-9-tetrahydro-cannabinol (THC). Because every part of the plant contains THC, cannabis can be prepared for consumption in several ways. **Marijuana** refers to the dried leaves and flowers, which can be smoked in a cigarette or pipe. It can also be baked in brownies and ingested orally. **Hashish** refers to the dried resin from the top of the female cannabis plant. It can be smoked or eaten after being baked in cookies or brownies.

Oral administration of cannabis material leads to slow and incomplete absorption. Therefore the dose must be two or three times larger to achieve the same subjective effect as when it is smoked. Most of the drug is metabolized in the liver.

**Short-Term Effects** The subjective effects of marijuana are almost always pleasant. "Getting high" on marijuana refers to a pervasive sense of well-being and happiness. Laboratory research has shown that marijuana can have variable effects on a person's mood. Many people begin to feel happy, but some become anxious and paranoid. The mood of other people seems to be especially important. After smoking marijuana, a person's mood may become more easily influenced by how other people are behaving.

Cannabis intoxication is often accompanied by *temporal disintegration*, a condition in which people have trouble retaining and organizing information, even over relatively short periods of time. Conversations may become disjointed because the drug interferes with the people's ability to recall what they have said or planned to say. Lapses in attention and concentration problems are frequent.

**Consequences of Prolonged Use and Abuse** Research in Ontario has shown that people who begin marijuana use at an early age are more likely to develop abuse or dependence (DeWit et al., 2000). Some tolerance effects to THC have been observed in laboratory animals. Tolerance effects in humans remain ambiguous. Most evidence suggests that people do not develop tolerance to THC unless they are exposed to high doses over an extended period of time. Some people actually report that they become more sensitive (rather than less sensitive) to the effects of marijuana after repeated use. This phenomenon is called *reverse tolerance*. Although reverse tolerance has been reported casually by frequent users, it has not been demonstrated in a laboratory situation, where dosage levels can be carefully controlled.

Withdrawal symptoms are unlikely to develop among occasional smokers of marijuana. People who have been exposed to continuous, high doses of THC may experience withdrawal symptoms, such as irritability, restlessness, and insomnia.

Prolonged heavy use of marijuana may lead to certain types of performance deficits on neuropsychological tests, especially those involving sustained attention, learning, and decision making (Pope & Yurgelun-Todd, 1996). These effects should be interpreted cautiously. Follow-up studies of adults who used cannabis over a period of several years did not find evidence of cognitive decline associated with the drug (Lyketsos et al., 1999).

### Hallucinogens and Related Drugs

Drugs that are called **hallucinogens** cause people to experience hallucinations. Although many other types of drugs can lead to hallucinations at toxic levels, hallucinogens cause hallucinations at relatively low doses. There are many different types of hallucinogens, and they have very different neurophysiological effects. The molecular structure of many hallucinogens is similar to the molecular structure of various neurotransmitters, such as serotonin and norepinephrine. The most common hallucinogen is a synthetic drug called LSD (D-lysergic acid diethylamide), which bears a strong chemical resemblance to serotonin. It achieves its effect by interacting with certain types of serotonin receptors in the brain. *Psilocybin* is another type of hallucinogen whose chemical structure resembles that of serotonin. It is found in different types of mushrooms, which grow in the southern United States and Mexico, and, to a lesser extent, in some regions of Canada. Mescaline is a type of hallucinogen that resembles norepinephrine. It is the active ingredient in a small, spineless cactus called peyote. Mescaline and psilocybin have been used in religious ceremonies by various First Nations people for many centuries.

MDMA (methylene-dioxy-methamphetamine, also known as ecstasy) is one of several synthetic amphetamine derivates. It could be classified as a stimulant but most texts list it as a type of hallucinogen (Julien, 2001). MDMA is also known as a "club drug" because it is popular among people who attend "raves" and dance clubs (LSD and methamphetamine are also known as club drugs). MDMA is usually taken as a tablet, but the powder form can be inhaled or injected. Within half an hour of ingesting MDMA orally, the person begins to experience an enhanced mood state and a feeling of well-being that often lasts several hours. Although it does not produce vivid hallucinations, MDMA does lead to changes in perceptual experiences, such as distortions in the sense of time and space, as well as increased sensory awareness. It also produces changes in blood pressure and can interfere with the body's ability to regulate its temperature.

*Phencyclidine* (PCP) is another synthetic drug that is often classified with the hallucinogens, although its effects are very different than those associated with LSD and mescaline. Small doses of PCP lead to relaxation, warmth, and numbness. At higher doses, PCP can induce psychotic behaviour, including delusional thinking, catatonic motor behaviour, manic excitement, and sudden mood changes. The drug is typically sold in a crystallized form that can be sprinkled on leaves, such as tobacco, marijuana, or parsley, and then smoked. Some people snort it or inject it after dissolving the crystals in water.

*MDMA is known as a "club drug" because it is popular among people who attend "raves" and dance clubs. It causes changes in perceptual experiences, such as distortions in the sense of time and space as well as increased sensory awareness.*

**Short-Term Effects** The effects of hallucinogenic drugs are difficult to study empirically because they are based primarily in subjective reports. They typically induce vivid, and occasionally spectacular, visual images. During the early phase of this drug experience, the images often take the form of colourful geometric patterns. The later phase is more likely to be filled with meaningful images of people, animals, and places. The images may change rapidly, and they sometimes follow an explosive pattern of movement.

Although these hallucinatory experiences are usually pleasant, they are occasionally frightening. "Bad trips" are a decidedly unpleasant experience that can lead to panic attacks and the fear of losing one's mind. People can usually be talked through this process by constantly reminding them that the experience is drug-induced and will be over soon.

Most hallucinogens are not particularly toxic. People do not die from taking an overdose of LSD, psilocybin, or mescaline. However, PCP is much more toxic. High doses can lead to coma, convulsions, respiratory arrest, and brain hemorrhage.

**Consequences of Prolonged Use and Abuse** The use of hallucinogens follows a different pattern than that associated with most other drugs. Hallucinogens, with the possible exception of PCP, are used sporadically and on special occasions rather than continuously. Tolerance develops very quickly to hallucinogens such as LSD, psilocybin, and mescaline (but not to PCP). If these drugs are taken repeatedly within two or three days, their effects disappear. Most people do not increase their use of hallucinogens over time. People who stop taking hallucinogens after continued use do not experience problems; there seem to be no withdrawal symptoms associated with the hallucinogens that resemble serotonin and norepinephrine. The perceptual effects of hallucinogenic drugs almost always wear off after several hours. There are cases, however, in which these drugs have induced persistent psychotic states. Most experts interpret these examples as an indication that the drug experience can trigger the onset of psychosis in people who were already vulnerable to that type of disorder. This is a difficult hypothesis to test because we do not have any independent tests to determine whether a person is vulnerable to psychosis. We can only look back, after the seemingly drug-induced onset of psychotic symptoms, and speculate that some type of predisposition must have been present.

Some people who have taken hallucinogens experience *flashbacks*—brief visual aftereffects that can occur at unpredictable intervals long after the drug has been cleared from the person's body. Scientists do not understand the mechanisms that are responsible for flashbacks. Flashbacks may be more likely to occur when the person is under stress or after the person has used another drug, such as marijuana.

The long-term effects of MDMA (ecstasy) have drawn particular attention because this drug is repeatedly used by some people who regularly attend "raves" and dance clubs. Research shows that it can damage serotonin neurons on a permanent basis, and it has been associated with some fatalities (Gold et al., 2001). Research by Konstantine Zakzanis and colleagues from the University of Toronto suggests that prolonged used of MDMA causes neuropsychological deficits characterized by impairments in learning and memory (Zakzanis & Young, 2001; Zakzanis et al., 2003).

## Classification

Substance dependence represents an extremely diverse set of problems. Everyone—clinicians and researchers, as well as those who abuse drugs and their families—seems to recognize the existence of a serious psychological disorder. But does it have a core? What is the best way to define it? In the following pages we briefly review some of the ways in which alcoholism and drug abuse have been defined.

### DSM-IV-TR

As we noted at the beginning of this chapter, DSM-IV-TR divides addictions into two categories: substance abuse and substance dependence, with the latter being the more severe and advanced form of disorder. This distinction is based, in part, on the recognition that many people who suffer serious impairment from substance abuse do not progress to the level of dependence (Bucholz, 1999). The manual lists 11 types of drugs that can lead to problems of abuse and dependence (refer to Table 11–2). Rather than including separate definitions of dependence and abuse for each class of substance, the manual provides one generic set of criteria for substance dependence and another for substance abuse. These criterion sets can be applied to any type of drug.

The DSM-IV-TR criteria for substance dependence are presented in Table 11–3. Tolerance and withdrawal are listed along with five other problems that describe a pattern of compulsive use and loss of control. The person has to exhibit at least three of the seven criteria for a diagnosis of substance dependence to be made. Tolerance and withdrawal are not required for the person to meet this definition of dependence. Their importance is recognized with a subtype designation. If there is evidence of either tolerance or withdrawal (or both), the additional specification of *physiological dependence* is made. Symptoms of withdrawal seem to be more important than symptoms of tolerance in this regard. People with a history of physiological dependence report more severe drug-related problems, greater intensity of exposure to drugs, and more comorbid conditions such as anxiety and depression (Schuckit et al., 1998a, 1998b).

This approach to the definition of substance dependence is convenient because it points to a unified view of addiction. However, it also has some disadvantages. Perhaps most important is the fact that the use of a single definition of dependence may conceal differences between the kinds of problems that are associated with various classes of drugs (Frances, First, & Pincus, 1995). For example, dependence on opiates almost always involves physiological symptoms of tolerance and withdrawal, whereas dependence on cannabis or hallucinogens almost never does.

Substance abuse is defined in terms of harmful consequences that appear in the absence of tolerance, withdrawal, or a pattern of compulsive use (dependence). The DSM-IV-TR definition of substance abuse is presented in Table 11–4. One difficult issue in defining this condition involves the identification of a boundary between substance abuse and the recreational use of drugs. The diagnostic manual emphasizes the terms *recurrent* and *maladaptive pattern* for this purpose. The problem must be persistent before this diagnosis would be considered. Someone involved in a single drug-related incident would not meet the criteria for this disorder, regardless of how serious the incident might have been (Frances, First, & Pincus, 1995).

Important questions have been raised about the validity of the DSM-IV-TR substance abuse category, especially with regard to alcoholism (Winters et al., 1999). Many people who receive a diagnosis of alcohol abuse do so on the basis of a single symptom—hazardous use—which usually involves driving while intoxicated. This is certainly a grave problem with major consequences, but it is not clear whether this form of maladaptive behaviour should be considered a mental disorder if it occurs in the absence of other symptoms of alcohol abuse. Perhaps the drunk driver would be better viewed as a person who has persistently chosen, for whatever reason, to engage in reckless and illegal behaviour that ignores the safety of other people. One group of investigators has recommended that the alcohol abuse category be retained but with the stipulation that people cannot meet the criteria for this disorder if the diagnosis is based

**TABLE 11–3 DSM-IV-TR Criteria for Substance Dependence**

**A. A maladaptive pattern of substance use, leading to clinically significant impairment or distress, as manifested by three (or more) of the following, occurring at any time in the same 12-month period:**

1. Tolerance, as defined by either of the following:
   a. A need for markedly increased amounts of the substance to achieve intoxication or desired effect.
   b. Markedly diminished effect with continued use of the same amount of the substance.
2. Withdrawal, as manifested by either of the following:
   a. The characteristic withdrawal syndrome for the substance (criteria sets for withdrawal are listed separately for specific substances).
   b. The same (or a closely related) substance is taken to relieve or avoid withdrawal symptoms.
3. The substance is often taken in larger amounts or over a longer period than was intended.
4. There is a persistent desire or unsuccessful efforts to cut down or control substance use.
5. A great deal of time is spent in activities necessary to obtain the substance (for example, visiting multiple doctors or driving long distances), use the substance (for example, chain-smoking), or recover from its effects.
6. Important social, occupational, or recreational activities are given up or reduced because of substance use.
7. The substance use is continued despite knowledge of having a persistent or recurrent physical or psychological problem that is likely to have been caused or exacerbated by the substance (for example, current cocaine use despite recognition of cocaine-induced depression, or continued drinking despite recognition that an ulcer was made worse by alcohol consumption).

only on driving after drinking (Hasin et al., 1999).

## Proposed Subtypes

DSM-IV-TR does not recognize any systems for subtyping substance dependence, other than the presence or absence of physiological symptoms (tolerance or withdrawal). Nevertheless, procedures for subdividing alcoholism have been employed extensively in research studies (Bucholz et al., 1996; Sher, 1991). One influential system was proposed by Cloninger and colleagues (1996).

Cloninger suggested that there are two prototypical varieties of alcoholism. According to this system, Type 1 alcoholism is characterized by a somewhat later onset, prominent psychological dependence (loss-of-control drinking), and the absence of antisocial personality traits. It is found in both men and women. Type 2 alcoholism, found almost exclusively among men, typically has an earlier onset and is associated with the co-occurrence of persistent antisocial behaviours. This proposed distinction has been useful in many research studies. On the other hand, the difference between Type 1 and Type 2 alcoholism

**TABLE 11–4 DSM-IV-TR Criteria for Substance Abuse**

**A. A maladaptive pattern of substance use leading to clinically significant impairment or distress, as manifested by one (or more) of the following, occurring within a 12-month period:**

1. Recurrent substance use resulting in a failure to fulfill major role obligations at work, school, or home.
2. Recurrent substance use in situations in which it is physically hazardous.
3. Recurrent substance-related legal problems.
4. Continued substance use despite having persistent or recurrent social or interpersonal problems caused or exacerbated by the effects of the substance.

**B. The symptoms have never met the criteria of substance dependence for this class of substance.**

Dalhousie University psychologist **Sherry Stewart** is a leading researcher on the factors that contribute to alcohol problems.

may be more quantitative than qualitative in nature (Vaillant, 1994). We return to a discussion of these two types when we consider the influence of genetic factors on the etiology of alcoholism.

### Course and Outcome

It is impossible to specify a typical course for substance dependence, especially alcoholism. Age of onset varies widely, ranging from childhood and early adolescence throughout the lifespan. Although we can roughly identify stages that intervene between initial exposure to a drug and the eventual onset of tolerance and dependence, the timing with which a person moves through these phases can vary enormously. The best available information regarding the course of substance use disorders comes from the study of alcoholism. The specific course of this problem varies considerably from one person to the next. The only thing that seems to be certain is that periods of heavy use alternate with periods of relative abstinence, however short-lived they may be (Schuckit et al., 2002).

Many important questions remain to be answered about the relapse process. Is there a "safe point" that separates a period of high risk for relapse from a period of more stable change? Data from one longitudinal study suggest that the six-year mark may be important for men who abuse alcohol (Vaillant, 1996). But does this generalize to other drugs? Do relapse rates stabilize over time? Is an addicted person more likely to succeed on a later attempt to quit than on an early attempt? Answers to these questions will be useful in the development of more effective treatment programs.

### Other Disorders Commonly Associated with Addictions

People with substance use disorders often exhibit other forms of mental disorder. Most prominent among these are antisocial personality disorder, mood disorders, and anxiety disorders (Kushner, Sher, & Erickson, 1999; Merikangas et al., 1998a). The complexity of the association among these problems makes them difficult to untangle. In some cases, prolonged heavy drinking or use of psychoactive drugs can result in feelings of depression and anxiety. The more the person drinks or uses drugs, the guiltier the person feels about his or her inability to control the problem. In addition, continued use of alcohol and drugs often leads to greater conflict with family members, coworkers, and other people. Sometimes the depression and anxiety precede the onset of the substance use problem. In fact, some people seem to use alcohol and drugs initially in a futile attempt to self-medicate for these other conditions. Ultimately, the drugs make things worse.

Another possibility is that addictions and other disorders may share a common diathesis; the factors contributing to alcohol abuse, for example, may also contribute to other disorders. Consistent with this possibility, research by Sherry Stewart (Dalhousie University) and colleagues has shown that the risk of developing an eating disorder (as indicated by chronic, rigorous dieting) was associated with the risk of developing an alcohol problem (as indicated by a pattern of heavy drinking). This suggests that for some people, drinking problems and eating disorders may develop at the same time (Stewart et al., 2000), and therefore might have some etiological factors in common. What those factors might be is currently unknown.

## Epidemiology

Drug-related problems are found in most countries. There are noteworthy variations, however, in patterns of use for specific types of drugs. The use of specific drugs is determined, in part, by their availability. For example, opium is used most heavily in Southeast Asia and in some Middle Eastern countries, where the opium poppy is cultivated. Cocaine is used frequently in certain countries of South America where coca trees grow; it is also imported into North America. Cocaine is less frequently used, and abused, in Canada compared to the United States (APA, 2000; CCSA/CAMH, 1999). Use of cannabis is widespread around the world, in part because the plants can grow in many different climates. In contrast, in Japan, where the amount of land available for cultivation is severely limited, the largest drug problem involves amphetamine, a synthetic drug.

The fact that people in some regions are frequent drug users does not necessarily imply that a particular population will have a high rate of substance dependence. Culture shapes people's choices about the use of drugs and the ways in which they are used. It influences such factors as the amount of a drug that is typically ingested, the route of administration, and the person's beliefs about drug effects (Pihl, 1999). These considerations, in turn, influence the probability that serious problems will develop. Consider, for example, the Indians of South America who produce coca for market. They have traditionally used the leaves as medicines and in religious ceremonies. They also roll the leaves into a ball that can be tucked in the cheek and sucked for an extended period of time. This form of use relieves cold, hunger, and thirst. It does not produce the severe dependence problems that are associated with the use of refined cocaine, a much more potent drug that can be sniffed or injected.

Dependence almost always develops slowly after extended exposure to a drug. The average time between initial use of illicit drugs and the onset of symptoms of dependence is between two and three years (Anthony & Helzer, 1991). The distinction between people who eventually become addicted and those who use drugs without becoming addicted is an important consideration in the study of psychopathology.

### Prevalence of Alcohol Abuse and Dependence

Alcohol, not cocaine or other drugs, is the drug of choice among young Canadians today and is the leading drug of abuse (CCSA/CAMH, 1999; Gliksman et al., 2000). According to a 1999 survey of Ontario high school students in Grades 7 to 13, conducted by Edward Adlaf and colleagues at Toronto's Centre for Addiction and Mental Health, 66 percent of high school students consumed alcohol, and 42 percent reported episodes of binge drinking (i.e., five or more drinks on a single occasion). Other research reveals that 90 percent of Canadian university students report using alcohol within the past year, as compared to 25 to 33 percent who report using any illicit drug (CCSA/CAMH, 1999; Gliksman et al., 2000). Binge drinking is widespread on Canadian campuses. A 1998 survey of 16 Canadian universities found that 63 percent of students reported having five or more drinks on a single occasion, and 35 percent had eight or more drinks. On average, students consumed five or more drinks about twice a month (Gliksman et al., 2000). In other words, the average university student was binge drinking every two weeks. The prevalence of binge drinking is higher in male than in female students (Wechsler et al., 1994).

For the population at large, approximately two out of every three males in Western countries drink alcohol regularly, at least on a social basis; less than 25 percent abstain from drinking completely. Among all men and women who have ever used alcohol, roughly 20 percent will develop serious problems—abuse or dependence—at some point in their lives as a consequence of prolonged alcohol consumption (Anthony, Warner, & Kessler, 1994).

According to the DSM-IV-TR (APA, 2000), which synthesizes data from many studies, the lifetime prevalence of alcohol dependence is approximately 15 percent of the general population. Similar findings were reported in an Ontario epidemiologic study by Ross (1995). Prevalence estimates of alcohol abuse have varied widely from study to study and region to region. Therefore, its prevalence is difficult to estimate. Nevertheless, it appears to be quite common.

Some occupations are associated with higher rates of alcoholism than others, perhaps because they provide for regular exposure to alcohol throughout the day or because they lack structured hours, which precludes excessive drinking for other people. The rate of alcoholism among professional writers, especially males, may be higher than that in other professions. A number of men who have been awarded the Nobel Prize in literature, for example, have struggled with serious drinking problems. In addition to Hemingway, others include Eugene O'Neill, William Faulkner, Sinclair Lewis, and John Steinbeck (Goodwin, 1991). Other writers who have struggled with alcohol problems include some of Canada's most respected and influential authors, such as Margaret Laurence, Alden Nowlan, and John Thompson (Crozier & Lane, 2001). Several have written about their struggles with alcoholism. Lois Simmie, for example, described how it was the dread of what might happen to her children that motivated her to quit drinking; "Did I really drive 150 miles home from Regina after drinking all night, no sleep, at eighty-five, ninety miles an hour, waking up twice heading for the ditch, the ten-year-old son I adored asleep on the back seat?" (2001, p. 39).

**Gender Differences** Among people who abuse alcohol or have alcohol dependence,

*When it comes to abusing alcohol, men outnumber women five to one, though this number may be narrower than it was 20 years ago.*

men outnumber women by a ratio of approximately five to one, but this ratio varies substantially depending on the age group. In general, women start to drink several years later than men, but once alcohol abuse or dependence develops in women, the disorder seems to progress somewhat more rapidly in them than in men (APA, 2000).

Western culture traditionally has held a negative view of intoxication among women. This pervasive attitude is reflected in opinions voiced by both men and women, including those who are dependent on alcohol (Gomberg, 1988). Social disapproval probably explains why women are more likely than men to drink in the privacy of their own homes, either alone or with another person. Women may be less likely than men to drink heavily because the range of situations in which they are expected to drink, or in which they can drink without eliciting social disapproval, is narrower.

There are also important gender differences in alcohol metabolism. A single standard dose of alcohol, measured in proportion to total body weight, will produce a higher peak blood alcohol level in women than in men. One explanation for this difference lies in the fact that men have a higher average content of body water than women do. A standard dose of alcohol will be less diluted in women because alcohol is distributed in total body water. This may help to explain the fact that women who drink heavily for many years are more vulnerable to liver disorders.

### Prevalence of Drug and Nicotine Dependence

The lifetime prevalence of dependence or abuse of various drugs is shown in Table 11–5. The table shows the estimates reported in DSM-IV-TR, which includes surveys from across Canada and the United States. For comparison purposes, the table also shows results from an epidemiological survey in Edmonton (Russell, Newman, & Bland, 1994). Notice that the Edmonton results are broadly similar to those reported in DSM-IV-TR. The Edmonton results also replicate other surveys by finding that drug abuse and dependence tends to be more common in men than women. Note the prevalence of cocaine dependence is lower in the Edmonton survey, corresponding to the lower prevalence of cocaine problems in Canada, compared to the United States (APA, 2000; CCSA/CAMH, 1999). Conversely, cannabis dependence is the most common form of dependence on illicit drugs in Canada and the United States.

Observe that the figures in this table are much lower than the estimated lifetime prevalence of nicotine dependence (25 percent: APA, 2000). This suggests that many more people are addicted to nicotine than to street drugs such as cannabis, cocaine, and opiates such as heroin. Indeed, as noted earlier in this chapter, nicotine may be among the most addicting drugs in our society.

Tobacco use has declined somewhat over the past few decades in Canada (CCSA/CAMH, 1999; Health Canada, 2001). In 1965, 61 percent of men and 38 percent of women were smokers. In 2001, these figures dropped to 25 percent and 20 percent respectively (Health Canada, 2001).The decline is likely due to a range of factors, including government legislation banning smoking in various public places, restrictions on the sale of tobacco to minors, warnings on tobacco packages, and public health campaigns emphasizing the harmful effects of smoking.

### Risk for Addiction across the Lifespan

Older people do not drink as much alcohol as younger people. The proportion of people who abstain from drinking alcohol is only 22 percent for people in their thirties, goes up to 47 percent for people in their sixties, and is approximately 80 percent for people over 80 years of age. Prevalence rates for alcohol dependence are highest among young adults and lowest among the elderly. Most elderly alcohol abusers are people who have had drinking problems for many years (Gomberg, 1999).

**TABLE 11–5 Estimated Lifetime Prevalence of Drug Abuse or Dependence (Percentage of Population)**

| Drug Group | Edmonton Survey (Russell, Newman, & Bland, 1994) | | | Surveys across the United States and Canada (APA, 2000) |
|---|---|---|---|---|
| | Men | Women | Both | Both Men & Women |
| Cannabis | 9.1 | 2.6 | 5.9 | 5.0 |
| Amphetamines | 2.5 | 0.4 | 1.5 | 1.5 |
| Opiates | 1.2 | 0.2 | 0.7 | 0.7 |
| Barbiturates/sedatives | 0.8 | 0.6 | 0.7 | <1.0 |
| Hallucinogens | 1.0 | 0.1 | 0.5 | 0.6 |
| Cocaine | 0.9 | 0.1 | 0.5 | 2.0 |

*Source:* Based on American Psychiatric Association, 2000, *Diagnostic and statistical manual of mental disorders,* 4th ed., text revision. Washington, DC: Author; J.M. Russell, S.C. Newman, and R.C. Bland, 1994, Drug abuse and dependence. *Acta Psychiatrica Scandinavica, 376 (Suppl.),* 54–62.

The use of illegal drugs is relatively infrequent among the elderly, but there is a problem associated with their abuse of, and dependence on, prescription drugs and over-the-counter medications, especially hypnotics, sedatives, anxiolytics, and painkillers. The elderly use more legal drugs than do people in any other age group. One estimate suggested that 25 percent of all people over the age of 55 use psychoactive drugs of one kind or another (Koch & Knapp, 1987). The risk for substance dependence among the elderly is increased by frequent use of multiple psychoactive drugs combined with enhanced sensitivity to drug toxicity (caused by slowed metabolic breakdown of alcohol and other drugs).

The following case illustrates several issues that are associated with substance use disorders among the elderly, including the abuse of alcohol together with abuse of prescription medications, the presence of prominent symptoms of anxiety and depression, and the tendency to deny the extent of their use or abuse of drugs.

## BRIEF CASE STUDY

### Ms. E's Drinking

Ms. E is an 80-year-old woman who was brought in for an evaluation by her daughters because they noticed depressive symptoms, appetite disturbance, and memory deficits. She denied all problems related to her daughters' concerns. She had a depressed affect, mild psychomotor agitation, and decrements of recent and remote memory. She was disoriented to time. She verbalized statements of guilt and self-deprecation. She denied ever drinking alcohol, which was corroborated by the daughter with whom she lived but was refuted by her other daughter, who stated that Ms. E drank one or two glasses of brandy almost every day. She had been taking various barbiturates for "nerves" for over 30 years. The dosage she ingested gradually increased over the years, and she frequently took more medications than were prescribed. Because it was unclear if her symptoms were related to her barbiturate use, she reluctantly agreed to be slowly and gradually detoxified. She refused a dementia workup. Once detoxification was complete, her affect and appetite were improved, but her cognitive deficits were unchanged. Several months later, she and her family dropped out of treatment. She was reportedly drinking brandy, wine, and "hard liquor" every afternoon and evening, with her hired caregiver mixing the drinks (Solomon et al., 1993). ◆

Diagnostic criteria for substance dependence and abuse are sometimes difficult to apply to the elderly, primarily because drug use has somewhat different consequences in their lives. Tolerance for many drugs is reduced among the elderly, and the symptoms of withdrawal may be more severe and prolonged. They are less likely to suffer occupational impairment because they are less frequently employed than younger people. The probability of social impairment may be reduced because elderly people are more likely to live apart from their families.

# Etiological Considerations and Research

Our discussion of etiology will focus primarily on alcohol dependence and abuse. We have chosen this approach because clinical scientists know more about alcohol and its abuse than about any of the other drugs. Research on alcohol abuse illustrates the factors that are also important in the etiology of other forms of substance dependence.

Most contemporary investigators consider the development of alcoholism in terms of multiple systems (Schuckit, 1999a). Biological factors obviously play an important role. The addicting properties of certain drugs are crucial: People become addicted to drugs like heroin, nicotine, and alcohol, but they do not become addicted to drugs like the antidepressants or to food additives like Nutrasweet. We must, therefore, understand how addicting drugs affect the brain in order to understand the process of dependence. At the same time, we need to understand the social and cultural factors that influence how and under what circumstances an individual first acquires and uses drugs. Our expectations about the effects of drugs are shaped by our parents, our peers, and the media. These are also important etiological considerations.

The etiology of alcoholism is best viewed within a developmental framework that views the problem in terms of various stages: (1) initiation and continuation, (2) escalation and transition to abuse, and (3) development of tolerance and withdrawal (Kandel & Yamaguchi, 1999; Leonard et al., 2000). In the following pages we review some of the social, psychological, and biological factors that explain why people begin to drink, how their drinking behaviours are reinforced, and how they develop tolerance after prolonged exposure.

## Social Factors

People who don't drink obviously won't develop alcoholism, and culture can influence that decision. Some cultures prohibit or actively discourage alcohol consumption. Many Muslims, for example, believe that drinking alcohol is sinful. Other religions encourage the use of small amounts of alcohol in religious ceremonies—such as Jews drinking wine at Passover seders—while also showing disdain for those who drink to the point of intoxication (Westermeyer, 1999). This type of cultural constraint can decrease rates of substance dependence. In one study, for example, Jews had significantly lower rates of alcohol abuse than Catholics and Protestants (Yeung & Greenwald, 1992).

Although Canada's Aboriginal or First Nations population is highly diverse, alcohol and drug dependence tend to be more common among Aboriginal than non-Aboriginal people (Tjepkema, 2002). Alcohol abuse in Aboriginal communities often co-occurs with other forms of substance abuse, such as inhalant abuse (Gfellner & Hundelby, 1995). Aboriginal Canadians, compared to their non-Aboriginal counterparts, are no more likely to drink alcohol. But those who do drink are more likely to drink more heavily, even when socioeconomic status is taken into consideration (Haggarty et al., 2000; Lavallee & Bourgault, 2000; Tjepkema, 2002). One view is that the prevalence of alcoholism among Aboriginals is a consequence of the forced attempt by European colonists to eradicate tribal language and culture, leading to a loss of cultural identity and social disorganization. It turn, this may have led to hopelessness and depression, which sets the stage for alcoholism and drug abuse (Berlin, 1987; Kahn, 1982).

Despite the role that cultural factors might play in alcoholism, many First Nations people who do drink, just like many people from other cultures, do not develop alcohol problems. Among those Canadians who choose to drink alcohol (or smoke cigarettes, or consume other addictive substances), which ones will eventually develop problems? The development of drug dependence requires continued use, and it is influenced by the manner in which the drug is consumed. In other words, with regard to alcohol, will the person's initial reaction to the drug be pleasant, or will he or she become sick and avoid alcoholic beverages in the future? If the person continues drinking, will he or she choose strong or weak drinks, with or without food, with others or alone, and so on? A variety of factors are at work here.

Initial experimentation with drugs is most likely to occur among those individuals who are rebellious and extroverted and whose parents and peers model or encourage use (Chassin & DeLucia, 1996; Stice, Barrera, & Chassin, 1998). The relative influence of parents and friends varies according to the gender and age of the adolescent as well as the drug in question. For example, parents may have a greater influence over their children's decision to drink alcohol, whereas peers seem to play a more important role in the initial exposure to marijuana.

Parents can influence their children's drinking behaviours in many ways (Pihl, 1999). They can serve as models for using drugs to cope with stressful circumstances. They may also help promote attitudes and expectations regarding the benefits of drug consumption, or they may simply provide access to licit or illicit drugs (Jacob & Johnson, 1997; Lang & Stritzke, 1993). Adolescents with alcoholic parents are more likely to drink alcohol than those whose parents do not abuse alcohol. This increased risk seems to be due to several factors, including the fact that alcoholic parents monitor their children's behaviour less closely, thereby providing more opportunities for illicit drinking. The level of negative affect is also relatively high in the families of alcoholic parents. This unpleasant emotional climate, coupled with reduced parental monitoring, increases the probability that an adolescent will affiliate with peers who use drugs (Chassin et al., 1999; Hussong & Chassin, 2002). Taken together, these considerations indicate that parents' drinking has a definite influence on their children's use of alcohol and that the mechanisms involved in this relationship are quite complex.

### Biological Factors

Initial physiological reactions to alcohol can have a dramatic negative influence on a person's early drinking experiences. For example, millions of people are unable to tolerate even small amounts of alcohol. These people develop flushed skin, sometimes after only a single drink. They may also feel nauseated, and some experience an abnormal heartbeat. This phenomenon is most common among people of Asian ancestry and may affect 30 to 50 percent of this population. Not coincidentally, the prevalence of alcoholism is unusually low among Asian populations. Research studies indicate a link between these two phenomena. For example, Japanese people who experience the fast-flushing response tend to drink less than those who do not flush (Wall & Ehlers, 1995; Yamashita, Koyama, & Ohmori, 1995). The basic evidence suggests that in addition to looking for factors that make some individuals especially vulnerable to the addicting effects of alcohol, it may also be important to identify protective factors that reduce the probability of substance dependence.

*The circumstances in which an adolescent is initially exposed to alcohol can influence the person's pattern of drinking. Drinking small amounts of wine with meals or during religious ceremonies may be less likely to lead to alcohol dependence than the sporadic consumption of hard liquor for the purpose of becoming intoxicated.*

A person's initial use of addictive drugs is obviously one important step toward the development of substance dependence, but the fact remains that most people who drink alcohol do not develop alcoholism. What accounts for the next important phase of the disorder? Why do some people abuse the drug while others do not? In the following pages we outline several additional biological variables. We begin by examining genetic factors, and then we consider the neurochemical effects of the drugs themselves.

**Genetics of Alcoholism** An extensive literature attests to the fact that patterns of alcohol consumption, as well as psychological and social problems associated with alcohol abuse, tend to run in families. The lifetime prevalence of alcoholism among the parents, siblings, and children of people with alcoholism is at least three to five times higher than the rate in the general population (Bierut et al., 1998; Merikangas et al., 1998b). Of course, this elevated risk among first-degree relatives could reflect the influence of either genetic or environmental factors, because families share both types of influence. Therefore we must look to the results of twin and adoption studies in an effort to disentangle these variables.

*Twin Studies* Several twin studies have examined patterns of alcohol consumption in nonalcoholic twins. The evidence from studies, such as those conducted by psychologist Kerry Jang at the University of British Columbia, indicates that both genetic factors and environmental factors play an important role in shaping the risk for alcohol problems (Jang, Livesley, & Vernon, 1997; Jang, Vernon, & Livesley, 2000).

Some studies have examined twin concordance rates when the proband meets diagnostic criteria for substance dependence. Here the focus is on severely disabling drinking problems rather than simply the consumption of alcohol. Several studies have found that concordance rates are higher among MZ than among DZ twin pairs. In some earlier studies, this finding was limited to male subjects. Recent data indicate a genetic influence on alcoholism for both men and women (McGue, 1999). For example, data from a large sample of Australian twins revealed concordance rates for alcohol dependence of 56 percent in male MZ twins and 33 percent in male DZ twins (Heath et al., 1997). Corresponding figures for MZ and DZ female twin pairs were 30 percent and 17 percent. Differences between MZ and DZ concordance rates were significant for both genders. The fact that concordance rates were higher for men than for women reflects the much higher prevalence rate for alcoholism among men. Heritability estimates were the same for both men and women, with approximately two-thirds of the variance in risk for alcoholism being produced by genetic factors.

*Adoption Studies* As discussed in Chapter 2, the strategy followed in an adoption study allows the investigator to separate relatively clearly the influence of genetic and environmental factors. The probands in this type of study are individuals who meet two criteria: (1) They had a biological parent who was alcoholic, and (2) they were adopted from their biological parents at an early age and raised by adoptive parents.

Two adoption studies were conducted in Sweden by Robert Cloninger and his colleagues (see Research Close-Up). The results of these investigations are consistent with the data from twin studies and point toward the influence of genetic factors in the etiology of alcohol abuse and dependence. They also indicate, however, that the manner in which genetic and environmental events combine probably differs from one type of alcoholism to another.

## RESEARCH CLOSE-UP

### The Swedish Adoption Studies

Two influential adoption studies suggest that Type 1 and Type 2 alcoholism are distinct forms of disorder that follow different etiological pathways. Genetic and environmental factors apparently interact in different ways for these separate forms of alcohol abuse. The investigations were conducted in Sweden by Robert Cloninger, a psychiatrist at Washington University, Michael Bohman, a Swedish psychiatrist, and Soren Sigvardsson, a Swedish psychologist. The first study included people from Stockholm (Cloninger, 1987). The second study followed the same procedures with men and women from Gottenburg (Sigvardsson, Bohman, & Cloninger, 1996). The fact that the same pattern of findings emerged from both studies lends a great deal of credibility to the investigators' conclusions regarding the etiology of alcoholism.

We will describe the procedures and results of the first study in some detail. The investigators began their initial study with a list of all male children who were born out of wedlock in Stockholm between 1930 and 1949 and who were also adopted away from their biological parents at an early age. At the time of the study, these men were between the ages of 23 and 43. The investigators collected information about the men's adjustment by using official records of local temperance boards, hospital and insurance records, and the national criminal register. They expected this procedure to identify about 70 percent of all people in this population who had a serious drinking problem.

The adoptees were divided into two groups on the basis of the type of alcohol abuse exhibited by their biological parents, using Cloninger's system of Type 1 and Type 2 alcoholism. The subject was considered to have a Type 1 genetic background if the biological father or mother had an adult (later) onset of drinking problems and had not engaged in severe criminal behaviour. The subject was classified as having a Type 2 genetic background if the biological father had undergone extensive treatment for alcoholism or had shown evidence of serious criminal behaviour beginning in adolescence or early adulthood.

The top panel of Table 11–6 summarizes the results for adoptees with a Type 1 genetic background. Preliminary analyses indicated that, by itself, the presence

*continued*

*cont.*

of treated alcoholism in the adoptive parents did not increase the risk for alcoholism in the adoptees. The results were different, however, when the investigators combined the effects of an alcoholic parent with family income and social class. The investigators assumed that, in Sweden during that particular time, children who were raised by adoptive fathers with unskilled occupations would be exposed to a pattern of heavy recreational drinking. When the groups were subdivided in this way, Cloninger and his colleagues found that both a genetic predisposition and environmental factors were necessary to increase the risk for severe alcohol abuse in the offspring of people with Type 1 alcoholism. The presence of either a genetic background for the disorder or a lower social class background did not significantly increase the adoptees' risk for alcoholism. But when an individual experienced both of these vulnerability factors, the risk for alcoholism was significantly increased—approximately double that expected in the general population.

**TABLE 11–6 Analysis of Severe Alcohol Abuse in the Swedish Adoption Study**

| | | Male Adoptees Observed | |
|---|---|---|---|
| **Type 1 Genetic Background** | **Environmental Background** | **Total Sample Size** | **Severe Abuse (%)** |
| No | No | 376 | 4.3 |
| No | Yes | 72 | 4.2 |
| Yes | No | 328 | 6.7 |
| Yes | Yes | 86 | 11.6 |
| | | **Male Adoptees Observed** | |
| **Type 2 Genetic Background** | **Environmental Background** | **Total Size Sample** | **Type 2 Abuse (%)** |
| No | No | 567 | 1.9 |
| No | Yes | 196 | 4.1 |
| Yes | No | 71 | 16.9 |
| Yes | Yes | 28 | 17.9 |

A different pattern emerged among the adoptees with a genetic background associated with Type 2 alcoholism, the more antisocial manifestation of the disorder (see the bottom panel of Table 11–6). Here the genetic component was more pronounced. Regardless of the environment provided by the adoptive family, the male offspring in this group were much more likely to abuse alcohol.

Cloninger and his colleagues also examined rates of alcohol abuse among the daughters of biological parents with both types of alcoholism. Female adoptees with a genetic predisposition to Type 1 alcoholism (where either the father or the mother may have abused alcohol) were three times more likely to abuse alcohol than were women in the control group. It therefore appears that genetic factors influence the development of this form of alcoholism in both men and women. A completely different pattern emerged in daughters of Type 2 alcoholic fathers. They were not more likely than the control subjects to abuse alcohol (although they did show an increased risk for somatic anxiety). On the basis of this result, Cloninger and his colleagues have argued that Type 2 alcoholism may be "male-limited."

The distinction between people with Type 1 and Type 2 alcoholism has been incorporated into many other studies. Some aspects of the study have been criticized, however (McGue, 1993; Searles, 1988, 1990). For example, the examination of environmental circumstances in the adoptive homes was quite limited in scope. The interaction of genes and environment in the Type 1 families was based primarily on socioeconomic status, which is a rather crude measure. The investigators were not able to measure specific drinking patterns or attitudes toward alcohol among the adoptive parents. Still, the Swedish adoption studies have generated enormous interest and have served as a catalyst for many other investigations. ◆

What can we conclude from the adoption studies? There are obviously some differences in both methods and results from one study to the next, but there are also consistent indications that genetic factors play some role in the etiology of alcohol abuse and dependence. McGue (1993) conducted a comprehensive review of the adoption study evidence and reached the following general conclusions:

- The offspring of alcoholic parents who are reared by nonalcoholic adoptive parents are more likely than people in the general population to develop drinking problems of their own. Thus the familial nature of alcoholism is at least partially determined by genes.
- Being reared by an alcoholic parent, in the absence of other etiological factors, does not appear to be a critical consideration in the development of the disorder.
- The etiology of alcoholism is probably heterogeneous in nature; that is, there are several pathways to the disorder.

- There is an association between antisocial personality traits, or "behavioural undercontrol," and alcohol abuse or dependence. The exact nature of this relation and the direction of effect have not been determined.

**Neuroanatomy and Neurochemistry** All of the addicting drugs produce changes in the chemical processes by which messages are transmitted in the brain, including systems that involve catecholamines (for example, dopamine, norepinephrine, and serotonin), as well as the neuropeptides. In the following sections, we will outline some of the ways in which psychoactive drugs influence neural transmission and the areas of the brain in which these effects are most pronounced.

*Dopamine and Reward Pathways* Scientists who study the biological basis of addiction have devoted a considerable amount of their attention to understanding the rewarding or reinforcing properties of drugs (Koob, 2000; Ritz, 1999). People may become dependent on psychoactive drugs because they stimulate areas of the brain that are known as "reward pathways" (see Figure 11–2). One primary circuit in this pathway is the medial forebrain bundle, which connects the ventral tegmental area to the nucleus accumbens. Connections from these structures to the frontal and prefrontal cortex as well as areas of the limbic system, such as the amygdala, also moderate the influence of reward. For many years, scientists have known electrical stimulation of the medial forebrain bundle can serve as a powerful source of positive reinforcement for animals as they perform an operant learning task (Olds & Milner, 1954). Natural rewards, such as food and sex, increase dopamine levels in certain crucial sections of this pathway, which is also known as the *mesolimbic dopamine pathway*.

Drugs of abuse have a dramatic effect on brain reward pathways. Some points at which different drugs influence the dopamine pathway between the ventral tegmental area and the nucleus accumbens are illustrated in Figure 11–3. For example, stimulants such as amphetamine and cocaine affect reward pathways by inhibiting the reuptake of dopamine into nerve terminals. Brain imaging studies with human participants have found that the administration of cocaine increases dopamine concentrations in limbic areas of the brain as well as the medial prefrontal cortex (Tomkins & Sellers, 2001). Furthermore, when people who are dependent on cocaine are exposed to cues that have previously signalled drug use, their medial prefrontal cortex becomes activated, suggesting that this area of the brain is involved in feelings of drug craving.

The effects of alcohol on reward pathways in the brain are more complex and less clearly understood than the effects of many other drugs (Julien, 2001). McGill University researchers Isabelle Boileau, Jean-Marc Assaad, Robert Pihl and their colleagues, conducted the first brain imaging of humans to demonstrate that alcohol promotes dopamine release in the brain, specifically in the nucleus accumbens (Boileau et al., 2003). The findings are consistent with the hypothesis that mesolimbic dopamine activation mediates the reinforcing effects of abused substances. Alcohol may stimulate the mesolimbic dopamine pathway directly, or it may act indirectly by decreasing the activity of GABA neurons (which normally inhibit dopamine neurons).

**Reward Pathways in the Brain**

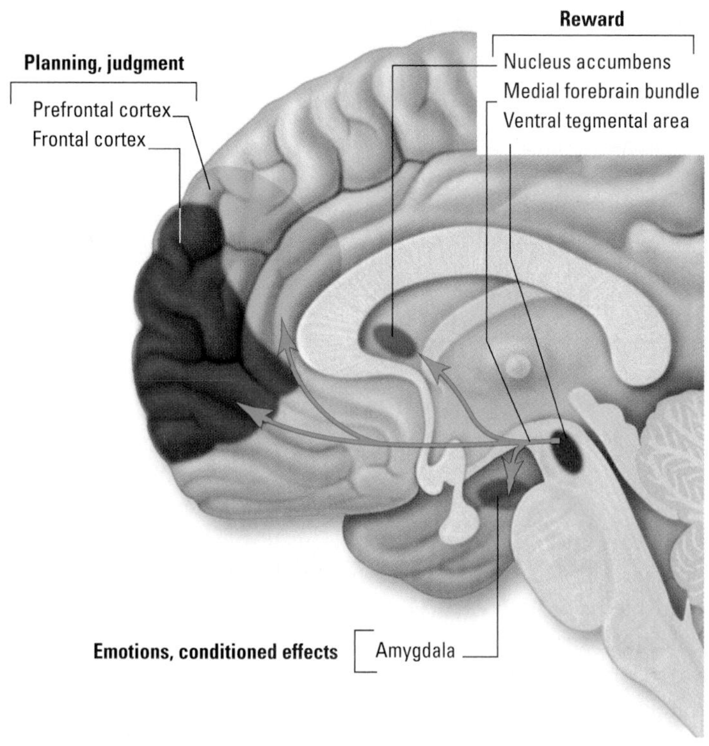


**FIGURE 11–2: The limbic dopamine reward pathways include connections from the ventral tegmental area to the nucleus accumbens and the frontal cortex.**

*Source:* After D.M. Tomkins and E.M. Sellers, 2001, Addiction and the brain: The role of neurotransmitters in the cause and treatment of drug dependence. *Canadian Medical Association Journal, 164,* 817–821.

**Neurochemical Mechanisms of Drug Action**

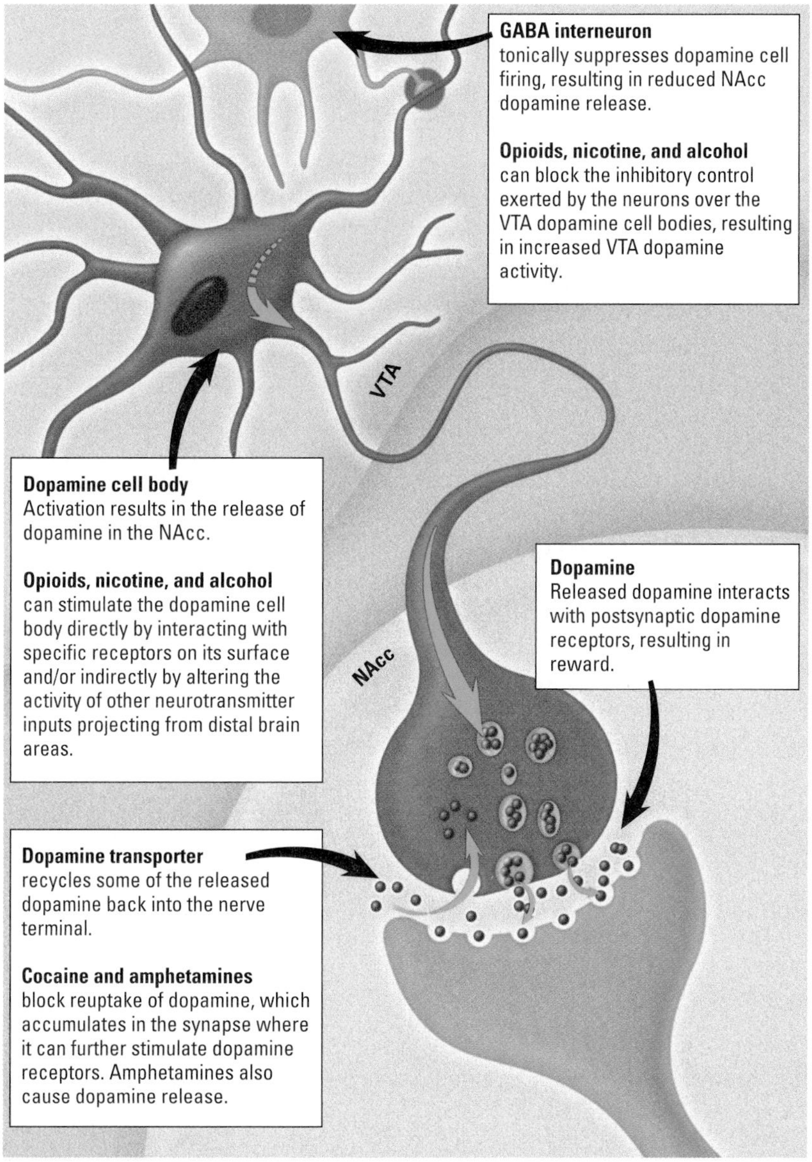
GABA interneuron
tonically suppresses dopamine cell firing, resulting in reduced NAcc dopamine release.
Opioids, nicotine, and alcohol
can block the inhibitory control exerted by the neurons over the VTA dopamine cell bodies, resulting in increased VTA dopamine activity.
VTA
Dopamine cell body
Activation results in the release of dopamine in the NAcc.
Opioids, nicotine, and alcohol
can stimulate the dopamine cell body directly by interacting with specific receptors on its surface and/or indirectly by altering the activity of other neurotransmitter inputs projecting from distal brain areas.
Dopamine
Released dopamine interacts with postsynaptic dopamine receptors, resulting in reward.
NAcc
Dopamine transporter
recycles some of the released dopamine back into the nerve terminal.
Cocaine and amphetamines
block reuptake of dopamine, which accumulates in the synapse where it can further stimulate dopamine receptors. Amphetamines also cause dopamine release.

**FIGURE 11–3: Effects of psychoactive drugs on dopamine activity in reward pathway from the ventral tegmental area (VTA) to the nucleus accumbens (NAcc).**

*Source:* After D.M. Tomkins and E.M. Sellers, 2001, Addiction and the brain: The role of neurotransmitters in the cause and treatment of drug dependence. *Canadian Medical Association Journal, 164,* 817–821.

*Endogenous Opioid Peptides* One of the most important advances in neuroscience research was the discovery of the endogenous opioids known as **endorphins** and enkephalins. These relatively short chains of amino acids, or *neuropeptides*, are naturally synthesized in the brain and are closely related to morphine in their pharmacological properties. Opioid peptides possess a chemical affinity for specific receptor sites, in the same way that a key fits into a specific lock. Several types of opioid peptides are distributed widely throughout the brain. They appear to be especially important in the activities associated with systems that control pain, emotion, stress, and reward, as well as such biological functions as feeding and growth (Froehlich, 1997; Julien, 2001).

Research studies have demonstrated many interesting features of the endorphins. Laboratory animals can develop tolerance to injections of endorphins, just as they develop tolerance to addicting drugs like morphine, and they also exhibit symptoms of withdrawal if the injections are suddenly discontinued. These studies confirm the pharmacological similarity between endogenous and exogenous opioids.

Some theorists associate alcoholism with exaggerated activation of the endogenous opioid system in response to alcohol stimulation (Gianoulakis, DeWaele, & Thavundayil, 1996). Several lines of evidence support this hypothesis. One is that opioid receptor antagonists (drugs that block the effects of opioid peptides) produce a decrease in alcohol self-administration in laboratory animals. Another important bit of information comes from drug trials with human participants: when alcoholic patients take naltrexone, an antagonist of endogenous opioids, they drink less alcohol and report that the subjective "high" associated with drinking is noticeably diminished (see the section on treatment with medication, later in this chapter). Finally, in both rodents and humans, a genetic predisposition toward increased consumption of alcohol is associated with high levels of opioid system response to the ingestion of alcohol (Froehlich, 1997). For all of these reasons, it seems likely that endogenous opioid peptides are somehow involved in mediating alcohol dependence.

*The Serotonin Hypothesis* Although alcohol does not bind directly to any receptor sites in the brain, it does alter the permeability of neuronal membranes (Roberts & Koob, 1997; Valenzuela, 1997). Channels for potassium and chlorine ions are opened, and corresponding channels for sodium and calcium are closed, thus depressing the central nervous system. Concentrations of neurotransmitters, such as serotonin and dopamine, are initially increased. If the person continues to drink heavily over an extended period of time, the alcohol produces many effects that are opposite to those of short-term intoxication: the central nervous system becomes excited rather than depressed, and the ion channel events are reversed.

The serotonin theory of the etiology of alcoholism assumes that alcohol dependence is caused by a genetically determined deficiency in serotonin activity in certain areas of the limbic system of the brain (Lovinger, 1997; Wallis, Rezazadeh, & Lal, 1993). Some studies have reported that acute intoxication is accompanied by an increase in serotonin activity. When the person sobers up, serotonin activity is reduced to subnormal levels. The serotonin theory suggests that some people begin with a deficiency in serotonin, and the consumption of alcohol initially helps to correct for this deficiency. Unfortunately, prolonged consumption further depletes the system. Therefore the person initially drinks to feel good—alcohol stimulates activity in the reward systems of the brain—but after a while he or she must drink more to avoid feeling worse when serotonin levels are reduced below their initial point.

Evidence supporting this theory comes primarily from two kinds of investigation. First, animals that are bred to exhibit high and low preferences for alcohol exhibit differences in serotonin levels. Those with a high preference for alcohol have lower levels of serotonin in areas of the brain that regulate emotional responses (McBride et al., 1993). Second, drugs that enhance serotonin transmission (such as selective serotonin reuptake inhibitors or SSRIs; see Chapter 5) can decrease voluntary alcohol consumption in human subjects.

*Common expectations about the effects of drinking alcohol include the notion that it enhances sexual arousal and experience.*

## Psychological Factors

Genetic factors and neurochemistry undoubtedly account for many of the problems associated with addictive drugs, but as the systems perspective indicates, biological explanations are not incompatible with psychological ones. In fact, extensive research over the past several decades has found that the progression of substance dependence depends on an interaction between environmental and biological events. One time-honoured perspective on the development of alcoholism is the tension-reduction hypothesis. At its most general level, this viewpoint holds that people drink alcohol in an effort to reduce the impact of a stressful environment.

The tension-reduction hypothesis became the focal point for scientific investigation when Conger (1956) adapted formal learning theory to the problem and proposed that alcohol consumption is reinforced by its ability to relieve unpleasant emotional states, especially fear and anxiety. Laboratory studies have provided inconsistent support for this hypothesis (Pihl & Smith, 1983), possibly because the stressors examined were not sufficiently intense. Studies of traumatic stressors, such as sexual assault or combat, provide stronger support for the tension-reduction hypothesis. To illustrate, in an extensive review of the literature, Dalhousie University psychologist Sherry Stewart found that for alcohol-abusing women seen in clinical settings, 24 to 85 percent have a history of sexual abuse. The sexual abuse typically preceded alcohol abuse. Similar links between trauma and alcohol have been found for combat veterans (Stewart, 1996).

Although stress may be one factor contributing to alcohol consumption, we will see in the following pages that the relation between stress and alcohol is more complex than the tension-reduction theory suggests. Drug effects interact with the person's beliefs and attitudes, as well as with the social context in which the drugs are taken.

**Expectations about Drug Effects** Placebo effects demonstrate that expectations are an important factor in any study of drug effects (see Chapter 3). During the 1970s and 1980s, several research studies sought to evaluate the influence of alcohol on various facets of behaviour using the *balanced placebo design*. This procedure allows the investigator to separate the direct, biological effects of the drug from the subjects' expectations about how the drug should affect their behaviour. The results indicated that expectations can account for many effects that have often been attributed to the drug itself, such as increased aggression and reported enhanced feelings of sexual arousal (Goldman, Brown, & Christiansen, 1987; Goldman et al., 1991; Hull & Bond, 1986). The following anecdote by McGill University psychologist Robert Pihl vividly illustrates the role of expectations. Students were served nonalcoholic beer, thinking it was real beer:

> Experienced drinkers quickly realized that something was wrong [i.e., that they had been served nonalcoholic beer]. . . . However, many individuals, particularly freshmen, displayed drunken behaviour, incoordination, falling down, loud exuberance, and some nausea and vomiting—all of this on a placebo. For these individuals, their expectations and milieu determined their behaviour and physical state. (Pihl, 1999, p. 253)

Much less is known about expectancies for drugs other than alcohol, but there is good reason to believe that these cognitive factors also influence the ways in which people respond to cannabis, nicotine, stimulants, anxiolytics, and sedatives (e.g., Brandon, Wetter, & Baker, 1996; Brown, 1993; Stark-Adamec, Pihl, & Adamec, 1981).

The results of experiments using the balanced placebo design stimulated considerable thought about the role that alcohol expectancies—expectations about alcohol or drug effects—may play in the etiology of drinking problems. These studies do not manipulate expectancies directly, however. They only lead subjects to believe that they have consumed alcohol when, in fact, they have not. The investigators infer that the subjects believed that alcohol would make them aggressive.

But is that really the case? Subsequent investigations began to examine alcohol expectancies directly (e.g., MacLatchy-Gaudet & Stewart, 2001). Investigators asked people, Why do you drink? What do you expect to happen after you have consumed a few beers or a couple of glasses of wine? Subjects' answers to these questions fit into six primary categories:

1. Alcohol transforms experiences in a positive way (for example: Drinking makes the future seem brighter).
2. Alcohol enhances social and physical pleasure (for example: Having a few drinks is a nice way to celebrate special occasions).
3. Alcohol enhances sexual performance and experience (for example: After a few drinks, I am more sexually responsive).
4. Alcohol increases power and aggression (for example: After a few drinks it is easier to pick a fight).
5. Alcohol increases social assertiveness (for example: Having a few drinks makes it easier to talk to people).

*McGill University psychologist **Robert Pihl** is a leading expert on the causes of alcohol use and abuse.*

6. Alcohol reduces tension (for example: Alcohol enables me to fall asleep more easily).

These expectations may constitute one of the primary reasons for continued and increasingly heavy consumption of alcoholic beverages. In fact, expectancy patterns can help predict drinking behaviours. Longitudinal studies have found that adolescents who are just beginning to experiment with alcohol and who initially have the most positive expectations about the effects of alcohol go on to consume greater amounts of alcoholic beverages (Smith et al., 1995). This type of demonstration is important because it indicates that, in many cases, the expectations appear before the person begins to drink heavily. Therefore, they may play a role in the onset of the problem rather than being consequences of heavy drinking (see Research Methods).

Where do these expectations come from, and when do they develop? In some cases they may arise from personal experiences with alcohol, but they can also be learned indirectly. Many adolescents hold strong beliefs about the effects of alcohol long before they take their first drink. These expectations may be influenced by parental and peer attitudes and by the portrayal of alcohol in the mass media (Brown et al., 1999; Walters, 1998). Follow-up studies have demonstrated that adolescents' expectations about the effects of alcohol are useful in predicting which individuals will later develop drinking problems (Kilbey, Downey, & Breslau, 1998; Stacy, Newcomb, & Bentler, 1991). Positive expectancies about alcohol,

## RESEARCH METHODS

### Risk, Risk Factors, and Studies of High-Risk Samples

In scientific research, a *risk* is a statement about the probability that a certain outcome will occur. For example, the risk that a person in Canada will develop alcohol dependence at some point in his or her life is about 15 in 100 (APA, 2000). The concept of risk implies only probability, not certainty. Someone who is "at risk" may or may not suffer harm, depending upon many other events and circumstances.

The concept of relative risk can be used to indicate that people with certain characteristics are more likely than others to develop a disorder. Relative risk (or a risk ratio) refers to the probability that someone with a certain characteristic will develop a disorder divided by the probability that someone without the same characteristic will develop the same disorder. The higher the number, the greater the risk. For example, the risk for developing alcohol dependence is approximately five times higher among men than among women; thus the relative risk for male gender is 5. This statistic suggests that male gender is a fairly strong risk factor for the development of alcohol dependence. *Risk factors* are variables that are associated with a higher probability of developing a disorder. Notice that this use of the term *risk* implies association, not causality. The concept of risk simply reflects a correlation between the risk factor (in this case, gender) and the disorder.

Some risk factors are demographic variables, such as gender and race. Others are biological or psychological variables, including the presence or absence of disorders. For example, the Ontario Child Health Study revealed that the development of childhood conduct disorder, assessed by teachers, predicted whether the child or adolescent had begun experimenting with alcohol use four years later (Boyle et al., 1993).

In order to determine whether certain risk factors actually play a causal role in the development of the disorder, it is often necessary to conduct longitudinal studies. The investigator collects information about each person before the onset of the disorder. He or she can therefore determine whether the risk factor is present before or only after the onset of symptoms. Studies of this sort can be extremely expensive and time-consuming. They take several years to complete. Longitudinal studies also require large numbers of participants because everyone in the study will not go on to develop the disorder in question and because some people inevitably will drop out or be lost from the study before all the follow-ups can be completed.

Some of the shortcomings of longitudinal studies are especially relevant to research on substance abuse disorders. The risk for developing such disorders is quite low in the general population. For example, even though alcohol dependence is one of the most prevalent mental disorders, a longitudinal study that follows the development of 100 randomly selected people from childhood to middle age will find only about 15 alcoholic adults. Thus, to collect a useful amount of data, researchers need to study a large population, which can be very expensive.

Recognition of this problem led scientists to develop special methods to increase the productivity of longitudinal research. One important technique is the **high-risk research design.** In high-risk research, subjects are selected from the general population based on some identified risk factor that has a fairly high risk ratio. A number of risk factors might be used to select subjects: positive family history for a given disorder, the presence of certain psychological characteristics, or perhaps a set of demographic variables such as age, gender, and/or race. ◆

which are likely to encourage people to drink, are especially influential. Negative expectancies are associated with diminished use but seem to be less powerful.

**Attention Allocation** Scientists have studied the behavioural effects of alcohol extensively, especially its influence on anxiety, aggression, sexual responsiveness, and mood. There is substantial evidence that the use of alcohol increases the likelihood of aggression (Pihl, Peterson, & Lau, 1993; Pihl, Lau, & Assaad, 1997). But there are many other inconsistencies in the literature. Some studies report that alcohol reduces tension; others conclude that it increases anxiety. Some investigators have found that drinking alcohol can increase self-esteem, whereas others have concluded that it can increase depression. Steele and Josephs' (1988, 1990) attention-allocation model of alcohol effects may explain these apparent inconsistencies.

Steele and Josephs' theory is based on two general factors. First, when alcohol reaches the brain, it interferes with the capacity for controlled and effortful cognitive activities. Intoxicated people focus their attention, by necessity, on immediate internal and external cues and are less able to consider subtle or complex aspects of a problem. Steele and Josephs (1990) call this process *alcohol myopia*—a marked tendency to engage in short-sighted information processing. The second component of the attention-allocation model involves the nature of the immediate environment. The impact of drinking on an intoxicated person's behaviour will depend on the specific situation with which the person is confronted.

Steele and Josephs have used this model to study the effects of alcohol on several aspects of human behaviour, including drunken excess—the tendency for social behaviour to become more extreme under the influence of alcohol. The attention-allocation model predicts that alcohol myopia will lead to drunken excess only in situations in which strong cues are pulling for a particular response, but in which that response is also inhibited by higher level cognitive processing. Suppose, for example, that somebody insults you. If you are sober, you might be tempted to respond by punching or slapping the person, but you would also anticipate several negative consequences that might be associated with this choice of action. If you are intoxicated, however, you will be cognitively impaired and therefore less able to invoke these inhibitory cues. Therefore you are more likely to respond in an excessively aggressive fashion.

*The attention-allocation model predicts that drinking alcohol will lead to drunken excess when strong cues pull for a particular response. In the photograph, a soccer fan in a sports bar reacts with rage after watching his national team lose an important game.*

The attention-allocation theory is an intriguing explanation for the short-term effects of alcohol on human behaviour. Of course, as with all theoretical models of psychopathology, the theory conflicts with certain facts. The most important point to be emphasized in considering this approach is that the short-term effects of alcohol on the behaviour of nonalcoholic subjects is determined, at least in part, by the disruptive effects of alcohol consumption on cognitive processes (Sayette, 1999).

### Integrated Systems

Alcoholism and other forms of addiction clearly result from an interaction among several types of systems. Various social, psychological, and biological factors influence the person's behaviour at each stage in the cycle, from initial use of the drug through the eventual onset of tolerance and withdrawal. The process seems to progress in the following way. Initial experimentation with drugs is influenced by the person's family and peers, who serve as models for the use of drugs. Other people also influence the person's attitudes and expectations about the effects of drugs. Access to drugs, in addition to the patterns in which they are originally consumed, is determined, in part, by cultural factors.

For many people, drinking alcohol leads to short-term positive effects that reinforce continued consumption. The exact psychological mechanisms that are responsible for reinforcing heavy drinking may take several different forms. They may involve diminished self-awareness, stress reduction, or improved mood. These effects of alcohol are determined, in part, by the person's expectations about the way in which the drug will influence his or her feelings and behaviour (Goldman, 1994).

Genetic factors play an important role in the etiology of alcoholism (Crabbe, 2002; Jang et al., 2000). There are most likely several different types of genetic influence, as illustrated by the results of the Swedish adoption studies. Genes interact strongly with environmental events for certain types of the disorder. A genetic predisposition to alcohol dependence probably causes the person to react to alcohol in an abnormal fashion. It is not clear whether those who are vulnerable to alcoholism are initially more or less sensitive than other people to the reinforcing effects of alcohol. Research studies have demonstrated both patterns of response (Sher, 1993).

The biological mechanisms responsible for abnormal reactions to alcohol seem to involve several interrelated neurotransmitter systems (Hyman & Malenka, 2001). Dopamine activity in the brain's reward pathway is stimulated by alcohol as well as other drugs of abuse. Another important consideration may be a deficiency in serotonin activity in certain areas of the limbic system. Drinking alcohol initially corrects this problem and increases serotonin activity, but the person eventually begins to feel worse after tolerance develops.

Drinking gradually becomes heavier and more frequent. The person becomes tolerant to the effects of alcohol and must drink larger quantities to achieve the same reinforcing effects. After he or she becomes addicted to alcohol, attempts to quit drinking are accompanied by painful withdrawal symptoms. Prolonged abuse can lead to permanent neurological impairment, as well as the disruption of many other organ systems.

# Treatment

The treatment of alcoholism and other types of substance use disorders is an especially difficult task. Many people with substance use disorders do not acknowledge their difficulties, and only a relatively small number seek professional help. When they do enter treatment, it is typically with reluctance or at the insistence of friends, family members, or legal authorities. Adherence with treatment recommendations is often low, and dropout rates are high. The high rate of comorbidity with other forms of mental disorder presents an additional challenge, complicating the formulation of a treatment plan. Treatment outcome is likely to be least successful with those people who have comorbid conditions.

The goals of treatment for substance use disorders are a matter of controversy. Some clinicians believe that the only acceptable goal is total abstinence from drinking or drug use. Others have argued that, for some people, a more reasonable goal is the moderate use of legal drugs (see Canadian Focus on p. 400). Important questions have also been raised about the scope of improvements that might be expected from a successful treatment program. Is the goal simply to minimize or eliminate drug use, or should we expect that treatment will also address the social, occupational, and medical problems that are typically associated with drug problems? If these associated problems are the result of the person's prolonged abuse of alcohol or other drugs, the problems may improve on their own if the person becomes abstinent. However, to the extent that family problems or interpersonal difficulties contribute to the person's use of drugs, it may be necessary to address these difficulties before the drug problem can be resolved (McLellan, Woody, & Metzger, 1996).

## Detoxification

Alcoholism and related forms of drug abuse are chronic conditions. Treatment is typically accomplished in a sequence of stages, beginning with a brief period of **detoxification**—the removal of a drug on which a person has become dependent—for three to six weeks. This process is often extremely difficult, as the person experiences marked symptoms of withdrawal and gradually adjusts to the absence of the drug. For many types of CNS depressants, such as alcohol, hypnotics, and sedatives, detoxification is accomplished gradually. Stimulant drugs, in contrast, can be stopped abruptly (Schuckit, 1999a). During the detoxification period, medical staff closely monitor the patient's vital signs to prevent seizures and delirium. Although detoxification usually takes place in a hospital, some evidence indicates that it can be accomplished with close supervision on an outpatient basis.

People who are going through alcohol detoxification are often given various types of medication, including benzodiazepines, primarily as a way of minimizing withdrawal symptoms (Gallant, 1999). This practice is controversial, in part because many people believe that it is illogical to use one form of drug, especially one that can be abused itself, to help someone recover from dependence on another drug.

### Medications during Remission

Following the process of detoxification, treatment efforts are aimed at helping the person maintain a state of remission. The best outcomes are associated with stable, long-term abstinence from drinking. Several forms of medication are used to help the person achieve this goal.

Disulfiram (Antabuse) is a drug that can block the chemical breakdown of alcohol. It was introduced as a treatment for alcoholism in Europe in 1948 and is still used fairly extensively (Brewer, 1996). If a person who is taking disulfiram consumes even a small amount of alcohol, he or she will become violently ill. The symptoms include nausea, vomiting, profuse sweating, and increased heart rate and respiration rate. People who are taking disulfiram will stop drinking alcohol in order to avoid this extremely unpleasant reaction. Unfortunately, voluntary adherence with this form of treatment is poor. Many patients discontinue taking disulfiram, usually because they want to resume drinking or because they believe that they can manage their problems without the drug. Research studies report inconsistent results regarding outcome for patients who are treated with disulfiram (Garbutt et al., 1999). It may be most useful when used in combination with one of the other, more recently developed forms of medication for treating alcoholism (Besson et al., 1998).

Another medication to be approved in Canada for the treatment of alcoholism is an antagonist of endogenous opioids known as naltraxone (Gianoulakis, 2001). Double-blind, placebo-controlled outcome studies demonstrated that patients who received naltraxone and psychotherapy were less likely to relapse than patients who received psychotherapy plus a placebo (Garbutt et al., 1999; Litten & Allen, 1998). Among those who do drink some alcohol during recovery, people taking naltraxone are less likely to lose control and return to heavy drinking. Some patients report that, if they drink while also taking naltraxone, they do not feel as "high" as they would without naltraxone. Naltraxone may dampen the person's craving by blocking alcohol's ability to stimulate the opioid system. In other words, it works by reducing the rewarding effects of alcohol rather than by inducing illness if the person drinks. The best effects for naltraxone are found with patients who are compliant with the medication (take it at least 80 percent of the time) and are also involved in a psychological treatment program.

Another promising medication for treating alcoholism is acamprosate (Campral). It is used in Europe but is currently not available in Canada or the United States (Richardson, 2004). An extensive body of evidence indicates that people taking acamprosate are able to reduce their average number of drinking days by 30 to 50 percent (Litten & Allen, 1998). It also increases the proportion of people who are able to achieve total abstinence (approximately 22 percent among people taking acamprosate and 12 percent taking placebo after 12 months of treatment). Its mechanism of action is not entirely clear, but acamprosate appears to reduce symptoms of acute alcohol withdrawal. It is particularly effective with people who drink in order to neutralize symptoms of withdrawal and to reduce anxiety. Like naltrexone, acamprosate is intended to be used in conjunction with a psychological treatment program. The dropout rate is very high without these added features (Gallant, 1999).

SSRIs, such as fluoxetine, have also been used for the long-term treatment of alcoholic patients. Outcome studies suggest that SSRIs have small and inconsistent effects in reducing drinking among those patients who are not also depressed. They do seem to be effective, however, for the treatment of people with a dual diagnosis of alcohol dependence and major depression (Cornelius et al., 1997). Among these patients, fluoxetine can reduce drinking levels as well as symptoms of depression.

### Self-Help Groups: Alcoholics Anonymous

One of the most widely accepted forms of treatment for alcoholism is Alcoholics Anonymous (AA). Organized in 1935, this self-help program is maintained by alcohol abusers for the sole purpose of helping other people who abuse alcohol become and remain

*Group therapy, like this session from the movie* Clean and Sober, *is an important part of most inpatient treatment programs. It offers an opportunity for patients to acknowledge and confront openly the severity of their problems.*

sober. Because it is established and active in virtually all communities in North America and Europe, as well as in many other parts of the world, AA is generally considered to be "the first line of attack against alcoholism" (Nathan, 1993). Surveys conducted by AA indicate that its membership increased considerably during the 1970s and 1980s. By the late 1990s, worldwide membership in AA was approximately 1.8 million people (Wallace, 1999). Many members of AA are also involved in other forms of treatment offered by various types of mental health professionals, but AA is not officially associated with any other form of treatment or professional organization. Similar self-help programs have been developed for people who are dependent on other drugs, such as opioids (Narcotics Anonymous) and cocaine (Cocaine Anonymous).

The viewpoint espoused by AA is fundamentally spiritual in nature. AA is the original "12-step program." In the first step, the person must acknowledge that he or she is powerless over alcohol and unable to manage his or her drinking. The remaining steps involve spiritual and interpersonal matters such as accepting "a Power greater than ourselves" that can provide the person with direction; recognizing and accepting personal weaknesses; and making amends for previous errors, especially instances in which the person's drinking caused hardships for other people. One principal assumption is that people cannot recover on their own (Emrick, 1999).

The process of working through the 12 steps to recovery is facilitated by regular attendance at AA meetings, as often as every day of the first 90 days after the person stops drinking. Most people choose to attend less frequently if they are able to remain sober throughout this initial period. Meetings provide chronic alcohol abusers with an opportunity to meet and talk with other people who have similar problems, as well as something to do instead of having a drink. New members are encouraged to call older members for help at any time if they experience an urge to drink. There is enormous variability in the format and membership of local AA meetings (Montgomery, Miller, & Tonigan, 1993).

It is difficult to evaluate the effectiveness of AA, for a number of reasons. Long-term follow-up is difficult, and it is generally impossible to employ some of the traditional methods of outcome research, such as random assignment to groups and placebo controls. Early dropout rates are relatively high: About half of all the people who initially join AA leave in less than three months. On the other hand, survival rates (defined in terms of continued sobriety) are much higher for those people who remain in AA. About 80 percent of AA members who have remained sober for between two and five years will remain sober in the next year (Mäkelä, 1994).

Although AA does seem to help people, it is not clear how it helps, or why. Several mechanisms are possible. One explanation centres on the personal growth process that is described in the 12-step program, but the active ingredients may be more social than spiritual. Membership in AA provides people with a stable social network that discourages rather than encourages the use of drugs. It also provides training in communication skills and cognitive coping strategies for stressful life events (Wallace, 1999). Another possible explanation involves personality traits that are present before the person enters treatment. Those people with traits that are compatible with continued membership in a group like AA may be most likely to recover. People who exhibit antisocial traits of the type associated with Cloninger's Type 2 alcoholism, who also presumably have an earlier onset and more difficulty abstaining from drinking, may be least likely to benefit from AA (Galaif & Sussman, 1995).

## Cognitive Behaviour Therapy

Psychological approaches to substance use disorders have often focused on cognitive and behavioural responses that trigger episodes of drug abuse. In the case of alcoholism, heavy drinking has been viewed as a learned, maladaptive response that some people use to cope with difficult problems or to reduce anxiety. Cognitive behaviour therapy teaches people to identify and respond more appropriately to circumstances that regularly precipitate drug abuse (Kadden, 1999).

**Coping Skills Training** One element of cognitive behaviour therapy involves training in the use of social skills, which might be used to resist pressures to drink heavily. It also includes problem-solving procedures, which can help the person both to identify situations that lead to heavy drinking and to formulate alternative courses of action. Anger management is one example. Some people drink in response to frustration. Through careful instruction and practice, people can learn to express negative emotions in constructive ways that will be understood by others. The focus in this type of treatment is on factors that initiate and maintain problem drinking rather than the act of drinking itself.

Cognitive events also play an important part in this approach to treatment. Expectations about the effects of alcohol are challenged, and more adaptive thoughts are rehearsed. Negative patterns of thinking about the self and events in the person's environment are also addressed because they are linked to unpleasant emotions that trigger problem drinking.

**Relapse Prevention** Most people who have been addicted to a drug will say that quitting is the easy part of treatment. The more difficult challenge is to maintain this change after it has been accomplished. Unfortunately, most people will slip up and return to drinking soon after they stop. The same thing can be said for people who stop smoking or using any other drug of abuse. These slips often lead to a full-scale return to excessive and uncontrolled use of the drug. Successful treatment, therefore, depends on making preparations for such incidents.

Marlatt and colleagues proposed a cognitive behavioural view of the relapse process (Marlatt, 1985; Marlatt, Blume, & Parks, 2001). This process applies to all forms of substance dependence, ranging from alcoholism to nicotine dependence (Shiffman et al., 1996). It has also been applied to other disorders associated with impulsive behaviour, such as bulimia and inappropriate sexual behaviours (see Chapters 10 and 12). It places principal emphasis on events that take place after detoxification and the initial efforts at intensive treatment.

The relapse prevention model addresses several important issues that confront the addict in trying to deal with the challenges of life without drugs. The model emphasizes increasing people's belief that they will be able to control their own behaviour and events in their lives. The therapist also helps patients learn more adaptive coping responses, such as applied relaxation and social skills, which can be used in situations that formerly might have triggered drug use.

Another important feature of the relapse prevention model is concerned with the **abstinence violation effect**, which refers to the guilt and perceived loss of control that the person feels whenever he or she slips and finds himself or herself having a drink (or a cigarette or whatever drug is involved) after an extended period of abstinence. People typically blame themselves for failing to live up to their promise to quit. They also interpret the first drink or use of the drug as a signal that further efforts to control their drinking will be useless. The following brief case study describes one man's thoughts and feelings, shortly after he returned to the use of heroin. Just prior to this relapse, he had been actively involved in a treatment program and had stayed "clean" for several months:

***Alan Marlatt**, a leading authority on psychological treatments for substance dependence, has promoted the use of relapse prevention methods.*

## BRIEF CASE STUDY

### Relapse to Heroin Use

"It was like goin' home," he tells me later, "and mom's got your favourite dish on the stove, and you smell it, to the back of your tongue, way back. That's the rush of the dope. It's right there, and for like two, three minutes I'm floating. But it was just a quarter of a bag, a baby rush. So I get up and lay down in my bed, put on the (music) again. And I'm feeling dirty, man. I'm thinking, that wasn't nothing, it wasn't worth it. Two, three minutes of this hot euphoria and then I just nod off to sleep."

He slams his fist on his knee. "I can't believe how bad I (screwed) up," Mike wails through his tears. "Damn! I know what happened ain't nobody's fault but mine, and I'm eating myself up over it. I'm scared out of my mind. I mean, it's like I'm afraid of myself. I really see it now, there's so much (stuff) inside me from my past that I ain't worked out yet that I scare even me. So where do I go with

*continued*

*cont.*

that if they kick me out? How do I stay off the dope if I'm alone again?"

Mike looks up, his eyes wide, wet with tears. "Maybe what they say is true, I'm already a junkie again. It's too late. But I did just one hit, that's all. And I can't be doing more dope, I know that. If I go on a real run of heroin this time, I won't come back, ever. I've seen it now—I *can* blow it, I *can* relapse, I *can* die. Damn! This is the time I need help more than ever, and this is when they're going to kick me out" (Shavelson, 2001, pp. 161 and 166). ◆

Relapse prevention programs are aimed at exactly this type of conflict. They teach patients to expect that they may slip occasionally and to interpret these behaviours as a temporary "lapse" rather than a total "relapse."

**Short-Term Motivational Therapy** Many people with substance use disorders do not seek or take full advantage of treatment opportunities because they fail to recognize the severity of their problems. Motivational interviewing is a nonconfrontational procedure that can be used to help people resolve their ambivalence about using drugs and make a definite commitment to change their behaviour (Maisto, Wolfe, & Jordan, 1999; Miller, 1995). It is based on the notion that in order to make a meaningful change, people must begin by recognizing the inconsistency between their current behaviour and their long-term goals. For example, chronic heavy drinking is not compatible with academic or occupational success.

Motivational interviewing begins with a discussion of problems—issues reported by the patient as well as concerns that have been expressed by others such as friends and family members. The person is asked to reflect on feedback that is provided in a nonthreatening way. Rather than confronting the person, arguing about the reasons for drinking, or demanding action, the therapist responds empathically in an effort to avoid or minimize defensive reactions that will interfere with attempts to change.

The primary goal of this process is to increase the person's awareness of the nature of his or her substance use problems. Central features of motivational interviewing include a comprehensive assessment of the situation and personalized feedback. Emphasis is placed on ways in which the person sees his or her problems rather than assigning diagnostic labels, such as "alcoholism." Various options for creating change are discussed. The therapist and the patient work together to select the most appropriate method to follow. This stage of the interaction is designed to encourage the person's belief in his or her own ability to accomplish positive change.

## Outcome Results and General Conclusions

A growing number of studies, including research by Curtis Breslin and colleagues at Toronto's Centre for Addiction and Mental Health, have shown that brief (e.g., four-session) motivationally based interventions can reduce substance abuse problems (Breslin et al., 2002). Motivational interviewing may be most helpful to people whose substance abuse problems are not yet severe or chronic. It can be used as a stand-alone intervention or in combination with other approaches to treatment. If the person is not ready to abstain completely, short-term motivational therapy can be used to help the person reduce the frequency or intensity of alcohol consumption (Roberts & Marlatt, 1999).

Although there has been a good deal of research on the effects of more intensive alcohol treatment programs, two set of studies deserve special attention because of their large sample sizes and the rigorous methods that the investigators employed. One is known as Project MATCH because it was designed to test the potential value of matching certain kinds of clients to specific forms of treatment (Project MATCH Research Group, 1998a, 1998b). In other words, would the outcomes associated with different forms of intervention be related to certain characteristics of the patients (such as the presence or absence of antisocial personality traits)?

The study evaluated three forms of psychological treatment: cognitive behaviour therapy (12 sessions focused on coping skills and relapse prevention), 12-step facilitation therapy (12 sessions designed to help patients become engaged in AA), and motivational enhancement therapy (4 sessions over 12 weeks designed to increase commitment to change). Most of the people in all three groups attended at least some AA meetings in addition to their assigned form of treatment. More than 1700 patients were randomly assigned to one of these three conditions. Outcome measures were collected for three years after the end of treatment.

Results indicated that all three forms of treatment led to major improvements in amount of drinking as well as other areas of life functioning. Before treatment, patients in this study averaged 25 drinking days per month. After treatment, they averaged less than 6 days per month (across all forms of treatment). Patients who did drink decreased their average number of drinks from 15 to 3 drinks per day. Very few differences were found between the different treatment methods. The one exception favoured 12-step facilitation therapy, in which 24 percent of patients were completely abstinent one year after treatment, compared to approximately 15 percent in the other two groups. Analyses that focused on the characteristics of individual clients suggested that there is relatively little reason to try to match certain kinds of patients to specific forms of treatment.

The second set of studies reported more encouraging findings for matching clients to treatments. This research focused specifically on personality patterns theoretically linked to various types of substance abuse. Preliminary results were recently reported by a group of investigators led by Patricia Conrod, who until recently was at the University of British Columbia. These researchers focused on four personality risk factors, which were assessed in a sample of 293 substance-abusing women: anxiety sensitivity (fear of anxiety: see Chapter 6), sensation seeking, impulsivity, and introversion-hopelessness. Cluster analyses reliably identified five personality subtypes. The subtypes differed in the lifetime risk for various disorders. An *anxiety-sensitive subtype* had a greater lifetime risk (compared to the other subtypes) for dependence on anti-anxiety drugs, and also a greater risk for somatization disorder and specific phobia. An *introverted-hopeless* subtype had greater lifetime risk for opioid dependence, social phobia, panic disorder, and mood disorders. An *impulsive subtype* was associated with higher rates of antisocial personality disorder, cocaine dependence, and alcohol dependence. A fourth subtype was identified as being high in sensation seeking but not impulsivity. This group reported the highest rates of lifetime alcohol dependence, and the lowest rates of other substance use disorders and other forms of psychopathology. The fifth group was a *low personality risk subtype*, which had lower lifetime rates of substance dependence and psychopathology (Conrod et al., 2000).

In their second study, Conrod, Stewart et al. (2000) randomly assigned approximately 200 substance-abusing women to one of three brief (90-minute) interventions that differentially targeted the client's personality subtype (as identified in their previous study). The treatments were (1) a motivation-matched intervention involving personality-specific motivational and coping skills training, (2) a motivational control intervention, involving a motivational film and supportive discussion with a therapist, and (3) a motivation-mismatched intervention targeting a theoretically different personality subtype. An assessment six months later revealed that only the matched intervention was more effective than the motivational control intervention in terms of reducing the frequency and severity of substance abuse.

These findings provide encouraging news for therapists trying to determine which treatment is likely to be most beneficial for which type of client. An important next step in matching research is to see whether Conrod's findings can be replicated in fresh samples of female substance abusers, and in males with substance use problems.

Comprehensive reviews of these studies and the rest of the research literature regarding treatment of alcoholism and drug abuse (e.g., Donavan, 1999) point to several general conclusions:

- People who enter treatment for various types of substance abuse and dependence typically show improvement in terms of reduced drug use that is likely to persist for several months following the end of treatment. Unfortunately, relapse is also relatively common.
- There is little evidence to suggest that one form of treatment (inpatient or outpatient, professional or self-help, individual or group) is more effective than another. When differences have been found, they tend to favour self-help groups, such as AA, particularly in terms of success in achieving abstinence.
- Apart from Conrod's findings, there is limited support for the assumption that certain kinds of patients do better in one kind of treatment than another (the matching hypothesis).

- Increased amount of treatment and greater frequency of attendance in self-help meetings and after-care counselling are associated with better outcomes.
- Among those people who are able to reduce their consumption of drugs, or abstain altogether, improvements following treatment are usually not limited to drug use alone but extend to the person's health in general as well as his or her social and occupational functioning.

Long-term outcome for the treatment of alcoholism is best predicted by the person's coping resources (social skills and problem-solving abilities), the availability of social support, and the level of stress in the environment. These considerations appear to be more important than the specific type of intervention that people receive. Those individuals who are in less stressful life situations, whose families are more cohesive and less supportive of continued drinking, and who are themselves better equipped with active coping skills are most likely to sustain their improvement over several years (Finney & Moos, 1992; Roberts & Marlatt, 1999).

## CANADIAN FOCUS The Controlled Drinking Controversy

During the 1950s there was increasing acceptance of the view that alcohol problems arise from an underlying disease (Jellinek, 1960). This was a simplistic model that stated that alcoholism was all-or-nothing; you either had the disease or you didn't. There was no middle ground. Following from this view was the assumption that abstinence was the only possible remedy.

Findings later emerged to challenge this assumption. As we have seen earlier in this chapter, research indicates that alcohol problems exist on a continuum, ranging from mild to severe, and are influenced by a variety of psychological, social, and biological factors. Thus, alcoholism is not an all-or-nothing entity.

The abstinence approach to treatment was further challenged by naturalistic studies reporting that people with alcohol dependence sometimes reverted to patterns of normal drinking (e.g., Davies, 1962). These findings raised the possibility that some cases of alcoholism might be treated by teaching clients how to drink in moderation. Thus, controlled drinking programs were developed during the 1970s.

Controlled drinking was seen as an important treatment development because of the possibility of it being more effective and more acceptable to clients than abstinence-based programs. A person with alcohol dependence might refuse to enter an abstinence program, but might be willing to attempt a program of controlled drinking (Marlatt et al., 1993). Thus, controlled drinking was thought to be a promising way of helping clients who might otherwise refuse treatment. This approach is consistent with a *harm reduction model* of substance use, which states that it is better to have at least some reduction in drinking-related problems (e.g., due to a controlled drinking program) than to have no reduction at all (Marlatt et al., 1993).

Advocates of the disease model of alcoholism strongly opposed controlled drinking, arguing that it would be ineffective at best, and possibly even harmful because it encourages clients to continue drinking. The only way to tell whether the critics were correct was to conduct research into the safety and efficacy of controlled drinking.

The first controlled study of controlled drinking was conducted by psychologists Mark and Linda Sobell (e.g., Sobell & Sobell, 1978). Their research was initially conducted at Patton State Hospital in California, although most of their subsequent work was done at Toronto's Addiction Research Foundation (which is now part of the Centre for Addiction and Mental Health). In their initial study, the Sobells carefully assessed 70 men who were admitted to hospital for treatment of alcohol dependence. Clients were considered to be good candidates for controlled drinking if (a) they had requested limited drinking as a goal, (b) they had shown some evidence of previous self-control in moderating their drinking, and (c) after leaving hospital they were expected to return to a supportive environment. Of the 70 men, 40 were considered to be good candidates. Of these, 20 were randomly assigned to a controlled drinking program, and the other 20 received the traditional abstinence program offered by the hospital. (The other 30, who will not be discussed here, also received the traditional abstinence program.)

Controlled drinking consisted of 17 sessions designed to help clients identify situations in which problem drinking was likely to occur, and to develop strategies to limit their drinking in those situations. Treatment included problem-solving training, developing alternatives to drinking in problem situations, training in drinking moderation skills, and other interventions.

After completing either the controlled drinking or the abstinence program, the 40 clients were followed for two years. Clients were assessed, via telephone interviews, approximately every two months, in which they provided information on a number of variables, including drinking frequency and the occurrence of drinking-related problems such as incarceration or hospitalization. Information was also collected from collateral sources (e.g., the client's spouse) and public records (e.g., hospital records, driving records).

*continued*

*cont.*

The results indicated that during the first year of follow-up, the controlled drinking group were "functioning well" for a mean of 71 percent of all days (i.e., not drunk and not incarcerated or in hospital), compared to only 35 percent of days for the abstinence group. At the end of the second year, the results were 85 and 42 percent, respectively. Thus, the controlled drinking program seemed superior to the abstinence program.

Controversy erupted in 1982 with a publication by Mary Pendery, Irving Maltzman, and L. Jolyn West in the prestigious journal *Science*. These investigators conducted a 10-year follow-up of Sobells' clients. In their article, Pendery et al. reported results for the controlled drinking group. They found that only 1 of the 20 clients had maintained a pattern of controlled drinking. Eight continued to have drinking problems, 6 abandoned their attempts at controlled drinking and became abstinent, 4 died from alcohol-related causes, and 1 client could not be contacted. Pendery et al. gave sensational descriptions of their findings (e.g., one deceased client was reported as being found floating face down in a lake). Pendery and colleagues seemed to imply that the deaths were *caused* by the Sobells' controlled drinking program.

The article created a huge scandal. TV programs and newspaper articles widely condemned the Sobells' study as fraudulent, and the Sobells were accused of professional misconduct. Two independent investigations were conducted to examine the validity of these charges. One investigation was ordered by the Addiction Research Foundation, and was chaired by Bernard Dickens, Professor of Law at the University of Toronto. Dickens and the rest of his committee reviewed the published articles and examined a good deal of the data collected by the Sobells. In their 123-page report the committee concluded that there was "no reasonable cause to doubt the scientific or personal integrity of either Dr. Mark Sobell or Dr. Linda Sobell" (Dickens et al., 1982, p. 109). Another independent investigation reached the same conclusion.

As part of these investigations, attention was also focused on the validity of the Pendery et al. study. It was revealed that all the client interviews were conducted by Mary Pendery, who was well known for her bias against controlled drinking (Marlatt et al., 1993). A serious flaw was also identified in Pendery et al.'s research design: they reported results only for the controlled drinking group. Without a control group it is difficult to interpret the effects of controlled drinking. Although most of the controlled drinking group did not fare well during the 10-year follow-up, it is possible that the abstinence group fared just as bad or even worse. Consistent with this possibility, Dickens et al. (1982) reported that at 10-year follow-up there were more deaths in the abstinence group (30 percent mortality) than in the controlled drinking group (20 percent mortality).

With the passing of time the debate over controlled drinking has gradually abated, although there are still people who staunchly believe that abstinence is the only treatment. Those beliefs are not supported by the data. Studies conducted since the Sobells' landmark investigation have found that controlled drinking is an effective treatment for many people with drinking problems, and is no less effective than abstinence-based treatments (e.g., Rychtarick et al., 1987). Although much work needs to be done to identify people most likely to benefit from controlled drinking programs, available evidence suggests that one of the most important variables is the client's treatment goals; those choosing abstinence are most likely to benefit from abstinence-based programs (such as Alcoholics Anonymous), whereas those choosing moderation are most likely to benefit from a controlled drinking program (Marlatt et al., 1993). ◆

# Summary

DSM-IV-TR uses two terms to describe substance use disorders. **Substance dependence**, the more severe of the two forms, refers to a pattern of repeated self-administration that often results in **tolerance**, **withdrawal**, or compulsive drug-taking behaviour. **Substance abuse** describes a more broadly conceived, less severe pattern of drug use that is defined in terms of interference with the person's ability to fulfill major role obligations at work or at home, recurrent use of a drug in dangerous situations, or repeated legal difficulties that are associated with drug use.

A **drug of abuse**—sometimes called a *psychoactive substance*—is a chemical substance that alters a person's mood, level of perception, or brain functioning. The list of chemicals on which people become dependent includes drugs that are legally available in Canada as well as many that are illegal. Although the patterns of dependence are similar in some ways for all drugs, each type of drug also has some unique features.

Prolonged abuse of alcohol can have a devastating impact on social relationships and occupational functioning while disrupting the functions of several important organ systems. Alcohol dependence has more negative health consequences than does abuse of almost any other drug, with the possible exception of nicotine.

Nicotine is one of the most harmful addicting drugs. Recognizing the serious long-term health consequences of exposure to nicotine, the Canadian government has prohibited the sale and distribution of tobacco products to children and adolescents. This policy attempts to prevent the development of nicotine addiction rather than trying to ban use of the drug completely.

The **psychomotor stimulants**, such as amphetamine and cocaine, activate the sympathetic nervous system and induce a positive mood state. High doses of amphetamines and cocaine can lead to the onset of psychosis. The most devastating effects of stimulant drugs involve the disruption of occupational and social roles.

**Opiates** have properties similar to those of opium and can induce a state of dreamlike euphoria. Tolerance develops quickly to opiates. After repeated use, their positive emotional effects are replaced by long-term negative changes in mood and emotion. Many of the severe health consequences of opiate use are the result of the lifestyle of the addict rather than the drug itself.

**Barbiturates** and **benzodiazepines** can be used, as prescribed by a physician, to decrease anxiety (tranquilizers) or help people sleep (hypnotics). They can also lead to a state of intoxication that is identical to that associated with alcohol. People who abruptly stop taking high doses of benzodiazepines may experience withdrawal symptoms, including a return of the original anxiety symptoms. Tolerance and withdrawal can develop after using barbiturates for several weeks.

**Marijuana** and **hashish** can induce a pervasive sense of well-being and happiness. People do not seem to develop tolerance to THC (the active ingredient in marijuana and hashish) unless they are exposed to high doses over an extended period of time. Withdrawal symptoms are unlikely to develop among people who smoke marijuana occasionally.

**Hallucinogens** induce vivid visual images that are usually pleasant but occasionally frightening. Unlike other drugs of abuse, hallucinogens are used sporadically rather than continuously. Most people do not increase their use of hallucinogens over time, and withdrawal symptoms are not observed.

It is impossible to specify a typical course for substance dependence. The specific pattern varies from one person to the next. In the case of alcoholism, the only thing that seems certain is that periods of heavy use alternate with periods of relative abstinence. Among alcoholic men in one long-term follow-up study, the proportion who become completely abstinent went up slowly but consistently over a period of many years. Relapse to alcohol abuse was unlikely among men who were able to remain abstinent for at least six years.

Alcohol dependence and abuse are among the most common forms of mental disorder, with a lifetime prevalence of 15 percent. Among people with alcohol use disorders, men outnumber women by a ratio of approximately five to one. Prevalence rates for alcohol dependence are highest among young adults and lowest among the elderly. The lifetime prevalence for dependence or abuse of other drugs is 25 percent (nicotine), 5 to 6 percent (cannabis), and less than 2 percent for each of the other drugs (e.g., amphetamines, opiates, cocaine).

Research on the etiology of alcoholism illustrates the ways in which various systems interact to produce and maintain drug dependence. The etiology of alcoholism is probably heterogeneous in nature. There are several pathways to the disorder. Social factors are particularly influential in the early phases of substance use. Initial experimentation with drugs is most likely to occur among those adolescents whose parents and peers model or encourage drug use. The culture in which a person lives influences the types of drugs that are used, the purposes for which they are used, and the expectations that people hold for the ways in which drugs will affect their experiences and behaviour.

Considerable attention has been paid to the role of biological factors in the etiology of alcoholism, particularly the influence of genetic factors and neurochemical processes. Twin studies indicate that genetic factors influence patterns of social drinking as well as the onset of alcohol dependence. Adoption studies indicate that the offspring of alcoholic parents who are raised by nonalcoholic parents are more likely than people in the general population to develop drinking problems of their own. Genetic factors may be more influential in the development of alcoholism among men than among women.

The influence of genetic factors may vary in different subtypes of alcoholism. The Swedish adoption studies illustrate this possibility, focusing on the proposed distinction between Type 1 and Type 2 alcoholism. The combination of a genetic predisposition to alcoholism and environmental circumstances that encourage heavy drinking may lead to the onset of Type 1 alcoholism (late onset, no antisocial personality). In the case of Type 2 alcoholism (early onset, accompanied by antisocial personality), a genetic contribution increases risk for the disorder regardless of the type of environment in which the person is raised.

All of the psychoactive drugs cause increased dopamine activity in the reward pathways of the brain. Alcohol may stimulate the mesolimbic dopamine pathway directly, or it may act indirectly by inhibiting GABA neurons. Another focus of neurochemical research has been the role of endogenous opioids known as **endorphins**. Some theorists have argued that alcoholism is associated with excessive production of endorphins. A third neurochemical hypothesis suggests that alcohol dependence is caused by a genetically determined deficiency in serotonin activity in certain limbic areas of the brain.

Psychological explanations for the etiology of substance use disorders have often focused on the ability of drugs to relieve unpleasant emotional states. Expectations about drug effects have an important influence on the ways in which people respond to alcohol and other drugs. People who believe that alcohol enhances pleasure, reduces tension, and increases social performance are more likely than other people to drink frequently and heavily. The attention-allocation theory is based on the recognition that alcohol reduces a person's capacity for cognitive activity. This process helps to explain the short-term effects of alcohol on mood and behaviour, which may be reinforcing for some people.

Treatment of substance use disorders is an especially challenging and difficult task in light of the fact that many people with these problems do not recognize or acknowledge their own difficulties. Recovery begins with a process of detoxification. Self-help programs, such as Alcoholics Anonymous, are the most widely used and probably one of the most beneficial forms of treatment.

# Critical Thinking

1. What is the difference between the rituals characteristic of obsessive–compulsive disorders and the compulsive drug-taking behaviours associated with substance dependence? Are there any similarities? Do you think that these disorders should be classified together?
2. Some drugs of abuse are illegal in Canada, whereas others are legally available. What impact does this legal policy have on the definition of substance dependence, as well as on the probability that a person will receive a DSM-IV-TR diagnosis?
3. Most adults in Western countries drink alcohol on a fairly regular basis, yet relatively few develop alcoholism. Why? There are gender differences and age differences in the prevalence of alcohol dependence. Why would women be less likely than men to become dependent on alcohol?
4. Although most people believe that alcohol makes them feel more relaxed, experimental studies indicate that it sometimes makes people more anxious or more aggressive. Why?
5. What are the risks and benefits of controlled drinking programs? When should a person choose abstinence instead of trying to drink in moderation?

# Key Terms

**barbiturates** 375
**benzodiazepines** 375
**detoxification** 394
**drug of abuse** 366
**endorphins** 389
**hallucinogens** 376
**hashish** 375
**high-risk research design** 392
**marijuana** 375
**opiates** 373
**polysubstance abuse** 366
**psychological dependence** 368
**psychomotor stimulants** 372
**substance abuse** 366
**substance dependence** 366
**tolerance** 368
**withdrawal** 369

# 12 Sexual and Gender Identity Disorders

Overview

Sexual Dysfunctions

Paraphilias

Gender Identity Disorders

**Should sexual problems be defined primarily in terms of difficulty reaching orgasm?**

**How is sexual arousal measured in the lab?**

**Is Viagra only a partial solution to arousal disorders?**

**Can sex offenders be treated successfully?**

Sex is often a perplexing area of our lives. Sexual experience can be a source of extreme pleasure while also providing for the development and expression of intimacy with one's partner. From an evolutionary point of view, reproduction is the key to our survival. But sexual behaviour also provides fertile ground for intense feelings of fear and guilt.

When something interferes with our ability to function sexually, it can be devastating both to the person who is affected and to the person's partner. Sometimes a person's inability to enjoy sexual experiences becomes so pervasive or so personally distressing that the person seeks professional help—alone or more often with his or her partner. In other instances, a person may enjoy sex but his or her sexual interest may be triggered by unusual stimuli, or it may involve nonconsenting partners or the pain and suffering of themselves or others. The point at which occasional sexual difficulties become a "sexual dysfunction" is quite subjective and may say as much about sexual norms and expectations as anything else. Similarly, the definition of sexual conduct that is considered deviant has also changed over time. This chapter explores the mix of factors that influence what it means to be a man or a woman and the ways in which we engage in sexual relationships. It also offers a picture of the shifting ground that surrounds what mental health professionals consider to be normal and abnormal sexual practices.

## Overview

Any discussion of sexual disorders requires some frank consideration of normal sexuality. Such openness has been encouraged and promoted by mental health professionals who specialize in the study and treatment of sexual problems. On the basis of their observational and physiological data, pioneering sex therapists Masters and Johnson (1966) described the human sexual response cycle in terms of a sequence of overlapping phases: excitement, orgasm, and resolution. Analogous processes occur in both men and women, but the timing may differ. There are, of course, individual differences in virtually all aspects of this cycle. Variations from the most common pattern may not indicate a problem unless the person is concerned about the response.

Sexual *excitement* increases continuously from initial stimulation up to the point of orgasm. According to McGill University researchers Kenneth Mah and Yitzchak Binki (2001), the orgasm is a complex, multidimensional phenomenon, consisting of sensory components (bodily sensations), evaluative components (e.g., excitement, pleasure), and affective components (e.g., emotional intimacy, elation). The orgasm may last anywhere from a few minutes to several hours. Among the most dramatic physiological changes during sexual excitement are those associated with *vasocongestion*—engorgement of the blood vessels of various organs, especially the genitals. The male and female genitalia become swollen, reddened, and warmed. Sexual excitement also

*Sexual dysfunctions are best defined in terms of the couple rather than individual persons. They are frequently associated with marital distress.*

increases muscular tension, heart rate, and respiration rate. These physiological responses are accompanied by feelings of arousal, especially at more advanced stages of excitement.

The experience of *orgasm* is usually distinct from the gradual buildup of sexual excitement that precedes it. This sudden release of tension is almost always experienced as being intensely pleasurable, but the specific nature of the experience varies from one person to the next. The female orgasm occurs in three stages, beginning with a "sensation of suspension or stoppage," which is associated with strong genital sensations. The second stage involves a feeling of warmth spreading throughout the pelvic area. The third stage is characterized by sensations of throbbing or pulsating, which are tied to rhythmic contractions of the vagina, the uterus, and the rectal sphincter muscle.

The male orgasm occurs in two stages, beginning with a sensation of ejaculatory inevitability. This is triggered by the movement of seminal fluid toward the urethra. In the second stage, regular contractions propel semen through the urethra, and it is expelled through the urinary opening.

During the *resolution* phase, which may last 30 minutes or longer, the person's body returns to its resting state. Men are typically unresponsive to further sexual stimulation for a variable period of time after reaching orgasm. This is known as the refractory period. Women, on the other hand, may be able to respond to further stimulation almost immediately. They are capable of experiencing a series of distinct orgasmic responses that are not separated by a period of noticeably lowered excitement (Andersen & Cyranowski, 1995).

Sexual dysfunctions can involve a disruption of any stage of the sexual response cycle. The following case study is concerned with a man who had difficulty controlling the rate at which he progressed from excitement to orgasm.

## CASE STUDY Margaret and Bill's Sexual Communication

Margaret and Bill, both in their late twenties, had been married for two years, and they had intercourse frequently. Margaret seldom reached orgasm during these experiences, but she was orgasmic during masturbation. The central feature of their problem was the fact that Bill was unable to delay ejaculation for more than a few seconds after insertion.

During intercourse he tried to keep his leg muscles tense and think about sports as a way of keeping his arousal in check. Bill was unaware that Margaret felt emotionally shut out during the sex. Bill was becoming more sensitized to his arousal cycle and was worrying about erection. He was not achieving better ejaculatory control, and he was enjoying sex less. The sexual relationship was heading downhill, and miscommunication and frustration were growing.

Margaret had two secrets that she had never shared with Bill. Although she found it easier to be orgasmic with manual stimulation, she had been orgasmic during intercourse with a married man she'd had an affair with a year before meeting Bill. Margaret expressed ambivalent feelings about that relationship. She felt that the man was a very sophisticated lover, and she had been highly aroused and orgasmic with him. Yet the relationship had been a manipulative one. He'd been emotionally abusive to Margaret, and the relationship had ended when he accused Margaret of giving him herpes. In fact, it was probably he who gave Margaret the herpes. Margaret was only experiencing herpes outbreaks two or three times a year, but when they did occur, she was flooded with negative feelings about herself, sexuality, and relationships. She initially saw Bill as a loving, stable man who would help rid her of negative feelings concerning sexuality. Instead, he continually disappointed her with the early ejaculation. Bill knew about the herpes but not about her sexual history and strong negative feelings.

Bill was terribly embarrassed about his secret masturbation, which he engaged in on a twice-daily basis. From adolescence on, Bill had used masturbation as his primary means of stress reduction. For him, masturbation was a humiliating secret (he believed married men should not masturbate). The manner in which he masturbated undoubtedly contributed to the early ejaculation pattern. Bill focused only on his penis, using rapid strokes with the goal

continued

*cont.*

of ejaculating as quickly as he could. This was both to prevent himself from being discovered and from a desire to "get it over with" as soon as he could and forget about it.

When it came to his personal and sexual life, Bill was inhibited, unsure of himself, and had particularly low sexual self-esteem. As an adolescent, Bill remembered being very interested sexually, but very unsure around girls. Bill's first intercourse at 19 was perceived as a failure because he ejaculated before he could insert his penis in the woman's vagina. He then tried desperately to insert because the young woman urged him to, but he was in the refractory period (a phenomenon Bill did not understand), and so he did not get a firm erection and felt doubly humiliated (McCarthy, 1989, pp. 151–159). ◆

The case of Bill and Margaret illustrates several important points. First, many sexual problems are best defined in terms of the couple rather than each partner individually (Stayton, 1996). Second, although problems in sexual behaviour clearly involve basic physiological responses and behavioural skills, each person's thoughts about the meaning of sexual behaviour are also extremely important. Sexual behaviour usually takes place in the context of a close, personal relationship. A recent view of the sexual response cycle by sexologist Rosemary Basson at the University of British Columbia has expanded beyond a simple focus on the mechanisms related to excitement and orgasm (Basson, 2001). This model begins at an earlier point of sexual neutrality and considers factors that influence whether the person will seek or be receptive to stimuli that might lead to arousal. And it extends beyond the experience of arousal and orgasm to consider feelings of emotional and physical satisfaction, which ultimately serve to build intimacy. The partners need to talk to each other about the things they enjoy as well as about their worries. Failure to communicate is often motivated by feelings of guilt and frustration, which can easily escalate over time.

The classification of sexual disorders was revised dramatically during the twentieth century. This process reflects important changes in the way that our culture views various aspects of sexual behaviour. Before describing the disorders that are included in DSM-IV-TR, we outline briefly some of the clinical and scientific perspectives on sexuality that laid the foundation for our current system.

### Brief Historical Perspective

Early medical and scientific approaches to sexual behaviour were heavily influenced by religious doctrines and prevailing cultural values. The exclusive purpose of sexual behaviour was assumed to be biological reproduction; anything that varied from that narrow goal was considered a form of psychopathology and was usually subject to severe moral and legal sanctions. Medical authorities were more worried about excessive sexuality and inappropriate or unusual sexual activities than they were about a person's subjective dissatisfaction or impaired sexual performance.

The period between 1890 and 1930 saw many crucial changes in the ways in which society viewed sexual behaviour (D'Emilio & Freedman, 1988). A significant number of people were beginning to think of sex as something more than a simple procreative function. If the purpose of sexual behaviour was to foster marital intimacy or to provide pleasure, then interference with that goal might become a legitimate topic of psychological inquiry. Changes in prevailing social attitudes led to a change in the focus of systems for the classification of sexual problems. Over the course of the later twentieth century and into the twenty-first, there has been a trend toward greater tolerance of sexual variation among consenting adult partners and toward increased concern about impairments in sexual performance and experience.

Several leading intellectuals influenced public and professional opinions regarding sexual behaviour during the first half of the twentieth century (Hogan, 1990). The work of Alfred Kinsey (1894–1956), a biologist at Indiana University, was especially significant. In keeping with his conscious adherence to scientific methods, Kinsey adopted a behavioural stance, focusing specifically on those experiences that resulted in orgasm. In their efforts to describe human sexual behaviour, Kinsey and his colleagues interviewed 18 000 men and women between 1938 and 1956 (Jones, 1997). They asked each participant a standard series of questions such as, "How old were you the first time that you had intercourse with another person?" Or, "How many times a week do you masturbate?" Kinsey's research largely ignored the person's feelings about sexuality and sexual experiences.

The incredible diversity of experiences reported by his subjects led Kinsey to reject the distinction between normal and abnormal sexual behaviour (Robinson, 1976). He argued that differences among people are quantitative rather than qualitative. For example, Kinsey suggested that the distinction between heterosexual and homosexual persons was essentially arbitrary and fundamentally meaningless. This argument was later used in support of the decision to drop homosexuality from DSM-III (see Further Thoughts in Chapter 1) and to cease regarding homosexuality as a form of abnormal behaviour. Kinsey's comments regarding sexual dysfunction reflected a similar view. He believed that low sexual desire was simply a reflection of individual differences in erotic capacity rather than a reflection of psychopathology (Kinsey, Pomeroy, and Martin, 1948).

# Sexual Dysfunctions

Sexuality represents a complex behavioural process that can easily be upset. Inhibitions of sexual desire and interference with the physiological responses leading to orgasm are called **sexual dysfunctions**. Problems can arise anywhere, from the earliest stages of interest and desire through the climactic release of orgasm. Some people also experience pain during sexual intercourse.

**Sexual Response in Primary Partnership during Previous Year**

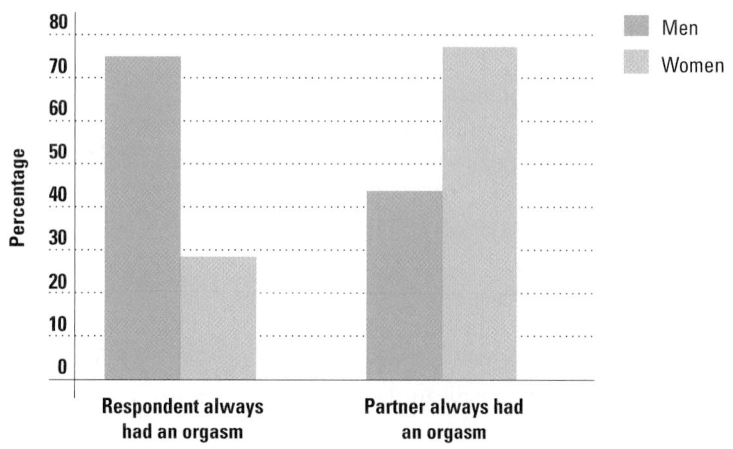


**FIGURE 12–1: This graph illustrates the frequency of orgasmic response as well as differences in perception by men and women in their partners' responses.**

*Source:* E.O. Laumann, J.H. Gagnon, R.T. Michael, and S. Michaels, 1994, *The Social Organization of Sexuality: Sexual Practices in the United States.* Chicago: University of Chicago Press.

## Typical Symptoms and Associated Features

How do people evaluate the quality of their sexual relationships? Subjective judgments obviously have an important impact on each person's commitment to a partnership. Dissatisfaction sometimes leads the couple to seek help from a mental health professional. It is useful, therefore, to know something about the ways in which normal couples evaluate their own sexual activities before we consider specific types of sexual dysfunction.

The National Health and Social Life Survey (NHSLS) collected extensive information about patterns of sexual activity and satisfaction in the general population (see Research Close-Up). Although the survey was conducted in the United States, the results are likely to generalize to other Western countries such as Canada. Figure 12–1 presents the NHSLS results on the proportion of people who said that they always had an orgasm during sexual activity with their primary partner during the past year. Several aspects of these data are worth mentioning. First, there is a very large difference between men and women with regard to the experience of orgasm. Only 29 percent of women reported that they always have an orgasm with a specific partner, compared to 75 percent of men. Second, notice that 44 percent of men reported that their partners always had orgasms during sex. This figure is much higher than the rate reported by women themselves. There are several plausible explanations for this discrepancy. Because female orgasm is sometimes less clearly defined than male orgasm, men may misinterpret some events as signs that their partners have had an orgasm. It may also be the case that women sometimes mislead their partners into thinking that they have reached orgasm so that their partners will feel better about their own sexual prowess (Wiederman, 1997).

Figure 12–2 depicts data on participants' ratings of physical and emotional satisfaction. Here the differences between men and women are less marked. Physical and emotional satisfaction in a sexual relationship might reasonably be expected to be influenced by the experience of orgasm, but the relations among these variables are complex. A relationship may be considered intimate and satisfying simply because sexual activity occurs, regardless of whether it always results in orgasm. In fact, a large proportion of both men and women indicated that they were extremely satisfied with their partners, on both the physical and emotional dimensions. Notice in particular that, although only 29 percent of women indicated that they always have an orgasm with their partner, 41 percent of women said that they were extremely physically satisfied with their partners. This pattern suggests that the experience of orgasm is only one aspect of sexual satisfaction, especially for women. Other aspects of the relationship, including tenderness, intimacy, and affection, are also critically important (Basson, 2001; Tiefer, 1999, 2001).

Strong negative emotions, such as anger, fear, and resentment, are often associated with

**Sexual Satisfaction in Primary Partnership during Previous Year**

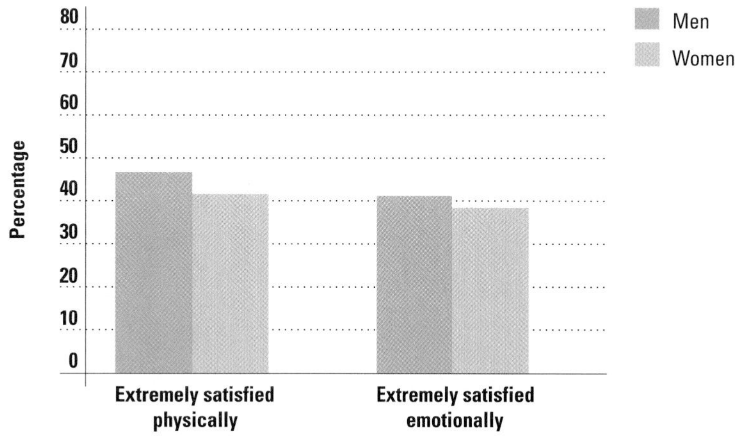


**FIGURE 12–2: This graph illustrates the physical and emotional satisfaction reported by men and women in their primary partnerships.**

*Source:* E.O. Laumann, J.H. Gagnon, R.T. Michael, and S. Michaels, 1994, *The Social Organization of Sexuality: Sexual Practices in the United States.* Chicago: University of Chicago Press.

# RESEARCH CLOSE-UP

## Sexual Activity in the General Population

What kinds of sexual behaviour do adults in our society typically practise? Many critical public health issues, including plans for preventing the spread of sexually transmitted diseases such as AIDS, hinge on answers to this question. Information about the sexual experiences of other people also helps us understand our own feelings and impulses. The most comprehensive information on this topic was collected by Laumann and colleagues (1994). Their study, known as the National Health and Social Life Survey (NHSLS), was the first large-scale follow-up to the Kinsey reports.

The NHSLS research team conducted detailed, face-to-face interviews with nearly 3500 men and women between the ages of 18 and 59. Several elements of research design contribute to the overall value of the NHSLS data. Perhaps most important, the investigators used a procedure known as *probability sampling*—sampling in which every member of a clearly specified population has a known probability of selection—to identify their participants. This procedure is absolutely essential in survey research. Without it, conclusions cannot be generalized to the population as a whole (see Research Methods in Chapter 16). Probability sampling provides much more useful information than *convenience sampling*, in which investigators rely on whatever group of participants is readily available (such as introductory psychology students, members of various organizations, or the readers of a magazine who voluntarily respond to a questionnaire). Most of the previously available evidence regarding normal sexual activities was based on convenience samples. Some of Kinsey's work, for example, relied heavily on data obtained from men in prison. The sexual experiences of these men are probably not representative of those of all men in the general population.

The results of the NHSLS survey paint a somewhat more conservative picture of sexual activity than some people may have expected. For example, monogamy is by far the most common pattern. In the year of the survey, only 16 percent of the participants had more than one sexual partner, 73 percent had only one partner, and 11 percent had no partner. Among the other key findings are the following:

- Married couples have sex more often than single people.
- Married couples reported more physical pleasure and emotional satisfaction from sex than single people did.
- People in younger generations were more likely than people in older generations to have had premarital sex (84 percent for men and 80 percent for women born between 1963 and 1974).
- One-third of the overall sample said they had sex with a partner at least twice a week; another third had sex with a partner a few times a month; and the remaining third had sex with a partner a few times a year or didn't have sexual partners at all.

Lifetime prevalence rates for specific forms of sexual activity are presented in Figure 12–3. Masturbation is relatively common among both men and women. Approximately 1 out of every 4 men and 1 out of every 10 women reported masturbating at least once a week. Approximately half of the men and women who masturbated indicated that they felt guilty about it. People without

*continued*

*cont.*

religious affiliations reported less guilt than people with strong religious connections. This pattern supports the argument that cultural factors play a role in shaping normal sexual activities and experiences.

The NHSLS questionnaire also asked about four basic sexual techniques involving partners: vaginal intercourse, fellatio, cunnilingus, and anal intercourse. The lifetime prevalence of these techniques for sexual activities with an opposite-gender partner are given in Figure 12–3 (data for same-gender sexual partnerships were analyzed separately). Virtually all of the men (95 percent) and women (97 percent) had experienced vaginal intercourse at some time during their lives. The investigators concluded that the vast majority of heterosexual encounters focus on vaginal intercourse.

Most of the men and women also reported that they had engaged in oral sexual activities (as both the person giving and receiving oral–genital stimulation). However, the percentage of men and women who indicated that their most recent sexual activity involved oral sex was much lower. This pattern suggests that although most people have some experience with oral sex, it is not sufficiently common to be considered a defining feature of sexual encounters between men and women (such as kissing and vaginal intercourse).

Regarding anal intercourse, most men and women in the study reported that they had never engaged in this activity.

**Lifetime Prevalence of Sexual Activities (with an Opposite-Gender Partner)**

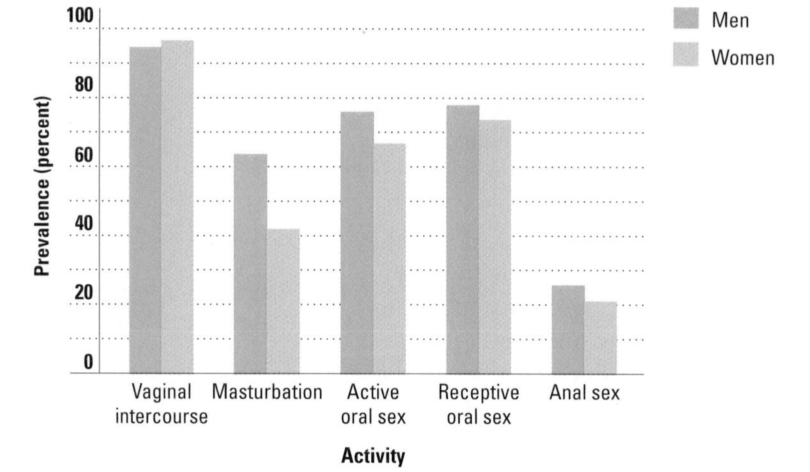


**FIGURE 12–3: This graph illustrates the prevalence of various types of sexual activities, based on responses to the NHSLS questionnaire. Note that vaginal intercourse is the most frequent activity, although masturbation and oral sex are also common.**

*Source:* E.O. Laumann, J.H. Gagnon, R.T. Michael, and S. Michaels, 1994, *The Social Organization of Sexuality: Sexual Practices in the United States.* Chicago: University of Chicago Press.

Anal sex has become a source of concern because it presents a relatively high risk for transmission of HIV. Among those people who had experimented with anal sex, relatively few had incorporated it into their usual sexual experiences.

The use of condoms was more frequent among younger, better-educated people. Men and women who had more than one sexual partner in the past year used condoms more frequently than people involved in stable, monogamous relationships. Nevertheless, some people still engaged in relatively high-risk behaviours. Only 40 percent of the people who had sex with four partners in the past year said that they used a condom during their most recent experience with vaginal intercourse. Many people were reluctant to use condoms during the initial stages of a new sexual relationship, even though this is a time when they are more vulnerable to exposure to sexually transmitted diseases. ◆

sexual dissatisfaction. In some cases, these emotional states appear before the onset of the sexual problem, and sometimes they develop later. Given the connection that many cultures make between virile sexual performance and "manhood," it is not surprising that men with erectile difficulties are often embarrassed and ashamed. Their humiliation can lead to secondary problems, such as anxiety and depression. Similar feelings frequently accompany premature ejaculation and the recognition that a partner's sexual expectations have not been fulfilled. Women who have trouble becoming aroused or reaching orgasm also frequently experience frustration and disappointment.

## Classification

DSM-IV-TR subdivides sexual dysfunctions into several types (see Table 12–1). The diagnostic criteria for these problems are much less specific than those used to define other kinds of disorders in DSM-IV-TR. Much is left to the judgment of the individual clinician. Failure to reach orgasm is not considered a disorder unless it is persistent or recurrent and results in marked distress or interpersonal difficulty. The DSM-IV-TR criteria also require that the sexual dysfunction is not better explained by another Axis I disorder (such as major depression) and is not the direct result of a chemical substance (such as alcohol) or a general medical condition. For many types of disorder, the clinician must decide whether the person has engaged in sexual activities that would normally be expected to produce sexual arousal or orgasm. Diagnostic judgments must take into consideration the person's age, as well as the circumstances in which the person is living, such as the presence of a partner, access to privacy, and so on. For all of these reasons, the reliability of diagnostic decisions for sexual dysfunctions is probably quite low (McConaghy, 1999a; Williams & Leiblum, 2002).

One diagnostic criterion that is required for all forms of sexual dysfunction defined in DSM-IV-TR is the demonstration that the problem in question leads to marked distress or interpersonal difficulty. In other words, someone who is not interested in sex or who experiences problems in sexual responsiveness would not qualify for a diagnosis of sexual dysfunction unless this circumstance is upsetting to him or her or causes interpersonal problems. Subjective distress and relationship problems will be evident in many of the brief case studies that are included in this chapter. We must be cautious, however, in weighing the diagnostic importance of relationship problems and the feelings of the person's partner. A panel of leading experts on women's reproductive health recently recommended that the only consideration in this regard should be personal distress experienced by the woman (Basson et al., 2000; Leiblum, 2001). The satisfaction and concerns of her partner might be an important consideration in terms of their relationship itself, but it should not be grounds for assigning to the woman a diagnosis of sexual dysfunction unless she is personally dissatisfied with her own sexual experience.

**TABLE 12–1 Sexual Dysfunctions Listed in DSM-IV-TR**

**Hypoactive Sexual Desire Disorder:** Persistently or recurrently deficient (or absent) sexual fantasies and desire for sexual activity.

**Sexual Aversion Disorder:** Persistent or recurrent extreme aversion to, and avoidance of, all (or almost all) genital sexual contact with a sexual partner.

**Female Sexual Arousal Disorder:** Persistent or recurrent inability to attain, or to maintain until completion of the sexual activity, an adequate lubrication–swelling response of sexual excitement.

**Male Erectile Disorder:** Persistent or recurrent inability to attain or maintain until completion of the sexual activity, an adequate erection.

**Female Orgasmic Disorder:** Persistent or recurrent delay in, or absence of, orgasm following a normal sexual excitement phase.

**Male Orgasmic Disorder:** Persistent or recurrent delay in, or absence of, orgasm following a normal sexual excitement phase during sexual activity.

**Premature Ejaculation:** Persistent or recurrent ejaculation with minimal sexual stimulation before, during, or shortly after penetration and before the person wishes it.

**Dyspareunia:** Recurrent or persistent genital pain associated with sexual intercourse in either a male or a female.

**Vaginismus:** Recurrent or persistent involuntary spasm of the musculature of the outer third of the vagina that interferes with sexual intercourse.

**Hypoactive Sexual Desire Disorder** Sexual desire sets the stage for sexual arousal and orgasm. Some clinicians refer to sexual desire as the person's willingness to approach or engage in those experiences that will lead to sexual arousal. Inhibited, or **hypoactive sexual desire** is defined in terms of subjective experiences, such as lack of sexual fantasies and lack of interest in sexual experiences. The absence of interest in sex must be both persistent and pervasive to be considered a clinical problem.

The absolute frequency with which a person engages in sex cannot be used as a measure of inhibited sexual desire because the central issue is *interest*—actively seeking out sexual experiences—rather than participation (Beck, 1995; Klein, 1997). For example, some people acquiesce to their partners' demands, even though they would not choose to engage in sexual activities if it were left up to them. In the absence of any specific standard, the identification of hypoactive sexual desire must depend on a clinician's subjective evaluation of the level of desire that is expected given the person's age, gender, marital status, and many other relevant considerations.

Almost everyone recognizes that sexual desire fluctuates in intensity over time, sometimes dramatically and frequently, for reasons that we do not understand. The fact that hypoactive sexual desire is listed in DSM-IV-TR as a type of disorder should not lead us to believe that it is a unitary condition with a simple explanation. It is, in fact, a collection of many different kinds of problems. People who suffer from low levels of sexual desire frequently experience other mental and medical disorders. Perhaps as many as 85 percent of males and 75 percent of women seeking treatment for hypoactive sexual desire report other forms of sexual dysfunction (Donahey & Carroll, 1993), such as problems with arousal or genital pain. Men and women with low sexual desire also have high rates of mood disorders. The mood disorder typically appears before the onset of low sexual desire. It appears likely, therefore, that many cases of low sexual desire develop after the person has experienced other forms of psychological distress.

**Sexual Aversion Disorder** Some people develop an active aversion to sexual stimuli and begin to avoid sexual situations altogether. Some people avoid only certain aspects of sexual behaviour, such as kissing, intercourse, or oral sex. This reaction is stronger than a simple lack of interest. Fear of sexual encounters can occasionally reach intense proportions, at which point it may be better characterized as **sexual aversion disorder**. This problem might be viewed as a kind of phobia because it extends well beyond anxiety about sexual performance (Berman, Berman, & Goldstein, 1999). Consider, for example, the following case from our files. The couple sought help at a psychological clinic in the hope that they might improve their sexual relationship.

## BRIEF CASE STUDY

### Sexual Aversion Disorder

Doug and Jennifer were both 32 years old. They had been married for five years, but they had never had sexual intercourse. They cared for each other very much and described themselves as being like brother and sister. Their inability to have intercourse was upsetting to them both for many reasons. Most important was their mutual desire to have children. Doug also felt that their marriage would be stronger and more enjoyable if they were sexually intimate. Jennifer wasn't interested in sexual activity; she never experienced sexual fantasies or erotic thoughts. She did view sex as her duty, however, and she felt guilty about not fulfilling that part of her "marital obligation." Jennifer's primary concern about the relationship involved a different kind of intimacy; she wished that Doug would spend more time with her talking, taking walks, and doing things together that did not involve sex.

Neither Doug nor Jennifer had been experienced sexually at the time of their marriage. Jennifer was clearly anxious in the presence of stimuli that were sexual in nature, such as movies or books with a sexual theme, but she did not avoid these situations or sexual interactions altogether. She and Doug had engaged in kissing and gentle touching early in their marriage. Jennifer masturbated Doug to orgasm several times, but she felt disgusted at the sight of semen when he ejaculated. Doug had persuaded her to engage in oral sex on a few occasions. She found it unpleasant and was unable to continue long enough for Doug to reach orgasm. They attempted intercourse once, but Jennifer was unable to become aroused and insertion had been impossible.

Doug and Jennifer gradually lost interest in sexual activities. He was extremely busy with his work and said that he no longer thought about sex very often, although he continued to masturbate. Since their failed attempt at intercourse, Doug had also begun to feel less sexually attracted to Jennifer. They eventually entered treatment in order to explore their feelings for each other and to see if they could do anything to salvage their sexual relationship, primarily in the hope that they would be able to have children.

Several weeks after entering therapy, Jennifer reluctantly confided in her therapist that she had been sexually abused by an uncle with whom she had lived for two years as a child. He had forced her to perform oral sex several times when she was about nine years old. She had never told anyone about the abuse—her parents, her aunt, or Doug—for many reasons. She was ashamed of the experience and frightened of what her uncle might do to her. The memories of this experience were still vivid, especially when she attempted to have sex with her husband. ◆

Jennifer's aversion to sexual activity was easily understandable in the context of previous abuse. The symptoms of sexual aversion disorder are often more pronounced than those that were exhibited by Jennifer. In some people, full-blown symptoms of a panic attack may be triggered by exposure to sexual stimuli.

**Male Erectile Disorder** Many men experience difficulties either in obtaining an erection that is sufficient to accomplish intercourse or maintaining an erection long enough to satisfy themselves and their partners during intercourse. Both problems are examples of **erectile dysfunction**. Men with this problem may report feeling subjectively aroused, but the vascular reflex mechanism fails, and sufficient blood is not pumped to the penis to make it erect (Korenman, 1998). These difficulties can appear at any time prior to orgasm. Some men have trouble achieving an erection during sexual foreplay, whereas others lose their erection around the time of insertion or during intercourse. This phenomenon used to be called *impotence*, but the term has been dropped because of its negative implications.

Erectile dysfunctions can be relatively transient, or they can be more chronic. Occasional experiences of this type are not considered unusual. When they persist and become a serious source of distress to the couple, however, erectile difficulties can lead to serious problems. Consider, for example, the feelings expressed by the man and woman in our next case study, who were treated by Zilbergeld (1995), an expert in the treatment of sexual dysfunction.

## BRIEF CASE STUDY

### Male Erectile Disorder

Norm and Linda are both 44 and have been married 15 years, the first marriage for him, the second for her. Linda called to ask if I would be available immediately to work with her and her husband, who had low sexual desire and erection problems. Individually, they are very different. Linda is attractive, vivacious, impulsive, and very critical. Norm . . . seemed generally timid and reluctant to express his feelings in front of his wife, spoke slowly and usually only after some time, and then said only nice things in a nice way, and he struck me as being depressed. [They] had a serviceable relationship in many ways. Neither had close friends and tended to rely on each other for support and companionship. They shared a number of common interests and held similar values about most things.

The only problem, as far as they were concerned, was sex. When they first met, Linda was far more sexually experienced than Norm. She was surprised that a man could have had so little knowledge and experience. He, on the other hand, was somewhat intimidated by her experience and knowledge. But he tried to be a good student and they enjoyed frequent lovemaking at the beginning, although not as frequent or as passionate as she would have liked.

Over the years, however, Norm gradually lost interest in sex and developed erection problems. Either he wouldn't get an erection or he would lose it before or during insertion. Norm sought help from a urologist who, although he found nothing physically wrong, gave him an injection in his penis, which produced an erection that lasted for three hours.

But neither Norm nor Linda was overjoyed by the idea of him taking injections. Norm had always been fearful of needles and almost fainted when the urologist gave him the first injection. Linda didn't like the needles either. In her mind, they weren't "natural or normal." For Norm to have to take shots to get erections meant that he didn't love her or wasn't aroused by her.

Linda appeared to be hurt and angry in my individual session with her. "I know you're sympathetic toward men with erection problems. But what about me? I feel totally defeminized. How can I feel loved or desirable when he can't get it up for me? You don't have any idea what that's like. Even with the help of modern chemistry, he can't do it for me. It's obvious he doesn't want me, doesn't desire me. Even at my age, other men look at me and want me. But not my husband. I feel awful."

In my session with Norm, he repeated several times that he loved Linda and wanted to stay with her. When I asked if he found her sexually attractive, he hesitated and then said yes. When I asked about the hesitation, he was silent for a few moments and then said, "No, it's nothing. I am turned on to her." Further prodding on my part yielded nothing, but I thought his arousal was not as unambivalent as he said. As we continued our discussion, I asked how he felt when he was first dating her. He began by saying how beautiful he found her and how surprised he was that a woman like her would take an interest "in a nerd like me." When I asked what else he felt at that time, he answered, "To tell the truth, I was frightened by her experience and sexual openness. It was like I was in kindergarten and she was a professor. I'm not sure I've ever gotten over that. I've always felt at least a little inadequate. And things really got bad after I started having trouble with erections." I wanted to know more about how their sex had been before the erection problem. He said that it had been good and added in a voice so low I could barely hear his words, "She was always teaching and correcting me. Somehow I wasn't able to do exactly what she wanted. I didn't touch her right, my erections were never as hard as she liked, and when we had intercourse, I wasn't passionate enough" (Zilbergeld, 1995, pp. 315–316). ◆

*Sexual arousal is somewhat more difficult to measure for women than for men. Women's feelings of arousal are not always directly connected to physiological responses.*

Norm and Linda experienced the frustrations and anxiety that often accompany sexual arousal difficulties. Their relationship also illustrates the marital distress that can develop when people begin to have problems with self-esteem and doubts about the affection of their partner.

**Female Sexual Arousal Disorder** Sexual arousal can also be impaired in women, but it is somewhat more difficult to describe and identify than is erectile dysfunction in men. Put simply, a woman is said to experience **inhibited sexual arousal** if she cannot either achieve or maintain genital responses, such as lubrication and swelling, which are necessary to complete sexual intercourse. The desire is there, but the physiological responses that characterize sexual excitement are inhibited (Leiblum, 1999).

The capacity for intercourse is somewhat less obvious and more difficult to measure for a woman than for a man, whose erect penis usually serves as a signal of readiness (see Research Methods). Investigators who have studied sexual responses in normal women have reported low correlations between self-reports of subjective arousal and physiological measures, such as the amount of vaginal lubrication or vasocongestion (Leiblum, 2001; Segraves & Blindt-Segraves, 2001). Among women who experience sexual difficulties, the problem may more often be decreased subjective arousal rather than impaired physiological responses. Therefore, inhibitions in sexual arousal must be defined in terms of this self-report dimension as well as in terms of specific genital responses.

***Karl Freund** was a leading sexologist who conducted pioneering research on penile plethysmography. He also developed the courtship disorder theory of paraphilias.*

**Premature Ejaculation** Many men experience problems with the control of ejaculation. They are unable to prolong the period of sexual excitement long enough to complete intercourse. This problem is known as **premature ejaculation**. Once they become intensely sexually aroused, they reach orgasm very quickly.

There have been many attempts to establish specific, quantitative criteria for premature ejaculation. None have been entirely satisfactory, but certain boundaries identify conditions that can be problematic. If the man ejaculates before or immediately upon insertion, or after only three or four thrusts, almost all clinicians will identify his response as premature ejaculation (Grenier & Byers, 1995). Research by Guy Grenier and Sandra Byers (2001) at the University of New Brunswick reveals that for men who identify rapid ejaculation as a problem, the average ejaculation latency (i.e., the mean time from insertion to ejaculation) was eight minutes, which is consistent with findings by other investigators (Kameya et al., 1997). Byers and Grenier (2003) found that for most couples, the effects of premature ejaculation can reduce sexual satisfaction, but does not impair overall personal functioning or the quality of the couple's relationship.

**Female Orgasmic Disorder** Some women are unable to reach orgasm even though they apparently experience uninhibited sexual arousal. Women who experience orgasmic difficulties may have a strong desire to engage in sexual relations, they may find great pleasure in sexual foreplay, and they may show all the signs of sexual arousal. Nevertheless, they cannot reach the peak erotic experience of orgasm. Women whose orgasmic impairment is *generalized* have never experienced orgasm by any means. *Situational* orgasmic difficulties occur when the woman is able to reach orgasm in some situations but not in others. That might mean that she is orgasmic during masturbation but not during intercourse, or perhaps she is orgasmic with one partner but not with another (Basson et al., 2000).

**Orgasmic disorder** in women is somewhat difficult to define in relation to inhibited

## RESEARCH METHODS

### Hypothetical Constructs: The Case of "Sexual Arousal"

The term *sexual arousal* refers to the state that precedes orgasm. It is defined in terms of two factors: physiological responses, such as vascular engorgement of the genitals; and feelings of pleasure and excitement. Psychologists refer to sexual arousal as a **hypothetical construct**. Many of the concepts that we have discussed in this book are hypothetical constructs: anxiety, depression, psychopathy, and schizophrenia. Hypothetical constructs are theoretical devices. In the field of psychopathology, they refer to events or states that reside within the person and are proposed to help us understand or explain a person's behaviour.

Constructs cannot be observed directly, but in order to be scientifically meaningful they must be defined in terms of observable responses (Cronbach & Meehl, 1955). These responses are all associated with the construct, but they are not perfectly related, and the construct is not exhaustively defined by them. For example, an erect penis is not always accompanied by feelings of sexual excitement, and feelings of arousal are not always associated with physiological responses. In other words, the construct of sexual arousal is anchored by feelings and responses that can be measured directly, but it is more than the sum of these parts.

An **operational definition** is a procedure that is used to measure a theoretical construct. Such a definition usually includes measures of the different components of the construct. For men, one obvious component of sexual arousal is penile erection. The most widely accepted procedure for measuring male sexual arousal uses a device called a *penile plethysmograph*, which has been used in research of normal and abnormal sexual behaviour, such as in the work of Ontario researchers Grant Harris and Marnie Rice (1996). In this procedure, the man places a thin elastic strain gauge around his penis, underneath his clothing. The rubber loop is filled with a column of mercury that changes in its electrical conductance as the circumference of the penis changes. The wire extending from the strain gauge is connected to a plethysmograph, which amplifies the electrical signal passing through the strain gauge and produces a record reflecting changes in penile tumescence.

Research using this technique was pioneered by the late Kurt Freund who worked in Czechoslovakia during the early 1950s, and later in Toronto during the 1960s. The Kurt Freund Phallometric Laboratory, at Toronto's Centre for Addiction and Mental Health, is a leading centre for penile plethysmography. There, the method is used mainly to assess sex offenders, but is also provided to men who have questions or concerns about their sexual behaviour or sexual orientation. Plethysmography is useful in assessing erotic preferences but it may not be sensitive enough to diagnose a man's proclivity for committing sexual offences (Freund & Blanchard, 1989).

To measure female sexual arousal, a device known as the *vaginal photometer* is used. It is shaped like a tampon and inserted into the vagina. Like the penile strain gauge, the photometer can be placed in position in private and worn underneath clothing during the assessment procedure. As the woman becomes sexually aroused, the walls of the vagina become congested with blood. Vasocongestion causes changes in the amount of red light that can be transmitted through the tissue. The photometer is sensitive to subtle changes in vaginal tissue and is probably most useful in measuring moderate to low levels of sexual arousal (Heiman, 1998).

Clinical scientists must always think carefully about the meaning of their operational definitions. Although the penile strain gauge and the vaginal photometer measure physiological events that are directly related to sexual arousal, the responses that they measure are not the same thing as sexual arousal. They are reflections of the construct, which has many dimensions (Berman et al., 1999). One important goal of scientific studies is to determine more specifically how (and when) these physiological measures are related to the other observable referents of sexual arousal. This process will determine the **construct validity** of the penile strain gauge and the vaginal photometer—that is, the extent to which these specific measures produce results that are consistent with the theoretical construct. ◆

sexual arousal because the various components of female sexual response are more difficult to measure than are erection and ejaculation in the male. One experienced researcher described this issue in the following way:

> In my experience, many women who have never reached orgasm present the following set of symptoms: They report that when engaging in intercourse they do not have difficulty lubricating and experience no pain. However, they report no genital sensations (hence the term genital anesthesia) and do not appear to know what sexual arousal is. Typically they do not masturbate and often have never masturbated. They do not experience the phenomenon that a sexually functional woman would call sexual desire. . . . Most of these women seek therapy because they have heard from others or have read that they are missing something, rather than because they themselves feel frustrated. (Morokoff, 1989, p. 74)

*McGill University psychologist **Yitzchak Binik** is a leading expert on dyspareunia. He argues that it is fundamentally a pain disorder rather than a form of sexual dysfunction.*

**Pain During Sex** Some people experience persistent genital pain during or after sexual intercourse, which is known as **dyspareunia**. The problem can occur in either men or women, although it is considered to be much more common in women (Binik, 2004; Meana & Binik, 1994). The severity of the discomfort can range from mild irritation following sexual activity to searing pain during insertion of the penis or intercourse. The pains may be sharp and intense, or they may take the form of a dull, aching sensation; they may be experienced as coming from a superficial area near the barrel of the vagina or as being located deep in the lower abdominal area; they may be intermittent or persistent. The experience of severe genital pain is often associated with other forms of sexual dysfunction. Not surprisingly, many women with dyspareunia develop a disinterest in, or an aversion toward, sexual activity.

The following first-person account was written by a 40-year-old woman who had been experiencing vaginal pain for several months. She had consulted several different health professionals about the problem, and none of their treatments had relieved her discomfort. This passage describes her experience one night when she and the man with whom she had been living seemed to be on the brink of enjoying a renewed interest in their sexual relationship.

## BRIEF CASE STUDY

### Genital Pain

We went to bed. For a while it was nice—more than nice. It was novel and thrilling, as if we had just met. We hadn't approached each other in more than a month. I was surprised by how wonderful I could feel. I was used to feeling lousy most of the time. The sensations of excitement were overwhelming. I'd forgotten about that. Then he pushed himself into me and it was horrible.

First I felt as if I were being torn or sliced. As he settled into a rhythm, I felt that something was scraping me over and over in the same raw spot, until the rawness and soreness were all I could feel. He didn't notice. He was intent on what he was doing. I decided to let him get on with it, but the pain was really bothering me. I pulled away inside myself, so that the events on the bed were far from where "I" was, and the pain was far away also. That worked, but I didn't like doing it. There was something nasty about it. I had the thought, People who don't like sex must feel this way. Then I realized that now I was somebody who didn't like sex (Kaysen, 2001, pp. 60–61).

Access to the vagina is controlled by the muscles surrounding its entrance. Some women find that whenever penetration of the vagina is attempted, these muscles snap tightly shut, preventing insertion of any object. This involuntary muscular spasm, known as **vaginismus**, prevents sexual intercourse as well as other activities, such as vaginal examinations and the insertion of tampons. Women with vaginismus may be completely sexually responsive in other respects, fully capable of arousal and orgasm through manual stimulation of the clitoris.

Research by McGill University psychologist Yitzchak Binik and colleagues indicates that vaginismus is a multidimensional disorder, consisting of pain, fear of pain, pelvic floor dysfunction (e.g., increased tone or tension in the pelvic floor muscles), and behavioural avoidance (e.g., avoiding intercourse or medical pelvic examinations) (Reissing, Binik, & Khalife, 1999; Reissing et al., 2004).

It is currently unclear whether dyspareunia is best regarded as a sexual dysfunction or as some other type of disorder. Binik and colleagues have argued that dyspareunia is primarily a pain syndrome rather than a sexual dysfunction (Binik, 2004; Meana et al., 1997). Consistent with this, many women experience genital pain during sexual stimulation other than intercourse. Thus one recommendation made by the Consensus Development Conference on Female Sexual Dysfunction was the addition of a new category for noncoital sexual pain (Basson et al., 2000).

### Epidemiology

The best available estimates of the lifetime prevalence of sexual problems are summarized in Figure 12–4. The figure suggests that these problems are quite common, although the prevalence of some sexual disorders, such as sexual aversion disorder and vaginismus, is unknown. Note that in survey data such as these, some of the sexual problems counted as "sexual dysfunctions" may not have met DSM-IV-TR diagnostic criteria (APA, 2000). To diagnose these disorders, one needs to take into account the person's age, the context of the person's life, and whether the person had experienced stimulation that would ordinarily be expected to lead to sustained arousal and orgasm. Clinicians would also take into consideration the amount of distress and interpersonal difficulty associated with the problem before arriving at a diagnosis of sexual dysfunction. Therefore, we must be cautious in our interpretations of these survey data.

Survey data can be supplemented with information on the prevalence of specific types of sexual dysfunction among people who seek professional treatment for sexual problems (Benet & Melman, 1995; Spector & Carey, 1990). These reports indicate several trends over the past 30 years:

- Orgasmic and erectile dysfunction have become more frequent complaints among people seeking treatment.
- Premature ejaculation has become less common as the presenting problem among people seeking treatment for sexual dysfunction.
- The frequency of desire disorders as presenting problems in sex clinics has increased.
- Recently, males have outnumbered females as the person with the presenting problem when couples seek treatment.

**Lifetime Prevalence of Sexual Dysfunctions**

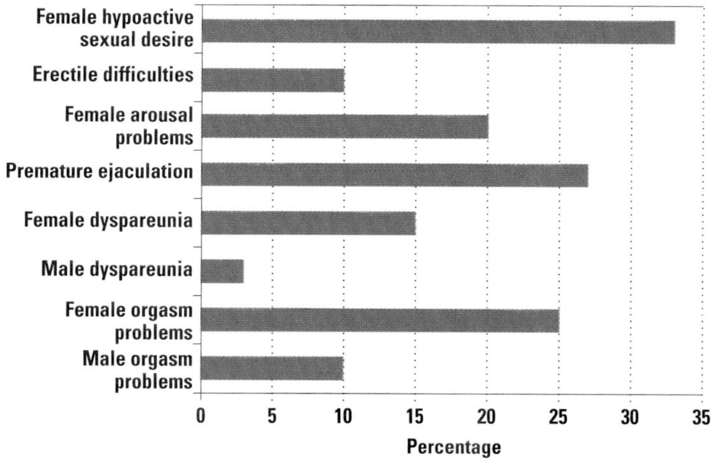


**FIGURE 12–4: This graph shows that sexual dysfunctions are very common in the general population.**

*Source:* Based on American Psychiatric Association, 2000, *Diagnostic and statistical maual of mental disorders,* 4th ed., text revision. Washington, DC: Author.

## Sexual Behaviour across the Lifespan

Sexual behaviour changes with age. Masters and Johnson devoted considerable attention to this topic in their original studies. Their data challenged the myth that older adults are not interested in, or capable of performing, sexual behaviours. The NHSLS data also indicate that many people remain sexually active later in life. Gender differences become marked in the late fifties, when rates of inactivity increase dramatically for women. Between ages 70 and 74, 65 percent of men are still sexually active, compared to only 30 percent of women. These differences may be, at least partly, the result of biological factors that are part of the aging process. They may also reflect the influence of a cultural prejudice against sexual activity among older women.

Differences between younger and older people are mostly a matter of degree. As men get older, they tend to achieve erections more slowly, but they can often maintain erections for longer periods of time. Older men find it more difficult to regain an erection if it is lost before orgasm. As women get older, vaginal lubrication may occur at a slower rate, but the response of the clitoris remains essentially unchanged. The intensity of the subjective experience of orgasm is decreased for older men and women. For both men and women, healthy sexual responsiveness is most likely to be maintained among those who have been sexually active as younger adults (Meston, 1997).

The prevalence of certain types of sexual dysfunction increases among the elderly, particularly among men (Gentili & Mulligan, 1998). The relation between sexual experience and aging is closely related to other health problems that increase with age. People who rate their health as being excellent have many fewer sexual problems than people who rate their health as being only fair or poor (Laumann et al., 1994).

*Many people remain sexually active later in life. Differences in sexual responsiveness between younger and older people are mostly a matter of degree.*

**Cross-Cultural Comparisons** Patients with sexual disorders seek treatment at clinics all over the world (Shokrollahi et al., 1999; Verma, Khaitan, & Singh, 1998). Therefore, these problems are not unique to any particular culture. Cultural and ethnic differences have been reported for sexual practices, beliefs about sexuality, and patterns of sexual decision making. For example, research conducted at the University of British Columbia indicates that Asians tend to be more conservative than Caucasians in many regards, such as in the prevalence and frequency of masturbation (Meston, Trapnell, & Gorzalka, 1996). Recent Asian immigrants were more likely than Canadian-born or long-term Canadian residents to hold conservative sexual attitudes (Meston, Trapnell, & Gorzalka, 1998). It is not clear whether variations in sexual behaviour are accompanied by cultural differences in the frequency and form of sexual dysfunctions. Cross-cultural studies of prevalence rates for specific sexual dysfunctions have not been reported. This kind of investigation may be difficult to perform because the DSM-IV-TR definitions of sexual dysfunctions may not be well suited to describing the sexual experiences and satisfaction of people living in non-Western cultures (Davis, 1998).

## Etiology

At each stage of the sexual response cycle, a person's behaviour is determined by the interaction of many biological and psychological factors, ranging from vasocongestion in the genitals to complex cognitive events involving the perception of sexual stimuli and the interpretation of sexual meanings. Interference with this system at any point can result in serious problems. In the following pages we review some of the factors that contribute to the etiology of various types of sexual dysfunction.

**Biological Factors** The experience of sexual desire is partly controlled by biological factors. Sexual desire is influenced by sex hormones for both men and women (Meston & Frohlich, 2000). Testosterone is particularly important for male sexual desire. Studies of men with inadequate levels of sex hormones show an inhibited response to sexual fantasies, but they are still able to have erections in response to viewing explicit erotic films. The influence of male sex hormones on sexual behaviour is, therefore, thought to be on sexual appetite rather than on sexual performance. This process probably involves a threshold level of circulating testosterone (Meston & Frohlich, 2000). In other words, sexual appetite is impaired if the level of testosterone falls below a particular point (close to the bottom of the laboratory normal range), but above that threshold, fluctuations in testosterone levels will not be associated with changes in sexual desire. The reduction of male sex hormones over the lifespan probably explains, at least in part, the apparent decline in sexual desire among elderly males.

Many cases of erectile dysfunction can be attributed to vascular, neurological, or hormonal impairment (Fowler, 1998; Korenman, 1998). Erection is the direct result of a threefold increase in blood flow to the penis. Thus it is not surprising that vascular diseases, which may affect the amount of blood reaching the penis, are likely to result in erectile difficulties. Neurological diseases, such as epilepsy and multiple sclerosis, can also produce erectile difficulties, because erection depends on spinal reflexes. Diabetes may be the most common neurologically based cause of impaired erectile responsiveness.

Various kinds of drugs can also influence a man's erectile response (Clayton & Shen, 1998; McCabe et al., 1996). Men who smoke cigarettes are more likely to experience erectile difficulties than are men in the general population. Many drugs, including alcohol and marijuana, may have negative effects on sexual arousal. Medication used to treat hypertension can impair erectile responsiveness, and so can various types of antipsychotic and antidepressant drugs (Gutierrez & Stimmel, 1999).

A number of biological factors and physiological diseases can impair a woman's ability to become sexually aroused (Graziottin, 1998). Various types of neurological disorder, pelvic disease, and hormonal dysfunction can interfere with the process of vaginal swelling and lubrication. Unfortunately, relatively little research has been conducted on problems of sexual arousal in women (Andersen & Cyranowski, 1995), and thus these mechanisms are not well understood.

Inhibited orgasm, in both men and women, is sometimes caused by the abuse of alcohol and other drugs. The problem may improve if the person is able to stop drinking and maintain a stable period of sobriety (Schiavi et al., 1995). Orgasm problems can also be associated with the use of prescribed forms of medication.

**Psychosocial Factors** Although sexual desire is rooted in a strong biological foundation, social and psychological variables also play an important role in the determination of which stimuli a person will find arousing.

Laumann and Gagnon (1995) argued that sexual desire and arousal are determined by mental scripts that we learn throughout childhood and adolescence. According to this view, the social meaning of an event is of paramount importance in releasing the biological process of sexual arousal. Both members of the potential couple must recognize similar cues, defining the situation as potentially sexual in nature, before anything is likely to happen.

Beliefs and attitudes toward sexuality, as well as the quality of interpersonal relationships, have an important influence on the development of low sexual desire, especially among women. Women seeking treatment for hypoactive sexual desire report negative perceptions of their parents' attitudes regarding sexual behaviour and the demonstration of affection. In comparison to a group of normal women, they also indicate that they feel less close to their husbands, have fewer romantic feelings, and are less attracted to their husbands. The quality of the relationship is an important factor to consider with regard to low sexual desire (Metz & Epstein, 2002).

Culturally determined attitudes toward sexual feelings and behaviours can also have a dramatic impact on women's ability to become sexually aroused (Al-Sawaf & Al-Issa, 2000; Haavio-Mannila & Kontula, 1997). Some societies openly encourage female sexuality; others foster a more repressive atmosphere. Within Canada, there are tremendous variations with regard to women's ability to experience and express their sexuality, and some studies have found that different attitudes are associated with different levels of sexual responsiveness. For example, many women feel guilty about having sexual fantasies, in spite of the fact that such fantasies are extremely common. Women who feel guilty about fantasizing while they are having intercourse are more likely to be sexually dissatisfied and to encounter sexual problems, including arousal difficulties (Cado & Leitenberg, 1990).

Social factors are also related to orgasmic difficulties. For example, women who were born in more recent decades (the 1950s and '60s) are more likely to reach orgasm successfully than are women born in previous decades (Read, 1995). This pattern reflects the fact that public attitudes toward female sexuality, and especially the expectation that women can and should experience orgasm, have changed progressively over the past several decades. Evidence that is consistent with this general hypothesis has been reported by a study that compared patterns of sexual arousal in anorgasmic women—those who experience inhibited orgasm—and orgasmic women (Kelly, Strassberg, & Kircher, 1990). The most important factors contributing to failure to reach orgasm involved negative attitudes, feelings of guilt, and failure to communicate effectively, rather than the simple practice of engaging in particular types of stimulation.

Among the psychological factors contributing to impaired sexual arousal, Masters and Johnson (1970) gave primary emphasis to *performance anxiety*, or fear of failure. People who have experienced inhibited sexual arousal on one or two occasions may be likely to have further problems to the degree that these difficulties make them more self-conscious or apprehensive regarding their ability to become aroused in future sexual encounters. Several prominent and experienced sex therapists have assumed that anxiety and sexual arousal are incompatible emotional states. People who are anxious will presumably be less responsive to sexual stimuli. And men who have sexual arousal disorders are more likely to report feeling high levels of performance anxiety (Ackerman & Carey, 1995).

Relationship factors represent another important consideration in the etiology of sexual dysfunction. Couples that experience communication problems, power conflicts, and an absence of intimacy and trust are more likely than others to experience sexual problems. Lack of assertiveness and lack of comfort in talking about sexual activities and pleasures are associated with various types of female sexual dysfunction (Rosen & Leiblum, 1995).

Low sexual desire in men has also been linked to various kinds of long-lasting, adverse relationships with adults during childhood (Kinzl et al., 1996). For example, boys who grow up in a home in which their father is physically abusive may learn to associate sex with violence and become convinced that they do not want to function—sexually or interpersonally—as their father had.

### Treatment

Masters and Johnson (1970) were pioneers in developing and popularizing a short-term, skills-based approach to the treatment of sexual dysfunctions. Hundreds of couples who visited their clinic in St. Louis went through a two-week course of assessment and therapy in which they became more familiar with their bodies, learned to communicate more effectively with their partners, and received training in procedures designed to help them diminish their fears about sexuality. The results of this treatment program were very positive and quickly spawned a burgeoning industry of psychosocial treatment for sexual dysfunction.

Therapeutic procedures developed and tested with middle-class Caucasian young adults may not be well suited for everyone (McCarthy, 1998). Treatment clinics in India, Iran, Japan, Saudi Arabia, and South Africa report that men and women from many different social traditions seek help for sexual dysfunctions (Osman & Al-Sawaf, 1995; Shokrollahi et al., 1999; Verma et al., 1998). Mental health professionals must give careful consideration to their clients' cultural background when they conduct an assessment and design a treatment program. For example, people in some Asian cultures believe that a man's health can be damaged through unnecessary loss of semen (Davis & Herdt, 1997). Such concerns may prohibit use of masturbation as a therapeutic exercise. Implicit rules governing communication patterns between partners are also determined by culture. Some societies value and encourage sharp differences in gender roles, with men being expected to make decisions about the timing and type of sexual activity (Quadagno et al., 1998). Therefore, communication training must be tailored to meet the expectations that each couple holds regarding the nature of their relationship.

**Psychological Procedures** Psychological treatments for sexual dysfunction address several of the etiological factors discussed earlier, especially negative attitudes toward sexuality, failure to engage in effective sexual behaviours, and deficits in communication skills. Sex therapy centres around three primary types of activity: sensate focus and scheduling; education and cognitive restructuring; and communication training (Rosen & Leiblum, 1995; Wiegel, Wincze, & Barlow, 2002).

The cornerstone of sex therapy is known as **sensate focus**, a procedure developed by Masters and Johnson. Sensate focus involves a series of simple exercises in which the couple spends time in a quiet, relaxed setting, learning to touch each other. They may start with tasks as simple as holding hands or giving each other back rubs. The rationale for sensate focus hinges on the recognition that people with sexual problems must learn to focus on erotic sensations rather than on performance demands. The goal is to help them become more comfortable with this kind of physical sharing and intimacy, to learn to relax and enjoy it, and to talk to each other about what feels good and what does not.

The related facet of psychological approaches to treating sexual dysfunction is *scheduling*. This is, in fact, closely related to sensate focus because the technique of sensate focus requires that people schedule time for sex. Couples need a quiet, relaxed, and private environment in order to engage in pleasurable and satisfying sexual behaviour.

The second major aspect of sex therapy involves education and cognitive restructuring—changing the way in which people think about sex. In many cases the therapist needs to help the couple correct mistaken beliefs and attitudes about sexual behaviour. Examples are the belief that intercourse is the only true form of sex, that foreplay is an adolescent interest that most adults can ignore, and that simultaneous orgasm is the ultimate goal of intercourse. Providing information about sexual behaviours in the general population can often help alleviate people's guilt and anxiety surrounding their own experiences. Some people are relieved to know that they are not the only ones who fantasize about various kinds of sexual experiences, or that the fact that they fantasize about these things does not mean that they are going to be compelled to behave in deviant ways.

The final element of treatment for sexual dysfunction is communication training. This is another technique that was emphasized by Masters and Johnson in their early work with sexually dysfunctional couples. Many different studies have indicated that people with sexual dysfunction often have deficits in communication skills (e.g., Kelly, Strassberg, & Kircher, 1990). They find it difficult to talk to their partners about matters involving sex, and they are especially impaired in the ability to tell their partners what kinds of things they find sexually arousing and what kinds of things turn them off. Therefore, sex therapists often employ structured training procedures aimed at improving the ways in which couples talk to each other. Of course, sex therapy techniques

*"Now, that's product placement!"*

©The New Yorker Collection, Robert Mankoff from cartoonbank.com. All Rights Reserved.

must be used with special care when the clients' communication problems are grounded in a cultural tradition that actively discourages discussion of sexual issues.

The outcome results of psychological treatment programs for sexual disorders, including research from McGill University, have generally been considered to be positive (Bergeron et al., 2001; McCabe, 2001; Segraves & Althof, 2002).

**Biological Treatments** Biological treatments are also useful in the treatment of sexual dysfunctions. This is especially true for severe forms of erectile disorder, the most frequent sexual problem for which men seek professional help. One procedure involves surgically inserting a penile implant (or prosthesis), which can be used to make the penis rigid during intercourse (Melman & Tiefer, 1992). Several devices have been used. One option is a semirigid silicone rod that the man can bend into position for intercourse. Another device is hydraulic and can be inflated for the purpose of sexual activity. The man squeezes a small pump, which forces fluid into the inflatable cylinder and produces an erection. The inflatable device is preferred by partners, but it is also more expensive and can lead to more frequent postsurgical complications, such as infection.

With regard to sexual dysfunctions in women, research from McGill University indicates that a surgical intervention called vestibulectomy may also be effective for treating dyspareunia (Bergeron et al., 2001). Vestibulectomy involves the surgical removal of the vulvar tissue that appears to the source of pain in dyspareunia.

Various medications have been used successfully in the treatment of sexual dysfunction, especially erectile disorder. Sildenafil citrate (Viagra) was the first oral drug approved in Canada for use in treating erectile dysfunction. Taken one hour before sexual activity, Viagra facilitates erection by increasing blood flow to certain areas of the penis. It facilitates the man's ability to respond to stimuli that he would ordinarily find sexually arousing, but it does not influence overall sexual desire.

Double-blind, placebo-controlled studies have evaluated the use of Viagra in men with erectile problems associated with various conditions, including hypertension, diabetes, and coronary artery disease. It is effective, increasing the number of erections for approximately two-thirds of men with severe erectile dysfunction (Fink et al., 2002). Viagra has also been used to treat women with sexual dysfunctions, but according to Rosemary Basson at the University of British Columbia, and her colleagues, so far the results suggest that it is no better than a placebo (Basson et al., 2002.)

Even for men with erectile problems, Viagra may not be a complete solution. Couples that have experienced sexual problems have often struggled with a number of difficult issues for several years, as illustrated by two of the brief case studies in this chapter. Increasing the man's capacity for erection may address only one part of the problem. Many experts recommend a treatment approach that combines the use of medication with cognitive behaviour therapy (McCarthy, 1998; Rosen, 2000). Therapists may need to work with couples to improve intimacy and communication while also helping them to overcome frustrations and anxiety that have accumulated over years (Lamberg, 1998).

Treatments for sexual dysfunction are certainly promising. Less promising are treatments for another group of sexual disorders known as paraphilias. They are less well understood, in comparison to the sexual dysfunctions, and they are also more difficult to treat. The next section of this chapter reviews the current state of our knowledge regarding these difficult problems.

## Paraphilias

For some people, sexual arousal is strongly associated with unusual things and situations, such as inanimate objects, sexual contact with children, exhibiting their genitals to strangers, or inflicting pain on another person. The person is preoccupied with or consumed by these interests and activities. These conditions are known as **paraphilias**. Literally translated, paraphilia means "love" (*philia*) "beyond the usual" (*para*). This term refers to conditions that were formerly called perversions or sexual deviations. According to DSM-IV-TR, the central features of all paraphilias are persistent sexual urges and fantasies that are associated with (1) nonhuman objects, (2) suffering or humiliation of oneself or one's partner, or (3) children or other nonconsenting persons. In the following pages we summarize a few of the most common types of paraphilias, and we consider some of the factors that might influence the development of unusual sexual preferences.

## Typical Symptoms and Associated Features

One hundred years ago, many experts considered any type of sexual behaviour other than heterosexual intercourse to be pathological. Contemporary researchers and clinicians have expanded the boundaries of normal behaviour to include a much broader range of sexual behaviour. A large proportion of men and women engage in sexual fantasies and mutually consenting behaviours such as oral sex. These experiences enhance their relationships without causing problems (Laumann et al., 1994).

Problems with sexual appetites arise when a pattern develops involving a longstanding, unusual erotic preoccupation that is highly arousing, coupled with a pressure to act on the erotic fantasy. DSM-IV-TR requires that the erotic preoccupation must have lasted at least six months before the person would meet diagnostic criteria for a paraphilia. Furthermore, the diagnosis of paraphilia is made only if the person's paraphilic urges lead to clinically significant distress or impairment. The person would be considered to be impaired if the urges have become compulsory, if they produce sexual dysfunction, if they require the participation of nonconsenting persons, if they lead to legal problems, or if they interfere with social relationships. For several specific types of paraphilias, the person would qualify for a diagnosis if he or she acted on the urge. These include pedophilia, exhibitionism, voyeurism, and frotteurism (see descriptions in the following pages). For sexual sadism, acting on the urge would qualify the person for a diagnosis only if the partner had not consented to the activity. Acting on the other forms of paraphilic urges (masochism, fetishism, and transvestic fetishism) would not be sufficient for a diagnosis unless the urges or fantasies lead to significant personal distress or interfere with the person's ability to function.

It is actually somewhat misleading, or imprecise, to say that paraphilias are defined solely in terms of reactions to unusual stimuli. The central problem is that sexual arousal is dependent on images that are detached from reciprocal, loving relationships with another adult (Levine, Risen, & Althof, 1990). As noted by University of Toronto researcher Ron Langevin, themes of aggression, violence, and hostility are common in paraphilic fantasies, as are impulses involving strangers or unwilling partners (Langevin, 1983). Rather than focusing on whether the stimuli are common or uncommon, some experts such as William Marshall at Queen's University place principal emphasis on the lack of human intimacy that is associated with many forms of paraphilias (Marshall et al., 1996; Moser, 2001).

Compulsion and lack of flexibility are also important features of paraphilic behaviours. Paraphilias may take up a lot of time and consume much of the person's energy. In that sense, they are similar to the addictions. People with paraphilic disorders are not simply aroused by unusual images or fantasies. They feel *compelled* to engage in certain acts that may be personally degrading or harmful to others, in spite of the fact that these actions are often repulsive to others and are sometimes illegal. The following case describes some of the central features of paraphilias.

### BRIEF CASE STUDY

**Paraphilia**

For the past 40 years, Jon has masturbated to images of barely clad women violently wrestling each other. Periodically throughout his marriage, he has tried to involve his wife in wrestling matches with her friends and, eventually, with their adolescent daughter. When Jon was drunk, he occasionally embarrassed his wife by trying to pick fights between her and other women. On

*continued*

cont.

summer vacations, he sometimes jokingly suggested the women wrestle. During much of his sober life, however, his daydreams of women wrestling were private experiences that preoccupied only him. He amassed a collection of magazines and videotapes depicting women wrestling, to which he would resort when driven by the need for excitement.

Jon presented for help with his inability to maintain his erection with his wife for intercourse. With the exception of procreational sex, he was not able to consummate his long marriage. He was able to become erect if his wife described herself wrestling other women while he stimulated his penis in front of her, but he always lost his erection when intercourse was attempted (Levine, Risen, & Althof, 1990).◆

This case illustrates the way in which paraphilias can interfere with a person's life, especially relationships with other people. Jon's preoccupation with fantasies of women wrestling led him to say and do things that disrupted his marriage and his friendships with other people. Many people with paraphilias experience sexual dysfunction involving desire, arousal, or orgasm during conventional sexual behaviour with a partner. The wives of men with paraphilias frequently protest that their husbands are not interested in their sexual relationship. In fact, the husband may be actively engaged in frequent masturbation to paraphilic fantasies. Cases of this sort present a diagnostic challenge to the clinician, who must distinguish a paraphilia from what might otherwise appear to be low sexual desire.

Several researchers, including Michael Seto and Howard Barbaree at the University of Toronto, have noted that men with paraphilias can typically be described as timid, low in self-esteem, and lacking in social skills (Seto & Barbaree, 2000). It is, of course, difficult to know whether these characteristics are traits that set the stage for the development of paraphilias or whether they are consequences associated with the performance of sexual behaviours that are considered repugnant by society.

## Classification

Although they are listed as distinct disorders, it might be more useful to think of the paraphilias as one diagnostic category, with the specific forms listed in DSM-IV-TR representing subtypes of this single disorder (Frances, First, & Pincus, 1995). The primary types of paraphilias described in the following pages are the ones most often seen in clinics that specialize in the treatment of sexual disorders. Not surprisingly, they are also the ones that frequently lead to a person being arrested.

**Fetishism** Anthropologists use the word *fetish* to describe an object that is believed to have magical powers to protect or help its owner. In psychopathology, **fetishism** refers to the association of sexual arousal with nonliving objects. The range of objects that can become associated with sexual arousal is virtually unlimited, but fetishism most often involves women's underwear, shoes and boots, or products made out of rubber or leather (Junginger, 1997; Mason, 1997). The person may go to great lengths, including burglary, to obtain certain kinds of fetish objects.

People who fit the description of fetishism typically masturbate while holding, rubbing, or smelling the fetish object. Particular sensory qualities of the object—texture, visual appearance, and smell—can be very important in determining whether or not the person finds it arousing. In addition to holding or rubbing the object, the person may wear, or ask his sexual partner to wear, the object during sexual activity. The person may be unable to become sexually aroused in the absence of the fetish object.

An intense sexual attraction to specific body parts (most often legs or feet, and excluding genitals, breasts, and buttocks) is known as *partialism*. Many experts believe that partialism is a form of fetishism (de Silva, 1993). In DSM-IV-TR, partialism is excluded from fetishism and listed in a miscellaneous category called "paraphilias not otherwise specified" (see Table 12–2).

**Transvestic Fetishism** A *transvestite* is a person who dresses in the clothing of the other gender. In DSM-IV-TR, **transvestic fetishism** is defined as cross-dressing for the purpose of sexual arousal. It has been described primarily among heterosexual men and should not be confused with the behaviour of some gay men known as *drag queens* (for whom cross-dressing has a very different purpose and meaning). DSM-IV-TR restricts the definition

**TABLE 12-2 Other Types of Paraphilias**

| Name | Focus of Sexual Urges and Fantasies |
|---|---|
| Telephone scatologia | Obscene phone calls |
| Necrophilia | Corpses |
| Partialism | One specific part of the body |
| Zoophilia | Animals |
| Coprophilia | Feces |
| Klismaphilia | Enemas |
| Urophilia | Urine |
| Stigmatophilia | Piercing; marking body; tattoos |

to heterosexual men, but research evidence suggests that a small proportion of transvestites are bisexual, homosexual, or not sexually active with another person (Bullough & Bullough, 1997).

People who engage in transvestic fetishism usually keep a collection of female clothes that are used to cross-dress. Some wear only a single article of women's clothing, such as female underwear, covered by male clothing. Others dress completely as women, including makeup, jewellery, and accessories. Cross-dressing may be done in public or only in private. The person masturbates while he is cross-dressed, often imagining himself to be a male as well as the female object of his own sexual fantasy. Aside from their interest in cross-dressing, men with transvestic fetishism are unremarkably masculine in their interests, occupations, and other behaviours. Most of these men get married and have children (Schott, 1995).

According to University of Toronto psychologists Ken Zucker and Ray Blanchard, for some men, transvestism may eventually lead to feelings of dissatisfaction with being male (Zucker & Blanchard, 1997). They may eventually want to live permanently as women. These men, who develop persistent discomfort with their gender role or identity, would be assigned a subtype diagnosis of *transvestic fetishism with gender dysphoria*.

**Sexual Masochism** People who become sexually aroused when they are subjected to pain or embarrassment are called masochists. DSM-IV-TR defines **sexual masochism** as recurrent, intense sexually arousing fantasies, urges, or impulses involving being humiliated, beaten, bound, or otherwise made to suffer. People may act on these impulses by themselves or with a partner. In some large cities, clubs cater to the sexual interests of masochistic men and women, who pay people to punish and abuse them (Ernulf & Innala, 1995).

The person may become aroused by being bound, blindfolded, spanked, pinched, whipped, verbally abused, forced to crawl and bark like a dog, or in some other way made to experience pain or feelings of shame and disgrace. One relatively common masochistic fantasy takes the form of being forced to display one's naked body to other people. Masochists desire certain types of pain (which are carefully controlled to remain within specified limits, usually unpleasant but not agonizing), but

*Some gay men who dress in women's clothes refer to themselves as "drag queens." This is different from transvestic fetishism, which applies only to heterosexual men whose cross-dressing is associated with intense, sexually arousing fantasies or urges.*

they also go to great lengths to avoid injury during their contrived, often ritualized experiences (Stoller, 1991). They do not enjoy, and are not immune to, painful experiences that lie outside these limited areas of their lives.

The following first-person account was written by Daphne Merkin (1996), an accomplished writer whose fascinating and controversial essay on masochism appeared in *The New Yorker*.

## BRIEF CASE STUDY

### Masochism

The fact is that I cannot remember a time when I didn't think about being spanked as a sexually gratifying act, didn't fantasize about being reduced to a craven object of desire by a firm male hand. Depending on my mood, these daydreams were marked by an atmosphere of greater or lesser ravishment, but all of them featured similar ingredients. Most important among them was a heightened—and deeply pleasurable—sense of exposure, brought about by the fact that enormous attention was being paid to my bottom, and by the fact that there was an aspect of helpless display attached to this particular body part. This scenario, in which my normally alert self was reduced to a condition of wordless compliance via a specific ritual of chastisement, exerted a grip that was the more strong because I felt it to be so at odds with the intellectually weighty, morally upright part of me. (p. 99)

These fantasies and urges made Merkin feel uncomfortable, and she kept them to herself for many years. Being cautious and somewhat inhibited—certainly not prone to illicit sexual adventures—she worried about the boundaries of her masochistic desires. If she ever acted on them, where would she stop? And how would her partner respond? After many years of privately harbouring masochistic sexual fantasies, Merkin finally described her fascination with spanking to a man whom she had been dating for several months. She was in her late twenties at the time, and eventually married this man.

The following paragraph describes what happened after her admission:

He appeared delighted at the prospect of implementing my wishes, and so it was that I found myself in the position I had been dreaming of for years: thrust over a man's knee, being soundly spanked for some concocted misdeed. The sheer tactile stimulation of it—the chastening sting—would have been enough to arouse me, but there was also, at last, the heady sense of emotional release: I was and was not a child; was and was not being reduced; was and was not being forced into letting go; was and was not the one in control. I had fantasized about this event for so long that in the back of my mind there had always lurked the fear that its gratification would prove disappointing. I needn't have worried; the reality of spanking, at least initially, was as good as the dream. (pp. 112–113)

Merkin tired of the spankings after she gave birth to her daughter, but the fantasies and urges returned several years later, after she had been separated from her husband. She eventually became involved in a relationship with another man that she described as "a fairly conventional romance that included some light (sadism and masochism)." After their mutual interests and consenting activities had escalated, Merkin found the relationship disturbing:

It occurred to me that underneath my own limited participation in this world I felt enormous resentment; I was following the steps in a dance I couldn't control. Spanking and its accoutrements may have helped to subdue my simmering rage toward men—as well as theirs toward me—but it also demonstrated how far I was from healthy intimacy, from the real give-and-take that makes a relationship viable. (p. 114) ◆

This case illustrates the compelling and often contradictory nature of the fantasies that are associated with paraphilias. This successful and independent woman, who did not believe in using corporal punishment with her own daughter, found great pleasure associated with fantasies of being spanked by a man. Merkin would not have qualified for a diagnosis of sexual masochism, even after she had acted on her fantasies, unless she experienced subjective distress or social impairment as a result.

*This photo shows the staff at a bondage club. The patrons of such clubs are often highly educated and occupationally successful.*

Like Daphne Merkin, many people who engage in masochistic sexual practices are highly educated and occupationally successful (Levitt, Moser, & Jamison, 1994). Masochists tend to be disproportionately represented among the privileged groups in society. This pattern leads to the suggestion that masochism may be motivated by an attempt to escape temporarily from the otherwise constant burden of maintaining personal control and pursuing self-esteem (Baumeister & Butler, 1997).

This may account for some masochistic behaviours but seems insufficient to explain a form of sexual masochism called *autoerotic asphyxia*. This involves deliberately depriving oneself of oxygen—often by strangulation or enclosing one's head in a plastic bag—to the point of unconsciousness. The person finds this to be sexually stimulating. According to a study of 19 cases of autoerotic asphyxial death that occurred between 1978 and 1989 in Alberta, the victim is usually (but not always) a single male aged 15 to 29 years. The autoerotic asphyxial activity was usually performed repetitively, and when the person was alone. Accidental death typically occurs when there is a failure in the "safety" mechanism design to alleviate neck compression. Friends and family usually do not find out about the fetish until some mishap has occurred (Tough, Butt, & Sanders, 1994). Toronto psychiatrist Stephen Hucker has further noted that people who practise autoerotic asphyxia also engage in other forms of sexual masochism, such as self-administered electric shocks (Hucker, 1995).

**Sexual Sadism** Someone who derives pleasure by inflicting physical or mental pain on other people is called a *sadist*. The term is based on the writings of the Marquis de Sade, whose novels describe the use of torture and cruelty for erotic purposes. DSM-IV-TR defines **sexual sadism** in terms of intense, sexually arousing fantasies, urges, or behaviours that involve the psychological or physical suffering of a victim. Sadistic fantasies often involve asserting dominance over the victim; the experience of power and control may be as important as inflicting pain (Hucker, 1997). Some people engage in sadistic sexual rituals with a consenting partner (who may be a sexual masochist) who willingly suffers pain or humiliation. Others act on sadistic sexual urges with nonconsenting partners. In some cases, the severity of the sadistic behaviours escalates over time.

**Exhibitionism** DSM-IV-TR defines **exhibitionism** in terms of the following criteria: "1. Over a period of at least 6 months, recurrent, intense sexually arousing fantasies, sexual urges, or behaviours involving exposure of one's genitals to an unsuspecting stranger. 2. The person has acted on these sexual urges, or the sexual urges or fantasies cause marked distress or interpersonal difficulty" (p. 569). This behaviour is also known as *indecent exposure*. Many different patterns of behaviour fit into this category. About half of these men have erections while exposing themselves, and some masturbate at the time. The others usually masturbate shortly after the experience while fantasizing about the victim's reaction. Their intent usually involves a desire to shock the observer, but sometimes they harbour fantasies that the involuntary observer will become sexually aroused. They rarely attempt to touch or otherwise molest their victims, who are usually women or children (Maletzky, 1997; Murphy, 1997).

Exhibitionism is almost exclusively a male disorder. Most exhibitionists begin to expose themselves when they are teenagers or in their early twenties. Over a third of all sexual offences in Canada and other countries involve exhibitionism (Rooth, 1973). Toronto researchers Ron Langevin and Rubin Lang (1987) found that most exhibitionists are married and most have satisfactory sexual relationships with adult women. Acts of exhibitionism seldom occur in isolation; men who engage in this type of behaviour tend to do it repeatedly (Abel & Osborn, 1992).

**Voyeurism** The focus of sexual arousal in **voyeurism** is the act of observing an unsuspecting person, usually a stranger, who is naked, in the process of disrobing, or engaging in sexual activity. Many people, especially men, are sexually aroused by the sight of people who are partially clad or naked. Voyeurs are not aroused by watching people who know that they are being observed. The process of looking ("peeping") is arousing in its own right. The person might fantasize about having a sexual relationship with the people who are being observed, but direct contact is seldom sought. In fact, the secret nature of the observation and the risk of discovery may contribute in an important way to the arousing nature of the situation. The voyeur reaches orgasm by masturbating during observation or later while remembering what he saw. Most keep their distance from the victim and are not dangerous, but there are exceptions to this rule (King, 1996).

**Frotteurism** In **frotteurism**, a person who is fully clothed becomes sexually aroused by touching or rubbing his genitals against other, nonconsenting people. The frotteur usually chooses crowded places, such as sidewalks and public transportation, so that he can easily escape arrest. He either rubs his genitals against the victim's thighs and buttocks or fondles her genitalia or breasts (Horley, 2001).

Like exhibitionism, frotteurism is a high-frequency form of paraphilia; interviews with people being treated for frotteurism indicate that they may engage in hundreds of individual paraphilic acts (Abel et al., 1987). People who engage in frotteurism seek to escape as quickly as possible after touching or rubbing against the other person. They do not want further sexual contact.

*Gary Blair Walker, age 50, is considered one of the worst pedophiles in Canada. He has admitted to sexually assaulting more than 200 boys over a period of 30 years. Four of his victims, all from a hockey team he coached, later took their own lives.*

**Pedophilia** People who persistently engage in sexual activities with children exhibit what is undoubtedly the most alarming and objectionable form of paraphilic behaviour: pedophilia. Every year, thousands of children in Canada are referred to child protective services because of suspected child abuse. Research conducted throughout the world, including investigations at universities in Ontario and Manitoba, indicates that there are many different long-term consequences of childhood sexual abuse, including problems in sexual functioning, anxiety disorders, mood disorders and suicidal behaviour (Abdulrehman & De Luca, 2001; Lipman et al., 2001; MacMillan et al., 2001; Rumstein-McKean & Hunsley, 2001). Martin Kruze is a tragic case in point. He, along with many other young hockey players, was sexually abused by pedophiles working in Toronto's Maple Leaf Gardens during the 1970s to 1990s (Vine & Challen, 2002). Many boys were traumatized. Martin, who as an adult blew the whistle on the abuse, later committed suicide.

**Pedophilia** entails recurrent, intense, sexually arousing fantasies, sexual urges, or behaviours involving sexual activity with a prepubescent child (generally age 13 years or younger). In order to qualify for a diagnosis of pedophilia in DSM-IV-TR, the person must be at least 16 years of age and at least 5 years older than the child. The terms *pedophile* and *child molester* are sometimes used interchangeably, but this practice confuses legal definitions with psychopathology. A child molester is a person who has committed a sexual offence against a child victim. Therefore the term depends on legal definitions of "sexual offence" and "child victim," which can vary from one state or country to another. In many locations, a child might be anyone under the age of consent, even if that person has reached puberty. Not all child molesters are pedophiles. Furthermore, as noted by University of Toronto researchers Howard Bararee and Michael Seto, some pedophiles may not have molested children, because the diagnosis can be made on the basis of recurrent fantasies in the absence of actual behaviour (Barbaree & Seto, 1997).

Pedophilia includes a great variety of behaviours and sexual preferences. Some pedophiles are attracted only to children, whereas others are sometimes attracted to adults. Most pedophiles are heterosexual, and the victims of pedophilia are more often girls than boys. Some offenders are attracted to both girls and boys. Sexual contact with children typically involves caressing and genital fondling. Vaginal, oral, and anal penetration are less common, and physical violence is relatively rare. In many cases, the child willingly and naively complies with the adult's intentions. In most cases, the child knows the person who molests him or her. More than half of all offences occur in the home of either the child or the offender. Research indicates that men with pedophilia, compared to other types of sex offenders, are more likely to have been themselves sexually abused as children (Freund & Kuban, 1994; Freund, Watson, & Dickey, 1990; Marshall, Serran, & Cortoni, 2000). This raises the possibility that early experiences may somehow contribute to pedophilia. However, note that the association is far from perfect; only some victims of sexual abuse develop pedophilia, and many people with this paraphilia have not been sexually abused. It is possible that childhood sexual abuse is a nonspecific factor that increases the risk for many kinds of psychological problems. Clearly, many factors are important in shaping pedophilia. Sexual abuse may be one of them.

Incestuous relationships, in which the pedophile molests his own children, should perhaps be distinguished from those in which the offender is only casually acquainted with the victim. **Incest** refers to sexual activity between close blood relatives, such as father–daughter, mother–son, or between siblings. The definition may also be expanded to include stepchildren and their stepparents in reconstituted families. Most reported cases of incest involve fathers and stepfathers sexually abusing daughters and stepdaughters (Cole, 1992). Many incest perpetrators would not be considered pedophiles, either because their victims are postpubescent adolescents or because they are also young themselves (such as male adolescents molesting their younger sisters). Perhaps as many as half of the men who commit incest have also engaged in sexual activity with children outside their own families (Abel & Osborn, 1992). This subgroup of pedophilic incest perpetrators may be the most harmful and the most difficult to treat. Their personality style is typically passive and dependent. They are unable to empathize with the plight of their victims, perhaps in part because they were absent or uninvolved in early child-care responsibilities (Williams & Finkelhor, 1990).

**TABLE 12–3 Prevalence of Forced Sexual Activity (Lifetime Occurrence)**

| Category | Men | Women |
|---|---|---|
| Never forced sexually | 96.1% | 77.2% |
| Forced by other gender person | 1.3 | 21.6 |
| Forced by same gender person | 1.9 | 0.3 |
| Forced by both men and women | 0.4 | 0.5 |

*Source:* E.O. Laumann, J.H. Gagnon, R.T. Michael, and S. Michaels, 1994, *The Social Organization of Sexuality: Sexual Practices in the United States.* Chicago: University of Chicago Press.

**Rape and Sexual Assault** The legal definition of **rape** includes "acts involving nonconsensual sexual penetration obtained by physical force, by threat of bodily harm, or when the victim is incapable of giving consent by virtue of mental illness, mental retardation, or intoxication" (Goodman et al., 1993). Rape and sexual assault are disturbingly common events. For example, in a survey of 551 women living in Winnipeg, 6 percent reported that they had been raped, and 21 percent reported having been sexually assaulted at some point in their lives (Brickman & Briere, 1984). In a large survey of over 3000 students from universities and colleges across Canada, 28 percent of women reported being sexually abused in the past year, whereas 11 percent of men reported having victimized a female dating partner in this way during the same period (DeKeseredy, 1997). For Canadians in general, it has been estimated that over 30 percent of men and over 50 percent of women have been sexually assaulted (Canadian Committee on Sexual Offences Against Children and Youth, 1984). In most cases the assaults occur before age 18. The impact of sexual assault on the victim is described in Chapter 7.

The frequency of coercive sex was studied as part of the NHSLS (Laumann et al., 1994). The 3500 participants were asked whether they had ever been forced to do something sexually that they did not want to do. The question was focused broadly and did not necessarily focus only on acts involving penetration or threats of violence. The prevalence of forced sex is presented separately for men and women in Table 12–3. Slightly more than one out of every five women in the sample reported that they had been forced by a man to engage in some kind of sexual activity against their will. Among those women who had experienced forced sex, 30 percent said that they had been forced sexually by more than one person.

Some rapes are committed by strangers, but many others—known as *acquaintance rapes*—are committed by men who know their victims (Wiehe & Richards, 1995). To illustrate, in a study of more than 1000 undergraduates at the University of Alberta, 44 percent of students who had experienced unwanted sexual experiences reported that the offender was a romantic partner (Elliot, Odynak, & Krahn, 1992). Also consider the evidence from women in the NHSLS who had been victims of forced sex (excluding those who had been forced by more than one person). Their relationship to the people who forced them to have sex is illustrated in Figure 12–5. Most reported that the person was either someone with whom they were in love or their spouse. Only 4 percent were forced to do something sexual by a stranger.

Rapes are committed by many different kinds of people for many different reasons (Newcomb, 1993). In DeKeseredy's (1997) survey of Canadian undergraduates, men who had sexually abused tended to hold a "patriarchal ideology," in which they believed that women should be obedient, respectful, dependent, and sexually submissive toward men. Such beliefs may increase the odds that a man will become sexually abusive. Many sex offenders were sexually abused themselves as children (Dhawan & Marshall, 1996), and may humiliate women as a way of expressing anger and power over women, and of taking revenge. For still other rapists, violent cues appear to enhance sexual arousal, so they are motivated to combine sex with aggression (Barbaree & Marshall, 1991; Marshall & Moulden, 2001). Exposure to pornography also appears to be a contributing factor. According to a recent review by Michael Seto and colleagues (2001), from the Centre for Addiction and Mental Health in Toronto, the evidence indicates that exposure to pornography may increase the odds of sexual aggression in people who are already predisposed to sexually offend.

The architects of DSM-IV-TR considered including rape as a type of paraphilia. This proposal was rejected, primarily because it might imply that rape is always motivated by sexual arousal, and it is not. Nevertheless, the behaviour of some rapists does include essential features of paraphilias: recurrent, intense sexually arousing fantasies and urges that involve the suffering of nonconsenting persons. Half the convicted rapists in one study reported a history of other types of paraphilia: pedophilia (24 percent), exhibitionism (19 percent), and voyeurism (17 percent) (Abel & Gouleau, 1990). Current efforts to classify sex offenders attempt to distinguish between those for whom deviant sexual arousal contributes to the act and those whose behaviour is motivated primarily by anger or violent impulses (Knight, 1999).

**Forced Sex: Relationship of Perpetrator to Victim**

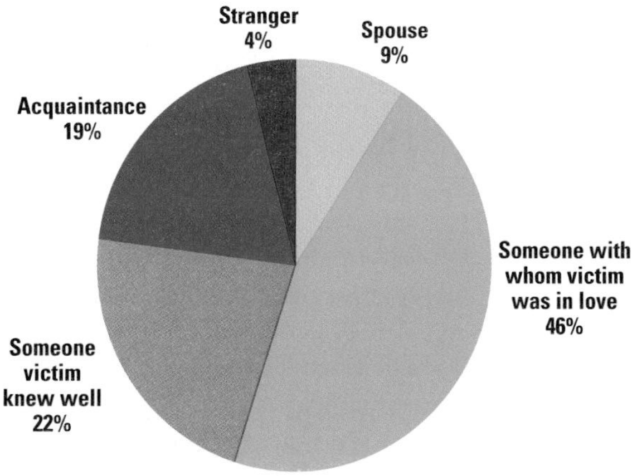


**FIGURE 12–5: As this chart shows, most NHSLS respondents who were forced into sexual activity knew the person who coerced them.**

*Source:* E.O. Laumann, J.H. Gagnon, R.T. Michael, and S. Michaels, 1994, *The Social Organization of Sexuality: Sexual Practices in the United States,* p. 338. Chicago: University of Chicago Press.

## Epidemiology

There is very little information about the frequency of various types of unconventional sexual behaviour. This is especially true for victimless or noncoercive forms of paraphilia, such as fetishism, transvestic fetishism, and sexual masochism, because most of these people seldom seek treatment or come to the attention of law enforcement officials. Furthermore, the fact that these forms of behaviour are considered deviant or perverse makes it unlikely that people who engage in them will readily divulge their secret urges and fantasies. The large commercial market for paraphilic pornography and paraphernalia suggests that paraphilias are not uncommon (APA, 2000).

The majority of all cases of pedophilia are men, although the disorder is occasionally seen in women (Denov, 2001; Fedoroff, Fishell, & Fedoroff, 1999). Research from Canada, England, and the United States suggests that paraphilias may have been overlooked in women (Denov, 2001; Fedoroff, Fishell, & Fedoroff, 1999). Although the prevalence of paraphilias in women is unknown, they are probably rare. In 1999 only 2 percent of convicted sex offenders in Canada were women (Canadian Centre for Justice Statistics, 1999). But in recent years there have been a number of widely publicized newspaper and TV reports of female high-school teachers, in their late twenties, thirties, or older, having affairs with their adolescent students (e.g., Denov, 2001). Reports have come from schools in B.C., Ontario, and elsewhere. Some of these may be cases of pedophilia, especially where the female teacher persistently seeks sexual encounters with young students.

The most common paraphilias seen in clinics specializing in these problems are pedophilia, voyeurism, and exhibitionism (APA, 2000). Sexual sadism and sexual masochism are much less commonly seen, at least among men. Research from Toronto's Centre for Addiction and Mental Health suggests that for those rare cases in which women have paraphilias, they are most likely to have pedophilia, sexual sadism, and/or exhibitionism (Fedoroff, Fishell, & Fedoroff, 1999).

Paraphilias are seldom isolated phenomena. People who exhibit one type of paraphilia often exhibit others. Gosselin and Wilson (1980) surveyed men who belonged to private clubs that cater to fetishists, sadomasochists, and transvestites, and they found that the members of different clubs often shared the same interests. This overlap is illustrated in Figure 12–6. This pattern has been called *crossing* of paraphilic behaviours.

There are limits to the amount of overlap among paraphilias. In a study of 117 fatal cases of autoerotic asphyxia, Blanchard and Hucker (1991) found that some people engaged in multiple fetishes such as autoerotic asphyxia, bondage, and transvestism. However, the greatest degree of transvestism was associated with intermediate rather than high levels of bondage, suggesting that "response competition" from bondage may limit the asphyxiator's involvement in a third paraphilia such as transvestism.

**Overlap among Three Major Types of Paraphilia**

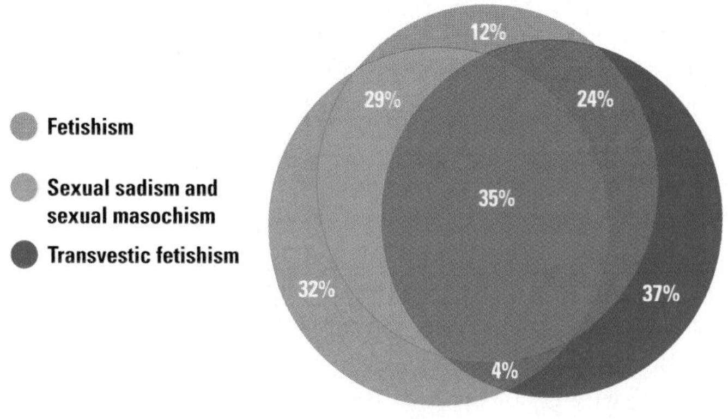


**FIGURE 12–6: The extent of overlap in the interests of three major types of paraphilias. Note that only 37 percent of men who practice fetishistic transvestism, 32 percent of men who practice sexual sadism and masochism, and 12 percent of those who practice fetishism exhibited those interests exclusively.**

*Source:* G.D. Wilson, 1987, An ethological approach to sexual deviation. In G.D. Wilson (Ed.), *Variant Sexuality: Research and Theory*, p. 92. London: Croom Helm.

## Etiology

The high rate of overlap among paraphilias indicates that the etiology of these behaviours might be most appropriately viewed in terms of common factors rather than in terms of distinct pathways that lead exclusively to one form of paraphilia or another. Those experiences and conditions that predispose an individual to one form of paraphilia are apparently also likely to lead to another. In the following pages we review a number of proposals regarding the etiology of paraphilias. Some of these have been associated with specific types of paraphilia. For the most part, however, they are concerned more generally with many forms of paraphilias.

The epidemiological evidence suggests another important pattern that must be explained by any theory of paraphilias: They are more prevalent among men than among women. The exception to this rule seems to be masochism, which may be equally common in both genders. We might conclude, therefore, that the development of masochism may be governed by different factors than those that account for the etiology of other types of paraphilias.

**Biological Factors** Vernon Quinsey (2003) at Queen's University argues that people *discover* rather than *choose* their sexual interests, typically beginning before puberty and associated with an increase in the secretion of sex hormones from the adrenal glands. According to Quinsey, the determinants of the direction of sexual interest (i.e., preference for the same or opposite sex) arise earlier, due to intrauterine hormonal effects.

## Further Thoughts The Classification of Rapists

Raymond Knight studied convicted rapists who were imprisoned at the Massachusetts Treatment Centre (MTC) for sexually dangerous persons (Knight, 1999; Knight, Prentky, & Cerce, 1994). His research indicates that rape is motivated by both aggressive and sexual components, in varying mixtures. Knight developed a classification system for rapists, known as the MTC-R3, which includes four main categories (see Table 12–4).

Two of the categories include men whose motivation for sexual assault is primarily sexual in nature. *Sadistic* rapists exhibit features that are close to the DSM-IV-TR definition of a paraphilia. Their behaviour is determined by a combination of sexual and aggressive impulses. The *nonsadistic* category also includes men who are preoccupied with sexual fantasies, but these fantasies are not blended with images of violence and aggression. The sexual aggression of these men may result, in part, from serious deficits in the ability to process social cues, such as the intentions of women (Lipton, McDonel, & McFall, 1987; McFall, 1990).

The other two categories in Knight and Prentky's system describe men whose primary motivation for rape is not sexual. *Vindictive* rapists seem intent on violence directed exclusively toward women. Their aggression is not erotically motivated, as with sadistic rapists. *Opportunistic* rapists are men with an extensive history of impulsive behaviour in many kinds of settings and who might be considered psychopaths (see Chapter 9). Their sexual behaviour is governed largely by immediate environmental cues. They will use whatever force is necessary to ensure compliance, but they express anger only in response to the victim's resistance.

The utility of the MTC-R3 typology has been examined in a study of rapists who were being treated at a sexual behaviour clinic (Barbaree et al., 1994). Most of these men could be placed reliably into one of Knight and Prentky's main categories. Overall, 22 of the men fit the description of the opportunistic rapist, 14 exhibited features of the vindictive type, 15 were described as nonsadistic rapists, and 8 fell into the sadistic category.

The investigators compared rapists in the four major categories on several laboratory measures. Deviant sexual arousal was measured using a penile strain gauge (see Research Methods on p. 415) while each subject listened to a series of audiotapes describing scenes of mutually consenting sex and of rape. Sadistic and nonsadistic rapists showed greater sexual arousal in response to the rape scenes than did the vindictive and opportunistic rapists. This pattern of results supports the validity of Knight and Prentky's classification system. It indicates that deviant patterns of sexual arousal may play a more important role in the sexual aggression displayed by the sadistic and nonsadistic rapists (see also Polaschek, 1997).

These studies help explain some of the factors that contribute to the disturbing rate of sexual aggression in our society. They may lay the foundation for efforts aimed at the prevention of this form of violence as well as the treatment of rapists. We must keep in mind, however, that this type of research is based almost exclusively on a small subset of rapists, those who have been convicted of their offences. It would be naive to generalize from this group to all rapists, for several reasons. Most instances of acquaintance rape are not reported. Among those rapes that are reported to the police, less than 10 percent ever lead to conviction. Therefore studies of convicted rapists must be interpreted with caution. We should not conclude that the motivations of all—or even most—rapists are accurately portrayed in these studies. ◆

**TABLE 12–4 Basic Structure of the MTC Typology for Rapists**

| Primary Motivation | General Category | Description of Rapists |
|---|---|---|
| **Aggressive** | Vindictive | Actions intended to degrade and humiliate the victim |
| | Opportunistic | Impulsive, unplanned actions; seeking immediate gratification; indifferent to the victim's plight |
| **Sexual** | Sadistic | Preoccupation with sadistic sexual fantasies; actions typically brutal and violent |
| | Nonsadistic | Distorted views of sexuality and women; feelings of inferiority; poor social skills |

*Source:* Adapted from R.A. Knight and R.A. Prentky, 1990, Classifying sexual offenders. In W. Marshall, D.R. Laws, and H.E. Barbaree (Eds.), *Handbook of Sexual Assault: Issues, Theories, and Treatment of the Offender*, p. 43. New York: Plenum.

Most of the research regarding the role of biological factors in the etiology of paraphilias has focused on the endocrine system (see Figure 2–4), the collection of glands that regulate sexual responses through the release of hormones (Collaer & Hines, 1995). Some studies of convicted sexually violent offenders have found evidence of elevated levels of testosterone. These reports must be viewed with some skepticism, however, for two reasons.

First, the participants in these studies are invariably convicted sexual offenders. Thus, it is not clear that the findings can be generalized to all people with paraphilias. Second, there is a high rate of alcoholism and drug abuse among men convicted of sexual crimes. For that reason, we do not know whether the biological abnormalities observed in these men are causes of their deviant sexual behaviour or consequences of prolonged substance abuse (Langevin, 1992).

Neurological abnormalities may also be involved in the development of paraphilias. Structures located in the temporal lobes of the brain, especially the amygdala and the hippocampus, appear to play an important role in the control of both aggression and sexual behaviour. These limbic structures, in conjunction with the hypothalamus, form a circuit that regulates biologically significant behaviours that sometimes are whimsically called the four Fs—feeding, fighting, fleeing, and sexual behaviour (Valenstein, 1973). In 1937, two scientists reported that after extensive bilateral damage to their temporal lobes, rhesus monkeys showed a dramatic increase in sexual activity, as well as a number of related behavioural and perceptual abnormalities. The monkeys apparently tried to copulate with a variety of inappropriate partners, including the investigators. This pattern has subsequently been called the Kluver–Bucy syndrome, named after the scientists who made the original observation.

Inspired by the suggestion that damage to the temporal lobe can lead to unusual patterns of sexual behaviour, clinical scientists have studied a number of neurological and neuropsychological factors in convicted sex offenders. Some reports indicate that men with pedophilia and exhibitionism show subtle forms of left temporal lobe dysfunction, as evidenced by abnormal patterns of electrophysiological response and impaired performance on neuropsychological tests (Flor-Henry, 1987; Murphy, 1997).

Some men with fetishism exhibit diffuse signs of neurological impairment, but these are also focused predominantly in the left temporal lobe. Similar findings have been reported for sexually sadistic criminals (Gratzer & Bradford, 1995). Before these results are interpreted too broadly, however, it should also be noted that most people who suffer from temporal lobe epilepsy do not engage in paraphilic behaviours. In fact, the most frequent result of temporal lobe epilepsy is a reduction in sexual activity (Huws, Shubsachs, & Taylor, 1991; Murphy, 1997). It seems reasonable to conclude that some cases of paraphilia are caused, at least in part, by endocrine and neurological abnormalities, but the relations among these factors are not entirely clear.

**Psychosocial Factors** Some types of paraphilias seem to be distortions of the normal mating process when viewed in a broad, evolutionary context. Kurt Freund at the Toronto's Centre for Addiction and Mental Health developed the notion of *courtship disorder* to explain paraphilias. Drawing an analogy between animal courtship rituals and human sexual behaviour, Freund described four phases of human mating: (1) looking for and evaluating the suitability of a potential partner, (2) pretactile interaction (e.g., smiling at, posturing for, or talking to a prospective partner), (3) tactile interaction (e.g., embracing, petting), and (4) sexual intercourse. Freund suggested that a particular class of erotic anomalies may be seen as distorted counterparts of the four normal phases: (1) voyeurism (a distortion of phase 1), (2) exhibitionism and obscene telephoning (distortions of phase 2), (3) frotteurism (distortion of phase 3), and (4) preferential rape—a paraphilic preference for coercive sex (distortion of phase 4). Freund and colleagues (e.g., Freund & Blanchard, 1986; Freund & Seto, 1998) presented data showing that two or more of these anomalies are often found in the same individual, suggesting that they are expressions of a common underlying problem known as courtship disorder. The strongest association is between voyeurism and exhibitionism (Freund, Seto, & Kuban, 1997). Courtship disorder is thought to arise from a disruption in whatever mechanisms facilitate the identification of a sexual partner and govern behaviours used to attract a partner.

If people with paraphilias have somehow failed to learn more adaptive forms of courtship behaviour, what sort of childhood experiences might have produced such unexpected results? Several background factors have been observed repeatedly among people who engage in atypical sexual behaviours (Wincze, 1989). These include the following:

- Early crossing of normative sexual boundaries through a direct experience (for example, sexual abuse by an adult)

*Frotteurs touch and rub against nonconsenting victims in crowded places. These offensive behaviours reflect problems achieving intimate relationships with other people.*

or an indirect experience (hearing about a father's atypical sexual behaviour). In other words, particular forms of classical conditioning or observational learning.

- Lack of a consistent parental environment in which normative sexual behaviour and values were modelled (i.e., observational learning).
- Lack of self-esteem.
- Lack of confidence and ability in social interactions.
- Ignorance and poor understanding of human sexuality.

All these factors may increase the probability that a person might experiment with unusual types of sexual stimulation or employ maladaptive sexual behaviours.

Researchers such as James Pfaus at Concordia University have reported that animal research supports the view that classical conditioning and observational learning could cause paraphilias (Pfaus, Kippin, & Centeno, 2001). Such forms of learning are probably important, although other factors may also be involved. If fetishes were acquired simply by conditioning, for example, then most of us should have fetishes to stimuli that are inadvertently and repeatedly connected with sexual activity, such as bedsheets, pillows, even ceilings (Breslow, 1989; Marshall & Eccles, 1993).

Although the most notable feature of paraphilias is sexual arousal, ultimately the paraphilias are problems in social relationships. Interpersonal skills may, therefore, play as important a role as sexual arousal. William Marshall, a psychologist at Queen's University, has argued that the risk for committing sexual offences is increased by early learning experiences that cause the person to have low self-confidence and poor social skills. These factors increase the likelihood that the person will engage in paraphilic behaviours, which require little in the way of social skills. Sexual offences also involve the domination or humiliation of victims, and thereby may give a sense of power to men who are otherwise lacking in power and self-confidence. Offensive sexual behaviours, such as those observed in pedophilia, are maladaptive attempts to achieve intimacy through sex. These efforts are invariably unsuccessful and self-defeating in the sense that they serve to isolate the person further from the rest of the community. Paradoxically, the pattern may become deeply ingrained because it results in the momentary pleasure associated with orgasm and because it offers the illusory hope of eventually achieving intimacy with another person. These and other factors are implicated in Marshall's theory (see Marshall & Barbaree, 1990; Marshall, Anderson, & Champagne, 1997; Marshall, Hudson, & Hodkinson, 1993).

### Treatment

The treatment of paraphilias is different from the treatment of sexual dysfunctions in several ways. Perhaps most important is the fact that most people with paraphilias do not enter treatment voluntarily. They are often referred to a therapist by the criminal justice system after they have been arrested for exposing themselves, peeping through windows, or engaging in sexual behaviours with children. Their motivation to change is, therefore, open to question. Participation in treatment may help them receive reduced sentences or avoid other legal penalties. In many cases, they are being asked to abandon highly reinforcing behaviours in which they have engaged for many years. Their families and other members of society may be much more concerned about change than they are. We mention this issue at the beginning of our discussion because the results of outcome studies in this area are typically less positive than are those concerning the treatment of sexual dysfunctions (McConaghy, 1999b; Prentky et al., 1997). In fact, some studies, such as Canadian research by Karl Hanson and colleagues, suggest that psychological treatments might be largely ineffective, at least for many sex offenders (Hanson et al., 2004). Sex offenders who are most likely to commit further offences when released from prison are those who are "career criminals" (i.e., have a history of numerous sexual assaults and other crimes, along with antisocial personality disorder), and continue to have deviant sexual preferences when released from prison (Hanson, 2004; Hanson & Bussiere, 1998). Details of specific interventions are discussed in the following sections.

**Aversion Therapy** For several decades, the most commonly used form of treatment for paraphilias was *aversion therapy*. In this procedure, the therapist repeatedly presents the stimulus that elicits inappropriate sexual arousal—such as slides of nude children—in association with an aversive stimulus, such as repulsive smells, electric shock, or chemically induced nausea. Revolting cognitive images are sometimes used instead of tangible aversive stimuli. Whatever the exact procedure, the rationale is to create a new association with the inappropriate stimulus so that the stimulus will no longer elicit sexual arousal. Some studies suggested that aversion therapy produces positive effects (Kilmann et al., 1982). This treatment has more recently fallen into disfavour, however, because the studies that were used to evaluate it suffered from design flaws.

**Cognitive Behavioural Treatment** Current cognitive behavioural treatment programs for paraphilia reflect a broader view of the etiology of these conditions. According to Marshall (1989, 1999), there is considerable reason to believe that paraphilias are based on a variety of cognitive and social deficits. Accordingly, treatment is multifaceted, including sex education, treatment of deviant sexual arousal, social skills training, and other interventions (Barbaree et al., 1998). Treatment is typically conducted in groups in clinics within the prison system (Marshall, 1999). For example, one of the major Canadian facilities is the Regional Treatment Centre, Ontario, a maximum-security inpatient facility located within the walls of Kingston Penitentiary (Barbaree et al., 1998). Sex offenders in Canadian penitentiaries are not required to submit to treatment. However, they are encouraged to do so, because they are more likely to receive parole if they enter treatment (Barbaree et al., 1998).

Regarding treatment efficacy, Marshall, Eccles, and Barbaree (1991) compared two approaches to the treatment of exhibitionists. One was based on aversion therapy and the other employed cognitive restructuring, social skills training, and stress management procedures. The men who received the second type of treatment were much less likely to return to their deviant forms of sexual behaviour than were the men who received aversion therapy. Treatment with aversion therapy was no more effective than was treatment with a placebo. These data suggest that broad-based cognitive and social treatment procedures may be useful in the treatment of paraphilias and sexual disorders (Marshall et al., 1996).

Unfortunately, other research results regarding the effectiveness of psychological treatment for sex offenders are discouraging. The only large-scale evaluation of such programs that has employed random assignment to treatment conditions was conducted by Marques et al. (1993). Treatment was designed for men convicted of either rape or child molestation. Men selected for this comprehensive treatment program were transferred to a special hospital unit, where they remained for several months. They received education in human sexuality as well as cognitive behaviour therapy, including applied relaxation and social skills training and stress and anger management. Treatment also included a relapse prevention component that was based on procedures used in the treatment of alcoholism (see Chapter 11). Relapse prevention procedures help the men confront personal, social, and sexual difficulties that may increase their risk of relapse after they are released from prison.

The men in the treatment group were compared to those in a control group. Outcome is measured in several ways, but the most important consideration is being arrested again for similar crimes. Figure 12–7 illustrates some of the results from this study, highlighting the comparison between 138 men who completed the treatment and 184 men who had originally volunteered to participate in the program but were assigned to a no-treatment control group (Marques, 1999). Within four years after their release from prison, the percentage of men who were arrested for another sexual offence was essentially identical to that of the men who had been treated and of the control group (13 percent). The rate of arrest for subsequent violent offences was somewhat lower for the treatment group than for the controls, but the difference was not significant.

**Outcome of Psychological Treatment for Sex Offenders**

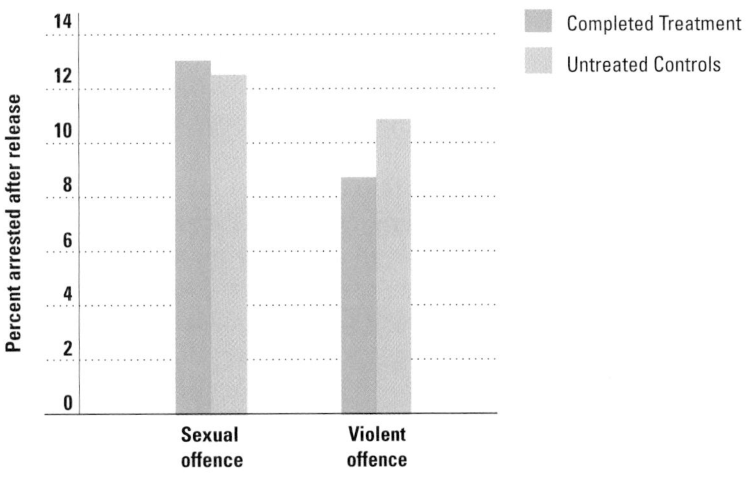


**FIGURE 12–7: Repeat arrest rates among male sex offenders (four years after treatment).**
*Source:* J.K. Marques, 1999, How to answer the question: Does sex offender treatment work? *Journal of Interpersonal Violence, 14,* 437–451.

Results were somewhat more encouraging with men convicted of rape than with those who had molested children. Nevertheless, the data from this study are discouraging. They suggest that a broadly based behavioural program focused on education, social skills, and relapse prevention procedures may not lead to obviously better outcomes than a routine period of incarceration (McConaghy, 1999a).

**Hormones and Medication** Another approach to the treatment of paraphilias involves the use of drugs that reduce levels of testosterone, on the assumption that male hormones control the sexual appetite (Bradford, 1997). One study reported that treatment of paraphilic men with cyproterone acetate, a drug that blocks the effects of testosterone, produced a significant reduction in some aspects of sexual behaviour, especially sexual fantasies (Bradford & Pawlak, 1993). Among men with pedophilia, the study found a greater reduction of sexual fantasies of children than of images of sex between consenting adults. Positive results have also been reported for use of triptorelin, which reduces testosterone secretion by inhibiting pituitary–gonadal function. In an uncontrolled trial, 30 male patients (25 with pedophilia) received monthly injections of triptorelin as well as supportive psychotherapy. All of the patients showed a reduction in deviant fantasies and in the number of incidents of paraphilic behaviours (Rosler & Witztum, 1998). We must remember, however, that the absence of double-blind, placebo-controlled studies leaves the efficacy of these drugs in doubt. One review of this literature concludes that treatment programs should never rely exclusively on the use of medications that reduce levels of testosterone (Prentky, 1997).

Antidepressants and antianxiety drugs have also been used to treat paraphilias. Case studies as well as some small uncontrolled outcome studies indicate that the SSRIs can have beneficial effects for some male patients (Balon, 1998). The process by which these drugs manage to alter sexual behaviour is open to question. For example, medication may work directly by decreasing deviant sexual interests without affecting other forms of sexual arousal. On the other hand, SSRIs may work by reducing social anxiety, which interferes with the ability to enjoy an intimate sexual relationship with another adult (Golwyn & Sevlie, 1992). This hypothesis is consistent with the approach taken by Marshall and his colleagues, whose psychological treatment program is aimed at similar types of social deficits.

***Ray Blanchard** is head of the Clinical Sexology Program at Toronto's Centre for Addiction and Mental Health. He is a leading expert on gender identity disorders.*

# Gender Identity Disorders

Our sense of ourselves as being either male or female is known as **gender identity**. Gender identity almost always reflects the child's physical anatomy: Toddlers who possess a penis learn that they are boys, and those with a vagina learn that they are girls. Gender identity is usually fixed by the time a child reaches two or three years of age (Parker & Aldwin, 1997).

Gender identity must be distinguished from *sex roles*, which are characteristics, behaviours, and skills that are defined within a specific culture as being either masculine or feminine. For example, certain aspects of appearance and behaviour are more often associated with men than with women. These are considered to be masculine. Those behaviours and appearances that are more often associated with women are considered feminine. In our own culture, masculine and feminine sex roles have changed considerably in recent years, and they overlap to a degree (Tiefer & Kring, 1995).

## Typical Symptoms and Associated Features

Some people are firmly convinced that their anatomy and their gender identity do not match up. In males, this means that they feel strongly that they are women trapped in a man's body. For females, the opposite pattern holds. DSM-IV-TR categorizes this sense of discomfort with one's anatomical sex as **gender identity disorder**. It has also been called *transsexualism* (Cohen-Kettenis & Gooren, 1999) or *gender dysphoria* (Blanchard, 1989). People with gender identity disturbances do not literally believe that they are members of the other gender. Rather, they feel that, with the exception of their physical anatomy, they are more like the other gender.

*Transsexual Christine Jorgenson (right) in 1952 and the former George Jorgenson (left), an Army veteran from New York. Jorgenson's sex-reassignment surgery, performed in Denmark, attracted worldwide attention.*

Most transsexuals report that they were aware of these feelings very early in childhood. Many report that they dressed in clothing and adopted sex-role behaviours of the other gender during childhood and adolescence. The intensity of the person's discomfort varies from one individual to the next. Invariably it becomes more intense during adolescence, when the person develops secondary sexual characteristics, such as breasts and wider hips for girls, and facial hair, voice changes, and increased muscle mass for boys. These characteristics make it more difficult for a person to pass for the other gender. Many transsexuals become preoccupied with the desire to change their anatomical sex through surgical procedures.

Gender identity disorders should be distinguished from transvestic fetishism, which is a form of paraphilia in which a heterosexual man dresses in the clothing of the other gender in order to achieve sexual arousal. These are, in fact, very different conditions. Transvestic fetishists do not consider themselves to be women, and transsexuals are not sexually aroused by cross-dressing. Even so, the two disorders appear to be connected; gender identity disorder is generally preceded by transvestic fetishism (Freund, Watson, & Dickey, 1991). According to Ray Blanchard, who is head of the Clinical Sexology Program at Toronto's Centre for Addiction and Mental Health, and a leading researcher in the field, gender identity disorders may be uncommon in women because their precursor—transvestic fetishism—is rare in women (Blanchard, 1989).

The relation between gender identity disorder and sexual orientation has been a matter of some controversy. Homosexual men with gender identity disorder feel that, deep down, they are actually women, and so they may regard their attraction to other men as heterosexual (Blanchard, 1989). Yet some clinicians have suggested that transsexuals are essentially homosexuals who claim to be members of the other gender as a way to avoid cultural and moral sanctions that discourage engaging in sexual relationships with members of their own sex. This proposal doesn't make sense for two reasons. First, lesbians and gay men are not uncomfortable with their own gender identity. This observation suggests that transsexuals are not simply escaping the stigma of homosexuality. Second, laboratory studies suggest that transsexual and nontranssexual homosexual subjects exhibit different patterns of sexual arousal in response to erotic stimuli (Bradley & Zucker, 1997).

## BRIEF CASE STUDY

### Transsexualism

Holly Devor was, by Aaron Devor's account, a strange, conspicuous woman. Even though she did a pretty good "woman" act, it became increasingly like contortionist's work and, ultimately, not very persuasive to others. "I never fit well as a girl or woman," said Mr. Devor, whose announcement that he was going to live as a man recently swept the University of Victoria campus.

Today, the university's Dean of Graduate Studies appears happy to conform to a conservative image more typical of men who run $3-million enterprises: Striding into his spare, elegant office, Mr. Devor projects confidence and control. He wears a dark grey suit and black tie with a blue shirt just over-large enough to hide any shape that might suggest he was once a woman.

He looks much younger than 51, with smooth skin, thick hair and light blue eyes that appraise from behind large-lensed glasses. In the manner of men used to commanding space, even at 5-feet-6, his hand gestures are expansive, the right leg crosses the left widely as he sits, he shrugs his shoulders loosely. Aaron Devor is a man in full, if not in anatomy.

Like many hitting 50, Holly Devor wanted sweeping changes in her life. So the sociologist was thrilled last spring to win her big, new job as graduate studies dean at UVic. Recently, she announced her name would be Aaron H. Devor and she would be living as a man.

Holly Devor always dressed in pants and presented herself as a masculine woman: the only change people on campus say they have seen in the dean lately is a shorter haircut. His voice is clearly male. Mr. Devor wouldn't reveal whether he is undergoing surgery for his transition, which can include anything from removal of breast tissue to construction of a penis. He would say only that he is transgendered and making physical changes. "Those are intimate details," he said.

Only one thing seems to prevent life as a man from being a totally happy thing for Mr. Devor: he will miss the intimate friendships women have in which they talk about their feelings openly. "Men are simply not accustomed to [doing] that," he says. "That's a big price to pay." ◆

*Source:* Excerpted from V. Smith, 2003, I never did fit well as a girl. *Globe and Mail*, January 4. Reprinted with permission of the author.

## Epidemiology

Gender identity disorders are rare in comparison to most of the other disorders that we have considered in this book. Male-to-female transsexuals are apparently more common than female-to-male transsexuals, at least based on the numbers of people who seek treatment at clinics. One study estimated the prevalence figures to be 1 person with gender identity disorder for every 12 000 males and 30 000 females (Kesteren, Gooren, & Megens, 1996).

Deeply ingrained cross-gender behaviours and attitudes among children occur infrequently in the general population (Bradley & Zucker, 1997; Zucker, 2000). Mild forms of cross-gender behaviour, such as dressing up in the clothes of the other gender or expressing a desire to be a member of the other sex, are relatively common during the preschool years. Extreme forms of these behaviours are relatively rare, however. Although gender identity disorders seem to be more common in children than in adults, they occur in only 3 percent of boys and 1 percent of girls (Green & Blanchard, 1995).

## Etiology

Very little is known about the origins of gender identity in normal men and women, so it is not surprising that the etiology of gender identity disorders is also poorly understood. There is some reason to believe that gender identity is strongly influenced by sex hormones, especially during the prenatal period (LeVay, 1993; Swaab & Gofman, 1995). Much of the research in this area has been done with animals, but an important set of data comes from studies of people with a condition that is sometimes called *pseudohermaphroditism*. Individuals with this condition are genetically male, but they are unable to produce a hormone that is responsible for shaping the penis and scrotum in the fetus. Therefore the child is born with external genitalia that are ambiguous in appearance—thus the term *pseudohermaphrodite*.[1]

Many of these children are raised as girls by their families. When they reach puberty, a sudden increase in testosterone leads to dramatic changes in the appearance of the adolescent's genitals. The organ that had previously looked more like a clitoris becomes enlarged and turns into a penis, and testicles descend into a scrotum. The child's voice becomes deeper, muscle mass increases, and the child quickly begins to consider himself to be a man (Imperato-McGinley et al., 1974). The speed and apparent ease with which people with these conditions adopt a masculine gender identity suggest that their brains had been prenatally programmed for this alternative (Hoenig, 1985). The importance of biological factors is further suggested by a tragic case of a Canadian boy, Bruce, who was raised as a girl (see Canadian Focus).

[1]A hermaphrodite has both male and female reproductive organs.

## CANADIAN FOCUS Nature and Nurture in Gender Identity

Gender identity and gender identity disorders are multifaceted phenomena, which likely arise from complex interactions among genes and environmental events. The latter include things that take place in the womb, such as the exposure to intrauterine sex hormones by the developing fetus. The fact that learning experiences are insufficient to determine gender identity has been underscored by the tragic case of a Winnipeg boy, originally named Bruce, who was raised as a girl. Bruce had an identical twin brother. When the twins were eight months old, a doctor badly botched Bruce's circumcision, leaving Bruce with a charred stump of a penis. The distraught parents were persuaded by a leading sexologist, John Money, to raise Bruce as a girl. Money reasoned, erroneously as it turned out, that Bruce's gender identity could be changed from male to female simply as a result of raising Bruce in the female gender role, supplemented with female hormones and, during adolescence, by sexual reassignment surgery (e.g., surgically creating a vagina). The fact that Bruce had an identical twin brother provided a scientifically important case control; if gender identity was largely due to environmental influences such as being raised in a female gender role, then it should be possible to take two people with identical genes (i.e., Bruce and his twin) and to successfully raise one as a girl and one as a boy.

Accordingly, Bruce was renamed Brenda and for the next 13 years the family struggled to raise him as a girl. The results were disastrous. Even though he was named Brenda and wearing a dress, he was clearly masculine in his appearance, interests, and behaviour, and he always felt that he was really a boy. His masculinity was clearly evident from an early age. Even in kindergarten there was a "rough-and-tumble rowdiness, an assertive, pressing dominance, and a complete lack of any demonstrable feminine interests" (Colapinto, 2000, p. 61). A female classmate came up to the kindergarten teacher and said "How come Brenda stands *up* when she goes to the bathroom?" No amount of coaxing from her mother could persuade Brenda to consistently sit down to urinate.

At age 11, Brenda continued to have clearly masculine interests; she had "marvellous plans for building tree houses, go-carts with CB radios, model gas airplanes . . . [and] appears to be more competitive and aggressive than her brother" (Colapinto, 2000, p. 112). Brenda had a very masculine gait, looked quite masculine, and was being teased by the other children who called her "cavewoman." Life for Brenda was miserable. She fought with boys who teased her. Brenda was ostracized, and had few friends apart from her twin brother.

Brenda steadfastly refused to have surgery to create a vagina, and complied with great reluctance to take the feminizing hormones. At age 14 Brenda was told of the botched operation, and shortly thereafter changed her name to David and began living in the male role. Later, David had reconstructive surgery to remove the breasts that had grown as a result of estrogen therapy, and had multiple operations to create an artificial penis and testicles. David also received testosterone injections to make his physique more masculine. David married and helped raise three adopted children, and worked for many years in a Winnipeg abattoir. The work was tough and physically demanding, but he enjoyed it. Thus, years of socialization into the female gender role were unsuccessful in altering his gender identity.

David had survived many hardships throughout his troubled life, and had had thoughts of killing himself during his years as Brenda. Life as David seemed to be an improvement, but he remained prone to bouts of depression, and quite likely brooded about what had been done to him. And then a series of stressful events unfolded that proved too much for him; his twin brother died from an overdose of antidepressant medication, then his marriage fell apart and he was laid off from his job. David committed suicide in May 2004, at the age of 38. ◆

*Sources:* CBC News Online (2004), Colapinto (2000, 2004), Diamond (1982), Diamond and Sigmundson (1997).

### Treatment

There are two obvious solutions to problems of gender identity: Change the person's identity to match his or her anatomy, or change the anatomy to match the person's gender identity. Various forms of psychotherapy have been used in an effort to alter gender identity, but the results have been fairly negative.

One alternative to psychological treatment is *sex-reassignment surgery*, in which the person's genitals are changed to match the gender identity (Hage, 1995). Medical science can construct artificial male and female genitalia. The artificial penis is not capable of becoming erect in response to sexual stimulation, but structural implants can be used to obtain rigidity. These surgical procedures have been used with thousands of patients over the past 50 or 60 years. Clinics that perform these operations, such as the Gender Identity Clinic at Toronto's Centre for Addiction and Mental Health, employ stringent selection procedures, and patients are typically required to live for several months as a member of the other gender before they can undergo the surgical procedure.

The results of sex-reassignment surgery have generally been positive (Carroll, 1999; Smith, van Goozen, & Cohen-Kettenis, 2001). Interviews with patients who have undergone surgery indicate that most are satisfied with the results, and the vast majority believe that they do not have trouble passing as a member of their newly assumed gender. Psychological tests obtained from patients who have completed surgery indicate reduced levels of anxiety and depression.

# Summary

DSM-IV-TR recognizes two major forms of sexual disorders. **Sexual dysfunctions** involve an inhibition of sexual desire or disruption of the physiological responses leading to orgasm. **Paraphilias** are defined in terms of extreme forms of unusual sexual behaviour, in which sexual arousal is associated with atypical stimuli. The central problem in paraphilias is that sexual arousal has become detached from a reciprocal, loving relationship with another adult.

Sexual dysfunctions are subdivided into several types, based on the stages of the sexual response cycle. These include problems related to sexual desire, sexual arousal, and orgasm. Related difficulties include **sexual aversion disorder** and **premature ejaculation**. **Dyspareunia** is defined in terms of persistent genital pain during or after sexual intercourse. **Vaginismus** is an involuntary spasm of the muscles surrounding the entrance to the vagina. All forms of sexual dysfunction can lead to personal distress, including anxiety and depression, as well as interpersonal and marital difficulties.

Sexual behaviour is dependent on a complex interaction among biological, psychological, and social factors. These factors include cognitive events related to the perception of sexual stimuli, social factors that influence sexual meanings or intentions, and physiological responses that cause vasocongestion of the genitals during sexual arousal.

Biological factors that contribute to sexual dysfunction include inadequate levels of sex hormones, which can contribute to diminished sexual desire, and a variety of medical disorders. Vascular and neurological diseases are important factors in many cases of erectile disorder. The effects of alcohol, illicit drugs, and some forms of medication can also contribute to **erectile dysfunction** in men and to **orgasmic disorder** in both men and women.

Several psychological factors are involved in the etiology of sexual dysfunction. Prominent among these are performance anxiety and guilt. Communication deficits can also contribute to sexual dysfunction. Previous experiences, including sexual abuse, play an important role in some cases of sexual dysfunction.

Psychological treatments for sexual dysfunction are quite successful. They focus primarily on negative attitudes toward sexuality, failure to engage in effective sexual behaviours, and deficits in communication skills.

Common characteristics of paraphilias include lack of human intimacy and urges toward sexual behaviours that the person feels compelled to perform. Many people with paraphilias experience sexual dysfunctions during conventional sexual behaviour with an adult partner. The diversity and range of paraphilic behaviour are enormous. DSM-IV-TR describes a few of the most prominent forms, such as **exhibitionism**, **fetishism**, **frotteurism**, **pedophilia**, **sexual masochism**, **sexual sadism**, **transvestic fetishism**, and **voyeurism**. These are not typically isolated preferences or patterns of behaviour; people who exhibit one form of paraphilia often exhibit others.

Treatment outcome is generally less successful with paraphilias than with sexual dysfunction. Currently, the most promising approaches to the treatment of paraphilias use a combination of cognitive and behavioural procedures to address a broad range of etiological factors, including deficits in social skills and stress and anger management, as well as knowledge and attitudes regarding sexuality.

**Gender identity disorder** is a disturbance in the person's sense of being either a man or a woman. People with this problem, which is also known as *transsexualism*, have developed a **gender identity** that is inconsistent with their physical anatomy. These disorders are extremely rare, and very little is known about their etiology. Gender identity seems to be strongly influenced by sex hormones, perhaps during the process of fetal development. Treatment of gender identity disorders may involve sex-reassignment surgery.

# Critical Thinking

1. Do you think sexual dysfunctions should be classified as mental disorders? How else might they be defined?
2. Suppose that you're a therapist who has been contacted by a couple who are concerned that the woman is unable to reach orgasm. What are the first things you would want to know? Would you want to see each partner alone?
3. Drag queens are gay men who dress up in women's clothing. Their masquerade balls are typically a source of pride and enjoyment. Why isn't this type of behaviour considered a sexual disorder? How is their behaviour different from transvestic fetishism?
4. Do you think rape or some specific subtype of rape should have been included in DSM-IV-TR under paraphilias? Why or why not?
5. Should sex offenders such as people with pedophilia be required to accept treatment for their disorder?

# Key Terms

**construct validity** 415
**dyspareunia** 416
**erectile dysfunction** 412
**exhibitionism** 426
**fetishism** 423
**frotteurism** 427
**gender identity** 436
**gender identity disorder** 436
**hypoactive sexual desire** 411
**hypothetical construct** 415
**incest** 428
**inhibited sexual arousal** 414
**operational definition** 415
**orgasmic disorder** 414
**paraphilias** 422
**pedophilia** 427
**premature ejaculation** 414
**rape** 428
**sensate focus** 420
**sexual aversion disorder** 412
**sexual dysfunction** 408
**sexual masochism** 424
**sexual sadism** 426
**transvestic fetishism** 423
**vaginismus** 416
**voyeurism** 426

# 13 Schizophrenic Disorders


Overview
Typical Symptoms and Associated Features
Classification
Epidemiology
Etiological Considerations and Research
Treatment

**What is the difference between hallucinations and delusions?**

**Why do clinical scientists say that schizophrenia is a "heterogeneous" disorder?**

**Why can't we use brain imaging to diagnose schizophrenia?**

**Are newer antipsychotic medications more effective than older drugs?**

**Schizophrenia** is a severe form of abnormal behaviour that encompasses what most of us have come to know as "madness." It is the fifth leading cause of disability worldwide (Bland, 1998). An estimated 221 000 Canadians suffered from schizophrenia in 1996; that year, its associated costs (direct healthcare costs and other costs) were estimated to be $2.35 billion (Goeree et al., 1999). People with schizophrenia exhibit many different kinds of psychotic symptoms, indicating that the person has lost touch with reality. They may hear voices that aren't there or make comments that are difficult, if not impossible, to understand. Their behaviour may be guided by absurd ideas and beliefs. For example, a person might believe that spaceships from another planet are beaming thoughts into his brain and controlling his behaviour. Some people with schizophrenia recover fairly quickly, whereas others deteriorate progressively after the initial onset of symptoms. It is a disorder with "many different faces" (Andreasen, 2001). Because of the diversity of symptoms and outcomes shown by these patients, many clinicians believe that schizophrenia, or "the group of schizophrenias," may actually include several forms of disorder that have different causes. Others contend that schizophrenia is a single pathological process and that variations from one patient to the next in symptoms and course of the disorder reflect differences in the expression or severity of this process.

## Overview

Many of the disorders that we have discussed in this book strike us as being familiar, at least in form if not in severity. For example, depression and anxiety are experiences with which we can easily empathize. Short-lived versions of these emotions help to shape our responses to daily events. Some clinical scientists speculate that mood and anxiety disorders may be viewed as evolved adaptations or mechanisms that can serve a useful purpose, but the symptoms of schizophrenia represent a different kind of problem. It is much harder for us to understand when someone hears voices that aren't there or speaks sentences that are meaningless. These symptoms seem to stem from a fundamental breakdown in basic cognitive functions that govern the way the person perceives and thinks about the world (McGuire & Troisi, 1998; Tsuang, 2001).

The most common symptoms of schizophrenia include changes in the way a person thinks, feels, and relates to other people and the outside environment. No single symptom or specific set of symptoms is characteristic of all forms of schizophrenia. All of the individual symptoms of schizophrenia can also be associated with other psychological and medical conditions. Schizophrenia is officially defined by various combinations of psychotic symptoms in the absence of other forms of disturbance, such as mood disorders (especially manic episodes), substance dependence, delirium, or dementia (see Chapter 14).

Schizophrenia is a devastating disorder for both the patients and their families. It can disrupt many aspects of the person's life, well beyond the experience of psychotic symptoms. The impact of this disorder is felt in many different ways. For people who develop schizophrenia, it often has a dramatic and lasting impact on their quality of life, both in terms of their own satisfaction and their ability to complete an education, hold a job, and develop social relationships with other people. About 40 to 60 percent of people with schizophrenia attempt suicide, and about 10 percent will die from suicide. They are 15 to 25 times more likely than the general population to die from a suicide attempt (Health Canada, 2002a). Most people who develop the disorder do not recover completely, and many become homeless because long-term institutional care is not available (see Chapter 18).

For family members of patients with schizophrenia, the consequences can also be cruel. They must come to grips with the fact that their son or daughter, or brother or sister, has developed a severe disorder that may change his or her life forever. One woman, whose daughter, then in her mid-thirties, had exhibited symptoms of schizophrenia for 17 years, described her feelings in the following way: "Nothing in (our daughter's) growing up years could have prepared us for the shock and devastation of seeing this normal, happy child become totally incapacitated by schizophrenia" (Smith, 1991, p. 691).

In the following case studies we describe the experiences of two people who exhibited symptoms of schizophrenia. DSM-IV-TR divides schizophrenic disorders into several subtypes, based primarily on the type of symptoms that the patient exhibits. Our first case illustrates the paranoid subtype of schizophrenia, which is characterized by a preoccupation with one or more delusions or by frequent auditory hallucinations, most often persecutory.

## CASE STUDY Marilyn's Paranoid Schizophrenia

For someone who lives in total isolation, Marilyn R. has a lot of company. She's got the Cabir brothers. All five of them, all abusive, callous and unrelenting in their insults. Marilyn recalls a beating she suffered at the hands of a Cabir: "He just went crazy and said, 'I hate you.' And he grabbed an ashtray and just—pow!—hit me over the head with it. Put his teeth in my face and was going for the knife . . ."

Marilyn starts to weep. It's a memory so vivid, so real, that the Cabirs' place of residence comes as a shock. "They're all in the wall. They just stand there and keep giving me slurs all the time. They say am I ever ugly, say 'I can't stand the sight of her,'" she explains. "Strange, isn't it?"

Marilyn finds a bi-weekly injection she gets at a downtown Toronto drop-in centre helps quiet the Cabirs. But it doesn't make them go away. They're in the walls every day and every night. They even follow her on the bus. The Cabirs—very real to Marilyn but invisible to a visitor—are only part of the story. The room she lives in is just as surreal—and far more frightening. It is crawling with cockroaches.

A swarm of hatchlings has taken over the table—probing every square millimetre of the surface. Marilyn sits, fly swatter in hand, trying to get as many as she can. Her conversation is interrupted frequently by the slap of her weapon. "I wish they'd go away," she says of the Cabirs. (swat!) "He just stands there in the wall. He just stands there with his hands on his hips. He's there now. The whole family's there." (swat!) In addition to the cockroaches, Marilyn has caught nine mice in her room. Scattered rodent droppings dot the thick shag carpet, a rug so heavily infested with insects, a visitor is grateful the room is partially dark.

The date is December 17, 1997. Marilyn has no plans for Christmas. And despite her appalling living conditions, she has no hope of finding anything better. She's been there five years. "I guess I'll be here the rest of my life," she says. In the spring of 1998, however, the City of Toronto got a look at 136 Jones Ave.—a look that convinced inspectors it was unfit for human habitation.

Marilyn was hooked up with a mental health worker, a woman who was astonished at the conditions in which she lived. The worker helped find her a new place; a considerable feat in a city where people like Marilyn languish on waiting lists for up to five years. Marilyn moved to a self-contained subsidized apartment in the Sherbourne–Dundas Sts. area. Not exactly prime real estate, but conditions are a world apart from her old place. "It was awful. Unbearable. I left a lot behind because those cockroaches used to get in my clothes." For her new apartment, Marilyn pays $300 a month—$30 less than her old place. And she says the surroundings have made a tremendous improvement in her mental health. "Oh, 100 per cent better!" she smiles. And she's still got company. "The Cabirs are here," she says. "There's five of them in the wall." ◆

*Source:* S. Simmie, 1998, I'd sit in the kitchen and just shake. *Toronto Star*, October 4. Reprinted with permission of the author and the Atkinson Charitable Foundation.

The onset of schizophrenia typically occurs during adolescence or early adulthood. The period of risk for the development of a first episode is considered to be between the ages of 15 and 35. The number of new cases drops off slowly after that, with very few people experiencing an initial episode after the age of 55 (Gottesman, 1991).

The subsequent course of the disorder can follow many different patterns. The problems of most patients can be divided into three phases of variable and unpredictable duration: prodromal, active, and residual. Symptoms such as hallucinations, delusions, and disorganized speech are characteristic of the *active phase* of the disorder. The **prodromal phase** precedes the active phase and is marked by an obvious deterioration in role functioning as a student, employee, or homemaker. The person's friends and relatives often view the beginning of the prodromal phase as a change in his or her personality. Prodromal signs and symptoms are similar to those associated with schizotypal personality disorder (see Chapter 9). They include peculiar behaviours (such as talking to oneself in public), unusual perceptual experiences, outbursts of anger, increased tension, and restlessness. Social withdrawal, indecisiveness, and lack of willpower are often seen during the prodromal phase (Gross, 1997).

The **residual phase** follows the active phase of the disorder and is defined by signs and symptoms that are similar in many respects to those seen during the prodromal phase. At this point, the positive symptoms of psychosis have improved, but the person continues to be impaired in various ways. Negative symptoms, such as impoverished expression of emotions, may remain pronounced during the residual phase (McGlashan, 1998).

After the onset of schizophrenia, many people do not return to expected levels of social and occupational adjustment. Some prefer social isolation and avoid contact with other people. The man in our second case illustrates this pattern. He is also an example of the disorganized type of schizophrenia. Patients who fit criteria for this category say things that are difficult to understand, behave in a disorganized way, and fail to express expected emotions.

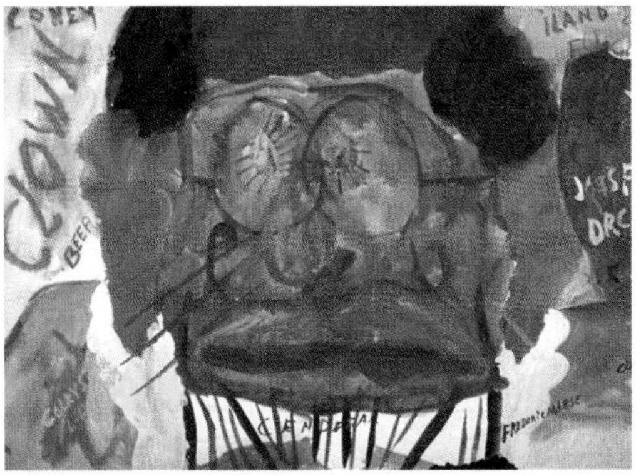


*Painting by a young schizophrenic patient, illustrating his hallucinations. He saw monsters, like the one painted here, crawling on the floor. He also believed that the chairs next of his bed had turned into devils. Patient's description of the picture: "I was very sick at the time I painted this picture. The head represents my fragmented personality and a feeling of being helpless, hopeless, and off balance and of being in a cocoon of unreality. The bright coloured rain and outlines represent the level of intensity of myself. The bright colours provided insulation and protected me. The colours felt like microwaves passing through my control centre."*

## CASE STUDY Edward's Disorganized Schizophrenia

Edward was 39 years old and had lived at home with his parents since dropping out of school after Grade 10. Edward worked on and off as a helper in his father's roofing business prior to his first psychotic episode at the age of 26. After that time, he was socially isolated and unable to hold any kind of job. He was hospitalized in psychiatric facilities 10 times in the next 14 years. When he was not in the hospital, most of his time at home was spent watching television or sitting alone in his room.

The tenth episode of psychosis became evident when Edward told his mother that he had seen people arguing violently on the sidewalk in front of their house. He believed that this incident was the beginning of World War II. His mother tried to persuade him that he had witnessed an ordinary, though perhaps heated, disagreement between two neighbours, but Edward could not be convinced. He continued to mumble about the fight and became increasingly agitated over the next few days. When he wasn't pacing back and forth from his bedroom to the living room, he could usually be found staring out the front window. Several days after witnessing the argument, he took curtains from several windows in the house and burned them in the street at 2 A.M. A neighbour happened to see what Edward was doing and called the police. When they arrived, they found Edward wandering in a snow-covered vacant lot, talking incoherently to himself. Recognizing that Edward was psychotic, the police took him to the psychiatric hospital.

Although his appearance was somewhat dishevelled, Edward was alert and cooperative. He knew the current date and recognized that he was in a psychiatric hospital. Some of his speech was incoherent, and his answers to questions posed by the hospital staff were frequently irrelevant. For example, the following exchange occurred during a structured diagnostic interview. The

*continued*

*cont.*

psychologist asked Edward whether he had any special powers or abilities that other people do not have. He responded by saying that he didn't know because he didn't date women. Puzzled by this tangential response, the psychologist asked him to explain what he meant. Edward responded by asking his own question, "If you had a star in the middle of your head, would you swallow marbles?"

Edward's expressive gestures were severely restricted, and he sat in a relatively motionless position. Although he said that he was frightened by the recent events that he reported to his mother, his face did not betray any signs of emotion. He mumbled slowly in a monotonous tone of voice that was difficult to understand. He said that he could hear God's voice telling him that his father was "the Master of the universe" and he claimed that he had "seen the shadow of the Master."

Other voices seemed to argue with one another about Edward's special calling and whether he was worthy of this divine power. The voices told him to prepare for God's return to earth. At times Edward said that he was a Nazi soldier and that he was born in Germany in 1886. He also spoke incoherently about corpses frozen in Greenland and maintained that he was "only half a person." ◆

## Typical Symptoms and Associated Features

In this section we describe in greater detail various types of symptoms that are commonly observed among schizophrenic patients and that are currently emphasized by official diagnostic systems, such as DSM-IV-TR. Remember that all of these symptoms can fluctuate in severity over time. Some patients exhibit persistent psychotic symptoms. Others experience symptoms during acute episodes and are better adjusted between episodes.

The symptoms of schizophrenia can be divided into three dimensions: positive symptoms, negative symptoms, and disorganization (Andreasen et al., 1995; Lenzenweger, 1999). **Positive symptoms,** which are sometimes called *psychotic symptoms,* include hallucinations and delusions. **Negative symptoms** include characteristics such as lack of initiative, social withdrawal, and deficits in emotional responding. Some additional symptoms of schizophrenia, such as incoherent or disorganized speech, do not fit easily into either the positive or negative types. Verbal communication problems and bizarre behaviour represent this third dimension, which is sometimes called *disorganization.* Note that these symptom dimensions overlap and combine in various ways within individual patients.

*Many of the symptoms of schizophrenia, including hallucinations and delusions, can be extremely distressing.*

### Positive Symptoms

The term *positive symptoms* of schizophrenia does not imply that these symptoms are beneficial or adaptive. Rather, it suggests that they are characterized by the *presence* of an aberrant response (such as hearing a voice that is not really there). Negative symptoms, on the other hand, are characterized by the *absence* of a particular response (such as emotion, speech, or willpower).

**Hallucinations** Our senses provide us with basic information that is vital to our notions of who we are, what we are doing, and what others think of us. Many people with schizophrenia experience perplexing and often frightening changes in perception. The most obvious perceptual symptoms are **hallucinations**, or sensory experiences that are not caused by actual external stimuli. Although hallucinations can occur in any of the senses, those experienced by schizophrenic patients are most often auditory. Many patients hear voices that comment on their behaviour or give them instructions. Others hear voices that seem to argue with one another. Edward heard the voice of God talking to him. Like Edward, most patients find such voices to be frightening (Delespaul et al., 2002). In some cases, however, hallucinations can be comforting or pleasing to the patient.

Hallucinations should be distinguished from the transient mistaken perceptions that most people experience from time to time (Ohayon, 2000). Have you ever turned around after thinking you heard someone call your name, to find that no one was there? You probably dismissed the experience as "just your imagination." Hallucinations, in contrast, strike the person as being real, in spite of the fact that they have no basis in reality. They are also persistent over time. Patients who experience auditory hallucinations often hear the voice (or voices) speaking to them throughout the day and for many days at a time.

Hallucinations are typically associated with other symptoms, particularly delusional beliefs. This relation makes considerable intuitive sense. Because hallucinations are vivid perceptual experiences, people who experience them need to explain their origin. These "explanations" often involve delusional beliefs. A patient, like Edward, who hears the voice of God telling him that he has been given divine powers may conclude that he is an important religious figure; this conclusion would be considered a *delusion*.

**Delusional Beliefs** Many schizophrenic patients express **delusions**, or idiosyncratic beliefs that are rigidly held in spite of their preposterous nature (Maher, 2001). Delusions have sometimes been defined as false beliefs based on incorrect inferences about reality. This definition has a number of problems, including the difficulty of establishing the ultimate truth of many situations. In the most obvious cases, delusional patients express and defend their beliefs with utmost conviction, even when presented with contradictory evidence. Preoccupation is another defining characteristic of delusional beliefs. Delusional patients typically are unable to consider the perspective that other people hold with regard to their beliefs.

Although delusional beliefs can take many forms, they are typically personal. They are not shared by other members of the person's family or cultural group. Common delusions include the belief that thoughts are being inserted into the patient's head, that other people are reading the patient's thoughts, or that the patient is being controlled by mysterious, external forces (Frith & Dolan, 2000; Gutierrez-Lobos et al., 2001). Many delusions focus on grandiose or paranoid content. For example, Edward expressed the grandiose belief that his father was the Master of the universe.

Delusions are often fragmented, especially among severely disturbed patients. In other words, delusions are not always coherent belief systems that are consistently expressed by the patient. At various times, for example, Edward talked about being a Nazi soldier and half a person. Connections among these fragmented ideas are difficult to understand.

## Negative Symptoms

Negative symptoms of schizophrenia are defined in terms of responses or functions that appear to be missing from the person's behaviour. In that sense, they may initially be more subtle or difficult to recognize than the positive symptoms of this disorder. Negative symptoms tend to be more stable over time than positive symptoms, which fluctuate in severity as the person moves in and out of active phases of psychosis (Earnst & Kring, 1997).

**Affective and Emotional Disturbances** One of the most common symptoms of schizophrenia involves a flattening or restriction of the person's nonverbal display of emotional responses. This symptom, called **blunted affect**, or *affective flattening*, was clearly present in Edward's case. Blunted patients fail to exhibit signs of emotion or feeling. They are neither happy nor sad, and they appear to be completely indifferent to their surroundings. The faces of blunted patients are apathetic and expressionless. Their voices lack the typical fluctuations in volume and pitch that other people use to signal changes in their mood. Events in their environment hold little consequence for them. They may demonstrate a complete lack of concern for themselves and for others (Dworkin et al., 1998).

Another type of emotional deficit is called **anhedonia**, which refers to the inability to experience pleasure. Whereas blunted affect refers to the lack of outward expression, anhedonia is a lack of positive feelings. People who experience anhedonia typically lose interest in recreational activities and social relationships, which they do not find enjoyable. They may also be unable to experience pleasure from physical sensations, such as taste and touch. Longitudinal studies indicate that anhedonia associated with both social and physical experiences is an enduring feature of the disorder for many people with schizophrenia (Blanchard, Horan, & Brown, 2001; Herbener & Harrow, 2002). For some people, it may also be an early marker, signalling the onset of the prodromal phase of the disorder (Kwapil, 1998). Like other symptoms of schizophrenia, anhedonia is not unique to this disorder; it is also found among people who are severely depressed (Romney & Candido, 2001).

**Apathy, Avolition, and Alogia** One of the most important and seriously debilitating aspects of schizophrenia is a malfunction of interpersonal relationships (Meehl, 1993). Many people with schizophrenia become socially withdrawn. In many cases, social isolation develops before the onset of symptoms, such as hallucinations and delusions. It can be one of the earliest signs that something is wrong. Social withdrawal appears to be both a symptom of the disorder and a strategy that is actively employed by some patients to deal with their other symptoms. They may, for example, attempt to minimize interactions with other people in order to reduce levels of stimulation that can exacerbate perceptual and cognitive disorganization (Walker, Davis, & Baum, 1993).

The withdrawal seen among many schizophrenic patients is accompanied by indecisiveness, ambivalence, and a loss of willpower. This symptom is known as **avolition** (lack of volition or will). A person who suffers from avolition becomes apathetic and ceases to work toward personal goals or to function independently. He or she might sit listlessly in a chair all day, not washing or combing his or her hair for weeks.

Another negative symptom involves a form of speech disturbance called **alogia**, which refers to impoverished thinking. Literally translated, it means "speechlessness." In one form of alogia, known as *poverty of speech*, patients show remarkable reductions in the amount of speech. They simply don't have anything to say. In another form, referred to as *thought blocking*, the patient's train of speech is interrupted before a thought or idea has been completed.

## Disorganization

Some symptoms of schizophrenia do not fit easily into either the positive or negative type. Thinking disturbances and bizarre behaviour represent a third symptom dimension, which is sometimes called *disorganization* (Grube, Bilder, & Goldman, 1998; Peralta & Cuesta, 1999).

**Thinking Disturbances** One important set of schizophrenic symptoms, known as **disorganized speech**, involves the tendency of some patients to say things that don't make sense. Signs of disorganized speech include making irrelevant responses to questions, expressing disconnected ideas, and using words in peculiar ways (Berenbaum & Barch, 1995). This symptom is also called *thought disorder*, because clinicians have assumed that the failure to communicate successfully reflects a disturbance in the thought patterns that govern verbal discourse. The woman described in the following case exhibited signs of disorganized speech.

## CASE STUDY Marsha's Disorganized Speech and Bizarre Behaviour

Marsha was a 32-year-old graduate student in political science. She had never been treated for psychological problems.

Marsha called Dr. Higgins, a clinical psychologist who taught at the university, to ask if she could speak with him about her twin sister's experience with schizophrenia. When she arrived at his office, she was neatly dressed and had a bible tucked tightly under her arm. The next three hours were filled with a rambling discussion of Marsha's experiences during the past 10 years. She talked about her education, her experience as a high school teacher before returning to graduate school, her relationships with her parents, and most of all her concern for her identical twin sister, Alice, who had spent 6 of the last 10 years in psychiatric hospitals.

Marsha's emotional expression vacillated dramatically throughout the course of this conversation, which was punctuated by silly giggles and heavy sighs. Her voice would be loud and emphatic one moment as she talked about her stimulating ideas and special talents. At other moments, she would whisper in a barely audible voice or sob quietly as she described the desperation, fear, and frustration that she had experienced watching

continued

*cont.*

the progression of her sister's disorder. She said that she had been feeling very uptight in recent months, afraid that she might be "going crazy" like her sister. She had been scared to death to go home because her parents might sense that something was wrong with her. Her behaviour was frequently inconsistent with the content of her speech. As she described her intense fears, for example, Marsha occasionally giggled uncontrollably.

Dr. Higgins also found Marsha's train of thought difficult to follow. Her speech rambled illogically from one topic to the next, and her answers to his questions were frequently tangential. For example, when Dr. Higgins asked what she meant by her repeated use of the phrase "the ideal can become real," Marsha replied, "Well, after serving the Word of Christ for three years, making a public spectacle of myself, someone apparently called my parents and said I had a problem. I said I can't take this anymore and went home. I perceived that Mom was just unbelievably nice to me. I began to think that my face was changing. Something about my forehead resembled the pain of Christ. I served Christ, but my power was not lasting."

At the end of this three-hour interview, Dr. Higgins was convinced that Marsha should be referred to the mental health centre for outpatient treatment. He explained his concerns to Marsha, but she refused to follow his advice, insisting that she did not want to receive the medication with which her sister had been treated. She agreed to return to Dr. Higgins's office in three days for another interview, but she did not keep that appointment.

Two weeks later, Marsha called Dr. Higgins to ask if he would talk with her immediately. It was very difficult to understand what she was saying, but she seemed to be repeating in a shrill voice "I'm losing my mind." The door to his office was closed when she arrived, but he could hear her shuffling awkwardly down the hallway, breathing heavily. He opened his door and found Marsha standing in a rigid posture, arms stiffly at her sides. Her eyes were opened wide, and she was staring vacantly at the nameplate on his door. In contrast to her prim and neat appearance at their first meeting, Marsha's hair and clothes were now in disarray. She walked stiffly into the office without bending her knees and sat, with some difficulty, in the chair next to Dr. Higgins's desk. Her facial expression was rigidly fixed. Although her eyes were open and she appeared to hear his voice, Marsha did not respond to any of Dr. Higgins's questions. Recognizing that Marsha was experiencing an acute psychotic episode, Dr. Higgins and one of the secretaries took her to the emergency room at the local hospital. ◆

Marsha's speech provides one typical example of disorganized speech. She was not entirely incoherent, but parts of her speech were difficult to follow. Connections between sentences were sometimes arbitrary, and her answers to the interviewer's questions were occasionally irrelevant.

The following excerpt from an interview with another patient illustrates a more extreme form of disorganized speech.

> **Interviewer:** Have you been nervous or tense lately?
>
> **Patient:** No, I got a head of lettuce.
>
> **Interviewer:** You got a head of lettuce? I don't understand.
>
> **Patient:** Well, it's just a head of lettuce.
>
> **Interviewer:** Tell me about lettuce. What do you mean?
>
> **Patient:** Well, . . . lettuce is a transformation of a dead cougar that suffered a relapse on the lion's toe. And he swallowed the lion and something happened. The . . . see, the . . . Gloria and Tommy, they're two heads and they're not whales. But they escaped with herds of vomit, and things like that. (Neale & Oltmanns, 1980, p. 102)

When speech becomes this disrupted, it is considered incoherent. Notice that this patient did not string words together in a random fashion. His speech followed grammatical rules. He was placing nouns and verbs together in an appropriate order, but they didn't make any sense. His speech conveyed little, if any, meaning, and that is the hallmark of disorganized speech.

Common features of disorganized speech in schizophrenia include shifting topics too abruptly, called *loose associations* or *derailment*; replying to a question with an irrelevant response, called *tangentiality*; or persistently repeating the same word or phrase over and over again, called *perseveration*. We all say things from time to time that fit these descriptions. It is not the occasional presence of a single feature but, rather, the accumulation of a large number of such features that defines the presence of disorganized speech.

**Bizarre Behaviour** Schizophrenic patients may exhibit various forms of unusual motor behaviour, such as the rigidity displayed by Marsha when she appeared for her second interview with Dr. Higgins. *Catatonia* most often refers to immobility and marked muscular

*These dementia praecox patients, treated by Emil Kraepelin in the late nineteenth century, display "waxy flexibility," a feature of catatonic motor behaviour. "They were put without difficulty in the peculiar positions and kept them, some with a sly laugh, others with rigid seriousness."*

rigidity, but it can also refer to excitement and overactivity. For example, some patients engage in apparently purposeless pacing or repetitious movements, such as rubbing their hands together in a special pattern for hours at a time. Many catatonic patients exhibit reduced or awkward spontaneous movements. In more extreme forms, patients may assume unusual postures or remain in rigid standing or sitting positions for long periods of time. For example, some patients will lie flat on their backs in a stiff position with their heads raised slightly off the floor as though they were resting on a pillow. Catatonic patients typically resist attempts to alter their position, even though maintaining their awkward postures would normally be extremely uncomfortable or painful.

Catatonic posturing is often associated with a *stuporous state*, or generally reduced responsiveness. The person seems to be unaware of his or her surroundings. For example, during her acute psychotic episode, Marsha refused to answer questions or to make eye contact with others. Unlike people with other stuporous conditions, however, catatonic patients seem to maintain a clear state of consciousness, and it is likely that Marsha could hear and understand everything that Dr. Higgins said to her. Many patients report after the end of a catatonic episode that they were perfectly aware of events that were taking place around them, in spite of their failure to respond appropriately.

Another kind of bizarre behaviour involves affective responses that are obviously inconsistent with the person's situation. This symptom is particularly difficult to describe in words. The most remarkable features of **inappropriate affect** are incongruity and lack of adaptability in emotional expression. For example, when Marsha described the private terror that she felt in the presence of her family, she giggled in a silly fashion. The content of Marsha's speech was inconsistent with her facial expression, her gestures, and her voice quality.

## Classification

The specific organization of symptoms of schizophrenia has been a matter of some controversy for many years. Schizophrenic disorders have been defined in many different ways. In the following pages we briefly review some of the more prominent trends that led to the DSM-IV-TR description of these disorders.

### Brief Historical Perspective

Descriptions of schizophrenic symptoms can be traced far back in history, but they were not considered to be symptoms of a single disorder until late in the nineteenth century (Gottesman, 1991). At that time, Emil Kraepelin, a German psychiatrist, suggested that several types of problems that previously had been classified as distinct forms of disorder should be grouped together under a single diagnostic category called *dementia praecox*. This term referred to psychoses that ended in severe intellectual deterioration (dementia) and that had an early or premature (praecox) onset, usually during adolescence. Kraepelin argued that these patients could be distinguished from those suffering from other disorders (most notably manic–depressive psychosis) largely on the basis of changes that occurred as the disorder progressed over time, primarily those changes involving the integrity of mental functions.

In 1911, Eugen Bleuler (1857–1939), a Swiss psychiatrist and a contemporary of Kraepelin, published an influential monograph in which he agreed with most of Kraepelin's suggestions about this disorder. He did not believe, however, that the disorder always ended in profound deterioration or that it always began in late adolescence. Kraepelin's term *dementia praecox* was, therefore, unacceptable to him. Bleuler suggested a new name for the disorder—*schizophrenia*. This term referred to the *splitting of mental associations*, which Bleuler believed to be the fundamental disturbance in schizophrenia. One unfortunate consequence of this choice of terms has been the confusion among laypeople of schizophrenia with dissociative identity disorder (also known as multiple personality), a severe form of dissociative disorder (see Chapter 7). The two disorders actually have very little in common.

Many other suggestions have been made in subsequent years regarding the description and diagnosis of schizophrenia (Gottesman, 1991; Neale & Oltmanns, 1980). Some clinicians have favoured a broader definition, whereas others have argued for a more narrow approach. These differences of opinion have focused on a number of issues.

One such issue has been the relative importance of specific types of symptoms in establishing a diagnosis of schizophrenia. Are some symptoms more useful than others in predicting the course of the disorder or the patient's response to treatment? Many clinicians have disagreed with Bleuler's choice of fundamental symptoms. One prominent alternative opinion was offered by Kurt Schneider (1959), a German psychiatrist, whose diagnostic system for schizophrenia placed primary emphasis on a set of specific types of hallucinations, delusions, and perceptual distortions that he considered to be "first-rank symptoms" (Carpenter et al., 1996). Examples include *thought broadcasting*, in which the person believes that his or her thoughts are being transmitted so that others know what he or she is thinking; *voices commenting*, in which the person hears someone else's voice provide a running commentary that describes or criticizes his or her behaviour; and *somatic passivity*, in which the person believes that he or she is a passive, unwilling recipient of physical sensations imposed by some outside force.

## DSM-IV-TR

The current North American approach to the diagnosis of schizophrenic disorders gives primary consideration to three types of symptoms: positive symptoms, negative symptoms, and disorganized speech and behaviour. The DSM-IV-TR definition includes a more restricted range of symptoms than Bleuler's description of the disorder, which placed less emphasis on the presence of persistent positive symptoms such as hallucinations and delusions. The inclusion of negative symptoms does represent, however, a remnant of Bleuler's influence.

DSM-IV-TR lists several specific criteria for schizophrenia (see Table 13–1). The first requirement (Criterion A) is that the patient must exhibit two (or more) active symptoms for at least one month. Notice that only one of the characteristic symptoms is required if that symptom is a bizarre delusion or hallucination that fits Schneider's description of first-rank symptoms. Negative symptoms, such as blunted affect, avolition, and social withdrawal, play a relatively prominent role in the DSM-IV-TR definition of schizophrenia, although some concern has been expressed about the reliability with which they are measured. The work group that developed DSM-IV-TR considered negative symptoms vital both to determining the causes of the disorder and to treating it successfully (Andreasen & Carpenter, 1993).

The DSM-IV-TR definition also takes into account social and occupational functioning as well as the duration of the disorder (Criteria B and C). These criteria reflect the influence of Kraepelin, who argued that the disorder is accompanied by marked impairment in

The Swiss psychiatrist **Eugen Bleuler** coined the term schizophrenia in his 1911 monograph on the disorder.

**TABLE 13–1 DSM-IV-TR Diagnostic Criteria for Schizophrenia**

**A. Characteristic Symptoms: Two (or more) of the following, each present for a significant portion of time during a one-month period (or less if successfully treated):**

1. Delusions
2. Hallucinations
3. Disorganized speech (such as frequent derailment or incoherence)
4. Grossly disorganized or catatonic behaviour
5. Negative symptoms, such as affective flattening, alogia, or avolition

(*Note:* Only one A symptom is required if delusions are bizarre or hallucinations consist of a voice keeping up a running commentary on the person's behaviour or thoughts, or two or more voices conversing with each other.)

**B. Social/Occupational Dysfunction: For a significant portion of the time since the onset of the disturbance, one or more major areas of functioning such as work, interpersonal relations, or self-care is markedly below the level achieved prior to the onset.**

**C. Duration: Continuous signs of the disturbance persist for at least six months. This six-month period must include at least one month of symptoms that meet Criterion A (active phase symptoms), and may include periods of prodromal or residual symptoms. During these prodromal or residual periods, the signs of the disturbance may be manifested by only negative symptoms or two or more symptoms listed in Criterion A present in an attenuated form (such as odd beliefs, unusual perceptual experiences).**

functioning as well as a chronic, deteriorating course. The DSM-IV-TR definition requires evidence of a decline in the person's social or occupational functioning as well as the presence of disturbed behaviour over a continuous period of at least six months. Active phase symptoms do not need to be present for this entire period. The total duration of disturbance is determined by adding together continuous time during which the person has exhibited prodromal, active, and residual symptoms of schizophrenia. If the person displays positive symptoms for at least one month but less than six months, the diagnosis would be *schizophreniform disorder*. The diagnosis would be changed to schizophrenic disorder if the person's problems persisted beyond the six-month limit.

The final consideration in arriving at a diagnosis of schizophrenia involves the exclusion of related conditions, especially mood disorders. According to DSM-IV-TR, active phase symptoms of schizophrenia must appear in the absence of a major depressive or manic episode. If symptoms of depression or mania are present, their duration must be brief relative to the duration of the active and residual symptoms of schizophrenia.

## Subtypes

Schizophrenia is a heterogeneous disorder with many different clinical manifestations and levels of severity. The title of Bleuler's classic text referred to "the group of schizophrenias" in an effort to draw attention to the varied presentations of the disorder. It is not clear, however, how best to think about the different forms of schizophrenia. Many clinicians and investigators, such as York University psychologist R. Walter Heinrichs (2001), believe that schizophrenia is a general term for a group of disorders, each of which may be caused by a completely different set of factors. Other clinicians believe that the numerous symptoms of schizophrenia are most likely varying manifestations of the same underlying condition (Gottesman, 1991). Given the current state of evidence, it is not possible to choose between these conceptual options. Nevertheless, most investigators agree that we should at least consider the possibility that there are several distinct forms.

**DSM-IV-TR Subcategories** DSM-IV-TR recognizes five subtypes of schizophrenia. The subtypes are used to describe the clinical state of the patient during the most recent examination. Only one subtype can be assigned at any point in time. The five subtypes are arranged in a hierarchy so that patients who exhibit symptoms of different subtypes can be diagnosed. The catatonic type is at the top of the hierarchy. Patients who fit this description are diagnosed as catatonic even if they show additional symptoms that are characteristic of other subtypes. The remaining subtypes, in descending order, are the disorganized subtype, the paranoid subtype, the undifferentiated subtype, and the residual subtype.

The **catatonic type** is characterized by symptoms of motor immobility (including rigidity and posturing) or excessive and purposeless motor activity. In some cases, the person may be resistant to all instructions or refuse to speak, for no apparent reason. Catatonic patients may also show a decreased awareness of their environment and a lack of movement and activity. If her disorder lasted more than six months, Marsha probably would have received a diagnosis of schizophrenic disorder, catatonic type, on the basis of her prominent motor symptoms and stuporous behaviour.

The **disorganized type** of schizophrenia is characterized by disorganized speech, disorganized behaviour, and flat or inappropriate affect. All three features must be present to make this diagnosis. Social impairment is usually quite marked in these patients. The patient's speech is frequently incoherent, and if delusions or hallucinations are present, their content is usually not well organized. Consider, for example, the delusions expressed by Edward. At various times, he talked about Nazi soldiers and World War II, frozen corpses in Greenland, being "half a person," and having special powers because he was the son of God. These fragmented and bizarre ideas were clearly delusional, but they were not woven into a coherent framework.

The most prominent symptoms in the **paranoid type** are systematic delusions with persecutory or grandiose content. Preoccupation with frequent auditory hallucinations can also be associated with the paranoid type. Patients who exhibit disorganized speech, disorganized behaviour, flat or inappropriate affect, or catatonic behaviour are excluded from a diagnosis of paranoid schizophrenia and would fall into one of the other subtypes.

Two additional subtypes are described in DSM-IV-TR, presumably to cover those patients who do not fit one of the traditional types. The **undifferentiated type** of schizophrenia includes schizophrenic patients who display prominent psychotic symptoms and either meet the criteria for several subtypes or otherwise do not meet the criteria for the catatonic, disorganized, or paranoid types. They often exhibit some disorganized symptoms together with hallucinations and/or delusions.

The **residual type** includes patients who no longer meet the criteria for active phase symptoms but nevertheless demonstrate continued signs of negative symptoms or attenuated forms of delusions, hallucinations, or disorganized speech. They are in "partial remission."

**Evaluation of Traditional Subtypes** The usefulness of the traditional subtypes has been debated extensively. Clinicians who advocate the use of subtype diagnoses claim that these categories are moderately stable over time (Fenton, 2000). Although traditional subtypes do not strongly predict either the course of the disorder or the response to treatment, there is some evidence indicating that patients who fit descriptions of the catatonic and paranoid subtypes have the best prognosis, whereas those in the disorganized subtype may have the worst prognosis (McGlashan & Fenton, 1991).

Critics respond by noting that the subtypes have relatively poor diagnostic reliability and are frequently unstable over time. Patients who fit a traditional subcategory during one psychotic episode may satisfy criteria for a different subtype diagnosis during a subsequent disturbance (Kendler, Gruenberg, & Tsuang, 1985). Perhaps most important is the fact that studies of extended families suggest that the traditional subtypes of schizophrenia are not etiologically distinct syndromes (Cardno et al., 1998; Kendler et al., 1994). If several members of a family—or two members of a monozygotic twin pair—have developed symptoms of schizophrenia, they will not necessarily exhibit symptoms of the same subtype.

Manfred Bleuler, a Swiss psychiatrist and the son of Eugen Bleuler, treated and observed more than 200 schizophrenic patients over a long period of time. His experience suggested that distinctions among subtypes become blurred over time. Bleuler's follow-up data and much of the other research evidence support the hypothesis that symptomatic subtypes are a reflection of varying stages of a single disorder or varying levels of severity of the disorder (Goldberg & Weinberger, 1995; Gottesman, 1991).

## Related Psychotic Disorders

The North American concept of schizophrenia is relatively narrow. The boundaries of the disorder have been refined by excluding patients with certain types of psychotic symptoms from a diagnosis of schizophrenic disorder. Immediately after its description of schizophrenia, DSM-IV-TR lists three additional disorders that are characterized by prominent psychotic symptoms.

**Schizoaffective disorder** is an ambiguous and somewhat controversial category (Frances, First, & Pincus, 1995). It describes the symptoms of patients who fall on the boundary between schizophrenia and mood disorder with psychotic features. This diagnosis applies only to the description of a particular episode of disturbance; it does not describe the overall lifetime course of the person's disorder. Schizoaffective disorder is defined by an episode in which the symptoms of schizophrenia partially overlap with a major depressive episode or a manic episode. The key to making this diagnosis is the presence of delusions or hallucinations for at least two weeks in the absence of prominent mood symptoms. If the delusions and hallucinations are present only during a depressive episode, for example, the diagnosis would be major depressive episode with psychotic features. Schizoaffective disorder will continue to be a vague diagnostic category until progress is made in unravelling the different causal mechanisms that might be involved in mood disorders and schizophrenia.

People with **delusional disorder** do not meet the full symptomatic criteria for schizophrenia, but they are preoccupied for at least one month with delusions that are not bizarre. These are beliefs about situations that could occur in real life, such as being followed or poisoned. The presence of hallucinations, disorganized speech, catatonic behaviour, or negative symptoms rules out a diagnosis of delusional disorder. The definition of delusional disorder also holds that the person's behaviour is not bizarre and that social and occupational functioning are not impaired except for those areas that are directly affected by the delusional belief.

**Brief psychotic disorder** is a category that includes those people who exhibit psychotic symptoms—delusions, hallucinations, disorganized speech, or grossly disorganized or catatonic behaviour—for at least one day but no more than one month. An episode of this sort is typically accompanied by confusion and emotional turmoil, often (but not necessarily) following a markedly stressful event. After the symptoms are resolved, the person returns to the same level of functioning that had been achieved prior to the psychotic episode. The long-term outcome is good for most patients who experience a brief episode of psychosis (Susser et al., 1998). This diagnosis is not assigned if the symptoms are better explained by a mood disorder, schizophrenia, or substance abuse. This category is used infrequently, and very little research has been conducted with people who have this disorder.

**Course and Outcome in Schizophrenia (8 Types)**

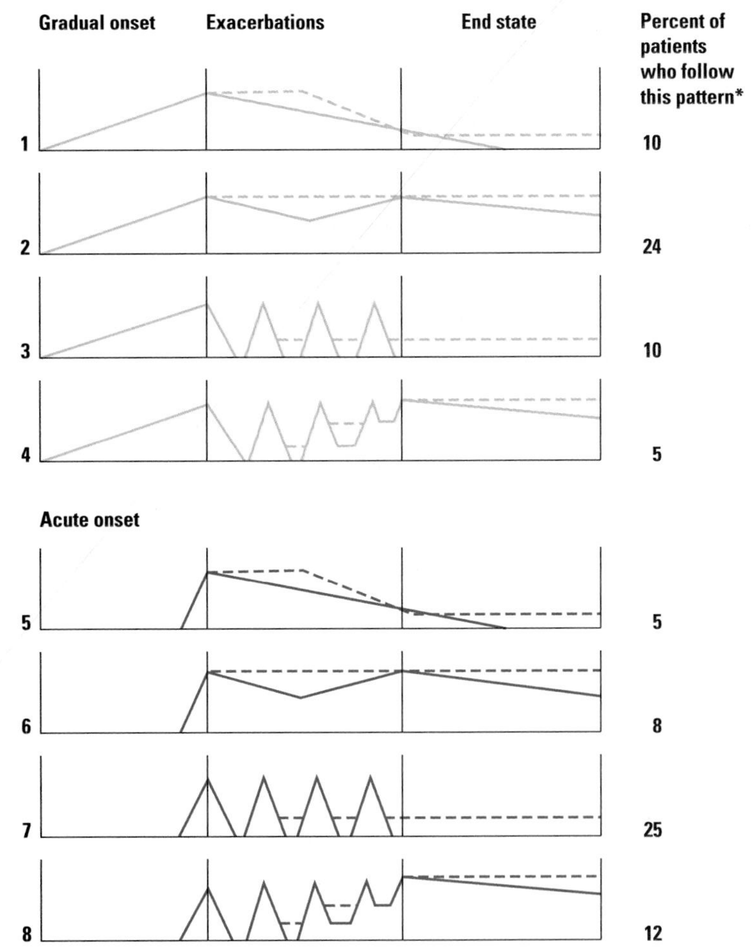


**FIGURE 13–1: Patterns identified in long-term follow-up studies. The horizontal axis represents time and the vertical axis represents severity of disturbance. Dotted lines represent slight variations on the overall pattern.**

*Data from Ciompi, 1980.

*Source:* C.M. Harding, 1988, Course types in schizophrenia: An analysis of European and American studies. *Schizophrenia Bulletin, 14,* 633–643.

## Course and Outcome

Schizophrenia is a severe, progressive disorder that most often begins in adolescence and typically has a poor outcome. However, many patients experience a good outcome. For example, Manfred Bleuler (1978) studied a sample of 208 schizophrenic patients who had been admitted to his hospital in Switzerland during 1942 and 1943. After a follow-up period of 23 years, 53 percent of the patients were either recovered or significantly improved.

In order to describe more completely the various patterns that patients followed over time, Bleuler identified two types of onset (sudden or gradual), two types of course (undulating or simple), and two types of outcome (recovered/mild impairment or moderate/severe impairment). When combined, these elements form eight basic patterns for the onset and course of schizophrenic disorders, as illustrated in Figure 13–1.

A long-term follow-up study of schizophrenia, reported by the Swiss psychiatrist Luc Ciompi (1980), provided useful information about the proportion of patients whose disorder fits into the types of onset, course, and outcome that Bleuler proposed. Ciompi found that approximately half of the 228 patients in his study suffered an acute onset of symptoms during their initial episode. Again, during the intermediate stages of the disorder, half of the patients followed an undulating course, whereas the others exhibited relatively stable symptoms. By the time the patients had reached the end state of their disorder, half had recovered (or showed only mild residual symptoms), whereas the other half continued to experience moderate or severe impairment. The proportions of patients in Ciompi's study who fit different combinations of onset, course, and outcome are indicated in Figure 13–1.

Follow-up studies of schizophrenic patients have found that the description of outcome can be a complicated process. Many factors must be taken into consideration other than whether the person is still in the hospital. Is the person still exhibiting symptoms of the disorder? Does he or she have any other problems, such as depression or anxiety? Is the person employed? Does she have any friends? How does he get along with other people? The evidence indicates that different dimensions of outcome, such as social adjustment, occupational functioning, and symptom severity, are only loosely correlated. As in most situations where psychologists attempt to predict future behaviour, the outcome data regarding schizophrenia suggest that the best predictor of future social adjustment is previous social adjustment. Similarly, the best predictor of symptom severity at follow-up is severity of psychotic symptoms at initial assessment (Carpenter & Strauss, 1991).

Research conducted at the University of British Columbia also indicates that the greater the number of friends and acquaintances in the schizophrenic patient's social network, the better the level of his or her adaptive functioning at follow-up (Erickson, Beiser, & Iacono, 1998; Erickson et al., 1989). The results further suggest that it is the supportive social environment present during the period prior to the development of schizophrenia—not the person's longstanding social competence—that predicts long-term adjustment. Note that these findings represent trends; they apply to most patients, but there are exceptions.

In order to better appreciate the course of schizophrenia over the lifespan, consider the case examples of Sue and Joe in the Canadian Focus box.

## CANADIAN FOCUS Long-Term Course of Schizophrenia: Two Examples

Sue and Joe were among a series of patients in a 20- to 30-year follow-up study by Mary V. Seeman, a psychiatrist at the University of Toronto. They were first treated during the early 1970s at Toronto's Clarke Institute of Psychiatry. In 1997 these patients were still being treated at the Clarke, at which point they were evaluated for Seeman's study. Seeman (1998) assessed these patients with structured clinical interviews, and also obtained information from the patients' clinical records and from interviews with their case managers.

Note that the following case descriptions of Sue and Joe refer to "depot" injections of antipsychotic medication. This is a form of slow-release medication given every two to four weeks (Kane, 1996). One case also refers to the use of electroconvulsive therapy (ECT). ECT is a safe and effective treatment that is sometimes used to treat acute psychotic episodes for patients who have not responded to, or cannot tolerate, antipsychotic medications (Working Group for the Canadian Psychiatric Association and Canadian Alliance for Research on Schizophrenia, 1998).

### Sue

Sue was born in 1943 in Western Canada but has lived in Toronto since her late teens. In 1997 she was 54 years old. Although Sue does not regularly attend treatment appointments, she is well known to the Clarke staff, especially the staff in the emergency room. Her pattern over the last 10 years has been to drop into the Clarke unexpectedly, either to quarrel with staff or to ask for a depot injection of antipsychotic medication. Sometimes, when it is cold outside, she visits the emergency room asking for directions to a hostel bed. On other occasions she is brought in by police because of aggressive behaviour. Sue is frequently verbally loud, irritable, and insulting.

There is a strong history of schizophrenia in Sue's family. Her father and two of her five siblings were diagnosed with schizophrenia, and each spent long periods in psychiatric hospitals.

Before developing schizophrenia, Sue had superior academic skills and a large network of friends and acquaintances. She left school and began work when she was 16. Sue had various office jobs, and was regularly promoted and received substantial salary increases. Before her first hospital admission, at age 28, she had been married and divorced, and had used hashish and LSD on several occasions. Over the course of the year prior to admission, she developed fears that television personalities were interfering with her life. Despite these fears, she was working regularly until the very day she was admitted to the hospital.

During the first decade of her schizophrenia (1971–81), Sue was treated with daily oral doses of chlorpromazine, which managed to keep her symptoms under control. During that period she continued to work steadily. Sue was well dressed, elegant, well spoken, and led an active life. She had a job, had intimate relationships, had contact with her family, and was independent. After her first hospital admission, she was re-hospitalized only once during these 10 years, and for only a short period. Sue changed jobs frequently, but always managed to find employment because of her excellent office skills. Sue's last paid job ended in 1981. She has never worked again.

After 1981, when she was 38, Sue's psychotic symptoms progressively worsened. Other problems also worsened, including increasing substance abuse, alienation from her family, fights with boyfriends, and frequent changes in

*continued*

*cont.*

residence. Since 1981 she has had more and more frequent hospital admissions. From 1971 to 1997 she had 37 psychiatric hospitalizations, some short, some very long. During this period Sue became increasingly inconsistent in her treatment contacts.

From a handsome, well-groomed, competent woman, Sue has become an exceptionally ill-kempt street-person dressed in rags. She is now continuously psychotic and difficult to understand. Sue is very delusional, but in a disorganized way, so it is impossible to know what she is delusional about. She is usually homeless, although residences are found for her. She has become raucous, disruptive, and verbally abusive, probably due to her addiction to street drugs. On several occasions, while living on the streets, she has been physically and sexually assaulted. Sue is frequently suicidal. She sometimes threatens to harm other people, and so she has become the object of fear. As mentioned earlier, she occasionally comes to the emergency room for an injection of depot medication, but seems unable to keep regular appointments.

Looking back over Sue's life, Seeman (1998) observed that Sue's good premorbid skills—that is, her social, financial, and occupational skills—probably shielded her from trouble during the first decade of her illness. The schizophrenia vulnerability, evident in her family history, may have then overpowered her compensatory abilities. When assessed in 1997 she had become one of the most seriously ill of all the Clarke's outpatients. Sue's social supports have disappeared over time, her parents have died, and her one healthy sister refuses to have any contact with her. As Sue grew less and less attractive, there were fewer boyfriends. Seeman notes that the loss of these social resources may have contributed to Sue's profound deterioration.

### Joe

Joe, a Portuguese Canadian, was born in 1949. He was not a good student and left school when he was 14 to work at a manual job. He worked until age 23, when he was abruptly admitted to hospital with psychotic symptoms that had developed over the previous year. Joe believed he was Satan. His delusional symptoms resulted in violent behaviour and did not respond to medication. He therefore received seven sessions of ECT and was subsequently discharged from hospital on depot antipsychotic medication.

After this episode Joe was never able to return to work. He lived with his parents and had no friends. During the first decade of his illness he was periodically hospitalized, which seemed to be a result of his noncompliance with depot injections. Whenever he stopped coming in for injections, he was re-hospitalized within several months.

After his last hospital admission in 1988, Joe's parents refused to allow him to return home because they had become afraid of his violence. Joe went to live in a boarding home, where he met and married the housekeeper. She has continued to work and support the household. She looks after Joe, and ensures that he never misses an injection. Currently, he has few symptoms. Despite a family history of schizophrenia (he has a brother diagnosed with it), things have turned out reasonably well for him. Joe is neatly groomed, well dressed, and more sociable than before. He is pleased to do the domestic work in the house, occasionally obtains a paying job to supplement the family income, and appears to be very happy. Seeman notes that Joe's good outcome is clearly attributable to the influence of his wife, and to the accompanying adherence to treatment. ◆

## Epidemiology

About 1 percent of adult Canadians will develop schizophrenia, diagnosed according to DSM-IV-TR (Health Canada, 2002a). The lifetime prevalence of DSM-IV-TR schizophrenia is broadly similar throughout the world, estimates being around 1 to 2 percent. Of course, prevalence rates depend on the diagnostic criteria that are used to define schizophrenia in any particular study, as well as the methods that are used to identify cases in the general population. Investigators who have employed more narrow or restrictive criteria for the disorder typically report lower lifetime prevalence (Haefner & Heiden, 1997; Jones & Cannon, 1998). The mean age of onset is 20 years, and 71 percent of the people who develop schizophrenia will experience their first symptoms by the age of 25 (Keith, Regier, & Rae, 1991).

### Gender Differences

Most epidemiological studies indicate that men and women are equally likely to be affected by schizophrenia (Gottesman, 1991; Keith, Regier, & Rae, 1991). This conclusion has been challenged by a few studies (e.g., Iacono & Beiser, 1992) that suggest that among new cases of schizophrenia men may outnumber women by a ratio of at least two to one. This pattern seems to depend on the breadth of the diagnostic criteria that are employed to identify cases of the disorder, as studies that use broader, more inclusive sets of diagnostic criteria are more likely to find equivalent rates of schizophrenia in men and women (Cannon et al., 1998; Goldstein, 1997).

The controversy surrounding gender differences in incidence may reflect, at least in part, gender differences in more specific aspects of schizophrenia. There are some widely recognized differences between male and female patients with regard to patterns of onset, symptoms, and course of the disorder. For example, the average age at which schizophrenic males begin to exhibit overt symptoms is younger by about four or five years than the average age at which schizophrenic women first experience problems (Tamminga, 1997). A summary of proposed gender differences in schizophrenia is presented in Table 13–2. Male patients are more likely than female patients to exhibit negative symptoms, and they are also more likely to follow a chronic, deteriorating course.

Gender differences in the age of onset and symptomatic expression of schizophrenia can be interpreted in several ways. The alternatives fall into two types of hypotheses. One approach assumes that schizophrenia is a single disorder and that its expression varies in men and women. A common, genetically determined vulnerability to schizophrenia might be expressed differently in men than in women. Mediating factors that might account for this difference could be biological differences between men and women—perhaps involving certain hormones—or different environmental demands, such as the timing and form of stresses associated with typical male and female sex roles. An alternative approach suggests that there are two qualitatively distinct subtypes of schizophrenia: one with an early onset that affects men more often than women, and another with a later onset that affects women more often than men. Both approaches fit the general diathesis-stress model. The available evidence does not allow us to favour one of these explanations over the other (Haefner et al., 1998; Lewine & Seeman, 1995; Salem & Kring, 1998).

**TABLE 13–2 Typical Gender Differences in Schizophrenia**

| Variable | Men | Women |
|---|---|---|
| Age of onset | Earlier (18–25) | Later (25–35) |
| Premorbid functioning; adjustment | Poor social functioning; more schizotypal traits | Good social functioning; fewer schizotypal traits |
| Typical symptoms | More negative symptoms; more withdrawn and passive | More hallucinations and paranoia; more emotional and impulsive |
| Course | More often chronic; poorer response to treatment | Less often chronic; better response to treatment |

*Source:* Based on J.M. Goldstein, 1995, The impact of gender on understanding the epidemiology of schizophrenia. In M.V. Seeman (Ed.), *Gender and Psychopathology*, pp. 159–199. Washington, DC: American Psychiatric Press.

## Cross-Cultural Comparisons

Schizophrenia has been observed in virtually every culture that has been subjected to careful scrutiny. Of course, the formal term *schizophrenia* is not used in all societies, but the symptoms of the disorder are nevertheless present.

Two large-scale epidemiological studies, conducted by teams of scientists working for the World Health Organization (WHO), indicate that the incidence of schizophrenia is relatively constant across different cultural settings. The International Pilot Study of Schizophrenia (IPSS) began in the 1960s and was conducted in nine countries in Europe, North America, South America, Africa, and Asia. It included 1200 patients who were followed for five years after their initial hospitalization. The Collaborative Study on the Determinants of Outcome of Severe Mental Disorders (DOS) was conducted a few years later in six of the same countries that had participated in the IPSS, plus four others. The DOS study included more than 1500 patients. Both the IPSS and DOS projects examined rural and urban areas in both Western and non-Western countries. For purposes of cultural comparison, countries can be divided into those that are "developing" (e.g., Nigeria) and those that are already "developed" on the basis of prevailing socioeconomic conditions (e.g., Canada). All the interviewers were trained in the use of a single, standardized interview schedule, and all employed the same sets of diagnostic criteria.

The IPSS results indicated that patients who exhibited characteristic signs and symptoms of schizophrenia were found in all of the study sites. Comparisons of patients across research centres revealed more similarities than differences in clinical symptoms at the time of entry into the study, which was always an active phase of disorder that required psychiatric treatment. Using a relatively narrow set of diagnostic criteria, scientists found that the incidence of schizophrenia did not differ significantly among the research centres. The IPSS investigators also found that clinical and social outcomes at two- and five-year follow-up were significantly better for schizophrenic patients in developing countries than in developed countries (Leff et al., 1992). The DOS study confirmed those results (Craig et al., 1997; Jablensky et al., 1992).

Taken together, the WHO studies provide compelling support for the conclusion that schizophrenia occurs with similar frequency and presents with similar symptoms in different cultures. Most experts believe that the more favourable clinical outcome that was observed in India and Nigeria is a product of the greater tolerance and acceptance extended to people with psychotic symptoms in developing countries. This conclusion is consistent with evidence regarding the relationship between frequency of relapse and patterns of family communication, which we consider later in this chapter in the section on expressed emotion. These cross-cultural data certainly testify to the important influence of culture in shaping the experience and expression of psychotic symptoms (Thakker & Ward, 1998).

Although the prevalence of schizophrenia is stable across most countries and cultures, there are some noteworthy exceptions. For example, the 12-month prevalence of schizophrenia is somewhat lower among people living in Hutterite colonies in Manitoba compared to the prevalence elsewhere in Canada (Nimgaonkar et al., 2000). Differences in prevalence may be due to some combination of cultural and genetic factors.

# Etiological Considerations and Research

## Biological Factors

Research in the areas of molecular genetics and the neurosciences has progressed at an explosive rate in the past decade.

**Genetics** The cumulative weight of this evidence points clearly toward some type of genetic influence in the transmission of schizophrenia (Gottesman & Moldin, 1997; Kendler, 1997; Tsuang, 2000).

*Family Studies* Figure 13–2 illustrates the lifetime risk for schizophrenia for various types of relatives of a person with schizophrenia. These data, compiled by Gottesman (1991), are the pooled results of 40 European studies published between 1920 and 1987. All the studies employed conservative diagnostic criteria for the disorder.

Consider the data for first-degree relatives and second-degree relatives. On average, siblings and children share 50 percent of their genes with the schizophrenic proband; nieces, nephews, and cousins share only 25 percent. The lifetime morbid risk for schizophrenia is much greater among first-degree relatives than it is among second-degree relatives. The risk in the second-degree relatives is greater than the 1 percent figure that is typically reported for people in the general population. As the degree of genetic similarity increases between an individual and a schizophrenic patient, the risk to that person increases. The family history data are consistent with the hypothesis that the transmission of schizophrenia is influenced by genetic factors. They do not prove the point, however, because family studies do not separate genetic and environmental events (see Chapter 2).

*Twin Studies* Several twin studies have examined concordance rates for schizophrenia. The results of these studies are also summarized in Figure 13–2. The average concordance rate for MZ twins is 48 percent, whereas the comparable figure for DZ twins is 17 percent. One study from Finland, published after Gottesman computed average rates for his figure, found a concordance rate of 46 percent among MZ twins and only 9 percent among DZ twins (Cannon et al., 1998). Although the specific rates vary somewhat from study to study, all of the published reports have found that MZ twins are significantly more likely than DZ twins to be concordant for schizophrenia. This pattern suggests strongly that genetic factors play an important role in the development of the disorder.

It should also be pointed out, however, that none of the twin studies of schizophrenia has found a concordance rate that even approaches 100 percent, which would be expected if genetic factors were entirely responsible for schizophrenia. Thus the twin studies also provide compelling evidence for the importance of environmental events. Some people, like Marsha in the case presented earlier, apparently inherit a predisposition to the development of schizophrenia. Among that select group of vulnerable individuals, certain environmental events must determine whether a given person will eventually exhibit the full-blown symptoms of the disorder.

*Adoption Studies* Studies of children who were adopted away from their biological parents and reared by foster families provide this type of clear distinction between genetic and environmental influence. The first adoption study of schizophrenia was reported by Heston (1966). He began by identifying records for a group of 49 children who were born between 1915 and 1945 while their mothers were hospitalized for schizophrenia. All the children were apparently normal at birth and were separated from their mothers within three days of birth. To rule out possible exposure to the environment associated with the mother's psychosis, any child who had been in contact with maternal relatives was excluded from the study. A control group of children was selected using the admission records of foundling homes where many of the target children had originally been placed. These children were matched to the patients' children on a number of variables, including age, sex, type of eventual placement, and amount of time spent in institutions.

Heston was able to locate and interview most of the offspring, the majority of whom were then in their mid-thirties. Five of the adult offspring of schizophrenic mothers received a diagnosis of schizophrenia. Correcting for the fact that most of the participants were still within the period of risk for the disorder, this resulted in a lifetime morbidity risk for schizophrenia of 16.6 percent in the target group, which is almost exactly the rate observed among children of schizophrenic parents who were raised by their biological parents (see Figure 13–2). In contrast, none of the adult offspring in the control group received a diagnosis of schizophrenia. Because the only difference between the two groups was the genetic relationship between the target offspring and their schizophrenic biological mothers, Heston's data indicate that genetic factors play a role in the development of the disorder. Several other adoption studies have been concerned with schizophrenia, and all reach the same conclusion as Heston's original report (see Gottesman, 1991, and Kendler & Diehl, 1993, for reviews of this literature).

**Average Risk of Developing Schizophrenia**

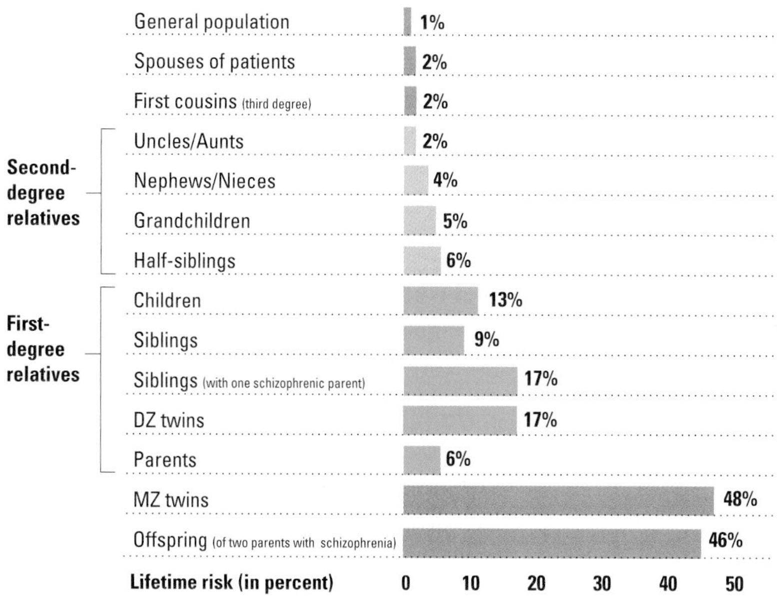


**FIGURE 13–2: Average risk of schizophrenia among biological relatives of a schizophrenic proband.**

*Source:* I.I. Gottesman, 1991, *Schizophrenia Genesis: The Origins of Madness*, p. 96. New York: Freeman.

*The Spectrum of Schizophrenic Disorders* Results from adoption and twin studies have provided clues regarding the boundaries of the concept of schizophrenia. Several types of psychotic disorders and personality disorders resemble schizophrenia in one way or another, including schizoaffective disorder, delusional disorder, and schizotypal personality disorder (discussed in Chapter 9). Are these conditions a reflection of the same genetically determined predisposition as schizophrenia, or are they etiologically distinct disorders? If they are genetically related, then investigators should find that the biological relatives of schizophrenic adoptees are more likely to exhibit these conditions as well as schizophrenia. The overall pattern of results suggests that vulnerability to schizophrenia is sometimes expressed as schizophrenia-like personality traits and other types of psychosis that are not specifically included in the DSM-IV-TR definition of schizophrenia (Kendler & Gardner, 1997).

*Linkage Studies* The combined results from twin and adoption studies indicate that genetic factors are involved in the transmission of schizophrenia. This conclusion does not imply, however, that the manner in which schizophrenia develops is well understood. We know little beyond the fact that genetic factors are involved in some way. The mode of transmission has not been identified. Some clinical scientists believe that a single dominant gene is involved. Others believe that schizophrenia is a polygenic characteristic, which means that it is the product of a reasonably large number of genes rather than a single gene (see Chapter 2).

One of the most exciting areas of research on genetics and schizophrenia focuses on the search for genetic linkage (see Research Methods in Chapter 14 for an explanation of this process). Studies of this type are designed to identify the location of a specific gene that is responsible for the disorder (or some large component of the disorder).

Linkage analysis has been unable to identify a *specific gene* for schizophrenia, but it has implicated *regions* on a small number of chromosomes that may contribute to the etiology of the disorder. Researchers, such as Anne Bassett and colleagues at the University of Toronto, have been searching for genetic subtypes of schizophrenia. It may be that there are several different sets of genetic anomalies; each set might independently give rise to schizophrenia.

Research on the genetics of schizophrenia is an important, ongoing endeavour. The results so far are suggestive, but not conclusive. Reports of positive linkage on regions of chromosomes 6, 8, and 22 have been verified by more than one laboratory (Gottesman & Moldin, 1999; Kendler, 1997; Shastry, 1999). To illustrate, one form of schizophrenia appears to be associated with small deletions on chromosome 22 (Bassett & Chow, 1999; Bassett et al., 1998). Approximately 25 percent of people with this genetic abnormality develop a psychotic disorder such as schizophrenia. These people also tend to have characteristic facial features (e.g., long, narrow face, prominent nose, small ears and mouth) and congenital defects (e.g., heart defects). A challenge for further research is to establish whether the chromosome 22 abnormalities are causes of schizophrenia, or whether they are simply correlates. It could be that people with abnormalities on this chromosome also tend to have other, undetected genetic abnormalities. The latter might be the true genetic cause of their schizophrenia.

We must remember that the identification of chromosome regions is only one step in the direction of finding specific genes. The region that has been implicated on the short arm of chromosome 6, for example, probably contains between 2000 and 4000 genes. Supporters of linkage analysis contend that the absence of more definitive discoveries is not surprising when we consider the complexity of this process and the magnitude of the search. They feel that the search for a particular gene that causes schizophrenia will simply take more time (Kidd, 1997; Waterworth, Bassett, & Brzustowicz, 2002). Critics respond that schizophrenia is a polygenic disorder, and therefore we will never trace its etiology to a single gene. There is good reason to believe that polygenic models provide the best explanation for the distribution of the disorder within families (Gottesman & Moldin, 1997).

**Pregnancy and Birth Complications** People with schizophrenia are more likely than the general population to have been exposed to various problems during their mother's pregnancy and to have suffered birth complications. Birth records, for example, indicate that the mothers of people who later develop schizophrenia experienced more complications at the time of labour and delivery (Cannon, Jones, & Murray, 2002; McNeil & Cantor-Graae, 1999).Problems during pregnancy include the mother's contracting various types of diseases and infections. Birth complications include extended labour, breech delivery, forceps delivery, and the umbilical cord wrapped around the baby's neck. Consistent with these findings, a Canadian team of investigators found that schizophrenia tends to be associated with poor fetal growth, premature birth, and low birth weight (Smith et al., 2001). Complications during pregnancy and birth may be harmful, in part, because they impair circulation or otherwise reduce the availability of oxygen to developing brain regions.

It is not clear whether the effects of pregnancy and birth complications interact with genetic factors. They may produce neurodevelopmental abnormalities that result in schizophrenia regardless of family history for the disorder. Conversely, a fetus that is genetically predisposed to schizophrenia may be more susceptible to brain injury following certain kinds of obstetric difficulties (Cannon, 1997; Walker & Diforio, 1997).

**Viral Infections** Some speculation has focused on the potential role that viral infections may play in the etiology of schizophrenia (Brown et al., 2001; Munk-Jorgensen, 2001). One indirect line of support for this hypothesis comes from studies indicating that people who develop schizophrenia are somewhat more likely than other people to have been born during the winter months (McGrath & Welham, 1999; Narita et al., 2000). Some clinicians interpret this pattern to mean that, during their pregnancies, the mothers were more likely to develop viral infections, which are more prevalent during the winter. Exposure to infection presumably interferes with brain development in the fetus. This possibility has received considerable attention in the research literature and remains an important topic of debate. Research support for the hypothesis remains inconsistent (Westergaard et al., 1999).

**Neuropathology** One important step toward understanding the etiology of schizophrenia would be to identify its neurological underpinnings. If people with schizophrenia suffer from a form of neurological dysfunction, shouldn't it be possible to observe differences between the structure of their brains and those of other people? This is a very challenging task. Scientists have invented methods to create images of the living human brain (see Chapter 4). Some of these procedures provide static pictures of various brain structures at rest, just as an X-ray provides a photographic image of a bone or some other organ of the body. More recently, sophisticated methods have enabled us to create functional images of the brain while a person is performing different tasks. Studies using these techniques have produced evidence indicating that a number of brain areas are involved in schizophrenia (Andreasen, 2001; Shenton et al., 2001). You may want to review the description of brain structures in Chapter 2 (Figure 2–3) before reading the next sections of this chapter.

*Structural Brain Imaging* Many investigations of brain structure in people with schizophrenia have employed magnetic resonance imaging (MRI; see Chapter 4 for an explanation of this process). The disorder is not associated with abnormalities in one specific brain region or in one particular type of nerve cell. Rather, it seems to affect many different regions of the brain and the ways in which they connect or communicate with each other (McGlashan & Hoffman, 2000). Most MRI studies have reported a decrease in total volume of brain tissue among schizophrenic patients. Another consistent finding is that some people with schizophrenia have mildly to moderately enlarged lateral ventricles, the cavities on each side of the brain that are filled with cerebrospinal fluid (Lawrie & Abukmeil, 1998; Pearlson & Marsh, 1999).

These differences seem to reflect a natural part of the disorder rather than a side effect of treatment with antipsychotic medication. In fact, some studies have found enlarged ventricles in young schizophrenic patients before they have been exposed to any form of treatment (Lieberman et al., 2001). One important study has also found enlarged ventricles prior to the onset of symptoms (see Research Close-Up). Significantly, these differences do not appear to become more marked as time goes on. The structural changes seem to occur early in the development of the disorder and therefore may play a role in the onset of symptoms (Cannon, 1998; Weinberger & McClure, 2002).

## RESEARCH CLOSE-UP

### The Danish High-Risk Project

Our ability to understand the etiology of schizophrenia is limited by a lack of information regarding patients' developmental histories. Once a person has become psychotic, it is difficult to reconstruct events from previous years. Furthermore, comparisons between schizophrenic patients and other groups are difficult to interpret because the patients have already been exposed to treatment. For these reasons, it would be extremely useful if systematic data could be collected before the onset of the disorder. Accordingly, researchers have conducted high-risk studies, such as the Danish project (Mednick & Schulsinger, 1968) and the McMaster–Waterloo project (Steffy et al., 1984). To date, the longest and most informative study has been the Danish project.

In 1962, Mednick and Schulsinger began in Denmark a longitudinal study of biological children of parents with schizophrenia. These people were selected because, in comparison to members of the general population, they were at high risk for schizophrenia. Roughly 13 percent of the high-risk group would be expected to develop the disorder as adults (see Figure 13–2). The project included 207 high-risk children whose biological mothers had been diagnosed as schizophrenic and 104 low-risk children to serve as a comparison group. The families of the low-risk children had been free of mental illness for at least

*continued*

*cont.*

three generations. When the study was begun, none of the children had exhibited any overt signs of psychological disorder. The family environments (for example, social class, rural or urban residence) were similar in both groups.

Mednick and his colleagues have collected an enormous amount of information in order to describe the developmental histories of children in both groups, from birth to adulthood. They relied on hospital records to determine the frequency of pregnancy and delivery complications associated with each subject's birth. The investigators conducted follow-up assessments, including structured diagnostic interviews, with each person at two principal times: in the early 1970s and again in the late 1980s, when the participants' average age was 42 years. The latter assessment included the use of CT scans to detect structural brain pathology.

It has been more than 30 years since the Danish study began, and 31 of the high-risk offspring have developed schizophrenia (Parnas et al., 1993). Age-corrected morbid risk rates for schizophrenia in the high- and low-risk groups are 17 percent and 3 percent, respectively. The high-risk offspring were also more likely than the low-risk offspring to meet the criteria for schizotypal personality disorder (18 percent compared to 5 percent). Rates of mood disorders were similar in both groups, suggesting that the high-risk group was predisposed to schizophrenia-spectrum disorders in particular rather than to serious mental disorders in general.

The most important data in this project involve factors that may precede the onset of schizophrenic symptoms. Several intriguing findings have been reported. For example, researchers noted a correlation between delivery complications and enlarged ventricles among people in the high-risk group but not among people in the low-risk group (Cannon et al., 1993). In addition, an earlier report indicated that, in comparison to members of the high-risk group who did not become schizophrenic, those high-risk individuals who did develop schizophrenia had experienced more pregnancy and birth complications (Cannon, Mednick, & Parnas, 1990). This was especially true for people who developed negative symptoms of the disorder. Thus far, the overall pattern of results suggests that vulnerability to schizophrenia may be associated with a pattern of fetal brain development that is especially sensitive to disruptions caused by delivery complications. The combination of genetic risk and problems in delivery seems to be especially relevant. Data from the Danish high-risk project are also consistent with the hypothesis that neurodevelopmental problems in schizophrenia are antecedents rather than consequences of the disorder. ◆

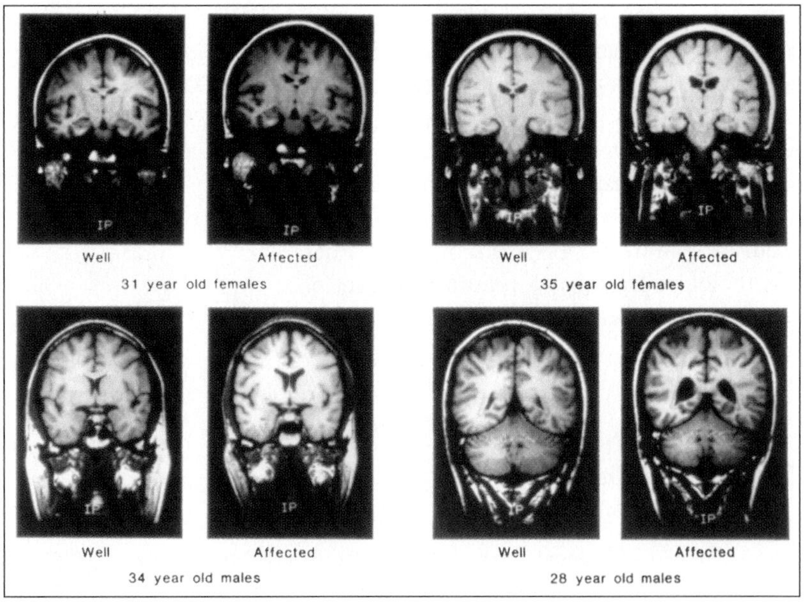


*MRI scans from four identical twin pairs discordant for schizophrenia showing varying degrees of increased ventricular size in the twin with the disorder compared to the twin who is well.*

The temporal lobes have also been studied extensively using MRI scans. Several studies have reported decreased size of the hippocampus, the parahippocampus, the amygdala, and the thalamus, all of which are parts of the limbic system (Altshuler et al., 2000; Copolov et al., 2000). These areas of the brain (see Figure 13–3) play a crucial role in the regulation of emotion as well as the integration of cognition and emotion. Decreased size of these structures in the limbic area of the temporal lobes may be especially noticeable on the left side of the brain, which plays an important role in the control of language. Schizophrenic patients who exhibit the greatest degree of disorganized speech may be most likely to show a decrease in the size of left temporal lobe structures (Shenton, 1996).

Another set of findings is focused on the planum temporale, an area of the temporal cortex that is involved in the processing of auditory stimuli (Hirayasu et al., 2000; see Figure 2–3). Normal men show marked hemispheric asymmetry for this structure; it is larger in the left hemisphere of the brain than in the right hemisphere. Women are less likely to show asymmetry with regard to the size of the planum temporale. Studies using MRI technology indicate that hemispheric asymmetry in the size of this brain structure may be reversed in men with schizophrenia; that is, it is larger in the right hemisphere. In comparison to people without the disorder, patients with schizophrenia show a reduction in the volume of the left planum temporale. This neurological irregularity may be related to their difficulties in verbal communication, as language skills seem to be regulated by the left hemisphere of the brain (Pearlson, 1997; Petty et al., 1995).

Many questions remain to be answered regarding the relation between structural brain abnormalities and schizophrenia. Does the pattern reflect a generalized deterioration of the brain, or is it the result of a defect in specific brain sites? We don't know. Is the presence of enlarged ventricles and cortical atrophy consistently found in some subset of schizophrenic patients? Some investigators have reported an association between this type of neuropathology and other factors, such as negative symptoms, poor response to medication, and absence of family history of the disorder. These are all possibilities, but none has been firmly established.

**Areas of the Brain Implicated in Schizophrenia**

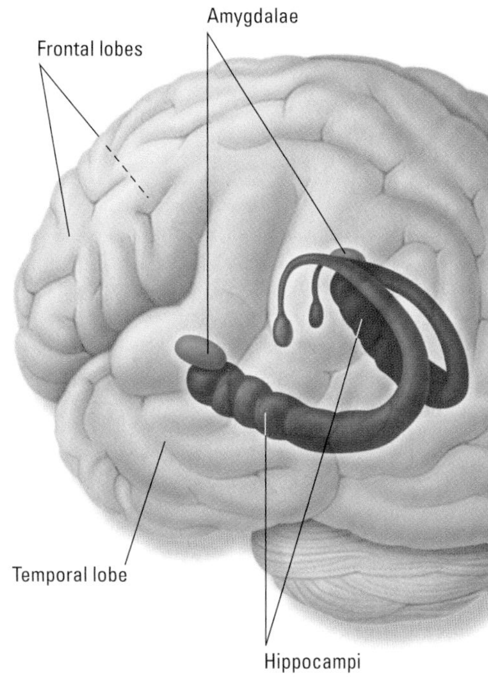


**FIGURE 13–3: Structural imaging procedures indicate reduced size of temporal lobe structures, such as the hippocampi and amygdalae, among some patients with schizophrenia.**

*Functional Brain Imaging* In addition to static pictures of brain structures, clinical scientists use techniques that provide dynamic images of brain functions. One dynamic brain imaging technique, known as positron emission tomography (PET), can reflect changes in brain activity as the person responds to various task demands. Visual stimulation will produce increased cerebral blood flow in the visual cortex; people performing a simple motor task exhibit increased flow in the motor cortex. Functional MRI is another tool that can be used to observe brain activity. The results of studies using these techniques suggest dysfunction in various neural circuits, including some regions of the prefrontal cortex (see Figure 13–4) and several regions in the temporal lobes (Barch et al., 2001; Harrison, 1999; Zakzanis & Heinrichs, 1999). The problems seem to involve activities within, as well as integration between, a variety of functional circuits rather than a localized abnormality in one region of the brain. Research from the University of Toronto and York University indicates that only some people with schizophrenia seem to have abnormalities in the functioning of the frontal or temporal lobes (Zakzanis et al., 2000; Zakzanis & Heinrichs, 1999), which suggests that there may be a specific subtype of schizophrenia that is associated with these abnormalities.

*General Conclusions* The primary conclusion that can be drawn from existing brain imaging studies is that schizophrenia is associated with diffuse patterns of neuropathology. The most consistent findings point toward structural as well as functional irregularities in the frontal cortex and limbic areas of the temporal lobes, which play an important role in cognitive and emotional processes. The neural networks connecting limbic areas with the frontal cortex may be fundamentally disordered in schizophrenia.

Speculation regarding disruptions in neural circuitry must also be tempered with caution. Evidence of neuropathology does not seem to be unique to schizophrenic patients. Many patients with other psychiatric and neurological disorders show similar changes in brain structure and function. Furthermore, a specific brain lesion has not been identified, and it is unlikely that one will be found. As Meehl (1990) has argued, it is unlikely that a disorder as complex as schizophrenia will be traced to a single site in the brain. The various symptoms and cognitive deficits that have been observed in schizophrenic patients may be linked to a host of subtle disruptions in neurological functions (Andreasen, 2001; Green, 2001).

It should also be emphasized that brain imaging procedures are not diagnostically meaningful tests for mental disorders. For

**Areas of the Brain Implicated in Schizophrenia**

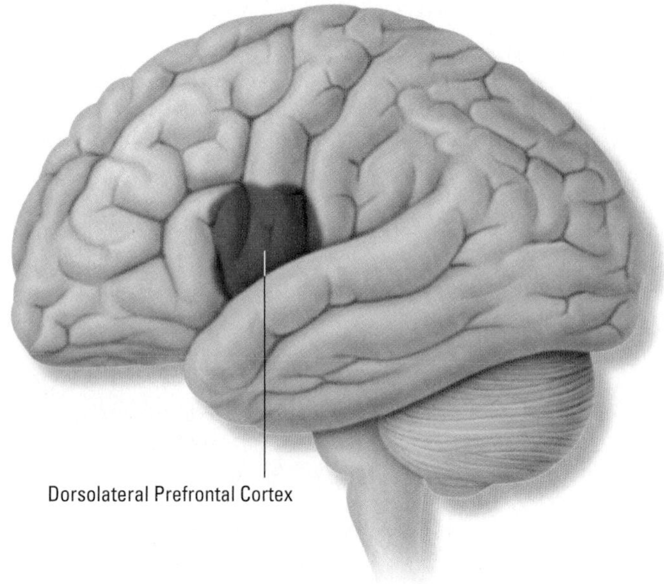


**FIGURE 13-4: Functional imaging procedures indicate abnormal activity levels in the dorsolateral prefrontal cortex.**

example, an MRI showing enlarged ventricles does not prove that a patient has schizophrenia. Brain imaging procedures have identified group differences, but they do not predict the presence of schizophrenia for individuals. The group differences that have been observed are very subtle in comparison to the levels of neuropathology found in disorders such as Alzheimer's disease and Huntington's disease (see Chapter 14). As noted earlier, some schizophrenic patients do not show abnormalities in brain structure or function.

**Neurochemistry** The neurological underpinnings of schizophrenia may not take the form of changes in the size or organization of brain structures. They may be even more subtle, involving alterations in the chemical communications among neurons within particular brain circuits.

*The Dopamine Hypothesis* Scientists have proposed various neurochemical theories to account for the etiology of schizophrenia. The most influential theory, known as the *dopamine hypothesis*, focuses on the function of specific dopamine pathways in the limbic area of the brain. The original version of the dopamine hypothesis proposed that the symptoms of schizophrenia are the product of excessive levels of dopaminergic activity. This hypothesis grew out of attempts to understand how antipsychotic drugs improve the adjustment of many schizophrenic patients. Animals who receive doses of antipsychotic drugs show a marked increase in the production of dopamine. In 1963, Arvid Carlsson, a Swedish pharmacologist, suggested that antipsychotic drugs block postsynaptic dopamine receptors. The presynaptic neuron recognizes the presence of this blockade and increases its release of dopamine in a futile attempt to override it (Carlsson & Lindqvist, 1963).

If the dopamine system is dysfunctional in schizophrenic patients, what is the specific form of this problem? One possibility is that certain neural pathways have an elevated sensitivity to dopamine because of increased numbers of postsynaptic dopamine receptors. The potency of various types of antipsychotic drugs is specifically related to their ability to block one type of dopamine receptor, known as $D_2$ receptors. Autopsy studies of schizophrenic patients' brains have found that some patients have an excessive number of $D_2$ receptors in the striatum (Roberts et al., 1996). The etiological significance of this finding is not clear because treatment with antipsychotic drugs produces an increase in the number of $D_2$ receptors. The density of dopamine receptors can be measured in the brains of living patients using PET. One laboratory has reported that untreated, first-episode schizophrenic patients have significantly more $D_2$ receptors when compared to a group of normal volunteers, but other studies have failed to replicate this result (Farde et al., 1995).

*Interactions of Multiple Neurotransmitters* A dysregulation and exaggerated response of certain dopamine pathways is certainly involved in schizophrenia, at least for some patients. On the other hand, experts now agree that several other neurotransmitters also play an important role. A neurochemical model focused narrowly on dopamine fails to explain many different aspects of the disorder, including the following: Some patients do not respond positively to drugs that block dopamine receptors; the effects of antipsychotic drugs require several days to become effective, but dopamine blockage begins immediately; research studies that examined the by-products of dopamine in cerebrospinal fluid were inconclusive at best.

Current neurochemical hypotheses regarding schizophrenia focus on a broad array of neurotransmitters (Carlsson et al., 2001). Special interest has been focused on serotonin pathways since the introduction of a new class of antipsychotic drugs such as clozapine (Clozaril) that are useful in treating patients who were resistant to standard antipsychotic drugs. (See the section on treatment.) These "atypical" antipsychotics produce a strong blockade of serotonin receptors and only a weak blockade of $D_2$ receptors. Several studies have found decreased serotonin receptor density in cortical areas of schizophrenic patients (Harrison, 1999). This pattern leads to speculation that the neurochemical substrates of schizophrenia may involve a complex interaction between serotonin and dopamine pathways in the brain (Kapur & Remington, 1996).

Brain imaging studies that point to problems in the prefrontal cortex have also drawn attention to glutamate and GABA (gamma-aminobutyric acid), the two principal neurotransmitters in the cerebral cortex. To illustrate, brain imaging research from investigators at the University of Western Ontario has shown that schizophrenia is associated with higher than normal glutamate levels in the left anterior cingulate cortex and thalamus, thereby providing evidence that schizophrenia is associated with elevated glutamatergic activity (Theberge et al., 2002). Glutamate is an excitatory neurotransmitter, and GABA is an inhibitory neurotransmitter. As in the case of serotonin, hypotheses regarding the role of glutamate and GABA focus on their interactions with dopamine pathways, especially those connecting temporal lobe structures with the prefrontal and limbic cortexes.

## Social Factors

There is little question that biological factors play an important role in the etiology of schizophrenia, but twin studies also provide compelling evidence for the importance of environmental events. The disorder is expressed in its full-blown form only when vulnerable individuals experience some type of environmental event, which might include anything from prenatal variables to stressful life events (McDonald & Murray, 2000). What sorts of nongenetic events interact with genetic factors and other biological factors to produce schizophrenia? Specific answers are not available at the present time. We can, however, review some of the hypotheses that have been proposed and studied.

**Social Class** One general indicator of a person's status within a community's hierarchy of prestige and influence is social class. People from different social classes are presumably exposed to different levels of environmental stress, with those people in the lowest class being subjected to the most hardships. In fact, the highest prevalence of schizophrenia is found in neighbourhoods of the lowest socioeconomic status (Brown et al., 2000; Mulvany et al., 2001).

There are two ways to interpret the relationship between social class and schizophrenia. One holds that harmful events associated with membership in the lowest social classes, which might include many factors ranging from stress and social isolation to poor nutrition, play a causal role in the development of the disorder. This is often called the *social causation hypothesis*. It is also possible, however, that low social class is an outcome rather than a cause of schizophrenia. Those people who develop schizophrenia may be less able than others to complete a higher-level education or to hold a well-paying job. Their cognitive and social impairments may cause downward social mobility. In other words, regardless of the social class of their family of origin, many schizophrenic patients may gradually drift into the lowest social classes. This view is sometimes called the *social selection hypothesis*.

Research studies have found evidence supporting both views. The social selection hypothesis is supported by studies that have compared the occupational roles of male schizophrenic patients with those of their fathers. The patients are frequently less successful than their fathers, whereas the opposite pattern is typical of men who do not have schizophrenia (Goldberg & Morrison, 1963; Jones et al., 1993).

It is also true, however, that a disproportionately high percentage of the fathers of schizophrenic patients were from the lowest social class (Turner & Wagonfeld, 1967). This finding is consistent with the social causation hypothesis. Additional support for the social causation hypothesis has been found using different research strategies. For example, a unique study considered the relation between economic conditions (employment rates) and rates of psychiatric hospitalization in the state of New York between 1852 and 1967 (Brenner, 1973). Throughout this extended period of time, increases in the rate of unemployment were followed closely, usually within a year, by sharp increases in the number of patients admitted to mental hospitals. The strongest relationship was found for schizophrenia and bipolar mood disorders.

In general, the evidence regarding socioeconomic status and schizophrenia indicates that the disorder is, to a certain extent, influenced by social factors. Adverse social and economic circumstances may increase the probability that persons who are genetically predisposed to the disorder will develop its clinical symptoms (Cohen, 1993; Schiffman et al., 2001).

### Psychological Factors

Most of the attention devoted to psychological factors and schizophrenia has focused on patterns of behaviour and communication within families. Research evidence indicates that family interactions and communication problems are not primarily responsible for the initial appearance of symptoms. They may help to trigger the onset of the disorder among those who were already genetically predisposed to its development, and they also influence the *course* of the disorder after the symptoms have appeared.

In order to place current thinking about these issues in historical perspective, consider the sort of causal pathways that were imagined by therapists in the 1960s. One influential hypothesis was concerned with the relationship between thought disorder in schizophrenic patients and communication problems exhibited by their parents (Wynne & Singer, 1963). According to this theory, the parents of schizophrenic patients are often unable to communicate clearly. This deficiency results in disrupted conversations and confusion on the part of their children. The child is caught between parents who are locked in conflict and subsequently fails to develop either a secure identity or conventional forms of thinking and speaking. Over an extended period of time, these problems presumably lead to the onset of schizophrenic symptoms. Hypotheses of this kind were tested extensively during the 1960s and 1970s, and the results were negative (Goldstein, 1988; Miklowitz, 1995; Neale & Oltmanns, 1980). Disturbed patterns of communication among family members do not cause people to develop schizophrenia. This knowledge is important to parents of schizophrenic patients. They experience enough emotional anguish without also being made to feel that something they did or said was the primary cause of their child's problems.

**Expressed Emotion** The family environment does have a significant impact on the course (as opposed to the etiology) of schizophrenia. Studies that point to this conclusion do not address the original onset of symptoms. Instead, they are concerned with the adjustment of patients who have already been treated for schizophrenic symptoms.

This effect was discovered by people who were interested in the adjustment of patients who were discharged after being treated in a psychiatric hospital. Men with schizophrenia were much more likely to return to the hospital within the next nine months if they went to live with their wives or parents than if they went to live in other lodgings or with their siblings. The patients who relapsed seemed to react negatively to some feature of their close relationship with their wives or mothers.

Subsequent research confirmed this initial impression (Brown, Birley, & Wing, 1972; Vaughn & Leff, 1976). Relatives of schizophrenic patients were interviewed prior to the patients' discharge from the hospital, and many of the relatives made statements that reflected negative or intrusive attitudes toward the patient. These statements were used to create a measure of **expressed emotion (EE)**. For example, many of the relatives expressed hostility toward the patient or repeatedly criticized the patient's behaviour. The following comments, made by the stepfather of a young man with schizophrenia, illustrate generalized, hostile criticisms of the patient's behaviour:

> **Interviewer:** What seemed different about Stephen's behaviour?
>
> **Stepfather:** Everything and anything. In other words, he's the type of person, you don't tell him, he tells you.
>
> **Interviewer:** You say that he spent time in a juvenile facility?
>
> **Stepfather:** Yeah. This kid is a genuine con artist, believe me. I spent time in the service and I've been around con artists. This kid is a first-class, genuine con artist, bar none. (Leff & Vaughn, 1985, p. 42)

Other family members appeared to be overprotective or too closely identified with the patient. Of course, a certain amount of worrying and concern should be expected from a parent whose child has developed a severe disorder such as schizophrenia. In the assessment of expressed emotion, relatives were considered to be emotionally overinvolved if they reported responses such as extreme anxiety or exaggerated forms of self-sacrifice. For example, the following exchange illustrates emotional overinvolvement by the mother of a 24-year-old male patient who had his first onset of the disorder when he was 22:

> **Mother:** He talked to me a lot—because I was his therapist—the person he shared with more than anybody else. He involves me, ruminates with me, because I allow him to do it.
>
> **Interviewer:** How frequently?
>
> **Mother:** He would do it constantly. He would do it as much as I would be there with him.
>
> **Interviewer:** Once or twice a week?
>
> **Mother:** No, it happened daily. All the time I was with him, particularly in the last four or five months. He would talk to me for hours at a time, worrying and sharing how bad he felt . . . reporting to me every change in mood or feeling from 5-minute to 5-minute period. (Leff & Vaughn, 1985, p. 51).

Patients who returned to live in a home with at least one member who was high in EE were more likely than patients from low EE families to relapse in the first nine months after discharge.

This result has been replicated many times. Approximately half of schizophrenic patients live in families that would be rated as being high in EE. Average relapse rates—defined primarily in terms of the proportion of patients who show a definite return of positive symptoms in the first year following hospital discharge—are 52 percent for patients in high EE families and 22 percent for patients in low EE families. Among the various types of comments that can contribute to a high EE rating, criticism is usually most strongly related to patients' relapse (Hooley & Gotlib, 2000).

Close contact with relatives increases the risk of relapse for schizophrenic patients living with a high EE relative. The opposite pattern is seen in low EE families, where increased contact with relatives seems to have a protective influence. The relationship between family contact and patients' relapse rates is illustrated in Figure 13–5. This figure is based on a reanalysis of data from 25 studies, with a combined sample of more than 800 patients (Bebbington & Kuipers, 1994). Patients who spent more than 35 hours per week in face-to-face contact with a high EE relative were placed in the "high-contact" category; less than 35 hours per week was considered "low contact." These data indicate that the effect of close contact with relatives depends on the emotional climate of the family.

High EE seems to be related, at least in part, to relatives' knowledge and beliefs about their family member's problems. Relatives find it easier to accept the most obvious positive symptoms as being the product of a mental disorder (Brewin et al., 1991). They show less tolerance toward negative symptoms, such as avolition and social withdrawal, perhaps because the patient may appear to be simply lazy or unmotivated.

**Understanding Family Attitudes** The influence of expressed emotion is not unique to schizophrenia. Patients with mood disorders, eating disorders, panic disorder with agoraphobia, and obsessive–compulsive disorder are also more likely to relapse following discharge if they are living with a high EE relative (Wearden et al., 2000). The extension of this phenomenon to other disorders should not be taken to mean that it is unimportant or that the social context of the family is irrelevant to

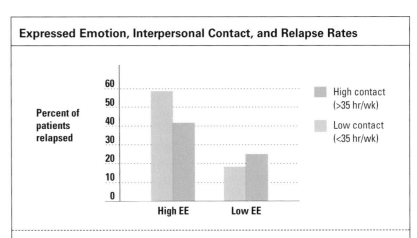

**Expressed Emotion, Interpersonal Contact, and Relapse Rates**

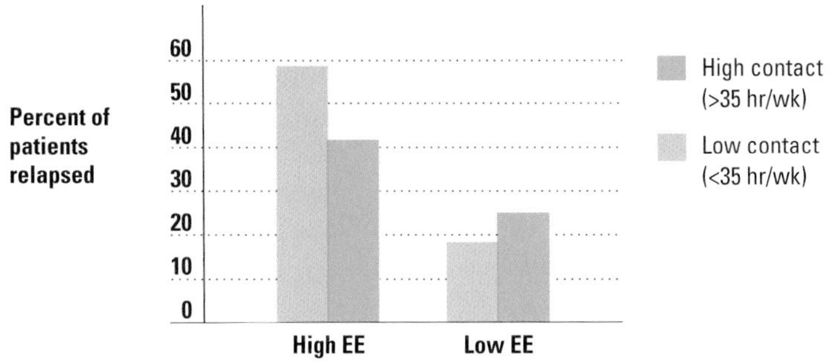


**FIGURE 13–5: Close contact increases the risk of relapse for schizophrenic patients living with a high EE relative. In low EE families, increased contact has a protective effect.**

*Source:* P. Bebbington and L. Kuipers, 1994, The predictive utility of expressed emotion in schizophrenia: An aggregate analysis. *Psychological Medicine, 24,* 707–718.

our understanding of the maintenance of schizophrenia (see Research Methods). It may indicate, however, that this aspect of the etiological model is shared with other forms of psychopathology. The specific nature of the person's symptoms may hinge on the genetic predisposition.

Cross-cultural studies suggest that high EE may be more common in Western or developed countries than in non-Western or developing countries (Hashemi & Cochrane, 1999; Lefley, 1992). This observation might help explain why the long-term course of schizophrenia is typically less severe in developing countries. Some speculation has focused on family members' attitudes and beliefs; people in developing countries may be more tolerant of eccentric behaviour among their extended family members. These attitudes may create environments similar to those found in

## RESEARCH METHODS

### Comparison Groups in Psychopathology Research

Research studies in the field of psychopathology typically involve comparisons among two or more groups of participants. One group, sometimes called "cases," includes people who already meet the diagnostic criteria for a particular mental disorder, such as schizophrenia. Comparison groups are composed of people who do not have the disorder in question. This approach is sometimes called the *case control design* because it depends on a contrast between cases and control participants. If the investigators find a significant difference between groups, they have demonstrated that the dependent variable is correlated with the disorder. They hope to conclude that they have identified a variable that is relevant to understanding the etiology of this condition. Causal inferences are risky, however, in correlational research. Our willingness to accept these conclusions hinges in large part on whether the investigators selected an appropriate comparison group.

People conducting correlational research, then, must make every effort to identify and test a group of people who are just like the cases except that they do not have the disorder in question. This typically means that the people in both groups should be similar with regard to such obvious factors as age, gender, and socioeconomic background. If the investigators find differences between people who have the disorder and those who do not, they want to attribute those differences to the disorder itself. Two main types of comparison groups are used in psychopathology research: people with no history of mental disorder, sometimes called "normal participants," and people who have some other form of mental disorder, sometimes called "patient controls." An example of this research approach is the work by Richard Neufeld and colleagues at the University of Western Ontario. These psychologists have compared the performance on cognitive processing tasks for people with paranoid schizophrenia, people with other types of schizophrenia (included as a patient control group), and normal participants (Carter & Neufeld, 1999).

Selecting normal comparison groups is not as simple as it might seem. In fact, researchers must make several basic decisions. Does "normal" mean that the person has never had the disorder in question, or does it mean a complete absence of any type of psychopathology? Should people be included as normal control participants if they have a family history of the disorder, even though they do not have the disorder themselves?

A second research strategy involves comparing patients with one type of disorder to those who have another form of psychopathology. Investigators usually employ this strategy to determine whether the variable in question is specifically related to the disorder they are studying. Are enlarged lateral ventricles or family communication problems unique to people with schizophrenia? Lack of specificity may raise questions about whether this variable is related to the cause of the disorder. It might suggest that this particular variable is, instead, a general consequence of factors such as hospitalization, which the patient control group has also experienced.

Many of the etiological variables examined by researchers are not unique to given disorder. Expressed emotion predicts relapse among patients with mood disorders as well as among those with schizophrenia. Should this result be taken to mean that EE does not play an important role in the etiology of schizophrenia? Not necessarily. The answer to this question depends on the specific causal model that is being considered (Garber & Hollon, 1991). All forms of psychopathology depend on the interaction of multiple factors spanning biological, social, and psychological systems. Some of these may be specific to the disorder being studied, and others may be general. The development of schizophrenia may depend on a specific genetically determined predisposition. The environmental events that are responsible for eventually causing vulnerable people to express this disorder might be nonspecific. The course of schizophrenia is clearly influenced by the social context in which the patient lives. The fact that similar factors influence people with mood disorders should not be taken to mean that EE is not an important factor in the complex chain of events that explain the etiology and maintenance of schizophrenia.

For all these reasons, the selection of meaningful comparison groups can be a complex and difficult process. There are no perfect solutions to these issues. The research strategy selected in any particular study will depend on the specific questions that the investigators are trying to answer. ◆

low EE homes in the West. An alternative view places greater emphasis on the culturally determined relationships between patients and other members of their families (Jenkins, 1993; Jenkins & Karno, 1992). In some cultures, family warmth serves as a protective factor and reduces the probability of patients' relapse (Lopez et al., 1999).

We must be cautious to avoid a narrow view of this phenomenon. The concept of expressed emotion raises extremely sensitive issues for family members, who have too frequently been blamed for the problems of people with schizophrenia. Expressed emotion is not the only factor that can influence the course of a schizophrenic disorder. Some patients relapse in spite of an understanding, tolerant family environment. Furthermore, research studies have shown that the relationship between patients' behaviour and relatives' expressed emotion is a transactional or reciprocal process. In other words, patients influence their relatives' attitudes at the same time that relatives' attitudes influence patients' adjustment. Persistent negative attitudes on the part of relatives appear to be perpetuated by a negative cycle of interactions in which patients play an active role (Goldstein et al., 1997).

## Integration and Multiple Pathways

A useful etiological model for schizophrenia must provide for the interaction of genetic factors and environmental events. According to University of Western Ontario psychologist Richard W.J. Neufeld, genetic factors and environmental stressors interact in complex, mutually reinforcing ways (e.g., Neufeld, 1999; Nicholson & Neufeld, 1992). Neufeld proposes that a genetic vulnerability to schizophrenia influences the person's ability to cope as well as the way that he or she appraises stressful events. In turn, schizophrenic symptoms, stressors, and the appraisal of stressors influence the person's ability to cope with symptoms and stressors. Coping is also thought to influence the genetically mediated vulnerability to develop schizophrenic symptoms. Cognitive dysfunctions associated with schizophrenia—such as impairments in memory, thinking, and language (Carter & Neufeld, 1999)—arise from both a genetic vulnerability for schizophrenia and from the direct effects of stress.

To illustrate some of these interactions, a genetic predisposition to develop schizophrenic symptoms can cause the person to behave in an unusual manner (e.g., talking to oneself in public). This can lead to environmental stressors (e.g., getting fired from one's job). In turn, this leads to anxiety, which interferes with coping and thereby exacerbates schizophrenic symptoms.

The heterogeneous nature of schizophrenia, in terms of symptoms as well as course, further suggests that the disorder should be explained in terms of multiple pathways. Some forms of schizophrenia may be the product of a strong genetic predisposition acting in combination with relatively common psychosocial experiences, such as stressful life events or disrupted communication patterns. For other people, relatively unusual circumstances—such as severe malnutrition during pregnancy—may be responsible for neurodevelopmental abnormalities that eventually lead to the onset of psychotic symptoms in the absence of genetic vulnerability.

***Richard W.J. Neufeld*** *is a psychologist at the University of Western Ontario. He is a leading schizophrenia researcher, who in 1992 received the Tannenbaum Schizophrenia Research Distinguished Scientist Award.*

**Schizotaxia: Inherited Vulnerability** Meehl proposed a theory of schizophrenia that provides another useful guide to understanding this complex disorder. According to Meehl (1993), individuals who are predisposed to schizophrenia inherit a subtle neurological defect of unknown form. Meehl referred to this condition as **schizotaxia**. As a result of the interaction between this defect and inevitable learning experiences, schizotaxic individuals develop odd or eccentric behaviours, which he called *schizotypic signs*. Most prominent among these behaviours are "associative loosening," which is similar to the cognitive symptoms emphasized by Bleuler, and "aversive drift," in which the individual withdraws from interpersonal relationships because they are associated with negative affect. These are relatively subtle behaviours in comparison to the full-blown symptoms of psychosis. Only a small proportion of schizotypic persons will eventually become overtly schizophrenic.

Various kinds of environmental events have been linked to the etiology of schizophrenia. Some may operate in interaction with the genotype for schizophrenia; others may be sufficient to produce the disorder on their own. Considerable speculation has focused recently on biological factors, such as viral infections and nutritional deficiencies.

Psychosocial factors, such as adverse economic circumstances, may also be involved. These events may be particularly harmful to people who are genetically predisposed to the disorder.

**A Threshold Model** Individual cases of schizophrenia undoubtedly represent various combinations of these genetic and environmental factors. Irving Gottesman (1991) has developed a sketch of hypothetical trajectories that might be followed by people who eventually develop symptoms of the disorder (see Figure 13–6). The horizontal axis represents time, beginning at the point of conception. The vertical axis represents the person's "combined liability" to the disorder—the probability of exhibiting overt symptoms of the disorder. Liability is determined by ongoing interactions between genotype and environment. Figure 13–6 is based on a *threshold model*, in which liability is viewed as lying along a continuum, but the probability that certain symptoms will be present changes dramatically as the person crosses a threshold. Two thresholds are represented in the figure: one for symptoms of schizophrenia spectrum disorders (which might also be viewed as prodromal and residual symptoms) and a second for active symptoms of schizophrenia, such as delusions and hallucinations.

**The Interaction between Heredity and Environment in Cases of Schizophrenia**

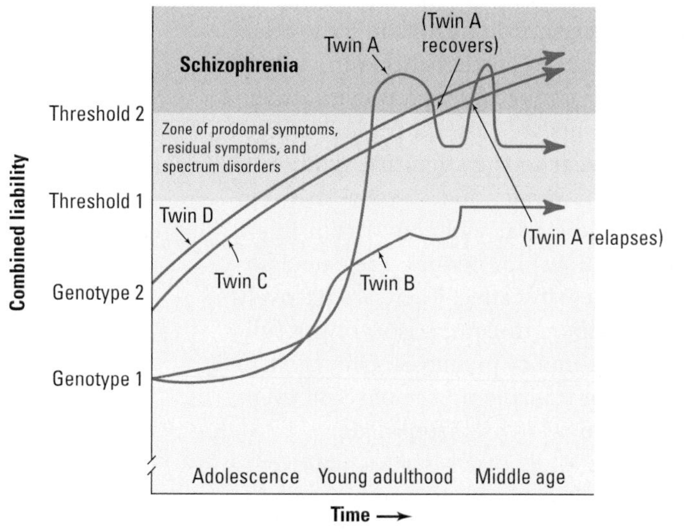


**FIGURE 13–6: Hypothetical pathways illustrating interactions between genetic predisposition and environmental factors in schizophrenia over time. The lines show a discordant MZ twin pair (Twins A and B) and a concordant MZ pair (Twins C and D).**

*Source:* I.I. Gottesman, 1991, *Schizophrenia Genesis: The Origins of Madness*, p. 244. New York: Freeman.

The figure illustrates two hypothetical genotypes (two twin pairs) and the trajectories that they might follow over the lifespan. Consider first the simplest case, which involves twins C and D. They both start life with a genetic predisposition ($G_2$) that places them relatively close to the threshold for schizophrenia. Both develop schizoid personality disorder and become concordant for schizophrenia during adolescence. Moderately stressful experiences, which might be relatively harmless for other people, may help to precipitate their disorder.

The second situation illustrated in Figure 13–6 involves identical twins A and B, who begin life with a genotype ($G_1$) that places them at average risk for schizophrenia. Twin A experiences more stress during infancy, moving her closer than twin B to the first threshold. The onset of her first psychotic episode occurs after she experiments with hallucinogenic drugs in college. Successful treatment leads to improvement in her condition (with residual symptoms), followed by relapse when she discontinues her medication. Her twin sister never develops the disorder, in spite of the fact that her combined liability brings her close to the threshold for prodromal symptoms.

Gottesman's sketch and hypothetical cases illustrate the need to consider multiple pathways to schizophrenia, as well as the many ways in which genetic and environmental events can interact to produce this disorder.

## The Search for Markers of Vulnerability

Some people apparently inherit a predisposition to schizophrenia. Obviously it would be useful to be able to identify those people. Genetic linkage studies may provide the answer, if one gene (or a small set of genes) is found to be responsible for the disorder. But that possibility is open to question.

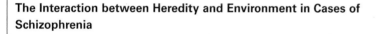

If we are looking for observable signs of vulnerability that can be detected among individuals who are genetically predisposed to schizophrenia, where should we look? What form will these signs take? We might also frame this question in terms of liability to the disorder (see Figure 13–6). Is it possible to detect signs of vulnerability among individuals who approach the threshold for schizophrenia spectrum disorders but have not exhibited any kind of overt symptoms? This issue has attracted considerable attention, but we don't have firm answers to these questions (Gooding & Iacono, 1995; Tsuang & Faraone, 1999).

According to Meehl's model, people who are vulnerable to schizophrenia might be identified by developing measures that could detect the underlying biological dysfunction (schizotaxia) or by developing sensitive measures of their subtle eccentricities of behaviour (schizotypal traits). The range of possible markers is, therefore, quite large.

Assume that we have selected a specific measure, such as a biochemical assay or a psychological test, and we are interested in knowing whether it might be useful in identifying people who are vulnerable to schizophrenia. What criteria should a **vulnerability marker** fulfill? First, the proposed marker must distinguish between people who already have schizophrenia and those who do not. Second, it should be a stable characteristic over time. Third, the proposed measure of vulnerability should identify more people among the biological relatives of schizophrenic patients than among people in the general population. For example, it should be found among the discordant MZ twins of schizophrenic patients, even if they don't exhibit any symptoms of schizophrenia. Finally, the proposed measure of vulnerability should be able to predict the future development of schizophrenia among those who have not yet experienced a psychotic episode (Adler et al., 1999; Iacono, 1998).

Although reliable measures of vulnerability have not been identified, they are being actively pursued by many investigators with a wide variety of measurement procedures. In the following pages we will outline some of the psychological procedures that have been shown to be among the most promising.

**Attention and Cognition** Many investigators have pursued the search for signs of vulnerability by looking at measures of performance in which schizophrenic patients differ from other people. Some of these studies have focused on cognitive tasks that evaluate information processing, selective attention, and working memory (Holzman, 1994; Park, Holzman, & Goldman-Rakic, 1995).

One important set of results regarding attentional dysfunction is based on use of the Continuous Performance Task (CPT). In one version of this task, the subject is required to pick out a letter or sequence of letters from among a larger sequence of letters that is presented very briefly (less than one second per letter) on a computer screen. Whenever the subject notices the target, he or she is supposed to press a button. The CPT is one of the most frequently used measures of sustained attention and is sensitive to various kinds of neurological impairment (Riccio et al., 2002).

Many studies have demonstrated that schizophrenic patients are less accurate than normal people and other psychiatric patients in their performance on the CPT. This seems to be a stable characteristic that does not fluctuate over time. Furthermore, the attentional deficits tapped by the CPT are found with increased prevalence among the unaffected first-degree relatives of schizophrenic persons (Chen et al., 1998; Finkelstein et al., 1997; Nuechterlein et al., 1998).

These data suggest that the CPT measure fulfills several of the criteria for an index of vulnerability. The research indicates that problems in sustained attention may be useful signs of vulnerability to schizophrenia (Nuechterlein et al., 2002).

**Eye-Tracking Dysfunction** Another promising line of work involves impairments in eye movements—specifically, difficulty in tracking the motion of a pendulum or a similarly oscillating stimulus while the person's head is held motionless. When people with schizophrenia are asked to track a moving target, like an oscillating pendulum, with their eyes, a substantial number of them show dysfunctions in smooth-pursuit eye movement (Holzman, 2000; Levy & Holzman, 1997). Instead of reproducing the motion of the pendulum in a series of smooth waves, their tracking records show frequent interruptions of smooth-pursuit movements by numerous rapid movements. Examples of normal tracking records and those of schizophrenic patients are presented in Figure 13–7. Only about 8 percent of normal people exhibit the eye-tracking dysfunctions illustrated in part (C) of Figure 13–7, although some studies have reported higher figures.

Approximately 50 percent of the first-degree relatives of schizophrenic persons show similar smooth-pursuit impairments (Avila et al., 2002; Curtis, Calkins, & Iacono, 2001). The overall pattern of results seen in people with

**Eye-Tracking Patterns**

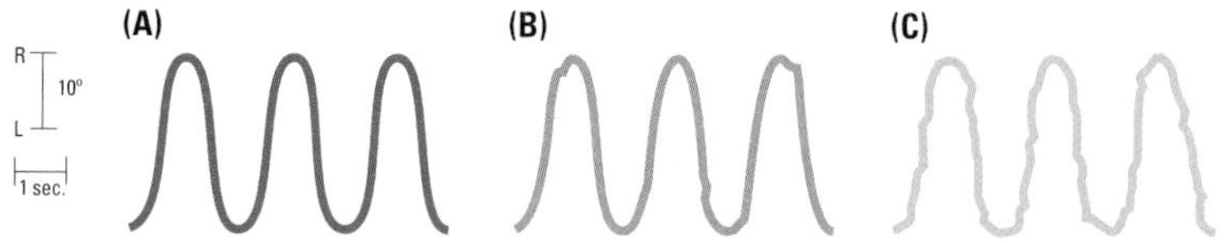


**FIGURE 13–7: This illustration contrasts smooth-pursuit eye-tracking patterns of normal subjects with those of schizophrenic patients. Part (A) shows the actual target. Part (B) illustrates the pattern for people without schizophrenia, and part (C) shows the pattern for people with schizophrenia.**

*Source:* From D.L. Levy et al., Eye-tracking dysfunction and schizophrenia: A critical perspective. *Schizophrenia Bulletin, 19,* 462.

schizophrenia and their families suggests that poor tracking performance may be associated with the predisposition to schizophrenia. That conclusion becomes even more important in light of evidence from additional studies suggesting that tracking ability is stable over time, influenced by genetic factors, and found among people who exhibit features associated with schizotypal personality disorder (Gooding, Miller, & Kwapil, 2000; Iacono & Clementz, 1993).

It is not yet possible to identify people who are specifically predisposed to the development of schizophrenia, but research studies have identified potential vulnerability markers. The real test, of course, will centre around predictive validity. Can any of these measures, such as smooth-pursuit eye-tracking impairment or attentional dysfunction, predict the later appearance of schizophrenia in people whose scores indicate possible vulnerability? High-risk studies will be useful in providing this type of evidence (see Research Close-Up on p. 461).

*This woman is attached to equipment used to record smooth-pursuit eye movements. Sensors inside the helmet are positioned in front of her right eye. Eye movements are recorded while she watches a dot of light move back and forth on a computer screen. The electronic equipment behind her records and amplifies the ocular signals.*

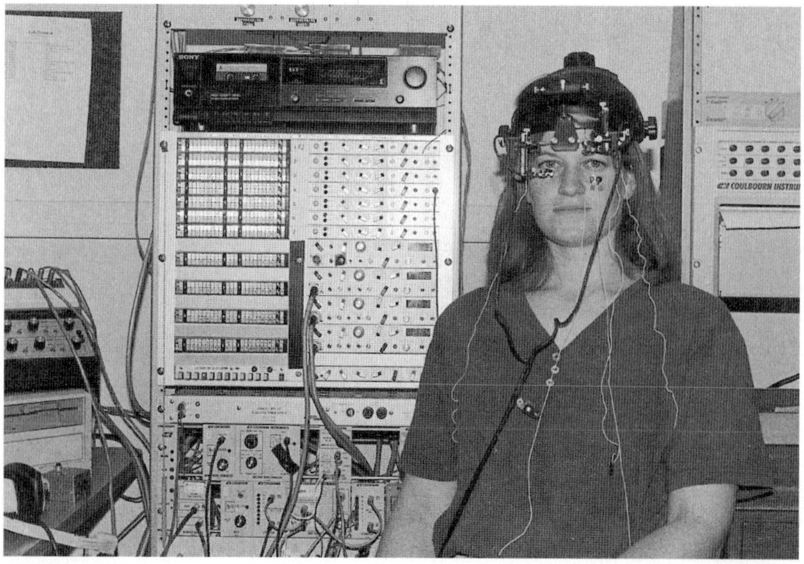

# Treatment

Schizophrenia is a complex disorder that often must be treated over an extended period of time. Clinicians must be concerned about the treatment of acute psychotic episodes as well as the prevention of future episodes. A panel of Canadian experts on schizophrenia—composed of psychologists and psychiatrists—recently published a set of clinical practice guidelines for the treatment of schizophrenia (Working Group for the Canadian Psychiatric Association and Canadian Alliance for Research on Schizophrenia, 1998). The guidelines, based on the best available evidence, are similar to guidelines published in other countries. The Canadian guidelines state that "antipsychotic medications are currently the most effective treatment available for schizophrenia, especially when combined with psychosocial treatments" (p. 29S). Antipsychotic medications are the primary way of treating this disorder. Because many patients remain impaired between episodes, long-term care must often involve the provision of housing and social support. People with impaired occupational and social skills need special types of training. The treatment of schizophrenia requires attention on all of these fronts and is necessarily concerned with the cooperative efforts of many types of professionals (Kopelowicz, Liberman, & Zarate, 2002). Schizophrenia also takes its toll on families.

## Antipsychotic Medication

The first effective antipsychotic drugs to be discovered were the phenothiazines. Their antipsychotic properties were discovered accidentally in the early 1950s by a French neurosurgeon who was using these drugs as a supplement to anesthesia. They were not effective for the purpose he intended, but did have a calming effect on the patients. This experience prompted psychiatrists to use the same drugs with their patients. Early reports of success in treating chronic psychotic patients quickly led to the widespread use of phenothiazines, such as chlorpromazine (Thorazine), in psychiatric hospitals throughout Europe. McGill University psychiatrist Heinz Lehmann learned of these developments and was the first physician in North America to publish on the merits of using chlorpromazine to treat schizophrenia (Lehmann & Hanrahan, 1954). The discovery of phenothiazines quickly changed the way in which schizophrenia was treated. Large numbers of patients who had previously been institutionalized could be discharged to community care (but see Chapter 18 on the effects of deinstitutionalization).

Several related types of drugs were developed in subsequent years. They are called **antipsychotic drugs** because they have a relatively specific effect—to reduce the severity of, and sometimes eliminate, psychotic symptoms. Classical antipsychotics are also known as *neuroleptic* drugs because they also induce side effects that resemble the motor symptoms of Parkinson's disease (see Chapter 14). Beneficial effects are sometimes noticed within a week after the patient begins taking antipsychotic medication, but it often takes several weeks before improvement is seen. Positive symptoms, such as hallucinations, respond better to antipsychotic medication than negative symptoms, such as alogia and blunted affect (Kane, 1999). This differential effect is not entirely clear-cut, however. For example, some patients who are socially withdrawn become less isolated when taking antipsychotic medication. Among the classical or typical antipsychotics, there is no convincing evidence to indicate that one is more effective than another (Bradford, Stroup, & Lieberman, 2002).

Double-blind, placebo-controlled studies have confirmed the effectiveness of antipsychotic medication in the treatment of patients who are acutely disturbed. Literally thousands of studies have addressed this issue over a period of more than 40 years (Marder et al., 1993). These studies provide substantial support for the effectiveness of antipsychotic medication. Most studies find that about half of the patients who receive medication are rated as being much improved after 4 to 6 weeks of treatment. Further improvements may continue beyond that point for some patients. In contrast, patients treated with placebos exhibit much smaller rates of improvement, and many of them actually deteriorate.

Unfortunately, a substantial minority of schizophrenic patients, perhaps 25 percent, do not improve on classical antipsychotic drugs (Conley & Kelly, 2001). Another 30 to 40 percent might be considered partial responders: Their condition improves, but they do not show a full remission of symptoms. Investigators have not been able to identify reliable differences between patients who improve on medication and those who do not. Some experts have suggested that treatment-resistant patients may have more prominent negative symptoms, greater disorganization, and more evidence of neurological abnormalities (Hellewell, 1999; McMahon et al., 2002).

**Maintenance Medication** After patients recover from acute psychotic episodes, there is a high probability that they will have another episode. The relapse rate may be as high as 65 to 70 percent in the first year after hospital discharge if patients discontinue medication. Continued treatment with antipsychotic drugs can reduce this rate to approximately 40 percent (Hogarty, 1993; Kane, 2001b). Therefore the great majority of schizophrenic patients continue to take medication after they recover from psychotic episodes, although usually at lower dosages. The need for maintenance medication is less clearly defined among patients who have had only one episode of schizophrenia. The relapse rate for these patients is lower than among those who have had multiple episodes.

Figure 13–8 illustrates general relapse rates for schizophrenic outpatients. The estimated rates presented in this figure were generated by analyzing data from several outcome studies (Weiden & Olfson, 1995). They apply to outpatients who have experienced more than one episode, have responded positively to classical antipsychotic drugs, and are not receiving active psychosocial treatments (discussed later in the chapter). The best-case scenario represents expected relapse rates for patients who are receiving an optimal dose of medication and who continue taking the medication on a regular basis. Under these circumstances, slightly more than half of schizophrenic outpatients will relapse and require re-hospitalization within two years of discharge. The real-world scenario in Figure 13–8 indicates that actual relapse rates are even higher because some patients stop taking medication, often to avoid unpleasant side effects (Glick & Berg, 2002).

**Motor Side Effects** Antipsychotic drugs produce several unpleasant side effects. They come

***Heinz Lehmann*** *(1911–1999), a McGill University psychiatrist, became world-famous in the 1950s as a result of his pioneering work on drug treatments. He was the first physician in North America to publish on the use of chlorpromazine to treat schizophrenia.*

**Relapse Rates for Schizophrenic Patients Taking Maintenance Medication**

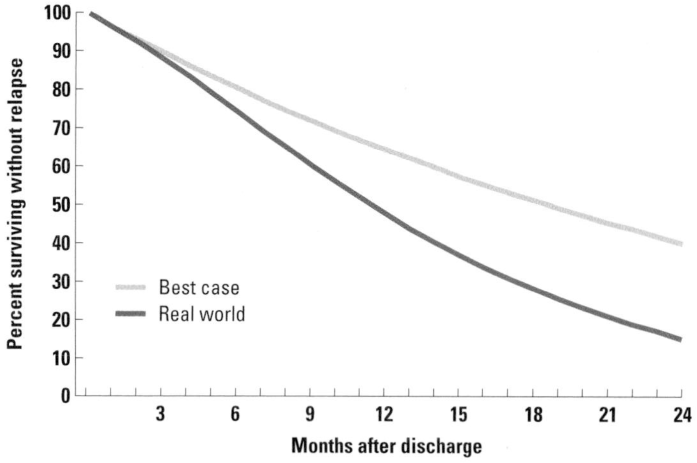


**FIGURE 13–8: Estimated relapse rates for patients receiving optimal doses of standard neuroleptic medication while not receiving active psychosocial treatments. Real world: Assumes some noncompliance with medication. Best case: Assumes complete compliance with medication.**

*Source:* P.J. Weiden and M. Olfson, 1995, Cost of relapse in schizophrenia. *Schizophrenia Bulletin, 21,* 425.

in varying degrees and affect different patients in different ways. In the case of classical or first-generation antipsychotic drugs, the most obvious and troublesome are called *extrapyramidal symptoms (EPS)* because they are mediated by the extrapyramidal neural pathways that connect the brain to the motor neurons in the spinal cord. These symptoms include an assortment of neurological disturbances, such as muscular rigidity, tremors, restless agitation, peculiar involuntary postures, and motor inertia. EPS may diminish spontaneously after three or four months of continuous treatment. Additional drugs, such as benztropine (Cogentin), can be used to minimize the severity of EPS during the first few months of treatment. Unfortunately, some patients exhibit persistent signs of EPS in spite of these efforts (Kane, 2001a).

Prolonged treatment with classical antipsychotic drugs frequently leads to the development of *tardive dyskinesia (TD).* This syndrome consists of abnormal involuntary movements of the mouth and face, such as tongue protrusion, chewing, and lip puckering, as well as spasmodic movements of the limbs and trunk of the body. The latter include writhing movements of the fingers and toes and jiggling of the legs, as well as jerking movements of the head and pelvis. Taken as a whole, this problem is distressing to patients and their families. The TD syndrome is induced by antipsychotic treatment, and it is irreversible in some patients, even after the medication has been discontinued. In fact, in some patients, TD becomes worse if antipsychotic medication is withdrawn (Lauterbach et al., 2001; Walters et al., 1997).

**Atypical Antipsychotics** The second generation of antipsychotic medications began to be introduced in the 1990s and stimulated what some people have called a "second revolution" in the care of patients with schizophrenia. These drugs have come to be known as **atypical antipsychotics** because they are much less likely than the classical antipsychotics to produce unpleasant motor side effects (Kapur & Remington, 2001). Clinical trials indicate that atypical antipsychotics are at least as effective as the first-generation drugs for the treatment of positive symptoms of schizophrenia, and they are generally more effective than classical antipsychotics in the treatment of negative symptoms (Leucht et al., 2002; Volavka et al., 2002).

The best known of the atypical drugs, clozapine (Clozaril), has been used extensively throughout Europe since the 1970s. Its use was delayed for several years in North America because the drug can produce a lethal blood condition known as agranulocytosis in about 1 percent of patients. It has since been approved for use by Health Canada. For patients taking this drug, it is necessary that they receive regular monitoring of their white blood cell levels. The second generation of antipsychotic medications also includes risperidone (Risperdal), olanzapine (Zyprexa), quetiapine (Seroquel). Some of these drugs are listed in Table 13–3.

Patients are more compliant with medication and less likely to drop out of treatment when taking one of the atypical antipsychotic drugs because of their decreased motor side effects. It should be noted, however, that atypical antipsychotics also produce side effects, and some of them are serious. For example, many of the second-generation antipsychotics lead to weight gain and obesity. These problems increase the person's risk for additional medical problems, such as diabetes, hypertension, and coronary artery disease.

At least 30 percent of schizophrenic patients who were previously treatment-resistant improve after taking atypical antipsychotic

**TABLE 13–3 Examples of Medications Used to Treat Schizophrenic Disorders**

| | | Selected Side Effects | | Modes of Action (Selected Receptors) | |
|---|---|---|---|---|---|
| **Drug Class** | **Generic Name (Trade Name)** | **EPS** | **Weight Gain** | **$D_2$** | **$5HT_{2a}$** |
| First-generation antipsychotics | chlorpromazine (Largactil) | ++ | + | ++ | + |
| | haloperidol (Haldol) | ++++ | + | ++++ | + |
| Atypical antipsychotics | clozapine (Clozaril) | +/– | ++++ | ++ | ++++ |
| | risperidone (Risperdal) | ++ | ++ | +++ | +++++ |
| | olanzapine (Zyprexa) | + | ++++ | +++ | ++++ |
| | quetiapine (Seroquel) | +/– | ++ | ++ | +++ |
| | amisulpride (Solian)* | + | ++ | ++++ | – |

$D_2$ = dopamine receptors; $5HT_{2a}$ = serotonin receptors.

*Amisulpride is not yet available in North America (as of 2004). It has been used for more than 10 years in France (Leucht et al., 2002).

*Source:* S. Kapur and G. Remington, 2001, Atypical antipsychotics: new directions and new challenges in the treatment of schizophrenia. *Annual Review of Medicine, 52,* 503–517.

drugs (Chakos et al., 2001; Kapur & Remington, 2001). Treatment resistance is usually defined as failure to improve on at least three different types of classical antipsychotic medication after six weeks on moderate to high doses. Most of the research evidence regarding the efficacy of atypical antipsychotic medication with treatment-resistant patients is based on the use of clozapine because it has been available longer than the other drugs. Future studies will determine whether medications such as olanzapine and resperidone are also more effective than traditional antipsychotics with such patients.

All antipsychotic medications—both traditional and atypical forms—act by blocking $D_2$ dopamine receptors in the cortical and limbic areas of the brain (Factor, 2002). They also affect a number of other neurotransmitters, including serotonin, norepinephrine, and acetylcholine. Table 13–3 includes a comparison of two traditional and five atypical antipsychotic drugs in terms of their ability to block specific types of dopamine and serotonin receptors. Most atypical antipsychotics produce a broader range of neurochemical actions in the brain than do the standard neuroleptic drugs, which act primarily on dopamine receptors. Clozapine and olanzapine, for example, produce a relatively strong blockade of $5HT_{2a}$ serotonin receptors and a relatively weaker blockade of $D_2$ dopamine receptors (Richelson, 1999). This increased affinity of some atypical drugs for serotonin receptors might explain why they can have a beneficial effect on symptoms of schizophrenia without producing marked motor side effects (EPS). This hypothesis is contradicted, however, by the modes of action associated with a newer form of atypical drug, amisulpride, which does not affect serotonin receptors (Leucht et al., 2002). Neurochemical differences between traditional and atypical antipsychotic drugs are not clearly understood and are currently the topic of debate (Seeman, 2002).

Further progress in the pharmacological treatment of schizophrenia will undoubtedly produce new drugs that have varying mechanisms of neurochemical action. The rate of

*The life of John Forbes Nash, a mathematician, was portrayed in the film* A Beautiful Mind. *Nash won the Nobel Prize for Economics in 1994. His thesis, written at the age of 21, revolutionized the field of game theory. He has recovered from paranoid schizophrenia, after experiencing psychotic symptoms for more than 20 years.*

progress in this field is very rapid. You can obtain regularly updated reviews of evidence regarding the treatment of schizophrenia from the Cochrane Library at its Web site: www.cochrane.org.

### Psychosocial Treatment

Optimal management of schizophrenia requires the integration of medical treatment with psychosocial interventions (Working Group for the Canadian Psychiatric Association and Canadian Alliance for Research on Schizophrenia, 1998). Several forms of psychological treatment have proved to be effective for schizophrenic patients. These procedures address a wide range of problems that are associated with the disorder. In contrast to pharmacological approaches, psychological approaches place relatively little emphasis on the treatment of acute psychotic episodes. Instead, they concentrate on long-term strategies (Kopelowicz, Liberman, & Zarate, 2002).

**Family-Oriented Aftercare** Studies of expressed emotion have inspired the development of innovative family-based treatment programs (Hooley, 1998). Family treatment programs attempt to improve the coping skills of family members, recognizing the burdens that people often endure while caring for a family member with a chronic mental disorder. Patients are maintained on antipsychotic medication on an outpatient basis throughout this process. There are several different approaches to this type of family intervention. Most include an educational component that is designed to help family members understand and accept the nature of the disorder. One goal of this procedure is to eliminate unrealistic expectations for the patient, which may lead to harsh criticism. Behavioural family management also places considerable emphasis on the improvement of communication and problem-solving skills, which may enhance the family members' ability to work together and thereby minimize conflict.

Several empirical studies have evaluated the effects of family interventions. Most have found reductions in relapse rates for people receiving family treatment. In the first year of treatment, relapse rates for patients who receive family treatment plus medication are typically below 20 percent, compared with 40 or 50 percent for those receiving medication alone (Tarrier & Barrowclough, 1995). Relapse rates increase in the next year for both groups. Family-based treatment programs can delay relapse, but they do not necessarily prevent relapse in the long run. The beneficial effects of treatment may be lost shortly after treatment ends (Hogarty, 1993), and intensive family programs may not be cost-effective (Bellack et al., 2000; Schooler et al., 1997). In the case of a disorder such as schizophrenia, which is often chronic, difficult decisions have to be made about priorities and the availability of services. Family-based programs can have a positive effect, but we need to find more efficient and more effective ways to integrate this aspect of treatment into an overall treatment program.

**Social Skills Training** Many patients who avoid relapse and are able to remain in the community continue to be impaired in terms of residual symptoms. They also experience problems in social and occupational functioning. For these patients, drug therapy must be supplemented by psychosocial programs that address residual aspects of the disorder. The need to address these problems directly is supported by evidence that shows that deficits in social skills are relatively stable in schizophrenic patients and relatively independent of other aspects of the disorder, including both positive and negative symptoms (Mueser et al., 1991).

*Social skills training (SST)* is a structured, educational approach to these problems that involves modelling, role playing, and the provision of social reinforcement for appropriate behaviours (Heinssen, Liberman, & Kopelwicz, 2000). A general description of this type of approach to treatment is provided in Chapter 3. Controlled-outcome studies indicate that, in combination with neuroleptic medication, SST leads to improved performance on measures of social adjustment. It is not clear, however, that SST has any beneficial effects on relapse rates (Bustillo et al., 2001). Moreover, Calgary researchers found that the benefits of a short (nine-week) social skills training program tended to be lost over time (Dobson et al., 1995), suggesting that long-term programs may be required, at least for some people with schizophrenia.

**Cognitive Behaviour Therapy** A promising method for treating schizophrenia is *cognitive behaviour therapy* (CBT). Research from investigators at the University of Western Ontario and the University of Toronto indicate that multifaceted cognitive behavioural interventions, which can include social skills training, stress management, and other techniques, appear to be helpful, particularly for patients who fail to benefit fully from antipsychotic medication (Norman et al., 2002; Norman & Townsend, 1999; Rector & Beck, 2001).

**Assertive Community Treatment** The treatment of a chronic disorder such as schizophrenia clearly requires an extensive range of comprehensive services that should be fully integrated and continuously available. *Assertive community treatment (ACT)* is a psychosocial intervention that is delivered by an interdisciplinary team of clinicians (Greenley, 1995; Stein & Santos, 1998). They provide a combination of psychological treatments—including education, support, skills training, and rehabilitation—as well as medication. Services are provided on a regular basis throughout the week and during crisis periods (any time of day and any day of the week). The program represents an intensive effort to maintain seriously disordered patients in the community and to minimize the need for hospitalization. It differs from more traditional outpatient services in its assertive approach to the provision of services; members of an ACT team go to the consumer rather than expecting the consumer to come to them.

Outcome studies indicate that ACT programs can effectively reduce the number of days that patients spend in psychiatric hospitals while also improving their level of functioning (Phillips et al., 2001; Thornicroft & Susser, 2001). One study found that only 18 percent of the people in the ACT group were hospitalized during the first year of treatment compared to 89 percent of the people in the control group. ACT is an intensive form of treatment that requires a well-organized and extensive network of professional services. In spite of the expense that is required to maintain this kind of program, empirical studies indicate that it is more cost-effective than traditional services provided by community mental health centres (Lehman et al., 1999). Reduction in costs of inpatient care offsets the expense of the ACT program.

**Institutional Programs** Although schizophrenic persons can be treated with medication on an outpatient basis, various types of institutional care continue to be important. Most patients experience recurrent phases of active psychosis. Brief periods of hospitalization (usually two or three weeks) are often beneficial during these times.

Some patients are chronically disturbed and require long-term institutional treatment. Social learning programs, sometimes called *token economies*, can be useful for these patients. In these programs specific behavioural contingencies are put into place for all of the patients on a hospital ward. The goal is to increase the frequency of desired behaviours, such as appropriate grooming and participation in social activities, and to decrease the frequency of undesirable behaviours, such as violence or incoherent speech. Staff members monitor patients' behaviour throughout the day. Each occurrence of a desired behaviour is praised and reinforced by the presentation of a token, which can be exchanged for food or privileges, such as time to watch television. Inappropriate behaviours are typically ignored, but occasional punishment, such as loss of privileges, is used if necessary.

Paul and colleagues conducted an extensive evaluation of behavioural treatment with chronic schizophrenic patients (Paul & Lentz, 1977). They compared two inpatient programs in the treatment of severely disturbed patients who had been continuously hospitalized for many years. One program followed a carefully designed and closely supervised social learning model, and the other followed a more traditional approach. These experimental treatments were compared to a group of similar patients who continued to reside in their original hospital wards. The patients' adjustment was evaluated at six-month intervals over a period of approximately six years.

Both groups of patients who received treatment showed significant improvement, especially during the first six months of the study. This finding highlights the possibility for improvement, even among chronically disturbed patients. Patients in the social learning program showed even more improvement than those in the traditional group, especially with regard to social functioning and self-care. These benefits were maintained throughout the duration of the treatment program. Perhaps most impressive was the fact that by the end of the first four years of active treatment, 11 percent of the patients in the social learning program were discharged to independent living in the community without being readmitted to the hospital. In contrast, none of the patients in the standard hospital comparison group was released to independent living. This study indicates that carefully structured inpatient programs, especially those that follow behavioural principles, can have important positive effects for chronic schizophrenic patients.

# Summary

People who meet the diagnostic criteria for **schizophrenia** exhibit many types of symptoms that represent impairments across a broad array of cognitive, perceptual, and interpersonal functions. These symptoms can be roughly divided into three types. **Positive symptoms** include **hallucinations** and **delusions**. **Negative symptoms** include **blunted affect**, **alogia**, **avolition**, and social withdrawal. Symptoms of disorganization include verbal communication problems and bizarre behaviour.

The onset of schizophrenia is typically during adolescence or early adulthood. The disorder can follow different patterns over time. Some people recover fairly quickly from schizophrenia, whereas others deteriorate progressively after the initial onset of symptoms.

The disorder was originally defined by Emil Kraepelin, who emphasized the progressive course of the disorder in distinguishing it from manic–depressive psychosis. Eugen Bleuler coined the term *schizophrenia*, proposing that disturbances in speech and emotion are the fundamental symptoms of the disorder. Many clinicians believe that schizophrenia actually includes several types of disorder with different causes. Others believe that it is a single pathological process with variations in symptomatic expression and course.

The negative symptoms of schizophrenia have been given increased emphasis in DSM-IV-TR. The manual requires evidence of a decline in the person's social or occupational functioning, as well as the presence of disturbed behaviour over a continuous period of at least six months. DSM-IV-TR recognizes several subtypes of schizophrenia, such as **paranoid**, **catatonic**, and **disorganized types**, that are based on prominent symptoms. These subtypes have relatively poor diagnostic reliability and are frequently unstable over time.

The lifetime prevalence of schizophrenia is approximately 1 or 2 percent in virtually all areas of the world. Men and women are equally likely to be affected, although the onset of the disorder appears at an earlier age in males. Male patients are more likely than female patients to exhibit negative symptoms, and they are also more likely to follow a chronic, deteriorating course.

Genetic factors clearly play a role in the development of schizophrenia. Risk for developing the disorder is between 10 and 15 percent among first-degree relatives of schizophrenic patients. Concordance rates are approximately 48 percent in MZ twins compared to only 17 percent in DZ pairs. Adoption studies have found that approximately 15 percent of the offspring of a schizophrenic parent will eventually develop the disorder themselves, even if they are separated from their biological parent at an early age and are raised by adoptive families. Twin and adoption studies also indicate that the disorder has variable expressions, sometimes called the *schizophrenia spectrum*. Related disorders include schizotypal personality disorder and **schizoaffective disorder**. Linkage studies have not found consistent evidence for a specific gene of major influence.

Advances in brain imaging technology have allowed extensive study of structural and functional brain abnormalities in schizophrenia. A specific brain lesion has not been identified, and it is unlikely that a disorder as complex as schizophrenia will be traced to a single site in the brain. Structural images of schizophrenic patients' brains reveal enlarged ventricles as well as decreased size of parts of the limbic system. Studies of brain metabolism and blood flow have identified functional changes in the frontal lobes, temporal lobes, and basal ganglia in many persons with schizophrenia. Current evidence points toward a subtle and diffuse type of neuropathology in schizophrenia.

The discovery of antipsychotic medication stimulated interest in the role of neurochemical factors in the etiology of schizophrenia. The dopamine hypothesis provided the major unifying theme in this area for many years, but it is now considered too simple to account for the existing evidence. Current neurochemical hypotheses regarding schizophrenia focus on a broad array of neurotransmitters, with special emphasis on serotonin.

The importance of environmental events in the etiology of schizophrenia is evident in the results of twin studies, which show that concordance rates in MZ twins do not approach 100 percent. Several social and psychological factors have been shown to be related to the disorder. Social class is inversely related to the prevalence of schizophrenia. In some cases, low levels of socioeconomic achievement represent a consequence of the disorder. Several kinds of research studies have also found, however, that social factors appear to make a causal contribution to the disorder. Disturbed patterns of family communication have been presumed to be related to the etiology of schizophrenia for many years. There is no evidence to indicate that the behaviour of family members contributes to the original onset of schizophrenic symptoms. Recent efforts on this topic have examined the relation between the social context of the family and the long-term course of the disorder. Patients from families that are high in **expressed emotion** are more likely to relapse than those from low EE families. Expressed emotion is the product of an ongoing interaction between patients and their families, with patterns of influence flowing in both directions.

The evidence regarding etiology supports a diathesis-stress model. It should be possible to develop **vulnerability markers** that can identify individuals who possess the genetic predisposition to the disorder. Promising research in this area is concerned with a broad range of possibilities, including smooth-pursuit eye-tracking movements and laboratory measures of sustained attention.

The central aspect of treatment for schizophrenia is antipsychotic medication. These drugs help to resolve acute psychotic episodes. They can also delay relapse and improve the level of patients' functioning between episodes. Unfortunately, they often produce troublesome side effects, and a substantial minority of schizophrenic patients are resistant to classic types of antipsychotic medication. The **atypical antipsychotics** are able to help some patients who do not respond to other drugs, and they produce fewer unpleasant motor side effects.

Various types of psychosocial treatment also provide important benefits to schizophrenic patients and their families. Prominent among these are family-based treatment for patients who have been stabilized on medication following discharge from the hospital. Social skills training can also be useful in improving the level of patients' role functioning.

# Critical Thinking

1. The typical course of schizophrenia may be less chronic in developing countries than in developed countries. How would you explain these differences? Why would the disorder tend to be more long-lasting among people living in Canada than in people living in rural India, for example?
2. Clinical scientists have been unable to identify a specific type of environmental event that is responsible for triggering the original onset of symptoms of schizophrenia. Where would you look if you were conducting research on the "stress" end of the diathesis-stress model?
3. How can we identify people who are vulnerable to schizophrenia? Would you place greater emphasis on behavioural markers or biological markers?
4. Imagine that you are the director of a large mental health centre that provides services for all types of disorders. If you have limited resources, which aspects of schizophrenia would receive highest priority in your programs? Medication for the resolution of acute psychotic episodes? Support to family members? Alternative housing? Social skills training?

# Key Terms

**alogia** 448
**anhedonia** 447
**antipsychotic drugs** 473
**atypical antipsychotics** 474
**avolition** 448
**blunted affect** 447
**brief psychotic disorder** 454
**catatonic type** 452
**delusions** 447
**delusional disorder** 453
**disorganized speech** 448
**disorganized type** 452
**expressed emotion (EE)** 466
**hallucination** 446
**inappropriate affect** 450
**negative symptoms** 446
**paranoid type** 452
**positive symptoms** 446
**prodromal phase** 445
**residual phase** 445
**residual type** 453
**schizoaffective disorder** 453
**schizophrenia** 443
**schizotaxia** 469
**undifferentiated type** 453
**vulnerability marker** 471

# 14 Dementia, Delirium, and Amnestic Disorders

Overview

Typical Symptoms and Associated Features

Classification

Epidemiology of Delirium and Dementia

Etiological Considerations and Research

Treatment and Management

**In what ways is delirium different from dementia?**

**Why is depression in an elderly person sometimes confused with dementia?**

**Are there cross-cultural differences in the incidence of dementia?**

**Can cognitive loss be prevented with the use of medication?**

Most of us are absentminded from time to time. We may forget to make a phone call, run an errand, or complete an assignment. Occasional lapses of this sort are part of normal experience. Unfortunately, some people develop severe and persistent memory problems that disrupt their everyday activities and their interactions with other people. Imagine that you have lived in the same house for many years. You go for a short walk, and then you can't remember how to get home. Suppose you are shown a photograph of your parents, and you don't recognize them. These are some of the fundamental cognitive problems discussed in this chapter.

# Overview

Dementia and delirium are the most frequent disorders found among elderly psychiatric patients. Both conditions involve memory impairments, but they are quite different in other ways. **Dementia** is a gradual worsening loss of memory and related cognitive functions, including the use of language, as well as reasoning and decision making. It is a clinical syndrome that involves progressive impairment of many cognitive abilities (Ross & Bowen, 2002). **Delirium** is a confusional state that develops over a short period of time and is often associated with agitation and hyperactivity. The most important symptoms of delirium are disorganized thinking and a reduced ability to maintain and shift attention (Foreman et al., 2001). Delirium and dementia are produced by very different processes. Dementia is a chronic, deteriorating condition that reflects the gradual loss of neurons in the brain. Delirium is usually the result of medical problems, such as infection, or of the side effects of medication. If diagnosed and properly treated, delirium is typically short-lived. It can, however, result in serious medical complications, permanent cognitive impairment, or death if the causes go untreated.

People with **amnestic disorders** experience memory impairments that are more limited than those seen in dementia or delirium. The person loses the ability to learn new information or becomes unable to recall previously learned information, but other higher-level cognitive abilities—including the use of language—are unaffected.

Dementia, delirium, and amnestic disorders are listed as Cognitive Disorders in DSM-IV-TR. Cognitive processes, including perception and attention, are related to many types of mental disorders that we have already discussed, such as depression, anxiety, and schizophrenia. In most forms of psychopathology, however, the cognitive problems are relatively subtle—mediating factors that help us understand the process by which clinical symptoms are produced. In the case of depression, for example, self-defeating biases may contribute to the onset of a depressed mood. These cognitive schemas are not used, however, as part of the diagnostic criteria for major depression in DSM-IV-TR. They are not considered to be the central, defining features of the disorder. Problems in sustained attention may represent vulnerability markers for schizophrenia, but again, they are not considered symptoms of the disorder. In dementia, memory and other cognitive functions are the most obvious manifestations of the problem. They are its defining features. As dementia progresses, the person's attention span,

*Confusion and disorientation are common symptoms of dementia. This elderly woman may not have been aware that she was walking in front of a line of riot police sent to control demonstrators in Moscow.*

concentration, judgment, planning, and decision making become severely disturbed.

Dementia and amnestic disorders are often associated with specific identifiable changes in brain tissue (Volicer, McKee, & Hewitt, 2001). Many times these changes can be observed only at autopsy, after the patient's death. For example, in Alzheimer's disease, which is one form of dementia, microscopic examination of the brain reveals the presence of an unusual amount of debris left from dead neurons, called *plaque*, and neurofibrillary tangles indicating that the connections between nerve cells had become disorganized. We describe the neuropathology of Alzheimer's disease later in this chapter.

Because of the close link between cognitive disorders and brain disease, patients with these problems are often diagnosed and treated by **neurologists**, physicians who deal primarily with diseases of the brain and the nervous system. Multidisciplinary clinical teams study and provide care for people with dementia and amnestic disorders. Direct care to patients and their families is usually provided by nurses and social workers. **Neuropsychologists** have particular expertise in the assessment of specific types of cognitive impairment. This is true for clinical assessments as well as for more detailed laboratory studies for research purposes.

The following two case studies illustrate the variety of symptoms and problems that are included in the general category of dementia. The first case describes the early stages of dementia.

Jonathan's case illustrates many of the early symptoms of dementia, as well as the ways in which the beginnings of memory problems can severely disrupt a person's life.

## CASE STUDY A Physician's Developing Dementia

Jonathan was a 61-year-old physician who had been practising family medicine for the past 30 years. His wife, Alice, worked as his office manager. A registered nurse, Kathryn, had worked with them for several years. Four months earlier, Alice and Kathryn both noticed that Jonathan was beginning to make obvious errors at work. On one occasion, Kathryn observed Jonathan prescribe the wrong medication for a patient's condition. At about the same time, Alice became concerned when she asked Jonathan about a patient whom he had seen the day before. Much to her surprise, he did not remember having seen the patient, in spite of the fact that he spent almost half an hour with her, and she was a patient whom he had treated for several years.

Jonathan's personality also seemed to change in small but noticeable ways. For example, Jonathan had always been a gentle and easygoing man. He had a special fondness and tolerance for small children. One day, one of his patients was accompanied to the office by her two-year-old son. As Jonathan was talking with the mother, the little boy accidentally pushed some bottles of pills off a counter. No harm was done, but Jonathan screamed loudly at the boy, chastising him for being so clumsy and careless. The mother was quite embarrassed. So were Kathryn and Alice, who witnessed Jonathan's sudden and uncharacteristic display of temper.

Although Alice tried to convince herself that these were isolated incidents, she finally decided to discuss them with Kathryn. Kathryn agreed that Jonathan's memory was failing. He had trouble recognizing patients whom he had known for many years, and he had unusual difficulty making treatment decisions. These problems had not appeared suddenly. Over the past year or two, both women had been doing more things for Jonathan than they had ever done in the past. They needed to remind him about things that were routine parts of his practice. As they pieced together various incidents, the pattern of gradual cognitive decline became obvious.

Alice talked seriously with Jonathan about the problems that she and Kathryn had observed. He said that he felt fine, but he reluctantly allowed her to make an appointment for him to be examined by a neurologist, who also happened to be a friend. Jonathan admitted to the neurolo-

*continued*

cont.

gist that he had been having difficulty remembering things. He believed that he had been able to avoid most problems, however, by writing notes to himself—directions, procedures, and so on. The results of psychological testing and brain imaging procedures, coupled with Jonathan's own description of his experiences and Alice's account of his impaired performance at work, led the neurologist to conclude that Jonathan was exhibiting early signs of dementia, perhaps Alzheimer's disease. He spoke directly with Jonathan regarding his diagnosis and recommended firmly that Jonathan retire immediately. A malpractice suit would be devastating to his medical practice. Jonathan agreed to retire.

Although Jonathan was no longer able to cope with his demanding work environment, his adjustment at home was not severely impaired. The changes in his behaviour remained relatively subtle for many months. In short conversations, his cognitive problems were not apparent to his friends, who still did not know the real reason for his retirement. His speech was fluent, and his memory for recent events was largely intact, but his comprehension was diminished. Alice noticed that Jonathan's emotional responses were occasionally flat or restricted. At other times, he would laugh at inappropriate times when they watched television programs together. If Alice asked him about his reaction, it was sometimes apparent that Jonathan did not understand the plot of even the simplest television programs.

Jonathan had become increasingly literal-minded. If Alice asked him to do something for her, she had to spell out every last detail. For example, he began to have trouble selecting his clothes, which had been a source of pride before the onset of his cognitive problems. Alice found that she had to sew labels into Jonathan's collars to distinguish for him the clothes that he wore to work in the yard from those that he wore if they were going shopping or out to eat. His judgment about what was appropriate to wear in different situations had disappeared altogether.

It had also become difficult for Jonathan to do things that required a regular sequence of actions or decisions, even if they were quite simple and familiar. Routine tasks took longer than before, usually because he got stuck part of the way through an activity. He had, for example, always enjoyed making breakfast for Alice on weekends. After his retirement, Alice once found him standing in the kitchen with a blank expression on his face. He had made a pot of coffee and some toast for both of them, but he ran into trouble when he couldn't find coffee cups. That disrupted his plan, and he was stymied. ◆

The onset of the disorder is often difficult to identify precisely because forgetfulness increases gradually. Problems are most evident in challenging situations, as in Jonathan's medical practice, and least noticeable in familiar surroundings.

Changes in emotional responsiveness and personality typically accompany the onset of memory impairment in dementia (Finkel et al., 1996). These changes may be consequences of the cognitive problems. Jonathan's irritability might easily have been aggravated by his own frustration with himself for being forgetful and indecisive. His emotional responses may have seemed unusual sometimes because he failed to comprehend aspects of the environment that were obvious to his wife and other people.

Our next case illustrates more advanced stages of dementia, in which the person can become extremely disorganized. Memory impairment progresses to the point where the person no longer recognizes his or her family and closest friends. People in this condition are unable to care for themselves, and they become so disoriented that the burden on others is frequently overwhelming. This case also provides an example of delirium superimposed on dementia. Up to 50 percent of dementia patients who are admitted to a hospital are also delirious. It is important for the neurologist to recognize the distinction between these conditions because the cause of the delirium (which might be an infection or a change in the patient's medications) must be treated promptly (Inouye, Schlesenger, & Lydon, 1999).

## CASE STUDY Dementia and Delirium—A Niece's Terrible Discoveries

Mary was an 84-year-old retired schoolteacher who had grown up in the same small rural community in which she still lived. Never married, she lived with her parents most of her life, except for the years when she was in college. Her parents had died when Mary was in her early sixties. After her retirement at age 65, Mary continued living in her parents' farmhouse. She felt comfortable there, in spite of its relative isolation, and liked the

continued

*cont.*

fact that it had plenty of space for animals, including her dog, which she called "my baby," several cats, and a few cows that were kept in the pasture behind the house. Mary's niece, Nancy, who was 45 years old and lived an hour's drive away, stopped to visit her once every two or three months.

Over the past year, Nancy had noticed that Mary was becoming forgetful, as well as more insistent that her routines remain unchanged. Bills went unpaid—in fact, the telephone had been disconnected for lack of payment—and the mail wasn't brought in from the roadside box. Nancy had suggested to Mary that she might be better off in a nursing home, but Mary was opposed to that idea.

At her most recent visit, Nancy was shocked to find that conditions at Mary's home had become intolerable. Most distressing was the fact that some of her animals had died because Mary forgot to feed them. The dog's decomposed body was tied to its house, where it had starved. Conditions inside the house were disgusting. Almost 30 cats lived inside the house, and the smell was unbearable. Mary's own appearance was quite dishevelled. She hadn't bathed or changed her clothes for weeks. Nancy contacted people at a social service agency, who arranged for Mary's admission to a nursing home. Mary became furious, refusing to go and denying that there was anything wrong with her own home. Nancy was soon declared her legal guardian because Mary was clearly not competent to make decisions for herself.

Mary grew progressively more agitated and belligerent during the few weeks that she lived at the nursing home. She was occasionally disoriented, not knowing where she was or what day it was. She shouted and sometimes struck people with her cane. She had trouble walking, a problem that was compounded by visual and spatial judgment difficulties. After she fell and broke her hip, Mary was transferred to a general hospital.

Mary became delirious in the hospital, apparently as a result of medication she was given for her injury. She appeared to be having visual hallucinations and often said things that did not make sense. These periods of incoherence fluctuated in severity throughout the course of the day. During her worse moments, Mary did not respond to her name being spoken, and her speech was reduced primarily to groans and nonsense words. This clouding of consciousness cleared up a few days after her medication was changed. She became less distractible and was once again able to carry on brief conversations. Unfortunately, her disorientation became more severe while she was immobilized in the hospital. When her hip eventually healed, she was moved to a psychiatric hospital and admitted to the geriatric ward.

Although Mary was no longer aware of the date or even the season of the year, she insisted that she did not have any problems with her mind. For the first six weeks at the psychiatric hospital, she would be surprised that she was not in her own home when she woke up each morning. After that time, she acknowledged that she was in a hospital, but she did not know why she was there, and she did not understand that the other patients on the unit were also demented. She didn't recognize hospital staff members from one day to the next. She was completely unable to remember anything that had happened recently. Nevertheless, her memory for events that had happened many years earlier was quite good. Mary repeated stories about her childhood over and over again.

Nurses on the unit were bombarded continuously with her complaints about being removed from her home. Every 20 minutes or so, Mary would approach the nurses' station, waving her cane and shouting, "Nurse, I need to go home. I have to get out of here. I have to go home and take care of my dog." The hospital staff would explain to her that she would have to stay at the hospital, at least for a while longer, and that her dog had died several months earlier. This news would usually provoke sadness, but she seemed unable to remember it long enough to complete the grieving process. Several minutes later, the whole scene would be repeated. Mary also became paranoid, claiming to anyone who would listen that people were trying to steal her things. The most common focus of her concern was her purse. If it was out of her sight, she would announce loudly that someone had stolen it.

In the midst of these obvious problems, Mary retained many other intellectual abilities. She was a well-educated and intelligent woman. Her attention span was reduced, but she was still able to do crossword puzzles and enjoyed reading short stories. Poetry had always been one of her special interests, and she was still able to recite many of her favourite poems beautifully from memory. In a quiet room, it was often possible to talk with her and pursue a meaningful conversation. Unfortunately, these lucid periods were interspersed with times of restless pacing and shouting. Her agitation would escalate rapidly unless staff members distracted her, taking her to a quiet room, talking to her, and getting her to read or recite something out loud. ◆

## Typical Symptoms and Associated Features

The symptoms of cognitive disorders are often overlooked in elderly patients. It can be difficult to distinguish the onset of dementia from patterns of modest memory decline that are an expected part of the aging process. Different forms of cognitive disorder can also be confused with one another. Recognition of these disorders and the distinctions among them carries important treatment implications for patients and their families.

## Delirium

The DSM-IV-TR criteria for delirium are listed in Table 14–1. The primary symptom of delirium is clouding of consciousness in association with a reduced ability to maintain and shift attention. The disturbance in consciousness might also be described as a reduction in the clarity of a person's awareness of his or her surroundings. Memory deficits may occur in association with impaired consciousness and may be the direct result of attention problems. The person's thinking appears disorganized, and he or she may speak in a rambling, incoherent fashion. Fleeting perceptual disturbances, including visual hallucinations, are also common in delirious patients (Cole et al., 2002).

The symptoms of delirium follow a rapid onset—from a few hours to several days—and typically fluctuate throughout the day. The person may alternate between extreme confusion and periods in which he or she is more rational and clearheaded. Symptoms are usually worse at night. The sleep/wake cycle is often disturbed. Daytime drowsiness and lapses in concentration are often followed by agitation and hyperactivity at night. If the condition is allowed to progress, the person's senses may become dulled, and he or she may eventually lapse into a coma. The delirious person is also likely to be disoriented with relation to time ("What day, month, or season is it?") or place ("Where are we? What is the name of this place?"). However, identity confusion ("What is your name?") is rare.

It isn't always easy to recognize the difference between dementia and delirium, especially when they appear simultaneously in the same patient. Table 14–2 summarizes several considerations that are useful in making this diagnostic distinction (Insel & Badger, 2002). One important consideration involves the period of time over which the symptoms appear. Delirium has a rapid onset, whereas dementia develops in a slow, progressive manner. In dementia, the person usually remains alert and responsive to the environment. Speech is most often coherent in demented patients, at least until the end stages of the disorder, but it is typically confused in delirious patients. Finally, delirium can be resolved, whereas dementia cannot.

## Dementia

The cases at the beginning of this chapter illustrate the changing patterns that emerge as dementia unfolds. Jonathan's cognitive symptoms were recognized at a relatively early stage of development, in part because of his occupational situation and because of his close relationships with other people. Mary's situation was much different because she lived in a relatively isolated setting without close neighbours or friends. By the time Nancy recognized the full severity of Mary's problems, the cognitive impairment had progressed so far that Mary was no longer able to appreciate the nature of her own difficulties. In the following pages we describe in more detail the types of symptoms that are associated with dementia.

**Cognitive Symptoms** Dementia appears in people whose intellectual abilities have previously been unimpaired. Both of the people in our case studies were bright, well educated, and occupationally successful before the onset of their symptoms. The earliest signs of dementia are often quite vague. They include difficulty remembering recent events and the names of people and familiar objects. These are

**TABLE 14–1 DSM-IV-TR Criteria for Delirium**

**A. Disturbance of consciousness (i.e., reduced clarity of awareness of the environment) with reduced ability to focus, sustain, or shift attention.**

**B. A change in cognition (such as memory deficit, disorientation, language disturbance) or the development of a perceptual disturbance that is not better accounted for by a pre-existing, established, or evolving dementia.**

**C. The disturbance develops over a short period of time (usually hours to days) and tends to fluctuate during the course of the day.**

**TABLE 14–2 Distinguishing Features of Dementia and Delirium**

| Characteristic | Delirium | Dementia |
|---|---|---|
| Onset | Sudden (hours to days) | Slow (months to years) |
| Duration | Brief | Long/lifetime |
| Course | Fluctuating | Stable, with downward trajectory over time |
| Attention | Impaired | Intact |
| Hallucinations | Visual/tactile/vivid | Rare |
| Insight | Lucid intervals | Consistently poor |
| Sleep | Disturbed | Less disturbed |

*Source:* K.C. Insel and T.A. Badger, 2002, Deciphering the 4 D's: cognitive decline, delirium, depression and dementia—a review. *Journal of Advanced Nursing, 38*, 360–368.

all problems that are associated with normal aging, but they differ from that process in order of magnitude (see Further Thoughts). The distinguishing features of dementia include cognitive problems in a number of areas, ranging from impaired memory and learning to deficits in language and abstract thinking. By the final stages of dementia, intellectual and motor functions may disappear almost completely (Rosenstein, 1998).

## Further Thoughts Memory Changes in Normal Aging

Changes in cognitive abilities are part of the normal aging process. One of the first people to investigate this phenomenon was London, Ontario, psychiatrist Vojtech A. Kral during the 1950s and 1960s (Eastwood & Merskey, 1996). Most elderly adults complain more frequently about memory problems than younger adults do, and they typically perform less efficiently than younger adults on laboratory tests of memory. There are, of course, individual differences in the age at which cognitive abilities begin to decline, as well as in the rate at which these losses take place. Nevertheless, some types of memory impairment are an inevitable consequence of aging (Christensen, 2001; Luszcz & Bryan, 1999).

In order to understand more clearly the cognitive changes associated with aging, it is useful to distinguish between two aspects of mental functioning: *mechanics* (also known as fluid intelligence) and *pragmatics* (sometimes called crystallized intelligence) (Baltes, 1993; Salthouse, 1999). The computer can be used as a metaphor to explain this distinction. Cognitive mechanics are "the hardware of the mind." These functions are concerned with the speed and accuracy of such basic processes as perception, attention, and memory. The proficiency of mechanics depends on neurophysiological processes and on the structural integrity of the person's brain.

Cognitive pragmatics represent the "culture-based software of the mind." Reading and writing skills, as well as knowledge about the self and ways of coping with environmental challenges, are examples of pragmatics. They represent information about the world that is acquired continually throughout the person's lifetime. Wisdom is a reflection of cognitive pragmatics.

Mechanics and pragmatics follow different trajectories over the normal human lifespan (Baltes, 1993, 1997). Both develop continuously during childhood and adolescence, reaching a point of optimal efficiency during young adulthood. After that point, mechanics follow a gradual pattern of decline. Pragmatics, on the other hand, remain unimpaired as the person reaches old age. The erosion of cognitive mechanics over time is presumably due to subtle atrophy of brain regions, such as the hippocampus, that take place during normal aging (Small et al., 1999).

Several research studies support this general conclusion. One laboratory task designed to measure cognitive mechanics requires subjects to remember long lists of words in their correct order. Even after many training and practice sessions, most adults in their sixties and seventies are unable to achieve the level of performance shown by young adults after a small number of practice sessions (Lindenberger & Baltes, 1997). Age-related deficits are found even among those normal elderly persons who are selected for study because of their experience with and talent for similar cognitive tasks.

Different measurement procedures have been used to explore the relationship between aging and cognitive pragmatics. In one procedure, subjects are presented with a life dilemma, such as "A 15-year-old girl wants to get married right away. What should she consider and do?" The subjects' task is to think aloud about each dilemma. Responses are scored in terms of the amount of knowledge that the person displays with regard to facts, values, and procedures that must be considered in each circumstance. In contrast to the results of research on mechanics, studies of pragmatics have found no change in performance between the ages of 30 and 70. Elderly people are just as likely as younger adults to produce the best scores on this type of task.

*Arthur Rubenstein (1887–1982) was one of the greatest pianists of the twentieth century.*

The aging mind apparently depends on the coordination of gains and losses. The elderly person strikes a balance through a process that involves *selection, optimization*, and *compensation* (Freund & Baltes, 2002). Arthur Rubinstein, the brilliant pianist who performed concerts well into his eighties, provides an example of this process. Rubinstein described three strategies that he employed in his old age: (1) He was selective, performing fewer pieces; (2) he optimized his performance by practising each piece more frequently; and (3) he compensated for a loss of motor speed by utilizing pieces that emphasized contrast between fast and slow segments so that his playing seemed faster than it really was. Successful aging is based on this dynamic process. The person compensates for losses in cogni-

continued

*cont.*

tive mechanics by taking advantage of pragmatics—increased knowledge and information.

The fact that an older person begins to experience subtle memory problems does not necessarily indicate that he or she is becoming demented. Where can we find the line between normal aging and dementia? Is this distinction simply a matter of degree, or is there a qualitative difference between the expected decline in cognitive mechanics and the onset of cognitive pathology? These issues present an important challenge for future research. ◆

*Memory and Learning* The diagnostic hallmark of dementia is memory loss. In order to describe the various facets of memory impairment, it is useful to distinguish between old memories and the ability to learn new things. **Retrograde amnesia** refers to the loss of memory for events prior to the onset of an illness or the experience of a traumatic event. **Anterograde amnesia** refers to the inability to learn or remember new material after a particular point in time.

Anterograde amnesia is usually the most obvious problem during the beginning stages of dementia. Consider, for example, the case of Jonathan. Alice eventually noticed that he sometimes could not remember things that he had done the previous day. Mary, the more severely impaired person, could not remember for more than a few minutes that her dog had died. Long-term memories are usually not affected until much later in the course of the disorder. Even in advanced stages of dementia, a person may retain some recollections of the past. Mary was able to remember, and frequently described, stories from her childhood.

*Verbal Communication* Language functions can also be affected in dementia. **Aphasia** is a term that describes various types of loss or impairment in language that are caused by brain damage (Saffran, 2000). Language disturbance in dementia is sometimes relatively subtle, but it can include many different kinds of problems. Patients often remain verbally fluent, at least until the disorder is relatively advanced. They retain their vocabulary skills and are able to construct grammatical sentences. They may have trouble finding words, naming objects, and comprehending instructions.

In addition to problems in understanding and forming meaningful sentences, the demented person may also have difficulty performing purposeful movements in response to verbal commands, a problem known as **apraxia**. The person possesses the normal strength and coordination to carry out the action and is able to understand the other person's speech, but is nevertheless unable to translate the various components into a meaningful action (Koski, Iacoboni, & Mazziotta, 2002).

*Perception* Some patients with dementia have problems identifying stimuli in their environments. The technical term for this phenomenon is **agnosia**, which means "perception without meaning." The person's sensory functions are unimpaired, but he or she is unable to recognize the source of stimulation (Farah, 1992). Agnosia can be associated with visual, auditory, or tactile sensations, and it can be relatively specific or more generalized. For example, visual agnosia is the inability to recognize certain objects or faces. Some people with visual agnosia can identify inanimate stimuli but are unable to recognize human faces.

It is sometimes difficult to distinguish between aphasia and agnosia. Imagine, for example, that a clinician shows a patient a toothbrush and asks, "What is this object?" The patient may look at the object and be unable to name it. Does that mean that the person cannot think of the word "toothbrush"? Or does it mean that the person cannot recognize the object at all? In this case, the distinction could be made by saying to the person, "Show me what you do with this object." A person suffering from aphasia would take the toothbrush in his hand and make brushing movements in front of his mouth, thereby demonstrating that he recognizes the object but cannot remember its name. A person with agnosia would be unable to indicate how the toothbrush is used.

*Abstract Thinking* Another manifestation of cognitive impairment in dementia is loss of the ability to think in abstract ways. The person may be bound to concrete interpretations of things that other people say. It may also be difficult for the person to interpret words that have more than one meaning (for example, "pen") or to explain why two objects are alike

("Why are a basketball and a football helmet alike?" Because they are both types of sporting equipment.)

In our opening case, Jonathan became increasingly literal-minded in his conversations with other people. After he retired, he had much more time to become involved in routine tasks around the home. Alice found that she had to give him very explicit instructions if she wanted him to do anything. For example, if she asked him to mow the grass, he would do exactly that—nothing more. This was unusual for Jonathan, because he had always enjoyed taking care of their lawn and took great pride in their bushes and flower gardens. Previously, "mowing the grass" would have been taken to include trimming, pulling weeds, raking leaves from under bushes, and all sorts of related details. Now Jonathan interpreted this instruction in concrete terms.

*Judgment and Social Behaviour* Related to deficits in abstract reasoning is the failure of social judgment and problem-solving skills. In the course of everyday life, we must acquire information from the environment, organize and process it, and then formulate and perform appropriate responses by considering these new data in the light of past experiences. The disruption of short-term memory, perceptual skills, and higher-level cognitive abilities obviously causes disruptions of judgment. Examples from Jonathan's case include problems deciding which clothes to wear for working around his home as opposed to going out in public, as well as his inability to understand the humour in some television programs. Impulsive and careless behaviours are often the product of the demented person's poor judgment. Activities such as shopping, driving, and using tools can create serious problems.

**TABLE 14–3 Mini–Mental State Examination**

1. What is the (year, season, date, day, month)?
2. Where are we (province, city, hospital)?
3. Name three objects (pen, sky, dog), then ask patient to repeat them.
4. Spell "world" backwards.
5. Ask for names of three objects given in question #3.
6. Point to a pencil and a watch. Ask the patient to name each as you point.
7. Ask the patient to repeat, "No ifs, ands, or buts."
8. Three-stage command: "Take this paper in your right hand. Fold the paper in half. Put the paper on the floor."
9. Ask the patient to read and obey the following (write on card in large letters): "CLOSE YOUR EYES."
10. Have the patient write a sentence of his or her choice.
11. Have the patient copy two intersecting pentagons.

*Source:* M.F. Folstein, S.E. Folstein, and P.R. McHugh, 1975, Mini–Mental State: A practical method for grading the cognitive state of patients for the clinician. *Journal of Psychiatric Research, 2,* 189–198.

### Assessment of Cognitive Impairment

There are many ways to measure a person's level of cognitive impairment. One is the Mini–Mental State Examination, which is outlined in Table 14–3. We include it here to give you an idea of the types of questions that a clinician might ask in order to elicit the cognitive problems of dementia. Some are directed at the person's orientation to time and place. Others are concerned with anterograde amnesia, such as the ability to remember the names of objects for a short period of time (items 3 and 5). Agnosia, aphasia, and apraxia are addressed by items 6, 7, and 8, respectively. Perceptual difficulties are tapped by the last item (11).

**Neuropsychological assessment** can be used as a more precise index of cognitive impairment. This process involves the evaluation of performance on psychological tests to indicate whether a person has a brain disorder (Morgan & Baade, 1997). Neuropsychological tests can sometimes be used to infer the location of a brain lesion. The best-known neuropsychological assessment procedure is the Halstead-Reitan Neuropsychological Test Battery, which includes an extensive series of tests that tap sensorimotor, perceptual, and speech functions. For example, in the tactile performance test, the person is blindfolded and then required to fit differently shaped blocks into spaces in a form board. The time needed to perform this test reflects one specific aspect of the person's motor skills.

Some neuropsychological tasks require the person to copy simple objects or produce drawings. The drawings illustrated in Figure 14–1 illustrate the Clock Test, which can be used to assess planning problems and apraxia, and is a useful tool for screening for dementia (Shulman, 2000; Tuokko & Hadjistavropoulos, 1998). In this test the person is presented with a piece of paper containing a circle and asked to draw a clock showing a particular time (e.g., 10 minutes to 3). The quality of the person's performance is then scored; e.g., in terms of

**Neuropsychological Test Performance: The Clock Test**

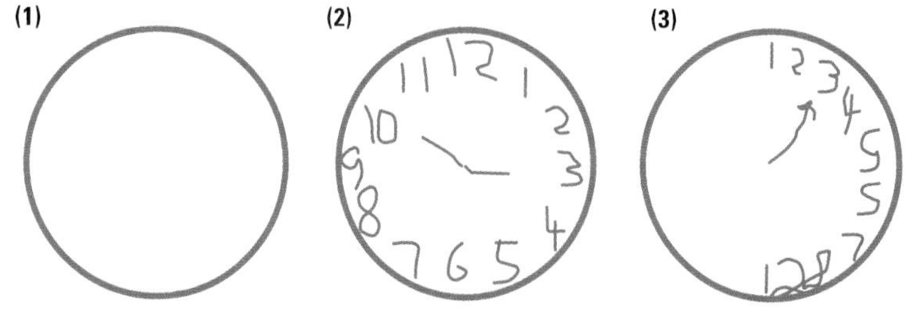


**FIGURE 14–1: The Clock Test is a commonly used method for screening dementia. The person is presented with (1) a circle and asked to draw a clock, with the hands set to a specific time (e.g., 10 minutes to 3). Drawing (2) is from an 87-year-old cognitively unimpaired woman. Drawing (3) is from a 66-year-old man with Alzheimer's disease. Notice that drawing (3), compared to drawing (2), is poorly organized. Drawing (3) also contains numerous omissions (numbers and a hand are missing) and a perseveration ("5" is repeated).**

whether the numbers are properly located on the clock face, and whether there are any errors of omission (e.g., missing numbers) or errors of commission (e.g., repeated numbers). Several scoring systems have been developed (Spreen & Strauss, 1998). One of the most useful systems was developed by a group of researchers led by Holly Tuokko at the University of Victoria, and Thomas Hadjistavropoulos at the University of Regina (e.g., Tuokko et al., 2000).

**Personality and Emotion** Personality changes, emotional difficulties, and motivational problems are frequently associated with dementia. These problems may not contribute to the diagnosis of the disorder, but they do have an impact on the person's adjustment. They can also create additional burdens for people who care for demented patients.

Hallucinations and delusions are seen in at least 20 percent of dementia cases and are more common during the later stages of the disorder (Stoppe, Brandt, & Staedt, 1999). The delusional beliefs are typically understandable consequences of the person's disorientation or anterograde amnesia. They are most often simple in nature and are relatively short-lived. Mary's frequent insistence that someone had stolen her purse is a typical example. Other common themes are phantom houseguests and personal persecution (Harvey, 1996).

The emotional consequences of dementia are quite varied. Some demented patients appear to be apathetic or emotionally flat. Their faces are less expressive, and they appear to be indifferent to their surroundings. Alice noticed, for example, that something seemed a bit vacant in Jonathan's eyes. At other times, emotional reactions may become exaggerated and less predictable. The person may become fearful or angry in situations that would not have aroused strong emotion in the past. Jonathan's sudden rage at the boy who pushed bottles off the counter in his office is one example. Changes like this often lead others to believe that the person's personality has changed.

Depression is another problem that is frequently found in association with dementia (Jorm, 2001; Migliorelli et al., 1995). In many ways, feelings of depression are understandable. The realization that your most crucial cognitive abilities are beginning to fail, that you can no longer perform simple tasks or care for yourself, would obviously lead to sadness and depression. Mary's case illustrates one way in which cognitive impairment can complicate depression: Her inability to remember from one day to the next that her dog had died seemed to interfere with her ability to grieve for the loss of her pet. Each time that she was reminded of his death was like the first time that she had heard the news.

**Motor Behaviours** Demented persons may become agitated, pacing restlessly or wandering away from familiar surroundings. In the later stages of the disorder, patients may develop problems in the control of the muscles by the central nervous system. Some patients develop muscular rigidity, which can be accompanied by painful cramping. Others experience epileptic seizures, which consist of involuntary, rapidly alternating movements of the arms and legs.

Some specific types of dementia are associated with involuntary movements, or **dyskinesia**—tics, tremors, and jerky movements of the face and limbs called *chorea*. These motor symptoms help to distinguish among different types of dementia. We return to this area later in the chapter when we discuss the classification of differentiated and undifferentiated dementias.

## Amnestic Disorder

Some cognitive disorders involve more circumscribed forms of memory impairment than those seen in dementia. In amnestic disorders, a person exhibits a severe impairment of memory while other higher-level cognitive abilities are unaffected. The memory disturbance interferes with social and occupational functioning and represents a significant decline from a previous level of adjustment. Subtypes of amnestic disorder are diagnosed on the basis of evidence, acquired from the patient's history, from a physical examination, or from laboratory tests, regarding medical conditions or substance use that is considered to be related to the onset of the memory impairment.

The following case, written by Oliver Sacks (1985), illustrates a form of amnestic disorder, involving severe anterograde amnesia, which developed after the patient had been dependent on alcohol for several years.

## CASE STUDY **Alcohol-Induced Persisting Amnestic Disorder—19 Going on 45**

Jimmie G. was admitted to our Home for the Aged near New York City early in 1975, with a cryptic transfer note saying, "Helpless, demented, confused and disoriented." Jimmie was a fine-looking man, with a curly bush of grey hair, a healthy and handsome 49-year-old. He was cheerful, friendly, and warm.

"Hiya, Doc!" he said. "Nice morning! Do I take this chair here?" He was a genial soul, very ready to talk and to answer any questions I asked him. He told me his name and birth date, and the name of the little town in Connecticut where he was born. He described it in affectionate detail, even drew me a map. He spoke of the houses where his family had lived—he remembered their phone numbers still. He spoke of school and school days, the friends he'd had, and his special fondness for mathematics and science. He talked with enthusiasm of his days in the navy—he was 17, had just graduated from high school when he was drafted in 1943. With his good engineering mind he was a "natural" for radio and electronics, and after a crash course in Texas found himself assistant radio operator on a submarine. He remembered the names of various submarines on which he had served, their missions, where they were stationed, the names of his shipmates. He remembered Morse code, and was still fluent in Morse tapping and touch-typing.

A full and interesting early life, remembered vividly, in detail, with affection. But there, for some reason, his reminiscences stopped. He recalled, and almost relived, his war days and service, the end of the war, and his thoughts for the future. He had come to love the navy, thought he might stay in it. But with the GI Bill, and support, he felt he might do best to go to college.

With recalling, reliving, Jimmie was full of animation; he did not seem to be speaking of the past but of the present, and I was very struck by the change of tense in his recollections as he passed from his school days to his days in the navy. He had been using the past tense, but now used the present and (it seemed to me) not just the formal or fictitious present tense of recall, but the actual present tense of immediate experience.

A sudden, improbable suspicion seized me. "What year is this, Mr. G.?" I asked, concealing my perplexity under a casual manner.

"Forty-five, man. What do you mean?" He went on, "We've won the war, FDR's dead, Truman's at the helm. There are great times ahead."

"And you, Jimmie, how old would you be?"

Oddly, uncertainly, he hesitated a moment, as if engaged in calculation. "Why, I guess I'm 19, Doc. I'll be 20 next birthday."

Looking at the grey-haired man before me, I had an impulse for which I have never forgiven myself—it was, or would have been, the height of cruelty had there been any possibility of Jimmie's remembering it.

"Here," I said, and thrust a mirror toward him. "Look in the mirror and tell me what you see. Is that a 19-year-old looking out from the mirror?"

He suddenly turned ashen and gripped the sides of the chair. "Jesus Christ," he whispered. "Christ, what's going on? What's happened to me? Is this a nightmare? Am I crazy? Is this a joke?" and he became frantic, panicked.

"It's okay, Jimmie," I said soothingly. "It's just a mistake. Nothing to worry about. Hey!" I took him to the window. "Isn't this a lovely spring day. See the kids there playing baseball?" He regained his colour and started to smile, and I stole away, taking the hateful mirror with me.

Two minutes later I re-entered the room. Jimmie was still standing by the window, gazing with pleasure at the kids playing baseball below. He wheeled around as I opened the door, and his face assumed a cheery expression.

"Hiya, Doc!" he said. "Nice morning! You want to talk to me—do I take this chair here?" There was no sign of recognition on his frank, open face.

"Haven't we met before, Mr. G.?" I asked casually.

"No, I can't say we have. Quite a beard you got there. I wouldn't forget you, Doc!"

"Why do you call me 'Doc'?"

"Well, you are a doc, ain't you?"

"Yes, but if you haven't met me, how do you know what I am?"

"You talk like a doc. I can see you're a doc."

"Well, you're right, I am. I'm the neurologist here."

"Neurologist? Hey, there's something wrong with my nerves? And 'here'—where's 'here'? What is this place anyhow?"

"I was just going to ask you—where do you think you are?"

"I see these beds, and these patients everywhere. Looks like a sort of hospital

*continued*

*cont.*

to me. But hell, what would I be doing in a hospital and with all these old people, years older than me. I feel good, I'm strong as a bull. Maybe I work here . . . Do I work? What's my job? . . . No, you're shaking your head, I see in your eyes I don't work here. If I don't work here, I've been put here. Am I a patient, am I sick and don't know it, Doc? It's crazy, it's scary . . . Is it some sort of joke?" (Sacks, 1985, pp. 22–25). ◆

The preceding case illustrates the most common type of amnestic disorder, alcohol-induced persisting amnestic disorder, also known as Korsakoff's syndrome. In this disorder, which is caused by chronic alcoholism, memory is impaired but other cognitive functions are not. More detailed examinations of the patient's cognitive abilities, using neuropsychological tests, have found evidence of more widespread cognitive deficits, especially those related to visuoperceptual skills and abstract thinking (Kopelman, 1995).

One widely accepted theory regarding this condition holds that lack of vitamin $B_1$ (thiamine) leads to atrophy of the medial thalamus, a subcortical structure of the brain, and mammillary bodies (MB). Support for one aspect of this theory comes from studies that used magnetic resonance imaging to compare brain structures in alcoholic patients with amnesia, alcoholic patients without amnesia, and normal controls. Deficits in MB volume occur in both types of alcoholics, and greater volume deficits are found in alcoholic patients with amnesia (Sullivan et al., 1999). Other data suggest, however, that these problems cannot be traced exclusively to thiamine deficiency (Homewood & Bond, 1999). In fact, prolonged exposure to alcohol may have direct toxic effects on cortical and subcortical tissue that are independent of vitamin deficiencies. Alcohol apparently can cause brain damage regardless of the person's nutritional habits (Fadda & Rosetti, 1998; Langlais, 1995).

# Classification

Cognitive disorders have been classified by a somewhat different process than most other forms of psychopathology because of their close link to specific types of neuropathology. Description of specific cognitive and behavioural symptoms has not always been the primary consideration. In the following pages we describe the ways in which these disorders have been defined and some of the considerations that influence the way in which they are classified.

## Brief Historical Perspective

Alois Alzheimer (1864–1915), a German psychiatrist, worked closely in Munich with Emil Kraepelin, who is often considered responsible for modern psychiatric classification (see Chapters 4, 5, and 12). Alzheimer's most famous case involved a 51-year-old woman who had become delusional and also experienced a severe form of recent memory impairment, accompanied by apraxia and agnosia. This woman died four years after the onset of her dementia. Following her death, Alzheimer conducted a microscopic examination of her brain and made a startling discovery: bundles of neurofibrillary tangles and amyloid plaques. Alzheimer presented the case at a meeting of psychiatrists in 1906 and published a three-page paper in 1907. Emil Kraepelin began to refer to this condition as Alzheimer's disease in the eighth edition of his famous textbook on psychiatry, published in 1910. He distinguished between this form of dementia, which is characterized by early onset, and senile dementia, which presumably has an onset after the age of 65 (Fox, Kelly, & Tobin, 1999).

For many years, there was an argument about the distinction between senile and

*Alois Alzheimer (left) on a pleasure cruise with his friend Emil Kraepelin. The form of dementia that Alzheimer described in his famous case was named after him in part because of the influence of Kraepelin's textbook.*

presenile dementia. As more and more evidence accumulated regarding these conditions, questions were raised about the value of the distinction. For example, several cases were reported in which two siblings developed dementia, but one had the presenile form and the other had the senile form. Clinical symptoms and brain pathology in the siblings were often the same. Katzman (1976) proposed that both types are forms of Alzheimer's disease, which may have either an early or a late onset, and that they are distinctly different from normal aging. Age of onset may be a reflection of the severity of the disorder. Most clinicians and researchers still believe that Alzheimer's disease is a heterogeneous category, and the genetic literature supports that contention.

Until recently, the diagnostic manual classified the various forms of dementia as Organic Mental Disorders because of their association with known brain diseases. That concept has fallen into disfavour because it is founded on an artificial dichotomy between biological and psychological processes. If we call dementia an organic mental disorder, does that imply that other types of psychopathology are not organically based (Spitzer et al., 1992)? Obviously not. Therefore, in order to be consistent with the rest of the diagnostic manual, and so as to avoid falling into the trap of simplistic mind–body dualism, dementia and related clinical phenomena are now classified as Cognitive Disorders in DSM-IV-TR. These disorders are divided into three major headings: deliria, dementias, and amnestic disorders (see Table 14–4).

**TABLE 14–4 Cognitive Disorders Listed in DSM-IV-TR**

| | |
|---|---|
| **Delirium** | Delirium due to a general medical condition<br>Substance-induced delirium<br>Delirium due to multiple etiologies |
| **Dementia** | Dementia of the Alzheimer's type<br>Vascular dementia<br>Dementia due to other general medical conditions<br>HIV disease<br>Head trauma<br>Parkinson's disease<br>Huntington's disease<br>Pick's disease<br>Creutzfeldt-Jakob disease<br>Substance-induced persisting dementia<br>Dementia due to multiple etiologies |
| **Amnestic Disorders** | Amnestic disorder due to a general medical condition<br>Substance-induced persisting amnestic disorder |

## Specific Disorders Associated with Dementia

Many specific disorders are associated with dementia. They are distinguished primarily on the basis of known neuropathology—specific brain lesions that have been discovered throughout the twentieth century. DSM-IV-TR lists several categories of dementia. The criteria for cognitive deficits of dementia are the same for each type, and they are listed in Table 14–5 as they relate to Dementia of the Alzheimer's Type. The only part of this definition that changes from one type of dementia to the next is the description listed under "C" (gradual onset and continuing cognitive decline). In order to qualify for a diagnosis of dementia, the person must exhibit memory impairment (either anterograde or retrograde amnesia) and at least one other type of cognitive disturbance, such as aphasia, apraxia, agnosia, or problems in abstract thinking. There must also be evidence that the person's cognitive impairment interferes with his or her social or occupational functioning. Finally, for all forms of dementia, DSM-IV-TR notes that the cognitive problems must be above and beyond anything that could be attributed solely to delirium.

**Dementia of the Alzheimer's Type** The speed of onset serves as the main feature to distinguish **Alzheimer's disease** from the other types of dementia listed in DSM-IV-TR. In this disorder, the cognitive impairment appears gradually, and the person's cognitive deterioration is progressive (Cummings & Cole, 2002). If the person meets these criteria, the diagnosis is then made on the basis of excluding other conditions, such as vascular disease, Huntington's disease, Parkinson's disease, or chronic substance abuse.

A definite diagnosis of Alzheimer's disease can only be determined by autopsy because it requires the observation of two specific types of brain lesions: neurofibrillary tangles and amyloid plaques (see Figure 14–2 on p. 494). The brain is composed of millions of neurons. The internal structure of branches that extend from each neuron includes microtubules, which provide structural support for

**TABLE 14-5 DSM-IV-TR Criteria for Dementia of the Alzheimer's Type**

**A. The development of multiple cognitive deficits manifested by both:**

1. Memory impairment (impaired ability to learn new information or to recall previously learned information)
2. One (or more) of the following cognitive disturbances:
   a. Aphasia (language disturbance)
   b. Apraxia (impaired ability to carry out motor activities despite intact motor function)
   c. Agnosia (failure to recognize or identify objects despite intact sensory function)
   d. Disturbance in executive functioning (that is, planning, organizing, sequencing, abstracting)

**B. The cognitive deficits each cause significant impairment in social or occupational functioning and represent a significant decline from a previous level of functioning.**

**C. The course is characterized by gradual onset and continuing cognitive decline.**

the cell and help transport chemicals used in the production of neurotransmitters (Blennow & Cowburn, 1996; Cummings et al., 1998). These microtubules are reinforced by tau proteins, which are organized symmetrically. Tau proteins are proteins associated with the assembly and stability of microtubules. In patients with Alzheimer's disease, enzymes loosen tau from their connections to the microtubule, and they break apart. The microtubules disintegrate in the absence of tau proteins, and the whole neuron shrivels and dies. The disorganized tangles of tau that are left at the end of this process are known as **neurofibrillary tangles**. They are found in both the cerebral cortex and the hippocampus. Neurofibrillary tangles have also been found in adults with Down syndrome and patients with Parkinson's disease.

The other type of lesion in Alzheimer's disease is known as **amyloid plaques**, which consist of a central core of homogeneous protein material known as **beta-amyloid** surrounded by clumps of debris left over from destroyed neurons. These plaques are located primarily in the cerebral cortex. They are found in large numbers in the brains of patients with Alzheimer's disease, but they are not unique to that condition. The brains of normal elderly people, especially after the age of 75, often contain some neurofibrillary tangles and amyloid plaques. A few widely scattered cells of this type do not appear to interfere with normal cognitive functioning.

### Frontotemporal Dementia (Pick's Disease)

A rare form of dementia associated with circumscribed atrophy of the frontal and temporal lobes of the brain is known as *frontotemporal dementia* (*FTD*). This syndrome is very similar to Alzheimer's disease in terms of both behavioural symptoms and cognitive impairment. Patients with both disorders display problems in memory and language. Early personality changes that precede the onset of cognitive impairment are more common among FTD patients. Impaired reasoning and judgment are more prominent than anterograde amnesia in FTD. In comparison to Alzheimer patients, patients with FTD are also more likely to engage in impulsive sexual actions, roaming and aimless exploration, and other types of disinhibited behaviour (Hodges, 2001; Knopman, 2001).

Another, more traditional diagnostic term that has been used to describe many patients who exhibit the behavioural syndrome of FTD is *Pick's disease* (Rossor, 2001). This term refers to a unique form of neural pathology that is found among some, but not all, patients with FTD. Detailed examination of brain tissue from patients with FTD often reveals the presence of unusual protein deposits, called *Pick's bodies*, within nerve cells (Hardin & Schooley, 2002). The loss and degeneration of neurons are usually concentrated in structures associated with the limbic system, such as the hippocampus and amygdala. The neurofibrillary tangles and amyloid plaques found in Alzheimer's disease are no more common in patients with Pick's disease than in normal people of the same age (Dickson, 2001). The more recent diagnostic term, FTD, is preferred by many neurologists because it describes a behavioural syndrome (deterioration of personality, antisocial behaviour, abnormal sense of humour, and memory disorder) rather than a specific form of neural pathology that is not found in all FTD patients.

**Forms of Brain Tissue Damage Associated with Alzheimer's Disease**

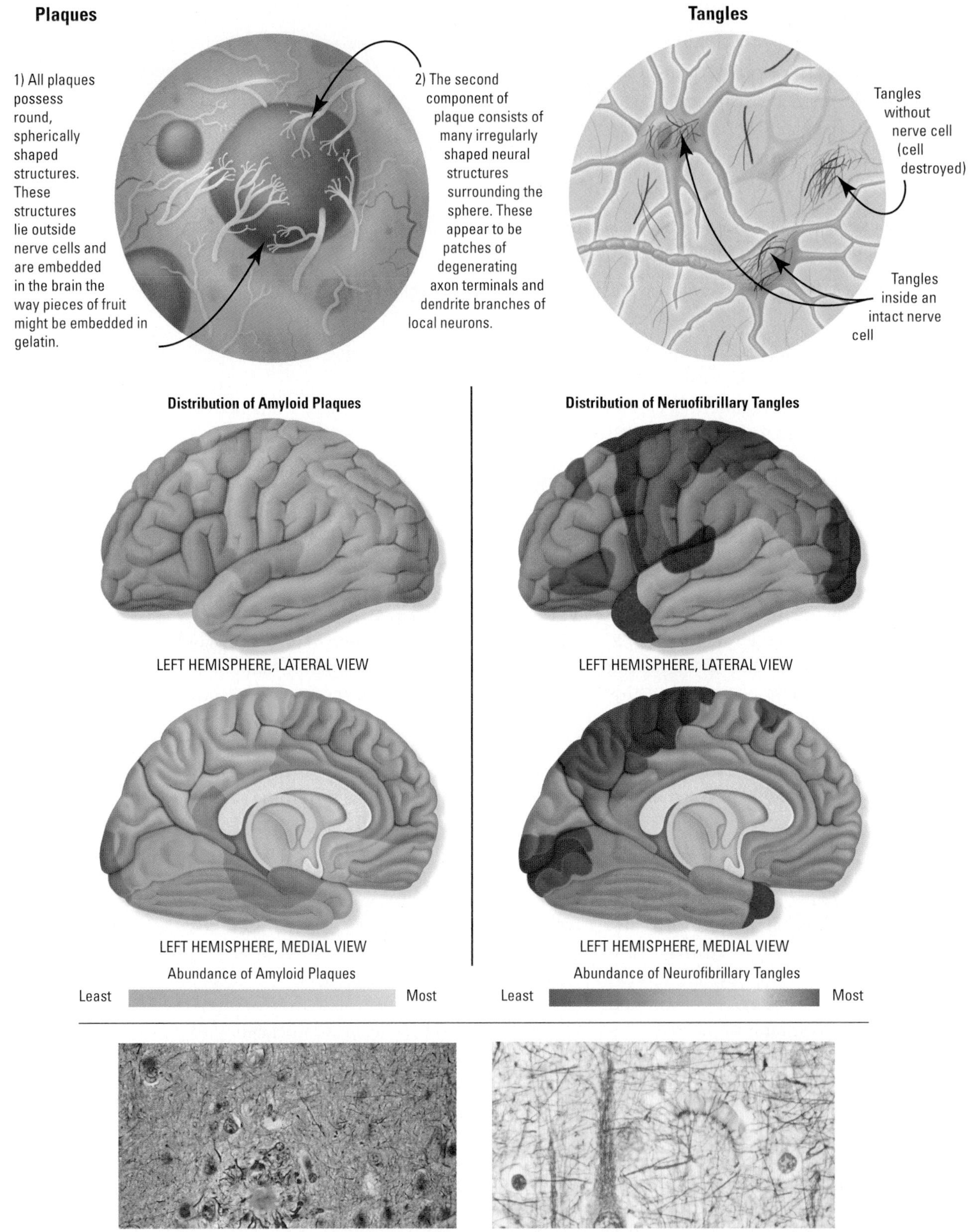
Plaques
1) All plaques possess round, spherically shaped structures. These structures lie outside nerve cells and are embedded in the brain the way pieces of fruit might be embedded in gelatin.
2) The second component of plaque consists of many irregularly shaped neural structures surrounding the sphere. These appear to be patches of degenerating axon terminals and dendrite branches of local neurons.
Tangles
Tangles without nerve cell (cell destroyed)
Tangles inside an intact nerve cell
Distribution of Amyloid Plaques
LEFT HEMISPHERE, LATERAL VIEW
LEFT HEMISPHERE, MEDIAL VIEW
Abundance of Amyloid Plaques
Least
Most
Distribution of Neruofibrillary Tangles
LEFT HEMISPHERE, LATERAL VIEW
LEFT HEMISPHERE, MEDIAL VIEW
Abundance of Neurofibrillary Tangles
Least
Most

**FIGURE 14–2: The top panel illustrates the appearance of amyloid plaques and neurofibrillary tangles. The middle panels illustrate the areas of the brain in which each type of lesion is most likely to appear.**

*Source:* J. Medina, 1999, *What You Need to Know About Alzheimer's*. Oakland, CA: New Harbinger Publications, and J.L. Cummings, 2002, Alzheimer's disease. *Journal of the American Medical Association, 287*, 2335–2338.

**Huntington's Disease** Unusual involuntary muscle movements known as **chorea** (from the Greek word meaning "dance") represent the most distinctive feature of **Huntington's disease**. These movements are relatively subtle at first, with the person appearing to be merely restless or fidgety. As the disorder progresses, sustained muscle contractions become difficult. Movements of the face, trunk, and limbs eventually become uncontrolled, leaving the person to writhe and grimace. A large proportion of Huntington's patients also exhibit a variety of personality changes and symptoms of mental disorders, primarily depression and anxiety. Between 5 and 10 percent develop psychotic symptoms. The symptoms of mental disorder may be evident before the appearance of motor or cognitive impairment (Haddad & Cummings, 1997).

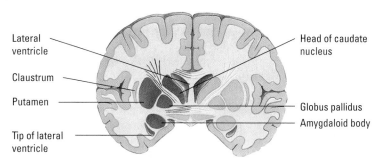

**Areas of the Brain Implicated in Huntington's Disease**

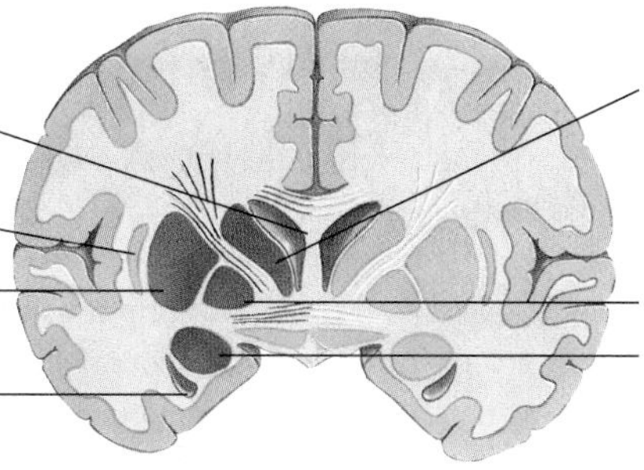


**FIGURE 14–3: Huntington's disease involves deterioration of the basal ganglia (also known as the cerebral nuclei). The primary units of this system are the caudate nucleus, putamen, globus pallidus, and the claustrum.**

*Source:* Adapted from R. Martini and M. Timmons, 1995, *Human Anatomy*, p. 378. Upper Saddle River, NJ: Prentice Hall.

The movement disorder and the cognitive deficits are produced by progressive neuronal degeneration in the basal ganglia (Chesselet & Delfs, 1996). This is a group of nuclei, including the caudate nucleus, the putamen, and the globus pallidus, that form a collaborative system of connections between the cerebral cortex and the thalamus (see Figure 14–3).

Dementia appears in all Huntington's disease patients, although the extent of the cognitive impairment and the rate of its progression vary widely. Impairments in recent memory and learning are the most obvious cognitive problems. Patients have trouble encoding new information. Higher-level cognitive functions are typically well preserved, and insight is usually intact. Unlike the pattern of dementia seen in Alzheimer's disease, patients with Huntington's do not develop aphasia, apraxia, or agnosia (Morris, 1995).

The diagnosis of Huntington's disease depends on the presence of a positive family history for the disorder. It is one of the few disorders that are transmitted in an autosomal dominant pattern with complete penetrance. In other words, the person must only inherit one gene—from either parent—to be vulnerable, and an individual who inherits the problematic gene will always develop the disorder (see Research Methods).

## RESEARCH METHODS

### Genetic Linkage Analysis

It is one thing to say that genetic factors "are involved" in the transmission of a disorder, and quite another to identify the specific mode of inheritance. Discovery of the gene that is responsible for a disorder would be an exciting step toward explaining the etiology of the disorder. It would also have crucial implications for people who are known to be at increased risk for the disorder. Developments in the field of molecular genetics have allowed scientists to begin the search for such genes and, in some cases, to find them. The dementias, especially Huntington's disease, are one area in which important advances have been made in this regard.

The mode of inheritance in Huntington's disease has been relatively clear for many years because it follows an obvious Mendelian pattern: Almost exactly 50 percent of an affected person's first-degree relatives will also have the disorder. It is, therefore, considered to be an *autosomal dominant trait*. The term *autosomal* means that the gene is not located on one of the sex chromosomes. The knowledge that one gene, or a single locus on a particular chromosome, is apparently responsible for Huntington's disease made it an obvious candidate for genetic linkage analysis.

A gene is a strand of DNA, composed of a vast sequence of pairs of nucleic acid bases. These are the rods that lend a stair-like appearance to the familiar double helix structure of DNA, described by James Watson and Francis Crick in 1953. We all possess 46 chromosomes (23 pairs), which, taken together, contain 3 billion of these base pairs. Locating a gene on a chromosome can be accomplished by demonstrating **genetic linkage** between the genetic locus associated with the disorder and the locus for a known gene, a

*continued*

cont.

chromosome marker. Two loci are said to be linked when they are sufficiently close together on the same chromosome. Because of this physical association, the alleles at the two loci do not segregate independently during meiosis, the cell division process that results in the formation of sperm and egg cells.

In order to identify linkage, an investigator must study a large extended family in which several members have been affected by the disorder in question. Samples of cells are collected from everyone in the family. If all (or almost all) of the family members who have the disorder also have the marker in question, and if all (or almost all) of the unaffected members do not have the marker, then genetic linkage has been established (Heston & White, 1991).

The concept of genetic linkage was introduced early in the twentieth century by Thomas Hunt Morgan. Progress toward establishing genetic linkage in human disorders was extremely limited, however, because very few markers were available. In the late 1970s, recombinant DNA procedures led to the discovery of *restriction fragment-length polymorphisms (RFLPs)*, fragments of DNA that are not associated with any recognized phenotypic trait but nevertheless provide useful landmarks for DNA segments. RFLPs are scattered across all the chromosomes.

In 1983, a group of scientists reported that the gene responsible for Huntington's disease was located on the short arm of chromosome 4 (Gusella et al., 1983). The data for their investigation came from a large extended family living in several remote villages on the northern coast of Venezuela. An unusually large number of the people in this family are victims of Huntington's disease. This is exactly the kind of pedigree required for genetic linkage analysis. Using blood samples collected from affected and unaffected members of the Venezuelan family, the investigators began looking for linkage with approximately a dozen RFLP markers. They were extremely lucky. The third marker that they tested produced a score indicating that the odds in favour of linkage between the Huntington's disease gene and this probe were over 200 million to 1. The probe was obviously located in very close proximity to the gene for which they were searching. Ten years later, the Huntington's Disease Collaborative Research Group (1993) announced that it had found the specific gene. Now researchers across the world, including Michael Hayden and colleagues at the University of British Columbia, are seeking to understand exactly how the gene leads to Huntington's disease, and how to inhibit this process (Leavitt, Wellington, & Hayden, 1999). ◆

**Parkinson's Disease** A disorder of the motor system, known as *Parkinson's disease*, is caused by a degeneration of a specific area of the brain stem known as the substantia nigra and loss of the neurotransmitter dopamine, which is produced by cells in this area. Typical symptoms include tremors, rigidity, postural abnormalities, and reduction in voluntary movements (Kontakos & Stokes, 1999). Unlike people with Huntington's disease, most patients with Parkinson's disease do not become demented. Follow-up studies suggest that approximately 20 percent of elderly patients with Parkinson's disease will develop symptoms of dementia. Their risk is approximately double the risk of dementia found among people of similar age who do not have Parkinson's disease (Marder et al., 1995; Tison et al., 1995).

**Vascular Dementia** Many conditions other than those that attack brain tissue directly can also produce symptoms of dementia. The central agent in these problems can be either medical conditions or other types of mental disorder. Diseases that affect the heart and lungs, for example, can interfere with the circulation of oxygen to the brain. Substance abuse can also interfere with brain functions.

One cause of dementia is vascular or blood vessel disease, which affects the arteries responsible for bringing oxygen and sugar to the brain (Roman, 2002). A *stroke*, the severe interruption of blood flow to the brain, can produce various types of brain damage, depending on the size of the affected blood vessel and the area of the brain that it supplies. The area of dead tissue produced by the stroke is known as an *infarct*. The behavioural effects of a stroke are usually obvious and can be distinguished from dementia on several grounds: (1) They appear suddenly rather than gradually; (2) they affect voluntary movements of the limbs and gross speech patterns, as well as more subtle intellectual abilities; and (3) they often result in unilateral rather than bilateral impairment, such as paralysis of only one side of the body.

There are instances, however, in which the stroke affects only a very small artery and may not have any observable effect on the person's behaviour. If several of these small strokes occur over a period of time, and if their sites are scattered in different areas of the brain, they may gradually produce cognitive impairment. DSM-IV-TR refers to this condition as **vascular dementia**. Another commonly used term for this condition is *multi-infarct dementia*. The cognitive symptoms of vascular dementia that are listed in the diagnostic manual are the same as those for Alzheimer's disease, but DSM-IV-TR does not require a gradual onset for vascular dementia, as it does for dementia of the Alzheimer's type. In addition, the diagnosis of vascular dementia depends on the presence of either focal neurological signs and symptoms associated with the experience of stroke, such as gait abnormalities or weakness in the extremities, or laboratory evidence of blood vessel disease (Caplan, Geldmacher, & Nyenhuis, 1999; Scheltens & Hijdra, 1998).

**Dementia with Lewy Bodies** *Lewy bodies* (also called *intracytoplasmic inclusions*) are rounded deposits found in nerve cells. Named after F.H. Lewy, who first described them in 1912, Lewy bodies are often found in the brain-stem nuclei of patients with Parkinson's disease (Kalra, Bergeron, & Lang, 1996). Neurologists later discovered occasional cases of progressive dementia in which autopsies revealed Lewy bodies widespread throughout the brain. The development of more sensitive staining techniques that can identify cortical Lewy bodies led to greatly increased interest in this phenomenon during the 1990s.

Clinicians have defined a syndrome known as **dementia with Lewy bodies (DLB)**, but the boundaries of DLB are not entirely clear. It overlaps, both in terms of clinical symptoms and brain pathology, with other forms of dementia such as Alzheimer's disease and Parkinson's disease. An international workshop established consensus criteria for the diagnosis of DLB in 1995. Many experts now agree that DLB may be the second most common form of dementia, after Alzheimer's disease. Among patients who meet diagnostic criteria for Alzheimer's disease, 30 percent also have evidence of diffuse Lewy bodies in cortical neurons (McKeith, 2002; Simard et al., 2000).

Symptoms of DLB typically begin with memory deficits followed by a progressive decline to dementia. Patients' cognitive impairment includes problems in attention, executive functions, problem solving, and visuospatial performance. Unlike patients with Alzheimer's disease, patients with DLB often show a fluctuation in cognitive performance, alertness, and level of consciousness. Their episodic confusional states sometimes resemble delirium. These changes may be evident over a period of hours or several days.

*Boxing legend Muhammed Ali and Alberta-born actor Michael J. Fox joke around before testifying at a government hearing on Parkinson's disease. Both men have the disorder, and they encouraged the committee to increase funds for research.*

The symptom that is most likely to distinguish DLB from Alzheimer's disease and vascular dementia is the presence of recurrent and detailed visual hallucinations. The patient usually recognizes that the hallucinations are not real. Many patients with DLB also develop Parkinsonian features, such as muscular rigidity, which appear early in the development of the disorder (Ballard et al., 2001).

The course of dementia appears to be different between patients with Alzheimer's disease and DLB. Patients with DLB show a more rapid progression of cognitive impairment, and the time from onset of symptoms to death is also shorter. They are also likely to develop adverse reactions to neuroleptic medication, which is sometimes used to treat their psychotic symptoms, such as hallucinations (Rojas-Fernandez & MacKnight, 1999).

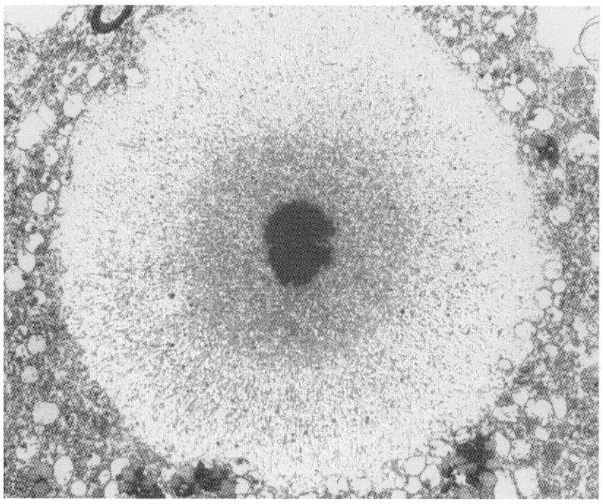

*Electron micrograph of a section through a Lewy body in a nerve cell in the brain. Lewy bodies are largely made up of filaments of a specific brain protein (shown here in blue), and these filaments are presumably responsible for degeneration of nerve cells.*

**Dementia versus Depression** Another condition that can be associated with symptoms of dementia, especially among the elderly, is depression. There are, indeed, many areas of overlap between these disorders, but the nature of the relationship is not yet clear. Approximately 25 percent of patients with a diagnosis of dementia also exhibit symptoms of major depressive disorder (Meyers, 1998). The symptoms of depression include a lack of interest in, and withdrawal of attention from, the environment. People who are depressed often have trouble concentrating, they appear preoccupied, and their thinking is laboured. These cognitive problems closely resemble some symptoms of dementia. Some depressed patients exhibit poverty of speech and restricted or unchanging facial expression. A dishevelled appearance, due to self-neglect and loss of weight, in an elderly patient may contribute to the impression that the person is suffering from dementia.

Despite the many similarities, there are important differences between depression and dementia. These are summarized in Table 14–6. Experienced clinicians can usually distinguish between depression and dementia by considering the pattern of onset and associated features (Insel & Badger, 2002). In those cases where the distinction cannot be made on the basis of these characteristics, response to treatment may be the only way to establish a differential diagnosis. If the person's condition, including cognitive impairments, improves following treatment with antidepressant medication or electroconvulsive therapy, it seems reasonable to conclude that the person was depressed. These procedures can also be somewhat dangerous, because the cognitive symptoms of patients who are actually suffering from dementia may become exaggerated in response to medication.

**TABLE 14–6 Signs and Symptoms Distinguishing Depression from Dementia**

| Depression | Dementia |
|---|---|
| Uneven progression over weeks | Even progression over months or years |
| Complains of memory loss | Attempts to hide memory loss |
| Often worse in morning, better as day goes on | Worse later in day or when fatigued |
| Aware of, exaggerates disability | Unaware or minimizes disability |
| May abuse alcohol or other drugs | Rarely abuses drugs |

*Source:* Adapted from I.I. Heston and J.A. White, 1991, *The Vanishing Mind: A Practical Guide to Alzheimer's Disease and Other Dementias.* New York: Freeman.

The relationship between depression and dementia has been the topic of considerable debate. Is depression a consequence of dementia, or are the symptoms of dementia a consequence of depression? Some clinicians have used the term *pseudodementia* to describe the condition of patients with symptoms of dementia whose cognitive impairment is actually produced by a major depressive disorder. There is no doubt that cases of this sort exist (Raskind, 1998). In fact, depression and dementia are not necessarily mutually exclusive disorders. We know that these conditions co-exist more often than would be expected by a major depressive disorder. There is no doubt that cases of this sort exist (Raskind, 1998). In fact, depression and dementia are not necessarily mutually exclusive disorders. We know that these conditions co-exist more often than would be expected by chance, but we do not know why (Jorm, 2001).

# Epidemiology of Delirium and Dementia

Cognitive disorders represent one of the most pressing health problems in our society. Detailed evidence regarding the prevalence of delirium is not available, but it does seem to be one of the most frequent symptoms of disease among elderly people. At least 15 percent of elderly hospitalized medical patients exhibit symptoms of delirium (Fann, 2000). The rate is much higher among nursing home patients, where delirium is often combined with dementia (as in the case study at the beginning of this chapter).

Dementia is an especially important problem among elderly people. Although it can appear in people as young as 40 to 45, the average age of onset is much later. The incidence of dementia will be much greater in the near future, because the average age of the population is increasing steadily (see Chapter 17). People over the age of 80 represent one of the fastest-growing segments of our population. In 1997 there were about 322 000 Canadians affected by dementia. By the year 2016, it is estimated that this figure will grow to 548 000, a 70 percent increase over 20 years (Bland, 1998). The personal and economic impact of dementia on patients, their families, and our society clearly warrants serious attention from healthcare professionals, policymakers concerned with healthcare reform, and clinical scientists seeking more effective forms of treatment.

Epidemiological studies must be interpreted with caution, of course, because of the problems associated with establishing a diagnosis of dementia. Mild cases are difficult to identify reliably. At the earliest stages of the disorder, symptoms are difficult to distinguish from forgetfulness, which can increase in normal aging (see Further Thoughts on p. 486). Definitive diagnoses depend on information collected over an extended period of time so that the progressive nature of the cognitive impairment, and deterioration from an earlier, higher level of functioning, can be documented. Unfortunately, this kind of information is often not available in a large-scale epidemiological study.

Also bear in mind the fact that the diagnosis of specific subtypes of dementia, such as dementia of the Alzheimer's type and dementia due to Pick's disease, requires microscopic examination of brain tissue after the person's death. Again, these data are not typically available to epidemiologists. With these limitations in mind, we now consider what is known about the frequency of dementia in the general population.

### Prevalence of Dementia

Approximately 8 percent of Canadians aged 65 and older have dementia, and the prevalence of this disorder increases dramatically with age (see Canadian Focus). Survival rates are reduced

## CANADIAN FOCUS **The Canadian Study of Health and Aging**

To date, the largest epidemiological study of dementia in Canada has been the Canadian Study of Health and Aging (CSHA, 1994a,b,c). In 1991 and 1992, researchers at 18 sites across Canada conducted a large survey of Canadians aged 65 years and older. The researchers trained interviewers to assess a randomly selected sample of over 9000 people living in the community and a random sample of over 1200 people living in residential care facilities. A multi-step assessment procedure was used, beginning with a screening interview for dementia that contained items similar to the Mini–Mental State Examination (Table 14–3). A subgroup of participants also completed a series of neuropsychological tests such as the Clock Test (Figure 14–1), and received a physical and neurological evaluation by a physician. In cases where one of the study participants was being cared for by an informal caregiver (i.e., family members or friends), the caregiver was also interviewed. (Informal caregivers differ from formal caregivers in that the latter are paid helpers, such as nurses.) The CSHA had four major objectives:

- To estimate the prevalence of dementias among the Canadian elderly
- To determine risk factors for dementia of the Alzheimer's type
- To identify the types of care received by people with dementia and to assess the burden on informal caregivers
- To establish a uniform database for future incidence and longitudinal studies of dementias

Approximately 8 percent of Canadians aged 65 and older met the criteria for dementia (CSHA, 1994a). Similar to findings of other studies, the prevalence of dementia increased with age, beginning at 2 percent for 65 to 74 years of age and rising to 35 percent for those 85 and over (CSHA, 1994a). The prevalence rates increase sharply among the very old; for people aged 100 to 106 years, the prevalence of dementia was 85 percent! This led some CSHA investigators to conclude that "dementia approaches universality when sufficient aging has taken place" (Ebly et al., 1994, p. 1598).

Dementia of the Alzheimer's type (AD) was the most common form of dementia (64 percent), followed by vascular dementia (19 percent) and other types of dementia (17 percent) (Hill et al., 1996). Vascular dementia was more common in men than in women, whereas AD was more common in women than men.

Several risk factors were identified for AD (CSHA, 1994b). Higher risk for AD was associated with age, a family history of dementia (the more relatives with dementia, the greater the risk), a history of head injury, and occupational exposure to glues, pesticides, or fertilizers. Greater educational attainment was associated with lower risk for AD. Lower risk for AD was also associated with the use of non-steroidal anti-inflammatory drugs. This finding is consistent with the theory, described later in this chapter, that dysfunction of the immune system plays a role in AD (McGeer & McGeer, 1996). Many of the risk factors identified in the CSHA had been reported in previous studies. However, in contrast to some

*continued*

*cont.*

other studies, there was no clear evidence that exposure to aluminum increases risk for AD, and no support that smoking decreases the risk for AD. The findings regarding glues, pesticides, and fertilizers were new findings that need to be replicated (CSHA, 1994b).

More than half of the people with dementia were living in institutions, such as long-term care facilities. The likelihood of living in an institution was influenced by the availability of an informal caregiver, who was typically a spouse, daughter, or son. Half of the informal caregivers were over 60 years of age, and frequently had health problems of their own. Many also had symptoms of depression, possibly because of the burden of caring for someone with dementia. Few informal caregivers made use of paid support services such as home nurses or cleaning/laundry services. This seemed to be because informal caregivers viewed these services as a last resort rather than as a way of alleviating their own stress (CSHA, 1994c). Informal caregivers were likely to feel more burdened and more depressed when the demented person had more disturbing behavioural problems (e.g., aggression) and greater functional limitations, and when the informal caregiver had few other family members or friends to draw on for assistance (Clyburn et al., 2000). ◆

**Gender Differences in the Incidence of Alzheimer's Disease and Vascular Dementia**

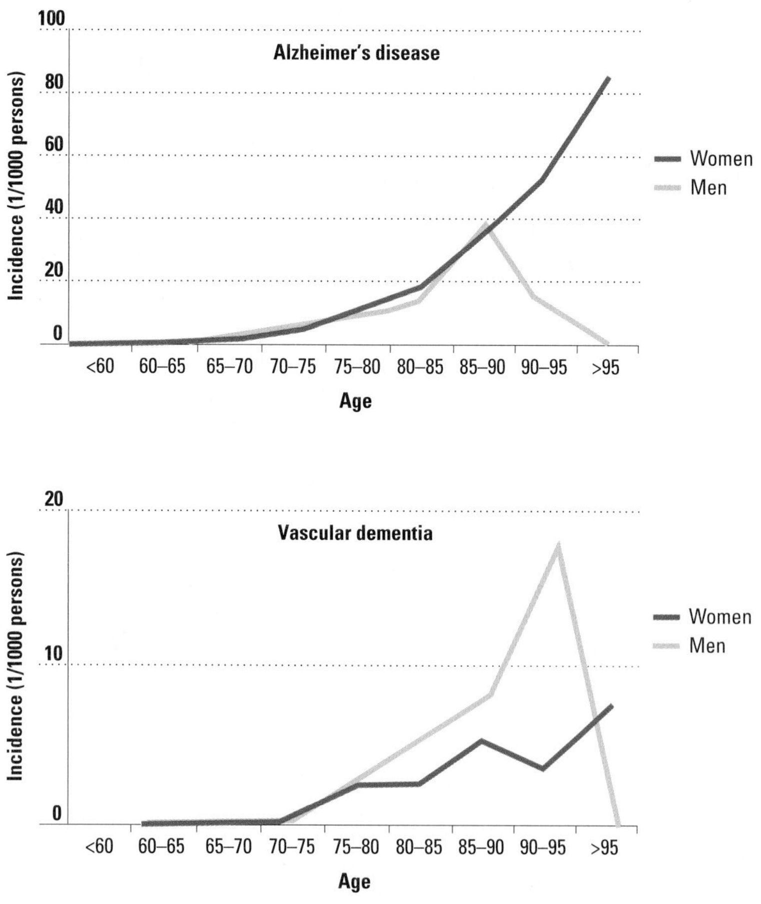


**FIGURE 14–4: This figure shows the number of new cases of dementia that appeared among people in specific age groups. The participants included 7000 people, 55 years and older, in the Netherlands.**

*Source:* A. Ruitenberg et al., 2001, Incidence of dementia: does gender make a difference? *Neurobiology of Aging, 22,* 575–580.

among demented patients. In Alzheimer's disease, for example, the average time between onset of the disorder and the person's death is less than 6 years. Higher mortality rates are found for men and for patients with extrapyramidal symptoms (Stern et al., 1997). There is considerable variability in these figures. Some patients have survived more than 20 years after the first appearance of obvious symptoms.

There are no obvious differences between men and women with regard to the overall prevalence of dementia, broadly defined. It seems, however, that dementia in men is more likely to be associated with vascular disease or to be secondary to other medical conditions or to alcohol abuse. The incidence of Alzheimer's disease is the same in men and women up to age 90; after that, the number of new cases continues to increase for women while it apparently declines for men (Lerner, 1999; Ruitenberg et al., 2001). Figure 14–4 illustrates gender differences in the number of new cases of Alzheimer's disease and vascular dementia that appear in different age groups. The incidence of vascular dementia is generally lower in women than in men at all age groups.

## Prevalence by Subtypes of Dementia

The studies we have already reviewed refer to cross-sectional examinations of populations, which do not allow diagnosis of specific subtypes of dementia. Some clinical studies, based on hospital populations, have allowed investigators to look at the frequency of specific subtypes of dementia. Alzheimer's disease appears to be the most common form of dementia (Breteler, Ott, & Hofman, 1998; Kaye, 1995), accounting for perhaps half of all cases (depending on the diagnostic criteria employed and the geographic location of the study). Dementia with Lewy bodies may be the second leading cause of dementia; studies report prevalence rates between 12 and 27 percent for DLB among patients with primary dementia (Kalra, Bergeron, & Lang, 1996). Prevalence rates for vascular dementia are similar to those for DLB (Leys, Pasquier, & Parnetti, 1998). Pick's disease is much less common than Alzheimer's disease, vascular dementia, or DLB. Huntington's disease is rare by comparison. It affects only 1 person in every 20 000 (Shoulson, 1990).

### Cross-Cultural Comparisons

Several issues make it difficult to collect cross-cultural data regarding the prevalence of dementia. Tests that are used to measure cognitive impairment must be developed carefully to be sure that they are not culturally or racially biased (see Chapter 4 on the validity of assessment procedures). Elderly people in developing countries who have little formal education pose a special challenge, since most cognitive tasks have been developed for use with a different population. Those who follow more traditional ways of life, such as the Australian aboriginal people, may have very different views of old age and its problems. For all of these reasons, we must interpret preliminary results on this topic with great caution (Pollit, 1997; Woodard et al., 1998).

Some studies have reported that prevalence rates for dementia vary geographically. Alzheimer's disease may be more common in North America and Europe, whereas vascular dementia may be more common in Japan and China (Chiu et al., 1998). There are also some tentative indications that prevalence rates for dementia may be significantly lower in developing countries than in developed countries (e.g., Hendrie et al., 1995). These differences may be influenced by many factors, including both genetic and environmental considerations. Dietary practices and educational opportunities are examples of environmental risk factors that may account for these patterns.

*Prevalence rates for Alzheimer's may be lower in developing countries than in developed countries. For example, Alzheimer's disease is more prevalent among African North Americans than among sub-Saharan Africans.*

## Etiological Considerations and Research

Delirium and dementia are clearly associated with brain pathology. Damage to various brain structures and neurotransmitter pathways can be the product of various biological and environmental events. In the following pages, we review some of the considerations that guide current thinking about the causes of these disorders.

### Delirium

The underlying mechanisms responsible for the onset of delirium undoubtedly involve neuropathology and neurochemistry (Flacker & Lipsitz, 1999; Trzepacz, 1999). The incidence of delirium increases among elderly people, presumably because the physiological effects of aging make elderly people more vulnerable to medication side effects and cognitive complications of medical illnesses (Jacobson, 1997). Delirium can be caused by many different kinds of medication, including the following:

- Psychiatric drugs (especially antidepressants, antipsychotics, and benzodiazepines)
- Drugs used to treat heart conditions
- Painkillers
- Stimulants (including caffeine)

Delirium also develops in conjunction with a number of metabolic diseases, including pulmonary and cardiovascular disorders (which can interfere with the supply of oxygen to the brain), as well as endocrine diseases (especially thyroid disease and diabetes mellitus). Various kinds of infection can lead to the onset of delirium. Perhaps the most common among elderly people is urinary tract infection, which can result from the use of an indwelling urinary catheter (sometimes necessary with incontinent nursing home patients).

## Dementia

In discussing the classification of dementia, we have touched on many of the factors that contribute to the etiology of these problems. Most of the other disorders listed in DSM-IV-TR are classified on the basis of symptoms alone. The classification of dementia is sometimes determined by specific knowledge of etiological factors, even though these may be determined only after the patient's death, as in Alzheimer's disease. In the following discussion we consider in greater detail a few of the specific pathways that are known to lead to dementia.

**Genetic Factors** Neurologists who treat demented patients have recognized for many years that the disorder often runs in families. Until recently, twin studies have not been used extensively to evaluate the influence of genetic factors in dementia because of the comparatively late age of onset of these disorders. By the time a proband develops symptoms of dementia, his or her co-twin may be deceased. A few studies have capitalized on national samples to find an adequate number of twin pairs. They confirm the impression, based on family studies, that genetic factors play an important role in the development of dementia. One Swedish study, for example, found that the concordance rate in monozygotic twins was over 50 percent, more than double the dizygotic rate (Pedersen & Gatz, 1991). One study, based on a registry of aging twin veterans of World War II and the Korean War, found an MZ concordance rate of 35 percent in 24 male pairs. None of the 16 DZ pairs was concordant at the time of the report (Breitner et al., 1993).

Most of the research concerned with genetic factors and Alzheimer's disease has focused on genetic linkage strategies. The astounding advances that have been made in molecular genetics since 1980 have been applied to Alzheimer's disease with fruitful results. Experts now agree that Alzheimer's disease is genetically heterogeneous. In other words, there are several forms of the disorder, and each seems to be associated with a different gene or set of genes. Three genes (located on chromosomes 21, 14, and 1) have been identified that, when mutated, cause early-onset forms of Alzheimer's disease. A fourth gene, located on chromosome 19, serves as a risk factor for late-onset forms of the disorder (Cummings & Cole, 2002; Holmes, 2002). The locations of these genes are illustrated in Figure 14–5, along with graphs that indicate the average age of onset for dementia associated with the different genes.

It has been known for many years that amyloid plaques and neurofibrillary tangles are found in the brains of all people who have Down syndrome (see Chapter 15), as well as in people with Alzheimer's disease. This similarity led investigators to search for a link between the gene for Alzheimer's disease and known markers on chromosome 21, because people with Down syndrome possess three copies of chromosome 21 in every cell instead of the normal two. In fact, the gene responsible for producing proteins (amyloid precursor protein, or APP) that serve as precursors to beta-amyloid, found in the core of amyloid plaques, is located on chromosome 21. Several research groups have independently confirmed this association. Therefore, within some families, the gene for Alzheimer's disease is located on chromosome 21.

Mutations on chromosome 14 (presenilin 1, or PS1) and chromosome 1 (presenilin 2, or PS2) have also been found to be associated with early-onset forms of Alzheimer's disease (Plassman & Breitner, 1997). Like the APP gene, both of the presenilin genes are inherited in an autosomal dominant mode of transmission and cause overproduction of beta-amyloid. Mutations in the PS1 gene are probably responsible for 50 percent of early-onset cases of the disorder (which represent less than 10 percent of all patients with Alzheimer's disease).

A fourth gene produces vulnerability to late-onset Alzheimer's disease without having a direct or necessary effect on the development of dementia. In other words, people who carry this gene have an increased risk for Alzheimer's disease, but many people without the gene develop the disorder, and some people who do have the gene do not develop the disorder. The apolipoprotein E (APOE) gene is located on chromosome 19. There are three common alleles (forms) of APOE, called e-2, e-3, and e-4. The APOE-2 allele is correlated with a de-

**Genes Associated with Alzheimer's Disease**

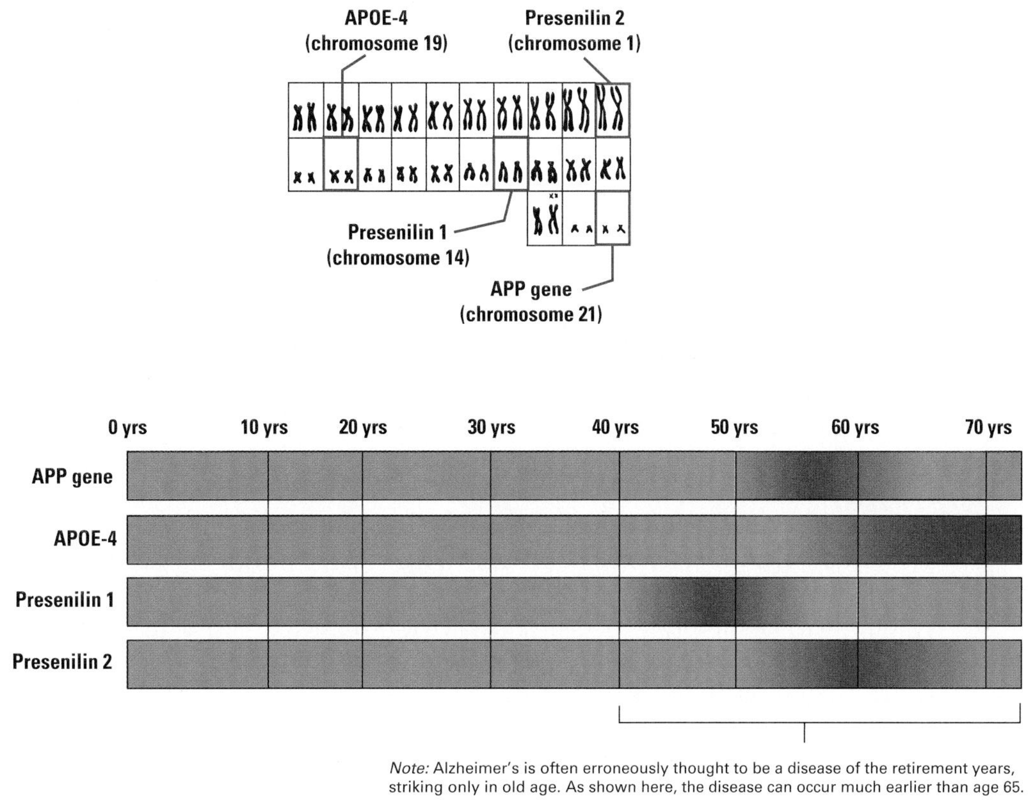


**FIGURE 14–5: Four different genes are associated with the creation of plaques found in Alzheimer's disease (AD). The top panel, which illustrates the 23 pairs of human chromosomes, identifies which chromosome carries which AD-related gene. The bottom panel indicates that average age of onset of the disorder depends, in part, on the gene that is involved. The age of first diagnosis is illustrated in red.**

*Source:* J. Medina, 1999, What You Need to Know About Alzheimer's, pp. 94–95. Oakland, CA: New Harbinger Publications.

creased risk for Alzheimer's disease. People who have the APOE-4 allele at this locus have an increased probability of developing the disorder (Farrer et al., 1997). The finding has been replicated in more than 100 different laboratories. The risk for Alzheimer's disease is between 25 and 40 percent among people who have at least one APOE-4 allele (Mayeux & Ottman, 1998). Because most cases of Alzheimer's disease have a late onset, the APOE gene is probably involved in more cases of the disorder than the genes on chromosomes 21, 14, and 1.

**Neurotransmitters** In patients suffering from dementia, the process of chemical transmission of messages within the brain is probably disrupted, but the specific mechanisms that are involved have not been identified. We know that Parkinson's disease, which is sometimes associated with dementia, is caused by a degeneration of the dopamine pathways in the brain stem. This dysfunction is responsible for the motor symptoms seen in patients with that disorder. It is not entirely clear, however, that the intellectual problems experienced by patients with Parkinson's disease are directly related to dopamine deficiencies.

Other types of dementia have also been linked to problems with specific neurotransmitters. Huntington's disease may be associated with deficiencies in gamma-aminobutyric acid (GABA). A marked decrease in the availability of acetylcholine (ACh), another type of neurotransmitter, has been implicated in Alzheimer's disease. Reductions in ACh levels, especially in the temporal lobes, are correlated with the severity of dementia symptoms (Newhouse, 1997; Raskind & Peskind, 1997).

**Viral Infections** Some forms of primary dementia are known to be the products of "slow" viruses—infections that develop over a much more extended period of time than do most viral infections. Creutzfeldt-Jakob disease is one example. Susceptibility to infection by a specific virus can be influenced by genetic factors. The demonstration that a condition is transmitted in a familial fashion does not rule out the involvement of viral infection. In fact, familial transmission has been demonstrated for the forms of dementia that are known to be associated with a specific virus.

**Immune System Dysfunction** The immune system is the body's first line of defence against infection. It employs antibodies to break down foreign materials, such as bacteria and viruses, which enter the body. The regulation of this system allows it to distinguish between foreign bodies that should be destroyed and normal body tissues that should be preserved. The production of these antibodies may be dysfunctional in some forms of dementia, such as Alzheimer's disease. In other words, the destruction of brain tissue may be caused by a breakdown in the system that regulates the immune system.

The presence of beta-amyloid at the core of amyloid plaques is one important clue to the possible involvement of immune system dysfunction. This protein is the breakdown product of a structural component of brain cells. It is made and eliminated constantly as part of normal brain functioning. For some reason, which probably involves genetic factors, some people develop problems with the elimination of beta-amyloid. Clumps of beta-amyloid accumulate. Some clinical scientists believe that immune cells in the brain attempt to destroy these amyloid plaques and inadvertently harm neighbouring, healthy brain cells. Some research evidence supports this hypothesis, such as the findings of studies by Patrick and Edith McGeer, conducted at the University of British Columbia (e.g., McGeer & McGeer, 1996).

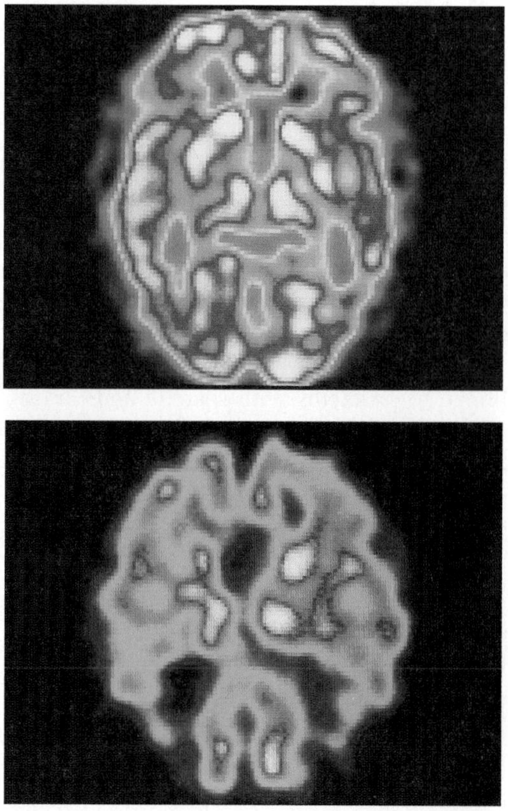

*PET scan of the brain (basal ganglia level) of a normal person and a patient with Alzheimer's disease. The scans show brain activity from low (blue) to high (yellow). Normal metabolic activity produces a roughly symmetrical pattern in the left and right hemispheres (top). The patchy appearance of the patient's scan indicates degeneration of brain tissue.*

**Environmental Factors** Epidemiological investigations have discovered several interesting patterns that suggest that some types of dementia, especially Alzheimer's disease, may be related to environmental factors. One example is head injury, which can cause a sudden increase of amyloid plaque. Elderly people who have been knocked unconscious as adults have an increased risk of developing Alzheimer's disease, compared to people with no history of head injury (O'Meara et al., 1997; Schofield et al., 1997).

Another example of an environmental risk factor is exposure to aluminum, an element that is abundant in the natural environment. Experimental studies with animals have demonstrated that exposure to aluminum can induce brain lesions that resemble the neurofibrillary tangles found in victims of Alzheimer's disease. Excess levels of aluminum have also been found at autopsy in the brains of some victims of Alzheimer's disease. Some epidemiological evidence indicates a correlation between levels of aluminum in the water supply and rates of dementia and cognitive impairment in the local population. Other studies have failed to replicate this result. The possible link between aluminum and dementia is both questionable and controversial, but it is still a topic of serious research efforts (Graves et al., 1998; Martyn et al., 1997; Murayama et al., 1999; Singer et al., 1997).

Some studies have reported significant relationships between Alzheimer's disease and variables that seem to protect the person from developing dementia. People who have achieved high levels of education are less likely to develop Alzheimer's disease than are people with less education (Johnson et al., 1997; Stern et al., 1994). For example, one fascinating study has reported that elderly Catholic nuns those who graduated from college were much less likely to be cognitively impaired than were those who had less than a college education (Butler, Ashford, & Snowdon, 1996). This finding may be interpreted to mean that increased "brain work" leads to a facilitation of neuronal activation, increased cerebral blood flow, and higher levels of glucose and oxygen consumption in the brain. All of this may increase the density of synaptic connections in the person's cortex and reduce risk for later neuronal deterioration.

A similar conclusion was drawn from a longitudinal study conducted at the University of Victoria. David Hultsch and colleagues (1999) evaluated 250 middle-aged and older adults three times over a six-year period. Changes in intellectually related activities predicted changes in cognitive functioning. In other words, the results were consistent with the idea that intellectually engaging activities (e.g., reading, crossword puzzles, and other intellectually engaging hobbies) serve to buffer or protect the person against cognitive decline.

Although findings with regard to environmental events are thought-provoking, a strong word of caution is in order. It is not clear whether these correlations indicate a causal relationship between these variables and dementia (Heston & White, 1991; Katzman, 1993). Indeed, Hultsch and colleagues acknowledged that their results are consistent with the notion that high-ability people lead intellectually active lives until cognitive decline in old age limits their activities.

# Treatment and Management

The most obvious consideration with regard to treatment of the cognitive disorders is accurate diagnosis (Cummings & Cole, 2002). The distinction between delirium and dementia is important because many conditions that cause delirium can be treated. Delirium must be recognized as early as possible so that the source of the problem, such as an infection or some other medical condition, can be treated. Some types of secondary dementia can also be treated successfully. For example, if the patient's cognitive symptoms are the products of depression, there is a relatively good chance that he or she will respond positively to antidepressant medication or electroconvulsive therapy.

When the person clearly suffers from a primary type of dementia, such as dementia of the Alzheimer's type, a return to previous levels of functioning is extremely unlikely. Currently, no form of treatment is capable of producing sustained and clinically significant improvement in cognitive functioning for patients with Alzheimer's disease (Tune, 2002). Realistic goals include helping the person to maintain his or her level of functioning for as long as possible in spite of cognitive impairment and minimizing the level of distress experienced by the person and the person's family. Several treatment options are typically used in conjunction, including medication, management of the patient's environment, behavioural strategies, and providing support to caregivers (Daly, 1999; Mayeux & Sano, 1999).

## Medication

Some drugs are designed to relieve cognitive symptoms of dementia by boosting the action of acetylcholine (ACh), a neurotransmitter that is involved in memory and whose level is reduced in patients with Alzheimer's disease. Two drugs that have been approved for use with Alzheimer's patients—tacrine (Cognex) and donepezil (Aricept)—increase ACh activity by inhibiting acetylcholinesterase, the enzyme that breaks down ACh in the synapse. Random controlled trials have demonstrated that these drugs can provide temporary symptomatic improvement for some patients (Rojas-Fernandez et al., 2001). Unfortunately, tacrine and donepezil usually work for only six to nine months; they are not able to reverse the relentless progression of the disease. Furthermore, their use has been seriously questioned because of the magnitude of the effects on memory that they produce (Pryse-Phillips, 1999). A statistically significant change in scores on a cognitive task does not necessarily imply a clinically significant improvement in overall clinical condition (see Research Methods in Chapter 6).

New drug treatments are being pursued that are aimed more directly at the processes by which neurons are destroyed (Bullock, 2002; Sramek & Cutler, 1999). One possibility involves the use of synthetic peptides and natural proteins that inhibit the formation of amyloid plaques. Others focus on blocking the construction of neurofibrillary tangles by keeping tau protein anchored to microtubules. These alternatives are being developed and tested at a rapid pace. Recent evidence regarding these new treatment options can be obtained on the Web from the Cochrane Library.

Although the cognitive deficits associated with primary dementia cannot be completely reversed with medication, neuroleptic medication can be used to treat some patients who develop psychotic symptoms (Devanand & Levy, 1995). These are the same drugs that are used to treat schizophrenia. Low doses are preferable because demented patients are especially vulnerable to the side effects of neuroleptics. Care must be taken to avoid use of these drugs with patients suffering from dementia with Lewy bodies because they may experience a severe negative reaction.

## Environmental and Behavioural Management

Patients with dementia experience fewer emotional problems and are less likely to become agitated if they follow a structured and predictable daily schedule (Stewart, 1995). Activities such as eating meals, exercising, and going to bed are easier and less anxiety-provoking if they occur at regular times. The use of signs and notes may be helpful reminders for patients who are in the earlier stages of the disorder. As the patient's cognitive impairment becomes more severe, even simple activities, such as getting dressed or eating a meal, must be broken down into smaller and more manageable steps. Directions have to be adjusted so that they are appropriate to the patient's level of functioning. Patients with apraxia, for example, may not be able to perform tasks in response to verbal instructions. Caregivers need to adjust their expectations and assume increased responsibilities as their patients' intellectual abilities deteriorate.

Severely impaired patients often reside in nursing homes and hospitals. The most effective residential treatment programs combine the use of medication and behavioural interventions with an environment that is specifically designed to maximize the level of functioning and minimize the emotional distress of patients who are cognitively impaired. Several goals guide the design of such an environment (Kettl, 1993; Lawton, 1989). These include considerations that enhance the following aspects of the patient's life.

- *Knowledge of the environment:* For example, rooms and hallways must be clearly labelled, because patients frequently cannot remember directions.
- *Negotiability:* In the case of dementia, psychological accessibility is at least as important as physical accessibility. For example, spaces that the person would use (a commons area or the dining room) should be visible from the patient's room if they cannot be remembered.
- *Safety and health:* For example, access to the setting must be secured so that patients who would otherwise wander away can remain as active as possible.

One important issue related to patient management involves the level of activity expected of the patient. It is useful to help the person remain active and interested in everyday events. Patients who are physically active are less likely to have problems with agitation, and they may sleep better. Engaging in pleasant activities may also minimize the frequency and severity of depression among patients with dementia (Pulsford, 1997; Teri & Gallagher-Thompson, 1991). Nevertheless, expectations regarding the patient's activity level may have to be reduced in proportion to the progression of cognitive impairment. Efforts should be made to preserve familiar routines and surroundings in light of the inevitable difficulties that are associated with learning new information and recalling past events. Helping the person to cope with these issues may minimize the emotional turmoil associated with the increasing loss of cognitive abilities.

Social interactions are often troublesome for patients with dementia. An example of this type of problem was described in the case of Mary at the beginning of this chapter. After Mary had been admitted to the hospital, she frequently approached the nurses, insisting that she had to go home to take care of her dog, which had, in fact, died. Creative problem-solving strategies that accommodate the patient's distorted view of reality are sometimes useful in this type of situation. Imagine, for example, a patient who continually insists that he must go to his former place of employment. It might be more effective to inform him each morning that his office called to say that he was not needed until the next day, rather than engaging in futile and upsetting arguments about whether he had, in fact, retired for medical reasons—a fact that he is incapable of remembering (Zarit, Zarit, & Rosenberg-Thompson, 1990).

## Support for Caregivers

A final area of concern is the provision of support to people who serve as caregivers for demented patients. In North America, spouses and other family members provide primary care for more than 80 percent of people who have dementia of the Alzheimer's type (Rabins, 1997). Their burdens are often overwhelming, both physically and emotionally. Consider, for example, the situation vividly described by Bernlef (1988) in his novel, *Out of Mind*. In the following passage, Maarten, who is dementing, describes the experience of listening to his wife, Vera, describe to a young woman (whom Vera has hired to help care for Maarten) how she has felt while attempting to cope with his progressive cognitive deterioration:

> I hear Vera. "More than 40 years I have been married to him. And then suddenly this. Usually these things happen more slowly, gradually. But with him it came all at once. I feel it has been sprung on me. It's cruel and unfair. Sometimes I get so angry and rebellious when I see him looking at me as if from another world. And then again I feel only sad and I would so much like to understand him. Or I just talk along with him and then I feel ashamed afterwards. I'm glad you're here because it really gets on top of me at times, when I just can't bear watching it any more. At least now I'll be able to get out occasionally."
>
> There is a moment of silence. I feel the tears running under my eyelids and down my cheeks.
>
> "And sometimes, sometimes his face radiates perfect peace. As if he's happy. Like a child can be. Those moments are so brief I sometimes think I imagine them. But I know only too well what I see at such moments: someone who looks exactly like my husband of long ago. At your age it's difficult to understand that. But people like us live by their memories. If they no longer have those there's nothing left. I am afraid he is in the process of forgetting his whole life. And to live alone with those memories while he sits there beside me . . . empty." (Bernlef, 1988, pp. 80–81)

In addition to the profound loneliness and sadness that caregivers endure, they must also learn to cope with more tangible stressors, such as the patient's incontinence, functional deficits, and disruptive behaviour. Relationships among other family members and the psychological adjustment of the principal caregiver are more disturbed by caring for a demented person than by caring for someone who is physically disabled. Guilt, frustration, and depression are common reactions among the family members of patients (Dunkin & Anderson-Hanley, 1998; Winslow & Carter, 1999).

Some treatment programs provide support groups, as well as informal counselling and ad hoc consultation services, for spouses caring for patients with Alzheimer's disease. The New York University Aging and Dementia Research Center has evaluated the effects of this approach, which attempts to help the caregiver survive the spouse's illness and to postpone the need to place the patient in a nursing home (Mittelman et al., 1997). Compared to caregivers in a control group, those who participated in the special support program were able to delay for a longer time placing the Alzheimer's patient in a nursing home. They were also less likely to become depressed and more likely to express satisfaction with the social support that they received from their families.

Some treatment programs arrange for direct assistance in addition to social support. Respite programs provide caregivers with temporary periods of relief away from the patient. One model program was designed and evaluated by M. Powell Lawton and his colleagues at the Philadelphia Geriatric Center (Brody, Saperstein, & Lawton, 1989). They either would send someone to the patient's home to relieve the caregiver or, in more severe cases, would temporarily institutionalize the patient if the caregiver needed to be away from home for an extended period. In some cases, these services were planned in advance so that the caregiver could take a short vacation, attend special events, or make his or her own medical appointments. Respite care was also available in response to unexpected circumstances, such as the illness of the caregiver. This type of flexible, comprehensive program is clearly needed to relieve the enormous burden that is faced by people who care for demented patients (Grasel, 1997).

## Summary

Dementia, delirium, and amnestic disorders are listed as Cognitive Disorders in DSM-IV-TR. Disruptions of memory and other cognitive functions are the most obvious symptoms of these disorders. Dementia and amnestic disorders are often associated with specific forms of neuropathology. These changes in brain tissue can often be observed only at autopsy, after the person's death. Until recently, the DSM referred to the Cognitive Disorders as Organic Mental Disorders because of their association with known brain diseases. That expression has been abandoned because it implies an artificial dichotomy between biological and psychological processes.

**Dementia** is defined as a gradually worsening loss of memory and related cognitive functions, including the use of language as well as reasoning and decision making. **Aphasia** and **apraxia** are among the most obvious problems in verbal communication. Perceptual difficulties, such as **agnosia,** are also common.

In amnestic disorder, the memory impairment is more circumscribed. The person may experience severe **anterograde amnesia,** but other higher-level cognitive abilities remain unimpaired. **Delirium** is a confusional state that develops over a short period of time and is often associated with agitation and hyperactivity.

Dementia can be associated with many different kinds of neuropathology. The most common form of dementia is associated with **Alzheimer's disease**, which accounts for approximately half of all diagnosed cases of dementia. **Dementia with Lewy bodies** and vascular dementia each account for 15 to 20 percent of cases. Less common forms of dementia include frontotemporal dementia (sometimes called Pick's disease), as well as dementia associated with **Huntington's disease**, and Parkinson's disease.

A definitive diagnosis of Alzheimer's disease can be made only after the patient's death. It requires the observation of two specific types of brain lesions: **neurofibrillary tangles** and **amyloid plaques**, which are found throughout the cerebral cortex. Neurofibrillary tangles are also found in the hippocampus, an area of the brain that is crucial for memory.

The incidence and prevalence of dementia increase dramatically with age. The annual incidence of dementia is 1.4 percent in people over the age of 65 and 3.4 percent for people over the age of 75. Almost 40 percent of people over 90 years of age exhibit symptoms of moderate or severe dementia. Men are more likely than women to develop vascular dementia. Men and women are equally vulnerable to Alzheimer's disease up to the age of 90, when the rate for women increases.

The etiology of dementia depends on many different factors. Some types of dementia are produced by viral infections and dysfunction of the immune system. Environmental toxins also may contribute to the onset of cognitive impairment.

Genetic factors clearly play a role in the etiology of some forms of dementia. Considerable research efforts have been devoted to the study of **genetic linkage** in Alzheimer's disease. Chromosome 21 has been examined closely because people with Down syndrome, who possess three copies of chromosome 21 in every cell, also have amyloid plaques and neurofibrillary tangles like those found in the brains of Alzheimer's patients. Within some families, the gene for Alzheimer's disease is located on chromosome 21. This pattern of linkage is not found for all families, however. Experts now assume that there are several forms of Alzheimer's disease, and each may be associated with a different gene or set of genes.

Delirium can often be resolved successfully by treating the medical condition. In some types of secondary dementia, the person can be restored to his or her original level of cognitive functioning. The intellectual deficits in primary forms of dementia are progressive and irreversible. The treatment goals in these disorders are more limited. They include maintaining the person's level of functioning for as long as possible while minimizing the level of distress experienced by the patient and the family, especially caregivers. Medication can produce modest cognitive benefits for some patients with dementia, but not all patients respond to such treatment, and the clinical significance of these changes is extremely limited. Drugs can be used to control motor dysfunctions associated with primary differentiated forms of dementia, such as Huntington's disease and Parkinson's disease.

Behavioural and environmental management are important aspects of any treatment program for demented patients. They allow patients to reside in the least restrictive and safest possible settings. Respite programs provide much-needed support to caregivers, usually spouses and other family members, who can easily be overwhelmed by the demands of caring for a person with dementia.

# Critical Thinking

1. Suppose you know an elderly person who is beginning to show memory problems. Does that necessarily mean that he or she is developing dementia? What measures might be used to distinguish normal aging from dementia?
2. Dementia and amnestic disorders are classified as Cognitive Disorders in DSM-IV-TR. Many clinicians also talk about the role of cognitive factors in the development of disorders such as anxiety and depression. What is the difference between cognitive impairments seen in dementia and those seen in other forms of psychopathology?
3. Why has the etiology of Alzheimer's disease received increased attention in recent years? Why do clinical scientists consider this disorder to be one of the most pressing health problems in our society?
4. If dementia is an irreversible process, how can it be treated? To which considerations would you give the highest priority in addressing the needs of patients and their families?

# Key Terms

**agnosia** 487
**Alzheimer's disease** 492
**amnestic disorder** 481
**amyloid plaques** 493
**anterograde amnesia** 487
**aphasia** 487
**apraxia** 487
**beta-amyloid** 493
**chorea** 495
**delirium** 481
**dementia** 481
**dementia with Lewy bodies (DLB)** 497
**dyskinesia** 489
**genetic linkage** 495
**Huntington's disease** 495
**neurofibrillary tangles** 493
**neurologists** 482
**neuropsychological assessment** 488
**neuropsychologists** 482
**retrograde amnesia** 487
**vascular dementia** 496

# 15 Mental Retardation and Pervasive Developmental Disorders

Overview

Mental Retardation

Autistic Disorder and Pervasive Developmental Disorders

**What is intelligence, and how is it measured?**

**How can mental retardation be prevented?**

**What is autism, and what causes it?**

**Do people with autism have exceptional intelligence?**

Mental retardation is a common and familiar concern. You may have attended a school where students with mental retardation were "mainstreamed" into regular classes, and we all encounter people with mental retardation in everyday life. Mental retardation also touches the life of expecting mothers, who must practise good health care to protect their developing fetus and who may consider genetic testing for mental retardation. Mental retardation affects many areas of an individual's functioning, and, sadly, this can prevent us from seeing the person behind the disorder. As a reminder that people with mental retardation are *people* first, we follow the convention of putting the "person first" in our writing. We refer to the "person with mental retardation," not to the "mentally retarded person."

## Overview

Too often, people with mental retardation are defined in terms of what they cannot do. This is a mistake. Today, the emphasis is on what the person with mental retardation *can* do. Christopher Burke, who has Down syndrome—one of the most common forms of mental retardation—represents a real-life triumph of ability over disability. From 1989 to 1993, Burke played the role of Corky Thatcher in the television series *Life Goes On*. Burke, now in his thirties, lectures on mental retardation, and performs as a singer and dancer as well. A decade ago, Burke wrote this about his condition:

> My name is Chris Burke and I live an exciting and happy life. That's because I am living my dreams. I love entertaining people and being an actor, and I like to help my fellow handi-capables. Many people recognize me from my role as Corky Thatcher on "Life Goes On," an ABC-TV series for many years. Corky has Down syndrome and so do I. Only I call it Up syndrome, because having Down syndrome has never made me feel down. I'm always up. One reason it is uplifting is because of the tremendous support I have received from my family and all the people in my life. My teachers, my friends, and the people I have worked with are very important to me, just like I am important to them. (Burke, 1995, p. ix)

Many people would not consider someone like Chris Burke to have mental retardation, apparently including Chris Burke. When people with significantly subaverage intelligence are able to adapt well in everyday life, we recognize their strengths and no longer label them as having a mental disorder.

*Pervasive developmental disorders* are far less common than mental retardation; thus, few of us encounter these disturbances in everyday life. Pervasive developmental disorders are distinguished by unusual symptoms that affect most areas of functioning. The person's ability to communicate and interact socially is severely impaired. In addition, she or he exhibits unusual repetitive behaviour, like needing to preserve rigid routines or rocking back and forth endlessly. Dustin Hoffman's role as Raymond in the movie *Rain Man* is perhaps the most familiar portrayal of a pervasive developmental disorder (autism).

*Christopher Burke, who has Down syndrome, starred as Corky Thatcher in the television show* Life Goes On.

Both mental retardation and pervasive developmental disorders typically either are present at birth or begin early in life. Both disorders are characterized by serious disruptions in many areas of functioning, sometimes including the ability to care for oneself and live independently. For these reasons we consider the two conditions together. We discuss mental retardation before reviewing the pervasive developmental disorders, because, contrary to some theories, most people with pervasive developmental disorders also have mental retardation (Volkmar et al., 1994).

# Mental Retardation

Some clinicians and researchers use terms like *intellectual disability* or *developmental disability* to describe mental retardation (e.g., Roeher Institute, 1993). These alternatives have been used because of concerns that the term *mental retardation* has pejorative overtones. Although it is important to ensure that people with intellectual disabilities are not stigmatized or denigrated, the use of alternative diagnostic terms creates confusion in the treatment and research literature, and confusion when clinicians communicate with one another to discuss how a patient's problems might best be managed. For example, two clinicians might use the term *intellectual disability* in different ways: one might use it to refer to a specific learning disability, while the other might use it to refer to general intellectual disabilities (as in mental retardation). To reduce confusion, the present chapter uses the term *mental retardation*, which is the most widely used diagnostic term. Note, however, that this term describes only one aspect of the person—his or her intellectual and adaptive functioning. It should not be used to label the whole person. Accordingly, the phrase "person with mental retardation" is more accurate and less stigmatizing than terms such as "mentally retarded person."

Mental retardation is a diverse diagnostic category. All people with mental retardation have impaired intellectual abilities, but they vary widely in academic ability and functioning. People with mental retardation also differ substantially in their ability to communicate, to master social situations, and to participate in their own care. Some people with profound retardation require total care and live their entire lives in institutions. However, the vast majority of people with mental retardation learn the self-care and vocational skills that allow them to live in the community.

Despite stereotypes to the contrary, much can be done about mental retardation. Although there are limits, early intervention can bring about substantial improvements in the lives of people with mental retardation, and many cases of mental retardation can be prevented by careful planning and health care. We begin our consideration of this important problem with a case from our files.

The case of Karen Cross and her family illustrates some important features of mental retardation. One issue is the adequacy of her functioning. Despite her recent struggles, Karen Cross had succeeded in living a happy, productive life. Many people in her community would not consider her to have mental retardation. Another feature is Karen Cross's depression. Many people with mental retardation suffer from emotional difficulties, a fact that is overlooked all too often. A review by Quebec researchers Lacharité, Boutet, and Proulx (1995) indicates that people with mental retardation, compared with people from the general population, are twice as likely to develop emotional and behavioural problems, such as depression or excessive aggression. These problems vary with the nature of the developmental disorder; people with Down syndrome, for example, have fewer emotional and behavioural problems than people with other developmental disorders (Grizenko et al., 1991).

## Typical Symptoms and Associated Features

The American Association on Mental Retardation (AAMR), which has chapters throughout Canada, is the leading organization for professionals concerned with mental retardation. It offers the following definition of **mental retardation:**

> Mental retardation is a disability characterized by significant limitations both in intellectual functioning and in adaptive behaviour as expressed in conceptual, social, and practical adaptive skills. This disability originates before age 18. (AAMR, 2002, p. 8)

The AAMR's definition of mental retardation differs somewhat from that of DSM-IV-

## CASE STUDY A Mother with Mild Mental Retardation

Karen Cross was a 41-year-old woman with three children when child protective services referred her and her husband, Mark, for a family evaluation. Two months earlier, the Crosses' 16-year-old daughter, Lucy, had called the police following a family fight. Lucy and her mother had been arguing about Lucy's excessive use of the telephone, and when Mr. Cross entered the dispute, he cuffed Lucy across her mouth in anger. Lucy was not seriously hurt, and the social workers who visited with the Cross family following the incident found no history of physical abuse. They were concerned about the adequacy of the Crosses' parenting, however, and the agency strongly recommended an evaluation for the family.

At the time of the referral, Mr. Cross was employed as a custodian at an elementary school where he had been working for 15 years. Testing indicated that he had an IQ of 88, and there was no sign of serious psychopathology based on a diagnostic interview or an MMPI. Both Mr. Cross and his wife admitted that he had exhibited increasingly frequent, angry outbursts, but they both denied any history of violence toward the children or Mrs. Cross.

Mrs. Cross was a homemaker who cared for Lucy and a 12-year-old daughter, Sue. The Crosses' 19-year-old son was serving in the Army. Mrs. Cross had a tested IQ of 67, and she reported that she had attended special education classes throughout her schooling. She married at the age of 19 and lived a normal life with her husband and children, but their low income barely kept the family out of poverty. Although Mrs. Cross demonstrated many adaptive skills in caring for her family, her coping currently was impaired by a severe depression. During the interview, Mrs. Cross's speech and body movements were slowed, and she reported feeling constantly tired. She did not describe herself as "depressed," but she felt unhappy and unable to cope with her children. She was not sure what had caused her troubles, but Mr. Cross traced the onset of her problems to her mother's death a year earlier.

Mrs. Cross cried repeatedly when recalling the loss of her mother. She described her mother as her best friend. They had lived in the same trailer park, and mother and daughter spent most of their days together. Mrs. Cross's mother offered her much practical support, especially in raising the children. Now the children ignored their mother's directions, and Mr. Cross was of little help. Mrs. Cross felt that her husband was too harsh, and she often contradicted him when he tried to punish the girls.

A family interview with the parents and the two teenagers together confirmed the impressions given by the parents. Lucy looked distracted and bored throughout the interview, and Sue frequently looked toward and imitated her older sister. The girls paid more attention briefly when their father got angry, but this ended when Mr. and Mrs. Cross started fighting over his tone of voice.

School records indicated that the girls were obtaining mostly C grades. Standardized test scores from the school indicated that the girls' academic abilities were in the normal range, although their scores were below average. Telephone calls to their teachers indicated that Sue was not much of a behaviour problem in school, but Lucy had lately become very disruptive.

Based on the data obtained from multiple sources, the psychologists made several recommendations to the family and to child protective services. They suggested an evaluation for antidepressant medication for Mrs. Cross, a referral to the school counsellor for Lucy, and a brief course of family therapy that would always include Mr. Cross and Mrs. Cross and sometimes would include the girls. The family therapy was designed to help the parents agree on a set of rules for the girls and enforce discipline with a clear system of rewards and punishments that would focus on the loss of privileges. Therapy also would be used to evaluate Mr. Cross's anger further and to monitor Mrs. Cross's depression. Finally, an attempt would be made to identify services in the community for Mrs. Cross with the goal of helping her build a new system of support. ◆

TR (see Table 15–1), and we highlight some of the differences and controversies between the two systems later in the chapter. Both definitions generally agree on the major criteria for mental retardation. Each definition has three major parts:

- *Significant limitations in intellectual functioning.* This criterion refers to an IQ of approximately 70 or below, as measured by an individually administered intelligence test. A score of 70 is two standard deviations below the average IQ score (see Research Methods on p. 515), and it is best viewed as an approximate cutoff for mental retardation. Even the best measures of intelligence are subject to minor errors, and the difference between an IQ of 71 and 69 is trivial practically.
- *Significant limitations in adaptive functioning.* This criterion refers to deficits in life skills. People who have an IQ below 70 but who function well in life are not considered to have mental retardation.
- *Onset before age 18 years.* This criterion excludes people whose deficits begin during adult life. When factors such as injury

**TABLE 15–1 DSM-IV-TR Diagnostic Criteria for Mental Retardation**

| |
|---|
| **A.** Significantly subaverage intellectual functioning: an IQ of approximately 70 or below on an individually administered IQ test (for infants, a clinical judgment of significantly subaverage intellectual functioning). |
| **B.** Concurrent deficits or impairments in present adaptive functioning (i.e., the person's effectiveness in meeting the standards expected for his or her age by his or her cultural group) in at least two of the following areas: communication, self-care, home living, social/interpersonal skills, use of community resources, self-direction, functional academic skills, work, leisure, health and safety. |
| **C.** Onset is before age 18 years. |

or degenerative brain disease produce significantly subaverage IQ after the age of 18, dementia, and not mental retardation, may be the appropriate diagnosis (see Chapter 14).

**Significantly Subaverage IQ** The AAMR and DSM-IV-TR both define subaverage intellectual functioning in terms of a score on an individualized *intelligence test*, a standardized measure for assessing intellectual ability. Commonly used intelligence tests include the Wechsler Intelligence Scale for Children—Third Edition (WISC-III) and the Wechsler Adult Intelligence Scale—Third Edition (WAIS-III). Intelligence tests yield a score called the **intelligence quotient**, or **IQ**, the test's rating of an individual's intellectual ability.

*Measurement of Intelligence* Defining *intelligence* can be controversial, and definitions and measures of intellectual ability have changed over the years. Early versions of intelligence tests derived an IQ by dividing the individual's "mental age" by his or her chronological age. Mental age was determined by comparing an individual's test results with the average obtained for various age groups. For example, someone who answered the same number of items correctly as the average 10-year-old would be given a mental age of 10. After mental age was divided by chronological age, the ratio was multiplied by 100 to yield an IQ score. According to this system, an 8-year-old with a mental age of 10 would have an IQ of 125, calculated as $10/8 \times 100$.

Contemporary intelligence tests have abandoned the concept of mental age and instead have adopted the concept of the "deviation IQ." According to this theory, intellectual ability follows the **normal distribution** in the population, a bell-shaped frequency distribution that is illustrated in Figure 15–1. As is the case with height and weight, both of which follow the normal distribution, most people are assumed to be near average in intelligence, and a few people are thought to be exceptionally low or exceptionally high in their intellectual abilities. The individual's IQ is determined based on how the person scores on an intelligence test relative to the norms for his or her age group. Narrow age ranges are used in creating norms for children, because cognitive abilities and knowledge acquisition change rapidly with age. In contrast, all adults are treated as a part of the same age group.

Intelligence tests are normed to have a *mean* (average) IQ score of 100 and a *standard deviation* of 15 (see Research Methods). Thus, given a normal distribution of IQ scores, about two-thirds of the population has an IQ within one standard deviation of the mean—between 85 and 115. The cutoff score for mental retardation is approximately two standard deviations below the average. About 2 percent of the population falls below this cutoff in the normal distribution (see Figure 15–1).

IQ tests are widely used, and they have demonstrated value for predicting performance in school. Moreover, IQ is a trait that is stable over time. Preschool measures of intelligence tend to be unstable, but the IQ scores of school-age children are good predictors of IQ scores later in life. This is true for people with mental retardation as well as for those with IQs in the normal range (Baroff & Olley, 1999). A school-age child who has a significantly subaverage IQ is likely to continue to score below

**The Normal Distribution of IQ Scores and the IQ Cutoff Score for Mental Retardation**

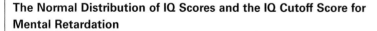

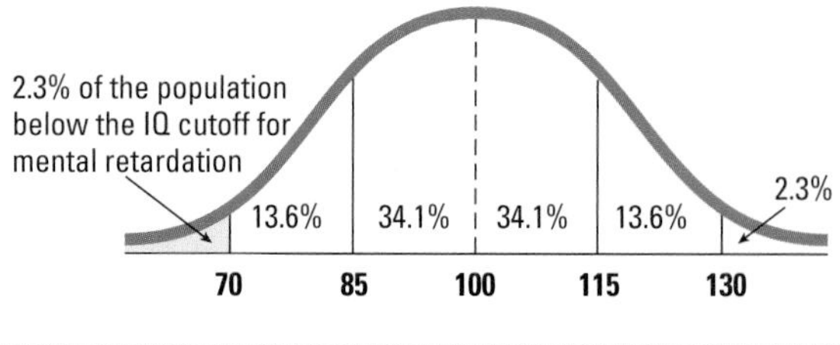


**FIGURE 15–1: Many theories assume a normal distribution of intelligence in the population. Contemporary IQ tests have a mean of 100 and a standard deviation of 15. The IQ cutoff for mental retardation is two standard deviations below the mean.**

# RESEARCH METHODS

## Central Tendency, Variability, and Standard Scores

We can explain the nature and meaning of IQ scores more fully by describing a few basic statistics. A *frequency distribution* is simply a way of arranging data according to the frequencies of different possible scores. For example, we might obtain the following frequency distribution of ages in a group of 10 university students:

| Age | Frequency |
|---|---|
| 17 | 1 |
| 18 | 4 |
| 19 | 1 |
| 20 | 2 |
| 21 | 2 |

The **mean** is the arithmetic average of a distribution of scores, as defined by the formula:

$$M = \frac{\text{sum of scores}}{N}$$

where $M$ is the mean, and $N$ is the number of scores. Thus, the mean of the frequency distribution of ages listed above is

$$M = \frac{17+18+18+18+18+19+20+20+21+21}{10} = 19$$

The mean is the most commonly used of various *measures of central tendency,* which are single scores that summarize and describe a frequency distribution.

Other important and commonly used measures of central tendency are the median and the mode. The **median** is the midpoint of a frequency distribution—that is, the score that half of all subjects fall above and half of all subjects fall below. In the above example, 19 is the median age. Finally, the **mode** is the most frequent score in a distribution. In our example, the mode is 18.

Measures of variability also provide useful summary information about a frequency distribution. The *range* is a simple measure of variability that includes the lowest and highest scores in a frequency distribution. In our example, the range of ages is 17 to 21. As a more complex measure of variability, we may wish to compute the average distance of each individual score from the overall mean (21–19, 17–19, etc.). However, when we subtract each score in a frequency distribution from the mean of the distribution, the positive and negative numbers always add up to zero. (Try this in our example.) As a way of compensating for this inevitability, statisticians have created a statistic called the **variance**, in which the differences from the mean are squared (to eliminate negative numbers) before they are added together. The variance is a very useful measure of variability that is defined by the following formula:

$$V = \frac{\text{sum of (score} - M)^2}{(N - 1)}$$

where $V$ is the variance, $M$ is the mean, and $N$ is the number of scores. We use $N - 1$ instead of $N$ in the equation because the –1 is a correction factor required for statistical reasons. The variance in our example is 2.0. You may want to calculate this statistic yourself to aid your understanding.

The variance is an extremely useful measure, but the variance is expressed as a different unit of measurement from the mean because the scores have been squared. This problem is easily solved by taking the square root of the variance, which results in a statistic called the **standard deviation**. The standard deviation is defined by the formula:

$$SD = \sqrt{V}$$

where $SD$ is the standard deviation and $V$ is the variance. In our example, the standard deviation is 1.4, or the square root of 2.0 (the variance).

**Standard scores** are created by subtracting each score in a frequency distribution from the mean and dividing the difference by the standard deviation. Standard scores, or *z*-scores, as they are often called, are computed according to the following formula:

$$z = \frac{(\text{score} - M)}{SD}$$

where $z$ is the standard score, $M$ is the mean, and $SD$ is the standard deviation. Because of the nature of the statistic, *z*-scores always have a mean of zero and a standard deviation of 1.

This brings us back to the deviation IQ, which is a type of standard score. The reason why IQ scores have a mean of 100 and a standard deviation of 15 is because the *z*-scores are first multiplied by 15 and then a constant of 100 is added to the product. For example, a standard score of 1 translates into a deviation IQ score of 115 ($[1 \times 15] + 100$), or a standard score of 22 translates into a deviation IQ score of 70 ($[-2 \times 15] + 100$).

The mean and the standard deviation are basic statistics for creating deviation IQ scores. The statistics also are central to understanding numerous other psychological concepts. For example, you should now be better able to understand the discussion of standard deviation units in relation to the meta-analysis. We recommend that you read back through the discussion and calculate the statistics yourself if you are at all confused about these concepts. ◆

the cutoff point for mental retardation throughout life.

*Controversies About Intelligence Tests* Despite the value of IQ tests in predicting academic performance, a number of important questions have been raised about them. One of the most controversial questions is whether intelligence tests are "culture-fair." That is, whether an IQ test produces lower scores in some cultural groups than in others. This would happen if the test contained items geared toward the language and experiences of one cultural group but not the other. **Culture-fair tests** contain material that is equally familiar to people who differ in their ethnicity, native language, or immigrant status. Tests that are *culturally biased* contain language, examples, or other assumptions that favour one ethnic group, particularly members of the majority group, over another. Because of the possibility of cultural bias, the AAMR (2002) explicitly notes that the valid assessment of intelligence should consider cultural and linguistic diversity.

Another controversy about intelligence tests is how well intelligence is measured among people with mental retardation. Many people with mental retardation have sensory or physical disabilities that impede their performance on standard IQ tests; thus they must take tests that are not influenced by their particular disability. Despite the difficulties involved in assessment, evidence indicates that, if anything, the IQ test scores of people with mental retardation are more reliable and more valid than IQ scores in the normal range (Baroff & Olley, 1999).

The most basic concern about intelligence tests is the most important one: What is intelligence? Intelligence tests measure precisely what their original developer, Alfred Binet, intended them to measure: potential for school achievement. And IQ tests predict school achievement fairly well. In fact, IQ scores correlate 0.4 to 0.7 with school achievement (Baroff & Olley, 1999). However, school achievement is not the same as "intelligence." Common sense, social sensitivity, and "street smarts" are also part of what most of us would consider to be intelligence, and they are not measured by IQ tests. There would be less controversy if IQ tests were labelled, more appropriately, as measures of academic aptitude.

**Limitations in Adaptive Skills** Both the AAMR and DSM recognize that intelligence is more than an IQ score; thus they include adaptive behaviour as a part of their definitions of mental retardation. The AAMR (2002) suggests that adaptive behaviour includes conceptual, social, and practical skills, while the DSM-IV-TR lists 10 specific adaptive skills (see Table 15–1). Fortunately, the AAMR suggests how the two definitions can be combined. *Conceptual skills* focus largely on community self-sufficiency, and incorporate communication, functional academics, self-direction, and health and safety from DSM-IV-TR. *Social skills* focus on understanding how to conduct oneself in social situations and include social skills and leisure from the DSM-IV-TR list. Finally, *practical skills* focus on the tasks of daily living and include self-care, home living, community use, health and safety, and work from the DSM-IV-TR.

Adaptive skills are difficult to quantify. How would *you* define and measure social skills? Despite the challenge, some useful, standardized instruments have been developed, such as the Vineland Social Maturity Scale—Revised (see Table 15–2). As with academic aptitude, adaptive skills must be judged within the context of age. Among preschoolers, adaptive skills include the acquisition of motor abilities, language, and self-control. Key skills during the school-age years include adequate academic performance and developing social relationships with peers. In adult life, adaptive skills include the ability to manage oneself, live independently, and assume adult interpersonal roles.

As with the definition of IQ, the AAMR (2002) now defines a significant limitation in adaptive behaviour as a score that is two standard deviations below the mean on a standardized measure of adaptive behaviour in conceptual, social, *or* practical skills. Significant limitation in one area alone is enough to meet this part of the definition of mental retardation.

An argument has been made for defining retardation solely on the basis of intelligence testing, because current measures of adaptive skills are imprecise (MacMillan, Gresham, & Siperstein, 1995). Moreover, the intellectual limitations of mental retardation imply that adaptive skills will necessarily be limited (Zigler & Hodapp, 1986). Since 1959, however, deficits in adaptive behaviour have been an essential part of the AAMR's definition of mental retardation (Heber, 1959). The adaptive skills criterion highlights the importance of assessing life functioning in borderline cases, as well as the need for services among people with mental retardation (AAMR, 2002). Many people with significantly subaverage IQs, like Chris Burke, lead lives that are not only normal but exciting. Moreover, deficits in adaptive behaviour are less stable over time than are IQ limitations, especially as life demands change from school to the more diverse world of work. Thus mental retardation can be "cured" in the sense that adaptive skills can be taught or environmental demands can be shaped to match an individual's unique abilities and experiences.

**Onset before Age 18 Years** The third criterion for defining mental retardation is onset before 18 years of age. This criterion excludes people whose deficits in intellect and adaptive skills begin later in life as a result of brain injury or disease. Besides differences in etiology, the most important aspect of this criterion is the experience of normal development. The cognitive development, social relationships, and life experiences of people who have lived normal lives into adulthood differentiate them from people with mental retardation in numerous important ways. People with mental retardation have not lost skills they once had mastered, nor have they experienced a notable change in their condition. Unfortunately, this means that their retardation may be perceived as "who they are" and not as something that has "happened to them." This is why we put the "person first" in writing about mental retardation, as a small but constant reminder of the person behind the disorder.

## Classification

Academic aptitude was less necessary to successful living in earlier, agrarian societies than it is in our modern, technological world. Thus many people seen as having mild mental retardation today would not have been viewed as having notable problems in the past. Even today, mental retardation is defined differently in more industrialized countries than in less industrialized ones because of the educational and technological requirements for work in the industrialized countries (Scheerenberger, 1982).

**Brief Historical Perspective** Severe mental retardation has been recognized as an abnormality throughout history, but few special efforts were made to help people with the disorder. Both "lunatics" and "idiots," as people with mental illness and mental retardation were called from the Middle Ages until the twentieth century, were either abandoned to roam the streets, sheltered inadequately in poorhouses, or warehoused in institutions (see Chapter 18). Socially, people with mental retardation often were derided because of their disabilities. Such pejorative terms as "idiot," "fool," "moron," and "imbecile" actually were used in formal diagnostic or legal terminology well into the twentieth century (Volkmar & Dykens, 2002).

The work of the French physician Jean Marc Itard (1774–1838) was instrumental in spurring efforts to develop special education programs for children with mental retardation. Itard worked extensively with a feral child, whom he named "Victor," found living in the woods near Aveyron, France, in 1799. Itard worked with the "wild boy of Aveyron" for five years in an attempt to educate and socialize him. In the end, Itard felt that he had failed in his efforts, but his work nevertheless encouraged others to develop special programs for educating children with mental retardation (Patton, Beirne Smith, & Payne, 1990).

**TABLE 15-2 Sample Items from the Vineland Adaptive Behaviour Scales**

| | | |
|---|---|---|
| **Daily Living Skills** | | |
| Age | 1: | Drinks from a cup. |
| Age | 5: | Bathes or showers without assistance. |
| Age | 10: | Uses a stove for cooking. |
| Age | 15: | Looks after own health. |
| **Socialization** | | |
| Age | 1: | Imitates simple adult movements like clapping. |
| Age | 5: | Has a group of friends. |
| Age | 10: | Watches television about particular interests. |
| Age | 15: | Responds to hints or indirect cues in conversation. |

*Source:* S.S. Sparrow, D.A. Balla, and D.V. Cicchetti, 1984, *Vineland Adaptive Behavior Scales.* Circle Pines, MN: American Guidance Service.

*This girl with Down syndrome shows that children with mental retardation can join in many normal childhood activities.*

In Canada, the first separate "asylum for idiots," as it was then called, was established in 1872 in Orillia, Ontario. This formed the basis of what later became a province-wide system of residential facilities for people with mental retardation (Goldberg, 1996). With the deinstitutionalization movement, which began in the 1960s (see Chapter 18), many of these facilities subsequently closed or decreased the number of people they housed.

*Early Classification Efforts* The beginnings of contemporary classifications of mental retardation date to the second half of the nineteenth century. In 1866, the British physician Langdon Down first described a subgroup of children with mental retardation who had a characteristic appearance. Their faces reminded Down of the appearance of Mongolians, and he used the term *mongolism* to describe them. Despite this offensive terminology, Down's classification helped subsequent scientists to establish a specific etiology for what we now know as Down syndrome.

The creation of IQ tests in the early twentieth century also greatly furthered the classification of mental retardation. The French psychologists Alfred Binet (1856–1911) and Theophile Simon (1873–1961) developed the first successful intelligence test in 1905 in response to a French government effort to identify children in need of special educational services. The Binet scale was refined further by psychologist Lewis Terman of Stanford University, and these efforts resulted in the Stanford–Binet intelligence tests. The first Wechsler intelligence test was developed by David Wechsler in 1939, and revisions of Wechsler's individualized intelligence tests continue to dominate contemporary intellectual assessment.

Once academic potential could be measured, controversy grew about what IQ score cutoff should define mental retardation. The debate reached a climax in 1959 when the AAMR greatly expanded the definition of retardation. In an attempt to help more people in need of services, the IQ cutoff was shifted from two standard deviations below the mean to one standard deviation below the mean. Anyone who scored 85 or lower was considered to have mental retardation, a criterion that included almost 15 percent of the population. This well-intentioned change included far too many well-functioning individuals, and it distracted attention from those most in need of help. Thus, in 1973, the AAMR returned to the cutoff of 70 (Grossman, 1983).

**Contemporary Classification** Today, mental retardation can be classified according to two different criteria. One criterion is based on IQ scores; the other is according to known or presumed etiology. Both approaches are reliable, and each is valid for different purposes, demonstrating that different classification systems can have value for different purposes (see Chapter 4). In fact, the AAMR (2002) uses a multiaxial diagnosis of mental retardation in which health, including etiological factors, is rated on a separate axis.

A more controversial aspect of the AAMR subclassification is the ratings of four levels of "intensity of needed support" across nine different areas of functioning (see Table 15–3). The laudable goal in rating support intensities is to convey the diversity of skills and needs among people with mental retardation both as people and for treatment planning. For example, one person with an IQ of 65 may need more assistance with self-care, whereas a second person with the same IQ may need more help with employment. This approach is designed to be sensitive to individual needs, but some professionals question its reliability and validity (MacMillan, Gresham, & Siperstein, 1995).

In adopting the support intensities approach, AAMR (2002) abandoned a long tradition still followed in DSM-IV-TR of dividing mental retardation into four levels based primarily on IQ scores: mild, moderate, severe, and profound (see Table 15–4). Although the AAMR's concerns about individualized assessment are important, they have proven to be difficult to use and have not been widely adopted (AAMR, 2002). Thus, we highlight the DSM-IV-TR subclassification, which has been the focus of considerable research.

*Mild mental retardation* is the designation for those with IQ scores between 50–55 and 70. This category accounts for about 85 percent of people with mental retardation. People with mild mental retardation typically have few, if any, physical impairments, generally reach the sixth-grade level in academic functioning, acquire vocational skills, and typically live in the community with or without special supports.

People with *moderate mental retardation* have IQs between 35–40 and 50–55; they make up about 10 percent of those with mental retardation. They may have obvious physical abnormalities such as the features of Down syndrome. Academic achievement generally reaches second-grade level, work activities require close training and supervision, and special supervision in families or group homes is needed for living in the community.

*Severe mental retardation* is defined by IQ scores between 20–25 and 35–40. This category accounts for 3 to 4 percent of people with mental retardation. At this severity level, motor development typically is abnormal, communicative speech is sharply limited, and close supervision is needed for community living.

About 1 to 2 percent of people with mental retardation have *profound mental retardation*. This severity level is characterized by an IQ below 20–25. Motor skills, communication, and self-care are severely limited, and constant supervision is required in the community or in institutions.

**TABLE 15-3 AAMR Definitions of Intensities of Needed Support**

**Intermittent**

Supports on an "as needed basis." Characterized by episodic nature (person not always needing the support[s]) or short-term nature (supports needed during lifespan transitions, e.g., job loss or acute medical crisis). Intermittent supports may be high or low intensity when provided.

**Limited**

An intensity of supports characterized by consistency over time, time-limited but not of an intermittent nature, may require fewer staff members and less cost than more intense levels of support (e.g., time-limited employment training or transitional supports during the school-to-adult provided period).

**Extensive**

Supports characterized by regular involvement (e.g., daily) in at least some environments (school, work, or home) and not time-limited nature (e.g., long-term support and long-term home living support).

**Pervasive**

Supports characterized by their constancy, high intensity, provision across environments, potential life-sustaining nature. Pervasive supports typically involve more staff members and intrusiveness than do extensive or time-limited supports.

*Source:* From American Association on Mental Retardation, 2002, *Mental Retardation: Definition, Classification, and Systems of Support*, 10th ed., p. 152. Washington, DC: AAMR.

## Epidemiology

Theoretically, IQ is distributed according to the normal curve, so 2.3 percent of the population should have IQs of 70 or below. In reality, however, more than the expected 2.3 percent of people have IQs below 70. Very low IQ scores, in particular, are found more often than expected, a result of the various biological conditions that produce mental retardation (Volkmar & Dykens, 2002). We, therefore, can think of there being two IQ distributions. One is the normal distribution of IQ scores. The other is the distribution of IQs of people with biological disorders that cause mental retardation (Zigler, 1967). These two theoretical distributions are portrayed in Figure 15–2.

Even though more than 2.3 percent of people have IQs below the 70 cutoff, the best estimate is that only 1 percent of the population has mental retardation (Volkmar & Dykens, 2002). The prevalence of mental retardation is lower than the prevalence of IQs below 70 because: (1) IQs cannot be adequately assessed among very young children, who therefore are omitted from prevalence figures; and (2) many adults with low IQs are not considered to have mental retardation because they have adaptive skills. As an indication of these two facts, studies show that twice as many school-age children as preschoolers have mental retardation, but the prevalence rates drop again among adults (Grossman, 1983).

Mental retardation is more common among the poor and, as a result, among certain ethnic groups. However, the increased prevalence is not found for all subtypes of retardation. Mental retardation with a specific, known organic cause (for example, Down syndrome) generally has an equal prevalence among all social classes, whereas retardation of nonspecific etiology is more common among families living in poverty (Patton, Beirne-Smith, & Payne, 1990). This epidemiological fact is the source of much controversy, as we discuss in the following sections.

**TABLE 15-4 Levels of Mental Retardation**

| Level | Approximate IQ Range | Adult Mental Age of an Average | Percent of People with Mental Retardation |
|---|---|---|---|
| Mild | 50–55 to 70 | 9 to 12 year old | 85 |
| Moderate | 35–40 to 50–55 | 6 to 9 year old | 10 |
| Severe | 20–25 to 35–40 | 3 to 6 year old | 3–4 |
| Profound | Below 20–25 | 3 year old or younger | 1–2 |

DSM-IV-TR follows the tradition of classifying mental retardation into levels. The AAMR and some others have rejected the levels approach, but the classification has predictive value and is useful for planning interventions.

**The Two-Curve Model of Mental Retardation**

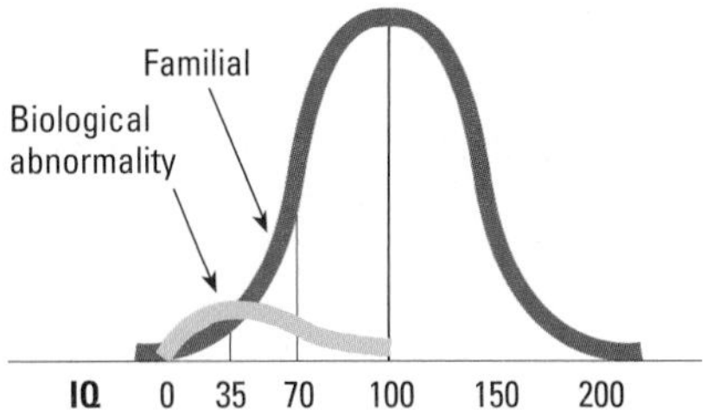


**FIGURE 15–2: The two-curve model of mental retardation distinguishes between people who score below 70 in the normal distribution of IQ scores (familial retardation) and the IQ scores for people below 70 with known biological causes of mental retardation.**

*Source:* Adapted from E. Zigler, 1967, Familial mental retardation: a continuing dilemma. *Science 155*, 292–298. Copyright 1967 by the American Association for the Advancement of Science.

## Etiological Considerations and Research

As we have noted, the etiology of mental retardation can be grouped into two broad categories: cases caused by known biological abnormalities and cases resulting from normal variations in IQ. We review known biological causes before considering the debate about the causes of the largest category of mental retardation, those cases at the extreme end of the normal IQ distribution.

**Biological Factors** About one-half of all cases of mental retardation are caused by known biological abnormalities (Volkmar & Dykens, 2002). In contrast to cases of unknown origin, known biological causes more often lead to retardation of moderate to profound severity and are associated with physical handicaps. Of the over 250 known biological causes (AAMR, 2002), we focus only on some major ones here.

*Christopher Murray, Marisol Pulido, Belinda Alexander, and Kim McKeon (left to right) assemble bandages for the military at a workshop at residential facility for people with mental retardation.*

*Chromosomal Disorders* The most common known biological cause of mental retardation is the chromosomal disorder **Down syndrome**. People with Down syndrome have a distinctively abnormal physical appearance. They have slanting eyes with an extra fold of skin in the inner corner, a small head and short stature, a protruding tongue, and a variety of organ, muscle, and skeletal abnormalities. They also have physical handicaps and limited speech (Thapar et al., 1994).

The cause of Down syndrome is the presence of an extra chromosome. Children with Down syndrome have 47 chromosomes instead of the normal 46. The extra chromosome is attached to the twenty-first pair; thus the disorder often is referred to as *trisomy 21*.

The incidence of Down syndrome is related to maternal age. For women under the age of 30, about 1 in 1000 births are Down syndrome infants. The incidence rises to 1 in 750 births for mothers between ages 30 and 34, 1 in 300 between 35 and 39, and over 1 in 100 after age 40. Increasing paternal age also is associated with Down syndrome and is thought to cause about 25 percent of the cases (Magenis et al., 1977). Down syndrome can be detected by testing during pregnancy.

In general, children and adults with Down syndrome function within the moderate to severe range of mental retardation. They exhibit substantial variation in their intellectual level, however, and research suggests that intensive intervention can lead to higher achievement and greater independence. Institutionalization once was commonly recommended, but home or community care is now the rule. In fact, many experts who have worked with people with Down syndrome report that they are especially sociable and eager to help, although research findings on their distinctive personality traits are not conclusive (Cicchetti & Beegly, 1990).

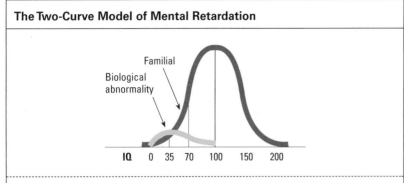

A potentially important recent discovery is that, by their thirties, the majority of adults with Down syndrome develop brain pathology similar to that found in Alzheimer's disease. About one-third also exhibit the symptoms of dementia (Salvatori et al. 1998). University of Guelph researchers have found that the risk of developing dementia is greatest in Down syndrome people with lower cognitive ability (Temple et al., 2001). Death in mid-adult life is common, although some adults with Down syndrome live into their fifties and sixties. According to a review by Penny Salvatori at McMaster University and her colleagues, recent evidence suggests that the lifespan of people with mental retardation is increasing (Salvatori et al., 1998). This may be associated with improvements in care and living conditions.

Another chromosomal abnormality, **fragile-X syndrome** (Lubs, 1969), is the second most common known biological cause of mental retardation. Fragile-X syndrome is indicated by a weakening or break on one arm of the X sex chromosome; and it is transmitted genetically. In fact, the specific gene responsible for the disorder, the fragile-X mental retardation (FMR-1) gene, was identified not long ago (Warren & Ashley, 1995). The disorder occurs in 1 out of every 1500 male births and about 1 in 2500 females (Bregman et al., 1987; Warren & Ashley, 1995). Recent advances have made it possible to detect fragile-X in the fetus during pregnancy.

Not all children with the fragile-X abnormality have mental retardation. Girls with fragile-X syndrome are considerably less likely to have mental retardation than are boys (Moldavsky et al., 2001; Warren & Ashley, 1995). Among those with normal intelligence, learning disabilities are common. Most of those with mental retardation have a characteristic facial appearance that includes an elongated face, high forehead, large jaw, and large, underdeveloped ears (Bregman et al., 1987). Children with fragile-X tend to be socially anxious, to avoid eye contact, and to have stereotypic hand movements; and some (approximately 15 percent) display the symptoms of autism (Rogers et al., 2001).

Several other chromosomal abnormalities have been linked to mental retardation. As in fragile-X syndrome, abnormalities of the sex chromosomes are particularly notable. *Klinefelter syndrome*, found in about 1 in 1000 live male births, is characterized by the presence of one or more extra X chromosomes. The most common chromosome configuration is XXY. With Klinefelter syndrome, IQ functioning typically is in the low normal to the mild range of mental retardation. Another chromosomal abnormality, *XYY syndrome*, once was thought to increase criminality, but the syndrome is now recognized to be linked with only minor social deviance and a mean IQ about 10 points lower than average. The syndrome occurs in 1 to 2 out of 2000 male births. *Turner syndrome*, the XO configuration in females, is characterized by a missing X chromosome. Girls with Turner syndrome are small, fail to develop sexually, and generally have intelligence near or within the normal range. The disorder occurs in about 1 in every 2200 live female births (Thapar et al., 1994).

*Genetic Disorders* Few cases of mental retardation result from dominant genetic inheritance, because such a mutation is unlikely to remain in the gene pool. However, mental retardation is known to be caused by several recessive gene pairings. **Phenylketonuria**, or **PKU**, is one of these. Geneticists estimate that about 1 in every 54 normal people carries a recessive gene for PKU, but the two genes are paired only in 1 of every 15 000 live births (NIH, 2000).

PKU is caused by abnormally high levels of the amino acid *phenylalanine*, usually due to the absence of or an extreme deficiency in *phenylalanine hydroxylase*, an enzyme that metabolizes phenylalanine. Children with PKU have normal intelligence at birth. However, as they eat foods containing phenylalanine early in life, the amino acid builds up in their system. This *phenylketonuria* produces brain damage that eventually results in mental retardation. Retardation typically progresses to the severe to profound range. PKU sometimes results in the behavioural symptoms of autism, as does the extremely rare dominant-gene disorder *tuberous sclerosis*, characterized by white growths in the ventricles of the brain that appear tuberous.

Fortunately, PKU can be detected by blood testing in the first several days after birth. (The musty odour of the infant's urine is a much less exact but notable clinical indicator of PKU.) Early detection is very important, because intellectual and behavioural impairments are diminished dramatically if the child maintains a diet low in phenylalanine. In such cases the child is likely to have normal to mildly impaired intelligence. For this reason, all provinces have laws that require routine screening of newborns for PKU. In order to maximize the benefits of the diet, the child should be maintained on it for as long as possible—certainly until age 10 and preferably throughout his or her life (*Lancet*, 1991; NIH,

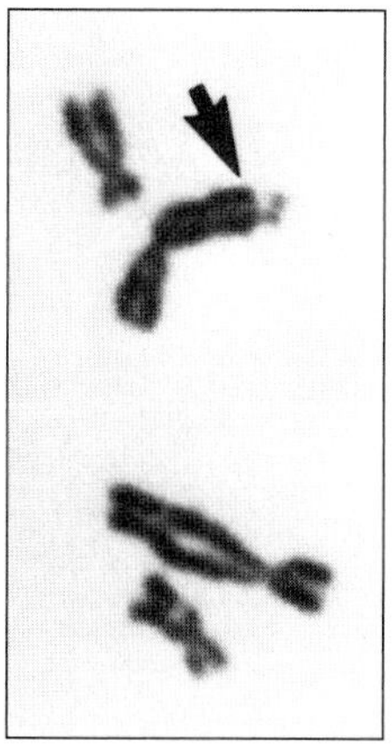

*Top: Fragile-X syndrome can be identified by a gap (arrow) near the distal end of the long arm of the X chromosome. Bottom: This adolescent boy with mental retardation suffers from fragile-X syndrome. He has an elongated face and prominent forehead and ears, features that characterize many people with this disorder.*

Source (top): S.T. Warren and D.L. Nelson, 1994, *Advances in molecular analysis of fragile-X syndrome. JAMA, 271*, 536–542.

2000). It also is very important for adult women with PKU to regulate their diet shortly during pregnancy in order to avoid damage to the fetus. Otherwise, high levels of phenylalanine in the mother's bloodstream can damage the developing brain of the fetus and cause mental retardation (NIH, 2000). Maintaining a diet low in phenylalanine is very difficult because phenylalanine is found in most foods and many food additives. Take a look at the labels of some of the foods you have at home (such as diet sodas). You will notice a warning about phenylalanine on many of the labels.

Other relatively rare recessive-gene disorders can also cause mental retardation. *Tay-Sachs disease* is a particularly severe disorder that eventually results in death during the infant or preschool years. The recessive gene that causes Tay-Sachs is particularly common among Jews of Eastern European heritage. *Hurler syndrome*, or *gargoylism*, results in gross physical abnormalities, including dwarfism, humpback, bulging head, and clawlike hands. Children with this disorder usually do not live past the age of 10. *Lesch-Nyhan syndrome* is most notable for the self-mutilation that accompanies the mental retardation. Children with this disorder bite their lips and fingers, often causing tissue loss. As with Down syndrome and fragile-X syndrome, many of these genetic abnormalities can be detected during pregnancy.

*Infectious Diseases* Mental retardation can also be caused by various infectious diseases. Damaging infections may be contracted during pregnancy, at birth, or in infancy to early childhood. Among the diseases passed from mother to fetus during pregnancy are *cytomegalovirus*, the most common fetal infection (and one that is usually harmless), and *toxoplasmosis*, a protozoan infection contracted from ingestion of infected raw meats or from contact with infected cat feces. No widely accepted treatments for these diseases exist.

*Rubella* (German measles) is a viral infection that may produce few symptoms in the mother but can cause severe mental retardation and even death in the developing fetus, especially if it is contracted in the first three months of pregnancy. Fortunately, rubella can be prevented by vaccination of prospective mothers before pregnancy. Vaccination against rubella is now a part of routine health care.

The *human immunodeficiency virus (HIV)* can be transmitted from an infected mother to a developing fetus. Fortunately, only about one-third of children who contact HIV prenatally develop *acquired immune deficiency syndrome (AIDS)*, but those who do, develop AIDS rapidly. The effects on the child are profound, including mental retardation, visual and language impairments, and eventual death (Baroff & Olley, 1999).

*Syphilis* is a bacterial disease that is transmitted through sexual contact. Infected mothers can pass the disease to the fetus. If untreated, syphilis produces a number of physical and sensory handicaps in the fetus, including mental retardation. The adverse consequences are avoided by testing the mother and administering antibiotics when an infection has been detected. Because penicillin crosses the placental barrier, treating the mother will also cure the disease in the fetus.

Another sexually transmitted disease, *genital herpes*, can be transmitted to the infant during birth. Herpes is a viral infection that produces small lesions on the genitals immediately following the initial infection and intermittently thereafter. Generally, the disease can be transmitted only when the lesions are present. If there is an outbreak of genital lesions near or at the time of delivery, a cesarean section can be performed, thus preventing infection of the newborn. About half of all infants delivered genitally in the presence of active lesions are infected, resulting in very serious problems, including mental retardation, blindness, and possible death.

Two infectious diseases that occur after birth, primarily during infancy, can cause mental retardation. *Encephalitis* is an infection of the brain that produces inflammation and permanent damage in about 20 percent of all cases. *Meningitis* is an infection of the *meninges*, the three membranes that line the brain. The inflammation creates intracranial pressure that can irreversibly damage brain tissues. Encephalitis and meningitis can be caused by a variety of infectious diseases. Cases resulting from bacterial infections can usually be treated successfully with antibiotics. In other cases, the outcome of both encephalitis and meningitis is unpredictable. Neuromuscular problems, sensory impairments, and mental retardation are possible.

*Toxins* Exposure to a variety of environmental toxins can also cause mental retardation.

Like infectious diseases, toxic chemicals can produce mental retardation when exposure occurs either before or after birth, but exposure during pregnancy creates the greatest risk.

Both legal and illegal drugs pose a risk to the developing fetus. Because of its frequent use, alcohol presents the greatest threat. About 1 to 2 of every 1000 births is a baby with **fetal alcohol syndrome**. This disorder is characterized by retarded physical development, a small head, narrow eyes, cardiac defects, and cognitive impairment. Intellectual functioning ranges from mild mental retardation to normal intelligence accompanied by learning disabilities.

Women who drink heavily during pregnancy (an average of 150 mL or 5 drinks of alcohol per day) are twice as likely to have a child with the syndrome as are women who average 30 mL of alcohol (1 drink) per day or less (Baroff & Olley, 1999). Controversy continues about the risk for difficulties associated with drinking in the intermediate range. Because of possible adverse effects of even low or moderate consumption, most experts recommend that pregnant women abstain from alcohol altogether.

Although heroin and methadone addiction have not been directly linked with mental retardation, they do result in the serious problems of low birth weight and drug addiction for the newborn. Particular concern has been raised about the use of crack cocaine by pregnant women. "Crack babies" are more likely to be born prematurely, to have a lower than normal birth weight, and to have a smaller than normal head circumference. Although greatly distressed at birth, the majority of these infants "catch up" with expected physical growth, while a third show a variety of behavioural and learning problems that may be attributable to cocaine exposure (Baroff & Olley, 1999).

Toxins also present a potential hazard to intellectual development after birth. *Mercury poisoning* is known to produce severe physical, emotional, and intellectual impairments, but it does not present a major public health problem because few children are exposed to mercury. Much more threatening to public health is **lead poisoning**. Until banned by federal legislation, the lead commonly used in paint and produced by automobile emissions exposed hundreds of thousands of children to a potentially serious risk. Although controversy continues about the effects of exposure to low levels of lead, at toxic levels lead poisoning can produce a number of adverse behavioural and cognitive impairments, including mental retardation. Despite federal bans on lead-based paints and leaded gasoline, lead poisoning continues to pose a particular risk to children reared in dilapidated housing who may eat peeling, lead-based paint chips (Tesman & Hills, 1994).

*Other Biological Abnormalities* A variety of pregnancy and birth complications also can cause mental retardation. One major complication is *Rh incompatibility*. The Rh factor is a protein found on the surface of red blood cells, and it is a dominant hereditary trait. People who possess this protein are Rh-positive; people who don't are Rh-negative. Rh incompatibility can occur when the mother is Rh-negative and the father is Rh-positive. In such cases the mother can develop antibodies that attack the blood cells of her Rh-positive fetus. The antibodies destroy oxygen-carrying red blood cells in the developing fetus, with a number of adverse consequences, including possible mental retardation.

Rh-negative women develop antibodies only after exposure to their infant's Rh-positive blood. If this exposure occurs at all, it usually does not happen until delivery. Thus the risk of Rh incompatibility in first births is minimal; the greatest risk is for subsequent pregnancies. This risk can be largely prevented, however, by the administration of the antibiotic RhoGAM to the mother within 72 hours after the birth of the first child. RhoGAM prevents the mother's body from developing internal antibodies against the Rh-positive factors, thus eliminating most of the risk for a future pregnancy. In the event that an Rh-negative mother develops antibodies against

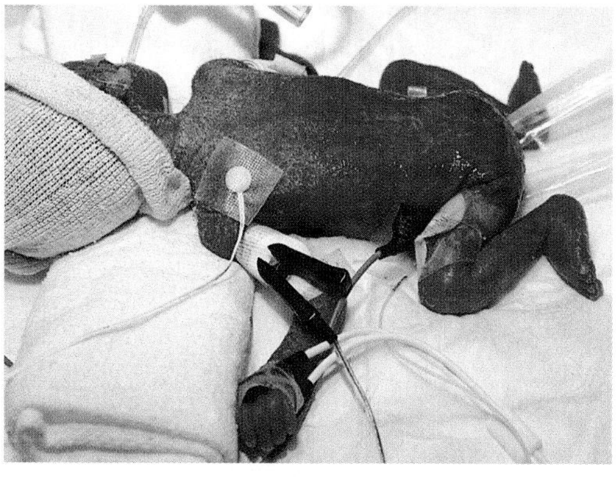

*A newborn of a mother who used crack cocaine. "Crack babies" often are premature and have low birth weights, and they are typically irritable and difficult to soothe.*

Rh-positive factors during pregnancy, a fetal blood transfusion must be carried out to replace the destroyed red blood cells.

Another pregnancy and birth complication that can cause intellectual deficits is *premature birth*. Premature birth is defined either as birth before 38 weeks of gestation or a birth weight of less than $5\frac{1}{2}$ pounds. There are many potential causes of prematurity, including the hereditary, infectious, and toxic factors already discussed. Other risk factors include poor maternal nutrition, maternal age of less than 18 years or more than 35 years, maternal hypertension or diabetes, and damage to the placenta. The effects of prematurity on the infant vary, ranging from few or no deficits to sensory impairments, poor physical development, and mental retardation. More serious consequences occur at lower birth weights, and infant mortality is common at very low weights.

Other known biological causes of mental retardation include extreme difficulties in delivery, particularly *anoxia*, or oxygen deprivation; severe *malnutrition* (which is rare in Canada but a major problem in less developed countries); and the seizure disorder *epilepsy*. The intellectual difficulties associated with each of these causes vary but are potentially significant.

*Normal Genetic Variation* All of the biological causes of mental retardation discussed so far are clear abnormalities in development. The last biological factor we consider, however, focuses on the tail of the normal IQ distribution (see Figure 15–1). These are the cases of mental retardation of unknown etiology—what is often referred to as **cultural-familial retardation**. As the term suggests, cultural-familial retardation tends to run in families and is linked with poverty. A controversial issue is whether this typically mild form of mental retardation is caused primarily by genes or by psychosocial disadvantage.

Normal genetic variation clearly contributes to individual differences in intelligence (Thapar et al., 1994). As summarized in Table 15–5, numerous family, twin, and adoption studies have been conducted on IQ. All of this research points to a substantial genetic contribution to intelligence. For example, the IQs of adopted children are more highly correlated to the IQs of their biological parents than to those of their adoptive ones (Horn, Loehlin, & Willerman, 1979; Plomin & Daniels, 1987).

How much of intelligence is inherited? Behaviour geneticists have calculated indices to measure the extent of genetic contribution to a characteristic, called *heritability ratios*. Estimates generally indicate that 75 percent of the normal range of intelligence is attributable to genetics, but there has been no good research on genetic contributions to cultural-familial retardation (Thapar et al., 1994). We should note, moreover, that heritability ratios can be misleading, because genes and the environment work together, not separately (Dickens & Flynn, 2001; see Research Methods in Chapter 17).

The concept of **reaction range** better conveys how genes and environment interact to determine IQ (Gottesman, 1963). The reaction range concept proposes that heredity determines the upper and lower limits of IQ, and experience determines the extent to which people fulfill their genetic potential. Figure 15–3 portrays some theoretical reaction ranges for children with Down syndrome, cultural-familial retardation, normal intelligence, and superior intelligence. This figure illustrates the key point that genetics and environment determine intelligence together, not independently (Turkheimer, 1991).

**Psychological Factors** Many people misinterpret evidence on the genetic contributions to intelligence and mistakenly conclude that environment matters little or not at all. Environment does matter, not only in influencing the normal range of intelligence but also as a potential cause of mental retardation (Dickens & Flynn, 2001). Grossly abnormal environments can produce gross abnormalities in intelligence, as occurred with Itard's "wild boy."

Other environmentally caused cases of mental retardation have been suggested in more modern studies. For example, Ames and colleagues at Simon Fraser University conducted research into the effects of adoption from Romanian orphanages (Ames & Carter, 1992; Morison, Ames, & Chisholm, 1995). The orphanages were colourless and very quiet, with little visual or auditory stimulation. Children generally spent their days lying or sitting immobile in their cribs. Some of these children were adopted, mostly by families in British Columbia. Some of these adoptees were also enrolled in the B.C. Infant Development Program, which is a province-wide home-based service that offers parents support and suggestions for facilitating their child's development. All of the adopted children were developmentally delayed at the time of the adoption. Once adopted and placed in a more stimulating environment, the majority of children improved in their intellectual and adaptive functioning, although many continued to have academic and behavioural problems at school.

Another example of environmental effects is Koluchova's (1972) case study of the abuse and deprivation experienced by two identical twin boys. Until they were discovered at the age of six, the twins lived in a closet in almost total isolation. Apparently, they were beaten regularly throughout their early life. When discovered, the twins could barely walk, had extremely limited speech, and showed no understanding of abstractions, like photographs. Over several years of intervention, however, their measured intelligence moved from moderate mental retardation when first discovered to the normal range by the age of 11.

Fortunately, cases of such torturous abuse are rare. They illustrate the theoretical contribution of experience to intelligence more than the actual contribution, because most children growing up in Canada live in decent environments, if far from perfect ones. As a social ideal, Canadians hope to provide all citizens with an equally advantaged environment. In working toward this laudable goal, we can overlook the fact that the influence of genes *increases* as environmental variation *decreases*. In fact, *all* individual differences in IQ would be caused by genes if everyone had exactly the same environmental advantages, just like all individual differences would be caused by the environment if everyone had the same genes (see Research Methods in Chapter 17). Ironically, as we succeed in creating a more nurturing and stimulating world for every child, we run the risk of concluding that "environment doesn't matter" unless we remember our successes—and how truly wretched environments can devastate children's intellectual development.

**TABLE 15-5 Correlations between the IQ Scores of Pairs of Relatives Reared Together or Apart**

| | Reared Together | | Reared Apart | |
|---|---|---|---|---|
| **Type of Relative** | **Correlation** | **(N)** | **Correlation** | **(N)** |
| Monozygotic twins | .86 | (4672) | .72 | (65) |
| Dizygotic twins | .60 | (5546) | — | |
| Biological siblings | .47 | (26 473) | .24 | (203) |
| Adoptive siblings | .34 | (369) | — | |
| Parent–child | .42 | (8633) | .22 | (814) |
| Adoptive parent–child | .19 | (1397) | — | |

*Source:* Adapted from T.J. Bouchard, Jr., and M. McGue, 1981, Familial studies of intelligence: A review. *Science, 212,* 1055–1059. Copyright © 1981 by the American Association for the Advancement of Science.

**Theoretical Reaction Ranges of IQ Scores for Groups with Differing Genetic Predispositions**

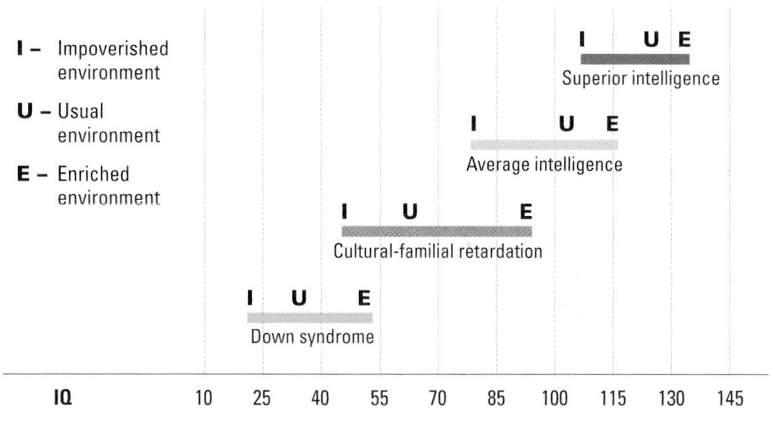


**FIGURE 15-3: According to the reaction range concept, genes set the limit on IQ and environment determines variation within the limits. Note that the usual environmental contributions to IQ differs among the four groups.**

*Source:* G.S. Baroff, 1986, *Mental retardation: Nature, cause, and management,* p. 151. Washington, DC: Hemisphere.

**Social Factors** Today, the range of environments in Canada still includes many undesirable circumstances for children. Tens of thousands of children are reared in psychosocial disadvantage in our cities and in the equally unstimulating environments found among the rural poor. To give you an idea of the scope of the problem, a large survey of major Canadian cities found that 30 percent of children aged 14 or younger were living in poverty (Lee, 2000).

Cultural-familial retardation is found far more frequently among the poor. Part of this association certainly is due to the fact that lower intelligence can cause lower social status. People with a below-average IQ will generally make less money in our society; thus they will remain in, or move into, lower socioeconomic classes. However, part of the link between poverty and cultural-familial retardation is caused by the effects of psychosocial disadvantage in lowering IQ scores.

Impoverished environments lack the *stimulation* and *responsiveness* required to promote children's intellectual and social skills throughout their development (Floyd, Costigan, & Phillippe, 1997). A stimulating environment challenges children's developing intellectual skills. Toys and other playthings make the toddler's environment interesting to explore. A responsive environment offers encouragement for their pursuits. Parents or siblings mimic the infant's first sounds and words.

Studies of adopted children demonstrate the positive effects of stimulating and responsive environments (Turkheimer, 1991). A famous early study by Skodak and Skeels (1949) demonstrated that children who were adopted away from unfortunate circumstances early in life achieved IQ scores at least 12 points higher on average than those of their biological mothers. More recent studies have found similarly dramatic increases (Capron & Duyme, 1989; Schiff et al., 1982). The potential for increasing IQ by 10 to 15 points obviously holds important implications for prevention and intervention. Many people with cultural-familial retardation could function normally if stimulating and responsive environments helped them to achieve their potential to function near the upper end of their reaction range.

## Treatment: Prevention and Normalization

Three major categories of intervention are essential in the treatment of mental retardation. First, many cases of both organic and cultural-familial mental retardation can be prevented through adequate maternal and child health care, as well as early psychoeducational programs. Second, educational, psychological, and biomedical treatments can help people with mental retardation to raise their achievement levels. Third, the lives of people with mental retardation can be normalized through mainstreaming in public schools and promoting care in the community.

**Primary Prevention** The availability and use of good maternal and child health care is one major step toward the primary prevention of many biological causes of mental retardation. Healthcare measures include specific actions, such as vaccinations for rubella and the detection and treatment of infectious diseases like syphilis. In addition, an adequate diet and abstinence from alcohol, cigarettes, and other drugs are essential to the health of pregnant women and the welfare of the developing fetus.

## CANADIAN FOCUS Involuntary Sterilization and the Eugenics Movement

During the late nineteenth and early twentieth centuries, the **eugenics** movement gained popularity throughout Canada and the United States. This movement was based on the belief that crimes, sexually transmitted disease, unwanted pregnancies, and other social problems were largely a result of mental retardation and other forms of psychopathology. It was believed that these disorders were primarily a result of heredity. In hindsight, these ideas are simplistic and flawed. But given the current state of knowledge at the time the views seemed convincing, both to professionals and the public. Sexual sterilization of people with mental retardation and other disorders was seen as a way improving the gene pool and reducing crime and other social problems.

In the early 1900s the United States began to implement legislation to sexually sterilize people considered to be "mentally defective" or suffering from other major mental disorders. The primary focus was on people considered to be mentally retarded. In 1928 Alberta passed the Sexual Sterilization Act and began sterilizing people deemed to be in danger of transmitting mental deficiency to their children, or incapable of intelligent parenthood. The act was later strengthened so that it was not necessary to obtain informed consent from the person or from his or her parents. A similar act was introduced in 1933 in British Columbia (Park & Radford, 1998). A leading figure in promoting sterilization was Dr. Clarence Hincks. Writing in *Maclean's* magazine in 1946, he asserted that:

> Subnormality and mental unfitness seem to be on the increase in Canada . . . we can expect the percentage to mount unless we act soon to improve the mental quality of our stock. For the mentally unfit are apparently breeding faster than the fit, and will continue to do so until we prevent those with undesirable hereditary traits from passing their disabilities on to their children . . . we have abundant evidence in Canada that the free propagation of mental subnormals is carrying us far in the direction of race deterioration. . . . It is my conviction that highly selective eugenical

*continued*

*cont.*

sterilisation should be part of our expanding health programs. (Cited in Park & Radford, 1998, p. 319)

Between 1928 and 1972 more than 4000 Canadians were forcibly sexually sterilized, mostly in Alberta but also in B.C. (Woodill, 1992). Several surgical methods were used. Males received either a vasectomy (removal of the vas deferens, which is the sperm duct from the testicle to the urethra) or an orchidectomy (removal of the testicles). Orchidectomy served a dual purpose of preventing procreation and supposedly reducing sexually aggressive behaviour. Females received either a salpingectomy (removal of the fallopian tube) or an oophorectomy (removal of ovaries) (Park & Radford, 1998). Some of the victims were misinformed about the operation (e.g., told they were having their appendix removed).

The eugenics movement gradually lost favour in Canada and other Western countries, partly in reaction to the barbaric Nazi eugenic policies, and partly because the basic tenets of eugenics were found to be flawed: for example, mental retardation is not entirely due to genes; eugenic policies do not necessarily improve the gene pool; and social problems are a result of many factors interacting in complex ways, and cannot be blamed on mental retardation. The sterilization acts were repealed in the 1970s. The Canadian Charter of Rights and Freedoms was later revised (e.g., in 1992) to firmly establish the rights of people with mental retardation. Effective specialized training programs were also developed to help them with their parenting skills (e.g., Tymchuk, Andron, & Tymchuk, 1990).

In a precedent-setting lawsuit, sterilization victim Leilani Muir received a government settlement of $750 000 in 1996. She was sterilized in 1959 at age 14, without her knowledge or consent, after being misdiagnosed as mentally retarded. Later IQ testing revealed that her intelligence was, in fact, in the low-normal range (*Edmonton Journal,* September 9, 1995, p. B2). Lawsuits were subsequently filed by other victims of involuntary sterilization. In Alberta, the government agreed to pay $140 million to more than 800 victims (*Edmonton Journal,* February 13, 2000, p. A6). Government officials issued a statement of profound regret for what had happened to these people. ◆

Planning for childbearing can also help prevent mental retardation. Pregnancy and birth complications are notably more common among mothers younger than 18 and older than 35. Although most babies born to women outside this age range are healthy and normal, many women are aware of the statistical risks and attempt to time their pregnancies accordingly. Children of teenage mothers also face a much greater threat of a life of poverty—a pressing issue, given the high percentage of children born to adolescent mothers. To illustrate, 11 percent of children in Saskatchewan and 17 percent of children in the Northwest Territories are born to adolescent mothers (Statistics Canada, 1999).

A more controversial means of preventing retardation is through diagnostic testing and selective abortion. One diagnostic procedure is **amniocentesis**, in which fluid is extracted from the amniotic sac that protects the fetus during pregnancy. Some chromosomal and genetic defects in the fetus can be determined from testing the amniotic fluid, leaving parents with the extremely difficult decision of whether to terminate the pregnancy if an abnormality is found. In the future, *gene therapy* may instead offer the opportunity for treating the developing fetus.

At present, many parents opt for amniocentesis despite the emotional turmoil created by the possibility of selective abortion. The procedure is particularly common among older women, whose infants are at a greatly increased risk for Down syndrome. Because amniocentesis increases the risk of miscarriage, there has been a search for noninvasive tests for Down syndrome. It is now possible to diagnosis the disorder by examining the flat nose that is characteristic of Down syndrome with *ultrasound*, a technique that uses harmless sound waves to create an image of the fetus during pregnancy (Cuckle, 2001). Ultrasound also has the advantage of being able to detect Down syndrome in the first trimester of pregnancy versus the second trimester with amniocentesis. Unfortunately, the specialized skills needed to use ultrasound to detect Down syndrome are not yet widespread.

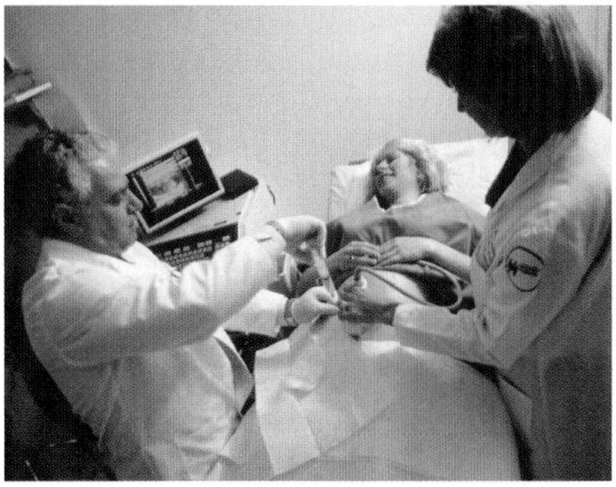

*During amniocentesis, amniotic fluid is extracted from the sac protecting the fetus. Tests of the amniotic fluid can detect some genetic and chromosomal defects that cause mental retardation.*

**Secondary Prevention** In addition to medical and healthcare measures, early social and educational interventions can lead to the secondary prevention of cultural-familial retardation. The most important current secondary prevention effort is Head Start, an American intervention program begun in 1964. The goals of Head Start include providing preschool children living in poverty with early educational experiences, nutrition, and healthcare monitoring. Evidence indicates that Head Start produces short-term increases in IQ (5 to 10 points) and achievement. The academic advantages diminish or disappear within a few years after intervention ends, but data indicate that children who participate in Head Start are less likely to repeat a grade or to be placed in special education classes. They also are more likely to graduate from high school (McKey et al., 1985; Zigler & Styfco, 1993). These data indicate that Head Start undoubtedly reduces the prevalence of cultural-familial retardation through its influence on adaptive behaviour if not on IQ itself. Recently in Canada, an Aboriginal Head Start program has been developed and implemented. Similar to the American counterpart, the results of the Canadian program have been promising (Health Canada, 2002b).

More specific evidence on preventing mental retardation through early intervention comes from two research programs (Garber, 1988; Ramey & Bryant, 1982). Both interventions offered a variety of services to children of mothers with below-average IQs, and both used control groups to assess the effectiveness of intervention. Gains of 20 or more points in IQ have been reported for experimental versus control children in one program (Garber, 1988), but questions about the methods of this study suggest that they be interpreted with caution (Baroff & Olley, 1999). More modest gains of 5 to 10 IQ points have been reported for the Abcedarian Project. Regardless of the magnitude of change, these projects, together with adoption studies and findings from Head Start, indicate that at least some cases of familial retardation can be prevented by increasing environmental stimulation and responsiveness.

**Tertiary Prevention** A huge array of services has been developed for the tertiary prevention and treatment of the various cognitive, socioemotional, and medical difficulties faced by people with mental retardation from birth through adult life. Given the volume of work devoted to the subject, we can only touch on a few treatments here.

One of the most important aspects of tertiary prevention is careful assessment early in life. Medical screening is essential for certain conditions such as PKU, as is the early detection of mental retardation through cognitive tests. Unfortunately, many cases of mental retardation are not detected early, as the doubling in prevalence during the school years indicates. Public screening of children's academic potential typically is not conducted until school age, and as we have noted, the intelligence tests available for infants and preschoolers are of questionable reliability and validity.

Accurate detection is important, because early interventions can benefit children diagnosed with mental retardation. Intervention with infants typically takes place in the home and focuses on stimulating the infant, educating parents, and promoting good parent–infant relationships (Shearer & Shearer, 1976). During the preschool years, special instruction may take place in child development centres, which also offer respite care for the parents who need relief from the added demands of rearing a child with mental retardation.

Treatment of the social and emotional needs of people with mental retardation is an essential component of their care. Treatment may include teaching basic self-care skills, such as feeding, toileting, and dressing, during the younger ages and various "life-survival" skills at later ages. Children with mental retardation may also need treatment for unusual behaviours, such as self-stimulation or aggressiveness. In general, research indicates that operant behaviour therapy is the most effective treatment approach (Bernard, 2002). Still, the effectiveness of behavioural approaches in absolute terms has been questioned, because problem behaviour may remain despite some improvements (Schotti et al., 1991).

Medical care for physical and sensory handicaps is critical in the treatment of certain types of mental retardation. In addition, medications are helpful in treating disorders such as epilepsy that may co-occur with mental retardation.

Medication is not especially helpful in treating the intellectual or socioemotional problems of people with mental retardation. Nevertheless, estimates indicate that 30 to 50 percent of institutionalized people with mental retardation are prescribed medication, often inappropriately, to control their behaviour problems (Singh, Guernsey, & Ellis, 1992). Neuroleptics (discussed in Chapter 13) are used with particular frequency to treat aggressiveness and other uncontrolled behaviour in institutions (Grossman, 1983). In some institutional settings, these drugs have been used primarily to sedate patients, and various public exposés have raised broad questions about their misuse (Scheerenberger, 1982). The use of neuroleptics with mental retardation is especially questionable because behaviour therapy provides a safe treatment alternative (Matson & Frame, 1986).

**Normalization** **Normalization** is a major focus of the treatment of mental retardation. Normalization means that people with mental retardation are entitled to live as much as possible like other members of society. Major goals of normalization include mainstreaming children into public schools and promoting a role in the community for adults with mental retardation.

Schooling is of great importance to children with mental retardation. According to legislation in Canada and in some other countries, all handicapped children have a right to a free and appropriate education in the least restrictive environment. Within the limits set by the handicapping condition, services should be provided in a setting that restricts personal liberty as little as possible.

For many children with mental retardation, particularly those with mild retardation, providing the least restrictive environment means **mainstreaming** them into regular classrooms. Rather than being taught in special classes, children with mental retardation enter the mainstream and receive as much of their education as possible in normal classrooms. Unfortunately, there are broad inconsistencies in the extent of mainstreaming and in the quality of support services provided to children with mental retardation across school districts (Robinson et al., 2000). The lack of consistent quality is a matter of concern, because some evidence indicates that children with mental retardation who are mainstreamed into regular classrooms learn as much as or more than they do in special classes. Advocates argue that children with mental retardation have a right to education in the least restrictive environment, regardless of the academic outcome of mainstreaming (Baroff & Olley, 1999; see also Chapter 18).

*A mother with her son who has Down syndrome. The two-year-old was receiving speech, physical, and occupational therapy as a part of tertiary prevention efforts.*

The *deinstitutionalization* movement that began in mental hospitals in the 1960s (see Chapter 18) also has greatly helped to normalize the lives of people with mental retardation. Between 1970 and 1981, the number of people with mental retardation living in institutions significantly dropped throughout Canada and the United States. For example, before 1974 Ontario had more than 10 000 individuals living in these institutions. In 1996 there were fewer than 2500 (Goldberg, 1996). Deinstitutionalization has been particularly rapid for those with milder forms of mental retardation. Of those now living in institutions, it is estimated that 7 percent have mild, 13 percent have moderate, 24 percent have severe, and 56 percent have profound levels of retardation (Baroff, 1986; Baroff & Olley, 1999). Evidence indicates that people with mental retardation who move from institutions to the community receive better care and function at a higher level. Despite some continued fear and prejudice, it is clear that people with mental retardation contribute to communities through their work, their play, and their relationships with all of us.

## Autistic Disorder and Pervasive Developmental Disorders

The **pervasive developmental disorders** are unusual problems that begin early in life and involve severe impairments in a number of areas of functioning. People with pervasive developmental disorders exhibit profound disturbances in relationships, engage in unusual behaviours, and typically have substantial communication difficulties. These difficulties are pronounced in **autistic disorder** (also known as **autism**), the most thoroughly researched form of pervasive developmental disorder. In fact, some experts prefer the term *autistic spectrum disorders* over *pervasive developmental disorders* (Lord & Bailey, 2002). The dictionary definition of the word *autism* is "absorption in one's own mental activity," but the term grossly understates the profound social disturbances that accompany the disorder.

Autistic disorder was brought to the public's awareness by Dustin Hoffman's stirring portrayal of Raymond in the movie *Rain Man*. The portrayal misrepresented some aspects of autism; for example, no one with autism can count hundreds of toothpicks as they fall to the floor. As we discuss shortly, however, some people with autism have highly unusual, specialized talents, and the character of Raymond was an accurate portrait of other aspects of a *good* adult outcome for autism. Because pervasive developmental disorders have been the subject of considerable theorizing and research, most of our discussion focuses on autistic disorder. We begin with a case study.

## Typical Symptoms and Associated Features

Like John, most children with autistic disorder are normal in physical appearance. Some observers have even suggested that they are especially attractive youngsters. Although they sometimes have unusual actions and postures (Wing, 1988), their body movements are not grossly uncoordinated, and their physical

## CASE STUDY A Child with Autistic Disorder

John was $3\frac{1}{2}$ years old when he was first seen at a treatment centre that specialized in autism. He spoke very little, and most of what he said wasn't meaningful. He used no names for himself or for others. If asked "What is your name?" he repeated "Name?" rather than answering "John." John would sometimes respond "you, you" as an affirmative answer to the question "Do you want something to eat?" This odd response was one of his few verbalizations that conveyed any meaning.

John's relationships were equally troubling. He literally showed no interest in other people. His parents reported that he never did such everyday things as seeking them out for play or sitting in their laps just to cuddle. In fact, John sometimes would throw a violent tantrum when he was touched. His mother said that when she tried to hug him, John frequently screamed in apparent pain and twirled away from her. She touched him rarely because of these horrible reactions. John was equally uninterested in his six-year-old sister, who was functioning normally. He didn't tease her or follow her around like most little brothers. In fact, he didn't even seem to know she existed. John also was terrified of the gentle family dog. The dog was kept tied up when John was awake, because its attempts to play with John provoked fearful tantrums.

According to his parents, John was most content when he was by himself in the family room at home. He liked to have the television set turned on, although his parents felt that he didn't really watch or understand the shows. He would sit on the floor near the set and rock back and forth for hours. He spent several hours like this every day.

John's parents could remember no particular incident that marked the beginning of his problems. They became aware of them gradually as John failed to meet some normal developmental milestones. They recalled that John had been an easy baby, but they now felt that his meagre need for attention may have been an early sign of his problems. His parents were concerned by his very limited speech and odd behaviour as a toddler, but they were reassured by the fact that he had learned to walk at the appropriate age and otherwise seemed normal physically. John's pediatrician also had been reassuring about the boy's apparently delayed development, until his annual checkup at age three. That was when the pediatrician suggested that John might have mental retardation. After subsequent visits to several mental health professionals in their community, John's parents were referred to a treatment centre that specialized in autism.

John was diagnosed by members of the centre staff as suffering from autistic disorder. The centre had an inpatient program for children with autism that used intensive behaviour modification, but John's parents wanted him to remain with them. The centre staff gave the parents extensive information about autism and about behaviour modification programs, and they referred the family to a child development centre in their community. The centre offered preschool programs for children with mental retardation, and the staff would help the parents attempt to teach John language and self-care skills. The centre also would give John's parents a break from the demands of caring for him. The staff warned John's parents, however, that without intensive inpatient treatment or truly heroic efforts on their part, John would continue to have severe difficulties with language, social relationships, and age-appropriate activities. ◆

growth and development is generally normal. Judging from physical appearance alone, you would not expect children with autistic disorder to have severe psychological impairments.

Early onset is another feature of autism illustrated by the case of John. Autism begins early in life, and in retrospect many parents recall abnormalities that seem to date back to birth. Other children seem to be developing normally, but they either stop learning new skills like speaking a few words or may lose the skills they have acquired. Because very young children with autism look normal and typically make few demands, the condition may not be accurately diagnosed for a few years. In the majority of cases, however, parents become aware that their child is profoundly disturbed by the age of three (Short & Schopler, 1988). By this time, parents have noted the child's impaired communication abilities, one of the three classic symptoms of autism. The other two central symptoms are impairments in social interaction and stereotyped patterns of behaviour, interests, and activities.

In the following sections we discuss these three defining symptoms. We also discuss other notable symptoms commonly found among people with autism and other pervasive developmental disorders, specifically apparent sensory deficits, self-injurious behaviour, and savant performance—highly specialized abilities found in some rare but fascinating cases.

**The Sally–Ann Task**

**FIGURE 15–4: Where will Sally (on left) look for the marble? Many children with autism answer "in the box," evidence that they may lack a "theory of mind."**

*Source:* U. Frith, 1989, *Autism: Explaining the Enigma*, p. 41. Oxford: Basil Blackwell.

**Impaired Social Interaction** Many mental health professionals view the inability to relate to others as the central feature of autistic disorder. Social impairments range from relatively mild oddities, such as a lack of social or emotional reciprocity, to extreme difficulties in which there is little awareness of the existence of others, let alone of their perspective. Some children and adults with pervasive developmental disorders treat other people as if they were confusing and foreign objects rather than as sources of protection, comfort, and reciprocal stimulation.

A contemporary viewpoint argues that people with autism lack a **theory of mind**—that is, they fail to appreciate that other people have a point of reference that differs from their own (Baron-Cohen, Tager-Flusberg, & Cohen, 1993). The concept of theory of mind is best illustrated by the "Sally–Ann task" (see Figure 15–4). In the Sally–Ann task, the test child is shown two dolls, Sally, who has a basket, and Ann, who has a box. Sally puts a marble in her basket and then leaves. While Sally is gone, Ann takes the marble out of Sally's basket and puts it into her own box. When Sally returns, the question is: Where will she look for her marble?

Sally should look for the marble in her basket, where she left it, because she did not see Ann hide it. However, children with autism typically fail to appreciate Sally's perspective—they lack a theory of mind. In one early study, 80 percent of children with autism said Sally would search in Ann's box, whereas only 14 percent of children with Down syndrome made the same error (Baron-Cohen, Leslie, & Frith, 1985).

Theory of mind has proved to be a useful, overarching concept for understanding social disturbances in autistic disorder (Happe, 1995; Rutter, 1996), but the problems are emotional as well as cognitive. In fact, many people with pervasive developmental disorders appear to be missing the basic, inborn tendency to form attachments with other people. As infants, they do not show the attachment behaviours that help normal children form a special bond with their caregivers. In retrospect, many parents remember that their children did not seek them out in times of distress, nor were they comforted by physical contact. Social impairments continue as children with pervasive developmental disorder show little interest in their peers. They do not engage in spontaneous social play, and they fail to develop friendships as they grow older. They also exhibit *gaze aversion*; that is, they actively avoid eye contact.

Even those adults who achieve exceptionally good outcomes continue to show severely disturbed social emotions and understanding. Consider the remarkable case of Temple Grandin, a woman who achieved what may be the most successful outcome of autism on record.

## CASE STUDY Temple Grandin: An Anthropologist on Mars

Temple Grandin, a woman who is now in her forties, suffered from the classic symptoms of autism as a child. She had not developed language by the age of three, and she threw wild tantrums in response to social initiations, even gentle attempts to give her a hug. Grandin spent hours staring into space, playing with objects, or simply rocking or spinning herself. She also engaged in other unusual behaviours, such as repeatedly smearing her own feces. With the extensive help of her parents and teachers, and with her own determination, however, Grandin developed complex strategies to help her compensate for, and cope with, her severe psychological impairments. Remarkably, she even earned a Ph.D. in animal science and has developed widely used techniques for managing cattle. In stark contrast to Grandin, the majority of people with autism spend most of their adult life in institutions.

One of Grandin's most complex coping strategies is "computing" how other people feel and how she should react in social circumstances. Like the characters of Data or Mr. Spock from the *Star Trek* series, with whom she identifies, Grandin does not experience normal human emotions and motivations. Rather, she describes herself as "an anthropologist on Mars." Like an anthropologist in a strange culture, she has had to learn how to relate to the human species through careful observation of "their" behaviour. Grandin details her struggles with social situations and other aspects of autism in two autobiographies, *Emergence: Labelled Autistic* and *Thinking in Pictures*. The neurologist Oliver Sacks has also written a detailed case study about Grandin. The following excerpt from Sacks's observations illustrates some of Grandin's social struggles.

> "I can tell if a human being is angry," she told me, "or if he's smiling." At the level of the sensorimotor, the concrete, the unmediated, the animal, Temple has no difficulty. But what about children, I asked her. Were they not intermediate between animals and adults? On the contrary, Temple said, she had great difficulties with children—trying to talk with them, to join in their games (she could not even play peekaboo with a baby, she said, because she would get the timing all wrong)—as she had had such difficulties herself as a child. Children, she feels, are already far advanced, by the age of three or four, along a path that she, as an autistic person, has never advanced far on. Little children, she feels, already "understand" other human beings in a way she can never hope to. (Sacks, 1995, p. 270)

Although she feels that she lacks even children's understanding of social motivations, Grandin apparently has residual traces of human needs, such as the need for physical contact. Still, she finds human touch—hugging—overwhelming. As a result, Grandin developed another remarkable strategy to compensate for her

deep-seated aversion to human touch. She developed a "squeeze machine," a device that gives her a soothing, mechanical hug. In *Thinking in Pictures*, Grandin describes her development of her squeeze machine:

> From as far back as I can remember, I always hated to be hugged. I wanted to experience the good feeling of being hugged, but it was just too overwhelming. It was like a great all-engulfing tidal wave of stimulation, and I reacted like a wild animal .... After visiting my aunt's ranch in Arizona . . . I watched cattle being put in the squeeze chute for their vaccinations, I noticed some of them relaxed. . . . I asked Aunt Ann to press the squeeze sides against me and to close the head restraint bars around my neck. I hoped it would calm my anxiety. At first there were a few moments of sheer panic as I stiffened up and tried to pull away from the pressure. . . . Five seconds later I felt a wave of relaxation. . . . I copied the design and built the first human squeeze machine out of plywood panels when I returned to school. (Grandin, 1995, pp. 62–63)

We have numerous descriptions of the unusual behaviour of people with autistic disorder. But social and communicative impairments typically prevent us from learning about the inner world of autism. Temple Grandin offers us a compelling exception to the rule. Throughout the remainder of this chapter, we quote from *Thinking in Pictures* in an attempt to offer some insight into autism from the inside.

**Impaired Communication** In addition to their dramatic social isolation, people with pervasive developmental disorders suffer from a variety of impairments in communication. The communication problems often are severe, but there can be a range of difficulties. Some children fail to speak at all between the ages of one and two, the time when normal children typically learn their first words. Others learn a few rudimentary words such as "Mama" and then suddenly lose their language abilities. Still other children progress further in acquiring language, but they either lose their abilities or stop progressing at the normal rate of language acquisition (Schreibman, 1988). Many children with autism remain mute, and about half never acquire functional language (Volkmar et al., 1994). According to field studies conducted for DSM-IV, 54 percent of patients with autism remain mute, compared with 35 percent of patients with other pervasive developmental disorders (Volkmar et al., 1994).

Many unusual features are found in the language of people with pervasive developmental disorders who do learn to speak. For one, the subtleties of speaking style often are unusual, a problem referred to as *dysprosody*. In dysprosody, speech production is disturbed in its rate, rhythm, and intonation. This makes the disturbed child or adult sound highly unusual to the normal listener, even when the speech content is normal.

*Echolalia* is another common language problem. People with autism or other pervasive developmental disorders frequently repeat phrases that are spoken to them, or sometimes repeatedly echo a phrase they heard at an earlier time. As with other problems, there is a dramatic contrast with normal development. When the mother of a 1½-year-old points to herself and says, "Who is this?" normal toddlers will respond with "Mama." A 10-year-old child with autism and echolalia will respond to the same question by repeating "Who is this?"

Another common language problem is *pronoun reversal*. Children and adults with pervasive developmental disorder are especially likely to confuse the pronoun "you" with the pronoun "I." They say "You want a cookie" when they mean "I want a cookie." According to one interpretation, pronoun reversal indicates that children with autism have failed to *individuate*, that is, to become a separate person (Bettelheim, 1967). A simpler explanation is that pronoun reversal demonstrates a lack of understanding of speech. Lacking a deeper understanding of the meaning of pronouns, some people with pervasive developmental disorders refer to themselves as "you," not "I."

The speech difficulties are not the products of auditory or other sensory problems, nor are they simply disturbances in the mechanics of speech. Rather, the difficulties stem from basic disturbances in the ability to communicate and, even more basically, in the ability to imitate or reciprocate interactions. Unlike infants and toddlers who are deaf or mute, children with autism do not easily use gestures as substitutes for speech. In fact, some children do not engage in the social imitation that is essential for learning basic skills. Once again, theory of mind offers a possible explanation for these deficits. In many respects, children with autism seem to lack the essential motivation for communicating with others. Their communication difficulties convey the failure to appreciate the perspective—or even the existence—of other minds (Tager-Flusberg, 1996).

Even high-functioning people with pervasive developmental disorders like Temple Grandin who have relatively well-developed language skills nevertheless demonstrate a limited ability to communicate about or understand abstractions. They may fail to generate unique or imaginative speech, and they have difficulty comprehending abstractions like metaphors. Thus the language problems in the pervasive developmental disorders apparently involve restrictions in thinking, not just in expression. Here is how Temple Grandin describes her struggles with language and abstraction:

> I can remember the frustration of not being able to talk at age three. This caused me to throw many a tantrum. I could understand what people said to me, but I could not get my words out. It was like a big stutter, and starting words was

> difficult. My first few words were very difficult to produce and generally had only one syllable, such as "bah" for "ball." (1995, p. 45)
>
> Autistics have problems learning things that cannot be thought about in pictures. The easiest words for an autistic child to learn are nouns, because they are directly related to pictures. . . . Spatial words such as "over" and "under" had no meaning for me until I had a visual image to fix them in my memory. Even now, when I hear the word "under" by itself, I automatically picture myself getting under the cafeteria tables at school during an air-raid drill, a common occurrence on the East Coast during the early fifties. . . . When I read, I translate written words into colour movies or I simply store a photo of the written page to be read later. When I retrieve material, I see a photocopy of the page in my imagination. I can then read it like a TelePrompTer. . . . When I am unable to convert text to pictures, it is usually because the text has no concrete meaning. Some philosophy books and articles about the cattle futures market are simply incomprehensible. (pp. 29–31)

**Stereotyped Behaviour, Interests, and Activities** The third major symptom of autism and other pervasive developmental disorders is restricted, repetitive, and stereotyped patterns of behaviour, interests, and activities. Many children with autistic disorder literally spend hours spinning a top or flapping a string in front of their eyes. Others might become uncontrollably agitated if the arrangement of furniture in a room is changed even slightly. Compulsively rigid adherence to daily routines is yet another aspect of these restricted activities and interests.

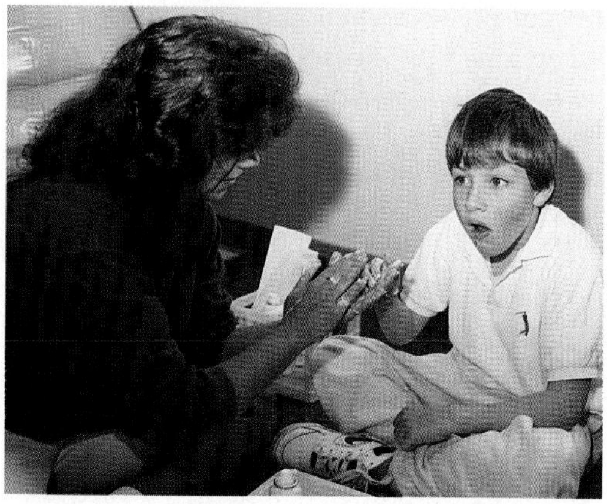

*Children with autistic disorder, like the child in this picture, are normal in physical appearance. The communication problems, autistic aloneness, and need to preserve sameness are readily apparent among children with autism, however.*

Not surprisingly, these odd preoccupations and rituals create social complications. People unfamiliar with the disorder are likely to find such behaviour bizarre and perhaps frightening. The ritualistic behaviour also causes numerous problems for those who are trying to manage and educate children with autism. How do you educate a child who is totally preoccupied with flapping a string in front of his or her face for hours?

What purpose does such stereotyped behaviour serve for the disturbed individual? Rituals such as flapping a string or spinning a top seem to serve no other function than to provide sensory feedback. Thus they are often referred to as *self-stimulation*. The common interpretation of self-stimulation is that the child with autism receives too little sensory input, and that ritual self-stimulation increases sensation to a more desirable level. We prefer an alternative interpretation. The stimulation of everyday environments has been described as overwhelming by several high-functioning people with pervasive developmental disorders. Perhaps self-stimulation reduces rather than increases sensory input by making the stimulation monotonously predictable. In fact, all of the stereotyped behaviour found in pervasive developmental disorders may serve the function of making a terrifying world more constant and predictable and therefore less frightening. Again, here are some comments by Temple Grandin on the topic:

> When left alone, I would often space out and become hypnotized. I could sit for hours on the beach watching sand dribbling through my fingers. I'd study each individual grain of sand as it flowed between my fingers. Each grain was different, and I was like a scientist studying the grains under a microscope. As I scrutinized their shapes and contours, I went into a trance which cut me off from the sights and sounds around me.
>
> Rocking and spinning were other ways to shut out the world when I became overloaded with too much noise. Rocking made me feel calm. It was like taking an addictive drug. The more I did it, the more I wanted to do it. My mother and my teachers would stop me so I would get back in touch with the rest of the world. (pp. 44–45)

**Apparent Sensory Deficits** Some people with pervasive developmental disorders respond to auditory, tactile, or visual sensations in a highly unusual and idiosyncratic manner. For example, some people with autistic disorder occasionally respond as if they were deaf, even though their hearing is intact. This unresponsiveness is an example of an *apparent sensory deficit* (Lovaas et al., 1971). There is no impairment in the sense organ, but the individual's responding makes it appear otherwise. Even more puzzling is that the same person who fails to be startled by a sudden crack of thunder may scream in apparent pain in reaction to a small sound like the scratch of chalk on a blackboard (Schreibman, 1988). This inconsistency suggests that the problem lies at some higher level of perception rather than at a lower level of sensation. The sensory apparatus is intact, but some cortical abnormality in integrating and perceiving sensory input creates these unusual reactions to sounds, sights, and touches. Temple Grandin has argued that psychological researchers have not paid sufficient attention to this aspect of autistic disorder. Here are some of her comments on her own experience:

> When I was little, loud noises were also a problem, often feeling like a dentist's drill hitting a nerve. They actually caused pain. I was scared to death of balloons popping, because the sound was like an explosion in my ear. Minor noises that most people can tune out drove me to distraction. When I was in college, my roommate's hair dryer sounded like a jet plane taking off. (p. 67)

**Self-Injury** *Self-injurious behaviour* is one of the most bizarre and dangerous difficulties that can accompany autism and other pervasive developmental disorders. The most common forms of self-injury are repeated head banging and biting the fingers and wrists (Rutter, Greenfield, & Lockyer, 1967). The resultant injuries may involve only minor bruises, or they can be severe enough to cause broken bones, brain damage, and even death. It is important that this self-injury not be misinterpreted as suicidal behaviour. The child with autism does not have enough self-awareness to be truly suicidal. Instead, self-injury seems to have several possible causes, the most widely accepted of which is self-stimulation (Carr, 1977). Fortunately, self-injury can be treated effectively with behaviour modification techniques, as we discuss later.

**Savant Performance** One of the most intriguing characteristics of pervasive developmental disorders is when a child occasionally shows **savant performance**—an exceptional ability in a highly specialized area of functioning. Savant performance typically involves artistic, musical, or mathematical skills. The image on this page portrays the savant artistic abilities of Nadia, a girl with autism who drew this picture when she was just five years old (Selfe, 1977).

No one has an adequate theory, let alone an explanation, for savant performance. Unfortunately, one aspect does seem clear: Despite what many people had hoped, the existence of savant performance does not indicate that children with autistic disorder have superior intelligence. Most people with autism do not show savant performance, and most autistics also have mental retardation. According to McGill University researchers, IQs may be somewhat higher when the disorder is defined more broadly (Chakrabarti & Fombonne, 2001), although the best estimates are that about a quarter of children with autism have IQs below 55, about half have IQs between 55 and 70, and only one-quarter have IQs over 70 (Volkmar et al., 1994; see Table 15–6).

*Nadia, a girl with autistic disorder, drew this picture when she was about five years old. Like Nadia, some children with autistic disorder demonstrate savant performance, typically in drawing ability, musical performance, mathematical calculations, or feats of memory.*

**TABLE 15-6 IQ Scores for Patients with Autism and Other Pervasive Developmental Disorders**

| | Autism | | Other Pervasive Developmental Disorders | |
|---|---|---|---|---|
| IQ Score | *N* | Percent | *N* | Percent |
| >70 | 118 | 26.0 | 122 | 50.8 |
| 55–70 | 197 | 43.4 | 61 | 25.4 |
| <20–54 | 114 | 25.1 | 53 | 22.1 |
| Unspecified | 25 | 5.5 | 4 | 1.7 |

Data from the DSM-IV field trials confirmed that most people with autism also have mental retardation.

*Source:* Based on F.R. Volkmar et al., 1994, Field trial for autistic disorder in DSM-IV. *American Journal of Psychiatry, 151,* 1361–1367.

Moreover, the IQ scores of children with autistic disorder are stable over time, and they predict future educational attainment (Schreibman, 1988).

## Classification

**Brief Historical Perspective** The history of the classification of the pervasive developmental disorders is very brief. The syndrome of "early infantile autism" was first described in 1943 by psychiatrist Leo Kanner (1894–1981). Among the characteristics that Kanner (1943) noted were an inability to form relationships with others, delayed or noncommunicative speech, a demand for sameness in the environment, stereotyped play activities, and lack of imagination. To Kanner's credit, contemporary diagnostic criteria are very similar to the symptoms he described.

*Psychiatrist **Leo Kanner** (1894–1981) promoted the study of psychological problems among children. Kanner was noted for his identification of autism as a distinct psychological disorder.*

Whereas Kanner's contributions are well known, mental health professionals have only recently recognized that the Viennese psychiatrist Hans Asperger (1944/1991) identified a very similar condition at virtually the same time as Kanner. One important difference, however, was that Asperger's patients exhibited higher intellectual functioning. The distinction between Kanner's and Asperger's patients was introduced into the formal diagnostic nomenclature in DSM-IV. **Asperger's disorder** is now listed as a subtype of pervasive developmental disorder. Descriptively, it is identical to autism, with the exception that the disorder involves no clinically significant delay in language. A recent review from Mary Konstantereas (2001) at the University of Guelph indicates that Asperger's syndrome is quite different from autism, even high-functioning autism.

Kanner's and Asperger's observations have stood the test of time. In contrast, another event is memorable for the misunderstanding that it caused. For several decades, the term *childhood schizophrenia* was used to classify autism and other severe forms of childhood psychosis (Bender, 1947). However, as shown by various researchers, including University of Guelph psychologist Mary Konstantareas, the symptoms of autism and schizophrenia differ dramatically, and evidence indicates that autism and schizophrenia remain different over time (Konstantareas & Hewitt, 2001). Thus, the misleading term *childhood schizophrenia* has been appropriately abandoned by experts.

**Contemporary Classification** The diagnostic criteria for autistic disorder have evolved somewhat in DSM (Volkmar, 1996), but the basic diagnostic criteria for the disorder have remained the same (see Table 15–7). However, DSM-IV introduced some important changes for other pervasive developmental disorders that are retained in DSM-IV-TR.

The new diagnosis for *Asperger's disorder* refers to people who show the symptoms of autism but do not have major problems in communication and generally function higher in other areas as well. Professionals differ about whether Asperger's disorder really is a separate disorder or merely a label for high-functioning individuals with autistic disorder (Volkmar et al., 1994). In support of the latter view, a recent study of 157 children with pervasive developmental disorder found *no* cases of Asperger's disorder, because all children had at least some communication problems (Mayes, Calhoun, & Crites, 2001).

*Childhood disintegrative disorder* refers to a poorly understood and somewhat controversial condition (Rutter, 1996) characterized by severe problems in social interaction and communication, in addition to stereotyped behaviour. The onset occurs after at least two years of normal development, and previously acquired skills are lost. Finally, *Rett's disorder* is a clearly distinct condition characterized by at least five months of normal development followed by (1) a deceleration in head growth, (2) loss of purposeful hand movements, (3) loss of social engagement, (4) poor coordination, and (5) a marked delay in language.

**TABLE 15–7 DSM-IV-TR Diagnostic Criteria for Autistic Disorder**

**A. A total of six (or more) items from (1), (2), and (3), with at least two from (1) and one each from (2) and (3):**

1. Qualitative impairments in social interaction, as manifested by at least two of the following:
   a. marked impairment in the use of multiple nonverbal behaviours such as eye-to-eye gaze, facial expression, body postures, and gestures to regulate social interaction
   b. failure to develop peer relationships appropriate to developmental level
   c. a lack of spontaneous seeking to share enjoyment, interests, or achievements with other people
   d. lack of social or emotional reciprocity
2. Qualitative impairments in communication as manifested by at least one of the following:
   a. delay in, or total lack of, the development of spoken language (not accompanied by an attempt to compensate through alternative modes of communication such as gesture or mime)
   b. in individuals with adequate speech, marked impairment in the ability to initiate or sustain a conversation with others
   c. stereotyped and repetitive use of language or idiosyncratic language
   d. lack of varied, spontaneous make-believe play or social imitative play appropriate to developmental level
3. Restricted repetitive and stereotyped patterns of behaviour, interests, and activities, as manifested by at least one of the following:
   a. encompassing preoccupation with one or more stereotyped and restricted patterns of interest that is abnormal either in intensity or focus
   b. apparently inflexible adherence to specific, nonfunctional routines or rituals
   c. stereotyped and repetitive motor mannerisms
   d. persistent preoccupation with parts of objects

**B. Delays or abnormal functioning in at least one of the following areas, with onset prior to age three years: (1) social interaction, (2) language as used in social communication, or (3) symbolic or imaginative play**

According to DSM-IV-TR, Rett's disorder has been found only among females. However, the mapping of gene mutations that can cause Rett's has led to the recent identification of at least a few cases among men (Dotti et al., 2002).

Inexperienced clinicians are not especially reliable in distinguishing among various pervasive developmental disorders, and, in fact, may misdiagnose them as cases of mental retardation. However, experienced clinicians make very reliable diagnoses for different subtypes of pervasive developmental disorders (Volkmar et al., 1994).

## Epidemiology

Autism is a rare disorder. Traditional estimates indicate that about 5 of every 10 000 children qualify for the diagnosis, although recent research by Dalhousie University psychologist Susan Bryson suggests that 10 in 10 000 children may be affected by the disorder (Bryson, 1996). Even the combined prevalence of autism and other pervasive developmental disorders is extremely low, perhaps 20 out of every 10 000 children (Lord & Bailey, 2002).

The majority of autistic children seen at prestigious specialty clinics have wealthy, educated parents, and thus it may seem that the disorder is related to social class. However, research reveals that this is a false correlation created by referral bias (Gillberg & Schaumann, 1982). No association is found between autism and social class in the general population. Apparently, parents with fewer resources sometimes accept an initial misdiagnosis of mental retardation, but wealthier and better-educated parents continue to seek opinions until specialists eventually recognize the autism (Schopler, Andrews, & Strupp, 1979). Referral bias is important to note, because the incorrect "evidence" on the relation between autism and social status has been used to support the false view that children with autism have superior intellects that are masked by their psychological problems.

The risk for autism increases dramatically among the siblings of children with autistic disorder. The prevalence of autism among the overall population is about .05 percent, whereas the prevalence among children with a sibling with autism is 2 to 5 percent, a 50- to 100-fold increase (Smalley, Asarnow, & Spence, 1988; Smalley & Collins, 1996). Although these statistics do not prove that autism has a genetic cause, they have encouraged research in this area. Finally, the fact that autism is three to four times more common among boys than among girls has prompted a search for a gender-linked etiology.

## Etiological Considerations and Research

Several problems discussed as causes of mental retardation also appear to cause autism in certain cases. In addition, recent findings suggest that genetic factors play an important role in the etiology of the disorder. Before discussing evidence on biological etiologies of autism, we first briefly consider—and reject—environmental explanations.

**Psychological and Social Factors** Theories of parental causation of autism have included purely psychoanalytic speculations that autism results from the infant's defence against maternal hostility (Bettelheim, 1967) to purely behavioural views that the disorder was caused by inappropriate parental reinforcement (Ferster, 1961). Most views shared the common belief that the disorder is caused by parents who are cold, distant, and subtly rejecting of their children. This view was once so popular that, in 1960, *Time* magazine published an account of these "refrigerator parents." The article claimed that the parents of children with autism "just happened to defrost long enough to produce a child" (Schreibman, 1988).

Such bold and harmful assertions are unsupported by evidence. Researchers have found no differences in the child-rearing styles of the parents of children with autism when compared with those of the parents of normal children (Cantwell, Baker, & Rutter, 1979). And even if differences existed, common sense would force us to challenge the "refrigerator parent" interpretation. How could a parent's emotional distance create such an extreme disturbance so early in life? As we saw in our discussion of mental retardation, even the heinous abuse of infants does not cause symptoms that approach the form or severity of the problems found among children with autism. Moreover, if parents are emotionally distant from their disordered children, could this be a reaction to their children's gross disturbances? Attachment behaviours are maintained by reciprocal interaction. If an infant shows no normal interest in cuddling or mimicking, is it surprising if the parent becomes a bit distant?

Speculation that autism is caused by poor parenting can never be completely disproved. However, logic, the lack of empirical support for psychological hypotheses, and mounting research on biological causes suggest with virtual certainty that autism does not have a psychological cause. More basically, the rules of science require scientists to prove their hypotheses and not to force others to disprove them. Parents have been unfairly blamed for causing autism, and we greet further assertions that poor parenting causes autism with extreme skepticism.

**Biological Factors** A number of findings indicate that biological abnormalities play an important role in the etiology of autism. These include the following:

- Nearly half of all children with autistic disorder develop seizure disorders by adolescence or early adult life (Tsai, 1996; Wing, 1988).
- Substantial increases in the prevalence of autism are found among children who have certain known genetic and infectious diseases (Reiss, Feinstein, & Rosenbaum, 1986).
- The prevalence of autism is higher among immediate relatives of individuals with autism than among the general population. Prevalence is particularly high among twin pairs (Bailey et al., 1995; Smalley et al., 1988).
- A disproportionate number of neurological abnormalities have been identified among children with autism by a variety of techniques ranging from evidence of pregnancy and birth complications to abnormal EEGs to findings based on postmortem examination of the brain (Bauman, 1996; Schreibman, 1988).

*Autism as a Consequence of Known Biological Disorders* One view of these diverse findings is that autism has several different biological causes (Reiss, Feinstein, & Rosenbaum, 1986). In support of this view, one epidemiological study found that over half the cases of autism were associated with various known biological difficulties or disorders (Wing, 1988). These illnesses include many established causes of mental retardation, in particular fragile-X syndrome, tuberous sclerosis, PKU, rubella, and encephalitis (Reiss, Feinstein, & Rosenbaum, 1986). Other causes of mental retardation, however, are not associated with an increased prevalence of autism. For example, autism is not related to Down syndrome. Thus there are many brain pathologies that cause mental retardation but only a few specific disturbances that may cause both mental retardation and autism.

*A Strongly Genetic Disorder?* In recent years a handful of studies have suggested that genetic factors also play an important role in the etiology of many, if not all, cases of autism. The prevalence of autism is as much as 100 times higher among the siblings of a proband with autism, and researchers have found higher concordance rates for autism among MZ than DZ twins (Smalley et al., 1988; Smalley & Collins, 1996; Steffenburg et al., 1989).

In the largest twin study to date, concordance rates for autism were 60 percent for MZ twins and 0 percent for DZ twins. Concordance rates for a social or cognitive disorder were 92 percent for MZ pairs and 10 percent for DZ pairs, suggesting that autism may be the extreme manifestation of an underlying cognitive disorder (Bailey et al., 1995). Importantly, all twins in this new study were carefully screened for known heritable conditions (like fragile-X) that may have distorted the results of earlier studies. The fact that only a few conditions were detected by screening suggests that most cases of autism are caused by a genetic abnormality that has yet to be detected, not by known genetic or infectious illnesses (Bailey et al., 1995). If so, autism is strongly but not completely genetic.

*Integration: Multiple Pathways to a Brain Disorder* Even if autism does not have a single specific etiology, it still may be produced by a common underlying brain pathology. That is, genetics, PKU, and tuberous sclerosis may be different routes to the same destination in that they produce similar abnormalities in brain function, structure, or development. In fact, different brain abnormalities may cause different symptoms of the disorder, and perhaps this accounts for differences in the presentation of pervasive developmental disorders (for example, autism versus Asperger's disorder). Detecting a common pathology could lead to the development of more effective means of preventing or treating the disorder. Toward these ends, researchers have developed several promising leads in understanding the neurophysiology and neuroanatomy of autism (Waterhouse, Fein, & Modahl, 1996).

*Neurophysiology and Autism* Different theorists have argued that autism is due to deficits in various neurochemicals. Currently, the most promising research focuses on endorphins and *neuropeptides*, substances that affect the action of neurotransmitters, as mediators of symptoms of the disorder.

*Endorphins* are internally produced opioids that have effects similar to those of externally administered opiate drugs like morphine (see Chapter 11). One endorphin theory of autism asserts that, in essence, individuals with autism behave like addicts high on heroin. They lack interest in others, because their excessive internal rewards reduce the value of the external rewards offered by relationships (Panksepp & Sahley, 1987). Other symptoms of autism, such as language problems, are hypothesized to stem from this core deficit.

Some research indicates that endorphin levels are elevated among people with autistic disorder, but critics argue that endorphin theory focuses too narrowly on only one area of functioning. More recent theorizing has expanded to include deficits in various neuropeptides, particularly oxytocin and vasopression, which are known to directly affect attachment and social affiliation in other animals (Waterhouse, Fein, & Modahl, 1996). Still, elevated endorphin levels may help explain some unusual symptoms exhibited by children with autism, particularly their self-destructive behaviour (Gillberg, 1988).

*Neuroanatomy and Autism* Other research has searched for abnormalities in brain structure, not function, among people with autism. Early theorizing suggested that the left cerebral hemisphere was a likely site of brain damage in autism, because speech typically is controlled by left hemisphere structures. Many experts have rejected this view, however, because the communication deficits that characterize autism are more basic than problems in language expression or comprehension. Based on this observation, it has been suggested that damage is more likely to be found in subcortical brain structures (Waterhouse, Fein, & Modahl, 1996; Wing, 1988).

Consistent with this reasoning, some research suggests that people with autism may have abnormalities in parts of the limbic system—the area of the brain that regulates emotions—and also in areas of the cerebellum, where sensorimotor input is integrated (Bauman, 1996; Courchesne et al., 2001; Schreibman, 1988; Waterhouse, Fein, & Modahl, 1996). It should be noted, however, that identified abnormalities are considerably more subtle than the brain damage associated with most known organic causes of mental retardation or with Rett's disorder, where the brain is approximately 25 percent smaller than its expected size (Bauman, 1996). Moreover, the search for structural abnormalities may be complicated by the likelihood that several different brain sites, not just one, are damaged in autism (Waterhouse, Fein, & Modahl, 1996).

*A Disorder of Brain Development* As investigators search for sites of brain damage, one thing seems clear: Any structural abnormalities are likely to be the result of abnormal brain development, not of specific damage or lesions. This is because *plasticity* is a basic characteristic of the development of the infant's brain. If damage occurs in one area of the infant's brain, another area often takes over the function of the damaged site. Because most cases of autism begin at an age when the brain is still plastic, specific brain damage or lesions are unlikely causes (Rutter, 1996).

In support of this view, some recent research using MRI suggests that brain growth may be unusually rapid in children with autism until the age of two or three, and then is arrested, so that cerebral and cerebellar brain volume are smaller than normal at later ages (Courchesne et al., 2001). Other researchers have found that a mutation of a gene critical to brain development, HOXA1, was found in 40 percent of a sample of autistics, suggesting that this mutation plays a role in the etiology of at least some cases of autistic disorder (Ingram et al., 2000).

## Treatment

Some controversy exists about the degree to which treatment can alter the prognosis for children with autistic disorder. Some researchers are optimistic about the possibilities of new treatments, whereas others are far more skeptical, especially because a large number of dubious treatments have been promoted. Everyone acknowledges, however, that there is no cure for autism (Rogers, 1998). Thus the effectiveness of treatment must be compared against the natural course and outcome of the disorder.

**Course and Outcome** Unfortunately, autism is a lifelong disorder. In one study of 63 children with autism who were followed into adulthood, only one person was functioning in what could be considered the normal range. Another 22 children achieved fair to good adjustment as adults. Even this group exhibited social isolation and odd behaviour, however, and required some form of specialized supervision. The remainder of the people with autism in the study (over 60 percent) were living in institutions or other special settings at the time of follow-up (Rutter, 1970). This gloomy picture is consistent with the findings painted by several similar longitudinal investigations (Schreibman, 1988). Note, though, that Asperger's disorder has a more optimistic prognosis because of the better communication abilities (Gillberg, 1991).

Two developmental periods are especially important to the course of autism: the early preschool years and early adolescence. Children who have developed language skills by the age of five or six have a significantly more positive prognosis than do those who have no or severely limited speech at this age (Sigman, 1999). Not surprisingly, higher IQ as measured during the early school years also is a positive prognostic indicator (Schreibman, 1988). The other key developmental period in autism is early adolescence. During the early teen years, the cognitive and social skills of some children with autism improve notably, whereas those of others decline. Scientists cannot yet predict which path any given child will follow. Adolescence is also important because as many as half of all teenagers with autism develop seizure disorders (Wing, 1988).

Case studies offer a sobering view of even good outcomes for autism. Temple Grandin is perhaps the most notable case of a successful outcome, but as her biographies reveal, even she still struggles in many areas of functioning. Nonetheless, she achieved a life that is far superior to the typical course of autism. Can treatment help others with pervasive developmental disorders to lead more normal lives?

**Medication** A huge variety of medications have been used to treat autism, including antipsychotics, antidepressants, amphetamines, psychedelics, and megavitamins. Unfortunately, none of these medications is an effective treatment for autism, and few show much promise.

In recent years, considerable excitement was generated by the medication *secretin* in treating autism. Secretin is a neurotransmitter that constitutes one of the hormones controlling digestion. In the late 1990s, widespread interest in the drug was sparked by publicity about a single case of a child with autism who responded to secretin with remarkable improvement. (Secretin is used to test for certain gastrointestinal problems, which are common among people with autism, which is why the child was given the medication in the first place.) Based on publicity about the single case, which was rapidly spread on the Internet, thousands of desperate parents across the country sought out secretin.

Scientists quickly responded to the public's intense interest in secretin, and unfortunately, the news was not good. A double-blind study using random assignment found no improvement over placebo in 58 autistic children treated with a single dose of secretin (Sandler et al., 1999). As with other "miracle" treatments for autism, the effects of secretin are not miraculous. Ongoing research will determine whether secretin has any benefit at all.

The medication *fenfluramine* rode a similar wave of enthusiasm followed by disappointment. Once the drug was avidly embraced, but experts now recommend against further use of fenfluramine in treating autistic disorder, because of limited effectiveness and potential side effects (McDougle, Price, & Volkmar, 1994).

Other medications may help alleviate aspects of some symptoms of autism. Certain antipsychotic medications, particularly the atypical antipsychotic risperidone, help the management and education of children with autism. Recently, medications used in treating obsessive–compulsive disorder (e.g., the SSRIs; see Chapter 6) have been found to help with some stereotyped behaviour in autistic disorder (Lewis, 1996). However, all medications fall far short of "curing" autism (Lewis, 1996; Lord & Bailey, 2002).

**Psychotherapy: Intensive Behaviour Modification** Intensive behaviour modification using operant conditioning techniques is the most promising approach to treating autism. Behaviour therapists focus on treating the specific symptoms of autism, including communication deficits, lack of self-care skills, and self-stimulatory or self-destructive behaviour. Even within these different symptom areas, behaviour modification emphasizes very specific and small goals. In attempting to teach language, for example, the therapist might spend hours, days, or weeks teaching the pronunciation of a specific syllable. Months of intensive effort may be needed to teach a small number of words and phrases. The lack of imitation among many children with autism is one reason why so much effort goes into achieving such modest goals.

If the first goal of behaviour modification is to identify very specific target behaviours, the second is to gain control over these behaviours through the use of reinforcement and punishment. Unlike normal children, who are reinforced by social interest and approval, children with autism do not understand ordinary praise, or they may find all social interaction unpleasant. For these reasons, the child's successful efforts must be rewarded repeatedly with primary reinforcers such as a favourite food, at least in the beginning phases of treatment.

An example helps to illustrate the level of detail of behaviour modification programs. A common goal in treating echolalia is to teach the child to respond by answering questions rather than repeating them. As an early step in treatment, a target behaviour might be to teach the child to respond to the question "What is your name?" with the correct answer "Joshua."

In order to bring this specific response under the control of the therapist, initially it may be necessary to reward the child for simply echoing. Therapist: "What is your name?" Child: "What is your name?" Reward. This first step may have to be repeated hundreds of times over the course of several days.

A logical next step would be to teach the child to echo both the question and the response. Therapist: "What is your name? . . . Joshua." Child: "What is your name? . . . Joshua." Reward. Again, hundreds of repetitions may be necessary.

Gradually, the behaviour therapist sets slightly more difficult goals, rewarding only increasingly accurate approximations of the correct response. One such intermediate step might be to echo the question "What is your name?" in a whisper and repeat the response "Joshua" in a normal tone of voice. Over a period of days, even weeks, the child learns to respond "Joshua" to the question "What is your name?"

Similar detailed strategies are used to teach children with autism other language skills. In the hope of speeding the process, some therapists have used sign language to teach communication to children with autism (Carr, 1982). Unfortunately, this method has not led to a breakthrough. The communication deficits in autism apparently are more basic than receptive or expressive problems with spoken language. Behaviour modification remains a painfully slow process that differs greatly from the way in which children normally learn to speak. The intensity and detail of these necessary efforts remind us that normal children come into the world remarkably well equipped to acquire language.

In addition to teaching communication skills, behaviour therapists who work with children with pervasive developmental disorders have concentrated on reducing the excesses of self-stimulation, self-injurious behaviour, and general disruptiveness, as well as teaching new skills to eliminate behavioural deficits in self-care and social behaviour (Schreibman, 1988). Behaviour modification programs have been successful with some behavioural excesses, particularly self-injury, but the treatments are controversial because they typically rely on punishment. A slap or a mild electric shock can reduce or eliminate such potentially dangerous behaviours as head banging, but are such aversive treatments justified? This is a question that confronts therapists, parents, and others concerned with the treatment and protection of children with autism.

In other areas of intervention, behaviour therapists have been fairly successful in teaching self-care skills and less successful in teaching social responsiveness, although treatment outcomes for children with autism are especially positive when social responsiveness improves (Koegel, Koegel, & McNerney, 2001). As Schreibman (1988) noted in her review of attempts to modify the social isolation of children with autistic disorder, "It is perhaps prophetic that the behaviour characteristic which most uniquely defines autism is also the one that has proven the most difficult to understand and treat" (p. 118).

Although behaviour therapy often focuses on specific target behaviours, ultimately the important question is: To what extent does treatment improve the entire syndrome of autism? Research has demonstrated that children with autism can learn specific target behaviours, but do intensive training efforts bring about improvements that are clinically significant?

An optimistic answer to this question has been provided by O. Ivar Lovaas, a psychologist at UCLA who is an acknowledged leader in behaviour modification for autism. In a comprehensive report on the efforts of his research team, Lovaas (1987) compared the outcomes of three groups of children with autism: 19 children who received intensive behaviour modification; 19 children who were referred to the program but who received less intensive treatment due to the unavailability of therapists; and 21 children who were treated elsewhere. In this study, all children received independent diagnoses of autism. Children with extremely low IQ scores were excluded, and treatment began before the children were four years of age. The children in the treatment group received the types of interventions described above, including both reinforcement and punishment procedures. In fact, they were treated 40 hours a week for more than 2 years.

No differences among the three groups of children were found before treatment began. Assessments following treatment were conducted between the ages of six and seven at the time when the children ordinarily would have finished Grade 1. In the intensive behaviour modification group, nine children (47 percent) completed Grade 1 in a normal school. Eight more children (42 percent) passed Grade 1 in a special class for children who cannot speak. In comparison, only one child (2 percent) in the two control groups completed Grade 1 in a normal classroom. In addition, 18 children (45 percent) in the control groups completed Grade 1 classes for apha-

*Psychologist* ***O. Ivar Lovaas*** *is a leader in using behaviour modification to treat children with autistic disorder.*

TABLE 15–8 **Educational Placement and IQ of Children with Autistic Disorder Following Behaviour Modification or Alternative Treatments**

| Group | Classroom | *N* | (%) | Mean IQ |
|---|---|---|---|---|
| **Intensive Behaviour Modification** | Normal | 9 | (47) | 107 |
| | Aphasic | 8 | (42) | 74 |
| | Retarded | 2 | (11) | 30 |
| **Limited Treatment** | Normal | 0 | (0) | — |
| | Aphasic | 8 | (42) | 74 |
| | Retarded | 11 | (58) | 36 |
| **No Treatment** | Normal | 1 | (5) | 99 |
| | Aphasic | 10 | (48) | 67 |
| | Retarded | 10 | (48) | 44 |

*Source:* From O.I. Lovaas, 1987, Behavioral treatment and normal educational and intellectual functioning in young autistic children. *Journal of Consulting and Clinical Psychology, 55*, 3–9.

sic children. Data on these findings are portrayed in Table 15–8. In examining this table, you should note the strong relation between IQ and classroom placement. You also should note the low mean IQ levels of the children, despite the investigators' attempts to screen out the most severely impaired children.

These data are reason for some optimism, and a follow-up study of the same sample indicated that many gains continued into late childhood and adolescence (McEachin, Smith, & Lovaas, 1993). Other research also showed significant but smaller gains of very intensive behaviour therapy over parent training approaches, with fewer children restored to normal functioning (Smith, Groen, & Wynn, 2000). We applaud the efforts of Lovaas and others who have used behaviour therapy to teach skills to children with autism. Despite the fact that autism seems to be caused by neurological abnormalities, the most effective treatment for the disorder is highly structured and intensive operant behaviour therapy (Rogers, 1998; Rutter, 1996). Still, cautions must be raised: Are the children who passed Grade 1 functioning normally in other respects? Would treatment have been as effective if it had not begun so early in life? Because pretreatment IQ predicted outcome (Lovaas, 1987), does behaviour modification produce dramatic changes only with children who are high-functioning? What about the 53 percent of children who received intensive therapy but who were not in normal classrooms?

Perhaps the most important question about the effectiveness of behaviour modification is its cost. Remember that the children in the intensive behaviour modification group were treated for 40 hours per week for more than 2 years. At the same time, children in the "limited treatment" control group received almost 10 hours of weekly treatment, yet they showed few improvements. The expenses associated with early but effective treatment clearly are far less than those involved in a lifetime of care (Lovaas, 1987). Still, our question is this: How do we, as a society, justify devoting large amounts of resources to the rare problem of autism, when in comparison we neglect intervention efforts with the much more common—and in many ways more treatable—problems of mental retardation?

# Summary

**Mental retardation** is defined by (1) significantly subaverage intellectual functioning, (2) deficits in adaptive skills, and (3) an onset before age 18. Intellectual functioning must be determined by an individualized IQ test. Many important criticisms have been raised about IQ tests, but the tests are reliable and valid (if imperfect) predictors of academic performance. Many people who have significantly subaverage IQs function adequately in the world, however, because they show no deficits in adaptive behaviour. Such people are not considered to have mental retardation.

DSM-IV-TR divides mental retardation into four levels based on **IQ** scores. People with mild mental retardation complete their education at the sixth-grade level and live in the community with little or no support. This is by far the most common category of mental retardation. People with moderate mental retardation reach a second-grade level of academic performance and require careful supervision in independent living. Severe mental retardation is characterized by major limitations in development and communication and necessitates close supervision. Finally, profound mental retardation often is accompanied by many physical handicaps and sharply restricted development, and it demands constant supervision in the community or in institutions.

The etiology of mental retardation can be grouped into cases caused by known biological abnormalities and cases resulting from normal variations in IQ. **Down syndrome**, which is caused by an extra chromosome on the twenty-first pair, is the most common of the known biological causes of mental retardation. **Fragile-X syndrome**, the second leading biological cause, is a genetic disorder indicated by a weakening of the X sex chromosome. Other known biological causes include **phenylketonuria (PKU)**, an inherited metabolic deficiency; infectious diseases transmitted to the fetus during pregnancy or birth, such as rubella, syphilis, and genital herpes; excessive maternal alcohol consumption or drug use during pregnancy; Rh incompatibility; and malnutrition, premature birth, and low birth weight.

So-called **cultural-familial retardation** comprises most cases of mental retardation. Retardation typically is mild, and there is no known specific etiology. An important debate about cultural-familial retardation is the relative importance of normal genetic variation and deprived psychosocial environments in its development. Our shameful history of **eugenics** is one reason why people worry about emphasizing genetic contributions to intelligence.

Many cases of mental retardation can be prevented by adequate health care before and during pregnancy. Testing for chromosomal or genetic abnormalities in the fetus and considering selective abortion are more controversial means of preventing retardation. Early psychoeducational programs also may prevent some cases of mental retardation by improving adaptive behaviour and perhaps by increasing IQ scores. Treatments for mental retardation include preschool stimulation programs, medical treatment of physical handicaps, and specialized educational services in school. Finally, a major policy goal is **normalization** of the lives of people with mental retardation through **mainstreaming** in public schools and promoting care in the community.

The **pervasive developmental disorders**, or autistic spectrum disorders, as some prefer to call these conditions, involve profound disturbances in relationships, stereotyped activities, and communication difficulties. **Autistic disorder** is the most widely researched pervasive developmental disorder. Social impairments in autism may be relatively mild oddities, but they also may include extreme difficulties in which there is little awareness of the existence of others. One unifying perspective on the social deficits suggests that children with autism lack a **theory of mind**. About half of all children with autism fail to develop communicative speech, and the remainder have either highly restricted language abilities or striking oddities in speech. Finally, many people with autism spend hours engaging in self-stimulation or compulsively adhere to rigid daily routines.

Other difficulties associated with autism and the pervasive developmental disorders include apparent sensory deficits and self-injurious behaviour. **Savant performance** is an exceptional ability at performing mental feats such as rapid mathematical calculations. Despite such unusual abilities, most people with pervasive developmental disorders do not have exceptional intelligence; rather, they have mental retardation. One exception is **Asperger's disorder**, characterized by the same difficulties that are found in autism except that language acquisition is not impaired.

The pervasive developmental disorders are rare conditions, and they almost certainly are caused by biological abnormalities. Several known causes of mental retardation may also cause pervasive developmental disorders (for example, fragile-X syndrome). Recent evidence also suggests that genetics plays an important role. At this time, there is no easy, effective treatment for these conditions. Intensive behaviour modification has promise as a treatment, but the expense and effort involved are considerable. Without intensive treatment over a prolonged period of time, the prognosis for the pervasive developmental disorders is a gloomy one. The majority of people with these conditions require intensive, lifelong care, often within an institution.

# Critical Thinking

1. The concept of intelligence can be controversial. Is academic performance the same thing as intelligence? How would you define practical, social, or emotional intelligence?
2. What could we—and should we—do as individuals and as a society to help normalize the lives of people with mental retardation?
3. Children with autism often receive more services than do children with mental retardation. In part, this is because autism is viewed as a mental illness, whereas mental retardation is seen as a developmental disability. Do you agree? Do you think it is justifiable to spend more money per child to treat autism than to treat mental retardation?

# Key Terms

**amniocentesis** 527
**Asperger's disorder** 536
**autistic disorder (autism)** 530
**cultural-familial retardation** 524
**culture-fair tests** 516
**Down syndrome** 520
**eugenics** 526
**fetal alcohol syndrome** 523
**fragile-X syndrome** 521
**intelligence quotient (IQ)** 514
**lead poisoning** 523
**mainstreaming** 529
**mean** 515
**median** 515
**mental retardation** 512
**mode** 515
**normal distribution** 514
**normalization** 529
**pervasive developmental disorders** 529
**phenylketonuria (PKU)** 521
**reaction range** 524
**savant performance** 535
**standard deviation** 515
**standard scores** 515
**theory of mind** 531
**variance** 515

# 16 Psychological Disorders of Childhood

Overview

Externalizing Disorders

Internalizing and Other Disorders

**Do children have the same kinds of psychological problems as adults?**

**Do children learn to be aggressive or do they learn to control inborn aggression?**

**Should disruptive schoolchildren be treated with stimulant medication?**

**How do young children experience and express sadness and anxiety?**

Is it normal to lie on the floor and kick, scream, and cry if you don't get your way? This certainly is not normal behaviour for a 19-year-old university student. However, it is normal, though sometimes obnoxious, for a 2-year-old child to throw a temper tantrum. Similarly, fears of monsters are developmentally normal at the age of 4, but not at the age of 14. We judge abnormal behaviour by making comparisons with normal behaviour, but what is considered normal changes rapidly during the first 20 years of life. Thus, in evaluating whether a child's behaviour is normal or abnormal, the first question we must ask is: How old is the child? Psychologists become concerned only when a child's behaviour deviates substantially from *developmental norms*.

## Overview

Viewing abnormal behaviour within the context of the course of normal development is important to understanding *all* abnormal behaviour (see Chapter 2). However, **developmental psychopathology** is absolutely essential to understanding psychological disorders of childhood, because children change rapidly during the first 20 years of life (Mash & Dozois, 2003). Psychologists become concerned only when a child's behaviour deviates substantially from **developmental norms**, behaviour that is typical for children of a given age. We cannot assess deviations from normal development as precisely as we can calculate the deviation IQ (see Chapter 15), but the idea is the same. We must compare children against narrowly defined age groups to determine whether their behaviour is normal or abnormal.

Children and adolescents may suffer from most of the disorders we have covered in earlier chapters. For example, children sometimes develop mood disorders, anxiety disorders, or schizophrenia. With the exception of mental retardation and pervasive developmental disorders, however, all of the psychological disorders we have discussed so far are much more prevalent among adults than children.

Psychological problems that arise more commonly among children than adults are listed in the DSM-IV-TR category Disorders Usually First Diagnosed in Infancy, Childhood, or Adolescence. According to University of British Columbia researchers who conducted a recent review of studies from Ontario, Quebec, England, and the United States, approximately 14 percent of children and adolescents (1.1 million people) suffer from a mental disorder, the most common being particular internalizing disorders (anxiety disorders and mood disorders) and externalizing disorders (conduct disorder and attention deficit hyperactivity disorder) (Waddell & Shepherd, 2002; Waddell et al., 2002). Less than one-third of children and adolescents with a mental

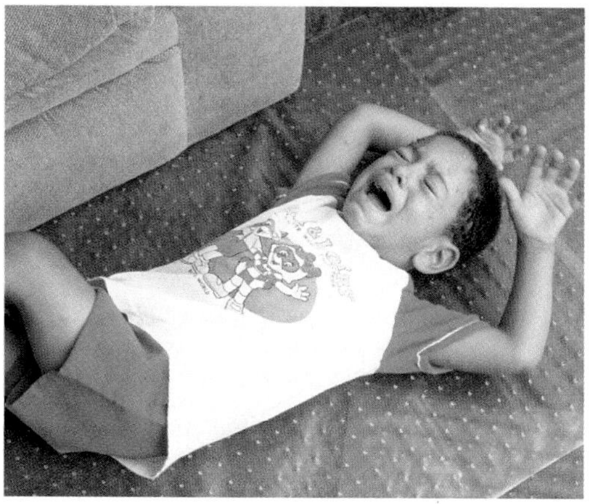


*Temper tantrums are a normal, if trying, part of child development during the "terrible twos" (and beyond). Awareness of such developmental norms is essential to evaluating abnormal behaviour in children.*

disorder receive specialized treatment (Waddell et al., 2002).

**Internalizing disorders** are psychological problems that primarily affect the child's internal world—for example, excessive anxiety or sadness. DSM-IV-TR does not list internalizing disorders as separate psychological disorders of childhood; rather, the manual notes that children may qualify for many "adult" diagnoses, such as anxiety or mood disorders. However, we think it is essential to take a developmental psychopathology approach and highlight children's unique experience of anxiety and depression. Children do not interpret events or express emotions in the same manner as adults; emotional experiences and expressions change rapidly with age; and the family, peer, and school contexts typically affect children more dramatically than they affect adults. Thus we suggest that children's mood and anxiety disorders are *not* simply miniature versions of adult diagnoses.

Together with our consideration of internalizing disorders, we introduce many of the 26 *additional* diagnoses included in DSM-IV-TR's list of disorders usually first diagnosed during childhood. Our coverage of these other childhood disorders is necessarily limited, not only by their sheer number but also by questions we have about the appropriateness of some of the diagnostic categories (Taylor & Rutter, 2002). We begin our review of psychological disorders of childhood with a discussion of externalizing disorders.

## Externalizing Disorders

Few children or adolescents identify themselves as having an **externalizing disorder**. Instead, some adult, often a parent or teacher, decides that a child has a behaviour problem. In some cases, children are unable to recognize or admit to their difficult behaviour. In other cases, however, the problem may be with the adult not the child (Yeh & Weisz, 2001). For example, an intolerant parent or teacher may see normal misbehaviour as a sign of a psychological problem. Different adults also frequently disagree in evaluating children's behaviour as disturbed or normal. Conflicting perceptions challenge the assessment of externalizing disorders, because it is often unclear who is objective and who is biased, as illustrated in the following case study.

The case of Jeremy W. illustrates many of the complicated issues in assessing and treating children's externalizing disorders. Is Jeremy

### CASE STUDY Bad Boy, Troubled Boy, or All Boy?

Jeremy W. was eight years old when his mother brought him to a clinical psychologist on the recommendations of his second-grade teacher and a school counsellor. Mrs. W. came to the psychologist reluctantly, because she was not sure if she agreed with the suggestions of the school personnel. In fact, Mrs. W. wasn't sure if she agreed with her husband about what was going on with Jeremy.

According to Mrs. W., Jeremy was constantly in trouble at school. His teacher reprimanded Jeremy daily for disrupting the class, not paying attention, and failing to finish his work. The teacher felt that her attempts at discipline had little effect. Sometimes Jeremy would listen for awhile, but soon he was pestering another child, talking out of turn, or simply staring off into space. Lately, Jeremy had begun to talk back when he was disciplined, and his teacher had sent him to the principal's office several times in the past month.

The psychologist confirmed this information in a subsequent telephone call to the school. At that time, the teacher also noted that Jeremy had no close friends in school, and that other kids thought of him as a "pain." The teacher had referred Jeremy to a school psychologist, who gave him several academic tests. According to an individualized intelligence test, Jeremy had an IQ of 108. However, his achievement test scores indicated performance at a Grade 1 level, almost a year behind his current grade. The school psychologist suspected that Jeremy had a learning disorder, but thought that his behaviour problems also were interfering with his learning. She concluded that Jeremy should remain in his regular classroom for the present. As a first step, she recommended therapy for Jeremy and perhaps for his parents. After treatment, she would re-evaluate him for possible placement in a "resource room," a special class for students with learning problems.

Mrs. W. was frightened by the suggestion that Jeremy might be "emotionally disturbed" or "learning disordered." According to his mother, Jeremy could be difficult to manage at home, but she had never considered the possibility that he needed psychological help. Jeremy had always been a handful, but in her view, he had never been a bad child. Instead, Mrs. W. thought that Jeremy expressed himself better through actions than words. In

continued

*cont.*

this respect, he was the opposite of his 11-year-old sister, who was an A and B student. Mrs. W. was not convinced that Jeremy's teacher was the best person to work with him, but she did agree that he was having problems in school. In her mind, Jeremy was developing low self-esteem, and many of his actions were attempts to get attention.

According to Mrs. W., Jeremy's father spent very little time with him. Mr. W. worked long hours on his construction job, and he often was off with his friends on weekends. Mrs. W. said that her husband was of little help even when he was home. He would tell his wife that it was her job to take care of the kids—he needed his rest. With tears in her eyes, Mrs. W. said that she needed a rest, too.

In any case, Mr. W. was not concerned about Jeremy's behaviour or his schoolwork. Instead, he thought that Jeremy was just "all boy" and not much of a student—just like Mr. W. was as a child. He refused to take time off from work to see a psychologist.

In confidence, Mrs. W. said that she, too, saw a lot of his father in Jeremy—too much of him, in fact. She got no support from her husband in disciplining Jeremy or in encouraging him in his schoolwork. She blamed her husband for Jeremy's problems, and she was secretly furious with him.

She knew that Jeremy had to do well in school in order to live a better life, and she felt like a failure as a mother. She was willing to try anything to help Jeremy, but she doubted that there was anything she could do without her husband's support. ◆

a disobedient child, as his teacher thinks? A learning-disordered child, as suggested by the school psychologist? Suffering from low self-esteem, as his mother fears? Or is he simply "all boy," as his father claims? What about Jeremy? How does he feel about himself, his family, his schoolwork, and his friendships at school?

Mental health professionals who treat children are constantly vexed by such difficult questions, and treatment often begins with an attempt to achieve consensus about the nature of a child's problem (Yeh & Weisz, 2001). The overriding goal is to reach an accurate diagnosis, but another goal is to get adults working together as a team. In Jeremy's case, Mr. and Mrs. W. may need to present a united front to Jeremy, and to do so they may need to resolve issues in their marriage. Because of such conflicts, many psychologists prefer to see children in *family therapy* rather than treat children alone (see Chapter 3). Many psychologists also work to establish better communication and cooperation between parents and teachers.

Of course, Jeremy is also at least part of the problem. If we can trust his teacher's report—and experienced child clinical psychologists do trust teachers—Jeremy clearly has some type of externalizing problem. Perhaps Jeremy's behaviour is simply a reaction to his parents' conflicts, and he will get better if they work out their differences. Or perhaps Jeremy is a troubled child who is causing some of these conflicts, not just reacting to them. Mr. and Mrs. W. both felt that Jeremy and his father were a lot alike. Could Jeremy have learned or inherited some of his father's characteristics? We can better answer these questions by considering the typical symptoms of externalizing disorders.

## Typical Symptoms of Externalizing Disorders

Children with externalizing disorders may demonstrate many different problem behaviours, including rule breaking, anger and aggression, impulsive actions, overactivity, and trouble paying attention. These different kinds of troublesome actions tend to occur together. As we will see, however, different clusters of problem behaviours have different implications for the etiology, treatment, and course of children's externalizing disorders.

**Rule Violations** Many externalizing symptoms are characterized by violations of age-appropriate social rules. Rule violations may include disobeying parents or teachers, violating social or peer group norms (e.g., annoying others), and perhaps violating the law. All children break at least some social rules, of course, and we often admire an innocent and clever rule breaker. For example, we see Calvin of the Calvin and Hobbes cartoons as devilish, but he is not really "bad," and we certainly do not view him as "sick."

*How Serious Is the Violation?* Some misconduct is normal, perhaps even healthy, for children. However, the rule violations found in externalizing disorders are not trivial and are far from "cute." Many schoolteachers lament that they spend far too much time disciplining children, a circumstance that also is unfair to the well-behaved youngsters in the classroom.

CALVIN AND HOBBES © Watterson. Reprinted with permission of UNIVERSAL PRESS SYNDICATE. All Rights Reserved.

Even more serious, evidence indicates that the worst 5 percent of juvenile offenders account for about half of all juvenile arrests (Farrington, Ohlin, & Wilson, 1986).

Several factors influence how we evaluate the seriousness of children's rule violations. Externalizing behaviour is a far greater concern when it is frequent, intense, lasting, and pervasive. That is, externalizing behaviour is more problematic when it is part of a *syndrome*, or cluster of problems, than when it is a *symptom* that occurs in isolation. The existence of an externalizing syndrome has been demonstrated consistently by statistical analysis (factor analysis) of checklists on which parents or teachers rate children's psychological symptoms. Moreover, agreement among adult raters typically is high for the externalizing dimension (Duhig et al., 2000).

*Children's Age and Rule Violations* Children of different ages are likely to violate very different rules (Lahey et al., 2000). A preschooler with an externalizing problem is likely to be disobedient to his parents and aggressive with other children. During the school years, he or she is more likely to be disruptive in the classroom, uncooperative on the playground, or defiant at home. By adolescence, the problem teenager may be failing in school, ignoring all discipline at home, hanging out with delinquent peers, and perhaps violating the law.

Children's age is important to consider in relation to the timing as well as the nature of rule violations. All children violate rules, but children with externalizing problems violate rules at a younger age than is developmentally normal (Loeber, 1988). For example, most young people experiment with smoking, alcohol, or sexuality, but children with externalizing disorders do so at a notably younger age.

Developmental norms for committing rule violations are important to consider for the teen years, as adolescence is a stage of normal development that borders on the abnormal from the perspective of adults. Teenagers often violate the rules laid down by parents, teachers, and society as a means of asserting their independence and perhaps of conforming to the rules of their peer group. Because of this, it is essential to distinguish between externalizing behaviour that is *adolescent-limited*—that ends along with the teen years—and *life-course-persistent* antisocial behaviour that continues into adult life (Moffitt, 1993).

In fact, externalizing problems that begin *before* adolescence are more likely to persist over the individual's life course than are problems that begin *during* adolescence. It is counterintuitive, but true, that scientists are better able to predict adult antisocial behaviour from information obtained during childhood than from information obtained during adolescence (Moffitt, 1993). This is because so many teenagers violate rules that, in order to distinguish life-course-persistent antisocial behaviour, scientists need to look back in time to a stage of development (childhood) when conformity was the norm (Moffitt, 1993).

Can adolescent-limited and life-course-persistent antisocial behaviour be distinguished in other ways? Many investigators are searching for symptoms among young people that will predict adult antisocial behaviour, particularly *antisocial personality disorder* (see Chapter 9). Evidence indicates that callousness and lack of emotional response in young people may be early indicators of this lifelong pattern of rule violations (Frick, Bodin, & Barry, 2000). For example, young people with antisocial tendencies do not readily recognize sadness and fear in other people's facial expressions (Blair et al., 2001).

**Negativity, Anger, and Aggression** Children with externalizing problems often are negative, angry, and aggressive. Their actions can range from stubbornness and uncooperativeness, particularly among younger children, to hostility and physically injuring others, particularly among adolescents. In addition to the harmful effects of aggression, these symptoms shed light on the motivations of a child with an externalizing disorder. We chuckle at the innocent adventures of a Calvin, but as in our legal system, we judge externalizing behaviour harshly when children's *intent* is selfish and they show little *remorse*. You might wonder about Jeremy W.'s private motivations, for example, and judge him differently based on whether he is an angry child who cares little about being "bad" or an impulsive child who wants to but just cannot consistently be "good."

**Impulsivity** Children who want to but fail to control their behaviour suffer from impulsivity; they act before thinking. Impulsive children seem unable, not unwilling, to control their disruptive actions, and the absence of negativity and aggression is of key importance to diagnosing attention-deficit/hyperactivity disorder (ADHD). Children with ADHD have trouble waiting their turn, blurt out answers in class, intrude into the activities of other children, or cause accidents around the house. Such actions certainly are annoying and disruptive to others, but the motivation behind them is innocent. Children with ADHD generally want to be "good," not "bad," but they seem unable to control their behaviour according to situational demands.

Research by Russell Schachar at Toronto's Hospital for Sick Children, and his colleagues, have shown that in ADHD, the deficit in impulse control is a problem in its own right; it is not simply caused by other problems associated with this disorder, such as attention deficits (e.g., Schachar, Tannock, & Logan, 1993; Schachar et al., 2000).

The difference between impulsivity and negativity suggests one reason for the enduring but misguided view that ADHD is biological and ODD and conduct disorder are environmental. Children with ADHD try but fail to control their behaviour, but children with ODD or conduct disorder seem as if they are not trying to control their behaviour. Such symptoms may seem to be related to biological versus psychological causation, but the relationship is only a superficial one.

**Hyperactivity** **Hyperactivity** involves squirming, fidgeting, and restless behaviour. Hyperactive children are in constant motion, and they often have trouble sitting still, even during leisure activities like watching television. Hyperactivity is found across situations, even during sleep, but it is more obvious in structured settings than in unstructured ones (Mash & Barkley, 2003). In particular, hyperactive behaviour is much more noticeable in the classroom than in other circumstances. Because of this, reports from teachers are critical in identifying hyperactive behaviour. The Conners Teacher Rating Scale is a measure commonly used by pediatricians and other professionals in order to assess teacher ratings of hyperactivity and other symptoms of ADHD in the classroom (see Figure 16–1).

*McGill University researcher **Virginia Douglas** was among the first to identify that attention deficits are a central feature of what is now known as ADHD.*

**Attention Deficits** Virginia Douglas and colleagues at McGill University were among the first to establish that attention deficits are important problems in ADHD children (e.g., Douglas, 1972, 1983). **Attention deficits** are characterized by distractibility, frequent shifts from one uncompleted activity to another, careless mistakes, poor organization or effort, and general "spaciness"—for example, not listening well or responding to questions. A particular attentional problem in ADHD is

**Brief Conners Teacher Rating Scale for Attention-Deficit/Hyperactivity Disorder**

| Observation | Degree of Activity | | | |
|---|---|---|---|---|
| CLASSROOM BEHAVIOUR | (0) Not At All | (1) Just a Little | (2) Pretty Much | (3) Very Much |
| Constantly fidgeting | | | | |
| Demands must be met immediately—easily frustrated | | | | |
| Restless or overactive | | | | |
| Excitable, impulsive | | | | |
| Inattentive, easily distracted | | | | |
| Fails to finish things he starts—short attention span | | | | |
| Cries often and easily | | | | |
| Disturbs other children | | | | |
| Mood changes quickly and drastically | | | | |
| Temper outbursts; explosive and unpredictable behaviour | | | | |

**FIGURE 16–1: Psychologists often ask teachers to complete this 10-item scale as a screening device for ADHD. A total score of 15 or greater suggests that a child may have ADHD.**

*Source:* C.K. Conners, 1969, A teacher rating scale for use with drug studies with children. *American Journal of Psychiatry, 126*, 884–888.

difficulty "staying on task," or what is called difficulty with *sustained attention* (Douglas & Peters, 1979). Numerous studies have documented that children with ADHD perform poorly on the *continuous performance test,* a laboratory task that requires the participant to monitor and respond to numbers or letters presented on a computer screen (Douglas, 1983). As with impulsivity, inattention is not intentional or oppositional; rather, it reflects an inability to maintain a focus despite an apparent desire to do so. Note also that hyperactivity is not merely a consequence of inattention, or vice versa; each is an independent symptom (Schachar et al., 2000).

## Classification of Externalizing Disorders

Theorists have debated how or whether externalizing disorders should be subclassified, and as we will see, the topic continues to be controversial. The DSM-IV-TR divides externalizing disorders into three major subtypes. Attention-deficit/hyperactivity disorder (ADHD) is the problem that you may have heard called "hyperactivity" or perhaps "ADD." Oppositional defiant disorder (ODD) includes a wide range of problem behaviour generally found among school-aged children. Conduct disorder is a lot like what you may think of as juvenile delinquency, because conduct disorder involves rule violations that also are violations of the law.

**Brief Historical Perspective** The first major subcategory of externalizing disorder, dividing hyperactivity from ordinary misbehaviour, was proposed about 100 years ago by British physician George Still (1902). He wrote about some children seen in his practice and speculated that their overactivity might be due to biological as well as moral "defects." Since then, professionals have debated whether the misbehaviour of school-aged children should be divided into two types. Children with what we now call ADHD often are assumed to have a biological problem best treated with medication. Children with what we now call ODD commonly are assumed to have a psychological problem requiring psychological treatment. Many years have been devoted to controversies about this diagnostic distinction. Opposing sides debated whether ADHD and ODD were the same or separate problems, were caused by biology or the environment, and whether medication should be used as a treatment (Schachar & Tannock, 2002).

Interest in what DSM-IV calls conduct disorder, which involves violations of the law, also is about 100 years old but has a very different origin. Even before Canadian Confederation, young offenders received special treatment within the criminal justice system. This approach was later taken in the 1908 Juvenile Delinquents Act, which declared that "as far as practicable every juvenile delinquent shall be treated not as a criminal, but as a misdirected child, and one needing aid, encouragement, help, and assistance" (McGuire, 1997, p. 187). Thus, the law in Canada—and in other Western countries—took a compassionate view of juvenile delinquency, which was seen as a result of a troubled upbringing, and the state adopted a parental role toward wayward youth. The criminal behaviour of juveniles therefore became of special interest as a psychological problem, not just a legal one.

### Attention-Deficit/Hyperactivity Disorder

**Attention-deficit/hyperactivity disorder (ADHD)** is characterized by hyperactivity, attention deficit, and impulsivity. According to DSM-IV-TR, at least some symptoms must begin before the age of 7, they must persist for at least 6 months, and there must be evidence of consistency in symptoms across situations. The manual takes a quantitative "checklist" approach to counting symptoms, implying that the underlying problem is dimensional even though the diagnosis is categorical (see Table 16–1). The quantitative threshold for making a diagnosis was based on empirical evidence from the DSM-IV field trials (Lahey et al., 1994).

At different times, the symptoms of hyperactivity and attention deficit each have been viewed as being the core characteristics of ADHD. In fact, DSM-II called the disorder *hyperkinesis*, a synonym for "hyperactivity," whereas DSM-III referred to it as *attention-deficit disorder*, or *ADD*. Now, much theorizing focuses on impulsivity as the core characteristic (Nigg, 2001). We are not concerned whether "attention deficit" or "hyperactivity"—or "impulsivity" in DSM-IV-TR—gets top billing as a label for a problem with an ever-changing series of names. Some children have problems primarily with only one of the two symptoms, as is evident in the subtypes of ADHD listed in DSM-IV-TR (see Table 16–1).

**Oppositional Defiant Disorder** **Oppositional defiant disorder (ODD)** is defined by a pattern of negative, hostile, and defiant behaviour. The symptoms must last for at least six months, and, as with other diagnoses, they must cause clinically significant impairment in life functioning. As you can see from Table 16–2, the rule violations in ODD typically involve minor transgressions, such as refusing to obey adult requests, arguing, and acting angry. Such misbehaviour is a cause for concern among school-aged children, and it often foreshadows the development of much more serious antisocial behaviour during adolescence and adult life. However, these types of rule violations fit within developmental norms for adolescents, who are typically somewhat rebellious. Thus, a problem with the DSM-IV-TR diagnostic criteria for ODD—and for virtually every childhood disorder—is that the diagnostic criteria need to reflect developmental norms better and offer different criteria for children of different ages.

**ADHD versus ODD** As we noted, professionals have long debated whether ADHD and ODD are the same or separate disorders. Some professionals have argued that the two conditions are distinct not only in symptoms but also in terms of etiology and treatment. Others have asserted that the distinction between ADHD and ODD is false and is wrongly used to justify treating troubled children with medication. Testing these widely opposing viewpoints was hampered by the fact that a differential diagnosis between ADHD and ODD could not be made with a high level of reliability (Hinshaw, 1994).

This debate has subsided considerably in recent years. The current consensus is that the two disorders are separate but overlapping problems (Hinshaw, 1994; see Figure 16–2). ODD and ADHD can be differentiated, but they frequently are comorbid conditions. Approximately half of all children with one disorder also have the other problem (Schachar & Tannock, 2002). Because researchers have only recently recognized the comorbidity, past research often is difficult to interpret. For example, are the long-term problems in school or with substance abuse among externalizing children due to ADHD, ODD, the overlap between the two conditions, or the presence of either problem? Scientists are hopeful that future researchers will move the field forward by studying children with "pure" ODD and ADHD—that is, cases where there is no comorbidity (Hinshaw, 1994).

**TABLE 16–1 DSM-IV-TR Diagnostic Criteria for Attention-Deficit/Hyperactivity Disorder**

**A. Either (I) or (II):**

**(I) Inattention:** Six (or more) of the following symptoms of inattention have persisted for at least six months to a degree that is maladaptive and inconsistent with developmental level:

1. Often fails to give close attention to details or makes careless mistakes in schoolwork, work, or other activities.
2. Often has difficulty sustaining attention in tasks or play activities.
3. Often does not seem to listen when spoken to directly.
4. Often does not follow through on instructions and fails to finish schoolwork, chores, or duties in the workplace.
5. Often has difficulty organizing tasks and activities.
6. Often avoids, dislikes, or is reluctant to engage in tasks that require sustained mental effort.
7. Often loses things necessary for tasks or activities.
8. Is often easily distracted by extraneous stimuli.
9. Is often forgetful of daily activities.

**(II) Hyperactivity and Impulsivity:** Six (or more) of the following symptoms of hyperactivity-impulsivity have persisted for at least six months to a degree that is maladaptive and inconsistent with developmental level:

**Hyperactivity**

1. Often fidgets with hands or feet or squirms in seat.
2. Often leaves seat in classroom or in other situations in which remaining seated is expected.
3. Often runs about or climbs excessively in situations in which it is inappropriate.
4. Often has difficulty playing or engaging in leisure activities quietly.
5. Is often "on the go" or often acts as if "driven by a motor."
6. Often talks excessively.

**Impulsivity**

7. Often blurts out answers before questions have been completed.
8. Often has difficulty waiting turn.
9. Often interrupts or intrudes on others.

**B. Some hyperactive-impulsive or inattentive symptoms that caused impairment were present before the age of seven.**

**C. Some impairment from the symptoms is present in two or more settings.**

**D. There must be clear evidence of clinically significant impairment in social, academic, or occupational functioning.**

***Code* Based on Type**

**Combined Type:** Criteria for I and II are met for past six months.

**Predominantly Inattentive Type:** Criteria for I are met but Criteria for II are not met for past six months.

**Predominantly Hyperactive-Impulsive Type:** Criteria for II are met but Criteria for I are not met for past six months.

**TABLE 16–2 DSM-IV-TR Diagnostic Criteria for Oppositional Defiant Disorder**

**A. A pattern of negativistic, hostile, and defiant behaviour lasting at least six months, during which four (or more) of the following are present:**

1. Often loses temper.
2. Often argues with adults.
3. Often actively defies or refuses to comply with adults' requests or rules.
4. Often deliberately annoys people.
5. Often blames others for his or her mistakes or misbehaviour.
6. Is often touchy or easily annoyed by others.
7. Is often angry and resentful.
8. Is often spiteful and vindictive.

**B. The disturbance in behaviour causes clinically significant impairment in social, academic, or occupational functioning.**

*Note:* Consider a criterion only if the behaviour occurs more frequently than is typically observed in individuals of comparable age and developmental level.

**Comorbidity** Not only are ADHD and ODD highly comorbid, but, as illustrated in Figure 16–2, about 25 percent of children with each problem also have a learning disorder. To a lesser extent, ADHD also is comorbid with internalizing disorders such as depression and anxiety (Schachar & Tannock, 2002). Comorbid internalizing disorders are particularly common among girls with ADHD (Rucklidge & Tannock, 2001).

**Comorbidity among ADHD, ODD, and Learning Disorder**

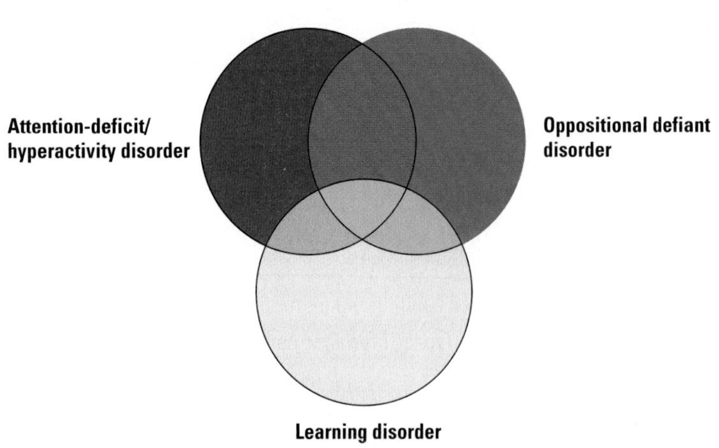


**FIGURE 16–2: ADHD and ODD are distinct but overlapping conditions. As many as half of all children with one disorder also suffer from the other problem. To a lesser extent, ADHD and ODD also overlap with learning disorders.**

**Subtypes of ADHD** The subtyping of ADHD into the predominantly inattentive, predominantly hyperactive-impulsive, or combined types is another important and sometimes controversial distinction. The predominantly inattentive subtype generally is accepted as an important diagnosis. Some children with ADHD have considerable difficulty with inattention and information processing, but they exhibit little or no hyperactivity (Milich, Balentine, & Lynam, 2001). Their struggles focus primarily on issues related to learning rather than behaviour control. Some parents and professionals still use the DSM-III term ADD for this subtype of ADHD, because they find it to be less stigmatizing.

There is less support for the predominantly hyperactive-impulsive subtype, which might best be classified with the combined subtype in future revisions of the DSM. In studies of these subtypes, preschool children generally are classified in the predominantly hyperactive-impulsive group, while school-aged children fall into the combined type. This implies that the two subtypes actually involve the same problems but are developmentally related. Problems with hyperactivity and impulsivity are evident during the preschool years, but attention deficits begin (or are first noticed) during the early school years (Mash & Barkley, 2003).

**Conduct Disorder** **Conduct disorder** is defined primarily by a persistent and repetitive pattern of serious rule violations, most of which are illegal as well as antisocial—for example, assault or robbery (see Table 16–3). Consistent with the research that we reviewed earlier, DSM-IV-TR notes that ODD and conduct disorder often are developmentally related. Oppositional defiant disorder is diagnosed primarily among school-aged children and may develop into a more serious conduct disorder during preadolescence or adolescence (Loeber, Lahey, & Thomas, 1991). You should note that DSM-IV-TR also includes a notation for age of onset in defining conduct disorder—a distinction between the adolescent-limited versus life-course patterns of antisocial behaviour, we discussed earlier (see Table 16–3).

You may think of what DSM-IV calls conduct disorder as being roughly equivalent to juvenile delinquency. Many of the symptoms of conduct disorder do indeed involve illegal acts against people or property. However, juvenile delinquency is a *legal* classification, not a mental health term. Adolescents who repeatedly break the law have conduct disorders whether or not they get arrested and convicted.

## Epidemiology of Externalizing Disorders

According to recent estimates (APA, 2000)—based on epidemiological studies conducted in Canada, the United States, and other countries—ADHD occurs in 3 to 7 percent of school-age children. The prevalence of conduct disorder seems to have increased over the past few decades. Estimates suggest that its prevalence is approximately 3 percent in Canada (Waddell & Shepard, 2002). In mental health facilities for children, conduct disorder is one of the most frequently diagnosed mental disorders. The prevalence of ODD is estimated in the vicinity of 2 to 16 percent. For each of these disorders, the estimated prevalences vary as a result of differences across studies in terms of the methods of assessment and the populations that are sampled. Even so, the percentages suggest that children's mental health is a major problem. How do researchers arrive at such conclusions? Important issues regarding the collection of such samples are discussed in the Research Methods box.

Factors correlated with higher prevalence rates identify subgroups of children at risk, and this information suggests possible causes of children's psychological disorders (see Canadian Focus on p. 575). After the first few years of life, boys have far more externalizing disorders than girls—from 2 to 10 times as many boys as girls have an externalizing

**TABLE 16–3 DSM-IV-TR Diagnostic Criteria for Conduct Disorder**

**A. A repetitive and persistent pattern of behaviour in which the basic rights of others or major age-appropriate societal norms or rules are violated, as manifested by the presence of three (or more) of the following criteria in the past 12 months, with at least one criterion present in the past 6 months:**

**Aggression to People and Animals**

1. Often bullies, threatens, or intimidates others.
2. Often initiates physical fights.
3. Has used a weapon that can cause serious physical harm to others.
4. Has been physically cruel to people.
5. Has been physically cruel to animals.
6. Has stolen while confronting a victim.
7. Has forced someone into sexual activity.

**Destruction of Property**

8. Has deliberately engaged in fire setting with the intention of causing serious damage.
9. Has deliberately destroyed others' property.

**Deceitfulness or Theft**

10. Has broken into someone else's house, building, or car.
11. Often lies to obtain goods or favours to avoid obligations.
12. Has stolen items of nontrivial value without confronting a victim.

**Serious Violations of Rules**

13. Often stays out at night despite parental prohibitions, beginning before age 13 years.
14. Has run away from home overnight at least twice while living in parental or parental surrogate home.
15. Is often truant from school, beginning before age 13 years.

**B. The disturbance in behaviour causes clinically significant impairment in social, academic, or occupational functioning.**

***Code* Type Based on Age at Onset**

**Conduct disorder Childhood-Onset Type:** Onset of at least one criterion characteristic of Conduct Disorder prior to age 10 years.

**Conduct disorder Adolescent-Onset Type:** Absence of any criteria characteristic of Conduct Disorder prior to age 10 years.

## RESEARCH METHODS

### Samples and Sampling

Psychologists often describe their samples in great detail—a fact attested to by numerous examples throughout this text. However, psychologists typically do not consider it necessary to obtain a **representative sample**—a sample that accurately represents some larger group of people. Instead, mental health researchers commonly obtain *convenience samples*—groups of people who are easily recruited and studied. In research in abnormal psychology, people who have sought psychological treatment often comprise the convenience sample.

The use of a convenience sample does not create problems for many of the questions that psychologists wish to study. For example, there is no need to obtain a representative sample to study the effectiveness of medication for treating most psychological disorders. For other purposes, obtaining representative samples is essential. To illustrate, Brian Cox and colleagues at the University of Manitoba have been interested in identifying the basic types of fears or phobias as they occur in Canadian and U.S. populations. Accordingly, they have been using nationally

*continued*

*cont.*

representative epidemiologic samples (e.g., Cox et al., 2003).

Our concern with sampling is one reason why we have systematically addressed the topic of epidemiology throughout this text. When studying risk factors like family status, often it is informative to be able to *generalize*—to make accurate statements that extend beyond a specific sample to a larger population group. How do scientists select representative samples that allow them to generalize to a larger population? Theoretically, the methods for obtaining a representative sample are straightforward. First, the researcher must identify the *population* of interest, the entire group of people to whom the researcher wants to generalize—for example, children under the age of 18 living in Canada. Second, the researcher must *randomly select* research subjects from the sample and obtain a large enough sample to ensure that the results are statistically reliable. These two procedures allow researchers to make generalizations that sometimes seem remarkable, such as when the outcome of a political election is accurately predicted by polling a relatively small number of voters.

Errors can occur in either step of the process of selecting a representative sample. Therefore, when you read about psychological research, we urge you to think critically about samples and sampling methods. A fortunate trend in the study of child psychopathology is that psychologists and psychiatrists often work with epidemiologists to design and implement epidemiological surveys. Clinical and convenience samples are decidedly not representative of the general population. There often are compelling reasons for studying these unrepresentative groups, but researchers who rely on such samples must exercise great caution in generalizing to the larger population. ◆

disorder (Keenan & Shaw, 1997; National Academy of Sciences, 1989). Except for the normative increase during adolescence, the prevalence of externalizing behaviour generally declines with age, although it declines at much earlier ages for girls (age four or five) than for boys (after age five) (Keenan & Shaw, 1997).

**Family Risk Factors** The prevalence of externalizing disorders is associated with various indicators of family adversity (Johnston & Mash, 2001). Rutter's (1989) Family Adversity Index includes six family predictors of behaviour problems among children: (1) low income, (2) overcrowding in the home, (3) maternal depression, (4) paternal antisocial behaviour, (5) conflict between the parents, and (6) removal of the child from the home. Rutter found that the risk for externalizing problems did not increase substantially when only one family risk factor was present. However, the risk increased fourfold when two family adversity factors were present. The risk for children's antisocial behaviour increased even further with three or more sources of family adversity.

Other epidemiological findings underscore the relationship between children's externalizing problems and social disadvantage (Earls & Mezzacappa, 2002). For example, psychological disorders are associated with divorce and single parenting (National Academy of Sciences, 1989; and see Canadian Focus on p. 575). For these reasons, family adversity is a substantial concern in the etiology of children's externalizing disorders.

## Etiology of Externalizing Disorders

During the course of normal development, children's inherent predispositions toward aggression, selfishness, or impulsivity are modified initially by the social consequences and instruction offered by parents and teachers. Peers and broader social influences like the media also teach children to control their behaviour. Eventually, children are expected to control their behaviour internally, and this self-control itself is a product of biological predispositions and social learning. Externalizing problems can result when any of these key developmental influences go awry. Some children are especially difficult from birth; some parents fail to control their children's selfish behaviour; peers, the media, and troubled family life can encourage rather than inhibit children's misbehaviour; and some children fail to develop the necessary internal controls over their behaviour.

**Biological Factors** All children require some external limits in order to learn to control their selfish or aggressive behaviour. If you doubt the truth of this statement, we urge you to spend some time observing a preschool where children continually need to be reminded to share, to cooperate, to be nice, and not to hit, push, scratch, or bite. The natural behaviour we observe in children is wonderful—preschoolers also make friends, exchange favours, and show empathy when others are hurt—but children's behaviour is far from perfect naturally. Of course, different children show different tendencies, as any parent of two children will attest.

*Temperament* One important biological contribution to individual differences is a child's **temperament**, his or her inborn characteristics, such as activity level, emotionality, and sociability (Buss, 1991). Theorists disagree about what qualities comprise children's temperamental characteristics, but Thomas and Chess's (1977) long-standing grouping into easy, difficult, and slow-to-warm-up categories is one clear categorization of temperamental styles. *Easy* children quickly form social relationships and follow discipline; *difficult* children challenge parental authority; *slow-to-warm-up* children tend to be shy and withdrawn. Many theorists have argued that a difficult temperament is a risk factor for later externalizing disorders, an assertion that has been supported by some research on infants and toddlers (Shaw, Keenan, & Vondra, 1994; Shaw et al., 1997).

*Behaviour Genetics* Theorists have long speculated that genetic factors play a central role in the etiology of ADHD, but until recently the theory has not been tested adequately. Several behaviour genetic studies have demonstrated, however, that genetic factors strongly contribute to ADHD. For example, a study of almost 4000 Australian twins found concordance rates for ADHD among MZ twins of roughly 80 percent, whereas DZ twins had concordance rates of approximately 40 percent (Levy et al., 1997). These concordances are close to what one would expect for a *purely* genetic disorder (where the concordances would be 100 percent for MZ and 50 percent for DZ twins). In fact, genetic factors explained 90 percent of the variance in ADHD symptoms, a much higher proportion than is the case for most behaviour disorders (Plomin, Owen, & McGuffin, 1994).

Behaviour genetic research demonstrates the influence of genes on behaviour, but it provides little information about specific genetic mechanisms. Other researchers are searching for particular genes that influence ADHD. Toronto researchers including Russell Schachar (at Toronto's Hospital for Sick Children) and colleagues have conducted a number of studies of the candidate genes for ADHD (e.g., Adams et al., 2004; Barr et al., 2002; Misener et al., 2004; Quist et al., 2003). Their findings suggest that there are probably many genes involved in the disorder, including genes that play a role in regulating the dopamine and serotonin neurotransmitter systems. Thus, ADHD is a heterogeneous disorder with multiple causes and presentations.

This conclusion has practical as well as theoretical implications. Although we often treat them as such, children do not simply have ADHD or not. In fact, genetic analysis in the major Australian twin study supported a dimensional, not a categorical, conceptualization of ADHD (Levy et al., 1997). While genetics strongly contributes to ADHD, scientists are unlikely to find a simple genetic cause or cure. Furthermore, we will continually be vexed by the question of where to draw the line between "normal" overactivity (or inattention) and "abnormal" ADHD. As we will see, this question becomes particularly important when we consider whether or not medication is overused in treating the disorder.

Genetic factors influence the development of antisocial behaviour as well as ADHD (Burt et al., 2001). Importantly, however, the role of genes is less substantial for ODD, and especially for conduct disorder, than for ADHD (Rutter et al., 1999), while genes are very important in the development of adult antisocial behaviour. The best explanation for this pattern is that rule violations are so common during adolescence that genetic effects are obscured until "pure" cases of antisocial behaviour emerge in adult life (Gottesman & Goldsmith, 1994). Genetic influences also are stronger in early rather than late onset delinquent behaviour, consistent with evidence that adult antisocial behaviour is more strongly associated with child than with adolescent externalizing problems (Taylor, Iacono, & McGue, 2000).

If genes contribute to the development of ODD or conduct disorder, an essential question is: What is the inherited mechanism? Hyperactivity or inattention may be directly inherited, but rule violations surely are not (Earls & Mezzacappa, 2002). No one has suggested that there is a "crime gene," let alone an "argue with your teacher gene"! One inherited tendency that may contribute to conduct disorder, and eventually to antisocial personality disorder (see Chapter 9), is chronic underarousal of the autonomic nervous system. That is, adolescents with conduct disorder may experience generally low levels of arousal and are less anxious about being punished. As a result, they engage in more stimulation-seeking, including risky, behaviours, and do not change their behaviour when their actions bring about adverse consequences (Quay, 1993).

*Neuropsychological Abnormalities* Findings from neuropsychological research suggest other biological contributions to externalizing disorders, particularly to ADHD. Brain damage can produce overactivity and inattention, but *hard signs* of brain damage, such as an abnormal CT scan, are found in less than 5 percent of cases of ADHD (Rutter, 1983). Neurological *soft signs*, such as delays in fine motor coordination (as may be evident in poor penmanship), also have been found with greater frequency among children with ADHD. However, many children with ADHD do not show soft signs, while many normal children do (Barkley, 1998). Thus the implications of the presence of soft signs are unclear.

Minor anomalies in physical appearance, delays in reaching developmental milestones, and a history of mothers' pregnancy and birth complications also appear more commonly among children with ADHD than normal children. Thus several findings suggest that neuropsychological problems contribute to ADHD, but no clear marker of biological vulnerability has been identified. Two promising avenues for further investigation are the search for reliable subtypes of ADHD associated with specific etiologies and the possibility that different contributing factors lead to a common final causal pathway. One candidate for a final causal pathway is impairment in the prefrontal cortical-striatal network, an area of the brain that may underlie the regulation of attention, inhibition, and emotion (Barkley, 1998).

*Food Additives and Sugar* A number of people have speculated that diet and food additives can cause ADHD. However, with the exception of lead poisoning (see Chapter 15), research has failed to find a relation between diet and ADHD. In the 1970s, it was argued that ADHD is caused by the ingestion of food additives, particularly the *salicylates*, which are commonly found in processed foods. A natural-foods diet based on this assertion became so popular that Congress considered a ban on salicylates—until researchers showed that the whole idea was wrong (Conners, 1980).

*Too much sugar can cause stomachaches and cavities, but too much sugar does not cause ADHD.*

Food additives are not the only aspect of children's diets, or the only misguided theory, proposed to be the cause of ADHD. Parents and teachers often blame refined sugar, and physicians often recommend sugar-restricted diets for children with ADHD (Bennett & Sherman, 1983). Existing studies indicate that sugar does not cause hyperactive behaviour, however; nor does the restriction of sugar lead to improved behaviour (Milich, Wolraich, & Lindgren, 1986).

**Social Factors** **Socialization** is the process of shaping children's behaviour and attitudes to conform to the expectations of parents, teachers, and society as a whole. Many psychologists believe that parental explanation, example, and appropriate discipline are most important in socializing children, but other influences cannot be ignored. Peer groups exert strong if sometimes subtle conformity pressures that increase as children grow older. School and television also are powerful socialization agents.

*Parenting Styles* Parental discipline is sometimes mistakenly viewed as the opposite of loving children, but parents need not choose between being strict and being loving. Warm parent–child relationships make discipline both less necessary and more effective (Shaw & Bell, 1993). In fact, **authoritative parenting**, parenting that is both loving and firm, is most effective in rearing well-adjusted children. Warmth and control are so important that developmental psychologists classify parenting into four styles based on these dimensions (see Figure 16–3). In contrast to authoritative parents, *authoritarian* parents lack warmth, and their strict discipline is often harsh and autocratic. Children of authoritarian parents generally are compliant, but they also may be anxious. *Indulgent* parents are the opposite of authoritarian parents: affectionate but lax in discipline. The children of indulgent parents tend to be impulsive and noncompliant, but they are not extremely antisocial. Finally, *neglectful* parents are unconcerned either with their children's emotional needs or with their needs for discipline. Children with serious conduct problems often have neglectful parents (Maccoby & Martin, 1983).

*Coercion* More specific problems in parenting also appear to contribute to the development of children's externalizing problems. One of the most important is Patterson's (1982) concept of **coercion**, which occurs when parents *positively* reinforce a child's misbehaviour by giving in to the child's demands. The child, in turn, *negatively* reinforces the parents by ending his or her obnoxious behaviour as soon as the parents capitulate. Thus coercion describes a system of interaction in which parents and children reciprocally reinforce child misbehaviour and parent capitulation. The concept is illustrated in the following brief case study.

**Classification of Parenting Styles**

| | Accepting, responsive, child-centred | Rejecting, unresponsive, parent-centred |
|---|---|---|
| **Demanding, controlling** | Authoritative | Authoritarian |
| **Undemanding, low in control attempts** | Indulgent | Neglectful |

**FIGURE 16–3: Four styles of parenting, based on dimensions of parental warmth and discipline efforts.**

*Source:* E.E. Maccoby and J.A. Martin, 1983, Socialization in the context of the family: Parent–child interaction. In E.M. Hetherington (Ed.), *Socialization, Personality, and Social Development: Vol. 4. Handbook of Child Psychology*, pp. 1–101. New York: Wiley.

## BRIEF CASE STUDY

### Ms. B's Son

Ms. B. finally admitted that she had lost all control of her four-year-old son, Billy. Ms. B. was a single parent who was exhausted by her routine of working from 8 to 5:30 every day and managing Billy and the household in the evenings and on weekends. She had no parenting or financial support from Billy's father or anyone else, and Ms. B. was worn down. When it came time to discipline Billy, she usually gave in—either because this was the easiest thing to do or because she felt too guilty to say no.

Ms. B. described many difficult interactions with Billy. One example stood out in the mind of the psychologist she consulted. Ms. B. would often stop at the grocery store with Billy after work, and he inevitably gave her trouble while they were shopping. Dealing with the candy aisle was a recent problem. Billy had asked for some candy when they first approached the aisle. Ms. B. told him no, but in an increasingly loud voice Billy protested, "I WANT CANDY!" Ms. B. attempted to stick to her guns, but soon she was embarrassed by the disapproving looks on the faces of other mothers. Feeling both resentful and resigned, she grabbed a bag of M&Ms and gave it to Billy. This gave her a few minutes of peace and quiet while she completed her shopping. ◆

Clearly, Ms. B. rewarded Billy for his misbehaviour in this interaction. Billy also negatively reinforced his mother by quieting down when she gave in to his demands. Because both parties were reinforced, the coercive interaction is predicted to continue over time (Patterson, 1982).

The coercion concept is appealing, in part because it has direct, practical implications. Parents need to break the pattern of interaction by ignoring the misbehaviour (extinction), punishing it, or rewarding more positive actions (Herbert, 2002). We discuss such treatments of noncompliant behaviour later in the chapter. In Billy's case, the psychologist recommended the use of **time-out**, the technique of briefly isolating a child following misbehaviour. The next time Billy acted up in the grocery store, Ms. B. left her shopping cart, and she and Billy sat in the car until he quieted down. She then completed her shopping. Several trips to the car were needed the first day, but Billy's behaviour improved as a result. He quickly was earning rewards for being good—not for being bad—while shopping.

*Love and Discipline* The coercion concept underscores the importance of parental discipline in managing children's behaviour. As we have noted, however, children are better behaved when their parents are loving as well as firm. Why is this so? Attachment theory suggests that children who feel secure and valued by their parents are more compliant because they value their parents in return. That is, children *identify* with parents who are loving to them (Waters, Hay, & Richters, 1986).

More generally, children's noncompliance may not always stem from a lack of discipline. Sometimes children misbehave as a way of getting attention rather than as a way of getting what they want. Consider the concept of *negative attention*, the idea that attempts at punishment sometimes accidentally reinforce children's misbehaviour. Imagine, for example, the teacher who scolds the "class clown" for misbehaving. In some circumstances, the scolding increases rather than decreases the child's misbehaviour; that is, the attempt at punishment actually serves as a reinforcement. Rather than trying to find a truly effective punishment, we think it is essential to understand *why* negative attention is reinforcing. We believe that many children are reinforced by negative attention because they are not getting enough positive attention—enough love. If so, increasing parental affection should be a better way of treating their externalizing behaviour than increasing parental discipline (Emery, 1992).

*Conflict and Inconsistent Discipline* Inconsistent discipline is another common correlate of children's externalizing problems (Patterson, De Baryshe, & Ramsey, 1989). Inconsistency can involve frequent changes in the style and standards of one parent, or two parents may be inconsistent in their differing expectations and rules for a child. For example, inconsistency between mothers and fathers often becomes a problem when parents have conflicts in their own relationship—as when they are unhappily married, divorced, or experiencing other forms of family adversity (Emery, 1999; Repetti, Taylor, & Seeman, 2002). In these circumstances, parents may deliberately undermine each other's discipline.

Yet another problem occurs when parents' actions are inconsistent with their words. For example, consider the contradiction inherent in angry and harsh physical punishment (Gershoff, 2002). On the one hand, such discipline teaches children to follow the rules. On the other hand, it teaches children that anger and aggression are acceptable means of solving problems. Parents socialize children by modelling appropriate behaviour as well as by disciplining them, and children often imitate what their parents do, not what they say.

*Broader Social Influences: Peers, Neighbourhoods, Television, and Society* Parents are not solely responsible for socializing children. Violence is continually modelled on television, for example, and longitudinal evidence indicates that children learn aggression from television programs (Eron, 1982). Youth who witness violence in their communities also are more likely to be violent themselves (Shahinfar, Kupersmidt, & Matza, 2001). Peer groups can teach antisocial behaviour (Dishion, McCord, & Poulin, 1999). In fact, some researchers have suggested that socialized delinquency, in which criminal acts occur in the company of others, is an important subtype of externalizing disorders (Kazdin, 1995). Others have argued that peers are *more* important agents of socialization than parents (Harris, 1995).

A number of neighbourhood and societal factors play a role in the etiology of externalizing problems. For example, more psychological problems are found among children who grow up in poor, inner-city neighbourhoods (Rutter, 1989; Shaw et al., 1994). Professionals concerned with children's mental health, therefore, need to be concerned about poverty, inadequate schooling, and violence (Caspi & Moffitt, 1995; Dishion, French, & Patterson, 1995).

Cross-cultural evidence also points to broad societal influences on externalizing behaviour. The crime rate in the United States is higher than the crime rates in Canada, Japan, and Europe (Jones & Krisberg, 1994). As we have noted, many crimes are committed by juveniles. It has been suggested that some aspects of U.S. culture, such as higher poverty rates or lack of gun control, may account for the societal influences on juvenile crime (Jones & Krisberg, 1994).

**Social Factors in Attention-Deficit/Hyperactivity Disorder** When discussing the etiology of externalizing disorders, we have not distinguished between the development of ODD or conduct disorder and ADHD. In fact, there are essentially no theories of how social factors might play a unique role in the development of ADHD (Hinshaw, 1994). However, some recent research found that shared environmental factors largely account for the *comorbidity* of ADHD and other externalizing disorders, suggesting that family and social adversity may explain why these disorders often occur together (Burt et al., 2001).

Some researchers have found that the parents of children with ADHD are less effective than other parents. For example, Charlotte Johnston at the University of British Columbia, and Eric Mash at the University of Calgary, have shown that mothers of children with ADHD tend to be more critical, demanding, and controlling when compared to the mothers of normal children (Mash & Johnston, 1982). Mothers find it stressful to raise an ADHD child, and often feel that their parenting is inadequate (e.g., Johnston & Mash, 1989; Mash & Johnston, 1990). However, problems in parenting appear to be a reaction to the children's troubles and not a cause of them. Researchers have used a clever technique to document that mothers do react negatively to their children's ADHD. Scientists have compared the interactions between mothers and their children under two conditions: placebo versus medication. The experimenter administers either a psychostimulant medication (discussed shortly) or a placebo (neither the child, the mother, nor the experimenter knows who received the real medication), and mother–child interactions are subsequently observed. Because psychostimulant medication directly alters children's hyperactive behaviour, any differences between mother–child interactions in the two conditions must be caused by changes in the children's behaviour.

In fact, children with ADHD become more attentive and compliant while on medication, and their mothers' behaviour "improves" as well. In comparison to the placebo group, mothers become less negative and less controlling when their children are medicated (Barkley et al., 1984; Danforth, Barkley, & Stokes, 1991). Children with ADHD make social interactions more difficult. Still, ineffective parenting surely intensifies their problems. This is why parent training is often used in the treatment of ADHD, as discussed in a later section of this chapter.

**Psychological Factors** *Self-control*, the internal regulation of behaviour, is the ultimate goal of socialization. Not surprisingly, several investigators have found problems with self-control among children with externalizing disorders.

One area of research on self-control has focused on *delay of gratification*—the adaptive ability to defer smaller but immediate rewards for larger, long-term benefits. An example of delay of gratification is studying for an exam rather than going out with friends. In general, children with externalizing problems are less able to delay gratification and are more oriented to the present than are other children. They opt for immediate rewards rather than for long-term goals, a maladaptive characteristic for achieving educational and career goals (Nigg, 2001).

Children with externalizing problems also may fail to exert self-control because they misinterpret the intentions of others, particularly in ambiguous social situations. Several studies by the psychologist Ken Dodge and his colleagues have indicated that aggressive children overinterpret the aggressive intentions of their peers (Crick & Dodge, 1994). That is, children with externalizing problems are likely to view other children as threatening them. As a result, some of their aggression may be an attempt to "get you before you get me."

Psychologists also have studied the moral reasoning of children with externalizing problems. Kohlberg (1985) created a hierarchy of moral reasoning based on the explanations children give to justify their actions. Research indicates that children use increasingly abstract and sophisticated moral principles as they grow older. For example, a young boy may say that the reason he behaves well is because "Mommy will get mad." An older boy may explain that the reason he behaves well is because "You need to follow the rules." A teenager might explain that he behaves well because "It is the right thing to do."

According to Kohlberg, higher moral principles are based on values regarding appropriate conduct rather than on the immediate consequences of misbehaviour. He hypothesized that these more sophisticated guidelines, in turn, lead to more prosocial behaviour. In support of his theorizing, some evidence indicates that aggressive children follow the hedonic principles commonly used by children at younger ages (Kohlberg, 1985). They exhibit less self-control, or, to put it in familiar terms, they may have less of a "conscience" than their peers.

**Integration and Alternative Pathways** How can we integrate evidence on the diverse contributions to the development of externalizing? Two conclusions seem clear. First, externalizing disorders have many etiological pathways, not one. Obviously, different factors contribute to causing ADHD, ODD, and conduct disorder, but different pathways also can lead to the development of the *same* disorder. For example, although life-course-persistent and adolescent-limited antisocial behaviour cannot be distinguished during adolescence, the two problems clearly reflect different etiological pathways: long-standing biological and socialization problems in the former case, and short-term rebellion and peer influences in the latter (Moffitt, 1993).

Second, biological, psychological, and social factors clearly interact in causing externalizing disorders. Temperament theorists note, for example, that the *goodness of fit* between a child's temperament and the family environment may be of greatest importance to healthy psychological development (Shaw & Bell, 1993). The combination of a difficult temperament and family adversity may result in ODD and eventually conduct disorder, while a temperamentally "easy" child might turn out well-behaved despite growing up in difficult family circumstances (Kasen et al., 1996). Similarly, recent evidence indicates that impulsive youth have unusually high rates of juvenile offending when they grow up in poor versus better-off neighbourhoods. However, whether the neighbourhood is poor or better off has no effect on offending for nonimpulsive youth (Lynam et al., 2000).

## Treatment of Externalizing Disorders

Numerous treatments have been developed for children's externalizing disorders, but unfortunately the problems are difficult to change (Kazdin, 1997). The most promising treatments include psychostimulants for ADHD, behavioural family therapy for ODD, and certain intensive programs for treating conduct disorder and delinquent youth.

**Psychostimulants and ADHD** **Psychostimulants** such as *Ritalin* are medications that increase central nervous system activity, and in appropriate dosages, the medications increase alertness, arousal, and attention. Psychostimulants are the most commonly used treatment for ADHD.

The frequent use of psychostimulants to control children's behaviour is a legitimate cause for concern. Perhaps the diagnosis of ADHD is overused. As we have noted, the diagnosis is used far less commonly in other countries, and ADHD appears to be a dimensional not a categorical problem. Perhaps mental health professionals should raise the threshold for making the diagnosis. Pills also can be overused as a "quick fix" not only for troubled children but for troubled schools. Many public schools are underfunded, overcrowded, and inadequately staffed. Moreover, the competitiveness in private schools can encourage the use of psychostimulants to push marginal or untroubled students to "get an edge" by heightening their attention and alertness.

Still, these important concerns should not cloud the facts about psychostimulants. The medications offer an inexpensive, carefully researched, and effective treatment for ADHD (MTA Cooperative Group, 1999). Psychostimulants produce immediate and noticeable improvements in the behaviour of about 75 percent of children with ADHD. At the same time, psychostimulants have only limited effects on learning; it is not clear whether they produce long-term benefits; and they have several side effects. We examine each of these issues, but first we must consider a long-held, and mistaken, view about psychostimulants and ADHD.

*The "Paradoxical Effect" Paradox* Psychostimulants heighten energy and alertness, and they lead to restless, even frenetic, behaviour when abused. These effects are accurately conveyed by a street name for the drugs, "speed." The psychiatrist Charles Bradley (1937) was one of the first to observe that stimulants seem to have a "paradoxical effect" on overactive children: The medication slows them down. For many years, professionals believed that this was proof of abnormal brain functioning in ADHD. The real irony, however, is that the idea of a paradoxical effect was wrong.

One reason for the enduring "paradoxical effect" paradox is that it was deemed unethical to experiment with psychostimulants on normal children, even though the medication was given regularly to millions of "abnormal" children. A group of researchers eventually found a clever way to address the ethical problem. They obtained permission from colleagues in the medical and mental health communities to study the effects of psychostimulants on their exceptionally competent children. The researchers found that the psychostimulants affected the normal children in the same way that they affected overactive children. The medication improved attention and decreased motor activity (Rapoport et al.,

1978). In fact, psychostimulants have the same effects on adults when taken in comparably small dosages. There is no paradoxical effect of psychostimulants on children with ADHD.

*Usage and Effects* The most commonly prescribed psychostimulants are known by the trade names of Ritalin (the most commonly used psychostimulant), Dexedrine, and Adderall. Each has the effect of increasing alertness and arousal. Another widely prescribed stimulant, Cylert (pemoline), was recalled from pharmacies across Canada once it was discovered that it could lead to serious liver complications (Health Canada, 1999a).

Psychostimulants usually are prescribed by pediatricians, who typically are consulted following a child's difficulties in the early years of school. The fact that behaviour problems in school are the main concern about children with ADHD is demonstrated in how psychostimulants are prescribed. A pill is taken in the morning before school, and because the effects of most psychostimulants last only three or four hours, another pill is taken at the lunch hour. A third pill may or may not be taken after school, but the medication typically is not taken on weekends or during school vacations because of concerns about side effects.

Children take psychostimulants for years, not days or weeks. Traditionally, medication was discontinued in early adolescence, because it was believed that the problem was "outgrown" by that age. However, research shows that, while hyperactivity usually improves during the teen years, problems with inattention and impulsivity often continue (Schachar & Tannock, 2002). Thus psychostimulants now are taken through the teen years, and perhaps into adulthood, as interest has grown in "adult ADHD" (Barkley, 1998).

Numerous double-blind, placebo-controlled studies have demonstrated that psychostimulants indisputably improve children's attentiveness and decrease their hyperactivity (Barkley, 1998; Pelham et al., 1993), with gains maintained at follow-up periods of at least five years (Charach, Ickowicz, & Schachar, 2004). In the largest treatment study to date, which involved six research sites including one in Canada, 579 children with ADHD were randomly assigned to one of four treatments: (1) controlled medication management, (2) intensive behaviour therapy, (3) the two treatments combined, or (4) uncontrolled community care (which typically included medication). A 14-month follow-up assessment showed that the controlled medication and combined treatments produced significantly more improvements in ADHD symptoms than the alternatives. Intensive behaviour therapy (part of the combined treatment) added only a slight improvement over medication for ADHD symptoms (see Figure 16–4) but may have modestly helped comorbid symptoms of aggressive behaviour (MTA Cooperative Group, 1999; Swanson et al., 2001). Russell Schachar and colleagues recently reviewed 14 studies involving almost 1400 participants and similarly concluded that the combination of medication and behavioural interventions is more effective than either treatment alone (Schachar et al., 2002).

More aggressive behaviour therapies, including summer treatment programs, may produce much more notable benefits (Pelham et al., 2002). Still, this evidence indisputably establishes psychostimulant medication as the first-line treatment for ADHD. However, the findings also indicate that improvements are needed in standard community medication management, which was much less effective than carefully controlled medication use. Unfortunately, standard community practice often involves little ongoing monitoring of ADHD children.

***Russell Schachar*** *at Toronto's Hospital for Sick Children is a leading expert on the nature and treatment of ADHD.*

**Overall Success Rates for Alternative ADHD Treatments in the MTA Study**

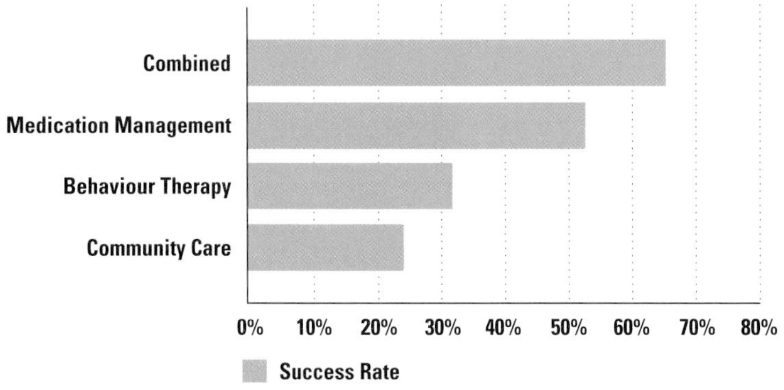


**FIGURE 16–4: Carefully monitored use of psychostimulants produces notable benefits for ADHD. Adding behaviour therapy to medication produces a small but significant increase in success rates. Behaviour therapy alone and community care—typically involving medication prescribed with little follow-up—produce much lower rates of improvement.**

*Source:* Based on J.M. Swanson et al., 2001, Clinical relevance of the primary findings of the MTA: Success rates based on severity of ADHD and ODD symptoms at the end of treatment. *Journal of the American Academy of Child and Adolescent Psychiatry, 40,* 168–179.

Although psychostimulants improve hyperactivity and impulsivity, their effects on attention and learning are less certain. Children on medication complete more reading, spelling, and arithmetic assignments with somewhat improved accuracy (Pelham et al., 1985), but their grades and achievement test scores improve little if at all (Henker & Whalen, 1989). This pattern of improvement in behaviour but not in learning was observed again in the recent, large-scale MTA Cooperative Study (1999).

Research on **dose–response effects**, the response to different dosages of medication, was once thought to explain the different effects on behaviour and learning. Sprague and Sleator (1977) found that a low dosage of psychostimulants produced gains in learning, but the medication *interfered* with learning at higher dosages. Higher dosages produced more improvements in behaviour, however, suggesting that some children received too much medication, because medication typically is increased gradually or *titrated* based on improvements in behaviour.

Subsequent evidence on dose–response effects is mixed, and it now appears that different children respond uniquely to different dosages (Tannock, Schachar, & Logan, 1995). Thus, it remains unclear why improved attention and behaviour in the classroom do not translate into improved grades and achievement. An even more troubling and puzzling fact is that psychostimulants have not been found to lead to *long-term* improvements in behaviour, learning, or any other areas of functioning (Barkley, 1998; Schachar & Tannock, 2002; see Table 16–4).

*Side Effects* The side effects of psychostimulants can be troubling. Some side effects are relatively minor, such as decreased appetite, increased heart rate, and sleeping difficulties. Others are more serious, such as an increase in motor tics in a small percentage of cases. Evidence that psychostimulants can slow physical growth is also an important concern. Children maintained on psychostimulants fall somewhat behind expected gains in height and weight, although rebounds in growth occur when the medication is stopped. This is one reason why the medication often is discontinued when children are out of school. Still, careful monitoring of cases is necessary because of possible individual differences in growth effects (Campbell, Green, & Deutsch, 1985).

Another side effect that concerns some psychologists is that parents, teachers, and children may credit the pills, not the child, for the improved behaviour (Whalen et al., 1991). When they are having an "off" day, for example, many children with ADHD are asked, "Did you take your pill today?" Research indicates that ADHD children on psychostimulants do not credit "the pill"; they make internal attributions for their positive behaviour (Pelham et al., 2002). Still, we face the question: Should children's misbehaviour be corrected with medication? This is an important and reasonable question to ask. Many parents are reluctant to use psychostimulants for various reasons, and, in fact, the medications are used about 3 to 10 times more often in the United States as in Europe, Canada, and Australia (Heyman & Santosh, 2002; Schachar & Tannock, 2002). Psychostimulants are an inexpensive and effective treatment for ADHD, especially in comparison with the alternatives. Still, the benefits of medication are limited, various side effects are a source of concern, and, most importantly, there is no bright line between normal and abnormal behaviour in diagnosing ADHD. Thus, it is reasonable to ask whether we are overdiagnosing ADHD and overmedicating schoolchildren.

**TABLE 16–4 Short-Term and Long-Term Effects of Psychostimulants on ADHD**

| | Hyperactivity/Impulsivity | Inattention/Learning |
|---|---|---|
| Short-term | Dramatic improvements; less active and more focused; fewer social problems | More work completed, but no change in grades or standardized test scores |
| Long-term | No demonstrated benefit | No demonstrated benefit |

*Antidepressant Medication for ADHD* A number of children with ADHD who fail to respond to psychostimulants have been treated with antidepressant medication in recent years. Although depression and ADHD often co-occur, this is not the rationale for the treatment. Rather, the antidepressants are thought to affect ADHD symptoms directly for reasons that are not yet clear. What is clear, however, is that antidepressants are a second-line treatment for ADHD. Their use is justified only following the failure of psychostimulants (DeVane &

Sallee, 1996; Spencer, Biederman, & Wilens, 1998).

**Behavioural Family Therapy** **Behavioural family therapy (BFT)** is a treatment based on learning theory principles that teaches parents to be very clear and specific about their expectations for children's behaviour, to monitor children's actions closely, and to systematically reward positive behaviour while ignoring or mildly punishing misbehaviour. BFT is sometimes used as an adjunct or alternative to medication in treating ADHD, although it offers limited benefits for ADHD symptoms (MTA Cooperative Study, 1999). However, BFT is more promising as a treatment of ODD (Brestan & Eyberg, 1998).

BFT typically begins with *parent training*. Parents are taught to identify specific problematic behaviours such as fighting with siblings, to list preferred alternative behaviours like speaking nicely, and to set consequences for appropriate and inappropriate behaviour. Parents may also make a "star chart" for recording children's progress and perhaps develop a "daily report card" that the child will carry home from school as a way of coordinating discipline in both settings (Scott, 2002).

Other aspects of parent training may include teaching parents about punishment strategies, such as the time-out technique. Conventional wisdom holds that punishment should be firm but not angry, and that rewards should far outweigh punishments as a strategy of discipline. Some experts believe that parent training should directly emphasize increasing warmth as well as discipline in parent–child relationships (Cavell, 2001). From this perspective, the goal of parent training is to teach parents to be authoritative.

Research on children with behaviour problems supports the short-term effectiveness of BFT (Patterson, 1982). Other studies demonstrate that parent training can be effectively delivered in groups or through the use of videotapes (Webster-Stratton, 1994) or based on an exciting series of studies conducted in Australia, through the various popular media (Sanders, Montgomery, & Brechman-Toussaint, 2000). However, evidence on long-term effectiveness is less certain, and benefits generally are limited to children under the age of 12 (Kazdin, 1997). In considering the challenges for BFT, you should recall that the parents of children with

The Scary Truth About Stock Options
U.S.News
& WORLD REPORT
Paxil, Prozac, Ritalin...
Are These Drugs Safe for Kids?
Many parents are using powerful pills to control behavior
Amy Coburn
A former Paxil user

*Psychostimulants are effective treatments of ADHD, but concern is rising that medication may be given too quickly to too many children.*

externalizing problems often live in adverse circumstances that make it difficult to alter their parenting (Emery, Fincham, & Cummings, 1992). Parents can be effective in changing children's behaviour, but psychologists need to develop more ways to help parents who live in difficult circumstances (Scott, 2002).

Some behavioural therapies also include direct training of children as well as parents. *Problem-solving skills training* (PSST) is one commonly used technique in which children are taught to slow down, evaluate a problem, and consider alternative solutions before acting. Some evidence indicates that the combination of PSST and parent training leads to more improvement than either therapy alone in the treatment of the problems found in ODD (Kazdin, Siegel, & Bass, 1992). As with behavioural family therapy, however, PSST offers only minimal help to children with ADHD.

**Treatment of Conduct Disorder and Juvenile Delinquency** Numerous programs have been developed to treat conduct disorder and juvenile delinquency. In fact, exciting claims about the effectiveness of new programs for difficult youth are commonly reported in the popular media. You should be cautious about these new approaches. Research indicates that conduct disorder among adolescents is even more resistant to treatment than are externalizing problems among younger children (Kazdin, 1995, 1997).

Some BFT approaches have shown promise in treating young people with family or legal problems (Alexander & Parsons, 1982). These treatments are based on principles similar to those in programs for younger children, except that *negotiation*—actively involving young people in setting rules—is central to BFT with adolescents. An obvious reason for the negotiation strategy is that parents have less direct control over adolescents than over younger children. Because of diminishing parental control, many mental health professionals also advocate treating externalizing problems prior to adolescence.

*Multisystemic Therapy* *Multisystemic therapy* is another intervention with conduct disorder that has received increasing attention (Henggeler & Borduin, 1990). In recognition of the diverse causes of externalizing behaviour, multisystemic therapy combines family treatment with coordinated interventions in other important contexts of the troubled child's life, including peer groups, schools, and neighbourhoods. Multisystemic therapy has not yet been adequately evaluated by independent research groups, but initial evidence is promising for improving family relationships and school attendance while reducing arrest rates among youth with conduct disorder (Borduin et al., 1995; Henggeler, 1994). Positive findings also have been reported for a similar intervention for delinquent youth placed in foster care (Chamberlain & Reid, 1998).

*Residential Programs and Juvenile Courts* Many adolescents with serious conduct problems or especially troubled families are treated in residential programs outside the home. One of the most actively researched residential programs is *Achievement Place*, a group home that operates according to highly structured behaviour therapy principles. Achievement Place homes, like many similar residential programs, are very effective in improving aggression and noncompliance while the adolescent is living in the treatment setting. For this reason, professionals working in residential or inpatient settings are wise to adopt similar behavioural strategies. Unfortunately, the programs do not prevent **recidivism**, or repeat offending, once the adolescent leaves the residential placement (Bailey, 2002; Kazdin, 1995). Delinquent adolescents typically return to family, peer, and school environments that do not consistently reward prosocial behaviour or monitor and punish antisocial behaviour.

Of course, many delinquent youths are treated in the juvenile justice system, and treatment, or *rehabilitation*, is the explicit goal of most legal interventions with minors. The philosophy of the juvenile justice system in Canada is based on the principle of *parens patriae*—the state as parent. In theory, juvenile courts are designed to help troubled youth, not to punish them. This lofty goal is belied by research indicating that diversion—keeping problem youths out of the juvenile justice system—is a promising "treatment" (Davidson et al., 1987). The juvenile justice system often seems to create delinquency instead of curing it, and evidence indicates that recidivism is lower when delinquents are diverted away from the courts.

The struggles involved in treating conduct disorder have led some to question the *parens patriae* philosophy of the juvenile justice system. Under the current laws in Canada, minors can be transferred out of the juvenile justice system and tried as adults (McGuire, 1997). Thus, in some cases the aim is primarily punishment rather than rehabilitation. Given that this occurs, we wish to add a caveat in concluding our overview of the difficulties in treating externalizing disorders: Our intention is to be realistic, not pessimistic, about treatment. Externalizing disorders are of vast importance to children, families, and society, and the difficulties in treating problem youth should be seen as a challenge and not a defeat.

As noted by Marlene Moretti (Simon Fraser University) and colleagues, Canada, like many other countries, places greater emphasis on the treatment rather than prevention of conduct disorder. This means that by the time many conduct disordered children or adolescents are referred for treatment, their behavioural problems have been entrenched and are resistant to treatment. Accordingly, interventions for conduct disorder are more effective for younger children than for adolescents (Moretti et al., 1997). Perhaps the best hope is to prevent the problems from developing by intervening early, and by helping to ease some of the family adversity that helps to create these problems in the first place.

To illustrate one prevention program, psychologist Richard Tremblay at the University of Montreal and his colleagues identified disruptive boys from an inner-city, low socioeconomic neighbourhood school. These children were at high risk for later antisocial behaviour. The boys were randomly assigned to a preventive intervention or a control condition. The intervention involved home-based parent training in behavioural strategies for managing problem child behaviours, and school-based social skills training. The boys were followed from early childhood through to mid-adolescence, where it was found that the intervention was associated with significantly less delinquent behaviour (Tremblay et al., 1995). These findings encourage early identification and treatment of problem behaviours.

**Course and Outcome** Do children "outgrow" externalizing disorders? Parents ask this question frequently, and the answer, obviously, is important for treatment planning. Longitudinal studies suggest that externalizing problems are often, but not always, chronic. For example, consider the research by Gabrielle Weiss and Lilly Hechtman at Montreal Children's Hospital, who conducted a long-term follow-up study of ADHD children. When these children were reassessed as adults, aged 25 to 30 years, many of them continued to have problems. More than 20 percent developed antisocial personality disorder (Herrero, Hechtman, & Weiss, 1994), and many had other problems such as substance abuse and ongoing difficulties in occupational and school functioning. Only one-third no longer had ADHD symptoms (Weiss & Hechtman, 1993).

With regard to the time-course of specific features of ADHD and other externalizing disorders, hyperactivity generally declines during adolescence, while attention deficits and impulsivity are more likely to continue. The continuity of some symptoms into adult life is evident in the recently growing interest in adult ADHD. Importantly, the prognosis of ADHD depends substantially on whether there is comorbid ODD or conduct disorder. If so, youth are more likely to develop problems with substance abuse, criminality, and other forms of antisocial behaviour (Hinshaw, 1994). In fact, roughly half of all children with ODD or conduct disorder continue to have problems with antisocial behaviour into adulthood (Hinshaw, 1994; Kazdin, 1995). As has been noted, however, antisocial behaviour that begins during adolescence is more likely to be transient than antisocial behaviour that begins during childhood (Moffit, 1993).

The continuity of externalizing disorders clearly underscores the need for prevention and early intervention. If we can do better in helping troubled children and their families, we will succeed in preventing antisocial behaviour not only during childhood but into adult life.

## Internalizing and Other Disorders

Teachers cannot ignore disruptive children in the classroom, but they may overlook anxious or depressed children who sit quietly and unhappily alone. The negative effect of externalizing disorders is an important reason why we have focused on these problems, but like schoolteachers, we do not want to overlook children whose troubles are *not* disruptive. In the following sections, we consider special issues related to children's internalizing disorders, even though there are no separate DSM-IV-TR categories for anxiety or mood disorders of childhood. We also briefly introduce—and raise some questions about—some of the many other psychological disorders of childhood included in DSM-IV-TR. We begin with a case study.

### CASE STUDY **Turning the Tables on Tormentors**

Mark was 12 years old when his mother brought him to see a new psychologist. Both Mark and his mother agreed that he had been depressed for well over a year, and nine months of "play therapy" resulted in little or no improvement. Mark felt sad most of the time, cried often, and felt helpless and hopeless about the future. He had withdrawn from his usual activities, and his straight As had fallen to Bs, Cs, and even a few Ds—despite an IQ of 145. Teasing was a particular problem, one that when talking about it brought Mark to tears during the first

continued

*cont.*

appointment. A group of boys at his school constantly tormented Mark, calling him the "little professor." As in the office, their teasing frequently brought Mark to the point of tears.

Mark's family was well functioning, and there was no family history of depression. Mark's mother was a homemaker, and his father made an adequate living as a police officer. His parents were happily married, and his two younger brothers were doing well. Mark's mother attributed many of his problems to his unusual intelligence and to the fact that Mark had played with few children during the first years of his life because the family lived in an apartment in an unsafe neighbourhood before the birth of his brothers.

The new treatment followed a cognitive behaviour therapy approach, but began with a careful period of building rapport. Establishing a good therapeutic relationship was very important to Mark who was socially isolated and unhappy with his previous therapy. Treatment eventually focused on skills training and behavioural activation. Mark was encouraged to rejoin various activities and to initiate relationships with his peers. His parents were told to treat Mark normally. In particular, they were encouraged to hold the same high (but not demanding) expectations for Mark's schoolwork as they did for their other sons.

A special emphasis of treatment was how Mark could deal with his tormentors. As a step, the therapist began to tease Mark playfully at times and to encourage teasing back in return. This was viewed both as a way of teaching Mark some skills and of desensitizing him to teasing, which is normative if often vicious among 12-year-old boys. Given the strong therapeutic relationship that had developed, Mark quickly learned not only to accept this game but to relish it. With his high IQ, he soon became devastatingly clever in his banter.

The benefits clearly generalized outside of the therapy session. Mark no longer cried when he was teased; instead, he learned retorts that set his tormentors on their heels. In fact, Mark did not limit his self-defence to words. He punched one particularly mean boy in the nose one day—a response that was *not* encouraged in therapy but one that did not upset his father, the police officer (or, privately, the therapist).

Over the course of about three months of therapy, Mark's mood improved considerably. He started getting A's again, he was re-engaged in various activities, and the teasing was no longer an issue. He remained himself—a quiet, intelligent, and introspective boy—but he had learned to have more rational expectations for himself, the importance of staying involved, and how to handle his tormentors. ◆

The case of Mark provides a clear illustration that children do suffer from "adult" disorders such as depression. Yet the diagnosis is not always so clear. Imagine, for example, if Mark were six years old. Although he might act and look sad, he certainly would be less able to express or reflect on his feelings at this young age or feel hopeless about the future. Moreover, his parents would have difficulty interpreting his crying, withdrawal, and falling grades without a good awareness of how Mark himself felt. Even if six-year-old Mark could tell them that he was sad, the meaning of his words would be difficult to interpret. At young ages, children do not have the same ability to experience and express their thoughts and emotions as adults. This is why we consider internalizing disorders among children separately from adult mood and anxiety disorders.

## Typical Symptoms of Internalizing and Other Disorders

Children's internalizing symptoms include sadness, fears, and somatic complaints, as well as other indicators of mood and anxiety disorders—for example, feeling worthless or tense. DSM-IV-TR does not have a separate category for children's internalizing disorders, but the manual does identify some unique ways in which children experience the symptoms of mood and anxiety disorders. When diagnosing major depressive episodes among children and adolescents, for example, the clinician is allowed to substitute "irritable mood" for "depressed mood." The manual recognizes that children sometimes act angry when they are feeling sad, and, more generally, that children may express their feelings in unique ways, or they may hide their true emotions, especially when talking to adults.

The diagnosis of phobia offers another example of how the DSM-IV-TR deals with symptoms in children. In contrast to adults, children are not required to recognize that their fears are excessive or unreasonable, because children often have limited insight into their problems. In fact, children may lack the *cognitive capacity* to experience some of the internalizing symptoms found among adults with the same disorder. Self-awareness emerges across the course of development, and it is not until adolescence that children develop the cognitive abilities necessary for "adult" insight.

These provisions in DSM-IV-TR recognize that children's capacity to experience and recognize emotions emerges over the course of development, as does their ability to express—and to mask—their own feelings. Unfortunately, the manual offers only a few, scattered developmental considerations. This is in large part due to the fact that the course of children's normal emotional development is not well charted, because it is extremely difficult to assess children's feelings. Children, especially at younger ages, typically are not reliable or valid informants about their internal life. It is much more difficult for adults to evaluate children's inner experiences than it is to observe their externalizing behaviour.

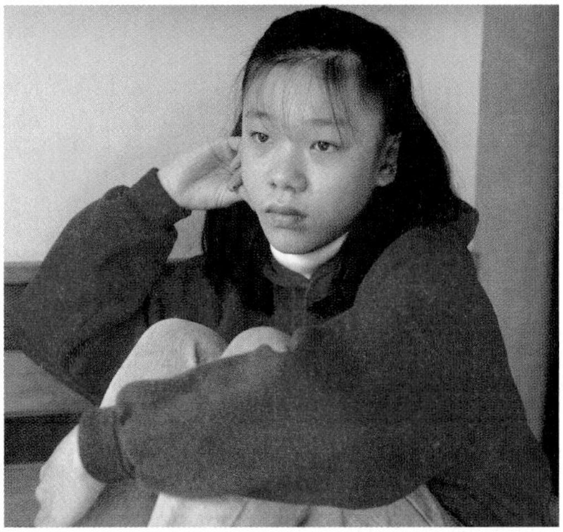

*Depression becomes much more common during adolescence, especially among teenage girls.*

**Depressive Symptoms** As illustrated by Mark, children can experience the adult symptoms of depression, but unlike the case of Mark, the assessment of depression in children can be difficult. For example, in one study of children hospitalized for depression, clinicians found a correlation of *zero* between children's and parents' ratings on identical measures of the children's depression (Kazdin, French, & Unis, 1983). The means that what adults said about the children was completely different from what the children said about themselves. In another study, children's and parents' ratings of depression were correlated with very different factors. Children's ratings of their own depression were associated with their other ratings of their internal distress—feelings of hopelessness, low self-esteem, internal attributions for negative events, and external locus of control. In contrast, parents' ratings of children's depression were associated with how they rated children's externalizing behaviour, not their internal distress (Kazdin, 1989). Finally, and perhaps of greatest concern, evidence indicates that parents systematically underestimate the extent of depression reported by their children and adolescents (Kazdin & Petti, 1982; Rutter, 1989).

Given parents' and children's widely differing perceptions, psychologists are rightly concerned about a child's depression if *either* a parent *or* a child notes problems. In assessing children's internalizing problems, mental health professionals must obtain information from *multiple informants*—parents, teachers, and the children themselves (Harrington, 2002).

When assessing children directly, child clinical psychologists are sensitive to different signs that may be indicative of depression at different ages: unresponsiveness to caregivers under the age of two; sad expressions and social withdrawal in preschoolers; somatic complaints in young school-age children; more direct admission of sad feelings or marked irritability in older school-age children or early adolescents; and full-blown depression, including suicide risk, among adolescents of all ages.

Sound research on depression in children awaits a better definition of the disorder and better methods of assessment. Currently, it is clear that depression in children and adolescents often is comorbid both with externalizing problems and with anxiety. Depression in children also may differ from depression in adolescents, not only in how it is expressed but also in its lower prevalence, equal frequency among boys and girls, stronger relation with family dysfunction, and less persistent course (Harrington, 2002).

**Children's Fears and Anxiety** *Anxiety* is a general and diffuse emotional reaction that often is linked with anticipation of future and perhaps unrealistic threats. In contrast, *fear* is an emotional reaction to real and immediate danger (see Chapter 6). As with depression, children often have trouble identifying their anxiety, but they are more aware of their fears, which are immediate and have a clear environmental referent. Also, adults can observe much of children's fearful behaviour for the same reasons. Thus research on the development of children's fears is more advanced than it is for their anxiety.

Three findings from fear research are especially helpful. First, children develop different fears for the first time at different ages, and the onset of new fears may be sudden and have

CALVIN AND HOBBES © Watterson. Reprinted with permission of UNIVERSAL PRESS SYNDICATE. All Rights Reserved.

no apparent cause in the child's environment. For example, infants typically develop a fear of strangers in the months just before their first birthday; preschoolers develop fears of monsters and the dark between the ages of two and six; and children between ages three and six often develop fears related to kindergarten or school (Cox & Taylor, 1999). (To cite one curious example, if you ever dreamed of going to school in your underwear or partially dressed, you are not alone. Such dreams are surprisingly common among school-age children.) In short, many fears, even those that seem odd or arise suddenly, are developmentally normal, a conclusion that can be reassuring to parents and perhaps to children. A second finding of importance is that some fears, particularly fears of uncontrollable events, are both common and relatively stable across different ages. Third, many other fears, especially specific ones, decline in frequency as children grow older (Cox & Taylor, 1999). Apparently, children "outgrow" many of their fears, probably by gradually confronting them in everyday life.

**Separation Anxiety Disorder and School Refusal** We can illustrate the importance of evidence on children's fears by considering the special case of separation anxiety. **Separation anxiety** is distress expressed following separation from an attachment figure, typically a parent or other close caregiver. It is a normal fear that begins to develop around 8 months and peaks around 15 months. An infant who has tolerated separations in the past may suddenly start to cling, cry, and scream whenever a parent tries to leave, even for a brief separation. Children's upset lessens over time, but even toddlers and preschoolers typically experience distress upon separation, particularly when left in an unfamiliar circumstance.

Although it is a normal response at younger ages, excessive separation anxiety can become a serious problem at older ages if children fail to "outgrow" the reaction. In fact, DSM-IV-TR contains a diagnosis for **separation anxiety disorder**, which is defined by symptoms such as persistent and excessive worry for the safety of an attachment figure, fears of getting lost or being kidnapped, nightmares with separation themes, and refusal to be alone. For a child to be diagnosed with this disorder, he or she must exhibit three or more of these symptoms for at least four weeks.

Separation anxiety disorder is especially problematic when it interferes with school attendance. **School refusal**, also known as *school phobia*, is characterized by an extreme reluctance to go to school, and is accompanied by various symptoms of anxiety, such as stomachaches and headaches. Some children are literally school phobic—they are afraid of school or specific aspects of attending school. But in many cases, school refusal can be traced to separation anxiety disorder (Last & Strauss, 1990). In such cases, it often appears that the parent, as well as the child, has difficulty separating. Whatever its origins, school refusal is a serious problem that has been reported to account for more than two-thirds of referrals to an anxiety disorders clinic for children.

**Troubled Peer Relationships** Children with internalizing or externalizing problems often have troubled peer relationships. In fact, research shows that peer relationship difficulties predict future, as well as current, psychological problems among children (Parker & Asher, 1987; Rutter, 1989). Simply put, children who are aggressive and disobedient or shy and withdrawn often are not well liked by their peers. However, different patterns of difficulties relating to peer relationships have been found among children with internalizing and externalizing problems.

Many recent findings on psychological problems and peer relationships have used the peer sociometric method to assess children's relationships. *Peer sociometrics* evaluate children's relationships by obtaining information on who is "liked most" and who is "liked least" from a large group of children who know one another (for example, children in a classroom). Statistical procedures are then used to group children into one of five categories based on the ratings of their peers (Coie & Kupersmidt, 1983; Newcomb, Bukowski, & Pattee, 1993):

- *Popular* children receive many "liked most" and few "liked least" ratings.
- *Average* children also receive few "liked least" ratings, but they receive fewer "liked most" ratings than popular children.
- *Neglected* children receive few of either type of rating.
- *Rejected* children receive many "liked least" ratings and few "liked most" nominations.
- *Controversial* children receive many positive and many negative ratings from their peers.

The neglected and rejected classifications are especially relevant to the present discussion. Rejected children are considerably more likely to have externalizing problems in comparison to the other four peer status groups (Patterson, Kupersmidt, & Griesler, 1990). Children with ADHD may be rejected because their symptoms impede social relationships (Greene et al., 2001), whereas children with ODD and conduct disorder are likely to have a few close friends—friends who, unfortunately, also engage in antisocial behaviour (Olweus, 1984).

Neglected children also have more troubles than popular, average, and controversial children. Not surprisingly, neglected children are likely to have internalizing symptoms such as loneliness (Asher & Wheeler, 1985). An optimistic research finding about the neglected status is that it is not particularly stable over time and across situations (Coie & Kupersmidt, 1983; Newcomb, Bukowski, & Pattee, 1993). Apparently, children who are left out of one social group often succeed in finding friends as they grow older or move to a new school or participate in new activities.

**Specific Developmental Deviations** A number of troubling symptoms of children's psychological disorders are best understood as specific **developmental deviations**, significant departures from age-appropriate norms in some specific area of functioning. In fact, some developmental deviations are considered disorders in their own right. Specific deviations in reading (*dyslexia*), writing (*dysgraphia*), or arithmetic (*dyscalulia*) are considered to be learning disorders if the deviation is substantial, as judged against both peer norms and the individual child's intellectual ability (see Further Thoughts). Similarly, once a child is past the age when most children toilet appropriately, delays in developing bladder or bowel control are considered to be abnormal. Of course, we can only determine if a child is delayed if we have good development norms for the behaviour of concern.

*Separation anxiety is a normal fear that typically develops just before a baby's first birthday. Toddlers and preschoolers continue to show a degree of distress even during routine separations from their attachment figures.*

## Further Thoughts **Learning Disorders**

The classification **learning disorder** (or *learning disability,* according to educational terminology) refers to a heterogeneous group of problems in which academic performance differs noticeably from academic aptitude. There are numerous ways of defining learning disabilities more specifically, but each method presents difficulties (Wicks-Nelson & Israel, 2000). The most common definition compares scores on intelligence tests, which measure academic aptitude, with scores on *academic achievement tests*—measures of performance in some academic subject area. Typically, a learning disorder is defined as a difference of one or two standard deviations between aptitude and achievement. Thus, a child would be considered to have a learning disorder (dyslexia) if he or she scored a standard deviation above the mean on an intelligence test (an IQ of 115) but a standard deviation below the mean in reading.

*continued*

*cont.*

Learning disorders typically are diagnosed by school professionals, and they almost always are treated in academic settings. Thus mental health professionals typically work with children with learning disorders only when the problems co-occur with other psychological disorders. In fact, there is a high degree of comorbidity between learning disabilities and both ADHD and ODD (Barkley, 1998).

The origins of learning disorders have been traced to a number of problems, including perceptual distortions, attentional problems, language difficulties, and poor cognitive strategies. Typically, etiology is attributed to some biological cause, and considerable research has been conducted on brain functions in learning disorders. Research, however, has not identified any psychological deficit or biological cause that is common to all learning disorders (Wicks-Nelson & Israel, 2000).

Tremendous efforts have gone into attempts to identify and treat learning disorders. However, it is not clear that the identification of students with learning problems has led to more effective education for these students. Numerous interventions have been attempted, including intensive tutoring, individually or in small groups; behaviour therapy programs in which academic success is systematically rewarded; psychostimulant medication; counselling for related problems (for example, low self-esteem); and various special efforts such as training in visual-motor skills. Unfortunately, no treatment has demonstrated consistent success (Wicks-Nelson & Israel, 2000).

Approximately 2 to 10 percent of children are thought to suffer from learning disorders (APA, 2000). These disorders tend to be chronic. As noted by University of Victoria psychologist Otfried Spreen (1988), the greater the severity of the disorder in childhood, the most likely it is to interfere with functioning in adulthood. These disorders are "real" in the sense that these children seem to have the ability and motivation to perform better in school, yet they still perform well below their abilities. Nevertheless, the identification of the discrepancy between ability and performance has not solved the puzzle of learning disorders. Controversy and uncertainty remain about their definition, cause, and treatment. ◆

## Classification of Internalizing and Other Disorders

**Brief Historical Perspective** The beginnings of child clinical psychology as a discipline can be traced back to 1896. In that year, the psychologist Lightner Witmer (1867–1956), of the University of Pennsylvania, established one of the earliest psychological clinics for children. Despite the early origins of child clinical psychology, children were largely ignored in early classifications of mental disorders (Garber, 1984). DSM-I (1952) contained only two separate diagnoses for children, and DSM-II (1968) listed only seven childhood disorders. DSM-III (1980) recognized a much wider range of childhood disorders. In fact, DSM-III contained a proliferation of diagnostic categories for children, 40 in all. Although laudable, the new effort was overly ambitious. Many of the new diagnoses were severely criticized and subsequently were dropped.

**Contemporary Classification** Table 16–5 summarizes the childhood disorders contained in DSM-IV-TR. Many of these diagnoses may be unfamiliar to you, in part because some of them are rare and unusual problems. We can consider most of these disorders only briefly.

*Pica and Rumination Disorder* Pica is the persistent eating of nonnutritive substances, such as paint or dirt. Many infants and toddlers put nonnutritive substances in their mouths, but the feeding disorder pica is rarely diagnosed, except among mentally retarded children. *Rumination disorder*, the repeated regurgitation and rechewing of food, is another infrequent feeding disorder. Rumination disorder is found primarily among infants, and it can be a serious problem that causes very low weight gain and can even lead to death.

*Tourette's Disorder and Stereotypic Movement Disorder* *Tourette's disorder* is a rare problem (4 to 5 cases per 10 000 people) that is characterized by repeated motor and verbal tics. The tics can be voluntarily suppressed only for brief periods of time, and they can interfere substantially with life functioning. Other tic disorder classifications reflect the facts that children may develop verbal or motor tics in isolation, and that children's tics often last for only a brief period of time (see Table 16–5). *Stereotypic movement disorder* is self-stimulation or self-injurious behaviour that is serious enough to require treatment, as may be the case in mental retardation or pervasive developmental disorder (see Chapter 15).

*Selective Mutism and Reactive Attachment Disorder* *Selective mutism* involves the consistent failure to speak in certain social situations (for example, in school) while speech is unrestricted in other situations (for example, at home). Selective mutism is found among less than 1 percent of the children treated for mental health disorders. *Reactive attachment disorder* is another rarely diagnosed problem, although it may be more prevalent than we would hope. Reactive attachment disorder is characterized by severely disturbed and developmentally inappropriate social relationships. Children may resist comfort and cuddling, for example, or they may "freeze" and watch others from a safe distance. Reactive attachment disorder is caused by parenting that is so grossly neglectful that the infant or preschooler fails to develop a selective attachment relationship. (In Chapter 18, we discuss the topics of child abuse and neglect, social problems that, unfortunately, are not rare.)

*Enuresis and Encopresis* **Encopresis** and **enuresis** are common problems. The terms refer, respectively, to inappropriately controlled defecation and urination. According to DSM-IV-TR, enuresis may be considered abnormal beginning at age 5, as most children have developed bladder control by this age. Bedwetting is found among approximately 5 percent of 5-year-olds, 2 to 3 percent of 10-year-olds, and 1 percent of 18-year-olds. Encopresis, a much less common problem, may be diagnosed beginning at age 4. Encopresis is found among approximately 1 percent of all 5-year-olds and fewer older children.

Encopresis and enuresis typically are causes of, not reactions to, psychological distress. That is, symptoms that sometimes accompany enuresis or encopresis—for example, shyness or social anxiety—generally disappear once children learn to control their bowels and bladders. Encopresis and especially enuresis can be effectively treated with various biofeedback devices. The best-known such treatment is the *bell and pad*, a device that awakens children by setting off an alarm as they begin to wet the bed during the night. Research indicates that the bell and pad is about 75 percent effective in treating bedwetting among young school-age children (Houts, 1991).

**TABLE 16–5 DSM-IV-TR Disorders Usually First Diagnosed in Infancy, Childhood, or Adolescence**

| |
|---|
| **Attention-Deficit and Disruptive Behaviour Disorders** |
| Attention-deficit/hyperactivity disorder |
| Combined type |
| Predominantly inattentive type |
| Predominantly hyperactive-impulsive type |
| Conduct disorder |
| Oppositional defiant disorder |
| **Learning Disorders** |
| Reading disorder |
| Mathematics disorder |
| Disorder of written expression |
| **Motor Skills Disorder** |
| Developmental coordination disorder |
| **Communication Disorders** |
| Expressive language disorder |
| Mixed receptive-expressive language disorder |
| Phonological disorder |
| Stuttering |
| **Feeding and Eating Disorders of Infancy or Early Childhood** |
| Pica |
| Rumination disorder |
| Feeding disorder of infancy or early childhood |
| **Tic Disorders** |
| Tourette's disorder |
| Chronic motor or vocal tic disorder |
| Transient tic disorder |
| **Elimination Disorders** |
| Encopresis |
| With constipation and overflow incontinence |
| Without constipation and overflow incontinence |
| Enuresis |
| **Other Disorders of Infancy, Childhood, and Adolescence** |
| Separation anxiety disorder |
| Selective mutism |
| Reactive attachment disorder of infancy or early childhood |
| Stereotypic movement disorder |

*Note:* This listing does not include mental retardation or pervasive developmental disorders, which we discussed in Chapter 15. It also does not include "Not Otherwise Specified" (NOS) subtypes of the diagnoses. NOS subtypes exist for many of the disorders listed here, and they are used when a child meets many but not all of the diagnostic criteria for the specific disorder.

**Overinclusive Listing of Disorders** Many of the disorders listed in Table 16–5 are unfamiliar because they are rare problems; others may be unfamiliar because of their questionable status as "mental disorders." A number of commentators believe that, beginning with DSM-III, the manual became overinclusive in its listing of childhood disorders. That is, the manual included too many "disorders" that are not in fact mental disorders (Garmezy, 1978). Many disorders were dropped from the manual, but there seem to be other ways in which the list should be shortened further.

"Developmental coordination disorder" is perhaps the most obvious example of overinclusion in DSM-IV-TR. The manual defines this problem as follows: "Performance in daily activities that require motor coordination is substantially below that expected given the person's chronological age and measured intelligence" (p. 58). In poking fun at such diagnostic overzealousness, two pediatricians proposed a new diagnostic category they called "sports deficit disorder." The major diagnostic criterion for this "disorder" is always being the last one chosen for a sports team (Burke & McGee, 1990).

The "learning disorders" and "communication disorders" are more controversial examples of possible overinclusion in DSM-IV-TR. Educators call these childhood problems *learning disabilities* and *speech and hearing problems*, respectively. Learning disabilities and speech and hearing problems are common and serious difficulties experienced by children, but we question their status as mental disorders. We view both problems as involving educational more than mental health concerns.

**Contextual Classifications?** As a final note, we remind you that children's behaviour is intimately linked with the family, school, and peer contexts. Because of this, some experts have suggested that diagnosing individual children is misleading and misguided. Instead, children's psychological problems could be classified within the context of key interpersonal relationships, particularly the family (Group for the Advancement of Psychiatry, 1995). As you saw in the case of Jeremy, parents, teachers, and peers often are part of a child's "individual" problem. Given current research and theory, we have followed the traditional approach to classification. However, future research should attempt to classify children's problem behaviour contextually in an attempt to improve upon the individual approach used in the DSM.

*Mourners at the wake of three teenagers who committed suicide together.*

## Epidemiology of Internalizing and Other Disorders

The prevalence of externalizing disorders generally decreases as children grow older, but the opposite is true for internalizing disorders. In particular, the prevalence of depression increases dramatically during preadolescence and adolescence, especially among girls (Hankin et al., 1998). More than 2 percent of Canadian children are diagnosed as having a mood disorder (Waddell & Shepard, 2002). For Canadian adolescents aged 15 to 19 years, up to 6 percent of males and 12 percent of females are diagnosed as having major depressive disorder (Shaw & Grenier, 2001).

Anxiety disorders also are very common, and are found among as many of 5 to 10 percent of all young people. Unlike depression, anxiety disorders are equally prevalent among children and adolescents (Klein & Pine, 2002). Precise estimates of the prevalence of both anxiety and depression are controversial, however, because of limited data and uncertainties about the best methods for diagnosing children and adolescents (Harrington, 2002). Much lower rates of clinically significant anxiety and depression certainly are suggested by the relatively small numbers of young people in treatment for internalizing problems.

The fact that boys have more externalizing disorders while girls have more internalizing problems leads to an interesting pattern in child treatment referrals across different ages. Parents, teachers, and other adults seek treatment for children with externalizing problems, especially during the school-age years. Thus, among children under 12 years old, boys are much more likely to be treated than girls. The increase in depression among girls begins to balance the gender ratio of treatment referrals during the teenage years (Lewinsohn et al., 1994), and by early adult life, more females than males are identified with psychological problems.

**Suicide** As we have noted, adults need to be sensitive to children's levels of distress, as evidence on the epidemiology of suicide underscores in a dramatic fashion. For example, in an epidemiological survey in Canada for the period 1989–1991, suicide was the second leading cause of death in teenagers, second only to traffic accidents (Task Force on Suicide in Canada, 1994). Although adolescents in the general population complete suicide at a lower rate than many other age groups, they are of particular concern because of the dramatic upward trend in adolescent suicide rate over the past 40 years (see Figure 16–5). The figure shows that suicide has remained rare among younger adolescents (10- to 14-year-olds), whereas it has increased considerably among older adolescents (15- to 19-year-olds). The rate of suicide among Canadian First Nations youth is three to four times higher than that of youth in the Canadian general population (Health Canada, 1999b).

In comparison to adult suicide attempts, suicide attempts among adolescents are more impulsive, are more likely to follow a family conflict, and are more often motivated by anger rather than depression (Hawton, 1986). Availability of firearms is an important factor, especially among male substance abusers. For Canadians under age 20 who commit suicide, firearms are used by 45 percent of males compared with 18 percent of females (Task Force on Suicide in Canada, 1994). Cluster suicides are also more common among teenagers than among adults (Spirito et al., 1989). When one teenager commits suicide, his or her peers are at an increased risk for suicide attempts. The risk sometimes stems from suicide pacts, but in addition, the death may make suicide seem more acceptable to other teenagers. As suggested by some accounts of reactions to the 1994 suicide of rock star Kurt Cobain, some adolescents may view a peer's suicide as understandable, even romantic.

**Suicide Rates in Canada: 1950 to 1992**

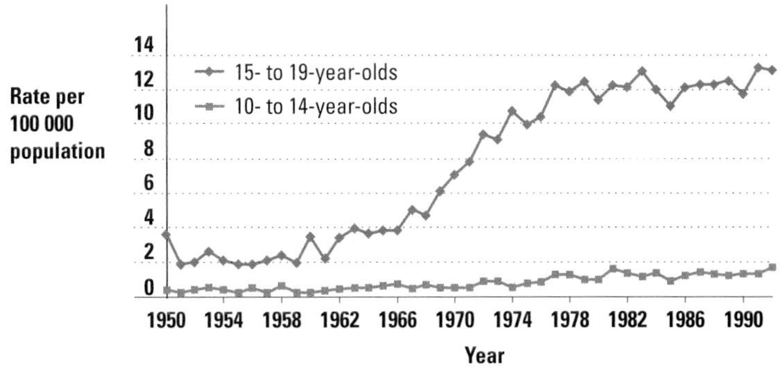


**FIGURE 16–5: Since 1950, suicide rates have increased substantially among older adolescents, but have remained consistently rare among younger adolescents.**
*Source:* Based on Task Force on Suicide in Canada, 1994, *Suicide in Canada.* Ottawa: Health Canada.

## CANADIAN FOCUS The Ontario Child Health Study

The Ontario Child Health Study (OCHS: Boyle et al., 1987; Offord et al., 1987, 1989) is the largest epidemiological study of children in Canada, and one of the largest, most detailed studies of its kind in the world. The OCHS has provided valuable information about the prevalence, co-occurrence, risk factors, and long-term outcome of mental disorders. We will describe the nature of this project and some of the major findings here.

In 1980, a team of investigators at McMaster University, led by David R. Offord and Michael H. Boyle, was commissioned by the Ontario government to design and implement the OCHS, a province-wide child health survey. The goal was to obtain information helpful in planning for more effective, comprehensive services. The researchers interviewed 1869 families, including 3294 children aged 4 to 16 years. Through careful sampling procedures, the researchers ensured that their sample was representative of children living in Ontario. Four types of mental health problems were assessed, based loosely on DSM-III criteria:

- *Hyperactivity.* This was said to be present if the child's behaviour in the past six months was characterized by inattention, impulsivity, and overactivity. The criteria are similar to the DSM-IV criteria for Attention-Deficit/Hyperactivity Disorder.
- *Conduct disorder.* This was characterized by physical violence against others, property damage, or severe violation of social norms over the past six months. The criteria for this disorder were similar to those in DSM-IV, although DSM-IV requires that the problems be present for at least 12 months.

continued

cont.

- *Emotional disorder.* This was defined by anxiety and depression over the past six months. This broad category encompasses all the DSM-IV mood and anxiety disorders, as well as milder conditions such as adjustment disorders.
- *Somatization.* This was said to be present if, during the past six months, the child's behaviour had been characterized by distressing, recurrent somatic symptoms with no known organic cause, and by the perception of oneself as sickly. This category includes DSM-IV somatoform disorders such as somatization disorder and hypochondriasis (see Chapter 7).

These disorders were assessed because previous studies suggest they are common, costly to assess and treat, and are associated with considerable suffering and hardship for the child and the family.

Interviewers collected information from the female head of the household, from teachers, and from youths aged 12 to 16 years. With the exception of the school information, all data were collected during a home visit. In addition to data on the four mental disorders, a wealth of other information was collected, including data on the use of mental health services and information on the child's use of substances, such as alcohol, tobacco, marijuana, and hard drugs such as heroin and amphetamines. Note that the interviewers did not assess the presence or absence of substance use disorders; they simply assessed the use of substances.

Results revealed a high prevalence of mental disorders: 18 percent of children had one or more of these disorders in the past six months. The prevalence of disorders was lower if more stringent diagnostic criteria were applied (e.g., Fleming, Offord, & Boyle, 1989), such as by strictly applying DSM-IV criteria (see the Epidemiology sections elsewhere in this chapter). Nevertheless, the OCHS results still indicate that emotional and behavioural problems are very common in children aged 4 to 16 years.

A detailed breakdown of prevalence results is shown in Figure 16–6. As the figure shows, conduct disorder was more frequent in boys than in girls, regardless of age, and most common of all in the older (12- to 16-year-old) boys. Hyperactivity was more prevalent in boys than in girls, regardless of age. For younger (4- to 11-year-old) children, emotional disorder was equally prevalent for boys and girls. Emotional disorder was least common in older boys. Somatization was more common in older girls than in older boys. The prevalence of somatization in younger children could not be estimated because the disorder was so rare in these groups.

**Prevalence of Mental Disorders over the Past Six Months**

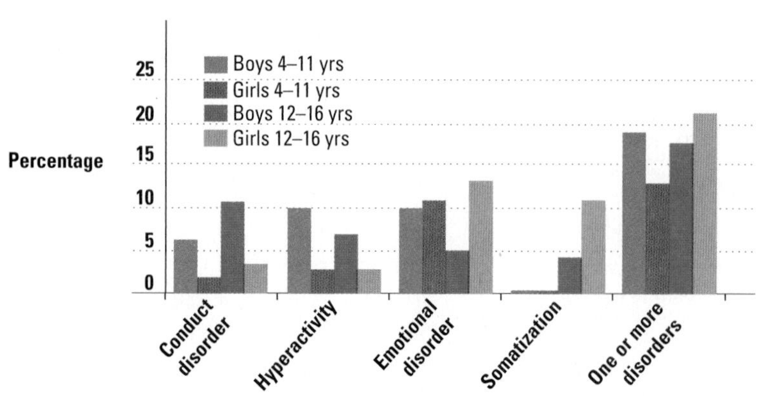


**FIGURE 16–6: The Ontario Child Health Study found that mental disorders were generally common among children, although the prevalence of specific disorders varied with age and gender.**

*Source:* Based on D.R. Offord, M.H. Boyle, J.E. Fleming, H. Monroe Blum, and N.I. Rae Grant, 1989, Ontario Child Health Study: Summary of selected results. *Canadian Journal of Psychiatry, 34,* 483–491.

As in studies discussed elsewhere in this chapter, the OCHS found evidence for considerable comorbidity among disorders. Most (68 percent) of children with one mental disorder also had one or more of the other disorders. Co-occurrence was particularly high between the two externalizing disorders (conduct disorder and hyperactivity) and between the two internalizing disorders (emotional disorder and somatization). That is, 40 percent of children with one externalizing disorder also had the other externalizing disorder. Similarly, 40 percent of children with one internalizing disorder also had the other internalizing disorder.

The high degree of comorbidity raises the question of whether these disorders are separate entities (Offord, 1995). It may be that there is a mix of common and specific factors causing these disorders; some causes may be specific to a given disorder, while other causes may be common to most disorders (see Taylor, 2000).

The presence of one or more of the four disorders was associated with poor school performance, substance use, and suicidal behaviour. Children with one or more of the four disorders tended to come from single-parent families subsisting on social assistance (e.g., welfare), and living in government-subsidized housing. Having one or more of the four disorders was also associated with greater use of mental health and social services, and with greater use of special education services. Surprisingly, specialized mental health or social service programs reached only 16 percent of children suffering from one or more of the four mental disorders.

Offord and colleagues also conducted a four-year follow-up of children assessed in the OCHS (e.g., Boyle et al., 1992; Offord et al., 1992; Lipman et al., 1998). Among the many important findings to emerge from this research, the investigators found that conduct disorder is moderately stable over time (Offord et al., 1992). Almost one in two children who had conduct problems when first assessed also had conduct problems when assessed four years later. However, of the children having conduct problems at follow-up, only 36 percent had conduct

continued

*cont.*

problems four years earlier. Thus, although conduct problems tend to be longstanding for some children, many children with early conduct problems appear to grow out of them, and many children with later conduct problems did not show early conduct problems (Lipman et al., 1998).

Substance use, as assessed in 12- to 16-year-olds in the initial assessment, predicted substance use four years later. Of the four mental disorders evaluated in the initial assessment, only conduct disorder predicted the use of marijuana and hard drugs four years later, after controlling for initial substance use and for the presence of coexisting disorders (Boyle et al., 1992).

Findings from the OCHS help us to understand how childhood disorders develop over time, and how they are linked to other behavioural and emotional problems. The findings also shed light on potential risk factors for mental disorders. The low percentage of children treated for their disorders is alarming, given that the disorders can be chronic. Findings such as these suggest that further efforts are needed to develop programs for treating mental disorders in children. ◆

## Etiology of Internalizing and Other Disorders

Most research on the causes of mood and anxiety disorders among children is based on the same theories of etiology we have discussed in relation to adults (Puig-Antich, 1986). Evidence simply is lacking or inadequate on the development of many other psychological problems of childhood. Thus, our discussion of the etiology of these problems must be limited.

**Biological Factors** Except for some research documenting genetic influences on childhood onset obsessive–compulsive disorder (March, Leonard, & Swedo, 1995), few behaviour genetic studies have been conducted on children's internalizing disorders. Moreover, existing research once again calls attention to the problems in classifying and assessing anxiety and depression among children. In the few studies completed to date, widely different estimates of genetic contributions are obtained based on children's versus parents' reports (Rutter et al., 1998).

Jerome Kagan and colleagues (Kagan & Snidman, 1991) have conducted some important basic research that suggests a more general, biological predisposition to anxiousness. These psychologists have identified a temperamental style that they call *inhibited to the unfamiliar*. Infants with this temperamental style cry easily and often in response to novel toys, people, or circumstances, and their psychophysiological responses (e.g., heart rate acceleration) also indicate their fearfulness. About 10 percent of babies consistently show inhibition to unfamiliar circumstances during the first two years of life (Kagan & Snidman, 1991). Researchers have found that children who are inhibited to the unfamiliar are more likely to develop anxiety disorders as they grow older (Schwartz et al., 1999; Klein & Pine, 2002).

**Social Factors: A Focus on Attachments** The major task of social development during the first year of life is the formation of a close bond, an *attachment*, between an infant and his or her caregivers. Extending the theories of John Bowlby (1969, 1973, 1980), the Canadian-American psychologist Mary Ainsworth (1913–1999) developed methods to test various propositions based on *attachment theory*, a set of proposals about the normal development of attachments and the adverse consequences of troubled attachment relationships. Troubled attachments may include the failure to develop a selective attachment early in life; the development of an insecure attachment; or multiple, prolonged separations from (or the permanent loss of) an attachment figure.

*Reactive Attachment Disorder* Extreme parental neglect deprives infants of the opportunity to form a selective attachment. Such neglect can cause *reactive attachment disorder*, or what attachment researchers sometimes call *anaclitic depression*—the lack of social responsiveness found among infants who do not have a consistent attachment figure (Sroufe & Fleeson, 1986). Research on the consequences of extreme neglect for children is strongly buttressed by evidence from animal analogue research. Nonhuman primates who are raised in isolation without a parent or a substitute attachment figure have dramatically troubled social relationships (Suomi & Harlow, 1972).

*Insecure Attachments* Attachment theory also predicts that variations in the quality of early attachments are associated with children's

*McMaster University psychiatrist **David R. Offord** (1933–2004) conducted some of the most important epidemiological studies in Canada. His findings from the Ontario Child Health Study have provided a great deal of valuable information on the prevalence, risk factors, and course of childhood disorders.*

*Canadian-American psychologist **Mary Ainsworth** (1913–1999) was an internationally renowned expert on infant–caregiver attachments. Her empirical studies grounded and expanded attachment theory.*

psychological adjustment. Attachment quality can be broadly divided into secure (healthy) and anxious attachments. Infants with *secure attachments* separate easily and explore away from their attachment figures, but they quickly seek comfort from their attachment figures when they are threatened or distressed. Infants with **anxious attachments** are fearful about exploration and are not easily comforted by their attachment figures, who respond inadequately or inconsistently to the child's needs (Carlson & Sroufe, 1995). Anxious attachments are further subcategorized into (1) *anxious avoidant attachments*, where the infant is generally unwary of strange situations and shows little preference for the attachment figure over others as a source of comfort; (2) *anxious resistant attachments*, where the infant is wary of exploration, not easily soothed by the attachment figure, and angry or ambivalent about contact; and (3) *disorganized attachments*, where the infant responds inconsistently because of conflicting feelings toward an inconsistent caregiver who is the potential source of either reassurance or fear (Carlson & Sroufe, 1995).

A number of longitudinal studies have demonstrated that secure versus anxious attachments during infancy foreshadow difficulties in children's social and emotional adjustment throughout childhood. However, an insecure attachment does not seem to result in the development of any particular emotional disorder. Rather, insecure attachments predict a number of internalizing and social difficulties, including lower self-esteem, less competence in peer interaction, and increased dependency on others (Carlson & Sroufe, 1995; Cassidy, 1988; Sroufe & Fleeson, 1986). Research demonstrates, moreover, that stable, anxious attachments during infancy also predict externalizing behaviour at three years of age (Shaw & Vondra, 1995). Thus, anxious attachments appear to be a general rather than a specific risk factor for children's subsequent psychological problems.

*Separation and Loss* Separation or loss is another disruption in attachment, one that clearly causes distress among children, at least in the short run. Children move through a four-stage process akin to grief when they are separated from or lose an attachment figure. The process includes (1) numbed responsiveness, (2) yearning and protest, (3) disorganization and despair, and ultimately (4), reorganization and detachment or loss of interest in the former attachment figure (Bowlby, 1979). However, there is considerable controversy about the consequences of separation, loss, and detachment. Bowlby (1973) asserted that detachment causes dependence, which, in turn, increases the risk for depression as the child's needs go unfulfilled in subsequent relationships. Critics have suggested, however, that what Bowlby called detachment is really an indication of children's adjustment to the new circumstances (Rutter, 1981). This interpretation highlights children's **resilience**—their ability to "bounce back" from adversity (Masten, 2001). The resilience interpretation of children's coping with loss is consistent with research that has failed to find a relationship between childhood loss and depression during adult life (Harrington & Harrison, 1999).

**Psychological Factors** As with children's conduct, the regulation of children's emotions also progresses from external to internal control across the course of development. For example, attachment relationships offer security and sooth anxiety for infants and toddlers. As they grow older, however, children develop *internal working models* or expectations about relationships as extensions of their early attachment experiences (Carlson & Sroufe, 1995). **Emotion regulation** is a more general process as children learn to identify, evaluate, and control their feelings based on the reactions, attitudes, and advice of their parents and others in their social world. The ability to recognize and regulate emotions appears to be of considerable importance to children's healthy development. For example, knowledge about emotions at age five predicts both positive and negative social behaviour at age nine (Izard et al., 2001).

As noted earlier, our understanding of children's emotional development is far from complete, and only scattered research has linked troubles with emotion regulation to children's internalizing disorders. One exciting area of investigation focuses on the interactions of children and their depressed mothers. *Role reversal*, where children care for the parent rather than vice versa, may be a particular problem in these interactions. Children may attempt, and inevitably fail, to alleviate a parent's depression, leaving them feeling excessively guilty and responsible. In fact, researchers have found excessive guilt among five- to six-year-old children of depressed mothers, as well as defensiveness against guilt among seven- to nine-year-olds (Zahn-Waxler et al., 1990). Other researchers have found increased depression among adolescent girls who responded to parental depression either by trying to be helpful or by becoming depressed themselves (Davis et al., 2000).

### Treatment of Internalizing Disorders

Relatively few treatments for anxiety or mood disorders have been developed or studied specifically as they apply to children. For example, it may surprise you to learn that biological treatments known to alleviate depression in adults (see Chapter 5) have rarely been studied among children and adolescents, and may be no more effective than placebos in treating their depression (Garland, 2004). The virtually unstudied treatments for depression among young people not only include ECT but also various antidepressant medications—SSRIs, tricyclics, and venlafaxine (Effexor, an atypical antidepressant). The lack of research is particularly troubling, since antidepressants are second only to psychostimulants as the most commonly prescribed psychotropic drugs for children and adolescents (Zito et al., 2000).

As noted by psychiatrist Jane Garland (2004) at the University of British Columbia, a more disturbing finding is that SSRIs can have dangerous side effects in depressed children and adolescents, including increased suicidal ideation and suicide attempts, and increased aggression. The combined lack of efficacy and serious side effects of SSRIs have led Health Canada (2004) and advisory bodies in other countries to issue warnings about these medications. Health Canada advises that patients under 18 years of age who are currently being treated with SSRIs should consult their treating physician to confirm that the benefits of the drug still outweigh its potential risks in light of recent safety concerns. Note that Health Canada has not approved these drugs for use in patients under 18 years of age. Health Canada does not advise that pediatric patients discontinue use of antidepressant medications without first consulting their treating physician. Treatment with these drugs should not be abruptly stopped due to the risk of withdrawal symptoms.

Some forms of cognitive behaviour therapy and interpersonal therapy show promise for treating children's depression (Harrington, 2002), and cognitive behaviour therapy and family therapy have produced positive results in treating children's anxiety in several studies (Barrett, 1996, 2001; Beidel, Turner, & Morris, 2000; Kendall, 1994; Silverman et al., 1999). Manassis and Monga (2001) from Toronto's Hospital for Sick Children have pointed out that it is important to involve the family in the treatment of childhood anxiety disorders. Parents can be helped to reduce their own anxiety (if they have an anxiety problem), so that they do not become anxious role models for their children. Parents can also be trained in skills that help them cope with their frustration with their child's anxiety, because parental frustration can worsen the child's anxiety.

Recently, imipramine in combination with cognitive behaviour therapy was found to be more effective in treating school refusal than therapy alone (Bernstein et al., 2000), and Luvox was shown to produce notably more benefit than placebo in treating mixed anxiety in children (RUPP Anxiety Group, 2001). Perhaps the most clearly established finding is that both clomipramine and SSRIs are helpful in treating children with obsessive–compulsive disorders (Rapoport & Swedo, 2002).

**Course and Outcome** Until recently, psychologists believed that children outgrew internalizing problems, which is one reason why few treatments have been developed and tested. Prospective research demonstrates, however, that certain internalizing disorders often persist over time. Specific fears tend to be relatively short-lived, but more complex disorders, such as depression (Harrington et al., 1990; Kovacs et al., 1984) and obsessive–compulsive disorder (March, Leonard, & Swedo, 1995), are likely to continue from childhood into adolescence and adult life. Childhood depression also predicts a six-fold increase in the risk for suicide in young adults (Harrington, 2002). Thus the prognosis is not optimistic for a child who has a full-blown mood or anxiety disorder, and the need to develop more effective treatments is pressing.

# Summary

Psychological problems that arise more commonly among children than adults are listed in the DSM-IV-TR category "Disorders Usually First Diagnosed in Infancy, Childhood, or Adolescence." The most important disorders in this category are the various **externalizing disorders**. Externalizing disorders create difficulties for the child's external world. They are characterized by children's failure to control their behaviour according to the expectations of others. The most familiar externalizing disorder is **attention-deficit/hyperactivity disorder (ADHD)**, a prevalent behaviour problem that is particularly noticeable in school and is characterized by inattention, overactivity, and impulsivity. ADHD often is contrasted with **oppositional defiant disorder (ODD)**, an externalizing disorder characterized by negative, hostile, and defiant behaviour that is also prevalent among school-age children. **Conduct disorder** is similar to ODD, except the rule violations are much more serious and conduct disorder is more common among adolescents than younger children.

**Internalizing disorders** are psychological problems that primarily affect the child's internal world—for example, excessive anxiety or sadness. DSM-IV-TR does not list internalizing disorders as separate psychological disorders of childhood but instead notes that children may qualify for many "adult" diagnoses, such as anxiety or mood disorders. DSM-IV-TR does include 26 additional childhood disorders, such as **learning disorder** and **separation anxiety disorder**. Some of these disorders are relatively rare; other categories are questionable in terms of their status as "mental disorders."

Epidemiological studies show that emotional and behavioural problems are common among children. Gender is one risk factor noted in epidemiological research: Boys are more likely to be identified as having psychological problems during childhood, but girls are found to have more difficulties in adolescence and early adult life. Apparently, adults seek treatment for children's externalizing behaviour, which is more common among boys, but the increase in depression among teenagers, especially adolescent girls, begins to balance the relationship between gender and the prevalence of psychological problems. Family adversity is a particularly important risk factor for externalizing problems, and epidemiological data indicate that suicide has been a growing problem among teens.

Research indicates that parents are most effective in socializing children when they are **authoritative**: loving and firm in disciplining their children. **Coercion** is a more specific parenting problem that occurs when parents reinforce children's misbehaviour by giving in to their demands. Conflict and inconsistent discipline are other parenting problems that may arise when parents are unhappily married or divorced. Other social factors that contribute to the etiology of externalizing problems include television violence, deviant peer groups, poverty, and societal attitudes. The etiology of internalizing disorders in children has been studied inadequately, but various problems in attachments have been implicated.

Biological factors appear to be more critical to attention-deficit/hyperactivity disorder than to oppositional defiant disorder; these include **temperament**, genetics, and neuropsychological abnormalities. Despite recent evidence on the strong role of genetic factors in ADHD, researchers are unlikely to identify a specific biological etiology of the disorder. The comorbidity of ADHD and ODD makes it difficult to interpret past research, and both problems are heterogeneous disorders that may require further subclassification.

Biological risks and problems in **socialization** may combine to produce psychological factors that cause or maintain children's psychological disorders. Lack of self-control, a tendency to overattribute aggressive intentions to others, and less developed moral reasoning are some of the psychological characteristics related to externalizing disorders. Insecure working models of attachment or problems with emotion regulation may foreshadow the development of internalizing problems.

The most promising treatments for externalizing disorders include **psychostimulants** for attention-deficit/hyperactivity disorder, **behavioural family therapy** for oppositional defiant disorder, and multisystemic family therapy for treating conduct disorder and delinquent youth. The difficulty in alleviating externalizing problems is underscored by the limited success of numerous attempts to treat conduct disorder and **juvenile delinquency** in families, in group homes, and in the juvenile justice system. Few treatments for anxiety or mood disorders have been developed or tested specifically for children, although recent research shows that cognitive behaviour therapy and perhaps some medications can help children's anxiety disorders. Data demonstrating the continuity of both externalizing and internalizing disorders underscore the need to develop more effective treatments for troubled children.

# Critical Thinking

1. Do you think depressed, anxious, or angry parents or teachers sometimes project their own concerns onto children? How could you detect such biases, either for individual cases or on standardized instruments?
2. Family adversity is a risk factor for various externalizing problems, but many children are resilient in the face of adversity. What factors do you think help to make children resilient in the face of difficult life circumstances?
3. What are your thoughts on the use of psychostimulant medication? Is ADHD overdiagnosed, and are medications overused, or are we simply employing the best treatment for a widespread problem?
4. What symptoms would you assess at different ages in order to create a developmentally sensitive measure of depression in children? Reflect on your own childhood in coming up with ideas.

# Key Terms

**anxious attachment** 578
**attention deficits** 551
**attention-deficit/hyperactivity disorder (ADHD)** 552
**authoritative parenting** 558
**behavioural family therapy (BFT)** 565
**coercion** 559
**conduct disorder** 554
**developmental deviations** 571
**developmental norms** 547
**developmental psychopathology** 547
**dose–response effects** 564
**emotion regulation** 578
**encopresis** 573
**enuresis** 573
**externalizing disorders** 548
**hyperactivity** 551
**internalizing disorders** 548
**learning disorder** 571
**oppositional defiant disorder (ODD)** 553
**psychostimulants** 562
**recidivism** 566
**representative sample** 555
**resilience** 578
**school refusal** 570
**separation anxiety** 570
**separation anxiety disorder** 570
**socialization** 558
**temperament** 557
**time-out** 559

# 17 Adjustment Disorders and Life-Cycle Transitions

Overview
The Transition to Adulthood
Family Transitions
Aging and the Transition to Later Life

**Can psychologists help people negotiate normal but difficult problems in living?**

**Is it normal to have—or not have—an "identity crisis"?**

**Where do troubled couples and families go wrong with their communication?**

**What psychological issues do older adults typically confront?**

Throughout the text, we have repeatedly noted that understanding abnormal behaviour is relevant to all of us. This certainly is true for the topics we consider in this chapter—major transitions in development beginning in young adult life and continuing through mid- and later life. These topics also are relevant to abnormal and clinical psychology, even though they clearly involve *normal* life challenges. Consistent with our developmental psychopathology perspective, we believe that abnormal behaviour among adults—not just children—must be understood within the context of normal development. The problems in living we consider in this chapter also are relevant to abnormal psychology because these troubles frequently cause people to seek treatment. Young adults may seek help when struggling with major conflicts with their parents or uncertainties about essential values and goals. In midlife, many people seek help for family problems such as an unhappy marriage, a divorce, or living an alternative lifestyle. Older adults sometimes consult therapists about such problems as adjusting to later life, bereavement, and loneliness. In fact, you may be surprised to learn that at least one out of every four people in psychotherapy has *never* had a mental disorder (Kessler et al., 1994).

## Overview

The reason these clients receive no diagnosis is that their problems do not fit neatly into an individual DSM diagnostic category. DSM-IV-TR does recognize the clinical importance of various problems in living. The manual includes a diagnostic category for *adjustment disorders*, the development of clinically significant symptoms in response to stress that are not severe enough to warrant classification as a mental disorder. DSM-IV-TR also includes a diverse list of *other conditions that may be a focus of clinical attention*, including such difficulties as "partner relational problem," "bereavement," and "phase of life problem." However, DSM provides only brief descriptions for both adjustment disorders and other conditions that may be the focus of treatment; it does not offer a common set of symptoms for problems, and it includes little in the way of an empirical or theoretical rationale for the classifications.

Clearly, we need to improve the classification of clinically significant interpersonal problems, yet there are some good reasons for the current shortcomings. Different people face a wide array of different life problems, and psychologists have not reached a consensus about how best to classify either difficult life events or people's reactions to stress (see Chapter 8). Still, increasingly scientists from a number of disciplines are documenting the course of **lifespan development**, continuities and changes in behaviour from infancy through the last years of life. A unique aspect of this field is its emphasis on *adult development*, the occurrence of fairly predictable challenges in relationships, work, life goals, and personal identity during adult life.

Several theorists divide adult development into three periods—early, middle, and later life. Consistent with this division, we highlight

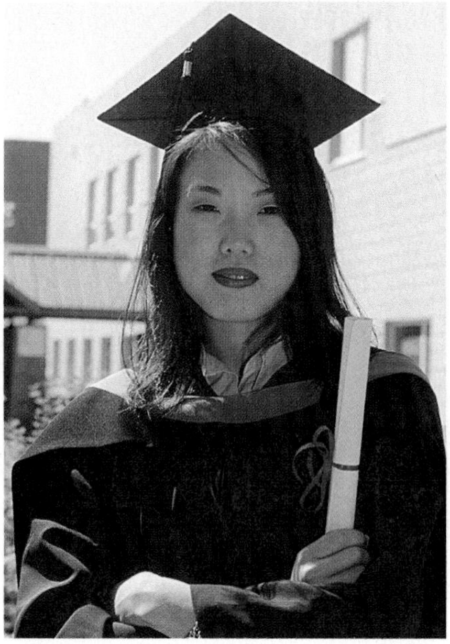
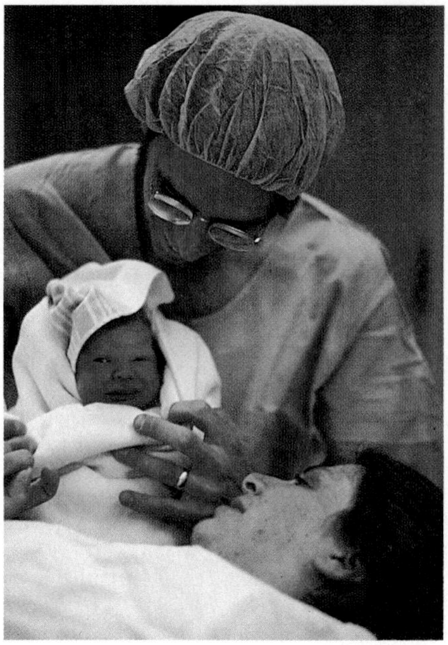

*Development continues throughout the adult life cycle. Stages of adult development often are marked by key transitions in family relationships and academic or work roles.*

three major life-cycle transitions in this chapter. **Life-cycle transitions** are struggles in the process of moving from one social or psychological stage of adult development into a new one. They are times of change that often cause interpersonal conflict and emotional distress. The *transition to adult life* in the late teens and early twenties is a time for grappling with the major issues related to identity, career, and relationships. *Family transitions* in the middle years may include very happy events, like the birth of the first child, or very unhappy ones, like a difficult divorce. The *transition to later life* may involve major changes in life roles (e.g., retirement), grief over the death of loved ones, and more abstract issues that accompany the inevitable processes of aging and facing our own mortality. We begin our consideration of the broad topic of adjustment disorders and life-cycle transitions with a case study from our files.

## CASE STUDY **Divorce in Midlife**

Chuck M. was 51 years old when his wife told him she wanted a divorce. Chuck and his wife had been married for 27 years, and he was totally unprepared for her pronouncement. He knew that his marriage was not perfect, but he had thought of his wife's complaints as normal "nagging." He had never thought of his marriage as either particularly troubled or particularly happy. He just had not thought about his marriage much at all. Chuck was content in his lifestyle, and he could not fathom what his wife was thinking. After serving in the Navy for 20 years, Chuck was collecting a pension and working as a technician for an electronics company. His two children were grown, the family was financially secure, and Chuck was planning to retire in another 10 or 15 years. His life was on the course he had set long ago.

At first, Chuck simply did not believe what was happening. His wife said that she had been unhappy for years, and that she only recently got the courage to leave him. This account clashed with Chuck's view of the history of their marriage. He openly wondered if the real problem was his wife's menopause, or what he called "the change of life."

Reality began to hit Chuck a few weeks after his wife moved out of their house and into an apartment. Chuck's wife said that she wanted a friendly divorce, and she telephoned him a few times a week just to talk. Chuck did not want a divorce, and if it was going to come to a divorce, he certainly did not want to be "friends." He was furious with his wife, but he still worked to avoid conflicts and keep his anger under control. Chuck wanted to avoid hard feelings, at least until he figured out what was going on with his wife and his marriage. Although he saw no need for it, he consulted a clinical psychologist at his wife's suggestion. She had been seeing a counsellor, and she had found their discussions very helpful.

Chuck remained stoic throughout the first several therapy sessions. He freely discussed the events of his life and admitted that he now realized that he had taken his wife for granted. He grudgingly acknowledged that he was a "little upset" and "pretty angry," but he could not or would not describe his emotions with

*continued*

*cont.*

more intensity or much more detail. Mostly, he wanted the therapist to try to help him to figure out what was really going on with his wife.

Chuck's feelings came flooding out in therapy a few weeks later when his wife told him that she was in love with another man. Chuck raged to the therapist about how he felt used and cheated. He was stunned, but he was not going to let his wife get away with this. He immediately contacted a lawyer. He wanted to make sure that his wife "didn't get a dime" out of the divorce settlement. Chuck also called his children and told them all of the details about what had happened. He seemed bent on revenge.

Chuck admitted to his therapist that, in addition to anger, he felt intense hurt and pain: real, physical pain as though someone had just punched him in the chest. When the therapist asked Chuck if any of these emotions were familiar to him, Chuck eventually recalled his feelings when he was 17 years old. His father died suddenly that year, and Chuck remembered feeling intense grief over the loss. He had controlled his feelings at the time, so he was surprised by the strong emotions he now felt in recalling the unfortunate event over 30 years later. His current feelings about his marital separation reminded him a lot of his sadness at his father's death, but his present grief was more volatile and he was much more angry than before.

Chuck began to talk more about his intense loneliness and sadness as therapy continued over the next few months and as it became clearer that his marriage really was ending. He kept up his daily routine at home and at work, but he said that it seemed as if he was living in a dream. In the midst of his grief, he sometimes wondered if his entire marriage, maybe his entire life, had been a sham. How could he have been so blind? Who was this woman he had been married to? What was he supposed to do with himself and his life plans if the divorce really happened? ◆

## Typical Experiences

Are Chuck's reactions typical "symptoms" of adjustment to divorce?[1] Various life-cycle transitions differ greatly, and it is also true that different people respond to the same stressor in different ways (see Chapter 8). Thus Chuck's particular reactions may have little in common with the feelings of other people who are getting divorced, let alone with people who are experiencing other major life changes.

At a more abstract level, however, there are some similarities across diverse life-cycle transitions. The psychologist Erik Erikson (1902–1994) highlighted *conflict* as the common theme. In fact, Erikson organized each of his eight stages of psychosocial development around a central conflict, or what he termed a *crisis of the healthy personality* (Erikson, 1959, 1980). According to Erikson, the conflict inherent in change creates both intrapsychic and interpersonal tension, as the comfortable but predictable known is pitted against the fearsome but exciting unknown.

Like Erikson, we also view conflict as a commonality across different life-cycle transitions. By definition, transitions involve change, and conflict is a frequent consequence of change. Conflict is not necessarily bad; in fact, conflict may be necessary in order for change to occur. Nevertheless, conflict and change often are psychologically distressing.

Thus we view conflict as a common "symptom" or theme across very different life-cycle transitions. In discussing conflict in this chapter, we often consider its behavioural, emotional, and cognitive components. At a behavioural level, interpersonal conflicts often increase in frequency during life-cycle transitions, particularly conflicts in close relationships. Chuck's growing conflict with his former wife is an obvious example. Emotional conflicts are characterized by uncertain and opposing feelings. Chuck felt many contradictory emotions, especially conflicts between holding on to hope for his marriage, becoming angry with his wife, and feeling sad over the separation and loss. Cognitive conflicts may involve a number of challenges to self-esteem, including broad doubts about what Erikson (1968) called *identity*, our global sense of self. Psychologists typically associate identity conflicts with adolescence and early adult life, but different life-cycle transitions can cause people of any age to re-examine basic assumptions about who they are (Waterman & Archer, 1990). Chuck certainly faced an identity crisis, as the marital separation undercut many of his assumptions about his wife, his life course, and, ultimately, his sense of self.

*The psychologist* ***Erik Erikson*** *(1902–1994) characterized development in terms of stages extending throughout the lifespan. A central conflict defines the transition between each of his stages of psychosocial development.*

## Classification of Life-Cycle Transitions

DSM-IV-TR includes two ways of classifying life issues that are not considered to be mental disorders but bring people to the attention of mental health professionals. **Adjustment**

[1] We discuss normal reactions to life-cycle transitions in this chapter, so we use the term *experience* instead of *symptom*.

**TABLE 17–1 DSM-IV-TR Diagnostic Criteria for Adjustment Disorder**

**A. The development of emotional or behavioural symptoms in response to an identifiable stressor(s) occurring within three months of the onset of the stressor(s).**

**B. These symptoms or behaviours are clinically significant as evidenced by either of the following:**

1. Marked distress that is in excess of what would be expected from exposure to the stressor
2. Significant impairment in social or occupational (academic) functioning

**C. The stress-related disturbance does not meet the criteria for another specific Axis I disorder and is not merely an exacerbation of a pre-existing Axis I or Axis II disorder.**

**D. The symptoms do not represent bereavement.**

**E. Once the stressor (or its consequences) has terminated, the symptoms do not persist for more than an additional six months.**

**disorders** are defined by the development of clinically significant symptoms in response to stress, but the symptoms are not severe enough to warrant classification as a mental disorder (see Table 17–1). Adjustment disorders are similar to acute stress disorders and posttraumatic disorders (see Chapter 7), because stress is an etiological factor in all three conditions. However, an adjustment disorder can be a reaction to a stressor of *any* severity, not just traumatic stress. In addition, the traumatic stress disorders share a common set of symptoms, but adjustment disorders may involve a wide array of different symptoms—anxiety, depression, conduct disturbance, or some other symptom may predominate (Frances, First, & Pincus, 1995). In fact, DSM-IV-TR offers only a very general description of the symptoms needed for a diagnosis.

DSM-IV-TR also contains a list of *other conditions that may be a focus of clinical attention*, sometimes referred to as "V codes."[2] This list is not a conceptually coherent summary of life difficulties (see Table 17–2), and DSM-IV-TR offers only very brief descriptions of each problem. For example, here is the manual's *entire* coverage of *partner relational problem*: "This category should be used when the focus of clinical attention is a pattern of interaction between spouses or partners characterized by negative communication (e.g., criticisms), distorted communication (e.g., unrealistic expectations), or noncommunications (e.g., withdrawal) that is associated with clinically significant impairment in individual or family functioning or the development of symptoms in one or both partners" (p. 737). Because of such limited coverage in DSM-IV-TR, we focus on other attempts to categorize major life-cycle transitions.

**TABLE 17–2 DSM-IV-TR Listing of Other Conditions That May Be a Focus of Clinical Attention***

**Relational Problems**

Relational problem related to a mental disorder or general medical condition
Parent–child relational problem
Partner relational problem
Sibling relational problem

**Additional Conditions That May Be a Focus of Clinical Attention**

Noncompliance with treatment
Malingering
Adult antisocial behaviour
Child or adolescent antisocial behaviour
Borderline intellectual functioning
Age-related cognitive decline
Bereavement
Academic problem
Occupational problem
Identity problem
Religious or spiritual problem
Acculturation problem
Phase of life problem

*The category also includes the subgroups of *psychological factors affecting medical conditions* (see Chapter 8), *medication-induced movement disorders* (see Chapter 13), and *problems related to abuse or neglect* (see Chapter 18).

**Brief Historical Perspective** Erik Erikson (1959, 1980) was the first to highlight that development does not end with childhood but continues throughout adult life. His model outlining the eight stages of psychosocial development from birth until death (see Table 2–5) includes four stages of adult development: (1) identity versus role confusion, (2) intimacy versus self-absorption, (3) generativity versus stagnation, and (4) integrity versus despair. Erikson viewed *identity versus role confusion* as the major challenge of adolescence and young adulthood. The young person's goal is to integrate various role identities into a global sense of self. The resolution of the

[2]The term *V code* has no special meaning. It refers to the letter of an appendix in the International Classification of Disease where the codes were once located.

**identity crisis**, this period of basic uncertainty about self, provides the first complete answer to the question "Who am I?" In Erikson's view, the resolution of the identity crisis allows young adults to embark on a journey toward achieving long-term life goals.

According to Erikson, one life goal is to form an intimate relationship early in adulthood. In his second stage of adult development, *intimacy versus self-absorption*, Erikson described the challenge in establishing intimate relationships as achieving a balance between closeness and independence. Self-absorption characterizes people who either become dependent in intimate relationships or remain aloof from others. Of course, people can remain aloof either inside or outside of close relationships.

People who succeed in establishing a truly intimate relationship are better prepared for their family and work lives. According to Erikson, they nevertheless eventually encounter the third crisis of adult life, *generativity versus stagnation*. Generativity is defined by accomplishments in middle adult life. These accomplishments include career achievements, but success in rearing children also is critical from Erikson's perspective. People who stagnate may have both a family and a job, but they steer their life course without a sense of purpose or direction in either of these principal areas of adult life.

Erikson's last stage of psychosocial development involves the conflict between *integrity and despair*. People can look back on their lives either with a sense of accomplishment or a sense of despair or anger. Integrity comes from pride in life accomplishments and, more importantly, from the acceptance of personal history. Despair comes from the impossible desire to change the past and from yearning for a second chance at life.

**Contemporary Classification of Life-Cycle Transitions** Erikson's views continue to be used to classify and comprehend life-cycle transitions. He focused largely on the psychological side of psychosocial development, however, whereas many contemporary approaches emphasize the social aspects of lifespan changes. For example, the psychologist Daniel Levinson (1986) emphasized three major (and many more minor) transitions between broad "eras" or "seasons" in adult life. The *early adult transition* involves moving away from family and assuming adult roles. In Levinson's view, the *midlife transition* is a time for becoming less driven by internal and external demands and for developing more compassion for ourselves and others. This is his somewhat controversial idea of a "midlife crisis." The *late adult transition*, according to Levinson, is characterized by the changing roles and relationships of later life (see Figure 17–1).

Models of adult development are intriguing, but they must be considered with some caution. One caution is that history, ethnicity, gender, culture, and personal values strongly influence what tasks are "normal" during the course of adult development. One reflection of cultural and historical influences on Erikson's model is that he assumed that normal adult development included forming an intimate heterosexual relationship and remaining in a lifelong partnership. We can readily question his assumption by pointing to the more diverse lifestyles and demographics of our times. In contrast to Erikson's perspective, contemporary lifespan psychology notes that many paths may be travelled in the journey through normal adult life.

**Life Transitions during the Adult Year**

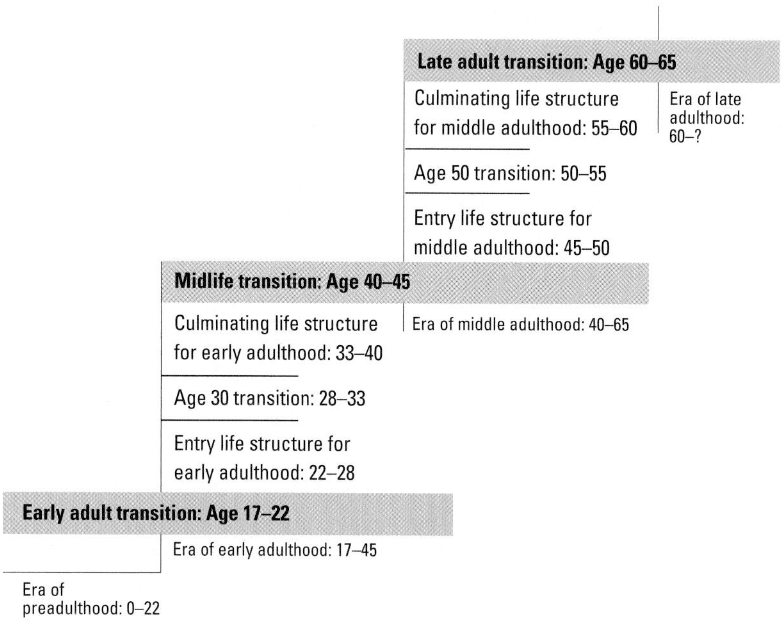


**FIGURE 17–1: Levinson's three major transitions between different "eras" of adult life, and smaller changes within each "era."**

*Source:* D.J. Levinson et al., 1978, The conception of adult development. In *The Seasons of a Man's Life.* New York: Knopf.

Another caution is that transitions or "crises" may not be as predictable as the models imply. Some people may not pass through a particular stage of development. For example, not everyone experiences an identity crisis during the transition to adult life, nor do all people have a midlife crisis when they turn 40. In addition, once a crisis is resolved, it is not necessarily resolved permanently. Furthermore, women confront different issues than men in physical changes, relationships, and values (Stewart & Ostrove, 1998). Still, the outlines offered by Erikson and Levinson do capture broad commonalities in the experiences of a great many people. At the very least, we all develop **social clocks**—age-related goals for ourselves—and we evaluate our achievements to the extent that we are "on time" or "off time," according to our individual social clocks.

## The Transition to Adulthood

In Canada, as in many other countries, the transition to adult life typically begins in the late teen years, and it may continue into the middle twenties or even later (Furstenberg, 2000). During this age range, young adults assume increasing independence, and many leave their family home. By the end of the transition, young adults have begun life roles in the central areas of adult development: love and work.

### Typical Experiences of the Adult Transition

In writing about the transition to adult life, Erikson (1959, 1980) argued that, in order to assume successful and lasting adult roles, young people need a **moratorium**, a time of uncertainty about themselves and their goals. In his words:

> The period can be viewed as a *psychosocial moratorium* during which the individual through free role experimentation may find a niche in some section of his society, a niche which is firmly defined and yet seems to be uniquely made for him. In finding it the young adult gains an assured sense of inner continuity and social sameness which will bridge what he *was* as a child and what he is *about to become*, and will reconcile his *conception of himself* and his community's recognition of him. (pp. 119–120, italics in original)

**Identity Crisis** As conveyed by this quotation, Erikson focused on the identity crisis as the central psychological conflict during the transition to adult life. Identity conflicts are epitomized by the searching question "Who am I?" Erikson's focus on identity captures many familiar experiences. In fact, the identity crisis is a frequent theme in novels like J.D. Salinger's *The Catcher in the Rye* and movies such as *Reality Bites*. At this time of multiple changes in life roles, many of us feel unable to decide on a career, and our tentative choices are uncertain and volatile. We question our values about religion, sex, and morality. We often doubt our ability to succeed in work or in relationships. Significantly, we also lack perspective on our experience. We feel as though we are confronting fundamental questions about who we are, not merely passing through a "stage."

During our twenties, we construct a "life story," an informal autobiography that gives the time we spend questioning and searching a consistent theme. By telling our life story, we make our new identity concrete and public (Pasupathi, 2001), and perhaps oversimplify the answer to the question, "Who am I?," to make our narrative clear, concise, and compelling.

**Changes in Roles and Relationships** Other things besides a person's identity change during the transition to adulthood. Young adults must make decisions about whether and where to go to university and what career paths to pursue. Such major decisions can permanently alter the course of life.

New boundaries also must be negotiated in the relationships between young adults and their parents. Finding the right balance between autonomy and relatedness is difficult (Allen et al., 2002). Conflicts in parent–child relationships increase during adolescence, as young people interpret parental control as an infringement on their independence (Smetana, 1989).

The theories of the ego psychologist Karen Horney (1939) are helpful to understanding the conflicted relationships between parents and young adults, as well as other relationship difficulties throughout the adult life cycle. Horney theorized that people have competing needs to move toward, to move away from, and to move against others. *Moving toward* others fulfills needs for love and acceptance. *Moving away* from others is a way of establishing independence and efficacy. *Moving against* others meets the individual's need for power and dominance. According to Horney, relationship difficulties come from conflicts among these three basic needs. Young adults want their parents' support; they also want their own independence; and at the same time, they may also want to outdo their parents.

Conflicts often increase in relationships with peers as well as with parents during the transition to adult life. Young adults become less certain about their friends as they become less certain about themselves. In fact, a sense of certainty about personal identity is correlated with both greater intimacy and the relative lack of conflict in peer relationships, including loving relationships (Fitch & Adams, 1983). Another important change is that intimate relationships take on new meanings during the transition to adult life. Young adults seriously consider the possibility of making a lifelong commitment, a prospect that puts new pressures on love relationships.

The number of changing roles and relationships suggests that the search for self during the transition to adulthood may be less of an attempt to define a single "me" and more of a struggle to integrate new role identities with old ones. Given all of the real and practical changes during the transition to adult life, it is not surprising that many of us ask: "Who am I?"

**Emotional Turmoil** Emotional conflicts also mark the transition to adult life, as well as earlier adolescent transitions (Paikoff & Brooks-Gunn, 1991). Research has shown that young people experience more intense and volatile emotions than adults do. In a clever series of studies, "beepers" were used to signal adolescents and adults at various times during the day and night in order to assess their activities and emotional states. In comparison to adults, young people between the ages of 13 and 18 reported emotions that were more intense, shorter lived, and more subject to change (Csikszentmihalyi & Larson, 1984; Larson, Csikszentmihalyi, & Graef, 1980).

Anxiety and depression often increase somewhat during the transition to adult life, but in our view, many emotional conflicts stem from uncertainty about relationships. In particular, Horney's conflicting needs to move toward, away from, and against others may be experienced as emotional conflicts. That is, young people often experience the conflicting feelings of love (moving toward), sadness (moving away from), and anger (moving against). Their emotional struggles may stem from both conflicts among these competing feelings and the intensity with which young people feel each of these emotions.

## Classification of Identity Conflicts

DSM-III-R listed "identity disorder" as a mental disorder, but DSM-IV-TR wisely places identity problems in the section on "other conditions that may be a focus of clinical attention" (see Table 17–2). As with all of these life problems, the description of identity problems in DSM-IV-TR is much briefer than the detailed consideration of mental disorders. There is one sentence: "This category can be used when the focus of clinical attention is uncertainty about multiple issues relating to identity such as long-term goals, career choice, friendship patterns, sexual orientation and behaviour, moral values, and group loyalties" (p. 741).

Other classification efforts have divided identity conflicts according to a progression of stages in achieving an independent sense of self. Based on Erikson's concepts, James Marcia (1966) at Simon Fraser University proposed several categories of identity conflict.

- *Identity diffusion:* Young people who have questioned their childhood identities but who are not actively searching for new adult roles.
- *Identity foreclosure:* Young adults who never question themselves or their goals

*Uncertainty about identity, relationships, and life goals is common during the transition to adult life. The movie* Reality Bites *offered a contemporary portrayal of the struggles involved in assuming adult roles.*

©The New Yorker Collection, Barbara Smaller from cartoonbank.com. All Rights Reserved.

*"O.K., here I am in the fourth grade, but is that really what I want to be doing with my life?"*

but who instead proceed along the predetermined course of their childhood commitments.

- *Identity moratorium:* People who are in the middle of an identity crisis and who are actively searching for adult roles.
- *Identity achievement:* Young people who have questioned their identities and who have successfully decided on their own long-term goals.

Some research supports the validity of these categories (Marcia, 1994). For example, the percentage of students classified as identity achievers increases between the first and last years of college (Waterman, Geary, & Waterman, 1974), and the percentage continues to increase in the years after college graduation (Waterman & Goldman, 1976). Consistent with Erikson's theory, identity achievers also are less conforming and more confident in social interaction than others are (Adams et al., 1985; Adams, Abraham, & Markstrom, 1987). Still, the expected developmental progression from identity diffusion to identity achievement may not be accurate for many people, as the different identity statuses reflect differences in age, personality, and cultural expectations (Bosma & Kunnen, 2001).

## Epidemiology of Identity Conflicts

The epidemiology of the transition to adult life is easy to characterize. Given sufficient time, everyone eventually becomes an adult! However, it takes *more* time to become an adult in Canada today, even in comparison to a few decades ago. The delay in the adult transition is indicated by average increases in the years young people spend in school, the later age at first marriage, and lower rates of fertility today (Furstenberg, 2000). Other questions are important to ask about the transition to adulthood: How many people experience significant distress during this phase of development? How many people never fully assume the responsibility of adult roles? To what extent are identity conflicts influenced by cultural expectations?

Unfortunately, psychologists have few empirical answers to these crucial questions. Perhaps the most important epidemiological evidence pertains to cultural influences on identity formation. For example, research conducted during the 1960s, a time of social and political strife, particularly for university students, suggested that a new identity status was common during this historical period: *alienated identity achievement*. Young people with this status assumed an adult identity (they were identity achievers), but their definition of self was alienated; it conflicted with many values held by the larger society (Marcia, 1994). These people chose new adult roles that differed from traditional ones.

University students may be less alienated today than they were in the 1960s, but demographic data suggest more reasons for alienation among a different group of young adults. In 1988, the William T. Grant Foundation's Commission on Work, Family, and Citizenship refocused attention on the "forgotten half"—youth who do not attend university and who often assume marginal roles in society. Although this study was conducted in the United States, the findings are equally applicable to Canada. The commission concluded:

> Our two-year study of 16- to-24-year-olds has convinced us that, as young Americans navigate the passage from youth to adulthood, far too many flounder and ultimately fail in their efforts. Although rich in material resources, our society seems unable to ensure that *all* our youth will mature into young men

> and women able to face their futures with a sense of confidence and security. This is especially true of the 20 million non-university-bound young people we have termed the Forgotten Half. . . . Opportunities for today's young workers who begin their careers with only a high school diploma or less are far more constrained than were those of their peers of 15 years ago. Typically, they cope with bleak job prospects by delaying marriage and the formation of their families. Many stop looking for work altogether. Disappointed in their ambitions and frustrated in their efforts to find a satisfying place in their communities, an unacceptably high number of young Americans give little in return to their families, their schools, and their work. (p. 1)

Consideration of the "forgotten half" reminds us that young adults cannot form an enduring identity in their occupations if there are few attractive job opportunities. Identity diffusion may be a consequence of unresolved psychological conflicts, but delays in making commitments to work and family can also result from the limited opportunities available to some members of society. The problems of the forgotten half have not been solved in a little over a decade, and they still merit our attention in research and in policy (Blustein et al., 2000).

## Etiological Considerations and Research on the Adult Transition

Few psychologists have attempted to predict empirically who will have more difficulties with the transition to adulthood. Nevertheless, the broad influences of family and society appear to be of central importance (Oosterwegel & Wicklund, 1995). Psychological research suggests that the most successful young adults have parents who strike a balance between continuing to provide support and supervision of their children and allowing them increasing independence (Hill & Holmbeck, 1986). Identity achievers often grow up in such families, whereas identity diffusers may have rejecting and distant families, and identity foreclosers may have overprotective families (Adams & Adams, 1989; Marcia, 1994). Moreover, young people who come from troubled families are more successful when they have developed a close and supportive relationship with some other adult (Werner & Smith, 1982).

*Job prospects are limited for the "forgotten half," young people who seek employment with only a high-school education or less.*

Is the absence of an identity crisis a problem that foreshadows identity conflicts later in life? Little research has been conducted on this important question, but cross-cultural considerations imply that avoiding an identity crisis may not be a problem. In fact, some evidence indicates that the "storm and stress" of the transition to adult life is a consequence of the affluence, education, and independence available to young people in Western, industrialized societies (Arnett, 1999). In other cultures, people's life course may be determined by parental authority or economic necessity, neither of which allows for an identity crisis. In considering this, you should also note that adult roles were assumed at much younger ages in Canada in the not too distant past, as they still are in many nonindustrialized societies.

Gender roles also appear to influence the resolution of the identity crisis and the formation of identity. Erikson's theories have been criticized for focusing on men to the exclusion of women. As an alternative, it has been suggested that women often form identities based more on family relationships than on instrumental success in a career (Gilligan, 1982). Consistent with this perspective, some evidence indicates that the process of developing an identity is different among women with traditional gender-role orientations than it is among others. Men may form an identity *before* entering into lasting relationships with others. Women in traditional roles, however, may define themselves in terms of their significant relationships with other people; that is, their identity develops out of their relationships, not vice versa. For these women, relationship intimacy may be fused with identity rather than being a consequence of it (Dyk & Adams, 1990).

### Treatment during the Transition to Adult Life

No research has been conducted on alternative treatments for people who are experiencing distress during the transition to adult life. Clinical reports indicate that many young adults seek therapy at this time, an observation bolstered by the frequent utilization of university counselling services. As discussed in the clinical literature, treatment goals include validating the young person's distress and helping him or her to understand and clarify difficult life choices. In addition, it may be helpful to "normalize" the experience of identity conflict—that is, to conceptualize the individual's struggle as a part of the difficult but normal confusion that results from the search for self. Finally, many clinicians suggest that supportive, nondirective therapy is a particularly appropriate treatment approach, because seeking autonomy is a recurring theme of the transition to adulthood. The following brief case illustrates the approach.

## BRIEF CASE STUDY

### Samantha's Life Story Is Rewritten

Samantha was stunned when she first came to see a clinical psychologist. Samantha was a 21-year-old undergraduate, and her birth mother had recently contacted her for the first time in Samantha's life. Samantha had not yet met her biological mother, and she was pretty certain that she did not want to meet her. Samantha had always known that she was adopted, yet she deeply loved her parents—parents, not adoptive parents, she insisted. Samantha had never yearned to meet her biological parents, and she did not welcome this unexpected intrusion in her life. Moreover, she did not want to do anything that would seem slightly disloyal to her parents, who also were surprised and distraught about the sudden appearance of Samantha's birth mother.

Apart from this recent shock, Samantha was a happy, well-adjusted, and successful young woman. She reported no history of emotional problems, talked at length about her close friends and boyfriend for the past year, seemed thoroughly attached to her parents, and was a successful psychology major who maintained good grades. Yet, she was understandably distraught about the appearance of her birth mother. She cried at length, but her tears and her overall affect were angry, not sad. She half shouted questions at her therapist like, "How could she do this to me?" "Why now?" "What right does this stranger have to intrude in my life?"

The therapist was empathic, and encouraged Samantha to explore and give voice to her many feelings. Samantha was uncomfortable being angry; thus she felt guilty as well as angry and confused. She also was frightened to meet her biological mother, in large part because she felt she might be meeting part of herself. What if this woman was mean? Ugly? Unpleasant? What if Samantha didn't like her? What if she did? Who would her mother be then? Who would Samantha be then?

With the psychologist's support and guidance, Samantha continued to explore her feelings and her options in therapy and on her own. She read about the experiences of other adopted young people who met their birth parents, and even chatted with some people in similar circumstances via the Internet. The sharing of their trying experiences "normalized" Samantha's feelings in a much more direct way than the psychologist's reassuring comments that her many conflicting feelings *were* normal.

Eventually, Samantha decided that she did want to meet her birth mother after all. Despite her initial apprehension, Samantha was exuberant after the meeting. Samantha *liked* her birth mother, who was apologetic, sad, eager to get to know Samantha, but understanding of Samantha's ambivalent feelings and not at all pushy. Moreover, Samantha's mother, like Samantha herself, was relieved when the known proved to be far less frightening than the unknown. Samantha ended therapy before she had figured out who she was—now. Still, she was confident that she was going to be able to answer that question. ◆

## Family Transitions

*Family transitions* are major changes in family life and family relationships. They typically involve the addition or loss of members of a family household. Among the major transitions are the transitions to marriage, parenting, and the *empty nest*—the adjustment that occurs when adult children leave the family home. Other family transitions may involve only changes in relationships and not in household composition, such as when an adolescent assumes more independence. Divorce and remarriage also are common family transitions in Canada today, an observation that underscores the fact that families extend beyond the boundaries of one household.

Social scientists find it helpful to consider the **family life cycle**—the developmental course of family relationships throughout life. Table 17–3 outlines one construction of the family life cycle. This outline, like most, bases family life cycle tasks on major changes in children's developmental status, because shifts in children's development create marked changes not only for children but also for the whole family. Of course, the family developmental tasks are not the same for all families. Clearly, there are many different types of families, including childless families, married families, single-parent families, divorced families, remarried families, gay and lesbian families, and extended family groups. Furthermore, all of these family types differ for families of different racial and ethnic backgrounds.

## Typical Experiences of Family Transitions

All family transitions are characterized by change—changes in time demands, changing expectations, and changes in the degree of control or warmth in family relationships. Early in marriage, newlyweds must directly or indirectly negotiate their expectations about time together, emotional closeness, and who will assume authority and responsibility for performing different tasks inside and outside the household. The roles that couples assume in the first years of their marriage often set a pattern that lasts for a lifetime. Nevertheless, aspects of the marital roles must be renegotiated when children are born. Children place numerous demands on each partner's time, energy, and patience. Although it is a joyous event for many young couples, the birth of the first child also challenges the marital relationship. A spouse's needs may become second priority to the demands of parenting, and the birth of children also confronts young adults with the substantial dilemma of choosing between priorities in work and family (Cowan & Cowan, 1992).

As children grow older, parents must gradually allow their relationships with their children to change in order to meet the children's developmental needs. Maintaining warmth while loosening the reins of control is the overriding theme of change in parent–child relationships. When children leave the family home, adults must discover or rediscover interests inside their marriage and outside the home. These patterns are again altered

**TABLE 17–3 The Family Life Cycle**

| Stage | Family Developmental Tasks |
|---|---|
| **1. Married Couple** | Establishing a mutually satisfying marriage; adjusting to pregnancy and the promise of parenthood; fitting into kin network |
| **2. Childbearing** | Having, adjusting to, and encouraging the development of infants; establishing a satisfying home for both parents and infants |
| **3. Preschool Age** | Adapting to the critical needs and interests of preschool children in stimulating, growth-promoting ways; coping with energy depletion and lack of privacy as parents |
| **4. School Age** | Fitting into the community of school-age families in constructive ways; encouraging children's educational achievement |
| **5. Teenage** | Balancing freedom with responsibility as teenagers mature and emancipate themselves; establishing post-parental interests and careers |
| **6. Launching Centre** | Releasing young adults into work, military service, university, marriage, and so forth with appropriate rituals and assistance; maintaining a supportive home base |
| **7. Middle-Aged Parents** | Rebuilding the marriage relationship; maintaining kin ties with older and younger generations |
| **8. Aging Family Members** | Coping with bereavement and living alone; closing the family home or adapting to aging; adjusting to retirement |

*Source*: E.M. Duvall and B.C. Miller, 1985, *Marriage and Family Development*, p. 62. New York: Harper & Row.

©The New Yorker Collection, Weber from cartoonbank.com. All Rights Reserved.

*"Do you want to tell him he's taking all the fun out of our marriage or shall I?"*

by the birth of grandchildren, retirement, and other family transitions of later life.

**Family Conflict** Increased family conflict is a common consequence of changing family relationships. The increase in conflict is illustrated by research on the relationship between children's age and parents' marital satisfaction. On average, marital satisfaction declines following the birth of the first child and does not rise again until the family nest begins to empty (Rutter & Rutter, 1993).

Family members may fight about hundreds of different issues. However, psychologists generally have been more concerned with the process than with the content of family conflicts. One analysis suggests that all disputes during family transitions ultimately involve either power struggles or intimacy struggles. *Power struggles* are attempts to change dominance relations, whereas *intimacy struggles* are attempts to alter the degree of closeness in a relationship (Emery, 1992). Uncertainty about **boundaries**, rules that mark the psychological territory of an individual or a relationship, may make conflicts particularly difficult during family transitions. For example, a newly married husband who surprises his wife by bringing friends home for dinner—unannounced—might soon learn that he has crossed a boundary. Disputes like this take on added importance during family transitions, because their resolution sets a precedent for defining new rules and roles in family relationships. As family members move through the transition, they eventually negotiate the boundaries of their relationship, and their conflict is reduced as they define and accept their roles.

Increased conflict may be a normal part of family transitions, but conflict creates great difficulties for some families. One of the most consistent findings in the study of family interactions concerns the **reciprocity**, or social exchange, of cooperation and conflict (Bradbury, Fincham, & Beach, 2000; Gottman & Notarious, 2000). Family members who have happy relationships reciprocate each other's positive actions, but they overlook negative behaviour. A grouchy remark is dismissed as part of a "bad day," whereas a compliment is readily returned. In contrast, family members who have troubled relationships are caught in negative cycles of interaction. They ignore positive initiations but reciprocate negative ones. For example, an unhappily married wife might ask her husband to stop reading the paper during dinner, and instead of putting the paper down, he sarcastically tells her not to nag him. In an instant, the couple is off into yet another fight. In fact, the reciprocity of conflict can escalate into episodes of family violence (Cordova et al., 1993; see Chapter 18).

A particular problem in marital conflict is the *demand and withdrawal* pattern, where the wife (more commonly) becomes increasingly demanding and the husband withdraws further and further. Conflicts go unresolved, and the couple's relationship grows increasingly distant. Evidence indicates that demand and withdrawal interactions predict future marital dissatisfaction, especially among women (Heavey, Christensen, & Malamuth, 1995). Other evidence indicates that conflicts in troubled families are more likely to continue over time and to spill over into other family relationships (Margolin, Christensen, & John, 1996). For example, marital conflicts may lead to fights between parents and children, perhaps because of the parents' negative affect or because the children become another focus of an ongoing marital dispute.

**Emotional Distress** Whether family conflict is expressed through explosive outbursts, constant bickering, or the "silent treatment," fighting often causes emotional distress for all family members. In fact, differences in emotional arousal between men and women may explain the demand and withdrawal pattern of interaction. Research on psychophysiological arousal during marital conflict indicates that men experience high psychophysiological (emotional) arousal as negative, whereas women do not (e.g., Levenson, Carstensen, & Gottman, 1994). That is, women appear to be comfortable with the emotion produced by marital disputes, but men are uncomfortable with their strong emotions. As a result, men may withdraw from marital disagreements as a way of regulating their own affect. The reduction in emotional arousal, in turn, negatively reinforces men's disengagement; thus the pattern of withdrawal is likely to continue. In contrast, women's emotions do not interfere with marital interaction; thus they may appear demanding as they continue to attempt to resolve the dispute (Gottman & Levenson, 1988).

Arguments not only upset the opponents in a dispute, but they can reverberate throughout the family (Cummings & Davies, 1994). For example, children are often upset by their parents' conflicts even when there is no spillover of marital hostility. In fact, researchers have found that children's psychophysiological arousal increases in response to observing their parents' fighting (Gottman & Katz, 1989).

Increased emotional distress may be only a temporary, if trying, consequence of family transitions. However, unresolved conflicts may lead to more serious emotional problems (Whisman et al., 2000). Ongoing family conflict, particularly marital conflict, is closely linked with depression, especially among women (Beach, Sandeen, & O'Leary, 1990). Marital distress also predicts increased behaviour problems among children (Emery, 1999). As we saw in the case of Chuck M., moreover, emotional turmoil is a clear and painful consequence of separation and divorce. Significantly, women are more likely to become depressed in response to marital conflict, whereas men are more likely to experience depression following a divorce (Waite & Gallagher, 2000).

**Cognitive Conflicts** Cognitive conflicts may also accompany difficult family transitions. Attribution of blame for family distress is one specific source of cognitive conflict. For example, happily married couples tend to blame their marital disputes on difficult but temporary circumstances. In contrast, among unhappily married couples each partner tends to blame the conflict on difficulties in the other partner's personality (Bradbury & Fincham, 1990).

*The movie* Mrs. Doubtfire *conveyed some of the emotional conflict of divorce. In order to maintain contact with his children, the title character, played by Robin Williams, dressed as an older woman and became a housekeeper for his children and former wife.*

Family transitions also can cause broader cognitive conflicts. Identity conflicts may be renewed, especially because identity often is closely linked with family roles. For example, a divorce may challenge a woman's identity, especially if much of her sense of self is based on her roles as wife and mother. Marriage, childbirth or infertility, and the empty nest also lead to role changes that may necessitate a broad redefinition of self.

In addition to challenges to personal identity, we often are confronted by a fundamental conflict between *acceptance and change* when moving through a life transition or when attempting to reconcile ongoing problems with a family member (Jacobson & Christensen, 1996). Our ability to mould our children, parents, partners, or ourselves is not limitless. We all must learn to accept those things we cannot change in our loved ones if we want to maintain harmony and happiness within our families and ultimately within ourselves.

## Classification of Troubled Family Relationships

Family transitions can be classified according to the major issue the family is facing, such as divorce, remarriage, or negotiating a new task in the family life cycle. However, this approach provides no information on the unique problems of an individual family. As an alternative, a more clinical approach categorizes families based on patterns of family relationships. One example is *scapegoating*, when one family member is held to blame for all of a family's troubles. The concept of scapegoating is akin to the idea of the "common enemy" in international relations. Common enemies can create alliances between enemies, as occurred in World War II when Canada, the Soviet Union, and other countries joined forces in opposing Nazi Germany. Scapegoating in families is thought to serve a similar function. For example, unhappily married parents may unite in blaming their difficulties on a troubled child. The scapegoat is treated like an outsider in a family, as illustrated in Figure 17–2, which portrays one boy's view of his family.

Some theorists have argued that the classification of troubled relationships should be used not only for categorizing family transitions but also to replace the diagnosis of individuals in general. According to this reasoning, psychological problems do not reside within the individual but, rather, in the individual's relationship with his or her world. Thus, these theorists have developed *interpersonal diagnoses*, classifications of troubled close relationships, not just troubled individuals (Group for the Advancement of Psychiatry, 1996; McLemore & Benjamin, 1979). This approach has some appeal, but the accurate diagnosis of troubled relationships is only in its early stages.

**Miguel's "Sculpture" of His Family**

**FIGURE 17–2: Miguel arranged family members in this way when asked to make a "sculpture" of his family during a family therapy session. Miguel put himself behind the table and apart from his siblings and parents, a clue to his status as the family scapegoat.**

*Source:* Illustration by Gaston Weisz. In R. Sherman and N. Fredman, 1986, *Handbook of Structured Techniques in Marriage and Family Therapy*, p. 76. New York: Brunner/Mazel.

## Epidemiology of Family Transitions

Epidemiological evidence is scant on the percentage of families that have difficulties with many life transitions. However, sound data are available on the number of people who pass through various family transitions with or without troubles. In fact, such data are considered to be so important to national wellbeing that they often are collected by census agencies such as Statistics Canada.

Alternative lifestyles notwithstanding, most adults in Canada will either formally marry or live in common-law (cohabiting) relationships during their adult lives, and most eventually have children. Age at first marriage has increased in recent years (Milan, 2000), and many people who get married today report a history of cohabitation prior to marriage (e.g., Le Bourdais, Neill, & Turcotte, 2000). Although probably very few people live "happily ever after," at any point in time most people report that their marriage and family relationships are a source of happiness and fulfillment (Milan, 2000; Zill, 1978). The extent to which marital happiness fluctuates is not known, nor do we know the number of couples who become extremely dissatisfied with their marriage at some point.

Divorce rates increased dramatically in Canada from the early 1970s to the early 1980s (see Figure 17–3). This was largely due to the 1968 Divorce Act, which made it considerably easier to obtain a divorce. Since then, divorce rates peaked in the mid-1980s and then stabilized or declined somewhat (Gentleman & Park, 1997; Milan, 2000). Estimates indicate that the lifetime rates of divorce are high. For example, based on the 1998 divorce rates, 36 percent of marriages are expected to end in divorce within 30 years of marriage (Statistics Canada, 2000). The chance of divorce increases rapidly in the early years of marriage, peaking at five years and then decreasing after that (Gentleman & Park, 1997). Divorce is likely to be followed by remarriage or a common-law relationship (Emery, 1999).

## Etiological Considerations and Research on Family Transitions

Most theories of the causes of difficulties in family transitions emphasize psychological and social factors. This focus is not surprising, given that family life obviously is an environmental event. However, it is also true that individuals make their own environments; thus environments are partially *heritable* (see Research Methods). For these reasons, it is important that we briefly examine biological contributions to family transitions after we consider psychological and social factors.

**Psychological Factors** Researchers often blame difficulties in negotiating family transitions on problems with *communication*. Family members must be able to communicate their feelings and wishes in order to renegotiate family roles and relationships during routine times as well as during times of change. Communication includes not only direct conversation but also nonverbal behaviours, such as posture, voice tone, and affect, that can convey hidden meanings. Think of the different meanings you can attach to a simple statement like "You look great today." Depending on your tone of voice, emphasis, and nonverbal gestures, the same statement might be an honest

**Annual Canadian Divorce Rates per 10 000 Population**

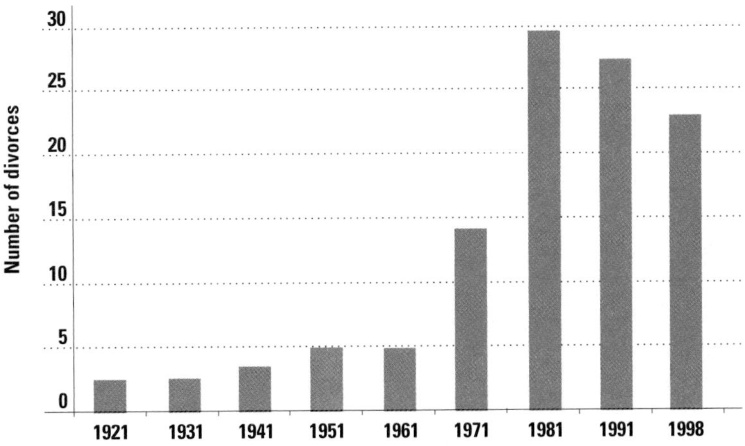


**FIGURE 17–3: Canadian divorce rates have risen since the introduction of the Divorce Act in 1968. Based on 1998 divorce rates, 36 percent of marriages are expected to end in divorce within 30 years of marriage.**

*Source:* Based on Statistics Canada, 2000, Divorces, *The Daily,* September 28; and A. Milan, 2000, One hundred years of families. *Canadian Social Trends,* Spring, 2–12.

# RESEARCH METHODS

## The Concept of Heritability

The twin study is the most common method used in behaviour genetics. This approach has been used to study a variety of disorders, such as in the research conducted by Kerry Jang in his University of British Columbia twin project (for example, Jang et al., 2002). When researchers find that identical (monozygotic: MZ) twins have higher concordance rates than do fraternal (dizygotic: DZ) twins for a particular characteristic, they rightly conclude that genes contribute to its development. Twin studies also yield important information about environmental contributions. In particular, environmental factors are implicated when the concordance rate for MZ twins is less than 100 percent. Concordance rates for MZ twins would have to be perfect if a disorder was purely genetic, because MZ twins are genetically identical. Thus imperfect MZ concordance rates demonstrate environmental contributions to the development of a behavioural characteristic—provided that the characteristic has been measured reliably and validly.

Because twin studies yield information about the contributions of both genes and environments, behaviour geneticists have developed ways of measuring **heritability**, the relative contribution of genes to a characteristic. Defined more formally, heritability is the proportion of variance in a trait that is attributable to genetic factors. Researchers often measure heritability by a statistic called the **heritability ratio**, which can be described according to the following simple formula:

$$\text{Heritability ratio} = \frac{\text{Variance due to genetic factors}}{\text{Total variance of a characteristic}}$$

where

Total variance = Variance due to genetic factors + Variance due to environmental factors + Variance due to the interaction of genes and environment[3]

The heritability ratio is a commonly used statistic for summarizing the genetic contributions to behavioural characteristics. It can be a useful summary when it is interpreted cautiously. You should particularly note two cautions. First, recall that the systems perspective indicates that genes and environments work together, not separately. Thus, in one sense it is erroneous even to attempt to calculate heritability because all behaviour is the product of genes *and* environments. That is, some experts view the heritability ratio as representing a false dichotomy. Second, any estimate of heritability is necessarily limited to the particular sample in a study. That is, we cannot generalize heritability estimates from one investigation to the population as a whole. When a researcher finds a heritability of 50 percent for some trait, it does not mean that the trait has the same heritability in the population as a whole or that heritability ratios are unchangeable.

This second point leads into a broader caution. Heritability estimates do not reflect the range of environments that are *theoretically* possible. Consider this point. One political goal in Canada is to provide everyone with the same rich and fulfilling

[3]The variance due to environments can be further divided into shared and nonshared environmental components. An example of a shared environment is family income; an example of a nonshared environment is being the favourite child.

*continued*

*cont.*

environment. If we ever achieved the goal of providing everyone with the identical environment, all differences between people would be caused by genetics. You can see this by setting the variance due to environmental factors to zero in the above equation. In this case, heritability always equals 1.0. In short, heritability estimates in contemporary studies underestimate potential environmental contributions to behaviour (Stoolmiller, 1999). Although there are dramatic and frightening exceptions, contemporary environments vary relatively little from one another compared to what is possible in theory.

The practical implication of this theoretical point is that environments may matter more than we are able to detect in contemporary research. Consider, for example, that the environmental variation found in today's research does not include those historical changes in the average expected environment that have produced notable increases in life expectancy, education, and material resources for the population as a whole. Dramatic changes have occurred in the average expected environment in Canada in the past century. Thus estimates of heritability in today's samples may be high, in part because there is relatively limited environmental variation—notwithstanding ongoing social problems like poverty, racism, and sexism. ◆

compliment, a sarcastic insult, a sexual innuendo, or a disinterested observation.

*Communication Problems* There are many potential problems in communication. Based on his extensive studies of marital interaction, John Gottman (1994), a clinical psychologist and noted marital interaction researcher, has identified four basic communication troubles:

- *Criticism* involves attacking someone's personality rather than his or her actions, for example, "You're boring!" instead of "Can we do something different?"
- *Contempt* is an insult that may be motivated by anger and is intended to hurt the other person, for example, "I wish I had a different mother!"
- *Defensiveness* is a form of self-justification, such as, "I understand how you feel, but. . . ."
- *Stonewalling* is a pattern of isolation and withdrawal—for example, verbally or nonverbally saying, "I don't want to talk about this any more!"

Gottman's research has focused on married couples, but similar patterns of problematic communication would seem to apply to other intimate partners, to parents and children, and even to divorced partners. Other researchers in the area of family interaction have focused on different problems in communication, but their findings share a basic conclusion: Communication difficulties distinguish distressed from nondistressed family relationships.

*Family Roles* Broader family roles may also be responsible for the development of some distressed family relationships. Many people believe, for example, that pressures to fulfill traditional marital roles—the wife as homemaker and the husband as breadwinner—cause difficulties in some marriages. In studies of unhappily married couples, women often complain of feeling unsupported in their marriages, whereas men often report feeling disengaged from their family life. In contrast, one study found that *androgynous* couples—those husbands and wives who scored high on measures of masculinity and femininity—had marriages that were happier and less distressed than more traditional unions (Baucom et al., 1990). Although nontraditional gender roles may lead to better long-term outcomes, it probably is also true that androgyny creates more conflict during the transition to marriage. Nontraditional couples must define the terms of their own relationship rather than assume clearly defined social roles; that is, the

*Many religious groups have long required couples to participate in counselling prior to marriage. Today, some government organizations are encouraging premarital counselling from religious figures, lay leaders, or therapists in the hope of strengthening marriage and reducing divorce rates.*

boundaries of their relationship are not defined by tradition.

**Social Factors** Gender roles can be conceptualized in psychological terms, but they also reflect the influence of society on family relationships. Numerous other social influences contribute to the development of marital and family distress (Karney & Bradbury, 1995). Poverty, unemployment, crowded living conditions, and limited social support systems all can cause substantial distress in family life and family relationships. In fact, many family problems are major social concerns in Canada today. Teenage pregnancy, nonmarital childbirth, divorce, and family violence are social issues, not just psychological ones.

**Biological Factors** Although their importance may be less obvious, biological factors also contribute to problematic family transitions (Booth et al., 2000). In fact, the potential contribution of biological factors to difficult family transitions bears on a central debate about individual development and family distress: Is family distress caused by dysfunctional individuals, or do troubled family relationships cause individual psychological problems? Clearly, family and individual problems are correlated, but it is not easy to determine the direction of causality or to rule out third variables. For example, people who have never been married, who are divorced or widowed, or who have conflicted marital relationships have more psychological problems than happily married partners. However, this correlation has several potential explanations. Marital distress may cause psychopathology, or marital happiness might protect individuals against it. Or people with emotional disorders may be less likely to get or remain married (Waite & Gallagher, 2000).

Psychological research has not yet untangled the correlation between individual and family distress, but doing so is a new and challenging area of research. It is undeniable, moreover, that biological factors contribute to family distress. For example, twin studies indicate that even divorce is partly explained by genetic factors (McGue & Lykken, 1992; see also Research Close-Up). As we discuss in the Research Close-Up, this empirical finding should lead you not only to think more deeply about the causes of family distress but also to rethink the meanings and the methods of behaviour genetic research.

## RESEARCH CLOSE-UP The Heritability of Divorce

Family transitions like marriage and divorce are commonly assumed to be determined purely by psychological and social factors. However, behaviour geneticists have emphasized that environmental events do not occur at random (Scarr & McCartney, 1983). Rather, there is a **gene–environment correlation**, a nonrandom association between inborn propensities and environmental experience. The gene–environment correlation can be *active*, because different people seek out different environments. For example, risk takers constantly seek thrills, even danger; risk adverse people, in contrast, seek stable, predictable environments. Gene–environment correlations can also be *passive*, because parents provide children both with their genes and their family environment. For example, a divorce may be partially determined by person's impulsivity, which, in turn, is influenced by genes. Thus, children's experience of divorce is correlated with their genes. Because of gene–environment correlations, family transitions may be partly determined by biology; divorce may be heritable.

In fact, researchers have found genetic contributions to numerous environmental experiences. One provocative example is a study conducted by the psychologists Matt McGue and David Lykken (1992) of the University of Minnesota. In a sample of more than 1500 MZ and DZ twin pairs, these psychologists found dramatically higher concordance rates for divorce among MZ than among DZ twin pairs. MZ twins with divorced co-twins were more than six times as likely to be divorced in comparison to MZ twins with never-divorced co-twins. DZ twins with divorced co-twins were less than two times as likely to be divorced in comparison to DZ twins with a never-divorced co-twin. Based on these findings, the investigators calculated that the heritability of divorce was .525 in their sample. This estimate is all the more remarkable because the researchers studied only one marital partner. Presumably, the twins' various spouses also contributed to marital longevity or divorce.

How could divorce be genetic? Clearly, there is no divorce gene. Rather, McGue and Lykken speculated that divorce may be a consequence of personality factors that are partially shaped by genetics—for example, a tendency toward antisocial behaviour. This is a very important suggestion. It implies, for instance, that researchers who compare children from married and divorced families are, to some extent, comparing apples and oranges. Divorce does not occur at random; thus

*continued*

*cont.*

children from divorced and married families differ in more ways than their parents' marital status. In fact, recent evidence demonstrates that mothers' delinquent behaviour predicts both divorce and externalizing behaviour among children 14 years in the future (Emery et al., 1999).

These findings show that gene–environment correlations are more than theoretical. At the same time, however, the research also illustrates important issues about the interpretation of behaviour genetics research. One question concerns the separation of genetic and environmental variance in the calculation of heritability. Divorce rates in Canada 100 years ago were close to zero, and they still are in some parts of the world (Emery, 1999). We certainly would be hard-pressed to explain such historical and cultural changes in divorce rates in terms of genetics. What does it mean to calculate the heritability of divorce when historical changes in the course of 100 years can change divorce rates from zero to rates that reached close to 50 percent in recent years? Genes may be important in determining who gets divorced, but environmental thresholds can eliminate divorce, or perhaps even increase divorce rates to 100 percent! It does, indeed, seem to be a false dichotomy to separate genes from the environment.

The research also highlights the importance of explaining the *mechanisms* of genetic effects. Genetically influenced personality characteristics may explain part of the heritability, but so may a host of other genetically influenced factors ranging from physical attractiveness to age at menarche. Finally, the findings raise questions about whether MZ and DZ twins always share the same trait-relevant environment, an essential assumption of the twin study method (see Chapter 2). In comparison to DZ twins, MZ twins may be more likely to get divorced following the divorce of their co-twin for social, not biological, reasons. Divorce is hard, but probably more acceptable if your identical twin has already been through it.

These observations are not intended as specific criticisms of the study by McGue and Lykken. In fact, the investigators themselves raised several of these issues. Rather, the observations are intended to encourage you to think more deeply both about genetic contributions to environmental events and about environmental contributions to behaviour genetic findings. ◆

*Psychologist **John Gottman** has elegantly documented some of the central communication problems and adverse emotional reactions between partners in distressed marriages.*

## Treatment during Family Transitions

A wide array of therapies has been developed for the treatment of family distress. They include both marital and family therapies and various community action projects designed to prevent family problems. In the following sections we introduce a few of these efforts.

**Prevention Programs** Programs designed to prevent marital distress have a long and informal history. Perhaps the most common attempts to promote successful marriages have been offered by various religious groups. As a requirement before performing a wedding, some religions encourage or require engaged couples to attend counselling sessions or discussion groups about family life. Unfortunately, little systematic research has been conducted on the effectiveness of most of these programs, and available data indicate that traditional efforts offer modest benefits at best (Sullivan & Bradbury, 1996, 1997).

Some research has been conducted on more psychologically oriented prevention efforts. One example is the Premarital Relationship Enhancement Program (PREP), a program originally designed from research with university students. PREP participants meet in small groups of couples, where they freely discuss their expectations about marital relationships, including difficult topics such as sexuality. Couples also learn specific communication and problem-solving skills as a part of the training. In one study, couples randomly assigned to participate in PREP maintained their marital satisfaction three years later, while the marital happiness of control couples declined during this time (Markman et al., 1988). Even five years after the intervention, PREP couples maintained their improved communication and reported lower rates of marital violence than control couples (Markman et al., 1993). Researchers reported similar benefits for a variation on the program implemented in Germany (Hahlweg et al., 1998).

The evidence on the success of the PREP is encouraging for the prevention of marital distress, but the systematic research illustrated by this study is of broader importance. Formal and informal prevention programs have been developed to help family members at nearly every transition in the family life cycle. There are childbirth programs, parenting programs, and support groups for parents whose children are infants, preschoolers, school-aged, or teenagers. Courts have programs for helping parents cope with separation, divorce, and remarriage. Creativity in developing programs is not lacking. What is often missing, however, is systematic research on the effectiveness of prevention efforts.

### Couples Therapy and Family Therapy

*Couples therapy* and *family therapy* both focus on changing relationships rather than changing individuals (Gurman & Jacobson, 2002). The couples or family therapist acts as an objective outsider who helps family members to identify and voice their disagreements, improve their communication, solve some specific problems, and ultimately alter and enhance troubled family relationships. This very different approach to therapy is illustrated in the following brief case study.

## BRIEF CASE STUDY

### Jan and Bill: Learning to Listen

Jan and Bill were seeking therapy for long-standing troubles in their marriage. Jan, a wife and homemaker, complained that Bill did not give her enough help with running the household or raising the couple's three children. More poignantly, Jan felt unloved because Bill did not seem to enjoy being around her and the children. Bill countered that he loved being with his children, but that Jan was a constant nag who did not appreciate the demands of his job as an insurance salesman. He also said that she was a "bottomless pit" in demanding his love and attention. The couple had been seen for several sessions when the following interaction occurred:

**Jan:** As you suggested, Bill and I were supposed to be working on a schedule so that he would only call on clients two evenings last week. But just like I knew would happen, Bill didn't follow through. (Jan begins to cry.) I just knew you wouldn't do it! Is that so much to ask? Couldn't you be home a few evenings during the week? Couldn't you at least tell me when you have to go out?

**Bill:** (in a monotone) I got some new clients this week, and there's a sales push on. I couldn't reschedule. Next week will be better.

**Jan:** Next week won't be any different! Or the week after that. You aren't going to change. Why should you? You have everything your way!

**Therapist:** I can see you're upset, Jan, but let's give Bill a chance. Do you know your schedule for next week?

**Bill:** Pretty much, but you never know.

**Therapist:** Do you want to make a commitment to Jan right now about what nights you will be home in the evening next week?

**Bill:** I suppose I can be home around six or so on Tuesday . . .

**Jan:** You suppose! Go ahead and . . .

**Therapist:** One second, Jan. OK, Bill. Tuesday is a start, but do you see what your tone of voice says to Jan?

**Bill:** But she's always complaining about something! I said that I'd be home, OK? What else do you want me to do?

**Jan:** I want you to want to be home.

**Therapist:** Now we're getting to the real issue. Part of this is about schedules and time together, but part of this is about what it means to fight about these things. Jan, when it seems like Bill doesn't want to be around you and the kids, you feel unloved.

**Jan:** That's what I just said. You heard me, but he didn't.

**Therapist:** Bill, you feel controlled when Jan asks you about your work schedule. You have a lot to balance between work and home, and maybe you really don't want to be with Jan when you feel like she's forcing you to come home.

**Bill:** That's exactly how I feel.

**Therapist:** I want the two of you to talk with each other about these feelings. Then we will get back to work on the schedule that might help to solve some practical problems. Jan, tell Bill how you feel—and Bill, I only want you to listen to her feelings. Try to understand what she says, and don't worry about rebuttal. In a few minutes, we'll try this the other way around. ◆

Several aspects of marital therapy are evident in this brief exchange with Jan and Bill. At the most specific level, the goal was to help them solve the important problem of work and family schedules. Even an imperfect schedule might reduce some of the couple's conflict because it would give them some clarity. Another goal was to break the couple's negative cycle of interaction by interrupting some fights, ignoring provocations, and encouraging Jan and Bill to talk about their own, deeper feelings. The discussion of feelings should be helpful in its own right. It also might allow the couple to develop a schedule, which, in turn, would alleviate some hard feelings. If they could mutually agree on a plan, Jan would have one less reason to feel rejected, and Bill would have one less reason to feel dominated.

***Behavioural Marital Therapy*** Most research on marital therapy has examined behaviour therapy approaches, the approach illustrated in the case of Bill and Jan. **Behavioural marital therapy** emphasizes the couple's moment-to-moment interaction, particularly their exchange of positive and negative behaviours, their style of communication, and their strategies for solving problems (Baucom et al., 2002). Systematic research comparing the effectiveness of behavioural marital therapy versus no treatment indicates that marital therapy leads to significant short-term improvements in marital satisfaction in about half of all couples treated. Still, approximately half of couples seen in behavioural marital therapy do not improve significantly. Relapse at follow-up is also common, and other treatment approaches appear to be about as effective as behavioural marital therapy (Alexander, Holtzworth-Munroe, & Jameson, 1994).

There clearly is a need to expand on behavioural marital therapy and perhaps to integrate it with other approaches. Clinically, marital therapists are beginning to address emotion, the core issue for Jan and Bill (Snyder, 1999), and the acceptance of disputes or differences that cannot be changed (Jacobson & Christensen, 1996). These innovations bode well for future treatment research. There is also a need to extend research efforts to include treatments for other difficult family transitions—for example, coping with divorce (Emery, 1994).

*Treating Individual Problems with Couples Therapy or Family Therapy* Couples therapy increasingly has been used not only to improve marriages but also as an alternative to individual therapy in the treatment of psychological disorders. As discussed in earlier chapters, couples or family therapy has been attempted as a treatment for almost every mental disorder, but most empirical work has focused on couples treatment for depression, anxiety, alcoholism, and psychological disorders of childhood. In each area, research suggests that an improved marriage helps to alleviate individual disorders, particularly depression (Beach, Sandeen, & O'Leary, 1990; Jacobson, Holtzworth-Munroe, & Schmaling, 1989). These findings are not only important for treatment outcome, but they also underscore the reciprocal nature of individual and family relationships. In some cases, successful marital therapy removes the cause of an individual spouse's psychopathology. In other cases, successful marital therapy enables well-adjusted spouses to understand and cope with their partner's psychological troubles.

## Aging and the Transition to Later Life

In Canada today, we commonly think of "old" as beginning at the age of 65, but aging and the transition to later life do not begin or end at this age. In fact, the aging transition extends over many years, and such issues as changes in appearance, health, family, friendships, work, and living arrangements become more or less important at different ages. In addition, the nature, timing, and meaning of the transition to later life often differ for men and women.

Typically, adults become increasingly aware of aging in their forties and fifties. Middle-aged men often worry about their physical performance in athletics and sex. Men in their forties and fifties also become more concerned about their physical health, especially as they learn of events like a friend's unexpected heart attack. Women also worry about their physical performance and appearance in middle age, but women often are more concerned with their husbands' than with their own physical health. Men have a notably shorter life expectancy than women—seven years shorter on average. Thus, even as they encourage their husbands to follow good health practices, many middle-aged wives begin a mental "rehearsal for widowhood" (Neugarten, 1990).

Concerns about physical health increase for both men and women in their sixties, seventies, and eighties. Chronic diseases such as hypertension become common, all five sensory systems decline in acuity, and some cognitive abilities diminish with advancing age (see Chapter 14). All of these physical changes occur gradually throughout adult life, although the decline in functioning accelerates, on average beginning around the age of 75. Major social transitions also take place during the later adult years. Most people retire from lifelong occupations in their early to late sixties, a transition that is eagerly anticipated by many people but dreaded by some. Whether retirement is seen as the end of a valued career or the beginning of a new life, it requires a redefinition of family roles as husbands and wives have more time and new expectations for each other. Parent–child relationships also change with age. Parents become more of a "friend" as their children become adults, and as parents become grandparents, older adults offer children and grandchildren practical support and a sense of continuity in family life. As older adults move through their seventies and enter into their eighties, children who are now middle-aged themselves increasingly find themselves worrying about and caring for their parents.

Death is an inevitability that confronts all of us but is especially relevant for older adults. With advancing age, we must face both the abstraction of our own mortality and our specific fears about a painful and prolonged death. Bereavement is a part of life for older adults, as friends fall ill and die. Because of differences in life expectancy, women are particularly likely to become widows in their sixties, seventies, and eighties (see Figure 17–4).

**Gap in Life Expectancy between Canadian Women and Men**

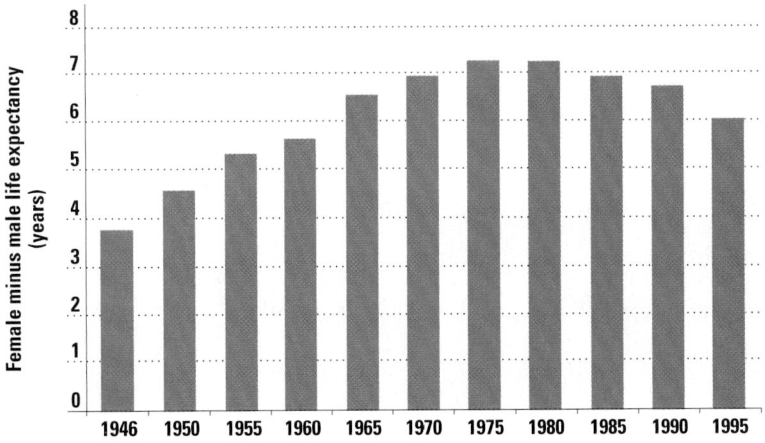


**FIGURE 17–4: Most older Canadians are women, since women tend to outlive men. However, this is changing as the life expectancies of women and men become increasingly similar.**

*Source:* Based on F. Nault, 1997, Narrowing mortality gaps, 1978 to 1995. *Health Reports, 9,* 35–41.

## Ageism

In considering the transition to later life, we must be careful not to fall prey to stereotypes about "old people." Older adults confront a form of social prejudice known as **ageism**, a term that encompasses a number of misconceptions and prejudices about aging (Pasupathi, Carstensen, & Tsai, 1995). For example, young Americans, even mental health professionals, tend to view older adults as stubborn, irritable, bossy, and complaining. Some research does indicate that adults become more inwardly focused as they enter later life. Still, the major finding is that personality is consistent from middle age to old age (Magai, 2001). Some older adults *are* stubborn and irritable, much like they were as younger adults! Older adults experience the full range of human personalities, interests, and concerns, and we must guard against forming stereotypes based on our prejudices or fears about aging. In fact, evidence indicates that, if any differences exist, older adults report *less* anxiety, depression, and especially anger than younger adults (Magai, 2001).

## Typical Experiences of Aging

We must be selective in reviewing typical experiences related to aging, because later life encompasses a large age range as well as numerous social and psychological transitions. In the following sections, we highlight only a few of the more important topics, including changes in physical functioning and health; general psychological well-being, work, and relationships; bereavement and grief; and mental health.

**Physical Functioning and Health** Physical functioning and health decline with age, but the loss of health and vigour is not nearly as rapid as stereotypes suggest. Men and women can and do remain healthy and active well into their seventies and eighties. In fact, physical activity and physical health are among the better predictors of psychological well-being among older adults.

*Menopause* **Menopause**, the cessation of menstruation, is an important physical focus for middle-aged women. (Men do not experience a similar change in reproductive functioning.) Women in Canada have their last period at an average age of 51 years, although menstruation typically is erratic for at least two or three years prior to its complete cessation. Many women experience physical symptoms such as "hot flashes" during menopause, and some experience emotional swings as well. For example, they may find themselves crying for no apparent reason. Episodes of depression also increase during menopause.

*The transition to later life is not a time of despair for most people. Older adults who remain physically active and socially involved have better mental and physical health.*

Psychological adjustments to aging and the loss of fertility contribute to emotional volatility during menopause, but so do the physical symptoms that result from fluctuations in the female sex hormone **estrogen**. In fact, *hormone replacement therapy*, the administration of artificial estrogen, alleviates many of the adverse physical symptoms of menopause. The alleviation of symptoms, in turn, eases some of the psychological strains of menopause. Hormone replacement therapy also reduces the subsequent risk for heart and bone disease, but it is a controversial treatment because it simultaneously increases the risk for cancer.

Hormone replacement therapy has no direct effect on depression, which is unrelated to estrogen levels during menopause, or on other broad psychological consequences of the "change of life" (Rutter & Rutter, 1993). Many women must redefine their identity as they face changes in their bodies, appearance, and family lives near the time of menopause. Still, we should note that for many other women menopause is *not* a trying time. For example, women may find the freedom from fear of pregnancy liberating. Moreover, many middle-aged women enjoy the "empty nest"—they value the increased time they have for themselves as children move away from home (Rutter & Rutter, 1993).

*Sensation and Physical Movement* Menopause is a rather "sudden" event in comparison to other physical changes that occur with age. For example, the functioning of all sensory systems declines gradually throughout adult life. Visual acuity declines slowly with age, as does the ability of the lens to accommodate from focusing on an object that is near to one that is far away. The eye also adapts to darkness or to light more slowly with age. In addition, hearing loss is gradual throughout adult life, particularly the ability to hear high tones. Sensitivity to taste, smell, and touch also decreases with advancing age. As with losses in vision and hearing, however, declines in these senses typically are gradual until the seventies, when loss of sensitivity may accelerate notably (Fozard & Gordon-Salant, 2001).

The amount of muscle in our bodies also declines with age, but, like sensory function, the loss is gradual until advanced age. A 70-year-old retains 80 percent of his or her young adult muscle strength, but the loss may double in the next 10 years. Bone loss also occurs with advancing age, with women experiencing bone loss at twice the rate of men. After menopause, women are especially susceptible to the development of *osteoporosis*, a condition in which bones become honeycombed and can be broken easily. Many older adults develop other chronic illnesses, especially arthritis, cardiovascular diseases, cancer, diabetes, and sleep disorders (Longino & Mittelmark, 1996).

### Life Satisfaction, Work, and Relationships

The fact that aging is accompanied by gradual declines in physical health does *not* mean that older adults experience similar declines in psychological well-being. In fact, older adults report more positive relationships and a greater sense of mastery over their environment than do adults who are young or in midlife. On the other hand, older adults do report feeling less of a sense of purpose in life and less satisfaction with personal growth in comparison to younger adults (Ryff et al., 2001).

Older adults also report greater satisfaction with their jobs than younger people, but this may be a result of self-selection. Older adults remain in a satisfying occupation, while younger adults struggle to find the right job. Despite their generally positive appraisal of work, most adults view retirement positively, even though retirement can be a mixed blessing. Retirement clearly leads to a loss of income and perhaps of status, and this makes retirement a very difficult transition for some older adults. On average, however, these costs are outweighed by the added benefits of increased leisure and freedom, especially for people with adequate financial resources (Kim & Moen, 2001).

*Integrity versus Despair* Erik Erikson suggested that the conflict between integrity and despair was a common psychological struggle during the transition to later life. Experience suggests that many older adults do struggle with the broad issue of the meaning of their lives when they look back from the perspective of their later years. Identity conflicts also may accompany less monumental tasks, such as the changes that come from becoming a grandparent or retiring from a long-term occupation. Unfortunately, little research has been conducted on Erikson's interesting conceptualization of the major psychosocial conflict of later life (see Canadian Focus).

*Relationships* People have more friendships as young adults than during later life, but the quality of relationships is more important than the number (Antonucci, 2001). The presence of a supportive close relationship is an important predictor of psychological well-being during adult life. In fact, one reason why older adults have fewer friendships is because they become more selective in their companions. That is, older adults actively choose to spend their time with only the people they care for most, perhaps because they believe their time is limited and more precious (Carstensen, Isaacowitz, & Charles, 1999).

Family relationships are of key importance to psychological well-being throughout the lifespan. Relationships with children are very important, and in addition, sibling relationships often take on renewed practical and emotional importance later in life (Cohler & Nakamura, 1996). Of course, the marital relationship remains centrally important. If anything, marital satisfaction increases in later life, and conflicts become less embedded or intense. This, too, may be related to the foreshortened sense of time. The belief that "this may be the last time" encourages older adults to focus on the positive and overlook or forgive the negative (Carstensen, Isaacowitz, & Charles, 1999). Unfortunately, the loss of loved ones, including the loss of a spouse, is a fact of life for older adults, particularly for older women, as illustrated in the following case study.

## BRIEF CASE STUDY

### Mrs. J's Loss

Mrs. Sylvia J. was 78 years old when she consulted a clinical psychologist for the first time in her life. Mrs. J. was physically fit, intellectually sharp, and emotionally vital. However, she remained terribly distressed by her husband's death. Eighteen months earlier, the 83-year-old Mr. J. had suffered a stroke. After a few weeks in the hospital, he was transferred to a nursing home, where his recuperation progressed slowly over the course of several months. According to his wife, Mr. J.'s care in the nursing home bordered on malpractice. He died as a result of infections from pervasive bedsores that he developed lying in the same position for hours on end. The staff was supposed to shift his position frequently in order to prevent bedsores from developing, but according to Mrs. J., they simply ignored her husband.

Mrs. J. was uncertain how to handle her grief, because she was stricken by many conflicting emotions. She had literally waited a lifetime to find the right man—she had married for the first time at the age of 71 after a long and successful career as a schoolteacher. She had been content throughout her life, but her marriage was bliss. She felt intensely sad over the loss of her husband, and she continued to make him part of her life. She would talk aloud to his picture when she awoke in the morning, and she visited his grave daily except when the weather was very bad.

Mrs. J. cried freely when discussing her loss, but she also chastised herself for not doing better in "getting on with her life." She had several female friends with whom she played bridge several times a week. Mrs. J. enjoyed the company of her friends, who also were widowed and who seemed more accepting of their losses.

*continued*

*cont.*

A greater problem than acceptance was the intense anger Mrs. J. often felt but rarely acknowledged. She was furious at the nursing home, and she was vaguely considering legal action against the institution. During her career as a teacher, she had never tolerated incompetence, and the incompetence of the nursing home had robbed her of her happiness. She was confused, however, because her minister said that her anger was wrong. He said that she should forgive the nursing home and be happy to know that her husband was in heaven. Mrs. J. wanted to follow her minister's advice, but her emotions would not allow it. She wanted the psychologist to tell her if her feelings were wrong. ◆

Clearly, it was not wrong for Mrs. J. to be distraught over her husband's death, but were some of her other reactions abnormal? Having constant thoughts of another person might seem obsessional in some circumstances, and talking out loud to a picture might indicate delusions or hallucinations. Mrs. J. was showing normal reactions to grief, however, as similar responses are common among other grief-stricken older people. Frequent thoughts of a loved one are a normal part of grief, and it also is normal for intense grief to continue for a year or two, or perhaps longer. But what about Mrs. J.'s anger? Whether she should forgive the nursing home or sue depends on many factors, of course, but she was not wrong—abnormal—for feeling angry. Evidence indicates that anger, too, is a common part of grief.

*Grief is a part of life for older adults.*

**Grief and Bereavement** **Grief** is the emotional and social process of coping with a separation or a loss. **Bereavement** is a specific form of grieving in response to the death of a loved one. The process of grieving in bereavement is commonly described as proceeding in a series of stages. For example, Elisabeth Kübler-Ross (1969) developed a popular model of bereavement in her work with terminally ill medical patients. She described their grief as occurring in five stages: (1) denial, (2) anger, (3) bargaining, (4) depression, and (5) acceptance.

Kübler-Ross's model is similar to Bowlby's (1979) four-stage outline of children's responses to separation or loss (see Chapter 16). The stage of bargaining, a period of attempting to negotiate for a longer life, is the only major difference between the two models. Perhaps bargaining is a unique reaction found among terminally ill patients, who, understandably, hope for some miracle cure. To understand Mrs. J's grief, you should note that anger is a part of both models. Importantly, Bowlby's attachment theory offers an explanation for why someone might feel angry in the middle of intense sadness over a loss. Yearning and searching (his second stage of grief) is a pursuit of, and a signal to, the missing attachment figure—an attempt to bring about reunion. A child who is separated from a parent cries, screams angrily, and searches for the parent in order to get her or him back. Of course, a reunion is impossible following the death of a loved one, as bereaved people understand intellectually. However, emotions are not rational, particularly at a time of loss.

Stage theories of grief have considerable intuitive appeal, but researchers have questioned whether bereavement follows any clear-cut series of stages. According to available evidence, few people experience grief in a fixed sequence of stages. Rather, mourners vacillate among different emotions—for example, moving back and forth between sadness and anger. Many people apparently do not experience several of the stages described by Bowlby or Kübler-Ross, and still other people show few observable reactions to bereavement—they suffer in silence. In short, although denial, sadness, and anger may be normal reactions to loss, there is no one "right" way to grieve, nor should people be forced to express their unexpressed grief. In fact, research indicates that *less* intense bereavement predicts *better* long-term adjustment (Wortman & Silver, 2001). In general, bereavement is more intense when a loss is "off time"—for example, when the loss of a mate occurs early in adult life or when a child dies before a parent (Cohler & Nakamura, 1996). There is no "good" time to lose a loved one, of course, but we all are more prepared for the death of aged family members, and we often can find some solace in their long life.

Returning to the case study, we believe that Mrs. J's grief *was* a normal reaction to the loss of her husband, but there are cases where grief becomes problematic. Theorists have created some systems for classifying normal and abnormal grief. For example, Worden (1986) divided bereavement responses into normal, chronic, delayed, exaggerated, and masked grief. One study found that clinicians were more reliable when using this system to classify case vignettes than when applying potentially appropriate DSM diagnoses to the same cases (e.g., depression, PTSD) (Marwit, 1996). Others have proposed a new DSM diagnosis called "complicated grief disorder" (Horowitz et al., 1997). These are only preliminary steps toward studying abnormal grief, but we are encouraged to see new work on this important topic.

**Mental Health** Although cognitive disorders do increase with age (see Chapter 14), a number of epidemiological studies suggest that the prevalence of other mental disorders, such as anxiety and mood disorders, are less common among older adults compared with younger adults (e.g., Bland, Newman, & Orn, 1988; Gurland, 1996). However, recent research suggests that the prevalence of mood disorders has been underestimated in the elderly (Newman, Bland, & Orn, 1998). Clearly, more research is needed to accurately estimate the prevalence of mental disorders among older people.

Regardless of the eventual outcome of this research, suicide risk remains a particular concern; Canadian males over the age of 80 have the highest rate of completed suicide of any age and gender group (Task Force on Suicide in Canada, 1994). Similar findings have been reported in other industrialized countries. In fact, suicide is one of the top 10 causes of death among older adults (Koenig & Blazer, 1990). Many experts view the increase in suicide as a consequence not only of the emotional problems and adverse social circumstances found among older adults but also as a result of chronic pain, physical disease, and the prospect of a long terminal illness. In fact, *rational suicide* is a controversial term for the decision some severely ill older adults make in ending their lives (Gallagher-Thompson & Osgood, 1997). Even more controversial is *assisted suicide*, a hotly debated procedure where a medical professional helps disabled people to end their own lives.

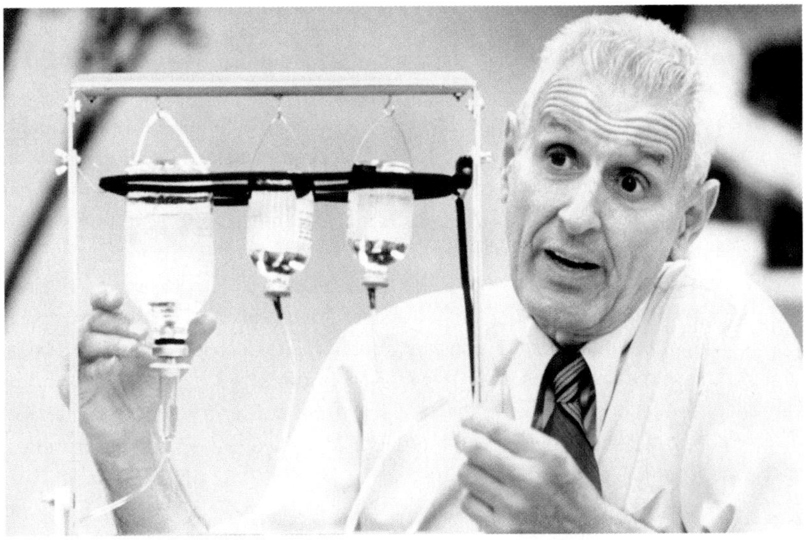

*Dr. Jack Kevorkian with his suicide machine. Kevorkian is an outspoken advocate of assisted suicide. He is currently in prison for helping severely ill patients to take their own life.*

## CANADIAN FOCUS Reminiscence among Older Adults

It is difficult to operationalize and conduct research on the abstractions of Erikson's stages of psychosocial development, including his stage of integrity versus despair. Some researchers have made innovative attempts in this direction, however, by studying a common phenomenon among older adults: *reminiscence*—the recounting of personal memories of the distant past. In fact, reminiscence may be helpful in facilitating adjustment during later life, and many senior centres in the community offer life-history discussion groups as a part of their services.

All memories of the past are not equal, as suggested by Erikson's conflict between integrity and despair. Older adults may recall their journey through life with

*continued*

*cont.*

pride and acceptance or with disappointment and regret. As a way of studying the manner in which memories of the past mark adjustment during later life, researchers Paul Wong and Lisa Watt, working at Trent University in Ontario, developed a taxonomy of six different categories of reminiscence (Watt & Wong, 1991; Wong & Watt, 1991).

*Integrative reminiscence* is an attempt to achieve a sense of self-worth, coherence, and reconciliation with the past. It includes a discussion of past conflicts and losses, but it is characterized by an overriding acceptance of events. *Instrumental reminiscence* involves the review of goal-directed activities and attainments. It reflects a sense of control and success in overcoming life's obstacles. *Transitive reminiscence* serves the function of passing on cultural heritage and personal legacy, and includes both direct moral instruction and storytelling that has clear moral implications. *Escapist reminiscence* is full of glorification of the past and deprecation of the present, a yearning for the "good old days." *Obsessive reminiscence* includes preoccupation with failure, and is full of guilt, bitterness, and despair. Finally, *narrative reminiscence* is descriptive rather than interpretive. It involves "sticking to the facts" and does not serve clear intrapsychic or interpersonal functions.

Each of these styles of discussing the past has been found among older adults. In fact, evidence indicates that integrative reminiscence and instrumental reminiscence are related to successful aging, whereas obsessive reminiscence is associated with less successful adjustment in later life (Wong & Watt, 1991). Reminiscence may have limited value as an intervention, however, because researchers have not found any differences in the amount of time that successful and unsuccessful older adults spend discussing the past. Perhaps we are limited in the extent to which we can "rewrite" our personal histories in a more favourable light. ◆

## Classification of Aging

Classification of adults in later life typically divides categories based on age and health status. In **gerontology**, the multidisciplinary study of aging, it is common to distinguish among the young-old, the old-old, and the oldest-old.

The *young-old* are adults roughly between the ages of 65 and 75. However, the category is defined less by age than by health and vigour. Notwithstanding the normal physical problems of aging, the young-old are in good health and are active members of their communities. The majority of older adults belong to this group.

The *old-old* are adults between the ages of approximately 75 and 85 who suffer from major physical, psychological, or social (largely economic) problems. They require some routine assistance in living, although only about 6 percent of Americans in this age group live in a nursing home. Despite advanced age, a healthy and active 80-year-old adult would be considered to be young-old instead of old-old.

Finally, the *oldest-old* are adults 85 years old or older. People in this category are a diverse group and include some adults who maintain their vigour and others in need of constant assistance. Widowed women and low-income groups are found disproportionately among the oldest-old. Twenty-two percent of the oldest-old live in nursing homes (Neugarten, 1990).

## Epidemiology of Aging

Over 12 percent of people living in Canada are 65 years of age or older. More than 10 percent of these adults are 80 years or older (Moore & Rosenberg, 1997). Figure 17–5 shows that the life expectancy of Canadians has been steadily increasing. This is at least partly due to advances in medical technology and improvements in public health programs, but is also due to the large cohort of baby boomers. Similar statistics have been reported for other industrialized countries. Given these trends, both the proportion and the absolute number of older Canadians are expected to increase in the coming decades. By 2031, approximately one in five Canadians will be at least 65 years old (Statistics Canada, 1994). Increases in the prevalence of older adults in Canada will be most dramatic among the oldest of the old.

Most older Canadians are women, since women tend to outlive men (see Figure 17–4). Even though the longevity gap has been narrowing in recent years, a significant gap still remains. An important consequence of the longevity gap is that the majority of older men (75 percent) are married, whereas the majority of older women (60 percent) live alone (Longino & Mittelmark, 1996). Poverty rates tend to be higher among older than among younger adults, and the percentage of older adults living in poverty increases with advancing age. This is due, in part, to the lower economic status of widowed women.

## Etiological Considerations and Research on the Aging Transition

Biological, psychological, and social factors all contribute to the quality of adjustment during the transition to later life. There is little doubt that the most important biological contribution to psychological well-being in later life is good physical health (Cohler & Nakamura, 1996). In fact, a study of adults over the age of 70 found that both men and women listed poor health as the most common contribution to a negative quality of life in their later years (Flanagan, 1982).

*Health behaviour* is particularly important to the physical well-being of older adults. Increased vigour and good health in later life are associated with proper diet, continued exercise, weight control, and the avoidance of cigarette smoking and excessive alcohol use (Leventhal et al., 2001). More generally, it has been suggested that the overriding goal of gerontology in industrialized societies should be to promote healthy and active lifestyles among older adults and to decrease the period of illness and infirmity that precedes death (Fries, 1990). In industrialized societies, current life expectancies probably are very close to the biological limits of the human species; therefore, increasing longevity may not be a realistic goal. Still, it may be possible to extend the number of vigorous and healthy years of life.

In addition to appropriate health behaviour, important psychological contributions to adjustment in later life include the availability of close relationships and the experience of loss. Among men over the age of 70, the most frequently listed positive contributions to quality of life include relationships with spouses, friends, and children. Because so many women over the age of 70 are widowed, women mention relationships with spouses far less frequently than men in describing contributions to their positive quality of life. However, they list relationships with friends and children, as well as general socializing (Flanagan, 1982).

As we discussed earlier in this chapter, among younger adults marital satisfaction is more closely related to women's than to men's mental health, whereas marital status is more closely linked with men's than women's emotional well-being. Evidence on widowhood suggests that the pattern continues into later life. Bereavement and living alone are more strongly related to depression among men than among women (Siegel & Kuykendall, 1990). Men apparently benefit more from marriage, and women benefit more from happy relationships.

**The Growing Number of Older Adults**

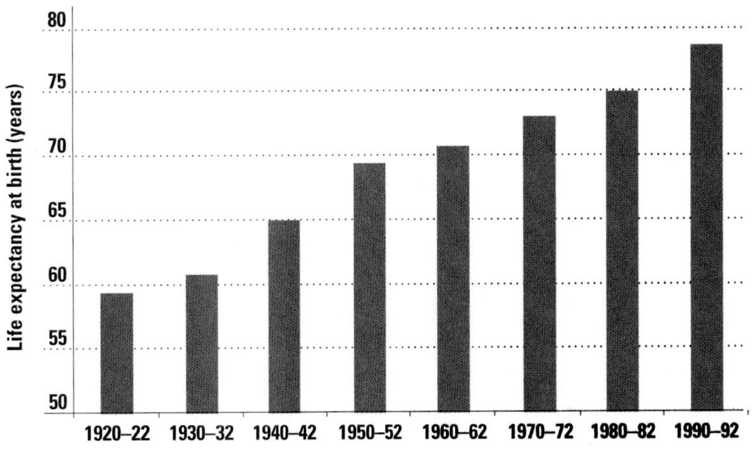


**FIGURE 17–5: The life expectancy of Canadians, like the life expectancies of people in other industrialized countries, has steadily increased over the past century.**

*Source:* Based on Statistics Canada, Catalogue No. 82F0075XCB.

Numerous social factors are linked with a happier transition to later life, especially material well-being and participation in recreational activities. Religion is also very important to many older adults, and religious affiliations have been found to moderate the ill effects of bereavement, particularly among men (Siegel & Kuykendall, 1990). Other research indicates that integration into the community is a major contribution to adjustment to later life.

## Treatment of Psychological Problems in Later Life

The availability and adequacy of medical care are of great importance to older adults, not only for treating disease but also for promoting physical health and psychological well-being. Because health behaviour is critical to the quality of life among older adults, experts view health psychology and behavioural medicine as central components of medical care. In fact, a new subdiscipline of these fields, called **behavioural gerontology**, has been developed specifically for studying and treating the behavioural components of health and illness among older adults (Bromley, 1990).

The same psychological and biological therapies used to treat emotional disorders among younger adults can be used to treat these problems among the aged. However, older adults may have misconceptions about psychotherapy. Thus education about the therapeutic process can be critical to its success. Some evidence also indicates that certain biological treatments may be more effective among older than among younger adults, particularly electroconvulsive therapy in the treatment of unremitting depression. Recent evidence also indicates that a combination of interpersonal therapy and medication is the best intervention for preventing relapse among older adults with recurrent depression (Reynolds et al., 1999). In general, however, research is insufficient on the effectiveness of alternative treatments for mental disorders among older adults. Mental services designed specifically for this population also are inadequately developed.

Finally, healthcare professionals increasingly focus not only on improving quality of life among older adults but also on maintaining integrity in death. *Living wills* are legal documents that direct healthcare professionals not to perform certain procedures in order to keep a terminally ill or severely disabled patient alive. Older adults often are much better at accepting death than are younger people, and living wills and other efforts to humanize dying allow dignity to be maintained through the end of life (Lawton, 2001).

# Summary

One out of every four people who sees a mental health professional has never met the criteria for the diagnosis of a mental disorder, and many of these people are seeking help with some difficult life problem. DSM-IV-TR categorizes such problems either as **adjustment disorders**, as clinically significant symptoms in response to stress, or as part of a general list of other conditions that may be a focus of clinical attention. We prefer to view life problems in terms of **life-cycle transitions**, struggles in moving from one stage of adult development into a new one.

The experiences associated with diverse life-cycle transitions differ greatly, but conflict is one common theme. Many conflicts during life-cycle transitions are interpersonal; others reflect a search for identity, our global sense of self; and still others involve emotional conflicts such as grieving. The concept of adult development was first highlighted by Erik Erikson's work on psychosocial development.

The transition to adult life begins late in the teen years and may continue through the twenties. The **identity crisis** is a central psychological conflict at this time, epitomized by the question "Who am I?" Many other things change during the transition to adulthood, including parent–child relationships, educational and career paths, and peer relationships. Emotional conflicts also mark the transition to adult life, as young people experience more intense and rapidly changing emotions than adults.

Family transitions are major changes in family relationships that often involve the addition or loss of members of a family household. Ongoing family conflict is closely linked with individual psychological problems, especially among women and children. Epidemiological evidence on family transitions indicates that over 90 percent of people get married; five out of six married people have children; a third of children are born outside of marriage; and divorce (which occurs in 40 percent of marriages) and remarriage are common. Family researchers often blame difficulties in negotiating family transitions on problems with communication, but broader family roles, such as traditional gender roles, also may be responsible for distressed family relationships. Social factors like poverty and even genetics also contribute to difficulties in family transitions. Both marital and family therapies and a variety of community action projects have been used to treat or prevent family problems.

Declining physical health and death are inevitabilities of aging. Older adults also confront a form of social prejudice known as **ageism**, a number of misconceptions and prejudices about aging. **Menopause**, the cessation of menstruation, is an important physical focus for middle-aged women. The functioning of all sensory systems also declines gradually throughout adult life, as do physical strength and general health. Gradual declines in physical health do not mean that older adults experience similar declines in psychological well-being. The prevalence of most mental disorders is lower, not higher, among adults 65 years of age and older. Most adults also view retirement positively, and relationships with children, siblings, and partners take on renewed importance. Unfortunately, the loss of loved ones, including the loss of a spouse, is a fact of life for older adults, particularly for older women. **Bereavement** is **grief** in response to the death of a loved one; it is commonly described as proceeding in a series of stages.

Young-old adults are between the ages of 65 and 75, are in good health, and are active members of their communities. The old-old are between 75 and 85, and may suffer from major physical, psychological, or social problems. The oldest-old are adults 85 years old or older. Approximately one out of every eight persons living in Canada is 65 years of age or older, and both the proportion and the absolute number of older Americans are expected to increase through the middle of the twenty-first century.

The most important biological factor in psychological well-being in later life is good physical health. Psychological factors include the availability of close relationships and the experience of loss. Social factors include material well-being, participation in recreational activities, religious affiliation, and integration into the community. **Behavioural gerontology** is a central component of medical care for older adults, and the same therapies can be used to treat psychological disorders among older as younger adults.

# Critical Thinking

1. What are some of the limitations of a broad model like Erikson's stages of psychosocial development? Can psychologists develop a clear model of adult development, or are the tasks of adult life too diverse to study systematically?
2. What are your personal thoughts about, and experience of, identity conflicts? Do you think a moratorium is necessary for healthy development? Do you think that people who vigorously pursue their childhood career paths have foreclosed their identity?
3. Is communication overrated by psychologists? Are some things better left unsaid and some conflicts better left unresolved? Do gender differences exist in communication interests and styles?
4. What can Canada do to prepare for the aging of its population? Are the country's social, medical, and economic resources sufficient to provide for the coming "boom" in the population of older adults?

# Key Terms

**adjustment disorders** 585
**ageism** 603
**behavioural gerontology** 609
**behavioural marital therapy** 602
**bereavement** 606
**boundaries** 594
**estrogen** 603
**family life cycle** 593
**gene–environment correlation** 599
**gerontology** 608
**grief** 606
**heritability** 597
**heritability ratio** 597
**identity crisis** 587
**life-cycle transitions** 584
**lifespan development** 583
**menopause** 603
**moratorium** 588
**reciprocity** 594
**social clocks** 588

# 18 Mental Health and the Law


Overview

Mental Health, Criminal Responsibility, and Procedural Rights

Mental Health and Civil Law

Mental Health and Family Law

Professional Responsibilities and the Law

**Under what circumstances are people with mental disorders acquitted of crimes?**

**When can people be committed against their will to a psychiatric hospital?**

**How do courts know what family arrangements meet children's "best interests"?**

**Can the confidentiality of psychotherapy ever be broken?**

Sometimes, people with DSM disorders are seen, in the eyes of the law, as being not criminally responsible for their crimes, because they are suffering from a mental disorder. This judgment was made, for example, in the case of André Dallaire, who attempted to assassinate Prime Minister Jean Chrétien in 1995. Dallaire was suffering from paranoid schizophrenia at the time. In other cases, however, people are judged as being criminally responsible for their crimes even if they suffered from a mental disorder at the time. This highlights a basic and essential point. The legal system views abnormal behaviour very differently from the way it is understood by mental health professionals.

## Overview

In this chapter we consider a number of important topics that lie at the intersection of mental health and the law. These topics underscore the different goals and values of the two professions. We begin with a discussion of mental health in the criminal law that focuses on the mental disorder defence. Then we discuss mental health issues in the civil law, including involuntary commitment, deinstitutionalization, and the rights of patients with mental disorders. The confinement of the mentally ill against their will is a serious action that must balance broad societal values against the needs and rights of the individual. To illustrate one extreme of these concerns, recall that many political dissidents in the former Soviet Union were confined to institutions to "treat" their "mental illnesses." At the other extreme, some seriously mentally ill people in Canada today do not receive therapy because they have the right to refuse treatment—a right they often exercise due to mental illness (lack of insight), not due to philosophical objections.

We also discuss legal intervention in families in this chapter, with an emphasis on the issues of child abuse and child custody disputes. Concerns about serious mental illness are the exception, not the rule, in custody and abuse cases. However, predictions about children's emotional well-being often are vital in these cases. The legal decisions can have far-reaching implications for children's emotional and physical health.

Finally, we consider some of the legal responsibilities of mental health professionals to their clients, especially the two topics of professional negligence and confidentiality. All these issues are not only of interest to professionals; they also have broad implications for society. Our most basic legal rights and responsibilities are reflected, and defined, by the manner in which we treat the mentally ill. The legal issues discussed in this chapter are considered largely in terms of Canadian law. Even so, our laws regarding mental illness are in many ways similar to the laws of other Western countries.

The mental disorder defence, in its various forms, is an area where there is often conflict between mental health and the law. One conflict arises when different mental health experts disagree about whether a given defendant has a mental disorder. This can lead to a "battle of the experts" (Low, Jeffries, & Bonnie, 1986). This occurs sometimes but not always. A more basic conflict concerns the difference between the legal concept of mental disorder

*Should people suffering from serious mental illnesses, like Edmond Yu, be required to receive treatment?*

and the psychological concept of mental disorder, as we discuss shortly.

We begin this chapter with the tragic case of Edmond Yu, which raises many important issues discussed in this chapter. As you read about Edmond, ask yourself the following questions: Do people with severe, debilitating mental disorders have the right to refuse treatment? Does society have the responsibility to impose treatment upon such people, such as antipsychotic medication and involuntary hospitalization? What if the person is homeless or disruptive because of a mental disorder?

## CASE STUDY The Tragic Case of Edmond Yu

As a youngster, Edmond Yu showed he had the drive to achieve great things. He was an excellent student, leaving home early for classes and studying in his room late every night. Yet he balanced his rigorous academic work with a variety of hobbies. After emigrating from Hong Kong to Canada, Edmond spent two years at York University in pre-med classes, and later earned a scholarship to study medicine at the University of Toronto.

In his first term, Edmond's marks were excellent. But during the second term, he started to become reclusive; he began studying from home, avoiding campus except for exams or group projects. The initial signs that all was not well were detected an ocean away by his sister, Katherine Yu, who was living in Hong Kong. She got a phone call saying there had been a serious fight between Edmond and his elder brother. Edmond had been asked to leave the house. There were other calls, too, from Edmond, in which he would ramble about someone stealing his wallet at university. He sounded incoherent, illogical, not himself. "I realized at that point there was something wrong with him," his sister recalls. She flew to Canada.

Things began to quickly spiral downward. Katherine remembers going to his apartment to check up on him. "He said the people in his building, as well as in nearby buildings, were spies," she says. "He believed there were satellites planted in his building—even in his own apartment—watching him." Likely unaware he was suffering from an illness, Edmond rejected Katherine's attempts to get him to seek help.

Katherine went to Edmond, demanding he accept help, see a doctor, take medication. He refused. "I knew there was something wrong with him. He asked me to leave, but I insisted and kept on talking. And then he slapped me in the face." It was painful for Katherine to use the incident against her brother, but she felt his best interests were at stake. The police apprehended Edmond and he was taken to the Clarke Institute of Psychiatry, where he was diagnosed as having paranoid schizophrenia. He was persuaded that, if he accepted treatment, he might still be able to return to medical school. He consented.

At least initially, Edmond tried to stick with the treatment, which consisted of antipsychotic drugs to quell the delusions. Unfortunately, some people experience severe side effects with psychotropic drugs. Edmond was one of them. "When he was on medication, he seemed to be a totally different person," Katherine says. "All he could do was eat and sleep. He was completely noncommunicative. His hands were so shaky he couldn't even hold a bowl of soup properly. The soup would always spill."

It was clear to Edmond he would not be able to attend school while on medication. It was equally clear he would not be able to attend school without it. Edmond requested that a doctor certify him fit for medical school. But because he would not take his medication, the doctor refused.

With no classes to attend, no career as a doctor, Edmond again flew back to Hong Kong. Within a month, he was picked up by police on a charge of disturbing the peace. Edmond was sent to a psychiatric hospital. The hospital then decided to impose treatment on Edmond—to force medication. When he returned to Canada, he immediately stopped taking the drugs. His noncompliance marked the start of a long struggle with his family over treatment.

Edmond's illness deepened, and his behaviour worsened. He was overtaken by paranoia and suspicion. He would talk nonstop. He felt he had special influence over world affairs. He feared those around him were conspiring to harm him. On occasion, he would be verbally abusive. And he began burning things—clothes, books, photographs. He would take them out on to the driveway and put a match to them. Edmond also started to meditate in front of the family's Scarborough home, sometimes for hours. On two occasions, he threw a knife at a dartboard he set up outside the garage door. Neighbours called the police both times. Other times, they just stared from their windows.

Edmond began to drift, from housing to hostels—where he says he was beaten and robbed—to the street. He made the occasional visit home, his deterioration

continued

*cont.*

more evident each time. His clothes were becoming ragged. The family later found him living in a public washroom in Grange Park, behind the Art Gallery of Ontario. His family managed to obtain a court order for him to be assessed by a psychiatrist. As a result he was involuntarily admitted to the Clarke Institute of Psychiatry for more than three months. Doctors declared him incapable of making his own treatment decisions, and his mother was appointed a substitute decision-maker. She had the power to authorize forced medication.

Over the next few years, a pattern set in: arrest, often for some form of assault, incarceration, release. The combination of winter, homelessness and illness were beginning to wear Edmond down. Late one afternoon, he was at the bus loop at the foot of Spadina Ave. Unaccountably, he struck a woman in the face, then boarded a bus. The police were called. The driver ordered everyone off the bus and left Edmond alone with the doors locked. Three police officers boarded the bus and tried to persuade Edmond to leave with them. At one point, he did agree to leave, but then took a hammer out of his jacket.

"I watched while he waggled his right wrist with the hammer in it," said a witness, who watched from an adjacent streetcar. "Then the movement of his wrist stopped, and seconds passed, when I heard what I thought initially was a cap gun. I could see the red flash of the gun, and the body slumped."

Constable Lou Pasquino fired six shots. One hit Edmond in the throat, his head twisting as the shots continued. A second hit his ear and entered the side of his head. The third hit the back of his skull. Edmond was dead before he hit the floor. ◆

*Source:* Scott Simmie, 1998, Reality is sometimes painful. *Toronto Star*, October 3. Reprinted with permission of the author and the Atkinson Charitable Foundation.

Should she be required to have treatment? When a person commits a crime as a result of a mental illness, such as an assault on another person, should he be held to be criminally responsible?

# Mental Health, Criminal Responsibility, and Procedural Rights

The law assumes that mental disorders may affect an individual's capacity to exercise his or her rights and responsibilities. Defendants are *unfit to stand trial* if they are judged to be unable to responsibly exercise their right to participate in their own trial defence.

## Mental Disorder and Criminal Responsibility

The idea that mental disability should limit **criminal responsibility** dates back to ancient Greek and Hebrew traditions and was evident in early English law. Records indicate cases where English kings pardoned murderers because of "madness," and later judicial decisions similarly excused some criminals who were "madmen" or "idiots" (Reisner & Slobogin, 1990). The emerging rationale underlying many of these **insanity** acquittals was that the defendant lacked the capacity to distinguish "good from evil" or what eventually became known as the inability to distinguish right from wrong. This ground for the **mental disorder defence** was codified in 1843, after Daniel M'Naghten was found not guilty of murder by reason of insanity.

**M'Naghten Test** M'Naghten was a British subject who attempted to kill Prime Minister Robert Peel, but who mistakenly murdered Peel's private secretary instead. The jury considered M'Naghten to be insane, because he believed he was being persecuted by various enemies, including the prime minister. His acquittal raised considerable controversy and caused the House of Lords to devise the following insanity test:

> To establish a defence on the ground of insanity, it must be clearly proved that, at the time of the committing of the act, the party accused was labouring under such a defect of reason, from disease of the mind, as not to know the nature and quality of the act he was doing; or, if he did know it, that he did not know he was doing what was wrong. (*Regina v. M'Naghten*, 1843)

Subsequently known as the *M'Naghten test*, this rule clearly articulated the "right from wrong" principle for determining insanity. If at the time a criminal act is committed a mental disease or defect prevented a criminal from knowing the wrongfulness of his or her actions, the person would be judged "not guilty by reason of insanity." For about a century, the "right from wrong" ground established in the *M'Naghten* case continued to be the major focus of the mental disorder defence in the laws of Canada and in many other Western countries.

**Irresistible Impulse Test** Later in the nineteenth century, the mental disorder defence was broadened in the United States when a second ground for determining insanity was introduced—the so-called *irresistible impulse test*. The irresistible impulse test determined that defendants also could be found insane if they were unable to control their actions because of mental disease. The rationale for the irresistible impulse test was that when people are unable to control their behaviour, the law can have no effect on deterring crimes. *Deterrence*, the idea that people will avoid committing crimes because they fear being punished for them, is a major public policy goal of criminal law. Although this test was used in the United States, it did not gain popularity in Canada.

**Not Criminally Responsible on Account of a Mental Disorder (NCRMD)** Under the provisions of the 1985 Canadian Criminal Code, a person found to be either not guilty by reason of insanity (NGRI) or unfit to stand trial because of a mental disorder would be automatically detained, indefinitely, in a psychiatric institution, "until the pleasure of the Lieutenant Governor is known." In other words, the person was detained until the mental disorder improved sufficiently to either justify release (in the case of NGRI) or to render the person fit to stand trial (if the mental disorder had previously rendered the person unfit to participate in his or her trial). Detention was intended to protect the public and to enable the person to recover from his or her mental disorder. But concerns arose because sometimes the period of detention was considerably longer than the period of time the person would have served in prison if convicted for the offence (Gélinas, 1994). A further concern was that some people judged to be NGRI were held in psychiatric hospitals without receiving adequate treatment.

This situation changed with a ruling by the Supreme Court of Canada in 1991, which stated that the treatment of mentally disordered criminal offenders was contrary to Canada's Charter of Rights and Freedoms. The court ruling required Parliament to amend the Criminal Code to give the accused person greater procedural and civil rights. Some of the major changes included reductions in how long an accused person could be detained in a psychiatric facility, and changes in the procedures for making appeals (e.g., the person could now obtain legal counsel to present his or her case for release). There were also changes in the mental disorder defence. The NGRI defence was changed to the "not criminally responsible on account of a mental disorder" (NCRMD) defence. According to the current Canadian Criminal Code:

> No person is criminally responsible for an act committed or an omission made while suffering from a mental disorder that rendered the person incapable of appreciating the nature and quality of the act or omission or of knowing that it was wrong.

The definitions of NGRI and NCRMD are similar in many ways, although there are some differences. They differ in that the term "insanity" has been replaced by "mental disorder." Another difference is that the defendant is now considered to be "not criminally responsible" instead of "not guilty." This change more explicitly recognizes that the defendant committed the offence, as opposed to being "not guilty" (Davis, 1993). A third difference between NGRI and NCRMD is that the meaning of "wrong" has been changed. The NGRI definition was concerned with legal wrongs, whereas a judgment of NCRMD is made if the person is incapable of knowing that an act or omission is *either* legally or morally wrong. To illustrate the difference between the two sorts of wrongs, if a person murdered someone under the delusion that the victim was Satan, then this would be legally wrong but perhaps morally justifiable (Davis, 1993).

The following Canadian Focus box illustrates Canada's mental disorder defence by describing the conditional discharge of André Dallaire. In 1995, Dallaire attempted to assassinate Prime Minister Jean Chrétien. Dallaire was suffering from paranoid schizophrenia, and was legally judged to be not criminally responsible for the assassination attempt because he was suffering from a mental disorder that prevented him from appreciating the nature and wrongfulness of his actions.

**Burden of Proof** The *burden of proof* substantially influences the meaning and likely success of the mental disorder defence. According to the current Canadian law, the defendant (or his or

## CANADIAN FOCUS The Mental Disorder Defence: Not Criminally Responsible on Account of a Mental Disorder (NCRMD)

During the early hours of November 5, 1995, 34-year-old André Dallaire, a thin, bespectacled former convenience store worker, broke into the residence of Prime Minister Jean Chrétien. Armed with a knife, Dallaire climbed the fence surrounding Chrétien's residence, smashed a window, and entered the house with the intention of slitting the prime minister's throat. Outside the bedroom, where the prime minister was sleeping, Dallaire encountered Chrétien's wife, Aline. She fled to the bedroom, locked the door, and called the police. While waiting for help to arrive, Jean Chrétien brandished a stone sculpture, just in case Dallaire broke through the door. Shortly afterwards, the RCMP arrived and took Dallaire into custody.

A psychiatric assessment revealed that Dallaire was delusional and hallucinating. He heard an inner voice commanding him to kill Chrétien, while another voice told him to stop. Dallaire believed he was a secret agent whose mission was to avenge the "No" side's victory in the Quebec referendum on independence (Fisher, 1996). Dallaire believed he would be glorified for liberating Canada from a "traitorous" prime minister. Thus, he was suffering from delusions of grandeur.

Dallaire had been suffering from paranoid schizophrenia since the age of 16. The judge ruled that Dallaire's intent to kill was the product of a severe mental disorder. Although Dallaire was found guilty of attempted murder, he was not held criminally responsible for his actions because he was suffering from a mental disorder at the time, which prevented him from appreciating the nature and wrongfulness of his actions. As a result, Dallaire was judged to be NCRMD. This is Canada's mental disorder defence, which is similar to the "not guilty by reason of insanity" defence used in other countries.

After being sent to the Royal Ottawa Hospital and placed on antipsychotic medication, Dallaire was no longer delusional or hearing voices, and expressed remorse for his actions. The court ordered a conditional discharge in which Dallaire was released to an Ottawa-area group home and allowed to come and go as long as he was escorted by a group home staff member (Fisher, 1996). He remained there until August 1996. At that point a review board decided that he was no longer a threat and so was free to move about unsupervised. However, he was not permitted to go within 500 m of the prime minister or his residence, and was required to continue seeing a psychiatrist and to take antipsychotic medication.

The mental disorder defence is not often used in Canada or in other countries. Even when it is used few people are judged to be NCRMD. In British Columbia in 1994, for example, only 60 people were NCRMD (Grant, 2001). Thus, in any given year there are not many people who are judged, like André Dallaire, to be NCRMD. ◆

her legal representative) may raise the issue of NCRMD at any time. In contrast, in order to protect the rights of the defendant, the prosecution may raise the possibility of NCRMD only after the defendant has been found guilty. The side raising the possibility of NCRMD bears the responsibility for proving the person is NCRMD.

*André Dallaire was found guilty of attempting to assassinate Prime Minister Jean Chrétien in 1995. Dallaire was also found to be not criminally responsible, however, because he was psychotic at the time.*

**Legal Definitions of Mental Disorder: Broad versus Narrow** An issue of obvious importance to mental health professionals is the precise legal definition of mental disorder, as used in the NCRMD defence. Some jurisdictions do not rely on an explicit definition, whereas the definitions in other jurisdictions differ to some extent from one another. Some definitions are quite broad and open to interpretation. For example, in British Columbia the legal definition of mental disorder is as follows:

> A disorder of the mind that seriously impairs [the person's] ability to react appropriately to his environment or to associate with others; and that requires medical treatment or makes care, supervision and control of the person necessary for his protection or for the protection of others. (Gaudet, 1994, p. 20)

Some jurisdictions specifically exclude certain mental disorders from being legally included as mental disorders, such as antisocial personality disorder. Thus, the legal definition of mental disorder generally is more restrictive than the DSM.

Some legal and mental health professionals argue that any disorder listed in the DSM should qualify for a mental disorder defence. Others have argued that some especially difficult circumstances—for example, being a victim of repeated violence—should also qualify defendants for the mental disorder defence, even if the problems are not listed as DSM diagnoses (see Further Thoughts). Still other commentators would sharply restrict the mental disorders that can be used as a part of the mental disorder defence. One suggestion is to confine the defence to mental retardation, schizophrenia, mood disorders, and cognitive disorders, excluding cognitive disorders induced by substance use or abuse (Appelbaum, 1994).

## Further Thoughts The Battered Woman Syndrome as a Defence

One-quarter of all violent crimes reported to police involve cases of family violence. Of these, two-thirds are violence committed by a spouse or ex-spouse, and 85 percent of the victims are women (Statistics Canada, 2003a). For centuries large numbers of women have been physically beaten by their husbands or lovers. In fact, wife battering has been institutionalized for much of Western history, and it remains an accepted practice in parts of the world today. The familiar phrase "rule of thumb" refers to the size of the stick, no thicker than a man's thumb, with which men were allowed to beat their wives according to common law. In the last few decades, spouse abuse finally has been recognized as a social and legal problem. Laws have been passed that protect wives from their husbands' physical and sexual abuse.

Battered women often remain in an abusive relationship for incomprehensibly long periods of time. To outsiders, the battered woman's reluctance to leave the relationship can seem foolish, even masochistic. To the battered woman, however, leaving the relationship often seems wrong or impossible. She may feel trapped by finances or out of concern for her children; chronic abuse may cause her to lose perspective on the extent of her maltreatment; or she simply may see no viable alternatives. She may fear for her life if she leaves. Some of these fears are realistic. An Ontario study found that up to 78 percent of murdered women are killed by their intimate partners (Crawford & Gartner, 1992).

Some women who have been constantly threatened, intimidated, and beaten by their husbands or boyfriends eventually escape the abuse by killing their tormentors. Surveys suggest that in North America, more than 1000 women kill their current or former batterer each year (e.g., American Psychological Association, 1995). Is this violence in response to violence ever justified?

The killing of an abuser clearly is justified in Canadian law when the victim's life is in immediate danger. In this case, the action is committed in self-defence. In many battering cases, however, the killing takes place when the threat of abuse is looming in the future but is not immediate. In this situation, a woman still might plead self-defence. According to contemporary trial practice, the defence may depend heavily on the battered woman syndrome.

The **battered woman syndrome** is a term coined by the psychologist Lenore Walker (1979) to describe her observations about the psychological effects of chronic abuse on victims. Two aspects of the syndrome are crucial to its use as a defence. First, Walker postulates a "cycle of violence," which includes three stages: (1) a tension-building phase leading up to violence; (2) the battering incident itself; and (3) a stage of loving contrition, during which the batterer apologizes and attempts to make amends. A second crucial aspect is Walker's assertion that the abused woman experiences learned helplessness. These two assertions are essential to a successful legal defence, because they imply that the battered woman expects to be beaten repeatedly but becomes immobilized and unable to leave the relationship.

The battered woman syndrome became a legitimate defence in Canadian law in 1990, with the Supreme Court ruling for the case of *Regina* v. *Lavallée*. Angelique Lavallée, a 22-year-old Winnipeg woman, had been living with her common-law partner, Kevin Rust, for a number of years. During their relationship she was beaten many times by Rust, which sent her to hospital at least eight times, with injuries including bruises, cuts, a broken nose, and a black eye. After a party one evening the two had a heated argument. Lavallée hid in the upstairs closet but was dragged out by Rust. He gave her his .303 calibre rifle, stating "Either you kill me or I'll kill you," and then he "kind of smiled and turned around." Although Lavallée said she aimed the gun above his head, she killed Rust with a single shot to the back of the head (Regehr & Glancy, 1995).

A psychiatrist called as an expert witness stated that Lavallée had been terrorized to the point of feeling trapped, vulnerable, worthless, and unable to escape from her relationship with Rust, despite the violence. In the psychiatrist's opinion, the shooting was a final, desperate act of a woman who genuinely believed she would be killed that night. The case eventually made its way to the Supreme Court of Canada, which acquitted Lavallée. The judgment was that Lavallée, suffering from the battered woman syndrome, was acting in self-defence (Regehr & Glancy, 1995).

*continued*

*cont.*

Expert testimony on the battered woman's syndrome has been used successfully to acquit many other battered women, or in other cases, to reduce their sentence. For example, in 1992 a Brampton, Ontario, woman drugged her husband and then cut off his penis while he slept. She was acquitted on the basis of having the battered woman's syndrome (Sillars, 1995).

Not surprisingly, the battered woman defence is controversial (Follingstad, 2003); some refer to it as the "abuse excuse." Criminal lawyer Alan Dershowitz (1994) is a notably vocal critic. He writes:

> On the surface, the abuse excuse affects only a few handfuls of defendants. . . . But at a deeper level, the abuse excuse is a symptom of a general abdication of responsibility. . . . It also endangers our collective safety by legitimating a sense of vigilantism. (p. 4)

Some courts have determined that expert testimony on the battered woman syndrome is inadmissible on various grounds, although the trend has been toward increasing acceptance of the defence (Brown, 1990; Faigman et al., 1997). Given the growing use of the defence, it may surprise you to learn that several commentators have argued that the scientific evidence supporting the battered woman syndrome is weak (Faigman et al., 1997; Schopp, Sturgis, & Sullivan, 1994). One question that has been asked, for example, is: How can someone who is suffering from learned helplessness bring herself to kill? Questions like this can make it difficult to plead self-defence based on the battered woman syndrome. ◆

**Mental Health Professionals as Expert Witnesses** **Expert witnesses** are specialists who the law allows to testify about specific matters of opinion (not just fact) that lie within their area of expertise. Unfortunately, mental health professionals sometimes present conflicting testimony when serving as expert witnesses. The resulting "battle of the experts" can be confusing and embarrassing, and can raise questions about professional ethics. For example, a commonly asked question is whether an expert's testimony has been "bought" by one side or the other. This possibility seems more feasible when expert witnesses are employed by either the prosecution or the defence rather than serving as a neutral *friend of the court*.

Some critics have argued that the mental health questions posed by the legal system cannot be answered with adequate reliability or validity, and therefore mental health professionals should not be allowed to offer expert testimony (Faust & Ziskin, 1988). The adequacy of expert opinion certainly is an important concern, especially when mental health professionals testify beyond their area of expertise or offer opinions that are not grounded in scientific evidence (Coles, 2000; Coles & Grant, 1999; Hoffman & Spiegel, 1989). However, we must recognize that the procedures and goals of the legal system differ from those of science. Expert witnesses are expected to offer informed opinion, not the "truth." In the law, it is the duty of the judge or a jury to reach a conclusion about truth. Furthermore, the law expects, and encourages, conflict during the process of reaching a judgment. Lawyers are duty-bound to present the most convincing case for their side, not the most objective case. As such, they expect challenges to an expert witness's testimony, and they expect conflicting testimony to be presented by the opposing side's experts (Fitch, Petrella, & Wallace, 1987). Legal rules do not excuse inaccurate or overblown "expert testimony," but they do leave room for opinion, particularly in the face of imperfect empirical evidence.

As noted by the University of Toronto psychiatrist Brian F. Hoffman (1997), mental health expert witnesses serve their profession and the legal system best if their testimony adheres closely to their expertise and to established knowledge. In cases of NCRMD, mental health experts are expected to testify about defendants' mental health and state of mind, but they are not expected to determine whether or not the person meets criteria for NCRMD. That is a decision to be made by a judge or a jury, not by the expert.

**Use and Consequences of the Mental Disorder Defence** Given the intensive media coverage of high-profile cases, as well as the important philosophical issues noted here, you might be surprised to learn that it was uncommon for the old (NGRI) mental disorder defence to be used in Canadian courts. It appears that the NCRMD defence is being used somewhat more frequently (Roesch et al., 1997). This may be because NCRMD, unlike NGRI, does not entail automatic detention in a psychiatric hospital.

Do defendants "walk" or "get away with murder" if they are found NCRMD? Some are incarcerated in psychiatric institutions for much shorter periods of time than if they had been sentenced to prison, while others actually are incarcerated for much longer periods. The duration of incarceration depends on a number of factors, including the seriousness of the offence and the extent to which the defendant is judged to be dangerous to self or others (Davis, 1993; Holley, Arboleda-Flórez, & Crisanti, 1998). Under the current law, a review board decides what will happen to the defendant who is judged to be NCRMD. The board can make its decisions without the need for approval from the Lieutenant-Governor. There are several possible outcomes, which take into consideration the person's mental condition, his or her needs for treatment, and the protection of society. The person judged NCRMD can be (1) absolutely discharged (if judged to be no longer a threat to self or others), (2) detained in a psychiatric hospital (with periodic evaluation by a review board and the right to appeal the decision), or (3) conditionally discharged. The latter might include some form of mandatory outpatient treatment, such as receiving medication while living in a group home (which may be subject to periodic review). The goal of the review board is to select an option that is appropriate and entails the least amount of restriction on the defendant's rights and freedoms.

In the event of detainment in a psychiatric hospital, government legislation requires that the duration of the stay is set, at least initially, such that the period of detention cannot exceed the maximum sentence that would have been applied if the person had been found guilty of the crime without being NCRMD. However, the duration of hospitalization can be extended for a further period if, for example, the person is judged to be dangerous to self or others. Under these circumstances, the person would be placed under civil commitment (Greenberg & Gratzer, 1994; see below for a discussion of civil commitment).

As noted by Davis (1993), there has been some controversy about the way NCRMD defendants are handled. Victims' rights groups have argued that the current Criminal Code does not adequately ensure protection of the public. On the other hand, civil rights advocates have argued that the old system of having the Lieutenant-Governor approve the review board decisions meant that people could be detained for political reasons that have nothing to do with the mental state of the defendant. (Concerns have also been raised that the Lieutenant-Governor's decision about whether or not to release a person could be politically motivated; Davis, 1994).

## Criminal Proceedings and Fitness to Stand Trial

Many people are institutionalized because they are unfit to stand trial as a result of a mental disorder. **Fitness to stand trial** refers to the defendants' ability to participate in their own defence. In order to participate, they must be able to understand the legal proceedings (Bal & Koenraadt, 2000)). Under section 2 of the current Canadian Criminal Code, a person is considered unfit to stand trial under the following conditions:

> "Unfit to stand trial" means unable on account of mental disorder to conduct a defence at any stage of the proceedings before a verdict is rendered or to instruct counsel to do so, and, in particular, unable on account of a mental disorder to: (a) understand the nature or object of the proceedings, (b) understand the possible consequences of the proceedings, or (c) communicate with counsel.

Notice that the question of fitness versus unfitness refers to the defendant's current mental state at the time of the trial, not to the mental state at the time of the alleged crime. A person is assumed fit unless there are reasonable grounds to suggest otherwise. A person can be fit to stand trial, yet found to be NCRMD. This would happen, for example, if a person was psychotic when a crime was committed, and then became nonpsychotic (e.g., with the help of medication) by the time he or she went to trial. Note also that the legal definition of "unfitness" is not the same as the psychologist's definition of mental disorder. Even a psychotic individual may possess enough rational understanding to be deemed fit in the eyes of the law. A person may be deemed fit even if he or she is unwilling to stand trial. For example, a defendant who simply refuses to consult with a court-appointed lawyer could still be fit to stand trial. The standard for fitness is fairly low. Only people suffering from severe mental disorders are likely to be found unfit (Melton et al., 1997).

If there are reasonable grounds to suggest that the defendant is unfit to stand trial, a physician (typically a psychiatrist) is asked to conduct an evaluation. If the defendant is determined to be unfit, legal proceedings must be suspended until the defendant is able to participate in them. The goal is to ensure that the legal proceedings are carried out fairly. As noted by Whittemore, Ogloff, and Roesch (1997), fitness is multifaceted; although a person can be fit to participate in some aspects of the criminal proceedings, he or she may be unfit to participate in other stages of the process. Thus, judges are faced with the task of determining whether the person is sufficiently competent to participate in the entire proceedings.

If the defendant is found unfit, then he or she may be sent for some form of therapy, such as inpatient or outpatient treatment, with the hope that the person will eventually become fit. Treatment is periodically reviewed and the accused person can lodge an appeal against any treatment plans. Treatment for people unfit to stand trial should take place in the least restrictive environment and should focus on the needs specific to the individual. If treatment efforts are not effective after a reasonable period of time, mental health practitioners and the court should find alternative options for the defendant, such as dismissal of charges and release, or civil commitment (Roesch, Ogloff, & Golding, 1993).

Under the old Canadian Criminal Code, an unfit person could be detained indefinitely in a psychiatric facility. Under the new code there are strict guidelines on how such people are treated and for how long they can be detained. The person's mental health status is periodically evaluated by a review board. In the case of involuntary hospitalization, the duration of detention is set so that it approximately matches the duration of detention for a criminal sentence (Davis, 1994). For example, if a person committed murder and was unlikely to ever become fit to stand trial, then he or she may be held in a psychiatric facility for life (i.e., corresponding to a life sentence when a sane person is found guilty of murder). A person who committed a minor crime (e.g., shoplifting), was not considered dangerous to self or others, and was unlikely to become fit to stand trial, might not be detained at all. He or she might receive a conditional discharge. For example, the person might be required to live in a group home and receive ongoing psychiatric treatment.

# Mental Health and Civil Law

Mental health issues are important in civil law as well as in criminal law. In particular, the involuntary hospitalization of the severely mentally impaired raises questions of major importance in civil law. Three issues are of special relevance: (1) civil commitment, the legal process of sending someone to a psychiatric hospital against his or her will; (2) patients' rights, especially their right to treatment, their right to treatment in the least restrictive alternative environment, and their right to refuse certain treatments; and (3) deinstitutionalization, the movement to treat patients in their communities instead of in psychiatric hospitals.

## Libertarianism versus Paternalism in Treating Patients Who Have Mental Disorders

What are society's legal and philosophical rationales for hospitalizing people against their will? Debates about involuntary hospitalization highlight the philosophical tension between *libertarian views*, which emphasize protecting the rights of the individual, and *paternalist* approaches, which emphasize the state's duty to protect its citizens. For example, the involuntary hospitalization of someone who appears to be dangerous to others serves a protective, paternalist goal. Yet civil libertarians note that *preventive detention*—confinement before a crime is committed—can lead to substantial abuse. Our laws prohibit the confinement of someone simply on the suspicion that he or she is about to commit a crime, with a single exception: **civil commitment**, the involuntary hospitalization of the mentally ill.

The debate between the libertarian and paternalist philosophies regarding civil commitment is very much alive today. Increased libertarianism has been the major trend since the 1960s, including a closer scrutiny of civil commitment procedures, an increasing recognition of patients' rights, and the deinstitutionalization movement.

## Civil Commitment

Canadian law contains two broad rationales for civil commitment. The first is based on the state's *parens patriae* authority, the philosophy that the government has a humanitarian responsibility to care for its weaker members. (The literal translation of the Latin phrase *parens patriae* is the "state as parent.") The concept of *parens patriae* dates back to ancient Rome and has influenced Canadian law through English traditions. Under the state's *parens patriae* authority, civil commitment may be justified when the mentally disturbed are either dangerous to themselves or unable to care for themselves. In addition to the confinement of the mentally ill, the concept of *parens patriae* is used to justify the state's supervision of minors and physically incapacitated adults.

The second rationale for civil commitment is based on the state's *police power*—its duty to protect the public safety, health, and welfare. Our government restricts individual liberties for the public good in many ways. For the safety of others, we are restricted from yelling "Fire!" in a crowded theatre or from driving a car at 180 km an hour. The civil commitment of people who are dangerous to others is justified by similar police power rationales. Civil commitment obviously involves a dramatic restriction in individual liberty, however, as it constitutes confinement without having committed a crime. Thus this severe restriction on individual liberty requires the highest degree of scrutiny. The police power rationales for civil commitment have been invoked throughout the history of Canadian law. Even in colonial times the mentally ill could be detained in order to prevent them from doing harm to others.

**Grounds and Procedures** Most jurisdictions provide two types of civil commitment procedures: emergency procedures and formal procedures. *Emergency commitment procedures* allow an acutely disturbed individual to be temporarily confined in a psychiatric hospital, typically for no more than a few days. Physicians determine whether an emergency commitment is required. Obviously, such action is taken only when a mental disorder is very serious, and the risk that the patient is dangerous to self or others appears to be very high.

*Formal commitment procedures* can lead to involuntary hospitalization for much longer periods of time than an emergency commitment, and formal commitment can be ordered only by a court. A hearing must be available to patients with mental disorders who object to involuntary hospitalization, and their rights must be protected. Typically, the need for hospitalization must be demonstrated by "clear and convincing" evidence. Following involuntary commitment, cases typically must be reviewed after a set period of time—for example, every six months.

Because civil commitment is a matter of provincial law, the specific grounds for involuntary hospitalization vary from jurisdiction to jurisdiction. However, all require that the person have a mental disorder *and* pose an *imminent* risk of harm or danger to themselves or others (Schuller & Ogloff, 2000).

In some jurisdictions, patients with mental disorders may be hospitalized against their will if they are unable to care for themselves adequately in the community or if they do not have family or friends who will care for them. The intention of this commitment standard is benevolent, but because it has been abused in some cases, legislation now exists to protect these rights, and advocacy programs have been developed to apply and enforce this legislation (Olley & Ogloff, 1995). Debates continue in courtrooms and in provincial legislatures. Should we be paternalist and sacrifice some individual rights by involuntarily committing patients with mental disorders who do not want, but who clearly need, inpatient treatment? Or do we run the danger of trampling on civil liberties if we hospitalize nondangerous people against their will?

The two other grounds for justifying civil commitment generally have not been attacked on philosophical grounds. Few civil libertarians object to hospitalizing people against their will when they clearly are either *dangerous to self* or *dangerous to others*, provided that the danger is "imminent." Thus a commonly accepted standard for civil commitment is "clear and convincing evidence of imminent danger to oneself or others."

**Assessing Dangerousness to Self and Others** The first question to ask about civil commitment and the assessment of dangerousness is: Are mentally disturbed people more dangerous than other people? According to Monahan (1992), recent, methodologically sophisticated research shows a relationship between violence and serious mental illness. Monahan draws this conclusion both from the rate of violence among the mentally ill and from the rate of mental disorder among criminals. Among prison inmates, the prevalence of bipolar disorder, major depression, and schizophrenia is several times as high as in the general population. Similarly, the rate of violence is about five times higher among people diagnosed with one of these major mental disorders than among those with no diagnosis. Of particular note, people who abuse alcohol or drugs are even more likely to engage in violent behaviour (see Table 18–1). This last finding is underscored by a recent study revealing that substance abuse symptoms increased the risk of violence in both former psychiatric inpatients and a comparison community sample (Steadman et al., 1998).

**TABLE 18–1 Mental Illness and Violence**

**Prevalence of Mental Disorders among a Sample of Convicted Criminals and Community Controls**

| | ***Percentage with Diagnosis*** | |
|---|---|---|
| ***Diagnosis*** | ***Jail Detainees*** | ***Controls*** |
| Schizophrenia | 2.7 | 0.9 |
| Major depression | 3.9 | 1.1 |
| Mania or bipolar disorder | 1.4 | 0.1 |
| Any severe disorder | 6.4 | 1.8 |

**Prevalence of Violence among People with or without a Mental Disorder**

| ***Diagnosis*** | ***Percentage Violent*** |
|---|---|
| No disorder | 2.1 |
| Schizophrenia | 12.7 |
| Major depression | 11.7 |
| Mania or bipolar disorder | 11.0 |
| Alcohol abuse/dependence | 24.6 |
| Substance abuse/dependence | 34.7 |

*Sources:* Adapted from J. Monahan, 1992, Mental disorder and violent behavior: Perceptions and evidence. *American Psychologist, 47,* 516, 518; L. Teplin, 1990, The prevalence of severe mental disorder among male urban jail detainees. *American Journal of Public Health, 80,* 665; and J. Swanson et al., 1990, Violence and psychiatric disorder in the community. *Hospital and Community Psychiatry, 41,* 765.

This evidence is informative, but it does not translate into a blanket policy for confining the mentally ill for several reasons. First, the risk for violence among the mentally ill is far lower than is publicly perceived. In fact, approximately 90 percent of the mentally disturbed have no history of violence (Monahan, 1992). Second, and most importantly, numerous factors other than mental illness are known to predict violence, but they obviously do not justify involuntary confinement. For example, research has documented that people who have a history of childhood maladjustment at home or school are more likely to be violent. Would anyone suggest that such a statistical risk justifies involuntary hospitalization?

*Clinical Assessment and the Prediction of Dangerous Behaviour* If mental illness is a philosophically problematic and not strong predictor of violence, our second question becomes: Can clinical assessments improve prediction? Researchers have concluded that clinical predictions that someone will be violent are wrong approximately two out of three times (Ennis & Emery, 1978; Monahan, 1981; also see Research Close-Up). That is, the false-positive rate of a prediction of violence is about 67 percent. In fact, several commentators have asserted that it is unethical for mental health experts to offer specific predictions about dangerous behaviour to the courts, because the clinical prediction of violence is so inaccurate (Ewing, 1991; Foot, 1990; Melton et al., 1997).

## RESEARCH CLOSE-UP

### The Accuracy of Predictions of Violence

The clinical prediction of violence often is inaccurate, but many studies of this topic are flawed in various ways. For example, many studies have assumed violence was predicted only in cases where a patient was committed to a hospital. Clinicians do not commit every potentially violent patient, however, and they sometimes commit patients who have a low likelihood of violence. Moreover, some dangerous patients allow themselves to be hospitalized voluntarily. Another problem with past research is the measurement of violence. Studies have relied upon police reports, court records, and medical files to assess subsequent violence, but many acts of violence are not documented in these official records.

An important study by Lidz, Mulvey, and Gardner (1993) sought to assess clinical predictions of violence more thoroughly than in past research. These investigators studied 714 cases seen in the psychiatric emergency room of a large teaching hospital in an urban area. Half the cases were predicted to have some potential for violence by two clinicians who interviewed them (including at least one

continued

*cont.*

psychiatrist), and the other half were comparison cases that were not predicted to be violent by the clinicians. Clinicians were asked directly about their predictions, and the two groups of patients were matched on their age, sex, and race, as well as on whether they were admitted to the hospital. Thus any differences in actual violence between the groups had to be a result of the predictions, not of either the background factors or whether the patient was hospitalized.

The investigators later interviewed the patients and someone who knew them about subsequent episodes of violence. This step represented another improvement over past research, which had used only official records of hospitals, courts, and/or the police to document violence. (These records were also checked in the present study.) The investigators conducted at least three interviews with all 714 cases in the six months following their contact with the emergency room. Violence was judged to have occurred if, according to any source of information, a patient laid hands on another person with a violent intent or threatened another person with a weapon.

The investigators found that 53 percent of the predicted cases engaged in a subsequent episode of violence versus 36 percent of the comparison cases, a statistically significant difference. Clinicians were equally good at predicting violence among members of different ethnic groups and among people of different ages. However, predictions of violence among women were less accurate than predictions for men. In fact, the clinical predictions of violence among women were no better than chance, as the clinicians greatly underestimated the base rate of violence among women (see Research Methods).

Among patients who had no prior history of violent behaviour, clinical prediction still was found to be above chance levels. Apparently the clinicians made some accurate judgments based on information other than past behaviour. Surprisingly, however, the accuracy of the clinical predictions was no greater when the risk of violence in a patient was judged to be higher versus lower. The critical distinction was the decision of whether the potential for violence was present or absent.

This research indicates that the clinical prediction of violence does have some value after all. Many inaccuracies are found in clinical prediction, but at least among men, clinicians were able to beat chance in predicting the potential for violence. A challenge for future research will be to find ways to improve the prediction of violence. Recent methods developed by University of Toronto psychologist Christopher Webster and colleagues (1997) are important in this regard (see the section titled Clinical Assessment and the Prediction of Dangerous Behaviour). Improving the accuracy of violence prediction is an especially important goal given the damage wrought by both false positives—wrongly hospitalizing someone who is not dangerous—and by false negatives—releasing someone who is dangerous to others. ◆

In support of clinical assessment, other commentators have noted that the prediction of violence is imperfect but well above chance levels (Monahan, 1981). At first glance, being wrong in predicting violence two out of three times may seem worse than chance. This is not the case, however, as one must take **base rates** or population frequencies into account. When predicting an event that has a very low frequency, a false-positive rate of two-thirds is, in fact, better than chance (see Research Methods). This is an important, if somewhat difficult, point to understand.

# RESEARCH METHODS

## Base Rates and Predictions

The validity with which an outcome like violence can be predicted depends on a number of factors. One obvious influence is the magnitude of the relation between the predictor and the outcome. The stronger the relation, the better the prediction. Thus the clinical prediction of violence seems highly flawed when we learn that clinicians are wrong two-thirds of the time that they predict that a patient will be violent. However, the validity of prediction also is affected by some conditions that are not obvious. Base rates or population frequencies are another very important influence (Meehl & Rosen, 1955).

We can use the prediction of violence to illustrate the general influence of base rates on the validity of prediction. We construct a hypothetical example in which we assume that (1) future, serious violence in our population has a base rate of 3 percent, (2) clinicians predict that violence will occur among 6 percent of the population, and (3) the clinical prediction of violence is wrong two-thirds of the time. These assumptions are portrayed in the following contingency table:

| | **Actually Violent** | **Actually Not Violent** |
|---|---|---|
| **Predicted Violent** | 2% (true positive) | 4% (false positive) |
| **Predicted Not Violent** | 1% (false negative) | 93% (true negative) |

*continued*

*cont.*

A quick check of the figures will confirm that they meet all our assumptions. The base rate of actual violence is 3 percent; the clinicians predict violence in 6 percent of the cases; and the prediction that patients will be violent is wrong two-thirds of the time. But let us examine the prediction a bit more closely. The hypothetical example yields a *sensitivity* (true positives over the sum of true positives and false negatives) of 67 percent and a *specificity* (true negatives divided by the sum of the true negatives and false positives) of 96 percent. Even though the predictions of violence are wrong two-thirds of the time, it is also true that the clinicians *correctly* detect 67 percent of violent patients and 96 percent of nonviolent patients in our hypothetical example.

Now let us compare these figures with another hypothetical example: Let's assume that a critic of psychological testing claimed that a coin flip is just as accurate as the clinical prediction of violence. The critic assumes that a coin flip would be right half of the time—it would come up heads or tails—while clinical prediction was right only one-third of the time. The statistics are not as simple as the critic, however, as we can easily illustrate. For this example, we will assume that (1) the base rate of future, serious violence remains at 3 percent, (2) the coin will predict violence (heads) 50 percent of the time, and (3) the coin flip produces random predictions. These assumptions are portrayed in the following contingency table:

| | Actually Not Violent | Actually Violent |
|---|---|---|
| **Predicted Violent** | 1.5% | 48.5% |
| **Predicted Not Violent** | 1.5% | 48.5% |

Unlike what the critic asserts, the coin flip does not beat clinical prediction in these hypothetical examples. Both the sensitivity and specificity of the coin flip are 50 percent. These figures indicate random prediction, and they are considerably lower than those obtained for clinical prediction. The coin flip method correctly detected only 50 percent of violent patients. In the real world, violence is a low-frequency event, and for statistical reasons alone, this makes it more difficult to predict validly (Meehl & Rosen, 1955). The clinical prediction of violence is far from perfect, but it is better than chance. Our critic did not understand the influence of base rates. We hope that you do now. ◆

Another consideration is that the prediction of violence is better in the short term than in the long run. This is an important distinction, because most research examines long-term outcomes (Monahan, 1981). Specifically, research indicates that two out of three people who are involuntarily hospitalized are not violent after they are released. However, this does not mean that they would not have been violent without the commitment. Clinicians commit only those patients who they strongly believe will become violent imminently, and they release the same patients only if they are convinced that they will not become violent. Such urgent, real-life decisions make it impossible to conduct unequivocal research. For obvious ethical reasons, no one will ever do the true, unequivocal experiment: release or confine potentially violent people at random and compare clinical predictions with actual acts of violence.

In reconciling the conflicting viewpoints, it is essential to consider again the differences between the goals of the legal and the mental health systems. Research and clinical evidence can be used to determine a reasonable assessment of the likelihood of violence. However, it is the job of the legal system, not the mental health profession, to translate such probabilities into decisions about whether a given individual is "dangerous" in the legal sense of the term (Grisso & Appelbaum, 1992). It also seems just—and helpful—to include the patient in the decision-making process. In clinical settings, evidence indicates that patients perceive hospital admissions to be less coercive if they feel they have a greater voice in the decision. That is, even if patients object to the ultimate decision, they are more likely to accept hospitalization if they feel they have been respectfully included in the decision-making process (Lidz et al., 1995; Monahan et al., 1999).

How can we improve the chances of accurately assessing a mentally disordered person's risk for violence? Researchers have been developing devices for risk assessment that combine the most promising violence predictors. These devices have been developed for predicting risk in psychiatric and criminal populations (see Borum, 1996). Some are highly specific measures, such as scales assessing the risk for spousal assault (Kropp & Hart, 1997).

A leading expert in the development of methods of risk assessment is Christopher D. Webster, a psychologist affiliated with the University of Toronto. Webster and colleagues have developed a number of methods, including the Violence Prediction Scheme (VPS: Webster et al., 1994) and the 20-item

*Psychologist* ***Christopher Webster,*** *from the University of Toronto, is an internationally recognized authority on the assessment of risk for violent behaviour.*

Historical/Clinical/Risk Management Scheme (HCR-20: Webster et al., 1997). Another promising risk assessment instrument is the Violence Risk Assessment Guide, developed and evaluated by researchers at the Penetanguishene Mental Health Center in Ontario, and Queen's University (Harris et al., 2003; Harris, Rice, & Quinsey, 1993).

To illustrate one of these approaches, the HCR-20 contains 10 items assessing historical variables, 5 items assessing clinical variables, and 5 items assessing future risk variables (see Table 18–2). The items were selected on the basis of a comprehensive review of the literature and from the clinical experience of experts on violence prediction.

Historical variables are those that are unlikely to change over time. These variables receive the greatest weighting because research to date suggests that they are the strongest known predictors of violence (Webster et al., 1997). For example, they include psychopathy (see Chapter 9), which is a form of personality disturbance that has been shown to predict violence. To underscore the importance of assessing psychopathy in risk assessment, consider the research by Dalhousie University psychologist Stephen Porter. Porter, Birt, and Boer (2001) assessed 317 Canadian federal offenders with the Psychopathy Check List-Revised (224 low scorers and 93 scoring within the psychopathic range). Criminal records and community release records were also examined. The investigators had access to the criminal records for offenders aged 20 to 81 years. Thus, in many cases the criminal records spanning over several decades. Consistent with previous research, the offenders classified as psychopaths consistently committed more violent and nonviolent crimes, compared to their counterparts. From the perspective of violence prediction and risk management, offenders with low psychopathy scores were increasingly less likely to commit further crimes as they got older. The opposite pattern was found for offenders classified as psychopaths. Other research by Porter and colleagues shows that psychopathy is associated with premeditated, "cold-blooded" homicide (Woodworth & Porter, 2002), and with severe sexual violence, including sadistic violence, that involves assaults upon multiple victims (Porter et al., 2000; Porter et al., 2001). Taken together, these findings offer further support for the importance of psychopathy in risk assessment.

Returning our attention specifically to the HCL-30, its clinical variables section refers to current signs and symptoms of psychopathology. Some of these clinical variables, which are listed in Table 18–2, require clarification. "Lack of insight" occurs when mentally disordered people are unable to rationally understand why they act the way they do. This may include a lack of awareness that one has a mental disorder in need of treatment. "Negative attitudes" refers to the extent to which the person holds antisocial, hostile, or angry attitudes. "Impulsivity" refers to erratic or unstable emotions and behaviours.

Risk management variables refer to existing circumstances in the community or to future situations that the individual may en-

**TABLE 18–2 Assessing the Risk for Violence: Items from the 20-Item Historical/Clinical/Risk Management Scheme (HCR-20)**

**Historical Variables (Including Historical Clinical Variables)**

- Previous violence
- Young age at the time of first violent incident
- Instability of personal relationships
- Employment problems
- Alcohol or drug problems
- History of a serious mental disorder (particularly psychotic or mood disorders)
- Early maladjustment at home or school
- Psychopathy
- Other personality disorders (aside from psychopathy)
- Prior supervision failure

**Clinical Variables (Current Status)**

- Lack of insight
- Negative attitudes
- Current symptoms of a serious mental disorder (particularly psychotic or mood disorders)
- Impulsivity
- Unresponsive to treatment

**Risk Management Variables**

- Plans for the future are unrealistic or lack feasibility
- Exposure to events that trigger relapse (destabilizers)
- Lack of personal support (from friends, relatives, etc.)
- Failure to comply with treatment
- Presence of stressful events

*Source:* Based on C.D. Webster, K.S. Douglas, D. Eaves, and S.D. Hart, 1997, Assessing risk of violence to others. In C.D. Webster and M.A. Jackson (Eds.), *Impulsivity: Theory, assessment, and treatment,* pp. 251–276. New York: Guilford.

counter after release from a psychiatric or forensic institution, for example, the person's living circumstances, the occurrence of stressful events, and his or her plans for dealing with stressors. It may not be possible to accurately assess the risk management variables until the person is released into the community. Clinical and risk management variables may change over time, with corresponding changes in the person's risk for violence. Therefore, it is important that these variables be periodically reassessed.

The HCR-20 is completed by collecting information from a variety of sources, including interviews with the patient, reports from social workers, police reports, and observations made when the person is in psychiatric care. There is a growing body of evidence to suggest that the HCR-20 is a useful method for assessing the risk of violence (Douglas et al., 1999; Douglas & Webster, 1999; Webster et al., 1997). In a recent review of the literature on violence prediction, Borum (1996) noted that the HCR-20 has several strengths, including the fact that it is based on empirical research, its items are clearly defined so they can be reliably rated, and it is brief and practical to use. Thus, the HCR-20 (and related devices) hold great promise for improving the accuracy in estimating the risk for violence.

*Assessing Suicide Risk* Identical concerns apply to civil commitment and the assessment of suicide risk as to the assessment of violence to others. As we discussed in Chapter 5, mental disorders, particularly depression, are related to an increased risk of suicide, but the risk of suicide clearly is far too small to justify civil commitment simply because of the presence of a mental disorder. Similarly, evidence on the clinical prediction of suicidal behaviour also indicates very high false-positive rates (Pokony, 1983). These findings again raise concerns about the accuracy of clinical prediction. Still, involuntary hospitalization is justified in cases in which the patient seems to be imminently at risk for harming themselves or others.

## The Rights of Patients with Mental Disorders

Like other democratic countries, Canada has constitutional provisions to protect the rights of its citizens. However, it was not until the past two decades that these rights and protections have been adequately extended to people in psychiatric care facilities. As a result of landmark court cases and the efforts of patient advocacy activists, several important rights have been established, including the right to treatment, the right to treatment in the least restrictive environment, and the right to refuse treatment (Olley & Ogloff, 1995).

Treatment in the least restrictive environment involves, for example, not hospitalizing a patient when he or she can be appropriately treated as an outpatient (and therefore able to remain living in the community). In theory, treatment in the least restrictive setting can be seen as an attempt to balance paternalist and libertarian concerns in the involuntary treatment of the mentally ill. The state provides mandatory care, but that care must restrict individual liberties to the minimal degree possible. However, questions arise about how to implement the theory. Who should determine what alternative is the least restrictive? Should the court monitor the consideration of alternatives? Should an independent party supervise these decisions? The practical answer to these important questions generally has been to place the decisions in the hands of mental health professionals.

Perhaps the most important issue about the least restrictive alternative concerns the problem that less restrictive alternatives to institutionalization, such as community care, often are not available. If a less restrictive alternative treatment is not available, must such treatment be developed and provided by the community? The development of community resources has not kept up with the release of patients from psychiatric hospitals (Hoffman & Foust, 1977). This is especially unfortunate, given that data suggest that community treatment can be more effective than inpatient care (Kiesler, 1982).

Another important and contentious patient rights issue concerns the right for involuntarily committed patients to refuse treatment, particularly the right to refuse psychoactive medication. The very concept of a patient refusing treatment is problematic in that involuntary hospitalization itself is treatment against a patient's will. The patient who is committed to a psychiatric hospital has refused inpatient treatment but is receiving it anyway. On what grounds can subsequent

*Dalhousie University psychologist **Stephen Porter** is a leading forensic investigator who has made important contributions to understanding psychopathy, in addition to his research on false memories and the recovered memory debate (see Chapter 7).*

treatment decisions be refused if the decision about hospitalization already has been taken out of the patient's hands? Many mental health professionals have noted this contradiction, and they argue that patients lose their right to refuse treatment once they are involuntarily hospitalized (Appelbaum, 1994; Gutheil, 1986; Torrey, 1997). After all, a mental health professional is in an awkward position if a patient is committed to a hospital for treatment yet retains the right to refuse medication.

On the other hand, it can be argued that it is unethical to force treatment upon competent patients who are involuntarily hospitalized; that is, on patients who are mentally competent to make decisions about their treatment. Competency involves the ability to understand that one has a mental disorder, and to understand the nature of the treatment and the risks and benefits involved. Thus, the question of the right to refuse treatment often turns on the issue of informed consent, one of several legal doctrines that can be used to justify a patient's refusal of mental health (or medical) treatments (Hermann, 1990). **Informed consent** requires that (1) a clinician tell a patient about a treatment and its associated risks, (2) the patient understands the information and freely consents to the treatment, and (3) the patient is competent to give consent. When the patient's competence to provide consent is in question, a common approach is to appoint an independent guardian who offers a substituted judgment, deciding not what is best for the patient but what the patient would have been likely to do if he or she were competent (Gutheil, 1986).

With the advent of the 1992 Canadian Charter of Rights and Freedoms, some provinces (e.g., Manitoba, Ontario) have recognized the right of competent, involuntary patients to refuse treatment (Gratzer & Matas, 1994). Other provinces, such as British Columbia, do not recognize this right. Instead, the treatment decision rests in the hands of the treating physician. Today, provincial mental health legislation generally does not allow for institutionalization and compulsory treatment of people who refuse treatment, unless they pose a threat to themselves or to the general public (Steller, 2003). A person like Edmond Yu, who was discussed at the beginning of this chapter, would not be involuntarily hospitalized and treated unless he was judged to be at imminent risk for harming himself or others. As we saw earlier, Edmond refused treatment and was generally allowed to do so, even though his schizophrenia could have been effectively treated.

Gratzer and Matas (1994) observe that legal developments on provincial and federal levels indicate a continuing trend for allowing involuntary patients the right to refuse treatment. These authors, however, note that most involuntary patients accept treatment; less than 10 percent persist in refusing treatment.

The right to refuse treatment raises concerns for some mental health practitioners. There is evidence that sometimes the right to refuse treatment is not in the patient's best interests. For example, consider the following patient, who was hospitalized in a province granting the right for involuntary patients to refuse treatment:

> A man with auditory hallucinations and paranoid delusions who previously had responded well to antipsychotic medication was involuntarily detained. He continually appealed treatment authorization [i.e., exercised his right to refuse treatment], so he was detained for 2 years without treatment. This could not have occurred in B.C. or Saskatchewan because treatment refusal is not permitted. (Gray & Keegan, 1999, p. 395)

As this example shows, a patient may be competent to refuse treatment, yet be involuntarily committed because he or she is a danger to self or others, or is unable to care for him- or herself. The only option in these cases is to detain the patient without treatment (or perhaps for the psychiatric institution to appeal the right of refusal to the court). This raises the complex issue of how to balance patients' rights with responsible caring: Should we allow patients to refuse treatment even when that means that they are unable or unsafe to live in the community?

## Deinstitutionalization

**Deinstitutionalization** became possible when effective medications, such as antipsychotic drugs, were developed to treat mental disorders (see Chapter 13). With the benefit of these medications, patients could function in the community (while receiving ongoing outpatient treatment), rather than being treated as inpatients in psychiatric hospitals. The deinstitutionalization movement embraces the philosophy that such outpatient treatment is often better than inpatient care, because it allows the person to become integrated into society. The goals of deinstitutionalization are (1) the prevention of inappropriate psychiatric hospital admissions through the provision of community alternatives for treatment, (2) the release to the community of all institutionalized patients who have been given adequate preparation for such a change, and (3) the establishment and maintenance of community support systems for noninstitutionalized people receiving mental health services in the community (Braun et al., 1981).

The establishment of mental health centres in communities was part of the effort to achieve these three goals. Deinstitutionalization throughout Canada and the United States occurred in a dramatic fashion, with many psychiatric hospitals either closing or drastically reducing the number of patients staying there. To illustrate, from 1962 to 1977 the population of provincial psychiatric hospitals fell by 78 percent, despite the fact that the number of mentally ill people continued to rise as the Canadian population grew (Freeman, 1994).

Unfortunately, the savings from closing or downsizing psychiatric hospitals were not used to develop adequate community support programs such as case management services, patient housing, vocational and educational rehabilitation, and so forth. As a result, most regions are still struggling to bring community mental health services up to standard (Freeman, 1994). There are still not enough community mental health centres, and many existing centres do not even offer services for the seriously mentally ill, such as emergency treatment or inpatient care (Torrey, 1997). Other community resources, such as halfway houses, simply have not been implemented in adequate numbers. Associated problems include an increase in homelessness among the mentally ill (Bachrach, 1994). Many seriously mentally ill individuals are living on streets and in shelters instead of receiving psychiatric inpatient care (Torrey, 1988). In addition, a *revolving door* phenomenon has developed in which more patients are admitted to psychiatric hospitals more frequently but for shorter periods of time (Karras & Otis, 1987). Some seriously mentally ill people are released from hospital with little or no provision for aftercare or follow-up treatment, and some people with serious mental disorders end up in the prison system instead of being treated in psychiatric hospitals (Torrey, 1988).

**The Case for Paternalism** Some of the problems of deinstitutionalization are compounded by restrictive civil commitment laws. One commentary graphically described the situation as one in which patients were "rotting with their rights on" (Appelbaum & Gutheil, 1979). Torrey (1988) argued, "Freedom to be insane is an illusory freedom, a cruel hoax perpetrated on those who cannot think clearly by those who will not think clearly" (p. 34).

**Outpatient** or **community commitment** is one important alternative that can balance some of these paternalist concerns against the libertarian fears of restricted freedom. Community commitment is a form of involuntary commitment where the person is required to undergo mental health treatment or care in an outpatient setting. This may involve attendance at an outpatient clinic, participation in individual or group therapy, educational and vocational activities (e.g., work experience programs), supervision, an obligation to stay in a recommended living situation (e.g., a group

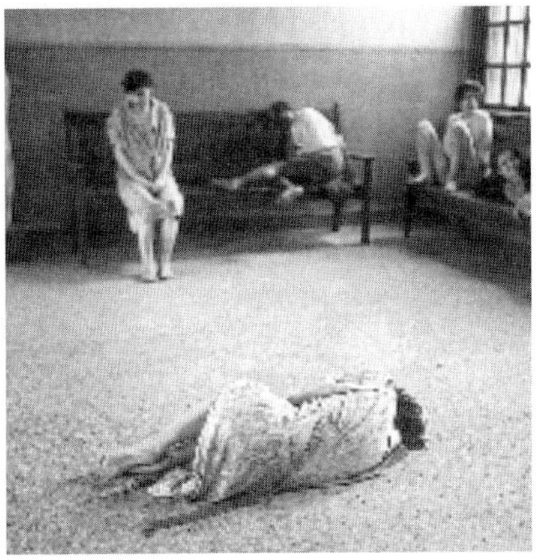

*These contrasting photos illustrate how mentally disordered patients often are neglected both inside and outside of institutions. The photo on the left, taken several decades ago, shows some of the depressing and dehumanizing conditions that characterized many institutions for the mentally ill. The photo on the right depicts the contemporary problem of homelessness. Many homeless people are deinstitutionalized patients suffering from mental disorders.*

home), the non-use of alcohol and illegal drugs, and money management (Boudreau & Lambert, 1993).

Some commentators call for the involuntary treatment of inpatients but only following careful review. In addition to providing procedural safeguards, the increased supervision of treatment decisions should benefit patients in psychiatric institutions where care often is less than ideal (Appelbaum, 1994). Others support more paternalism in civil commitment laws but argue that a broader reorientation is needed in the thinking—and funding—of mental health professionals.

# Mental Health and Family Law

Both the mental disorder defence and civil commitment primarily involve people who have a serious mental illness. In contrast, mental health professionals who are involved with *family law* issues typically work with people whose problems are less severe, and they often are consulted about issues related to normal development. This is evident in the major issues that form the focus of family law: divorce, spousal abuse, foster care, adoption, juvenile delinquency, child custody disputes, and child abuse and neglect. Any one of these problems can involve serious psychopathology, but they more commonly involve family members who are only mildly disturbed or are functioning normally.

We consider both family law and mental health law issues together in this chapter, because the opinions and advice of mental health professionals are frequently sought by legal professionals working in both areas. However, family and mental health law are distinct in the legal system. The two areas have different historical roots and practices. Much of mental health law is based on the state's police power obligations, but virtually all of family law is premised on the government's *parens patriae* duties.

In theory, the functions of juvenile and family courts are to help and protect children and families. Thus the goals of family courts historically have been more psychological than legal. The importance of mental health professionals is particularly evident in the two family law topics considered in this chapter—child custody disputes following divorce (or separation), and cases of child abuse and neglect. Psychological findings carry great weight not only because of the family court's philosophy but also because family laws often are vague. The guiding principle for judicial decision-making in custody and abuse cases is the very general directive to make determinations according to what is in the "child's best interest" (Mnookin, 1975). Not surprisingly, family court judges frequently turn to mental health professionals for practical guidance in defining a given child's "best interests."

## Children, Parents, and the State

A general dilemma in family law is how to balance the potentially competing interests of children, parents, and the state (Mnookin, 1985). Are children entitled to the same rights as adults? Should parental authority be respected above and beyond the wishes of either children or the state? Or should the state's *parens patriae* obligation overrule the desires of both children and parents?

The tension among children, parents, and the state pervades controversies about child custody and child abuse. Advocates for children's rights want children to have a voice in the outcome of custody disputes and the disposition of abuse cases. Advocates for family autonomy want parents to resolve custody disputes themselves, and want to narrow the definition of abuse and neglect in order to minimize state intervention in the family. Advocates for state intervention want judges to determine custody arrangements, and they argue for earlier and more vigorous intervention in cases of child abuse. Like other issues we have considered in this chapter, specific controversies about child custody or child abuse often reflect broad philosophical concerns about the sometimes conflicting interests of children, parents, and the state.

## Child Custody Disputes

Parental divorce is a common experience for children. In 2002, for example, there were over 70 000 divorces in Canada (Statistics Canada, 2004). Estimates indicate that about 40 percent of children today will experience their parents' divorce (Emery, 1999a), and child custody disputes also commonly occur between cohabiting couples and even between other family members.

**Child custody** is one of the issues that must be decided when parents divorce (or separate). Although the legal terminology differs from jurisdiction to jurisdiction, custody decisions involve two determinations: *physical custody,* or where the children will live at what times; and *legal custody*, or how the parents will make separate or joint decisions about their children's lives. *Sole custody* refers to a situation in which only one parent retains physical or legal custody of the children; in contrast, in *joint custody* both parents retain custody. The test determining the right to custody and access is: What custody or access disposition will serve the best interests of the child? The issue of custody is not framed as a question of what rights the parents or other claimants may have; it is always framed in terms of the rights and needs of the child (McHale, 1991).

The majority of custody decisions are made outside of court by lawyers who negotiate for the parents. A growing number of custody decisions are being made by the parents themselves, however, typically with the help of a *mediator*—a neutral third party who facilitates the parents' discussions. Finally, a small but significant percentage of custody disputes are decided in court by a judge (Maccoby & Mnookin, 1992). Mental health professionals may be involved in providing recommendations during lawyer negotiations, they may provide expert testimony in court, or they may act as mediators themselves.

**Expert Witnesses in Custody Determinations** Over the past two decades the Canadian legal system has been turning more frequently to mental health professionals for their assistance in resolving custody disputes (Austin, Jaffe, & Friedman, 1994). Mental health professionals who conduct custody evaluations typically consider a number of factors in evaluating a child's best interests. These include the quality of the child's relationship with each parent, the family environment provided by each parent, each parent's mental health, the relationship between the parents, and the child's expressed wishes, if any (Emery, 1994; Emery & Rogers, 1990). Evaluating these broad family circumstances and drawing implications for child custody is a precarious task. Concerns have been raised about the objectivity and reliability of custody evaluations from mental health professionals (Bala, 1994). In fact, some skeptics have argued that, because of inexact scientific knowledge, mental health professionals should refrain from conducting custody evaluations (O'Donohue & Bradley, 1999).

Others suggest that the problem lies as much with the system for determining child custody as with psychological evaluations (Emery, 1999b). The law that governs custody disputes, the *child's best interests standard,* is unclear about what a child's future best interests are, how they can be determined, or how they can be achieved. As law professor Robert Mnookin (1975) has pointed out:

> Deciding what is best for a child poses a question no less ultimate than the purposes and values of life itself. Should the judge be primarily concerned with the child's happiness? Or with the child's spiritual and religious training? Should the judge be concerned with the economic "productivity" of the child when he grows up? Are the primary values of life in warm interpersonal relationships, or in discipline and self-sacrifice? Is stability and security for a child more desirable than intellectual stimulation? These questions could be elaborated endlessly. And yet, where is the judge to look for the set of values that should inform the choice of what is best for the child? (pp. 260–261)

Mnookin argues that the child's best interests standard increases conflict between a child's parents, because the directive is so vague. Virtually any information that makes one parent look bad and the other look good may be construed as helping a parent's case—and people who have been married have much private and potentially damaging information about each other. The likelihood that the best interests standard increases acrimony is a particular problem, because a wide range of research indicates that conflict between parents is strongly related to maladjustment among children following divorce (Emery, 1982, 1999a; Grych & Fincham, 1990). This raises the sad irony that parents and the legal system may be undermining a child's best interests by fighting for them in a custody battle. For this reason, many mental health professionals feel that they serve children and the legal system better if they help parents to settle custody disputes outside of court rather than providing testimony in court.

**Divorce Mediation** Mental health professionals, as well as many family lawyers, are now serving a new role as mediators to help parents settle custody disputes. In **divorce mediation**, parents meet with a neutral third party who helps them to identify, negotiate, and ultimately resolve their disputes. The role of mediator is very different from the evaluation role of mental health professionals, and mediation also is a major change in the practice of the law. Mediators adopt a cooperative approach to dispute resolution rather than the usual adversary procedures (Emery, 1994).

Evidence consistently indicates that mediation dramatically reduces the number of custody hearings in court, helps parents reach decisions more quickly, and is viewed more favourably than litigation by parents, especially fathers (Emery, 1994; Emery, Matthews, & Kitzmann, 1994). Importantly, recent evidence demonstrates that an average of five hours of mediation causes nonresidential parents to remain substantially more involved in their children's lives and improves the co-parenting relationship—12 years after mediation (Emery et al., 2001). More generally, the custody mediation movement shows that mental health professionals need not limit their involvement in the legal system to evaluations. Rather, mental health professionals can help to develop alternatives to legal procedures when these procedures create undue distress for the people involved, as illustrated in the following brief case study.

## BRIEF CASE STUDY

### A Custody Dispute

Jim and Suzanne had been divorced for two years when they first came to a mediator. At the time, the parents were disputing custody of their 8-year-old daughter, Ellen, and 10-year-old son, Will. The parents had maintained a tense and uneasy joint physical custody arrangement. Every other week the children alternated between each of their parents' homes. However, Suzanne recently decided to sue for sole custody of the children. She said did this because she was worried about Will's increasingly difficult behaviour in school and at home with her, as well as Ellen's reluctance to talk about her feelings or her activities with her father. Jim argued that the real problem was his recent remarriage to Adriana. He said that he was eager to get on with his life, but Suzanne insisted on hanging on to the past. He did not want anything more to do with her.

Suzanne and Jim were referred to mediation by their lawyers, who urged their clients to avoid renewing the long, contentious, and expensive negotiations that had surrounded their divorce. Suzanne and Jim had decided on joint custody as a last-minute compromise. They reached this decision literally on the courthouse steps.

During the course of mediation, the mediator urged Suzanne and Jim to see their children's perspective on their divorce and, for the children's sake, to cooperate as parents even though they no longer were spouses. Privately, the mediator also encouraged Suzanne to face her grief over the end of her marriage, as well as her fears of losing her children to Jim's new family. In private, the mediator also urged Jim to recognize that, like it or not, Suzanne *was* a part of his life. After all, she was the mother of his two children, and he claimed to love them above all else.

With the guidance of the mediator, and following several frank discussions about their feelings, their preferences, and their past problems with joint custody, Suzanne and Jim reached a settlement out of court. They would return to the week-to-week joint physical custody schedule but with a new commitment to communicate better, to support each other's efforts in parenting, and to work together to be both more flexible with the schedule and to make routines more consistent across their homes. Adriana came for one of the last mediation sessions, and all of the adults agreed that Adriana should be an important part of raising Will and Ellen, but that no one could or wanted to replace Suzanne or Jim as the children's parents. ◆

### Child Abuse

Child abuse has been going on for centuries, although consistent public attention to the problem did not begin until 1962, when the physician Henry Kempe wrote about the "battered child syndrome." Kempe documented tragic cases of child abuse in which children suffered repeated injuries, fractured bones, and, in a substantial number of cases, death

(Kempe et al., 1962). Reporting laws have since then been developed to make it mandatory for any citizen, including mental health professionals, to report child abuse to the authorities (Thompson-Cooper, Fugère, & Cormier, 1993). Such laws are in place throughout Canada, except for the Yukon, where reporting is permitted but not legally required (Thompson-Cooper et al., 1993). Thus, in most places in Canada, mental health professionals not only can but must break the confidentiality of psychotherapy if they suspect child abuse.

Four forms of **child abuse** generally are distinguished: physical abuse, sexual abuse, neglect, and psychological abuse (American Psychological Association, 1995). *Physical child abuse* involves the intentional use of physically painful and harmful actions. The definition of physical abuse is complicated by the fact that corporal punishments like spanking are widely accepted discipline practices (Emery & Laumann-Billings, 1998; Wolfe, 1987). Only about 10 percent of physically abused children whose caretakers are reported to social service agencies sustain injuries serious enough to require professional care, but the danger to children can be considerable nevertheless. Estimates indicate that thousands of children in North America die every year because of maltreatment (Emery & Laumann-Billings, 1998).

*Child sexual abuse* involves sexual contact between an adult and a child. This form of abuse is a worldwide problem of alarming proportions. An international study of 21 countries, including Canada, the United States, and countries in Europe, found that the prevalence of child sexual abuse ranged from 7 to 36 percent for girls, and 3 to 29 percent for boys. The prevalence in Canada was estimated to be 18 percent for girls and 8 percent for boys (Finkelhor, 1994).

*Child neglect*, the most commonly reported form of child abuse, involves placing children at risk for serious physical or psychological harm by failing to provide basic and expected care. Some children are severely neglected, and they experience extreme failure in their growth and development as a result (Wolfe, 1987). Some children also suffer *psychological abuse*—repeated denigration in the absence of physical harm.

**Munchausen-by-Proxy syndrome (MBPS)** is a unique but potentially very harmful syndrome that merits special note. This form of child abuse is apparently rare, although it is being increasingly recognized and reported in Canada and throughout the world (Feldman & Brown, 2002). In MBPS, a parent feigns, exaggerates, or induces illness in a child. In benign cases, the parent simply fabricates the child's illness; in more serious cases, the parent actually induces illness. One study used covert video surveillance to monitor parents suspected of MBPS (Southall et al., 1997). Of 39 children, video recordings captured 30 parents' attempts to intentionally suffocate the child, one mother's attempt to break her child's arm, and another mother's attempt to poison her child with disinfectant. These results clearly illustrate that MBPS can be associated with severe and potentially deadly child abuse.

With regard to child abuse in general, the number of reported cases has steadily increased since the 1970s (Dezwirek, Wolfe, & Gowdey, 1996; Lang & Daro, 1996; Wang & Harding, 1999). Experts debate the reasons for the increased number of reports. The rate of child abuse could be increasing, but the real increase may be in reports of abuse (Besharov, 1992; Besharov & Laumann, 1996; Emery & Laumann-Billings, 1998). Over half of all reports of abuse are found to be unsubstantiated after an investigation (e.g., Thompson-Cooper et al., 1993), and some experts have suggested that the percentage of unsubstantiated reports is growing. One reason for this, according to some critics, is that the concept of neglect is applied too broadly (Besharov, 1986, 1988, 1992).

The increasing number of reports of child abuse and the large percentage of less severe cases that are unsubstantiated create two problems. First, social service agencies are overwhelmed with more minor cases, and they are less able to deal with children who are living in circumstances of clear danger. Second, intervention in less severe cases may actually do more harm than good. Overwhelmed social service agencies may stigmatize and disrupt families that are troubled but coping—and offer them relatively little treatment in return (Emery & Laumann-Billings, 1998).

When an allegation of abuse is substantiated, one of the major questions is whether to remove the child from the home. Tens of thousands of maltreated children in North America are placed in *foster care* each year. Foster care obviously benefits children who are in physical danger, but as many as half of all children placed in foster care are in no immediate danger of physical injury (Besharov, 1988). Stable foster care can offer children psychological benefits, as well as physical protection (Wald, Carlsmith, & Leiderman, 1988). However, half of the children placed in foster care remain there for at least two years, almost one-third are separated from their parents for over six years, and a substantial proportion live in many different foster homes during this time (Besharov, 1986).

Children who are likely to be placed in foster care for long periods of time may be adopted instead. However, this raises an even more controversial issue, the *termination of parental rights,* that is, the nonvoluntary removal of any right a parent has to care for and supervise his or her child. Obviously, this is an extreme step, and one that the courts have taken only with great reluctance.

As with child custody decisions, judicial determinations about foster care and other possible dispositions of child abuse cases are guided by the child's best interest standard. Psychologists frequently play a role in these legal proceedings by investigating allegations of abuse in interviews with children, making recommendations to the court about appropriate placements for children, and providing treatment to children and families (Becker et al., 1995; Melton & Limber, 1989). Some have argued that too many of our legal and mental health efforts have been devoted to identifying families as abusive, while not enough resources are available for helping families afterwards. While coercive intervention and removal from the home is justified in serious cases of abuse, in more moderate cases, treatment of families under stress is a role that requires more attention in both psychology and the law (Emery & Laumann-Billings, 1998).

## Professional Responsibilities and the Law

The regulation of the mental health professions is the last area of psychology and the law that we consider in this chapter. Clinical psychologists, psychiatrists, and social workers all have **professional responsibilities** to meet the ethical standards of their profession and to uphold the law. The duties of mental health professionals are numerous and varied. Here we focus on two important and illustrative professional issues: negligence and confidentiality.

### Professional Negligence and Malpractice

*Negligence* occurs when a professional fails to perform in a manner that is consistent with the level of skill exercised by other professionals in the field. Simply put, negligence is substandard professional service. *Malpractice* refers to situations in which professional negligence results in harm to clients or patients. In the law, malpractice is demonstrated when (1) a professional has a duty to conform to a standard of conduct, (2) the professional is negligent in that duty, (3) the professional's client experiences damages or loss, and (4) it is reasonably certain that the negligence caused the damages (Evans, 1997; Ogloff & Olley, 1998; Reisner & Slobogin, 1990). When professionals are found guilty of malpractice, they are subject to disciplinary action from their professional organizations and licensing boards, and run the risk of civil suits and criminal actions.

Medical malpractice claims are common, but malpractice claims against mental health professionals are relatively infrequent. The inappropriate use of electroconvulsive therapy (ECT) and medication are two of the more common reasons for malpractice claims against mental health professionals. These treatments are clearly defined, research on their appropriate use is more clear-cut than is psychotherapy research, and the treatments can result in physical as well as psychological damages. In other words, malpractice is easier to demonstrate for these treatments.

The existence of a sexual relationship between therapists and their clients is another common ground for successful malpractice suits. Although specific damages can be difficult to prove, it is commonly accepted that sexual relationships between therapists and their clients are harmful in and of themselves. This is evident in the ethical codes of the Canadian Psychological Association and the Canadian Psychiatric Association, both of which prohibit sexual relationships between therapists and their clients. Other claims of professional negligence stem from the failure to prevent suicide, failure to prevent violence against others, and violations of confidentiality (Leesfield,

1987). As the field continues to evolve, a new area of professional negligence may become important: the failure to offer adequate treatment and to inform clients about treatment alternatives.

**Informed Consent on the Efficacy of Alternative Treatments** Patients may receive any of a wide range of alternative treatments for the same mental disorder. From the patient's perspective, the choice of treatment hinges, in part, on chance factors such as the profession of the therapist or his or her "theoretical orientation." In Canada, only psychiatrists can prescribe medication, and they surely are more likely to recommend this treatment than are psychologists and social workers. Similarly, behaviour therapists are likely to offer behaviour therapy, and psychoanalysts to offer psychoanalysis.

As we have argued throughout this text, however, the goal of research is to identify specific treatments for specific disorders. This scientific approach has been successful in identifying some approaches that are more effective than others in treating particular disorders. If evidence points to the superiority of one treatment over another, several questions arise. Does the mental health professional have an obligation to offer the more effective treatment, make a referral to another professional who can provide it, or, at a minimum, obtain informed consent to pursue an alternative course of therapy?

It is likely that mental health professionals will be held to increasingly higher standards in offering alternative treatments, or at least in informing patients about the risks and benefits of various treatments. As researchers demonstrate that certain approaches are more or less effective in treating particular disorders, offering informed consent about treatment alternatives is likely to become a routine practice for mental health professionals. Informed consent means providing full and accurate information about risks and benefits in an understandable and noncoercive manner (Crowhurst & Dobson, 1993; Evans, 1997; Ogloff, 1995).

When the client is a person under the age of 18, the legal requirements for informed consent vary from jurisdiction to jurisdiction. In some jurisdictions there is an age limit placed on when consent can be given, whereas other jurisdictions use criteria based on the person's capacity for understanding. To illustrate the latter, in British Columbia the Infants Act (1996) stipulates that a child can give informed consent provided that he or she is able to understand the nature, risks, and benefits of treatment, and if the mental health practitioner believes that the treatment would be in the best interests of the child. If the child does not display this sort of understanding, then consent must be obtained from the next of kin (e.g., parent) or legal guardian.

**Who Is the Client?** An issue closely related to the choice of a therapeutic approach is the choice of who is to receive treatment. Many psychological problems are closely linked with family difficulties, and researchers continue to debate whether particular disorders cause family distress or whether family distress causes particular disorders. This raises the question of who should be targeted to receive psychological treatment, as well as what sort of treatment they should receive.

The issue is not a minor one. The choice of a treatment can convey subtle but important messages about the cause of psychological problems and the responsibility for changing them. For example, individual therapy with a troubled child or a depressed wife can communicate both to the clients and their families that the problem rests within the individual, even though the difficulties might be a reaction to poor parenting or to an abusive marriage. Similarly, family therapy can falsely convey the impression that schizophrenia is

*"First, we'll look for repressed memories of malpractice suits."*

©The New Yorker Collection, Frank Cotham from cartoonbank.com. All rights reserved.

caused by inadequate child rearing. Some of these impressions can be corrected by direct feedback from a therapist, but some are unavoidable consequences of the focus of treatment.

Another problem arises when therapists are unclear about therapeutic alliance. To whom do therapists owe confidentiality? If a couple divorces after marital therapy, can a therapist testify at the request of one spouse and over the objection of the other? If a therapist sees a client in court-ordered treatment, must (or can) information on therapy be shared with the court? There are no easy solutions to such dilemmas. Clearly, the best approach is for therapists to decide who their client is before the question of disclosure arises and to share their position on confidentiality with all involved parties.

### Confidentiality

**Confidentiality**—the ethical obligation not to reveal private communications—is basic to psychotherapy. The therapist's guarantee of privacy is essential to facilitating the disclosure of important, clinically relevant information, and the maintenance of confidentiality with past clients is essential to gaining the trust of future clients. For these reasons, confidentiality standards are a part of the professional ethics of all the major mental health professions, and are frequently addressed in licensing regulations as well.

Despite the overriding importance of confidentiality, mental health professionals sometimes may be compelled by law to reveal confidential information. For example, mental health professionals are usually required to break confidentiality and report suspected cases of child abuse. This requirement can create dilemmas for therapists (Smith & Meyer, 1985). In order to provide fully informed consent, must a therapist make the limits on confidentiality clear before beginning therapy? If therapists tell their clients that their disclosures of child abuse will be reported, does this encourage clients to be something less than honest? Does reporting child abuse undermine the therapeutic relationship that might benefit an abused child?

Tatiana Tarasoff and Prosenjit Poddar, the man who killed her. The California Supreme Court ruled that Poddar's therapist should have warned Tarasoff that her life might be in danger.

There are other limits to confidentiality. *Privileged communications*—such as communications between a lawyer and his or her client—are confidential exchanges that legislation explicitly protects from being revealed. Mental health practitioners in Canada do not have this privilege, and so the practitioner may be required to break confidentiality if this is ordered by the courts (Cram & Dobson, 1993). The therapist, for example, might be required to provide the court with details about the client's psychological problems and their treatment.

Confidentiality also must be broken when clients are dangerous to themselves or others, so that civil commitment can proceed. The case of *Tarasoff* v. *Regents of the University of California* (1976) raised the important possibility that mental health practitioners might have to break confidentiality when a client expresses violent intentions. In other words, the practitioner may have an obligation to warn the potential victim.

***Tarasoff* and the Duty to Protect Potential Victims** On October 27, 1969, a young woman named Tatiana Tarasoff was killed by Prosenjit Poddar, a foreign student at the University of California at Berkeley. Poddar had pursued a romantic relationship with Tarasoff, but after having been repeatedly rejected by her, he sought treatment at the Berkeley student health facility. Poddar was diagnosed as suffering from paranoid schizophrenia, and the clinical psychologist who treated Poddar concluded that he was dangerous to himself and others. After consulting with two psychiatrists, the psychologist decided to pursue civil commitment. He notified the campus police of his concerns, and asked them to detain Poddar for the purpose of an emergency commitment. The police concluded that Poddar was not dangerous, however, and released him after he agreed to stay away from Tarasoff. Poddar subsequently discontinued therapy, and no one notified Tarasoff that Poddar posed a threat to her life. Poddar had never mentioned Tatiana Tarasoff by name, but the information he related to the psychologist was sufficient to deduce her identity. Two months after the police had questioned him, Poddar murdered Tarasoff after being rejected by her once more.

Tarasoff's parents sued the university, the therapists, and the police for negligence. The California Supreme Court ruled that the defendants were liable for failing to warn the woman of the impending danger. Specifically, the court ruled that therapists are liable if (1) they should have known about the dangerousness based on accepted professional standards of conduct, and (2) they failed to exercise reasonable care in warning the potential victim. Subsequent California cases have limited the duty to protect to cases that involve a specific, identifiable target of potential violence. A general statement of intended violence invokes no duty to protect (Goodman, 1985).

The *Tarasoff* case prompted subsequent litigation, and almost 20 U.S. states have enacted laws that outline therapists' duty to protect potential victims of violence (Appelbaum, 1994; Geske, 1989). Guidelines for evaluating and documenting assessments of dangerousness to others are rapidly becoming as important as policies for assessing suicide risk (Monahan, 1993).

While both U.S. and Canadian law have their roots in English law, U.S. court decisions do not apply in Canada, and so the legal reasoning that led to the *Tarasoff* decision does not necessarily apply in Canada (Truscott & Crook, 1993). Some civil lawsuits in Canada have raised arguments similar to those in the *Tarasoff* case, although we have yet to see a legal precedent like the *Tarasoff* ruling (Birch, 1992; Schuller & Ogloff, 2000). Nevertheless, it could be argued that it is ethical for mental health practitioners to warn third parties of impending harm. Indeed, this is present in the code of ethics for the Canadian Psychological Association (1991). As Ogloff and Olley (1998) recently pointed out, the code of ethics for Canadian psychologists is quite similar to the legal requirements imposed by the *Tarasoff* ruling. According to the code, psychologists should:

> Do everything reasonably possible to stop or offset the consequences of actions by others when these actions are likely to cause serious physical harm or death. This may include reporting to appropriate authorities (e.g., the police) or an intended victim, and would be done even when a confidential relationship is involved. (Canadian Psychological Association, 1991)

The code of ethics in its entirety can be found at **www.cpa.ca/ethics.html**.

***James Ogloff*** *is a professor of law and forensic psychology, who until recently was at Simon Fraser University in British Columbia. He is a leader in the study of psychology and the law.*

# Summary

The *M'Naghten* test is one rule for finding a person not guilty by reason of **insanity**. According to this rule, legal insanity is established if a mental disease or defect prevents a criminal from knowing the wrongfulness of his or her actions. Canada's **mental disorder defence** was derived from the *M'Naghten* test. A person can be found to be not criminally responsible on account of a mental disorder (NCRMD) if a crime is committed while the person is suffering from a mental disorder that renders him or her incapable of appreciating the nature of the crime or of knowing that it was wrong. The NCRMD defence entails the recognition that the person is guilty of committing the crime, but also acknowledges that the offence occurred under circumstances of a mental disorder.

**Fitness** to stand trial is the defendant's ability to understand legal proceedings and to participate in his or her own defence. Many people accused of crimes are institutionalized because they are unfit to stand trial.

The issue of **civil commitment**—hospitalizing people against their will—reflects philosophical tensions within the law. Libertarian views, which emphasize protecting the rights of the individual, often conflict with paternalist approaches, which emphasize the state's duty to protect its citizens. Three grounds dominate commitment laws: (1) unable to care for self, (2) dangerous to self, and (3) dangerous to others. Controversies abound, but a relation between mental illness and "dangerousness" does exist, and mental health professionals can predict violence with some accuracy. The fact that violence has a low **base rate** in the population is a major contributor to inaccurate prediction.

The rights of patients with mental disorders have received increased attention since the

1970s. The right to treatment indicates that hospitalized patients must receive therapy and not just custodial care. The right to treatment in the least restrictive environment indicates that therapy should be provided in community settings when it is possible and appropriate. The right to refuse treatment indicates that patients cannot be forced to receive certain treatments (for example, taking medications) without **informed consent**. Concerns about patients' rights also have given impetus to the **deinstitutionalization** movement, the philosophy that many of the mentally ill and mentally retarded can be better cared for in their community than in large psychiatric hospitals. Unfortunately, the lack of follow-up care in the community has undermined this laudable goal. Paternalist concerns about the failure to treat those in need must be balanced against concerns for patient rights. A procedure called **outpatient commitment** may help to balance concerns about offering treatment while protecting liberties.

A general dilemma in family law is how to balance the potentially competing interests of children, parents, and the state. **Child custody** must be decided when parents divorce (or separate). These decisions involve determinations about both physical custody—where the children will live—and legal custody—how the parents will make decisions about their children. Custody decisions are based on the child's best interests standard, a vague directive that requires judgments as to what the child's best interests are and what the future will bring. Parents often make determinations about their own children's best interests privately in **divorce mediation** or elsewhere.

Child abuse may involve physical abuse, sexual abuse, neglect, or psychological abuse. A rare but potentially dangerous form of abuse is associated with **Munchausen-by-Proxy syndrome.** Reports of child abuse have increased greatly in recent years, but neither the law nor mental health professionals have reached consensus on how best to fulfill children's best interests in these cases. Currently, agencies are overloaded simply investigating abuse allegations.

Clinical psychologists, psychiatrists, and social workers all have **professional responsibilities** to meet the ethical standards of their profession and to uphold the laws of the jurisdictions in which they practise. Key professional issues include obtaining informed consent, clearly identifying whom the professional is serving, and maintaining **confidentiality**. A relatively new concern is the ethical obligation to warn potential victims when a client reveals violent intentions.

# Critical Thinking

1. What is your view on the mental disorder defence? Should we hold mentally ill criminals fully responsible for all their actions? What about battered women who kill their husbands? Is the "abuse excuse" dangerous?
2. What is your position on the libertarian versus paternalist debate about serious mental illness? Do we need to protect rights vigorously or is the duty to treat a greater obligation?
3. Are too many patients with mental disorders released into communities with inadequate services? How would you feel if a group home for the mentally ill were being planned for your neighbourhood?
4. Is it unethical for mental health professionals to offer a given treatment when research indicates that other approaches are more effective?

# Key Terms

**base rates** 624
**battered woman syndrome** 618
**child abuse** 633
**child custody** 631
**civil commitment** 621
**community commitment** 629
**confidentiality** 636
**criminal responsibility** 615
**deinstitutionalization** 628
**divorce mediation** 632
**expert witness** 619
**fitness to stand trial** 620
**informed consent** 628
**insanity** 615
**mental disorder defence** 615
**Munchausen-by-Proxy syndrome (MBPS)** 633
**outpatient commitment** 629
**professional responsibilities** 634

# Glossary

**Abnormal psychology** The application of psychological science to the study of mental disorders. Includes investigation of the causes and treatment of psychopathological conditions.

**Abstinence violation effect** The guilt and perceived loss of control that the person feels whenever he or she slips and finds himself or herself returning to drug use after an extended period of abstinence.

**Acquired immune deficiency syndrome (AIDS)** A disease caused by the human immunodeficiency virus (HIV) that attacks the immune system and leaves the patient susceptible to unusual infections.

**Actuarial interpretation** Analysis of test results based on an explicit set of rules derived from empirical research.

**Acute stress disorder (ASD)** A new category of mental disorder in DSM-IV that is defined as a reaction occurring within four weeks following a trauma and is characterized by dissociative symptoms, re-experiencing, avoidance, and marked anxiety or arousal. Contrasts with posttraumatic stress disorder, which either lasts longer or has a delayed onset.

**Adjustment disorder** A DSM-IV classification designating the development of clinically significant symptoms in response to stress in which the symptoms are not severe enough to warrant classification as another mental disorder.

**Affect** The pattern of observable behaviours that are associated with subjective feelings. People express affect through changes in their facial expressions, the pitch of their voices, and their hand and body movements.

**Ageism** A number of misconceptions and prejudices about aging and older adults.

**Agnosia** ("perception without meaning") The inability to identify objects. The person's sensory functions are unimpaired, but he or she is unable to recognize the source of stimulation.

**Agoraphobia** An excessive fear of being in situations from which escape might be difficult in the event of a panic attack or panic-like symptoms. Literally means "fear of the marketplace," and is sometimes described as fear of public spaces.

**Allegiance effect** A characterization of psychotherapy outcome research such that investigators commonly find the most effective treatment is the one to which they hold a theoretical allegiance.

**Alogia** A form of speech disturbance found in schizophrenia. Can include reductions in the amount of speech (poverty of speech) or speech that does not convey meaningful information (poverty of content of speech).

**Alzheimer's disease** A form of dementia in which cognitive impairment appears gradually and deterioration is progressive. A definite diagnosis of Alzheimer's disease requires the observation of two specific types of brain lesions: neurofibrillary tangles and senile plaques.

**Amenorrhea** The absence of at least three consecutive menstrual cycles; a defining symptom of anorexia nervosa in females.

**Amnestic disorder** A form of cognitive disorder characterized by memory impairments that are more limited or circumscribed than those seen in dementia or delirium.

**Amniocentesis** The extraction of fluid from the amniotic sac in order to test for chromosomal and genetic defects in the developing fetus.

**Amyloid plaques** A central core of homogeneous protein material know as beta-amyloid found in large numbers in the cerebral cortex of patients with Alzheimer's disease, but they are not unique to that condition.

**Analogue study** A research procedure in which the investigator studies behaviours that resemble mental disorders or isolated features of mental disorders. Usually employed in situations in which the investigator hopes to gain greater experimental control over the independent variable.

**Androgyny** The possession of both "female" and "male" gender-role characteristics.

**Anhedonia** The inability to experience pleasure. In contrast to blunted affect, which refers to the lack of outward expression, anhedonia is a lack of positive subjective feelings.

**Anorexia nervosa** A type of eating disorder characterized by the refusal to maintain a minimally normal body weight along with other symptoms related to body image.

**Anterograde amnesia** The inability to learn or remember new material after a particular point in time.

**Antisocial personality disorder** A pervasive and persistent disregard for, and frequent violation of, the rights of other people. Also known as *psychopathy*. In DSM-IV, it is defined in terms of a persistent pattern of irresponsible and antisocial behaviour that begins during childhood or adolescence and continues into the adult years.

**Anxiety** A diffuse emotional reaction that is out of proportion to threats from the environment. Rather than being directed toward the person's present, anxiety is typically associated with the anticipation of future problems.

**Anxious attachment** An insecure relationship in which an infant or child shows ambivalence about seeking reassurance or security from an attachment figure.

**Aphasia** The loss or impairment of previously acquired abilities in language comprehension or production that cannot be explained by sensory or motor defects or by diffuse brain dysfunction.

**Apraxia** The loss of a previously acquired ability to perform purposeful movements in response to verbal commands. The problem cannot be explained by muscle weakness or simple incoordination.

**Asperger's disorder** A subtype of pervasive developmental disorder (new in DSM-IV) that is identical to autism (oddities in social interaction, stereotyped behaviour) with the exception that there is no clinically significant delay in language.

**Assessment** The process of gathering and organizing information about a person's behaviour.

**Attachments** Selective bonds that develop between infants and their caregivers, usually their parents, and are theorized to be related to later development. Analogous to the process of imprinting, which has been observed in many animals.

**Attention deficit** Inattention characterized by distractibility, frequent shifts from one uncompleted activity to another, careless mistakes, and/or poor organization or effort. A key symptom of attention-deficit/hyperactivity disorder.

**Attention-deficit/hyperactivity disorder** A psychological disorder of childhood characterized by hyperactivity, inattention, and impulsivity. Typically has an onset by the early school years.

**Attribution** Perceived causes; people's beliefs about cause–effect relations.

**Atypical antipsychotic** A type of medication that is beneficial for psychotic patients but does not produce extrapyramidal motor side effects and may not be associated with increased risk of tardive dyskinesia.

**Authoritative parenting** A style of parenting that is both loving and firm and is often used by parents of well-adjusted children.

**Autism** Literally, "absorption in one's own mental activity." Formally, a severe pervasive developmental disorder characterized by profound problems in social interaction, communication, and stereotyped behaviour, interests, and activities (see also *autistic disorder*).

**Autistic disorder** A severe form of pervasive developmental disorder characterized by oddities in social interaction (autistic aloneness), communication impairments, and stereotyped behaviour, interests, and activities.

**Autonomic nervous system** The division of the peripheral nervous system that regulates the functions of various bodily organs such as the heart and stomach. The actions of the autonomic nervous system are largely involuntary, and it has two branches, the sympathetic and parasympathetic nervous systems.

**Aversion therapy** A classical conditioning technique for attempting to eliminate unwanted behaviour by pairing an unpleasant (aversive) stimulus with the behaviour—for example, inducing nausea when alcohol is consumed.

**Avoidant personality disorder** An enduring pattern of thinking and behaviour that is characterized by pervasive social discomfort, fear of negative evaluation, and timidity. People with this disorder tend to be socially isolated outside of family circles. They want to be liked by others, but they are easily hurt by even minimal signs of disapproval from other people.

**Avolition** (lack of volition or will) A negative symptom of schizophrenia involving a loss of willpower, indecisiveness, and ambivalence. The person becomes apathetic and ceases to engage in purposeful actions.

**Balanced placebo design** A research design that combines the placebo and antiplacebo methods. It can be used to assess the effect of alcohol, the effect of expectations, and the interaction of alcohol by expectation.

**Barbiturates** Drugs that depress activities of the central nervous system; mostly for sedation.

**Base rates** Population frequencies. Relative base rates set statistical limits on the degree to which two variables can be associated with each other.

**Battered woman syndrome** A controversial classification of the common psychological effects of spousal abuse. Includes a tension-building phase leading up to violence, the battering incident itself, and a stage of loving contrition, during which the batterer apologizes. According to some experts, this induces learned helplessness in battered women.

**Behaviour genetics** The study of broad genetic contributions to the development of normal and abnormal behaviour.

**Behavioural coding system** (also known as a *formal observation schedule*) An observational assessment procedure that focuses on the frequency of specific behavioural events.

**Behavioural family therapy (BFT)** A form of family treatment that may include several variations, but always trains parents to use operant conditioning as a way of improving child discipline.

**Behavioural gerontology** A subspecialty within behavioural medicine developed specifically for studying and treating the behavioural components of illness among older adults.

**Behavioural marital therapy** A variation on couples therapy that emphasizes the partners' moment-to-moment interaction, particularly their exchange of positive and negative behaviours, their style of communication, and their strategies for solving problems.

**Behavioural medicine** A multidisciplinary field concerned with studying and treating the behavioural components of physical illness.

**Behaviourism** The belief within scientific psychology that observable behaviours, not unobservable cognitive or emotional states, are the appropriate focus of psychological study.

**Benzodiazepines** Group of drugs that have potent hypnotic, sedative, and anxiolytic action (also called antianxiety drugs).

**Bereavement** Grieving in response to the death of a loved one.

**Beta-amyloid** Protein material that forms the core of senile plaques, a type of brain lesion found in patients with Alzheimer's disease.

**Binge eating** Eating an amount of food in a fixed period of time that is clearly larger than most people would eat under similar circumstances. One part of the eating disorder of bulimia nervosa.

**Binge eating disorder** A controversial diagnosis defined by repeated episodes of binge eating but in the absence of compensatory behaviour; included in an appendix of DSM-IV.

**Biofeedback** Behavioural medicine treatment that uses laboratory equipment to monitor physiological processes (that generally occur outside of conscious awareness) and provide feedback about them. Hypothesized to help patients to gain conscious control over problematic physiological processes such as hypertension.

**Biological reductionism** The assumption that biological explanations are more useful than psychological explanations because they deal with smaller units—with brain chemistry, for example, instead of emotional experience.

**Biopsychosocial model** A view of the etiology of mental disorders that assumes that disorder can best be understood in terms of the interaction of biological, psychological, and social systems.

**Bipolar mood disorder** A form of mood disorder in which the person experiences episodes of mania as well as episodes of depression.

**Blunted affect** A flattening or restriction of the person's nonverbal display of emotional responses. Blunted patients fail to exhibit signs of emotion or feeling.

**Body dysmorphic disorder** A type of somatoform disorder characterized by constant preoccupation with some imagined defect in physical appearance.

**Body image** A cognitive and affective evaluation of one's weight and shape, often a critical one.

**Borderline personality disorder** An enduring pattern of thinking and behaviour whose essential feature is a pervasive instability in mood, self-image, and interpersonal relationships. Manifestations of this disorder include frantic efforts to avoid real or imagined abandonment. People who fit this description frequently hold opinions of significant others that vacillate between unrealistically positive and negative extremes.

**Boundaries** Rules defining a relationship, particularly the rules that separate a third person from an individual or another relationship. For example, the boundary of the marital relationship is defined, in part, by the limited discussion of intimate topics outside the relationship.

**Brief psychotic disorder** A diagnostic category in DSM-IV that includes people who exhibit psychotic symptoms for at least one day but no more than one month. After the symptoms are resolved, the person returns to the same level of functioning that had been achieved prior to the psychotic episode.

**Bulimia nervosa** A type of eating disorder characterized by repeated episodes of binge eating followed by inappropriate compensatory behaviours (such as self-induced vomiting) together with other symptoms related to eating and body image.

**Cardiovascular disease (CVD)** A group of disorders that affect the heart and circulatory system. Hypertension (high blood pressure) and coronary heart disease are the most important forms of CVD.

**Cardiovascular reactivity** A measure of the intensity of an individual's cardiovascular reactions to stress in the laboratory; a predictor of future cardiovascular disease.

**Case study** A careful description and analysis of the problems experienced by one person.

**Catatonia** Motor symptoms that can include either immobility and marked muscular rigidity or excitement and overactivity.

**Catatonic type** A subtype of schizophrenia that is characterized by symptoms of motor immobility (including rigidity and posturing) or excessive and purposeless motor activity.

**Categorical approach to classification** A view of classification based on the assumption that there are qualitative differences between normal and abnormal behaviour as well as between one form of abnormal behaviour and other forms of abnormal behaviour.

**Central nervous system** The major communication system in the body, comprising the brain and the spinal cord.

**Cerebral cortex** The uneven surface of the brain that lies just underneath the skull and controls and integrates sophisticated memory, sensory, and motor functions.

**Cerebral hemispheres** The two major structures of the forebrain and the site of most sensory, emotional, and cognitive processes. The functions of the cerebral hemispheres are lateralized. In general, the left cerebral hemisphere is involved in language and related functions, and the right side is involved in spatial organization and analysis.

**Child abuse** A legal decision that a parent or other responsible adult has inflicted damage or offered inadequate care to a child; may include physical abuse, sexual abuse, neglect, and psychological abuse.

**Child custody** A legal decision, especially common in separation and divorce, that involves determining where children will reside and how parents will share legal rights and responsibilities for child rearing.

**Chorea** Unusual, involuntary muscle movements associated with disorders such as Huntington's disease.

**Chromosomes** Chainlike structures found in the nucleus of cells that carry genes and information about heredity. Humans normally have 23 pairs of chromosomes.

**Civil commitment** The involuntary hospitalization of the mentally ill; the decision typically is justified based on dangerousness to self or others (or inability to care for self).

**Classical conditioning** Pavlov's form of learning through association. A conditioned response eventually is elicited by a conditioned stimulus after repeated pairings with an unconditioned stimulus (which produces an unconditioned response).

**Classification system** A system for grouping together objects or organisms that share certain properties in common. In psychopathology, the set of categories in DSM-IV that describes mental disorders.

**Client-centred therapy** Carl Rogers's humanistic therapy that follows the client's lead. Therapists offer warmth, empathy, and genuineness, but clients solve their own problems.

**Clinical depression** A syndrome of depression in which a depressed mood is accompanied by several other symptoms, such as fatigue, loss of energy, difficulty in sleeping, and changes in appetite. Clinical depression also involves a variety of changes in thinking and overt behaviour.

**Clinical psychology** The profession and academic discipline that is concerned with the application of psychological science to the assessment and treatment of mental disorders.

**Coercion** A pattern of interaction in which unwitting parents positively reinforce children's misbehaviour (by giving in to their demands), and children negatively reinforce parents' capitulation (by ending their obnoxious behaviour).

**Cognitive behaviour therapy** The expansion of the scope of behaviour therapy to include cognition and research on human information processing. Includes various general techniques, such as Beck's cognitive therapy and Ellis's RET.

**Cognitive therapy** A psychotherapy technique and important part of cognitive behaviour therapy that was developed specifically as a treatment by Aaron Beck. Beck's cognitive therapy involves challenging negative cognitive distortions through a technique called collaborative empiricism.

**Cohort** A group whose members share some feature in common, particularly their date of birth.

**Cohort effect** Differences that distinguish one cohort from another. Cohorts share some feature in common, especially their date of birth, and cohort effects often distinguish people born in one time period (e.g., the 1980s) from those born in another.

**Comorbidity** The simultaneous manifestation of more than one disorder.

**Competence** Defendants' ability to understand legal proceedings and act rationally in relation to them. Competence evaluations can take place at different points in the legal process, but competence to stand trial (the ability to participate in one's own defence) is particularly important.

**Compulsion** A repetitive, ritualistic behaviour that is aimed at the reduction of anxiety and distress or the prevention of some dreaded event. Compulsions are considered by the person to be senseless or irrational. The person feels compelled to perform the compulsion; he or she attempts to resist but cannot.

**Concordance** Agreement. In behaviour genetic studies, concordance occurs when a relative has the same disorder as a proband (index case); for example, when twin pairs either both have the same disorder or both are free from the disorder.

**Conduct disorder** A psychological disorder of childhood that is defined primarily by behaviour that is illegal as well as antisocial.

**Confidentiality** The ethical obligation not to reveal private communications in psychotherapy and in other professional contacts between mental health professionals and their clients.

**Construct validity** The overall strength of the network of relations that have been observed among variables that are used to define a construct. The extent to which the construct possesses some systematic meaning.

**Contingency management** A form of operant behaviour therapy that focuses on directly changing rewards and punishments in order to increase desired and decrease undesired behaviour. A contingency is the relationship between a behaviour and its consequences; contingency management involves changing this relationship.

**Control group** The group of participants in an experiment that receives no treatment or perhaps a placebo treatment. Participants in the control group are compared with participants in the experimental group (who are given an active treatment).

**Controlled drinking** A controversial goal for some alcohol abusers. This concept refers to moderate consumption of alcohol in a pattern that avoids drinking to the point of intoxication.

**Conversion disorder** A type of somatoform disorder characterized by physical symptoms that often mimic those found in neurological diseases, such as blindness, numbing, or paralysis. The symptoms often make no anatomic sense.

**Coping** An attempt to adapt to stress by changing the stressor or by altering one's thinking or emotional response.

**Coronary heart disease (CHD)** A group of diseases of the heart that includes angina pectoris (chest pains) and myocardial infarction (heart attack).

**Correlational study** A scientific research method in which the relation between two factors (their co-relation) is studied in a systematic fashion. Has the advantage of practicality, as correlations between many variables can be studied in the real world, but also has the disadvantage that "correlation does not mean causation."

**Correlation coefficient** A number that always ranges between −1.00 and +1.00 and indicates the strength and direction of the relation between two variables. A higher absolute value indicates a stronger relation, while a correlation coefficient of 0 indicates no relation. The sign indicates the direction of the correlation.

**Cortisol** A corticosteroid secreted by the adrenal cortex. Cortisol is known as the "stress hormone" because its release is so closely linked with stress.

**Countertransference** The therapist's own feelings toward the client, particularly as described in psychoanalysis.

**Couples therapy** Partners who are involved in an intimate relationship are seen together in psychotherapy; sometimes called *marital therapy* or *marriage counselling*. Improving communication and negotiation are common goals.

**Creutzfeldt-Jakob disease** A type of dementia caused by a specific viral infection.

**Criminal responsibility** A legal concept that holds a person responsible for committing a crime if he or she (a) has been proven to have committed the act and (b) was legally sane at the time.

**Critical incident stress debriefing** An early intervention following trauma involving a single one- to five-hour group meeting offered within one to three days following a disaster. CISD is used frequently, although data supporting its effectiveness are limited.

**Cross-cultural psychology** The scientific study of ways that human behaviour and mental processes are influenced by social and cultural factors.

**Cross-sectional study** A research design in which subjects are studied only at one point in time. (Contrast with *longitudinal study*.)

**Culture-bound syndrome** Patterns of erratic or unusual thinking and behaviour that have been identified in diverse societies around the world and do not fit easily into the other diagnostic categories that are listed in the main body of DSM-IV-TR.

**Cultural-familial retardation** Typically mild mental retardation that runs in families and is linked with poverty. Thought to be the most common cause of mental retardation. There is controversy about the relative roles of genes or psychosocial disadvantage.

**Culture** The shared way of life of a group or people; a complex system of accumulated knowledge that helps the people in a particular society adapt to their environment.

**Cybernetics** A communication and control process that uses feedback loops in order to adjust progress toward a goal—for example, the operation of a thermostat.

**Cyclothymia** A chronic, less severe form of bipolar disorder. The bipolar equivalent of dysthymia.

**Defence mechanisms** Unconscious processes that service the ego and reduce conscious anxiety by distorting anxiety-producing memories, emotions, and impulses—for example, projection, displacement, or rationalization.

**Deinstitutionalization** The movement to treat the mentally ill and mentally retarded in communities rather than in large mental hospitals.

**Delirium** A confusional state that develops over a short period of time and is often associated with agitation and hyperactivity. The primary symptom is clouding of consciousness or reduced awareness of one's surroundings.

**Delusion** An obviously false and idiosyncratic belief that is rigidly held in spite of its preposterous nature.

**Delusional disorder** Describes persons who do not meet the full symptomatic criteria for schizophrenia, but who are preoccupied for at least one month with delusions that are not bizarre.

**Dementia** A gradually worsening loss of memory and related cognitive functions, including the use of language as well as reasoning and decision making.

**Dependent personality disorder** An enduring pattern of dependent and submissive behaviour. These people are exceedingly dependent on other people for advice and reassurance. Often unable to make everyday decisions on their own, they feel anxious and helpless when they are alone.

**Dependent variable** The outcome that is hypothesized to vary according to manipulations in the independent variable in an experiment.

**Depersonalization disorder** A type of dissociative disorder characterized by severe and persistent feelings of being detached from oneself (depersonalization experiences). For example, the repeated and profound sensation of floating above your body and observing yourself act.

**Depressed mood** Depressed feelings such as of disappointment and despair, but which are not yet necessarily part of a clinical syndrome.

**Depression** Can refer to a *symptom* (subjective feelings of sadness), a *mood* (sustained and pervasive feelings of despair), or to a clinical *syndrome* (in which the presence of a depressed mood is accompanied by several additional symptoms, such as fatigue, loss of energy, sleeping difficulties, and appetite changes).

**Determinism** The philosophical assumption (made by all psychologists except humanistic psychologists) that behaviour is a potentially predictable consequence of biological, psychological, and social factors. Contrasts with the assumption that behaviour is the product of free will.

**Detoxification** The process of short-term medical care (medication, rest, diets, fluids, and so on) during removal of a drug upon which a person has become dependent. The aim is to minimize withdrawal symptoms.

**Developmental deviation** Significant departures from age-appropriate norms in some specific area of functioning. Some developmental deviations are considered disorders in their own right.

**Developmental norms** Behaviour that is typical for children of a given age.

**Developmental psychopathology** A new approach to abnormal psychology that emphasizes the importance of normal development to understanding abnormal behaviour.

**Developmental stage** A distinct period of development focused on certain central "tasks" and marked by boundaries defined by changing age or social expectations.

**Diagnosis** The process of determining the nature of a person's disorder. In the case of psychopathology, deciding that a person fits into a particular diagnostic category, such as schizophrenia or major depressive disorder.

**Diathesis** A predisposition to disorder. Also known as *vulnerability*. A diathesis only causes abnormal behaviour when it is combined with a stress or challenging experience.

**Dimensional approach to classification** A view of classification based on the assumption that behaviour is distributed on a continuum from normal to abnormal. Also includes the assumption that differences between one type of behaviour and another are quantitative rather than qualitative in nature.

**Disorganized speech** (also known as *formal thought disorder*) Severe disruptions of verbal communication, involving the form of the person's speech.

**Disorganized type** A subtype of schizophrenia (formerly known as *hebephrenia*) that is characterized by disorganized speech, disorganized behaviour, and flat or inappropriate affect. If delusions or hallucinations are present, their content is not well organized.

**Dissociation** The separation of mental processes such as memory or consciousness that normally are integrated. Normal dissociative experiences include fleeting feelings of unreality and *déjà vu* experiences—the feeling that an event has happened before. Extreme dissociative experiences characterize dissociative disorders.

**Dissociative amnesia** A type of dissociative disorder characterized by the sudden inability to recall extensive and important personal information. The onset often is sudden and may occur in response to trauma or extreme stress.

**Dissociative disorders** A category of psychological disorders characterized by persistent, maladaptive disruptions in the integration of memory, consciousness, or identity. Examples include dissociative fugue and dissociative identity disorder (multiple personality).

**Dissociative fugue** A rare dissociative disorder characterized by sudden, unplanned travel, the inability to remember details about the past, and confusion about identity or the assumption of a new identity. The onset typically follows a traumatic event.

**Dissociative identity disorder (DID)** An unusual dissociative disorder characterized by the existence of two or more distinct personalities in a single individual (also known as *multiple personality disorder*). At least two personalities repeatedly take control over the person's behaviour, and some personalities have limited or no memory of the other.

**Distorted body image** A perceptual inaccuracy in evaluating body size and shape that sometimes is found in anorexia nervosa.

**Diversion** A practice of directing problem youth away from the juvenile justice system and into some alternative treatment or program. For example, a juvenile offender may be referred to counselling instead of having a hearing held in court.

**Divorce mediation** A procedure in which former partners attempt to resolve child custody or other disputes that arise from a divorce with the help of an impartial third party (a mediator).

**Dizygotic (DZ) twins** Fraternal twins produced from separate fertilized eggs. Like all siblings, DZ twins share an average of 50 percent of their genes.

**Dominance** The hierarchical ordering of a social group into more and less powerful members. Dominance rankings are indexed by the availability of uncontested privileges.

**Dose-response effects** Different treatment responses to different dosages of a medication.

**Double-blind, placebo-controlled study** A study in which neither the therapist nor the patient knows whether the patient receives the real treatment (for example, a medication) or a placebo.

**Down syndrome** A chromosomal disorder that is the most common known biological cause of mental retardation. It is caused by an extra chromosome (usually on the twenty-first pair) and associated with a characteristic physical appearance.

**Drug of abuse** (also called a *psychoactive substance*) A chemical substance that alters a person's mood, level of perception, or brain functioning.

**Dualism** The philosophical view that the mind and body are separate. Dates to the writings of the philosopher René Descartes, who attempted to balance the dominant religious views of his times with emerging scientific reasoning. Descartes argued that many human functions have biological explanations, but some human experiences have no somatic representation. Thus, he argued for a distinction—a dualism—between mind and body.

**Dyskinesia** Involuntary movements, such as tics, chorea, or tremors, that are often associated with certain types of dementia.

**Dyspareunia** Persistent genital pain during or after sexual intercourse. The problem can occur in either men or women.

**Dysphoria** Unpleasant mood, often associated with depression.

**Dysthymia** One of the mood disorders; a form of mild depression characterized by a chronic course (the person is seldom without symptoms).

**Eating disorders** A category of psychological disorders characterized by severe disturbances in eating behaviour, specifically anorexia nervosa and bulimia nervosa.

**Eclectic** The term used to describe the therapeutic approach of a group of mental health proefessionals who do not identify themselves with a specific paradigm, but instead use different treatments for different disorders.

**Ego** One of Freud's three central personality structures. In Freudian theory, the ego must deal with reality as it attempts to fulfill id impulses as well as superego demands. The ego operates on the reality principle, and much of the ego resides in conscious awareness.

**Ego analysis** Originated in the work of different therapists trained in Freudian psychoanalysis, but who focus much more on the ego than on the id. Ego analysts are concerned with the patient's dealings with the external world.

**Electroconvulsive therapy (ECT)** A treatment that involves the deliberate induction of a convulsion by passing electricity through one or both hemispheres of the brain. Modern ECT uses restraints, medication, and carefully controlled electrical stimulation to minimize adverse consequences. Can be an effective treatment for severe depression, especially following the failure of other approaches.

**Emotion** A state of arousal that is defined by subjective feeling states, such as sadness, anger, and disgust. Emotions are often accompanied by physiological changes, such as in heart rate and respiration rate.

**Emotion-focused coping** Internally oriented coping in an attempt to alter one's emotional or cognitive responses to a stressor.

**Emotional processing** A process of facing and coming to accept powerful emotions following trauma. Emotional processing involves confronting fear, diminishing its intensity, and coming to some new understanding of the trauma and its consequences.

**Emotion regulation** The process of learning to control powerful emotions according to the demands of a situation. Children learn to regulate their emotions initially through interactions with their parents and others in their social world, and eventually children learn to regulate their own emotions.

**Empathy** Emotional understanding. Empathy involves understanding others' unique feelings and perspectives. Highlighted by Rogers but basic to most forms of psychotherapy.

**Encopresis** Inappropriately controlled defecation among children old enough to maintain control of their bowels.

**Endocrine system** A collection of glands found at various locations throughout the body, including the ovaries or testes and the pituitary, thyroid, and adrenal glands. Releases hormones that sometimes act as neuromodulators and affect responses to stress. Also important in physical growth and development.

**Endorphin** The term is a contraction formed from the words *endogenous* (meaning "within") and *morphine*. Endorphins are relatively short chains of amino acids, or neuropeptides, that are naturally synthesized in the brain and are closely related to morphine (an opioid) in terms of their pharmacological properties.

**Enmeshed family** Families whose members are overly involved in one another's lives.

**Enuresis** Inappropriately controlled urination (during sleep or while awake) among children old enough to maintain control of their bladder.

**Epidemiology** The scientific study of the frequency and distribution of disorders within a population.

**Equifinality** A concept from systems theory that states that the same outcome (e.g., a psychological disorder) may have different causes. That is, there may be not one cause but multiple pathways that lead to a given outcome (disorder).

**Erectile dysfunction** Difficulty experienced by a man in obtaining an erection that is sufficient to accomplish intercourse or maintaining an erection long enough to satisfy himself or his partner during intercourse.

**Essential hypertension** A form of high blood pressure in which the hypertension is the principal disorder, as opposed to hypertension that is secondary to a known illness such as a kidney disorder.

**Estrogen** The female sex hormone.

**Etiology** The causes or origins of a disorder.

**Euphoria** An exaggerated feeling of physical and emotional well-being, typically associated with manic episodes in bipolar mood disorder.

**Exhibitionism** One of the paraphilias, characterized by distress over, or acting on, urges to expose one's genitals to an unsuspecting stranger.

**Experiment** A powerful scientific method that allows researchers to determine cause-and-effect relations. Key elements include random assignment, the manipulation of the independent variable, and careful measurement of the dependent variable.

**Experimental group** The group of participants in an experiment that receives a treatment that is hypothesized to cause some measured effect. Participants in the experimental group are compared with untreated participants in a control group.

**Experimental hypothesis** A new prediction made by an investigator to be tested in an experiment.

**Experimental method** The powerful scientific method that allows researchers to determine cause and effect by randomly assigning participants to experimental and control groups. In an experiment, researchers systematically manipulate independent variables and observe their effects on dependent variables.

**Expert witness** An individual stipulated as an expert on some subject matter who, because of his or her expertise, is allowed to testify about matters of opinion and not just matters of fact. For example, mental health professionals may serve as expert witness concerning a defendant's sanity.

**Expressed emotion (EE)** A concept that refers to a collection of negative or intrusive attitudes sometimes displayed by relatives of patients who are being treated for a disorder. If at least one of a patient's relatives is hostile, critical, or emotionally overinvolved, the family environment typically is considered high in expressed emotion.

**Externalizing disorders** An empirically derived category of disruptive child behaviour problems that create problems for the external world (for example, attention-deficit/hyperactivity disorder).

**External validity** Whether the findings of an experiment generalize to other people, places, and circumstances, particularly real-life situations.

**Extinction** The gradual elimination of a response when learning conditions change. In classical conditioning, extinction occurs when a conditioned stimulus no longer is paired with an unconditioned stimulus. In operant conditioning, extinction occurs when the contingent is removed between behaviour and its consequences.

**Factitious disorder** A feigned condition that, unlike malingering, is motivated by a desire to assume the sick role, not by a desire for external gain.

**Family life cycle** The developmental course of family relationships throughout life; most family life cycle theories mark stages and transitions with major changes in family relationships and membership.

**Family therapy** Treatment that might include two, three, or more family members in the psychotherapy sessions. Improving communication and negotiation are common goals, although family therapy also may be used to help well members adjust to a family member's illness.

**Fear** An unpleasant emotional reaction experienced in the face of real, immediate danger. It builds quickly in intensity and helps to organize the person's responses to threats from the environment.

**Fetal alcohol syndrome** A disorder caused by heavy maternal alcohol consumption and repeated exposure of the developing fetus to alcohol. Infants have retarded physical development, a small head, narrow eyes, cardiac defects, and cognitive impairments. Intellectual functioning ranges from mild mental retardation to intelligence with learning disabilities.

**Fetishism** The use of nonliving objects as a focus of sexual arousal.

**Fight or flight response** A response to a threat in which psychophysiological reactions mobilize the body to take action against danger.

**Fixation** The psychodynamic concept that psychological development is arrested at a particular age or stage. The person stops growing emotionally.

**Flashbacks** Re-experienced memories of past events, particularly as occurs in posttraumatic stress disorder or following use of hallucinogenic drugs.

**Flooding** A treatment for fears and phobias that involves exposure to the feared stimulus at full intensity. Works through extinction.

**Fragile-X syndrome** The second most common known biological cause of mental retardation. Transmitted genetically and indicated by a weakening or break on one arm of the X sex chromosome.

**Free association** A basic technique in Freudian psychoanalysis in which patients are encouraged to speak freely about whatever thoughts cross their mind; presumed to give insight into the unconscious.

**Free will** The capacity to make choices and freely act upon them. A philosophical counterpoint to determinism, which is the scientific assumption that behaviour is a predictable consequence of internal and external events. Humanistic psychology and the legal system assume people act out of free will.

**Frotteurism** One of the paraphilias, characterized by recurrent, intense sexual urges involving touching and rubbing against a nonconsenting person; it often takes place in crowded trains, buses, and elevators.

**Gender identity** A person's sense of himself or herself as being either male or female.

**Gender identity disorder** A strong and persistent identification with the opposite sex coupled with a sense of discomfort with one's anatomic sex.

**Gender roles** Roles associated with social expectations about gendered behaviour—for example, "masculine" or "feminine" activities.

**General adaptation syndrome (GAS)** Selye's three stages in reaction to stress: alarm, resistance, and exhaustion.

**Generalization** Making accurate statements that extend beyond a specific sample to a larger population.

**Generalized anxiety disorder** One of the anxiety disorders, which is characterized by excessive and uncontrollable worry about a number of events or activities (such as work or school performance) and associated with symptoms of arousal (such as restlessness, muscle tension, and sleep disturbance).

**General paresis** (general paralysis) A set of severe symptoms including dementia, delusions of grandeur, and paralysis caused by the sexually transmitted disease syphilis. Discovery of the cause of general paresis spurred the biological model of mental illness.

**Genes** Ultramicroscopic units of DNA that carry information about heredity. Located on the chromosomes.

**Genetic linkage** A close association between two genes, typically the genetic locus associated with a disorder or a trait and the locus for a known gene. Two loci are said to be linked when they are sufficiently close together on the same chromosome.

**Genotype** An individual's actual genetic structure, most of which cannot be observed directly at this time.

**Gerontology** The multidisciplinary study of aging and older adults.

**Gestalt therapy** A variation of the humanistic approach to psychotherapy that underscores affective awareness and expression, genuineness, and experiencing the moment (living in the "here and now").

**Grief** The emotional and social process of coping with a separation or a loss, often described as proceeding in stages.

**Group therapy** The treatment of three or more people in a group setting, often using group relationships as a central part of therapy.

**Hallucination** A perceptual experience in the absence of external stimulation, such as hearing voices that aren't really there.

**Hallucinogens** Drugs that produce hallucinations.

**Harmful dysfunction** A concept used in one approach to the definition of mental disorder. A condition can be considered a mental disorder if it causes some harm to the person and if the condition results from the inability of some mental mechanism to perform its natural function.

**Hashish** The dried resin from the top of the female cannabis plant. Ingestion of hashish leads to a feeling of being "high" (see *marijuana*).

**Health behaviour** A wide range of activities that are essential to promoting good health, including positive actions such as proper diet and the avoidance of negative activities such as cigarette smoking.

**Health psychologist** A psychologist who specializes in reducing negative health behaviour (e.g., smoking) and promoting positive health behaviour (e.g., exercise). Health psychology is a part of the interdisciplinary field of behavioural medicine.

**Heritability** The variability in a behavioural characteristic that is accounted for by genetic factors.

**Heritability ratio** A statistic for computing the proportion of variance in a behavioural characteristic that is accounted for by genetic factors in a given study or series of studies.

**High-risk research design** A longitudinal study of persons who are selected from the general population based on some identified risk factor that has a fairly high risk ratio.

**Histrionic personality disorder** An enduring pattern of thinking and behaviour that is characterized by excessive emotionality and attention-seeking behaviour. People with this disorder are self-centred, vain, and demanding. Their emotions tend to be shallow and may vacillate erratically.

**Human Immunodeficiency Virus (HIV)** The virus that causes AIDS and attacks the immune system, leaving the patient susceptible to infection, neurological complications, and cancers that rarely affect those with normal immune function.

**Holism** The assumption that the whole is more than the sum of its parts. A central tenet of systems theory, and counterpoint to reductionism.

**Homeostasis** The tendency to maintain a steady state. A familiar concept in biology that also is widely applicable in psychology.

**Hopelessness theory** A theory regarding the role of cognitive events in the etiology of depression; depression is associated with the expectation that very desirable events probably will not occur and that aversive events probably will occur regardless of what the person does.

**Hormones** Chemical substances that are released into the bloodstream by glands in the endocrine system. Hormones affect the functioning of distant body systems and sometimes act as neuromodulators.

**Humanistic psychotherapy** An approach that assumes that the most essential human quality is the ability to make choices and freely act on them (free will). Promoted as a "third force" to counteract the deterministic views of psychodynamic and the behavioural approaches to psychotherapy.

**Huntington's disease** A primary, differentiated dementia characterized by the presence of unusual involuntary muscle movements. Many Huntington's patients also exhibit a variety of personality changes and symptoms of mental disorders, including primarily depression and anxiety.

**Hyperactivity** A symptom of attention-deficit/hyperactivity disorder (ADHD), often manifested as squirming, fidgeting, or restless behaviour. Found across but particularly notable in structured settings.

**Hypertension** High blood pressure.

**Hypnosis** An altered state of consciousness during which hypnotized subjects are particularly susceptible to suggestion. There is considerable debate as to whether hypnosis is a unique state of consciousness or merely a form of relaxation.

**Hypoactive sexual desire** Diminished desire for sexual activity and reduced frequency of sexual fantasies.

**Hypochondriasis** A type of somatoform disorder characterized by a person's preoccupying fear or belief that he or she is suffering from a physical illness.

**Hypomania** An episode of increased energy that is not sufficiently severe to qualify as a full-blown manic episode.

**Hypothalamus** A part of the limbic system that plays a role in sensation, but more importantly it controls basic biological urges, such as eating, drinking, and activity, as well as much of the functioning of the autonomic nervous system.

**Hypothesis** A prediction about the expected findings in a scientific study.

**Hypothetical construct** A theoretical device that refers to events or states that reside within a person and are proposed to help understand or explain a person's behaviour.

**Hysteria** An outdated but influential diagnostic category that included both somatoform and dissociative disorders. Attempts to treat hysteria had a major effect on Charcot, Freud, and Janet, among others. In Greek, *hysteria* means "uterus," a reflection of ancient speculation that hysteria was restricted to women and caused by frustrated sexual desires.

**Iatrogenesis** A creation of a disorder by an attempt to treat it.

**Id** One of Freud's three central personality structures. In Freudian theory, the id is present at birth and is the source of basic drives and motivations. The id houses biological drives (such as hunger), as well as Freud's two key psychological drives, sex and aggression. Operates according to the pleasure principle.

**Identification** A process wherein children not only imitate adults but also want to be like them and adopt their values. In Freudian theory, identification is the to the Oedipal and Electra conflicts. In developmental psychology, a similar but broader concept than modelling.

**Identity** Erikson's term for the broad definition of self; in his view, identity is the product of the adolescent's struggle to answer the question "Who am I?"

**Identity crisis** Erikson's period of basic uncertainty about self during late adolescence and early adult life. A consequence of the psychosocial stage of identity versus role confusion.

**Implicit memory** Implicit memory is indicated by changes in behaviour apparently based on a memory of prior event but with nonconscious remembering of the event. *Explicit memory* is the conscious recollection of a past event.

**Impulse control disorder** A disorder characterized by failure to resist an impulse or a temptation to perform some pleasurable or tension-releasing act that is harmful to oneself or others; examples are pathological gambling, setting fires, and stealing.

**Inappropriate affect** A form of emotional disturbance seen in schizophrenia. The central features of inappropriate affect are incongruity and lack of adaptability in emotional expression.

**Incest** Sexual activity between close blood relatives, such as father-daughter, mother-son, or siblings.

**Incidence** The number of new cases of a disorder that appear in a population during a specific period of time.

**Independent variable** The variable in an experiment that is controlled and deliberately manipulated by the experimenter (for example, whether or not a subject receives a treatment). Affects the dependent variable.

**Infarct** The area of dead tissue produced by a stroke.

**Informed consent** A legal and ethical safeguard concerning risks in research and in treatment. Includes (a) accurate information about potential risks and benefits, (b) competence on the part of subjects/patients to understand them, and (c) the ability of subjects/patients to participate voluntarily.

**Inhibited sexual arousal** Difficulty experienced by a woman in achieving or maintaining genital responses, such as lubrication and swelling, that are necessary to complete sexual intercourse.

**Insanity** A legal term referring to a defendant's state of mind at the time of committing a crime. An insane individual is not held legally responsible for his or her actions because of a mental disease or defect.

**Insanity defence** An attempt to prove that a person with a mental illness did not meet the legal criteria for sanity at the time of committing a crime. The inability to tell right from wrong and an "irresistible impulse" are the two most common contemporary grounds for the defence.

**Insight** Self-understanding; the extent to which a person recognizes the nature (or understands the potential causes) of his or her disorder. In psychoanalysis, insight is the ultimate goal, specifically, to bring formerly unconscious material into conscious awareness.

**Intelligence quotient (IQ)** A measure of intellectual ability that typically has a mean of 100 and a standard deviation of 15. An individual's IQ is determined by comparisons with norms for same-aged peers.

**Internalizing disorders** An empirically derived category of psychological problems of childhood that affect the child more than the external world (for example, depression).

**Internal validity** Whether changes in the dependent variable can be accurately attributed to changes in the independent variable in an experiment—that is, there are no experimental confounds.

**Interpretation** A tool in psychotherapy and psychoanalysis in which the therapist suggests new meanings about a client's accounts of his or her past and present life.

**Introceptive awareness** Recognition of internal cues, including various emotional states as well as hunger.

**In vivo desensitization** A treatment for overcoming fears and phobias that involves gradual exposure to feared stimuli in real life while simultaneously maintaining a state of relaxation. Contrast with *systematic desensitization*.

**Kappa** A statistical index of reliability (diagnostic agreement between clinicians) that reflects the proportion of agreement that occurred above and beyond that which would have occurred by chance.

**Korsakoff 's syndrome** An amnestic disorder sometimes associated with chronic alcoholism. Memory is impaired but other cognitive functions are not.

**Labelling theory** A perspective on mental disorders that is primarily concerned with the social context in which abnormal behaviour occurs. Labelling theory is more interested in social factors that determine whether or not a person will be given a psychiatric diagnosis than in psychological or biological reasons for the behaviours.

**La belle indifference** A flippant lack of concern about physical symptoms that may accompany somatoform disorders.

**Lateralization** The specialized functioning of each cerebral hemisphere. In general, the left hemisphere is involved in language and related functions, and the right side is involved in spatial organization and analysis.

**Lead poisoning** Ingestion of toxic levels of lead (mainly through environmental pollutants) that can cause brain damage and a number of adverse behavioural and cognitive impairments, including mental retardation.

**Learned helplessness theory** A theory that holds that depressed people do not recognize a contingency between their behaviour and outcomes in their environments.

**Learning disorders** A heterogeneous group of educational problems characterized by academic performance that is notably below academic aptitude.

**Life-cycle transitions** Movements from one social or psychological "stage" of adult development into a new one; often characterized by interpersonal, emotional, and identity conflict.

**Lifespan development** The study of continuities and changes in behaviour, affect, and cognition from infancy through the last years of life.

**Limbic system** A variety of brain structures, including the thalamus and hypothalamus, that are central to the regulation of emotion and basic learning processes.

**Linkage** A process used to locate the position of a gene on a particular chromosome. Two genetic loci are said to be linked if they are close together on the same chromosome.

**Longitudinal study** A type of research design in which subjects are studied over a period of time (contrasts with the cross-sectional approach of studying subjects at only one point in time). Longitudinal studies attempt to establish whether hypothesized causes precede their putative effects in time.

**Mainstreaming** The educational philosophy that mentally retarded children should be taught, as much as possible, in regular classrooms rather than in "special" classes.

**Malingering** Pretending to have a psychological disorder in order to achieve some external gain such as insurance money or avoidance of work.

**Mania** A disturbance in mood characterized by such symptoms as elation, inflated self-esteem, hyperactivity, and accelerated speaking and thinking. An exaggerated feeling of physical and emotional well-being.

**Marijuana** The dried leaves and flowers of the female cannabis plant. "Getting high" on marijuana refers to a pervasive sense of well-being and happiness.

**Mean** The arithmetic average of a distribution of scores; the sum of scores divided by the number of observations.

**Median** The midpoint of a frequency distribution; half of all subjects fall above and half fall below the median.

**Medulla** The part of the hindbrain that controls various body functions involved in sustaining life, including heart rate, blood pressure, and respiration.

**Melancholia** A particularly severe type of depression. In DSM-IV, melancholia is described in terms of a number of specific features, such as loss of pleasure in activities and lack of reactivity to events in the person's environment that are normally pleasurable.

**Menopause** The cessation of menstruation and the associated physical and psychological changes that occur among middle-aged women (the so-called "change of life").

**Mental retardation** Substantial limitations in present functioning characterized by significantly subaverage intellectual functioning (IQ of 70 to 75 or below), concurrent limitations in adaptive skills, and an onset before age 18.

**Meta-analysis** A statistical technique that allows the results from different studies to be combined in a standardized way.

**Midbrain** Part of the brain between the hindbrain and forebrain that is involved in the control of some motor activities, especially those related to fighting and sex.

**Minimal brain damage (MBD)** Damage to the brain too slight to be detected with objective instruments but sometimes inferred from behaviour. Was once held to be the cause of attention-deficit/hyperactivity disorder but now widely rejected.

**Mode** The most frequent score in a frequency distribution.

**Modelling** A social learning concept describing the process of learning through imitation. Contrasts with the broader concept of identification.

**Monoamine oxidase inhibitors (MAOI)** A group of antidepressant drugs that inhibit the enzyme monoamine oxidase (MAO) in the brain and raise the levels of neurotransmitters, such as norepinephrine, dopamine, and serotonin.

**Monozygotic (MZ) twins** Identical twins produced from a single fertilized egg; thus MZ twins have identical genotypes.

**Mood** A pervasive and sustained emotional response that, in its extreme, can colour the person's perception of the world.

**Mood disorders** A broad category of psychopathology that includes depressive disorders and bipolar disorders. These conditions are defined in terms of episodes in which the person's behaviour is dominated by either clinical depression or mania.

**Moral treatment** A historically important movement in the treatment of the mentally ill that led to improved hospital conditions. This movement was based on the belief that the mentally ill deserve adequate care and that good care would promote their recovery.

**Moratorium** A period of allowing oneself to be uncertain or confused about identity. Erikson advocated a moratorium as an important step in the formation of an enduring identity.

**Multiple personality disorder** An unusual dissociative disorder characterized by the existence of two or more distinct personalities in a single individual (called *dissociative identity disorder* in DSM-IV).

**Munchausen-by-proxy syndrome (MBPS)** A unique, rare, but potentially very harmful form of physical child abuse in which a parent feigns, exaggerates, or induces illness in a child.

**Myocardial infarction (MI)** Commonly known as a heart attack, this most deadly form of coronary heart disease is caused by oxygen deprivation to the heart and results in the death of at least some heart tissue.

**Narcissistic personality disorder** An enduring pattern of thinking and behaviour that is characterized by pervasive grandiosity. Narcissistic people are preoccupied with their own achievements and abilities.

**Nature–nurture controversy** The debate that pits genetic and biological factors against life experience as causes of abnormal behaviour.

**Negative affect** One of two mood dimensions (compare *positive affect*) employed by Tellegen as well as Watson and Clark in their theories of personality. Adjectives that describe negative affect include angry, guilty, afraid, and sad.

**Negative symptoms** (of schizophrenia) Include flat or blunted affect, avolition, alogia, and anhedonia.

**Neurofibrillary tangles** A type of brain lesion found in the cerebral cortex and the hippocampus in patients with Alzheimer's disease. A pattern of disorganized neurofibrils, which provide structural support for the neurons and help transport chemicals that are used in the production of neurotransmitters.

**Neuroleptic** A type of antipsychotic medication that also induces side effects that resemble the motor symptoms of Parkinson's disease.

**Neurologist** A physician who deals primarily with diseases of the brain and nervous system.

**Neuron** The nerve cells that form the basic building blocks of the brain. Each neuron is composed of the soma or cell body, the dendrites, the axon, and the terminal buttons.

**Neuropsychological assessment** Assessment procedures focused on the examination of performance on psychological tests to indicate whether a person has a brain disorder. An example is the Halstead-Reitan Neuropsychological Test Battery.

**Neuropsychologist** A psychologist who has particular expertise in the assessment of specific types of cognitive impairment, including those associated with dementia and amnestic disorders.

**Neurosis** A traditional term, often associated with psychoanalytic theory, that describes maladaptive behaviour resulting from the ego's failure to control anxiety resulting from unconscious conflicts. In DSM-I and DSM-II, neurotic disorders were defined as those in which anxiety is the chief characteristic. Anxiety presumably could be felt and expressed directly, or it could be controlled unconsciously by defence mechanisms.

**Neurotransmitters** Chemical substances that are released into the synapse between two neurons and carry signals from the terminal button of one neuron to the receptors of another.

**Nonshared environment** The component of a sibling's environment inside or outside the family that is unique to that sibling—for example, being a favourite child or one's best friend. Contrasts with the shared environment, family experiences that are common across siblings.

**Normal distribution** A frequency distribution represented by a bell-shaped curve—the normal curve—that is important for making statistical inferences. Many psychological characteristics (e.g., intelligence) are assumed to follow the normal distribution.

**Normalization** The philosophy that mentally retarded or mentally ill people are entitled to live as much as possible like other members of the society. Often deinstitutionalization involves providing custodial care and mainstreaming in education.

**Null hypothesis** The prediction that an experimental hypothesis is not true. Scientists must assume that the null hypothesis holds until research contradicts it.

**Obesity** Excess body fat, a circumstance that roughly corresponds with a body weight 20 percent above the expected weight.

**Obsession** A repetitive, unwanted, intrusive cognitive event that may take the form of thoughts, images, or impulses. Obsessions intrude suddenly into consciousness and lead to an increase in subjective anxiety.

**Obsessive–compulsive personality disorder** An enduring pattern of thinking and behaviour that is characterized by perfectionism and inflexibility. These people are preoccupied with rules and efficiency. They are excessively conscientious, moralistic, and judgmental.

**Operant conditioning** A learning theory asserting that behaviour is a function of its consequences. Specifically, behaviour increases if it is rewarded, and it decreases if it is punished.

**Operational definition** A procedure that is used to measure a theoretical construct.

**Opiates** (sometimes called *opioids*) Drugs that have properties similar to opium. The main active ingredients in opium are morphine and codeine.

**Oppositional defiant disorder** A psychological disorder of childhood characterized by persistent but relatively minor transgressions, such as refusing to obey adult requests, arguing, and acting angry.

**Optimism** A general and effective style of coping with stress involving a positive attitude when a stressor cannot be changed.

**Orgasmic disorder** A sexual disorder in which the person has recurrent difficulties reaching orgasm after a normal sexual arousal.

**Outpatient commitment** Outpatient commitment generally requires the same dangerousness standards as inpatient commitment, but the patient is court-ordered to comply with treatment in the community (e.g., making regular office visits, taking medication). Outpatient commitment is permitted in various jurisdictions, and because it involves less infringement on civil liberties, commitment criteria may be applied less stringently for outpatient versus inpatient commitment.

**Pain disorder** A type of somatoform disorder characterized by preoccupation with pain, and complaints are motivated at least in part by psychological factors.

**Panic attack** A sudden, overwhelming experience of terror or fright. While anxiety involves a blend of several negative emotions, panic is more focused.

**Panic disorder** A form of anxiety disorder in which a person experiences recurrent, unexpected panic attacks. At least one of the attacks must have been followed by a period of one month or more in which the person has either persistent concern about having additional attacks, worry about the implications of the attack or its consequences, or a significant change in behaviour related to the attacks. Panic disorder is divided into two subtypes, depending on the presence or absence of agoraphobia.

**Paradigm** A set of assumptions both about the substance of a theory and about how scientists should collect data and test theoretical propositions. The term was applied to the progress of science by Thomas Kuhn, an influential historian and philosopher.

**Paranoid personality disorder** An enduring pattern of thinking and behaviour characterized by a pervasive tendency to be inappropriately suspicious of other people's motives and behaviours. People who fit the description for this disorder expect that other people are trying to harm them, and they take extraordinary precautions to avoid being exploited or injured.

**Paranoid type** A subtype of schizophrenia that is characterized by systematic delusions with persecutory or grandiose content. Preoccupation with frequent auditory hallucinations can also be associated with the paranoid type.

**Paraphilias** Forms of sexual disorder that involve sexual arousal in association with unusual objects and situations, such as inanimate objects, sexual contacts with children, exhibiting their genitals to strangers, and inflicting pain on another person.

**Parkinson's disease** A disorder of the motor system that is caused by a degeneration of a specific area of the brain stem known as the *substantia nigra* and loss of the neurotransmitter dopamine, which is produced by cells in this area.

**Pedophilia** One of the paraphilias, characterized by marked distress over, or acting on urges involving, sexual activity with a prepubescent child.

**Peer sociometrics** A method of assessing children's social relationships and categorizing children's social standing by obtaining information on who is "liked most" and who is "liked least" from a group of children who know each other.

**Peripheral nervous system** Nerves that stem from the central nervous system and connect to the body's muscles, sensory systems, and organs. Divided into two subdivisions, the somatic and the autonomic nervous systems.

**Personality** The combination of persistent traits or characteristics that, taken as a whole, describe a person's behaviour. In DSM-IV, personality is defined as "enduring patterns of perceiving, relating to, and thinking about the environment and oneself, which are exhibited in a wide range of important social and personal contexts."

**Personality disorder** Inflexible and maladaptive patterns of personality that begin by early adulthood and result in either social or occupational problems or distress to the individual.

**Personality inventory** Sometimes called an *objective personality test*, it consists of a series of straightforward statements that the person is required to rate or endorse as being either true or false in relation to himself or herself.

**Pervasive developmental disorders** A category of unusual psychological problems that begin early in life and involve severe impairments in a number of areas of functioning. Autistic disorder is one example.

**Phenomenology** The study of events and symptoms (including subjective experiences) in their own right rather than in terms of inferred causes.

**Phenotype** The observed expression of a given genotype or genetic structure, for example, eye colour.

**Phenylketonuria (PKU)** A cause of mental retardation transmitted by the pairing of recessive genes that results in the deficiency of the enzyme that metabolizes phenylalanine. Infants have normal intelligence at birth, but the ingestion of foods containing phenylalanine causes phenylketonuria and produces brain damage. Can be prevented with a phenylalanine-free diet.

**Phobia** A persistent and irrational narrowly defined fear that is associated with a specific object or situation.

**Pick's disease** A form of primary dementia that is associated with atrophy of the frontal and temporal lobes of the brain. Very similar to Alzheimer's disease in terms of both behavioural symptoms and cognitive impairment.

**Placebo control group** A group of subjects given a treatment with no known specific ingredients for the purpose of comparison with alternative treatments that are thought to contain specific, therapeutic benefits.

**Placebo effect** The improvement in a condition produced by a placebo (sometimes a substantial change). An overriding goal of scientific research is to identify treatments that exceed placebo effects.

**Polygenic** Caused by more than one gene. Characteristics become normally distributed as more genes are involved in the phenotypic expression of a trait.

**Polysubstance abuse** (also known as *multidrug abuse*) A disorder characterized by the abuse of at least three different psychoactive drugs (not including nicotine or caffeine). No single substance predominates in the pattern of abuse.

**Polythetic class** A category that is defined in terms of a set of criteria that are neither necessary nor sufficient. Each member of the category must possess a certain minimal number of the defining features, but none of the features has to be found in each member of the category.

**Pons** Part of the hindbrain that serves various functions in regulating stages of sleep.

**Population** The entire group of people about whom a researcher wants to generalize.

**Positive affect** One of two mood dimensions (compare *negative affect*) employed by Tellegen as well as Watson and Clark in their theories of personality. Adjectives that describe positive affect include active, delighted, enthusiastic, and proud.

**Positive symptoms** (of schizophrenia) Include hallucinations, delusions, disorganized speech, inappropriate affect, and disorganized behaviour.

**Posttraumatic stress disorder (PTSD)** A psychological disorder characterized by recurring symptoms of numbing, avoidance, re-experiencing, and hyperarousal following exposure to a traumatic stressor.

**Prefrontal lobotomy** A psychosurgery technique introduced in 1935 by Egas Moniz in which the two hemispheres of the brain are severed. Moniz won a Nobel Prize for the treatment, which now is discredited.

**Premature ejaculation** A type of sexual disorder, in which a man is unable to delay ejaculation long enough to accomplish intercourse.

**Premorbid history** A pattern of behaviour that precedes the onset of an illness. Adjustment prior to the disorder.

**Preparedness theory** The notion that organisms are biologically prepared, on the basis of neural pathways in their central nervous systems, to learn certain types of associations (also known as *biological constraints on learning*).

**Prevalence** An epidemiological term that refers to the total number of cases that are present within a given population during a particular period of time.

**Primary appraisal** The cognitive evaluation of the challenge, threat, or harm posed by a stressful life event.

**Primary prevention** An attempt to prevent new cases of disorder by improving the environment; promotes health, not just the treatment of illness.

**Primary sleep disorder** A condition where a sleeping difficulty is the principal complaint. In DSM-IV, either a dyssomnia—a difficulty in the amount, quality, or timing of sleep, or a parasomnia—an abnormal event that occurs during sleep; for example, nightmares.

**Probands** Index cases. In behaviour genetic studies, probands are family members who have a disorder, and the relatives of the index cases are examined for concordance.

**Problem-focused coping** Externally oriented coping in an attempt to change or otherwise control a stressor.

**Prodromal phase** Precedes the active phase of schizophrenia and is marked by an obvious deterioration in role functioning. Prodromal signs and symptoms are less dramatic than those seen during the active phase of the disorder.

**Professional responsibilities** A professional's obligation to follow the ethical standards of his or her profession and to uphold the laws of the jurisdictions in which he or she practises, for example, confidentiality.

**Prognosis** Predictions about the future course of a disorder with or without treatment.

**Projective tests** Personality tests, such as the Rorschach inkblot test, in which the person is asked to interpret a series of ambiguous stimuli.

**Prospective design** A research design in which people are studied longitudinally and forward in time. Supposed causes of future outcomes are assessed in the present, and subjects are then followed to see if the hypothesized effects develop over time.

**Psychiatry** The branch of medicine that is concerned with the study and treatment of mental disorders.

**Psychoactive substance** A drug that alters a person's mood, level of perception, or brain functioning.

**Psychoanalysis** Freud's orthodox form of psychotherapy that is practised rarely today because of its time, expense, and questionable effectiveness in treating mental disorders. Freud viewed the task of psychoanalysis as promoting insight by uncovering the unconscious conflicts and motivations that cause psychological difficulties.

**Psychoanalytic theory** A paradigm for conceptualizing abnormal behaviour based on the concepts and writings of Sigmund Freud. Highlights unconscious processes and conflicts as causing abnormal behaviour and emphasizes psychoanalysis as the treatment of choice.

**Psychodynamic psychotherapy** A variation on the Freudian approach that searches for unconscious conflicts and motivations but does not adhere to Freud literally as in psychoanalysis. The process is considerably less lengthy than in psychoanalysis.

**Psychological dependence** A term used to describe forceful, subjective urges to use drugs, often as a means of relieving negative mood states. Contrasts with the term "physiological dependence," which involves symptoms of tolerance and withdrawal.

**Psychology** The science, profession, and academic discipline concerned with the study of mental processes and behaviour in humans and animals.

**Psychometric approach** A method of classification that forms diagnostic categories from statistical analysis of symptom checklists. Particularly used in classifying and internalizing disorders of childhood.

**Psychomotor retardation** A generalized slowing of physical and emotional reactions. The slowing of movements and speech; frequently seen in depression.

**Psychomotor stimulants** Drugs such as amphetamine and cocaine that produce their effect by simulating the effects of certain neurotransmitters, specifically norepinephrine, dopamine, and serotonin.

**Psychoneuroimmunology (PNI)** Research on the effects of stress on the functioning of the immune system.

**Psychopathology** The manifestations of (and the study of the causes of) mental disorders. Generally used as another term to describe abnormal behaviour.

**Psychopathy** Another term for *antisocial personality disorder*. Usually associated with Cleckley's definition of that concept, which included features such as disregard for the truth, lack of empathy, and inability to learn from experience.

**Psychopharmacology** The study of the effects of psychoactive drugs on behaviour. Clinical psychopharmacology involves the expert use of drugs in the treatment of mental disorders.

**Psychophysiology** The study of changes in the functioning of the body that result from psychological experiences.

**Psychosis** A term that refers to several types of severe mental disorder in which the person is out of contact with reality. Hallucinations and delusions are examples of psychotic symptoms.

**Psychosomatic disorder** A term indicating that a physical disease is a product both of the psyche (mind) and the soma (body).

**Psychostimulants** Medications that heighten energy and alertness when taken in small dosages, but lead to restless, even frenetic, behaviour when misused. Often used in the treatment of attention-deficit/hyperactivity disorder.

**Psychosurgery** A controversial treatment that involves the surgical destruction of specific regions of the brain. Modern psychosurgery involves relatively little destruction of brain tissue, unlike the discredited prefrontal lobotomy.

**Psychotherapy** The use of psychological techniques in an attempt to produce change in the context of a special, helping relationship.

**Psychotropic medications** Chemical substances that when taken internally affect a person's psychological state.

**Purging** An intentional act designed to eliminate consumed food from the body. Self-induced vomiting is the most common form.

**Random assignment** Any of several methods of ensuring that each subject has a statistically equal chance of being exposed to any level of an independent variable.

**Random selection** A method of selecting samples from a larger population that ensures that each subject has a statistically equal chance of being selected.

**Rape** An act involving nonconsensual sexual penetration obtained by physical force, by threat of bodily harm, or when the victim is incapable of giving consent by virtue of mental illness, mental retardation, or intoxication.

**Rating scale** An assessment tool in which the observer is asked to make judgments that place the person somewhere along a dimension.

**Rational–emotive therapy (RET)** A cognitive behaviour therapy technique designed to challenge irrational beliefs about oneself and the world. Developed by Albert Ellis as a treatment for anxiety, depression, and related problems. Ellis now calls this threatment rational–emotive behaviour therapy (REBT).

**Reaction range** A behaviour genetic concept for conceptualizing the joint influence of genes and environment; specifically, that heredity determines the upper and lower limits of a trait and experience determines the extent to which people fulfill their genetic potential.

**Reactivity** The influence of an observer's presence on the behaviour of the person who is being observed.

**Receptors** Sites on the dendrites or soma of a neuron that are sensitive to certain neurotransmitters.

**Recidivism** Repeat offending in violating the law.

**Reciprocal causality** The concept of causality as bidirectional (or circular). Interaction is a process of mutual influence, not separable causes and effects.

**Reciprocity** The social exchange of cooperation and conflict. Family members with happy relationships reciprocate positive actions; family members with troubled relationships reciprocate negative ones.

**Recovered memories** Dramatic recollections of long-forgotten traumatic experiences; a controversial topic because the "memories" often are impossible to validate and many such memories may be created rather than recovered.

**Reductionism** The scientific perspective that the whole is the sum of its parts, and that the task of scientists is to divide the world into its smaller and smaller components.

**Regression** A return or retreat to an earlier stage or style of coping or behaving.

**Relapse** The reappearance of active symptoms following a period of remission (such as a return to heavy drinking by an alcoholic after a period of sustained sobriety).

**Reliability** The consistency of measurements, including diagnostic decisions. One index of reliability is agreement among clinicians.

**Remission** A stage of disorder characterized by the absence of symptoms (i.e., symptoms that were previously present are now gone).

**Representative sample** A sample that accurately represents the larger population of an identified group (e.g., a representative sample of all children in Canada).

**Residual phase** Follows the active phase of a disorder such as schizophrenia. At this point, psychotic symptoms have improved, but the person continues to be impaired in various ways. Negative symptoms may be more pronounced during the residual phase.

**Residual type** A subtype of schizophrenia that includes patients who no longer meet the criteria for active phase symptoms but nevertheless demonstrate continued signs of negative symptoms or attenuated forms of delusions, hallucinations, or disorganized speech.

**Resilience** The ability to "bounce back" from adversity despite life stress and emotional distress.

**Retrograde amnesia** The loss of memory for events prior to the onset of an illness or the experience of a traumatic event.

**Retrospective reports** Recollections about past experiences that are often questioned in terms of reliability and validity.

**Reuptake** The process of recapturing some neurotransmitters in the synapse before they reach the receptors of another cell and returning the chemical substances to the terminal button. The neurotransmitter then is reused in subsequent neural transmission.

**Reverse causality** Indicates that causation could be operating in the opposite direction: Y could be causing X instead of X causing Y. A threat to interpretation in correlational studies, and a basic reason why correlation does not mean causation.

**Risk** A statement about the probability that a certain outcome will occur.

**Risk factor** A variable that is associated with a higher probability of developing a disorder.

**Role playing** Improvisational play acting that may be used in therapy to teach clients alternative ways of acting in problematic situations.

**Savant performance** An exceptional ability in a highly specialized area of functioning typically involving artistic, musical, or mathematical skills.

**Schema** A general cognitive pattern that guides the way a person perceives and interprets events in his or her environment.

**Schizoaffective disorder** A disorder defined by a period of disturbance during which the symptoms of schizophrenia partially overlap with a major depressive episode or a manic episode.

**Schizoid personality disorder** An enduring pattern of thinking and behaviour characterized by pervasive indifference to other people, coupled with a diminished range of emotional experience and expression. People who fit this description prefer social isolation to interactions with friends or family.

**Schizophrenia** A type of (or group of) psychotic disorders characterized by positive and negative symptoms and associated with a deterioration in role functioning. The term was originally coined by Eugen Bleuler to describe the *splitting of mental associations*, which he believed to be the fundamental disturbance in schizophrenia (previously known as *dementia praecox*).

**Schizophrenic spectrum** A group of disorders that, on the basis of family history and adoption study data, are presumed to be genetically related to schizophrenia. These disorders may include schizotypal personality disorder, schizoaffective disorder, and delusional disorder.

**Schizophreniform disorder** A condition characterized by the same symptoms as schizophrenia, in which the patient has exhibited symptoms for less than the six-month period required by DSM-IV for a diagnosis of schizophrenia.

**Schizotaxia** According to Paul Meehl's theoretical model for schizophrenia, a subtle neurological defect of unknown form that is inherited by all individuals who are predisposed to schizophrenia.

**Schizotypal personality disorder** An enduring pattern of discomfort with other people coupled with peculiar thinking and behaviour. The latter symptoms take the form of perceptual and cognitive disturbances. Considered by some experts to be part of the schizophrenic spectrum.

**School refusal** (*school phobia*) Extreme reluctance to go to school, accompanied by various symptoms of anxiety such as stomachaches and headaches. May be a fear of school or an expression of separation anxiety disorder.

**Seasonal affective disorder** A type of mood disorder (either unipolar or bipolar) in which there has been a regular temporal relation between onset (or disappearance) of the person's episodes and a particular time of the year. For example, the person might become depressed in the winter.

**Secondary appraisal** The assessment of one's abilities and resources for coping with a stressful life event.

**Secondary gain** The psychoanalytic concept that conversion (or other somatoform) symptoms can help a patient avoid responsibility or receive attention (reinforcement).

**Secondary prevention** Focuses on the early detection of emotional problems (for instance, "at-risk" groups) in an attempt to prevent problems from becoming more serious and difficult to treat.

**Selective serotonin reuptake inhibitors (SSRIs)** A group of antidepressant drugs that inhibit the reuptake of serotonin into the presynaptic nerve endings and therefore promote neurotransmission in serotonin pathways.

**Self-control** Appropriate behaviour guided by internal (rather than external) rules.

**Senile plaques** A type of brain lesion found in Alzheimer's disease that consists of a central core of homogeneous protein material known as *amyloid* surrounded by clumps of debris left over from destroyed neurons.

**Sensate focus** A procedure for the treatment of sexual dysfunction that involves a series of simple exercises in which the couple spends time in a quiet, relaxed setting, learning to touch each other.

**Separation anxiety** A normal fear that begins to develop around 8 months and peaks around 15 months. The infant expresses distress following separation from an attachment figure, typically a parent or other close caregiver.

**Separation anxiety disorder** A psychological disorder of childhood characterized by persistent and excessive worry for the safety of an attachment figure and related fears such as getting lost, being kidnapped, nightmares, and refusal to be alone. Distinct from normal separation anxiety, which typically develops shortly before an infant's first birthday.

**Sexual aversion disorder** A form of sexual dysfunction in which a person has an extreme aversion to, and avoids, genital sexual contact with a partner.

**Sexual dysfunctions** Forms of sexual disorder that involve inhibitions of sexual desire or interference with the physiological responses leading to orgasm.

**Sexual masochism** A form of paraphilia in which sexual arousal is associated with the act of being humiliated, beaten, bound, or otherwise made to suffer.

**Sexual sadism** A form of paraphilia in which sexual arousal is associated with desires to inflict physical or psychological suffering, including humiliation, on another person.

**Shared environment** The component of the family environment that offers the same or highly similar experiences to all siblings, for example, socioeconomic status. Stands in contrast to the nonshared environment, experiences inside and outside the family that are unique to one sibling.

**Social clocks** Age-related goals people set for themselves and later use to evaluate life achievements.

**Socialization** The process of shaping children's behaviour and attitudes to conform to the expectations of parents, teachers, and society.

**Social phobia** A type of phobic disorder in which the person is persistently fearful of social situations that might expose him or her to scrutiny by others, such as fear of public speaking.

**Social skills training** A behaviour therapy technique in which clients are taught new skills that are desirable and likely to be rewarded in the everyday world.

**Social support** The emotional and practical assistance received from others.

**Social work** A profession whose primary concern is how human needs can be met within society.

**Somatic symptoms** Symptoms of mood disorders that are related to basic physiological or bodily functions, including fatigue, aches and pains, and serious changes in appetite and sleep patterns.

**Somatization disorder** A type of somatoform disorder characterized by multiple, somatic complaints in the absence of organic impairments.

**Somatoform disorders** A category of psychological disorders characterized by unusual physical symptoms that occur in the absence of a known physical pathology. Examples include hypochondriasis and conversion disorder. Somatoform disorders are somatic in form only, thus their name (note the distinction from psychosomatic disorders, which do involve real physical pathology).

**Standard deviation** A measure of dispersion of scores around the mean. Technically, the square root of the variance.

**Standard scores** A standardized frequency distribution in which each score is subtracted from the mean and the difference is divided by the standard deviation.

**State-dependent learning** Learning that occurs in one state of affect or consciousness is best recalled in the same state of affect or consciousness.

**Statistically significant** A statistical statement that a research result has a low probability of having occurred by chance alone. By convention, a result is said to be statistically significant if the probably is 5 percent or less that it was obtained by chance. This probability is often written as $p<.05$.

**Stigma** A negative stamp or label that sets the person apart from others, connects the person to undesirable features, and leads others to reject the person.

**Stress** An event that creates physiological or psychological strain for the individual. Stress has been defined differently by various scientists.

**Stress management** A treatment used in behavioural medicine and health psychology to teach more effective coping skills, reduce adverse reactions to stress, and improve health behaviour.

**Substance abuse** The less severe form of substance use disorder listed in DSM-IV. Describes a pattern of drug use that is defined in terms of interference with the person's ability to fulfill major role obligations, the recurrent use of a drug in dangerous situations, or the experience of repeated legal difficulties that are associated with drug use.

**Substance dependence** The more severe form of substance use disorder listed in DSM-IV. Refers to a pattern of repeated self-administration that results in tolerance, withdrawal, or compulsive drug-taking behaviour.

**Superego** One of Freud's three central personality structures, roughly equivalent to the "conscience." In Freudian theory, the superego contains societal standards of behaviour, particularly rules that children learn from identifying with their parents. The superego attempts to control id impulses.

**Synapse** A small gap filled with fluid that lies between the axon of one neuron and a dendrite or soma of another neuron.

**Syndrome** A group of symptoms that appear together and are assumed to represent a specific type of disorder.

**Systematic desensitization** A treatment for overcoming fears and phobias developed by Joseph Wolpe. Involves learning relaxation skills, developing a fear hierarchy, and systematic exposure to imagined, feared events while simultaneously maintaining relaxation.

**Systems theory** An innovation in the philosophy of conceptualizing and conducting science that emphasizes interdependence, cybernetics, and especially holism—the idea that the whole is more than the sum of its parts. Often traced to the biologist and philosopher Ludwig von Bertalanffy.

**Temperament** Characteristic styles of relating to the world that are often conceptualized as inborn traits. Generally emphasizes the "how" as opposed to the "what" of behaviour.

**Tend and befriend** An alternative response to stress hypothesized to be more common among females. Tending involves caring for offspring in a way that protects them from harm, and also alters the offspring's neuroendocrine responses in a healthful manner. Befriending is responding to threat with social affiliation, thereby reducing the risk of physical danger and encouraging the exchange of resources.

**Tertiary prevention** Involves treatment for a disorder, but also attempts to address some of the adverse consequences of mental illness (such as unemployment).

**Thalamus** A part of the limbic system that is involved in receiving and integrating sensory information both from the sense organs and from higher brain structures.

**Therapeutic alliance** The emotional bond of confidence and trust between a therapist and client believed to facilitate therapy.

**Third variable** An unmeasured factor that may account for a correlation observed between any two variables. A threat to interpretation in correlational studies, and a basic reason why correlation does not mean causation.

**Threshold model** A perspective on etiology that holds that people can exhibit characteristics of a disorder without experiencing any adverse impact on their adjustment until they pass a critical threshold. Beyond that level, there is presumably a dramatic increase in the number of problems that are encountered.

**Time-out** A discipline technique that involves briefly isolating a child as a punishment for misbehaviour.

**Token economy** A type of contingency management program that has been adopted in many institutional settings. Desired and undesired behaviours are identified, contingencies are defined, behaviour is monitored, and rewards or punishments are given according to the rules of the economy.

**Tolerance** The process through which the nervous system becomes less sensitive to the effects of a psychoactive substance. As a result, the person needs to consume increased quantities of the drug to achieve the same subjective effect.

**Transference** In psychoanalysis, the process whereby patients transfer feelings about a key figure in their life onto the analyst. In psychotherapy, the client's feelings toward the therapist.

**Transsexualism** A severe form of gender identity disorder in adults.

**Transvestic fetishism** A form of paraphilia in which sexual pleasure is derived from dressing in the clothing of the opposite gender.

**Trauma desensitization** A treatment for posttraumatic stress disorder where the client is first taught to relax, and while maintaining a state of relaxation, he or she relives the traumatic event through discussions or fantasies.

**Traumatic stress** A catastrophic event that involves real or perceived threat to life or physical well-being.

**Tricyclics** A group of antidepressant drugs that block the uptake of neurotransmitters, such as norepinephrine and dopamine, from the synapse.

**Two-factor theory** A combination of classical conditioning and operant conditioning that is hypothesized to explain the acquisition and maintenance of fear. Fears are acquired through classical conditioning and maintained through operant conditioning (the reduction in anxiety that stems from avoidance).

**Type A behaviour pattern** A characterological response to challenge that is competitive, hostile, urgent, impatient, and achievement-striving. Linked to an increased risk for coronary heart disease.

**Undifferentiated type** A subtype of schizophrenia that includes patients who display prominent psychotic symptoms and either meet the criteria for several subtypes or otherwise do not meet the criteria for the catatonic, paranoid, or disorganized types.

**Unipolar mood disorder** A form of mood disorder in which the person experiences episodes of depression but has never experienced an episode of mania or hypomania.

**Vaginismus** A form of sexual dysfunction in which the outer muscles of the vagina snap tightly shut when penetration is attempted, thus preventing insertion of any object.

**Validity** The meaning or systematic importance of a construct or a measurement.

**Variance** A measure of dispersion of scores around the mean. Technically, the average squared difference from the mean (see also *standard deviation*).

**Vascular dementia** (also known as *multi-infarct dementia*) A type of dementia associated with vascular disease. The cognitive symptoms of vascular dementia are the same as those for Alzheimer's disease, but a gradual onset is not required.

**Ventricles** Four connected chambers in the brain filled with cerebrospinal fluid. The ventricles are enlarged in some psychological and neurological disorders.

**Voyeurism** A form of paraphilia (also known as *peeping*) in which a person becomes sexually aroused by observing unsuspecting people (usually strangers) while they are undressing or engaging in sexual activities.

**Vulnerability marker** A specific measure, such as a biochemical assay or a psychological test, which might be useful in identifying people who are vulnerable to a disorder such as schizophrenia.

**Weight set point** Fixed weights or small ranges of weight around which the body regulates weight, for example, by increasing or decreasing metabolism.

**Withdrawal** The constellation of symptoms that are experienced shortly after a person stops taking a drug after heavy or prolonged use.

**Worry** A relatively uncontrollable sequence of negative, emotional thoughts and images that are concerned with possible future threats or danger.

# References


Abdulrehman, R.Y., & De Luca, R.V. (2001). The implications of childhood sexual abuse on adult social behavior. *Journal of Family Violence, 16,* 193–203.

Abel, G.G., Becker, J.V., Mittelman, M., Cunningham-Rathner, J., et al. (1987). Self-reported sex crimes of nonincarcerated paraphiliacs. *Journal of Interpersonal Violence, 2,* 3–25.

Abel, G.G., & Gouleau, J.L. (1990). Male sex offenders. In M.E. Thase, B.A. Edelstein, & M. Hersen (Eds.), *Handbook of Outpatient Treatment of Adults: Nonpsychotic Mental Disorders* (pp. 271–290). New York: Plenum.

Abel, G.G., & Osborn, C. (1992). The paraphilias: The extent and nature of sexually deviant and criminal behavior. *Psychotic Clinics of North America, 15,* pp. 675–687.

Abela, J.R.Z. (2001). The hopelessness theory of depression: A test of the diathesis-stress and causal mediation components in third and seventh grade children. *Journal of Abnormal Child Psychology, 29,* 241–254.

Abela, J.R.Z. (2002). Depressive mood reactions to failure in the achievement domain: A test of the integration of the hopelessness and self-esteem theories of depression. *Cognitive Therapy and Research, 26,* 531–552.

Abela, J.R.Z., & Payne, A.V.L. (2003). A test of the integration of the hopelessness and self-esteem theories of depression in schoolchildren. *Cognitive Therapy and Research, 27,* 519–535.

Abela, J.R.Z., & Sarin, S. (2002). Cognitive vulnerability to hopelessness depression: A chain is only as strong as its weakest link. *Cognitive Therapy and Research, 26,* 811–829.

Adams, J., Crosbie, J., Wigg, K., Ickowicz, A., Pathare, T., Roberts, W., Malone, M., Schachar, R., Tannock, R., Kennedy, J.L., & Barr, C.L. (2004). Glutamate receptor, ionotropic, N-methyl D-aspartate 2A (GRIN2A) gene as a positional candidate for attention-deficit/hyperactivity disorder in the 16p13 region. *Molecular Psychiatry, 9,* 494–499.

Abrams, R. (1997). *Electroconvulsive Therapy.* New York: Oxford University Press.

Abramowitz, J.S. (1998). Does cognitive-behavioral therapy cure obsessive-compulsive disorder? A meta-analytic evaluation of clinical significance. *Behavior Therapy, 29,* pp. 339–355.

Abramson, L.Y., Metalsky, G.I., & Alloy, L.B. (1989). Hopelessness depression: A theory-based subtype of depression. *Psychological Review, 96,* 358–372.

Ackerman, M.D., & Carey, M.P. (1995). Psychology's role in the assessment of erectile dysfunction: Historical precedents, current knowledge, and methods. *Journal of Consulting and Clinical Psychology, 63,* 862–876.

Adams, G.R., Abraham, K.G., & Markstrom, C.A. (1987). The relation among identity development, self-consciousness and self-focusing during middle and late adolescence. *Developmental Psychology, 23,* 292–297.

Adams, G.R., & Adams, C.M. (1989). Developmental issues. In L.K.G. Hsu & M. Hersen (Eds.), *Recent Developments in Adolescent Psychiatry* (pp. 13–30). New York: Wiley.

Adams, G.R., Ryan, J.H., Hoffman, J.J., Dobson, W.R., & Nielsen, E.C. (1985). Ego identity status, conformity behavior and personality in late adolescence. *Journal of Personality and Social Psychology, 47,* 1091–1104.

Adlaf, E.M., & Paglia, A. (2001). *The mental health and well-being of Ontario students: 1991–1999.* Toronto, ON: CAMH.

Adler, C.M., McDonough-Ryan, P., Sax, K.W., Holland, S.K., Arndt, S., & Strakowski, S.M. (2000). fMRI of neuronal activation with symptom provocation in unmedicated patients with obsessive compulsive disorder. *Journal of Psychiatric Research, 34,* 317–324.

Adler, L.E., Freedman, R., Ross, R.G., Olincy, A., & Waldo, M.C. (1999). Elementary phenotypes in the neurobiological and genetic study of schizophrenia. *Biological Psychiatry, 46,* 8–18.

Adler, R. (2001). Psychoneuroimmunology. *Current Directions in Psychological Science, 10,* 94–98.

Agras, W.S. (1987). *Eating Disorders: Management of Obesity, Bulimia, and Anorexia Nervosa.* Elmsford, NY: Pergamon.

Agras, W.S., Walsh, B.T., Fairburn, C.G., Wilson, G.T., & Kraemer, H.C. (2002). A multicenter comparison of cognitive-behavioral therapy and interpersonal psychotherapy for bulimia nervosa. *Archives of General Psychiatry, 57,* 459–466.

Ainsworth, M.D.S. (1989). Attachments beyond infancy. *American Psychologist, 44,* 709–716.

Ainsworth, M.D.S., Blehar, M., Waters, E., & Wall, S. (1978). *Patterns of attachment.* Hillsdale, NJ: Erlbaum.

Akagi, H., & House, A. (2001). Epidemiology of Conversion Hysteria. In P. Halligan, C. Bass & J. Marshall (Eds.), *Contemporary Approaches to the Study of Hysteria* (pp. 73–86). Oxford: Oxford University Press.

Akiskal, H.S. (1992). Borderline: An adjective still in search of a noun. In D. Silver & M. Rosenbluth (Eds.), *Handbook of Borderline Disorders* (pp. 155–176). Madison, CT: International Universities Press.

Akyuz, G., Dogan, O., Sar, V., Yargic, L.I., & Tutkun, H. (1999). Frequency of dissociative identity disorder in the general population in Turkey. *Comprehensive Psychiatry, 40,* 151–159.

Alarcon, R.D., Foulks, E.F., & Vakkur, M. (1998). *Personality Disorders and Culture: Clinical and Conceptual Interactions.* New York: Wiley.

Aldridge-Morris, R. (1989). *Multiple Personality: An Exercise in Deception.* Hillsdale, NJ: Erlbaum.

Alexander, F. (1950). *Psychosomatic Medicine: Its Principles and Applications.* New York: Norton.

Alexander, F., & French, T.M. (1947). *Psychoanalytic therapy.* New York: Ronald Press.

Alexander, F., French, T.M., & Pollock, G.H. (1968). *Psychosomatic Specificity.* Chicago: University of Chicago Press.

Alexander, J.F., Holtzworth-Munroe, A., & Jameson, P.B. (1994). The process and outcome of marital and family therapy: Research, review, and evaluation. In A.E. Bergin & S.L. Garfield (Eds.), *Handbook of Psychotherapy and Behavior Change* (4th ed., pp. 595–630). New York: Wiley.

Alexander, J.F., Newell, R.M., Robbins, M.S., & Turner, C.W. (1995). Observational coding in family therapy process research. *Journal of Family Psychology, 9,* 355–365.

Alexander, J.F., & Parsons, B.V. (1982). *Functional Family Therapy.* Monterey, CA: Brooks/Cole.

Allen, J.P., et al. (2002). Attachment and autonomy as predictors of the development of social skills and delinquency during midadolescence. *Journal of Consulting and Clinical Psychology, 70,* 56–66.

Alloy, L.B., Abramson, L.Y., & Francis, E.L. (1999). Do negative cognitive styles confer vulnerability to depression? *Current Directions in Psychological Science, 8,* 128–132.

Alloy, L.B., Reilly-Harrington, N., Fresco, D.M., Whitehouse, W.G., & Zechmeister, J.S. (1999). Cognitive styles and life events in subsyndromal unipolar and bipolar disorders. *Journal of Cognitive Psychotherapy, 13,* 21–40.

Al-Sawaf, M., & Al-Issa, I. (2000). Sex and sexual dysfunction in an Arab-Islamic society. In I. Al-Issa (Ed.), *Mental Illness in the Islamic World* (pp. 295–311). Guilford, CT: International Universities Press.

Altshuler, L.L., Bartzokis, G., Grieder, T., Curran, J., Jimenez, T., Leight, K., Wilkins, J., Gerner, R., & Mintz, J. (2000). An MRI study of temporal lobe structures in men with bipolar disorder or schizophrenia. *Biological Psychiatry, 48,* 147–162.

American Association on Mental Retardation (2002). *Mental Retardation: Definition, Classification, and Systems of Supports* (10th ed.). Washington, DC: AAMR.

American Bar Association (1995). *Mental Disability Law,* 5th ed. Washington, DC.

American Psychiatric Association (1980). *Psychiatric Glossary.* Washington, DC: American Psychiatric Press.

American Psychiatric Association (1983). American Psychiatric Association statement on the insanity defense. *American Journal of Psychiatry, 140,* 681–688.

American Psychiatric Association (1994). *Diagnostic and Statistical Manual of Mental Disorders,* 1st ed. 1952; 2nd ed. 1968; 3rd ed. 1980; rev. 3rd ed. 1987; 4th ed. 1994. Washington, DC.

American Psychiatric Association. (2000). *Diagnostic and Statistical Manual of Mental Disorders* (DSM-IV-TR, 4th edition, text revision). Washington, DC.

American Psychological Association (1995). *Violence in the Family.* Washington, DC.

Ames, E.W., & Carter, M. (1992). Development of Romanian orphanage children adopted to Canada. *Canadian Psychology, 33,* 503.

Anda, R., Williamson, D., Jones, D., Macera, C., Eaker, E., Glasman, A., & Marks, J. (1993). Depressed affect, hopelessness, and the risk of ischemic heart disease. *Epidemiology, 4,* 285–294.

Andersen, A.E. (1995). Eating disorders in males. In K.D. Brownell & C.G. Fairburn (Eds.), *Eating Disorders and Obesity: A Comprehensive Handbook* (pp. 177–182). New York: Guilford.

Andersen, B.L., & Cyranowski, J.M. (1995). Women's sexuality: Behaviors, responses, and individual differences. *Journal of Consulting and Clinical Psychology, 63,* 891–906.

Anderson, A.E. (2002). Eating disorders in males. In C.G. Fairburn & K.D. Brownell (Eds.), *Eating Disorders and Obesity* (2nd ed., pp. 188–192). New York: Guilford.

Anderson, E.M., & Lambert, M.J. (1995). Short-term dynamically oriented psychotherapy: A review and meta-analysis. *Clinical Psychology Review, 9,* 503–514.

Anderson, B.L., Kiecolt-Glaser, J.K., & Glaser, R. (1994). A biobehavioral model of cancer stress and disease course. *American Psychologist, 49,* 389–404.

Anderson, N.B., & McNeilly, M. (1991). Age, gender, and ethnicity as variables in psychophysiological assessment: Sociodemographics in context. *Psychological Assessment, 3,* 376–384.

Andreasen, N.C. (2000). Schizophrenia: The fundamental questions. *Brain Research Reviews, 31,* 106–112.

Andreasen, N.C. (2001). *Brave New Brain: Conquering Mental Illness in the Era of the Genome.* New York: Oxford University Press.

Andreasen, N.C., Arndt, S., Alliger, R., Miller, D., & Flaum, M. (1995). Symptoms of schizophrenia: Methods, meanings, and mechanisms. *Archives of General Psychiatry, 52*, 341–351.

Andreasen, N.C., & Carpenter, W.T., Jr. (1993). Diagnosis and classification of schizophrenia. *Schizophrenia Bulletin, 19*, 199–214.

Andrews, A. (1999). *Be good, sweet maid: The trials of Dorothy Joudrie*. Ontario: Wilfrid Laurier Press.

Andrews, G. (1996). Comorbidity in neurotic disorders: The similarities are more important than the differences. In R.M. Rapee (Ed.), *Current Controversies in the Anxiety Disorders* (pp. 3–20). New York: Guilford.

Andrews, G., MacMahon, S.W., Austin, A., & Byrne, D.G. (1984). Hypertension: Comparison of drug and non-drug treatments. *British Medical Journal, 284*, 1523–1530.

Andrews, G., Slade, T., & Peters, L. (1999). Classification in psychiatry: ICD-10 versus DSM-IV. *British Journal of Psychiatry, 174*, 3–5.

Angst, J., Sellaro, R., & Angst, F. (1998). Long-term outcome and mortality of treated versus untreated bipolar and depressed patients: A preliminary report. *International Journal of Psychiatry in Clinical Practice, 2*, 115–119.

Angst, J., Sellaro, R., & Merikangas, K.R. (2000). Depressive spectrum diagnoses. *Comprehensive Psychiatry, 41*, 39–47.

Anisman, H., & Zul, M. (1999). Understanding stress: Characteristics and caveats. *Alcohol Research and Health, 23*, 241–249.

Anthony, J.C., & Helzer, J.E. (1991). Syndromes of drug abuse and dependence. In L.N. Robins & D.A. Regier (Eds.), *Psychiatric Disorders in America: The Epidemiologic Catchment Area Study* (pp. 116–154). New York: Free Press.

Anthony, J.C., Warner, L.A., & Kessler, R.C. (1994). Comparative epidemiology of dependence on tobacco, alcohol, controlled substances, and inhalants: Basic findings from the National Comorbidity Survey. *Experimental and Clinical Psychopharmacology, 2*, 1–24.

Antonucci, T.C. (2001). Social relations. In J.E. Birren & K.W. Schaie (Eds.), *Handbook of the Psychology of Aging* (5th ed., pp. 427–453). San Diego: Academic Press.

Antony, M.M., & Barlow, D.H. (2001). *Handbook of assessment and treatment planning for psychological disorders*. New York: Guilford.

Antony, M.M., & Barlow, D.H. (2002). Specific phobias. In D.H. Barlow, *Anxiety and its disorders: The nature and treatment of anxiety and panic* (2nd ed., pp. 380–417). New York: Guilford.

Antony, M.M., & Swinson, R.P. (2000). *Phobic Disorders and Panic Attacks in Adults: A Guide to Assessment and Treatment*. Washington, DC: American Psychological Association.

Appelbaum, P.S. (1994). *Almost a Revolution: Mental Health Law and the Limits of Change*. New York: Oxford University Press.

Appelbaum, P.S., & Gutheil, T.G. (1979). Rotting with their rights on: Constitutional theory and clinical reality in drug refusal by psychiatric patients. *Bulletin of the American Academy of Psychiatry and Law, 7*, 308–317.

Apter, J.T., & Allen, L.A. (1999). Buspirone: Future directions. *Journal of Clinical Psychopharmacology, 19*, 86–93.

Archer, R.P. (1992). Review of the Minnesota Multiphasic Personality Inventory-2. In J.J. Kramer & J.C. Conoley (Eds.), *The Eleventh Mental Measurements Yearbook* (pp. 558–561). Lincoln: University of Nebraska Press.

Arnett, J.J. (1999). Adolescent storm and stress, reconsidered. *American Psychologist, 54*, 317–326.

Arrigo, B.A., & Shipley, S. (2001). The confusion over psychopathy (I): Historical considerations. *International Journal of Offender Therapy and Comparative Criminology, 45*, 325–344.

Asberg, M. (1994). Monoamine neurotransmitters in human aggressiveness and violence: A selected review. *Criminal Behaviour and Mental Health, 4*, 303–327.

Asher, S.R., & Wheeler, V.A. (1985). Children's loneliness: A comparison of rejected and neglected peer status. *Journal of Consulting and Clinical Psychology, 53*, 500–505.

Asmundson, G.J.G., Carleton, R.N., Wright, K.D., & Taylor, S. (2004). Psychological sequelae of remote exposure to the September 11th terrorist attacks in Canadians with and without panic. *Cognitive Behaviour Therapy, 33*, 51–59.

Asmundson, G.J.G., Cox, B.J., Larsen, D.K., Frombach, I.K., & Norton, G.R. (1999). Psychometric properties of the Accident Fear Questionnaire: An analysis based on motor vehicle accident survivors in a rehabilitation setting. *Rehabilitation Psychology, 44*, 373–387.

Asmundson, G.J.G., Norton, P.J., & Norton, G.R. (1999). Beyond pain: The role of fear and avoidance in chronicity. *Clinical Psychology Review, 19*, 97–119.

Asmundson, G.J.G., Stein, M.B., & McCreary, D.R. (2002). Posttraumatic stress disorder symptoms influence health status of deployed peacekeepers and nondeployed military personnel. *Journal of Nervous and Mental Disease, 190*, 807–815.

Asmundson, G.J.G., & Taylor, S. (1996). Role of anxiety sensitivity in pain-related fear and avoidance. *Journal of Behavioral Medicine, 19*, 577–586.

Asperger, H. (1944/1991). "Autistic psychopathy" in childhood. In U. Frith (Ed. and Trans.), *Autism and Asperger Syndrome* (pp. 37–92). Cambridge: Cambridge University Press. (Original published in 1944).

Attie, I., & Brooks-Gunn, J. (1989). Development of eating problems in adolescent girls: A longitudinal study. *Developmental Psychology, 25*, 70–79.

Austin, G.W., Jaffe, P., & Friedman, B. (1994). Custody and access assessors: Effects of background and experience on analogue case judgement. *Canadian Journal of Behavioural Science, 26*, 463–475.

Avila, M.T., McMahon, R.P., Elliott, A.R., & Thaker, G.K. (2002). Neurophysiological markers of vulnerability to schizophrenia: Sensitivity and specificity of specific quantitative eye movement measures. *Journal of Abnormal Psychology, 111*, 259–267.

Ayres, J.J.B. (1998). Fear conditioning and avoidance. In W.T. O'Donohue (Ed.), *Learning and Behavior Therapy* (pp. 122–145). Needham Heights, MA: Allyn and Bacon.

Ayuso-Mateos, J.L., Vazquez-Barquero, J.L., Dowrick, C., Lehtinen, V., Dalgard, O.S., Casey, P.W., Wilkinson, C., Lasa, L., Page, H., Dunn, G., & Wilkinson, G. (2001). Depressive disorders in Europe: Prevalence figures from the ODIN study. *British Journal of Psychiatry, 179*, 308–316.

Babiak, P. (1995). When psychopaths go to work: A case study of an industrial psychopath. *Applied Psychology, 44*, 171–188.

Babiak, P., & Hare, R.D. (2003). *B-Scan*. Toronto: MultiHealth Systems.

Bachrach, L.L. (1994). Deinstitutionalization and service priorities in Canada and the United States. In L.L. Bachrach, P. Goering, & D. Wasylenki (Eds.), *Mental health care in Canada* (pp. 3–9). San Francisco: Jossey-Bass.

Baer, L., Rauch, S.L., Ballantine, T., et al. (1995). Cingulotomy for intractable obsessive–compulsive disorder: Prospective long-term follow-up of 18 patients. *Archives of General Psychiatry, 52*, 384–392.

Bailey, A., Le Couteur, A., Gottesman, I., Bolton, P., Simonoff, E., Yuzda, E., & Rutter, M. (1995). Autism as a strongly genetic disorder: Evidence from a British twin study. *Psychological Medicine, 25*, 63–77.

Bailey, S. (2002). Treatment of delinquents. In M. Rutter & E. Taylor (Eds.), *Child and Adolescent Psychiatry* (4th ed., pp. 1019–1037). Oxford, UK: Blackwell.

Baker, J.D., Capron, E.W., & Azorlosa, J. (1996). Family environment characteristics of persons with histrionic and dependent personality disorders. *Journal of Personality Disorders, 10*, 82–87.

Bal, P. & Koenraadt, F. (2000). Criminal law and mentally ill offenders in comparative perspective. *Psychology, Crime and Law, 6*, 219–250.

Bala, N. (1994). Children, psychiatrists and the courts: Understanding the ambivalence of the legal profession. Part I—General principles. *Canadian Journal of Psychiatry, 39*, 526–530.

Ballard, C.G., O'Brien, J.T., Swann, A.G., Thompson, P., Neill, D., & McKeith, I.G. (2001). The natural history of psychosis and depression in dementia with Lewy bodies and Alzheimer's disease: Persistence and new cases over 1 year of follow-up. *Journal of Clinical Psychiatry, 62*, 46–49.

Ballenger, J.C., et al. (2000). Consensus statement on posttraumatic stress disorder from the International Consensus on Depression and Anxiety. *Journal of Clinical Psychiatry, 61*, 60–66.

Balon, R. (1998). Pharmacological treatment of paraphilias with a focus on antidepressants. *Journal of Sex and Marital Therapy, 24*, 241–254.

Baltes, P.B. (1993). The aging mind: Potential and limits. *Gerontologist, 33*, 580–594.

Baltes, P.B. (1997). On the incomplete architecture of human ontogeny: Selection, optimization, and compensation as foundation of developmental theory. *American Psychologist, 52*, 366–380.

Bandura, A. (1977). Self-efficacy: Toward a unifying theory of behavior change. *Psychological Review, 84*, 191–215.

Bandura, A., & Walters, R.H. (1963). *Social learning and personality development*. New York: Ronald Press.

Banki, C.M. (1995). Prophylactic potential of selective reuptake inhibitors in suicidal patients. *International Clinical Psychopharmacology, 9* (suppl. 4), 61–65.

Bankier, B., Aigner, M., & Bach, M. (2001). Alexithymia in DSM-IV disorder: Comparative evaluation of somatoform disorder, panic disorder, obsessive–compulsive disorder, and depression. *Psychosomatics, 42*, 235–240.

Barbaree, H.E., Peacock, E.J., Cortoni, F., Marshall, W.L., & Seto M. (1998). Ontario penitentiaries' program. In W.L. Marshall, Y.M. Fernandez, S.M. Hudson, & T. Ward (Eds.), *Sourcebook of treatment programs for sexual offenders* (pp. 59–77). New York: Plenum.

Barbaree, H.E., & Seto, M.C. (1997). Pedophilia: Assessment and treatment. In D.R. Laws & W.T. O'Donohue (Eds.), *Handbook of Sexual Deviance: Theory and Application* (pp. 175–193). New York: Guilford.

Barbaree, H.E., Seto, M.C., Serin, R.C., Amos, N.L., & Preston, D.L. (1994). Comparisons between sexual and nonsexual rapist subtypes: Sexual arousal to rape, offense precursors, and offense characteristics. *Criminal Justice and Behavior, 21*, 95–114.

Barch, D.M., Carter, C.S., Braver, T.S., Sabb, F.W., MacDonald, A., Noll, D.C., & Cohen, J.D. (2001). Selective deficits in prefrontal cortex function in medication-naïve patients with schizophrenia. *Archives of General Psychiatry, 58*, 280–288.

Barkley, R.A. (1998). *Attention-Deficit/Hyperactivity Disorder* (2nd ed.). New York: Guilford.

Barkley, R.A., Karlsson, J., Strzelecki, E., & Murphy, J.V. (1984). Effects of age and Ritalin dosage on the mother-child interactions of hyperactive children. *Journal of Consulting and Clinical Psychology, 52*, 750–758.

Barlow, D.H. (2002). *Anxiety and its Disorders* (2nd ed.). New York: Guilford.

Barlow, D.H., Brown, T.A., & Craske, M.G. (1994). Definitions of panic attacks and panic disorder in the DSM-IV: Implications for research. *Journal of Abnormal Psychology, 103*, 553–564.

Barlow, D.H., & Campbell, L.A. (2000). Mixed anxiety-depression and its implications for models of mood and anxiety disorders. *Comprehensive Psychiatry, 41* (suppl. 1), 55–60.

Barnier, A.J. (2002). Posthypnotic amnesia for autobiographical episodes: A laboratory model of functional amnesia? *Psychological Science, 13*, 232–237.

Baroff, G.S. (1986). *Mental Retardation: Nature, Cause, and Management* (2nd ed.). Washington, DC: Hemisphere.

Baroff, G.S., & Olley, J.G. (1999). *Mental Retardation* (3rd ed). Philadelphia: Brunner/Mazel.

Baron-Cohen, S., Leslie, A.M., & Frith, U. (1985). Does the autistic child have a "theory of mind"? *Cognition, 21*, 37–46.

Baron-Cohen, S., Tager-Flusberg, H., & Cohen, D.J. (Eds.) (1993). *Understanding other Minds*. Oxford: Oxford University Press.

Barondes, S.H. (1993). *Molecules and mental illness*. New York: Scientific American.

Barr, C.L., Kroft, J., Feng, Y., Wigg, K., Roberts, W., Malone, M., Ickowicz, A., Schachar, R., Tannock, R., & Kennedy, J.L. (2002). The norepinephrine transporter gene and attention-deficit hyperactivity disorder. *American Journal of Medical Genetics, 8*, 255–259.

Barrett, J.E, Williams, J.W., Oxman, T.E, Frank, E., Katon, W., Sullivan, M., Hegel, M.T., Cornell, J.E, & Sengupta, A.S. (2001). Treatment of dysthymia and minor depression in primary care: A randomized trial in patients aged 18 to 59 years. *Journal of Family Practice, 50*, 405–412.

Barrett, M.S., & Berman, J.S. (2001). Is psychotherapy more effective when therapists disclose information about themselves? *Journal of Consulting and Clinical Psychology, 69*, 597–603.

Barrett, P.M., Dadds, M.R., & Rapee, R.M. (1996). Family treatment of childhood anxiety: A controlled trial. *Journal of Consulting and Clinical Psychology, 64*, 333–342.

Barrett, P.M. et al., (2001). Cognitive-behavioral treatment of anxiety disorders in children: Longterm (6-year) follow-up. *Journal of Consulting and Clinical Psychology, 69*, 135–141.

Bartlett, P. (2000). Structures of confinement in 19th-century asylums: A comparative study using England and Ontario. *International Journal of Law and Psychiatry, 23*, 1–13.

Basoglu, M., Mineka, S., Paker, M., Aker, T., Livanou, M., & Gok, S. (1997). Psychological preparedness for trauma as a protective factor in survivors of torture. *Psychological Medicine, 27*, 1421–1433.

Bass, C., Peveler, R., & House, A. (2001). Somatoform disorders: Severe psychiatric illnesses neglected by psychiatrists. *British Journal of Psychiatry, 179*, 11–14.

Bass, E., & Davis, L. (1988). *The Courage to Heal*. New York: Harper & Row.

Bassett, A.S. (1991). Linkage analysis of schizophrenia: Challenges and promise. *Social Biology, 38*, 189–196.

Bassett, A.S., & Chow, E.W.C. (1999). 22q11 deletion syndrome: A genetic subtype of schizophrenia. *Biological Psychiatry, 46*, 882–891.

Bassett, A.S., Hodgkinson, K., Chow, E.W.C., Correia, S., Scutt, L., & Weksberg, R. (1998). 22q11 deletion syndrome in adults with schizophrenia. *American Journal of Medical Genetics, 81*, 328–337.

Basson, R. (2001). Human sex-response cycles. *Journal of Sex and Marital Therapy, 27*, 33–43.

Basson, R., Berman, J., Burnett, A., Derogatis, L., Ferguson, D., Fourcroy, J., Goldstein, I., Graziottin, Al., Heiman, J., Laan, E., Leiblum, S., Padma-Nathan, H., Rosen, R., Segraves, K., Segraves, R.T., Shabsigh, R., Sipski, M., Wagner, G., & Whipple, B. (2000). Report of the international consensus development conference on female sexual dysfunction: Definitions and classification. *Journal of Urology, 163*, 888–896.

Basson, R., McInnes, R., Smith, M.D., Hodgson, G., & Koppiker, N. (2002). Efficacy and safety of sildenafil citrate in women with sexual dysfunction associated with female sexual arousal disorder. *Journal of Women's Health & Gender-Based Medicine, 11*, 367–377.

Bastiani, A.M., Rao, R., Weltzin, T., & Kaye, W.H. (1995). Perfectionism in anorexia nervosa. *International Journal of Eating Disorders, 17*, 147–152.

Bates, J.E., Wachs, T.D., & Emde, R.N. (1994). Toward practical uses for biological concepts of temperament. In J.E. Bates & T.D. Wachs (Eds.), *Temperament: Individual Differences at the Interface of Biology and Behavior* (pp. 275–306). Washington, DC: American Psychological Association.

Battaglia, M., & Torgersen, S. (1996). Schizotypal disorder: At the crossroads of genetics and nosology. *Acta Psychiatrica Scandinavica, 94*, 303–310.

Baucom, D.H., Epstein, N., & LaTaillade, J.J. (2002). Cognitive-behavioral couple therapy. In A. Gurman & N. Jacobson (Eds.), *Clinical Handbook of Couple Therapy* (3rd ed., pp. 26–58). New York: Guilford.

Baucom, D.H., Notarius, C.I., Burnett, C.K., & Haefner, P. (1990). Gender differences and sex-role identity in marriage. In F.D. Fincham & T.N. Bradbury (Eds.), *The Psychology of Marriage: Basic Issues and Applications* (pp. 150–171). New York: Guilford.

Baum, A., Davidson, L.M., Singer, J.E., & Street, S.W. (1987). Stress as a psychophysiological response. In A. Baum & J.E. Singer (Eds.), *Handbook of Psychology and Health. Stress* (Vol. 5, pp. 1–24). Hillsdale, NJ: Erlbaum.

Bauman, M.L. (1996). Neuroanatomic observations of the brain in pervasive developmental disorders. *Journal of Autism and Developmental Disorders, 26*, 199–203.

Baumeister, R.F. (1990). Suicide as escape from self. *Psychological Review, 97*, 90–113.

Baumeister, R.F. (1997). Identity, self-concept, and self-esteem: The self lost and found. In R. Hogan, J. Johnson, & S. Briggs (Eds.), *Handbook of Personality Psychology* (pp. 681–710). San Diego, CA: Academic Press.

Baumeister, R.F., & Butler, J.L. (1997). Sexual masochism. In D.R. Laws & W.T. O'Donohue (Eds.), *Handbook of Sexual Deviance: Theory and Application* (pp. 225–239). New York: Guilford.

Beach, S.R.H., Sandeen, E.E., & O'Leary, K.D. (1990). *Depression in Marriage: A Model for Etiology and Treatment*. New York: Guilford.

Beale, A.L., Dumont, R., Branche, A.-E.H., & Cruse, C.L. (1996). Practical implications of differences between the American and Canadian norms for WISC-III and a short form for children with learning disabilities. *Canadian Journal of School Psychology, 12*, 7–14.

Bebbington, P., & Kuipers, L. (1994). The predictive utility of expressed emotion in schizophrenia: An aggregate analysis. *Psychological Medicine, 24*, 707–718.

Beck, A.T. (1967). *Depression: Clinical, Experimental, and Theoretical Aspects*. New York: Harper & Row.

Beck, A.T. (1974). The development of depression. In R.J. Friedman & M.M. Katz (Eds.), *The Psychology of Depression: Contemporary Theory and Research* (pp. 3–20). New York: Winston-Wiley.

Beck, A.T. (1995). Cognitive therapy: Past, present, and future. In M.J. Mahoney (Ed.), *Cognitive and Constructive Psychotherapies: Theory, Research, and Practice* (pp. 29–40). New York: Springer.

Beck, A.T., & Emery, G. (1985). *Anxiety Disorders and Phobias: A Cognitive Perspective*. New York: Basic Books.

Beck, A.T., Rush, A.J., Shaw, B.F., & Emery, G. (1979). *Cognitive Therapy of Depression*. New York: Guilford.

Beck, J.G. (1995). Hypoactive sexual desire disorder: An overview. *Journal of Consulting and Clinical Psychology, 63*, 919–927.

Becker, D., & Lamb, S. (1994). Sex bias in the diagnosis of borderline personality disorder and posttraumatic stress disorder. *Professional Psychology: Research and Practice, 25*, 55–61.

Becker, J.V., Alpert, J.L., BigFoot, D.S., Bonner, B.L., Geddie, L.F., Henggeler, S.W., Kaufman, K.L., & Walker, C.E. (1995). Empirical research on child abuse treatment: Report by the Child Abuse and Neglect Treatment Working Group, American Psychological Association. *Journal of Clinical Child Psychology, 24*, 23–46.

Bechtoldt, H., Norcross, J.C., Wyckoff, L.A., Pokrywa, M.L., & Campbell, L.F. (2001). Theoretical orientations and employment settings of clinical and counseling psychologists: A comparative study. *The Clinical Psychologist, 54*, 3–6.

Beidel, D.C., Turner, S.M., & Cooley, M.R. (1993). Assessing reliable and clinically significant change in social phobia: Validity of the social phobia and anxiety inventory. *Behaviour Research and Therapy, 31*, 331–337.

Beidel, D.C., Turner, S.M., & Morris, T.L. (2000). Behavioral treatment of childhood social phobia. *Journal of Consulting and Clinical Psychology, 68*, 1072–1080.

Bellack, A.S., Haas, G.L., Schooler, N.R., & Flory, J.D. (2000). Effects of behavioural family management on family communication and patient outcomes in schizophrenia. *British Journal of Psychiatry, 177*, 434–439.

Bender, L. (1947). Childhood schizophrenia, clinical study of one hundred schizophrenic children. *American Journal of Orthopsychiatry, 17*, 40–56.

Benet, A.E., & Melman, A. (1995). The epidemiology of erectile dysfunction. *Urologic Clinics of North America, 22*, 699–709.

Benjamin, L.S. (1996). *Interpersonal Diagnosis and Treatment of Personality Disorders* (2nd ed.). New York: Guilford.

Bennett, F.C., & Sherman, R. (1983). Management of childhood "hyperactivity" by primary care physicians. *Journal of Developmental and Behavioral Pediatrics, 4*, 88–93.

Berenbaum, H., & Barch, D. (1995). The categorization of thought disorder. *Journal of Psycholinguistic Research, 24*, 349–376.

Bergeron, S., Binik, Y. M., Kalife, S., Pagidas, K., Glazer, H.I., Meana, M., & Amsel, R. (2001). A randomized comparison of group cognitive-behavioral therapy, surface electromyographic biofeedback, and vestibulectomy in the treatment of dyspareunia resulting from vulvar vestibulitis. *Pain, 91*, 297–306.

Berlin, I.N. (1987). Suicide among American Indian adolescents: An overview. *Suicide and Life-Threatening Behavior, 17*, 218–232.

Berman, A.L., & Jobes, D.A. (1994). Treatment of the suicidal adolescent. In A.A. Leenaars, J.T. Maltsberger, & R.A. Neimeyer (Eds.), *Treatment of Suicidal People* (pp. 89–100). Washington, DC: Taylor & Francis.

Berman, J.R., Berman, L., & Goldstein, I. (1999). Female sexual dysfunction: Incidence, pathophysiology, evaluation, and treatment options. *Urology, 54*, 385–391.

Berman, J.R., Berman, L.A., Werbin, T.J., Flaherty, E.E., Leahy, N.M., & Goldstein, I. (1999). Clinical evaluation of female sexual function: Effects of age and estrogen status on subjective and physiologic sexual responses. *International Journal of Impotence Research, 11* (suppl. 1), 31–38.

Bernard, S.H. (2002). Services for children and adolescents with severe learning disabilities (mental retardation). In M. Rutter & E. Taylor (Eds.), *Child and Adolescent Psychiatry* (4th ed., pp. 1114–1127). Oxford: Blackwell.

Bernlef, J. (1988). *Out of Mind*. London: Faber.

Bernstein, D.A., & Borkovec, T.D. (1973). *Progressive Relaxation training: A Manual for the Helping Professions*. Champaign, IL: Research Press.

Bernstein, D.P., Cohen, P., Velez, C.N., Schwab-Stone, M., Siever, L.J., & Shinsato, L. (1993). Prevalence and stability of the DSM-III-R personality disorders in a community-based survey of adolescents. *American Journal of Psychiatry, 150*, 1237–1243.

Bernstein, D.P., Useda, D., & Siever, L.J. (1995). Paranoid personality disorder. In W.J. Livesley (Ed.), *The DSM-IV Personality Disorders* (pp. 45–57). New York: Guilford.

Bernstein, G.A., Borchardt, C.M., Perwien, A.R., Crosby, R.D., Kushner, M.G., Thuras, P.D., & Last, C.G. (2000). Imipramine plus cognitive-behavioral therapy in the treatment of school refusal. *Journal of the American Academy of Child and Adolescent Psychiatry, 39*, 276–283.

Berrios, G.E. (1992). Research into the history of psychiatry. In C. Freeman & P. Tyrer (Eds.), *Research Methods in Psychiatry: A Beginner's Guide* (2nd ed.). London: Gaskell.

Berrios, G.E., & Hauser, R. (1988). The early development of Kraepelin's ideas on classification: A conceptual history. *Psychological Medicine, 18*, 813–821.

Berry, J.W., Poortinga, Y.H., Segall, M.H., & Dasen, P.R. (1992). *Cross-cultural psychology: Research and applications*. New York: Cambridge University Press.

Bersoff, D.N. (1999). *Ethical Conflicts in Psychology* (2nd ed.). Washington: American Psychological Association.

Bertelson, A., Harvald, B., & Hauge, M. (1977). A Danish twin study of manic-depressive disorders. *British Journal of Psychiatry, 130*, 330–351.

Besharov, D.J. (1992). A balanced approach to reporting child abuse. *Child, Youth, and Family Services Quarterly, 15*, 5–7.

Besson, J., Aeby, F., Kasas, A., Lehert, P., & Potgieter, A. (1998). Combined efficacy of acamprosate and disulfiram in the treatment of alcoholism: A controlled study. *Alcoholism: Clinical and Experimental Research, 22*, 573–579.

Bettelheim, B. (1967). *The Empty Fortress*. New York: Free Press.

Beumont, P.J.V., Garner, D.M., & Touyz, S.W. (1994). Diagnoses of eating or dieting disorders: What may we learn from past mistakes? *International Journal of Eating Disorders, 16*, 349–362.

Beutler, L.E., Crago, M., & Arizmendi, T.G. (1986). Therapist variables in psychotherapy process and outcome. In S.L. Garfield & A.E. Bergin (Eds.), *Handbook of psychotherapy and behavior change* (3rd ed., pp. 257–310). New York: Wiley.

Beutler, L.E., Machado, P.P.P., & Neufeldt, S.A. (1994). Therapist variables. In A.E. Bergin & S.L. Garfield, *Handbook of psychotherapy and behavior change* (4th ed., pp. 229–269). New York: Wiley.

Bickel, H. (1980). Phenylketonuria: Past, present, future. *Journal of Inherited Metabolic Disease, 3*, 123–312.

Bieling, P.J., Beck, A.T., & Brown, G.K. (2000). The sociotropy-autonomy scale: Structure and implications. *Cognitive Therapy and Research, 24*, 763–780.

Bienenfeld, L., Frishman, W., & Glasser, S.P. (1996). The placebo effect in cardiovascular disease. *American Heart Journal, 132*, 1207–1221.

Bierut, L.J., Heath, A.C., Bucholz, K.K., Dinwiddie, S.H., Madden, P.A.F., Statham, D.J., Dunne, M.P., & Martin, N.G. (1999). Major depressive disorder in a community-based twin sample: Are there different genetic and environmental contributions for men and women? *Archives of General Psychiatry, 56*, 557–563.

Bierut, L.M., Dinwiddie, S.H., Begleiter, H., Crowe, R.R., Hesselbrock, V., Nurnberger, J.I., Porjesz, B., Schuckit, M.A., & Reich, T. (1998). Familial transmission of substance dependence: Alcohol, marijuana, cocaine, and habitual smoking. *Archives of General Psychiatry, 55*, 982–988.

Binik, Y.M. (in press). Should dyspareunia be retained as a sexual dysfunction in DSM-V? A painful classification decision. *Archives of Sexual Behavior*.

Birch, D.E. (1992). Duty to protect: Update and Canadian perspective. *Canadian Psychology, 33*, 94–101.

Black, D.W., & Moyer, T. (1998). Clinical features and psychiatric comorbidity of subjects with pathological gambling behavior. *Psychiatric Services, 49*, 1434–1439.

Black, D.W., Noyes, R., Goldstein, R.B., & Blum, N. (1992). A family study of obsessive–compulsive disorder. *Archives of General Psychiatry, 49*, 362–368.

Black, P.H., & Garbutt, L.D. (2002). Stress, inflammation and cardiovascular disease. *Journal of Psychosomatic Research, 52*, 1–23.

Blair, R.J.R., et al. (2001). A selective impairment in the processing of sad and fearful expressions in children with psychopathic tendencies. *Journal of Abnormal Child Psychology, 29*, 491–498.

Blais, F.C., Gendron, L., Mimeault, V., & Morin, C.M. (1997). Evaluation de l'insomnie: Validation de trios questionnaires. *Encephale, 23*, 447–453.

Blanchard, D.C., Hebert, M., & Blanchard, R.J. (1999). Continuity versus (political) correctness: Animal models and human aggression. In M. Haug & R.E. Whalen (Eds.), *Animal models of human emotion and cognition* (pp. 297–316). Washington, DC: American Psychological Association.

Blanchard, E.B. (Ed.) (1992). Special issue on behavioral medicine. *Journal of Consulting and Clinical Psychology, 60*.

Blanchard, E.B. (1994). Behavioral medicine and health psychology. In A.E. Bergin & S.L. Garfield (Eds.), *Handbook of Psychotherapy and Behavior Change* (4th ed., pp. 701–733). New York: Wiley.

Blanchard, J.J., Horan, W.P., & Brown, S.A. (2001). Diagnostic differences in social anhedonia: A longitudinal study of schizophrenia and major depressive disorder. *Journal of Abnormal Psychology, 110*, 363–371.

Blanchard, R. (1989). The classification and labeling of nonhomosexual gender dysphorias. *Archives of Sexual Behavior, 18*, 315–334.

Blanchard, R., & Hucker, S.J. (1991). Age, transvestism, bondage, and concurrent paraphilic activities in 117 cases of autoerotic asphyxia. *British Journal of Psychiatry, 159*, 371–377.

Blanchard, R., Steiner, B.W., Clemmensen, L.H., & Dickey, R. (1989). Prediction of regrets in postoperative transsexuals. *Canadian Journal of Psychiatry, 34*, 43–45.

Bland, R.C. (1998). Psychiatry and the burden of mental illness. *Canadian Journal of Psychiatry, 43*, 801–810.

Bland, R.C., Newman, S.C., & Orn, H. (1988). Period prevalence of psychiatric disorders in Edmonton. *Acta Psychiatrica Scandinavica, 77* (suppl. 338), 33–42.

Bland, R.C., Newman, S.C., & Orn, H. (1990). Health care utilization for emotional problems: Results from a community survey. *Canadian Journal of Psychiatry, 35*, 397–400.

Bland, R.C., Newman, S.C., & Orn, H. (1997). Help-seeking for psychiatric disorders. *Canadian Journal of Psychiatry, 42*, 935–942.

Bland, R.C., Newman, S.C., Orn, H., & Stebelsky, G. (1993). Epidemiology of pathological gambling in Edmonton. *Canadian Journal of Psychiatry, 38*, 108–112.

Bland, R.C., Orn, H., & Newman, S.C. (1988). Lifetime prevalence of psychiatric disorders in Edmonton. *Acta Psychiatrica Scandinavica, 77* (suppl. 338), 24–32.

Blankstein, K.R., & Segal, Z.V. (2001). Cognitive assessment: Issues and methods. In K.S. Dobson (Ed.), *Handbook of cognitive-behavioral therapies* (2nd ed., pp. 40–85). New York: Guilford.

Blashfield, R.K., & McElroy, R.A. (1987). The 1985 literature on the personality disorders. *Comprehensive Psychiatry, 28*, 536–546.

Blashfield, R.K., & McElroy, R.A. (1989). Ontology of personality disorder categories. *Psychiatric Annals, 19*, 126–131.

Blatchford, C. (August 28, 2000). Montreux clinic shut but it could rise again. *National Post*.

Blazer, D.G. (1997). Generalized anxiety disorder and panic disorder in the elderly: A review. *Harvard Review of Psychiatry, 5*, 18–27.

Blennow, K., & Cowburn, R.F. (1996). The neurochemistry of Alzheimer's disease. *Acta Neurologica Scandinavia* (suppl. 168), 77–86.

Bleuler, M. (1978). *The Schizophrenic Disorders: Long-Term Patient and Family Studies*. New Haven, CT: Yale University Press.

Bliss, E.L. (1986). *Multiple Personality, Allied Disorders, and Hypnosis*. New York: Oxford University Press.

Bloch, S., & Crouch, E. (1987). *Therapeutic factors in group psychotherapy*. New York: Oxford University Press.

Blundell, J.E. (1995). The psychobiological approach to appetite and weight control. In K.D. Brownell & C.G. Fairburn (Eds.), *Eating Disorders and Obesity: A Comprehensive Handbook* (pp. 13–20). New York: Guilford.

Blustein, D.L., Juntunen, C.L., Worthington, R.L. (2000). The school-to-work transition: Adjustment challenges of the forgotten half. In S.D. Brown & R.W. Lent (Eds.), *Handbook of Counseling Psychology* (3rd ed., pp. 435–470). New York: Wiley.

Boileau, I., Assaad, J.-M., Pihl, R.O., Benkelfat, C., Leyton, M., Diksic, M., Tremblay, R.E., & Dagher, A. (2003). Alcohol promotes dopamine release in the human nucleus accumbens. *Synapse, 49*, 226–231.

Boland, R., & Keller, M.B. (1996). Outcome studies of depression in adulthood. In K.I. Shulman and M. Tohen (Eds.). *Mood Disorders Across the Life Span* (pp. 217–250). New York: Wiley-Liss.

Boland, R., & Keller, M.B. (2001). Chronic and recurrent depression: Pharmacotherapy and psychotherapy combinations. In J.F. Greden (Ed.), *Treatment of Recurrent Depression. Review of Psychiatry, 20* (pp. 59–80). Washington, DC: American Psychiatric Association.

Bolla, K.I., Cadet, J., & London, E.D. (1998). The neuropsychiatry of chronic cocaine abuse. *Journal of Neuropsychiatry and Clinical Neurosciences, 10*, 280–289.

Booth, A., et al. (2000). Biosocial perspectives on the family. *Journal of Marriage and the Family, 62*, 1018–1034.

Booth-Kewley, S., & Friedman, H.S. (1987). Psychological predictors of heart disease: A quantitative review. *Psychological Bulletin, 101*, 343–362.

Bootzin, R.R. (2000). Cognitive-behavioral treatment of insomnia: Knitting up the ravell'd sleave of care. In D.T. Kenny et al. (Eds.), *Stress and Health* (pp. 243–266). Sydney: Harwood Academic Press.

Borduin, C.M., Mann, B.J., Cone, L.T., Henggeler, S.W., Fucci, B.R., Blaske, D.M., & Williams, R.A. (1995). Multisystemic treatment of serious juvenile offenders: Long-term prevention of criminality and violence. *Journal of Consulting and Clinical Psychology, 63*, 569–578.

Borkovec, T.D., & Costello, E. (1993). Efficacy of applied relaxation and cognitive-behavioral therapy in the treatment of generalized anxiety disorder. *Journal of Consulting and Clinical Psychology, 61*, 611–619.

Borkovec, T.D., Newman, M.G., Pincus, A.L., & Lytle, R. (2002). A component analysis of cognitive-behavioral therapy for generalized anxiety disorder and the role of interpersonal problems. *Journal of Consulting and Clinical Psychology, 70*, 288–298.

Borkovec, T.D., Ray, W.J., & Stoeber, J. (1998). Worry: A cognitive phenomenon intimately linked to affective, physiological, and interpersonal behavioral processes. *Cognitive Therapy and Research, 22*, 561–576.

Bornstein, R.F. (1996). Dependency. In C.G. Costello (Ed.), *Personality characteristics of the personality disordered* (pp. 120–145). New York: Wiley-Interscience.

Bornstein, R.F. (1998). Dependency in the personality disorders: Intensity, insight, expression, and defense. *Journal of Clinical Psychology, 54*, 175–189.

Borum, R. (1996). Improving the clinical practice of violence risk assessment: Technology, guidelines, and training. *American Psychologist, 51*, 945–956.

Bosma, H.A., & Kunnen, E.S. (2001). Determinants and mechanisms in ego identity development: A review and synthesis. *Developmental Review, 21*, 39–66.

Bouchard, C. (2002). Genetic influences on body weight. In C.G. Fairbum & K.D. Brownell (Eds.), *Eating Disorders and Obesity* (2nd ed., pp.16–21). New York: Guilford.

Bouchard, S., Gauthier, J., Laberge, B., French, D., Pelletier, M.-H., & Godbout, C. (1996). Exposure versus cognitive restructuring in the treatment of panic disorder with agoraphobia. *Behaviour Research and Therapy, 34*, 213–224.

Bouchard, S., Payeur, R., Rivard, V., Allard, M., Paquin, B., Renaud, P., & Goyer, L. (2000). Cognitive behavior therapy for panic disorder with agoraphobia in videoconference: Preliminary results. *CyberPsychology and Behavior, 3*, 999–1007.

Boudreau, F., & Lambert, P. (1993). Compulsory community treatment? I. Ontario stakeholders' responses to "helping those who won't help themselves." *Canadian Journal of Community Mental Health, 12*, 57–78.

Bourin, M., Baker, G.B., & Bradwejn, J. (1998). Neurobiology of panic disorder. *Journal of Psychosomatic Research, 44*, 163–180.

Bower, G.H. (1990). Awareness, the unconscious, and repression: An experimental psychologist's perspective. In J.L. Singer (Ed.), *Repression and Dissociation* (pp. 209–232). Chicago: University of Chicago Press.

Bowlby, J. (1969). *Attachment*. New York: Basic Books.

Bowlby, J. (1973). *Separation: Anxiety and Anger*. New York: Basic Books.

Bowlby, J. (1979). *The Making and Breaking of Affectional Bonds*. London: Tavistock.

Bowlby, J. (1980). *Loss: Sadness and Depression*. New York: Basic Books.

Bowlby, J. (1982). Attachment and loss: Retrospect and prospect. *American Journal of Orthopsychiatry, 52*, 664–678.

Bowman, M.L. (1997). *Individual differences in posttraumatic response: Problems with the adversity-distress connection*. Mahwah, NJ: Erlbaum.

Bowman, M.L. (1999). Individual differences in posttraumatic distress: Problems with the DSM-IV model. *Canadian Journal of Psychiatry, 44*, 21–33.

Bowman, M.L. (2000). The diversity of diversity: Canadian-American differences and their implications for clinical training and APA accreditation. *Canadian Psychology, 41*, 230–243.

Boyd, C.P., Gullone, E., Needleman, G.L., & Burt, T. (1997). The Family Environment Scale: Reliability and normative data for an adolescent sample. *Family Process, 36*, 369–373.

Boyle, M.H., Offord, D.R., Hofmann, H.G., Catlin, G.P., Byles, J.A., Cadman, D.T., Crawford, J.W., Links, P.S., Rae-Grant, N.I., & Szatmari, P. (1987). Ontario Child Health Study: I. Methodology. *Archives of General Psychiatry, 44*, 826–831.

Boyle, M.H., Offord, D.R., Racine, Y.A., Fleming, J.E., et al. (1993). Predicting substance abuse in early adolescence based on parent and teacher assessments of childhood psychiatric disorder: Results from the Ontario Child Health Study follow-up. *Journal of Child Psychology and Psychiatry and Allied Disciplines, 34*, 535–544.

Boyle, M.H., Offord, D.R., Racine, Y.A., Szatmari, P., Fleming, J.E., & Links, P.S. (1992). Predicting substance use in late adolescence: Results from the Ontario Child Health Study follow-up. *American Journal of Psychiatry, 149*, 761–767.

Boyle, M.H., Offord, D.R., Racine, Y.A., Szatmari, P., Sanford, M., & Fleming, J.E. (1997). Adequacy of interviews vs checklists for classifying childhood psychiatric disorder based on parent reports. *Archives of General Psychiatry, 54*, 793–799.

Bradbury, T.N., & Fincham, F.D. (1990). Attributions in marriage: Review and critique. *Psychological Bulletin, 107*, 3–33.

Bradbury, T.N., Fincham, F.D., & Beach, S.R.H. (2000). Research on the nature and determinants of marital satisfaction: A decade in review. *Journal of Marriage and the Family, 62*, 964–980.

Bradford, D., Stroup. S., & Lieberman, J. (2002). Pharmacological treatments for schizophrenia. In P.E. Nathan and J.M. Gorman (Eds.), *A Guide to Treatments that Work* (2nd ed., pp. 169–199). London, England: Oxford University Press.

Bradford, J. (1997). Medical interventions in sexual deviance. In D.R. Laws & W.T. O'Donohue (Eds.), *Handbook of Sexual Deviance: Theory and Application* (pp. 449–464). New York: Guilford.

Bradford, J.M.W., & Pawlak, A. (1993). Double-blind placebo cross-over study of cyproterone acetate in the treatment of paraphilias. *Archives of Sexual Behavior, 22*, 383–402.

Bradley, C. (1937). The behavior of children receiving benzedrine. *American Journal of Psychiatry, 94*, 577–585.

Bradley, S.J., & Zucker, K.J. (1997). Gender identity disorder: A review of the past 10 years. *Journal of the American Academy of Child and Adolescent Psychiatry, 36*, 872–880.

Bradwejn, J., & Koszycki, D. (1995). Cholecystokinin and panic disorder. In G.M. Asnis & H.M. van Praag (Eds.), *Panic disorder: Clinical, biological, and treatment aspects* (pp. 233–254). New York: Wiley & Sons.

Brandon, T.H., Wetter, D.W., & Baker, T.B. (1996). Affect, expectancies, urges, and smoking: Do they conform to models of drug motivation and relapse? *Experimental and Clinical Psychopharmacology, 4*, 29–36.

Braun, B.G. (1989). Psychotherapy of the survivor of incest with a dissociative disorder. *Psychiatric Clinics of North America, 12*, 307–324.

Braun, D.L., Sunday, S.R., & Halmi, K.A. (1994). Psychiatric comorbidity in patients with eating disorders. *Psychological Medicine, 24*, 859–867.

Braun, P., Kochansky, G., Shapiro, R., et al. (1981). Overview: Deinstitutionalization of psychiatric patients: A critical review of outcome studies. *American Journal of Psychiatry, 138*, 736–749.

Breggin, P.R. (1994). *Talking back to Prozac*. New York: St. Martin's Press.

Bregman, J.D., Dykens, E., Watson, M., Ort, S.I., & Leckman, J.F. (1987). Fragile-X syndrome: Variability of phenotypic expression. *Journal of the American Academy of Child and Adolescent Psychiatry, 26*, 463–471.

Breitner, J.C.S., Gatz, M., Bergem, A.L.M., Christian, J.C., Mortimer, J.A., McClearn, G.E., Heston, L.L., Welsh, K.A., Anthony, J.C., Folstein, M.F., & Radebaugh, T.S. (1993). Use of twin cohorts for research in Alzheimer's disease. *Neurology, 43*, 261–267.

Brenner, M.H. (1973). *Mental Illness and the Economy*. Cambridge, MA: Harvard University Press.

Breslau, N., Davis, G.C., & Andreski, P. (1995). Risk factors for PTSD-related traumatic events: A prospective analysis. *American Journal of Psychiatry, 152*, 529–535.

Breslau, N., Davis, G.C., Andreski, P., and Peterson, E. (1991). Traumatic events and posttraumatic stress disorder in an urban population of young adults. *Archives of General Psychiatry, 48*, 216–222.

Breslau, N., Kessler, R.C., Chilcoat, H.D., Schultz, L.R., Davis, G.C., & Andreski, P. (1998). Trauma and post traumatic stress disorder in the community: The 1996 Detroit Area Survey of Trauma. *Archives of General Psychiatry, 55*, 626–632.

Breslin, C., Li, S., Sdao-Jarvie, K., Tupker, E., & Ittig-Deland, V. (2002). Brief treatment for young substance abusers: A pilot study in an addiction treatment setting. *Psychology of Addictive Behaviors, 16*, 10–16.

Breslow, N. (1989). Sources of confusion in the study and treatment of sadomasochism. *Journal of Social Behavior and Personality, 4*, 263–274.

Brestan, E.V., & Eyberg, S.M. (1998). Effective psychosocial treatments of conduct-disordered children and adolescents: 29 years, 82 studies, and 5, 272 kids. *Journal of Clinical Child Psychology, 27*, 180–189.

Breteler, M.M.B., Ott, A., & Hofman, A. (1998). The new epidemic: Frequency of dementia in the Rotterdam study. *Haemostasis, 28*, 117–123.

Brewer, C. (1996). On the specific effectiveness, and undervaluing, of pharmacological treatments for addiction: A comparison of methadone, naltrexone and disulfiram with psychosocial interventions. *Addiction Research, 3*, 297–313.

Brewerton, T.D., Lydiard, R.B., Herzog, D.B., Brotman, A.W., O'Neil, P.M., & Ballenger, J. (1995). Comorbidity of Axis I psychiatric disorders in bulimia nervosa. *Journal of Clinical Psychiatry, 56*, 77–80.

Brewin, C.R., Andrews, B., & Gotlib, I.H. (1993). Psychopathology and early experience: A reappraisal of retrospective reports. *Psychological Bulletin, 113*, 82–98.

Brewin, C.R., MacCarthy, B., Duda, K., et al. (1991). Attributions and expressed emotion in the relatives of patients with schizophrenia. *Journal of Abnormal Psychology, 100*, 546–554.

Brickman, J., & Briere, J. (1984). Incidence of rape and sexual assault in an urban Canadian population. *International Journal of Women's Studies, 7*, 195–206.

Brody, E.M., Saperstein, A.R., & Lawton, M.P. (1989). A multi-service respite program for caregivers of Alzheimer's patients. *Journal of Gerontological Social Work, 14*, 41–75.

Bromley, D.B. (1990). *Behavioral Gerontology: Central Issues in the Psychology of Ageing*. New York: Wiley.

Brown, A.S., Cohen, P., Harkavy-Friedman, J., Babulas, V., Malaspina, D., Gorman, J.M., & Susser, E.S. (2001). Prenatal rubella, premorbid abnormalities, and adult schizophrenia. *Biological Psychiatry, 49*, 473–486.

Brown, A.S., Susser, E.S., Jandorf, L., & Bromet, E.J. (2000). Social class of origin and cardinal symptoms of schizophrenic disorders over the early illness course. *Social Psychiatry and Psychiatric Epidemiology, 35*, 53–60.

Brown, G.W. (1998). Genetic and population perspectives on life events and depression. *Social Psychiatry and Psychiatric Epidemiology, 33*, 363–372.

Brown, G.W., Bifulco, A., & Harris, T.O. (1987). Life events, vulnerability and onset of depression: Some refinements. *British Journal of Psychiatry, 150*, 30–42.

Brown, G.W., Birley, J.L.T., & Wing, J.K. (1972). Influence of family life on the course of schizophrenic disorders: A replication. *British Journal of Psychiatry, 121*, 241–258.

Brown, G.W., & Harris, T.O. (1978). *Social origins of Depression: A Study of Psychiatric Disorder in Women*. London: Tavistock.

Brown, G.W., & Harris,T.O. (1993). Aetiology of anxiety and depressive disorders in an inner-city population. 1. Early adversity. *Psychological Medicine, 23*, 143–154.

Brown, L.S. (1992). A feminist critique of the personality disorders. In L.S. Brown & M. Ballou (Eds.), *Personality and Psychopathology: Feminist Reappraisals* (pp. 206–228). New York: Guilford.

Brown, P. (1994). Toward a psychobiological model of dissociation and post-traumatic stress disorder. In S.J. Lynn & J.W. Rhue (Eds.), *Dissociation: Clinical and Theoretical Perspectives* (pp. 94–122). New York: Guilford.

Brown, R. (1990). Limitations on expert testimony on the battered women syndrome in homicide cases: The return of the ultimate issue rule. *Arizona Law Review, 32*, 665–689.

Brown, S.A. (1993). Drug effect expectancies and addictive behavior change. *Experimental and Clinical Psychopharmacology, 1*, 55–67.

Brown, S.A., Tate, S.R., Vik, P.W., Haas, A.L., & Aarons, G.A. (1999). Modeling of alcohol use mediates the effect of family history of alcoholism on adolescent alcohol expectancies. *Experimental and Clinical Psychopharmacology, 7*, 20–27.

Brown, T.A., & Barlow, D.H. (1992). Comorbidity among anxiety disorders: Implications for treatment and DSM-IV. *Journal of Consulting and Clinical Psychology, 60*, 835–844.

Brown, T.A., Chorpita, B.F., & Barlow, D.H. (1998). Structural relationships among dimensions of the DSM-IV anxiety and mood disorders and dimensions of negative affect, positive affect, and autonomic arousal. *Journal of Abnormal Psychology, 107*, 179–192.

Brownell, K.D. (1995). Definition and classification of obesity. In K.D. Brownell & C.G. Fairburn (Eds.), *Eating Disorders and Obesity: A Comprehensive Handbook* (pp. 386–390). New York: Guilford.

Brownell, K.D., & Fairburn, C.G. (Eds.) (1995). *Eating Disorders and Obesity: A Comprehensive Handbook*. New York: Guilford.

Brownell, K.D., & Rodin, J. (1994). The dieting maelstrom: Is it possible and advisable to lose weight? *American Psychologist, 49*, 781–791.

Bruch, H. (1982). Anorexia nervosa: Therapy and theory. *American Journal of Psychiatry, 132*, 1531–1538.

Bryant, R.A., & Harvey, A.G. (2000). *Acute Stress Disorder: A Handbook of Theory, Assessment and Treatment*. Washington, DC: American Psychological Association.

Bryne, C.A., Resnick, H.S., Kilpatrick, D.G., Best, C.L., & Saunders, B.E. (1999). The socioeconomic impact of interpersonal violence on women. *Journal of Consulting and Clinical Psychology, 67*, 362–366.

Bryne, S.M. (2002). Sport, occupation, and eating disorders. In C.G. Fairburn & K.D. Brownell (Eds.), *Eating Disorders and Obesity* (2nd ed., pp. 256–259). New York: Guilford.

Bryson, S.E. (1996). Epidemiology of autism. *Journal of Autism and Developmental Disorders, 26*, 165–167.

Bucholz, K.K. (1999). Nosology and epidemiology of addictive disorders and their comorbidity. *Psychiatric Clinics of North America, 22*, 221–240.

Bucholz, K.K., Heath, A.C., Reich, T., Hesselbrock, V.M., et al. (1996). Can we subtype alcoholism? A latent class analysis of data from relatives of alcoholics in a multicenter family study of alcoholism. *Alcoholism: Clinical and Experimental Research, 20*, 1462–1471.

Bulik, C.M., Wade, T.D., & Kendler, K.S. (2000). Characteristics of monozygotic twins discordant for bulimia nervosa. *International Journal of Eating Disorders, 19*, 1–10.

Bullock, R. (2002). New drugs for Alzheimer's disease and other dementias. *British Journal of Psychiatry, 180*, 135–147.

Bullough, B., & Bullough, V. (1997). Are transvestites necessarily heterosexual? *Archives of Sexual Behavior, 26*, 1–11.

Burke, B.L., & McGee, D.P. (1990). Sports deficit disorder. *Pediatrics, 85*, 1118.

Burke, C. (1995). Foreword. In L. Nadel & D. Rosenthal (Eds.), *Down Syndrome: Living and Learning in the Community* (p. ix). New York: Wiley.

Burke, J.D., & Regier, D.A. (1996). Epidemiology of mental disorders. In R.E. Hales & S.C. Yudofsky (Eds.), *The American Psychiatric Press Synopsis of Psychiatry* (pp. 79–102). Washington, DC: American Psychiatric Press.

Burns, D.D. (1999). *Feeling Good: The New Mood Therapy* (revised edition). New York: Wholecare.

Burnside, S., & Cairns, A. (1995). *Deadly innocence: The true story of Paul Bernado, Karla Homolka, and the schoolgirl murders*. New York: Warner.

Burt, S.A., Krueger, R.F., McGue, M., & Iancono, W.G. (2001). Sources of covariation among attention-deficit/hyperactivity disorder, oppositional defiant disorder, and conduct disorder: The importance of shared environment. *Journal of Abnormal Psychology, 110*, 516–525.

Buss, A. (1991). The EAS theory of temperament. In J. Strelau & A. Angleitner (Eds.), *Explorations in Temperament* (pp. 43–60). New York: Plenum.

Buss, D.M. (1999). Human nature and individual differences: The evolution of human personality. In L.A. Pervin & O.P. John (Eds.), *Handbook of Personality: Theory and Research* (2nd ed., pp. 31–56). New York: Guilford.

Bustillo, J.R. Lauriello, J., Horan, W.P., & Keith, S.J. (2001). The psychosocial treatment of schizophrenia: An update. *American Journal of Psychiatry, 158*, 163–175.

Butcher, J.N., & Williams, C.L. (2000). *Essentials of MMPI-2 and MMPI-A Interpretation* (2nd ed.). Minneapolis, MN: University of Minnesota Press.

Butler, S.M., Ashford, J.W., & Snowdon, D.A. (1996). Age, education, and changes in the Mini-Mental State Exam scores of older women: Findings from the Nun Study. *Journal of the American Geriatrics Society, 44*, 675–681.

Byers, E.S., & Grenier, G. (2003). Premature or rapid ejaculation: Heterosexual couples' perceptions of men's ejaculatory behavior. *Archives of Sexual Behavior, 32*, 261–270.

Bystritsky, A., Pontillo, D., Powers, M., Sabb, F.W., Craske, M.G., & Bookheimer, S.Y. (2001). Functional MRI changes during panic anticipation and imagery exposure. *NeuroReport, 12*, 3953–3957.

Cacioppo, J.T., Bernston, G.G., Sheridan, J.F., & McClintock, M.K. (2000). Multilevel integrative analyses of human behavior: Social neuroscience and the complementing nature of social and biological approaches. *Psychological Bulletin, 126*, 829–843.

Cadieux, R.J. (1996). Azapirones: An alternative to benzodiazepines for anxiety. *American Family Physician, 53*, 2349–2353.

Cado, S., & Leitenberg, H. (1990). Guilt reactions to sexual fantasies during intercourse. *Archives of Sexual Behavior, 19*, 49–63.

Cadoret, R.J., Yates, W.R., Troughton, E., Woodworth, G., & Stewart, M.A. (1995). Genetic-environmental interaction in the genesis of aggressivity and conduct disorders. *Archives of General Psychiatry, 52*, 916–924.

Cairns, R.B., & Green, J.A. (1979). How to assess personality and social patterns: Observations or ratings? In R.B. Cairns (Ed.), *The Analysis of Social Interactions: Methods, Issues, and Illustrations* (pp. 209–226). Hillsdale, NJ: Erlbaum.

Cale, E.M., & Lilienfeld, S.O. (2002). Histrionic personality disorder and antisocial personality disorder: Sex-differentiated manifestations of psychopathy? *Journal of Personality Disorders, 16*, 52–72.

Calev, A., Guadino, E.A., Squires, N.K., & Zervas, I.M. (1995). ECT and memory cognition: A review. *British Journal of Clinical Psychology, 34*, 505–515.

Callahan, A.M., & Bauer, M.S. (1999). Psychosocial interventions for bipolar disorder. *Psychiatric Clinics of North America, 22*, 675–688.

Callahan, L.A., Steadman, H.J., McGreevy, M.A., & Robbins, P.C. (1991). The volume and characteristics of insanity defense pleas: An eight-state study. *Bulletin of the American Academy of Psychiatry and the Law, 19*, 331–338.

Callicott, J.H. (2001). Functional brain imaging in psychiatry: The next wave. In J.J. Morihisi (Ed.), *Advances in Brain Imaging. Review of Psychiatry, 20*, 1–24. Washington, DC: American Psychiatric Press.

Cameron, H.M., & McGoogan, E. (1981). A prospective study of 1152 hospital autopsies. II. Analysis of inaccuracies in clinical diagnoses and their significance. *Journal of Pathology, 133*, 285–300.

Cameron, N., & Rychlak, J.F. (1985). *Personality development and psychopathology: A dynamic approach*. Boston: Houghton Mifflin.

Campbell, E. (1990). The psychopath and the definition of "mental disease or defect" under the Model Penal Code test of insanity: A question of psychology or a question of law? *Nebraska Law Review, 69*, 190–229.

Campbell, M., Green, W.H., & Deutsch, S.I. (1985). *Child and Adolescent Psychopharmacology*. Beverly Hills, CA: Sage.

Campbell, R., Sefl, T., Barnes, H.E., Ahrens, C.E., Wasco, S.M., & Zaragoza-Diesfeld, Y. (1999). Community services for rape survivors: Enhancing psychological well-being or increasing trauma? *Journal of Consulting and Clinical Psychology, 67*, 847–858.

Canadian Cancer Society (2003a). *General cancer statistics*. Retrieved May 19, 2004, from http://www.cancer.ca/ccs/internet/standard/0,2283,3172_14423__langId-en,00.html

Canadian Cancer Society (2003b). *Lung cancer statistics*. Retrieved May 19, 2004, from http://www.cancer.ca/ccs/internet/standard/0,3182,3172_14459__langId-en,00.html

Canadian Centre for Justice Statistics (1999). Crime statistics in Canada. *Juristat, 20*(5), whole issue.

Canadian Committee on Sexual Offences Against Children and Youth (1984). *Report of the committee*. Ottawa: National Health and Welfare.

Canadian Pharmaceutical Association (2004). *Compendium of Pharmaceuticals and Specialties* (39th ed.). Ottawa: Author.

Canadian Psychological Association. (1991). *Canadian code of ethics for psychologists*. Ottawa: Author.

Canadian Study of Health and Aging (1994a). Canadian Study of Health and Aging: Study methods and prevalence of dementia. *Canadian Medical Association Journal, 150*, 899–913.

Canadian Study of Health and Aging (1994b). Risk factors for Alzheimer's disease in Canada. *Neurology, 44*, 2073–2080.

Canadian Study of Health and Aging (1994c). Patterns of caring for people with dementia in Canada. *Canadian Journal on Aging, 13*, 470–487.

Cannon, M., Jones, P.B., & Murray, R.M. (2002). Obstetric complications and schizophrenia: Historical and meta-analytic review. *American Journal of Psychiatry, 159*, 1080–1092.

Cannon, T.D. (1997). On the nature and mechanisms of obstetric influences in schizophrenia: A review and synthesis of epidemiologic studies. *International Review of Psychiatry, 9*, 387–397.

Cannon, T.D. (1998). Neurodevelopmental influences in the genesis and epigenesis of schizophrenia: An overview. *Applied and Preventive Psychology, 7*, 47–62.

Cannon, T.D., Kaprio, J., Loennqvist, J., Huttunen, M., & Koskenvuo, M. (1998). The genetic epidemiology of schizophrenia in a Finnish twin cohort: A population-based modeling study. *Archives of General Psychiatry, 55*, 67–74.

Cannon, T.D., Mednick, S.A., & Parnas, J. (1990). Antecedents of predominantly negative and predominantly positive-symptom schizophrenia in a high-risk population. *Archives of General Psychiatry, 47*, 622–632.

Cannon, T.D., Mednick, S.A., Parnas, J., Schulsinger, F., Praestholm, J., & Vestergaard, A. (1993). Developmental brain abnormalities in the offspring of schizophrenic mothers. I. Contributions of genetic and perinatal factors. *Archives of General Psychiatry, 50*, 551–564.

Cannon, W.B. (1935). Stress and strains of homeostasis. *American Journal of Medical Science, 189*, 1–14.

Cantwell, D.P., Baker, L., & Rutter, M. (1979). Families of autistic and dysphasic children. I. Family life and interactions patterns. *Archives of General Psychiatry, 36*, 682–687.

Caplan, L.R., Geldmacher, D.S., & Nyenuis, D.L. (1999). Distinguishing vascular dementia from Alzheimer's disease. *Patient Care, 33*, 71–79.

Caplan, P.J. (1995). *They Say You're Crazy: How the World's Most Powerful Psychiatrists Decide Who's Normal.* Reading: MA: Addison-Wesley.

Capron, C., & Duyme, M. (1989). Assessment of effects of socioeconomic status on IQ in a full cross-fostering study. *Nature, 340*, 552–554.

Cardno, A.G., Jones, L.A., Murphy, K.C., Sanders, R.D., Asherson, P., Owen, M.J., & McGuffin, P. (1998). Sibling pairs with schizophrenia or schizoaffective disorder: Associations of subtypes, symptoms and demographic variables. *Psychological Medicine, 28*, 815–823.

Carey, G., & Gottesman, I.I. (1996). Genetics and antisocial behavior: Substance versus sound bytes. *Politics and the Life Sciences*, March, 88–90.

Carlat, D.J., Camargo, C.A., & Herzog, D.B. (1997). Eating disorders in males: A report on 135 patients. *American Journal of Psychiatry, 154*, 1127–1132.

Carlson, E.A., & Sroufe, A. (1995). Contribution of attachment theory to developmental psychopathology. In D. Cicchetti & D.J. Cohen (Eds.), *Developmental Psychopathology* (Vol. 1, pp. 581–617). New York: Wiley.

Carlsson, A., Waters, N., Holm-Waters, S., Tedroff, J., Nilsson, M., & Carlsson, M.L. (2001). Interactions between monoamines, glutamate, and GABA in schizophrenia: New evidence. *Annual Review of Pharmacology and Toxicology, 41*, 237–260.

Carlsson, A., & Lindqvist, M. (1963). Effect of chlorpromazine and haloperidol on the formation of 3-methoxytyramine and normetanephrine in mouse brain. *Acta Pharmacology, 20*, 140.

Carmin, C.N., Pollard, C.A., & Gillock, K.L. (1999). Assessment of anxiety disorders in the elderly. In P.A. Lichtenberg (Ed.), *Handbook of Assessment in Clinical Gerontology* (pp. 59–90). New York: Wiley.

Carney, R.M., Freeland, K.E., Rich, M.W., & Jaffe, A.S. (1995). Depression as a risk factor for cardiac events in established coronary heart disease: A review of possible mechanisms. *Annals of Behavioral Medicine, 17*, 142–149.

Carpenter, W.T., McGuffin, P., Mellor, C.S., Torrey, E.F., et al. (1996). Commentaries on first-rank symptoms or rank-and-file symptoms? *British Journal of Psychiatry, 169*, 541–550.

Carpenter, W.T., & Strauss, J.S. (1991). The prediction of outcome in schizophrenia. IV. Eleven-year follow-up of the Washington IPSS cohort. *Journal of Nervous and Mental Disease, 179*, 517–525.

Carr. E.G. (1982). *How to Teach Sign Language to Developmentally Disabled Children.* Lawrence, KS: H & H Enterprises.

Carroll, R.A. (1999). Outcomes of treatment for gender dysphoria. *Journal of Sex Education and Therapy, 24*, 128–136.

Carstensen, L.L., Isaacowitz, D.M., & Charles, S.T. (1999). Taking time seriously: A theory of socioemotional selectivity. *American Psychologist, 54*, 165–181.

Carter, J.C., Olmsted, M.P., Kaplan, A.S., McCabe, R.E., Mills, J.S., & Aime, A. (2003). Self-help for bulimia nervosa: A randomized controlled trial. *American Journal of Psychiatry, 160*, 973–978.

Carter, J.R., & Neufeld, R.W.J. (1999). Cognitive processing of multidimensional stimuli in schizophrenia: Formal modeling of judgment speed and content. *Journal of Abnormal Psychology, 108*, 633–654.

Carver, C.S., &. Scheier, M.F. (1999). Optimism. In C.R. Snyder (Ed.), *Coping: The Psychology of What Works* (pp. 182–204). New York: Oxford University Press.

Carter, R. (1999). *Mapping the Mind.* Berkeley, CA: University of California Press.

Casey, P. (2001). Multiple personality disorder. *Primary Care Psychiatry, 7*, 7–11.

Cash, T.F., & Henry, P.E. (1995). Women's body images: The results of a national survey in the U.S.A. *Sex Roles, 33*, 19–28.

Caspi, A., Henry, B., McGee, R.O., Moffitt, T.E., et al. (1995). Temperamental origins of child and adolescent behavior problems: From age three to fifteen. *Child Development, 66*, 55–68.

Caspi, A., & Moffitt, T.E. (1995). The continuity of maladaptive behavior: From description to understanding in the study of antisocial behavior. In D. Cicchetti & D.J. Cohen (Eds.), *Developmental Psychopathology* (Vol. 1, pp. 472–511). New York: Wiley.

Cassidy, J. (1988). Child-mother attachment and the self in six-year-olds. *Child Development, 59*, 121–134.

Cassidy, J. (1995). Attachment and generalized anxiety disorder. In D. Cicchetti, S.L. Toth et al. (Eds.), *Emotion, Cognition, and Representation* (pp. 343–370). Rochester, NY: University of Rochester Press.

Cassidy, J., & Mohr, J.J. (2001). Unsolvable fear, trauma, and psychopathology: Theory, research, and clinical considerations related to disorganized attachment, across the life span. *Clinical Psychology: Science and Practice, 8*, 275–298.

Cattarin, J.A., & Thompson, J.K. (1994). A three-year longitudinal study of body image, eating disturbance, and general psychological functioning in adolescent females. *Eating Disorders: Journal of Treatment and Prevention, 2*, 114–125.

Cavell, T.A. (2001). Updating our approach to parent training. I: The case against targeting noncompliance. *Clinical Psychology: Science and Practice, 8*, 299–318.

CBC News Online (May 10, 2004). *David Reimer: The boy who lived as a girl.* http://www.cbc.ca/news/background/reimer/; retrieved June 30, 2004.

CCSA/CAMH (Canadian Centre on Substance Abuse and Centre for Addiction and Mental Health) (1999). *Canadian profile: Alcohol, tobacco and other drugs.* Ottawa: Author.

Chakos, M., Lieberman, J., Hoffman, E., Bradford, D., & Sheitman, B. (2001). Effectiveness of second-generation antipsychotics in patients with treatment-resistant schizophrenia: a review and meta-analysis of randomized trials. *American Journal of Psychiatry, 158*, 518–526.

Chakrabarti, S., & Fombonne, E. (2001). Pervasive developmental disorders in preschool children. *Journal of the American Medical Association 285*, 3093–3099.

Chamberlain, P., & Reid, J.B. (1998). Comparison of two community alternatives to incarceration for chronic juvenile offenders. *Journal of Consulting and Clinical Psychology, 66*, 624–633.

Chambless, D.L., & Ollendick, T.H. (2000). Empirically supported psychological interventions. Controversies and evidence. *Annual Review of Psychology, 52*, 685–716.

Charach, A., Ickowicz, A., & Schachar, R. (2004). Stimulant treatment over five years: Adherence, effectiveness, and adverse effects. *Journal of the American Academy of Child and Adolescent Psychiatry, 43*, 559–567.

Chassin, L., & DeLucia, C. (1996). Drinking during adolescence. *Alcohol Health and Research World, 20*, 175–180.

Chassin, L., Pitts, S.C., & DeLucia, C. (1999). The relation of adolescent substance use to young adult autonomy, positive activity involvement, and perceived competence. *Development and Psychopathology, 11*, 915–932.

Chen, W.J., Liu, S.K., Chang, C.J., Lien, Y.J., Chang, Y.H., & Hwu, H.G. (1998). Sustained attention deficit and schizotypal personality features in nonpsychotic relatives of schizophrenic patients. *American Journal of Psychiatry, 155*, 1214–1220.

Chess, S., & Thomas, A. (1984). *Origins and evolution of behavior disorders.* New York: Brunner-Mazel.

Chesselet, M., & Delfs, J.M. (1996). Basal ganglia and movement disorders: An update. *Trends in Neurosciences, 19*, 417–423.

Chiu, H.F.K., Lam, L.C.W., Chi, I., Leung, T., Li, S.W., Law, W.T., Chung, D.W.S., Fung, H.H.L, Kan, P.S., Lum, C.M., Ng, J., & Lau, J. (1998). Prevalence of dementia in Chinese elderly in Hong Kong. *Neurology, 50*, 1002–1009.

Chorpita, B.F., & Barlow, D.H. (1998). The development of anxiety: The role of control in the early environment. *Psychological Bulletin, 124*, 3–21.

Chorpita, B.F., Brown, T.A., & Barlow, D.H. (1998). Diagnostic reliability of the DSM-III-R anxiety disorders: Mediating effects of patient and diagnostician characteristics. *Behavior Modification, 22*, 307–320.

Christensen, A., & Jacobson, N.S. (1994). Who (or what) can do psychotherapy: The status and challenge of nonprofessional therapies. *Psychological Science, 5*, 8–14.

Christensen, H. (2001). What cognitive changes can be expected with normal ageing? *Australian and New Zealand Journal of Psychiatry 35*, 768–775.

Ciarnello, R.D., Aimi, J., Dean, R.R., Morilak, D.A., Porteus, M.H., & Cicchetti, D. (1995). Fundamentals of molecular neurobiology. In D. Cicchetti & D. Cohen (Eds.), *Developmental psychopathology* (pp. 109–160). New York: Wiley.

Cicchetti, D., & Beegly, M. (1990). *Children with Down Syndrome: A Developmental Perspective.* New York: Cambridge University Press.

Cicchetti, D., & Cohen, D. (Eds.) (1995). *Developmental psychopathology* (Vols. 1 & 2). New York: Wiley.

Ciompi, L. (1980). Catamnestic long-term study on the course of life and aging of schizophrenics. *Schizophrenia Bulletin, 6*, 606–618.

Cipparone, R.C. (1987). The defense of battered women who kill. *University of Pennsylvania Law Review, 135*, 427–452.

Clark, D.A. (1997). Twenty years of cognitive assessment: Current status and future directions. *Journal of Consulting and Clinical Psychology, 65*, 996–1000.

Clark, D. A. (2004). *Cognitive-behavior therapy for OCD.* New York: Guilford.

Clark, D.A., Beck, A.T., & Alford, B.A. (1999). *Scientific Foundations of Cognitive Theory and Therapy of Depression.* New York: Wiley.

Clark, D. A., & Purdon, C. L. (1995). The assessment of unwanted intrusive thoughts: A review and critique of the literature. *Behaviour Research and Therapy, 33*, 967–976.

Clark, D.C., & Goebel-Fabbri, A.E. (1999). Lifetime risk of suicide in major affective disorders. In D.G. Jacobs et al. (Eds.), *The Harvard Medical School Guide to Suicide Assessment and Intervention* (pp. 270–286). San Francisco: Jossey-Bass.

Clark, D.M. (1986). A cognitive approach to panic. *Behaviour Research and Therapy, 24*, 461–470.

Clark, D.M. (1999). Anxiety disorders: Why they persist and how to treat them. *Behaviour Research and Therapy, 37* (suppl.), 5–27.

Clark, L.A. (1999). Dimensional approaches to personality disorder assessment and diagnosis. In C.R. Cloninger (Ed.), *Personality and Psychopathology* (pp. 219–244). Washington, DC: American Psychiatric Press.

Clark, L.A., Livesley, W.J., & Morey, L. (1997). Personality disorder assessment: The challenge of construct validity. *Journal of Personality Disorders, 11*, 205–231.

Clark, L.A., & Watson, D. (1991). Tripartite model of anxiety and depression: Psychometric evidence and taxonomic implications. *Journal of Abnormal Psychology, 100*, 316–336.

Clark, R., Anderson, N.B., Clark, V.R., & Williams, D.R. (1999). Racism as a stressor for African Americans: A biopsychosocial model. *American Psychologist, 54*, 805–816.

Clarke, J.W. (1990). *On Being Mad or Merely Angry*. Princeton, NJ: Princeton University Press.

Clarkin, J.F., Foelsch, P.A., Levy, K.N., Hull. J.W., Delaney, J.C., & Kernberg, O.F., (2001). The development of a psychodynamic treatment for patients with borderline personality disorder: A preliminary study of behavioral change. *Journal of Personality Disorders, 15*, 487–495.

Clayton, D.O., & Shen, W.W. (1998). Psychotropic drug-induced sexual function disorders: Diagnosis, incidence and management. *Drug Safety, 19*, 299–312.

Cleckley, H. (1976). *The Mask of Sanity* (5th ed.). St. Louis: Mosby.

Cloninger, C.R. (1987). Neurogenetic adaptive mechanisms in alcoholism. *Science, 236*, 410–416.

Cloninger, C.R., Sigvardsson, S., & Bohman, M. (1996). Type I and type II alcoholism: An update. *Alcohol Health and Research World, 20*, 18–23.

Clyburn, L.D., Stones, M.J., Hadjistavropoulos, T., & Tuokko, H. (2000). Predicting caregiver burden and depression in Alzheimer's disease. *Journals of Gerontology: Series B: Psychological Sciences and Social Sciences, 55B*, S2–S13.

Cohen, C.I. (1993). Poverty and the course of schizophrenia: Implications for research and policy. *Hospital and Community Psychiatry, 44*, 951–958.

Cohen., J.G., Brown., J., Smailes, E.M., & Bernstein., D.P. (1999). Childhood maltreatment increases risk for personality disorders during early adulthood. *Archives of General Psychiatry, 56*, 600–606.

Cohen, M.S., & Bookheimer, S.Y. (1994). Localization of brain function using magnetic resonance imaging. *Trends in Neurosciences, 17*, 268–277.

Cohen, S., & Williamson. G.M. (1991). Stress and infectious disease in humans. *Psychological Bulletin, 109*, 5–24.

Cohen-Kettenis, P.T., & Gooren, L.J. (1999). Transsexualism: A review of etiology, diagnosis and treatment. *Journal of Psychosomatic Research, 46*, 315–333.

Cohler, B.J., & Nakamura, J.E. (1996). In J. Sadavoy, L.W. Lazarus, L.F. Jarvik, & G.T. Grossberg (Eds.), *Comprehensive Review of Geriatric Psychiatry II* (pp. 153–194). Washington, DC: American Psychiatric Press.

Coie, J., & Kupersmidt, J., (1983). A behavioral analysis of emerging social status in boys' groups. *Child Development, 54*, 1400–1416.

Colapinto, J. (2000). *As nature made him: The boy who was raised as a girl*. Toronto: HarperCollins.

Colapinto, J. (June 3, 2004). Gender gap: What were the real reasons behind David Reimer's suicide? *The Slate*. Extracted July 2, 2004, from http://slate.msn.com/id/2101678/

Cole, M.G., McCusker, J., Dendukuri, N., & Han, L. (2002). Symptoms of delirium among elderly medical inpatients with or without dementia. *Journal of Neuropsychiatry and Clinical Neuroscience 14*, 167–175.

Cole, W. (1992). Incest perpetrators: Their assessment and treatment. *Psychiatric Clinics of North America, 15*, 689–670.

Coles, E.M. (2000). The emperor in the courtroom: Psychology and pseudoscience. *Journal of Forensic Psychiatry, 11*, 1–6.

Coles, E.M., & Grant, F.E. (1999). The role of the expert witness in Canadian Dangerous Offender hearings. *Psychiatry, Psychology and Law, 6*, 13–21.

Collaer, M.L., & Hines, M. (1995). Human behavioral sex differences: A role for gonadal hormones during early development. *Psychological Bulletin, 118*, 55–107.

Collins, A. (1997). *In the sleep room: The story of the CIA brainwashing experiments in Canada*. Toronto: Key Porter.

Comas-Diaz, L. (2000). An ethnopolitical approach to working with people of color. *American Psychologist, 55*, 1319–1325.

Conduct Problems Prevention Research Group (1999). Initial impact of the Fast Track prevention trial for conduct problems: II. Classroom effects. *Journal of Consulting and Clinical Psychology, 67*, 648–657.

Conger, J.J. (1956). Alcoholism: Theory, problem, and challenge. II. Reinforcement theory and the dynamics of alcoholism. *Quarterly Journal of Studies on Alcohol, 17*, 296–305.

Conley, R.R., & Kelly, D.L. (2001). Management of treatment resistance in schizophrenia. *Biological Psychiatry, 50*, 898–911.

Conners, C.K. (1980). Artificial colors and the diet of disruptive behavior: Current status of research. In R.M. Knights & D.J. Bakker (Eds.), *Treatment of Hyperactive and Learning Disabled Children*. Baltimore: University Park Press.

*Consumer Reports* (1995, November). Mental health: Does therapy help?, 734–739.

Connor, T.J., Kelly, J.P., & Leonard, B.E. (1997). Forced swim test-induced neurochemical, endocrine, and immune changes in the rat. *Pharmacology, Biochemistry and Behavior, 58*, 961–967.

Conrod, P.J., Pihl, R.O., Stewart, S.H., & Dongier, M. (2000). Validation of a system of classifying female substance abusers on the basis of personality and motivational risk factors for substance abuse. *Psychology of Addictive Behaviors, 14*, 243–256.

Conrod, P.J., Stewart, S.H., Pihl, R.O., Cote, S., Fontaine, V., & Dongier, M. (2000). Efficacy of brief coping skills interventions that match different personality profiles of female substance abusers. *Psychology of Addictive Behaviors, 14*, 231–242.

Contrada, R.J. et al., (2001). Ethnicity-related sources of stress and their effects on wellbeing. *Current Directions in Psychological Science 9*, 136–139.

Cook, M., & Mineka, S. (1991). Selective associations in the origins of phobic fears and their implications for behavior therapy. In P.R. Martin (Ed.), *Handbook of Behavior Therapy and Psychological Science: An Integrative Approach* (pp. 413–434). New York: Pergamon.

Coons, P. (1986). The prevalence of multiple personality disorder. *Newsletter of the International Society for the Study of Multiple Personality and Dissociation, 4*, 6–8.

Coons, P.M., & Bowman, E.S. (2001). Ten-year follow-up study of patients with dissociative identity disorder. *Journal of Trauma and Dissociation, 2*, 73–89.

Coons, P., & Milstein, V. (1988). Psychogenic amnesia: A clinical investigation of 25 consecutive cases. Unpublished data cited in D. Spiegel & E. Cardena (1991). Disintegrated experience: The dissociative disorders revisited. *Journal of Abnormal Psychology, 100*, 366–378.

Cooper, P.J. (1995). Eating disorders and their relationship to mood and anxiety disorders. In K.D. Brownell & C.G. Fairburn (Eds.), *Eating Disorders and Obesity: A Comprehensive Handbook* (pp. 159–164). New York: Guilford.

Coovert, D.L., Kinder, B.N., & Thompson, J.K. (1989). The psychosexual aspects of anorexia nervosa and bulimia nervosa: A review of the literature. *Clinical Psychology Review, 9*, 169–180.

Copolov, D., Velakoulis, D., McGorry, P., Mallard, C., Yung, A., Rees, S., Jackson, G., Rehm, A., Brewer, W., & Pantelis, C. (2000). Neurobiological findings in early phase schizophrenia. *Brain Research Reviews, 31*, 157–165.

Corbitt, E.M. (2002). Narcissism from the perspective of the five-factor model. In P.T. Costa, Jr., & T.A. Widiger (Eds.), *Personality Disorders and the Five-Factor Model of Personality* (2nd ed., pp. 293–298). Washington, DC: American Psychological Association.

Cordova, J.V., Jacobson, N.S., Gottman, J.M., Rushe, R., & Cox, G. (1993). Negative reciprocity and communication in couples with a violent husband. *Journal of Abnormal Psychology, 102*, 559–564.

Cornelius, J.R., Salloum, I.M., Ehler, J.G., Jarrett, P.J., Cornelius, M.D., Perel, J.M, Thase, M.E., & Black, A. (1997). Fluoxetine in depressed alcoholics: A double-blind placebo-controlled trial. *Archives of General Psychiatry, 54*, 700–705.

Correctional Services Canada (2002). *Recidivism*. Ottawa: Author. Retrieved April 14, 2004 from http://www.csc-scc.gc.ca/text/pblct/forum/e052/e052h_e.shtml

Corse, C.D., Manuck, S.B., Cantwell, J.D., Giordani, B., & Matthews, K.A. (1982). Coronary-prone behavior pattern and cardiovascular response in persons with and without coronary heart disease. *Psychosomatic Medicine, 44*, 449–459.

Coryell, W., Endicott, J., Andreasen, N., & Keller, M. (1985). Bipolar I, bipolar II, and nonbipolar major depression among the relatives of affectively ill probands. *American Journal of Psychiatry, 142*, 817–821.

Coryell, W., Turvey, C., Endicott, J., Leon, A.C., Mueller, T., Solomon, D., & Keller, J. (1998). Bipolar I affective disorder: Predictors of outcome after 15 years. *Journal of Affective Disorders, 50*, 109–116.

Coryell, W., & Winokur, G. (1992). Course and outcome. In E.S. Paykel (Ed.), *Handbook of Affective Disorders* (2nd ed., pp. 89–110). New York: Guilford.

Coser, L.A. (1977). *Masters of Sociological Thought: Ideas in Historical and Social Context*. San Diego: Harcourt Brace Jovanovich.

Courchesne, E., et al. (2001). Unusual brain growth patterns in early life in patients with autistic disorder: An MRI study. *Neurology, 57*, 245–254.

Cowan, C.P., & Cowan, P.A. (1992). *When Partners Become Parents*. New York: Basic Books.

Cox, B.J., Enns, M.W., Walker, J.R., Kjernisted, K., & Pidlubny, S.R. (2001). Psychological vulnerabilities in patients with major depression vs panic disorder. *Behaviour Research and Therapy, 39*, 567–573.

Cox, B.J., Kwong, J., Michaud, V., & Enns, M.W. (2000). Problem and probable pathological gambling: Considerations from a community survey. *Canadian Journal of Psychiatry, 45*, 548–553.

Cox, B.J., McWilliams, L.A., & Clara, I.P. (2003). The structure of feared situations in a nationally representative sample. *Journal of Anxiety Disorders, 17*, 89–101.

Coyne, J.C. (1999). Thinking interactionally about depression: A radical restatement. In T. Joiner & J.C. Coyne (Eds.), *The Interactional Nature of Depression* (pp. 365–392). Washington, DC: American Psychological Association.

Coyne, J.C., Thompson, R., & Palmer, S.C. (2002). Marital quality, coping with conflict, marital complaints, and affection in couples with a depressed wife. *Journal of Family Psychology, 16*, 26–37.

Cox, B.J., & Taylor, S. (1999). Anxiety disorders: Panic and phobias. In T. Millon, P. Blaney, & R. Davis (Eds.), *Oxford textbook of psychopathology* (pp. 81–113). Oxford: Oxford University Press.

Crabbe, J.C. (2002). Genetic contributions to addiction. *Annual Review of Psychology, 53*, 435–462.

Craig, T.J., Siegel, C., Hopper, K., Lin, S., et al. (1997). Outcome in schizophrenia and related disorders compared between developing and developed countries: A recursive partitioning re-analysis of the WHO. *British Journal of Psychiatry, 170*, 229–233.

Craighead, W.E., & Miklowitz, D.J. (2000). Psychosocial interventions for bipolar disorder. *Journal of Clinical Psychiatry, 61* (suppl. 13), 58–64.

Cram, S.J., & Dobson, K.S. (1993). Confidentiality: Ethical and legal aspects for Canadian psychologists. *Canadian Psychology, 34*, 347–363.

Cramer, P. (2000). Defense mechanisms in psychology today: Further processes for adaptation. *American Psychologist, 55*, 637–646.

Craske, M. G., & Freed, S. (1995). Expectations about arousal and nocturnal panic. *Journal of Abnormal Psychology, 104*, 567–575.

Craske, M.G., & Rowe, M.K. (1997). Nocturnal panic. *Clinical Psychology: Science and Practice, 4*, 153–174.

Crawford, M., & Garnter, R. (1992). *Woman killing: Intimate femicide in Ontario, 1974–1990*. Toronto: Women We Honour Action Committee.

Crick, N.R., & Dodge, K.A. (1994). A review and reformulation of social information-processing mechanisms in children's social adjustment. *Psychological Bulletin, 115*, 74–101.

Crimlisk, H.L., Bhatia, K., Cope, H., David, A., Marsden, C.D., & Ron, M.A. (1998). Slater revisited: 6 year follow up of patients with medically unexplained motor symptoms. *British Medical Journal, 316*, 582–586.

Critelli, J.W., & Neumann, K.F. (1984). The placebo: Conceptual analysis of a construct in transition. *American Psychologist, 39*, 32–39.

Crits-Christoph, P. (1998). Psychosocial treatments for personality disorders. In P.E. Nathan & J.M. Gorman (Eds.), *A Guide to Treatments that Work* (pp. 544–553). New York: Oxford University Press.

Cronbach, L.J., & Meehl, P.E. (1955). Construct validity in psychological tests. *Psychological Bulletin, 52*, 281–302.

Cross-National Collaborative Panic Study. Second Phase Investigators. (1992). Drug treatment of panic disorder: Comparative efficacy of alprazolam, imipramine, and placebo. *British Journal of Psychiatry, 160*, 191–202.

Crowhurst, B., & Dobson, K.S. (1993). Informed consent: Legal issues and applications to clinical practice. *Canadian Psychology, 34*, 328–345.

Crozier, L., & Lane, P. (2001). *Addicted: Notes from the belly of the beast*. Vancouver, BC: Greystone Books.

Crozier, W.R., & Alden, L.E. (2001). *International handbook of social anxiety: Concepts, research, and interventions relating to the self and shyness*. New York: Wiley.

Csikszentmihalyi, M., & Larson, R. (1984). *Being Adolescent*. New York: Basic Books.

Cuckle, H. (2001). Time for a total shift to first trimester screening for Down syndrome. *The Lancet, 358*, 1658–1659.

Cummings, J.L., & Cole, G. (2002). Alzheimer disease. *Journal of the American Medical Association, 287*, 2335–2338.

Cummings, E.M., & Davies, P. (1994). *Children and Marital Conflict*. New York: Guilford.

Cummings, J.L., Vinters, H.V., Cole, G.M., & Khachaturian, Z.S. (1998). Alzheimer's disease: Etiologies, pathophysiology, cognitive reserve, and treatment opportunities. *Neurology, 51* (suppl. 1), S2–17.

Cunningham, D. (1997). Olson: From monster to moron. *Alberta Report*, 24(38), p. 27.

Cunningham, M.D., & Reidy, T.J. (1998). Antisocial personality disorder and psychopathy: Diagnostic dilemmas in classifying patterns of antisocial behavior in sentencing evaluations. *Behavioral Sciences and the Law, 16*, 333–351.

Curtis, C.E., Calkins, M.E., & Iacono, W.G. (2001). Saccadic disinhibition in schizophrenia patients and their first-degree biological relatives. *Experimental Brain Research, 137*, 228–236.

Dallaire, R. (2003). *Shake hands with the devil: The failure of humanity in Rwanda*. Toronto: Random House.

Daly, M.P. (1999). Diagnosis and management of Alzheimer disease. *Journal of the American Board of Family Practice, 12*, 375–385.

Danforth, J.S., Barkley, R.A., & Stokes, T.F. (1991). Observations of parent–child interactions with hyperactive children: Research and clinical implications. *Clinical Psychology Review, 11*, 703–727.

Davidson, J.R., DuPont, R.L., Hedges, D., & Haskins, J.T. (1999). Efficacy, safety, and tolerability of venlafaxine extended release and buspirone in outpatients with generalized anxiety disorder. *Journal of Clinical Psychiatry, 60*, 528–535.

Davidson, J.R.T. (2001). Pharmacotherapy of generalized anxiety disorder. *Journal of Clinical Psychiatry, 62* (suppl. 11), 46–50.

Davidson, J.R.T., & Meltzer-Brody, S.E. (1999). The underrecognition and undertreatment of depression: What is the breadth and depth of the problem? *Journal of Clinical Psychiatry, 60* (Suppl. 7), 4–9.

Davidson, P.R., & Parker, K.C.H. (2001). Eye movement desensitization and reprocessing (EMDR): A meta-analysis. *Journal of Consulting and Clinical Psychology, 69*, 305–316.

Davidson, R.J., Pizzagalli, D., Nitschke, J.B., & Putnam, K. (2002). Depression: Perspectives from affective neuroscience. *Annual Review of Psychology, 53*, 545–574.

Davidson, W.S., Redner, R., Blakely, C.H., Mitchell, C.M., & Emshoff, J.G. (1987). Diversion of juvenile offenders: An experimental comparison. *Journal of Consulting and Clinical Psychology, 55*, 68–75.

Davies, D.L. (1962). Normal drinking in recovered alcohol addicts. *Quarterly Journal of Studies on Alcohol, 23*, 94–104.

Davila, J. (2001). Refining the association between excessive reassurance seeking and depressive symptoms: The role of related interpersonal constructs. *Journal of Social and Clinical Psychology, 20*, 538–559.

Davis, B., Sheeber, L., Hops, H., & Tildesley, E. (2000). Adolescent responses to depressive parental behaviors in problem-solving interactions: Implications for depressive symptoms. *Journal of Abnormal Child Psychology, 28*, 451–465.

Davis, C., Shuster, B., Blackmore, E., & Fox, J. (2004). Looking good: Family focus on appearance and the risk for eating disorders. *International Journal of Eating Disorders, 35*, 136–144.

Davis, C., Shuster, B., Dionee, M., Claridge, G. (2001). Do you see what I see?: Facial attractiveness and weight preoccupation in college women. *Journal of Personality and Social Psychology, 20*, 147–160.

Davis, D., & Herdt, G. (1997). Cultural issues and sexual disorders. In T.A. Widiger, A.J. Frances, H.A. Pincus, R. Ross, M.B. First, and W. Davis (Eds.), *DSM-IV Sourcebook* (Vol. 3, pp. 951–958). Washington, DC: American Psychiatric Press.

Davis, D.L. (1998). The sexual and gender identity disorders. *Transcultural Psychiatry, 35*, 401–412.

Davis, G.C., & Akiskal, H.S. (1986). Descriptive, biological, and theoretical aspects of borderline personality disorder. *Hospital and Community Psychiatry, 37*, 685–692.

Davis, S. (1993). Changes to the *Criminal Code* provisions for mentally disordered offenders and their implications for Canadian psychiatry. *Canadian Journal of Psychiatry, 38*, 122–126.

Davis, S. (1994). Fitness to stand trial in Canada in light of the recent criminal code amendments. *International Journal of Law and Psychiatry, 17*, 319–329.

Dawson, D.A. (2000). Drinking patterns among individuals with and without DSM-IV alcohol use disorders. *Journal of Studies on Alcohol, 61*, 111–125.

de Beurs, E., Beekman, A., Geerlings, S., Deeg, D., van Dyck, R., & van Tilburg, W. (2001). On becoming depressed or anxious in late life: Similar vulnerability factors but different effects of stressful life events. *British Journal of Psychiatry, 179*, 426–431.

DeKeseredy, W.S. (1997). Measuring sexual abuse in Canadian university/college dating relationships. In M.D. Schwartz (Ed.), *Researching sexual violence against women* (pp. 43–53). Thousand Oaks, CA: Sage.

DeLeon, P.H., Sammons, M.T., & Sexton, J.L. (1995). Focusing on society's real needs: Responsibility and prescription privileges. *American Psychologist, 50*, 1022–1032.

Delespaul, P., deVries, M., & van Os, J. (2002). Determinants of occurrence and recovery from hallucinations in daily life. *Social Psychiatry and Psychiatry Epidemiology, 37*, 97–104.

DeLongis, A., Coyne, J.C., Dakof, G., Folkman, S., & Lazarus, R.S. (1982). Relationship of daily hassles, uplifts, and major life events to health status. *Health Psychology, 1*, 119–136.

DeLongis, A., Folkman, S., & Lazarus, R.S. (1988). The impact of daily stress on health and mood: Psychological and social resources as mediators. *Journal of Personality and Social Psychology, 54*, 486–495.

de Man, A.F., Gutierrez, B.I.B., & Sterk, N. (2001). Stability as a moderator of the relationship between level of self-esteem and depression. *North American Journal of Psychology, 3*, 303–308.

D'Emilio, J., & Freedman, E.B. (1988). *Intimate Matters: A History of Sexuality in America*. New York: Harper & Row.

Denov, M.S. (2001). Culture of denial: Exploring professional perspectives on female sex offending. *Canadian Journal of Criminology, 43*, 303–329.

DePaulo, J.R., & Horvitz, L.A. (2002). *Understanding Depression: What We Know and What You Can Do About it*. New York: Wiley.

Dershowitz, A.M. (1994). *The Abuse Excuse and Other Cop-outs, Sob Stories, and Evasions of Responsibility*. Boston: Little-Brown.

DeRubeis, R.J., Gelfand, L.A., Tang, T.Z., & Simons, A.D. (1999). Medications versus cognitive behavior therapy for severely depressed outpatients: Mega-analysis of four randomized comparisons. *American Journal of Psychiatry, 156*, 1007–1013.

Deschesnes, M. (1998). Étude de la validité et de la fidélité de l'Indice de détresse psychologique de Santé Québéc (IDPSQ-14), chez une population adolescente. *Canadian Psychology, 39*, 288–298.

de Silva, P. (1993). Fetishism and sexual dysfunction: Clinical presentation and management. *Sexual and Marital Theraphy, 8*, 147–155.

Dhawan, S., & Marshall, W.L. (1996). Sexual abuse histories of sexual offenders. *Sexual Abuse: Journal of Research and Treatment, 8*, 7–15.

Devanand, D.P., & Levy, S.T. (1995). Neuroleptic treatment of agitation and psychosis in dementia. *Journal of Geriatric Psychiatry and Neurology*, 8, (suppl. 1), S18–S27.

DeVane, C.L., & Sallee, F.R. (1996). Serotonin selective reuptake inhibitors in child and adolescent psychopharmacology: A review of published evidence. *Journal of Clinical Psychiatry*, 57, 55–66.

DeWit, D. J., Hance, J., Offord, D.R., & Ogborne, A. (2000). The influence of early and frequent use of marijuana on the risk of desistance and of progression to marijuana-related harm. *Preventive Medicine*, 31, 455–464.

Dezwirek, L., Wolfe, D.A., & Gowdey, K. (1996). Children and the courts in Canada. In B.L. Bottoms & G.S. Goodman (Eds.), *International perspectives on child abuse and children's testimony* (pp. 77–95). Thousand Oaks, CA: Sage.

Dhawan, S., & Marshall, W.L. (1996). Sexual abuse histories of sexual offenders. *Sexual Abuse: Journal of Research and Treatment*, 8, 7–15.

Diamond, M. (1982). Sexual identity, monozygotic twins reared in discordant sex roles and a BBC follow-up. *Archives of Sexual Behavior*, 11, 181–186.

Diamond, M., & Sigmundson, H.K. (1997). Sex reassignment at birth. Long-term review and clinical implications. *Archives of Pediatrics & Adolescent Medicine*. 151, 298–304.

Dick, L. (1995). "Pibloktoq" (arctic hysteria): A construction of European–Inuit relations? *Arctic Anthropology*, 32, 1–42.

Dickens, C. (1842/1970). *American Notes and Pictures from Italy*. New York: Oxford University Press.

Dickens, B.M., Doob, A.N., Warwick, O.H., & Winegard, W.C. (1982). *Report of the Committee of Enquiry into Allegations Concerning Drs. Linda and Mark Sobell*. Toronto: Addiction Research Foundation.

Dickens, W.T., & Flynn, J.R. (2001). Heritability estimates versus large environmental effects: The IQ paradox resolved. *Psychological Review*, 108, 346–369.

Dickson, D.W. (2001). Neuropathology of Alzheimer's disease and other dementias. *Clinics in Geriatric Medicine*, 17, 209–228.

Digman, J.M. (2002). Historical antecedents of the five-factor model. In P.T. Costa, Jr., & T.A. Widiger (Eds.), *Personality Disorders and the Five-Factor Model of Personality* (2nd ed., pp. 17–22). Washington, DC: American Psychological Association.

Dimeff, L.A., McDavid, J., & Linehan, M.M. (1999). Pharmacotherapy for borderline personality disorder: A review of the literature and recommendations for treatment. *Journal of Clinical Psychology in Medical Settings*, 6, 113–138.

Dineen, T. (August 15, 2002). Peggy Claude-Pierre: Angel for anorexics or misguided amateur? *Vancouver Sun*. Retrieved June 15, 2004, from http://tanadineen.com/columnist/columns/montreuxclinic.htm

Dingle, G., Samtani, P., Kraatz, J., & Solomon, R. (2002). *The real facts on alcohol use, injuries and deaths*. Mississauga, ON: MADD.

Dishion, T.J., French, D.C., & Patterson, G.R. (1995). The development and ecology of antisocial behavior. In D. Cicchetti & D.J. Cohen (Eds.), *Developmental Psychopathology* (Vol. 1, pp. 421–471). New York: Wiley.

Dishion, T.J, McCord, J., & Poulin, F. (1999). When interventions harm: Peer groups and problem behavior. *American Psychologist*, 54, 755–764.

Ditton, P.M. (1999). *Mental Health and Treatment of Inmates and Probationers*. Washington, DC: Bureau of Justice Statistics.

Dobson, D.J.G., McDougall, G., Busheikin, J., & Aldous, J. (1995). Effects of social skills training and social milieu treatment on symptoms of schizophrenia. *Psychiatric Services*, 46, 376–380.

Dobson, K.S. (2002). A national imperative: Public funding of psychological services. *Canadian Psychology*, 43, 65–75.

Dohrenwend, B.P., Link, B.G., Kern, R., Shrout, P.E., & Markowitz, J. (1990). Measuring life events: The problem of variability within event categories. *Stress Medicine*, 6, 179–187.

Dolan-Sewell, R.T., Krueger, R.F., & Shea, M.T. (2001). Co-occurrence with syndrome disorders. In W.J. Livesley (Ed.), *Handbook of Personality Disorders: Theory, Research, and Treatment* (pp. 84–104). New York: Guilford.

Donahey, K.M., & Carroll, R.A. (1993). Gender differences in factors associated with hypoactive sexual desire. *Journal of Sex and Marital Therapy*, 19, 25–40.

Donavan, D.M. (1999). Efficacy and effectiveness: Complementary findings from two multisite trials evaluating outcomes of alcohol treatments differing in theoretical orientations. *Alcoholism: Clinical and Experimental Research*, 23, 564–572.

Dorian, B.J., & Garfinkel, P.E. (1999). The contributions of epidemiologic studies to the etiology and treatment of the eating disorders. *Psychiatric Annals*, 29, 187–192.

Dotti, M.T., et al. (2002). A Rett syndrome MECP2 mutation that causes mental retardation in men. *Neurology*, 58, 226–230.

Douglas, K.S., Ogloff, J.R.P., Nicholls, T.L., & Grant, I. (1999). Assessing risk for violence among psychiatric patients: The HCR-20 violence risk assessment scheme and the Psychopathy Checklist: Screening Version. *Journal of Consulting and Clinical Psychology*, 67, 917–930.

Douglas, K.S., & Webster, C.D. (1999). The HCR-20 violence risk assessment scheme: Concurrent validity in a sample of incarcerated offenders. *Criminal Justice and Behavior*, 26, 3–19.

Douglas, V.I. (1972). Stop, look, and listen: The problem of sustained attention and impulse control in hyperactive and normal children. *Canadian Journal of Behavioural Science*, 4, 259–282.

Douglas, V.I. (1983). Attention and cognitive problems. In M. Rutter (Ed.), *Developmental Neuropsychiatry* (pp. 280–329). New York: Guilford.

Douglas, V.I., & Peters, K.G. (1979). Toward a clearer definition of the attentional deficit of hyperactive children. In G.A. Hale & M. Lewis (Eds.), *Attention and the development of cognitive skills* (pp. 173–248). New York: Plenum.

Dozois, D.J.A., Covin, R., & Brinker, J.K. (2003). Normative data on cognitive measures of depression. *Journal of Consulting and Clinical Psychology*, 71, 71–80.

Dozois, D.J.A., & Dobson, K.S. (1995a). Should Canadian psychologists follow the APA trend and seek prescription privileges?: A reexamination of the (r)evolution. *Canadian Psychology*, 36, 288–304.

Dozois, D.J.A., & Dobson, K.S. (1995b). Psychology's heritage and prescription privileges: An unconsummatable marriage. *Canadian Psychology*, 36, 327–332.

Dozois, D.J.A., & Dobson, K.S. (2001). Information processing and cognitive organization in unipolar depression: Specificity and comorbidity issues. *Journal of Abnormal Psychology*, 110, 236–246.

Dozois, D.J.A., & Dobson, K.S. (2002). Depression. In M.M. Antony & R.P. Swinson (Eds.), *Handbook of assessment and treatment planning for psychological disorders* (pp. 259–299). New York: Guilford Press.

Draguns, J.G. (1994). Pathological and clinical aspects. In L.L. Adler & U.P. Gielen (Eds.), *Cross-Cultural Topics in Psychology* (pp. 165–178). Westport, CT: Praeger.

Drevets, W.C. (1999). Prefrontal cortical-amygdalar metabolism in major depression. *Annals of the New York Academy of Sciences*, 877, 614–637.

Drevets, W.C., & Raichle, M.E. (1998). Reciprocal suppression of regional cerebral blood flow during emotional versus higher cognitive processes: Implications for interactions between emotion and cognition. *Cognition and Emotion*, 12, 353–385.

Drobes, D.J., Stritzke, W.G.K., & Coffey, S.F. (2000). Psychophysiological factors. In M. Hersen and A.S. Bellack (Eds.), *Psychopathology in Adulthood* (2nd ed., pp. 112–130). Needham Heights, MA: Allyn & Bacon.

Dugas, M.J., Gagnon, F., Ladouceur, R., & Freeston, M.H. (1998). Generalized anxiety disorder: A preliminary test of a conceptual model. *Behaviour Research and Therapy*, 36, 215–226.

Dugas, M.J., & Koerner, N. (in press). The cognitive-behavioral treatment of generalized anxiety disorder: Current status and future directions. *Journal of Cognitive Psychotherapy*.

Dugas, M., Ladouceur, R., Leger, E., Freeston, M.H., Langlois, F., Provencher, M.D., & Boisvert, J.-M. (2003). Group cognitive-behavioral therapy for generalized anxiety disorder: Treatment outcome and long-term follow-up. *Journal of Consulting and Clinical Psychology*, 71, 821–825.

Duhig, A.M., Renk, K., Epstein, M.K., & Phares, V. (2000). Interparental agreement on internalizing, externalizing, and total behavior problems: A meta-analysis. *Clinical Psychology: Science and Practice*, 7, 435–453.

Dunkin, J.J., & Anderson-Hanley, C. (1998). Dementia caregiver burden: A review of the literature and guidelines for assessment and intervention. *Neurology*, 51 (suppl. 1), 53–59.

Durham, M.L., & LaFond, J.Q. (1988). A search for the missing premise of involuntary therapeutic commitment: Effective treatment of the mentally ill. *Rutgers Law Review*, 40, 303–368.

Durkheim, E. (1897/1951). *Suicide: A Study in Sociology*. New York: Free Press.

Dusseldorp, E., van Elderen, T., Maes, S., Meulman, J., & Kraaij, V. (1999). A meta-analysis of psychoeducational programs for coronary heart disease patients. *Health Psychology*, 18, 506–519.

Dutton, D.G. (1995). *The batterer: A psychological profile*. New York: Basic Books.

Dworkin, R.H., Oster, H., Clark, S.C., & White, S.R. (1998). Affective expression and affective experience in schizophrenia. In M.F. Lenzenweger & R.H. Dworkin (Eds.), *Origins and Development of Schizophrenia: Advances in Experimental Psychopathology* (pp. 385–424). Washington, DC: American Psychological Association.

Dyk, P.H., & Adams, G.R. (1990). Identity and intimacy: An initial investigation of three theoretical models using cross-lag panel correlations. *Journal of Youth and Adolescence*, 19, 91–110.

D'Zurilla, T., & Goldfried, M. (1971). Problem solving and behavior modification. *Journal of Abnormal Psychology*, 78, 107–126.

Earls, F., & Mezzacappa, E. (2002). Conduct and oppositional disorders. In M. Rutter & E. Taylor (Eds.), *Child and Adolescent Psychiatry* (4th ed., pp. 419–436). Oxford, UK: Blackwell.

Earnst, K.S., & Kring, A.M. (1997). Construct validity of negative symptoms: An empirical and conceptual review. *Clinical Psychology Review*, 17, 167–190.

Eastwood, M.R., & Merskey, H. (1996). Dementia. In Q. Rae-Grant (Ed.), *Images in psychiatry: Canada* (pp. 241–243). Washington, DC: American Psychiatric Press.

Eaton, W.W., Anthony, J.C., Romanoski, A., Tien, A., Gallo, J., Cai, G., Neufeld, K., Schlaepfer, T., Laugharne, J., & Chen, L.S. (1998). Onset and recovery from panic disorder in the Baltimore Epidemiologic Catchment Area follow-up. *British Journal of Psychiatry*, 173, 501–507.

Ebly, E.M., Parhad, I.M., Hogan, D.B., & Fung, T.S. (1994). Prevalence and types of dementia in the very old: Results from the Canadian Study of Health and Aging. *Neurology, 44*, 1593–1600.

Eddy, K.T., Keel, P.K., Dorer, D.J., Delinsky, S.S., Franko, D.L., & Herzog, D.B. (2002). Longitudinal comparison of anorexia nervosa subtypes. *International Journal of Eating Disorders, 31*, 191–201.

Edwards, V. (2002). *Depression and bipolar disorders.* Toronto: Key Porter.

Egeland, J.D., & Sussex, J.N. (1985). Suicide and family loading for affective disorders. *Journal of the American Medical Association, 254*, 915–918.

Ehlers, A., & Clark, D.M. (2000). A cognitive model of persistent posttraumatic stress disorder. *Behaviour Research and Therapy, 38*, 319–345.

Ehlers, A., Mayou, R.A., & Bryant, B. (1998). Psychological predictors of chronic posttraumatic stress disorders after motor vehicle accidents. *Journal of Abnormal Psychology, 107*, 508–519.

Eich, E., Macaulay, D., Lowenstein, R.J., & Dihle, P.H. (1997). Memory, amnesia, and dissociative identity disorder. *Psychological Science, 8*, 417–422.

Eisenberg, N., Shepard, S.A., Fabes, R.A., Murphy, B.C., & Guthrie, I.K. (1998). Shyness and children's emotionality, regulation, and coping: Contemporaneous, longitudinal, and across-context relations. *Child Development 69*, 767–790.

Ekselius, L., Tillfors, M., Furmark, T., & Fredrikson, M. (2001). Personality disorders in the general population: DSM-IV and ICD-10 defined prevalence as related to sociodemographic profile. *Personality and Individual Differences, 30*, 311–320.

Ellason, J.W., & Ross, C.A. (1997).Two-year follow-up of inpatients with dissociative identity disorder. *American Journal of Psychiatry, 154*, 832–839.

Elliot, S., Odynak, D., & Krahn, H. (1992). *A survey of unwanted sexual experiences among University of Alberta students.* Research report prepared for the Council on Student Life. University of Alberta: Population Research Laboratory.

Ellis, A. (1962). *Reason and Emotion in Psychotherapy.* New York: Lyle Stuart.

Ellis, A. (1973). *Humanistic psychotherapy: The rational-emotive approach.* New York: McGraw-Hill.

Ellis, A. (1999). Early theories and practices of rational-emotive behavior therapy and how they have been augmented and revised during the last three decades. *Journal of Rational-Emotive and Cognitive Behavior Therapy, 17*, 69–93.

Emery, R.E. (1982). Interparental conflict and the children of discord and divorce. *Psychological Bulletin, 92*, 310–330.

Emery, R.E. (1992). Family conflict and its developmental implications: A conceptual analysis of deep meanings and systemic processes. In C.U. Shantz & W.W. Hartup (Eds.), *Conflict in Child and Adolescent Development* (pp. 270–298). London: Cambridge University Press.

Emery, R.E. (1994). *Renegotiating Family Relationships: Divorce, Child Custody, and Mediation.* New York: Guilford.

Emery, R.E. (1999a). *Marriage, Divorce, and Children's Adjustment* (2nd ed.). Thousand Oaks, CA: Sage.

Emery, R.E. (1999b). Changing the rules for determining child custody in divorce cases. *Clinical Psychology: Science and Practice, 6*, 323–327.

Emery, R.E., Fincham, F.D., & Cummings, E.M. (1992). Parenting in context: Systemic thinking about parental conflict and its influence on children. *Journal of Consulting and Clinical Psychology, 60*, 909–912.

Emery, R.E., & Laumann-Billings, L. (1998). An overview of the nature, causes, and consequences of abuse family relationships: Toward differentiating maltreatment and violence. *American Psychologist, 53*, 121–135.

Emery, R.E., & Laumann-Billings, L. (2002). In M. Rutter & E. Taylor (Eds.), *Child and Adolescent Psychiatry* (4th ed., pp. 325–339). Oxford, UK: Blackwell.

Emery, R.E., Laumann-Billings, L., Waldron, M., Sbarra, D.A., and Dillon, P. (2001). Child custody mediation and litigation: Custody, contact, and co-parenting 12 years after initial dispute resolution. *Journal of Consulting and Clinical Psychology, 69*, 323–332.

Emery, R.E., & Marholin, D. (1977). An applied behavior analysis of delinquency: The irrelevancy of relevant behavior. *American Psychologist, 32*, 860–873.

Emery, R.E., Matthews, S., & Kitzmann, K. (1994). Child custody mediation and litigation: Parents' satisfaction and functioning a year after settlement. *Journal of Consulting and Clinical Psychology, 62*, 124–129.

Emery, R.E., & Rogers, K.C. (1990). The role of behavior therapists in child custody cases. In M. Hersen & R.M. Eisler (Eds.), *Progress in Behavior Modification* (pp. 60–89). Beverly Hills: Sage.

Emery, R.E., Waldron, M.C., Kitzmann, K.M., & Aaron, J. (1999). Delinquent behavior, future divorce or nonmarital childbearing, and externalizing behavior among offspring: A 14-year prospective study. *Journal of Family Psychology, 13*, 1–12.

Emmanuel, J., Simmonds, S., & Tyrer, P. (1998). Systematic review of the outcome of anxiety and depressive disorders. *British Journal of Psychiatry, 173* (suppl. 34), 35–41.

Emmons, R.A. (1997). Motives and goals. In R. Hogan, J. Johnson, & S. Briggs (Eds.), *Handbook of Personality Psychology* (pp. 486–512). San Diego, CA: Academic Press.

Emrick, C.D. (1999). Alcoholics anonymous and other 12-step groups. In M. Galanter & H.D. Kleber (Eds.), *Textbook of Substance Abuse Treatment* (2nd ed., pp. 403–411). Washington, DC: American Psychiatric Press.

Endler, N.S. (1982). *Holiday of darkness: A psychologist's personal journey out of his depression.* Toronto: Wiley.

Endler, N.S. (1990). *Holiday of darkness: A psychologist's personal journey out of his depression (rev. ed.).* Toronto: Wall & Emerson.

Endler, N.S. (1997). Stress, anxiety and coping: The multidimensional interaction model. *Canadian Psychology, 38*, 136–153.

Endler, N.S., Crooks, D.S., & Parker, J.D.A. (1992). The interaction model of anxiety: An empirical test in a parachute jumping situation. *Anxiety, Stress, and Coping, 5*, 301–311.

Eng, W., Heimberg, R.G., Hart, T.A., Schneier, F.R., & Liebowitz, M.R. (2001). Attachment in individuals with social anxiety disorder: The relationship among adult attachment styles, social anxiety, and depression. *Emotion, 1*, 365–380.

Ennis, B., & Emery, R. (1978). *The Rights of Mental Patients.* New York: Avon.

Epstein, N.B., Baldwin, L.M., & Bishop, D.S. (1983). The McMaster Family Assessment Device. *Journal of Marital and Family Therapy, 9*, 171–182.

Epstein, S. (1994). Integration of the cognitive and the psychodynamic unconscious. *American Psychologist, 49*, 709–724.

Erdelyi, M.H. (1990). Repression, reconstruction, and defense: History and integration of the psychoanalytic and experimental frameworks. In J.L. Singer (Ed.), *Repression and Dissociation* (pp. 1–32). Chicago: University of Chicago Press.

Erickson, D.H., Beiser, M., & Iacono, W.G. (1998). Social support predicts 5-year outcome in first-episode schizophrenia. *Journal of Abnormal Psychology, 107*, 681–685.

Erickson, D.H., Beiser, M., & Iacono, W.G., Fleming, J.A.E., & Lin, T. (1989). The role of social relationships in the course of first-episode schizophrenia and affective psychosis. *American Journal of Psychiatry, 146*, 1456–1461.

Erikson, E.H. (1959, 1980). *Identity and the Life Cycle.* New York: Norton.

Erikson, E.H. (1968). *Identity: Youth and Crisis.* New York: Norton.

Erlenmeyer-Kimling, L., Squires-Wheeler, E., Adamo, U.H., Bassett, A.S., Cornblatt, B.A., Kestenbaum, C.J., Rock, D., Roberts, S.A., & Gottesman, I.I. (1995). The New York high-risk project: Psychoses and cluster: A personality disorders in offspring of schizophrenic parents at 23 years of follow-up. *Archives of General Psychiatry, 52*, 857–865.

Ernulf, K.E., & Innala, S.M. (1995). Sexual bondage: A review and unobtrusive investigation. *Archives of Sexual Behavior, 24*, 631–655.

Eron, L.D. (1982). Parent–child interaction, television violence, and aggression in children. *American Psychologist, 37*, 197–211.

Esterling, B.A., L'Abate, L., Murray, E.J., & Pennebaker, J.W. (1999). Empirical foundations for writing in prevention and psychotherapy: Mental and physical health outcomes. *Clinical Psychology Review, 19*, 79–96.

Evans, D.L., Leserman, J., Perkins, D.O., et al. (1997). Severe life stress as a predictor of early disease progression in HIV infection. *American Journal of Psychiatry, 154*, 630–634.

Evans, R.G., Lomas, J., Barer, M.L., Labelle, R.J., Fooks, C., Stoddart, G.L., Anderson, G.M., Feeny, D., Gafni, A., Torrance, G.W. (1989). Controlling health care expenditures: The Canadian reality. *New England Journal of Medicine, 320*, 571–577.

Ewing, C. (1991). Preventive detention and execution: The constitutionality of punishing future crimes. *Law and Human Behavior, 15*, 139–163.

Ewing, S.E., Falk, W.E., & Otto, M.W. (1996). The recalcitrant patient: Treating disorders of personality. In M.H. Pollack & M.W. Otto (Eds.), *Challenges in Clinical Practice: Pharmacologic and Psychosocial Strategies* (pp. 355–379). New York: Guilford.

Exner, J.E., Jr. (1993). *The Rorschach: A comprehensive system, Vol. 1: Basic foundations* (3rd ed.) New York: Wiley.

Exner, J.E., Jr. (1999). The Rorschach: Measurement concepts and issues of validity. In S.E. Embretson, & S.L. Hershberger (Eds.), *The New Rules of Measurement: What Every Psychologist and Educator Should Know* (pp. 159–183). Mahwah, NJ: Erlbaum.

Eysenck, H.J. (1952/1992). The effects of psychotherapy: An evaluation. *Journal of Consulting Psychology, 16*, 319–324.

Eysenck, H.J. (1979). The conditioning model of neurosis. *Behavioral and Brain Sciences, 2*, 155–199.

Factor, S.A. (2002). Pharmacology of atypical antipsychotics. *Clinical Neuropharmacology, 25*, 153–157.

Fadda, R., & Rosetti, Z.L. (1998). Chronic ethanol consumption: From neuroadaptation to neurodegeneration. *Progress in Neurology, 56*, 385–431.

Faigman, D.L., Kaye, D.H., Saks, M.J., & Sanders, J. (1997). *Modern Scientific Evidence: The Law and Science of Expert Testimony.* St. Paul, MN: West.

Fairburn, C.G. (1996). *Overcoming Binge Eating.* New York: Guilford.

Fairburn, C.G. (2002). Cognitive-behavioral therapy for bulimia nervosa. In C.G. Fairburn & K.D. Brownell (Eds.), *Eating Disorders and Obesity* (2nd ed., pp. 302–307). New York: Guilford.

Fairburn, C.G., & Brownell, K.D. (Eds.). *Eating Disorders and Obesity* (2nd ed.). New York: Guilford.

Fairburn, C.G., Hay, P.J., & Welch, S.L. (1993). Binge eating and bulimia nervosa: Distribution and determinants. In C.G. Fairburn & G.T. Wilson (Eds.), *Binge Eating: Nature, Assessment, and Treatment* (pp. 123–143). New York: Guilford.

Fairburn, C.G., Jones, R., Peveler, R.C., Carr, S.J., Solomon, R.A., O'Connor, M.E., Burton, J., & Hope, R.A. (1991). Three psychological treatments for bulimia nervosa. *Archives of General Psychiatry, 48*, 463–469.

Fairburn, C.G., Jones, R., Peveler, R.C., Hope, R.A., & O'Connor, M. (1993). Psychotherapy and bulimia nervosa: Longer-term effects of interpersonal psychotherapy, behavior therapy, and cognitive behavior therapy. *Archives of General Psychiatry, 50*, 419–428.

Fairburn, C.G., Welch, S.L., Doll, H.A., Davies, B.A., & O'Connor, M.E. (1997). Risk factors for bulimia nervosa: A community-based case-control study. *Archives of General Psychiatry, 54*, 509–517.

Fairburn, C.G., & Wilson, G.T. (Eds.) (1993). *Binge Eating: Nature, Assessment, and Treatment*. New York: Guilford.

Falk, A.J. (1999). Sex offenders, mental illness, and criminal responsibility: The constitutional boundaries of civil commitment after *Kansas v. Hendricks*. *American Journal of Law and Medicine, 25*, 117–147.

Fallon, P., Katzman, M.A., & Wooley, S.C. (1994). *Feminist Perspectives on Eating Disorders*. New York: Guilford.

Falloon, I., Boyd, J.L., & McGill, C.W. (1985). *Family care of schizophrenia*. New York: Guilford.

Fann, J.R. (2000). The epidemiology of delirium: A review of studies and methodological issues. *Seminars in Clinical Neuropsychiatry, 5*, 64–74.

Farah, M.J. (1992). Agnosia. *Current Opinion in Neurobiology, 2*, 162–164.

Farah, M.J., O'Reilly, R.C., & Vecera, S.P. (1993). Dissociated overt and covert recognition as an emergent property of a lesioned neural network. *Psychological Review, 100*, 571–588.

Faraone, S.V., Tsuang, M.T., & Tsuang, D.W. (1999). *Genetics of Mental Disorders*. New York: Guilford.

Faravelli, C., Paterniti, S., & Servi, P. (1997). Stressful life events and panic disorder. In T.W. Miller (Ed.), *Clinical Disorders and Stressful Life Events* (pp. 143–170). Madison, CT: International Universities Press.

Farde, L., Nordstrom, A., Karlsson, P., Halldin, C., & Sedvall, G. (1995). Positron emission tomography studies on dopamine receptors in schizophrenia. *Clinical Neuropharmacology, 18* (suppl. 1), S121–S129.

Farmer, A.E., & Griffiths, H. (1992). Labeling and illness in primary care: Comparing factors influencing general practitioners' and psychiatrists' decisions regarding patient referral to mental illness services. *Psychological Medicine, 22*, 717–723.

Farmer, A.E., McGuffin, P., & Gottesman, I.I. (1987). Twin concordance for DSM-III schizophrenia: Scrutinizing the validity of the definition. *Archives of General Psychiatry, 44*, 634–641.

Farquhar, J.W., Macoby, N., Wood, P.D., et al. (1977). Community education for cardiovascular health. *Lancet*, i, 1192–1195.

Farrer, L.A., Cupples, A., Haines, J.L., Hyman, B., Kukull, W.A., Mayeux, R., Myers, R.H., Pericek-Vance, M.A., Risch, N., & van Duijn, C.M. (1997). Effects of age, sex, and ethnicity on the association between apolipoprotein E genotype and Alzheimer disease: A meta-analysis. *Journal of the American Medical Association, 278*, 1349–1356.

Farrington, D., Ohlin, L., & Wilson, J.Q. (1986). *Understanding and Controlling Crime*. New York: Springer.

Faust, D., & Ziskin, J. (1988). The expert witness in psychology and psychiatry. *Science, 241*, 31–35.

Fawzy, F.I., Fawzy, N.W., Hyun, C.S., Gutherie, D., Fahey, J.L., & Morton, D. (1993). Malignant melanoma. Effects of an early structured psychiatric intervention, coping, and affective state on recurrence and survival six years later. *Archives of General Psychiatry, 50*, 681–689.

Fedoroff, I.C., & Taylor, S. (2001). Psychological and pharmacological treatments of social phobia: A meta-analysis. *Journal of Clinical Psychopharmacology, 21*, 311–324.

Fedoroff, I.C., Taylor, S., Asmundson, G.J.G., & Koch, W.J. (2000). Cognitive factors in traumatic stress reactions: Predicting PTSD symptoms from anxiety sensitivity and beliefs about harmful events. *Behavioural and Cognitive Psychotherapy, 28*, 5–15.

Fedoroff, J.P., Fishell, A., & Fedoroff, B. (1999). A case series of women evaluated for paraphilic sexual disorders. *Canadian Journal of Human Sexuality, 8*, 127–140.

Feingold, A., & Mazzella, R. (1998). Gender differences in body image are increasing. *Psychological Science, 9*, 190–195.

Feldman, M.D., & Brown, R.M.A. (2002). Munchausen by Proxy in an international context. *Child Abuse and Neglect, 26*, 509–524.

Felman, M.D., & Brown, R.M.A. (2002). Munchausen by proxy in an international context. *Child Abuse & Neglect, 26*, 509–524.

Fenton, W.S. (2000). Heterogeneity, subtypes, and longitudinal course in schizophrenia. *Psychiatric Annals, 30*, 638–644.

Fernandez, H. (1998). *Heroin*. Center City, MN: Hazeldon.

Ferster, C.B. (1961). Positive reinforcement and behavioral deficits of autistic children. *Child Development, 32*, 437–456.

Figley, C.R. (1978). *Stress Disorders Among Vietnam Veterans*. New York: Brunner/Mazel.

Fincham, F.D., Beach, S.R.H., Harold, G.T., & Osborne, L.N. (1997). Marital satisfaction and depression: Different causal relationships for men and women? *Psychological Science, 8*, 351–357.

Fink, H.A., MacDonald, R., Rutks, I.R., Nelson, D.B., & Wilt, T.J. (2002). Sildenafil for male erectile dysfunction: a systematic review and meta-analysis. *Archives of Internal Medicine, 162*, 1349–1360.

Fink, M. (2001). Convulsive therapy: A review of the first 55 years. *Journal of Affective Disorders, 63*, 1–15.

Fink, P.J., & Tasman, A. (Eds.) (1992). *Stigma and mental illness*. Washington, DC: American Psychiatric Press.

Finkel, S.I., Costa, S.J., Cohen, G., Miller, S., & Sartorius, N. (1996). Behavioral and psychological signs and symptoms of dementia: A consensus statement on current knowledge and implications for research and treatment. *International Psychogeriatrics, 8* (suppl. 3), 497–500.

Finkelhor, D. (1994). The international epidemiology of child sexual abuse. *Child Abuse & Neglect, 18*, 409–417.

Finkelstein, J.R., Cannon, T.D., Gur, R.E., Gur, R.C., & Moberg, P. (1997). Attentional dysfunctions in neuroleptic-naive and neuroleptic-withdrawn schizophrenic patients and their siblings. *Journal of Abnormal Psychology, 106*, 203–212.

Finlay-Jones, R., & Brown, G.W. (1981). Types of stressful life event and the onset of anxiety and depressive disorders. *Psychological Medicine, 11*, 803–815.

Finney, J.W., & Moos, R.H. (1992). The long-term course of treated alcoholism. II. Predictors and correlates of 10-year functioning and mortality. *Journal of Studies on Alcohol, 53*, 142–153.

Fischman, M.W., & Haney, M. (1999). Neurobiology of stimulants. In M. Galanter & H.D. Kleber (Eds.), *Textbook of Substance Abuse Treatment* (2nd ed., pp. 21–31). Washington, DC: American Psychiatric Press.

Fishbain, D.A., Cutler, R.B, Rosomoff, H.L., Rosomoff, R., & Steele, R. (1998). Do antidepressants have an analgesic effect in psychogenic pain and somatoform pain disorder? A meta-analysis. *Psychosomatic Medicine, 60*, 503–509.

Fisher, L. (1996). Bizarre right from Day 1. *MacLean's, 109*(28), p. 14.

Fisher, P.J., & Breakey, W.R. (1991). The epidemiology of alcohol, drug, and mental disorders among homeless persons. *American Psychologist, 46*, 1115–1128.

Fitch, S.A., & Adams, G.R. (1983). Ego-identity and intimacy status: Replication and extension. *Developmental Psychology, 19*, 839–845.

Fitch, W.L., Petrella, R.C., & Wallace, J. (1987). Legal ethics and the use of mental health experts in criminal cases. *Behavioral Sciences and the Law, 5*, 105–117.

Flacker, J.M., & Lipsitz, L.A. (1999). Neural mechanisms of delirium: Current hypotheses and evolving concepts. *Journals of Gerontology. Series A, Biological Sciences and Medical Sciences, 54*, 239–246.

Flanagan, J.C. (1982). *New Insights to Improve the Quality of Life at Age 70*. Palo Alto, CA: American Institutes for Research.

Fleming, J.E., Offord, D.R., & Boyle, M.H. (1989). Prevalence of childhood and adolescent depression in the community: Ontario Child Health Study. *British Journal of Psychiatry, 155*, 647–654.

Flett, G.L., Endler, N.S., & Fairlie, P. (1999). The interaction model of anxiety and the threat of Quebec's separation from Canada. *Journal of Personality and Social Psychology, 76*, 143–150.

Flett, G.L., & Hewitt, P.L. (2002). *Perfectionism: Theory, Research, and Treatment*. Washington, DC: American Psychological Association.

Flett, G.L., Vredenburg, K., & Krames, L. (1997). The continuity of depression in clinical and nonclinical samples. *Psychological Bulletin, 121*, 395–416.

Flint, A.J. (1994). Epidemiology and comorbidity of anxiety disorders in the elderly. *American Journal of Psychiatry, 151*, 640–649.

Flor-Henry, P. (1987). Cerebral aspects of sexual deviation. In G.D. Wilson (Ed.), *Variant Sexuality: Research and Theory* (pp. 49–83). Baltimore: Johns Hopkins University Press.

Floyd, F.J., Costigan, C.L., & Phillippe, K.A. (1997). Developmental change and consistency in parental interactions with school-age children who have mental retardation. *American Journal on Mental Retardation, 101*, 579–594.

Foa, E.B., & Riggs, D.S. (1995). Post traumatic stress disorder following assault: Theoretical considerations and empirical findings. *Current Directions in Psychological Science, 5*, 61–65.

Foa, E.B. & Street, G.P. (2001). Women and traumatic events. *Journal of Clinical Psychiatry, 62*, 29–34.

Fogarty, F., Russell, J.M., Newman, S.C., & Bland, R.C. (1994). Mania. *Acta Psychiatrica Scandinavica (suppl. 376)*, 16–23.

Folkman, S., & Moskowitz, J.T. (2000). Stress, positive emotion, and coping. *Current Directions in Psychological Science, 9*, 115–118.

Follette, W.C., & Houts, A.C. (1996). Models of scientific progress and the role of theory in taxonomy development: A case study of the DSM. *Journal of Consulting and Clinical Psychology, 64*, 1120–1132.

Follingstad, D.R. (2003). Battered woman syndrome in the courts. In A.M. Goldstein (Ed.), *Handbook of psychology: Forensic psychology* (Vol. 11, pp. 485–507). New York: Wiley.

Foot, P. (1990). Ethics and the death penalty: Participation of forensic psychiatrists in capital trials. In R. Rosner & R. Weinstock (Eds.), *Ethical Practice in Psychiatry and the Law* (pp. 202–217). New York: Plenum.

Fordyce, W.E. (1976). *Behavioral Methods for Chronic Pain and Illness*. St. Louis: Mosby.

Forehand, R., & McMahon, R.J. (1981). *Helping the noncompliant child: A clinician's guide to parent training*. New York: Guilford.

Foreman, M.C., Wakefield, B., Culp, K., & Milisen, K. (2001). Delirium in elderly patients: An overview of the state of the science. *Journal of Gerontological Nursing, 27*, 12–20.

Fornari, V., Wlodarczyk-Bisaga, K., Matthews, M., Sandberg, D., Mandel, F.S., & Katz, J.L. (1999). Perception of family functioning and depressive symptomatology in individuals with anorexia nervosa or bulimia nervosa. *Comprehensive Psychiatry, 40*, 434–444.

Forrest, K.A. (2001). Toward an etiology of dissociative identity disorder: A neurodevelopmental approach. *Consciousness and Cognition, 10*, 259–293.

Foster, S.L., & Cone, J.D. (1986). Design and use of direct observation procedures. In A.R. Ciminero, K.S. Calhoun, & H.E. Adams (Eds.), *Handbook of Behavioral Assessment*, (2nd ed., pp. 253–324). New York: Wiley.

Foster, S.L., & Cone, J.D. (1995). Validity issues in clinical assessment. *Psychological Assessment, 7*, 248–260.

Fowler, C.J. (1998). The neurology of male sexual dysfunction and its investigation by clinical neurophysiological methods. *British Journal of Urology, 81*, 785–795.

Fox, P.J., Kelly, S.E., & Tobin, S.L. (1999). Defining dementia: Social and historical background of Alzheimer disease. *Genetic Testing, 3*, 13–19.

Fozard, J.L., & Gordon-Salant, S. (2001). Changes in vision and hearing with aging. In J.E. Birren & K.W. Schaie (Eds.), *Handbook of the Psychology of Aging* (5th ed., pp. 241–266). San Diego: Academic Press.

Frances, A., First, M.B., & Pincus, H.A. (1995). *DSM-IV Guidebook*. Washington, DC: American Psychiatric Press.

Frances, A., Miele, G.M., Widiger, T.A., Pincus, H.A., Manning, D., & Davis, W.W. (1993). The classification of panic disorders: From Freud to DSM-IV. *Journal of Psychiatric Research, 27* (suppl. 1), 3–10.

Frank, E., Swartz, H.A., & Kupfer, D.J. (2000). Interpersonal and social rhythm therapy: Managing the chaos of bipolar disorder. *Biological Psychiatry, 48*, 593–604.

Frank, E., Swartz, H.A., Mallinger, A.G., Thase, M.E., Weaver, E.V., & Kupfer, D.J. (1999). Adjunctive psychotherapy for bipolar disorder: Effects of changing treatment modality. *Journal of Abnormal Psychology, 108*, 579–587.

Frank, E., & Thase, M.E. (1999). Natural history and preventative treatment of recurrent mood disorders. *Annual Review of Medicine, 50*, 453–468.

Frank, J.D. (1973). *Persuasion and healing* (2nd ed.). Baltimore: Johns Hopkins University Press.

Frank, J.D., & Frank, J.B. (1991). *Persuasion and healing* (3rd ed.). Baltimore: Johns Hopkins University Press.

Frankish, C.J. (1994). Crisis centers and their role in treatment: Suicide prevention versus health promotion. In A.A. Leenaars, J.T. Maltsberger, & R.A. Neimeyer (Eds.), *Treatment of Suicidal People* (pp. 33–44). Washington, DC: Taylor & Francis.

Franklin, J.A., & Andrews, G. (1989). Stress and the onset of agoraphobia. *Australian Psychologist, 24*, 203–219.

Franklin, M.E., & Foa, E.B. (2002). Cognitive behavioral treatments for obsessive compulsive disorder. In P.E. Nathan and J.M. Gorman (Eds.). *A Guide to Treatments that Work* (2nd ed., pp. 367–386). London: Oxford University Press.

Frasure-Smith, N., & Prince, R. (1985). Long-term follow-up of the ischemic heart disease life stress monitoring program. *Psychosomatic Medicine, 51*, 485–513.

Freeman, S.J.J. (1994). An overview of Canada's mental health system. In L.L. Bachrach, P. Goering, & D. Wasylenki (Eds.), *Mental health care in Canada* (pp. 11–20). San Francisco: Jossey-Bass.

Freud, S. (1912/1957). Recommendations for physicians on the psycho-analytic method for treatment. *Standard Edition* (Vol. 12, pp. 109–120). London: Hogarth Press.

Freud, S. (1917/1961). Mourning and melancholia. In J. Strachey (Ed. and Trans.), *The Standard Edition of the Complete Psychological Works of Sigmund Freud* (Vol. 14, pp. 239–258). London: Hogarth Press.

Freud, S. (1924/1962). The aetiology of hysteria. In J. Strachey (Ed. and Trans.), *The Standard Edition of the Complete Psychological Works of Sigmund Freud* (Vol. 3, pp. 191–221). London: Hogarth Press.

Freud, S. (1940/1969). *An Outline of Psycho-Analysis*. New York: Norton.

Freund, A.M., & Baltes, P.B. (2002). Life-management strategies of selection, optimization, and compensation: Measurement by self-report and construct validity. *Journal of Personality and Social Psychology, 82*, 642–662.

Freund, K., & Blanchard, R. (1986). The concept of courtship disorder. *Journal of Sex and Marital Therapy, 12*, 79–92.

Freund, K., & Blanchard, R. (1989). Phallometric diagnosis of pedophilia. *Journal of Consulting and Clinical Psychology, 57*, 100–105.

Freund, K., & Blanchard, R. (1993). Erotic target location errors in male gender dysphorics, paedophiles, and fetishists. *British Journal of Psychiatry, 162*, 558–563.

Freund, K., & Kuban, M. (1994). The basis of the abused abuser theory of pedophilia: A further elaboration on an earlier study. *Archives of Sexual Behavior, 23*, 553–563.

Freund, K., & Seto, M.C. (1998). Preferential rape in the theory of courtship disorder. *Archives of Sexual Behavior, 27*, 433–445.

Freund, K., & Seto, M.C., & Kuban, M. (1997). Frotteurism: The theory of courtship disorder. In. D.R. Laws, & W.T. O'Donohue (Eds.), *Sexual deviance: Theory, assessment, and treatment* (pp. 111–130). New York: Guilford.

Freund, K., Watson, R.J., & Dickey, R. (1990). Does sexual abuse in childhood cause pedophilia: An exploratory study. *Archives of Sexual Behavior, 19*, 557–568.

Freund, K., Watson, R.J., & Dickey, R. (1991). The types of gender identity disorder. *Annals of Sex Research, 14*, 93–105.

Frick, P.J., Bodin, S.D., & Barry, C.T. (2000). Psychopathic traits and conduct problems in community and clinic-referred samples of children: Further development of the psychopathy screening device. *Psychological Assessment, 12*, 382–393.

Friedman, M., & Rosenman, R.H. (1959). Association of specific overt behavior pattern with blood and cardiovascular findings: Blood cholesterol level, blood clotting time, incidence of arcus senilis and clinical coronary artery disease. *Journal of the American Medical Association, 169*, 1286–1296.

Friedman, M., Thoresen, C.D., Gill, J.J., et al. (1986). Alteration of Type A behavior and its effect on cardiac recurrences in post-myocardial infarction patients: Summary results of the recurrent coronary prevention project. *American Heart Journal, 112*, 653–665.

Friedman, R.A., & Kocsis, J.H. (1996). Pharmacotherapy for chronic depression. *Psychiatric Clinics of North America, 19*, 121–132.

Fries, J.F. (1990). Medical perspectives upon successful aging. In P.B. Baltes & M.M. Baltes (Eds.), *Successful Aging: Perspectives from the Behavioral Sciences* (pp. 35–49). Cambridge: Cambridge University Press.

Frith, C., & Dolan, R.J. (2000). The role of memory in the delusions associated with schizophrenia. In D.L. Schacter and E. Scarry (Eds.), *Memory, Brain, and Belief* (pp. 115–135). Cambridge, MA: Harvard University Press.

Froehlich, J.C. (1997). Opioid peptides. *Alcohol Health and Research World, 21*, 144–148.

Frueh, B.C., Turner, S.M., & Beidel, D.C. (1995). Exposure therapy for combat-related PTSD: A critical review. *Clinical Psychology Review, 15*, 799–817.

Funtowicz, M.N., & Widiger, T.A. (1999). Sex bias in the diagnosis of personality disorders: An evaluation of DSM-IV criteria. *Journal of Abnormal Psychology, 108*, 195–201.

Furer, P., Walker, J.R., & Freeston, M.H. (2001). Individual and group cognitive behaviour therapy for intense illness worry. In G.J.G. Asmundson, S. Taylor, & B.J. Cox (Eds.), *Health anxiety: Clinical and research perspectives on hypochondriasis and related disorders* (pp. 161–192). New York: Wiley.

Furniss, E. (1995). *Victims of Benevolence: The Dark Legacy of the Williams Lake Residential School*. Vancouver, BC: Arsenal Pulp Press.

Furstenberg, F.F. (2000). The sociology of adolescence and youth in the 1990s: A critical commentary. *Journal of Marriage and the Family, 62*, 896–910.

Fyer, A.J., Mannuzza, S., Chapman, T.F., Liebowitz, M.R., & Klein, D.F. (1993). A direct interview family study of social phobia. *Archives of General Psychiatry, 50*, 286–293.

Gabbard, G.O. (2000). Psychodynamic psychotherapy of borderline personality disorder: A contemporary approach. *Bulletin of the Menninger Clinic, 65*, 41–57.

Gabbard, G.O. (2001). Musings on the report of the international consensus development conference on female sexual dysfunction: Definitions and classification. *Journal of Sex and Marital Therapy, 27*, 145–147.

Gadde, K.M., & Krishman, R.R. (1997). Recent advances in the pharmacologic treatment of bipolar illness. *Psychiatric Annals, 27*, 496–506.

Gagne, F.F., Furman, M.J., Carpenter, L.L., & Price, L.H. (2000). Efficacy of continuation ECT and antidepressant drugs compared to long-term antidepressants alone in depressed patients. *American Journal of Psychiatry, 157*, 1960–1965.

Galaif, E.R., & Sussman, S. (1995). For whom does Alcoholics Anonymous work? *International Journal of the Addictions, 30*, 161–184.

Galea, S., Ahern, J., Resnick, H., Kilpatrick, D., Bucuvalas, M., Gold, J., & Vlahov, D. (2002). Psychological sequelae of the September 11 terrorist attacks. *New England Journal of Medicine, 346*, 982–987.

Gallagher-Thompson, D., & Osgood, N.J. (1997). Suicide in later life. *Behavior Therapy, 28*, 23–41.

Gallant, D. (1999). Alcohol. In M. Galanter & H.D. Kleber (Eds.), *Textbook of Substance Abuse Treatment* (2nd ed., pp. 151–164). Washington, DC: American Psychiatric Press.

Garber, H.I. (1988). *The Milwaukee Project: Preventing Mental Retardation in Children at Risk*. Washington, DC: American Association on Mental Retardation.

Garber, J. (1984). Classification of childhood psychopathology: A developmental perspective. *Child Development, 55*, 30–48.

Garber, J., & Hollon, S.D. (1991). What can specificity designs say about causality in psychopathology research? *Psychological Bulletin, 110*, 129–136.

Garbutt, J.C., West, S.L., Carey, T.S., Lohr, K.N., & Crews, F.T. (1999). Pharmacological treatment of alcohol dependence: A review of the evidence. *Journal of the American Medical Association, 281*, 1318–1326.

Garfield, S.L. (1989). *The practice of brief psychotherapy*. New York: Pergamon.

Garfinkel, P.E., & Garner, D.M. (1982). *Anorexia Nervosa: A Multidimensional Perspective*. New York: Basic Books.

Garfinkel, P.E., Kennedy, S.H., & Kaplan, A.S. (1995). Views on classification and diagnosis of eating disorders. *Canadian Journal of Psychiatry, 40*, 445–456.

Garfinkel, P.E., Lin, B., Goering, P., Spegg, C., Goldbloom, D.S., Kennedy, S., Kaplan, A.S., & Woodside, D.B. (1996). Purging and nonpurging forms of bulimia nervosa in a community sample. *International Journal of Eating Disorders, 20*, 231–238.

Garfinkel, P.E., Moldofsky, H., & Garner, D.M. (1980). The heterogeneity of anorexia nervosa. *Archives of General Psychiatry, 37*, 1036–1040.

Garfinkel, P.E., & Walsh, W.B. (1997). Drug therapies. In D.M. Garner & P.E. Garfinkel (Eds.), *Handbook of treatment for eating disorders* (2nd ed., pp. 372–380). New York: Guilford.

Garland, A.F., & Zigler, E. (1993). Adolescent suicide prevention: Current research and social policy implications. *American Psychologist, 48*, 169–182.

Garland, E.J. (2004). Facing the evidence: Antidepressant treatment in children and adolescents. *Canadian Medical Association Journal, 170*, 490–491.

Garmezy, N. (1978). DSM-III: Never mind the psychologists; Is it good for the children? *Clinical Psychologist, 31*, 1–6.

Garner, D.M. (1997). The 1997 body image survey results. *Psychology Today, 30*(1), 30–44.

Garner, D.M., & Bemis, K.M. (1982). A cognitive-behavioral approach to anorexia nervosa. *Cognitive Therapy and Research, 6*, 123–150.

Garner, D.M., Garfinkel, P.E., Schwartz, D., & Thompson, M. (1980). Cultural expectations of thinness in women. *Psychological Reports, 47*, 483–491.

Garner, D.M., Garner, M.V., & Rosen, L.W. (1993). Anorexia nervosa "restrictors" who purge: Implications for subtyping anorexia nervosa. *International Journal of Eating Disorders, 13*, 171–185.

Garner, D.M., & Needleman, L.D. (1996). Stepped-care and decision-tree models for treating eating disorders. In J.K.Thompson, *Body Image, Eating Disorders, and Obesity* (pp. 225–252). Washington, DC: American Psychological Association.

Garner, D.M., Olmsted, M.P., & Polivy, J. (1983). The Eating Disorder Inventory: A measure of cognitive-behavioral dimensions of anorexia nervosa and bulimia. In P.L. Darby, P.E. Garfinkel, D.M. Garner, & D.V. Coscina (Eds.), *Anorexia Nervosa: Recent Developments in Research* (pp. 173–184). New York: Liss.

Garssen, B., de Ruiter, C., & Van Dyck, R. (1992). Breathing retraining: A rational placebo? *Clinical Psychology Review, 12*, 141–153.

Garza-Trevino, E. (1994). Neurobiological factors in aggressive behavior. *Hospital and Community Psychiatry, 45*, 690–699.

Gatehouse, J. (2002). The echoes of terror. *Maclean's*, 115(37), p. 18.

Gater, R., Tansella, M., Korten, A., Tiemens, B.G., Mayreas, V.G., & Olatawura, M.O. (1998). Sex differences in the prevalence and detection of depressive and anxiety disorders in general health care settings. *Archives of General Psychiatry, 55*, 405–413.

Gatz, M., & Smyer, M.A. (2001). Mental health and aging at the outset of the twenty-first century. In J.E. Birren & K.W. Schaie (Eds.), *Handbook of the Psychology of Aging* (5th ed., pp. 523–544). San Diego: Academic Press.

Gaudet, M. A. (1994). *Overview of mental health legislation in Canada*. Ottawa, ON: Health Canada.

Gaulin, S.J.C., & McBurney, D.H. (2001). *Psychology: An Evolutionary Approach*. Upper Saddle River, NJ: Prentice-Hall.

Gazzaniga, M.S., Churchland, P.S., Sejnowski, T.J., Hillyard, S.A., & Raichle, M.E. (2000). History and methods of cognitive neuroscience. In M.S. Gazzaniga (Ed.), *Cognitive Neuroscience: A Reader* (pp. 1–54). Malden, MA: Blackwell Publishers.

Gélinas, L. (1994). The new rights of persons held in psychiatric institutions following the commission of a criminal offence: The Criminal Code revised and corrected. *Canada's Mental Health, Spring*, 10–16.

Geller, J.L., McDermeit, M., & Brown, J. (1997). Pyromania? What does it mean? *Journal of Forensic Sciences, 42*, 1052–1057.

Gemar, M.C., Segal, Z., Sagrati, S., & Kennedy, S.J. (2001). Mood-induced changes on the Implicit Association Test in recovered depressed patients. *Journal of Abnormal Psychology, 110*, 282–289.

Gentili, A., & Mulligan, T. (1998). Sexual dysfunction in older adults. *Clinics in Geriatric Medicine, 14*, 383–393.

Gentleman, J.F., & Park, E. (1997). Divorce in the 1990s. *Health Reports, 9*, 53–58.

Gershoff, E.T. (2002). Corporal punishment by parents and associated child behaviors and experience: A meta-analytic and theoretical review. *Psychological Bulletin, 128*, 539–579.

Geske, M.R. (1989). Statutes limiting mental health professionals' liability for the violent acts of their patients. *Indiana Law Journal, 64*, 391–422.

Gfellner, B.M., & Hundelby, J.D. (1995). Patterns of drug use among native and white adolescents: 1990–1993. *Canadian Journal of Public Health, 86*, 95–97.

Ghaemi, S.N., Lenox, M.S., & Baldessarini, R.J. (2001). Effectiveness and safety of long-term antidepressant treatment in bipolar disorder. *Journal of Clinical Psychiatry, 62*, 565–569.

Gianoulakis, C. (2001). Influence of the endogenous opioid system on high alcohol consumption and genetic predisposition to alcoholism. *Journal of Psychiatry and Neuroscience, 26*, 304–318.

Gianoulakis, C., DeWaele, J.P., & Thavundayil, J. (1996). Implications of the endogenous opioid system in excessive ethanol consumption. *Alcohol, 13*, 19–23.

Gibbs, N.A., & Oltmanns, T.F. (1995). The relation between obsessive–compulsive personality traits and subtypes of compulsive behavior. *Journal of Anxiety Disorders, 9*, 397–410.

Gilbert, P. (2001). Evolutionary approaches to psychopathology: The role of natural defences. *Australian and New Zealand Journal of Psychiatry, 35*, 17–27.

Gillberg, C. (1988). The role of the endogenous opioids in autism and possible relationships to clinical features. In L. Wing (Ed.), *Aspects of Autism: Biological Research* (pp. 31–37). London: Gaskell.

Gillberg, C., Rastam, M., & Gillberg, C. (1995). Anorexia nervosa 6 years after onset. I. Personality disorders. *Comprehensive Psychiatry, 36*, 61–69.

Gillberg, C., & Schaumann, H. (1982). Social class and infantile autism. *Journal of Autism and Developmental Disorders, 12*, 223–228.

Gilligan, C. (1982). *In a Different Voice*. Cambridge, MA: Harvard University Press.

Gillmor, D. (1987). *I Swear by Apollo: Dr. Ewen Cameron and the CIA-Brainwashing Experiments*. Montreal: Eden Press.

Glaser, D. (2002). Child sexual abuse. In M. Rutter & E. Taylor (Eds.), *Child and Adolescent Psychiatry* (4th ed., pp. 340–358). Oxford, UK: Blackwell.

Gleaves, D.H. (1996). The sociocognitive model of dissociative identity disorder: A reexamination of the evidence. *Psychological Bulletin, 120*, 42–59.

Glick, I.D., & Berg, P.H. (2002). Time to study discontinuation, relapse, and compliance with atypical or conventional antipsychotics in schizophrenia and related disorders. *International Clinical Psychopharmacology, 17*, 65–68.

Gliksman, L., Adlaf, E., Demers, A., Newton-Taylor, B., & Schmidt, K. (2000). *Canadian Campus Survey*. Toronto: CAMH.

Goddard, A.W., & Charney, D.S. (1997). Toward an integrated neurobiology of panic disorder. *Journal of Clinical Psychiatry, 58* (suppl. 2), 4–11.

Goeree, R., O'Brien, B.J., Goering, P., Blackhouse, G., Agro, K., Rhodes, A., & Watson, J. (1999). The economic burden of schizophrenia in Canada. *Canadian Journal of Psychiatry, 44*, 464–472.

Goering, P., Wasylenki, D., & Durbin, J. (2000). Canada's mental health system. *International Journal of Law and Psychiatry, 23*, 345–359.

Gold, M.S., Tabrah, H., Frost-Pineda, K. (2001). Psychopharmacology of MDMA (Ecstasy). *Psychiatric Annals, 31*, 675–681.

Goldapple, K., Segal, Z., Garson, C., Lau, M., Bieling, P., Kennedy, S., & Mayberg, H. (2004). Modulation of cortical-limbic pathways in major depression. *Archives of General Psychiatry, 61*, 34–41.

Goldberg, B. (1996). Developmental disabilities. In Q. Rae-Grant (Ed.), *Images in psychiatry: Canada* (pp. 39–43). Washington, DC: American Psychiatric Press.

Goldberg, E.M., & Morrison, S.L. (1963). Schizophrenia and social class. *British Journal of Psychiatry, 109*, 785–802.

Goldberg, L.R. (1993). The structure of phenotypic personality traits. *American Psychologist, 48*, 26–34.

Goldberg, T.E., & Weinberger, D.R. (1995). A case against subtyping in schizophrenia. *Schizophrenia Research, 17*, 147–152.

Goldfried, M.R. (1995). *From cognitive-behavior therapy to psychotherapy integration: An evolving view*. New York: Springer.

Goldfried, M.R., & Davison, G.C. (1994). *Clinical Behavior Therapy* (2nd ed). New York: Wiley-Interscience.

Goldman, H.H., Skodol, A.E., & Lave, T.R. (1992). Revising Axis V for DSM-IV: A review of measures of social functioning. *American Journal of Psychiatry, 149*, 1148–1156.

Goldman, M.S. (1994). The alcohol expectancy concept: Applications to assessment, prevention, and treatment of alcohol abuse. *Applied and Preventive Psychology, 3*, 131–144.

Goldman, M.S., Brown, S.A., & Christiansen, B.A. (1987). Expectancy theory: Thinking about drinking. In H.T. Blane & K.E. Leonard (Eds.), *Psychological Theories of Drinking and Alcoholism* (pp. 181–226). New York: Guilford.

Goldman, M.S., Brown, S.A., Christiansen, B.A., & Smith, G.T. (1991). Alcoholism and memory: Broadening the scope of alcohol-expectancy research. *Psychological Bulletin, 110*, 137–146.

Goldstein, J.J., Rosenfarb, I., Woo, S., & Nuechterlein, K. (1997). Transactional processes which can function as risk or protective factors in the family treatment of schizophrenia. In H.D. Brenner and W. Boeker (Eds.), *Towards a Comprehensive Therapy for Schizophrenia* (pp. 147–157). Kirkland, WA: Hogrefe & Huber.

Goldstein, J.M. (1997). Sex differences in schizophrenia: Epidemiology, genetics and the brain. *International Review of Psychiatry, 9*, 399–408.

Goldstein, M.J. (1988). The family and psychopathology. *Annual Review of Psychology, 39*, 283–299.

Golub, E.S. (1994). *The Limits of Medicine: How Science Shapes our Hope for the Cure*. New York: Random House.

Golwyn, D.H., & Sevlie, C.P. (1992). Paraphilias, nonparaphilic sexual addictions, and social phobia. *Journal of Clinical Psychiatry, 53*, 330.

Gomberg, E.S.L. (1988). Alcoholic women in treatment: The question of stigma and age. *Alcohol and Alcoholism, 23*, 507–514.

Gomberg, E.S.L. (1999). Substance abuse in the elderly. In P.J. Ott, R.E.Tarter, & R.T. Ammerman (Eds.), *Sourcebook on Substance Abuse: Etiology, Epidemiology, Assessment, and Treatment* (pp. 113–125). Boston: Allyn & Bacon.

Good, B., & Kleinman, A. (1985). Culture and anxiety: Cross-cultural evidence for the patterning of anxiety disorders. In A.H. Tuma & J. Maser (Eds.), *Anxiety and the Anxiety Disorders* (pp. 297–323). Hillsdale, NJ: Erlbaum.

Gooding, D.C., & Iacono, W.G. (1995). Schizophrenia through the lens of a developmental psychopathology perspective. In D. Cicchetti & D.J. Cohen (Eds.), *Developmental Psychopathology. Vol. 2, Risk, Disorder, and Adaptation* (pp. 535–580). New York: Wiley.

Gooding, D.G., Miller, M.D., & Kwapil, T.R. (2000). Smooth pursuit eye tracking and visual fixation in psychosis-prone individuals. *Psychiatry Research, 93*, 41–54.

Goodman, L.A., Koss, M.P., & Russo, N.F. (1993). Violence against women: Physical and mental health effects. Part I. Research findings. *Applied and Preventive Psychology, 2*, 79–89.

Goodman, L.A., Koss, M.P., Fitzgerald, L.F., Russo, N.F., & Keita, G.P. (1993). Male violence against women: Current research and future directions. *American Psychologist, 48*, 1054–1058.

Goodman, T.A. (1985). From Tarasoff to Hopper: The evolution of the therapist's duty to protect third parties. *Behavioral Sciences and the Law, 3*, 195–225.

Goodman, W.K., Price, L.H., Rasmussen, S.A., Mazure, C., Fleischman, R.L., Hill, C.L., Heninger, G.R., & Charmey, D.S. (1989). The Yale-Brown Obsessive–Compulsive Scale. 1. Development, use, and reliability. *Archives of General Psychiatry, 46*, 1006–1011.

Goodwin, D.W. (1991). The genetics of alcoholism. In P.R. McHugh & V.A. McKusick (Eds.), *Genes, Brain, and Behavior* (pp. 219–226). New York: Raven Press.

Goodwin, P.J. et al., (2001). The Effect of Group Psychosocial Support on Survival in Metastatic Breast Cancer. *New England Journal of Medicine, 345*, 1719–1726.

Gorman, J.M., Kent, J.M., Sullivan, G.M., & Coplan, J.D. (2000). Neuroanatomical hypothesis of panic disorder, revised. *American Journal of Psychiatry, 157*, 493–505.

Gosselin, C.C., & Wilson, G.D. (1980). *Sexual Variations*. London: Faber & Faber.

Gotlib, I.H., & Hammen, C. (1992). *Psychological Aspects of Depression: Toward a Cognitive-Interpersonal Integration*. New York: Wiley.

Gotlib, I.H., & Neubauer, D.L. (2000). Information-processing approaches to the study of cognitive biases in depression. In S.L. Johnson and A.M. Hayes (Eds.), *Stress, Coping, and Depression* (pp. 117–143). Mahwah, NJ: Erlbaum.

Gotlib, I.H., Lewinsohn, P.M., & Seeley, J.R. (1998). Consequences of depression during adolescence: Marital status and marital functioning in early adulthood. *Journal of Abnormal Psychology, 107*, 686–690.

Gotlib, I.H., & McCabe, S.B. (1990). Marriage and psychopathology. In F.D. Fincham & T.N. Bradbury (Eds.), *The Psychology of Marriage: Basic Issues and Applications* (pp. 226–257). New York: Guilford.

Gotowiec, A., & Beiser, M. (1993–1994). Aboriginal children's mental health: Unique challenges. *Canada's Mental Health, 41*, 7–11.

Gottesman, I.G. (1963). Genetic aspects of intelligent behavior. In N. Ellis (Ed.), *The Handbook of Mental Deficiency: Psychological Theory and Research* (pp. 253–296). New York: McGraw-Hill.

Gottesman, I.I. (1987). The psychotic hinterlands, or the fringes of lunacy. *British Medical Bulletin, 43*, 1–13.

Gottesman, I.I. (1991). *Schizophrenia Genesis: The Origins of Madness*. New York: Freeman.

Gottesman, I.I., & Goldsmith, H.H. (1994). Developmental psychopathology of antisocial behavior: Inserting genes into its ontogenesis and epigenesis. In C.A. Nelson (Ed.), *Threats to Optimal Development: Integrating Biological, Psychological, and Social Risk Factors* (pp. 69–104). Hillsdale, NJ: Erlbaum.

Gottman, J.M. (1985). Observational measures of behavior therapy outcome: A reply to Jacobsen. *Behavioral Assessment, 7*, 317–321.

Gottman, J.M. (1994). *Why Marriages Succeed or Fail*. New York: Simon & Schuster.

Gottman, J.M. (1999). *The Marriage Clinic: A Scientifically Based Marital Therapy*. New York: Norton & Co.

Gottman, J.M., & Katz, L.F. (1989). Effects of marital discord on young children's peer interaction and health. *Developmental Psychology, 25*, 373–381.

Gottman, J.M., & Levenson, R.W. (1986). Assessing the role of emotion in marriage. *Behavioral Assessment, 8*, 31–48.

Gottman, J.M., & Levenson, R.W. (1988). The social psychophysiology of marriage. In P. Noller & M.A. Fitzpatrick (Eds.), *Perspectives on Marital Interaction* (pp. 182–200). Clevedon, England: Multilingual Matters.

Gottman, J.M., & Levenson, R.W. (1992). Marital processes predictive of later dissolution: Behavior, physiology, and health. *Journal of Personality and Social Psychology, 63*, 221–233.

Gottman, J.M., & Levenson, R.W. (2000). The timing of divorce: Predicting when a couple will divorce over a 14-year period. *Journal of Marriage & the Family, 62*, 737–745.

Gottman, J.M., & Notarious, C.I. (2000). Decade review: Observing marital interaction. *Journal of Marriage and the Family, 62*, 927–947.

Gottman, J., Notarius, C., Gonso, J., & Markman, H. (1976). *A Couple's Guide to Communication*. Champaign, IL: Research Press.

Gove, W.R. (1990). Labeling theory's explanation of mental illness: An update of recent evidence. In M. Nagler (Ed.), *Perspectives on Disability* (pp. 75–85). Palo Alto, CA: Health Markets Research.

Grant, A. (1996). *No End of Grief: Indian Residential Schools in Canada*. Winnipeg, MB: Pemmican Publications.

Grant, I. (2001). The British Columbia Criminal Code Review Board: An empirical analysis. In D. Eaves, J.R.P. Ogloff, & R. Roesch (Eds.), *Mental disorders and the criminal code: Legal background and contemporary perspectives* (pp. 161–206). Burnaby, BC: SFU Mental Health, Law and Policy Institute.

Grant, W.T., Foundation. (1988). *The Forgotten Half: Pathways to Success for America's Youth and Young Families*. Washington, DC: Youth and America's Future: William T. Grant Foundation Commission on Work, Family and Citizenship.

Grasel, E. (1997). Temporary institutional respite in dementia cases: Who utilizes this form of respite care and what effect does it have? *International Psychogeriatrics, 9*, 437–448.

Gratzer, T.G., & Bradford, J.M.W. (1995). Offender and offense characteristics of sexual sadists: A comparative study. *Journal of Forensic Sciences, 40*, 450–455.

Gratzer, T.G., & Matas, M. (1994). The right to refuse treatment: Recent Canadian developments. *Bulletin of the American Academy of Psychiatry and Law, 22*, 249–256.

Graves, A.B., Rosner, D., Echeverria, D., Mortimer, J.A., & Larson, E.B. (1998). Occupational exposures to solvents and aluminum and estimated risk of Alzheimer's disease. *Occupational and Environmental Medicine, 55*, 627–633.

Gray, J.E., & Keegan, D. (1999). Re: Mental health legislation and the right to appropriate treatment [letter]. *Canadian Journal of Psychiatry, 44*, 394–395.

Graziottin, A. (1998). The biological basis of female sexuality. *International Clinical Psychopharmacology, 13* (suppl. 6), 15–22.

Greaves, G.B. (1980). Multiple personality disorder: 165 years after Mary Reynolds. *Journal of Nervous and Mental Disease, 168*, 577–596.

Green, B.L., Epstein, S.A., Krupnick, J.L., & Rowland, J.H. (1997). Trauma and medical illness: Assessing trauma-related disorders in medical settings. In J.P. Wilson & T.M. Keane (Eds.), *Assessing Psychological Trauma and PTSD* (pp. 160–191). New York: Guilford.

Green, M.F. (2001). *Schizophrenia Revealed: From Neurons to Social Interactions*. New York: Norton.

Green, R., & Blanchard, R. (1995). Gender identity disorders. In H.I. Kaplan & B.J. Sadock (Eds.), *Comprehensive textbook of psychiatry* (pp. 1345–1360). Baltimore, MD: Williams & Wilkins.

Greenberg, D.M., & Gratzer, T.G. (1994). The impact of the Charter of Rights and Freedoms on the mental disorder provisions of the Criminal Code. *Canada's Mental Health, Spring*, 6–9.

Greenberg, L.S. (2003). Integrating an emotion-focused approach to treatment into psychotherapy integration. *Journal of Psychotherapy Integration, 12*, 154–189.

Greenberg, L.S., Elliott, R.K., & Lietaer, G. (1994). Research on experimental psychotherapies. In A.E. Bergin & S.L. Garfield, *Handbook of psychotherapy and behavior change* (4th ed., pp. 509–542). New York: Wiley.

Greenberg, L.S., & Johnson, S.M. (1988). *Emotionally focused couples therapy*. New York: Guilford.

Greenberg, L.S., & Malcolm, W. (2002). Resolving unfinished business: Relating process to outcome. *Journal of Consulting and Clinical Psychology, 70*, 406–416.

Greenberg, L.S., Rice, L.N., Rennie, D.L., & Toukman, S.G. (1991). York University psychotherapy research program. In L.E. Beutler & M. Crago (Eds.), *Psychotherapy research: An international review of programmatic studies* (pp. 175–181). Washington, DC: American Psychological Association.

Greenberg, L.S., & Watson, J. (1998). Experiential therapy of depression: Differential effects of client-centered relationship conditions and process experiential interventions. *Psychotherapy Research, 8*, 210–224.

Greenberg, P.E., Sisitsky, T., Kessler, R.C., Finkelstein, S.N., Berndt, E.R., Davidson, J.R., Ballenger, J.C., & Fyer, A.J. (1999). The economic burden of anxiety disorders in the 1990s. *Journal of Clinical Psychiatry, 60*, 427–435.

Greenberg, R.P., Bornstein, R.F., Zborowski, M.J., Fisher, S., & Greenberg, M.D. (1994). A meta-analysis of fluoxetine outcome in the treatment of depression. *Journal of Nervous and Mental Disease, 182*, 547–551.

Greene, R.L. (2000). *The MMPI-2: An Interpretive Manual* (2nd ed.). Needham Heights, MA: Allyn & Bacon.

Greene, R.W. et al. (2001). Social impairment in girls with ADHD: Patterns, gender comparisons, and correlates. *Journal of the American Academy of Child and Adolescent Psychiatry, 40*, 704–710.

Greenley, J.R. (1995). Madison, Wisconsin, United States: Creation and implementation of the Program of Assertive Community Treatment (PACT). In R. Schulz & J.R. Greenley (Eds.), *Innovating in Community Mental Health: International Perspectives* (pp. 83–96). Westport, CT: Praeger.

Greenspan, E.L. (Ed.) (1998). *Annotations at Section 16 of Martin's Criminal Code*. Toronto: Canada Law Book Inc.

Grenier, G., & Byers, E.S. (1995). Rapid ejaculation: A review of conceptual, etiological and treatment issues. *Archives of Sexual Behavior, 24*, 447–471.

Grenier, G., & Byers, E.S. (2001). Operationalizing premature or rapid ejaculation. *Journal of Sex Research, 38*, 369–378.

Griffin, M.G., Resick, P.A., & Mechanic, M.B. (1997). Objective assessment of peritraumatic dissociation: Psychophysiological indicators. *American Journal of Psychiatry, 154*, 1081–1088.

Grisso, T., & Appelbaum, P.S. (1992). Is it unethical to offer predictions of future violence? *Law and Human Behavior, 16*, 621–633.

Grizenko, N., Cvejic, H., Vida, S., & Sayegh, L. (1991). Behaviour problems of the mentally retarded. *Canadian Journal of Psychiatry, 36*, 712–717.

Grob, G.N. (1994). *The Mad Among us: A History of the Care of America's Mentally Ill*. Cambridge, MA: Harvard University Press.

Gross, G. (1997). The onset of schizophrenia. *Schizophrenia Research, 28*, 187–198.

Grossman, H.J. (1983). *Classification in Mental Retardation*. Washington, DC: American Association on Mental Deficiency.

Grotevant, H.D., & Carlson, C.I. (1989). *Family Assessment: A Guide to Methods and Measures*. New York: Guilford.

Group for the Advancement of Psychiatry (1966). *Psychopathological Disorders of Childhood: Theoretical Considerations and a Proposed Classification. Report 62*. New York: Mental Health Memorials Center.

Group for the Advancement of Psychiatry. (1995). A model for the classification and diagnosis of relational disorders. *Psychiatric Services, 46*, 926–931.

Growe, S. J. (2000). PTSD. *Toronto Star*, September 24. Retrieved December 8, 2000, from http://www1.thestar.com/thestar/editorial/health/20000924BOD01_PTSD-MAIN.html.

Grube, B.S., Bilder, R.M., & Goldman, R.S. (1998). Meta-analysis of symptom factors in schizophrenia. *Schizophrenia Research, 31*, 113–120.

Grunau, R.V.E., & Craig, K.D. (1988). Pain. In W. Linden (Ed.), *Biological barriers in behavioral medicine* (pp. 257–279). New York: Plenum.

Grych, J.H., & Fincham, F.D. (1990). Marital conflict and children's adjustment: A cognitive-contextual framework. *Psychological Bulletin, 101*, 267–290.

Guarnaccia, P.J. (1997). A cross-cultural perspective on anxiety disorders. In S. Friedman (Ed.), *Cultural Issues in the Treatment of Anxiety*, 3–20. New York: Guilford.

Guarnaccia, P.J., & Rogler, L.H. (1999). Research on culture-bound syndromes: New Directions. *American Journal of Psychiatry, 156*, 1322–1327.

Gunderson, J. (1984). *Borderline Personality Disorder*. Washington, DC: American Psychiatric Press.

Gunderson, J.G. (1994). Building structure for the borderline construct. *Acta Psychiatrica Scandinavica, 89* (suppl. 379), 12–18.

Gureje, O., Simon, G.E., Ustun, T.B., & Goldberg, D.P. (1997). Somatization in cross-cultural perspective: A world health organization study in primary care. *American Journal of Psychiatry, 154*, 989–995.

Gurland, B. (1996). Epidemiology of psychiatric disorders. In J. Sadavoy, L.W. Lazarus, L.F. Jarvik, & G.T. Grossberg (Eds.), *Comprehensive review of geriatric psychiatry* (Vol. 2, pp. 3–42). Washington, DC: American Psychiatric Press.

Gurman, A., & Jacobson, N. (Eds.), (2002). *Clinical Handbook of Couple Therapy* (3rd ed.). New York: Guilford.

Gurman, A.S., & Kniskern, D.P. (Eds.) (1991). *Handbook of family therapy* (Vol. 2.). New York: Brunner/Mazel.

Gusella, J.F., Wexler, N.S., Conneally, P.M., Naylor, S.L., Anderson, M.A., Tanzi, R.E., Watkins, P.C., Ottina, K., Wallace, M.R., Sakaguchi, A.Y., Young, A.B., et al. (1983). A polymorphic DNA marker genetically linked to Huntington's disease. *Nature, 306*, 234–238.

Gussow, Z. (1985). Pibloktoq (hysteria) among the polar Eskimo. In R.C. Simons & C.C. Hughes (Eds.), *The culture-bound syndromes* (pp. 271–287). Dordrecht, The Netherlands: Kluwer.

Gutheil, T.G. (1986). The right to refuse treatment: Paradox, pendulum and the quality of care. *Behavioral Sciences and the Law, 4*, 265–277.

Gutierrez, M.A., & Stimmel, G.L. (1999). Management of and counseling for psychotropic drug-induced sexual dysfunction. *Pharmacotherapy, 19*, 823–831.

Gutierrez-Lobos, K., Schmid-Siegel, B., Bankier, B., & Walter, H. (2001). Delusions in first-admitted patients: Gender, themes, and diagnoses. *Psychopathology, 34*, 1–7.

Guzder, J., Paris, J., Zelkowitz, P., & Marchessault, K. (1996). Risk factors for borderline psychology in children. *Journal of the American Academy of Child and Adolescent Psychiatry, 35*, 26–33.

Haavio-Mannila, E., & Kontula, O. (1997). Correlates of increased sexual satisfaction. *Archives of Sexual Behavior, 26*, 399–416.

Haddad, M.S., & Cummings, J.L. (1997). Huntington's disease. *Psychiatric Clinics of North America, 20*, 791–807.

Hadjistavropoulos, H.D., MacLeod, F.K., & Asmundson, G.J.G. (1999). Validation of the Chronic Pain Coping Inventory. *Pain, 80*, 471–481.

Hadjistavropoulos, T., & Craig, K.D. (2002). A theoretical framework for understanding self-report and observational measures of pain: A communications model. *Behaviour Research and Therapy, 40*, 551–570.

Hadjistavropoulos, T., von Baeyer, C., & Craig, K.D. (2001). Pain assessment in persons with limited ability to communicate. In D.T. Turk (Ed.), *Handbook of pain assessment* (2nd ed., pp. 134–149). New York: Guilford.

Haefner, H., & Heiden, W. (1997). Epidemiology of schizophrenia. *Canadian Journal of Psychiatry, 42*, 139–151.

Haefner, H., Heiden, W., Behrens, S., Gattaz, W.F., Hambrecht, M., Loeffler, W., Maurer, K., Munk-Jorgensen, P., Nowotny, B., Riecher-Roessler, A., & Stein, A. (1998). Causes and consequences of the gender difference in age at onset of schizophrenia. *Schizophrenia Bulletin, 24*, 99–113.

Haggarty, J., Cernovsky, Z., Kermeen, P., & Merskey, H. (2000). Psychiatric disorders in an Arctic community. *Canadian Journal of Psychiatry, 45*, 357–362.

Hage, J.J. (1995). Medical requirements and consequences of sex reassignment surgery. *Medicine, Science and the Law, 35*, 17–24.

Hahlweg, K., Fiegenbaum, W., Frank, M., Schroeder, B., & Witzleben, I. (2001). Short- and long-term effectiveness of an empirically supported treatment for agoraphobia. *Journal of Consulting and Clinical Psychology, 69*, 375–382.

Hahlweg, K., Markman, H.J., Thurmaier, F., Engl, J., & Eckert, V. (1998). Prevention of martial distress: Results of a German prospective longitudinal study. *Journal of Family Psychology, 12*, 543–556.

Haig-Brown, C. (1988). *Resistance and Renewal: Surviving the Indian Residential School*. Vancouver, BC: Tillacum Library.

Haines, J., Josephs, S., Williams, C.L., & Wells, J.H. (1998). The psychophysiology of obsessive compulsive disorder. *Behaviour Change, 15*, 244–254.

Hall, G.C.N. (2001). Psychotherapy research with ethnic minorities: Empirical, ethical, and conceptual issues. *Journal of Consulting and Clinical Psychology, 69*, 502–510.

Hammen, C. (2002). Context of stress in families of children with depressed parents. In S.H. Goodman and I.H. Gotlib (Eds.), *Children of Depressed Parents: Mechanisms of Risk and Implications for Treatment* (pp. 175–199). Washington, DC: American Psychological Association.

Hammen, C., & Garber, J. (2001). Vulnerability to depression across the lifespan. In R.E. Ingram and J.M. Price (Eds.), *Vulnerability to Psychopathology: Risk Across the Lifespan* (pp. 258–267). New York: Guilford.

Hankin, B.L., & Abramson, L.Y. (2001). Development of gender differences in depression: An elaborated cognitive vulnerability-transactional stress theory. *Psychological Bulletin, 127*, 773–796.

Hankin, B.L. et al. (1998). Development of depression from preadolescence to young adulthood: Emerging gender differences in a 10-year longitudinal study. *Journal of Abnormal Pyschology, 107*, 128–140.

Hanson, R.K. (2004). Will they do it again? Predicting sex-offense revidivism. In T.F. Oltmanns & R.E. Emery (Eds.), *Current directions in abnormal psychology* (pp. 116–121). Upper Saddle River, NJ: Pearson Education.

Hanson, R.K., Broom, I., & Stephenson, M. (2004). Evaluating community sex offender treatment programs: A 12-year follow-up of 724 offenders. *Canadian Journal of Behavioural Science, 36*, 87–96.

Hanson, R.K., & Bussiere, M.T. (1998). Predicting relapse: A meta-analysis of sexual offender recidivism studies. *Journal of Consulting and Clinical Psychology, 66*, 348–362.

Happe, F. (1995). *Autism*. Cambridge, MA: Harvard University Press.

Hardin, S., & Schooley, B. (2002). A story of Pick's disease: A rare form of dementia. *Journal of Neuroscience Nursing, 34*, 117–122.

Harding, C.M. (1988). Course types in schizophrenia: An analysis of European and American studies. *Schizophrenia Bulletin, 14*, 633–643.

Hare, R.D. (1993). *Without Conscience: The Disturbing World of the Psychopaths Among Us*. New York: Pocket Books.

Hare, R.D. (1996). Psychopathy: A clinical construct whose time has come. *Criminal Justice and Behavior, 23*, 25–54.

Hare, R.D., Clark, D., Grann, M., & Thornton, D. (2000). Psychopathy and the predictive utility of the PCL-R: An international perspective. *Behavioral Sciences and the Law, 18*, 623–645.

Hare, R.D., Cooke, D.J., & Hart, S.D. (1999). Psychopathy and sadistic personality disorder. In T. Millon, P.H. Blaney, & R.D. Davis (Eds.), *Oxford textbook of psychopathology* (pp. 555–584). Oxford: Oxford University Press.

Hare, R.D., Hart, S.D., & Harpur, T.J. (1991). Psychopathy and the DSM-IV criteria for antisocial personality disorder. *Journal of Abnormal Psychology, 100*, 391–398.

Harkness, K.L., Frank, E., Anderson, B., Houck, P.R., Luther, J., & Kupfer, D.J. (2002). Does interpersonal psychotherapy protect women from depression in the face of stressful life events? *Journal of Consulting and Clinical Psychology, 70*, 908–915.

Harkness, K.L., Monroe, S.M., Simons, A.D., & Thase, M. (1999). The generation of life events in recurrent and non-recurrent depression. *Psychological Medicine, 29*, 135–144.

Harpur, T.J., & Hare, R.D. (1994). Assessment of psychopathy as a function of age. *Journal of Abnormal Psychology, 103*, 604–609.

Harrington, R. (2002). Affective disorders. In M. Rutter & E. Taylor (Eds.), *Child and Adolescent Psychiatry* (4th ed., pp. 463–485). Oxford, UK: Blackwell.

Harrington, R., Fudge, H., Rutter, M., Pickles, A., & Hill, J. (1990). Adult outcomes of childhood and adolescent depression. I. Psychiatric status. *Archives of General Psychiatry, 47*, 465–473.

Harrington, R.C., & Harrison, L. (1999). Unproven assumptions about the impact of bereavement on children. *Journal of the Royal Society of Medicine, 92*, 230–233.

Harris, G.T., & Rice, M.E. (1996). The science in phallometric measurement of male sexual interest. *Current Directions in Psychological Science, 5*, 156–160.

Harris, G.T., Rice, M.E., & Cormier, C.A. (1994). Psychopaths: Is a therapeutic community therapeutic? *Therapeutic Communities: International Journal for Therapeutic and Supportive Organizations*, 15, 283–299.

Harris, G.T., Rice, M.E., & Quinsey, V.L. (1993). Violent recidivism of mentally disordered offenders: The development of a statistical prediction instrument. *Criminal Justice and Behavior*, 20, 315–335.

Harris, G.T., Rice, M.E., Quinsey, V.L., Lalumiere, M.L., Boer, D., & Lang, C. (2003). A multisite comparison of actuarial risk instruments for sex offenders. *Psychological Assessment*, 15, 413–425.

Harris, J.R. (1995). Where is the child's environment? A group socialization theory of development. *Psychological Review*, 102, 458–489.

Harris, J.R. (1998). *The Nurture Assumption. Why Children Turn Out the Way they Do*. New York: Free Press.

Harrison, P.J. (1999). The neuropathology of schizophrenia: A critical review of the data and their interpretation. *Brain*, 122, 593–624.

Hart, A.B., Craighead, W.E., & Craighead, L.W. (2001). Predicting recurrence of major depressive disorder in young adults: A prospective study. *Journal of Abnormal Psychology*, 110, 633–643.

Hart, S.D., Cox, D.N., & Hare, R.D. (1995). *Manual for the Hare Psychopathy Checklist: Screening Version*. Toronto: Multi-Health Systems.

Hart, S.D., & Hare, R.D. (1997). Psychopathy: Assessment and association with criminal conduct. In D.M. Stoff, J. Breiling, & J. Maser (Eds.), *Handbook of Antisocial Behavior* (pp. 22–35). New York: Wiley.

Hartmann, H., Kris, E., & Loewenstein, R.W. (1947). Comments on the formation of psychic structure. In A. Freud et al. (Eds.), *The psychoanalytic study of the child*. New York: International Universities Press.

Harvey, A.G., & Bryant, R.A. (1998). The relationship between acute stress disorder and posttraumatic stress disorder: A prospective evaluation of motor vehicle accident survivors. *Journal of Consulting and Clinical Psychology*, 66, 507–512.

Harvey, A.G., & Bryant, R.A. (1999). The relationship between acute stress disorder and posttraumatic stress disorder: A 2-year prospective evaluation. *Journal of Consulting and Clinical Psychology*, 67, 985–988.

Harvey, A.G., Bryant, R.A., & Dang, S.T. (1998). Autobiographical memory in acute stress disorder. *Journal of Consulting and Clinical Psychology*, 66, 500–506.

Harvey, R.J. (1996). Review: Delusions in dementia. *Age and Ageing*, 25, 405–409.

Hashemi, A.J., & Cochrane, R. (1999). Expressed emotion and schizophrenia: A review of studies across cultures. *International Review of Psychiatry*, 11, 219–224.

Hasin, D., Paykin, A., Endicott, J., & Grant, B. (1999). The validity of DSM-IV alcohol abuse: Drunk drivers versus all others. *Journal of Studies on Alcohol*, 60, 746–755.

Haskett, R.F. (1993). The HPA axis and depressive disorders. In J. John Mann & David J. Kupfer (Eds.), *Biology of Depressive Disorders* (pp. 171–188). New York: Plenum.

Haugaard, J.J., & Reppucci, N.D. (1988). *The Sexual Abuse of Children*. San Francisco: Jossey-Bass.

Hawton, K. (1986). *Suicide and attempted suicide among children and adolescents*. Beverly Hills, CA: Sage.

Hayes, S.C., Nelson, R.O., & Jarrett, R.B. (1987). The treatment utility of assessment: A functional approach to evaluating assessment quality. *American Psychologist*, 42, 963–974.

Hayman-Abello, B.A., Hayman-Abello, S.E., & Rourke, B.P. (2003). Human neuropsychology in Canada: The 1990s (a review of research by Canadian neuropsychologists over the past decade). *Canadian Psychology*, 44, 100–138.

Haynes, S.G., & Feinleib, M. (1980). Women, work, and coronary heart disease: Prospective findings from the Framingham heart study. *American Journal of Public Health*, 70, 133–141.

Health Canada (1999a). Advisory. Liver complications result in withdrawal of Attention Deficit Hyperactivity Disorder drug Cylert. Ottawa: Author. Retrieved June 15, 2004, from http://www.hc-sc.gc.ca/english/protection/warnings/1999/99_113e.htm

Health Canada (1999b). Measuring up. A health surveillance update on Canadian children and youth. Suicide. Ottawa: Author. Retrieved June 15, 2004, from http://www.hc-sc.gc.ca/pphb-dgspsp/publicat/meas-haut/mu_y_e.html

Health Canada (2000a). *HIV and AIDS in Canada*. Epi Update, Division of HIV/AIDS Surveillance, Bureau of HIV/AIDS, STD and TB, LCDC. Ottawa: Author.

Health Canada (2000b). *HIV and AIDS among aboriginal people in Canada*. Epi Update, Division of HIV/AIDS Surveillance, Bureau of HIV/AIDS, STD and TB, LCDC. Ottawa: Author.

Health Canada (2001). *Canadian Tobacco Use Monitoring Survey*. Retrieved March 18, 2003, from www.hc-sc.gc.ca/hecs-sesc/tobacco/research/ctums/2001/2001overview.html

Health Canada (2002a). *A Report on Mental Illnesses in Canada* (Catalogue No. 0-662-32817-5). Ottawa: Health Canada Editorial Board Mental Illnesses in Canada.

Health Canada (2002b). *Aboriginal Head Start in Urban and Northern Communities*. Ottawa: Author. Retrieved October 18, 2003, from http://www.hc-sc.gc.ca/dca-dea/programs-mes/ahs_overview_e.html#top

Health Canada (2003a). *Deaths in Canada due to smoking*. Retrieved May 19, 2004, from http://www.hc-sc.gc.ca/english/media/releases/1996/deathe.htm

Health Canada (2003b). *Canada's report on HIV/AIDS 2002*. Retrieved May 19, 2004, from http://www.hc-sc.gc.ca/hppb/hiv_aids/report02/sec1.html#epidemic

Health Canada (2004). Advisory. Health Canada advises Canadians under the age of 18 to consult physicians if they are being treated with newer anti-depressants. Ottawa: Author. Retrieved June 15, 2004, from http://www.hc-sc.gc.ca/english/protection/warnings/2004/2004_02.htm

Health Reports (2002). *How healthy are Canadians? 2002 Annual Report* (Catalogue No. 82-003-SIE). *Health Reports*, 13(suppl.), 73–88.

Healy, D. (1997). *The Anti-Depressant Era*. Cambridge, MA: Harvard University Press.

Heath, A.C., Bucholz, I.I., Madden, P.A.F., Dinwiddie, S.H., Slutske, W.S., Bierut, L.J., Statham, D.J., Dunne, M.P., Whitfield, J.B., & Martin, N.G. (1997). Genetic and environmental contributions to alcohol dependence risk in a national twin sample: Consistency of findings in women and men. *Psychological Medicine*, 27, 1381–1396.

Heatherton, T.F., & Polivy, J. (1992). Chronic dieting and eating disorders: A spiral model. In J. Crowther, S.E. Hobfall, M.A.P. Stephens, & D.L. Tennenbaum (Eds.), *The Etiology of Bulimia: The Individual and Familial Context* (pp. 135–155). Washington, DC: Hemisphere.

Heavey, C.L., Christensen, A., & Malamuth, N.M. (1995). The longitudinal impact of demand and withdrawal during marital conflict. *Journal of Consulting and Clinical Psychology*, 63, 797–801.

Hebb, D.O. (1949). *The Organization of Behavior*. New York: Wiley.

Heber, R. (1959). A manual on terminology and classification in mental retardation. *American Journal on Mental Deficiency*, 64 (monograph suppl.).

Heiman, J.R. (1998). Psychophysiological models of female sexual response. *International Journal of Impotence Research*, 10 (suppl. 2), 94–97.

Heiman, J.R., & LoPiccolo, J. (1988). *Becoming Orgasmic: A Sexual and Personal Growth Program for Women*. New York: Fireside.

Heinberg, L.J., Thompson, J.K., & Stormer, S. (1995). Development and validation of the sociocultural attitudes towards appearance questionnaire. *International Journal of Eating Disorders*, 17, 81–89.

Heinrichs, R.W. (2001). *In search of madness: Schizophrenia and neuroscience*. London: Oxford University Press.

Heinssen, R.K., Liberman, R.P., & Kopelowicz, A. (2000). Psychosocial skills training for schizophrenia: Lessons from the laboratory. *Schizophrenia Bulletin* 26, 21–46.

Heitler, S.M. (1992). *From conflict to resolution: Strategies for diagnosis and treatment of distressed individuals, couples, and families*. New York: Norton.

Hellewell, J.S.E. (1999). Treatment-resistant schizophrenia: Reviewing the options and identifying the way forward. *Journal of Clinical Psychiatry*, 60 (suppl. 23), 14–19.

Helmes, E., & Reddon, J.R. (1993). A perspective on developments in assessing psychopathology: A critical review of the MMPI and MMPI-2. *Psychological Bulletin*, 113, 453–471.

Helzer, J.E., Robins, L.N., & McEvoy, L. (1987). Posttraumatic stress disorder in the general population: Findings of the Epidemiologic Catchment Area Survey. *New England Journal of Medicine*, 317, 1630–1634.

Hempel, C.G. (1961). Introduction to problems of taxonomy. In J. Zubin (Ed.), *Field Studies in the Mental Disorders* (pp. 3–22). New York: Grune & Stratton.

Hendin, H. (1995). *Suicide in America*. New York: Norton.

Hendricks, C.L. (1993–94). The trend toward mandatory mediation in custody and visitation disputes of minor children: An overview. *Journal of Family Law*, 32, 491–510.

Hendrie, H.C., Osuntokun, B.O., Hall, K.S., et al. (1995). Prevalence of Alzheimer's disease and dementia in two communities: Nigerian Africans and African Americans. *American Journal of Psychiatry*, 152, 1485–1492.

Henggeler, S.W. (1994). *Treatment Manual for Family Preservation Using Multisystemic Therapy*. Charleston: Medical University of South Carolina.

Henggeler, S.W., & Borduin, C.M. (1990). *Family Therapy and Beyond: A Multisystemic Approach to Treating the Behavior Problems of Children and Adolescents*. Pacific Grove, CA: Brooks/Cole.

Henker, B., & Whalen, C.K. (1989). Hyperactivity and attention deficits. *American Psychologist*, 44, 216–223.

Herbener, E.S., & Harrow, M. (2002). The course of anhedonia during 10 years of schizophrenic illness. *Journal of Abnormal Psychology*, 111, 237–248.

Herbert, M. (2002). Behavioural therapies. In M. Rutter & E. Taylor (Eds.), *Child and Adolescent Psychiatry* (4th ed., pp. 900–920). Oxford, UK: Blackwell.

Herman, C.P., & Polivy, J. (1988). Excess and restraint in bulimia. In K. Pirke, W. Vandereycken, & D. Ploog (Eds.), *The Psychobiology of Bulimia* (pp. 33–41). Munich: Springer-Verlag.

Hermann, D.H.J. (1990). Autonomy, self-determination, the right of involuntarily committed persons to refuse treatment, and the use of substituted judgment in medication decisions involving incompetent persons. *International Journal of Law and Psychiatry*, 13, 361–385.

Herpertz, S.C., Werth, U., Lucas, G., Qunaibi, M., Schuerkens, A., Kunert, H., Freese, R., Flesch. M., Mueller-Isberner, R., Osterheider, M., & Sass, H. (2001). Emotion in criminal offenders with psychopathy and borderline personality disorders. *Archives of General Psychiatry*, 58, 737–745.

Herrero, M.E., Hechtman, L., & Weiss, G. (1994). Antisocial disorders in hyperactive subjects from childhood to adulthood: Predictive factors and characterization of subgroups. *American Journal of Orthopsychiatry, 64*, 510–521.

Herzog, D.B., Dorer, D.J., Keel, P.K., Selwyn, S.E., Ekeblad, E.R., Flores, A.T., Greenwood, D.N., Burwell, R.A., & Keller, M.B. (1999). Recovery and relapse in anorexia and bulimia nervosa: A 75-year follow-up study. *Journal of the American Academy of Child & Adolescent Psychiatry, 38*, 829–837.

Heston, L.L. (1966). Psychiatric disorders in foster home reared children of schizophrenic mothers. *British Journal of Psychiatry, 112*, 819–825.

Heston, L.L., & White, J.A. (1991). *The Vanishing Mind: A Practical Guide to Alzheimer's Disease and Other Dementias*. New York: Freeman.

Hettema, J.M., Prescott, C.A., & Kendler, K.S. (2001). A population-based twin study of generalized anxiety disorder in men and women. *Journal of Nervous and Mental Disease, 189*, 413–420.

Hewitt, P.L., Flett, G.L., & Ediger, E. (1995). Perfectionism traits and perfectionistic self-presentation in eating disorder attitudes. *International Journal of Eating Disorders, 18*, 317–326.

Hewitt, P.L., Flett, G.L., Sherry, S.B., Habke, M., Parkin, M., Lam, R.W., McMurtry, B., Ediger, E., Fairlie, P., & Stein, M.B. (2003). The interpersonal expression of perfection: Perfectionistic self-presentation and psychological distress. *Journal of Personality and Social Psychology, 84*, 1303–1325.

Hewitt, P.L., Flett, G.L., Turnbull-Donovan, W., & Mikail, S.F. (1991). The Multidimensional Perfectionism Scale: Reliability, validity, and psychometric properties in psychiatric samples. *Psychological Assessment, 3*, 464–468.

Heyman, I., & Santosh, P. (2002). Pharmacological and other physical treatments. In M. Rutter & E. Taylor (Eds.), *Child and Adolescent Psychiatry* (4th ed., pp. 998–1018). Oxford, UK: Blackwell.

Hill, G., Forbes, W., Berthelot, J.-M., Lindsay, J., & McDowell, I. (1996). Dementia among seniors. *Health Reports, 8*, 7–10.

Hill, J., & Holmbeck, G. (1986). Attachment and autonomy during adolescence. In G. Whitehurst (Ed.), *Annals of Child Development* (Vol. 3, 145–189). Greenwich, CT: JAI.

Hill, M.A. (1992). Light, circadian rhythms, and mood disorders: A review. *Annals of Clinical Psychiatry, 4*, 131–146.

Hilsenroth, J.J., Ackerman, S.J., Blagys, M.D., Baumann, B.D., Baity, M.R., Smith, S.R., Price, J.L, Smith, C.L., Heindselman, T.L., Mount, M.K., & Holdwick, D.J. (2000). Reliability and validity of DSM-IV axis V. *American Journal of Psychiatry, 157*, 1858–1863.

Hinde, R.A. (1992). Developmental psychology in the context of other behavioral sciences. *Developmental Psychology, 28*, 1018–1029.

Hinshaw, S.P. (1994). *Attention Deficits and Hyperactivity in Children*. Thousand Oaks, CA: Sage.

Hinshaw et al. (2000). Family processes and treatment outcome in the MTA: Negative/ineffective parenting practices in relations to multimodal treatment. *Journal of Abnormal Child Psychology, 28*, 555–568.

Hirayasu, Y., McCarley, R.W., Salisbury, D.F., Tanaka, S., Kwon, J.S., Frumin, M., Snyderman, D., Yurgelun-Todd, D., Kikinis, R., Jolesz, F.A., & Shenton, M.E. (2000). Planum temporale and Heschl gyrus volume reduction in schizophrenia: a magnetic resonance imaging study of first-episode patients. *Archives of General Psychiatry, 57*, 692–699.

Hirschfeld, R.M.A., Shea, M.T., & Weise, R. (1995). Dependent personality disorder. In W.J. Livesley (Ed.), *The DSM-IV Personality Disorders* (pp. 239–256). New York: Guilford.

Hirschfeld, R.M.A. (2001). Antidepressants in the United States: Current status and future needs. In M.M. Weissman (Ed.), *Treatment of Depression: Bridging the 21st Century* (pp. 123–134). Washington, DC: American Psychiatric Press.

Hlastala, S.A., Frank, E., Kowalski, J., Tu, X.M., Anderson, B., & Kupfer, D.J. (2000). Stressful life events, bipolar disorder, and the "kindling model." *Journal of Abnormal Psychology, 109*, 777–786.

Hodges, J.R. (2001). Frontotemporal dementia (Pick's disease): Clinical features and assessment. *Neurology, 56* (suppl. 4), S6–S10.

Hoek, H.W. (1995). The distribution of eating disorders. In K.D. Brownell & C.G. Fairburn (Eds.), *Eating Disorders and Obesity: A Comprehensive Handbook* (pp. 207–211). New York: Guilford.

Hoek, H.W. (2002). Distribution of eating disorders. In C.G. Fairburn & K.D. Brownell (Eds.), *Eating Disorders and Obesity*, (2nd ed., pp. 233–237). New York: Guilford.

Hoenig, J. (1985). Etiology of transsexualism. In B.W. Steiner (Ed.), *Gender Dysphoria: Development, Research, Management* (pp. 33–74). New York: Plenum.

Hoffman, B.F. (1997). Courts and torts: The psychiatrist preparing for trial. *Canadian Journal of Psychiatry, 42*, 497–501.

Hoffman, B.F., & Spiegel, H. (1989). Legal principles in the psychiatric assessment of personal injury litigants. *American Journal of Psychiatry, 146*, 304–310.

Hoffman, P.B., & Foust, L.L. (1977). Least restrictive treatment of the mentally ill: A doctrine in search of its senses. *San Diego Law Review, 14*, 1100–1154.

Hogan, D.R. (1990). Sexual dysfunctions: A historical perspective. In C.E. Walker (Ed.), *History of Clinical Psychology* (pp. 279–309). Pacific Grove, CA: Brooks/Cole.

Hogarty, G.E. (1993). Prevention of relapse in chronic schizophrenic patients. *Journal of Clinical Psychiatry, 54* (suppl.), 18–23.

Hogben, D. (2003). Corporate psychos blend in well: Psychopaths are attracted to today's business climate. *Vancouver Sun*, January 24, p. B5.

Hole, J.W., Jr. (1984). *Human anatomy and physiology* (3rd ed.). Dubuque, IA: Wm. C. Brown.

Holland, J. (2001). *Ecstasy: The Complete Guide: A Comprehensive Look at the Risks and Benefits of MDMA*. Rochester, VT: Inner Traditions.

Hollander, E., & Rosen, J. (2000). Impulsivity. *Journal of Psychopharmacology, 14* (suppl. 1), S39–S44.

Holley, H., Arboleda-Flórez, J, & Crisanti, A. (1998). Do forensic offenders receive harsher sentences? *International Journal of Law and Psychiatry, 21*, 43–57.

Hollon, S.D. (1999). Allegiance effects in treatment research: A commentary. *Clinical Psychology: Science and Practice, 6*, 107–112.

Hollon, S.D., Shelton, R.C., & Davis, D.D. (1993). Cognitive therapy for depression: Conceptual issues and clinical efficacy. *Journal of Consulting and Clinical Psychology, 61*, 270–275.

Holmes, C. (2002). Genotype and phenotype in Alzheimer's disease. *British Journal of Psychiatry, 180*, 131–134.

Holmes, T.H., & Rahe, R.H. (1967). The Social Readjustment Rating Scale. *Journal of Psychosomatic Research, 11*, 213–218.

Holzman, P.S. (1994). Parsing cognition: The power of psychology paradigms. *Archives of General Psychiatry, 51*, 952–954.

Holzman, P.S. (2000). Eye movements and the search for the essence of schizophrenia. *Brain Research Reviews, 31*, 350–356.

Holtzman, S., Newth, S., & DeLongis, A. (in press). The role of social support in coping with daily pain among patients with rheumatoid arthritis. *Journal of Health Psychology.*

Homewood, J., & Bond, N.W. (1999). Thiamin deficiency and Korsakoff's syndrome: Failure to find memory impairments following nonalcoholic Wernicke's encephalopathy. *Alcohol, 19*, 75–84.

Hooley, J.M. (1998). Expressed emotion and psychiatric illness: From empirical data to clinical practice. *Behavior Therapy, 29*, 631–646.

Hooley, J.M., & Gotlib, I.H. (2000). A diathesis-stress conceptualization of expressed emotion and clinical outcome. *Applied and Preventive Psychology 9*, 135–151.

Horevitz, R., & Loewenstein, R.J. (1994). The rational treatment of multiple personality disorder. In S.J. Lynn & J.W. Rhue (Eds.), *Dissociation: Clinical and Theoretical Perspectives* (pp. 289–316). New York: Guilford.

Horley, J. (2001). Frotteurism: A term in search of an underlying disorder. *Journal of Sexual Aggression, 7*, 51–55.

Horn, J.M., Loehlin, J.C., & Willerman, L. (1979). Intellectual resemblance among adoptive and biological relatives: The Texas Adoption Project. *Behavior Genetics, 9*, 177–205.

Horney, K. (1939). *New Ways in Psychoanalysis*. New York: International Universities Press.

Horowitz, M.J., Siegel, B., Holen, A., Bonanno, G.A., Milbrath, C., & Stinson, C.H. (1997). Diagnostic criteria for complicated grief disorder. *American Journal of Psychiatry, 154*, 904–910.

Houezec, J.L. (1998). Pharmacokinetics and pharmacodynamics of nicotine. In J. Snel & M.M. Lorist (Eds.), *Nicotine, Caffeine and Social Drinking: Behaviour and Brain Function* (pp. 3–20). Amsterdam: Harwood.

Houts, A.C. (1991). Nocturnal enuresis as a biobehavioral problem. *Behavior Therapy, 22*, 133–151.

Houts, A.C. (2001). The diagnostic and statistical manual's new white coat and circularity of plausible dysfunctions: Response to Wakefield. *Behaviour Research and Therapy, 39*, 315–345.

Howard, K.I., Kopta, S.M., Krause, M.S., & Orlinsky, D.E. (1986). The dose-effect relationship in psychotherapy. *American Psychologist, 41*, 159–164.

Hsu, L.K.G. (1990). *Eating Disorders*. New York: Guilford.

Hsu, L.K.G. (1995). Outcome of bulimia nervosa. In K.D. Brownell & C.G. Fairburn (Eds.), *Eating Disorders and Obesity: A Comprehensive Handbook* (pp. 238–244). New York: Guilford.

Hucker, S.J. (1985). Self-harmful sexual behavior. *Psychiatric Clinics of North America, 8*, 323–328.

Hucker, S.J. (1997a). Impulsivity in DSM-IV impulse-control disorders. In C.D. Webster & M.A. Jackson (Eds.), *Impulsivity: Theory, Assessment, and Treatment* (pp. 195–211). New York: Guilford.

Hucker, S.J. (1997b). Sexual sadism: Theory and psychopathology. In D.R. Laws & W.T. O'Donohue (Eds.), *Handbook of Sexual Deviance: Theory and Application* (pp. 194–209). New York: Guilford.

Hughes, C.C. (1998). The glossary of culture-bound syndromes in DSM-IV: A critique. *Transcultural Psychiatry, 35*, 413–421.

Hughes, J.R., Oliveto, A.H., Liguori, A., Carpenter, J., & Howard, T. (1998). Endorsement of DSM-IV dependence criteria among caffeine users. *Drug and Alcohol Dependence, 52*, 99–107.

Hull, J.G., & Bond, C.F., Jr. (1986). Social and behavioral consequences of alcohol consumption and expectancy: A meta-analysis. *Psychological Bulletin, 99*, 347–360.

Hultsch, D.F., Hertzog, C., Small, B.J., & Dixon, R.A. (1999). Use it or lose it: Engaged lifestyle as a buffer of cognitive decline in aging? *Psychology & Aging, 14*, 245–263.

Human Capital Initiative. (1996). *Doing the Right Thing: A Research Plan for Healthy Living*. Washington, DC: American Psychological Society.

Humphrey, L.L. (1987). Comparison of bulimic-anorexic and nondistressed families using structural analysis of social behavior. *Journal of the American Academy of Child and Adolescent Psychiatry, 26*, 248–255.

Hunsley, J., & Bailey, J.M. (1999). The clinical utility of the Rorschach: Unfulfilled promises and an uncertain future. *Psychological Assessment, 11*, 266–277.

Hunsley, J., & Bailey, J.M. (2001). Whither the Rorschach? An analysis of the evidence. *Psychological Assessment, 13*, 472–485.

Hunsley, J., Dobson, K. S., Johnston, C., & Mikhail, S. F. (1999). Empirically supported treatments in psychology: Implications for Canadian professional psychology. *Canadian Psychology, 40*, 289–302.

Hunsley, J., & Johnston, C. (2000). The role of empirically supported treatments in evidence-based psychological practice: A Canadian perspective. *Clinical Psychology: Science and Practice, 7*, 269–272.

Hunsley, J., Lee, C.M., & Wood, J.M. (2003). Controversial and questionable assessment techniques. In S.O. Lilienfeld & S.J. Lynn (Eds.), *Science and pseudoscience in clinical psychology* (pp. 39–76). New York: Guilford.

Hunter, J.M., Shannon, G.W., & Sambrook, S.L. (1986). Rings of madness: Service areas of 19th-century asylums in North America. *Social Science and Medicine, 23*, 1033–1050.

Huntington's Disease Collaborative Research Group (1993). A novel gene containing a trinucleotide repeat that is expanded and unstable on Huntington's disease chromosomes. *Cell, 72*, 971–983.

Hurt, S.W., Reznikoff, M., & Clarkin, J.F. (1991). *Psychological Assessment, Psychiatric Diagnosis, and Treatment Planning*. New York: Brunner/Mazel.

Hussong, A.M., & Chassin, L. (2002). Parent alcoholism and the leaving home transition. *Development and Psychopathology, 14*, 139–157.

Huws, R., Shubsachs, A.P.W., & Taylor, P.J. (1991). Hypersexuality, fetishism and multiple sclerosis. *British Journal of Psychiatry, 158*, 280–281.

Hyman, S.E., & Malenka, R.C. (2001). Addiction and the brain: The neurobiology of compulsion and its persistence. *Nature Reviews Neuroscience, 2*, 695–703.

Hyman, S.E., & Moldin, S.O. (2001). Genetic science and depression: Implications for research and treatment. In M.M. Weissman (Ed.), *Treatment of Depression: Bridging the 21st Century* (pp. 83–103). Washington, DC: American Psychiatric Press.

Iacono, W.G. (1998). Identifying psychophysiological risk for psychopathology: Examples from substance abuse and schizophrenia research. *Psychophysiology, 35*, 621–637.

Iacono, W.G., & Beiser, M. (1992). Are males more likely than females to develop schizophrenia? *American Journal of Psychiatry, 149*, 1070–1074.

Iacono, W.G., & Clementz, B.A. (1993). A strategy for elucidating genetic influences on complex psychopathological syndromes. In L.J. Chapman, J.P. Chapman, & D. Fowles (Eds.), *Progress in Experimental Personality and Psychopathology Research* (pp. 11–65). New York: Springer.

Imperato-McGinley, J., Guerrero, L., Gautier, T., & Peterson, R.E. (1974). Steroid 5a-reductase deficiency in man: An inherited form of male pseudohermaphroditism. *Science, 186*, 1213–1215.

Ingram, J.L., Stodgell, C.J., Hyman, S.L., Figlewicz, D.A., Weitkamp, L.R., & Rodier, P.M. (2000). Discovery of allelic variants of HOXA1 and HOXB1: Genetic susceptibility to autism spectrum disorders. *Teratology, 62*, 396–409.

Ingram, R.E., Miranda, J., & Segal, Z. (1998). *Cognitive vulnerability to depression*. New York: Guilford.

Ingram, R.E., & Ritter, J. (2000). Vulnerability to depression: Cognitive reactivity and parental bonding in high-risk individuals. *Journal of Abnormal Psychology, 109*, 588–596.

Inouye, S.K., Schlesinger, M.J., & Lydon, T.J. (1999). Delirium: A symptom of how hospital care is failing older persons and a window to improve quality of hospital care. *American Journal of Medicine, 106*, 565–573.

Insel, K.C., & Badger, T.A. (2002). Deciphering the 4 D's: cognitive decline, delirium, depression and dementia–a review. *Journal of Advanced Nursing, 38*, 360–368.

Izard, C. et al. (2001). Emotion knowledge as a predictor of social behavior and academic competence in children at risk. *Psychological Science, 12*, 18–25.

Jablensky, A. (1985). Approaches to the definition and classification of anxiety and related disorders in European psychiatry. In A.H. Tuma & J. Maser (Eds.), *Anxiety and the Anxiety Disorders* (pp. 735–758). Hillsdale, NJ: Erlbaum.

Jablensky, A. (1999). The nature of psychiatric classification: Issues beyond ICD-10 and DSM-IV. *Australian and New Zealand Journal of Psychiatry, 33*, 137–144.

Jablensky, A. (2000). Epidemiology of schizophrenia: The global burden of disease and disability. *European Archives of Psychiatry and Clinical Neuroscience, 250*, 274–285.

Jablensky, A., Sartorius, N., Ernberg, G., Anker, M., Korten, A., Cooper, J.E., Day, R., & Bertelsen, A. (1992). Schizophrenia: Manifestations, incidence and course in different cultures: A World Health Organization ten-country study. *Psychological Medicine* (suppl. 20), 1–97.

Jackson, D.N. (1998). *Multidimensional aptitude battery-II*. London, ON: Research Psychologists Press.

Jackson, D.N., & Livesley, W.J. (1995). Possible contributions from personality assessment to the classification of personality disorders. In W.J. Livesley (Ed.), *The DSM-IV personality disorders* (pp. 459–481). New York: Guilford.

Jackson, D.N., & Livesley, W.J. (1999). *Dimensional assessment of personality pathology*. London, ON: Research Psychologists Press.

Jackson, D.N., & Paunonen, S.V. (1980). Personality structure and assessment. *Annual Review of Psychology, 31*, 503–582.

Jacob, T., & Johnson, S. (1997). Parenting influences on the development of alcohol abuse and dependence. *Alcohol Health and Research World, 21*, 204–209.

Jacobson, E. (1938). *Progressive Relaxation*. Chicago: University of Chicago Press.

Jacobson, N.S., & Christensen, A. (1996). *Integrative Couple Therapy: Promoting Acceptance and Change*. New York: Norton.

Jacobson, N.S., Holtzworth-Munroe, A., & Schmaling, K.B. (1989). Marital therapy and spouse involvement in the treatment of depression, agoraphobia, and alcoholism. *Journal of Consulting and Clinical Psychology, 57*, 5–10.

Jacobson, N.S., & Truax, P. (1991). Clinical significance: A statistical approach to defining meaningful change in psychotherapy research. *Journal of Consulting and Clinical Psychology, 59*, 12–19.

Jacobson, S.A. (1997). Delirium in the elderly. *Psychiatric Clinics of North America, 20*, 91–110.

Jaffe, J.H. (1995). Pharmacological treatment of opioid dependence: Current techniques and new findings. *Psychiatric Annals, 25*, 369–375.

Jaffe, J.H., & Jaffe, A.R. (1999). Neurobiology of opiates/opioids. In M. Galanter & H.D. Kleber (Eds.), *Textbook of Substance Abuse Treatment* (2nd ed., pp. 11–20). Washington, DC: American Psychiatric Press.

Jamison, K.R. (1995). *An Unquiet Mind: A Memoir of Moods and Madness*. New York: Knopf.

Jamison, K.R. (1999). *Night Falls Fast: Understanding Suicide*. New York: Knopf.

Janeck, A.S., Calamari, J.E., Riemann, B.C., & Heffelfinger, S.K. (2003). Too much thinking about thinking?: Metacognitive differences in obsessive–compulsive disorder. *Journal of Anxiety Disorders, 17*, 181–195.

Jang, K.L., Livesley, W.J., & Vernon, P.A. (1997). Gender-specific etiological differences in alcohol and drug problems: A behavioural genetic analysis. *Addiction, 92*, 1265–1276.

Jang, K L., Livesley, W.J., Vernon, P.A. (2002). The etiology of personality function: The University of British Columbia Twin Project. *Twin Research, 5*, 42–46.

Jang, K.L., Livesley, W.J., Vernon, P.A., Taylor, S., & Moon, E.C. (2004). Heritability of individual depressive symptoms. *Journal of Affective Disorders, 80*, 125–133.

Jang, K.., Paris, J., Zweig-Frank, H., & Livesley, W.J. (1998). Twin study of dissociative experience. *Journal of Nervous and Mental Disease, 186*, 345–351.

Jang, K.L., Stein, M.B., Taylor, S., Asmundson, G.J.G., & Livesley, W. J. (2003). Exposure to traumatic events and experiences: Aetiological relationships with personality function. *Psychiatry Research, 120*, 61–69.

Jang, K.L., Stein, M.B., Taylor, S., & Livesley, W.J. (1999). Gender differences in the etiology of anxiety sensitivity: A twin study. *Journal of Gender Specific Medicine, 2*, 39–44.

Jang, K.L., Vernon, P.A., & Livesley, W.J. (2000). Personality disorder traits, family environment, and alcohol misuse: A multivariate behavioural genetic analysis. *Addiction, 95*, 873–888.

Janoff-Bulman, R. (1992). *Shattered assumptions: Towards a new psychology of trauma*. New York: Free Press.

Jefferson, J.W. (1997). Antidepressants in panic disorder. *Journal of Clinical Psychiatry, 58* (suppl. 2), 20–24.

Jellinek, E.M. (1960). *The disease concept of alcoholism*. New Haven, CT: Hillhouse Press.

Jenkins, C.D. (1988). Epidemiology of cardiovascular diseases. *Journal of Consulting and Clinical Psychology, 56*, 324–332.

Jenkins, J.H. (1993). Too close for comfort: Schizophrenia and emotional overinvolvement among Mexican families. In A.D. Gaines (Ed.), *Ethnopsychiatry* (pp. 203–221). Albany: State University of New York Press.

Jenkins, J.H., & Karno, M. (1992). The meaning of expressed emotion: Theoretical issues raised by cross-cultural research. *American Journal of Psychiatry, 149*, 9–21.

Jiang, W., Babyak, M., Krantz, D.S., Waugh, R.A., et al. (1996). Mental stress-induced myocardial ischemia and cardiac events. *Journal of the American Medical Association, 275*, 1651–1656.

Joffe, R.T., & Gardner, D.M. (2000). *The Canadian psychotropic handbook*. Mississauga, ON: Sudler & Hennessey.

Joffres, M.R., Ghadirian, P., Fodor, J.G., Petrasovits, A., Chockalingam, A., & Hamet, P. (1997). Awareness, treatment, and control of hypertension in Canada. *American Journal of Hypertension, 10*, 1097–1102.

Johnson, C.C., Rybicki, B.A., Brown, G., D'Hondt, E., Herpolsheimer, B., Roth, D., & Jackson, C.E. (1997). Cognitive impairment in the Amish: A four county survey. *International Journal of Epidemiology, 26*, 387–394.

Johnson, G. (2002). Fear of fat. *Georgia Straight*, June 13–20, pp. 19–22.

Johnson, J.G., Cohen, P., Brown, J., Smailes, E.M., & Bernstein, D.P. (1999). Childhood maltreatment increases risk for personality disorders during early adulthood. *Archives of General Psychiatry, 56*, 600–606.

Johnson, J.G., Cohen, P., Skodol, A.E., Oldham, J.M., Kasen, S., & Brook, J.S. (1999). Personality disorders in adolescence and risk of major mental disorders and suicidality during adulthood. *Archives of General Psychiatry, 56*, 805–811.

Johnson, P. (1989). Hemingway: Portrait of the artist as an intellectual. *Commentary, 87*, 49–59.

Johnson, S.L., & Miller, I. (1997). Negative life events and time to recovery from episodes of bipolar disorder. *Journal of Abnormal Psychology, 106*, 449–457.

Johnson, S.L., & Roberts, J.E. (1995). Life events and bipolar disorder: Implications from biological theories. *Psychological Bulletin, 117*, 434–449.

Johnson, S.L, Sandrow, D., Meyter, B., Winters, R., Miller, I., Solomon, D., & Keitner, G. (2000). Increases in manic symptoms after life events involving goal attainment. *Journal of Abnormal Psychology, 109*, 721–727.

Johnson, S.L., Winett, C.A., Meyer, B., Greenhouse, W.J., & Miller, I. (1999). Social support and the course of bipolar disorder. *Journal of Abnormal Psychology, 108*, 558–566.

Johnson, S.M. (2000). Emotionally focused couples therapy. In F.M. Dattilio & L.J. Bevilacqua (Eds.), *Comparative treatments for relationship dysfunction* (pp. 163–185). New York: Springer.

Johnson, S.M., Hunsley, J., Greenberg, L., & Schindler, D. (1999). Emotionally focused couples therapy: Status and challenges. *Clinical Psychology: Science and Practice, 6*, 67–79.

Johnston, C., & Mash, E.J. (1989). A measure of parenting satisfaction and efficacy. *Journal of Clinical Child Psychology, 18*, 167–175.

Johnston, C., & Mash, E.J. (2001). Families of children with attention-deficit/hyperactivity disorder: Review and recommendations for future research. *Clinical Child and Family Psychology Review, 4*, 183–207.

Johnston, D.W. (1985). Psychological interventions in cardiovascular disease. *Journal of Psychosomatic Research, 29*, 447–456.

Johnston, D.W. (1989). Prevention of cardiovascular disease by psychological methods. *British Journal of Psychiatry, 154*, 183–194.

Joiner, R.E., & Metalsky, G.I. (1995). A prospective test of an integrative interpersonal theory of depression: A naturalistic study of college roommates. *Journal of Personality and Social Psychology, 69*, 778–788.

Joiner, T., Coyne, J.C., & Blalock, J. (1999). On the interpersonal nature of depression: Overview and synthesis. In T. Joiner & J.C. Coyne (Eds.), *The Interactional Nature of Depression* (pp. 3–20). Washington, DC: American Psychological Association.

Jones, D.M. (1985). Bulimia: A false self-identity. *Clinical Social Work, 13*, 305–316.

Jones, J.C., & Barlow, D.H. (1990). The etiology of posttraumatic stress disorder. *Clinical Psychology Review, 10*, 299–328.

Jones, J.H. (1997). *Alfred C. Kinsey: A Public/Private Life.* New York: Norton.

Jones, M.A., & Krisberg, B. (1994). *Images and Reality: Juvenile Crime, Youth Violence, and Public Policy.* San Francisco: National Council on Crime and Delinquency.

Jones, P., & Cannon, M. (1998). The new epidemiology of schizophrenia. *Psychiatric Clinics of North America, 21*, 1–25.

Jones, P.B., Bebbington, P., Foerster, A., Lewis, S.W., et al. (1993). Premorbid social underachievement in schizophrenia: Results from the Camberwell Collaborative Psychosis Study. *British Journal of Psychiatry, 162*, 65–71.

Jones, R.R., Reid, J.B., & Patterson, G.R. (1975). Naturalistic observation in clinical assessment. In P. McReynolds (Ed.), *Advances in Psychological Assessment* (Vol. 3, pp. 234–297). San Francisco: Jossey-Bass.

Jorm, A.F. (2001). History of depression as a risk factor for dementia: An updated review. *Australian and New Zealand Journal of Psychiatry, 35*, 776–781.

Josephs, L. (1994). Psychoanalytic and related interpretations. In B.B.Wolman & G. Stricker (Eds.), *Anxiety and Related Disorders: A Handbook* (pp. 11–29). New York: Wiley-Interscience.

Joyce, A. S., & McCallum, M. (2004). Assessing patient capacities for therapy: Psychological-mindedness and quality of object relations. In D.P. Charman (Ed.), *Core processes in brief psychodynamic psychotherapy: Advancing effective practice* (pp. 69–100). Mahwah, NJ: Erlbaum.

Julien, R.M. (2001). *A Primer of Drug Action: A Concise, Nontechnical Guide to the Actions Uses and Side Effects of Psychoactive Drugs* (9th ed.). New York: Worth.

Junginger, J. (1997). Fetishism: Assessment and treatment. In D.R. Laws & W.T. O'Donohue (Eds.), *Handbook of Sexual Deviance: Theory and Application* (pp. 92–110). New York: Guilford.

Just, N., & Alloy, L.B. (1997). The response styles theory of depression: Tests and an extension of the theory. *Journal of Abnormal Psychology, 106*, 221–229.

Kadden, R.M. (1999). Cognitive behavior therapy. In P.J. Ott, R.E. Tarter, & R.T. Ammerman (Eds.), *Sourcebook on Substance Abuse: Etiology, Epidemiology, Assessment, and Treatment* (pp. 272–283). Boston: Allyn & Bacon.

Kagan, J. (1998). *Three Seductive Ideas.* Cambridge, MA: Harvard University Press.

Kagan, J., & Snidman, N. (1991). Temperamental factors in human development. *American Psychologist, 46*, 856–862.

Kahn, M.W. (1982). Cultural clash and psychopathology in three aboriginal cultures. *Academic Psychology Bulletin, 4*, 553–561.

Kaihla, P. (1996). No conscience, no remorse: A British Columbian psychologist probes the inner workings of psychopaths' brains. *Maclean's, 109*(4), 50–51.

Kallman, W.M., & Feuerstein, M.J. (1986). Psychophysiological procedures. In A.R. Ciminero, K.S. Calhoun, & H.E. Adams (Eds.), *Handbook of Behavioral Assessment* (2nd ed., pp. 325–350). New York: Wiley-Interscience.

Kalra, S., Bergeron, C., & Lang, A.E. (1996). Lewy body disease and dementia: A review. *Archives of Internal Medicine, 156*, 487–493.

Kamarck, T., & Jennings, J.R. (1991). Biobehavioral factors in sudden cardiac death. *Psychological Bulletin, 109*, 42–75.

Kameya, Y., Deguchi, A., & Yokota, Y. (1997). Analysis of measured values of ejaculation time in healthy males. *Journal of Sex and Marital Therapy, 23*, 25–28.

Kandel, D.B., & Yamaguchi, K. (1999). Developmental stages of involvement in substance use. In P.J. Ott, R.E. Tarter, & R.T. Ammerman (Eds.), *Sourcebook on Substance Abuse: Etiology, Epidemiology, Assessment, and Treatment* (pp. 50–74). Boston: Allyn & Bacon.

Kane, J.M. (1996). Schizophrenia. *New England Journal of Medicine, 334*, 34–41.

Kane, J.M. (1999). Pharmacologic treatment of schizophrenia. *Biological Psychiatry, 46*, 1396–1408.

Kane, J.M. (2001a). Extrapyramidal side effects are unacceptable. *European Neuropsychopharmacology, 11*(suppl. 4), S397–S403.

Kane, J.M. (2001b). Long-term therapeutic management in schizophrenia. In A. Breier, and P.V. Tran (Eds.), *Current Issues in the Psychopharmacology of Schizophrenia* (pp. 430–446). Philadelphia, PA: Lippincott.

Kanner, L. (1943). Autistic disturbances of affective contact. *Nervous Child, 2*, 217–250.

Kaplan, A.S. (2002). Psychological treatments for anorexia nervosa: A review of published studies and promising new directions. *Canadian Journal of Psychiatry, 47*, 235–242.

Kaplan, A.S., & Garfinkel, P.E. (1999). Difficulties in treating patients with eating disorders: A review of patient and clinical variables. *Canadian Journal of Psychiatry, 44*, 665–670.

Kapur, S., & Remington, G. (2001). Antypical antipsychotics: New directions and new challenges in the treatment of schizophrenia. *Annual Review of Medicine, 52*, 503–517.

Kapur, S., & Remington, G. (1996). Serotonin-dopamine interaction and its relevance to schizophrenia. *American Journal of Psychiatry, 153*, 466–476.

Karasek, R.A., Theorell, T.G., Schwartz, J., Pieper, C., & Alfredsson, L. (1982). Job, psychological factors and coronary heart disease: Swedish prospective findings and U.S. prevalence findings using a new occupational inference method. *Advances in Cardiology, 29*, 62–67.

Karney, B.R., & Bradbury, T.N. (1995). The longitudinal course of marital quality and stability: A review of theory, method, and research. *Psychological Bulletin, 118*, 3–34.

Karno, M., & Golding, J.M. (1991). Obsessive–compulsive disorder. L.N. Robins & D.A. Regier (Eds.), *Psychiatric Disorders in America: The Epidemiologic Catchment Area Study* (pp. 204–219). New York: Free Press.

Karras, A., & Otis, D.B. (1987). A comparison of inpatients in an urban state hospital in 1975 and 1982. *Hospital and Community Psychiatry, 38*, 963–967.

Kasen, S., Cohen, P., Brook, J.S., & Hartmark, C. (1996). A multiple-risk interaction model: Effects of temperament and divorce on psychiatric disorders in children. *Journal of Abnormal Child Psychology, 24*, 121–150.

Kasvikis, Y.G., Tsakiris, F., Marks, I.M., Basogulu, M., & Noshirvani, H.V. (1986). Past history of anorexia nervosa in women with obsessive–compulsive disorders. *International Journal of Eating Disorders, 5*, 1069–1075.

Katschnig, H., & Amering, M. (1990). Panic attacks and panic disorder in cross-cultural perspective. In J.C. Ballenger (Ed.), *Clinical Aspects of Panic Disorder* (pp. 67–80). New York: Wiley.

Katschnig, H., & Amering, M. (1998). The long-term course of panic disorder and its predictors. *Journal of Clinical Psychopharmacology, 18* (suppl. 2), 6–11.

Katz, R., & McGuffin, P. (1993). The genetics of affective disorders. In D. Fowles (Ed.), *Progress in Experimental Personality and Psychopathology Research* (pp. 200–221). New York: Springer.

Katzman, R. (1976). The prevalence and malignancy of Alzheimer's disease. *Archives of Neurology, 33*, 217–218.

Katzman, R. (1993). Education and the prevalence of dementia and Alzheimer's disease. *Neurology, 43*, 13–20.

Kaul, T.J., & Bednar, R.L. (1986). Experimental group research: Results, questions, and suggestions. In S.L. Garfield & A.E. Bergin (Eds.), *Handbook of psychotherapy and behavior change* (3rd ed., pp. 671–714). New York: Wiley.

Kaye, D.W.K. (1995). The epidemiology of age-related neurological disease and dementia. *Reviews in Clinical Gerontology, 5*, 39–56.

Kaye, W.H., Weltzin, T.E., Hsu, L.K.G., McConahan, C.W., & Bolton, B. (1993). Amount of calories retained after binge eating and vomiting. *American Journal of Psychiatry, 150*, 969–971.

Kaysen, S. (2001). *The Camera My Mother Gave Me.* New York: Knopf.

Kazdin, A.E. (1989). Identifying depression in children: A comparison of alternative selection criteria. *Journal of Abnormal Child Psychology, 17*, 437–455.

Kazdin, A.E. (1994a). Methodology, design, and evaluation in psychotherapy research. In A.E. Bergin and S.L. Garfield (Eds.), *Handbook of Psychotherapy and Behavior Change* (4th ed., pp. 19–71), New York: Wiley.

Kazdin, A.E. (1994b). Psychotherapy for children and adolescents. In A.E. Bergin & S.L. Garfield (Eds.), *Handbook of Psychotherapy and Behavior Change* (4th ed., pp. 543–594). New York: Wiley.

Kazdin, A.E. (1995). *Conduct Disorders in Childhood and Adolescence* (2nd ed.). Thousand Oaks, CA: Sage.

Kazdin, A.E. (1997). Parent management training: Evidence, outcomes, and issues. *Journal of the American Academy of Child and Adolescent Psychiatry, 36*, 1349–1365.

Kazdin, A.E., French, N.H., & Unis, A.S. (1983). Child, mother, and father evaluations of depression in psychiatric inpatient children. *Journal of Abnormal Child Psychology, 11*, 167–180.

Kazdin, A.E., & Petti, T.A. (1982). Self-report and interview measures of childhood and adolescent depression. *Journal of Child Psychology and Psychiatry, 23*, 437–457.

Kazdin, A.E., Siegel, T.C., & Bass, D. (1992). Cognitive problem-solving skills training and parent management training in the treatment of antisocial behavior in children. *Journal of Consulting and Clinical Psychology, 60*, 753–747.

Kazdin, A.E., & Wilcoxin, L.A. (1976). Systematic desensitization and nonspecific treatment effects: A methodological evaluation. *Psychological Bulletin, 83*, 729–758.

Keane, T.M., Zimering, R.T., & Caddell, J.M. (1985). A behavioral formulation of posttraumatic stress disorder in Vietnam veterans. *The Behavior Therapist, 8*, 9–12.

Keel, P.K., & Mitchell, J.E. (1997). Outcome in bulimia nervosa. *American Journal of Psychiatry, 154*, 313–321.

Keel, P.K., Mitchell, J.E., Davis, T.L., & Crow, S.J. (2002). Long-term impact of treatment in women diagnosed with bulimia nervosa. *International Journal of Eating Disorders, 31*, 151–158.

Keel, P.K., et al., (2000). Predictive validity of bulimia nervosa as a diagnostic category. *American Journal of Psychiatry, 157*, 136–138.

Keel, P.K. et al. (2002). Predictors of treatment utilization among women with anorexia and bulimia nervosa. *American Journal of Psychiatry, 159*, 140–142.

Keenan, K., & Shaw, D. (1997) Developmental and social influences on young girls' early problem behavior. *Psychological Bulletin, 121*, 95–113.

Keesey, R.E. (1995). A set-point model of body weight regulation. In K.D. Brownell & C.G. Fairburn (Eds.), *Eating Disorders and Obesity: A Comprehensive Handbook* (pp. 46–50). New York: Guilford.

Keith, S.J., Regier, D.A., & Rae, D.S. (1991). Schizophrenic disorders. In L.N. Robins & D.A. Regier (Eds.), *Psychiatric Disorders in America: The Epidemiologic Catchment Area Study* (pp. 33–52). New York: Free Press.

Keller, J., Hicks, B.D., & Miller, G.A. (2000). Psychophysiology in the study of psychopathology. In J.T. Cacioppo, L.G. Tassinary, and G.G. Berntson (Eds.). *Handbook of Psychophysiology* (2nd ed., pp. 719–750). New York: Cambridge University Press.

Keller, M.B. (1987). Differential diagnosis, natural course and epidemiology of bipolar disorder. *American Psychiatric Association Annual Review, 6*.

Keller, M.B., Hirschfeld, R.M.A., & Hanks, D. (1997). Double depression: A distinctive subtype of unipolar depression. *Journal of Affective Disorders, 45*, 65–73.

Kellner, C.H. (1997). Left unilateral ECT: Still a viable option. *Convulsive Therapy, 13*, 65–67.

Kellner, R. (1985). Functional somatic symptoms in hypochondriasis. *Archives of General Psychiatry, 42*, 821–833.

Kelly, M.P., Strassberg, D.S., & Kircher, J.R. (1990). Attitudinal and experiential correlates of anorgasmia. *Archives of Sexual Behavior, 19*, 165–177.

Kelly, T. (1990). The role of values in psychotherapy: A critical review of process and outcome effects. *Clinical Psychology Review, 10*, 171–186.

Kelly, T., Soloff, P.H., Cornelius, J., George, A., Lis, J.A., & Ulrich, R. (1992). Can we study (treat) borderline patients? Attrition from research and open treatment. *Journal of Personality Disorders, 6*, 417–433.

Kempe, C.H., Silverman, F., Steele, B., Droegueller, W., & Silver, H. (1962). The battered child syndrome. *Journal of the American Medical Association, 181*, 17–24.

Kendall, P.C. (1994). Treating anxiety disorders in children: Results of a randomized clinical trial. *Journal of Consulting and Clinical Psychology, 62*, 100–110.

Kendall, P.C., & Watson, D. (Eds.) (1989). *Anxiety and Depression: Distinctive and Overlapping Features*. San Diego: CA: Academic Press.

Kendell, R.E. (1975). *The role of diagnosis in psychiatry*. Oxford: Blackwell.

Kendell, R.E. (1989). Clinical validity. *Psychological Medicine, 19*, 45–55.

Kendell, R.E. (1991). Relationship between the DSM-IV and the ICD-10. *Journal of Abnormal Psychology, 100*, 297–301.

Kendell, R.E. (2002) The distinction between personality disorder and mental illness. *British Journal of Psychiatry, 180*, 110–115.

Kendler, K.S. (1997). The genetic epidemiology of psychiatric disorders: A current perspective. *Social Psychiatry and Psychiatric Epidemiology, 32*, 5–11.

Kendler, K.S., & Diehl, S.R. (1993). The genetics of schizophrenia: A current, genetic-epidemiologic perspective. *Schizophrenia Bulletin, 19*, 261–285.

Kendler, K.S., & Gardner, C.O. (1997). The risk for psychiatric disorders in relatives of schizophrenic and control probands: A comparison of three independent studies. *Psychological Medicine, 27*, 411–419.

Kendler, K.S., Gruenberg, A.M., & Tsuang, M.T. (1985). Subtype stability in schizophrenia. *American Journal of Psychiatry, 142*, 827–832.

Kendler, K.S., Karkowski, L.M., & Prescott, C.A. (1999). Causal relationship between stressful life events and the onset of major depression. *American Journal of Psychiatry, 156*, 837–848.

Kendler, K.S., Kessler, R.C., Walters, E.E., MacLean, C., Neale, M.C., Heath, A.C., & Eaves, L.J. (1995). Stressful life events, genetic liability, and onset of an episode of major depression in women. *American Journal of Psychiatry, 152*, 833–842.

Kendler, K.S., MacLean, C., Neale, M., Kessler, R., Heath, A., & Eaves, L. (1991). The genetic epidemiology of bulimia nervosa. *American Journal of Psychiatry, 148*, 1627–1637.

Kendler, K.S., McGuire, M., Gruenberg, A.M., O'Hare, A., Spellman, M., & Walsh, D. (1993). The Roscommon Family Study. III. Schizophrenia-related personality disorders in relatives. *Archives of General Psychiatry, 50*, 781–788.

Kendler, K.S., McGuire, M., Gruenberg, A.M., & Walsh, D. (1994). Outcome and family study of the subtypes of schizophrenia in the west of Ireland. *American Journal of Psychiatry, 151*, 849–856.

Kendler, K.S., Myers, J., Prescott, C.A., & Neale, M.C. (2001). The genetic epidemiology of irrational fears and phobias in men. *Archives of General Psychiatry, 58*, 257–265.

Kendler, K.S., Neale, M.C., Kessler, R.C., Heath, A.C., & Eaves, L.J. (1992a). Generalized anxiety disorder in women: A population-based twin study. *Archives of General Psychiatry, 49*, 267–272.

Kendler, K.S., Neale, M.C., Kessler, R.C., Heath, A.C., & Eaves, L.J. (1992b). The genetic epidemiology of phobias in women: The interrelationship of agoraphobia, social phobia, situational phobia, and simple phobia. *Archives of General Psychiatry, 49*, 273–281.

Kendler, K.S., Walters, E.E., Neale, M.C., Kessler, R.C., Heath, A.C., & Eaves, L.J. (1995). The structure of the genetic and environmental risk factors for six major psychiatric disorders in women. *Archives of General Psychiatry, 52*, 374–383.

Kernberg, O.F. (1967). Borderline personality organization. *Journal of the American Psychoanalytic Association, 15*, 641–685.

Kernberg, O.F. (1975). *Borderline Conditions and Pathological Narcissism*. New York: Aronson.

Kessler, R.C. (1995). The national comorbidity survey: Preliminary results and future directions. *International Journal of Methods in Psychiatric Research, 5*, 139–151.

Kessler, R.C. (1997). The effects of stressful life events on depression. *Annual Review of Psychology, 48*, 191–214.

Kessler, R.C. (2000). Gender differences in major depression: Epidemiological findings. In E. Frank (Ed.), *Gender and its Effects on Psychopathology* (pp. 61–84). Washington, DC: American Psychiatric Press.

Kessler, R.C., Gillis-Light, J., Magee, W.J., Kendler, K.S., & Eaves, L.J. (1997). Childhood adversity and adult psychopathology. In I.H. Gotlib & B. Wheaton (Eds.), *Stress and Adversity over the Life Course: Trajectories and Turning Points* (pp. 29–49). New York: Cambridge University Press.

Kessler, R.C, Keller, M.B., Wittchen, H. (2001). The epidemiology of generalized anxiety disorder. *Psychiatric Clinics of North America, 24*, 19–39.

Kessler, R.C., McGonagle, K.A., Zhao, S., Nelson, C.R., Highes, M., Eshleman, S., Wittchen, H., & Kendler, K.S. (1994). Lifetime and 12-month prevalence of DSM-III-R psychiatric disorders in the United States: Results from the National Comorbidity Survey. *Archives of General Psychiatry, 51*, 8–19.

Kessler, R.C., Sonnega, A., Bromet, E., Hughes, M., & Nelson, C.B. (1995). Posttraumatic stress disorder in the National Comorbidity Survey. *Archives of General Psychiatry, 52*, 1048–1060.

Kessler, R.C., Stang, P.E., Wittchen, H., Ustun, T.B., Roy-Burne, P.P., & Walters, E. (1998). Lifetime panic-depression comorbidity in the National Comorbidity Survey. *Archives of General Psychiatry, 55*, 801–808.

Kessler, R.C., & Zhao, S. (1999). The prevalence of mental disorder. In A.V. Horwitz and T.L. Scheid (Eds.), *A Handbook for the Study of Mental Health: Social Contexts, Theories, and Systems*. Cambridge, UK: Cambridge University Press (pp. 58–78).

Kesteren, P.J. van, Gooren, L.J., & Megens, J.A. (1996). An epidemiological and demographic study of transsexuals in the Netherlands. *Archives of Sexual Behavior, 25*, pp. 589–599.

Kettl, P.A. (1993). 10 basic rules for managing dementia. *Patient Care, 27*, 79–86.

Keys, A., Brozek, J., Henschel, A., Mickelsen, O., & Taylor, H.L. (1950). *The Biology of Human Starvation* (2 vols.). Minneapolis: University of Minnesota Press.

Kidd, K.K. (1997). Can we find genes for schizophrenia? *American Journal of Medical Genetics, 74*, 104–111.

Kiecolt-Glaser, J.K. (1999). Stress, personal relationships, and immune function: Health implications. *Brain, Behavior, and Immunity, 13*, 61–72.

Kiecolt-Glaser, J.K., Malarkey, W.B., Chee, M., Newton, T., Cacioppo, J.T., Mao, H., & Glaser, R. (1993). Negative behavior during marital conflict is associated with immunological down-regulation. *Psychosomatic Medicine, 55*, 395–409.

Kiecolt-Glaser, J.K., & Newton, T.L. (2001). Marriage and health: His and hers. *Psychological Bulletin, 127*, 472–503.

Kiesler, C. (1982). Mental hospitals and alternative care: Coninstitutionalization as potential public policy for mental patients. *American Psychologist, 37*, 349–360.

Kihlstrom, J.F. (1998a). Exhumed memory. In S.J. Lynn & K.M. McConkey (Eds.), *Truth in Memory* (pp. 3–31). New York: Guilford.

Kihlstrom, J.F. (1998b). Dissociations and dissociation theory in hypnosis: A comment on Kirch and Lynn (1998). *Psychological Bulletin, 123,* 186–191.

Kihlstrom, J.F., Glisky, M.L., & Angiulo, M.J. (1994). Dissociative tendencies and dissociative disorders. *Journal of Abnormal Psychology, 103,* 117–124.

Kilbey, M.M., Downey, K., & Breslau, N. (1998). Predicting the emergence and persistence of alcohol dependence in young adults: The role of expectancy and other risk factors. *Experimental and Clinical Psychopharmacology, 6,* 149–156.

Kilmann, P.R., et al. (1982). The treatment of sexual paraphilias: A review of the outcome research. *Journal of Sex Research, 18,* 193–252.

Kilpatrick, D.G., Edmunds, C.N., & Seymour, A.K. (1992). *Rape in America: A Report to the Nation.* Arlington, VA: National Victim Center.

Kilpatrick, D.G., Saunders, B.E., Amick-McMullan, A., Best, C.L., Veronen, L.J., & Resnick, H.S. (1989). Victim and crime factors associated with the development of crime-related posttraumatic stress disorder. *Behavior Therapy, 20,* 199–214.

Kilzieh, N., & Akiskal, H.S. (1999). Rapid-cycling bipolar disorder: An overview of research and clinical experience. *Psychiatric Clinics of North America, 22,* 585–607.

Kim, J.E., & Moen, P. (2001). Is retirement good or bad for subjective well-being? *Current Directions in Psychological Science. 10,* 83–86.

King, B.M. (1996). *Human Sexuality Today.* Upper Saddle River, NJ: Prentice Hall.

King, R.A., Segman, R.H., & Anderson, G.M. (1994). Serotonin and suicidality: The impact of acute fluoxetine administration. I. Serotonin and suicide. *Israel Journal of Psychiatry and Related Sciences, 31,* 271–279.

Kinsey, A.C., Pomeroy, W.B., & Martin, C.E. (1948). *Sexual Behavior in the Human Male.* Philadelphia: Saunders.

Kinzl, J.F., Mangweth, B., Traweger, C., & Biebl, W. (1996). Sexual dysfunction in males: Significance of adverse childhood experiences. *Child Abuse and Neglect, 20,* 759–767.

Kirmayer, L.J. (2001). Cultural variations in the clinical presentation of depression and anxiety: Implications for diagnosis and treatment. *Journal of Clinical Psychiatry, 62* (suppl. 13), 22–28.

Kirmayer, L.J., Brass, G.M., & Tait, C.L. (2000). The mental health of Aboriginal peoples: Transformations of identity and community. *Canadian Journal of Psychiatry, 45,* 607–616.

Kirmayer, L.J., MacDonald, M.E., & Brass, G.M. (2001). *Proceedings of the Advanced Study Institute: The Mental Health of Indigenous Peoples.* Montreal, QC: McGill Summer Program in Social & Cultural Psychiatry.

Kirmayer, L.J., Robbins, J.M., & Paris, J. (1994). Somatoform disorders: Personality and the social matrix of somatic distress. *Journal of Abnormal Psychology, 103,* 125–136.

Kirmayer, L.J., & Young, A. (1998). Culture and somatization: Epidemiological and ethnographic perspectives. *Psychosomatic Medicine, 60,* 420–430.

Kirrane, R.M., & Siever, L.J. (2000). The biological basis of schizotypal personality disorder. *Irish Journal of Psychological Medicine, 17,* 106–109.

Kirsch, I., & Lynn, S.J. (1995). The altered state of hypnosis: Changes in the theoretical landscape. *American Psychologist, 50,* 846–858.

Kirsch, I., & Lynn, S.J. (1998). Dissociation theories of hypnosis. *Psychological Bulletin, 123,* 100–115.

Klein, D.F. (1981). Anxiety reconceptualized. In D.F. Klein & J. Rabkin (Eds.), *Anxiety: New Research and Changing Concepts* (pp. 235–263). New York: Raven Press.

Klein, D.F. (1999). Harmful dysfunction, disorder, disease, illness, and evolution. *Journal of Abnormal Psychology, 108,* 421–429.

Klein, R.G., & Pine, D.S. (2002). Anxiety disorders. In M. Rutter & E. Taylor (Eds.), *Child and Adolescent Psychiatry* (4th ed., pp. 486–509). Oxford, UK: Blackwell.

Klein, M. (1997). Disorders of desire. In R.S. Charlton and I.D. Yalom (Eds.), *Treating Sexual Disorders* (pp. 201–236). San Francisco, CA: Jossey-Bass.

Kleindienst, N., & Greil, W. (2000). Differential efficacy of lithium and carbamazepine in the prophylaxis of bipolar disorder. *Neuropsychobiology, 42,* 2–10.

Kleinman, A. (1988). *Rethinking Psychiatry: From Cultural Category to Personal Experience.* New York: Free Press.

Klerman, G.L. (1990a). History and development of modern concepts of anxiety and panic. In J. Ballenger (Ed.), *Clinical Aspects of Panic Disorder* (pp. 3–12). New York: Wiley.

Klerman, G. (1990b). The psychiatric patient's right to effective treatment: Implications of Osheroff vs. Chestnut Lodge. *American Journal of Psychiatry, 147,* 409–418.

Klerman, G.L., Weissman, M.M., Markowitz, J.C., Glick, I., Wilner, P.J., Mason, B., & Shear, M.K. (1994). Medication and psychotherapy. In A.E. Bergin & S.L. Garfield (Eds.), *Handbook of psychotherapy and behavior change* (4th ed., pp. 734–782). New York: Wiley.

Klerman, G.L., Weissman, M.M., Rounsaville, B.J., & Chevron, E.S. (1984). *Interpersonal Psychotherapy of Depression.* New York: Basic Books.

Kluft, R.P. (1987). An update on multiple personality disorder. *Hospital and Community Psychiatry, 38,* 363–373.

Klump, K.L., McGue, M., & Iacono, W.G. (2000). Age differences in genetic and environmental influences on eating attitudes and behaviors in preadolescent and adolescent female twins. *Journal of Abnormal Psychology, 109,* 239–251.

Kluznik, J.C., Speed, N., Van Valkenburg, C., & Magraw, R. (1986). Forty-year follow-up of United States prisoners of war. *American Journal of Psychiatry, 143,* 1443–1446.

Knight, R.A. (1999). Validation of a typology for rapists. *Journal of Interpersonal Violence, 14,* 303–330.

Knight, R.A., Prentky, R.A., & Cerce, D.D. (1994). The development, reliability, and validity of an inventory for the multidimensional assessment of sex and aggression. *Criminal Justice and Behavior, 21,* 72–94.

Knopman, D.S. (2001). An overview of common non-Alzheimer dementias. *Clinics in Geriatric Medicine, 17,* 281–301.

Koch, H., & Knapp, D.E. (1987). Highlights of drug utilization in office practice. National Ambulatory Medical Survey, 1885. *Advance Data from Vital and Health Statistics,* No. 134, U.S. Department of Health and Human Services Publication No. (PHS) 87–1250.

Koegel, R.L., Koegel, L.K., & McNerney, E.K. (2001). Pivotal areas intervention for autism. *Journal of Clinical Child Psychology, 30,* 19–32.

Koenig, H.G., & Blazer, D.G. (1990). Depression and other affective disorders. In C.K. Cassel, D.E. Riesenberg, L.B. Sorenson, & J.R. Walsh (Eds.), *Geriatric Medicine* (2nd ed., pp. 473–489). New York: Springer.

Koenigsberg, H.W., Woo-Ming, A.M., & Siever, L.J. (2002). Pharmacological treatments for personality disorders. In P.E. Nathan and J.M. Gorman (Eds.), *A Guide to Treatments that Work* (2nd ed., pp. 625–641). New York: Oxford University Press.

Kohlberg, L. (1985). *The Psychology of Moral Development.* San Francisco: Harper & Row.

Koluchova, J. (1972). Severe deprivation in twins: A case study of marked IQ change after age 7. *Journal of Child Psychology and Psychiatry, 13,* 107–114.

Konstantareas, M.M. (2001). How shall a thing be called? The overlap and differences between Asperger's disorder and high functioning autism. *Canadian Psychology, 42,* 146 (abstract).

Konstantareas, M.M., & Hewitt, T. (2001). Autistic disorder and schizophrenia: Diagnostic overlaps. *Journal of Autism and Developmental Disorders, 31,* 19–28.

Kontakos, N., & Stokes, J. (1999). Parkinson's disease—Recent developments and new directions. *Chronic Diseases in Canada, 20,* 58–76.

Koob, G.F. (2000). Neurobiology of addiction: Toward the development of new therapies. *Annals of the New York Academy of Sciences, 909,* 170–185.

Koons, C.R., Robins, C.J., Tweed, J.L., Lynch, T.R., Gonzales. A.M., Morse, J.Q., Bishop, G.K., Butterfield, M.I., & Bastian, L.A. (2001). Efficacy of dialectical behavior therapy in women veterans with borderline personality disorder. *Behavior Therapy, 32,* 371–390.

Kop, W.J. (1999). Chronic and acute psychological risk factors for clinical manifestations of coronary artery disease. *Psychosomatic Medicine, 61,* 476–487

Kopelman, M.D. (1995). The Korsakoff syndrome. *British Journal of Psychiatry, 166,* 154–173.

Kopelowicz, A., Liberman, R.P., & Zarate, R. (2002). Psychosocial treatments for schizophrenia. In P.E. Nathan and J.M. Gorman (Eds.), *A Guide to Treatments that Work* (2nd ed., pp. 201–228). London: Oxford University Press.

Koppel, T. (2002). *A good man in hell: General Romeo Dallaire and the Rwanda genocide* [interview]. Washington, DC: United States Holocaust Memorial Museum. Retrieved January 22, 2004, from http://www.ushmm.org/conscience/events/dallaire/dallaire.php.

Kopta, S.M., Howard, K.I., Lowry, J.L., & Beutler, L.E. (1994). Patterns of symptomatic recovery in psychotherapy. *Journal of Consulting and Clinical Psychology, 62,* 1009–1016.

Koranyi, E.K. (1989). Physiology of stress reviewed. In S. Cheren (Ed.), *Psychosomatic Medicine: Theory, Physiology, and Practice* (Vol. 1, pp. 241–278). Madison, CT: International Universities Press.

Korenman, S.G. (1998). New insights into erectile dysfunction: A practical approach. *American Journal of Medicine, 105,* 135–144.

Koskenvuo, M., Kaprio, J., Rose, R.J., Kesaniemi, A., Sarna, S., Heikkila, K., & Langinvainio, H. (1988). Hostility as a risk factor for mortality and ischemic heart disease in men. *Psychosomatic Medicine, 50,* 330–340.

Koski, L., Iacoboni, M., & Mazziotta, J.C. (2002). Deconstructing apraxia: Understanding disorders of intentional movement after stroke. *Current Opinion in Neurology, 15,* 71–77.

Koss, M.P., & Butcher, J.M. (1986). Research on brief psychotherapy. In S.L. Garfield & A.E. Bergin (Eds.), *Handbook of psychotherapy and behavior change* (3rd ed., pp. 627–670). New York: Wiley.

Koss, M.P., Tromp, S., & Tharan, M. (1995). Traumatic memories: Empirical foundations, forensic, and clinical implications. *Clinical Psychology: Science and Practice, 2,* 111–132.

Kovacs, M., Feinberg, T.L., Crouse-Novak, M.A., Paulaukas, S., Pollock, M., & Finkelstein, R. (1984). Depressive disorders in childhood. II. A longitudinal study of the risk for a subsequent major depression. *Archives of General Psychiatry, 41,* 643–649.

Kowalski, K.M. (1998). The dangers of alcohol. *Current Health, 24,* 6–13.

Kraepelin, E. (1921). *Manic-Depressive Insanity and Paranoia.* Edinburgh: Livingstone.

Krantz, D.S., Contrada, R.J., Hill, D.R., & Friedler, E. (1988). Environmental stress and biobehavioral antecedents of coronary heart disease. *Journal of Consulting and Clinical Psychology, 56*, 333–341.

Krantz, D.S., Gabbay, F.H., Hedges, S.M., Leach, S.G., Gottdiener, J.S., & Rozanski, A. (1993). Mental and physical triggers of silent myocardial ischemia: Ambulatory studies using self-monitoring diary methodology. *Annals of Behavioral Medicine, 15*, 33–40.

Kroenke, K., Spitzer, R.L., deGruy, F.V., Hahn, S.R., Linzer, M., Williams, J.B.W., Brody, D., & Davies, M. (1997). Multisomatoform disorder: An alternative to undifferentiated somatoform disorder for the somatizing patient in primary care. *Archives of General Psychiatry, 54*, 352–358.

Kroenke, K., & Swindle, R. (2000). Cognitive behavioural therapy for somatization and symptom syndromes: a critical review of controlled clinical trials. *Psychotherapy and Psychosomatics, 69*, 205–215.

Kroenke, K., West, S.L., Gilsenan, A., Eckert, G.J., Dolor, R., Stang, P. Zhou, X., Hays, R., & Weinberger, M. (2001). Similar effectiveness of paroxetine, fluoxetine, and sertraline in primary care: A randomized trial. *Journal of the American Medical Association, 286*, 2947–2955.

Kropp, P.R., & Hart, S.D. (1997). Assessing risk of violence in wife assaulters: The spousal assault risk assessment guide. In C. D. Webster & M. A. Jackson (Eds.), *Impulsivity: Theory, assessment, and treatment* (pp. 302–325). New York: Guilford.

Krueger, R.F. (1999). Personality traits in late adolescence predict mental disorders in early adulthood: A prospective-epidemiological study. *Journal of Personality, 67*, 39–65.

Kübler-Ross, E. (1969). *On Death and Dying*. New York: Macmillan.

Kubzansky, L.D., Sparrow, D., Vokonas, P., & Kawachi, I. (2001). Is the glass half empty or half full? A prospective study of optimism and coronary heart disease in the normative aging study. *Psychosomatic Medicine, 63*, 910–916.

Kuch, K., & Cox, B.J. (1992). Symptoms of PTSD in 124 survivors of the Holocaust. *American Journal of Psychiatry, 149*, 337–340.

Kuhn, T.S. (1962). *The Structure of Scientific Revolutions*. Chicago: University of Chicago Press.

Kuiper, N.A., Grimshaw, M., Leite, C., & Kirsh, I. (in press). Humor is not always the best medicine: Specific components of sense of humor and psychological well-being. *Humor: International Journal of Humor Research*.

Kuiper, N.A., & Martin, R.A. (1993). Humor and self-concept. *Humor: International Journal of Humor Research, 6*, 251–270.

Kuiper, N.A., & Nicholl, S. (in press). Thoughts of feeling better? Sense of humor and physical health. *Humor: International Journal of Humor Research*.

Kupfer, D.J., Chengappa, K.N.R., Gelenberg, A.J., Hirschfeld, R.M.A., Goldberg, J.F., Sachs, G.S., Grochocinski, V.J. Houck, P.R., & Kolar, A.B. (2001). Citalopram as adjunctive therapy in bipolar depression. *Journal of Clinical Psychiatry, 62*, 985–990.

Kupfer, D.J., & Frank, E. (2001). The interaction of drug- and psychotherapy in the long-term treatment of depression. *Journal of Affective Disorders, 62*, 131–137.

Kushner, M.B., Sher, K.J., & Beitman, B.D. (1990). The relation between alcohol problems and the anxiety disorders. *American Journal of Psychiatry, 147*, 685–695.

Kushner, M.G., Sher, K.J., & Erickson, D.J. (1999). Prospective analysis of the relation between DSM-III anxiety disorders and alcohol use disorders. *American Journal of Psychiatry, 156*, 723–732.

Kwapil, T.R. (1998). Social anhedonia as a predictor of the development of schizophrenia-spectrum disorders. *Journal of Abnormal Psychology, 107*, 558–565.

L'Abate, L., & Bagarozzi, D.A. (1993). *Sourcebook of Marriage and Family Evaluation*. New York: Brunner/Mazel.

Labronte, R., & Thompson, P. (1993). *Promoting heart health in Canada: A focus on heart health inequalities*. Ottawa: Minister of Supply and Services.

Lacey, J.I. (1967). Somatic response patterning and stress: Some revisions of activation theory. In M.H. Appley & R. Trumball (Eds.), *Psychological Stress* (pp. 14–42). New York: McGraw-Hill.

Lacharité, C., Boutet, M., & Proulx, R. (1995). Intellectual disability and psychopathology: Developmental perspective. *Canada's Mental Health, 43*, 2–8.

LaCroix, A.Z., & Haynes, S.G. (1987). Gender differences in the stressfulness of workplace roles: A focus on work and health. In R. Barnett, G. Baruch, & L. Biener (Eds.), *Gender and Stress* (pp. 96–121). New York: Free Press.

Ladouceur, R., & Dugas, M.J. (2002). Generalized anxiety disorder. In M. Hersen & L.K. Porzelius (Eds.), *Diagnosis, conceptualization, and treatment planning for adults: A step-by-step guide* (pp. 209–224). Mahwah, NJ: Erlbaum.

Ladouceur, R., Dugas, M.J., Freeston, M.H., Léger, E., Gagnon, F., & Thibodeau, N. (2000). Efficacy of a cognitive-behavioral treatment for generalized anxiety disorder: Evaluation in a controlled clinical trial. *Journal of Consulting and Clinical Psychology, 68*, 957–964.

Ladouceur, R., Sylvain, C., Letarte, H., Giroux, I., & Jacques, C. (1998). Cognitive treatment of pathological gamblers. *Behaviour Research and Therapy, 36*, 1111–1119.

Ladwig, K., Marten-Mittag, B., Erazo, N., & Guendel, H. (2001). Identifying somatization disorder in a population-based health examination survey: Psychosocial burden and gender differences. *Psychosomatics, 42*, 511–518.

Lahey, B.B. et al. (1994). DSM-IV field trials for attention deficit/hyperactivity disorder in children and adolescents. *Journal of the American Academy of Child and Adolescent Psychiatry, 151*, 1673–1685.

Lai, D.W.L. (2000). Measuring depression in Canada's elderly Chinese population: Use of a community screening instrument. *Canadian Journal of Psychiatry, 45*, 279–284.

Lalonde, J.K., Hudson, J.I., Gigante, R.A., & Pope, H.G. (2001). Canadian and American psychiatrists' attitudes toward dissociative disorders diagnoses. *Canadian Journal of Psychiatry, 46*, 407–412.

Lam, R.W., Gorman, C.P., Michalon, M., Steiner, M., Levitt, A.J., Corral, M.R., Watson, G.D., Morehouse, R.L., Tam, W., & Joffe, R.T. (1995). Multicenter, placebo-controlled study of fluoxetine in seasonal affective disorder. *American Journal of Psychiatry, 152*, 1765–1770.

Lam, R.W., & Levitt, A.J. (1999). *Canadian consensus guidelines for the treatment of seasonal affective disorder*. Vancouver, BC: Clinical and Academic Publishing.

Lamberg, L. (1998). New drug for erectile dysfunction boon for many, "viagravation" for some. *Journal of the American Medical Association, 280*, 867–869.

Lambert, M.J., Shapiro, D.A., & Bergin, A.E. (1986). The effectiveness of psychotherapy. In S.L. Garfield & A.E. Bergin (Eds.), *Handbook of psychotherapy and behavior change* (3rd ed., pp. 157–212). New York: Wiley.

Lamerson, C.D., & Kelloway, E.K. (1996). Towards a model of peacekeeping stress: Traumatic and contextual influences. *Canadian Psychology, 37*, 195–204.

*Lancet* (1991). Editorial. Phenylketonuria grows up. *Lancet, 337*, 1256–1257.

Landy, D. (1985). Pibloktoq (hysteria) and Inuit nutrition: Possible implications of hypervitaminosis A. *Social Science and Medicine, 21*, 173–185.

Lang, A.R., & Stritzke, W.G.K. (1993). Children and alcohol. In M. Galanter, H. Begleiter, R. Deitrich, et al. (Eds.), *Recent Developments in Alcoholism*. Vol. 11, *Ten Years of Progress* (pp. 73–85). New York: Plenum.

Lang, C.T., & Daro, D. (1996). *Current trends in Child Abuse Reporting and Fatalities: The Results of the 1995 Annual State Survey*. Working paper 808. Washington, DC: National Committee on the Prevention of Child Abuse.

Langevin, R. (1992). Biological factors contributing to paraphilic behavior. *Psychiatric Annals, 22*, 307–314.

Langevin, R. (1983). *Sexual strands: Understanding and treating sexual anomalies in men*. Hillsdale, NJ: Erlbaum.

Langevin, R. & Lang, R. (1987). The courtship disorders. In G.D. Wilson (Ed.), *Variant sexuality: Research and theory* (pp. 202–228). London: Croom Helm.

Langlais, P.J. (1995). Alcohol-related thiamine deficiency. *Alcohol Health and Research World, 19*, 113–122.

Lara, M.E., & Klein, D.N. (1999). Psychosocial processes underlying the maintenance and persistence of depression: Implications for understanding chronic depression. *Clinical Psychology Review, 19*, 553–570.

Larsen, R.J., & Buss, D.J. (2002). *Personality Psychology*. New York: McGraw-Hill.

Larson, R., Csikszentmihalyi, M., & Graef, R. (1980). Mood variability and the psychosocial adjustment of adolescents. *Journal of Youth and Adolescence, 9*, 469–490.

Last, C.G., & Strauss, C.C. (1990). School refusal in anxiety-disordered children and adolescents. *Journal of the American Academy of Child and Adolescent Psychiatry, 29*, 31–35.

Laumann, E.O., Gagnon, J.H., Michael, R.T., & Michaels, S. (1994). *The Social organization of Sexuality: Sexual Practices in the United States*, Chicago: University of Chicago Press.

Laumann, E.O., Paik, A., & Rosen, R. (1999). Sexual dysfunction in the United States: Prevalence and predictors. *Journal of the American Medical Association, 281*, 537–544.

Lauterbach, E.C., Carter, W.G., Rathke, K.M., Thomas, B.H., Shillcutt, S.D., Vogel, R.L., Moore, N.C., Mimbs, J.W., & Nelson, W.H. (2001). Tardive dyskinesia—Diagnostic issues, subsyndromes, and concurrent movement disorders. *Schizophrenia Bulletin 27*, 601–614.

Lavallee, C., & Bourgault, C. (2000). The health of Cree, Inuit and southern Quebec women: Similarities and differences. *Canadian Journal of Public Health, 91*, 212–216.

Lavori, P.W., Klerman, G.L., Keller, M.B., Reich, T., Rice, J., & Endicott, J. (1987). Age-period-cohort analysis of secular trends in onset of major depression: Findings in siblings of patients with major affective disorder. *Journal of Psychiatric Research, 21*, 23–35.

Lawrie, S.M., & Abukmeil, S.S. (1998). Brain abnormality in schizophrenia: A systematic and quantitative review of volumetric magnetic resonance imaging studies. *British Journal of Psychiatry, 172*, 110–120.

Lawton, M.P. (1989). Environmental approaches to research and treatment of Alzheimer's disease. In E. Light & B.D. Lebowitz (Eds.), *Alzheimer's Disease Treatment and Family Stress: Directions for Research* (pp. 340–362). U.S. Department of Health and Human Services, Publication No. (ADM) 89–1569.

Lawton, M.P. (2001). Quality of life and the end of life. In J.E. Birren & K. W. Schaie (Eds.), *Handbook of the Psychology of Aging* (5th ed., pp. 592–616). San Diego: Academic Press.

Lazarus, R.S. (1966). *Psychological Stress and the Coping Process*, New York: McGraw-Hill.

Lazarus, R.S. (2000). Toward better research on stress and coping. *American Psychologist* 55, 665–673.

Lazarus, R.S., & Folkman, S. (1984). *Stress, Appraisal, and Coping*, New York: Springer.

Lazoritz, S. (1990). What ever happened to Mary Ellen? *Child Abuse and Neglect*, 14, 143–149.

Leary, T. (1957). *Interpersonal diagnosis of personality*. New York: Ronald Press.

Leavitt, B.R., Wellington, C.L., & Hayden, M.R. (1999). Recent insights into the molecular pathogenesis of Huntington disease. *Seminars in Neurology*, 19, 385–395.

Le Bourdaise, C., Neill, G., & Turcotte, P. (2000). The changing face of conjugal relationships. *Canadian Social Trends*, Spring, 13–17.

LeDoux. J.E. (2000). Emotion circuits in the brain. *Annual Review of Neuroscience*, 23, 155–184.

Ledoux, J.E., & Gorman, J.M. (2001). A call to action: Overcoming anxiety through active coping. *American Journal of Psychiatry*, 158, 1953–1955.

Lee, K.K. (2000). *Urban Poverty in Canada: A Statistical Profile*. Ottawa, ON: Canadian Council on Social Development.

Leesfield, I.H. (1987). Negligence of mental health profesionals. *Trial*, 23, 57–61.

Lefebvre, J., Lesage, A., Cyr, M., Toupin, J., & Fournier, L. (1998). Factors related to utilization of services for mental health reasons in Montreal, Canada. *Social Psychiatry and Psychiatric Epidemiology*, 33, 291–298.

Leff, J. (1992). Transcultural aspects. In E.S. Paykel (Ed.), *Handbook of Affective Disorders* (2nd ed., pp. 539–550). New York: Guilford.

Leff, J., Sartorius, N., Jablensky, A., Korten, A., & Ernberg, G. (1992). The International Pilot Study of Schizophrenia: Five-year follow-up findings. *Psychological Medicine*, 22, 131–145.

Leff, J., & Vaughn, C. (1985). *Expressed Emotion in Families: Its Significance for Mental Illness*, New York: Guilford.

Leff, J. (1988). *Psychiatry Around the Globe: A Transcultural View*, London: Royal College of Psychiatrists.

Lefley, H.P. (1992). Expressed emotion: Conceptual, clinical, and social policy issues. *Hospital and Community Psychiatry*, 43, 591–598.

Lehman, A.F., Dixon, L.B., Hoch, J.S., DeForge, B., Kernan, E., & Frank, R. (1999). Cost-effectiveness of assertive community treatment for homeless persons with severe mental illness. *British Journal of Psychiatry*, 174, 346–352.

Lehmann, H.E., & Hanrahan, G.E. (1954). Chlorpromazine: New inhibiting agent for psychomotor excitement and manic states. *Archives of Neurology and Psychiatry*, 71, 227–237.

Lehrer, P., & Carr, R. (1997). Progressive relaxation. In W.T. Roth & I.D. Yalom (Eds.), *Treating Anxiety Disorders* (pp. 83–116). San Francisco: Jossey-Bass.

Leibenluft, E. (Ed.) (1999). *Gender Differences in Mood and Anxiety Disorders: From Bench to Bedside*. Washington, DC: American Psychiatric Press.

Leiblum, S.R. (1995). Relinquishing virginity: The treatment of a complex case of vaginismus. In R.C. Rosen & S.R. Leiblum (Eds.), *Case Studies in Sex Therapy* (pp. 250–263). New York: Guilford.

Leiblum, S.R. (1999). What every urologist should know about female sexual dysfunction. *International Journal of Impotence Research*, 11 (suppl. 1), 39–40.

Leiblum, S.R. (2001). Critical overview of the new consensus-based definitions and classification of female sexual dysfunction. *Journal of Sex and Marital Therapy*, 27, 159–168.

Leichtman, M. (1989). Evolving concepts of borderline personality disorders. *Bulletin of the Menninger Clinic*, 53, 229–249.

Lenzenweger, M.F. (1999). Schizophrenia: Refining the phenotype, resolving endophenotypes. *Behaviour Research and Therapy*, 37, 281–295.

Lenzenweger, M.R., Loranger, A.W., Korfine, L., & Neff, C. (1997). Detecting personality disorders in a nonclinical population. *Archives of General Psychiatry*, 54, 345–351.

Leon, G., Fulkerson, J.A., Perry, C.L., & Cudeck, R. (1993). Personality and behavioral vulnerabilities associated with risk status for eating disorders in adolescent girls. *Journal of Abnormal Psychology*, 102, 438–444.

Leon, G.R., Fulkerson, J.A., Perry, C.L., & Early-Zald, M.B. (1995). Prospective analysis of personality and behavioral vulnerabilities and gender influences in the later development of disordered eating. *Journal of Abnormal Psychology*, 104, 140–149.

Leonard, H.L., Swedo, S.E., Lenane, M.C., Rettew, D.C., Hamburger, S.D., Bartko, J.J., & Rapoport, J.L. (1993). A 2- to 7-year follow-up study of 54 obsessive–compulsive children and adolescents. *Archives of General Psychiatry*, 50, 429–439.

Leonard, K.E., Eiden, R.D., Wong, M.M., Zucker, R.A., Puttler, L.I., Fitzgerald, H.E., Hussong, A., Chassin, L., & Mudar, P. (2000). Developmental perspectives on risk and vulnerability in alcoholic families. *Alcoholism: Clinical and Experimental Research*, 24, 238–240.

Lerner, A.J. (1999). Women and Alzheimer's disease. *Journal of Clinical Endocrinology and Metabolism*, 84, 1830–1834.

Leserman, J., Jackson, E.D., Petitto, J.M., Golden, R.N., Silva, S.G., Perkins, D.O., Cai, J., Folds, J.D., & Evans, D.L. (1999). Progression to AIDS: The effects of stress, depressive symptoms, and social support. *Psychosomatic Medicine*, 61, 397–406.

Leshner, A.I. (1997). Addiction is a brain disease, and it matters. *Science*, 278, 45–47.

Lester, D. (1997). The effectiveness of suicide prevention centers: A review. *Suicide and Life-Threatening Behavior*, 27, 304–310.

Leucht, S., Pitschel-Walz, G., Engel, R.R., & Kissling, W. (2002). Amisulpride, an unusual "atypical" antipsychotic: A meta-analysis of randomized controlled trials. *American Journal of Psychiatry*, 159, 180–190.

Levav, M., Mirsky, A.F., French, L.M., & Bartko, J.J. (1998). Multinational neuropsychological testing: Performance of children and adults. *Journal of Clinical & Experimental Neuropsychology*, 20, 658–672.

LeVay, S. (1993). *The Sexual Brain*, Cambridge, MA: MIT Press.

Levenson, M.R. (1992). Rethinking psychopathy. *Theory and Psychology*, 2, 51–71.

Levenson, R.W., Carstensen, L.L., & Gottman, J.M. (1994). The influence of age and gender on affect, physiology, and their interrelations: A study of long-term marriages. *Journal of Personality and Social Psychology*, 67, 56–68.

Leventhal, H., et al. (2001). Heath risk behaviors and aging. In J.E. Birren & K.W. Schaie (Eds.), *Handbook of the Psychology of Aging* (5th ed., pp. 186–214). San Diego: Academic Press.

Levine, S.B., Risen, C.B., & Althof, S.E. (1990). Essay on the diagnosis and nature of paraphilia. *Journal of Sex and Marital Therapy*, 16, 89–102.

Levinson, D.J. (1986). A conception of adult development. *American Psychologist*, 41, 3–13.

Levitt, A.J., Boyle, M.H., Joffe, R.T., Baumal, Z. (2000). Estimated prevalence of the seasonal subtype of major depression in a Canadian community sample. *Canadian Journal of Psychiatry*, 45, 650–654.

Levitt, E.E., Moser, C., & Jamison, K.V. (1994). The prevalence and some attributes of females in the sadomasochistic subculture: A second report. *Archives of Sexual Behavior*, 23, 465–474.

Levy, D.L., & Holzman, P.S. (1997). Eye tracking dysfunction and schizophrenia: An overview with special reference to the genetics of schizophrenia. *International Review of Psychiatry*, 9, 365–371.

Levy, F., Hay, D.A., McStephen, M., Wood, C., & Waldman, I. (1997). Attention-deficit/hyperactivity disorder: A category or a continuum? Genetic analysis of a large-scale twin study. *Journal of the American Academy of Child and Adolescent Psychiatry*, 36, 737–744.

Lewine, R.R.J., & Seeman, M.V. (1995). Gender, brain, and schizophrenia. In M.V. Seeman (Ed.), *Gender and Psychopathology* (pp. 131–158). Washington, DC: American Psychiatric Press.

Lewinsohn, P.M., Gotlib, I.H., Lewinsohn, M., Seeley, J.R., & Allen, N.B. (1998). Gender differences in anxiety disorders and anxiety symptoms in adolescents. *Journal of Abnormal Psychology*, 107, 109–117.

Lewinsohn, P.M., Roberts, R.E., Seely, J.R., Rohde, P., Gotlib, I.H., & Hops, H. (1994). Adolescent psychopathology. II. Psychosocial risk factors for depression. *Journal of Abnormal Psychology*, 103, 302–315.

Lewis, M.H. (1996). Psychopharmacology of autism spectrum. *Journal of Autism and Developmental Disorders*, 26, 231–235.

Leys, D., Pasquier, F., & Parnetti, L. (1998). Epidemiology of vascular dementia. *Haemostasis*, 28, 134–150.

Liddle, P.F. (1997). Dynamic neuroimaging with PET, SPET or fMRI. *International Review of Psychiatry*, 9, 331–337.

Lidz, C.W., Hoge, S.K., Gardner, W., Bennett, N.S., Monahan, J., Mulvey, E.P., & Roth, L.H. (1995). Perceived coercion in mental hospital admission: Pressures and process. *Archives of General Psychiatry*, 52, 1034–1039.

Lidz, C.W., Mulvey, E.P., & Gardner, W. (1993). The accuracy of predictions of violence to others. *Journal of the American Medical Association* 269, 1007–1011.

Lieberman, J., Chakos, M., Wu, H., Alvir, J., Hoffman, E., Robinson, D., & Bilder R. (2001). Longitudinal study of brain morphology in first episode schizophrenia. *Biological Psychiatry*, 49, 487–499.

Lilienfeld, S.O. (1992). The association between antisocial personality and somatization disorders: A review and integration of theoretical models. *Clinical Psychology Review*, 12, 641–662.

Lilienfeld, S.O. (1994). Conceptual problems in the assessment of psychopathy. *Clinical Psychology Review*, 14, 17–38.

Lilienfeld, S.O., Lyn, S.J., Kirsch, I., Chaves, J.F., Sarbin, T.R., Ganaway, G.K., & Powell, R.A. (1999). Dissociative identity disorder and the sociocognitive model: Recalling lessons of the past. *Psychological Bulletin*, 125, 507–523.

Linden, W., Stossel, C., & Maurice, J. (1996). Psychosocial interventions for patients with coronary artery disease: A meta-analysis. *Archives of Internal Medicine*, 156, 745–752.

Lindenberger, U., & Baltes, P.B. (1997). Intellectual functioning in old and very old age: Cross-sectional results from the Berlin Aging Study. *Psychology and Aging*, 12, 410–432.

Lindsay, D.S., Hagen, L., Read, J.D., Wade, K.A. & Garry, M. (2004). True photographs and false memories. *Psychological Science*, 15, 149–154.

Linehan, M.M. (1993). *Cognitive-Behavioral Treatment of Borderline Personality Disorder*, New York: Guilford.

Linehan, M.M., Cochran, B.N., & Kehrer, C.A. (2001). Dialectical behavior therapy for borderline personality disorder. In D.H. Barlow (Ed.), *Clinical Handbook of Psychological Disorders: A Step By Step Treatment Manual* (3rd ed., pp. 470-522). New York: Guilford.

Linehan, M.M., Kanter, J.W., & Comtois, K.A. (1999). Dialectical behavior therapy for borderline personality disorder: Efficacy, specificity, and cost effectiveness. In D.S. Janowsky (Ed.), *Psychotherapy Indications and Outcomes* (pp. 93–118). Washington, DC: American Psychiatric Press.

Linehan, M.M., Tutek, D.A., Heard, H.L., & Armstrong, H.E. (1994). Interpersonal outcome of cognitive-behavioral treatment for chronically suicidal borderline patients. *American Journal of Psychiatry, 151*, 1771–1776.

Link, B., Cullen, F., & Andrews, H. (1990, August). *Violent and illegal behavior of current and former mental patients compared to community controls.* Paper presented at the meeting of the Society for the Study of Social Problems.

Link, B.G., & Phelan, J.C. (1999). The labeling theory of mental disorder (II): The consequences of labeling. In A.V. Horwitz and T.L. Scheid (Eds.), *A Handbook for the Study of Mental Health: Social Contexts Theories and Systems* (pp. 361–376). New York: Cambridge University Press.

Link, B.G., Struening, E., Rahav, M., Phelan, J.C., & Nuttbrock, L. (1997). On stigma and its consequences: Evidence from a longitudinal study of men with dual diagnoses of mental illness and substance abuse. *Journal of Health and Social Behavior, 38*, 177–190.

Links, P. S., Heslegrave, R., & van Reekum, R. (1998). Prospective follow-up study of borderline personality disorder: Prognosis, prediction of outcome, and Axis II Comorbidity. *Canadian Journal of Psychiatry, 43*, 265–270.

Links, P.S., Heslegrave, R., & Villella, J. (1998). Psychopharmacological management of personality disorders: An outcome-focused model. In K.R. Silk (Ed.), *Biology of Personality Disorders* (pp. 93–127). Washington, DC: American Psychiatric Press.

Lipman, E.L., Bennett, K.J., Racine, Y.A., Mazumdar, R., & Offord, D.R. (1998). What does early antisocial behaviour predict? A follow-up of 4- and 5-year-olds from the Ontario Child Health Study. *Canadian Journal of Psychiatry, 43*, 605–613.

Lipman, E.L., MacMillan, H.L., & Boyle, M.H. (2001). Childhood abuse and psychiatric disorders among single and married mothers. *American Journal of Psychiatry, 158*, 73–77.

Lipowski, Z.J. (1988). Somatization: The concept and its clinical applications. *American Journal of Psychiatry, 145*, 1358–1368.

Lipsey, M.W., & Wilson, D.B. (1993). The efficacy of psychological, educational, and behavioral treatment: Confirmation for meta-analysis. *American Psychologist, 48*, 1181–1209.

Lipton, D.N., McDonel, E.C., & McFall, R.M. (1987). Heterosocial perception in rapists. *Journal of Consulting and Clinical Psychology, 55*, 17–21.

Lisanby, S.H., Maddox, J.H., Prudic, J., Devanand, D.P., & Sackheim, H.A. (2000). The effects of electroconvulsive therapy on memory of autobiographical and public events. *Archives of General Psychiatry, 57*, 581–590.

Litten, R.Z., & Allen, J.P. (1998). Advances in development of medications for alcoholism treatment. *Psychopharmacology, 139*, 20–33.

Livesley, W.J. (1986). Trait and behavioral prototypes of personality disorder. *American Journal of Psychiatry, 143*, 728–732.

Livesley, W.J. (1995). Commentary on dependent personality disorder. In W.J. Livesley (Ed.), *The DSM-IV Personality Disorders* (pp. 257–260). New York: Guilford.

Livesley, W.J. (2000). A practical approach to the treatment of patients with borderline personality disorder. *Psychiatric Clinics of North America, 23*, 211–232.

Livesley, W.J. (2003). *Practical management of personality disorder.* New York: Guilford.

Livesley, W.J., Jackson, D.N., & Schroeder, M.L. (1991). Dimensions of personality pathology. *Canadian Journal of Psychiatry, 36*, 557–562.

Livesley, W.J., Jang, K.L., & Vernon, P.A. (1998). Phenotypic and genetic structure of traits delineating personality disorder. *Archives of General Psychiatry, 55*, 941–948.

Loeber, R. (1988). Natural histories of conduct problems, delinquency, and associated substance use: Evidence for developmental progression. In B.B. Lahey & A.E. Kazdin (Eds.), *Advances in Clinical Child Psychology* (Vol. 11, pp. 73–118). New York: Plenum.

Loeber, R., Lahey, B.B., & Thomas, C. (1991). Diagnostic conundrum of oppositional defiant disorder and conduct disorder. *Journal of Abnormal Psychology, 100*, 379–390.

Loftin, C., McDowall, D., Wiersema, B., & Cottey, T.J. (1991). Effects of restrictive licensing of handguns on homicide and suicide in the District of Columbia. *New England Journal of Medicine, 325*, 1615–1620.

Loftus, E.F. (1993). The reality of repressed memories. *American Psychologist, 48*, 518–537.

Loftus, E., & Ketcham, K. (1994). *The Myth of Repressed Memory.* New York: St. Martin's Press.

Loftus, E.F., & Klinger, M.R. (1992). Is the unconscious smart or dumb? *American Psychologist, 47*, 761–765.

Lohr, J.M., Kleinknecht, R.A., Conley, A.T., Dal Cerro, S., Schmidt, J., & Sonntag, M.E. (1992). A methodological critique of the current status of eye movement desensitization (EMD). *Behavior Therapy and Experimental Psychiatry, 23*, 159–167.

Longino, C.F., & Mittelmark, M.B. (1996). In J. Sadavoy, L.W. Lazarus, L.F. Jarvik, & G.T. Grossberg (Eds.), *Comprehensive Review of Geriatric Psychiatry—II* (pp. 135–152). Washington, DC: American Psychiatric Press.

Looper, K.J, Kirmayer, L.J. (2001). Hypochondriacal concerns in a community population. *Psychological Medicine 31*, 577–584.

Looper, K. J., & Paris, J. (2000). What dimensions underlie Cluster B personality disorders? *Comprehensive Psychiatry, 41*, 432–437.

Lopez, A.D., & Murray, C.J.L. (1998). The global burden of disease, 1990–2020. *Nature Medicine, 4*, 1241–1243.

Lopez, J.F., Vazquez, D.M., Chalmers, D.T., & Watson, S.J. (1997). Regulation of 5-HT receptors and the hypothalamic-pituitary-adrenal axis: Implications for the neurobiology of suicide. In D.M. Stoff & J.J. Mann (Eds.), *The Neurobiology of Suicide: From the Bench to the Clinic* (pp. 106–134). New York: New York Academy of Sciences.

Lopez, S.R., & Guarnaccia, P.J. (2000). Cultural psychopathology: Uncovering the social world of mental illness. *Annual Review of Psychology, 51*, 571–598.

Lopez, S.R., Nelson, K., Snyder, K., & Mintz, J. (1999). Attributions and affective reactions of family members and course of schizophrenia. *Journal of Abnormal Psychology, 108*, 307–314.

Loranger, A.W., Sartorius, N., Andreoli, A., Berger, P., Buchheim, P., Channabasavanna, S.M., Coid, B., Dahl, A., Diekstra, R.F., Ferguson, B., et al. (1994). The international personality disorders examination. *Archives of General Psychiatry, 51*, 215–224.

Lord, C., & Bailey, A. (2002). Autism spectrum disorders. In M. Rutter & E. Taylor (Eds.), *Child and Adolescent Psvchiatry* (4th ed., pp. 636–663). Oxford: Blackwell.

Lorion, R.P., & Felner, R.D. (1986). Research on psychotherapy with the disadvantaged. In S.L. Garfield & A.E. Bergin (Eds.), *Handbook of psychotherapy and behavior change* (3rd ed., pp. 739–776). New York: Wiley.

Lovaas, O.I. (1987). Behavioral treatment and normal educational and intellectual functioning in young autistic children. *Journal of Consulting and Clinical Psychology, 55*, 3–9.

Lovaas, O.I., Schreibman, L., Koegel, R.L., & Rehm, R. (1971). Selective responding by autistic children to multiple sensory input. *Journal of Abnormal Psychology, 77*, 211–222.

Lovinger, D.M. (1997). Serotonin's role in alcohol's effects on the brain. *Alcohol Health and Research World, 21*, 114–120.

Low, P.W., Jeffries, J.C., & Bonnie, R.J. (1986). *The trial of John W. Hinckley, Jr.: A Case Study in the Insanity Defense*, Mineola, NY: Foundation Press.

Luborsky, L., Barber, J.P., & Beutler, L. (1993). Introduction to special section: A briefing on curative factors in dynamic psychotherapy. *Journal of Consulting and Clinical Psychology, 61*, 539–541.

Luborsky, L., Diguer, L., Seligman, D.A., Rosenthal, R., Krause, E.D., Johnson, S., Halperin, G., Bishop, M., Berman, J.S., & Schweizer, E. (1999). The researcher's own therapy allegiances: A "wild card" in comparisons of treatment efficacy. *Clinical Psychology: Science and Practice, 6*, 95–106.

Lubs, H.A. (1969). A marker X chromosome. *American Journal of Human Genetics, 21*, 231–244.

Lucas, A.R., Crowson, C.S., O'Fallon, W.M., & Melton, L.J. (1999). The ups and downs of anorexia nervosa. *International Journal of Eating Disorders, 26*, 397–405.

Luszcz, M.A., & Bryan, J. (1999). Toward understanding age-related memory loss in late adulthood. *Gerontology, 45*, 2–9.

Lyketsos, C.G., Garrett, E., Liang, K., & Anthony, J.C. (1999). Cannabis use and cognitive decline in persons under 65 years of age. *American Journal of Epidemiology, 149*, 794–781.

Lykken, D.T. (1957). A study of anxiety in the sociopathic personality. *Journal of Abnormal and Social Psychology, 55*, 6–10.

Lynam, D.R., & Widiger, T.A. (2001). Using the five-factor model to represent the DSM-IV personality disorders: An expert consensus approach. *Journal of Abnormal Psychology, 110*, 401–412.

Lynam, D.R., et al. (2000). The interaction between impulsivity and neighborhood context on offending: The effects of impulsivity are stronger in poor neighborhoods. *Journal of Abnormal Psychology, 109*, 563–574.

Lyness, S.A. (1993). Predictors of differences between Type A and B individuals in heart rate and blood pressure reactivity. *Psychological Bulletin, 114*, 266–295.

Lyon, D.R., Hart, S.D., & Webster, C.D. (2000). Violence and risk assessment. In R.A. Schuller & J.R.P. Ogloff (Eds.), *Introduction to psychology and law: Canadian perspectives* (pp. 314–350). Toronto: University of Toronto Press.

Lyons, M.J. (1995). Epidemiology of personality disorders. In M.T. Tsuang, M. Tohen, & G.E.P. Zahner (Eds.), *Textbook in Psychiatric Epidemiology* (pp. 407–436). New York: Wiley.

Lyons, M.J., Goldberg, J., Eisen, S.A., True, W., Tsuang, M.T., Meyer, J.M., & Henderson, W.G. (1993). Do genes influence exposure to trauma? A twin study of combat. *American Journal of Medical Genetics (Neuropsychiatric Genetics)*, 48, 22–27.

Maccoby, E.E. (1992). The role of parents in the socialization of children: An historical overview. *Developmental Psychology, 28*, 1006–1017.

Maccoby, E.E. (1998). *The Two Sexes: Growing Up Apart, Coming Together.* Cambridge, MA: Harvard.

Maccoby, E.E., & Martin, J.A. (1983). Socialization in the context of the family: Parent–child interaction. In E.M. Hetherington (Ed.), *Socialization, Personality, and Social Development.* Vol. 4, *Handbook of Child Psychology* (pp. 1–101). New York: Wiley.

Maccoby, E.E., & Mnookin, R.H. (1992). *Dividing the Child: Social and Legal Dilemmas of Custody*, Cambridge, MA: Harvard University Press.

Mack, A.H., Forman, L., Brown, R., & Frances, A. (1994). A brief history of psychiatric classification: From the ancients to DSM-IV. *Psychiatric Clinics of North America*, 17, 515–523.

Mackay, R.D. (1988). Post-Hinckley insanity in the U.S.A. *Criminal Law Review*, 88–96.

MacLatchy-Gaudet, H.A., & Stewart, S.H. (2001). The context-specific positive alcohol outcome expectancies of university women. *Addictive Behaviors*, 26, 31–49.

MacLeod, C., Rutherford, E., Campbell, L., Ebsworthy, G., & Holker, L. (2002). Selective attention and emotional vulnerability: Assessing the causal basis of their association through the experimental manipulation of attentional bias. *Journal of Abnormal Psychology*, 111, 107–123.

Macklin, M.L., Metzger, L.J., McNally, R.J., Litz, B.T., Lasko, N.B., Orr, S.P., et al. (1998). Lower precombat intelligence is a risk factor for posttraumatic stress disorder. *Journal of Consulting and Clinical Psychology*, 66, 323–326.

MacMillan, D.L., Gresham, F.M., & Siperstein, G.N. (1995). Heightened concerns over the 1992 AAMR definition: Advocacy versus precision. *American Journal on Mental Retardation*, 100, 87–97.

MacMillan, H.L., Fleming, J.E., Streiner, D.L., Lin, E., Boyle, M.H., Jamieson, E., Duku, E.K., Walsh, C.A., & Wong, M.Y.Y. (2001). Childhood abuse and lifetime psychopathology in a community sample. *American Journal of Psychiatry*, 158, 1878–1883.

MacMillan, H.L., MacMillan, A.B., Offord, D.R., & Dingle, J.L. (1996). Aboriginal health. *Canadian Medical Association Journal*, 155, 1569–1578.

Maddi, S.R. (1980). *Personality theories: A comparative analysis* (4th ed.). Homewood, IL: Dorsey.

Magai. C. (2001). Emotions over the life span. In J.E. Birren & K.W. Schaie (Eds.), *Handbook of the Psychology of Aging* (5th ed., pp. 399–426). San Diego: Academic Press.

Magenis, R.E., Overton, K.M., Chamberlin, J., Brady, T., & Lovrien, E. (1977). Parental origin of the extra chromosome in Down's syndrome. *Human Genetics*, 37, 7–16.

Mah, K., & Binik, Y. M. (2001). The nature of human orgasm: A critical review of major trends. *Clinical Psychology Review*, 21, 823–856.

Mahe, V., & Balogh, A. (2000). Long-term pharmacological treatment of generalized anxiety disorder. *International Clinical Psychopharmacology*, 15, 99–105.

Maher, B.A. (2001). Delusions. In P.B. Sutker and H.E. Adams (Eds.), *Comprehensive Handbook of Psychopathology* (3rd ed., pp. 309–339). New York: Kluwer Academic/Plenum.

Mahoney, M.J. (1991). *Human change processes: The scientific foundations of psychotherapy*. New York: Basic Books.

Maier, S.F., Watkins, L.R., & Fleshner, M. (1994). Psychoneuroimmunology: The interface between behavior, brain, and immunity. *American Psychologist*, 49, 1004–1017.

Maisto, S.A., Wolfe, W., & Jordan, J. (1999). Short-term motivational therapy. In P.J. Ott, R.E. Tarter, & R.T. Ammerman (Eds.), *Sourcebook on Substance Abuse: Etiology, Epidemiology, Assessment, and Treatment* (pp. 284–292). Boston: Allyn & Bacon.

Mäkelä, K. (1994). Rates of attrition among the membership of Alcoholics Anonymous in Finland. *Journal of Studies on Alcohol*, 55, 91–95.

Malcolm, J.G. (1987). Treatment choices and informed consent in psychiatry: Implications of the Osheroff case for the profession. *Journal of Psychiatry and the Law*, 15, 9–81.

Maldonado, J.R., Butler, L.D., & Spiegel, D. (2001). Treatments for dissociative disorders. In P.E. Nathan & J.M. Gorman (Eds.), *A Guide to Treatments that Work* (pp. 463–469). London: Oxford University Press.

Maletzky, B.M. (1997). Exhibitionism: Assessment and treatment. In R.D. Laws & W.T. O'Donohue (Eds.), *Sexual deviance: Theory, assessment, and treatment* (pp. 40–74). New York: Guilford.

Malla, A.K., Norman, R.M.G., McLean, T.S., Cheng, S., Rickwood, A., McIntosh, E., Cortese, L., Diaz, K., & Voruganti, L.P. (1998). An integrated medical and psychosocial treatment program for psychotic disorders: Patient characteristics and outcome. *Canadian Journal of Psychiatry*, 43, 698–705.

Manassis, K., & Monga, S. (2001). A therapeutic approach to children and adolescents with anxiety disorders and associated comorbid conditions. *Journal of the American Academy of Child and Adolescent Psychiatry*, 40, 115–117.

Manderscheid, R.W., Henderson, M.J., Witkin, M.J., & Atay, J.E. (1999). Contemporary mental health systems and managed care. In A.V. Horwitz and T.L. Scheid (Eds.), *A Handbook for the Study of Mental Health: Social Contexts, Theories, and Systems* (pp. 412–426). Cambridge, UK: Cambridge University Press.

Manicavasagar, V., Silove, D., & Hadzi-Pavolvic, D. (1998). Subpopulations of early separation anxiety: Relevance to risk of adult anxiety disorders. *Journal of Affective Disorders*, 48, 181–190.

Mannuzza, S., Schneier, F.R., Chapman, T.F., Liebowitz, M.R., Klein, D.F., & Fyer, A.J. (1995). Generalized social phobia: Reliability and validity. *Archives of General Psychiatry*, 52, 230–237.

Manson, S.M. (1994). Culture and depression: Discovering variations in the experience of illness. In W.J. Lonner & R.S. Malpass (Eds.), *Psychology and Culture* (pp. 285–290). Boston: Allyn & Bacon.

Manson, S.M., & Kleinman, A. (1998). DSM-IV, culture and mood disorders: A critical reflection on recent progress. *Transcultural Psychiatry*, 35, 377–386.

March, J.S., Leonard, H.L., & Swedo, S.E. (1995). Obsessive–compulsive disorder. In J.S. March (Ed.), *Anxiety Disorders in Children and Adolescents* (pp. 251–275). New York: Guilford.

Marcia, J.E. (1966). Development and validation of ego-identity status. *Journal of Personality and Social Psychology*, 24, 551–558.

Marcia, J.E. (1994). The empirical study of ego identity. In H.A. Bosma, T.L.G. Graafsma, H.D. Grotevant, & D.J. de Levita (Eds.), *Identity and Development* (pp. 67–80). Thousand Oaks, CA: Sage.

Marder, K., Tang, M., Cote, L., & Stern, Y. (1995). The frequency and associated risk factors for dementia in patients with Parkinson's disease. *Archives of Neurology*, 52, 695–701.

Marder, S.R., Ames, D., Wirshing, W.C., & Van Putten, T. (1993). Schizophrenia. *Psychiatric Clinics of North America*, 16, 567–587.

Margolin, G., Christensen, A., & John, R.S. (1996). The continuance and spillover of everyday tensions in distressed and nondistressed families. *Journal of Family Psychology*, 10, 304–321.

Marin, A. (2001). *Report to the Minister of National Defence: Systematic treatment of CF members with PTSD*. Ottawa: Canadian Department of National Defence.

Markman, H.J., Floyd, F.J., Stanley, S.M., & Storaasli, R.D. (1988). Prevention of marital distress: A longitudinal investigation. *Journal of Consulting and Clinical Psychology*, 56, 210–217.

Markman, H.J., Leber, B.D., Cordova, A.D., & St. Peters, M. (1995). Behavioral observation and family psychology: Strange bedfellows or happy marriage? *Journal of Family Psychology*, 9, 371–379.

Markman, H.J., Renick, M.J., Floyd, F.J., Stanley, S.M., & Clements, M. (1993). Preventing marital distress throught communication and conflict management training: A 4- and 5-year follow-up. *Journal of Consulting and Clinical Psychology*, 61, 70–77.

Marks, I.M., & Nesse, R.M. (1994). Fear and fitness: An evolutionary analysis of anxiety disorders. *Ethology and Sociobiology*, 15, 247–261.

Marks, I.M., Swinson, R.P., Basoglu, M., Kuch, K., Noshirvani, H., O'Sullivan, G., Lelliott, P.T., Kirby, M., McNamee, G., Sengun, S., & Wickwire, K. (1993). Alprazolam and exposure alone and combined in panic disorder with agoraphobia: A controlled study in London and Toronto. *British Journal of Psychiatry*, 162, 776–787.

Marks, P.A., Seeman, W., & Haller, D.L. (1974). *The Actuarial Use of the MMPI with Adolescents and Adults*, New York: Oxford University Press.

Marlatt, G.A. (1985). Relapse prevention: Theoretical rationale and overview of the model. In G.A. Marlatt & J.R. Gordon (Eds.), *Relapse Prevention* (pp. 3–70). New York: Guilford.

Marlatt, G.A., Baer, J.S., Donovan, D.M., & Kivlahan, D.R. (1988). Addictive behaviors: Etiology and treatment. *Annual Review of Psychology*, 39, 223–252.

Marlatt, G.A., Blume, A.W., & Parks, G.A. (2001). Integrating harm reduction therapy and traditional substance abuse treatment. *Journal of Psychoactive Drugs*, 33, 13–21.

Marlatt, G.A., Larimer, M.E., Baer, J.S., & Quigley, L.A. (1993). Harm reduction for alcohol problems: Moving beyond the controlled drinking controversy. *Behavior Therapy*, 24, 461–504.

Marques, J.K. (1999). How to answer the question "Does sexual offender treatment work?" *Journal of Interpersonal Violence*, 14, 437–451.

Marques, J.K., Day, D.M., Nelson, C., & West, M.A. (1993). Findings and recommendations from California's experimental treatment program. In G.C.N. Hall, R. Hirschman, J.R. Graham, & M.S. Zaragoza (Eds.), *Sexual Aggression: Issues in Etiology, Assessment, and Treatment* (pp. 197–214). Washington, DC: Hemisphere.

Marshall, K., & Wynne, H. (2003). Fighting the odds. *Perspectives on Labour and Income*, 4(12), whole issue.

Marshall, W.L. (1989). Intimacy, loneliness, and sexual offenders. *Behaviour Research and Therapy*, 27, 491–503.

Marshall, W.L. (1999). Current status of North American assessment and treatment programs for sexual offenders. *Journal of Interpersonal Violence*, 14, 221–239.

Marshall, W.L., Anderson, D., & Champagne, F. (1997). Self-esteem and its relationship to sexual offending. *Psychology, Crime, and Law*, 3, 161–186.

Marshall, W.L., & Barbaree, H.E. (1990). An integrated theory of sexual offending. In W.L. Marshall, D.R. Laws, & H.E. Barbaree (Eds.), *Handbook of sexual assault* (pp. 257–275). New York: Plenum.

Marshall, W.L., Bryce, P., Hudson, S.M., Ward, T., & Moth, B. (1996). The enhancement of intimacy and the reduction of loneliness among child molesters. *Journal of Family Violence*, 11, 219–236.

Marshall, W.L., & Eccles, A. (1993). Pavlovian conditioning processes in adolescent sex offenders. In H.E. Barbaree, W.L. Marshall, & S.M. Hudson (Eds.), *The juvenile sex offender* (pp. 118–142). New York: Guilford.

Marshall, W.L., Eccles, A., & Barbaree, H.E. (1991). The treatment of exhibitionists: A focus on sexual deviance versus cognitive and relationship features. *Behaviour Research and Therapy*, 29, 129–135.

Marshall, W.L., Hudson, S.M., & Hodkinson, S. (1993). The importance of attachment bonds in the development of juvenile sex offending. In H.E. Barbaree, W.L. Marshall, & S.M. Hudson (Eds.), *The juvenile sex offender* (pp. 164–181). New York: Guilford.

Marshall, W.L., & Moulden, H. (2001). Hostility toward women and victim empathy of rapists. *Sexual Abuse: A Journal of Research and Treatment*, 13, 249–255.

Marshall, W.L., Serran, G.A., & Cortoni, F.A. (2000). Childhood attachments, sexual abuse, and their relationship to adult coping in child molesters. *Sexual Abuse: Journal of Research and Treatment, 12,* 17–26.

Martin, G. (1998). Media influence to suicide: The search for solutions. *Archives of Suicide Research, 4,* 51–66.

Martin, R. A. (1996). The situational humor response questionnaire (SHRQ) and coping humour scale (CHS): A decade of research findings. *Humor: International Journal of Humor Research, 9,* 251–272.

Martin, R. A. (2001). Humor, laughter, and physical health: Methodological issues and research findings. *Psychological Bulletin, 127,* 504–519.

Martin, R.A., & Lefcourt, H.M. (1983). Sense of humor as a moderator of the relation between stressors and moods. *Journal of Personality and Social Psychology, 45,* 1313–1324.

Martin, R.L., Roberts, W.V., & Clayton, P.J. (1980). Psychiatric status after hysterectomy: A one-year prospective follow-up. *Journal of the American Medical Association, 244,* 350–353.

Martyn, C.N., Coggon, D.N., Inskip, H., Lacey, R.F., & Young, W.F. (1997). Aluminum concentrations in drinking water and risk of Alzheimer's disease. *Epidemiology, 8,* 281–286.

Marwit, S.J. (1996). Reliability of diagnosing complicated grief: A preliminary investigation. *Journal of Consulting and Clinical Psychology, 64,* 563–568.

Mash, E.J., & Dozois, D.J.A. (2003). Child psychopathology: A developmental-systems perspective. In E. J. Mash & R. A. Barkley (Eds.), *Child psychopathology* (2nd ed., pp. 3–71). New York: Guilford.

Mash, E.J., & Johnston, C. (1982). A comparison of the mother–child interactions of younger and older hyperactive and normal children. *Child Development, 53,* 1371–1381.

Mash, E.J., & Johnston, C. (1990). Determinants of parenting stress: Illustrations from families of hyperactive children and families of physically abused children. *Journal of Clinical Child Psychology, 18,* 313–328.

Mash, E.J., & Terdal, L.G. (1997). *Assessment of childhood disorders* (3rd ed.). New York: Guilford.

Maslow, A.H. (1954). *Motivation and Personality.* New York: Harper & Row.

Maslow, A.H. (1970). *Motivation and Personality.* (2nd ed.). New York: Harper & Row.

Mason, F.L. (1997). Fetishism: Psychopathology and theory. In D.R. Laws & W.T. O'Donohue (Eds.), *Handbook of Sexual Deviance: Theory and Application* (pp. 75–91). New York: Guilford.

Mason, J.W. (1975). A historical view of the "stress" field. II. *Journal of Human Stress, 1,* 12–16.

Masand, P.S., & Gupta, S. (1999). Selective serotonin-reuptake inhibitors: An update. *Harvard Review of Psychiatry, 7,* 69–84.

Masters, W.H., & Johnson, V.E. (1966). *Human Sexual Response.* Boston: Little, Brown and Company.

Masters, W.H., & Johnson, V.E. (1970). *Human Sexual Inadequacy.* Boston: Little, Brown and Company.

Masten, A.S. (2001). Ordinary magic: Resilience processes in development. *American Psychologist, 56,* 227–238.

Matarazzo, J.D. (1983). The reliability of psychiatric and psychological diagnosis. *Clinical Psychology Review, 3,* 103–145.

Mate-Kole, C., Freschi, M., & Robin, A. (1988). Aspects of psychiatric symptoms at different stages in the treatment of transsexualism. *British Journal of Psychiatry, 152,* 550–553.

Mathews, A. (1990). Why worry: The cognitive function of anxiety. *Behaviour Research and Therapy, 28,* 455–468.

Mathews, A., & Mackintosh, B. (2000). Induced emotional interpretation bias and anxiety. *Journal of Abnormal Psychology, 109,* 602–615.

Mathis, J. (2001). Community integration of individuals with disabilities: An update on *Olmsted* implementation. *Journal of Poverty Law and Policy, 23,* 395–410.

Matson, J.L., & Frame, C.L. (1986). *Psychopathology Among Mentally Retarded Children and Adolescents.* Beverly Hills, CA: Sage.

Matthysse, S., & Pope, A. (1986). The neuropathology of psychiatric disorders. In P. Berger & K.H. Brodie (Eds.), *American Handbook of Psychiatry* (2nd ed., Vol. 8, pp. 151–159). New York: Basic Books.

Mattia, J.I., & Zimmerman, M. (2001). Epidemiology. In W.J. Livesley (Ed.). *Handbook of Personality Disorders: Theory, Research, and Treatment* (pp. 107–123). New York: Guilford.

Mavissakalian, M.R., & Ryan, M.T. (1998). Rational treatment of panic disorder with antidepressants. *Annals of Clinical Psychiatry, 10,* 185–195.

Mayes. S.D., Calhoun, S.L., & Crites, D.L. (2001). Does DSM-IV Asperger's Disorder exist? *Journal of Abnormal Child Psychology, 29,* 263–271.

Mayeux, R., & Ottman, R. (1998). Alzheimer's disease genetics: Home runs and strikeouts. *Annals of Neurology, 44,* 716–719.

Mayeux, R., & Sano, M. (1999). Treatment of Alzheimer's disease. *New England Journal of Medicine, 341,* 1670–1679.

Mayou, R.A., Ehlers, A., & Hobbs, M. (2000). Psychological debriefing for road traffic accident victims. *British Journal of Psychiatry, 176,* 589–593.

Mazure, C.M., Bruce, M.L., Maciejewski, P.K., & Jacobs, S.C. (2000). Adverse life events and cognitive-personality characteristics in the prediction of major depression and antidepressant response. *American Journal of Psychiatry, 157,* 896–903.

McBride, W.J., Murphy, J.M., Yoshimoto, K., Lumeng, L., & Li, T.K. (1993). Serotonin mechanisms in alcohol-drinking behavior. *Drug Development Research, 30,* 170–177.

McCabe, M.P. (2001). Evaluation of a cognitive behavior therapy program for people with sexual dysfunction. *Journal of Sex and Marital Therapy, 27,* 259–271.

McCabe, M.P., McDonald, E., Deeks, A., Vowels, L.M., & Cobain, M.J. (1996). The impact of multiple sclerosis on sexuality and relationships. *Journal of Sex Research, 33,* 241–249.

McCabe, R.E. (1999). Implicit and explicit memory for threat words in high- and low-anxiety-sensitive participants. *Cognitive Therapy and Research, 23,* 21–38.

McCann, U.D., Rossiter, E.M., King, R.J., & Agras, W.S. (1991). Nonpurging bulimia: A distinct subtype of bulimia nervosa. *International Journal of Eating Disorders, 10,* 679–687.

McCarroll, J.E., Ursano, R.J., Fullerton, C.S., Liu, X., & Lundy, A. (2002). Somatic symptoms in Gulf War mortuary workers. *Psychosomatic Medicine, 64,* 29–33.

McCarthy, B.W. (1989). Cognitive-behavioral strategies and techniques in the treatment of early ejaculation. In S.R. Leiblum & R.C. Rosen (Eds.), *Principles and Practice of Sex Therapy* (2nd ed., pp. 141–167). New York: Guilford.

McCarthy, B.W. (1998). Integrating Viagra into cognitive-behavioral couples sex therapy. *Journal of Sex Education and Therapy, 23,* 302–308.

McCarthy, B.W. (1998). Sex therapy workshops: The Indian experience. *Journal of Sex Education and Therapy, 23,* 309–311.

McCarty, D., Argeriou, M., & Huebner, R.B. (1991). Alcoholism, drug abuse, and the homeless. *American Psychologist, 46,* 1139–1148.

McConaghy, N. (1999a). Unresolved issues in scientific sexology. *Archives of Sexual Behavior, 28,* 285–318.

McConaghy, N. (1999b). Methodological issues concerning evaluation of treatment for sexual offenders: Randomization, treatment dropouts, untreated controls, and within-treatment studies. *Sexual Abuse: Journal of Research and Treatment, 11,* 183–193.

McCulloch, S. (April 26, 2002). Montreux offices searched. *Times Colonist,* p. D1.

McDavid, J.D., & Pilkonis, P.A. (1996). The stability of personality disorder diagnoses. *Journal of Personality Disorders, 10,* 1–15.

McDonald, C., & Murray, R.M. (2000). Early and late environmental risk factors for schizophrenia. *Brain Research Reviews, 31,* 130–137.

McDougle, C.J., Price, L.H., & Volkmar, F.R. (1994). Recent advances in the pharmacotherapy of autism and related conditions. *Child and Adolescent Psychiatric Clinics of North America, 3,* 71–89.

McEachin, J.J., Smith, T., & Lovaas, O.I. (1993). Long-term outcome for children with autism who received early intensive behavioural treatment. *American Journal on Mental Retardation, 97,* 359–372.

McElroy, S.L. (1999). Recognition and treatment of intermittent explosive disorder and explosivity. *Journal of Clinical Psychiatry Monograph Series, 17,* 8–11.

McFall, R.M. (1982). A review and reformulation of the concept of social skills. *Behavioral Assessment, 4,* 1–33.

McFall, R.M. (1990). The enhancement of social skills: An information-processing analysis. In W.L. Marshall, D.R. Laws, & H.E. Barbaree (Eds.), *Handbook of Sexual Assault: Issues, Theories, and Treatment of the Offender* (pp. 311–330). New York: Plenum.

McFall, R.M., & McDonel, E.C. (1986). The continuing search for units of analysis in psychology: Beyond persons, situations, and their interactions. In R.O. Nelson & S.C. Hayes (Eds.), *Conceptual Foundations of Behavioral Assessment* (pp. 201–241). New York: Guilford.

McGeer, P.L., & McGeer, E.G. (1996). Anti-inflammatory drugs in the fight against Alzheimer's disease. *Annals of the New York Academy of Sciences, 777,* 213–220.

McGlashan, T. (1986). The Chestnut Lodge follow-up study. III. Long-term outcome of borderline personalities. *Archives of General Psychiatry, 43,* 20–30.

McGlashan, T.H. (1992). The longitudinal profile of borderline personality disorder: Contributions from the Chestnut Lodge follow-up study. In D. Silver & M. Rosenbluth (Eds.), *Handbook of Borderline Disorders* (pp. 53–83). Madison, CT: International Universities Press.

McGlashan, T.H. (1998). The profiles of clinical deterioration in schizophrenia. *Journal of Psychiatric Research, 32,* 133–141.

McGlashan, T.H., & Fenton, W.S. (1991). Classical subtypes for schizophrenia: Literature review for DSM-IV. *Schizophrenia Bulletin, 17,* 609–623.

McGlashan, T.H., & Hoffman, R.E. (2000). Schizophrenia as a disorder of developmentally reduced synaptic connectivity. *Archives of General Psychiatry, 57,* 637–648.

McGrath, J.J., & Welham, J.L. (1999). Season of birth and schizophrenia: A systematic review and meta-analysis of data from the Southern Hemisphere. *Schizophrenia Research, 35,* 237–242.

McGue, M. (1993). From proteins to cognitions: The behavioral genetics of alcoholism. In R. Plomin & G.E. McClearn (Eds.), *Nature, Nurture, and Psychology* (pp. 245–268). Washington, DC: American Psychological Association.

McGue, M. (1999). The behavioral genetics of alcoholism. *Current Directions in Psychological Science, 8,* 109–115.

McGue, M., & Lykken, D.T. (1992). Genetic influence on risk of divorce. *Psychological Science, 3,* 368–373.

McGuire, M. (1987). C.19. An act to amend the Young Offenders Act and the Criminal Code: "Getting tougher?" *Canadian Journal of Criminology, 39*, 185–214.

McGuire, M. (1997). C.19. An act to amend the Young Offenders Act and the Criminal Code: "Getting tougher?" *Canadian Journal of Criminology, 39*, 185–214.

McGuffin, P., & Thapar, A. (1998). Genetics and antisocial personality disorder. In T. Millon and E. Simonsen (Eds.), *Psychopathy: Antisocial, Criminal, and Violent Behavior* (pp. 215–230). New York: Guilford.

McGuffin, P., Katz, R., Watkins, S., & Rutherford, J. (1996). A hospital-based twin register of the heritability of DSM-IV unipolar depression. *Archives of General Psychiatry, 53*, 129–136.

McGuire, M.T., & Troisi, A. (1998a). *Darwinian Psychiatry*. New York: Oxford University Press.

McGuire, M.T., & Troisi, A. (1998b). Prevalence differences in depression among males and females: Are there evolutionary explanations? *British Journal of Medical Psychology, 71*, 479–491.

McHale, M.J. (1991). Family law. In D. Turner & M.R. Uhlemann (Eds.), *A legal handbook for the helping professional* (pp. 93–113). Victoria, BC: Sedgewick Society for Consumer and Public Education.

McKeith, I.G. (2002). Dementia with Lewy bodies. *British Journal of Psychiatry, 180*, 144–147.

McKenna, M.C., Zevon, M.A., Corn, B., & Rounds, J. (1999). Psychosocial factors and the development of breast cancer: A meta-analysis. *Health Psychology, 18*, 520–531.

McKenna, S.P., Doward, L.C., Kohlmann, T., Mercier, C., Niero, M., Paes, M., Patrick, D., Ramirez, N., Thorsen, H., & Whalley, D. (2001). International development of the Quality of Life in Depression Scale (QLDS). *Journal of Affective Disorders, 63*, 189–199.

McKey, R.H., Condelli, L., Granson, H., Barrett, B., McConkey, C., & Plantz, M. (1985, June). *The Impact of Head Start on Children, Families, and Communities*. Final Report of the Head Start Evaluation, Synthesis and Utilization Project. Washington, DC: CSR.

McKim, W. (2000). *Drugs and Behavior: An Introduction to Behavioral Pharmacology* (4th ed). Upper Saddle River, NJ: Prentice Hall.

McLellan, A.T., Woody, G.E., & Metzger, D. (1996). Evaluating the effectiveness of addiction treatments: Reasonable expectations, appropriate comparisons. *Milbank Quarterly, 74*, p. 51.

McLemore, C.W., & Benjamin, L.A. (1979). Whatever happened to interpersonal diagnosis? A psychosocial alternative to DSM-III. *American Psychologist, 34*, 17–34.

McLintock, B. (2002). *Anorexia's fallen angel: The untold story of Peggy Claude-Pierre and the controversial Montreux clinic*. Toronto: HarperCollins.

McMahon, F.J., Simpson, S.G., McInnis, M.G., Badner, J.A., MacKinnon, D.F., & DePaulo, J.R. (2001). Linkage of bipolar disorder to chromosome 18q and the validity of bipolar II disorder. *Archives of General Psychiatry, 58*, 1025–1031.

McMahon, R.P., Kelly, D.L., Kreyenbuhl, J., Kirkpatrick, B., Love, R.C., & Conley, R.R. (2002). Novel factor-based symptom scores in treatment resistant schizophrenia: Implications for clinical trials. *Neuropsychopharmacology, 26*, 537–545.

McNally, R.J. (1994). Cognitive bias in panic disorder. *Current Directions in Psychological Science, 3*, 129–132.

McNally, R.J. (1998). Information-processing abnormalities in anxiety disorders: Implications for cognitive neuroscience. *Cognition and Emotion, 12*, 479–495.

McNeil, T.F., & Cantor-Graae, E. (1999). Does preexisting abnormality cause labor-delivery complications in fetuses who will develop schizophrenia? *Schizophrenia Bulletin, 25*, 425–435.

McSherry, B. (1998). Getting away with murder? Dissociative states and criminal responsibility. *International Journal of Law and Psychiatry, 21*, 163–176.

Meana, M., & Binik, Y.M. (1994). Painful coitus: A review of female dyspareunia. *Journal of Nervous and Mental Disease, 182*, 264–272.

Meana, M., Binik, Y.M., Khalife, S., & Cohen, D. (1997). Dyspareuia: Sexual dysfunction or pain syndrome? *Journal of Nervous and Mental Disease, 185*, 561–569.

Meaney, M.J. (2001). Nature, nurture, and the disunity of knowledge. *Annals of the New York Academy of Sciences, 935*, 50–61.

Medina, J. (1999). *What You Need to Know About Alzheimer's*. Oakland, CA: New Harbinger.

Mednick, S.A., & Schulsinger, F. (1968). Some premorbid characteristics related to breakdown in children with schizophrenic mothers. *Journal of Psychiatric Research 6* (suppl. 1), 354–362.

Meehl, P.E. (1990). Toward an integrated theory of schizotaxia, schizotypy, and schizophrenia. *Journal of Personality Disorders, 4*, 1–99.

Meehl, P.E. (1993). The origins of some of my conjectures concerning schizophrenia. In L.J. Chapman, J.P. Chapman, & D. Fowles (Eds.), *Progress in Experimental Personality and Psychopathology Research* (pp. 1–11). New York: Springer.

Meehl, P.E., & Rosen, A. (1955). Antecedent probability and the efficiency of psychometric signs, patterns, or cutting scores. *Psychological Bulletin, 52*, 194–216.

Meichenbaum, D. (1977). *Cognitive behavior modification*. New York: Plenum.

Meissner, D. (July 23, 2002). U.S. man paid Montreux $200,000 to treat wife. *Times Colonist*, p. B1.

Mejeur, J. (1999). There's more to TEA-21 than .08. *State Legislatures, 25*, p. 33.

Mellings, T.M.B., & Alden, L.E. (2000). Cognitive processes in social anxiety: The effects of self-focus, rumination and anticipatory processing. *Behaviour Research and Therapy, 38*, 243–257.

Melman, A., & Tiefer, L. (1992). Surgery for erectile disorders: Operative procedures and psychological issues. In R.C. Rosen & S.R. Leiblum (Eds.), *Erectile Disorders: Assessment and Treatment* (pp. 255–282). New York: Guilford.

Melton, G.B., & Limber, S. (1989). Psychologists' involvement in cases of child maltreatment: Limits of roles and expertise. *American Psychologist, 44*, 1225–1233.

Melton, G.B., Petrila, J., Poythress, N.G., & Slobogin, C. (1997). *Psychological Evaluations for the Courts* (2nd ed). New York: Guilford.

Melzack, R., & Wall, P. D. (1965). Pain mechanisms: A new theory. *Science, 150*, 971–979.

Mendlewicz, J., Souery, D., & Rivelli, S.K. (1999). Short-term and long-term treatment for bipolar patients: Beyond the guidelines. *Journal of Affective Disorders, 55*, 79–85.

Merikangas, K.R., Avenevoli, S., Acharyya, S., Zhang, H., & Angst, J. (2002). The spectrum of social phobia in the Zurich cohort study of young adults. *Biological Psichiatry, 51*, 81–91.

Merikangas, K.R., Stevens, D.E., Fenton, B., Stolar, M., O'Malley, S., Woods, S.W., & Risch, N. (1998a). Comorbidity and familial aggregation of alcoholism and anxiety disorders. *Psychological Medicine, 28*, 773–788.

Merikangas, K.R., Stolar, M., Stevens, D.E., Goulet, J., Preisig, M.A., Fenton, B., Zhang, H., O'Malley, S.S., & Rounsaville, B.J. (1998b). Familial transmission of substance use disorders. *Archives of General Psychiatry, 55*, 973–979.

Merkin, D. (1996). Unlikely obsession: Confronting a taboo. *The New Yorker*, February 26 and March 4, 98–115.

Merskey, H. (1992). The manufacture of personalities: The production of multiple personality disorder. *British Journal of Psychiatry, 160*, 327–340.

Meston, C.M. (1997). Aging and sexuality. *Western Journal of Medicine, 167*, 285–290.

Meston, C.M., & Frohlich, P.F. (2000). The neurobiology of sexual function. *Archives of General Psychiatry, 57*, 1012–1030.

Meston, C.M., Trapnell, P.D., & Gorzalka, B.B. (1996). Ethnic and gender differences in sexuality: Variations in sexual behavior between Asian and non-Asian university students. *Archives of Sexual Behavior, 25*, 33–72.

Meston, C.M., Trapnell, P.D., & Gorzalka, B.B. (1998). Ethnic, gender, and length-of-residency influences on sexual knowledge and attitudes. *Journal of Sex Research, 35*, 176–188.

Metalsky, G.I., Joiner, T.E., Hardin, T.S., & Abramson, L.Y. (1993). Depressive reactions to failure in a naturalistic setting: A test of the hopelessness and self-esteem theories of depression. *Journal of Abnormal Psychology, 102*, 101–109.

Metz, M.E., & Epstein, N. (2002). Assessing the role of relationship conflict in sexual dysfunction. *Journal of Sex and Marital Therapy, 28*, 139–164.

Meyer, G.J., & Archer, R.P. (2001). The hard science of Rorschach research: What do we know and where do we go? *Psychological Assessment, 13*, 486–502.

Meyers, B.S. (1998). Depression and dementia: Comorbidities, identification, and treatment. *Journal of Geriatric Psychiatry and Neurology, 11*, 201–205.

Mezzich, J.E., Berganza, C.E., & Ruiperez, M.A. (2001). Culture in DSM-IV, ICD-10, and evolving diagnostic systems. *Psychiatric Clinics of North America, 24*, 407–419.

Michelini, S., Cassano, G.B., Frare, F., & Perugi, G. (1996). Long-term use of benzodiazepines: Tolerance, dependence and clinical problems in anxiety and mood disorders. *Pharmacopsychiatry, 29*, 127–134.

Mickelson, K.D., Kessler, R.C., & Shaver, P.R. (1997). Adult attachment in a nationally representative sample. *Journal of Personality and Social Psychology, 73*, 1092–1106.

Migliorelli, R., Teson, A., Sabe, L., Petracchi, M., Leiguarda, R., & Starkstein, S.E. (1995). Prevalence and correlates of dysthymia and major depression among patients with Alzheimer's disease. *American Journal of Psychiatry, 152*, 37–45.

Miklowitz, D.J. (1995). The evolution of family-based psychopathology. In R.H. Mikesell, D. Losterman, & S.H. McDaniel (Eds.), *Integrating Family Therapy: Handbook of Family Psychology and Systems Theory* (pp. 183–197). Washington, DC: American Psychological Association.

Miklowitz, D.J. (2002). *The Bipolar Disorder Survival Guide: What You and Your Family Need to Know*. New York: Guilford.

Miklowitz, D.J., Goldstein, M.J., et al. (1988). Family factors and the course of bipolar affective disorder. *Archives of General Psychiatry, 45*, 225–231.

Miklowitz, D.J., Goldstein, M.J., & Nuechterlein, K.H. (1995). Verbal interactions in the families of schizophrenic and bipolar affective patients. *Journal of Abnormal Psychology, 104*, 268–276.

Milan, A. (2000). One hundred years of families. *Canadian Social Trends*, Spring, 2–12.

Milich, R., Balentine, A.C., & Lynam, D.R. (2001). ADHD combined type and ADHD predominantly inattentive type are distinct and unrelated disorders. *Clinical Psychology: Science and Practice, 8*, 463–488.

Milich, R., Wolraich, M., & Lindgren, S. (1986). Sugar and hyperactivity: A critical review of empirical findings. *Clinical Psychology Review, 6*, 493–513.

Millar, W.J. (1996). Chronic pain. *Health Reports, 7*, 47–53.

Miller, M., & Hemenway, D. (1999). The relationship between firearms and suicide: A review of the literature. *Aggression and Violent Behavior, 4*, 59–75.

Miller, T.Q., Smith, T.W., Turner, C.W., Guijarro, M.L., & Hallet, A.J. (1996). A meta-analytic review of research on hostility and physical health. *Psychological Bulletin, 119*, 322–348.

Miller, T.Q., Turner, C.W., Tindale, R.S., Posavac, E.J., & Dugoni, B.L. (1991). Reasons for the trend toward null findings in research on Type A behavior. *Psychological Bulletin, 110*, 469–485.

Miller, T.W. (1989). *Stressful Life Events.* Madison, CT: International Universities Press.

Miller, W.R. (1995). Increasing motivation for change. In R.K. Hester & W.R. Miller (Eds.), *Handbook of Alcoholism Treatment Approaches* (2nd ed., pp. 89–104). Boston: Allyn & Bacon.

Miller-Johnson, S., Emery, R.E., Marvin, R.S., Clarke, W., Lovinger, R., & Martin, M. (1994). Parent–child relationships and the management of insulin-dependent diabetes mellitus. *Journal of Consulting and Clinical Psychology, 62*, 603–610.

Millon, T., & Martinez, A. (1995). Avoidant personality disorder. In W.J. Livesley (Ed.), *The DSM-IV Personality Disorders* (pp. 218–233). New York: Guilford.

Mineka, S., & Cook, M. (1993). Mechanisms involved in the observational conditioning of fear. *Journal of Experimental Psychology: General, 122*, 23–38.

Mineka, S., & Kihlstrom, J.F. (1978). Unpredictable and uncontrollable events: A new perspective on experimental neurosis. *Journal of Abnormal Psychology, 87*, 256–271.

Mineka, S., & Ohman, A. (2002). Born to fear: Non-associative vs associative factors in the etiology of phobias. *Behaviour Research and Therapy, 40*, 173–184.

Mineka, S., & Thomas, C. (1999). Mechanisms of change in exposure therapy for anxiety disorders. In T. Dalgleish & M.J. Power (Eds.), *Handbook of Cognition and Emotion* (pp. 747–764). Chichester, England: Wiley.

Mineka, S., Watson, D., & Clark, L.A. (1998). Comorbidity of anxiety and unipolar mood disorders. *Annual Review of Psychology, 49*, 377–412.

Mineka, S., & Zinbarg, R. (1991). Animal models of psychopathology. In C.E. Walker (Ed.), *Clinical Psychology* (pp. 51–86). New York: Plenum Press.

Mineka S., & Zinbarg R. (1998). Experimental approaches to the anxiety and mood disorders. In J.G. Adair and D. Belanger (Eds.), *Advances in Psychological Science.* Vol. 1, *Social, Personal, and Cultural Aspects* (pp. 429–454). Hove, UK: Psychology Press.

Minton, H.L. (2002). *Departing from Deviance: A History of Homosexual Rights and Emancipatory Science in America.* Chicago, IL: University of Chicago Press.

Minuchin, P. (1985). Families and individual development: Provocations from the field of family therapy. *Child Development, 56*, 289–302.

Minuchin, S. (1974). *Families and family therapy.* Cambridge, MA: Harvard University Press.

Minuchin, S., Rosman, B.L., & Baker, L. (1978). *Psychosomatic Families.* Cambridge, MA: Harvard University Press.

Misener, V.L., Luca, P., Azeke, O., Crosbie, J., Waldman, I., Tannock, R., Roberts, W., Malone, M., Schachar, R., Ickowicz, A., Kennedy, J.L., & Barr, C.L. (2004). Linkage of the dopamine receptor D1 gene to attention-deficit/hyperactivity disorder. *Molecular Psychiatry, 9*, 500–509.

Mitchell, J., & Dyregrov, A. (1993). Traumatic stress in disaster workers and emergency personnel. In J.P. Wilson & B. Raphael (Eds.), *International Handbook of Traumatic Stress Syndromes* (pp. 905–914). New York: Plenum.

Mitchell, J.T., & Everly, G.S. (2000). Critical incident stress management and critical incident stress debriefings: Evolutions, effects and outcomes. In B. Raphael & J. P. Wilson (Eds.), *Psychological debriefing: Theory, practice and evidence* (pp. 71–90). NY: Cambridge University Press.

Mitchell, J.E., Pyle, R.L., Eckert, E.D., Hatsukami, D., Pomeroy, C., & Zimmerman, R. (1990). A comparison study of antidepressants and structured intensive group psychotherapy in the treatment of bulimia nervosa. *Archives of General Psychiatry, 47*, 149–157.

Mitchell, J.E., Raymond, N., & Specker, S. (1993). A review of controlled trials of pharmacotherapy and psychotherapy in the treatment of bulimia nervosa. *International Journal of Eating Disorders, 14*, 229–247.

Mitchell, P.B., & Malhi, G.S. (2002). The expanding pharmacopoeia for bipolar disorder. *Annual Review of Medicine, 53*, 173–188.

Mittelman, M.S., Ferris, S.H., Shulman, E., Steinberg, G., Ambinder, A., & Mackell, J. (1997). Effects of a multicomponent support program on spouse-caregivers of Alzheimer's disease patients: Results of a treatment/control study. In L. Heston (Ed.), *Progress in Alzheimer's Disease and Similar Conditions* (pp. 259–275). Washington, DC: American Psychiatric Press.

Mnookin, R.H. (1975). Child-custody adjudication: Judicial functions in the face of indeterminancy. *Law and Contemporary Problems, 88*, 226–293.

Mnookin, R.H. (1985). *In the Interest of Children: Advocacy, Law Reform, and Public Policy.* New York: Freeman.

Moffitt, T.E. (1993). Adolescence-limited and life-course-persistent antisocial behavior: A developmental taxonomy. *Psychological Review, 100*, 674–701.

Moffitt, T.E. (1997). Adolescence-limited and life-course-persistent offending: A complementary pair of developmental theories. In T.P. Thornberry (Ed.), *Developmental Theories of Crime and Delinquency. Advances in Criminological Theory* (Vol. 7, pp. 11–54). New Brunswick, NJ: Transaction.

Moldavsky, M., Dorit, L., & Lerman-Sagie, T. (2001). Behavioral phenotypes in genetic syndromes: A reference guide for psychiatrists. *Journal of the American Academy of Child and Adolescent Psychiatry, 40*, 749–761.

Moldin, S.O., & Gottesman, I.I. (1997). Genes, experience, and chance in schizophrenia: Positioning for the 21st century. *Schizophrenia Bulletin, 23*, 547–561.

Monahan, J. (1981). *The Clinical Prediction of Violent Behavior.* Rockville, MD: National Institute of Mental Health.

Monahan, J. (1992). Mental disorder and violent behavior: Perceptions and evidence. *American Psychologist, 47*, 511–521.

Monahan, J. (1993). Limiting therapist exposure to Tarasoff liability: Guidelines for risk containment. *American Psychologist, 48*, 242–250.

Monahan, J., et al. (2001a). Mandated community treatment: Beyond outpatient commitment. *Psychiatric Services, 52*, 1198–1205.

Monahan, J., et al. (2001b). *Rethinking Risk Assessment.* New York: Oxford.

Mongrain, M., Lubbers, R. & Struthers, W. (2004). The power of love: Mediation of rejection in roommate relationships of dependents and self-critics. *Personality and Social Psychology Bulletin, 30*, 94–105.

Mongrain, M., Vettese, L.C., Shuster, B., & Kendal, N. (1998). Perceptual biases, affect, and behavior in relationships of dependents and self-critics. *Journal of Personality and Social Psychology, 75*, 230–241.

Monroe. S.M., Rhode, P., Seeley, J.R., & Lewinsohn, P.M. (1999). Life events and depression in adolescence: Relationship loss as a prospective risk factor for first onset of major depressive disorder. *Journal of Abnormal Psychology, 108*, 606–614.

Monroe, S.M., & Simons, A.D. (1991). Diathesis-stress theories in the context of life stress research: Implications for the depressive disorders. *Psychological Bulletin, 110*, 406–425.

Montgomery, H.A., Miller, W.R., & Tonigan, J.S. (1993). Differences among AA groups: Implications for research. *Journal of Studies on Alcohol, 54*, 502–504.

Moore, E.G., & Rosenberg, M.W. (1997). *Growing old in Canada.* Toronto: ITP Nelson.

Moore, M. (1975). Some myths about "mental illness." *Inquiry, 18*, 233–240.

Moos, R.H. (1990). Conceptual and empirical approaches to developing family-based assessment procedures: Resolving the case of the Family Environment Scale. *Family Process, 29*, 199–208.

Moretti, M.M., Emmrys, C., Grizenko, N., Holland, R., Moore, K., Shamsie, J., & Hamilton, H. (1997). The Treatment of Conduct Disorder: Perspectives from across Canada. *Canadian Journal of Psychiatry, 42*, 637–648.

Morgan, C.D., & Baade, L.E. (1997). Neuropsychological testing and assessment scales for dementia of the Alzheimer's type. *Psychiatric Clinics of North America, 20*, 25–43.

Morin, C.M., Colecchi, C., Stone, J., Sood, R., Brink, D. (1999). Behavioral and pharmacological therapies for late-life insomnia: A randomized controlled trial. *Journal of the American Medical Association, 281*, 991–999.

Morin, C.M., Hauri, P.J., Espie, C.A., Spielman, A.J., Buysse, D.J., & Bootzin, R.R. (1999). Nonpharmacological treatment of chronic insomnia: An American Academy of Sleep Medicine review. *Sleep, 22*, 1134–1156.

Morin, D., & Maurice, P. (2001). Elaboration de le version scolaire de l'echelle Québecoise de comportements adaptatifs (EQCA-VS). *Revue Francophone de la Deficience Intellectuelle, 12*, 7–20.

Morison, S.J., Ames, E.W., & Chisholm, K. (1995). The development of children adopted from Romanian orphanages. *Merrill-Palmer Quarterly, 41*, 411–430.

Morokoff, P.J. (1989). Sex bias and POD. *American Psychologist*, 73–75.

Morris, J. (1995). Dementia and cognitive changes in Huntington's disease. In W.J. Weiner & A.E. Lang (Eds.), *Behavioral Neurology of Movement Disorders. Advances in Neurology* (Vol. 65, pp. 187–200). New York: Raven Press.

Morrison, J., & Herbstein, J. (1988). Secondary affective disorder in women with somatization disorder. *Comprehensive Psychiatry, 29*, 433–440.

Morse, K.L. (1990). A uniform testimonial privilege for mental health professionals. *Ohio State Law Journal, 51*, 741–757.

Moscicki, E.K. (1995). Epidemiology of suicidal behavior. *Suicide and Life-Threatening Behavior, 25*, 22–35.

Moser, C. (2001). Paraphilia: A critique of a confused concept. In P.J. Kleinplatz (Ed.), *New Directions in Sex Therapy: Innovations and Alternatives* (pp. 91–108). Philadelphia, PA: Brunner-Routledge.

Moskovitz, R.A. (1996). *Lost in the Mirror: An Inside Look at Borderline Personality Disorder.* Dallas, TX: Taylor Publishing.

MTA Cooperative Group. (1999). A 14-month randomized clinical trial of treatment strategies for attention-deficit/hyperactivity disorder. *Archives of General Psychiatry, 56*, 1073–1086.

Mueser, K.T., Bellack, A.S., Douglas, M.S., & Morrison, R.L. (1991). Prevalence and stability of social skill deficits in schizophrenia. *Schizophrenia Research, 5*, 167–176.

Mulder, R.T. (2002). Personality pathology and treatment outcome in major depression: A review. *American Journal of Psychiatry, 159*, 359–371.

Multiple Risk Factor Intervention Trial Research Group (1982). Multiple Risk Factor Intervention Trial: Risk factor changes and mortality results. *Journal of the American Medical Association, 248*, 1465–1477.

Mulvany, F., O'Callaghan, E., Takei, N., Byrne, M., Fearon, P., & Larkin, C. (2001). Effect of social class at birth on risk and presentation of schizophrenia: case control study. *British Medical Journal, 323*, 1398–1401.

Munk-Jorgensen, P., & Ewald, H. (2001). Epidemiology in neurological research: Exemplified by the influenza-schizophrenia theory. *British Journal of Psychiatry, 178* (suppl. 40), S30–S32.

Murayama, H., Shin, R.W., Higuchi, J., Shibuya, S., Muramoto, T., & Kitamoto, T. (1999). Interaction of aluminum with PHFtau in Alzheimer's disease neurofibrillary degeneration evidenced by desferrioxamine-assisted chelating autoclave method. *American Journal of Pathology, 155*, 877–885.

Muris, P., Merckelbach, H., & Clavan, M. (1997). Abnormal and normal compulsions. *Behaviour Research and Therapy, 35*, 249–252.

Murphy, J.M. (1976). Psychiatric labeling in cross-cultural perspective. *Science, 191*, 1019–1028.

Murphy, W.D. (1997). Exhibitionism: Psychopathology and theory. In D.R. Laws & W.T. O'Donohue (Eds.), *Handbook of Sexual Deviance: Theory and Application* (pp. 22–39). New York: Guilford.

Murray, C.J.L., & Lopez, A.D. (1997). Global mortality, disability, and the contribution of risk factors: Global Burden of Disease Study. *Lancet, 349*, 1436–1442.

Myers, J.E.B. (1983–84). Involuntary civil commitment of the mentally ill: A system in need of change. *Villanova Law Review, 29*, 367–433.

Myers, J.K., & Weissman, M.M. (1980). Screening for depression in a community sample: The use of a self-report scale to detect the depressive syndrome. *American Journal of Psychiatry, 137*, 1081–1084.

Myers, M. (2000). Suicide: From despair to hope. *Canadian Psychiatric Association Bulletin*, October.

Narita, K., Sasaki, T., Akaho, R., Okazaki, Y.I., Kusumi, I., et al. (2000). Human leukocyte antigen and season of birth in Japanese patients with schizophrenia. *American Journal of Psychiatry, 157*, 1173–1175.

Nathan, P.E. (1993). Alcoholism: Psychopathology, etiology, and treatment. In P.B. Sutker & H.E. Adams (Eds.), *Comprehensive Handbook of Psychopathology* (2nd ed., pp. 451–476). New York: Plenum.

Nathan, P.E., Gorman, J.M., & Salkind, N.J. (1999). *Treating mental disorders: A guide to what works.* New York: Oxford.

Nathan, P.E., Stuart, S.P., & Dolan, S.L. (2000). Research on psychotherapy efficacy and effectiveness: Between Scylla and Charybdis? *Psychological Bulletin, 126*, 964–981.

National Academy of Sciences, Institute of Medicine (1989). *Research on Children & Adolescents with Mental, Behavioral, and Developmental Disorders.* Washington, DC: National Academy Press.

National Advisory Mental Health Council. (1995). *Basic Behavioral Science Research for Mental Health: A National Investment.* Rockville, MD: National Institute of Mental Health.

National Cancer Institute of Canada (2003). *Canadian cancer statistics 2003, Toronto.* Retrieved May 19, 2004, from http://129.33.170.48/stats_en.pdf

National Institutes of Health (2000). Phenylketonuria (PKU): Screening and Management. *NIH Consensus Statement, 17*, 1–33.

National Institute of Mental Health. (1990). *Somatization Disorder in the Medical Setting.* Rockville, MD: NIMH.

Nault, F. (1997). Narrowing mortality gaps, 1978 to 1995. *Health Reports, 9*, 35–41.

Neale, J.M., & Oltmanns, T.F. (1980). *Schizophrenia.* New York: Wiley.

Nehlig, A. (1999). Are we dependent upon coffee and caffeine? A review on human and animal data. *Neuroscience and Biobehavioral Reviews, 23*, 563–576.

Nemeroff, C.B. (1998). Psychopharmacology of affective disorders in the 21st century. *Biological Psychiatry, 44*, 517–525.

Nesse, R.M. (1999). Proximate and evolutionary studies of anxiety, stress and depression: Synergy at the interface. *Neuroscience and Biobehavioral Reviews, 23*, 895–903.

Nestadt, G., Romanoski, A.J., Chahal, R., Merchant, A., Folstein, J.F., Gruenberg, E.M., & McHugh, P.R. (1990). An epidemiological study of histrionic personality disorder. *Psychological Medicine, 20*, 413–422.

Nestler, E.J. (1998). Antidepressant treatments in the 21st century. *Biological Psychiatry, 44*, 526–533.

Neufeld, R.W.J. (1999). Dynamic differentials of stress and coping. *Psychological Review, 106*, 385–397.

Neufeld, R.W.J., & Williamson, P. (1996). Neuropsychological correlates of positive symptoms: Delusions and hallucinations. In C. Pantelis, H.E. Nelson, & T.R.E. Barnes (Eds.), *Schizophrenia: A neuropsychological perspective* (pp. 205–235). London: Wiley.

Neugarten, B.L. (1990). The changing meanings of age. In M. Bergener & S.I. Finkel (Eds.), *Clinical and scientific psychogeriatrics* (pp. 1–6). New York: Springer.

Neugebauer, R. (1979). Medieval and early modern theories of mental illness, *Archives of General Psychiatry, 36*, 477–483.

Neuhaus, I.M., & Rosenthal, N.E. (1997). Light therapy as a treatment modality for affective disorders. In A. Honig and H.M. van Praag (Eds.), *Depression: Neurobiological, Psychopathological and therapeutic Advances* (pp. 591–605). New York: Wiley.

Newcomb, A.F., Bukowski, W.M., & Pattee, L. (1993). Children's peer relations: A meta-analytic review of popular, rejected, neglected, controversial, and average sociometric status. *Psychological Bulletin, 113*, 99–128.

Newcomb, M.D. (1993). Four theories of rape in American society. *Archives of Sexual Behavior, 22*, 373–377.

Newhouse, P.A. (1997). Alzheimer's disease and the cholinergic system: An introduction to clinical pharmacological research. In L. Heston (Ed.), *Progress in Alzheimer's Disease and Similar Conditions.* Washington, DC: American Psychiatric Press.

Newman, J.P., Schmitt, W.A., & Voss, W.D. (1997). The impact of motivationally neutral cues on psychopathic individuals: Assessing the generality of the response modulation hypothesis. *Journal of Abnormal Psychology, 106*, 563–575.

Newman, J.P., & Wallace, J.F. (1993). Psychopathy and cognition. In K.S. Dobson & P.C. Kendall (Eds.), *Psychopathology and Cognition* (pp. 293–349). San Diego, CA: Academic Press.

Newman, S.C., Bland, R.C., & Orn, H.T. (1998). The prevalence of mental disorders in the elderly in Edmonton: A community survey using GMS-AGECAT. *Canadian Journal of Psychiatry, 43*, 910–914.

Newport, D.J., & Nemeroff, C.B. (2000). Neurobiology of posttraumatic stress disorder. *Cognitive Neuroscience, 10*, 211–218.

Nicholson, I.R., & Neufeld, R.W.J. (1992). A dynamic vulnerability perspective on stress and schizophrenia. *American Journal of Orthopsychiatry, 62*, 117–130.

Nierenberg, A.A. (2001). Long-term management of chronic depression. *Journal of Clinical Psychiatry, 62* (suppl. 16), 17–21.

Nietzel, M.T., Bernstein, D.A., & Milich, R. (1994). *Introduction to Clinical Psychology* (4th ed.). Englewood Cliffs, NJ: Prentice Hall.

Nigg, J.T. (2001). Is ADHD a disinhibitory disorder? *Psychological Bulletin, 127*, 571–598.

Nigg, J.T., & Goldsmith, H.H. (1994). Genetics of personality disorders: Perspectives from personality and psychopathology research. *Psychological Bulletin, 115*, 346–380.

Nimgaonkar, V.L., Fujiwara, T.M., Dutta, M., Wood, J., Gentry, K., Maendel, S., Morgan, K., & Eaton, J. (2000). Low prevalence of psychoses among the Hutterites, an isolated religious community. *American Journal of Psychiatry, 157*, 1065–1070.

Ninan, P.T. (1999). The functional anatomy, neurochemistry, and pharmacology of anxiety. *Journal of Clinical Psychiatry, 60* (suppl. 22), 12–17.

Nisbett, R.E., & Wilson, T.D. (1977). Telling more than we can know: Verbal reports on mental processes. *Psychological Review, 84*, 231–259.

Nobler, M.S., & Sackeim, H. (1998). Mechanisms of action of electroconvulsive therapy: Functional brain imaging studies. *Psychiatric Annals, 28*, 23–29.

Nolen-Hoeksema, S. (1990). *Sex Differences in Depression.* Stanford, CA: Stanford University Press.

Nolen-Hoeksema, S. (1994). An interactive model for the emergence of gender differences in depressive in adolescence. *Journal of Research on Adolescence, 4*, 519–534.

Nolen-Hoeksema, S. (2000). The role of rumination in depressive disorders and mixed anxiety/depressive symptoms. *Journal of Abnormal Psychology, 109*, 504–511.

Norden, K.A., Klein, D.N., Donaldson, S.K., Pepper, C.M., et al. (1995). Reports of the early home environment in DSM-III-R personality disorders. *Journal of Personality Disorders, 9*, 213–223.

Nordstrom, P., Samuelsson, M., Asberg, M., Traskman-Bendz, L., et al. (1994). CSF-5-HIAA predicts suicide risk after attempted suicide. *Suicide and Life Threatening Behavior, 24*, 1–9.

Norman, R.M.G., Malla, A.K., McLean, T.S., McIntosh, E.M., Neufeld, R.W.J., Voruganti, L.P., & Cortese, L. (2002). An evaluation of a stress management program for individuals with schizophrenia. *Schizophrenia Research, 58*, 293–303.

Norman, R.M.G., & Townsend, L.A. (1999). Cognitive-behavioural therapy for psychosis: A status report. *Canadian Journal of Psychiatry, 44*, 245–252.

Norton, G.R., Cox, B.J., & Malan, J. (1992). Nonclinical panickers: A critical review. *Clinical Psychology Review, 12*, 121–139.

Noyes, R., Garvey, M.J., & Cook, B.L. (1989). Follow-up study of patients with panic disorder and agoraphobia with panic attacks treated with tricyclic antidepressants. *Journal of Affective Disorders, 16*, 249–257.

Noyes, R., Jr., Clarkson, C., Crowe, R.R., Yates, W.R., & McChesney, C.M. (1987). A family study of generalized anxiety disorder. *American Journal of Psychiatry, 144*, 1019–1024.

Nuechterlein, K.H., Asarnow, R.F., Subotnik, K.L., Fogelson, D.L., Payne, D.L., Kendler, K.S., Neale, M.C., Jacobson, K.C., & Mintz, J. (2002). The structure of schizotypy: Relationships between neurocognitive and personality disorder features in relatives of schizophrenic patients in the UCLA family study. *Schizophrenia Research 54*, 121–130.

Nuechterlein, K.H., Asarnow, R.F., Subotnik, K.L., Fogelson, D.L., Ventura, J., Torquato, R.D., & Dawson, M.E. (1998). Neurocognitive vulnerability factors for schizophrenia: Convergence across genetic risk studies and longitudinal trait-state studies. In M.F. Lenzenweger & R.H. Dworkin (Eds.), *Origins and Development of Schizophrenia: Advances in Experimental Psychopathology* (pp. 299–328), Washington, DC: American Psychological Association.

Nunes, E.V., Frank, K.A., & Kornfeld, J. (1987). Psychologic treatment for the Type A behavior pattern and for coronary heart disease: A meta-analysis of the literature. *Psychosomatic Medicine, 48*, 159–173.

Nutt, D.J. (2001). Neurobiological mechanisms in generalized anxiety disorder. *Journal of Clinical Psychiatry, 62* (suppl. 11), 22–27.

O'Brien, T.B., & DeLongis, A. (1997). Coping with chronic stress: An interpersonal perspective. In B. H. Gottlieb (Ed.), *Coping with chronic stress* (pp. 161–190). New York: Plenum.

O'Connor, G.T., Buring, J.E., Yusuf, S., Goldhaber, S.Z., Olmsted, E.M., Paffenbarger, R.S., & Hennekens, C.H. (1989). An overview of randomized trials of rehabilitation with exercise after myocardial infarction. *Circulation, 80*, 234–244.

O'Donohue, W., & Bradley, A.R. (1999). Conceptual and empirical issues in child custody evaluations. *Clinical Psychology: Science and Practice, 6*, 310–322.

Oei, T.P.S., Lim, B., & Hennessy, B. (1990). Psychological dysfunction in battle: Combat stress reactions and posttraumatic stress disorder. *Clinical Psychology Review, 10*, 355–388.

Offord, D.R., Boyle, M.H., Campbell, D., Goering, P., Lin, E., Wong, M., & Racine, Y.A. (1996). One-year prevalence of psychiatric disorder in Ontarians 15 to 64 years of age. *Canadian Journal of Psychiatry, 41*, 559–563.

Offord, D.R. (1995). Child psychiatric epidemiology: Current status and future prospects. *Canadian Journal of Psychiatry, 40*, 284–288.

Offord, D.R., Boyle, M.H., Fleming, J.E., Monroe Blum, H.M., & Rae Grant, N.I. (1989). Ontario Child Health Study: Summary of selected results. *Canadian Journal of Psychiatry, 34*, 483–491.

Offord, D.R., Boyle, M.H., Racine, Y.A., Fleming, J.E., Cadman, D.T., Munroe Blum, H., Byrne, C., Links, P.S., Lipman, E.L., MacMillan, H.L., Rae Grant, N.I., Sanford, M.N., Szatmari, P., Thomas, H., & Woodward, C.A. (1992). Outcome, prognosis, and risk in a longitudinal follow-up study. *Journal of the American Academy of Child and Adolescent Psychiatry, 31*, 916–923.

Offord, D.R., Boyle, M.H., Szatmari, P., Rae-Grant, N.I., Links, P.S., Cadman, D.T., Byles, J.A., Crawford, J.W., Munroe Blum, H., Byrne, C., Thomas, H., & Woodward, C.A. (1987). Ontario Child Health Study: II. Six-month prevalence of disorder and rates of service utilization. *Archives of General Psychiatry, 44*, 832–836.

Ogloff, J.R.P. (1995). Navigating the quagmire: Legal and ethical guidelines. In D. Martin & A. Moore (Eds.), *First steps in the art of intervention* (pp. 347–376). Pacific Grove, CA: Brooks/Cole.

Ogloff, J.R.P. (1997). A legal perspective on the concept of "impulsivity." In C.D. Webster & M.A. Jackson (Eds.), *Impulsivity: Theory, assessment, and treatment* (pp. 63–81). New York: Guilford.

Ogloff, J.R.P., & Olley, M.C. (1998). The interaction between ethics and the law: The ongoing refinement of ethical standards for psychologists in Canada. *Canadian Psychology, 39*, 221–230.

Ohayon, M.M. (2000). Prevalence of hallucinations and their pathological associations in the general population. *Psychiatry Research, 97*, 153–164.

Ohman, A. (1996). Preferential preattentive processing of threat in anxiety: Preparedness and attentional biases. In R.M. Rapee (Ed.), *Current Controversies in the Anxiety Disorders* (pp. 253–290). New York: Guilford.

Ohman, A., & Mineka, S. (2001). Fears, phobias, and preparedness: Toward an evolved module of fear and fear learning. *Psychological Review, 108*, 483–522.

Olds, J., & Milner, P. (1954). Positive reinforcement produced by electrical stimulation of septal area and other regions of rat brain. *Journal of Comparative and Physiological Psychology, 47*, 419–427.

O'Leary, K.D., & Wilson, G.T. (1987). *Behavior therapy: Application and outcome* (2nd ed.). Englewood Cliffs, NJ: Prentice Hall.

Oliver, J.M., & Simmons, M.E. (1984). Depression as measured by the DSM-III and the Beck Depression Inventory in an unselected adult population. *Journal of Consulting and Clinical Psychology, 52*, 892–898.

Olley, M.C., & Ogloff, J.R.P. (1995). Patients' rights advocacy: Implications for program design and implementation. *Journal of Mental Health Administration, 22*, 368–376.

Oltmanns, T.F., Melley, A.H., & Turkheimer, E. (2002). Impaired social functioning and symptoms of personality disorders in a non-clinical population. *Journal of Personality Disorders, 16*, 437–452.

Oltmanns, T.F., Turkheimer, E., & Strauss, M.E. (1998). Peer assessment of personality traits and pathology. *Assessment, 5*, 53–65.

Olweus, D. (1984). Aggressors and their victims: Bullying at school. In N. Frude & H. Gault (Eds.), *Disruptive Behavior in Schools* (pp. 57–76). New York: Wiley.

O'Meara, E.S., Kukull, W.A., Sheppard, L., Bowen, J.D., McCormick, W.C., Teri, L., Pfanschmidt, M., Thompson, J.D., Schellenberg, G.D., & Larson, E.B. (1997). Head injury and risk of Alzheimer's disease by apolipoprotein E genotype. *American Journal of Epidemiology, 146*, 373–384.

Oosterwegel, A., & Wicklund, R.A. (1995). *The Self in European and North American Culture: Development and Processes*. Boston: Kluwer.

Oren, D.A., & Rosenthal, N.E. (1992). Seasonal affective disorders. In E.S., Paykel (Ed.), *Handbook of Affective Disorders* (2nd ed., pp. 551–568). New York: Guilford.

Orne, M.T., Dingers, D.F., & Orne, E.C. (1984). On the differential diagnosis of multiple personality in the forensic context. *International Journal of Clinical and Experimental Hypnosis, 32*, 118–169.

Osman, A.K., & Al-Sawaf, M.H. (1995). Cross-cultural aspects of sexual anxieties and the associated dysfunction. *Journal of Sex Education and Therapy, 21*, 174–181.

Ostwald, P. F. (1997). *Glenn Gould: The Ecstasy and Tragedy of Genius*. New York: Norton.

O'Sullivan, R.L., Mansueto, C.S., Lerner, E.A., & Miguel, E.C. (2000). Characterization of trichotillomania: A phenomenological model with clinical relevance to obsessive–compulsive spectrum disorders. *Psychiatric Clinics of North America, 23*, 587–604.

Otto, R.K., Poythress, N.G., Nicholson, R.A., Edens, J.F., Monahan, J., Bonnie, R.J., Hoge, S.K., & Eisenberg, M. (1998). Psychometric properties of the MacArthur Competence Assessment Tool—Criminal Adjudication. *Psychological Assessment, 10*, 435–443.

Padilla, A.M. (2001). Issues in culturally appropriate assessment. In L.A. Suzuki, J.G. Ponterotto, & P.J. Metter (Eds.), *Handbook of Multicultural Assessment: Clinical Psychological, and Educational Applications* (2nd ed., pp. 5–27). San Francisco, CA: Jossey-Bass.

Pagliaro, L.A. (1995). "Should Canadian psychologists follow the APA trend and seek prescription privileges?": Of course they should! An invited commentary of Dozois and Dobson. *Canadian Psychology, 36*, 305–312.

Paikoff, R.L., & Brooks-Gunn, J. (1991). Do parent–child relationships change during puberty? *Psychological Bulletin, 110*, 47–66.

Paivio, S.C. (2001). Stability of retrospective self-reports of child abuse and neglect before and after therapy for child abuse issues. *Child Abuse & Neglect, 25*, 1053–1068.

Paivio, S.C., & Greenberg, L.S. (2000). Emotion focused therapy for interpersonal trauma. *National Center for PTSD Clinical Quarterly, 9*, 22–29.

Paivio, S.C., & Niewenhuis, J.A. (2001). Efficacy of emotion focused therapy for adult survivors of child abuse: A preliminary study. *Journal of Traumatic Stress, 14*, 115–133.

Palmer, R.L. (1995). Sexual abuse and eating disorders. In K.D. Brownell & C.G. Fairburn (Eds.), *Eating Disorders and Obesity: A Comprehensive Handbook* (pp. 230–233). New York: Guilford.

Panksepp, J. (1988). Brain emotional circuits and psychopathologies. In M. Clynes & J. Panksepp (Eds.), *Emotions and Psychopathology* (pp. 37–76). New York: Plenum.

Panksepp, J., & Sahley, T.L. (1987). Possible brain opioid involvement in disrupted social intent and language development of autism. In E. Schopler & G.B. Mesibov (Eds.), *Neurobiological issues in autism* (pp. 357–372). New York: Plenum.

Pantle, M., Pasewark, R., & Steadman, H. (1980). Comparing institutionalization periods and subsequent arrests of insanity acquittees and convicted felons. *Journal of Psychiatry and the Law, 8*, 305–316.

Parikh, S.V., Lesage, A.D., Kennedy, S.H., & Goering, P.N. (1999). Depression in Ontario: Undertreatment and factors related to antidepressant use. *Journal of Affective Disorders, 52*, 67–76.

Paris, J. (1998). Anxious traits, anxious attachment, and anxious-cluster personality disorders. *Harvard Review of Psychiatry, 6*, 142–148.

Paris, J. (2002a). Commentary on the American Psychiatric Association guidelines for the treatment of borderline personality disorder: Evidence-based psychiatry and the quality of evidence. *Journal of Personality Disorders, 16*, 130–134.

Paris, J. (2002b). Implications of long-term outcomes reseach for the management of patients with borderline personality disorder. *Harvard Review of Psychiatry, 10*, 315–323.

Paris, J., Brown, R., & Nowlis, D. (1987). Long-term follow-up of borderline patients in a general hospital. *Comprehensive Psychiatry, 28*, 530–535.

Paris, J., & Zweig-Frank, H. (2001). A 27-year follow-up of patients with borderline personality disorder. *Comprehensive Psychiatry, 42*, 482–487.

Paris, J., Zweig-Frank, H., Ng Ying Kin, N.M.K., Schwartz, G., Steiger, H., & Nair, N.P.V. (2004). Neurobiological correlates of diagnosis and underlying traits in patients with borderline personality disorder compared with normal controls. *Psychiatry Research, 121*, 239–252.

Park, D.C., & Radford, J.P. (1998). From the case files: Reconstructing a history of involuntary sterilisation. *Disability & Society, 13*, 317–342.

Park, S., Holzman, P.S., & Goldman-Rakic, P.S. (1995). Spatial working memory deficits in the relatives of schizophrenic patients. *Archives of General Psychiatry, 52*, 821–828.

Parker, G., Cheah, Y.C., Roy, K. (2001). Do the Chinese somatize depression? A cross-cultural study. *Social Psychiatry & Psychiatric Epidemiology, 36*, 287–293.

Parker, G., Hadzi-Pavlovic, D., Hickie, I., Brodaty, H., et al. (1995). Sub-typing depressing: III. Development of a clinical algorithm for melancholia and comparison with other diagnostic measures. *Psychological Medicine, 25*, 833–884.

Parker, G., Roussos, J., Mitchell, P., Wilhelm, K., et al. (1997). Distinguishing psychotic depression from melancholia. *Journal of Affective Disorders, 42*, 155–167.

Parker, J.D.A., Taylor, G.J., & Bagby, R.M. (2003). The 20-item Toronto Alexithymia Scale III. Reliability and factorial validity in a community population. *Journal of Psychosomatic Research, 55*, 269–275.

Parker, J.G., & Asher, S.R. (1987). Peer relations and later personality adjustment: Are low-accepted children at risk? *Psychological Bulletin, 102*, 357–389.

Parker, R.A., & Aldwin, C.M. (1997). Do aspects of gender identity change from early to middle adulthood? Disentangling age, cohort and period effects. In J.E. Lachman and J.B. James (Eds.), *Multiple Paths of Midlife Development* (pp. 67–107). Chicago: University of Chicago Press.

Parnas, J., Cannon T.D., Jacobsen, B., Schulsinger, H., Schulsinger, F., & Mednick, S.A. (1993). Lifetime DSM-III-R diagnostic outcomes in the offspring of schizophrenic mothers: Results from the Copenhagen high-risk study. *Archives of General Psychiatry, 50*, 707–714.

Parry-Jones, B. (1994). Merycism or rumination disorder: A historical investigation and current assessment. *British Journal of Psychiatry, 165*, 303–314.

Pasupathi, M. (2001). The social construction of the personal past and its implications for adult development. *Psychological Bulletin, 127*, 651–672.

Pasupathi, M., Carstensen, L.L., & Tsai, J.L. (1995). Ageism in interpersonal settings. In B. Lott & D. Maluso (Eds.), *The Social Psychology of Interpersonal Discrimination* (pp. 160–182). New York: Guilford.

Patelis-Siotis, I., Young, L.T., Robb, J.C., Marriott, M., Bieling, P.J., Cox, L.C., & Joffe, R.T. (2001). Group cognitive behavioral therapy for bipolar disorder: A feasibility and effectiveness study. *Journal of Affective Disorders, 65*, 145–153.

Paterson, R. J. (2000). *The assertiveness workbook*. Oakland, CA: New Harbinger.

Patrick, C.J., & Zempolich, K.A. (1998). Emotion and aggression in the psychopathic personality. *Aggression and Violent Behavior, 3*, 303–338.

Patterson, C.J., Kupersmidt, J.B., & Griesler, P.C. (1990). Children's perceptions of self and of relationships with others as a function of sociometric status. *Child Development, 61*, 1335–1349.

Patterson, C.M., & Newman, J.P. (1993). Reflectivity and learning from aversive events: Toward a psychological mechanism for the syndromes of disinhibition. *Psychological Review, 100*, 716–736.

Patterson, G.R. (1982). *Coercive Family Process*. Eugene, OR: Castalia.

Patterson, G.R. (Ed.) (1990). *Depression and Aggression in Family Interaction*. Hillsdale, NJ: Erlbaum.

Patterson, G.R., DeBaryshe, B.D., & Ramsey, E. (1989). A developmental perspective on antisocial behavior. *American Psychologist, 44*, 329–325.

Patterson, G.R., & Fleischman, M.J. (1979). Maintenance of treatment effects: Some considerations concerning family systems and follow-up data. *Behavior Therapy, 10*, 168–185.

Patton, J.R., Beirne-Smith, M., & Payne, J.S. (1990). *Mental Retardation* (3rd ed.). Columbus, OH: Merrill.

Paul, G.L., & Lentz, R.J. (1977). *Psychosocial Treatment of Chronic Mental Patients: Milieu Versus Social-Learning Programs*. Cambridge, MA: Harvard University Press.

Pauli, P., & Alpers, G.W. (2002). Memory bias in patients with hypochondriasis and somatoform pain disorder. *Journal of Psychosomatic Research, 52*, 45–53.

Pavlov, I.P. (1928). *Lectures on Conditioned Reflexes*. New York: International Publishers.

Payne, R.L. (1992). First person account: My schizophrenia. *Schizophrenia Bulletin, 18*, 725–728.

Pearlson, G.D. (1997). Superior temporal gyrus and planum temporale in schizophrenia: A selective review. *Progress in Neuro-Psychopharmacology and Biological Psychiatry, 21*, 1203–1229.

Pearlson, G.D., & Marsh, L. (1999). Structural brain imaging in schizophrenia: A selective review. *Biological Psychiatry, 46*, 627–649.

Pedersen, N.L., & Gatz, M. (1991). Twin studies as a tool for bridging the gap between genetics and epidemiology of dementia: The study of dementia in Swedish twins [abstract]. *Gerontologist, 31*, 333.

Pelham, W.E., et al. (1985). Methylphenidate and children with attention deficit disorder: Dose effects on classroom academic and social behavior. *Archives of General Psychiatry, 42*, 948–952.

Pelham, W.E., Carlson, C., Sams, S.E., Vallano, G., Dixon, M.J., & Hoza, B. (1993). Separate and combined effects of methylphenidate and behavior modification with attention deficit-hyperactivity disorder in the classroom. *Journal of Consulting and Clinical Psychology, 61*, 506–515.

Pelham, W.E., et al. (2000). Behavioral versus behavioral and pharmacological treatment in ADHD children attending a summer treatment program. *Journal of Abnormal Child Psychology, 28*, 507–525.

Pelham, W.E., et al. (2002). Effects of methylphenidate and expectancy on children with ADHD: Behavior, academic performance, and attributions in a summer treatment program and regular classroom settings. *Journal of Consulting and Clinical Psychology, 70*, 320–335.

Pendery, M.L., Maltzman, I.M., & West, L.J. (1982). Controlled drinking by alcoholics? New findings and a reevaluation of a major affirmative study. *Science, 217*, 169–175.

Pennebaker, J.W. (1990). *Opening up: The Healing Power of Confiding in Others*. New York: Morrow.

Pennebaker, J.W., Kiecolt-Glaser, J., & Glaser, R. (1988). Disclosure of traumas and immune function: Health implications for psychotherapy. *Journal of Consulting and Clinical Psychology, 56*, 239–245.

Pennix, B., Van Tilburg, T., Kriegsman, D., Deeg, D., Boeke, A., & Van Eijk, J. (1997). Effects of social support and personal coping resources on mortality in older age: The Longitudinal Aging Study of Amsterdam. *American Journal of Epidemiology, 146*, 510–519.

Peralta, V., & Cuesta, M.J. (1999). Dimensional structure of psychotic symptoms: An item-level analysis of SAPS and SANS symptoms in psychotic disorders. *Schizophrenia Research, 38*, 13–26.

Perls, F. (1969). *Gestalt therapy verbatim*. Lafayette, CA: Real People Press.

Perris, C. (1992). Bipolar-unipolar distinction. In E.S. Paykel (Ed.), *Handbook of Affective Disorders* (2nd ed., pp. 57–75). New York: Guilford.

Perry, C., & Laurence, J. (1984). Mental processing outside of awareness: The contributions of Freud and Janet. In K.S. Bowers & D. Meichenbaum (Eds.), *The Unconscious Reconsidered* (pp. 9–48). New York: Wiley.

Pescosolido, B., et al. (1999). The public's view of the competence, dangerousness, and need for legal coercion among persons with mental illness. *American Journal of Public Health, 89*, 1339–1345.

Pescosolido, B.A., & Georgianna, S. (1989). Durkheim, suicide, and religion: Toward a network theory of suicide. *American Sociological Review, 54*, 33–48.

Peters, K.D., Kochanek, K.D., and Murphy, S.L. (1998). Deaths: Final data for 1996. *National Vital Statistics Reports*, vol. 47, no. 9. Hyattsville, MD: National Center for Health Statistics.

Peterson, B.D., West, J., Tanielian, T.L., Pincus, H.A., Kohout, J., Pion, G.M., et al. (1998). Mental health practitioners and trainees. In R.W. Manderscheid and M.J. Henderson (Eds.), *Mental Health, United States* (pp. 214–246). Rockville, MD: U.S. Department of Health and Human Services.

Peterson, C., & Seligman, M.E.P. (1984). Causal explanations as a risk factor for depression: Theory and evidence. *Psychological Review, 91*, 347–374.

Petrie, K.J., Booth, R.J., Pennebaker, J.W., Davison, K.P., & Thomas, M.G. (1995). Disclosure of trauma and immune response to a Hepatitis B vaccination program. *Journal of Consulting and Clinical Psychology, 63*, 787–792.

Petty, R.G., Barta, P.E., Pearlson, G.D., McGilchrist, I.K., et al. (1995). Reversal of asymmetry of the planum temporale in schizophrenia. *American Journal of Psychiatry, 152*, 715–721.

Pfaus, J.G., Kippin, T.E., & Centeno, S. (2001). Conditioning and sexual behavior: A review. *Hormones and Behavior, 40*, 291–321.

Pfohl, B. (1995). Histrionic personality disorder. In W.J. Livesley (Ed.), *The DSM-IV personality disorders* (pp. 173–192). New York: Guilford.

Pfohl, B., Blum, N., & Zimmerman, M. (1995). *Structured Interview for DSM-IV Personality (SIDP-IV)*. Iowa City: University of Iowa.

Pfohl, B., Coryell, W., Zimmerman, M., & Stangl, D. (1986). DSM-III personality disorders: Diagnostic overlap and internal consistency of individual DSM-III-criteria. *Comprehensive Psychiatry, 27*, 21–34.

Phelan, J.C., & Link, B.G. (1999). The labeling theory of mental disorder (I): The role of social contingencies in the application of psychiatric labels. In A.V. Horwitz and T.L. Scheid (Eds.), *A Handbook for the Study of Mental Health: Social Contexts, Theories, and Systems* (pp. 139–150). New York: Cambridge University Press.

Phillips, E.L., Phillips, E.A., Wolf, M.M., & Fixsen, D.L. (1973). Achievement Place: Development of the elected manager system. *Journal of Applied Behavior Analysis, 6*, 541–561.

Phillips, K.A. (1991). Body dysmorphic disorder: The distress of imagined ugliness. *American Journal of Psychiatry, 148*, 1138–1149.

Phillips, K.A., Albertini, R.S., & Rasmussen, S.A. (2002). A randomized placebo-controlled trial of fluoxetine in body dysmorphic disorder. *Archives of General Psychiatry, 59*, 381–388.

Phillips, K.A., Grant, J., Siniscalchi, J., Albertini, R.S. (2001). Surgical and nonpsychiatric medical treatment of patients with body dysmorphic disorder. *Psychosomatics, 42*, 504–510.

Phillips, S.D., Burns, B.J., Edgar, E.R., Mueser, K.T., Linkins, K.W., Rosenheck, R.A., Drake, R.E., & McDonel Herr, E.C. (2001). Moving assertive community treatment into standard practice. *Psychiatric Services, 52*, 771–779.

Piasecki, T., Fiore, M.C., & Baker, T.B. (1998). Profiles in discouragement: Two studies of variability in the time course of smoking withdrawal symptoms. *Journal of Abnormal Psychology, 107*, 238–251.

Pigott, T.A. (1999). Gender differences in the epidemiology and treatment of anxiety disorders. *Journal of Clinical Psychiatry, 60* (suppl. 18), 4–15.

Pihl, R.O. (1999). Substance abuse: Etiological considerations. In T. Millon, P.H. Blaney, & R.D. Davis (Eds.), *Oxford textbook of psychopathology* (pp. 249–276). Oxford: Oxford University Press.

Pihl, R.O., Lau, M.L., & Assaad, J.M. (1997). Aggressive disposition, alcohol, and aggression. *Aggressive Behavior, 23*, 11–18.

Pihl, R.O., Paylan, S.S., Gentes-Hawn, A., & Hoaken, P.N.S. (2003). Alcohol affects executive cognitive functioning differentially on the ascending versus descending limb of the blood alcohol concentration curve. *Alcoholism: Clinical and Experimental Research, 27*, 773–779.

Pihl, R.O., Peterson, J.B., & Lau, M.A. (1993). A biosocial model of the alcohol-aggression relationship. *Journal of Studies on Alcohol* (suppl. 11), 128–139.

Pihl, R.O., & Smith, S. (1983). Of affect and alcohol. In L. A. Pohorecky & J. Brick (Eds.), *Stress and alcohol use* (pp. 203–228). New York: Elsevier.

Pincus, H.A., Tanielian, T.L., Marcus, S.C., Olfson, M., Zarin, D.A., Thompson, J., & Zito, J.M. (1998). Prescribing trends in psychotropic medications: Primary care, psychiatry, and other medical specialties. *Journal of the American Medical Association, 279*, pp. 526–531.

Pinker, S. (1997). *How the Mind Works*. New York: Norton.

Pinto, C., Dhavale, H.S., Nair, S., Patil, B., & Dewan, M. (2000). Borderline personality disorder exists in India. *Journal of Nervous and Mental Disease*, 188, 386–388.

Piper, A. (1994). Multiple personality disorder. *British Journal of Psychiatry*, 164, 600–612.

Piper, W.E., Azim, H.F.A., McCallum, M., & Joyce, A.S. (1991). The University of Alberta Psychotherapy Research Centre. In L.E. Beutler & M. Crago (Eds.), *Psychotherapy research: An international review of programmatic studies* (pp. 82–89). Washington, DC: American Psychological Association.

Pitman, R.K. (1997). Overview of biological themes in PTSD. In R. Yehuda & A.C. McFarlane (Eds.), *Psychobiology of Posttraumatic Stress Disorder* (pp. 1–9). New York: New York Academy of Sciences.

Pitts, F.N., Jr., & McClure, J.N., Jr. (1967). Lactate metabolism in anxiety neurosis. *New England Journal of Medicine*, 277, 1329–1336.

Plassman, B.L., & Breitner, J.C.S. (1997). The genetics of dementia in late life. *Psychiatric Clinics of North America*, 20, 59–76.

Plaut, S.M. (1995). Sex therapy following treatment by an exploitive therapist. In R.C. Rosen and S.R. Leiblum (Eds.), *Case Studies in Sex Therapy* (pp. 264–278). New York: Guilford.

Plomin, R., & Crabbe, J. (2000). DNA. *Psychological Bulletin*, 126, 806–828.

Plomin, R., & Daniels, D. (1987). Why are children in the same family so different from one another? *Behavioral and Brain Sciences*, 10, 1–60.

Plomin, R., DeFries, J.C., & McClearn, G.E. (1990). *Behavioral Genetics* (2nd ed.). New York: Freeman.

Plomin, R., Owen, M.J., & McGuffin, P. (1994). The genetic bases of complex human behaviors. *Science*, 264, 1733–1739.

Plotsky, P.M., Owens, M.J., & Nemeroff, C.B. (1998). Psychoneuroendocrinology of depression: Hypothalamic-pituitary-adrenal axis. *Psychiatric Clinics of North America*, 21, 293–307.

Pokony, A. (1983). Prediction of suicide in psychiatric patients: A prospective study. *Archives of General Psychiatry*, 40, 249–257.

Polaschek, D.L. (1997). New Zealand rapists: An examination of subtypes. In G.M. Habermann (Ed.), *Looking Back and Moving Forward: 50 Years of New Zealand Psychology* (pp. 224–231). Wellington, New Zealand: New Zealand Psychological Society.

Polivy, J., Heatherton, T.F., & Herman, C.P. (1988). Self-esteem, restraint, and eating behavior. *Journal of Abnormal Psychology*, 97, 354–356.

Polivy, J., & Herman, C.P. (1985). Dieting and binging: A causal analysis. *American Psychologist*, 40, 193–201.

Polivy, J., & Herman, C.P. (1991). Good and bad dieters: Self-perception and reaction to a dietary challenge. *International Journal of Eating Disorders*, 10, 91–99.

Polivy, J., & Herman, C.P. (2002). Causes of eating disorders. *Annual Review of Psychology*, 53, 187–213.

Polivy, J., Zeitlin, S.B., Herman, C.P., & Beal, A.L. (1994). Food restrictions and binge eating: A study of former prisoners of war. *Journal of Abnormal Psychology*, 103, 409–411.

Pollack, M.H. (2001). Comorbidity, neurobiology, and pharmacotherapy of social anxiety disorder. *Journal of Clinical Psychiatry*, 62 (suppl. 12), 24–29.

Pollit, P.A. (1997). The problem of dementia in Australian aboriginal and Torres Strait Islander communities: An overview. *International Journal of Geriatric Psychiatry*, 12, 155–163.

Pollitt, R.J. (1987). Amino acid disorders. In J.B. Holton (Ed.), *The inherited metabolic disease* (p. 96). Edinburgh: Churchill Livingstone.

Pomeroy, C. (1996). Anorexia nervosa, bulimia nervosa, and binge eating disorder: The assessment of physical status. In J.K. Thompson, *Body Image, Eating Disorders, and Obesity* (pp. 177–204). Washington, DC: American Psychological Association.

Poole, D.A., Lindsay, D.S., Memon, A., & Bull, R. (1995). Psychotherapy and the recovery of memories of childhood sexual abuse: U.S. and British practitioners' opinions, practices, and experiences. *Journal of Consulting and Clinical Psychology*, 63, 426–437.

Pope, H.G., & Yurgelun-Todd, D. (1996). The residual cognitive effects of heavy marijuana use in college students. *Journal of the American Medical Association*, 275, 521–527.

Porter, S., & Birt, A.R. (2001). Is traumatic memory special? A comparison of traumatic memory characteristics with memory for other emotional life experiences. *Applied Cognitive Psychology*, 15, S101–S117.

Porter, S., Birt, A.R., & Boer, D.P. (2001). Investigation of the criminal and conditional release profiles of Canadian federal offenders as a function of psychopathy and age. *Law and Human Behavior*, 25, 647–661.

Porter, S., Birt, A.R., Yuille, J.C., & Lehman, D.R. (2000). Negotiating false memories: Interviewer and rememberer characteristics relate to memory distortion. *Psychological Science*, 11, 507–510.

Porter, S., Campbell, M.A., Woodworth, M., & Birt, A.R. (2001). A new psychological conceptualization of the sexual psychopath. *Advances in Psychology Research* (Vol. 7). New York: Nova Science.

Porter, S., Fairweather, D., Drugge, J., Herve, H., Birt, A.R., & Boer, D. (2000). Profiles of psychopathy in incarcerated sexual offenders. *Criminal Justice and Behavior*, 27, 216–233.

Porter, S., Woodworth, M., Earle, J., Drugge, J., & Boer, D. (2003). Characteristics of sexual homicides committed by psychopathic and nonpsychopathic offenders. *Law and Human Behavior*, 27, 459–470.

Porter, S., Yuille, J.C., & Lehman, D.R. (1999). The nature of real, implanted, and fabricated childhood emotional events: Implications for the recovered memory debate. *Law and Human Behavior*, 23, 517–537.

Posner, M.I., & DiGirolamo, G.J. (2000). Cognitive neuroscience: Origins and promise. *Psychological Bulletin*, 126, 873-889.

Poulton, R., & Menzies, R.G. (2002). Non-associative fear acquisition: A review of the evidence from retrospective and longitudinal research. *Behaviour Research and Therapy*, 40, 127–149.

Prentky, R.A. (1997). Arousal reduction in sexual offenders: A review of antiandrogen interventions. *Sexual Abuse: Journal of Research and Treatment*, 9, 335–347.

Pressman, J.D. (1998). *Last resort: Psychosurgery and the limits of medicine*. New York: Cambridge University Press.

Presta, S., Marazziti, D., Dell'Osso, L., Pfanner, C., Pallanti, S., & Cassano, G.B. (2002). Kleptomania: Clinical features and comorbidity in an Italian sample. *Comprehensive Psychiatry*, 43, 7–12.

Price, J. (2000). Subordination, self-esteem, and depression. In Leon Sloman & Paul Gilbert (Eds.), *Subordination and Defeat: An Evolutionary Approach to Mood Disorders and their Therapy* (pp. 165–177). Mahwah, NJ: Lawrence Erlbaum Associates.

Prigerson, H.G., Maciejewski, P.K., & Rosenheck, R.A. (2002). Population attributable fractions of psychiatric disorders and behavioral outcomes associated with combat exposure among U.S. men. *American Journal of Public Health*, 92, 59–63.

Prkachin, K.M., Mills, D.E., Zwaal, C., & Husted, J. (2001). Comparison of hemodynamic responses to social and nonsocial stress: Evaluation of an anger interview. *Psychophysiology*, 38, 879–885.

Prkachin, K.M., Williams-Avery, R.M., Zwaal, C., & Mills, D.E. (1999). Cardiovascular changes during induced emotion: An application of Lang's theory of emotional imagery. *Journal of Psychosomatic Research*, 47, 255–267.

Prochaska, J.O., & Norcross, J.C. (1999). *Systems of psychotherapy* (4th. ed.). Pacific Grove, CA: Brooks/Cole.

Project Match Research Group. (1998a). Matching alcoholism treatments to client heterogeneity: Project Match three-year drinking outcomes. *Alcoholism: Clinical and Experimental Research*, 22, 1300–1311.

Project Match Research Group. (1998b). Matching alcoholism treatments to client heterogeneity: Treatment main effects and matching effects on drinking during treatment. *Journal of Studies on Alcohol*, 59, 631–639.

Pron, N. (1995). *Lethal marriage: The unspeakable crimes of Paul Bernado and Karla Homolka*. Toronto: Seal Books.

Prout, P.I., & Dobson, K.S. (1998). Recovered memories of childhood sexual abuse: Searching for the middle ground in clinical practice. *Canadian Psychology*, 39, 257–265.

Pryse-Phillips, W. (1999). Do we have drugs for dementia? *Archives of Neurology*, 56, 735–737.

Puig-Antich, J. (1986). Psychobiological markers: Effects of age and puberty. In M. Rutter, C. Izard, & P. Read (Eds.), *Depression in Young People* (pp. 341–382). New York: Guilford.

Pulsford, D. (1997). Therapeutic activities for people with dementia: What, why, and why not? *Journal of Advanced Nursing*, 26, 704–709.

Purdon, C. (1999). Thought suppression and psychopathology. *Behaviour Research and Therapy*, 37, 1029–1054.

Purdon, C. (2004). Empirical investigations of thought suppression in OCD. *Journal of Behavior Therapy and Experimental Psychiatry*, 35, 121–136.

Purdon, C., & Clark, D.A. (1993). Obsessive intrusive thoughts in nonclinical subjects. Part I. Content and relation with depressive, anxious and obsessional symptoms. *Behaviour Research and Therapy*, 31, 713–720.

Purdon, C., Rowa, K., & Antony, M.M. (in press). Thought suppression and its effects on thought frequency, appraisal and mood state in individuals with obsessive–compulsive disorder. *Behaviour Research and Therapy*.

Putnam, F.W., Curoff, J.J., et al. (1986). The clinical phenomenology of multiple personality disorder: Review of 100 recent cases. *Journal of Clinical Psychiatry*, 47, 285–293.

Quadagno, D., Sly, D.F., Harrison, D.F., Eberstein, I.W., & Soler, H.R. (1998). Ethnic differences in sexual decisions and sexual behavior. *Archives of Sexual Behavior*, 27, 57–75.

Quay, H.C. (1993). The psychobiology and undersocialized aggressive conduct disorder: A theoretical perspective. *Development and Psychopathology*, 5, 165–180.

Quinsey, V. L. (2003). The etiology of anomalous sexual preferences in men. *Annals of the New York Academy of Sciences*, 989, 105–117.

Quist, J.F., Barr, C.L., Schachar, R., Roberts, W., Malone, M., Tannock, R., Basile, V.S., Beitchman, J., & Kennedy, J.L. (2003). The serotonin 5-HT1B receptor gene and attention deficit hyperactivity disorder. *Molecular Psychiatry*, 8, 98–102.

Rabins, P.V. (1997). Caring for persons with dementing illnesses: A current perspective. In L. Heston (Ed.), *Progress in Alzheimer's Disease and Similar Conditions* (pp. 277–289). Washington, DC: American Psychiatric Press.

Radomsky, A.S., Gilchrist, P.T., & Dussault, D. (2003, November). *Repeated checking really does cause memory distrust*. Paper presented at the annual meeting of the Association for Advancement of Behavior Therapy, Boston, MA.

Radomsky, A.S., Rachman, S., & Hammond, D. (2002). Panic termination and the post-panic period. *Journal of Anxiety Disorders*, 16, 97–111.

Radomsky, A.S., Rachman, S., Teachman, B.A., & Freeman, W.S. (1998). Why do episodes of panic stop? *Journal of Anxiety Disorders, 12*, 263–270.

Raichle, M.E. (2001). Bold insights. *Nature, 412*, 128–130.

Ramey, C.T., & Bryant, D. (1982). Evidence for primary prevention of developmental retardation. *Journal of Early Childhood Development, 5*, 73–78.

Raphael, B., Wilson, J., Meldrum L., & McFarlane, A.C. (1996). Acute preventive interventions. In B.A. van der Kolk, A.C. McFarlane, & L.Weisaeth (Eds.), *Traumatic Stress* (pp. 463–479). New York: Guilford.

Rapoport, J.L., Buchsbaum, M.S., Zahn, T.P., Weingartner, H., Ludlow, C., & Mikkelsen, E.J. (1978). Dextroamphetamine: Cognitive and behavioral effects in normal prepubertal boys. *Science, 199*, 560–563.

Rapoport, J., & Swedo, S. (2002). Obsessive–compulsive disorders. In M. Rutier & E. Taylor (Eds.), *Child and Adolescent Psychiatry* (4th ed., pp. 571–592). Oxford, UK: Blackwell.

Raskind, M.A. (1998). The clinical interface of depression and dementia. *Journal of Clinical Psychiatry, 59* (suppl. 10), 9–12.

Raskind, M.A., & Peskind, E.R. (1997). Neurotransmitter abnormalities and the psychopharmacology of Alzheimer's disease. In L. Heston (Ed.), *Progress in Alzheimer's Disease and Similar Conditions* (pp. 245–257). Washington, DC: American Psychiatric Press.

Rastam, M., Gillberg, C., & Gillberg, C. (1995). Anorexia nervosa 6 years after onset. Part II. Cormorbid psychiatric problems. *Comprehensive Psychiatry, 36*, 70–76.

Rauch, S.L., Dougherty, D.D., Cosgrove, G.R., Cassem, E.H., Alpert, N.M., Price, B.H., Nierenberg, A.A., Mayberg, H.S., Baer, L., Jenike, M.A., & Fischman, A.J. (2001). Cerebral metabolic correlates as potential predictors of response to anterior cingulotomy for obsessive compulsive disorder. *Biological Psychiatry, 50*, 659–667.

Read, J. (1995). Female sexual dysfunction. *International Review of Psychiatry, 7*, 175–182.

Rector, N.A., & Beck, A.T. (2001). Cognitive behavioral therapy for schizophrenia: An empirical review. *Journal of Nervous and Mental Disease, 189*, 278–287.

Rector, N.A., Segal, Z., & Gemar, M. (1998). Schema research in depression: A Canadian perspective. *Canadian Journal of Behavioral Science, 30*, 213–224.

Regehr, C., & Glancy, G. (1995). Battered woman syndrome defense in Canadian courts. *Canadian Journal of Psychiatry, 40*, 130–135.

Regier, D.A., Kaelber, C.T., Rae, D.S., Farmer, M.E., Knauper, B., Kessler, R.C., & Norquist, G.S. (1998). Limitations of diagnostic criteria and assessment instruments for mental disorders. *Archives of General Psychiatry, 55*, 109–115.

*Regina v. Swain* (1991), 63 C.C.C. (3d) 481 (S.C.C.).

Reich, J. (1996). The morbidity of DSM-III-R dependent personality disorder. *Journal of Nervous and Mental Disease, 184*, 22–26.

Reid, W.H., & Gacono, C. (2000). Treatment of antisocial personality, psychopathy, and other characterologic antisocial syndromes. *Behavioral Sciences and the Law, 18*, 647–662.

Reis, H.T., Collins, W.A., & Berscheid, E. (2000). The relationship context of human behavior and development. *Psychological Bulletin, 6*, 844–872.

Reisner, R., & Slobogin, C. (1990). *Law and the mental health system* (2nd ed.). St. Paul, MN: West.

Reisner, R., Slobogin, C., & Rai, A. (1999). *Law and the Mental Health System. Civil and Criminal Aspects* (3rd ed.). St. Paul, MN: West.

Reiss, A.L., Feinstein, C., & Rosenbaum, K.N. (1986). Autism and genetic disorders. *Schizophrenia Bulletin, 12*, 724–738.

Reiss, S., & McNally, R.J. (1985). The expectancy model of fear. In S. Reiss & R. R. Bootzin (Eds.), *Theoretical issues in behavior therapy* (pp. 107–121). New York: Academic Press.

Reissing, E.D., Binik, Y.M., & Khalife, S. (1999). Does vaginismus exist? A critical review of the literature. *Journal of Nervous and Mental Disease, 187*, 261–274.

Reissing, E.D., Binik, Y.M., Khalife, S., Cohen, D., & Amsel, R. (2004). Vaginal spasm, pain, and behavior: An empirical investigation of the diagnosis of vaginismus. *Archives of Sexual Behavior, 33*, 5–17.

Repetti, R.L., Taylor, S.E., & Seeman, T.E. (2002). Risky families: Family social environments and the mental and physical health of offspring. *Psychological Bulletin, 128*, 330–366.

Research Units on Pediatric Psychopharmacology (RUPP) Anxiety Group (2001). *New England Journal of Medicine, 344*, 1279–1285.

Reynolds, C.F., et al. (1999). Nortriptyline and interpersonal psychotherapy as maintenance therapies for recurrent major depression. *Journal of the American Medical Association, 281*, 39–45.

Riccio, C.A., Reynolds, C.R., Lowe, P., & Moore, J.J. (2002). The continuous performance test: A window on the neural substrates for attention? *Archives of Clinical Neuropsychology, 17*, 235–272.

Rice, M.E., & Harris, G.T. (1997). The treatment of adult offenders. In D.M. Stoff, J. Breiling, & J. Maser (Eds.), *Handbook of Antisocial Behavior* (pp. 425–435). New York: Wiley.

Rice, M.E., Harris, G.T., & Cormier, C.A. (1992). An evaluation of a maximum security therapeutic community for psychopaths and other mentally disordered offenders. *Law and Human Behavior, 16*, 399–412.

Richardson, K. (2003). Only 40% of mentally ill get treatment: Survey. *Medical Post, 39*(33), September 16.

Richardson, K. (2004). Anti-craving medications coming soon? *Medical Post, 40*(20), May 18.

Richelson, E. (1999). Receptor pharmacology of neuroleptics: Relation to clinical effects. *Journal of Clinical Psychiatry, 60* (suppl. 10), 5–14.

Richters, J.E. (1993). Community violence and children's development: Toward a research agenda for the 1990s. *Psychiatry, 56*, 3–6.

Richters, J.E., & Hinshaw, S.P. (1999). The abduction of disorder in psychiatry. *Journal of Abnormal Psychology, 108*, 438–445.

Rieber, R.W. (1999). Hypnosis, false memory and multiple personality: A trinity of affinity. *History of Psychiatry, 10*, 3–11.

Rief, W., Hiller, W., & Margraf, J. (1998). Cognitive aspects of hypochondriasis and the somatization syndrome. *Journal of Abnormal Psychology, 107*, 587–595.

Rind, B., Tromovitch, P., & Bauserman, R. (1998). A meta-analytic examination of assumed properties of child sexual abuse using college samples. *Psychological Bulletin, 124*, pp. 22–53.

Ritz, M.C. (1999). Reward systems and addictive behavior. In R.J.M. Niesink, R.M.A. Jaspers, L.M.W. Kornet, & J.M. van Ree (Eds.), *Drugs of Abuse and Addiction: Neurobehavioral toxicology* (pp. 124–149). Boca Raton, FL: CRC Press.

Roberts, A.J., & Koob, G.F. (1997). The neurobiology of addiction: An overview. *Alcohol Health and Research World, 21*, 101–106.

Roberts, L.J., & Marlatt, G.A. (1999). Harm reduction. In P.J. Ott, R.E. Tarter, & R.T. Ammerman (Eds.), *Sourcebook on Substance Abuse: Etiology, Epidemiology, Assessment, and Treatment* (pp. 389–398). Boston: Allyn & Bacon.

Roberts, R.C., Conley, R., Kung, L., Peretti, F.J., & Chute, D.J. (1996). Reduced striatal spine size in schizophrenia: A postmortem ultrastructural study. *Neuroreport, 7*, 1214–1218.

Robertson, I., & Cairns, A. (2000). Horror on the subway: Toronto doctor throws herself and six-month-old son in front of moving train. *Toronto Sun*, August 12.

Robin, A.L., Koepke, T., & Nayar, M. (1986). Conceptualizing, assessing, and treating parent–adolescent conflict. In B. Lahey & A. Kazdin (Eds.), *Advances in Clinical Child Psychology* (Vol. 9, pp. 87–124).

Robin, A.L., Siegel, P.T., Moye, A.W., Gilroy, M., Dennis, A.B., & Sikand, A. (1999). A controlled comparison of family versus individual therapy for adolescents with anorexia nervosa. *Journal of the American Academy of Child & Adolescent Psychiatry, 38*, 1482–1489.

Robins, E., & Guze, S. (1989). Establishment of diagnostic validity in psychiatric illness. In L.N. Robins & J.E. Barrett (Eds.), *The Validity of Psychiatric Diagnosis* (pp. 177–197). New York: Raven Press.

Robins, L.N. (1966). *Deviant Children Grown Up: A Sociological and Psychiatric Study of Sociopathic Personality.* Baltimore: Williams & Wilkins.

Robins, L.N., & Regier, D.A. (1991). *Psychiatric Disorders in America: The Epidemiologic Catchment Area Study*. New York: Free Press.

Robins, L.N., Tipp, J., & Przybeck, T. (1991). Antisocial personality. In L.N. Robins & D.A. Regier (Eds.), *Psychiatric Disorders in America: The Epidemiologic Catchment Area Study* (pp. 258–290). New York: Free Press.

Robinson, N.M., Zigler, E., & Gallagher, J.J. (2000). Two tails of the normal curve: Similarities and differences in the study of mental retardation and giftedness. *American Psychologist, 55*, 1413–1424.

Robinson, P. (1976). *The Modernization of Sex: Havelock Ellis, Alfred Kinsey, William Masters and Virginia Johnson*. New York: Harper & Row.

Roeher Institute (1993). *Community living and intellectual disability in Canada*. Toronto: Author.

Roesch, R., Ogloff, J.R.P., & Golding, S.L. (1993). Competency to stand trial: Legal and clinical issues. *Applied and Preventive Psychology, 2*, 43–51.

Roesch, R., Ogloff, J.R.P., Hart, S.D., Dempster, R.J., Zapf, P.A., & Whittemore, K.E. (1997). The impact of Canadian Criminal Code changes on remands and assessments of fitness to stand trial and criminal responsibility in British Columbia. *Canadian Journal of Psychiatry, 42*, 509–514.

Rogers, C.R. (1957). The necessary and sufficient conditions of therapeutic personality change. *Journal of Consulting Psychology, 21*, 95–103.

Rogers, C.R. (1961). *On Becoming a Person: A Therapist's View of Psychotherapy*. Boston: Houghton Mifflin.

Rogers, D. D., & Abas, N. (1988). A survey of native mental health needs in Manitoba. *Arctic Medical Research, 47* (suppl. 1), 576–580.

Rogers, M.P., Weinshenker, N.J., Warshaw, M.G., et al. (1996). Prevalence of somatoform disorders in a large sample of patients with anxiety disorders. *Psychosomatics, 37*, 17–22.

Rogers, S., Wehner, E.A., & Hagerman, R. (2001). The behavioral phenotype in fragile X: Symptoms of autism in very young children with fragile X syndrome, idiopathic autism, and other developmental. *Journal of Developmental and Behavioral Pediatrics, 22*, 409–417.

Rogers, S.J. (1998). Empirically supported comprehensive treatments for young children with autism. *Journal of Clinical Child Psychology, 27*, 168–179.

Rojas-Fernandez, C.H., & MacKnight, C. (1999). Dementia with Lewy bodies: Review and pharmacotherapeutic implications. *Pharmacotherapy, 19*, 795–803.

Rojas-Fernandez, C.H., Lanctot, K.L., Allen, D.D., & MacKnight, C. (2001). Pharmacotherapy of behavioral and psychological symptoms of dementia: Time for a different paradigm? *Pharmacotherapy, 21*, 74–102.

Roman, G.C. (2002). Vascular dementia revisited: Diagnosis, pathogenesis, treatment, and prevention. *Medical Clinics of North America, 86,* 477–499.

Romney, D.M., & Candido, C.L. (2001). Anhedonia in depression and schizophrenia: A reexamination. *Journal of Nervous and Mental Disease, 189,* 735–740.

Ronningstam, E., & Gunderson, J. (1991). Differentiating borderline personality disorder from narcissistic personality disorder. *Journal of Personality Disorders, 5,* 225–232.

Rooth, F.G. (1973). Exhibitionism outside Europe and America. *Archives of Sexual Behavior, 2,* 351–363.

Rosen, J.C., Reiter, J., & Orosan, P. (1995). Cognitive-behavioral body image therapy for body dysmorphic disorder. *Journal of Consulting and Clinical Psychology, 63,* 263–269.

Rosen, R.C. (2000). Medical and psychological interventions for erectile dysfunction: Toward a combined treatment approach. In R.C. Rosen & S.R. Leiblum (Eds.), *Principles and Practice of Sex Therapy* (3rd ed., pp. 276–304). New York: Guilford.

Rosen, R.C., Lane, R.M., & Menza, M. (1999). Effects of SSRIs on sexual function: A critical review. *Journal of Clinical Psychopharmacology, 19,* 67–85.

Rosen, R.C., & Leiblum, S.R. (1995). Treatment of sexual disorders in the 1990s: An integrated approach. *Journal of Consulting and Clinical Psychology, 63,* 877–890.

Rosenhan, D.L. (1973). On being sane in insane places. *Science, 179,* 250–258.

Rosenstein, L.D. (1998). Differential diagnosis of the major progressive dementias and depression in middle and later adulthood: A summary of the literature of the early 1990s. *Neuropsychology Review, 8,* 109–167.

Rosenthal, D. (Ed.) (1963). *The Genain Quadruplets.* New York: Basic Books.

Rosenthal, N.E. (1998). *Winter Blues: Seasonal Affective Disorder.* New York: Guilford.

Rosenthal, R. (1966). *Experimenter Bias in Behavioral Research.* New York: Appleton-Century-Crofts.

Rosenthal, R. (1979). The "file drawer problem" and tolerance for null results. *Psychological Bulletin, 86,* 638–641.

Rosenthal, R. (1983). Assessing the statistical importance of the effects of psychotherapy. *Journal of Consulting and Clinical Psychology, 51,* 4–13.

Rosenthal, R., & Rosnow, R.L. (1969). *Artifact in behavioral science research.* New York: Academic Press.

Rosler, A., & Witztum, E. (1998). Treatment of men with paraphilia with a long-acting analogue of gonadotripin-releasing hormone. *New England Journal of Medicine, 338,* 416–422.

Ross, C.A. (1991). Epidemiology of multiple personality disorder and dissociation. *Psychiatric Clinics of North America, 14,* 503–516.

Ross, C.A. (1997). *Dissociative Identity Disorder: Diagnosis, Clinical Features, and Treatment of Multiple Personality.* New York: Wiley.

Ross, C.A., Duffy, C.M., & Ellason, J.W. (2002). Prevalence, reliability, and validity of dissociative disorders in an inpatient setting. *Journal of Trauma and Dissociation, 3,* 7–17.

Ross, C.A., Norton, G.R., & Wozney, K. (1989). Multiple personality disorder: An analysis of 236 cases. *Canadian Journal of Psychiatry, 34,* 413–418.

Ross, G.W., & Bowen, J.D. (2002). The diagnosis and differential diagnosis of dementia. *Medical Clinics of North America, 86,* 455–476.

Ross, H.E. (1995). DSM-III-R alcohol abuse and dependence and psychiatric comorbidity in Ontario: Results from the Mental Health Supplement to the Ontario Health Survey. *Drug and Alcohol Dependence, 39,* 111–128.

Rossor, M.N. (2001). Pick's disease: A clinical overview. *Neurology, 56* (suppl. 4), S3–S5.

Roth, D., & Bean, J. (1986). New perspectives on homelessness: Findings from a statewide epidemiological study. *Hospital and Community Psychiatry, 37,* 712–723.

Rothbart, M.K., & Bates, J.E. (1997). Temperament. In W. Damon and N. Eisenberg (Eds.), *Handbook of Child Psychology: Vol. 3. Social, Emotional, and Personality Development* (pp. 105–176). New York: Wiley.

Rothbaum, B.O., & Foa, E.B. (1996). Cognitive behavioral therapy for posttraumatic stress disorder. In B.A. van der Kolk, A.C., McFarlane, & L. Weisaeth (Eds.), *Traumatic Stress* (pp. 491–509). New York: Guilford.

Rourke, B.P. (2000). Neuropsychological and psychosocial subtyping: A review of investigations within the University of Windsor laboratory. *Canadian Psychology, 41,* 34–51.

Rourke, B.P., van der Vlugt, H., & Rourke, S.B. (2002). *Practice of child-clinical neuropsychology: An introduction.* Lisse, The Netherlands: Swets & Zeitlinger.

Roy, A., Rylander, G., & Sarchiapone, M. (1997). Genetics of suicide: Family studies and molecular genetics. *Annals of the New York Academy of Sciences, 836,* 135–157.

Roy-Byrne, P.P., & Cowley, D.S. (2002). Pharmacological treatments for panic disorder, generalized anxiety disorder, specific phobia, and social anxiety disorder. In P.E. Nathan and J.M. Gorman (Eds.), *A Guide to Treatments that Work* (2nd ed., pp. 337–365). London: Oxford University Press.

Rozanski, A., Blumenthal, J.A., & Kaplan, J. (1999). Impact of psychological factors on the pathogenesis of cardiovascular disease and implications for therapy. *Circulation, 99,* 2192–2217.

Rucklidge, J.J., & Tannock, R. (2001). Psychiatric, psychosocial, and cognitive functioning of female adolescents with ADHD. *Journal of the American Academy of Child and Adolescent Psychiatry, 40,* 530–540.

Rueter, M.A., Scaramella, L., Wallace, L.E., & Conger, R.D. (1999). First onset of depressive or anxiety disorders predicted by the longitudinal course of internalizing symptoms and parent–adolescent disagreements. *Archives of General Psychiatry, 56,* 726–732.

Ruitenberg, A., Ott, A.L, van Swieten, J.C., Hofman, A., & Breteler, M.M.B. (2001). Incidence of dementia: Does gender make a difference? *Neurobiology of Aging, 22,* 575–580.

Rumstein-McKean, O., & Hunsley, J. (2001). Interpersonal and family functioning of female survivors of childhood sexual abuse. *Clinical Psychology Review, 21,* 471–490.

Ruscio, A.M., Borkovec, T.D., & Ruscio, J. (2001). A taxometric investigation of the latent structure of worry. *Journal of Abnormal Psychology, 110,* 413–422.

Russell, D.E.H. (1984). *Sexual Exploitation: Rape, Child Sexual Abuse, and Workplace Harassment.* Beverly Hills, CA: Sage.

Russell, G.F.M. (1979). Bulimia nervosa: An ominous variant of anorexia nervosa. *Psychological Medicine, 9,* 429–448.

Russell, G.F.M., Szmukler, G.I., Dare, C., & Eisler, I. (1987). An evaluation of family therapy in anorexia nervosa and bulimia nervosa. *Archives of General Psychiatry, 44,* 1047–1056.

Russell, J.M., Newman, S.C., & Bland, R.C. (1994). Drug abuse and dependence. *Acta Psychiatrica Scandinavica* (suppl. 376), 54–62.

Rutherford, J., McGuffin, P., Katz, R.J., & Murray, R.M. (1993). Genetic influences on eating attitudes in a normal female twin population. *Psychological Medicine, 23,* 425–436.

Rutledge, T., & Linden, W. (2003). Defensiveness and 3-year blood pressure levels among young adults: The mediating effects of stress-reactivity. *Annals of Behavioral Medicine, 25,* 34–40.

Rutter, M. (1970). Autistic children: Infancy to adulthood. *Seminars in Psychiatry, 2,* 435–450.

Rutter, M. (1981). *Maternal Deprivation Reassessed* (2nd ed). London: Penguin.

Rutter, M. (1983). Introduction: Concepts of brain dysfunction syndromes. In M. Rutter (Ed.), *Developmental Neuropsychiatry* (pp. 1–14). New York: Guilford Press.

Rutter, M. (1989). Isle of Wight revisited: Twenty-five years of child psychiatric epidemiology. *Journal of the American Academy of Child & Adolescent Psychiatry, 28,* 633–653.

Rutter, M. (1996). Autism research: Prospects and priorities. *Journal of Autism and Developmental Disorders, 26,* 257–275.

Rutter, M. (1997). Nature–nurture integration: The example of antisocial behavior. *American Psychologist, 52,* 390–398.

Rutter, M., & Garmezy, N. (1983). Developmental psychopathology. In E.M. Hetherington (Ed.), *Handbook of Child Psychology* (Vol. 4, pp. 775–912). New York: Wiley.

Rutter, M., Greenfield, D., & Lockyer, L. (1967). A five- to fifteen-year follow-up study of infantile psychosis. II. Social and behavioral outcome. *British Journal of Psychiatry, 113,* 1187–1199.

Rutter, M., Pickles, A., Murray, R., & Eaves, L. (2001). Testing hypotheses on specific environmental causal effects on behavior. *Psychological Bulletin, 127,* 291–324.

Rutter, M., & Rutter, M. (1993). *Developing Minds.* New York: Basic Books.

Rutter, M., Silberg, J., O'Connor, T., & Simonoff, E. (1998). Genetics and child psychiatry. II Empirical research findings. *Journal of Child Psychology and Psychiatry, 40,* 19–55.

Ruyak, P.S., Bilsbury, C.D., & Rajda, M. (2004). A survey of insomnia treatment at Canadian sleep centres: Is there a role for clinical psychologists? *Canadian Psychology, 45,* 165–173.

Ryan, C.S. (1996). Battered children who kill: Developing an appropriate legal response. *Notre Dame Journal of Law, Ethics, and Public Policy, 10,* 301–339.

Rychtarick, R.G., Foy, D.W., Scott, T., Lokey, L., & Prue, D.M. (1987). Five- to six-year follow-up of broad-spectrum behavioral treatment for alcoholism: Effects of training controlled drinking skills. *Journal of Consulting and Clinical Psychology, 55,* 106–108.

Ryff, C.D., Kwan, C.M.L., & Singer, B.H. (2001). Personality and aging: Flourishing agendas and future challenges. In J.E. Birren & K.W. Schaie (Eds.), *Handbook of the Psychology of Aging* (5th ed., pp. 477–499). San Diego: Academic Press.

Saavedra, J.E,, Messich, J.E., Salloum, I.M., & Kirisci, L. (2001). Predictive validity of the physical disorders axis of the DSM multiaxial diagnostic system. *Journal of Nervous and Mental Disease, 189,* 435–441.

Sabshin, M. (1990). Turning points in twentieth-century American psychiatry. *American Journal of Psychiatry, 147,* 1267–1274.

Sacks, O. (1985). *The Man Who Mistook His Wife for a Hat and Other Clinical Tales.* New York: Summit.

Saffran, E.M. (2000). Aphasia and the relationship of language and brain. *Seminars in Neurology, 20,* 409–418.

Saklofske, D.H., & Hildebrand, D.K. (1999). The Weschler Adult Intelligence Scale—Third Edition: The Canadian standardization study. *Canadian Clinical Psychologist, 9*(2), 11–12.

Salekin, R.T. (2002). Psychopathy and therapeutic pessimism Clinical lore or clinical reality? *Clinical Psychology Review, 22,* 79–112.

Salem, J.E., & Kring, A.M. (1998). The role of gender differences in the reduction of etiologic heterogeneity in schizophrenia. *Clinical Psychology Review, 18,* 795–819.

Salthouse, T.A. (1999). Pressing issues in cognitive aging. In N. Schwarz and D.C. Park (Eds.), *Cognition, Aging, and Self-Reports* (pp. 185–198). Hove, England: Psychology Press.

Salvatori, P., Tremblay, M., Sandys, J., & Marcaccio, D.(1998). Aging with an intellectual disability: A review of Canadian literature. *Canadian Journal on Aging, 17*, 249–271.

Sanderlin, T.K. (2001). Anger management counseling with the antisocial personality. *Annals of the American Psychotherapy Association, 4*, 9–11.

Sanders, M.R., Montgomery, D.T., & Brechman-Toussaint, M.L. (2000), The mass media and the prevention of child behavior problems: The evaluation of a television series to promote better child and parenting outcomes. *Journal of Child Psychology and Psychiatry, 41*, 939–948.

Sanderson, W.C., & McGinn, L.K. (2001). Cognitive-behavioral therapy of depression. In M.M. Weissman (Ed.), *Treatment of Depression: Bridging the 21st Century* (pp. 249–279). Washington, DC: American Psychiatric Press.

Sanderson, W.C., Rapee, R.M., & Barlow, D.H. (1989). The influence of an illusion of control on panic attacks induced via inhalation of 5.5% carbon dioxide-enriched air. *Archives of General Psychiatry, 46*, 157–162.

Sandler, A.D., Sutton, K.A.., DeWeese, J., Girardi, M.A., Sheppard, V., & Bodfish, J.W. (1999). Lack of benefit of a single dose of synthetic human secretin in the treatment of autism and pervasive developmental disorder. *New England Journal of Medicine, 341*, 1801–1806.

Sanislow, C.A., & McGlashan, T.H. (1998). Treatment outcome of personality disorders. *Canadian Journal of Psychiatry, 43*, 237–250.

Sapolsky, R.M. (1992). Neuroendocrinology of the stress response. In J.B. Becker, S.M. Breedlove, & D. Crews (Eds.), *Behavioral Endocrinology* (pp. 288–324). Cambridge, MA: MIT Press.

Sartorius, N. (2001). The economic and social burden of depression. *Journal of Clinical Psychiatry, 62*, (suppl. 15), 8–11.

Sartorius, N., Kaelber, C.T., Cooper, J.E., Roper, M.T., Rae, D.S., Gulbinat, W., Ustun, B., & Regier, D.A. (1993). Progress toward achieving a common language in psychiatry: Results from the field trial of the clinical guidelines accompanying the WHO classification of mental and behavioral disorders in ICD-10. *Archives of General Psychiatry, 50*, 115–124.

Sayer, N.A., Sackeim, H.A., Moeller, J.R., Prudic, J., Devanand, D.P., Coleman, E.A., & Kiersky, J.E. (1993). The relations between observer-rating and self-report of depressive symptomatology. *Psychological Assessment, 5*, 350–360.

Sayette, M.A. (1999). Does drinking reduce stress? *Alcohol Research and Health, 23*, 250–255.

Sayette, M.A., Shiffman, S., Tiffany, S.T., Niaura, R.S., Martin, C.S., & Shadel, W.G. (2000). The measurement of drug craving. *Addiction, 95* (suppl. 2), S189–S210.

Scarr, S., & McCartney, K. (1983). How people make their own environments: A theory of genotype-environment effects. *Child Development, 54*, 424–435.

Schachar, R., Jadad, A.R., Gauld, M., Boyle, M., Booker, L., Snider, A., Kim, M., & Cunningham, C. (2002). Attention-deficit hyperactivity disorder: Critical appraisal of extended treatment studies. *Canadian Journal of Psychiatry, 47*, 337-348.

Schachar, R., & Tannock, R. (2002). Syndromes of hyperactivity and attention deficit. In M. Rutter & E. Taylor (Eds.), *Child and Adolescent Psychiatry* (4th ed., pp. 399–418). Oxford, UK: Blackwell.

Schachar, R.J., Tannock, R., & Logan, G. (1993). Inhibitory control, impulsiveness, and attention deficit hyperactivity disorder. *Clinical Psychology Review, 13*, 721–739.

Schachar, R.J., Mota, V.L., Logan, G.D., Tannock, R., & Klim, P. (2000). Confirmation of an inhibitory control deficit in attention-deficit/hyperactivity disorder. *Journal of Abnormal Child Psychology, 28*, 227–235.

Schacter, D.L. (1987). Implicit memory: History and current status. *Journal of Experimental Psychology: Learning, Memory, and Cognition, 13*, 501–518.

Schatzberg, A.F. (1999). Antidepressant effectiveness in severe depression and melancholia. *Journal of Clinical Psychiatry, 60*, 14–22.

Scheel, K.R. (2000). The empirical basis of dialectical behavior therapy: Summary, critique, and implications. *Clinical Psychology: Science and Practice, 7*, 68–86.

Scheerenberger, R.C. (1982). Public residential services, 1981: Status and trends. *Mental Retardation, 20*, 210–215.

Scheff, T.J. (1966). *Being mentally ill: A sociological theory*. Chicago: Aldine.

Scheffler, R.M., Ivey, S.L., & Garrett, A.B. (1998). Changing supply and earning patterns of the mental health workforce. *Administration and Policy in Mental Health, 26*, 85–99.

Scheltens, P., & Hijdra, A.H. (1998). Diagnostic criteria for vascular dementia. *Haemostasis, 28*, 151–157.

Schiavi, R.C., Stimmel, B.B., Mandeli, J., & White, D. (1995). Chronic alcoholism and male sexual function. *American Journal of Psychiatry, 152*, 1045–1054.

Schiff, M., Duyme, M., Dumaret, A., & Tomkiewicz, S. (1982). How much could we boost scholastic achievement and IQ scores? A direct answer from a French adoption study. *Cognition, 12*, 165–196.

Schiffman, J., Abrahamson, A., Cannon, T., LaBrie, J., Parnas, J., Schulsinger, F., & Mednick, S. (2001). Early rearing factors in schizophrenia. *International Journal of Mental Health, 30*, 3–16.

Schmidt, N.B. (1999). Prospective evaluations of anxiety sensitivity. In S. Taylor (Ed.), *Anxiety sensitivity: Theory, research, and treatment of the fear of anxiety* (pp. 217–235). Mahwah, NJ: Erlbaum.

Schneider, K. (1959). *Clinical Psychopathology* (M.W. Hamilton, Trans.). New York: Grune & Stratton.

Schneider, R.D., Glancy, G.D., Bradford, J. McD., & Seibenmorgen, E. (2000). Canadian landmark case, *Winko v. British Columbia*: Revisiting the conundrum of the mentally disordered accused. *Journal of the American Academy of Psychiatry and Law, 28*, 206–212.

Schneiderman, N., Chesney, M.A., & Krantz, D.S. (1989). Biobehavioral aspects of cardiovascular disease: Progress and prospects. *Health Psychology, 8*, 649–676.

Schneidman, E.S. (1996). *The Suicidal Mind*. New York: Oxford University Press.

Schneller, J. (1988). Terror on the A-train: Anatomy of a panic attack. *Mademoiselle, 94*, 148–159.

Schofield, P.W., Tang, M., Marder, K., Bell, K., Dooneief, G., Chun, M., Sano, M., Stern, Y., & Mayeux, B. (1997). Alzheimer's disease after remote head injury: An incidence study. *Journal of Neurology, Neurosurgery and Psychiatry, 62*, 119–124.

Schooler, N.R., Keith, S.J., Severe, J.B., et al. (1997). Relapse and rehospitalization during maintenance treatment of schizophrenia: The effects of dose reduction and family treatment. *Archives of General Psychiatry, 54*, 453–463.

Schopler, E.M., Andrews, C.E., & Strupp, K. (1979). Do autistic children come from upper-middle-class parents? *Journal of Autism and Developmental Disorders, 9*, 139–152.

Schopp, R.F., Sturgis, B.J., & Sullivan, M. (1994). Battered woman syndrome, expert testimony, and the distinction between justification and excuse. *University of Illinois Law Review, 54*, 45–113.

Schott, R.L. (1995). The childhood and family dynamics of tranvestites. *Archives of Sexual Behavior, 24*, 309–328.

Schotti, J.R., Evans, I.M., Meyer, L.H., & Walker, P. (1991). A meta-analysis of intervention research with problem behavior: Treatment validity and standards of practice. *American Journal on Mental Retardation, 96*, 233–256.

Schreibman, L. (1988). *Autism*. Beverly Hills, CA: Sage.

Schuckit, J.A., & Monteiro, J.G. (1988). Alcoholism, anxiety and depression. *British Journal of Addication, 83*, 1373–1380.

Schuckit, M. (1999). *Drug and Alcohol Abuse*. Norwell, MA: Kluwer.

Schuckit, M.A. (2000). *Drug and Alcohol Abuse: A Clinical Guide to Diagnosis and Treatment* (5th ed.). New York: Kluwer Academic/Plenum.

Schuckit, M.A., Smith, T.L., Danko, G.P., Reich, T., Bucholz, K.K., & Bierut, L.J. (2002). Similarities in the clinical characteristics related to alcohol dependence in two populations. *American Journal on Addictions, 11*, 1–9.

Schuckit, M.A., Daeppen, J., Danko, G.P., Tripp, M.L., Smith, T.L., Li, T.K., Hesselbrock, V.M., & Bucholz, K.K. (1998a). Clinical implications for four drugs of the DSM-IV distinction between substance dependence with and without a physiological component. *American Journal of Psychiatry, 156*, 41–49.

Schuckit, M.A., Smith, T.L., Daeppen, J., Eng, M., Li, T.K., Hesselbrock, V.M., Nurnberger, J.I., & Bucholz, K.K. (1998b). Clinical relevance of the distinction between alcohol dependence with and without a physiological component. *American Journal of Psychiatry, 155*, 733–740.

Schuepbach, W.M.M., Adler., R.H., Sabbioni, M.E.E. (2002). Accuracy of clinical diagnosis of psychogenic disorders' in the presence of physical symptoms suggesting a general medical condition: A 5-year follow-up in 162 patients. *Psychotherapy and Psychosomatics, 71*, 11–17.

Schulberg, H.C., Katon, W.J., Simon, G.E., & Rush, A.J. (1999). Best clinical practice: Guidelines for managing major depression in primary medical care. *Journal of Clinical Psychiatry, 60* (suppl. 7), 19–26.

Schuller, R.A., & Ogloff, J.R.P. (2000). *Introduction to psychology and law: Canadian perspectives*. Toronto: University of Toronto Press.

Schuyler, D. (1991). *A Practical Guide to Cognitive Therapy*. New York: Norton.

Schwartz, C.E., Snidman, N., & Kagan, J. (1999). Adolescent social anxiety as an outcome of inhibited temperament in childhood. *Journal of the American Academy of Child and Adolescent Psychiatry, 38*, 1008–1015.

Schwartz, G.E. (1982). Testing the biopsychosocial model: The ultimate challenge facing behavioral medicine. *Journal of Consulting and Clinical Psychology, 50*, 1040–1053.

Schwartz, G.E. (1989). Dysregulation theory and disease: Toward a general model for psychosomatic medicine. In S. Cheren (Ed.), *Psychosomatic Medicine: Theory, Physiology, and Practice* (Vol. 1, pp. 91–118). Madison, CT: International Universities Press.

Scott, S. (2002). Parent training programs. In M. Rutter & E. Taylor (Eds.), *Child and Adolescent Psychiatry* (4th ed., pp. 949–967). Oxford, UK: Blackwell.

Scroppo, J.C., Drob, S.L., Weinberger, J.L., & Eagle, P. (1998). Identifying dissociative identity disorder: A self-report and projective study. *Journal of Abnormal Psychology, 107*, 272–284.

Scurfield, R.M. (1985). Posttrauma stress assessment and treatment: Overview and formulations. In C.R. Figley (Ed.), *Trauma and its Wake* (pp. 219–259). New York: Brunner/Mazel.

Searles, J.S. (1988). The role of genetics in the pathogenesis of alcoholism. *Journal of Abnormal Psychology, 97*, 153–167.

Searles, J.S. (1990). Methodological limitations of research on the genetics of alcoholism. In C.R. Cloninger & H. Begleiter (Eds.), *Genetics and Biology of Alcoholism* (pp. 89–100). Cold Spring Harbor, NY: Cold Spring Harbor Laboratory Press.

Sechrest, L., Stickle, T.R., & Stewart, M. (1998). The role of assessment in clinical psychology. In A. Bellack, M. Hersen, & C.R. Reynolds (Eds.), *Comprehensive Clinical Psychology: Vol. 4. Assessment* (pp. 2–28). New York: Pergamon.

Sedgwick, P. (1981). Illness—Mental and otherwise. In A.L. Caplan, H.T. Engelhardt, Jr., & J.J. McCartney (Eds.), *Concepts of Health and Disease: Interdisciplinary Perspectives* (pp. 119–129). Reading, MA: Addison-Wesley.

Seeman, M.V. (1998). Narratives of twenty- to thirty-year outcomes in schizophrenia. *Psychiatry, 61*, 249–261.

Seeman, P. (2002). Atypical antipsychotics: Mechanisms of action. *Canadian Journal of Psychiatry, 47*, 27–38.

Segal, D.L. (1997). Structured interviewing and DSM classification. In S.M. Turner and M. Hersen (Eds.), *Adult Psychopathology and Diagnosis* (3rd ed., pp. 24–57). New York: Wiley.

Segal, Z., Gemar, M., & Williams, S. (1999). Differential cognitive response to a mood challenge following successful cognitive therapy or pharmacotherapy for unipolar depression. *Journal of Abnormal Psychology, 108*, 3–10.

Segal, Z., Williams, M., & Teasdale, J. (2002). *Mindfulness-based cognitive therapy for depression: A new approach to preventing relapse.* New York: Guilford.

Segraves, T., & Althof, S. (2002). Psychotherapy and pharmacotherapy for sexual dysfunctions. In P.E. Nathan and J.M. Gorman (Eds.), *A Guide to Treatments that Work* (2nd ed., pp. 497–524). London, England: Oxford University Press.

Segraves, R.T., & Blindt Segraves, K. (2001). Female sexual disorders. In N.L. Stotland and D.E. Stewart (Eds.), *Psychological Aspects of Women's Health Care: The Interface Between Psychiatry and Obstetrics and Gynecology* (2nd ed., pp. 379–400). Washington, DC: American Psychiatric Press.

Segrin, C., & Abramson, L.Y. (1994). Negative reactions to depressive behaviors: A communication theories analysis. *Journal of Abnormal Psychology, 103*, 655–668.

Seidman, B.T., Marshall, W.L., Hudson, S.M., & Robertson, P.J. (1994). An examination of intimacy and loneliness in sex offenders. *Journal of Interpersonal Violence, 9*, 518–534.

Selfe, L. (1977). *Nadia: A Case of Extraordinary Drawing Ability in an Autistic Child.* London: Academic Press.

Seligman, M.E.P. (1995). *What You Can Change, and What You Can't: The Complete Guide to Successful Self-Improvement.* Fawcett Books.

Selye, H. (1956). *The Stress of Life.* New York: McGraw-Hill.

Serdula, M.K., Collins, M.E., Williamson, D.F., Anda, R.F., Pamuk, E.R., & Byers, T.E. (1993). Weight control practices of U.S. adolescents and adults. *Annals of Internal Medicine, 119*, 667–671.

Seto, M.C., & Barbaree, H.E. (2000). Paraphilias. In V.B. Van Hasselt & M. Hersen (Eds.), *Aggression and Violence: An Introductory Text* (pp. 198–213). Boston: Allyn & Bacon.

Seto, M.C., & Kuban, M. (1996). Criterion-related validity of a phallometric test for paraphilic rape and sadism. *Behaviour Research and Therapy, 34*, 175–183.

Seto, M.C., Maric, A., & Barbaree, H.E. (2001). The role of pornography in the etiology of sexual aggression. *Aggression and Violent Behavior, 6*, 35–53.

Shadish, W.R., Matt, G.E., Navarro, A.N., & Phillips, G. (2000). The effects of psychological therapies under clinically representative conditions: A meta-analysis. *Psychological Bulletin, 126*, 512–529.

Shahinfar, A., Kupersmidt, J.B., & Matza, L.S. (2001). The relation between exposure to violence and social information processing among incarcerated adolescents. *Journal of Abnormal Psychology, 110*, 136–141.

Shalev, A.Y. (in press). Historical concepts and present patterns: Stress management and debriefing. In J.P. Wilson & B. Raphael (Eds.), *Stress Debriefing: Theory, Practice, and Challenge.* Cambridge, England: Cambridge University Press.

Shalev, A.Y. (1996). Stress versus traumatic stress: From acute homeostatic reactions to chronic psychopathology. In B.A. van der Kolk, A.C. McFarlane, & L. Weisaeth (Eds.), *Traumatic Stress* (pp. 77–101). New York: Guilford.

Shalev, A.Y., & Munitz, H. (1986). Conversion without hysteria: A case report and review of the literature. *British Journal of Psychiatry, 148*, 198–203.

Shalev, A.Y., Peri, T., Caneti, L., & Schreiber, S. (1996). Predictors of PTSD in injured trauma survivors. *American Journal of Psychiatry, 53*, 219–224.

Shapiro, A.K., & Morris, L.A. (1978). The placebo effect in medical and psychological therapies. In S.L. Garfield & A.E. Bergin (Eds.), *Handbook of psychotherapy and behavior change* (2nd ed., pp. 369–410). New York: Wiley.

Shapiro, D.A., & Shapiro, D. (1982). Meta-analysis of comparative psychotherapy outcome studies: A replication and refinement. *Psychological Bulletin, 92*, 581–604.

Shapiro, F. (1995). *Eye Movement Desensitization and Reprocessing.* New York: Guilford.

Sharpe, L. (2002). A reformulated cognitive-behavioral model of problem gambling: A biopsychosocial perspective. *Clinical Psychology Review, 22*, 1–25.

Shastry, B.S. (1999). Recent developments in the genetics of schizophrenia. *Neurogenetics, 2*, 149–154.

Shatte, A.J., Reivich, K., Gillham, J.E., & Seligman, M.E.P. (1999). Learned optimism in children. In C.R. Snyder (Ed.), *Coping: The Psychology of What Works* (pp. 165–181). New York: Oxford University Press.

Shavelson, L. (2001). *Hooked: Five Addicts Challenge our Misguided Drug Rehab System.* New York: New Press.

Shaw, D.S., & Bell, R.Q. (1993). Developmental theories of parental contributors to antisocial behavior. *Journal of Abnormal Child Psychology, 21*, 493–518.

Shaw, D.S., Keenan, K., & Vondra, J.I. (1994). Developmental precursors of externalizing behavior: Ages 1 to 3. *Developmental Psychology, 30*, 355–364.

Shaw, D.S., Vondra, J.I., Hommerding, K.D., Keenan K., & Dunn, M. (1994). Chronic family adversity and early child behavior problems: A longitudinal study of low income families. *Journal of Child Psychology and Psychiatry, 35*, 1109–1122.

Shaw, D.S., & Vondra, J.I. (1995). Infant attachment security and maternal predictors of early behavior problems: A longitudinal study of low-income families. *Journal of Abnormal Child Psychology, 23*, 335–357.

Shaw, D.S., Winslow, E.B., Owens, E.B., Vondra, J.I., Cohn, J.F., & Bell, R.Q. (1997). The development of early externalizing problems among children from low-income families: A transformational perspective. *Journal of Abnormal Child Psychology, 26*, 95–107.

Shaw, E. & Grenier, D. (2001). Taking the pulse of Canadian children – A health report card for the millennium. *Paediatrics & Child Health, 6*(4). Ottawa: Canadian Paediatric Association. Retrieved June 15, 2004, from http://www.pulsus.com/Paeds/06_04/shaw_ed.htm

Shea, M.T. (1995). Interrelationships among categories of personality disorders. In W.J. Livesley (Ed.), *The DSM-IV personality disorders* (pp. 397–406). New York: Guilford.

Shear, M.K. (1996). Factors in the etiology and pathogenesis of panic disorder: Revisiting the attachment-separation paradigm. *American Journal of Psychiatry, 153*, 125–135.

Shearer, D.E., & Shearer, M.S. (1976). The Portage Project: A model for early childhood intervention. In T.D. Tjossem (Ed.), *Intervention Strategies for High Risk Infants and Young Children.* Baltimore: University Park Press.

Shedler, J., Mayman, M., & Manis, M. (1993). The illusion of mental health. *American Psychologist, 48*, 1117–1131.

Sheffield, A. (1998). *How You Can Survive When They're Depressed: Living and Coping with Depression Fallout.* New York: Three Rivers Press.

Shenton, M.E. (1996). Temporal lobe structural abnormalities in schizophrenia: A selective review and presentation of new magnetic resonance findings. In S. Matthysse & D.L. Levy (Eds.), *Psychopathology: The Evolving Science of Mental Disorder* (pp. 51–99). New York: Cambridge University Press.

Shenton, M.E., Dickey, C.C., Frumin. M., & McCarley, R.W. (2001). A review of MRI findings in schizophrenia. *Schizophrenia Research, 49*, 1–52.

Sher, K.J. (1991). *Children of Alcoholics: A Critical Appraisal of Theory and Research.* Chicago: University of Chicago Press.

Sher, K.J. (1993). Children of alcoholics and the intergenerational transmission of alcoholism: A biopsychosocial perspective. In J.S. Baer, G.A. Marlatt, & R.J. McMahon (Eds.), *Addictive Behaviors Across the Life Span: Prevention, Treatment, and Policy Issues* (pp. 3–33). Newbury Park, CA: Sage.

Shiffman, S., Paty, J.A., & Gnys, M. (1996). First lapses to smoking: Within-subjects analysis of real-time reports. *Journal of Consulting and Clinical Psychology, 64*, 366–379.

Shipley, S., & Arrigo, B. A. (2001). The confusion over psychopathy (II): Implications for forensic (correctional) practice. *International Journal of Offender Therapy and Comparative Criminology, 45*, 407–420.

Shokrollahi, P., Mirmohamadi, M., Mehrabi, F., & Babaei, G. (1999). Prevalence of sexual dysfunction in women seeking services at family planning centers in Tehran. *Journal of Sex and Marital Therapy, 25*, 211–215.

Short, A.B., & Schopler, E. (1988). Factors relating to age of onset in autism. *Journal of Autism and Developmental Disorders, 18*, 207–216.

Shorter, E. (1992). *From Paralysis to Fatigue: A History of Psychosomatic Illness in the Modern Era.* New York: Free Press.

Shoulson, I. (1990). Huntington's disease: Cognitive and psychiatric features. *Neuropsychiatry, Neuropsychology, and Behavioral Neurology, 3*, 15–22.

Showalter, E. (1997). *Hystories: Hysterical Epidemics and Modern Medicine.* New York: Columbia University Press.

Shulman, K.I. (2000). Clock-drawing: Is it the ideal cognitive screening test? *International Journal of Geriatric Psychiatry, 15*, 548–561.

Siegel, J.M., & Kuykendall, D.H. (1990). Loss, widowhood, and psychological distress among the elderly. *Journal of Consulting and Clinical Psychology, 58*, 519–524.

Siegel, S. (2001). Pavlovian conditioning and drug overdose: When tolerance fails. *Addiction Research and Theory, 9*, 503–513.

Siegel, S., Baptista, M.A.S., Kim, J.A., McDonald, R.V., & Weise-Kelly, L. (2000). Pavlovian psychopharmacology: The associative basis of tolerance. *Experimental and Clinical Psychopharmacology, 8*, 276–293.

Siever, L.J., Bernstein, D.P., & Silverman, J.M. (1995). Schizotypal personality disorder. In W.J. Livesley, (Ed.), *The DSM-IV Personality Disorders* (pp. 71–90). New York: Guilford.

Sigman, M. (1999). Response to the commentary by Mervis and Robinson. *Monographs of the Society for Research in Child Development, 64*, 131–139.

Sigvardsson, S., Bohman, M., & Cloninger, C.R. (1996). Replication of the Stockholm adoption study of alcoholism: Confirmatory cross-fostering analysis. *Archives of General Psychiatry, 53*, 681–687.

Sillars, L. (1995). New hope for husband murderers. *Alberta Report, 22*(34), p. 18.

Silverman, W.K., et al. (1999). Contingency mangagement, self-control, and education support in the treatment of childhood phobic disorders. A randomized clinical trial. *Journal of Consulting and Clinical Psychology, 67*, 675–687.

Simard, M., van Reekum, R., & Cohen, T. (2000). A review of the cognitive and behavioral symptoms in dementia with Lewy bodies. *Journal of Neuropsychiatry and Clinical Neuroscience, 12*, 425–450.

Simmie, L. (2001). An open letter to Laura. In L. Crozier & P. Lane (Eds.), *Addicted: Notes from the belly of the beast* (pp. 35–46). Vancouver, BC: Greystone Books.

Simmie, S. (1998). I'd sit in the kitchen and just shake. *Toronto Star*, October 4.

Singer, S.M., Chambers, C.B., Newfry, G.A., Norlund, M.A., & Muna, N.A. (1997). Tau in aluminum-induced neurofibrillary tangles. *Neurotoxicology, 18*, 63–76.

Singh, N.N., Guernsey, T.F., & Ellis, C.R. (1992). Drug therapy for persons with developmental disabilities: Legislation and litigation. *Clinical Psychology Review, 12*, 665–679.

Skeem, J.L., Poythress, N., Edens, J.F., Lilienfeld, S.O., & Cale, E.M. (2003). Psychopathic personality or personalities? Exploring potential variants of psychopathy and their implications for risk assessment. *Aggression and Violent Behavior, 8*, 513–546.

Skilling, T.A., Harris, G.T., Rice, M.E., & Quinsey, V.L. (2002). Identifying persistently antisocial offenders using the Hare Psychopathy Checklist and DSM antisocial personality disorder criteria. *Psychological Assessment, 14*, 27–38.

Skinner, B.F. (1953). *Science and Human Behavior*. New York: Macmillan.

Skodak, M., & Skeels, H. (1949). A final follow-up study of one hundred adopted children. *Journal of Genetic Psychology, 75*, 85–125.

Skoog, G., & Skoog, I. (1999). A 40-year follow-up of patients with obsessive–compulsive disorder. *Archives of General Psychiatry, 56*, 121–127.

Skre, I., Onstad, S.I., Edvardsen, J., Torgersen, S., & Kringlen, E. (1994). A family study of anxiety disorders: Familial transmission and relationship to mood disorder and psychoactive substance use disorder. *Acta Psychiatrica Scandinavica, 90*, 366–374.

Slade, P.D., & Russell, G.F.M. (1973). Awareness of body dimensions in anorexia nervosa and bulimia nervosa: Cross-sectional and longitudinal studies. *Psychological Medicine, 3*, 188–199.

Slater, E. (1965). Diagnosis of hysteria. *British Medical Journal, 1*, 1395–1399.

Sloane, R.B., Staples, F.R., Cristo, A.H., Yorkston, N.J., & Whipple, K. (1975). *Psychotherapy versus behavior therapy*. Cambridge, MA: Harvard University Press.

Sloman, L., Gardner, R., & Price, J. (1989). Biology of family systems and mood disorders. *Family Process, 28*, 387–398.

Slutske, W.S., Eisen, S., True, W.R., Lyons, M.J., Goldberg, J., & Tsuang, M. (2000). Common genetic vulnerability for pathological gambling and alcohol dependence in men. *Archives of General Psychiatry, 57*, 666–673.

Slutske, W.S., Eisen, S., Xian, H., True, W.R., Lyons, M.J., Goldberg, J., & Tsuang, M. (2001). A twin study of the association between pathological gambling and antisocial personality disorder. *Journal of Abnormal Psychology, 110*, 297–308.

Small, S.A., Perera, G.M., DeLaPaz, R., Mayeux, R., & Stern, Y. (1999). Differential regional dysfunction of the hippocampal formation among elderly with memory decline and Alzheimer's disease. *Annals of Neurology, 45*, 466–472.

Small, S.A., Tsai, W.Y., DeLaPaz, R., Mayeux, R., & Stern, Y. (2002). Imaging hippocampal function across the human life span: Is memory decline normal or not? *Annals of Neurology, 51*, 290–295.

Smalley, S.L., Asarnow, R.F., & Spence, M.A. (1988). Autism and genetics: A decade of research. *Archives of General Psychiatry, 45*, 953–961.

Smalley, S.L., & Collins, F. (1996). Brief report: Genetic, prenatal, and immunologic factors. *Journal of Autism and Developmental Disorders, 26*, 195–197.

Smetana, J.G. (1989). Adolescents' and parents' reasoning about actual family conflict. *Child Development, 60*, 1052–1067.

Smith, D.A. (1999). The end of theoretical orientations? *Applied and Preventive Psychology, 8*, 269–280.

Smith, A.L., & Weissman, M.M. (1992). Epidemiology. In E.S. Paykel (Ed.), *Handbook of Affective Disorders* (2nd ed., pp. 111–130). New York: Guilford.

Smith, E. (1991). First person account: Living with schizophrenia. *Schizophrenia Bulletin, 17*, 689–691.

Smith, G. (2003). Prairies rife with addicts to gambling, study finds. *Globe and Mail*, December 13, p. A5.

Smith, G., & Hall, M. (1982). Evaluating Michigan's guilty but mentally ill verdict: An empirical study. *University of Michigan Journal of Law Reform, 16*, 77–114.

Smith, G.N., Flynn, S.W., McCarthy, N., Meistrich, B., Ehmann, T.S., MacEwan, W.G., Kopala, L.C., & Honer, W.G. (2001). Low birthweight in schizophrenia: Prematurity or poor fetal growth? *Schizophrenia Research, 47*, 177–184.

Smith, G.R., Monson, R.A., & Ray, D.C. (1986). Psychiatric consultation in somatization disorder: A randomized controlled study. *New England Journal of Medicine, 314*, 1407–1413.

Smith, G.T., Goldman, M.S., Greenbaum, P.E., & Christiansen, A. (1995). Expectancy for social facilitation from drinking: The divergent paths of high-expectancy and low-expectancy adolescents. *Journal of Abnormal Psychology, 104*, 32–40.

Smith, M.L., Glass, G.V., & Miller, T.I. (1980). *The benefits of psychotherapy*. Baltimore: Johns Hopkins University Press.

Smith, S.R., & Meyer, R.G. (1985). Child abuse reporting laws and psychotherapy: A time for reconsideration. *International Journal of Law and Psychiatry, 7*, 351–366.

Smith, T., Groen, AD., & Wynn, J.W. (2000). Randomized trial of intensive early intervention for children with pervasive developmental disorder. *American Journal of Mental Retardation, 105*, 269–285.

Smith, V. (2003). I never fit well as a girl. *Globe and Mail*, January 4.

Smith, Y.L.S., van Goozen, S.H.M., & Cohen-Kettenis, P.T. (2001). Adolescents with gender identity disorder who were accepted or rejected for sex reassignment surgery: A prospective follow-up study. *Journal of the American Academy of Child and Adolescent Psychiatry, 40*, 472–481.

Smyth, J.M., Stone, A.A., Hurewitz, A., & Kaell, A. (1999). Effects of writing about stressful experiences on symptom reduction in patients with asthma or rheumatoid arthritis: A randomized trial. *Journal of the American Medical Association, 281*, 1304–1309.

Snyder, C.R. (Ed.) (1999). *Coping: The Psychology of What Works*, 182–204. New York: Oxford University Press.

Snyder, D.K. (1999). Affective reconstruction in the context of a pluralistic approach to couple therapy. *Clinical Psychology: Science and Practice, 6*, 348–365.

Sobell, L.C., Agrawal, S., Annis, H., Ayala-Velazquez, H. Echeverria, L., Leo, G.I., Rybakowski, J.K., Sandahl, C., Saunders, B., Thomas, S., & Ziolkowski, M. (2001). Cross-cultural evaluation of two drinking assessment instruments: Alcohol Timeline Followback and Inventory of Drinking Situations. *Substance Use and Misuse, 36*, 313–331.

Sobell, L.C., Brown, J., Leo, G.I., & Sobell, M.B. (1996). The reliability of the Alcohol Timeline Followback when administered by telephone and by computer. *Drug & Alcohol Dependence, 42*, 49–54.

Sobell, M.B., & Sobell, L.C. (1978). *Behavioral treatment of alcohol problems*. New York: Plenum.

Solomon, A. (2001). *The Noonday Demon: An Atlas of Depression*. New York: Scribner.

Solomon, D.A., Keitner, G.I., Miller, I.W., Shea, M.T., et al. (1995). Course of illness and maintenance treatments for patients with bipolar disorder. *Journal of Clinical Psychiatry, 56*, 5–13.

Solomon, K., Manepalli, J., Ireland, G.A., & Mahon, G.M. (1993). Alcoholism and prescription drug abuse in the elderly: St. Louis University grand rounds. *Journal of the American Geriatrics Society, 41*, 57–69.

Somerfield, M.R., & McCrae, R.R. (2000). Stress and coping research: Methodological challenges, theoretical advances, and clinical applications. *American Psychologist, 55*, 620–625.

Song, C., & Leonard, B.E. (2000). *Fundamentals of Psychoneuroimmunology*. New York: Wiley.

Sonino, N., & Fava, G.A. (2001). Psychiatric disorders associated with Cushing's syndrome: Epidemiology, pathophysiology and treatment. *CNS Drugs, 15*, 361–373.

Souery, D., Rivelli, S.K., & Mendlewicz, J. (2001). Molecular genetic and family studies in affective disorders: State of the art. *Journal of Affective Disorders, 62*, 45–55.

Southall, D.P., Plunkett, M.C., Banks, M.W., Falkov, A.F., & Samuels, M.P (1997). Covert video recordings of life-threatening child abuse: Lessons for child protection. *Pediatrics, 100*, 735–774.

Spaner, D., Bland, R.C., & Newman, S.C. (1994). Major depressive disorder. *Acta Psychiatrica Scandinavica* (suppl. 376), 7–15.

Spanos, N.P. (1994). Multiple identity enactments and multiple personality disorder: A sociocognitive perspective. *Psychological Bulletin, 116*, 143–165.

Spanos, N.P., Weekes, J.R., & Bertrand, L.D. (1985). Multiple personality: A social psychological perspective. *Journal of Abnormal Psychology, 94*, 362–376.

Spanos, N.P., Weekes, J.R., Menary, E., & Bertrand, L.D. (1986). Hypnotic interview and age regression procedures in the elicitation of multiple personality symptoms: A simulation study. *Psychiatry, 49*, 298–311.

Spector, I.P., & Carey, M.P. (1990). Incidence and prevalence of the sexual dysfunctions: A critical review of the empirical literature. *Archives of Sexual Behavior, 19*, 389–408.

Spencer, T.J., Biederman, J., & Wilens, T. (1998). Pharmacotherapy of ADHD with antidepressants. In R.A. Barkley (Ed.), *Attention-Deficit/Hyperactivity Disorder* (2nd ed., 552–563). New York: Guilford.

Spiegel, D., & Cardena, E. (1991). Disintegrated experience: The dissociative disorders revisited. *Journal of Abnormal Psychology, 100*, 366–378.

Spirito, A., Brown, L., Overholser, J., & Fritz, G. (1989). Attempted suicide in adolescence: A review and critique of the literature. *Clinical Psychology Review, 9*, 335–363.

Spitzer, R.L., First, M.B., Williams, J.B.W., Kendler, K., Pincus, H.A., & Tucker, G. (1992). Now is the time to retire the term "organic mental disorders." *American Journal of Psychiatry, 149*, 240–244.

Spitzer, R.L., & Fleiss, J.L. (1974). A re-analysis of the reliability of psychiatric diagnosis. *British Journal of Psychiatry, 125*, 341–347.

Spivack, G., & Shure, M.B. (1974). *Social adjustment of young children: A cognitive approach to solving real-life problems.* Washington, DC: Jossey-Bass.

Sprague, R.L., & Sleator, E.K. (1977). Methlphenidate in hyperkinetic children: Differences in doses effects learning and social behavior. *Science, 198*, 1274–1276.

Spreen, O. (1988). Prognosis of learning disability. *Journal of Consulting and Clinical Psychology, 56*, 836–842.

Spreen, O., & Strauss, E. (1998). *A compendium of neuropsychological tests: Administration, norms, and commentary* (2nd ed.). London: Oxford University Press.

Sramek, J.J., & Cutler, N.R. (1999). Recent developments in the drug treatment of Alzheimer's disease. *Drugs and Aging, 14*, 359–373.

Sroufe, L.A., & Fleeson, J. (1986). Attachment and the construction of relationships. In W.W. Hartup & Z. Rubin (Eds.), *Relationships and Development* (pp. 51–72). Hillsdale, NJ: Erlbaum.

Stacy, A.W., Newcomb, M.D., & Bentler, P.W. (1991). Cognitive motivation and drug use: A 9-year longitudinal study. *Journal of Abnormal Psychology, 100*, 502–515.

Stanwick, R.S. (December, 1, 1999). *Decision in the matter of the Captial Health Region, Community Care Facilities Licensing and Montreux Specialized Residential Facility for Eating Disorders.* Victoria, BC: Author. Retrieved June 15, 2004, from http://www.viha.ca/mho/publications/montreux/pdf/montreux.pdf

Stark-Adamec, C., Pihl, R.O., & Adamec, R. (1981). The subjective marijuana experience: Great expectations. *International Journal of Addictions, 51*, 203–206.

Starr, P. (1982). *The Social Transformation of American Medicine.* New York: Basic Books.

Statistics Canada (1994). *Population projections 1993–2041.* Ottawa: Ministry of Industry, Science, and Technology.

Statistics Canada (1999). Births. *The Daily*, June 16, 1999.

Statistics Canada (2000). Divorces. *The Daily*, September 28.

Statistics Canada (2003a). Family violence. *The Daily*, June 23.

Statistics Canada (2003b). *Lifetime probability of developing and dying from cancer.* Retrieved May 19, 2004, from http://www.statcan.ca/english/Pgdb/health25a.htm

Statistics Canada (2004). Divorces. *The Daily*, May 4.

Stayton, W.R. (1996). Sexual and gender identity disorders in a relational perspective. In F.W. Kaslow (Ed.), *Handbook of Relational Diagnosis and Dysfunctional Family Patterns* (pp. 357–370). New York: Wiley.

Steadman, H., Pantle, R., & Pasewark, S. (1983). Factors associated with a successful insanity defense. *American Journal of Psychiatry, 140*, 401–405.

Steadman, H., et al. (1993). *Before and After Hinckley. Evaluating Insanity Defense Reform.* New York: Guilford.

Steadman, H.J., Mulvey, E.P., Monahan, J., Robbins, P.C., Appelbaum, P.S., Grisso, T., Roth, L.H., & Silver, E. (1998). Violence by people discharged from acute psychiatric inpatient facilities and by others in the same neighborhoods. *Archives of General Psychiatry, 55*, 393–401.

Steele, C.M., & Josephs, R.A. (1988). Drinking your troubles away. II. An attention-allocation model of alcohol's effect on psychological stress. *Journal of Abnormal Psychology, 97*, 196–205.

Steele, C.M., & Josephs, R.A. (1990). Alcohol myopia: Its prized and dangerous effects. *American Psychologist, 45*, 921–933.

Steffenburg, S., Gillberg, C., Hellgren, L., Andersson, L., Gillberg, I., Jakobsson, G., & Bohman, M. (1989). A twin study of autism in Denmark, Finland, Iceland, Norway and Sweden. *Journal of Child Psychology and Psychiatry, 30*, 405–416.

Steffy, R.A., Asarnow, R.F., Asarnow, J.R., MacCrimmon, D.J., & Cleghorn, J.M. (1984). The McMaster–Waterloo high-risk project: Multifaceted strategy for high-risk research. In N.F. Watt & E.J. Anthony (Eds.), *Children at risk for schizophrenia: A longitudinal perspective* (pp. 401–413). Cambridge: Cambridge University Press.

Steiger, H. (2003). Eating disorders and the serotonin connection: State, trait and developmental effects. *Journal of Psychiatry and Neuroscience, 29*, 20–29.

Steiger, H., Gauvin, L., Israel, M., Koerner, N., Kin, N., Paris, J., & Young, S.N. (2001). Association of serotonin and cortisol indices with childhood abuse in bulimia nervosa. *Archives of General Psychiatry, 58*, 837–843.

Steiger, H., Gauvin, L., Jabalpurwala, S., Seguin, J.R., & Stotland, S. (1999). Hypersensitivity to social interactions in bulimic syndromes: Relationship to binge eating. *Journal of Consulting & Clinical Psychology, 67*, 765–775.

Stein, D.J. (2000). Neurobiology of the obsessive–compulsive spectrum disorders. *Biological Psychiatry, 47*, 296–304.

Stein, L.I., & Santos, A.B. (1998). *Assertive Community Treatment of Persons with Severe Mental Illness.* New York: Norton.

Stein, M.B., Jang, K.L., Taylor, S., Vernon, P.A., & Livesley, W.J. (2002). Genetic and environmental influences on trauma exposure and posttraumatic stress disorder symptoms: A general population twin study. *American Journal of Psychiatry, 159*, 1675–1681.

Stein, M.., Torgrud, L.J., & Walker, J.R. (2000). Social phobia symptoms, subtypes, and severity: Findings from a community survey. *Archives of General Psychiatry, 57*, 1046–1052.

Steinhausen, H. (1996). The course and outcome of anorexia nervosa. In K.D. Brownell & C.G. Fairburn (Eds.), *Eating Disorders and Obesity: A Comprehensive Handbook* (pp. 234–237). New York: Guilford.

Steketee, G. (1993). Social support and treatment outcome of obsessive–compulsive disorder at 9-month follow-up. *Behavioral Psychotherapy, 21*, 81–95.

Steller, S. (2003). *Special study on mentally disordered accused in the criminal justice system.* Ottawa, ON: Statistics Canada.

Sterk, C.E. (1999). *Fast Lives: Women Who Use Crack Cocaine.* Philadelphia: Temple University Press.

Stermac, L., Blanchard, R., Clemmensen, L.H., & Dickey, R. (1991). Group therapy for gender-dysphoric heterosexual men. *Journal of Sex and Marital Therapy, 17*, 252–258.

Stern, Y., Gurland, B., Tatemichi, T.K., et al. (1994). Influence of education and occupation on the incidence of Alzheimer's disease. *Journal of the American Medical Association, 271*, 1004–1010.

Stern, Y., Tang, M., Albert, M.S., Brandt, J., Jacobs, D.M., Bell, K., Marder, K., Sano, M., Devanand, D., Albert, S.M., Bylsma, F., & Tsai, W. (1997). Predicting time to nursing home care and death in individuals with Alzheimer disease. *Journal of the American Medical Association, 277*, 806–812.

Stevens, S.E., Hynan, M.T., & Allen, M. (2000). A meta-analysis of common factors and specific treatment effects across the outcome domains of the phase model of psychotherapy. *Clinical Psychology: Science and Practice, 7*, 273–290.

Stevens, V.J., et al. (2001). Long-Term Weight Loss and Changes in Blood Pressure: Results of the Trials of Hypertension Prevention, Phase II. *Annals of Internal Medicine, 134*, 1–11.

Stewart, A.J., & Ostrove, J.M. (1998). Women's personality in middle age: Gender, history, and mid-course corrections. *American Psychologist, 53*, 1185–1194.

Stewart, J.T. (1995). Management of behavior problems in the demented patient. *American Family Physician, 52*, 231–240.

Stewart, S.E., Manion, I.G., & Davidson, S. (2002). Emergency management of the adolescent suicide attempter: A review of the literature. *Journal of Adolescent Health, 30*, 312–325.

Stewart, S.H. (1996). Alcohol abuse in individuals exposed to trauma: A critical review. *Psychological Bulletin, 120*, 83–112.

Stewart, S.H., Angelopoulos, M., Baker, J.M., & Boland, F.J. (2000). Relations between dietary restraint and patterns of alcohol use in young adult women. *Psychology of Addictive Behaviors, 14*, 77–82.

Stewart, S.H., Conrod, P.J., Gignac, M.L., & Pihl, R.O. (1998). Selective processing biases in anxiety-sensitive men and women. *Cognition and Emotion, 12*, 105–133.

Stewart, S.H., Taylor, S., Jang, K.L., Cox, B.J., Watt, M.C., Fedoroff, I.C., & Borger, S.C. (2001). Causal modeling of relations among learning history, anxiety sensitivity, and panic attacks. *Behaviour Research and Therapy, 39*, 443–456.

Stice, E. (2001). A prospective test of the dual-pathway model of bulimic pathology: Mediating effects of dieting and negative affect. *Journal of Abnormal Psychology, 110*, 124–135.

Stice, E., & Agras, W.S. (1999). Subtyping bulimic women along dietary restraint and negative affect dimensions. *Journal of Consulting & Clinical Psychology, 67*, 460–469.

Stice, E., Barrera, M., Jr., & Chassin, L. (1998). Prospective differential prediction of adolescent alcohol use and problem use: Examining the mechanisms of effect. *Journal of Abnormal Psychology, 107*, 616–628.

Stice, E., Schupak-Neuberg, E., Shaw, H.E., & Stein, R.I. (1994). Relation of media exposure to eating disorder symptomatology: An examination of mediating mechanisms. *Journal of Abnormal Psychology, 103*, 836–840.

Stice, E., Spangler, D., & Agras, W.S. (2001). Exposure to media-portrayed thin-ideal images adversely affects vulnerable girls: A longitudinal experiment. *Journal of Social & Clinical Psychology, 20*, 270–288.

Still, G.F. (1902). The Coulstonian Lectures on some abnormal physical conditions in children. *Lancet, 1*, 1008–1012, 1077–1082, 1163–1168.

Stokols, D. (1992). Establishing and maintaining healthy environments: Toward a social ecology of health promotion. *American Psychologist, 47*, 6–22.

Stoller, R.J. (1991). *Pain and Passion: A Psychoanalyst Explores the World of S & M.* New York: Plenum.

Stone, M.H. (1993). *Abnormalities of Personality: Within and Beyond the Realm of Treatment.* New York: Norton.

Stone, M.H. (2001). Natural history and long-term outcome. In W.J. Livesley (Ed.), *Handbook of Personality Disorders: Theory Research, and Treatment* (pp. 259–273). New York: Guilford.

Stoolmiller, M. (1999). Implications of the restricted range of family environments for estimates of heritability and nonshared environment in behavior-genetic adoptions studies. *Psychological Bulletin, 125*, 392–409.

Stoppe, G., Brandt, C.A., & Staedt, J.H. (1999). Behavioural problems associated with dementia: The role of newer antipsychotics. *Drugs and Aging, 14*, 41–54.

Stowe, R., & Taylor, S. (2001). Posttraumatic stress disorder. *Encyclopedia of life sciences*. London: Nature Publishing Group.

Stretch, R.H. (1991). Psychosocial adjustment of Canadian Vietnam veterans. *Journal of Consulting and Clinical Psychology, 59*, 188–189.

Stricker, G., & Gold, J.R. (1999). The Rorschach: Toward a nomothetically based, idiographically applicable configurational model. *Psychological Assessment, 11*, 240–250.

Striegel-Moore, R.H. (1995). A feminist perspective on the etiology of eating disorders. In K.D. Brownell & C.G. Fairburn (Eds.), *Eating Disorders and Obesity: A Comprehensive Handbook* (pp. 224–229). New York: Guilford.

Striegel-Moore, R.H., Silberstein, L.R., & Rodin, J. (1993). The social self in bulimia nervosa: Public self-consciousness, social anxiety, and perceived fraudulence. *Journal of Abnormal Psychology, 102*, 297–303.

Striegel-Moore, R.H., & Smolak, L. (2001). *Eating Disorders: Innovative Directions in Research and Practice*. Washington: American Psychological Association.

Strober, M. (1995). Family-genetic perspectives on anorexia nervosa and bulimia nervosa. In K.D. Brownell & C.G. Fairburn (Eds.), *Eating Disorders and Obesity: A Comprehensive Handbook* (pp. 212–218). New York: Guilford.

Strober, M., & Bulik, C.M. (2002). Genetic epidemiology of eating disorders. *Eating Disorders and Obesity*, (2nd ed.), 238–242. New York: Guilford.

Strunk, D.R., & DeRubeis, R.J. (2001). Cognitive therapy for depression: A review of its efficacy. *Journal of Cognitive Psychotherapy, 15*, 289–297.

Strupp, H.H. (1986). Psychotherapy: Research, practice, and public policy (how to avoid dead ends). *American Psychologist, 41*, 120–130.

Stuss, D.T. (2002). Adult clinical neuropsychology: Lessons from studies of the frontal lobes. *Annual Review of Psychology, 53*, 401–433.

Sullivan, E.V., Lane, B., Deshmukh, A., Rosenbloom, M.J., Desmond, J.E., Lim, K.O., & Pfefferbaum, A. (1999). In vivo mammillary body volume deficits in amnesic and nonamnesic alcoholics. *Alcoholism: Clinical and Experimental Research, 23*, 1629–1636.

Sullivan, K.T., & Bradbury, T.N. (1996). Preventing marital dysfunction: The primacy of secondary strategies. *The Behavior Therapist, 19*, 33–36.

Sullivan, P.F., Neale, M.C., & Kendler, K.S. (2000). Genetic epidemiology of major depression: Review and meta-analysis. *American Journal of Psychiatry, 157*, 1552–1562.

Suomi, S.J., & Harlow, H.F. (1972). Social rehabilitation of isolate-reared monkeys. *Developmental Psychology, 6*, 487–496.

Surgeon General (2001). *Mental Health: Culture, Race, and Ethnicity*. Washington: Department of Health and Human Services.

Susser, E., Varma, V.K., Mattoo, S.K., Finnerty, M., Mojtabi, R., Tripathi, B.M., Mistra, A.K., & Wig, N.N. (1998). Long-term course of acute brief psychosis in a developing country setting. *British Journal of Psychiatry, 173*, 226–230.

Sussman, N., & Ginsberg, D. (1998). Rethinking side effects of the selective serotonin reuptake inhibitors: Sexual dysfunction and weight gain. *Psychiatric Annals, 28*, 89–97.

Sussman, S. (1998). The first asylums in Canada: A response to neglectful community care and current trends. *Canadian Journal of Psychiatry, 43*, 260–264.

Sutandar-Pinnock, K., Woodside, D.B., Carter, J.C., Olmsted, M.P., & Kaplan, A.S. (2003). Perfectionism in anorexia nervosa: A 6- to 24-month follow-up. *International Journal of Eating Disorders, 33*, 225–229.

Swaab, D.F., & Gofman, M.A. (1995). Sexual differentiation of the human hypothalamus in relation to gender and sexual orientation. *Trends in Neurosciences, 18*, 264–270.

Swanson, J.M., et al. (2001). Clinical relevance of the primary findings of the MTA: Success rates based on severity of ADHD and ODD symptoms at the end of treatment. *Journal of the American Academy of Child and Adolescent Psychiatry, 40*, 168–179.

Swartz, M.S., Hughes, D., Blazer, D.G., & George, L.K. (1987). Somatization disorder in the community: A study of diagnostic concordance among three diagnostic systems. *Journal of Nervous and Mental Disorder, 175*, 26–33.

Swartz, M.S., Landerman, R., & Blazer, D. G. (1989). Somatization symptoms in the community: A rural/urban comparison. *Psychosomatics, 30*, 44–53.

Swartz, M.S., et al. (2001). Randomized controlled trial of outpatient commitment in North Carolina. *Psychiatric Services, 52*, 325–329.

Swendsen, J.D, & Merikangas, K.R. (2000). The comorbidity of depression and substance use disorders. *Clinical Psychology Review, 20*, 173–189.

Swinson, R.P., Antony, M.M., Rachman, S., & Richter, M.A. (1998). *Obsessive–compulsive disorder: Theory, research, and treatment*. New York: Guilford.

Swinson, R.P., Fergus, K.D., Cox, B.J., & Wickwire, K. (1995). Efficacy of telephone-administered behavioral therapy for panic disorder with agoraphobia. *Behaviour Research and Therapy, 33*, 465–469.

Szasz, T. (1960). *The Myth of Mental Illness*. New York: Harper & Row.

Szasz, T. (1963). *Law, Liberty, and Psychiatry: An Inquiry into the Social Uses of Mental Health Practices*. New York: Macmillan.

Szasz, T. (1970). *Ideology and Insanity: Essays on the Psychiatric Dehumanization of Man*. New York: Doubleday.

Tabakoff, B., & Hoffman, P.L. (1999). Neurobiology of alcohol. In M. Galanter & H.D. Kleber (Eds.), *Textbook of Substance Abuse Treatment* (2nd ed., pp. 3–10). Washington, DC: American Psychiatric Press.

Tager-Flusberg, H. (1996). Current theory and research on language and communication in autism. *Journal of Autism and Developmental Disorders, 26*, 169–171.

Tamminga, C.A. (1997). Gender and schizophrenia. *Journal of Clinical Psychiatry, 58* (suppl. 15), 33–37.

Tannock, R., Schachar, R., & Logan, G. (1995). Methylphenidate and cognitive flexibility: Dissociated dose effects in hyperactive children. *Journal of Abnormal Child Psychology, 23*, 235–266.

Tarrier, N., & Barrowclough, C. (1995). Family interventions in schizophrenia and their long-term outcomes. *International Journal of Mental Health, 24*, 38–53.

Taschentke, T.M. (2001). Pharmacology and behavioral pharmacology of the mesocortical dopamine system. *Progress in Neurobiology, 63*, 241–320.

Taylor, E., & Rutter, M. (2002). Classification: Conceptual issues and substantive findings. In M. Rutter & E. Taylor (Eds.), *Child and adoloscent Psychiatry* (4th ed., pp. 3–17), Oxford, UK: Blackwell.

Taylor, G.J., Bagby, R.M., Ryan, D.P., & Parker, J.D. (1990). Validation of the alexithymia construct: A measurement-based approach. *Canadian Journal of Psychiatry, 35*, 290–297.

Taylor, J., Iacono, W.G., & McGue, M. (2000). Evidence for a genetic etiology of early-onset delinquency. *Journal of Abnormal Psychology, 109*, 634–643.

Taylor, S. (1999). *Anxiety sensitivity*. Mahwah, NJ: Erlbaum.

Taylor, S. (2000). *Understanding and treating panic disorder: Cognitive-behavioural approaches*. New York: Wiley.

Taylor, S. (2003). Outcome predictors for three PTSD treatments: Exposure therapy, EMDR, and relaxation training. *Journal of Cognitive Psychotherapy, 17*, 149–161.

Taylor, S. (2004). *Advances in the treatment of posttraumatic stress disorder: Cognitive-behavioral perspectives*. New York: Springer.

Taylor, S., & Asmundson, G.J.G. (2004). *Treating Health Anxiety: A Cognitive-Behavioral Approach*. New York: Guilford.

Taylor, S., & Cox, B.J. (1998a). An expanded Anxiety Sensitivity Index: Evidence for a hierarchic structure in a clinical sample. *Journal of Anxiety Disorders, 12*, 463–484.

Taylor, S., & Cox, B.J. (1998b). Anxiety sensitivity: Multiple dimensions and hierarchic structure. *Behaviour Research and Therapy, 36*, 37–51.

Taylor, S., Fedoroff, I.C., Koch, W.J., Thordarson, D.S., Fecteau, G., & Nicki, R. (2001). Posttraumatic stress disorder arising after road traffic collisions: Patterns of response to cognitive-behaviour therapy. *Journal of Consulting and Clinical Psychology, 69*, 541–551.

Taylor, S., Koch, W.J., & McNally, R.J. (1992). How does anxiety sensitivity vary across the anxiety disorders? *Journal of Anxiety Disorders, 6*, 249–259.

Taylor, S., & Livesley, W.J. (1995). The influence of personality on the clinical course of neurosis. *Current Opinion in Psychiatry, 8*, 93–97.

Taylor, S., Thordarson, D. S., Maxfield, L., Fedoroff, I. C., Lovell, K., & Ogrodniczuk, J. (2003a). Comparative efficacy, speed, and adverse effects of three treatments for PTSD: Exposure therapy, EMDR, and relaxation training. *Journal of Consulting and Clinical Psychology, 71*, 330–338.

Taylor, S., Thordarson, D. S., Spring, T., Yeh, A., Corcoran, K., Eugster, K., & Tisshaw, C. (2003b). Telephone-administered cognitive-behaviour therapy for obsessive–compulsive disorder. *Cognitive Behaviour Therapy, 32*, 13–25.

Taylor, S., Woody, S., Koch, W.J., McLean, P., Paterson, R., & Anderson, K. (1997). Cognitive restructuring in the treatment of social phobia: Efficacy and mode of action. *Behavior Modification, 21*, 487–511.

Taylor, S.E. (1990). Health psychology: The science and the field. *American Psychologist, 45*, 40–50.

Taylor, S.E. (1995). *Health Psychology* (3rd ed.). New York: McGraw-Hill.

Taylor, S.E., Klein, L.C., Lewis, B.P., Gruenewald, T.L., Gurung, R.A.R., & Updegraff, J.A. (2000). Biobehavioral responses to stress in females: Tend-and-befriend, not fight-or-flight. *Psychological Bullettin, 107*, 411–429.

Telch, C.F., Agras, W.S., & Linehan, M.M. (2001). Dialectical behavior therapy for binge eating disorder. *Journal of Consulting and Clinical Psychology, 69*, 1061–1065.

Tellegen, A. (1985). Structures of mood and personality and their relevance to assessing anxiety, with an emphasis on self-report. In A.H. Tuma & J.D. Maser (Eds.), *Anxiety and the Anxiety Disorders* (pp. 681–706). Hillsdale, NJ: Erlbaum.

Temple, V., Jozsvai, E., Konstantareas, M.M., & Hewitt, T.-A. (2001). Alzheimer dementia in Down's syndrome: The relevance of cognitive ability. *Journal of Intellectual Disability Research, 45*, 47–55.

Teplin, L.A., Abram, K.M., & McClelland, G.M. (1994). Does psychiatric disorder predict violent crime among released jail detainees? A six-year longitudinal study. *American Psychologist, 49*, 335–342.

Teri, L., & Gallagher-Thompson, D. (1991). Cognitive-behavioral interventions for treatment of depression in Alzheimer's patients. *Gerontologist, 31*, 413–416.

Tesman, J.R., & Hills, A. (1994). Developmental effects of lead exposure in children. *Social Policy Report: Society for Research in Child Development*, 8, 1–16.

Thakker, J., & Ward, T. (1998). Culture and classification: The cross-cultural application of the DSM-IV. *Clinical Psychology Review*, 18, 501–529.

Thapar, A., Gottesman, I.I., Owen, M.J., O'Donovan, M.C., & McGuffin, P. (1994). The genetics of mental retardation. *British Journal of Psychiatry*, 164, 747–758.

Thase, M.E. (1989). Comparison between seasonal affective and other forms of recurrent depression. In N.E. Rosenthal et al. (Eds.), *Seasonal Affective Disorders and Phototherapy* (pp. 64–78). New York: Guilford.

Theberge, J., Bartha., R., Drost, D.J., Menon, R.S., Malla, A., Takhar, J., Neufeld, R.W., Rogers, J., Pavlosky, W., Schaefer, B., Densmore, M., Al-Semaan, Y., & Williamson, P. C. (2002). Glutamate and glutamine measured with 4.0 T proton MRS in never-treated patients with schizophrenia and healthy volunteers. *American Journal of Psychiatry*, 159, 1944–1946.

Thomas, A., & Chess, S. (1977). *Temperament and Development*. New York: Brunner/Mazel.

Thomas, C., Turkheimer, E., & Oltmanns, T.F. (2003). Factor structure of pathological personality traits as evaluated by peers. *Journal of Abnormal Psychology*, 112, 81–91.

Thomas, J., Turkheimer, E., & Oltmanns, T.F. (2000). Psychometric analysis of racial differences on the Maudsley Obsessional Compulsive Inventory. *Assessment*, 7, 247–258.

Thomas, K.M., Drevets, W.C., Dahl, R.E., Ryan, N.D., Birmaher, B., Eccard, C.H., Axelson, D., Whalen, P.J., & Casey, B.J. (2001). Amygdala response to fearful faces in anxious and depressed children. *Archives of General Psychiatry*, 58, 1057–1063.

Thomas, V.H., Melchert, T.P., & Banken, J.A. (1999). Substance dependence and personality disorders: Comorbidity and treatment outcome in an inpatient treatment population. *Journal of Studies on Alcohol*, 60, 271–277.

Thompson, J.K. (1996). *Body Image, Eating Disorders, and Obesity*. Washington, DC: American Psychological Association.

Thompson, J.K., & Stice, E. (2001). Thin-ideal internalization: Mounting evidence for a new risk factor for body-image disturbance and eating pathology. *Current Directions in Psychological Science*, 10, 181–183.

Thompson-Cooper, I., Fugère, R., & Cormier, B.M. (1993). The child abuse reporting laws: An ethical dilemma for professionals. *Canadian Journal of Psychiatry*, 38, 557–562.

Thoresen, C.E., & Powell, L.H. (1992). Type A behavior pattern: New perspectives on theory, assessment, and intervention. *Journal of Consulting and Clinical Psychology*, 60, 595–604.

Thornicroft, G., & Sartorius, N. (1993). The course and outcome of depression in different cultures: 10-year follow-up of the WHO Collaborative Study on the Assessment of Depressive Disorders. *Psychological Medicine*, 23, 1023–1032.

Thornicroft, G., & Susser, E. (2001). Evidence-based psychotherapeutic interventions in the community care of schizophrenia. *British Journal of Psychiatry*, 178, 2–4.

Tiefer, L. (1999). Challenging sexual naturalism, the shibboleth of sex research and popular sexology. In D. Bernstein (Ed.), *Gender and Motivation. Nebraska Symposium on Motivation* (Vol. 45, pp. 143–172). Lincoln, NE: University of Nebraska Press.

Tiefer, L. (2001). The "consensus" conference on female sexual dysfunction: Conflicts of interest and hidden agendas. *Journal of Sex and Marital Therapy*, 27, 227–236.

Tiefer, L., & Kring, B. (1995). Gender and the organization of sexual behavior. *Psychiatric Clinics of North America*, 18, 25–37.

Tison, F., Dartigues, J.F., Auriacombe, S., Letenneur, L., et al. (1995). Dementia in Parkinson's disease: A population-based study in ambulatory and institutionalized individuals. *Neurology*, 45, 705–708.

Tjepkema, M. (2002). The health of the off-reserve Aboriginal population. *Health Reports*, 13 (suppl.), 73–86.

Toffel, H. (1996). Crazy women, unarmed men, and evil children: Confronting the myths about battered people who kill their abusers, and the argument for extending battering syndrome self-defenses to all victims of domestic violence. *Southern California Law Review*, 70, 337–380.

Tombaugh, T.N. (2002). The Test of Memory Malingering (TOMM) in forensic psychology. *Journal of Forenic Neuropsychology*, 2, 69–96.

Tombaugh, T.N., Grandmaison, L.J., & Schmidt, J.P. (1995). Prospective memory: Relationship to age and retrospective memory in the learning and memory battery (LAMB). *Clinical Neuropsychologist*, 9, 135–142.

Tomkins, D.M., & Sellers, E.M. (2001). Addiction and the brain: The role of neurotransmitters in the cause and treatment of drug dependence. *Canadian Medical Association Journal*, 164, 817–821.

Tondo, L., Baldessarini, R.J., & Floris, G. (2001). Long-term clinical effectiveness of lithium maintenance treatment in types I and II bipolar disorders. *British Journal of Psychiatry*, 178 (suppl. 141), S184–S190.

Torgersen, S. (1986). Genetic factors in moderately severe and mild affective disorders. *Archives of General Psychiatry*, 43, 222–226.

Torgersen, S. (1994). Genetics in borderline conditions. *Acta Psychiatrica Scandinavica*, 89 (suppl. 379), 19–25.

Torgersen, S., Kringlen, E., & Cramer, V. (2001). The prevalence of personality disorders in a community sample. *Archives of General Psychiatry*, 58, 590–596.

Torrey, E.F. (1988). *Nowhere to Go: The Tragic Odyssey of the Homeless Mentally Ill*. New York: Harper & Row.

Torrey, E.F. (1997). *Out of the Shadows*. New York: Wiley.

Tough, S.C., Butt, J.C., & Sanders, G.L. (1994). Autoerotic asphyxial deaths: Analysis of nineteen fatalities in Alberta, 1978 to 1989. *Canadian Journal of Psychiatry*, 39, 157–160.

Tremblay, R.E., Pagani-Kurtz, L., Mâsse, L.C., Vitaro, F., & Pihl, R.O. (1995). A bimodal preventive intervention for disruptive kindergarten boys: Its impact through mid-adolescence. *Journal of Consulting and Clinical Psychology*, 63, 560–568.

Trials of the Hypertension Prevention Collaborative Research Group. (1992).The effects of nonpharmacologic interventions on blood pressure of persons with high normal levels: Results of the Trials of Hypertension Prevention, Phase I. *Journal of the American Medical Association*, 67, 1213–1220.

Triandis, H.C. (1994). Culture and social behavior. In W.J. Lonner & R.S. Malpass (Eds.), *Psychology and Culture* (pp. 169–174). Boston: Allyn & Bacon.

Trotter, M.A. & Endler, N.S. (1999). An empirical test of the interaction model of anxiety in a competitive equestrian setting. *Personality and Individual Differences*, 27, 861–875.

Truax, C., & Carkhuff, R. (1967). *Toward effective counseling and psychotherapy: Training and practice*. Hawthorne, NY: Aldine.

True, W.R., Rice, J., Eisen, S.A., Heath, A.C., Goldberg, J., Lyons, M.J., & Nowak, J. (1993). A twin study of genetic and environmental contributions to liability for posttraumatic stress symptoms. *Archives of General Psychiatry*, 50, 257–265.

Trull, T.J. (1995). Borderline personality disorder features in nonclinical young adults. 1. Identification and validation. *Psychological Assessment*, 7, 33–41.

Trull, T.J., & McCrae, R.R. (2002). A five-factor perspective on personality disorder research. In P.T. Costa, Jr., & T.A. Widiger (Eds.), *Personality Disorders and the Fivefactor Model of Personality* (2nd ed., pp. 45–58). Washington, DC: American Psychological Association.

Truscott, D., & Crook, K.H. (1993). *Tarasoff* in the Canadian context: *Wenden* and the duty to protect. *Canadian Journal of Psychiatry*, 38, 84–89.

Trzepacz, P.T. (1999). Update on the neuropathogenesis of delirium. *Dementia and Geriatric Cognitive Disorders*, 10, 330–334.

Tsai, J.L., Butcher, J.N., Munoz, R.F., & Vitousek, K. (2001). Culture, ethnicity, and psychopathology. In P.B. Sutker and H.E. Adams (Eds.), *Comprehensive Handbook of Psychopathology* (3rd ed., pp. 105–127). New York: Kluwer Academic/Plenum Publishers.

Tsai, L.Y. (1996). Comorbid psychiatric disorders of autistic disorder. *Journal of Autism and Developmental Disorders*, 26, 159–163.

Tsuang, M.T. (2000). Schizophrenia: Genes and environment. *Biological Psychiatry*, 47, 210–220.

Tsuang, M.T. (2001). Defining alternative phenotypes for genetic studies: What can we learn from studies of schizophrenia? *American Journal of Medical Genetics*, 105, 8–10.

Tsuang, M.T., & Faraone, S.V. (1999). The concept of target features in schizophrenia research. *Acta Psychiatrica Scandinavica*, 395 (suppl.), 2–11.

Tsuang, M.T., Simpson, J.C., & Fleming, J.A. (1992). Epidemiology of suicide. *International Review of Psychiatry*, 4, 117–129.

Tune, L. (2002). Treatments for dementia. In P.E. Nathan and J.M. Gorman (Eds.), *A Guide to Treatments that Work* (2nd ed., pp. 87–124). London: Oxford University Press

Tuokko, H., & Hadjistavropoulos, T. (1998). *An assessment guide to geriatric neuropsychology*. Mahwah, NJ: Erlbaum.

Tuokko, H., Hadjistavropoulos, T., Rae, S., & O'Rourke, N. (2000). A comparison of alternative approaches to the scoring of clock drawing. *Archives of Clinical Neuropsychology*, 15, 137–148.

Turkat, I.D., & Carlson, C.R. (1984). Data-based versus symptomatic formulation of treatment: The case of a dependent personality. *Journal of Behavior Therapy and Experimental Psychiatry*, 15, 153–160.

Turkheimer, E. (1991). Individual and group differences in adoption studies of IQ. *Psychological Bulletin*, 110, 392–405.

Turkheimer, E. (1998). Heritability and biological explanation. *Psychological Review*, 105, 782–791.

Turkheimer, E., & Waldron, M. (2000). Nonshared environment: A theoretical, methodological and quantitative review. *Psychological Bulletin*, 126, 78–108.

Turner, N.E., Annis, H.M., & Skar, S.M. (1997). Measurement of antecedents to drug and alcohol use: Psychometric properties of the Inventory of Drug-Taking Situations (IDST). *Behaviour Research and Therapy*, 35, 465–483.

Turner, R.J., & Wagonfield, M.O. (1967). Occupational mobility and schizophrenia: An assessment of the social causation and social selection hypotheses. *American Sociological Review*, 32, 104–113.

Turvey, C.L., Coryell, W.H., Solomon, D.A., Leon, A.C., Endicott, J., Keller, M.B., & Akiskal, H. (1999). Long-term prognosis of bipolar I disorder. *Acta Psychiatrica Scandinavica*, 99, 110–119.

Tymchuk, A., Andron, I., & Tymchuk, M. (1990). Training mothers with mental handicaps to understand behavioral and developmental principles. *Mental Handicap Research*, 3, 51–59.

Tyrer, P. (2001). The case for cothymia: Mixed anxiety and depression as a single diagnosis. *British Journal of Psychiatry, 179*, 191–193.

Uchino, B.N., Cacioppo, J.T., & Kiecolt-Glaser, J.K. (1996). The relationship between social support and physiological processes: A review with emphasis underlying mechanisms and implications for health. *Psychological Bullettin, 119*, 488–531.

Updegraff, J.A., & Taylor, S.E. (2000). From vulnerability to growth: Positive and negative effects of stressful life events. In J.H. Harvey and E.D. Miller (Eds.), *Loss and Trauma: General and Close Relationship Perspectives* (pp. 3–28). Philadelphia, PA: Brunner-Routledge.

U.S. Department of Justice, Bureau of Justice Statistics, (1999). *Special Report: Mental Health and Treatment of Inmates and Probationers*. Washington, DC: NCJ.

Uttal, W.R. (2001). *The New Phrenology: The Limits of Localizing Cognitive Processes in the Brain*. Cambridge, MA: MIT Press.

Vaillant, G.E. (1994). Evidence that the Type 1/Type 2 dichotomy in alcoholism must be re-examined. *Addiction, 89*, 1049–1057.

Vaillant, G.E. (1996). A long-term follow-up of male alcohol abuse. *Archives of General Psychiatry, 53*, 243–249.

Valenstein, E.S. (1973). *Brain Control*. New York: Wiley.

Valenstein, E.S. (1986). *Great and Desperate Cures*. New York: Basic Books.

Vallenstein, E.S. (1998). *Blaming the Brain*. New York: Free Press.

Valenzuela, C.F. (1997). Alcohol and neurotransmitter interactions. *Alcohol Health and Research World, 21*, 144–148.

Van Ameringen, M. (March, 2004). *Posttraumatic stress disorder in Canada: An epidemiological study*. Paper presented at the annual meeting of the Anxiety Disorders Association of America, Miami, FL.

van den Heuvel, O.A., van de Wetering, B.J.M. Veltman, D.J., & Pauls, D.L. (2000). *Journal of Clinical Psychiatry, 61*, 756–766.

Vandereycken, W. (2002.) Families of patients with eating disorders. In C.G. Fairburn & K.D. Brownell (Eds.), *Eating Disorders and Obesity*, (2nd ed., pp. 215–22). New York: Guilford.

van der Kolk, B.A., & McFarlane, A.C. (1996). The black hole of trauma. In B.A. van der Kolk, A.C. McFarlane, & L. Weisaeth (Eds.), *Traumatic Stress* (pp. 3–23). New York: Guilford.

van Emmerik, A.A.P., Kamphuis, J.H., Hulsbosch, A.M., & Emmelkamp, P.M.G. (2002). Single session debriefing after psychological trauma: A meta-analysis. *Lancet, 360*, 766–771.

van Etten, M., & Taylor, S. (1998). Comparative efficacy of treatments for posttraumatic stress disorder: A meta-analysis. *Clinical Psychology and Psychotherapy, 5*, 126–145.

Van Ommeren, M., de Jong, J., Sharma, B., Komproe, I., Thapa, S.B., & Cardena, E. (2001). Psychiatric disorders among tortured Bhutanese refugees in Nepal. *Archives of General Psychiatry*, 58, 475–482.

Vasey, M.W., & Borkovec, T.D. (1992). A catastrophizing assessment of worrisome thoughts. *Cognitive Therapy and Research, 16*, 505–520.

Vaughn, C.E., & Leff, J.P. (1976). The influence of family and social factors on the course of psychiatric illness: A comparison of schizophrenic and depressed neurotic patients. *British Journal of Psychiatry, 129*, 125–137.

Verma, K.K., Khaitan, B.K., & Singh, O.P. (1998). The frequency of sexual dysfunctions in patients attending a sex therapy clinic in North India. *Archives of Sexual Behavior, 27*, 309–314.

Vettese, L.C., & Mongrain, M. (2000). Communication about the self and partner in the relationships of dependents and self-critics. *Cognitive Therapy and Research, 24*, 609–626.

Vine, C., & Challen, P. (2002). *Gardens of shame: The tragedy of Martin Kruze and the sexual abuse at Maple Leaf Gardens*. Vancouver, BC: Greystone Books.

Visintainer, M.A., Seligman, M.E.P., & Volpicelli, J.R. (1982). Tumor rejection in rats after inescapable or escapable electric shock. *Science, 216*, 437–439.

Vitousek, K.B. (2002). Cognitive-behavioral therapy for anorexia nervosa. In C.G. Fairburn & K.D. Brownell (Eds.), *Eating Disorders and Obesity*, (2nd ed., pp. 308–313). New York: Guilford.

Vohs, K.D., Bardone, A.M., Joiner, T.E., & Abramson, L.Y. (1999). Perfectionism, perceived weight status, and self-esteem interact to predict bulimic symptoms: A model of bulimic symptom development. *Journal of Abnormal Psychology, 108*, 695–700.

Volavka, J., Czobor, P., Sheitman, B., Lindenmayer, J., Citrome, L., McEvoy, J.P., Cooper, T.B., Chakos, M., & Lieberman, J.A. (2002). Clozapine, olanzapine, risperidone, and haloperidol in the treatment of patients with chronic schizophrenia and schizoaffective disorder. *American Journal of Psychiatry, 159*, 255–262.

Volicer, L., McKee, A., & Hewitt, S. (2001). Dementia. *Neurologic Clinics, 19*, 867–885.

Volkmar, F., & Dykens, E. (2002). Mental retardation. In M. Rutter & E. Taylor (Eds.), *Child and Adolescent Psychiatry* (4th ed., pp. 697–710). Oxford: Blackwell.

Volkmar, F.R., Klin, A., Siegel, B., et al. (1994). Field trial for autistic disorder in DSM-IV. *American Journal of Psychiatry, 151*, 1361–1367.

von Bertalanffy, L. (1968). *General Systems Theory*. New York: Braziller.

von Ranson, K.M., Iacono, W.G., & McGue, M. (2002). Disordered eating and substance use in an epidemiological sample: I. Associations within individuals. *International Journal of Eating Disorders, 31*, 389–403.

von Ranson, K.M., McGue, M., & Iacono, W.G. (2003). Disordered eating and substance use in an epidemiological sample: II. Associations within families. *Psychology of Addictive Behaviors, 17*, 193–202.

Waddell, C., Lipman, E., & Offord, D. (1999). Conduct disorder: Practice parameters for assessment, treatment, and prevention. *Canadian Journal of Psychiatry, 44* (suppl. 2), 35S–40S.

Waddell, C., Offord, D. R., Shepherd, C.A., Hua, J.M., & McEwan, K. (2002). Child psychiatric epidemiology and Canadian public policy-making: The state of the science and the art of the possible. *Canadian Journal of Psychiatry, 47*, 825–832.

Waddell, C., & Shepherd, C. (2002). *Prevalence of mental disorders in children and youth. A research update prepared for the British Columbia Ministry of Children and Family Development: October 2002*. Vancouver: The University of British Columbia.

Wagner, W., Zaborny, B.A., & Gray, T.E. (1994). Fluvoxamine: A review of its safety profile in world-wide studies. *International Clinical Psychopharmacology, 9*, 223–227.

Waite, L.J., & Gallagher, M. (2000). *The Case for Marriage*. New York: Doubleday.

Wakefield, J.C. (1992a). Disorder as harmful dysfunction: A conceptual critique of DSM-III-R's definition of mental disorder. *Psychological Review, 99*, 232–247.

Wakefield, J.C. (1992b). The concept of mental disorder: On the boundary between biological facts and social values. *American Psychologist, 47*, 373–388.

Wakefield, J.C. (1999). The measurement of mental disorder. In A.V. Horwitz & T.L. Scheid (Eds.), *A Handbook for the Study of Mental Health: Social Contexts, Theories, and Systems* (pp. 29–57). Cambridge, UK, Cambridge University Press.

Wald, J., & Taylor, S. (2000). Efficacy of virtual reality exposure therapy to treat driving phobia: A case report. *Journal of Behavior Therapy and Experimental Psychiatry, 3–4*, 249–257.

Wald, J., & Taylor, S. (2003). Preliminary research on the efficacy of virtual reality exposure therapy to treat driving phobia. *Cyberpsychology and Behavior, 6*, 459–465.

Wald, M.S., Carlsmith, J.M., & Leiderman, P.H. (1988). *Protecting Abused and Neglected Children*. Stanford, CA: Stanford University Press.

Walden, J., Normann, C., Langosch, J., Berger, M., & Grunze, H. (1998). Differential treatment of bipolar disorder with old and new antiepileptic drugs. *Neuropsychobiology, 38*, 181–184.

Walker, E., Davis, D., & Baum, K. (1993). Social withdrawal. In C.G. Costello (Ed.), *Symptoms of Schizophrenia* (pp. 227–260). New York: Wiley.

Walker, E.F., & Diforio, D. (1997). Schizophrenia: A neural diathesis–stress model. *Psychological Review, 104*, 667–685.

Walker, L. (1979). *The Battered Woman*. New York: Harper & Row.

Walker, L. (1989). Psychology and violence against women. *American Psychologist, 44*, 695–702.

Wall, T.L., & Ehlers, C.L. (1995). Genetic influences affecting alcohol use among Asians. *Alcohol Health and Research World, 19*, 184–189.

Wallace, J. (1999). The twelve-step recovery approach. In P.J. Ott, R.E. Tarter, & R.T. Ammerman (Eds.), *Sourcebook on Substance Abuse: Etiology, Epidemiology, Assessment, and Treatment* (pp. 293–302). Boston: Allyn & Bacon.

Waller, N.G., & Ross, C.A. (1997). The prevalence and biometric structure of pathological dissociation in the general population: Taxometric and behavior genetic findings. *Journal of Abnormal Psychology, 106*, 499–510.

Wallis, C.J., Rezazadeh, S.M., & Lal, H. (1993). Role of serotonin in ethanol abuse. *Drug Development and Research, 30*, 178–188.

Walsh, B.T. (1995). Pharmacotherapy of eating disorders. In K.D. Brownell & C.G. Fairburn (Eds.), *Eating Disorders and Obesity: A Comprehensive Handbook* (pp. 313–317). New York: Guilford.

Walsh, T., Wilson, G.T., Loeb, K.L., et al. (1997). Medication and psychotherapy in the treatment of bulimia nervosa. *American Journal of Psychiatry, 154*, 523–531.

Walters, G.D. (1998). The alcohol expectancy process: Origins, structure, and change. *Alcoholism Treatment Quarterly, 16*, 25–38.

Walters, G.D. (1999). *The Addiction Concept: Working Hypothesis or Self-Fulfilling Prophesy?* Boston: Allyn & Bacon.

Walters, V.L., Tognolini, R.Z., Rueda, H.M., Rueda, R.M., & Torres, R.G. (1997). New strategies for old problems: Tardive dyskinesia. *Schizophrenia Research, 28*, 231–246.

Wang, C.T., & Harding, K. (1999). *Current trends in child abuse reporting and fatalities: The results of the 1998 Annual Fifty Sate Survey*. Chicago: National Center on Child Abuse Prevention Research.

Warren, S.T., & Ashley, C.T. (1995). Triplet repeat expansion mutations: The example of fragile X syndrome. *Annual Review of Neuroscience, 18*, 77–99.

Waterhouse, L., Fein, D., & Modahl, C. (1996). Neurofunctional mechanisms in autism. *Psychological Review, 103*, 457–489.

Waterman, A.S., & Archer, S. (1990). A life-span perspective on identity formation: Development in form, function, and process. In P.B. Baltes, D.L. Featherman, & R.M. Lerner (Eds.), *Life-Span Development and Behavior* (Vol. 10, pp. 29–57). Hillsdale, NJ: Erlbaum.

Waterman, A.S., & Goldman, J.A. (1976). A longitudinal study of changes in ego identity development at a liberal arts college. *Journal of Youth and Adolescence, 5*, 361–369.

Waterman, G., Geary, P., & Waterman, C. (1974). Longitudinal study of changes in ego identity status from the freshman to the senior year at college. *Developmental Psychology, 10*, 387–392.

Waters, E., Hay, D., & Richters, J. (1986). Infant–parent attachment and the origins of prosocial and antisocial behavior. In D. Olweus, J. Block, & M. Radke-Yarrow (Eds.), *Development of Antisocial and Prosocial Behavior: Research, Theories, and Issues* (pp. 97–126). Orlando, FL: Academic Press.

Waterworth, D.M., Bassett, A.S., & Brzustowicz, L.M. (2002). Recent advances in the genetics of schizophrenia. *Cellular and Molecular Life Sciences, 59*, 331–348.

Watkins, J.G. (1984). The Bianchi (L.A. Hillsdale Strangler) case: Sociopath or multiple personality. *International Journal of Clinical and Experimental Hypnosis, 32*, 67–101.

Watson, D., & Clark, L.A. (1990). *The Positive and Negative Affect Schedule—Expanded Form.* Unpublished manuscript. Southern Methodist University.

Watson, D., Clark, L.A., Weber, K., Assenheimer, J.S., Strauss, M.E., & McCormick, R.A. (1995). Testing a tripartite model. II. Exploring the symptom structure of anxiety and depression in student, adult, and patient samples. *Journal of Abnormal Psychology, 104*, 15–25.

Watson, D.C., & Sinha, B.K. (1999). A cross-cultural comparison of the Brief Symptom Inventory. *International Journal of Stress Management, 6*, 255–264.

Watt, L.M., & Wong, P.T.P. (1991). A taxonomy of reminiscence and therapeutic implications. *Journal of Gerontological Social Work, 16*, 37–57.

Watt, M.C., & Stewart, S.H. (2000). Anxiety sensitivity mediates the relationships between childhood learning experiences and elevated hypochondriacal concerns in young adulthood. *Journal of Psychosomatic Research, 49*, 107–118.

Watt, M.C., & Stewart, S.H. (2003). The role of anxiety sensitivity components in mediating the relationship between childhood exposure to parental dyscontrol and adult anxiety symptoms. *Journal of Psychopathology and Behavioral Assessment, 25*, 167–176.

Wearden, A.J., Tarrier, N., Barrowclough, C., Zastowny, T.R., & Rahill, A.A. (2000). A review of expressed emotion research in health care. *Clinical Psychology Review, 20*, 633–666.

Weaver, T.L., & Clum, G.A. (1993). Early family environments and traumatic experiences associated with borderline personality disorders. *Journal of Consulting and Clinical Psychology, 61*, 1068–1075.

Webster, C.D., Douglas, K.S., Eaves, D., & Hart, S.D. (1997). Assessing risk of violence to others. In C.D. Webster & M.A. Jackson (Eds.), *Impulsivity: Theory, assessment, and treatment* (pp. 251–276). New York: Guilford.

Webster, C.D., Harris, G.T., Rice, M.E., Cormier, C., & Quinsey, V.L. (1994). *The violence prediction scheme: Assessing dangerousness in high risk men.* Toronto: University of Toronto Centre of Criminology.

Webster-Stratton, C. (1994). Advancing videotape parent training: A comparison study. *Journal of Consulting and Clinical Psychology, 62*, 583–593.

Wechsler, H., Davenport, A., & Dowdall, G. (1994). Health and behavioral consequences of binge drinking in college: A national survey of students at 140 campuses. *Journal of the American Medical Association, 272*, 1672–1677.

Weekes, J.R., Morison, S.J., Millson, W.A., & Fettig, D.M. (1995). A comparison of Native, Metis, and Caucasin offender profiles on the MCMI. *Canadian Journal of Behavioural Science, 27*, 187–198.

Wegner, D.M. (1994). Ironic processes of mental control. *Psychological Review, 101*, 34–52.

Wehr, T.A. (1989). Seasonal affective disorder: A historical overview. In N.E. Rosenthal, & M.C. Blehar. (Eds.), *Seasonal Affective Disorders and Phototherapy* (pp. 11–32). New York: Guilford.

Weiden, P.J., & Olfson, M. (1995). Cost of relapse in schizophrenia. *Schizophrenia Bulletin, 21*, 419–429.

Weinberger, D.R., & McClure, R.K. (2002). Neurotoxicity, neuroplasticity, and magnetic resonance imaging morphometry: What is happening in the schizophrenic brain? *Archives of General Psychiatry, 59*, 553–558.

Weiner, H., & Fawzy, F.I. (1989). An integrative model of health, disease, and illness. In S. Cheren (Ed.), *Psychosomatic Medicine: Theory, Physiology, and Practice* (Vol. 1, pp. 9–44). Madison, CT: International Universities Press.

Weiner, I.B. (2000). Using the Rorschach properly in practice and research. *Journal of Clinical Psychology, 56*, 435–438.

Weiner, R.D., & Krystal, A.D. (1994). The present use of electroconvulsive therapy. *Annual Review of Medicine, 45*, 273–281.

Weinstein, H.M. (1990). *Psychiatry and the CIA: Victims of Mind Control.* Washington, DC: American Psychiatric Press.

Weishaar, M.E., & Beck A.T. (1992). Hopelessness and suicide. *International Review of Psychiatry, 4*, 177–184.

Weiss, G., & Hechtman, L. (1993). *Hyperactive children grown up: ADHD in children, adolescents, and adults* (2nd ed.). New York: Guilford.

Weiss, J.M., Cierpial, M.A., & West, C.H.K. (1998). Selective breeding of rats for high and low motor activity in a swim test: Toward a new animal model of depression. *Pharmacology Biochemistry and Behavior, 61*, 49–66.

Weissman, M.M. (1993). The epidemiology of personality disorders: A 1990 update. *Journal of Personality Disorders*, (suppl.), 44–62.

Weissman, M.M., Bland, R.C., Canino, G.J., Faravelli, C., Greenwald, S., Hwu, H.-G., Joyce, P.R., Karam, E.G., Lee, C.-K., Lellouch, J., Lépine, J.-P., Newman, S.C., Oakley-Browne, M.A., Rubio-Stipec, M., Wells, J.E., Wickramaratne, P.J., Wittchen, H.-U., & Yeh, E.-K. (1997). The cross-national epidemiology of panic disorder. *Archives of General Psychiatry, 54*, 305–309.

Weissman, M.M., Bland, R.C., Canino, G.J., Faravelli, C., Greenwald, S., Hwu, H.-G., Joyce, P.R., Karam, E.., Lee, C.-K., Lellouch, J., Lépine, J.-P., Newman, S. C., Rubio-Stipec, M., Wells, J.E., Wickramaratne, P.J., Wittchen, H.-U., & Yeh, E.-K. (1996a). Cross-national epidemiology of major depression and bipolar disorder. *Journal of the American Medical Association, 276*, 293–299.

Weissman, M.M., Bland, R.C., Canino, G.J., Greenwald, S., Hwu, H.-G., Lee, C.K., Newman, S.C., Oakley-Browne, M.A., Rubio-Stipec, M., Wickramaratne, P.J., Wittchen, H.-U., & Yeh, E.-K. (1994). The cross-national epidemiology of obsessive–compulsive disorder. *Journal of Clinical Psychiatry, 55* (suppl. 3), 5–10.

Weissman, M.M., Bland, R.C., Canino, G.J., Greenwald, S., Hwu, H.-G., Lee, C.K., Newman, S.C., Rubio-Stipec, M., & Wickramaratne, P.J. (1996b). The cross-national epidemiology of social phobia: A preliminary report. *International Clinical Psychopharmacology, 11* (suppl. 3), 9–14.

Weissman, M.M., Bruce, M.L., Leaf, P.J., Florio, L.P., & Holzer, C. (1991). Affective disorders. In L.N. Robins & D.A. Regier (Eds.), *Psychiatric Disorders in America: The Epidemiologic Catchment Area Study* (pp. 53–80). New York: Free Press.

Weissman, M.M., Markowitz, J.C., & Klerman, G.L. (2000). *Comprehensive Guide to Interpersonal Psychotherapy.* New York: Basic Books.

Weithorn, L.A. (1988). Mental hospitalization of troublesome youth: An analysis of skyrocketing admission rates. *Stanford Law Review, 40*, 773–838.

Werner, J.S., & Smith, R.S. (1982). *Vulnerable But Invincible: A Longitudinal Study of Resilient Children and Youth.* New York: McGraw-Hill.

Wesson, V.A., & Levitt, A.J. (1998). Light therapy for seasonal affective disorder.In R.W. Lam (Ed.), *Seasonal Affective Disorder and Beyond: Light Treatment for SAD and Non-SAD Conditions* (pp. 45–89). Washington, DC: American Psychiatric Press.

Westen, D. (1998). The scientific legacy of Sigmund Freud: Toward at psychodynamically informed psychological science. *Psychological Bulletin, 124*, 333–371.

Westen, D., & Arkowitz-Westen, L. (1998). Limitations of Axis II in diagnosing personality pathology in clinical practice. *American Journal of Psychiatry, 155*, 1767–1771.

Westen, D., & Morrison, K. (2001). A multidimensional meta-analysis of treatments for depression, panic, and generalized anxiety disorder: An empirical examination of the status of empirically supported therapies. *Journal of Consulting and Clinical Psychology, 69*, 875–899

Westergaard, T., Mortensen, P.B., Pedersen, C.B., Wohlfahrt, J., & Melbye, M. (1999). Exposure to prenatal and childhood infections and the risk of schizophrenia. *Archives of General Psychiatry, 56*, 993–998.

Westermeyer, J. (1999). Cross-cultural aspects of substance abuse. In M. Galanter & H.D. Kleber (Eds.), *Textbook of Substance Abuse Treatment* (2nd ed., pp. 75–88). Washington, DC: American Psychiatric Press.

Westling, B.E., & Öst, L. (1993). Relationship between panic attack symptoms and cognitions in panic disorder patients. *Journal of Anxiety Disorders, 7*, 181–194.

Westra, H.A., & Stewart, S.H. (1998). Cognitive behavioural therapy and pharmacotherapy: Complementary or contradictory approaches to the treatment of anxiety? *Clinical Psychology Review, 18*, 307–310.

Westra, H.A., Stewart, S.H., & Conrad, B.E. (2002). Naturalistic manner of benzodiazepine use and cognitive behavioral therapy outcome in panic disorder with agoraphobia. *Journal of Anxiety Disorders, 16*, 233–246.

Whalen, C., Henker, B., Hinshaw, S., Heller, T., & Huber-Dressler, A. (1991). Messages of medication: Effects of actual versus informed medication status on hyperactive boys's expectancies and self-evaluation. *Journal of Consulting and Clinical Psychology, 59*, 602–606.

Whisman, M.A., Sheldon, C.T., & Goering, P. (2000). Psychiatric disorders and dissatisfaction with social relationships: Does type of relationship matter? *Journal of Abnormal Psychology, 109*, 803–808.

Whittemore, K.E., Ogloff, J.R.P., & Roesch, R. (1997). An investigation of competency to participate in legal proceedings in Canada. *Canadian Journal of Psychiatry, 42*, 869–875.

Whybrow, P.C. (1997). *A Mood Apart: The Thinker's Guide to Emotion and its Disorders.* New York: HarperCollins.

Wicks-Nelson, R., & Israel, A.C. (2000). *Behavior Disorders of Childhood* (4th ed). Upper Saddle River, NJ: Prentice Hall.

Widiger, T.A. (1998). Sex biases in the diagnosis of personality disorders. *Journal of Personality Disorders, 12*, 95–118.

Widiger, T.A. (2001). Social anxiety, social phobia, and avoidant personality. In W.R. Crozier and L.E. Alden (Eds.), *International Handbook of Social Anxiety; Concepts, Research, and Interventions Relating to the Self and Shyness* (pp. 336–356), New York: Wiley.

Widiger, T.A., Cadoret, R., Hare, R., Robins, L., et al. (1996). DSM-IV antisocial personality disorder field trial. *Journal of Abnormal Psychology, 105*, 3–16.

Widiger, T.A., & Clark, L.A. (2000). Toward DSM-V and the classification of psychopathology. *Psychological Bulletin, 126*, 946–963.

Widiger, T.A., Costa, P.T., Jr., & McCrae, R.M. (2002a). A proposal for Axis II: Diagnosing personality disorders using the five-factor model. In P.T. Costa, Jr., & T.A, Widiger (Eds.), *Personality Disorders and the Five-Factor Model of Personality* (2nd ed., pp. 431–456). Washington, DC: American Psychological Association.

Widiger, T.A., Trull, T.J., Clarkin, J.F., Sanderson, C., & Costa, P.T., Jr. (2002b). A description of the DSM-IV personality disorders with the five-factor model of personality. In P.T. Costa, Jr., & T.A. Widiger (Eds.), *Personality Disorders and the Five-Factor Model of Personality* (2nd ed., pp. 89–102). Washington, DC: American Psychological Association.

Widiger, T.A., & Trull, T.J. (1993). Borderline and narcissistic personality disorders. In P.B. Sutker & H.E. Adams (Eds.), *Comprehensive Handbook of Psychopathology* (2nd ed., pp. 371–394). New York: Plenum.

Wiebe, J.M.D., & Cox, B.J. (2001). A profile of Canadian adults seeking treatment for gambling problems and comparisons with adults entering an alcohol treatment program. *Canadian Journal of Psychiatry, 46*, 418–421.

Wiederman, M.W. (1997). Pretending orgasm during sexual intercourse: Correlates in a sample of young adult women. *Journal of Sex and Marital Therapy, 23*, 131–139.

Wiegel, M., Wlncze, J.P., & Barlow, D.H. (2002). Sexual dysfunction. In M.M. Antony and D.H. Barlow (Eds.), *Handbook of Assessment and Treatment Planning for Psychological Disorders* (pp. 481–522). New York: Guilford.

Wiehe, V.R., & Richards, A.L. (1995). *Intimate Betrayal: Understanding and Responding to the Trauma of Acquaintance Rape*. Thousand Oaks, CA: Sage.

Wierzbicki, M. (1993). *Issues in Clinical Psychology: Subjective Versus Objective Approaches*. Boston: Allyn & Bacon.

Wildes, J.E., Emery, R.E., & Simons, A.D. (2001). The roles of ethnicity and culture in the development of eating disturbance and body dissatisfaction: A meta-analytic review *Clinical Psychology Review, 21*, 521–551.

Wileman, S.M., Eagles, J.M., Andrew, J.E., Howie, F.L., Cameron, I.M., McCormack, K., & Naji, S.A. (2001). Light therapy for seasonal affective disorder in primary care: Randomised controlled trial. *British Journal of Psychiatry, 178*, 311–316.

Wilkins, K., & Beaudet, M.P. (1998). Work stress and health. *Health Reports, 10*, 47–62.

Williams, L.M. (1994). Recall of childhood trauma: A prospective study of women's memories of child sexual abuse. *Journal of Consulting and Clinical Psychology, 62*, 1167–1176.

Williams, L.M., & Finkelhor, D. (1990). The characteristics of incestuous fathers: A review of recent studies. In W.L. Marshall, D.R. Laws, & H.E. Barbaree (Eds.), *Handbook of Sexual Assault: Issues, Theories, and Treatment of the Offender* (pp. 231–255). New York: Plenum.

Williams, N., & Leiblum, S.L. (2002). Sexual dysfunction. In G.M. Wlngood and R.J. DiClemente (Eds.), *Handbook of women's sexual and reproductive health* (pp. 303–328). New York: Kluwer Academic.

Williams, R.B., Barefoot, J.C., Califf, R.M., Haney, T.L., Saunders, W.B., et al. (1992). Prognostic importance of social and economic resources among medically treated patients with angiographically documented coronary artery disease. *Journal of the American Medical Association, 267*, 520–524.

Williams, S. (1996). *Invisible darkness: The horrifying case of Paul Bernado and Karla Homolka*. Toronto: McArthur & Co.

Williams, S. (2003). *Karla: A pact with the devil*. Toronto: Cantos.

Wilson, G.T., Loeb, K.L., Walsh, B.T., Labouvie, E., Petkova, E., Liu, X., & Waternaux, C. (1999). Psychological versus pharmacological treatments of bulimia nervosa: Predictors and processes of change. *Journal of Consulting & Clinical Psychology, 67*, 451–459.

Wilson, P. (2000). Keeping pain at a distance. *Hamilton Spectator*, May 16.

Wincze, J.P. (1989). Assessment and treatment of atypical sexual behavior. In S.R. Lieblum & R.C. Rosen (Eds.), *Principles and Practice of Sex Therapy* (2nd ed., pp. 382–404). New York: Guilford.

Wing, L. (1988). Autism: Possible clues to the underlying pathology. 1. Clinical facts. In L.Wing (Ed.), *Aspects of Autism: Biological Research* (pp.11–18). London: Gaskell.

Winograd, E., & Killinger, W.A. (1983). Relating age at encoding in early childhood to adult recall: Development of flashbulb memories. *Journal of Experimental Psychology: General, 112*, 413–422.

Winokur, G., Coryell, W., Keller, M., Endicott, J., & Leon, A. (1995). A family study of manic-depressive (bipolar I) disease. *Archives of General Psychiatry, 52*, 367–373.

Winslow, B.W., & Carter, P. (1999). Patterns of burden in wives who care for husbands with dementia. *Nursing Clinics of North America, 34*, 275–287.

Winter, D.G., John, O.P., Stewart, A.J., Klohnen, E.C., & Duncan, L.E. (1998). Traits and motives: Toward an integration of two traditions in personality research. *Psychological Review, 105*, 230–250.

Winters, K.C., Latimer, W., & Stinchfield, R.D. (1999). The DSM-IV criteria for adolescent alcohol and cannabis use disorders. *Journal of Studies on Alcohol, 60*, 337–344.

Wiseman, C.V., Gray, J.J., Mosimann, J.E., & Ahrens, A.H. (1992). Cultural expectations of thinness in women: An update. *International Journal of Eating Disorders, 11*, 85–89.

Wittchen, H., Holsboer, F., & Jacobi, F. (2001). Met and unmet needs in the management of depressive disorder in the community and primary care: The size and breadth of the problem. *Journal of Clinical Psychiatry, 62* (suppl. 26), 23–28.

Wittchen, H., & Hoyer, J. (2001). Generalized anxiety disorder: Nature and course. *Journal of Clinical Psychiatry, 62* (suppl. 11), 15–19.

Wittchen, H., Knauper, B., & Kessler, R.C. (1994). Lifetime risk of depression. *British Journal of Psychiatry, 165* (suppl. 26), 16–22.

Wittchen, H., Schuster, P., & Lieb, R. (2001). Comorbidity and mixed anxiety-depressive disorder: Clinical curiosity or pathophysiological need? *Human Psychopharmacology, 16* (suppl. 1), S21–S30.

Witvliet, C., Ludwig, T.W., & Vander Laan, K.L. (2001). Granting forgiveness or harboring grduges: Implications for emotion, physiology, and health. *Psychological Science, 12*, 117–124.

Wolfe, D. (1987). *Child Abuse: Implications for Child Development and Psychopathology*. Beverly Hills, CA: Sage.

Wolff, M., Alsobrook, J.P., & Pauls, D.L. (2000). Genetic aspects of obsessive–compulsive disorder. *Psychiatric Clinics of North America, 23*, 535–544.

Wolpe, J. (1958). *Psychotherapy and Reciprocal Inhibition*. Stanford, CA: Stanford University Press.

Wolpe, J. (1990). *The practice of behavior therapy* (4th ed.). New York: Pergamon.

Wong, P.T., & Watt, L.M. (1991). What types of reminiscence are associated with successful aging? *Psychology and Aging, 6*, 272–279.

Wood, J.M., Lilienfeld, S.O., Garb, H.N., & Nezworski, M.T. (2000). "The Rorschach test in clinical diagnosis": A critical review, with a backward look at Garfield (1947). *Journal of Clinical Psychology, 56*, 395–430.

Wood, J.M., Lilienfeld, S.O., Nezworski, M.T., & Garb, H.N. (2001). Coming to grips with negative evidence for the comprehensive system for the Rorschach. *Journal of Personality Assessment, 77*, 48–70.

Wood, J.M., Nezworski, M.T., & Stejskal, W.J. (1996). The comprehensive system for the Rorschach: A critical examination. *Psychological Science, 7*, 3–17.

Woodard, J.L., Auchus, A.P., Godsall, R.E., & Green, R.C. (1998). An analysis of test bias and differential item functioning due to race on the Mattis Dementia Rating Scale. *Journals of Gerontology. Ser. B, Psychological Sciences and Social Sciences, 53*, 370–374.

Woodill, G. (1992). Controlling the sexuality of developmentally disabled persons: Historical perspectives. *Journal of Developmental Disabilities, 1*, 1–14.

Woodside, D.B., Garfinkel, P.E., Lin, E., Goering, P., & Kaplan, A.S. (2001). Comparisons of men with full or partial eating disorders, men without eating disorders, and women with eating disorders in the community. *American Journal of Psychiatry, 158*, 570–574.

Woodside, D.B., & Kennedy, S.H. (1995). Gender differences in eating disorders. In M.V. Seeman (Ed.), *Gender and psychopathology* (pp. 253–268). Washington, DC: American Psychiatric Press.

Woodworth, M., & Porter, S. (2002). In cold blood: Characteristics of criminal homicides as a function of psychopathy. *Journal of Abnormal Psychology, 111*, 436–445.

Woody, E., & Sadler, P. (1998). On reintegrating dissociated theories: Comment on Kirsch and Lynn (1998). *Psychological Bulletin, 123*, 192–197.

Woody, S.R. (1996). Effects of focus of attention on anxiety levels and social performance of individuals with social phobia. *Journal of Abnormal Psychology, 105*, 61–69.

Worden, J.W. (1986). *Grief Counseling and Grief Therapy: A Handbook for the Mental Health Practitioner*. New York: Springer.

Working Group for the Canadian Psychiatric Association and Canadian Alliance for Research on Schizophrenia (1998). Canadian clinical practice guidelines for the treatment of schizophrenia. *Canadian Journal of Psychiatry, 43* (suppl. 2), 25S–39S.

Wortman, C.B., & Silver, R.C. (2001). The myths of coping with loss revisited. In M.S. Stroebe et al. (Eds.), *Handbook of Bereavement Research* (pp. 405–429). Washington, DC: American Psychological Association.

Wright, K.D., & Asmundson, G.J.G. (2003). Health anxiety in children: Development and psychometric properties of the childhood Illness Attitude Scales. *Cognitive Behaviour Therapy, 32*, 194–202.

Wynne, L.C., & Singer, M.T. (1963). Thought disorder and family relations of schizophrenics. II. A classification of forms of thinking. *Archives of General Psychiatry, 9*, 199–206.

Yalom, I.D. (1985). *Theory and practice of group psychotherapy* (3rd ed.). New York: Basic Books.

Yamashita, I., Koyama, T., & Ohmori, T. (1995). Ethnic differences in alcohol metabolism and physiological responses to alcohol: Implications in alcohol abuse. In B. Tabakoff & P.L. Hoffman (Eds.), *Biological Aspects of Alcoholism* (pp. 49–61). Seattle, WA: Hogrefe & Huber.

Yang, B., Stack. S., & Lester, D. (1992). Suicide and unemployment: Predicting the smoothed trend and yearly fluctuations. *Journal of Socio-Economics, 21*, 39–41.

Yang, J., McCrae, R.R., Costa, P.T., Yao, S., Dai, X, Cai, T., & Gao, B. (2000). The cross-cultural generalizability of Axis-II constructs: An evaluation of two personality disorder assessment instruments in the

People's Republic of China. *Journal of Personality Disorders*, 14, 249–263.

Yates, A. (1990). Current perspectives on the eating disorders. II. Treatment, outcome, and research directions. *Journal of the American Academy of Child and Adolescent Psychiatry*, 29, 1–9.

Yates, W.R., Cadoret, R.J., & Troughton, E.P. (1999). The Iowa adoption studies: Methods and results. In M.C. LaBuda & E.L. Grigorenko (Eds.), *On the Way to Individuality: Current Methodological Issues in Behavioral Genetics* (pp. 95–125). Huntington. NY: Nova Science Publishers.

Yeh, M., & Weisz, J.R. (2001). Why are we here at the clinic? Parent–child (dis)agreement on referral problems at outpatient treatment entry. *Journal of Consulting and Clinical Psychology*, 69, 1018–1025.

Yehuda, R. (2002). Current concepts: Posttraumatic stress disorder. *New England Journal of Medicine*, 346, 108–114.

Yeung, P.P., & Greenwald, S. (1992). Jewish Americans and mental health: Results of the NIMH Epidemiologic Catchment Area study. *Social Psychiatry and Psychiatric Epidemiology*, 27, 292–297.

Yonkers, K.A., Dyck, I.R., & Keller, M.B. (2001). An eight-year longitudinal comparison of clinical course and characteristics of social phobia among men and women. *Psychiatric Services*, 52, 637–643.

Yonkers, K.A., & Gurguis, G. (1995). Gender differences in the prevalence and expression of anxiety disorders. In M.V. Seeman (Ed.), *Gender and Psychopathology* (pp. 113–130). Washington, DC: American Psychiatric Press.

Zahn-Waxler, C., Cole, P.M., Barrett, K.C. (1991). Guilt and empathy: Sex differences and implications for the development of depression. In Judy Garber & Kenneth A. Dodge (Eds.), *The Development of Emotion Regulation and Dysregulation. Cambridge Studies in Social and Emotional Development* (pp. 243–272). New York: Cambridge University Press.

Zahn-Waxler, C., Kochanska, G., Krupnick, J., & McKnew, D. (1990). Patterns of guilt in children depressed and well mothers. *Developmental Psychology*, 26, 51–59.

Zakzanis, K.K. (2001). Statistics to tell the truth, the whole truth, and nothing but the truth: Formulae, illustrative numerical examples, and heuristic interpretation of effect size analyses for neuropsychological researchers. *Archives of Clinical Neuropsychology*, 16, 653–667.

Zakzanis, K.K., & Heinricks, R.W. (1999). Schizophrenia and the frontal brain: A quantitative review. *Journal of the International Neuropsychological Society*, 5, 556–566.

Zakzanis, K.K., Poulin, P., Hansen, K.T., & Jolic, D. (2000). Searching the schizophrenic brain for temporal lobe deficits: A systematic review and meta-analysis. *Psychological Medicine*, 30, 491–504.

Zakzanis, K.K., & Young, D.A. (2001). Memory impairment in abstinent MDMA ("Ecstasy") users: A longitudinal investigation. *Neurology*, 56, 966–969.

Zakzanis, K.K., Young, D.A., & Campbell, Z. (2003). Prospective memory impairment in abstinent MDMA ("Ecstasy") users. *Cognitive Neuropsychiatry*, 8, 141–153.

Zanarini, M.C., & Frankenburg, F.R. (2001). Olanzapine treatment of female borderline personality disorder patients: A double-blind, placebo-controlled pilot study. *Journal of Clinical Psychiatry*, 62, 849–854.

Zarate, C.A., & Tohen, M. (1996). Epidemiology of mood disorders throughout the life cycle. In K.I. Shulman, and M. Tohen (Eds.), *Mood Disorders Across Lifespan* (pp. 17–33). New York: Wiley.

Zarit, S.H., Zarit, J.M., & Rosenberg-Thompson, S. (1990). A special treatment unit for Alzheimer's disease: Medical, behavioral, and environmental features. *Clinical Gerontologist*, 9, 47–63.

Zebb, B.J., & Beck, J.G. (1998). Worry versus anxiety: Is there really a difference? *Behavior Modification*, 22, 45–61.

Zelkowitz, P., Paris, J., Guzder, J., & Feldman, R. (2001). Diathesis and stressors in borderline pathology of childhood: The role of neuropsychological risk and trauma. *Journal of the American Academy of Child & Adolescent Psychiatry*, 40, 100–105.

Zilbergeld, B. (1995). The critical and demanding partner in sex therapy. In R.C. Rosen and S.R. Leiblum (Eds.), *Case Studies in Sex Therapy* (pp. 311–330). New York: Guilford.

Zilbergeld, B. (1999). *The New Male Sexuality* (rev. ed.). New York: Bantam Doubleday Dell.

Zigler, E. (1967). Familial mental retardation: A continuing dilemma. *Science*, 155, 292–298.

Zigler, E., & Hodapp, R.M. (1986). *Understanding Mental Retardation*. New York: Cambridge University Press.

Zigler, E., & Styfco, S.J. (1993). Using research and theory to justify and inform Head Start expansion. *Social Policy Report for the Society Research in Child Development*, 7, 1–20.

Zill, N. (1978). *Divorce, Marital Happiness, and the Mental Health of Children: Findings from the FCD National Survey of Children*. Paper presented at the NIMH workshop on divorce and children. Bethesda, MD.

Zimmerman, M., & Coryell, W.H. (1989). DSM-III personality disorder diagnoses in a nonpatient sample. *Archives of General Psychiatry*, 46, 682–689.

Zito, J.M., Safer, D.J., dos Reis, S., Gardner, J.F., Boles, M., & Lynch, F. (2000). Trends in the prescribing of psychotropic medications to preschoolers. *Journal of the American Medical Association*, 283, 1025–1030.

Zoccolillo, M., & Cloninger, C.R. (1986). Somatization disorder: Psychologic symptoms, social disability, and diagnosis. *Comprehensive Psychiatry*, 27, 65–73.

Zoccolillo, M., Price, R., Ji, T.H.C., & Hwu, H. (1999). Antisocial personality disorder: Comparisons of prevalence, symptoms, and correlates in four countries. In P. Cohen and C. Slomkowski (Eds.), *Historical and Geographical Influences on Psychopathology* (pp. 249–277). Mahwah, NJ: Erlbaum.

Zohar, J., Sasson, Y., Chopra, M., Amital, D., & Iancu, I. (2000). Pharmacological treatment of obsessive–compulsive disorder: A review. In M. Maj and N. Sartorius (Eds.), *Obsessive–Compulsive Disorder* (pp. 43–92). New York: Wiley.

Zorn, C.A. (1998). My private disorder. *Groton School Quarterly*, 19–21.

Zucker K.J. (2000) Gender identity disorder. In A.J. Sameroff, M. Lewis, & S.M. Miller (Eds.), *Handbook of Developmental Psychopathology* (2nd ed., pp. 671–686). New York: Kluwer Academic.

Zucker, K.J., & Blanchard, R. (1997). Transvestic fetishism: Psychopathology and theory. In D.R. Laws & W.T. O'Donohue (Eds.), *Handbook of Sexual Deviance: Theory and Application* (pp. 253–279). New York: Guilford.

Zuckerman, M. (1991). *Psychobiology of Personality*. New York: Cambridge University Press.

Zuckerman, M. (1999). *Vulnerability to Psychopathology: A Biosocial Model*. Washington: American Psychological Association Press.

Zvolensky, M.J., Arrindell, W.A., Taylor, S., Bouvard, M., Cox, B.J., Stewart, S.H., Sandin, B., Cardenas, S.J., & Eifert, G.H. (2003). Anxiety sensitivity in six cultures. *Behaviour Research and Therapy*, 41, 841–859.

# Name Index


## A

Abdulrehman, R.Y., 427
Abel, G.G., 426, 427, 428, 429
Abela, J., 161
Abela, J.R.Z., 161
Abraham, K.G., 590
Abramowitz, J.S., 221
Abrams, R., 176
Abramson, L.Y., 151, 159, 160, 161, 162
Abukmeil, S.S., 461
Ackerman, M.D., 419
Adalf, E.M., 151
Adamec, R., 391
Adams, C.M., 591
Adams, G.R., 589, 590, 591
Adams, H.E., 131
Adams, J., 557
Adler, C.M., 135, 217
Adler, L.E., 471
Adler, R., 274
Agras, W.S., 324, 346, 348, 350, 353, 359, 360, 361
Ainsworth, M.D.S., 54, 333, 577
Akagi, H., 260
Akiskal, H.S., 149, 322
Akyuz, G., 255
Al-Issa, I, 419
Al-Sawaf, M., 419, 420
Alarcon, R.D., 314
Alden, L.E., 198, 199
Aldridge-Morris, R., 250, 252
Aldwin, C.M., 436
Alexander, F., 76, 94, 280
Alexander, J.F., 130, 566, 602
Alford, B.A., 158, 171
Allen, J.P., 395, 588
Allen, L.A., 223
Allen, M., 90–91
Alloy, L.B., 159, 160, 162
Alpers, G.W., 264
Althof, S., 421
Althof, S.E., 422, 423
Altshuler, L.L., 462
Alzheimer, A., 491
Amering, M., 200, 204
Ames, E.W., 524
Anda, R., 290
Andersen, B.L., 406, 418
Andersen-Hanley, C., 507
Anderson, A.E., 339
Anderson, B.L., 283–284
Anderson, D., 433
Anderson, E.M., 91, 339
Anderson, G.M., 184
Andreasen, N.C., 443, 446, 451, 461, 463
Andrews, A., 249
Andrews, B., 263
Andrews, G., 107, 200, 206, 210
Andrews, C.E., 537
Andrews, G., 293
Andron, I., 527
Angiulo, M.J., 255
Angst, F., 150
Angst, J., 148, 150
Anisman, H., 281
Annis, H.M., 133
Anserson, N.B., 132
Anthony, J.C., 381
Antonucci, T.C., 605
Antony, M.M., 67, 203–204, 208, 211, 213, 219, 220, 221, 222
Appelbaum, P.S., 618, 625, 628, 629, 630, 637
Apter, J.T., 223
Arboleda-Flarez, J., 620
Archer, R.P., 125, 129
Archer, S., 585
Arizmendi, T.G., 91, 92
Arnett, J.J., 591
Arrigo, B.A., 325, 326
Asarnow, R.F., 538
Asberg, M., 181
Asher, S.R., 570, 571
Ashford, J.W., 505
Ashley, C.T., 521
Asmundson, G.J.G., 133, 231, 241, 257, 263, 264, 285
Asperger, H., 536
Assaad, J.M., 393
Attie, I., 353
Austin, G.W., 631
Avila, M.T., 471
Ayres, J.J.B., 208
Ayuso-Mateos, J.L., 150
Azorlosa, J., 333

## B

Baade, L.E., 488
Babiak, P., 326–327
Bachrach, L.I., 629
Badger, T.A., 485, 498
Baer, J.S., 400
Baer, L., 73
Bagarozzi, D.A., 130
Bagby, R.M., 133
Bailey, A., 530, 537, 538, 539, 541
Bailey, J.M., 129, 133
Bailey, s., 566
Baker, J.D., 333
Baker, L., 349, 356, 538
Baker, T.B., 372, 391
Bal, P., 620
Bala, N., 631
Baldwin, L.M., 133
Balentine, A.C., 554
Balla, D.A., 517
Ballard, C.G., 497
Ballenger, J.C., 242
Balogh, A., 223
Balon, R., 435
Baltes, P.B., 486
Bandura, A., 55, 56
Banki, C.M., 184
Bankier, B., 263–264
Barbaree, H.E., 423, 427, 429, 431, 434
Barber, J.P., 78
Barch, D., 448
Barch, D.M., 463
Barkley, R.A., 551, 558, 561, 563, 564, 572
Barlow, D.H., 67, 192, 199, 201, 202–204, 208, 210, 212, 217, 420
Barnier, A.J., 247
Baroff, G.S., 516, 522, 523, 525, 528, 529
Baron-Cohen, S., 531
Barondes, S.H., 41
Barr, C.L., 557
Barrera, M.Jr., 385
Barrett, J.E., 68, 174, 579
Barrowclough, C., 476
Barry, C.T., 550
Bartlett, P., 18
Basoglu, M., 239
Bason, R., 421
Bass, C., 264, 265
Bass, D., 565
Bass, E., 248
Bassett, A.S., 460
Basson, R., 407, 409, 411, 414, 416
Bastiani, A.M., 352
Bates, J.E., 301, 329
Battaglia, M., 317
Baucom, D.H., 598, 602
Bauer, M.S., 176
Baum, A., 277, 279
Baum, a., 274, 276
Baum, K., 448
Bauman, M.L., 538, 540
Baumeister, R.F., 180, 300, 426
Beach, S.R.H., 594, 595, 602
Beal, A.L., 134, 354
Beaudet, M.P., 279
Bebbington, P., 467
Bechtoldt, H., 66
Beck, A., 82
Beck, A.T., 56, 83, 143, 158, 159, 171, 180, 212, 222, 332, 477
Beck, J.G., 411
Becker, D., 313
Becker, J.V., 634
Beckl, J.G., 192
Bednar, R.L., 95
Beegly, M., 520
Beggington, P., 467
Beidel, D.C., 242, 579
Beirne-Smith, M., 517, 519
Beiser, M., 60, 455, 456
Beitman, B.D., 203
Bell, R.Q., 558, 562
Bellack, A.S., 476
Bemis, K.M., 356
Bender, L., 536
Benet, A.E., 417
Benjamin, L.A., 596
Benjamin, L.S., 333
Bennett, F.C., 558
Bentler, P.W., 392
Berenbaum, H., 448
Berg, P.H., 473
Bergeron, C., 497, 501
Bergeron, S., 421
Bergin, A.E., 86–87
Berlin, I.N., 384
Berman, A.L., 183
Berman, J.R., 412, 415
Berman, J.S., 68
Bernard, S.H., 528
Bernlef, J., 507
Bernstein, D.A., 124, 221
Bernstein, D.P., 312, 313, 314, 317
Bernstein, E.M., 252
Bernstein, G.A., 579
Berrios, G.E., 105, 145
Berry, J.W., 316
Berscheid, E., 59
Bertelson, A., 164
Bertrand, L.D., 253
Besharov, D.J., 633, 634
Besson, J., 395
Bettelheim, B., 533, 538
Beumont, P.J.V., 337

Beutler, L.E., 91, 92
Bickel, H., 104
Biederman, J., 565
Bieling, P.J., 332
Bienenfeld, L., 87
Bierut, L.J., 164
Bierut, L.M., 385
Bifulco, A., 156
Bilder, R.M., 448
Bilsbury, C.D., 285
Binet, A., 518
Bini, l., 72
Binik, Y.M., 416
Binik, Y.S., 416
Binki, Y., 405
Birch, D.E., 637
Birley, J.L.T., 466
Birt, A.R., 248, 626
Bishop, D.S., 133
Black, D.W., 214, 321
Black, P.H., 288
Blair, R.J.R., 550
Blais, F.C., 134
Blalock, J., 162
Blanchard, D.C., 55, 436
Blanchard, E.B., 264
Blanchard, J.J., 448
Blanchard, R., 437
Blanchard, R.J., 55, 415, 424, 430, 432, 436, 437
Bland, R.C., 13, 15, 16, 17, 68, 150, 153, 320, 382, 383, 443, 499, 607
Blankstein, K.R., 133
Blashfield, R.K., 324
Blatchford, C., 358
Blazer, D.G., 203, 607
Blennow, K., 493
Bleuler, E., 451, 454, 478
Bleuler, M., 453
Blindt-Segraves, K., 414
Bliss, E.L., 255
Bloch, S., 94–95
Blum, N., 120
Blume, A.W., 397
Blumenthal, J.A., 286
Blumenthal, K., 279
Blundell, J.E., 354
Blustein, D.L., 591
Bodin, S.D., 550
Bohman, M., 386
Boileau, I., 388
Boland, R., 149, 174
Bolla, K.I., 373
Bond, C.F., Jr., 391
Bond, N.W., 491
Bonnie, R.J., 613
Bookheimer, S.Y., 135
Booth, A., 599
Booth-Kewley, S., 290, 291
Bootzin, R.R., 285
Borduin, C.M., 566
Borkovec, T., 97
Borkovec, T.D., 192, 212, 221
Bornstein, R.F., 332, 333
Borum, R., 625, 627
Bosma, H.A., 590
Bouchard, S., 96
Bouchard, T.J. Jr., 525
Boudreau, F., 629–630
Bourgault, C., 384
Bourin, M., 217
Boutet, M., 512
Bowen, J.D., 481
Bower, G.H., 254
Bowlby, J., 53, 54, 77, 207, 333, 577, 578, 606
Bowman, E.S., 256
Bowman, M., 240
Bowman, M.L., 134
Boyd, C.P., 130
Boyle, M.H., 68, 134, 392, 561, 575, 576, 577
Bradbury, T.N., 594, 595, 599, 600
Bradford, D., 473
Bradford, J.M.W., 432, 435
Bradley, A.R., 631
Bradley, C., 562
Bradley, S.J., 436, 437
Bradwejn, J., 217–218
Brandon, T.H., 391
Brandt, C.A., 489
Brass, G.M., 60
Braun, B.G., 254
Braun, D.L., 342, 345
Braun, P., 629
Brechman-Toussaint, M.L., 565
Breggin, P.R., 75
Bregman, J.D., 521
Breitner, J.C.S., 502
Brenner, M.H., 466
Breslau, N., 235, 236, 392
Breslin, C., 398
Breslow, N., 433
Brestan, E.V., 565
Breteler, M.M.B., 501
Breuer, J., 75
Brewer, C., 395
Brewerton, T.D., 345
Brewin, C.R., 263, 467
Brickman, J., 428
Briere, J., 428
Brink, D., 95
Brinker, J.K., 112
Brody, E.M., 507
Bromet, M., 237
Bromley, D.B., 609
Brooks, A.E., 275
Brooks-Gum, J., 353, 589
Brown, A.S., 460, 465
Brown, G.K., 332
Brown, G.W., 156, 157, 158, 161, 206, 207, 466
Brown, J., 320
Brown, L.S., 312
Brown, R., 313, 619
Brown, R.M.A., 633
Brown, S.A., 391, 448
Brown, T.A., 192, 199, 201, 203
Brown, S.A., 392
Brownell, K.D., 344, 345, 347, 354
Bruch, H., 342, 352, 356
Bryan, J., 486
Bryant, B., 239
Bryant, D., 528
Bryant, R.A., 236, 237, 239, 240, 242
Bryson, S.E., 537
Brzustowicz, L.M., 460
Bucholz, K.K., 370, 378, 379
Bukowski, W.M., 570, 571
Bulik, C.M., 355
Bullock, R., 505
Bullough, B., 424
Bullough, V., 424
Burke, B.L., 574
Burke, C., 511
Burke, J.D., 139
Burnside, S., 327, 328
Burt, S.A., 557, 560
Buss, A., 557
Buss, D.J., 53
Bussiere, M.T., 434
Bustillo, J.R., 476
Butcher, J.M., 91, 125
Butler, J.L., 426
Butler, S.M., 505
Butt, J.C., 426
Byers, E.S., 414
Bystritsky, A., 218

## C

Cacioppo, J.T., 37, 280
Caddell, J.M., 239
Cadet, J., 373
Cadieux, R.J., 223
Cado, S., 419
Cadoret, R.J., 329
Cairns, A., 177, 327, 328
Cairns, R.B., 122
Cale, E.M., 305–306
Calev, A., 176
Calhoun, K.S., 131
Calhoun, S.L., 536
Calkins, M.E., 471
Callahan, A.M., 176
Callicott, J.H., 134
Cameron, D., 23
Cameron, H.M., 112
Cameron, N., 54
Campbell, D., 68
Campbell, L.A., 202
Campbell, M., 564
Campbell, M.A., 626
Campbell, R., 236
Campbell, Z., 133
Candido, C.L., 448
Canino, G.J., 13
Cannon, M., 456, 460
Cannon, T.D., 456, 458, 460, 461, 462
Cannon, W., 273, 274, 276
Cantor-Graae, E., 460
Cantwell, D.P., 538
Caplan, L.R., 497
Caplan, P.J., 9, 312
Capron, C., 526
Capron, E.W., 333
Cardena, E., 247, 249
Cardno, A.G., 453
Carey, G., 329
Carey, M.P., 417, 419
Carkhuff, R., 85, 92
Carlat, D.J., 340
Carlsmith, J.M., 634
Carlson, C.I., 130
Carlson, C.R., 332
Carlson, E.A., 578
Carlsson, A., 464, 465
Carmin, C.N., 204
Carney, R.M., 294
Carpenter, W.T., 451, 455
Carr, E.G., 542
Carr, R., 221, 535
Carroll, R.A., 411, 439
Carstensen, L.L., 595, 603, 605
Carter, J.C., 359
Carter, J.R., 468, 469
Carter, M., 524
Carter, P., 507
Carter, R., 135, 169, 215, 216
Carver, C.S., 278, 279
Casey, P., 252, 255
Cash, T.F., 338
Caspi, A., 301, 560
Cassidy, J., 53, 207, 578
Cattarin, J.A., 353
Cavell, T.A., 565
Centeno, S., 433
Cerce, D.D., 431
Cerletti, U., 72
Chakos, M., 475
Chakrabarti, S., 535
Challen, P., 427

Chamberlain, P., 566
Chambless, D.L., 67
Champagne, F., 433
Charach, A., 563
Charcot, J., 32, 245, 264
Charles, S.T., 605
Charney, D.S., 217
Chassin, L., 385
Cheah, Y.C., 152
Chen, W.J., 471
Cheng, O., 141
Chesney, M.A., 287, 288, 290
Chess, S., 54, 557
Chesselet, M., 495
Chisholm, K., 524
Chiu, H.F.K., 501
Chorpita, B.F., 199, 203, 210
Chow, E.W., 460
Chretien, J., 613
Christensen, A., 93, 95, 594, 595, 602
Christensen, H., 486
Christiansen, B.A., 391
Ciaranello, R.D., 41
Cicchetti, D., 40, 517, 520
Cierpal, M.A., 170
Ciminero, K.S., 131
Ciompi. L., 454
Clark, D.A., 133, 158, 171, 194–195, 196, 203, 220, 221, 222, 224
Clark, D.C., 178
Clark, D.M., 210, 240
Clark, L.A., 114–115, 202, 203, 298
Clarkin, J.F., 128, 323
Clavan, M., 195–196
Clayton, D.O., 418
Clayton, P.J., 257
Cleckley, H., 298, 299, 325, 326, 330–331
Clementz, B.A., 472
Cloninger, C.R., 257, 379, 386, 387
Clum, G.A., 322
Clyburn, L.D., 500
Cochrane, R., 468
Coffey, S.F., 132
Cohen, C.I., 466
Cohen, D., 40
Cohen, D.J., 531
Cohen, J.G., 322
Cohen, M.S., 135
Cohen, S., 279
Cohen-Kettenis, P.T., 436, 439
Cohler, B.J., 605, 607, 609
Coie, J., 60, 570, 571
Colapimto, J., 438
Colapinto, J., 438
Cole, G., 492, 502, 505
Cole, M.G., 485
Cole, T.A., 275
Cole, W., 428
Colecchi, C., 95
Coles, E.M., 619
Collaer, M.L., 431
Collins, A., 23
Collins, F., 538, 539
Collins, W.A., 59
Cone, J.D., 118, 123, 124
Conger, J.J., 391
Conley, R.R., 473
Conners, C.K., 558
Connor, T.J., 170
Connors, C.K., 551
Conrod, P.J., 399
Contrada, D.R., 290
Contrada, R.J., 271
Cook, B.L., 224
Cook, M., 209
Cooke, D.J., 331
Coons, P., 249, 251, 256
Cooper, P.J., 342
Coovert, D.L., 349
Copolov, D., 462
Cordova, J.V., 594
Cormier, B.M., 633
Cormier, C.A., 331
Cornelius, J.R., 395
Cornille, T.A., 68
Corse, C.D., 288
Cortoni, F.A., 428
Coryell, W., 150
Coryell, W.H., 312
Coser, L.A., 178
Costa, P.T.Jr., 302, 308
Costello, E., 97
Costigan, C.L., 526
Cottey, T.J., 182
Courchesne, E., 540
Covin, R., 112
Cowan, C.P., 593
Cowan, P.A., 593
Cowburn, R.F., 493
Cowley, D.S., 223–224
Cox, 208
Cox, B.J., 133, 203, 208, 211, 241, 321, 555–556, 570
Coyne, J.C., 160–162
Crabbe, J., 52, 394
Crago, M., 91, 92
Craig, K.D., 133, 285
Craig, T.J., 458
Craighead, L.W., 150
Craighead, W.E., 149–150, 175
Cram, S.J., 636
Cramer, P., 277
Cramer, V., 311
Craske, M.G., 192, 210–211
Crawford, M., 618
Crick, F., 495
Crick, N.R., 561
Crimlisk, H.L., 262
Crisanti, A., 620
Cristo, N.J., 90
Critelli, J.W., 87
Crites, D.L., 536
Crits-Christoph, P., 319, 333
Cronbach, L.J., 415
Crook, K.H., 637
Crouch, E., 94–95
Crowhurst, B., 635
Crozier, L., 381
Crozier, W.R., 198, 199
Csikszentmihalyi, M., 589
Cuckle, H., 527
Cuesta, M.J., 448
Cummings, E.M., 565, 595
Cummings, J.L., 492–493, 495, 502, 505
Cunningham, M.D., 326
Curoff, J.J., 254, 255
Curtis, C.E., 471
Cutler, N.R., 505
Cvejic, H., 512
Cyr, M., 17
Cyranowski, J.M., 406, 418

## D

D'Emilio, J., 407
D'Zurilla, T., 81, 82
Dallaire, R., 231, 232
Daly, M.P., 505
Danforth, J.S., 561
Dang, S.T., 239
Daniels, D., 524
Daro, D., 633
David, D.L., 418
Davidson, J.R., 223
Davidson, J.R.T., 151
Davidson, L.M., 276
Davidson, P.R., 243
Davidson, R.J., 167, 168
Davidson, W.S., 566
Davies, P., 595
Davila, J., 332
Davis, B., 579
Davis, C., 351
Davis, D., 420, 448
Davis, G.C., 322
Davis, L., 248
Davis, S., 616, 620, 621
Davison, G.C., 333
Dawson, D.A., 368
de Beurs, E., 206
de Luca, R.V., 427
de Man, A.F., 143
de Ruiter, C., 222
de Silva, P., 423
deBaryshe, B.D., 560
deFries, J.C., 47, 48
deKeseredy, W.S., 428, 429
deLanney, L.E., 275
deLeon, P.H., 17
Delesoaul, P., 446
Delfs, J.M., 495
deLongis, A., 269, 279, 285
deLucia, C., 385
Denov, M.S., 430
dePaulo, J.R., 172
Dershowitz, A., 619
deRubeis, R.J., 172, 174
Descartes, R., 42
Deschesnes, M., 134
Deutsch, S.I., 564
Devanand, D.P., 506
deVane, C.L., 564
deWaele, J.P., 390
deWit, D.J., 376
Dezwirek, L., 633
Dhawan, S., 429
Diamond, M., 438
Dick, L., 111
Dickens, B.M., 401
Dickens, W.T., 524
Dickey, R., 428, 436
Dickson, D.W., 493
Diehl, S.R., 459
Diforio, D., 460
diGirolamo, G.J., 132
Digman, J.M., 301
Dimeff, L.A., 324
Dineen, T., 358
Dingers, D.F., 252
Dingle, G., 365
Dishion, T.J., 560
Dix, D., 19
Dobson, K., 17, 143, 174, 247
Dobson, K.S., 95, 112, 636
Dodge, K.A., 561
Dohrenwend, B.P., 271, 273
Dolan, R.J., 447
Dolan, S.L., 88
Dolan-Sewell, R.T., 311
Donahey, K.M., 411
Donavan, D.M., 399
Donbson, K.S., 635
Dongier, M., 399
Dorian, B.J., 355
Dotti, M.T., 537
Douglas, D., 551, 626
Douglas, K.S., 626, 627
Douglas, V.I., 552
Downey, K., 392

Dozois, D., 17, 143, 174
Dozois, D.J.A., 112, 547
Draguns, J.G., 14
Drevets, W.C., 168
Drobes, D.J., 132
Dugas, M., 79
Dugas, M.J., 199, 212
Duhig, A.M., 550
Dunkin, J.J., 507
Durbin, J., 15
Durkheim, D., 178, 179, 182
Durkheim, E., 178, 181
Dusseldorp, E., 292
Dutton, D.G., 298
Duyme, M., 526
Dworkin, R.H., 447
Dyk, P.H., 591
Dykens, E., 517, 519, 520
Dyregrov, A., 242

E

Earls, F., 556, 557
Easrnst, K.S., 447
Eastwood, M.R., 486
Eaton, W.W., 200
Eaves, D., 626
Ebbing, K., 32
Ebly, E.M., 499
Eccles, A., 433, 434
Eddy, K.T., 346
Ediger, E., 352
Egeland, J.D., 181
Ehlers, A., 239, 240
Ehlers, C.L., 385
Ehrlich, P., 32
Eich, E., 253
Eisenberg, N., 301
Ekselius, L., 311
Ellason, J.W., 256
Elliot, S., 429
Ellis, A., 222
Ellis, a., 83
Ellis, C.R., 529
Emde, R.N., 329
Emdler, N.S., 281
Emery, G., 212, 222
Emery, R.E., 38, 58, 81, 93, 94, 254, 350, 560, 565, 594, 595, 596, 600, 602, 623, 630, 631, 632, 633, 634
Emmanuel, J., 200
Emmons, R.A., 300
Emrick, C.D., 396
Endler, N.S., 281
Eng, W., 207
Ennis, B., 623
Epstein, N., 419
Epstein, N.B., 133
Epstein, S., 246
Erdelyi, M.H., 246
Erickson, D.H., 455
Erickson, D.J., 203, 380
Erikson, E., 56, 57t, 77, 585, 586, 587, 588, 605, 607
Erlenmeyer-Kimling, L., 318
Ernulf, K.E., 424
Eron, L.D., 560
Esquirol, J., 176
Esterling, B.A., 278
Evans, D.L., 284, 348, 634, 635
Evans, R.G., 95
Everly, G.S., 242
Ewing, C., 623
Ewing, S.E., 318
Exner, J.E., 129
Eyberg, S.M., 565
Eysenck, H., 86, 87

F

Factor, S.A., 475
Fadda, R., 491
Faigman, D.L., 619
Fairburn, C.G., 344, 345, 347, 348, 351, 353, 354, 359–360, 361
Fairlie, P., 281
Falk, W.E., 318
Fallon, P., 356
Falloon, I., 94
Fann, J.R., 498
Farah, M.J., 246, 487
Faraone, S.V., 51, 471
Faravelli, C., 13, 206
Farde, L., 464
Farmer, A.E., 106
Farquhar, J.W., 292
Farrer, L.A., 503
Farrington, D., 550
Faust, D., 619
Fava, G.A., 166
Fawzy, F.I., 269, 284
Federoff, B., 430
Federoff, J.P., 430
Fedoroff, I.C., 222, 223, 241
Fein, D., 539, 540
Feinleib, M., 289
Feinstein, C., 538, 539
Feldman, M.D., 633
Felner, R.D., 89
Fenton, W.S., 453
Fernandez, H., 403
Ferster, C.B., 538
Feuerstein, M.J., 131
Figley, C.R., 233
Fincham, F.D., 59, 565, 594, 595, 631
Fink, H.A., 421
Fink, M., 176
Fink, P.J., 106
Finkel, S.I., 483
Finkelhor, D., 428, 633
Finkelstein, J.R., 471
Finlay-Jones, R., 206
Finney, J.W., 400
Fiore, M.C., 372
First, M.B., 198, 306, 320, 378, 423, 453, 586
Fischman, M.W., 372
Fishbain, D.A., 264
Fishell, A., 430
Fisher, L., 617
Fitch, S.A., 589
Fitch, W.L., 619
Flacker, J.M., 501
Flanagan, J.C., 609
Fleeson, J., 577, 578
Fleiss, J.L., 106
Fleming, J.E., 576
Fleshner, M., 276
Flett, G., 38, 170, 281, 352
Flint, A.J., 203
Flor-Henry, P., 432
Floyd, F.J., 526
Flynn, J.R., 524
Foa, E.B., 220, 240, 242
Fogarty, F., 153
Folkman, S., 272, 276, 278, 279
Follette, W.C., 114
Follingstad, D.R., 619
Folstein, M.F., 488
Folstein, S.E., 488
Fombonne, E., 535
Foot, P., 623
Fordyce, W.E., 264
Forehand, R., 93
Foreman, M.C., 481
Fornari, V., 351
Forrest, K.A., 255
Foster, S.L., 118, 123, 124
Foulks, E.F., 314
Fournier, L., 17, 32
Foust, L.L., 627
Fowler, C.J., 418
Fox, P.J., 491
Fozard, J.L., 604
Frame, C.L., 529
Frances, A., 197, 198, 230, 233, 234, 306, 320, 378, 423, 453, 586
Francis, E.L., 160
Frank, E., 150, 174, 176
Frank, J.B., 87, 92
Frank, J.D., 71, 87, 92
Frank, K.A., 294
Frankenburg, F.R., 324
Frankish, C.J., 183
Franklin, J.A., 206
Franklin, M.E., 220
Frasure-Smith, N., 293
Fredman, N., 596
Freed, S., 211, 262
Freedman, E.B., 407
Freeman, S.J.J., 629
Freeston, M.H., 265
French, D.C., 560
French, N.H., 569
French, T.M., 76, 280
Freud, S., 34, 52, 56, 57t, 75, 76, 77, 91, 155, 229, 245, 255, 262
Freund, A.M., 486
Freund, K., 414, 415, 427–428, 432, 436
Frick, P.J., 550
Friedler, E., 290
Friedman, B., 631
Friedman, H.S., 289, 290
Friedman, M., 289, 294
Friedman, R.A., 174
Fries, J.F., 609
Frishman, W., 87
Frith, C., 447
Frith, U., 531
Froehlich, J.C., 389, 390
Frohlich, P.F., 418
Frueh, B.C., 242
Fung, T.S., 499
Funtowicz, M.N., 312
Furer, P., 265
Furniss, E., 61, 62
Furstenberg, F.F., 588, 590
Fyer, A.J., 214

G

Gabbard, G.O., 319, 323
Gacono, C., 331
Gadde, K.M., 175
Gagne, F.F., 176
Gagnon, R.T., 408, 409, 410, 419, 428
Galaif, E.R., 396
Galea, S., 238, 241
Gallagher, M., 595, 599
Gallagher-Thompson, D., 506, 607
Gallant, D., 395
Garaone, S.V., 48
Garb, H.N., 128
Garber, H.I., 528
Garber, J., 162, 468, 572
Garbutt, J.C., 395
Garbutt, L.D., 288
Gardner, C.O., 459
Gardner, D.M., 223–224
Gardner, R., 54
Gardner, W., 624
Garfield, S.L., 78

Garfinkel, P.E., 340, 341–342, 344, 346, 347, 348, 349, 350, 355, 359
Garland, E.J., 579
Garland, J., 173, 579
Garmezy, N., 40, 573
Garner, D.M., 337, 338, 342, 346, 349, 350, 352, 355, 356
Garrett, A.B., 16, 17
Garssen, B., 222
Gartner, R., 618
Garvey, M.J., 224
Garza-Trevino, E., 181
Gatehouse, J., 229
Gater, R., 203
Gatz, M., 502
Gaudet, M.A., 617
Gaulin, S.J.C., 53
Gazzaniga, M.S., 132
Geary, P., 590
Geldmacher, D.S., 497
Gelinas, L., 616
Geller, J.L., 320
Gemar, M., 96, 133
Gentili, A., 417
Gentleman, J.F., 596
Georgianna, S., 181
Geske, M.R., 637
Gfellner, B.M., 384
Ghaemi, S.N., 175
Gianoulakis, C., 390, 395
Gibbs, N.A., 307
Gillberg, C., 342, 352, 537, 539, 540
Gilligan, C., 60, 591
Gillmor, D., 23
Gillock, K.L., 204
Ginsberg, D., 173
Glancy, G., 618
Glaser, R., 278, 283
Glass, G.V., 86, 90
Glasser, S.P., 87
Gleaves, D.H., 247, 251, 253, 254
Glick, I.D., 473
Gliksman, L., 381
Glisky, M.L., 255
Goddard, A.W., 217
Goebel-Fabbri, A.E., 178
Goeree, R., 443
Goering, P.N., 151
Goering, P., 15, 59, 68, 347
Gofman, M.A., 437
Gold, J.R., 129
Gold, M.S., 377
Goldapple, K., 96, 168
Goldberg, B., 518, 529
Goldberg, D.P., 261
Goldberg, E.M., 465
Goldberg, L.R., 54
Goldberg. T.E., 453
Goldfried, M., 81, 82, 91
Goldfried, M.R., 333
Golding, J.M., 203
Golding, S.L., 621
Goldman, H.H., 109
Goldman, J.A., 590
Goldman, M.S., 391, 394
Goldman, R.S., 448
Goldman-Rakic, P.S., 471
Goldsmith, H.H., 317, 322, 557
Goldstein, I., 412
Goldstein, J.J., 456, 469
Goldstein, J.M., 457
Goldstein, M.J., 158, 466
Golub, E.S., 18
Golwyn, D.H., 435
Gomberg, E.S.L., 382
Good, B., 204
Gooding. D.C., 471
Gooding. D.G., 471–472
Goodman, L.A., 236, 428
Goodman, T.A., 637
Goodman, W.K., 122
Goodwin, D.W., 381
Goodwin, P.J., 284
Gooren, L.J., 436, 437
Gordon-Salant, S., 604
Gorman, J.M., 216, 242
Gorzalka, B.B., 418
Gosselin, C.C., 430
Gotlib, I.H., 58, 59, 160, 162, 263, 467
Gotowiec, A., 60
Gottesman, I., 470
Gottesman, I.G., 524
Gottesman, I.I., 48, 317, 329, 445, 450, 451, 452, 453, 456, 458, 459, 460, 470, 557
Gottman, J.M., 93, 124, 125, 132, 594, 595, 598, 600
Gouleau, J.L., 429
Gove, W.R., 106
Gowdey, K., 633
Graef, R., 589
Grandin, T., 533
Grandmaison, L.J., 133
Grant, A., 61, 62
Grant, F.E., 619
Grant, I., 617, 627
Grasel, E., 508
Gratzer, T.G., 432, 620, 628
Graves, A.B., 504
Gray, J.E., 628
Graziottin, A., 418
Greaves, G.B., 251
Green, B.L., 257
Green, J.A., 122
Green, M.L., 463
Green, R., 437
Green, W.H., 564
Greenberg, D.M., 360, 620
Greenberg, L.S., 96, 97, 243
Greenberg, P.E., 189
Greene, R.L., 125, 126
Greene, R.W., 571
Greenfield, D., 535
Greenley, J.R., 477
Greenwald, S., 13, 384
Greil, W., 175
Grenier, D., 574
Grenier, G., 414
Gresham, F.M., 516, 518
Grey, T.E., 184
Griesler, P.C., 571
Griffin, M.G., 233, 239
Griffiths, H., 106
Grisso, T., 625
Grizenko, N., 512
Grndin, T., 532
Grob, G.N., 19, 20, 31
Groen, A.D., 543
Gross, G., 445
Grossman, H.J., 518, 519, 529
Grotevant, H.D., 130
Growe, S.J., 231
Grube, B.M., 448
Gruenberg, A.M., 319, 453
Grunau, R.V.E., 285
Grych, J.H., 631
Guarnaccia, P.J., 9, 110, 204
Guerje, O., 261
Guernsey, T.F., 529
Gull, W.W., 345
Gunderson, J., 306, 321
Gupta, S., 173
Gureje, O., 261
Gurguis, G., 203
Gurland, B., 504, 607
Gurman, A., 601
Gurman, A.S., 94
Gusella, J.F., 496
Gussow, Z., 111
Gutheil, T.G., 628, 629
Gutierrez, B.I.B., 143
Gutierrez, M.A., 418
Gutierrez-Lobos, K., 447
Guzder, J., 322
Guze, S., 113

## H

Haavio-Mannila, E., 419
Haddad, M.S., 495
Hadjistavropoulos, T., 133, 488–489
Hadzi-Pavlovic, D., 207
Haefner, H., 456, 457
Hage, J.J., 439
Haggarty, J., 384
Hahlweg, K., 600
Haig-Brown, C., 61, 62
Haines, J., 131
Haller, D.L., 126
Halmi, K.A., 342, 345
Hammen, C., 160, 162
Haney, M., 372
Hankin, B.L., 151, 162, 574
Hanks, D., 146
Hanrahan, G.E., 473
Hanson, R.K., 434
Happe, F., 532
Hardin, S., 493
Harding, C.M., 454
Harding, K., 633
Hare, R.D., 134, 325, 326, 327, 328, 330, 331
Harkness, K.L., 160, 174
Harlow, H.F., 577
Harpru, T.J., 328
Harpur, T.J., 325
Harrington, R., 569, 574, 578, 579
Harris, G.T., 331, 626
Harris, J.R., 50, 560
Harris, T.O., 156, 158, 161, 206, 207
Harrison, L., 578
Harrison, P.J., 463, 465
Harrow, M., 448
Hart, A.B., 150
Hart, S., 133
Hart, S.D., 325, 326, 331, 625, 626
Hartmann, H., 77
Harvey, A.G., 234, 236, 237, 239, 240, 242
Harvey, R.J., 489
Hashemi, A.J., 468
Hasin, D., 379
Haskett, R.F., 167
Haslam, J., 32
Hathaway. S., 125
Hauser, R., 105
Hawton, K., 575
Hay, D., 559
Hay, P.J., 348
Hayden, M.R., 496
Hayman-Abello, B.A., 133
Hayman-Abello, S.E., 133
Haynes, S.G., 289
Healy, D., 168, 169, 173
Heath, A., 348
Heatherton, T.F., 352, 354
Heavey, C.L., 594
Hebb, D.O., 43, 52
Heber, R., 516
Hebert, M., 55
Hechtman, L., 567
Heiden, W., 456
Heiman, J.R., 415
Heinberg, L.J., 350
Heinrichs, R.W., 452, 463

Heinssen, R.K., 476
Heitler, S.M., 93
Hellewell, J.S.E., 473
Helm, C., 430
Helmes, E., 126
Helzer, J.E., 381
Hemenway, D., 182
Hempel, C.G., 113
Hendin, H., 179, 182, 183
Hendrie, H.C., 501
Henggeler, S.W., 566
Henker, B., 564
Hennessy, B.B., 238, 239
Henry, P.E., 338
Herbener, E.S., 448
Herbert, M., 559
Herbstein, J., 257
Herdt, G., 420
Herman, C.P., 350, 352, 353, 354
Hermann, D.H.J., 628
Herpertz, S.C., 330
Herrero, M.E., 567
Herzog, D.B., 340, 361
Heslegrave, R., 313, 333
Heston, I.I., 498
Heston, L.L., 459, 496, 505
Hettema, J.M., 214
Hewitt, P.L., 38, 133, 352
Hewitt, S., 482
Hewitt, T., 536
Heyman, I., 564
Hicks, B.D., 131
Hijdra, A.H., 497
Hildebrand, D.K., 134
Hill, D.R., 290
Hill, G., 499
Hill, J., 591
Hill, M.A., 177
Hiller, W., 264
Hills, A., 523
Hilsenroth, J.J., 114
Hinde, R.A., 37
Hines, M., 431
Hinshaw, S.P., 553, 560, 567
Hirayasu, Y., 462
Hirschfeld, R.M.A., 147, 172, 332
Hlastala, S.A., 157
Hodapp. R.M., 516
Hodges, J.R., 493
Hodkinson, S., 433
Hoek, H.W., 347, 348, 350
Hoenig, J., 438
Hoffman, B.F., 619
Hoffman, P.B., 627
Hoffman, P.L., 370
Hoffman, R.E., 461
Hofman, A., 501
Hogan, D.B., 499
Hogan, D.R., 407
Hogarty, G.E., 473, 476
Hogben, D., 327
Hole, J.W., Jr., 217
Hollander, E., 320
Holley, H., 620
Hollon, S.D., 87, 172, 468
Holmbeck, g., 591
Holmes, C., 502
Holmes, T.H., 271, 272
Holtzman, S., 285
Holtzworth-Munroe, A., 94, 602
Holzman, P.S., 471
Homewood, J., 491
Hooley, J.M., 467, 476
Hope, R.A., 361
Horan, W.P., 448
Horevitz, R., 256
Horley, J., 427
Horn, J.M., 524
Horney, K., 77, 588
Horowitz, M.J., 607
Horvitz, L.A., 172
Houezec, J.J., 371
House, A., 260
Houts, A.C., 114, 573
Howard, K.I., 68, 89
Hoyer, J., 200
Hsu, L.K.G., 338, 340, 342, 349, 350, 352, 357, 361
Hucker, S.J., 320, 426, 430
Hudson, S.M., 433
Hughes, C.C., 110, 369
Hughes, M., 237
Hull, J.G., 391
Hultsch, D., 505
Humphrey, L.L., 351
Hundelby, J.D., 384
Hunsley, J., 21, 129, 133, 427
Hunter, J.M., 19, 20
Hurt, S.W., 128
Hussong, A.M., 385
Huws, R., 432
Hwu, H.G., 13
Hyman, S.E., 165, 394
Hynan, M.T., 90

## I

Iacoboni, M., 487
Iacono, M., 39, 455, 456
Iacono, W.G., 355, 471, 557
Ickowicz, A., 563
Imperato-McGinley, J., 438
Infants Act, 635
Ingram, J.L., 540
Ingram, R.E., 158, 162
Innala, S.M., 424
Inouye, S.K., 483
Insel, K.C., 485, 498
Isaacowitz, D.M., 605
Israel, A.C., 571, 572
Itard, J.M., 517
Ivey, S.L., 16, 17
Izard, C., 578

## J

Jablensky, A., 15, 107, 196, 200, 458
Jackson, D.N., 133, 134, 309
Jackson, M.A., 626
Jacob, T., 385
Jacobson, N.S., 93, 95, 221, 595, 601, 602
Jacobson, S.A., 501
Jaffe, A.R., 366
Jaffe, J.H., 366, 373
Jaffe, P., 631
Jameson, P.B., 94, 602
Jamison, K.R., 140, 178, 180
Jamison, K.V., 426
Janeck, A., 213
Janeck, A.S., 213
Janet, P., 245, 255, 264
Jang, K.L., 50, 163, 164, 211, 214, 238, 255, 309, 386, 394, 597
Janoff-Bulman, R., 231
Jefferson, J.W., 224
Jeffries, J.C., 613
Jellinek, E.M., 400
Jenkins, C.D., 287, 289
Jenkins, J.H., 469
Jennings, J.R., 287
Jepson-Young, P., 284
Jiang, W., 288
Jobes, D.A., 183
Joffe, R.T., 223–224
Joffres, M.R., 287
John, R.S., 594
Johnson, C.C., 504–505
Johnson, J.G., 158, 298, 322, 329
Johnson, P., 367
Johnson, S.L., 157, 158, 385
Johnson, S.M., 96
Johnson, V.E., 419–420
Johnson, W.H., 275
Johnston, C., 21, 556, 561
Johnston, D.W., 292, 293, 294
Joiner, R.E., 162
Joiner, T., 162
Jones, M.A., 560
Jones, D.M., 353
Jones, J.H., 407–408
Jones, P., 456
Jones, P.B., 460, 465
Jones, R., 361
Jordan, J., 398
Jorm, A.F., 489, 498
Josephs, L., 197, 393
Josephs, R.A., 393
Joudrie, D., 249
Joyce, A.S., 96
Joyce, P.R., 13
Julien, R.M., 369, 376, 388, 389
Junginger, J., 423
Just, N., 162

## K

Kadden, R.M., 397
Kagan, J., 216, 577
Kahn, M.V., 384
Kaihla, P., 327
Kallman, W.M., 131
Kalra, S., 497, 501
Kamarck, T., 287
Kameya, Y., 414
Kandel, D.B., 384
Kane, J.M., 455, 473, 474
Kanner, L., 536
Kaplan, A.F., 340, 356
Kaplan, A.S., 341, 348, 356–357
Kaplan, J., 286
Kapur, S., 465, 474
Karam, E.G., 13
Karasek, R.A., 289, 290
Karkowski, L.M., 156
Karney, B.R., 599
Karno, M., 203, 468–469
Karras, A., 629
Kasen, S., 562
Kasnot, K., 41, 45
Kasvikis, Y.G., 342
Katsching, H., 204
Katschnig, H., 200
Katz, L.F., 595
Katz, R., 163, 164
Katzman, M.A., 356
Katzman, R., 492, 505
Kaufman, D.M., 258
Kaul, T.J., 95
Kaye, D.W.K., 501
Kaye, W.H., 344
Kaysen, S., 416
Kazdin, A.E., 67, 80, 560, 562, 565, 566, 567, 569
Keane, T.M., 239
Keegan, D., 628
Keel, P.K., 338, 356, 361
Keenan, K., 556, 557
Keesey, R.E., 354
Keith, S.J., 456
Keller, J., 131
Keller, M.B., 147, 149, 150, 174, 199
Kellner, C.H., 176
Kellner, R., 257
Kelloway, E.K., 231

Kclly, D.L., 473
Kelly, G., 56
Kelly, J.P., 170
Kelly, M.P., 419, 420
Kelly, S.E., 491
Kelly, T., 323
Kempe, C.H., 632–633
Kendal, N., 160
Kendall, P.C., 143, 579
Kendell, R.E., 105, 107, 113, 298
Kendler, K.S., 156, 163, 164, 165, 214, 215, 317, 319, 347, 348, 355, 453, 458, 459, 460
Kennedy, S.H., 14, 151, 340, 348
Kenrick, D.T., 47
Kernberg, O., 320
Kessler, R.C., 13, 17, 115, 151, 154, 155, 197, 199, 201–202, 207, 235, 236, 237, 312, 348, 381, 583
Kesteren, P.J. van, 437
Ketcham, K., 248
Kettl, P.A., 506
Keys, A., 341, 342, 354
Khaitan, B.K., 417
Khalife, S., 416
Kidd, K.K., 460
Kiecolt-Glaser, J.K., 275–276, 278, 280, 283
Kiesler, C., 627
Kihlstrom, J.F., 210, 247, 248, 255, 278
Kilbey, M.M., 392
Killinger, W.A., 248
Kilmann, P.R., 434
Kilpatrick, D.G., 235, 237
Kilzieh, N., 149
Kim, J.E., 605
Kinder, B.N., 349
King, B.M., 427
King, R.A., 184
Kinsey, A., 407
Kinsey, A.C., 408
Kinzl, J.F., 419
Kippin, T.E., 433
Kircher, J.R., 419, 420
Kirmayer, L.J., 60, 152, 260, 261, 264
Kirrane, R.M., 317
Kirsch, I., 247
Kitzmann, K., 632
Klein, D.N., 207
Klein, M., 411
Klein, R.G., 574, 577
Kleindienst, N., 175
Kleinman, A., 152, 204, 316
Klerman, G.L., 75, 172, 196
Klim, P., 551
Klinger, M.R., 246
Kluft, R.P., 254
Klump, K.L., 355
Kluznik, J.C., 237
Knapp, D.E., 383
Knauper, B., 154
Knight, R.A., 429, 431
Kniskern, D.P., 94
Knopman, D.S., 493
Koch, H., 383
Kocsis, J.H., 174
Koegel, L.K., 542
Koegel, R.L., 542
Koenig, H.G., 607
Koenigsberg, H.W., 318, 324
Koenraadt, F., 620
Koepke, T., 93
Koerner, N., 212
Kohlberg, L., 561
Kolb, B., 41
Koluchova, J., 525
Konstantareas, M., 536
Kontakos, N., 496
Kontula, O., 419
Koob, G.F., 388, 390
Koons, C.R., 324
Kop, W.J., 291
Kopelman, M.D., 491
Kopelowicz, A., 472, 476
Koppel, T., 231
Kopta, S.M., 89
Koranyi, E.K., 274
Korenman, S.G., 413, 418
Kornfeld, J., 294
Koskenvuo, M., 290
Koski, L., 487
Koss, M.P., 91, 236, 248
Koszycki, D., 218
Kovacs, M., 579
Kowalski, K.M., 370
Koyama, T., 385
Kraepelin, E., 105, 145, 151, 451, 478, 491
Krahn, H., 429
Krantz, D.S., 287, 288, 289, 290
Krantz, R.J., 290
Krause, M.S., 89
Kring, A.M., 447, 457
Kring, B., 436
Kringlen, E., 311
Kris, E., 77
Krisberg, B., 560
Krishnan, P.R., 175
Kroenke, K., 173, 260, 264
Kropp, P.R., 625
Krueger, R.F., 298, 311
Krystal, A.D., 73
Kuban, M., 134, 428, 432
Kübler-Ross, E., 606
Kubzansky, L.D., 278
Kuch, K., 241
Kuhn, T., 35, 36
Kuiper, N.A., 278, 279
Kuipers, L., 467
Kunnen, E.S., 590
Kupersmidt, J., 60, 570, 571
Kupersmidt, J.B., 560
Kupfer, D.J., 150, 174, 175
Kushner, M.B., 203, 380
Kuykendall, D.H., 609
Kwapil, T.R., 472
Kwapil. T.R., 448

## L

L'Abate, L., 130
Labronte, R., 286, 287–288
Lacey, J.I., 131
LaCroix, A.Z., 289
Ladouceur, R., 79, 95, 199, 212
Ladwig, K., 260
Lahey, B.B., 550, 552, 554
Lai, D.W.L., 134
Lal, H., 390
Lalonde, J.K., 250
Lam, R., 95
Lam, R.W., 151
Lamb, S., 313
Lamberg, L., 421
Lambert, M.J., 86–87, 91
Lambert, P., 630
Lamerson, C.D., 231
Landy, D., 111
Lane, P., 381
Lang, A.E., 497, 501
Lang, A.R., 385
Lang, C.T., 633
Lang, K.L., 310
Lang, R., 426
Langevin, R., 422, 426, 432
Langlais, P.J., 491
Lara, M.E., 207
Larimer, M.E., 400
Larsen, R.J., 53
Larson, R., 589
Last, C.G., 570
Lau, M.A., 393
Laumann, E.O., 408, 409, 410, 417, 419, 422, 428, 429
Laumann-Billings, L., 254, 633, 634
Laurence, J., 246
Lauterbach, E.C., 474
Lavallee, C., 384
Lave, T.R., 109
Lavori, P.W., 154
Lawrie, S.M., 461
Laws, D.R., 431
Lawton, M.P., 506, 507, 610
Lazarus, R.S., 269, 272, 276, 279
Le Bourdais, C., 596
Leary, T., 77
Leavitt, B.R., 496
LeDoux, J.E., 215
Ledoux, J.E., 242
Lee, C.-K, 13
Lee, C.-K., 13
Lee, C.M., 133
Lee, K.K., 60, 525
Leesfield, I.H., 634
Lefcourt, H.M., 278
Lefebvre, J., 17
Leff, J., 152, 458, 466, 467
Lefley, H.P., 468
Lehman, A.F., 477
Lehmann, H., 472–473
Lehrer, P., 221
Leibenluft, E., 203
Leiblum, S.L., 411
Leiblum, S.R., 411, 414, 419, 420
Leichtman, M., 320
Leiderman, P.H., 634
Leitemberg, H., 419
Lellouch, J.L., 13
Lentz, R.J., 81, 477
Lenzenweger, M.R., 307, 446
Leon, G., 352
Leon, G.R., 352
Leonard, B.E., 170, 274, 275
Leonard, H.L., 130, 577, 579
Leonard, K.E., 384
Lépine, J.-P., 13
Lerner, A.J., 500
Lesage, A.D., 151
Lesage, A., 17
Leserman, J., 284
Leshner, A.I., 365
Leslie, A.M., 531
Lester, D., 180, 183
Leucht, S., 474, 475
Levav, M., 134
LeVay, S., 437
Levenson, M.R., 331
Levenson, R.W., 132, 595
Leventhal, H., 609
Levine, S.B., 422, 423
Levinson, D., 587
Levinson, d., 587
Levitt, A.J., 151, 177
Levitt, E.E., 426
Levy, D.L., 471, 472, 557
Levy, S.T., 506
Lewine, R.R.J., 457
Lewinsohn, P.M., 59, 154, 203, 575
Lewis, M.H., 541
Leys, D., 501
Liberman, R.P., 472, 476
Liddle, P.F., 135
Lidz, C.W., 623, 625
Lieberman, J., 461, 473
Lilienfeld, S.O., 128, 247, 253, 261, 306, 326

Lim, B.B., 238, 239
Limber, S., 634
Lin, E., 68
Linden, W., 291, 293
Lindenberger, U., 486
Lindgren, S., 558
Lindqvist, M., 464
Lindsay, S., 248
Linehan, M.M., 323, 324
Link, B.G., 106
Links, P.S., 313, 333
Lipman, E.L., 427, 576–577
Lipowski, Z.J., 258, 261, 263
Lipsey, M.W., 86
Lipsitz, L.A., 501
Lipton, D.N., 431
Lisanby, S.H., 73
Litten, R.Z., 395
Livesley, J., 50, 309, 310, 311, 322, 386
Livesley, W.J., 133, 134, 211, 214, 255, 307, 332, 386
Lochlin, J.C., 524
Lockyer, L., 535
Loeber, R., 550, 554
Loewenstein, R.J., 256
Loewenstein, R.W., 77
Loftin, C., 182
Loftus, E.F., 246, 248
Logan, G., 551, 564
Lohr, J.M., 243
London, E.D., 373
Longino, C.F., 604, 608
Looper, K.J., 260
Loovas, O.I., 542
Lopez, A.D., 3, 13, 14, 139, 140, 366, 371, 372
Lopez, J.F., 181
Lopez, S.R., 9, 110, 469
Loranger, A.W., 307
Lord, C., 530, 537, 541
Lorion, R.P., 89
Lovaas, O.I., 535, 542, 543
Lovinger, D.M., 390
Low, P.W., 613
Lowenstein, R.J., 256
Lubbers, R., 160
Luborsky, L., 78, 87, 88
Lubs, H.A., 521
Lucas, A.R., 347
Ludwig, T.W., 277
Lueger, R.J., 68
Luszcz, M.A., 486
Lydon, T.J., 483
Lyketsos, C.G., 376
Lykken, D.T., 38, 58, 330, 599, 600
Lynam, D.R., 308, 554, 562
Lyness, S.A., 290
Lynn, S.J., 247
Lyons, J.T., 68
Lyons, M.J., 238, 311

## M

Maccoby, E.E., 39, 54, 56, 60, 559, 631
MacDonald, M.E., 60
Machado, P.P.P., 92
Mack, A.H., 200
Mackintosh, B., 212
Macklin, M.L., 241
MacKnight, C., 497
MacLatchy-Gaudet, H.A., 391
MacLean, C., 348
MacLeod, C., 212
MacLeod, F.K., 133
MacMillan, D.L., 516, 518
MacMillan, H.L., 60, 427
Maddi, S.R., 76
Magai, C., 603
Magenis, R.E., 520
Mah, K., 405
Mahe, V., 223
Maher, B.A., 447
Mahoney, M.J., 78, 91
Maier, S.F., 276, 311
Maisto, S.A., 398
Malamuth, N.M., 594
Malcolm, W., 96
Maldonado, J.R., 256
Malenka, R.C., 394
Maletzky, B.M., 426
Malhi, G.S., 175
Maltzman, I., 401
Manassis, K., 579
Manderscheid, R.W., 15, 17
Manicavasagar, V., 207
Manis, M., 277
Mannuzza, S., 214
Manson, S.M., 20, 152
March, J.S., 577, 579
Marcia, J., 589
Marcia, J.E., 590, 591
Marder, K., 496
Marder, S.R., 473
Margolin, G., 594
Margraf, J., 264
Marholin, D., 81
Marin, A., 231
Markman, H.J., 130, 600
Markowitz, J.C., 172
Marks, I., 95
Marks, I.M., 205, 223
Marks, P.A., 126
Markstrom, C.A., 590
Marlatt, G.A., 367, 397, 398, 400, 401
Marques, J.K., 434, 435
Marsh, L., 461
Marshall, D.R., 431
Marshall, K., 321, 429
Marshall, W.L., 422, 428, 429, 433, 434
Martin, C.E., 408
Martin, G., 182
Martin, J.A., 54, 559
Martin, R.A., 278
Martin, R.L., 257
Martinez, A., 306
Martini, R., 495
Martyn, C.N., 504
Marwit, S.J., 607
Masand, P.S., 173
Mash, C., 561
Mash, E.J., 133, 547, 551, 554, 556, 561
Maslow, A., 35
Mason, F.L., 423
Masten, A.S., 578
Masters, W.H., 419–420
Matarazzo, J.D., 112
Matas, M., 628
Mathews, A., 212
Matrshall, W.L., 433
Matson, J.L., 529
Matthews, K., 279
Matthews, S., 632
Matthysse, S., 43
Mattia, J.I., 311
Matza, L.S., 560
Maurice, J., 293
Maurice, P., 134
Mavissakalian, M.R., 224
Mayes, S.D., 536
Mayeux, R., 503, 505
Mayman, M., 277
Mayou, R.A., 239, 242
Mazure, C.M., 332
Mazzella, R., 349
Mazziotta, J.C., 487
McBride, W.J., 390
McBurney, D.H., 53
McCabe, M.P., 418, 421
McCabe, R.E., 211
McCabe, S.B., 58, 59
McCallum, M., 96
McCann, U.D., 347
McCarroll, J.E., 263
McCarthy, B.W., 407, 420, 421
McCartney, K., 599
McCarty, D., 365
McClearn, G.E., 47, 48
McClure, J.N. Jr., 217
McClure, R.K., 461
McConaghy, N., 411, 434, 435
McCord, J., 560
McCrae, R.M., 308
McCrae, R.R., 277, 301, 302
McCulloch, S., 358
McDavid, J., 324
McDermeit, M., 320
McDonald, C., 465
McDonel, E.C., 431
McDougle, C.J., 541
McDowall, D., 182
McEachin, J.J., 543
McElroy, R.A., 324
McElroy, S.L., 320
McFall, R.M., 81, 431
McFarlane, A.C., 233
McGee, D.P., 574
McGeer, E.G., 499–500, 504
McGeer, P.L., 499, 504
McGinn, L.K., 172
McGlashan, T., 322
McGlashan, T.H., 313, 318, 445, 453, 461
McGoogan, E., 112
McGrath, J.J., 461
McGue, M., 38, 58, 355, 386, 387, 525, 557, 599, 600
McGue, W.G., 39
McGuffin, P., 163, 164, 329, 557
McGuire, M., 566
McGuire, M.T., 154, 319, 443, 552
McHale, M.J., 631
McHugh, P.R., 488
McKee, A., 482
McKeith, I.G., 497
McKenna, M.C., 283
McKey, R.H., 528
McKim, W., 370
McLellan, A.T., 394
McLemore, C.W., 596
McLintock, B., 358
McMahon, F.J., 165
McMahon, R.J., 93
McMahon, R.P., 473
McNally, R.J., 210, 211, 216, 218
McNeil, T.F., 460
McNeilly, M., 132
McNerney, E.K., 542
Meana, M., 416
Meaney, M.J., 52
Mechanic, M.B., 233, 239
Medina, J., 494, 503
Mednick, S.A., 461, 462
Meehl, P.E., 415, 448, 463, 469, 624, 625
Megens, J.A., 437
Meichenbaum, D., 82, 222
Meissner, D., 358
Mejeur, J., 370
Melley, A.H., 298
Mellings, T.M.B., 198
Melman, A., 417, 421
Melton, G.B., 620, 623, 634
Meltzer-Brody, S.E., 151
Melzack, R., 285
Mendel, G., 47–48

Mendlewicz, J., 175
Menzies, R.G., 209
Merikangas, K.R., 145, 148, 200, 203, 380, 385
Merkelbach, H., 195
Merkin, D., 425
Merskey, H., 254, 255, 486
Meston, C.M., 417, 418
Metalsky, G.I., 159, 161, 162
Metz, M.E., 419
Metzger, D., 394
Meyer, G.J., 129
Meyer, R.G., 636
Meyers, B.S., 498
Mezzacappa, E., 556, 557
Mezzich, J.E., 111
Michael, R.T., 428
Michael, S., 408, 409
Michaels, S., 408, 409, 410, 428
Michelini, S., 223
Mickelson, K.D., 207
Migliorelli, R., 489
Miklowitz, D.J., 158, 175, 466
Milan, A., 596
Milich, R., 124, 554, 558
Millar, W.J., 285
Miller, G.A., 131
Miller, I., 158
Miller, M., 182
Miller, M.D., 472
Miller, T.I., 86, 90
Miller, T.Q., 290
Miller, T.W., 271
Miller, W.R., 396, 398
Miller-Johnson, S., 280
Millon, T., 306
Milner, P., 388
Milstein, V., 249
Mineka, S., 170, 203, 208, 209, 210, 216, 219, 278
Minton, H.L., 9
Minuchin, P., 94
Minuchin, S., 349, 351, 356
Miranda, J., 158, 162
Misener, V.L., 557
Mitchell, J., 242, 345, 352
Mitchell, J.E., 352, 359, 361
Mitchell, P.B., 175
Mittelman, M.S., 507
Mittelmark, M.B., 604, 608
Mnookin, R.H., 630, 631
Modahl, C., 539, 540
Moen, P., 605
Moffit, T.E., 567
Moffitt, T.E., 328, 550, 560, 562
Mohr, J.J., 53, 207
Moldavsky, M., 521
Moldin, S.O., 165, 458, 460
Moldofsky, H., 346
Monahan, J., 623, 624, 625, 637
Monga, S., 579
Mongrain, M., 160
Moniz, E., 21, 73
Monroe, S.M., 155, 156
Monroe-Blum, H., 576
Monson, R.A., 265
Montgomery, D.T., 565
Montgomery, H.A., 396
Moore, E.G., 608
Moos, R.H., 130, 400
Moretti, M.M., 566
Morey, L., 298
Morgan, C.D., 488
Morin, C.M., 95, 285
Morin, D., 134
Morison, S.J., 524
Morokoff, P.J., 415
Morris, J., 495
Morris, L.A., 87
Morris, T.L., 579
Morrison, J., 257
Morrison, K., 86, 90
Morrison, S.L., 465
Moser, C., 422, 426
Moskovitz, R.A., 321
Moskowitz, J.T., 278
Mota, V.L., 551
Moulden, H., 429
Moyer, T., 321
Mueser, K.T., 476
Mulder, R.T., 298
Mulligan, T., 417
Mulvany, F., 465
Mulvey, E.P., 623
Munitz, H., 262
Munk-Jorgensen, P., 460
Murayama, H., 504
Muris, P., 195
Murphy, J., 15
Murphy, W.D., 426, 432
Murray, C.J.L., 3, 13, 14, 139, 366, 371, 372
Murray, D.J.L., 140
Murray, R.M., 460, 465
Myers, J.K., 127
Myers, M., 177

## N

Nakamura, J.E., 605, 607, 609
Narita, K., 461
Nathan, P.E., 88, 98, 370, 396
Nayar, M., 93
Neale, J.M., 449, 458, 466
Neale, M.C., 163, 348
Needleman, L.D., 356
Nehlig, A., 369
Neill, G., 596
Nelson, C.B., 237
Nemeroff, C., 166
Nemeroff, C.B., 167, 169, 239, 242
Nesse, R.M., 154, 200, 205
Nestadt, G., 312
Nestler, E.J., 169
Neubauer, D.L., 160
Neuchterlein, K.H., 158
Neufeld, R.W.J., 468, 469
Neufeldt, S.A., 92
Neugarten, B.L., 602, 608
Neugebauer, R., 31, 71
Neuhaus, I.M., 177
Neumann, K.F., 87
Newcomb, A.F., 570, 571
Newcomb, M.D., 392, 429
Newhouse, P.A., 503
Newman, J.P., 330, 383
Newman, S.C., 13, 15, 16, 17, 68, 153, 330, 382, 383, 607
Newport, D.J., 239, 242
Newth, S., 285
Nezworski, M.T., 128, 129
Nicholl, S., 279
Nicholls, T.L., 627
Nicholson, I.R., 469
Nietzel, M.T., 124
Niewenhuis, J.A., 243
Nigg, J.T., 317, 322, 332, 552, 561
Nimgaonkar, V.L., 458
Ninan, P.T., 217
Nirenberg, A.A., 149
Nisbett, R.E., 55
Nobler, M.S., 176
Nolen-Hoeksema, S., 60, 162
Norcross, J.C., 67
Norden, K.A., 322
Nordstrom, P., 181
Norman, R.M.G., 477
Norton, G.R., 193, 251, 255, 285
Norton, P.J., 285
Notarious, C.I., 594
Nowlis, D., 313
Noyes, R. Jr., 213, 224
Nuechterlein, K.H., 471
Nunes, E.V., 294
Nutt, D.J., 217
Nyenhuis, D.L., 497

## O

O'Brien, T.B., 269
O'Connor, G.T., 293
O'Connor, M., 361
O'Donohue, W., 631
O'Hare, A., 319
O'Leary, K.D., 80, 82, 595, 602
O'Meara, E.S., 504
O'Reilly, R.C., 246
O'Rourke, N., 488
O'Sullivan, R.L., 320
Oakley-Browne, M.A., 13
Odynak, D., 429
Oei, T.P.S., 238, 239
Offord, D.R., 3, 12, 68, 189, 201, 203, 564, 575, 576, 577
Ogloff, J.R.P., 621, 622, 627, 634, 635, 637
Ohayon, M.M., 447
Ohlin, L., 550
Ohman, A., 208, 216
Ohmori, T., 385
Olds, J., 388
Olfson, M., 473, 474
Oliver, J.M., 127
Ollendick, T.H., 67
Olley, J.G., 516, 522, 523, 528, 529
Olley, M.C., 622, 627, 634, 637
Olmsted, M.P., 352
Oltmanns, T.F., 118, 298, 307, 449, 451, 466
Olweus, D., 571
Om, H., 68
Oosterweger, A., 591
Oren, D.A., 149
Orlinsky, D.E., 89
Orn, H., 15, 16, 17, 321, 607
Orne, E.C., 252
Orne, M., 252
Orosan, P., 264
Osborn, C., 426, 428
Osgood, N.J., 607
Osman, A.K., 420
Ostrove, J.M., 588
Ostwald, P.F., 22
Otis, D.B., 629
Ott, A., 501
Ottman, R., 503
Otto, M.W., 318
Owen, M.J., 557

## P

Padilla, A.M., 118
Paglia, A., 151
Pagliaro, L., 17
Paikoff, R.L., 589
Paivio, S.C., 243, 263
Palmer, R.L., 351
Panksepp, J., 55, 539
Parhad, I.M., 499
Parikh, S.V., 151
Paris, J., 255, 264, 310, 313, 323
Park, D.C., 526, 527
Park, E., 596
Park, S., 471
Parker, G., 148–149, 152
Parker, J.G., 570
Parker, J.G.A., 133
Parker, K.C.H., 243

Parker, R.A., 436
Parks, G.A., 397
Parnas, J., 462
Parnetti, L., 501
Parry-Jones, B., 345
Parsons, B.V., 566
Pasquier, F., 501
Pasupathi, M., 588, 603
Patelis-Siotis, I., 176
Paterniti, S., 206
Paterson, R.J., 81
Patrick, C.J., 330
Pattee, L., 570, 571
Patterson, C.J., 130, 571
Patterson, C.M., 330
Patterson, G.R., 93, 559, 560, 565
Patton, J.R., 517, 519
Paul, G.L., 81, 477
Pauli. P., 264
Paunonen, S.V., 133
Pavlov, I., 34, 35
Pawlak, A., 435
Payne, A.V.L., 161
Payne, J.S., 517, 519
Pearlson, G.D., 461, 463
Pedersen, N.L., 502
Pelham, W.E., 563, 564
Pendery, M.L., 401
Pennebaker, J.W., 277, 278
Pennix, B., 290
Peralta, V., 448
Perls, E., 84, 85
Perls, F., 35
Perris, C., 149
Perry, C., 245–246
Pescosolido, B.A., 181
Peskind, E.R., 503
Peters, K.D., 286
Peters, K.G., 552
Peters, L., 107
Peterson, B.D., 16, 17
Peterson, C., 56
Peterson, J.B., 393
Petrella, R.C., 619
Petrie, K.J., 277, 278
Petti, T.A., 569
Petty, R.G., 463
Peveler, R.A., 361
Pfaus, J.G., 433
Pfohl, B., 120, 306
Phelan, J.C., 106
Phillippe, K.A., 526
Phillips, E.L., 81
Phillips, K.A., 257, 259, 264, 477
Piasecki, T., 372
Pigott, T.A., 203
Pihl, R.O., 370, 381, 385, 391, 393, 399
Pincus, H.A., 74, 198, 306, 320, 378, 423, 453, 586
Pine, D.S., 574, 577
Pinel, P., 19
Pinker, S., 208
Pinto, C., 314
Piper, A., 254
Piper, W.E., 96
Pitman, R.K., 239
Pitts, F.N., Jr., 217
Plassman, B.L., 502
Plomin, R., 47, 48, 50, 51, 52, 524, 557
Plotsky, P.M., 167
Pokony, A., 627
Polaschek, D.L., 431
Polivy, J., 350, 351, 352, 353, 354
Pollack, M.H., 217
Pollard, C.A., 204
Pollitt, P.A., 501
Pollitt, R.J., 105
Pollock, G.H., 280
Pomeroy, C., 341, 345
Pomeroy, W.B., 408
Poole, D.A., 248
Pope, A., 43
Pope, H.G., 376
Porter, S., 248, 626, 627
Posner, M.I., 132
Poulin, F., 560
Poulton, R., 209
Powell, L.H., 294
Prentky, R.A., 431, 434, 435
Prescott, C.A., 156, 164, 214
Pressman, J.D., 73
Presta, S., 320
Price, J., 54, 154
Price, L.H., 541
Prince, R., 293
Prkachin, K.M., 134
Prochaska, J.O., 67
Pron, N., 327
Proulx, R., 512
Prout, P.I., 248
Pryse-Phillips, W., 505
Przybeck, T., 312
Puig-Antich, J., 577
Pulsford, D., 506
Purdon, C., 195–196, 213
Purdon, C.L., 133
Putnam, F.W., 254, 255, 267

## Q

Quadagno, D., 420
Quay, H.C., 558
Quigley, L.a., 400
Quinsey, V., 430
Quinsey, V.L., 626
Quist, J.F., 557

## R

Rabins, P.V., 507
Radford, J.P., 526, 527
Radomsky, A., 171, 211
Rae, D.S., 456
Rae-Grant, N.I., 576
Rahe, R.H., 271, 272
Raichle, M.E., 134, 168
Rajda, M., 285
Ramey, C.T., 528
Ramsey, E., 560
Rapee, R.M., 210
Raphael, B., 242
Rapoport, J.L., 562, 579
Raskind, M.A., 498, 503
Rastam, M., 342, 352
Rauch, S.L., 135, 217
Ray, D.C., 257, 265
Ray, W.J., 192
Raymond, N., 352
Read, J., 419
Rector, N.A., 133, 477
Rectorr, N.A., 96
Reddon, J.R., 126
Regehr, C., 618
Regier, D.A., 12–13, 139, 151, 202, 456
Reich, J., 332
Reid, J.B., 566
Reid, W.H., 331
Reidy, T.J., 326
Reiger, D.a., 59
Reis, H.T., 59
Reisner, R., 615, 634
Reiss, A.L., 538, 539
Reiss, S., 211
Reissing, E.D., 416
Reiter, J., 264
Remington, G., 22, 474, 475
Repetti, R.L., 560
Resick, P.A., 233, 239
Reynolds, C.F., 610
Rezazadeh, S.M., 390
Reznikoff, M., 128
Riccio, C.A., 471
Rice, M.E., 331, 415, 626
Richards, A.L., 429
Richardson, K., 67, 68, 395
Richelson, E., 475
Richters, J.E., 60, 559
Rieber, R.W., 250
Rief, W., 264
Riggs, D.S., 240
Rind, B., 254
Risen, C.B., 422, 423
Ritter, J., 162
Ritz, M.C., 388
Rivelli, S.K., 175
Robbins, J.M., 264
Roberts, R.C., 464
Roberts, A.J., 390
Roberts, J.E., 157
Roberts, L.J., 398, 400
Roberts, W.V., 257
Robertson, I., 177
Robin, A.L., 93, 356
Robins, E., 113
Robins, L.N., 12, 58, 151, 312, 313
Robinson, N.M., 529
Robinson, P., 408
Rodin, J., 347, 353
Roesch, R., 619, 621
Roesch, R.., 621
Rogers, C., 35, 56, 91, 92
Rogers, C.R., 84, 85, 91–92
Rogers, K.C., 631
Rogers, M.P., 261
Rogers, S., 521
Rogers, S.J., 540, 543
Rogler, L.H., 110
Rojas-Fernandez, C.H., 497, 505
Roman, G.C., 496
Romney, D.M., 448
Ronningstam, E., 306
Rooth, F.G., 426
Rorschach, H., 128, 129
Rosen, A., 624, 625
Rosen, J.C., 264, 320
Rosen, L.W., 342, 346
Rosen, R.C., 419, 420, 427
Rosenbaum, K.N., 538, 539
Rosenberg, M.W., 608
Rosenberg-Thompson, H., 507
Rosenman, R.H., 289
Rosenstein, L.D., 486
Rosenthal, N.E., 149, 177
Rosenthal, R., 58, 86, 87, 88
Rosetti, Z.L., 491
Rosler, A., 435
Rosman, B.L., 349, 356
Rosnow, R.L., 87
Ross, C.A., 251, 254, 255, 256
Ross, G.W., 481
Ross, H.E., 381
Rossor, M.N., 493
Rothbart, M.K., 301
Rothbaum, B.O., 242
Rourke, B.P., 133
Rourke, S.B., 133
Rowa, K., 213
Rowe, M.K., 210
Roy, A., 181
Roy, K., 152
Roy-Bryne, P.P., 223
Rozanski, A., 286, 288, 289, 290, 292
Rubio-Stipec, M., 13

Rucklidge, J.J., 554
Rueter, M.A., 206
Ruitenberg, A., 500
Rumstein-McKean, O., 427
Rush, B., 19
Russell, G.F.M., 340, 345, 356
Russell, J.M., 153, 382, 383
Russo, N.F., 236
Ruteledge, T., 291
Rutherford, J., 164, 355
Rutter, M., 30, 40, 47, 54, 532, 535, 536, 538, 540, 543, 548, 556, 557, 558, 560, 569, 570, 577, 578, 594, 604
Ruyak, P.S., 285
Ryan, M.T., 224
Rychlak, J.F., 54
Rychtarick, R.G., 401
Ryff, C.D., 604
Rylander, G., 181

## S

Saavedra, J.E., 109
Sabshin, M., 107
Sackeim, H., 176
Sacks, O., 490, 491
Sadler, P., 247
Saffran, E.M., 487
Sahley, T.L., 539
Saklofske, D.H., 134
Salekin, R.T., 331
Salem, J.E., 457
Sallee, F.R., 565
Salthouse, T.A., 486
Salvatori, P., 521
Sambrook, S.L., 19
Sammons, M.T., 17
Sandeen, E.E., 595, 602
Sanderlin, T.K., 331
Sanders, G.L., 426
Sanders, M.R., 565
Sanderson, W.C., 172, 210
Sandler, A.D., 541
Sanislow, C.A., 318
Sano, M., 505
Santos, A.B., 477
Santosh, P., 564
Sapolsky, R.M., 274, 276, 277, 278
Sarchiapone, M., 181
Sarin, S., 161
Sartorius, N., 149, 150
Saunders, S.M., 68
Sayegh, L., 512
Sayer, N.A., 128
Sayette, M.A., 368, 393
Scarr, S., 599
Schachar, R.J., 551, 552, 553, 554, 563, 564
Schacter, D.L., 246
Schatzberg, A.F., 148, 174
Schaumann, H., 537
Scheerenberger, R.C., 517, 529
Scheff, T., 106
Scheffler, R.M., 16, 17
Scheier, M.F., 278, 279
Scheltens, P., 497
Schiavi, R.C., 418
Schiff, M., 526
Schiffman, J., 466
Schlesenger, M.J., 483
Schmaling, K.B., 602
Schmidt, J.P., 133
Schmidt, N.B., 211
Schmitt, W.A., 330
Schneider, K., 451
Schneiderman, N., 287, 288, 290
Schneidman, E.S., 179, 180, 179
Schneller, J., 190
Schofield, P.W., 504
Schooler, N.R., 476
Schooley, B., 493
Schopler, E., 531
Schopler, E.M., 537
Schopp, R.F., 619
Schott, R.L., 424
Schotti, J.R., 528
Schreibman, L., 533, 535–536, 538, 540, 542
Schroeder, M.L., 309
Schuckit, 384, 394
Schuckit, M., 366
Schuckit, M.A., 378, 380
Schuepbach, W.M.M., 262
Schulberg, H.C., 172, 174
Schuller, R.A., 622, 637
Schulsinger, F., 461
Schuyler, D., 222
Schwartz, C.E., 577
Schwartz, G.E., 37, 277
Scott, S., 565
Scroppo, J.C., 253, 254
Scurfield, R.M., 242
Seamon, J.G., 47
Searles, J.S., 387
Sedgwick, P., 9
Seeley, J.R., 59
Seeman, M.V., 455, 456, 457, 475
Seeman, T.E., 560
Seeman, W., 126
Segal, Z., 95, 96, 133
Segal, Z.V., 158, 162
Segman, R.H., 184
Segraves, R.T., 414, 421
Segrin, C., 162
Selfe, L., 535
Seligman, M.E.P., 56, 88, 89, 283
Sellaro, R., 148, 150
Sellers, E.M., 388, 389
Selye, H., 276
Serdula, M.K., 338
Serran, G.A., 428
Servi, P., 206
Seto, M.C., 134, 423, 427, 429, 432
Sevlie, C.P., 435
Sexton, J.L., 17
Shadish, W.R., 89
Shahinfar, A., 560
Shalev, A.Y., 239, 262
Shannon, G.W., 19
Shapiro, A.K., 87
Shapiro, D.A., 86–87, 90
Shapiro, F., 243
Sharpe, L., 320
Shastry, B.S., 460
Shatte, A.J., 278
Shavelson, L., 398
Shaver, P.R., 207
Shaw, D., 556, 557, 558, 560, 562, 578
Shaw, E., 574
Shea, M.T., 311, 332
Shear, M.K., 207
Shearer, D.E., 528
Shearer, M.S., 528
Shedler, J., 277
Sheldon, C.T., 59
Shen, W.W., 418
Shenton, M.E., 461, 462
Shepard, C., 555
Shepherd, C., 547
Sher, K.J., 203, 379, 380, 394
Sherman, R., 558, 596
Shiffman, S., 397
Shipley, S., 325, 326
Shokrollahi, P., 417–418, 420
Short, A.B., 531
Shorter, E., 260, 264
Shoulson, I., 501
Showalter, E., 245, 254, 260, 261
Shubsachs, A.P.W., 432
Shulman, K.I., 488
Shure, M.B., 81, 82
Shusterm, B., 160
Siegel, J.M., 609
Siegel, S., 369
Siegel, T.C., 565
Siever, L.J., 312, 317, 318, 324
Sigman, M., 540
Sigvardsson, S., 386
Silberstein, L.R., 353
Sillars, L., 619
Silver, R.C., 607
Silverman, J.M., 317
Silverman, W.K., 579
Simard, M., 497
Simmie, S., 444, 615
Simmonds, S., 200
Simon, T.B., 261, 518
Simons, A.D., 156, 350
Singer, J.E., 276
Singer, M.T., 466
Singer, S.M., 504
Singh, N.N., 529
Singh, O.P., 417
Sinha, B.K., 134
Siperstein, G.N., 516, 518
Skeels, H., 526
Skeem, J.L., 325
Skilling, T.A., 326
Skinner, B.F., 34, 35
Sklar, S.M., 133
Skodak, M., 526
Skodol, A.E., 109
Skoog, G., 201
Skoog, I., 201
Skre, I., 213
Slade, P.D., 340
Slade, T., 107
Slater, E., 262
Sleator, E.K., 564
Sloane, R.B., 90
Slobogin, C., 615, 634
Sloman, L., 54
Slutske, W.S., 321
Small, S.A., 486
Smalley, S.L., 538, 539
Smetana, J.G., 588
Smith, A.L., 151
Smith, D.A., 67, 98
Smith, E., 444
Smith, G.N., 460
Smith, G.R., 257, 265, 321
Smith, G.T., 392
Smith, M.L., 86, 90
Smith, R.S., 59, 591
Smith, S., 391
Smith, S.R., 636
Smith, T., 543
Smith, V., 437, 543
Smith, Y.L.S., 439
Smolak, L., 345
Smyth, J.M., 278
Snidman, N., 577
Snowdon, D.A., 505
Snyder, J., 602
Sobell, L.C., 133, 400, 401
Sobell, M.B., 400
Solomon, D.A., 176
Solomon, K., 383
Somerfield, M.R., 277
Song, C., 274–275
Sonino, N., 166–167
Sonnega, E., 237
Sood, J., 95
Souery, D., 165

Southall, D.P., 633
Spaerstein, A.R., 507
Spaner, D., 153
Spangler, D., 350
Spanos, N.P., 252, 253, 255
Sparrow, S.S., 517
Specker, S., 352
Spector, I.P., 417
Spellman, J., 319
Spence, M.A., 538
Spencer, T.J., 565
Spiegel, D., 247, 249
Spiegel, H., 619
Spirito, A., 575
Spitzer, R.L., 106, 107, 492
Spivack, G., 81, 82
Sprague, R.L., 564
Spreen, O., 133, 488–489, 572
Sramek, J.J., 505
Sroufe, A., 578
Sroufe, L.A., 577
Stack, S., 180
Stacy, A.W., 392
Staedt, J.H., 489
Stanwick, R.S., 358
Staples, F.R., 90
Stark-Adamec, C., 391
Starr, P., 18, 279
Steadman, H.J., 623
Steele, C.M., 393
Steffenburg, S., 539
Steffy, R.A., 461
Steiger, H., 353, 355
Stein, 236
Stein, D.J., 217
Stein, L.I., 477
Stein, M., 198, 211
Stein, M.B., 214, 238
Steinhausen, H., 357
Stejskal, W.J., 129
Steketee, G., 130
Steller, S., 628
Sterk, N., 143
Stern, Y., 500, 505
Stevens, S.E., 90–91
Stevens, V.J., 293
Stewart, A.J., 588
Stewart, J.T., 506
Stewart, S., 211, 263, 380, 391, 399
Stewart, S.H., 224, 380, 391
Stice, E., 350, 353, 355, 385
Still, G., 552
Stimmel, G.L., 14
Stoeber, J., 192
Stokes, J., 496
Stokes, T.F., 561
Stokols, D., 291
Stoller, R.J., 425
Stone, J., 95
Stone, M.H., 305, 317, 319
Stoolmiller, M., 598
Stoppe, G., 489
Stormer, S., 350
Stossel, C., 293
Stowe, R., 241
Strassberg, D.S., 419, 420
Strauss, C.C., 570
Strauss, E., 133, 489
Strauss, J.S., 455
Street, G.P., 240
Street, S.W., 276
Stretch, R.H., 233
Stricker, G., 129
Striegel-Moore, R.H., 345, 349, 353
Stritzke, W.G.K., 132, 385
Strober, M., 352, 355
Stroup, S., 473
Strunk, D.R., 172
Strupp, H.H., 91
Strupp, K., 537
Struthers, W., 160
Stuart, S.P., 88
Sturgis, B.J., 619
Stuss, D.T., 133
Styfco, S.J., 528
Sullivan, 348, 361
Sullivan, E.V., 491
Sullivan, H., 77
Sullivan, H.S., 77
Sullivan, K.T., 600
Sullivan, P.F., 163
Sullivan. M., 619
Sunday, S.R., 342, 345
Suomi, S.J., 577
Susser, E., 454, 477
Sussex, J.N., 181
Sussman, N., 173
Sussman, S., 18, 396
Sutandar-Pinnock, K., 352
Swaab, D.F, 437
Swanson, J., 623
Swanson, J.M., 563
Swartz, F.E., 175
Swartz, H.A., 150
Swartz, M.S., 257, 260
Swedo, S.E., 577, 579
Swendsen, J.D., 145
Swindle, R., 264
Swinson, R., 95, 96
Swinson, R.P., 211, 219, 220, 221, 222, 223
Szasz, T., 62, 106

## T

Tabakoff, B., 370
Tager-Flusberg, H., 531, 533
Tamminga, C.A., 457
Tannock, R., 551, 552, 553, 554, 563, 564
Tarrier, N., 476
Tasman, A., 106
Taylor, E., 548
Taylor, G.J., 133, 280, 360
Taylor, J., 189, 203–204, 211, 557, 576
Taylor, P.J., 432
Taylor, S., 39, 96, 133, 200, 208, 211, 218, 220, 221, 222, 223, 231, 235, 241, 242, 243, 257, 263, 264, 273, 284, 285, 307, 570
Taylor, S.E., 206, 560
Teasdale, J., 96
Telch, C.F., 324
Tellegen, A., 202
Teplin, L., 623
Terdal, L.G., 133
Teri, L., 506
Tesman, J.R., 523
Thakker, J., 458
Thapar, A., 329, 520, 521, 524
Tharan, M., 248
Thase, M.E., 149
Thavundayil, J., 390
Theberge, J., 465
Thomas, A., 54, 557
Thomas, C., 219
Thomas, c., 554
Thomas, J., 118
Thomas, K.M., 218
Thomas, V.H., 311
Thompson, J.K., 349, 350, 353
Thompson, P., 286, 288
Thompson-Cooper, I., 633
Thoresen, C.E., 294
Thornicroft, G., 149, 477
Tiefer, L., 409, 421, 436
Timmnos, M., 495
Tipp, J., 312
Tison, F., 496
Tjepkema, M., 384
Tobin, S.L., 491
Tohen, M., 154
Tombaugh, T.N., 133
Tomkins, D.M., 388, 389
Tondo, L., 175
Tonigan, A.S., 396
Torgersen, S., 164, 311, 317, 322
Torrey, E.F., 628, 629
Tough, S.C., 426
Toupin, J., 17
Touyz, S.W., 337
Townsend, L.a., 477
Trapnell, P.D., 418
Tremblay, R.E., 567
Triandis, H.C., 314
Troisi, A., 443
Tromp, S., 248
Trotter, M.A., 281
Troughton, E.P., 329
Truax, C., 85, 92
Truax, P., 221
True, W.R., 238
Trull, T.J., 301, 321
Trusscott, D., 637
Trzepacz, P.T., 501
Tsai, J.L., 110, 603
Tsai, L.Y., 538
Tsuang, D.W., 48
Tsuang, M.T., 443, 453, 458, 471
Tuke, W., 19
Tune, L., 505
Tuokko, H., 133, 488–489
Turkat, I.D., 332
Turkheimer, E., 42, 50, 51, 118, 298, 524, 526
Turner, N.E., 133
Turner, R.J., 465
Turner, S.M., 242, 579
Turvey, C.L., 150
Tymchuk, A., 527
Tymchuk, M., 527
Tyrer, P., 200, 202

## U

Uchino, B.N., 280
Unis, A.S., 569
Updegraff, J.A., 206
Useda, D., 312
Ustun, T.B., 261
Uttal, W.R., 136

## V

Vaillant, G.E., 380
Vakkur, M., 314
Valenstein, E.S., 20, 42, 432
Valenzuela, C.F., 390
Van Amerigen, M., 231, 236
Van den Heuvel, O.A., 213
Van der Kolk, B.A., 233
Van der Vlugt, H., 133
Van Dyck, R., 222
Van Emmerik, A.A.P., 242
Van Etten, M., 242, 243
Van gogh, V., 56
Van Goozen, S.H.M., 439
Van Ommeren, M., 263
Van Reekum, R., 313
Vander Laan, K.L., 277
Vandereycken, W., 351
Vasey, M.W., 212
Vaughn, C.E., 466, 467
Vealenstein, E.S., 72
Vecera, S.P., 246
Verma, K.K., 417, 420
Vernon, P.A., 50, 310, 386
Vernon, P.L., 309

Vessey, R.J., 68
Vettess, L.C., 160
Vida, S., 512
Villella, J., 333
Vine, C., 427
Visintainer, M.A., 283
Vitousek, K.B., 356
Vohs, K.D., 353
Volavka, J., 474
Volicer, L., 482
Volkmar, F.R., 512, 517, 519, 520, 533, 536, 537, 541
Volpicelli, J.R., 283
Von Baeyer, C., 133
Von Bertalanffy, L., 39
Von Ranson, K.M., 39, 342
Vondra, J.I., 557, 578
Voss, W.D., 330

## W

Wachs, T.D., 329
Waddell, C., 547, 555
Wade, T.D., 355
Wagner, W., 184
Wagner-Jauregg, J., 21
Wagonfeld, M.O., 465
Waite, L.J., 595, 599
Wakefield, J., 9
Wald, J., 220
Wald, M.S., 634
Walden, J., 175
Waldron, M., 50
Walker, E., 448, 460
Walker, J.R., 265
Walker, L., 618
Wall, P.D., 285
Wall, T.L., 385
Wallace, J.F., 330, 396, 619
Waller, N.G., 251, 255
Wallis, C.J., 390
Walsh, D., 319
Walsh, W.B., 359
Walters, G.D., 368, 392
Walters, R., 55
Walters, V.L., 466
Wang. C.T., 633
Ward, T., 458
Warner, L.A., 381
Warren, S.T., 521
Wasylencki, D., 15
Waterhouse, L., 539, 540
Waterman, A.S., 585, 590
Waterman, G., 590
Waters, E., 559
Waterworth, D.M., 460
Watkins, J.G., 252
Watkins, L.R., 276
Watkins, S., 164
Watson, D., 143, 202, 203
Watson, D.C., 134
Watson, J.B., 35, 52, 78, 495
Watson, R.J., 428, 436
Watt, L.M., 608
Watt, M.C., 211
Wearden, A.J., 467
Weaver, T.L., 322
Webster, C., 624, 625, 626, 627
Webster, C.D., 626
Webster-Stratton, C., 565
Wechsler, D., 518
Wechsler, H., 381
Weekes, J.R., 134, 253
Wegner, D.M., 213
Wehr, T.A., 177
Weiden, P.J., 27, 474
Weinberger, D.R., 453, 461
Weiner, H., 269–270
Weiner, R.D., 73
Weinstein, H.M., 23
Weise, A., 332
Weishaar, M.E., 180
Weiss, G., 567
Weiss, J.M., 170
Weiss, S., 279
Weissman, M.M., 12, 13, 127–128, 151, 153, 172, 204
Weisz, J.R., 548, 549
Welch, S.L., 348, 351
Welham, J.I., 461
Wellington, C.L., 496
Wells, J.E., 13
Werner, J.S., 59, 591
Wesson, V.A., 177
West, C.H.K., 170
West, L.J., 401
Westen, D., 86, 90
Westergaard, T., 461
Westermeyer, J., 384
Weston, D., 34
Westra, H., 224
Wetter, D.W., 391
Whalen, C.K., 564
Wheeler, V.A., 571
Whipple, K., 90
Whislaw, I.Q., 41
Whisman, M.A., 58, 59, 595
White, J.A., 496, 498, 505
Whittemore, K.E., 621
Whybrow, P.C., 167, 168, 169, 177
Wicklund, R.A., 591
Wickramaratne, P.J., 13
Wicks-Nelson, R., 571, 572
Widiger, T.A., 114–115, 302, 308, 312, 321, 326
Wiebe, J.M.D., 321
Wiederman, M.W., 408
Wiegel, M., 420
Wiehe, V.R., 429
Wiersma, B., 182
Wierzbicki, M., 129
Wilcoxin, L.A., 80
Wildes, J.E., 350
Wileman, S.M., 177
Wilens, T., 565
Wilkins, K., 279
Willerman, L., 524
Williams, C.L., 125
Williams, L.M., 248, 428
Williams, M., 96
Williams, N., 411
Williams, R.B., 290
Williams, S., 96, 327, 328
Williams, s., 133
Williamson, G.M., 279
Wilson, D.B., 86
Wilson, G.D., 430
Wilson, G.T., 80, 82, 359
Wilson, J.Q., 550
Wilson, T.D., 55
Wincze, J.P., 420, 432
Wing, J.K., 466
Wing, L., 530, 539, 540
Wing, l., 538
Winograd, E., 248
Winokur, G., 150, 164
Winslow, B.W., 507
Winter, D.G., 300
Winters, K.C., 378
Wiseman, C.V., 349
Witmer, L., 572
Wittchen, H.-U., 13, 154, 199, 200
Witvliet, C., 277
Witztum, E., 435
Wolfe, D., 633
Wolfe, W., 398, 633
Wolff, M., 214
Wolpe, J., 78, 80, 219
Wolraich, M., 558
Wong, P.T.P., 608
Woo-Ming, A.M., 318, 324
Wood, J.M., 128, 129, 133
Woodard, J.L., 501
Woodill, G., 527
Woodside, D.B., 14, 339
Woodworth, M., 626
Woody, E., 247
Woody, G.E., 394
Woody, S.R., 198
Wooley, S.C., 356
Worden, J.W., 607
Wortman, C.B., 607
Wozney, K., 251, 255
Wright, K.D., 133
Wundt, W., 34
Wynn, J.W., 543
Wynne, H., 321
Wynne, L.C., 466

## Y

Yalom, I.D., 94–95
Yamaguchi, K., 384
Yamashita, I., 385
Yang, B., 180
Yang, J., 314
Yates, A., 355
Yates, W.R., 329
Yeh, E.-K., 13
Yeh, M., 548, 549
Yehuda, R., 239, 274
Yeung, P.P., 384
Yonkers, K.A., 200, 203
Yorkston, N.J., 90
Young, A., 261
Young, D.A., 133, 378
Yuokko, H., 488
Yurgelun-Todd, D., 376

## Z

Zaborny, B.A., 184
Zahn-Waxler, C., 163, 579
Zakzanis, K.K., 133, 377–378, 463
Zanarini, M.C., 324
Zarate, C.A., 154
Zarate, R., 472, 476
Zarit, J.M., 507
Zarit, S.H., 507
Zebb, B.J., 192
Zeitlin, S.B., 354
Zelkowitz, P., 323
Zempolich, K.A., 330
Zhao, S., 13
Zigler, E., 516, 519, 520, 528
Zill, N., 596
Zimmerman, M., 120, 311, 312
Zinbarg, R., 170, 210
Ziskin, J., 619
Zito, J.M., 74, 579
Zoccolillo, M., 257, 314
Zohar, J., 224
Zorn, C.A., 357
Zucker, K.J., 424, 436, 437
Zuckerman, M., 38, 54
Zul, M., 281
Zvolensky, M.J., 134, 211
Zweig-Frank, H., 255, 313

# Subject Index

Note: Entries for tables, figures, and footnotes are followed by "t," "f," "n," respectively.


A
abnormal behaviour
causes of. *See* systems theory
cross-cultural comparisons, 13–14
cultural considerations, 9–10
definitions of, 6–8
DSM-IV-TR definition, 8, 8t
harmful dysfunction, 7–8
individual experiences of personal distress, 6
multifactorial causes, 29
statistical norms, 7
subjective experience and social adjustment, 10–12
abnormal psychology
applied field, 8
defined, 3
Aboriginal peoples
alcohol and drug dependence, 384
depression, 152
poverty, 60
residential schools, 61–62
and suicide, 152
abreaction, 256
abstinence violation effect, 397
abstract thinking, loss of ability, 487–488
academic achievement tests, 571
acamprosate, 395
Achievement Place, 566
acquaintance rapes, 236, 421–429, 429f
acquired immune deficiency syndrome (AIDS), 284, 522
actuarial interpretation, 126
acute stress disorder (ASD)
and adjustment disorder, 235
alternative pathways, 240
anxiety, 233
arousal, 233
avoidance, 233
biological factors, 238–239
classification, 233–235
course and outcome, 236–237
described, 231
dissociative symptoms, 233
DSM-IV-TR diagnostic criteria, 234–235, 235t
epidemiology, 235–237
etiology, 237–240
exaggerated startle response, 233
historical perspective, 233
prevention, 241–243
psychological factors, 239–240
re-experiencing, 232
social factors, 237–238
symptoms and associated features, 230–233
treatment, 241–243
adaptive fears, 205
addiction, 366
*see also* substance dependence
adjustment disorders
*see also* life-cycle transitions
causes of, 235
definitions of, 585–586
described, 583
DSM-IV-TR diagnostic criteria, 586t
adolescent-limited externalizing behaviour, 550
adolescents
*see also* childhood psychological disorders
and contagious suicide, 182
eating disorders, 349–350
identity *vs.* role confusion, 586
pathological personality traits, 298
personality disorders, 314
adoption studies
alcoholism, 386–387, 387t
antisocial personality disorder (ASPD), 329
described, 50–51
mental retardation, 526
schizophrenia, 459
adrenalin, 274
adult development, 583
adult transition
case study, 592
classification of identity conflicts, 589–590
described, 584
emotional turmoil, 589
epidemiology of identity conflicts, 590–591
etiology, 591
"forgotten half," 590–591
identity crisis, 588
moratorium, 588
research, 591
role and relationship changes, 588–589
"storm and stress," 591
treatment during, 592
typical experiences, 588–589
affect, 139, 149n
affective disorders, 149n
*see also* mood disorders
affective flattening, 447
affiliation, 54, 300
age of onset
anorexia nervosa, 349
bipolar disorders, 150
bulimia nervosa, 349
mental retardation, 517
schizophrenia, 445
unipolar disorders, 149
ageism, 603
aggression, and externalizing disorders, 550
aging
bereavement, 606–607
case study, 605–606
classification, 608
described, 584, 602–603
epidemiology, 608
etiology, 609
grief, 606–607
integrity *vs.* despair, 587, 605
life satisfaction, 604–606
memory changes, 486–487
menopause, 603–604
mental health, 607
physical functioning and health, 603–604
relationships, 605–606
reminiscence, 607–608
research, 609
sensation and physical movement, 604
treatment during, 609–610
typical experiences, 603–607
work, 604–606
agnosia, 487
agoraphobia
case study, 190–191
described, 190, 193–194
diagnostic criteria, 198
insecure attachment, 207
stressful life events, 206
AIDS, 284, 522
alcohol, 370–371
alcohol-induced persisting amnestic disorder, 490–491
alcohol myopia, 393
alcohol withdrawal delirium, 369
Alcoholics Anonymous (AA), 395–396
alcoholism
Aboriginal peoples, 384
adoption studies, 386–387, 387t
Alcoholics Anonymous (AA), 395–396
associated occupations, 381
attention-allocation theory, 393
biological factors, 385–390
case study, 367
cognitive behaviour therapies, 396–398
controlled drinking controversy, 400–401
coping skills training, 397
and depression, 145
detoxification, 394–395
disease model, 400
dopamine and reward pathways, 388
endogenous opiod system, 390
etiology, 384–394
expectations about drug effects, 391–393
gender differences, 382
genetic factors, 394
genetics of, 385–387
integrated systems, 393–394
male deaths caused by, 371f
and marital status, 59
medications during remission, 395
neuroanatomy, 388–390
neurochemistry, 388–390
prevalence, 381
psychological factors, 390–393
relapse prevention, 397–398
serotonin hypothesis, 390
short-term motivational therapy, 398
social factors, 384–385
subtypes of, 379
tension-reduction hypothesis, 391
treatment, 394–400
twin studies, 386
alexithymia, 264
alienated identity achievement, 590
Allan Memorial Institute, 23
allegiance effect, 88, 360
alleles, 48
alliances, 94
alogia, 448
alternative pathways
acute stress disorder, 240
cardiovascular disease (CVD), 291–292
eating disorders, 355–356
externalizing disorders, 561–562
posttraumatic stress disorder, 240
altruistic suicide, 178
Alzheimer's disease
amyloid plaques, 493
brain lesions in, 492–493
brain tissue damage, 482, 494f
caregiver support, 507
diagnosis of, 492–493
DSM-IV-TR criteria, 493t
environmental factors, 504–505
gender differences, 500, 500f
genetic factors, 502–503, 502f
medication, 505–506
neurofibrillary tangles, 46, 492–493
neurotransmitters, 503
speed of onset, 492
survival rates, 500
treatment, 505

amenorrhea, 341
American Association on Mental Retardation, 512–514, 516, 518–519, 519t
amnesia
anterograde amnesia, 487
dissociative amnesia, 233, 249
interpersonality amnesia, 253
retrograde amnesia, 73, 487
selective amnesia, 249
amnestic disorders
*see also* cognitive disorders
alcohol-induced persisting amnestic disorder, 490–491
brain tissue changes, 482
case study, 490–491
described, 481
Korsakoff's syndrome, 490–491
symptoms and associated features, 489–491
amniocentesis, 527
amok, 110
amphetamine, 372–373
amyloid plaques, 493
anaclitic depression, 577
anal sex, 410
analogue studies, 170–171
anatomy, 40
androgynous couples, 598
anger, and externalizing disorders, 550
angina pectoris, 287
anhedonia, 447–448
animal models of psychopathology, 170–171, 209
animals
depression, 170
ethology, 53
imprinting, 53
anomic suicide, 178
anorexia nervosa
*see also* eating disorders
age of onset, 349–350
amenorrhea, 341
binge eating/purging type, 346
*vs.* bulimia nervosa, 338, 342, 345t
case study, 338–339
comorbidity, 342, 342f
control, struggle for, 341
course and outcome, 356–357
and depression, 342
described, 337
disturbance in weight or shape evaluation, 340
DSM-IV-TR criteria, 346, 346t
enmeshed families, 351
fear of gaining weight, 340
incidence, 347, 347f–348f
medical complications, 341
and obsessive-compulsive disorder (OCD), 342
and obsessive-compulsive personality disorder, 342
prevalence, 347
refusal to maintain normal weight, 340
restricting type, 346
sexual disinterest, 341
symptoms and associated features, 339–342
treatment, 356
anoxia, 524
anterograde amnesia, 487
antianxiety medications, 223–435
anticonvulsant medications, and bipolar mood disorder, 175
antidepressant medications
anxiety disorders, 223–224
attention-deficit/hyperactivity disorder (ADHD), 564
bulimia nervosa, 359
paraphilias, 435
posttraumatic stress disorder (PTSD), 242
somatoform disorders, 264
unipolar mood disorder, 172–174, 173t
antigens, 274
antihypertensives, 292
antipsychotic drugs
atypical antipsychotics, 474–475
and autistic disorders, 541
classical antipsychotics, 473
effectiveness of, 473
extrapyramidal symptoms (EPS), 474
maintenance medication, 473, 473f
motor side effects, 473–474
neuroleptic drugs, 473
relapse rates, 473, 473f
tardive dyskinesia (TD), 474
antisocial personality disorder (ASPD)
across the lifespan, 328
biological factors, 329
case study, 298, 299, 324
comorbidity, 326–327
and conduct disorder, 325
described, 304
DSM-IV-TR criteria, 326–327, 326t
etiology, 328–331
gender differences, 312
historical perspective, 325
impulse control problems, 320
Paul Bernardo and Karla Homolka, 327–328
prediction of, 550
psychological factors, 330–331
and psychopathy, 325, 326
social factors, 329–330
treatment, 331
anxiety
and acute stress disorder (ASD), 233
and cardiovascular disease (CVD), 290
in children, 569–570
and depression, 143, 202–203
described, 191
evolutionary significance of, 205
multidimensional interaction model, 281
and perception of control, 209–210
and posttraumatic stress disorder (PTSD), 233
anxiety disorders
across the lifespan, 203–204
agoraphobia, 190, 191, 193–194, 198
anxiety, 191
attention to threat, 212
biased information processing, 211–212
catastrophic misinterpretation, 210–211
classification, 196–200
comorbidity, 201–203
compulsions, 194, 196
course and outcome, 200–201, 201f
cross-cultural comparisons, 204
and depression, 143, 189–190, 199f, 202–203
DSM-IV-TR approach, 197–200, 197t
epidemiology, 201–205
etiology. *See* anxiety disorders (etiology)
excessive worry, 192
gender differences, 203
generalized anxiety disorder, 199, 213, 213f
historical perspective, 196–197
"lumpers," 200
obsessions, 194–196
obsessive-compulsive disorder. *See* obsessive-compulsive disorder (OCD)
overview, 189–190
panic attacks, 192–193, 192t
panic disorder, 197
phobias, 193–194, 208–209
prevalence, 201, 201t
research, 205–218
social phobia, 198–199, 212f, 214
specific phobia, 198
"splitters," 200
and substance dependence, 202–203
symptoms, 191–196
treatment. *See* anxiety disorders (treatment)
anxiety disorders (etiology)
adaptive fears, 205
anxiety sensitivity, 211
attachment relationships, 207
attention to threat, 212
biased information processing, 211–212
biological factors, 213–218
catastrophic misinterpretation, 210–211
childhood adversity, 206–207
cognitive factors, 209–212
family studies, 213–214
genetic factors, 213–215
learning processes, 208–209
maladaptive fears, 205
neuroanatomy, 215–217
neurochemistry, 217–218
observational learning, 208–209
perception of control, 209–210
preparedness model, 208
psychological factors, 207–213
separation anxiety, 207
social factors, 205–207
stressful life events, 205–206
thought suppression, 213
twin studies, 214–215, 215t
anxiety disorders (treatment)
antianxiety medications, 223
antidepressant medications, 223–224
biological interventions, 222–224, 224t
breathing retraining, 222
cognitive therapy, 222
exposure and response prevention, 220
interoceptive exposure, 219–220
medications, 222–224, 224t
psychological interventions, 219–222
relaxation training, 221
summary of, 224t
systematic desensitization, 219–220
anxiety-sensitive subtype, 399
anxiety sensitivity, 211
anxiolytics, 366
anxious attachments, 53, 578
apathy, 448
aphasia, 487
apparent sensory deficits, 535
applied relaxation (AR), 97
appraisal of life events, 272
apraxia, 487
arousal, 233
Asperger's disorder, 536
assertive community treatment (ACT), 477
assertiveness training, 81
assessment
assumptions about consistency of behaviour, 116–117
biological systems, 130–136
Canadian contributions and issues, 133–134
case study, 102–103
described, 101, 116–122
goals of, 116
levels of analysis, 117
psychological systems, 118–130
purposes of, 116
social systems, 130
assessment procedures
Beck Depression Inventory (BDI), 127, 127t
behavioural coding systems, 123–124
biological systems, 130–136
brain imaging techniques, 132–136
evaluation of, 117–118
Family Environment Scale (FES), 130
Family Interaction Coding System (FICS), 130
formal observation schedules, 123–124

functional MRI (fMRI), 135
interviews, 119–121
magnetic resonance imaging (MRI), 132–134
Minnesota Multiphasic Personality Inventory (MMPI-2), 125–127
objective tests, 124–127
observational procedures, 121–124
personality inventories, 124–127
personality tests, 124
positron emission tomography (PET), 134
projective personality tests, 128–130
psychological systems, 118–130
psychophysiological assessment, 131–132, 131t
rating scales, 122, 123t
self-monitoring, 123
self-report inventories, 127
single photon emission computed tomography (SPECT), 135
social systems, 130
structured interviews, 119–121, 120t
Thematic Apperception Test (TAT), 129
types of, 118
assisted suicide, 607
associative loosening, 469
asylum, 18–20
atherosclerosis, 288
attachment
agoraphobia, 207
and anxiety disorders, 207
described, 53
and panic disorder, 207
attachment theory, 53–54, 77, 577
attention-allocation theory, 393
attention-deficit disorder (ADD), 552
attention-deficit/hyperactivity disorder (ADHD)
*see also* externalizing disorders
antidepressant medication, 564
behavioural family therapy (BFT), 565
comorbidity, 554, 554f, 560
Conners Teacher Rating Scale, 551, 551f
continuous performance test, 552
diet and food additives, 558
DSM-IV-TR diagnostic criteria, 552, 553t
genetics, 557
neuropsychological abnormalities, 558
*vs.* oppositional defiant disorder (ODD), 553, 553f–554f
overall treatment success rates, 563f
prevalence, 555
problem-solving skills training (PSST), 565
psychostimulants, 562, 564t
social factors, 560–561
subtypes, 554
attention deficits, 551–552
attention to threat, 212
attentional dysfunction, and schizophrenia, 471
attribution errors, 56
attribution retraining, 82
attributions, 55, 82
atypical antipsychotics, 474–475
authoritarian parenting, 333
authoritative parenting, 54
autism. *See* autistic disorder
autistic disorder
*see also* pervasive developmental disorders
apparent sensory deficits, 535
biological factors, 538–540
case studies, 532
case study, 530
course and outcome, 540
described, 530
different biological causes, 539
disorder of brain development, 540
DSM-IV-TR diagnostic criteria, 536, 537t
epidemiology, 537–538
etiology, 538–540
gaze aversion, 532
genetic factors, 539
impaired communication, 533–534
impaired social interaction, 531–533
integration, 539
intensive behaviour modification, 541–543, 543t
IQ scores, 536t
medication, 541
and mental retardation, 535–536
multiple pathways, 539
neuroanatomy, 539–540
neurophysiology, 539
psychological factors, 538
psychotherapy, 541–543
self-injurious behaviour, 535
social factors, 538
stereotyped behaviour, interests and activities, 534
symptoms and associated features, 530–536
theory of mind, lack of, 531–532
treatment, 540–543
autoerotic asphyxia, 426
autonomic nervous system, 46–47, 131, 275f
autosomal dominant disorders, 48f
autosomal dominant trait, 495
autosomal gene, 48
autosomal recessive disorders, 48f
auxiliary axes, 114
aversion therapy, 80–434
aversive drift, 469
avoidance, 233
avoidance-oriented coping, 281
avoidant personality disorder, 199, 306
avolition, 448
axon terminal, 41
azapirones, 223


## B


B cells, 274
balanced placebo design, 391
barbiturates, 375
base rates, 624, 625
battered woman syndrome, 618–619
beauty standards, 348–349
Beck Depression Inventory (BDI), 127, 127t
Beck's cognitive therapy. *See* cognitive therapy
befriending, 273
behaviour genetics, 47
*see also* genetics
behaviour modification, 541–543, 543t
behaviour therapy. *See* cognitive behaviour therapies
behavioural coding systems, 123–124
behavioural conditioning mechanisms, 369
behavioural family therapy (BFT), 565, 566
behavioural gerontology, 609
behavioural management, and dementia, 506
behavioural marital therapy, 602
behavioural medicine
defined, 269
disease, 269–270
behavioural symptoms, 144–145
behaviourism, 35, 78
benzodiazepines, 222–375
bereavement, 606–607
Bernardo, Paul, 327–328
beta-amyloid, 493
beta blockers, 292
biased information processing, 211–212
bilateral ECT, 72
binge eating, 342, 343–344
binge eating disorder, 347
binge eating/purging type of anorexia nervosa, 346
biofeedback, 292–293
biological factors
acute stress disorder (ASD), 238–239
alcoholism, 385–390
antisocial personality disorder (ASPD), 329
anxiety disorders, 213–218
autistic disorder, 538–540
behaviour genetics, 47–52
brain structures, 43–46
cardiovascular disease (CVD), 288
cerebral hemispheres, 43–45
chromosomal disorders, 520–521
dementia, 502–504
dissociative disorders, 255
eating disorders, 354–355
externalizing disorders, 556–558
family transitions, 599
genetic disorders, 521–522
internalizing disorders, 577
mental retardation, 520–524
and mind-body dualism, 42
mood disorders, 163–169
neural networks, 42–43
neuron, 41, 41f
neurotransmitters, 41, 42
paraphilias, 430–432
posttraumatic stress disorder (PTSD), 238–239
pregnancy and birth complications, 460
psychophysiology, 46–47
receptors, 41
reuptake, 41
schizophrenia, 458–465
schizotypal personality disorder, 317–318
sexual dysfunctions, 418
somatoform disorders, 262
suicide, 181
synapse, 41
synaptic transmission, 41f
temperament, 557
trauma exposure, 239
viral infections, 461
biological paradigm, 32
biological systems, assessment of, 130–136
biological therapies
described, 69
psychopharmacology, 73–75
psychosurgery, 73
sexual dysfunctions, 421
symptom alleviation, 72, 75
biopsychosocial approach, 29
biopsychosocial model, 68
bipolar II disorder, 147
bipolar mood disorder
*see also* mood disorders
anticonvulsant medications, 175
classification, 147–148
cognitive therapy, 175–176
course and outcome, 150
cyclothymia, 148
described, 140
electroconvulsive therapy, 176
hypomania, 147
interpersonal therapy, 175–176
lithium, 175
manic episodes, 147–148t
psychotherapy, 175–176
social factors and, 157–158
treatment, 174–176
birth cohort trend, 154
birth complications
and mental retardation, 523–524
and schizophrenia, 460
bizarre behaviour, 448–449, 450
blunted affect, 447
body contour rating scale, 353f
body dysmorphic disorder, 259

body mass index, 340, 340n
borderline personality disorder (BPD)
case study, 305, 319
and childhood maltreatment, 322–323
comorbidity, 321–322
described, 305
DSM-IV-TR criteria, 321–322, 322t
etiology, 322–323
historical perspective, 320–321
impulse control problems, 320
treatment, 323–324
boundaries, 594
the brain
anxiety disorders, 215–217, 218
and autistic disorder, 540
brain tissue changes, and cognitive disorders, 482
externalizing disorders, 558
hard signs of brain damage, 558
and Huntington's disease, 495f
major brain structures, 43–46
mood disorders, 167–168, 167f–168f
plaque, 482
reward pathways, 388, 388f
and schizophrenia, 461–464, 462f–464f
soft signs of brain damage, 558
brain imaging techniques
described, 132–136
mood disorders, 167–168, 167f–168f
schizophrenia, 461–464
brainstorming, 82
breathing-related sleep disorder, 286
breathing retraining, 222
brief psychotic disorder, 454
Briquet's syndrome, 258
bulimia nervosa
*see also* eating disorders
age of onset, 349–350
*vs.* anorexia nervosa, 338, 342, 345t
antidepressant medications, 359
binge eating, 342, 343–344
case study, 10–11, 343
cognitive behaviour therapies, 359
comorbidity, 345
course and outcome, 361
and depression, 345
described, 337–338
DSM-IV-TR diagnostic criteria, 346–347t
excessive emphasis on weight and shape, 344
inappropriate compensatory behaviour, 342, 344
incidence, 347–348
interpersonal psychotherapy, 359–361
medical complications, 345
prevalence, 348, 348f
purging, 344
symptoms, 342–345
treatment, 359–361, 361f
twin studies, 355
burden of proof, 21, 616

## C

Cameron, Ewen, 23
Canada
anxiety sensitivity, and panic attacks, 211
assessment research, 133–134
depression, research in, 161
healthcare system, 95–96
leading causes of death, 282f
Montreaux residential program, 357–358
suicide rates, 575f
Canadian Charter of Rights and Freedoms, 628
Canadian Criminal Code, 616, 621
Canadian Psychological Association code of ethics, 637
Canadian Study of Health and Aging, 499–500
cancer, 282–284
cannabinoids, 366
cannabis, 375–376
cardiovascular disease (CVD)
alternative pathways, 291–292
angina pectoris, 287
and anxiety, 290
and behaviour, 287
biological factors, 288
cardiovascular reactivity to stress, 288–289
classification, 287
coronary heart disease (CHD), 286, 287
and depression, 290
epidemiology, 287–288
etiology, 288–292
hypertension, 286, 287–288
integration, 291
and job strain, 289
and life stressors, 289
myocardial infarction, 287
prevention, 292–294
psychological factors, 288–290
risk factors, 287
social factors, 290–291
stress and, 286, 288–290
sudden cardiac death, 287
symptoms, 286–287
treatment, 292
Type A behaviour pattern, 289–290
cardiovascular reactivity to stress, 288–289
caregiver support, 507
case control design, 468
case studies
adult transition, 592
aging, 605–606
agoraphobia, 190–191
alcohol dependence, 367
alcohol-induced persisting amnestic disorder, 490–491
anorexia nervosa, 338–339
antisocial personality disorder, 299, 324–325
anxiety disorder, treatment of, 218–219
autistic disorder, 530, 532
body dysmorphic disorder, 259
borderline personality disorder, 305, 319
bulimia nervosa, 10–11, 343
causes of abnormal behaviour, 30–31
custody dispute, 632
delirium, 483–484
dementia, advanced stages of, 483–484
dementia, early stages of, 482–483
dependent personality disorder (DPD), 331–332
depression, 69, 141
described, 22
diagnosis and assessment, 102–103
disorganized schizophrenia, 445–446
dissociative fugue, 244–245
dissociative identity disorder (DID), 250–251
divorce in midlife, 584–585
dyspareunia, 416
Edmund Yu, 614–615
externalizing disorders, 548–549, 559
heroin, 374
internalizing disorders, 567–568
male erectile disorder, 413
manic episodes, 142
marital therapy, 601
masochism, 425
mental retardation, 513
narcissistic personality disorder, 308–309
obsessive-compulsive disorder, 195
paranoid schizophrenia, 4–5, 444
paraphilia, 422–423
Paul Bernardo and Karla Homolka, 327–328
post-partum suicide, 177
posttraumatic stress disorder (PTSD), 231–232
relapse to heroin use, 397–398
schizophrenic disorders, 4–5, 444, 445–446, 448–449
schizotypal personality disorder, 315–317
sexual aversion disorder, 412
sexual communication, 406–407
stress, and heart attacks, 270–271
substance use disorders among the elderly, 383
transsexualism, 437
uses and limitations, 22–24
catastrophic misinterpretation, 210–211
catatonia, 449–450
catatonic type of schizophrenia, 452
categorical approach to classification, 103–104
catharsis, 75
causal attributions, 159
causality
correlation *vs.* causation, 37
and correlational study, 39
described, 37–38
diathesis-stress model, 38
equifinality, 38
homeostasis, 39–40
multifinality, 38
reciprocal causality, 39–40
reverse causality, 39
risk factors, 38
third-variable possibility, 39
central nervous system, 46, 131, 366
cerebellum, 43
cerebral cortex, 44
cerebral hemispheres, 43–45
chest pain, 287
child abuse
*see also* child sexual abuse
child neglect, 633
dispositions of substantiated cases, 633–634
and dissociative disorders, 254, 255t
forms of, 633
increased reports of, 633
Munchausen-by-Proxy syndrome (MBPS), 633
physical child abuse, 633
psychological abuse, 633
reporting requirements, 633
child custody, 630–632
child molester, 427
child neglect, 633
child sexual abuse
and borderline personality disorder, 322–323
described, 633
dissociative identity disorder (DID), 254
and eating disorders, 351
prevalence, 633
childhood adversity, and anxiety disorders, 206–207
childhood disintegrative disorder, 536
childhood psychological disorders
externalizing disorders. *See* externalizing disorders
internalizing and other disorders. *See* internalizing disorders
Ontario Child Health Study, 575–577
overview, 547–548
prevalence, 576f
childhood schizophrenia, abandonment of term, 536
children
*see also* childhood psychological disorders
and antisocial behaviour, 329–330
anxiety, 569–570
attachment theory, 53–54

conduct disorder, 325
and depression, 567–568, 569
developmental norms, 547
fears, 569–570
identity *vs.* role confusion, 586
inhibited to the unfamiliar, 577
neglected children, 571
parenting and, 54
poverty and, 60
rejected children, 571
resilience, 578
temperament, 54
chlorpromazine, 472
chorea, 495
chromosomal disorders, 520–521
chromosomes, 47
cingulotomy, 73
circadian rhythm sleep disorder, 286
civil commitment
base rates, 624, 625
clinical assessment, 623–627
community commitment, 629
dangerous to self and others, 622–623
defined, 621
grounds, 622
outpatient commitment, 629
prediction of dangerous behaviour, 623–627, 626t
procedures, 622
rationales for, 621–622
suicide, assessment of risk of, 627–636
civil law
civil commitment, 621, 627, 629–630
deinstitutionalization, 628–629
informed consent, 628
libertarian views, 621
paternalist approaches, 621, 629–630
patient rights, 627–628
right to refuse treatment, 628
classical conditioning, 34
classification
acute stress disorder (ASD), 233–235
aging, 608
anxiety disorders, 196–200
cardiovascular disease (CVD), 287
cognitive disorders, 491–498
dementia, 492–498
dissociative disorders, 247–250
eating disorders, 345–347
externalizing disorders, 552–555
identity conflicts, 589–590
illness, 280–282
internalizing and other disorders, 572–574
life-cycle transitions, 585–588
mental retardation, 517–519
mood disorders, 145–149
paraphilias, 423–429
personality disorders, 303–310
pervasive developmental disorders, 536–537
posttraumatic stress disorder (PTSD), 233–235
schizophrenic disorders, 450–455
somatoform disorders, 257–260
stress, 280–282
substance use disorders, 378–380
troubled family relationships, 595–596
classification systems
categorical approach to classification, 103–104
and cultural issues, 109–111
defined, 103
described, 101, 103
descriptive based classification, 104–105
diagnostic systems, 105
dimensional approach to classification, 104, 307–310
DSM-IV-TR. *See* DSM-IV-TR (*Diagnostic and Statistical Manual of Mental Disorders*)
evaluation of, 112–115
historical perspective, 105–107
multiaxial classification system, 108
need for, 105
reliability, 112
theoretically based classification, 104–105
unresolved questions, 114
validity, 112–114
client-centred therapy, 84
clinical assessment. *See* assessment
clinical depression. *See* depression
clinical importance, 221
clinical psychology, 16
clinical symptoms (Axis 1), 108–109
clinically significant finding, 79
clozapine, 474
cocaine, 372–373
code of ethics, 637
coercion, 559
cognition
assessment of cognitive impairment, 488–488t, 488f
dementia, and cognitive impairment, 485–488–489
intellectually engaging activities, effect of, 505
mechanics (fluid intelligence), 486
neuropsychological assessment, 488–488f
and normal aging, 486–487
pragmatics (crystallized intelligence), 486
and schizophrenia, 471
cognitive behaviour therapies
alcoholism, 396–398
anxiety disorders, 221–222
aversion therapy, 80
Beck's cognitive therapy, 82–83
beginnings of behaviour therapy, 78
breathing retraining, 222
bulimia nervosa, 359
cognitive behaviour therapy (CBT), 97, 476
cognitive techniques, 82
contingency management, 81
coping skills training, 397
definitions of, 90t
described, 70–71, 78
empiricism, commitment to, 83
experimental method, 78, 79–80
exposure therapies, 80
flooding, 80
paraphilias, 434–435, 435f
posttraumatic stress disorder (PTSD), 242–243
rational-emotive therapy, 83
relapse prevention, 397–398
relaxation training, 221
short-term motivational therapy, 398
social skills training, 81–82
somatoform disorders, 264
substance use disorders, 396–398
systematic desensitization, 78–80
in vivo desensitization, 80
cognitive behaviour therapy (CBT), 97, 476
cognitive behavioural paradigm, 34–35
cognitive biases, 56
cognitive conflicts, 595
cognitive disorders
*see also* amnestic disorders; dementia
aging and, 607
and brain disease, 482
classification, 491–498
diagnosis, accuracy of, 505
DSM-IV-TR, 492t
epidemiology, 498–501
etiology, 501–505
historical perspective, 491–492
symptoms and associated features, 484–491
treatment and management, 505–507
cognitive dysregulation, 309
cognitive factors
anxiety disorders, 209–212
attention to threat, 212
biased information processing, 211–212
catastrophic misinterpretation, 210–211
described, 55–56
panic attacks, 210–211
perception of control, 209–210
thought suppression, 213
unconscious mental processes, 245–247
cognitive symptoms, 143–144
cognitive techniques, 82
cognitive therapy
anxiety disorders, 222
bipolar mood disorder, 175–176
decatastrophisizing, 222
described, 82–83
and panic attacks, 218
Type A behaviour pattern, 294
unipolar mood disorder, 171–172
cognitive vulnerability, 158–160
cohort, 348
cohort effects, 348
collectivism, 314
communication, impaired, 533–534
communication problems, 598
communication skills, 93
community commitment, 629
community psychology, 96
comorbidity
anorexia nervosa, 342, 342f
antisocial personality disorder, 326–327
anxiety disorders, 199f, 201–203
attention-deficit/hyperactivity disorder (ADHD), 554, 553f–554f, 560
borderline personality disorder (BPD), 321–322
bulimia nervosa, 345
dependent personality disorder (DPD), 332
depression, 199f
described, 13, 115f
and DSM-IV-TR, 114–115
interpretation of, 115
oppositional defiant disorder (ODD), 554, 553f–554f
personality disorders, 311, 318
posttraumatic stress disorder (PTSD), 235
schizotypal personality disorder, 317
somatoform disorder, 261
substance dependence, 380
comparison groups, 468
compulsions, 194, 196
compulsivity, 310
conceptual skills, 516
concordance rate, 49
concurrent validity, 113
conditioned response, 34
conditioned stimulus, 34
condom use, 410
conduct disorder, 325, 552, 554–555, 555t, 566–567, 575
confidentiality, 636
conflict resolution, 93
confounded, 79
Conners Teacher Rating Scale, 551, 551f
construct validity, 415
*Consumer Reports* study, 88
contagious suicide, 182
contemporary diagnostic systems. *See* DSM-IV-TR (*Diagnostic and Statistical Manual of Mental Disorders*)
contempt, 598
context, and personality, 303

contingency, 81
contingency management, 81
Continuous Performance Task (CPT), 471
continuous performance test, 552
control group, 79, 278
controlled drinking controversy, 400–401
convenience sampling, 409
conversion disorder, 257, 257f
coping
avoidance-oriented coping, 281
control, importance of, 278
described, 269
emotion-focused coping, 277
emotion-oriented coping, 281
humour, 278–279
multidimensional interaction model, 281
optimism, 278, 279t
outlets for frustration, 277
predictability, importance of, 277
problem-focused coping, 276, 277
repression hypothesis, 277
task-oriented coping, 281
use of, 269
coping skills training, 397
coprophilia, 424
coronary heart disease (CHD), 286, 287
coronary occlusion, 288
corpus callosum, 43
correlation, *vs.* causation, 37
correlation coefficient, 39
correlational study, 39
corticotrophin-releasing factor (CRF), 274
cortisol, 274
counselling psychology, 16
countertransference, 76
couples therapy, 93, 601–602
course and outcome
acute stress disorder (ASD), 236–237
anorexia nervosa, 356–357
anxiety disorders, 200–201, 201f
autistic disorder, 540–541
bipolar mood disorder, 150
bulimia nervosa, 361
externalizing disorders, 567
internalizing disorders, 579
mood disorders, 149–150
posttraumatic stress disorder (PTSD), 236–237, 237f
schizophrenia, 445, 454–455, 454f, 455–456
substance dependence, 380
unipolar mood disorder, 149, 149f
courtship disorder, 432
Creutzfeldt-Jakob disease, 504
criminal responsibility, 615
*see also* mental disorder defence
crisis centres, 182–183
crisis of the healthy personality, 585
critical incident stress (CIS), 241–242
critical incident stress debriefing (CISD), 242
criticism, 598
cross-cultural comparisons
*see also* culture
anxiety disorders, 204–205
assessment procedures, validity of, 118
dementia, 501
expressed emotion (EE), 468–469
externalizing disorders, 560
incidence and prevalence of mental disorders, 13–14
mood disorders, 151–152
process of, 316
schizophrenia, 457–458
sexual dysfunctions, 417–418
"storm and stress" of adolescence, 591
cross-cultural psychology, 316
cross-generational comparisons, and mood disorders, 154
Cross-National Collaborative Panic Study, 204
Cross-National Collaborative Study, 12–13, 151, 204
cross-sectional study, 291
crossing of paraphilic behaviours, 430, 430f
crystallized intelligence, 486
cultural-familial retardation, 524, 524f, 526
culture
*see also* cross-cultural comparisons
and classification systems, 110–111
defined, 9, 316
diagnostic practice, impact on, 9
and female sexuality, 419
homosexuality, and diagnostic practice, 9
and personality, 313–315
and somatoform disorder, 261, 261f
culture-bound syndromes
amok, 110
described, 110–111
kayak angst, 204
neurasthenia, 152
pibloktoq, 111
culture-fair tests, 516
Cushing's syndrome, 166
custody disputes, 630–632
cyclothymia, 148
cytomegalovirus, 522

## D

dangerous to self and others, 622–623
Danish schizophrenia project, 461–462
death, leading causes of, 282f
decatastrophisizing, 222
defence mechanisms, 33, 34t, 70
defensiveness, 598
deinstitutionalization, 628–629
deinstitutionalization movement, 529
delay of gratification, 561
delirium
*see also* cognitive disorders
case study, 483–484
*vs.* dementia, 481
described, 481
distinguishing features, 485t
epidemiology, 498–501
etiology, 501–502
symptoms and associated features, 485
delirium tremens (DTs), 369
delusional disorder, 453
delusions, 447
demand and withdrawal pattern, 594
dementia
*see also* cognitive disorders
abstract thinking, loss of, 487–488
advanced stages of, 483–484
agnosia, 487
of Alzheimer's type, 492–493, 493t
anterograde amnesia, 487
apraxia, 487
assessment of cognitive impairment, 488–488t, 488f
associated disorders, 492–498
behavioural management, 506
biological factors, 502–504
brain tissue changes, 482
caregiver support, 507
case study, 482–483, 484
classification, 492–498
cognitive symptoms, 485–488
cross-cultural comparisons, 501
*vs.* delirium, 481
dementia with Lewy bodies (DLB), 497
and depression, 489
*vs.* depression, 498, 498f
described, 481
distinguishing features, 485t
DSM-IV-TR criteria, 492, 493t
dyskinesia, 489
early symptoms of, 482–483, 482–483
emotional difficulties, 489
environmental factors, 504–505
environmental management, 506
epidemiology, 498–501
etiology, 502–505
frontotemporal dementia (FTD), 493
gender differences, 500, 500f
Huntington's disease, 495, 495f, 496
immune system dysfunction, 504
incidence, 498–499
language disturbance, 487
medication, 505–506
memory loss, 487
motivational problems, 489
motor behaviours, 489
multi-infarct dementia, 496–497
neuropsychological assessment, 488–488f
neurotransmitters, 503
*vs.* normal aging, 486–487
Parkinson's disease, 496
perception, 487
personality changes, 489
Pick's disease, 493
prevalence, 499–500
prevalence by subtype, 500–501
problem-solving skills, loss of, 488
social interactions, 506–507
social judgment, failure of, 488
survival rates, 500
symptoms and associated features, 485–489
vascular dementia, 496–497, 500, 500f
viral infections, 504
dementia praecox, 105, 450
*see also* schizophrenia
dementia with Lewy bodies (DLB), 497
dendrites, 41
denial, 34t, 70
depatterning, 23
dependent personality disorder (DPD)
case study, 331–332
comorbidity, 332
described, 306–307
DSM-IV-TR criteria, 332, 333t
etiology, 332–333
gender differences, 314
historical perspective, 332
treatment, 333
dependent variable, 79
depersonalization, 233
depersonalization disorder, 249
depressed mood, 139, 142
depression
*see also* mood disorders
and Aboriginal peoples, 152
and alcoholism, 145
anaclitic depression, 577
and anorexia nervosa, 342
and anxiety, 143, 202–203
and anxiety disorders, 143, 189–190, 199f
and bulimia nervosa, 345
and cardiovascular disease (CVD), 290
case study, 69, 141
childhood incidences, 162
in children, 567–568, 569
clinical syndrome, 139
cognitive and interpersonal factors, integration of, 162–163
cognitive vulnerability, 158–160
course of, 149f
and dementia, 489
*vs.* dementia, 498, 498f

described, 139
double depression, 146
and eating disorders, 352–353
episodes of, 140
hopelessness, 159, 161
interpersonal perspective, 160–162
leading cause of disability, 139
mood, 139
and negative life events, 160
*vs.* normal sadness, 140, 141t
onset of, 162
postpartum onset, 149
psychomotor retardation, 144
response styles and gender, 162
risk factors, 165f
self-destructive impulses, 143
and social relationships, 160–162
and suicide, 143–144, 178
theoretical advances in understanding, 161
in women, social origins of, 156–157
depressive triad, 158
derailment, 449
derealization, 233
descriptive based classification, 104–105
determinism, 35
deterrence, 616
detoxification, 394–395
"developmental coordination disorder," 574
developmental deviations, 571
developmental norms, 40, 547, 550
developmental psychopathology, 547
developmental stages, 57–58, 57t
deviation IQ, 515
dexamethasone suppression test (DST), 167
diagnosis
case study, 102–103
cognitive disorders, 505
gender bias, and personality disorders, 312–313
kappa, 112
and labelling theory, 106–107
meaning of, 101
diagnosis by exclusion, 262
*Diagnostic and Statistical Manual of Mental Disorders. See* DSM-IV-TR (*Diagnostic and Statistical Manual of Mental Disorders*)
diagnostic reliability, 112
diagnostic systems, 105
dialectical behaviour therapy (DBT), 323–324
diastolic blood pressure, 287
diathesis, 38
diathesis-stress model, 38
dietary restraint, 354
"dieting disorder," 337
*see also* eating disorders
dimensional approach to classification, 104
Dimensional Assessment of Personality Pathology (DAPP), 309–310, 309f–310f
dimensional perspective on personality disorders, 307–310
diminished integration, 178
diminished regulation, 178
dis-ease, 269–270
disability, leading causes of, 139, 140t
discipline, and externalizing disorders, 559–560
discontinuance syndrome, 375
disease burden, 13
dismantling studies, 96
disorganization
bizarre behaviour, 448–449, 450
catatonia, 449–450
described, 446
disorganized speech, 448–449
inappropriate effect, 450
stuporous state, 450
thinking disturbances, 448–449
disorganized speech, 448–449
disorganized type of schizophrenia
case study, 445–446
described, 452
displacement, 34t
dissocial behaviour, 310
dissociation
described, 229
disagreements about, 229
dissociative amnesia, 233, 249
dissociative disorders
biological factors, 255
and child abuse, 254, 255t
classification, 247–250
depersonalization disorder, 249
described, 243
dissociative amnesia, 249
dissociative fugue, 244–245, 243–245, 249
dissociative identity disorder (DID), 250–251, 252–253
dissociative symptoms, 233, 247
DSM-IV-TR classification, 249–250
epidemiology, 251–254
etiology, 254–264
historical perspective, 247
hysteria, and unconscious mental processes, 245–247
pibloktoq and, 13
prevalence, 251
psychological factors, 254–255
research, 254–264
*vs.* role enactment, 252–253
social factors, 255
symptoms, 247
treatment, 256
Dissociative Experiences Questionnaire, 252, 252t
dissociative fugue, 244–245, 243–245, 249
dissociative identity disorder (DID)
case study, 250–251
correlates of, 255t
described, 249–250
frequency of diagnosis, 252
implicit memory, 253
*vs.* role enactment, 252–253
treatment, 256
dissociative state, 232–233
dissociative symptoms, 233, 247
distorted body image, 340, 353
distracting style, 162
disulfiram, 395
divorce, 584–585, 599–600
divorce mediation, 632
Dix, Dorothea, 19
dizygotic (DZ) twins, 49
dominance, 54
dominant/recessive inheritance, 48
dopamine, 42, 168, 388
dopamine hypothesis, 464
dose-response effects, 564
double-blind study, 87, 360
double depression, 146
down regulation, 369
Down syndrome, 520–521, 527
drag queens, 423–424
drug of abuse
*see also* substance abuse
alcohol, 370–371
amphetamine, 372–373
barbiturates, 375
benzodiazepines, 375
brain reward pathways, 388, 388f
cannabis, 375–376
cocaine, 372–373
commonly abused drugs, 366t
comparison of various psychoactive substances, 370t
described, 366
dopamine, 388, 388f
endorphins, 389–390
expectations about drug effects, 391–393
hallucinogens, 376–378
hashish, 375–376
heroin, 397–398
marijuana, 375–376
neuroanatomy, 388–390
neurochemical mechanisms of drug action, 389f
neurochemistry, 388–390
nicotine, 371–372
opiates, 373–375, 374
tolerance, buildup of, 369
DSM-IV-TR (*Diagnostic and Statistical Manual of Mental Disorders*)
abnormal behaviour, definition of, 8, 8t
acute stress disorder (ASD), 234–235, 235t
adjustment disorders, 586t
agoraphobia, 198
anorexia nervosa, 346, 346t
antisocial personality disorder, 326–327, 326t
anxiety disorders, 197–200, 197t
autistic disorder, 536, 537t
auxiliary axes, 114
binge eating, 343
binge eating disorder, 347
bipolar mood disorder, 147
borderline personality disorder (BPD), 321–322, 322t
bulimia nervosa, 346–347, 347t
clinical symptoms (Axis 1), 108–109
cluster A personality disorders, 303–304
cluster B personality disorders, 304–306
cluster C personality disorders, 306–307
cognitive disorders, 492t
comorbidity issue, 115
conduct disorder, 554–555, 555t
and conventional clinical wisdom, 113
cultural issues, 109–111
culture-bound syndromes, 110–111
cutoff points, 114
dementia, 492, 493t
dependent personality disorder (DPD), 332, 333t
described, 105–106, 107–108
dissociative disorders, 249–250
eating disorders, 346–347
evaluation of, 112–115
exclusion criteria, 107
gender identity disorders, 436
generalized anxiety disorder, 199
global assessment of functioning (Axis V), 109
and ICD-10, differences between, 107n
impulse control disorders, 320–321
inclusion criteria, 107
internalizing disorders, 572–573, 573t
major depressive episode, 147t
major domains of information, 109t
manic episodes, 148t
medical factors (Axis III), 109, 280–280t
mental retardation, 514t
mood disorders, 146–149, 146t, 147t, 148t
multiaxial classification system, 108
obsessive-compulsive disorder, 199–200
obsessive-compulsive disorder, criteria for, 108
oppositional defiant disorder (ODD), 553, 554t
other conditions that may be focus of clinical attention (V codes), 586, 586t
panic attacks, 192t
panic disorder, 197

paraphilias, 422, 423–429
personality disorder not otherwise specified (PD NOS), 307
personality disorders (Axis II), 108–109, 303t
pervasive developmental disorders, 536–537
posttraumatic stress disorder, 234t
posttraumatic stress disorder (PTSD), 233–235
problems and limitations, 114–115
psychosocial and environmental factors (Axis IV), 109
reliability, 112
schizophrenic disorders, 451–453, 451t
schizotypal personality disorder, 317, 318t
sexual dysfunctions, 410–411, 411t
social phobia, 198–199
specific phobia, 198
stressors, 282, 282t
substance abuse, 378, 379t
substance dependence, 378, 379t
suicidal ideation, 178
time periods, and definitions of disorders, 114
traumatic stress, 230
undefined concepts, 114
unipolar mood disorder, 146
unresolved questions, 114
validity, 112–114
dualism, 42
duty to protect potential victims, 636–637
dyscalulia, 571
dysgraphia, 571
dyskinesia, 489
dyslexia, 571
dyspareunia, 416
dysphoria, 353
dysphoric mood, 142
dysprosody, 533
dyssomnias, 285
dysthymia, 146, 151

E

early adult transition, 587
*see also* adult transition
eating disorders
*see also* anorexia nervosa; bulimia nervosa
adolescents, 349–350
alternative pathways, 355–356
binge eating disorder, 347
biological factors, 354–355
and child sexual abuse, 351
classification, 345–347
control, struggle for, 352
and depression, 352
described, 337
dietary restraint, 354
DSM-IV-TR classification, 346–347
dysphoria, 353
epidemiology, 347–350
etiology, 350–356
family relationships, 351
gender differences, 338, 348–349
historical perspective, 345–346
integration, 355–356
introceptive awareness, lack of, 352
low self-esteem, 353
in males, 339
Montreaux residential program, 357–358
negative body image, 353
overlap in symptoms, 342f
perfectionism, 352
psychological factors, 351–354
research, 350–356
social factors, 350
and standards of beauty, 348–349
echolalia, 533
eclectic approach, 67–68
ecstasy, 376–377
ego, 33
ego analysis, 77
ego-syntonic, 300
egoistic suicide, 178
the elderly, and substance use disorders, 383
Electra complex, 33
electroconvulsive therapy (ECT)
bipolar mood disorder, 176
described, 72–73
schizophrenia, 455
unipolar mood disorder, 176
use of, 23
electrolyte imbalance, 341
emergency commitment procedures, 622
emotion-focused coping, 276–277
*see also* coping
Emotion Focused Therapy, 243
emotion-oriented coping, 281
emotion regulation, 578
emotional awareness, 84
emotional disorder, 576
emotional dysregulation, 309
emotional problems, and dementia, 489
emotional processing, 239–240
emotional symptoms, 142–143
emotional systems, 55
emotional turmoil, 589, 595
emotional understanding, 84
emotions, 54–139
empathy, 84
empty chair technique, 85
encephalitis, 522
encopresis, 573
encounter group, 95
Endler's multidimensional interaction model, 281
endocrine system, 46, 46f
endogenous opiod peptides, 390
endorphins, 389–390, 539
enkephalins, 389–390
enmeshed families, 351
enuresis, 573
environmental factors, and dementia, 504–505
environmental management, and dementia, 506
environmental toxins, 522–523
Epidemiologic Catchment Area (ECA) study, 59
epidemiology
acute stress disorder (ASD), 235–237
aging, 608
anxiety disorders, 201–205
autistic disorder, 537–538
cardiovascular disease (CVD), 287–288
cognitive disorders, 498–501
defined, 12
delirium, 498–501
dementia, 498–501
dissociative disorders, 251–254
eating disorders, 347–350
externalizing disorders, 555–556
family transitions, 596
gender identity disorders, 437
identity conflicts, 590–591
internalizing disorders, 574–577
mental retardation, 519
mood disorders, 150–154
paraphilias, 429–430, 430f
posttraumatic stress disorder (PTSD), 235–237
schizophrenia, 456–458
sexual dysfunctions, 416–418
somatoform disorders, 260–261
substance use disorders, 380–383
suicide, 179
trauma, 235–237
epilepsy, 524
epinephrine, 274
episodes, 140
equifinality, 38
erectile dysfunctions, 413, 418
escapist reminiscence, 608
essential hypertension, 287
estrogen, 604
ethics. *See* professional responsibilities
ethnic differences, 316
ethology, 53
etiological theories, 178
etiological validity, 113
etiology
acute stress disorder (ASD), 237–240
adult transition, 591
aging, 609
alcoholism, 384–394
antisocial personality disorder (ASPD), 328–331
anxiety disorders, 205–218
autistic disorder, 538–540
and behaviour genetics, 52
borderline personality disorder (BPD), 322–323
cognitive disorders, 501–505
delirium, 501
dementia, 502–505
dependent personality disorder (DPD), 332–333
dissociative disorders, 254–264
eating disorders, 350–356
externalizing disorders, 556–562
family transitions, 596–600
gender identity disorders, 437–438
internalizing disorders, 577–579
levels of analysis, 155
major brain structures, 46
mental retardation, 520–526
mood disorders, 154–171
and neurotransmitters, 41–42
paraphilias, 430–433
posttraumatic stress disorder (PTSD), 237–240
and psychophysiology, 47
schizophrenia, 458–472
schizotypal personality disorder, 317–318
sexual dysfunctions, 418–419
somatoform disorders, 262–264
substance use disorders, 384–394
suicide, 179–182
eugenics movement, 526–527
euphoria, 140
evolutionary psychology, 52–53
evolved fear module, 208, 215
exaggerated startle response, 233
excessive integration, 178
excessive regulation, 178
excessive worry, 192
exhibitionism, 426
exorcism, 71
expectations about drug effects, 391–393
experiential group therapy, 94–95
experiential system, 246
experiment, 79
experimental group, 79
experimental hypothesis, 21
experimental method, 78, 79–80
experimental neurosis, 209
expert witnesses, 619, 631
explicit memory, 246
exposure and response prevention, 220
exposure therapies, 80
expressed emotion (EE), 466–467, 467f, 468–469
external validity, 79

externalizing disorders
aggression, 550–551
alternative pathways, 561–562
anger, 550
attention-deficit/hyperactivity disorder (ADHD). *See* attention-deficit/hyperactivity disorder (ADHD)
attention deficits, 551–552
biological factors, 556–558
case study, 548–549, 559
classification, 552–555
coercion, 559
conduct disorder, 554–555, 555t, 566–567
conflict and inconsistent discipline, 560
course and outcome, 567
cross-cultural comparisons, 560
described, 548–549
diet and food additives, 558
epidemiology, 555–556
etiology, 556–562
family risk factors, 556
genetics, 557
historical perspective, 552
hyperactivity, 551, 551f
impulsivity, 551
integration, 561–562
love and discipline, 559–560
negativity, 550–551
neighbourhood and societal factors, 560
neuropsychological abnormalities, 558
oppositional defiant disorder (ODD), 553, 554, 553f–554f, 554t
parenting styles, 558–559, 558f–559f
prevalence, 555–556
psychological factors, 561
rule violations, 549–550
social factors, 558–560
symptoms, 549–552
temperament, 557
treatment, 562–567
extinction, 34, 35
extrapyramidal symptoms (EPS), 474
eye movement desensitization and reprocessing (EMDR), 243
eye-tracking dysfunction, 471–472, 471f–472f

F
factitious disorder, 260
family
and externalizing disorders, 556
and schizophrenia, 466–469
family conflict, 594
Family Environment Scale (FES), 130
family incidence studies, 49
Family Interaction Coding System (FICS), 130
family law
child abuse, 632–634
child custody disputes, 630–632
competing interests, balancing, 630
issues, 630
family life cycle, 593, 593t
family-oriented aftercare, 476
family relationships, and eating disorders, 351
family roles, 598–599
family studies
anxiety disorders, 213–214
mood disorders, 163–164, 164f
schizophrenia, 458
family therapy, 93–94, 356, 549, 565, 601–602
family transitions
behavioural marital therapy, 602
biological factors, 599
classification of troubled family relationships, 595–596
cognitive conflicts, 595
communication problems, 598
couples therapy, 601–602
described, 584–593
emotional distress, 595
epidemiology, 596
etiology, 596–600
family conflict, 594
family roles, 598–599
family therapy, 601–602
prevention programs, 600
psychological factors, 597–599
research, 596–600
social factors, 599
treatment during, 600–602
typical experiences, 593–595
fatalistic suicide, 178
fear network, 239
fears, 191, 205, 208–209, 569–570
female orgasm, 406
female orgasmic disorder, 414–415
female sexual arousal disorder, 414
fenfluramine, 541
fetal alcohol syndrome, 523
fetishism, 423
fight or flight response, 273
file drawer problem, 88
First Nations people. *See* Aboriginal peoples
fitness to stand trial, 620–621
five-factor model of personality, 301, 302t, 308–309
flashbacks, 232
flooding, 80
fluid intelligence, 486
food additives, 558
forced sexual activity, 428t, 428–429
forebrain, 43
forgiveness, 277
"forgotten half," 590–591
formal commitment procedures, 622
formal observation schedules, 123–124
foster care, 634
fragile-X syndrome, 521
fraternal twins, 49
free association, 75
free will, 35
frequency distribution, 515
Freudian psychoanalysis, 75–77
Freudian slips, 75
frontal lobe, 45
frontotemporal dementia (FTD), 493
frotteurism, 427
functional MRI (fMRI), 135, 463

G
gargoylism, 522
gaze aversion, 532
gender, 60
gender bias in diagnosis, 312–313
gender differences
alcohol dependence, 381–382
Alzheimer's disease, 500, 500f
antisocial personality disorder, 312
anxiety disorders, 203
dementia, 500, 500f
dependent personality disorder, 314
eating disorders, 338, 348–349
life expectancy, 603f
mood disorders, 151
paraphilias, 430
pedophilia, 430
personality disorders, 312
response styles, 162
schizophrenia, 456–457, 457t
somatoform disorder, 260–261
vascular dementia, 500, 500f
gender dysphoria, 436
gender identity, 436
gender identity disorders
epidemiology, 437
etiology, 437–438
nature and nurture, 438
sex-reassignment surgery, 439
and sexual orientation, 436
symptoms and associated features, 436
*vs.* transvestic fetishism, 436
treatment, 439
gender roles, 60, 591
gene-environment correlation, 599
gene therapy, 527
general adaptation syndrome (GAS), 276, 276f
general distress, 202
general paresis, 32
generalization, 116–117
generalized anxiety disorder, 199, 213, 213f
generalized orgasmic difficulties, 414
generativity *vs.* stagnation, 587
genes, 47
genetic disorders, 521–522
genetic linkage analysis, 495–496
genetics
adoption studies, 50–51
alcoholism, 385–387
Alzheimer's disease, 502–503, 503f–502f
autistic disorder, 539
autosomal dominant trait, 495
basic principles of genetics, 47–48
contemporary behavioural genetics research, 50
dementia, 502–503
dominant/recessive inheritance, 48
and etiology of psychopathology, 52
externalizing disorders, 557
family incidence studies, 49
misinterpretation of findings, 51–52
mood disorders, 163–165
polygenic inheritance, 48, 49f
schizophrenia, 458–460
twin studies, 49–50, 50f
genital herpes, 522
genotype, 47
German measles (rubella), 522
gerontology, 608
Gestalt therapy, 84–85
global assessment of functioning (Axis V), 109
Global Burden of Disease Study, 13
goodness of fit, 54
Gould, Glenn, 22
Grandin, Temple, 532
Graves' disease, 46
Greek tradition, 18
grief, 606–607
group therapy, 94–95

H
hallucinations, 446–447
hallucinogens, 376–378
harm reduction model, 400
harmful dysfunction, 7–8
hashish, 375–376
health behaviour
described, 279
medical advice, 279–280
older adults, 609
health psychologists, 269–270
heart attacks, 270–271
Hemingway, Ernest, 367
heritability, 597–598
heritability of divorce, 599–600
heritability ratio, 597
hermaphrodite, 438n
heroin, 373, 374, 397–398
hierarchy of fears, 80
high-risk research design, 392

high risk samples, 392
hindbrain, 43
Hippocratic perspective, 18
Historical/Clinical/Risk Management Scheme (HCR-20), 626, 626t
historical perspective
  acute stress disorder (ASD), 233
  antisocial personality disorder, 325
  anxiety disorders, 196–197
  borderline personality disorder (BPD), 320–321
  classification system, 105–107
  cognitive disorders, 491–492
  dependent personality disorder (DPD), 332
  dissociative disorders, 247–249
  eating disorders, 345–346
  externalizing disorders, 552
  illness, 280
  internalizing disorders, 572
  life-cycle transitions, 586–587
  mental disorder defence, 615–616
  mental retardation, 517–518
  mood disorders, 145–146
  paradigms, 31–36
  posttraumatic stress disorder (PTSD), 233
  psychopathology, 17–20
  psychotherapy, 71–72
  schizophrenic disorders, 450–451
  schizotypal personality disorder, 317
  sexual behaviour, 407–408
  stress, 280
histrionic personality disorder, 305–306
histrionic style, 258
HIV, 284, 522
holism, 36–37
homeostasis, 39–40
homework, 70
Homolka, Karla, 327–328
homosexuality, 9–10
hopelessness, 159, 161
hormone replacement therapy, 604
hormones, 46, 435
hot lines, 182–183
human immunodeficiency virus (HIV), 284, 522
human motivations, 52–54
humanist psychotherapies
  client-centred therapy, 84
  described, 71
  emotional awareness, 84
  Gestalt therapy, 84–85
  psychotherapy process research, 85
  therapist-client relationship, 84
humanistic paradigm, 35
humour, 278–279
Huntington's disease, 495, 495f, 496, 503
Hurler syndrome, 522
hybristophilia, 328
hyperactivity, 551, 551f, 575
hyperkinesis, 552
hyperlipogenesis, 354
hypertension, 286, 287–288
hyperthyroidism, 46
hypnosis, 246–255
hypnotic method, 75
hypnotics, 366, 375
hypoactive sexual desire, 411
hypoactive sexual desire disorder, 411
hypochondriasis, 258–259
hypomania, 147
hypothalamic-pituitary-adrenal axis, 166, 166f, 239, 274
hypothalamus, 43
hypothesis, 79
hypothetical constructs, 415
hysteria, 245–247

## I

iatrogenesis, 255
id, 33
identical twins, 49
identity, 56
identity achievement, 590
identity conflicts
  classification, 589–590
  epidemiology, 590–591
identity crisis, 587, 588
identity diffusion, 589
identity foreclosure, 589
identity moratorium, 590
identity *vs.* role confusion, 586
idioms of distress, 111
idiosyncratic beliefs, 447
iindividuation, 533
illness. *See* physical illness
illness behaviour, 280
imipramine, 579
immune system responses to stress, 274–276
immunosuppression, 274
impaired communication, 533–534
impaired social interaction, 531–533
implicit memory, 246, 253
imprinting, 53
improvement without treatment, 86–87
impulse control disorders, 320–321
impulsive subtype, 399
impulsivity, and externalizing disorders, 551
in vivo desensitization, 80
inappropriate compensatory behaviour, 342, 344
inappropriate effect, 450
incest, 428
incidence
  anorexia nervosa, 347, 347f–348f
  bulimia nervosa, 347–348
  defined, 12
  dementia, 498–499
  mood disorders, 151
inclusive fitness, 52
inconsistent discipline, 560
indecent exposure, 426
independent variables, 79
index case, 49
individual differences, 54
individualism, 314
infectious diseases, and mental retardation, 522
informal counselling, 86–87
informed consent, 628, 635
inhibited sexual arousal, 414
inhibited sexual desire, 411
inhibited to the unfamiliar, 577
inhibitedness, 310
insanity acquittals, 615
insecure attachments, 53, 309, 577–578
insight, 75
institutional programs, and schizophrenia, 477
instrumental reminiscence, 608
integration
  acute stress disorder, 240
  alcoholism, 393–394
  autistic disorder, 539
  cardiovascular disease (CVD), 291–292
  eating disorders, 355–356
  externalizing disorders, 561–562
  posttraumatic stress disorder, 240
  schizophrenia, 469–470
integrative reminiscence, 608
integrity *vs.* despair, 587, 605
intelligence quotient (IQ), 514
intensive behaviour modification, 541–543, 543t
intermittent explosive disorder, 320
internal validity, 79
internalization, 56, 82, 350
internalizing disorders
  anxiety, 569–570
  biological factors, 577
  case study, 567–568
  classification, 572–574
  course and outcome, 579
  depression, 567–568, 569
  described, 548, 567–568
  developmental deviations, 571
  DSM-IV-TR classification, 572–573, 573t
  encopresis, 573
  enuresis, 573
  epidemiology, 574–577
  etiology, 577–579
  fears, 569–570
  historical perspective, 572
  insecure attachments, 577–578
  overinclusive listing of disorders, 573–574
  pica, 572
  psychological factors, 578
  reactive attachment disorder, 572–577
  rumination disorder, 572
  school refusal, 570
  selective mutism, 572
  separation anxiety, 570
  separation anxiety disorder, 570
  separation or loss, 578
  social factors, 577–578
  stereotypic movement disorder, 572
  suicide, 575
  symptoms, 568–572
  Tourette's disorder, 572
  treatment, 579
  troubled peer relationships, 570–571
*International Classification of Diseases* (ICD), 105–107n
International Pilot Study of Schizophrenia (IPSS), 457
interoceptive exposure, 219–220
interpersonal and social rhythm therapy, 175
interpersonal diagnoses, 596
interpersonal perspective, 160–162
interpersonal psychotherapy, 359–361
interpersonal therapy
  and bipolar mood disorder, 175–176
  and unipolar mood disorder, 172
interpersonality amnesia, 253
interpretation, 75
intersexual selection, 53
interviews, 119–121
intimacy struggles, 594
intimacy *vs.* self absorption, 587
intolerance of uncertainty, 212
intracytoplasmic inclusions, 497
intrasexual competition, 53
introceptive awareness, 352
introverted-hopeless subtype, 399
the Inuit, 15
involuntary hospitalization, 184
involuntary sterilization, 526–527
IQ tests, 514–516
irrational beliefs, 83
irresistible impulse test, 616

## J

job strain, 289
joint custody, 631
juvenile courts, 566–567
juvenile delinquency, 565–567

## K

kappa, 112
kayak angst, 204
kleptomania, 320
Klinefelter syndrome, 521
klismaphilia, 424
Korsakoff's syndrome, 490–491

L


la belle indifference, 258
labelling theory, 58, 106–107
lactic acid, 217n
language disturbance, and dementia, 487
lanugo, 341
late adult transition, 587
lateralized brain functions, 43
the law
  battered woman syndrome, 618–619
  burden of proof, 616
  civil law, 621–630
  *see also* civil law
  criminal responsibility, 615
  deterrence, 616
  expert witnesses, 619
  family law, 630–634
  *see also* family law
  fitness to stand trial, 620–621
  legal definitions of mental disorder, 617–618
  mental disorder defence, 615–620
  not criminally responsible on account of a mental disorder (NCRMD), 616, 617
  professional responsibilities and, 634–637
  unfit to stand trial, 615
lead poisoning, 523
leading causes of death, 282f
learned helplessness theory, 56
learning
  classical conditioning, 34
  and cognitive behavioural paradigm, 34–35
  fears, 208–209
  modelling, 55
  observational learning, 208–209
  operant conditioning, 34
  and phobias, 208–209
  preparedness model, 208
  state-dependent learning, 254
learning disorder, 554f, 571–572, 574
learning process, 80
left cerebral hemisphere, 43
legal custody, 631
Lesch-Nyhan syndrome, 522
levels of analysis, 37, 37t, 117, 155
Lewy bodies, 497
libertarian views, 621
libido, 33
life-course-persistent antisocial behaviour, 550
life-cycle transitions
  *see also* adjustment disorders
  adult transition, 583–584, 588–592
  classification, 585–588
  contemporary classification, 587–588
  described, 584
  divorce in midlife, 584–585
  early adult transition, 587
  family transitions, 584–602
  identity crisis, 587
  midlife transition, 587
  transition to later life, 584, 602–611
  transitions during adult years, 587f
  typical experiences, 585
life events, 271–272, 272t, 273t
life expectancy, 603f, 608
life-span development, 583
life stressors. *See* stressful life events
lifespan, risk factors across
  antisocial personality disorder, 328
  anxiety disorders, 203–204
  mood disorders, 152–154
  sexual behaviour, 417
  substance dependence, 382–383
lifetime prevalence, 12, 13t
  *see also* prevalence
light therapy, 177
limbic system, 43
linkage studies
  mood disorders, 165
  schizophrenia, 459–460
lithium, and bipolar mood disorder, 175
lobotomy, 20, 73
longitudinal design, 291
longitudinal study, 291
loose associations, 449
love, and externalizing disorders, 559–560
low personality risk subtype, 399
low self-esteem, 353
"lumpers," 200
lymphocytes, 274


M


magnetic resonance imaging (MRI), 132–134, 461
mainstreaming, 529
major depressive disorder, 146, 147t
major depressive episode, 147t
maladaptive fears, 205
male erectile disorder, 413
male orgasm, 406
malingering, 260
malnutrition, 524
malpractice, 634
mania, 140, 144–145
manic-depressive disorder. *See* bipolar mood disorder
manic-depressive psychosis, 105
  *see also* bipolar mood disorder
manic episodes, 142, 144, 148t
marijuana, 375–376
marital conflict, 594
marital status, and psychopathology, 58
marital therapy, 93, 601
  *see also* couples therapy
marriage, and mental health, 59
marriage and family therapy (MFT), 17
marriage counselling, 93
masochism, 424–426, 425
masturbation, 409–410
McMaster-Waterloo schizophrenia project, 461–462
MDMA (methylene-dioxy-methamphetamine), 376–378
meaning making, 240
mechanics, 486
median, 515
medical factors (Axis III), 109
medical malpractice, 634
medications. *See* psychopharmacology
medulla, 43
melancholia, 148
memory changes in normal aging, 486–487
men
  deaths caused by alcohol use, 371f
  and eating disorders, 339
meningitis, 522
menopause, 603–604
mental disorder defence, 615–616
  burden of proof, 616
  consequences of, 619–620
  expert witnesses, 619
  historical perspective, 615–616
  irresistible impulse test, 616
  legal definitions of mental disorder, 617–618
  M'Naghten test, 615–616
  not criminally responsible on account of a mental disorder (NCRMD), 616, 617
  use of, 619–620
mental disorders
  comorbidity, 13
  cross-cultural comparisons, 13–14
  culture, and diagnostic practices, 9
  definitions of, 5
  disease burden, 13
  frequency of, 12–13
  identification of presence of disorder, 5–6
  impact on community populations, 12–13
  impact on people's lives, 13f
  laboratory tests, lack of, 6
  and the law. *See* civil law; the law
  lifetime prevalence, 13t
  patient rights, 627–628
  prevalence of, 3
  scientific study methods, 20–24
  untreated, 68f
  and violence, 623t
mental health professions, 15–17, 619
mental retardation
  AAMR classification, 518–519, 519t
  adaptive skills, limitations in, 516
  age of onset, 517
  and autism, 535–536
  biological factors, 520–524
  case study, 513
  chromosomal disorders, 520–521
  classification, 517–519
  conceptual skills, 516
  cultural-familial retardation, 524, 524f, 526
  definitions of, 512–514
  deinstitutionalization movement, 529
  described, 512
  DSM-IV-TR diagnostic criteria, 514t
  environmental toxins, 522–523
  epidemiology, 519
  etiology, 520–526
  eugenics movement, 526–527
  genetic disorders, 521–522
  historical perspective, 517–518
  infectious diseases, 522
  intensities of needed support, 519t
  involuntary sterilization, 526–527
  IQ cutoff score, 514f
  levels of, 518–519, 519t
  mainstreaming, 529
  mild, 518
  moderate, 519
  normal genetic variation, 524, 524f
  normalization, 529
  overview, 511
  practical skills, 516
  pregnancy and birth complications, 523–524
  prevalence, 519
  prevention, 526–529
  primary prevention, 526–527
  profound, 519
  psychological factors, 524–525
  secondary prevention, 528
  severe, 519
  significantly subaverage IQ, 514–516
  social factors, 525–526
  social skills, 516
  symptoms and associated features, 512–517
  terminology, 512
  tertiary prevention, 528–529
  treatment, 526–529
  two-curve model, 520f
  Vineland Social Maturity Scale, 516, 517t
mercury poisoning, 523
meta-analysis, 85–86, 86f
metabolic rate, 354
metabolic tolerance, 369
midbrain, 43
midlife transition, 587
mild mental retardation, 518
mind-body dualism, 42
Mini-Mental State Examination, 488, 488t

Minnesota Multiphasic Personality Inventory (MMPI-2), 125–127
MMPI-2, 125–127
M'Naghten test, 615–616
mode of inheritance, and mode of inheritance, 165, 515
modelling, 55, 263
moderate mental retardation, 518–519
modules, 208
monoamine oxidase inhibitors (MAOs), 174
monozygotic (MZ) twins, 49
Montreaux residential program, 357–358
mood, 139, 149n
mood disorders
  *see also* depression
  anxiety, 143
  behavioural symptoms, 144–145
  bipolar II disorder, 147
  bipolar mood disorder. *See* bipolar mood disorder
  classification, 145–149
  cognitive symptoms, 143–144
  comorbidity, 145
  course and outcome, 149–150
  cross-cultural differences, 151–152
  cross-generational comparisons, 154
  cyclothymia, 148
  definitions of, 145
  described, 140
  DSM-IV-TR classification, 146–149, 146t, 147t, 148t
  dysthymia, 146, 151
  electroconvulsive therapy, 176
  emotional symptoms, 142–143
  epidemiology, 150–154
  episodes, 140
  etiological considerations. *See* mood disorders (etiology)
  gender differences, 151
  heterogeneity issue, 146
  historical perspective, 145–146
  hypomania, 147
  incidence, 151
  lifetime prevalence, 153f
  major depressive episode, 147t
  mania, 140, 144–145
  melancholia, 148
  prevalence, 151, 153f
  psychotic features, 149
  rapid cycling, 149
  research, 154–171
  risk across the lifespan, 152–154
  seasonal affective disorder, 149, 176–177
  somatic symptoms, 144
  symptoms of, 142–145
  theoretical advances in understanding, 161
  treatment, 171–177
  unipolar mood disorder. *See* unipolar mood disorder
mood disorders (etiology)
  behaviour genetics, 163–165
  biological factors, 163–169
  brain imaging studies, 167–168, 167f
  cognitive vulnerability, 158–160
  family history, 163–164, 164f
  genetic risk and stressful life events, 164
  interaction of factors, 169–170
  linkage studies, 165
  mode of inheritance, 165
  neuroendocrine system, 165–167
  psychological factors, 154–155, 158–163
  social factors, 155–158
  twin studies, 164
moral anxiety, 33
moratorium, 588
motivation, 300–301
motivational problems, and dementia, 489
multi-infarct dementia, 496–497
multi-site studies, 95
multiaxial classification system, 108
multifinality, 38
multiple pathways
  autistic disorder, 539
  described, 38
  and schizophrenia, 469–470
multiple personality disorder, 22, 250–251
Multiple Risk Factor Intervention Trial (MRFIT), 293
multiple risk factors, 38
multisomaform disorder, 260
multisystemic therapy, 566
Munchausen-by-Proxy syndrome (MBPS), 633
Munchausen syndrome, 260
myocardial infarction, 286, 287
myocardial ischemia, 288

## N

naltraxone, 395
narcissistic personality disorder, 306, 308–309
narcolepsy, 286
narcotic analgesics, 366
narrative reminiscence, 608
National Comorbidity Survey (NCS), 13, 237
National Health and Social Life Survey (NHSLS), 408, 409–410
natural selection, 52
naturalistic/scientific approaches, 72
nature and nurture, 438
necrophilia, 424
negative affect, 202
negative attention, 560
negative body image, 353
negative cognitive errors, 56
negative correlations, 39
negative emotionality, 240
negative life effects. *See* stressful life events
negative reinforcement, 35, 35n
negative symptoms
  affective disturbances, 447–448
  alogia, 448
  anhedonia, 447–448
  apathy, 448
  avolition, 448
  blunted affect, 447
  described, 446
  emotional disturbances, 447–448
negativity, and externalizing disorders, 550
neglected children, 571
negligence, 634–635
negotiation, 93
nervous system, 46, 131
neural networks, 42–43
neurasthenia, 152
neuroanatomy
  anxiety disorders, 215–217
  autistic disorder, 539–540
  described, 40
  drugs and, 388–390
neurochemistry
  anxiety disorders, 217–218
  dopamine hypothesis, 464
  drugs and, 388–390
  schizophrenia, 464–465
neuroendocrine system, 165–167
neurofibrillary tangles, 493
neuroleptic drugs, 473
neurologists, 482
neuromodulators, 41
neuron, 41, 41f
neuropeptides, 539
neurophysiology, 40, 539
neuropsychological assessment, 488–488f
neuropsychologists, 482
neuroscience
  described, 40
  endorphins, 389–390
  serotonin hypothesis, 390
neurosis, 197, 247
neuroticism, 240
neurotransmitters
  dementia, 503
  described, 41
  mood disorders, etiology of, 168–169, 169f
  psychopathology, etiology of, 41–42
  and schizophrenia, 464–465
New York University Aging and Dementia Research Center, 507
nicotine, 371–372, 382
nightmare disorder, 286
no-treatment control group, 86
nondirective therapy (ND), 97
nonsadistic rapists, 431
nonshared environment, 50
norepinephrine, 168, 274
normal aging process, and memory changes, 486–487
normal distribution, 514
normal genetic variation, and mental retardation, 524, 524f
normalization, 529
not criminally responsible on account of a mental disorder (NCRMD), 616, 617
  *see also* mental disorder defence
null hypothesis, 21
numbing of responsiveness, 233

## O

obesity, 347
objective tests, 124–127
observational learning, 208–209
observational procedures, 121–124
obsessions, 194–196
obsessive-compulsive disorder (OCD)
  analogue research, 171
  and anorexia nervosa, 342
  brain regions associated with, 135, 135f
  case study, 195
  course and outcome, 200–201, 201f
  diagnostic criteria, 199
  DSM-IV-TR criteria, 108
  exposure and response prevention, 220
  family studies, 214
  observational procedures, 122
  *vs.* obsessive-compulsive personality disorder, 307
  thought suppression, 213
obsessive-compulsive personality disorder, 307, 342
obsessive reminiscence, 608
occipital lobe, 45
occupational control and demand, 320f
Oedipal conflict, 33
old-old, 608
oldest-old, 608
onset. *See* age of onset
Ontario Child Health Study, 392, 575–577
operant conditioning, 34
operational definition, 415
opiates, 373–375, 374
opiods, 373–375, 374
opportunistic rapists, 431
oppositional defiant disorder (ODD), 553, 554, 553f–554f, 554t
optimism, 278, 279t
orgasm, 406
orgasmic disorder, 414–415
orgasmic response, 408f

other conditions that may be focus of clinical attention (V codes), 586, 586t
outcome. *See* course and outcome
outlets for frustration, 277
outpatient commitment, 629

**P**

pain disorder, 259
pain during sex, 416
pain management, 284–285
panic attacks, 192–193, 192t, 210–211, 218
panic disorder
  anxiety sensitivity, 211
  course and outcome, 200
  diagnostic criteria, 197
  family studies, 213, 213f
  insecure attachment, 207
  panic attacks, 192–193
panic induction procedures, 218
paradigms
  biological paradigm, 32
  cognitive behavioural paradigm, 34–35
  comparison of, 36t
  defined, 29
  historical perspective, 31–36
  humanistic paradigm, 35
  problem with, 35–36
  psychodynamic paradigm, 32–34
  treatment and, 68–71
  twentieth-century paradigms, 31–36
paradoxical effect paradox, 562
paranoid personality disorder, 303–304
paranoid type of schizophrenia
  case study, 4–5, 444
  described, 452
paraphilias
  autoerotic asphyxia, 426
  aversion therapy, 434
  biological factors, 430–432
  case studies, 422–423
  classification, 423–429
  cognitive behavioural treatment programs, 434–435, 435f
  compulsion, 422
  courtship disorder, 432
  crossing of paraphilic behaviours, 430, 430f
  described, 422
  DSM-IV-TR criteria, 422
  epidemiology, 429–430, 430f
  etiology, 430–433
  exhibitionism, 426
  fetishism, 423
  frotteurism, 427
  gender differences, 430
  lack of flexibility, 422
  medication, 435
  other types of, 424t
  partialism, 423
  pedophilia, 427–428
  psychosocial factors, 432–433
  and rape, 429
  sexual masochism, 424–426, 425
  sexual sadism, 426
  and social relationships, 433
  symptoms and associated features, 407–423
  transvestic fetishism, 423–424
  treatment, 434–435
  voyeurism, 426
paraprofessionals, 95
parasomnias, 285, 286
parasympathetic nervous system, 47, 275f
*parens patriae*, 566, 621–622
parent management training, 93
parenting styles, 558–559, 558f–559f
parietal lobe, 45
Parkinson's disease, 496, 503
partialism, 423, 424
paternalist approaches, 621, 629–630
pathological gambling, 320–321
patient rights, 627–628
pedophile, 427
pedophilia, 427–428
peer sociometrics, 570
penile plethysmograph, 415
penis envy, 33
perception, and dementia, 487
perception of control, 209–210
perfectionism, 352
performance anxiety, 419
peripheral nervous system, 46, 131
perseveration, 449
persistent maladaptive behaviours, 5
personality changes, and dementia, 489
personality disorder not otherwise specified (PD NOS), 307
personality disorders
  adolescents, 314
  antisocial personality disorder, 298, 299, 304, 324–331
  avoidant personality disorder, 306
  Axis II (DSM-IV-TR), 108–109, 303t
  borderline personality disorder, 305, 319–324
  classification, 303–310
  cluster A disorders, 303–304
  cluster B disorders, 304–306
  cluster C disorders, 306–307
  cognitive perspectives regarding self and others, 300–301
  comorbidity, 311, 318
  context, and personality, 303
  controversial category, 298
  and cultural expectations, 313–315
  dependent personality disorder, 306–307, 314, 331–333
  Dimensional Assessment of Personality Pathology (DAPP), 309–310, 309f–310f
  dimensional perspective, 307–310
  ego-syntonic, 300
  epidemiology, 311–315
  five-factor model of personality, 301, 302t
  gender bias in diagnosis, 312–313
  gender differences, 312
  general definition, 297–298
  histrionic personality disorder, 305–306
  narcissistic personality disorder, 306, 308–309
  obsessive-compulsive personality disorder, 307
  overview, 297–298
  paranoid personality disorder, 303–304
  and pathological gambling, 321
  personality disorder not otherwise specified (PD NOS), 307
  personality traits, 301
  prevalence, 203–311, 311f
  schizoid personality disorder, 304
  schizotypal personality disorder, 304, 315–318
  social dysfunction, 298
  social motivation, 300–301
  stability over time, 313, 314
  symptoms and associated features, 300–303
  temperament, 301
personality inventories, 124–127
personality tests, 124
personality traits, 301
pervasive developmental disorders
  *see also* autistic disorder
  Asperger's disorder, 536
  attachment behaviours, 532
  childhood disintegrative disorder, 536
  classification, 536–537
  described, 529–530
  DSM-IV-TR criteria, 536–537
  IQ scores, 536t
  overview, 511–512
  Rett's disorder, 536
  savant performance, 535
  symptoms and associated features, 530–536
perversions. *See* paraphilias
pharmacodynamic tolerance, 369
pharmacological challenge procedures, 217
phencyclidine (PCP), 377
phenothiazines, 472–473
phenotype, 48
phenylketonuria (PKU), 105, 521–522
phobias
  agoraphobia, 190, 191, 193–194, 198
  described, 193–194
  and learning processes, 208–209
  social phobia, 198–199, 212f
  specific phobia, 198
physical child abuse, 633
physical custody, 631
physical illness
  acquired immune deficiency syndrome (AIDS), 284
  cancer, 282–284
  cardiovascular disease (CVD), 286–294
  as cause of stress, 282
  and chronic stress, 276
  classification, 280–282
  general medical conditions (DSM-IV-TR), 280–280t
  historical perspective, 280
  human immunodeficiency virus (HIV), 284
  illness behaviour, 280
  pain management, 284–285
  psychological factors, role of, 282–286
physiological dependence, 368–369, 378
physiological hyperarousal, 202
physiology, 40
pibloktoq, 111
pica, 572
Pick's bodies, 493
Pick's disease, 493
placebo, 79, 360
placebo control groups, 87, 360
placebo effect, 87
plaque, 482
plasticity, 540
pleasure principle, 33
police power, 622
polygenic disorders, 49f
polygenic inheritance, 48, 49f
polysubstance abuse, 366
pons, 43
population, 556
positive affect, 202
positive correlations, 39
positive reinforcement, 35, 263
positive symptoms
  delusions, 447
  described, 446
  hallucinations, 446–447
positron emission tomography (PET), 134–463
post-partum suicide, 177
posttraumatic stress disorder (PTSD)
  and adjustment disorder, 235
  alternative pathways, 240
  antidepressant medication, 242
  anxiety, 233
  arousal, 233
  avoidance, 233
  biological factors, 238–239
  case study, 231–232
  classification, 233–235

cognitive behaviour therapies, 242–243
comorbidity, 235
course and outcome, 236–237, 237f
described, 231
dissociative symptoms, 233
DSM-IV-TR diagnostic criteria, 233–235, 234t
Emotion Focused Therapy, 243
emotional processing, 239–240
epidemiology, 235–237
etiology, 237–240
exaggerated startle response, 233
eye movement desensitization and reprocessing, 243
heritability coefficients, 238f
historical perspective, 233
interaction of risk factors, 240
prediction of, from ASD symptoms, 236f
prevention, 241–243
psychological factors, 239–240, 240f
re-experiencing, 232
sexual assault, 236
social factors, 237–238
and social support, 238
and stress, 240–241
symptoms and associated features, 230–233
treatment, 241–243
twin studies, 238–238t
two-factor theory, 239

poverty, 60
poverty of speech, 448
power, 300
power struggles, 594
practical skills, 516
pragmatics, 486
predictability, 277
predictive validity, 113
prefrontal lobotomy, 73
pregnancy
- amniocentesis, 527
- complications, and mental retardation, 523–524
- complications, and schizophrenia, 460
- infectious diseases during, 522

prejudice, 60–61
Premarital Relationship Enhancement Program (PREP), 600
premature birth, 524
premature ejaculation, 414
premenstrual dysphoric disorder, 9
premorbid history, 40
preparedness model, 208
prevalence
- acute stress disorder, 235–236
- alcohol abuse and dependence, 381
- anorexia nervosa, 347
- anxiety disorders, 201, 201t
- bulimia nervosa, 348, 348f
- child sexual abuse, 633
- childhood psychological disorders, 576f
- defined, 12
- dementia, 499–500
- dementia, by subtype, 500–501
- dissociative disorders, 251
- externalizing disorders, 555–556
- forced sexual activity, 428t
- lifetime prevalence, 12, 13t
- major depression, 151
- mental retardation, 519
- mood disorders, 151, 153f
- personality disorders, 203–311, 311f
- posttraumatic stress disorder, 235–236
- schizophrenia, 458
- sexual activity, specific forms, 409–410, 410f
- sexual dysfunctions, 416–417f
- somatoform disorders, 260
- substance dependence, 381, 382, 383t

prevention
- acute stress disorder (ASD), 241–243
- cardiovascular disease (CVD), 292–294
- described, 96–97
- mental retardation, 526–529
- posttraumatic stress disorder (PTSD), 241–243
- primary prevention, 96
- secondary prevention, 96
- tertiary prevention, 96–97

preventive detention, 621
primary appraisal, 272
primary hypersomnia, 285
primary insomnia, 285
primary prevention
- cardiovascular disease, 292
- described, 96
- mental retardation, 526–527

primary sleep disorder, 285
priming, 253
privileged communications, 636
probability sampling, 409
probands, 49
problem-focused coping, 276, 277
problem-solving skills training (PSST), 565
prodromal phase, 445
professional counsellors, 17
professional negligence and malpractice, 634
professional responsibilities
- child abuse reporting requirements, 633
- code of ethics, 637
- confidentiality, 636
- described, 634
- duty to protect potential victims, 636–637
- informed consent on efficacy of alternative treatments, 635
- professional negligence and malpractice, 634
- *Tarasoff* case, 636–637
- target of treatment, 635–636

profound mental retardation, 519
prognosis
- *see also* course and outcome
- bipolar disorders, 150
- meaning, 40
- unipolar disorders, 149

progressive muscle relaxation, 78
projection, 33, 34t, 70
projective personality tests, 128–130
prolonged exposure therapy, 242–243
pronoun reversal, 533
prosopagnosia, 246
prospective design, 291
prospective longitudinal research, 254
pseudodementia, 498
pseudohermaphroditism, 437
psilocybin, 376
psychiatric social workers, 16
psychiatry, 16
psychic driving, 23
psychoactive substance, 366
- *see also* drug of abuse

psychoanalysis, 75–77
psychoanalytic techniques, 75–76
psychoanalytic theory, 33
psychodynamic paradigm, 32–34
psychodynamic psychotherapy, 77–78
psychodynamic theory, 33
psychodynamic therapies
- described, 70
- ego analysis, 77
- Freudian psychoanalysis, 75–77
- psychodynamic psychotherapy, 77–78
- short-term psychodynamic psychotherapy, 78

psychoeducational groups, 94
psychological abuse, 633
psychological assessment. *See* assessment
psychological dependence, 368
psychological factors
- acquired immune deficiency syndrome (AIDS), 284
- acute stress disorder (ASD), 239–240
- alcoholism, 390–393
- antisocial personality disorder (ASPD), 330–331
- anxiety disorders, 207–213
- attachment theory, 53–54
- autistic disorder, 538
- cancer, 282–284
- cardiovascular disease (CVD), 288–290
- cognition, 55–56
- cognitive vulnerability, 158–160
- developmental stages, 57–58, 57t
- dissociative disorders, 254–255
- dominance, 54
- eating disorders, 351–354
- emotions and emotional systems, 54–55
- evolutionary psychology, 52–53
- externalizing disorders, 561
- family transitions, 597–599
- human immunodeficiency virus (HIV), 284
- human motivations, 52–54
- internalizing disorders, 578–579
- interpersonal perspective, 160–162
- learning, 55–56
- mental retardation, 524–525
- modelling, 55
- mood disorders, 154–155, 158–163
- paraphilias, 432–433
- physical illness, 282–286
- posttraumatic stress disorder (PTSD), 239–240, 240f
- schizophrenia, 466–469
- sense of self, 56–57
- sexual dysfunctions, 419
- social cognition, 55–56
- somatoform disorders, 262–264
- suicide, 179–181
- temperament, 54
- two-factor theory, 239

psychological systems, assessment of, 118–130
psychomotor retardation, 144
psychomotor stimulants, 372
psychoneuroimmunology (PNI), 275
psychopathology
- asylum, 18–20
- biological factors, 40–52
- defined, 3
- developmental psychopathology, 40
- etiology of. *See* etiology
- Greek tradition, 18
- historical context, 17–20
- psychological factors, 52–58
- social factors, 58–62

psychopathy, 325, 326, 327t
- *see also* antisocial personality disorder (ASPD)

Psychopathy Checklist (PCL), 326
psychopharmacology
- alcoholism, 395
- anxiety disorders, 222–224, 224t
- autistic disorder, 541
- bipolar mood disorder, 175
- borderline personality disorder (BPD), 324
- cardiovascular disease (CVD), 292
- dementia, 505–506
- described, 73–75
- dissociative disorders, 256
- externalizing disorders, 562, 564t
- major categories of medications, 74t
- paraphilias, 435
- posttraumatic stress disorder (PTSD), 242
- psychotropic medications, 73–74

schizophrenia, 472–476, 475t
sexual dysfunctions, 421
side effects, 75
success of, 74
suicidal behaviour, 184
symptom alleviation, 75
unipolar mood disorder, 172–174, 173t
psychophysiological assessment, 131–132, 131t
psychophysiological responses to stress, 274
psychophysiology
autonomic nervous system, 46–47
described, 46
endocrine system, 46, 46f
and etiology of psychopathology, 47
hormones, 46
psychosexual development, 33
psychosis, 5
psychosocial and environmental factors (Axis IV), 109
psychosocial interventions, and schizophrenia, 476–477
psychosocial moratorium, 588
psychosocial rehabilitation (PSR), 17
psychosomatic illnesses, 256n
psychostimulants, 562, 564t
psychosurgery, 73
psychotherapy
*see also* treatments
anxiety disorder, 219–222
autistic disorder, 541–543
bipolar mood disorder, 175–176
and borderline personality disorder (BPD), 323
defined, 67
definitions of, 90t
effectiveness of, 88
efficacy of, 88
humanist psychotherapy, 83–85
improvement and length of psychotherapy, 89f
integration, 91
psychodynamic psychotherapies, 75–78
psychotherapy outcome research, 85–89
psychotherapy process research, 89–92
research on, 85–92
roots of, 71–72
suicidal behaviour, 183–184
unipolar mood disorder, 174
psychotherapy outcome research
allegiance effect, 88
described, 68, 85
double-blind study, 87
efficacy *vs.* effectiveness, 87–88
factors predicting effective treatment, 89
improvement without treatment, 86–87
meta-analysis, 85–86, 86f
placebo control groups, 87
placebo effect, 87
psychotherapy process research
common factors, 90–91, 91t
described, 68, 89
effective brief psychotherapies, 91t
and humanistic psychotherapy, 85
social influence, psychotherapy as, 92
social support, psychotherapy as, 91–92
therapeutic alliance, 85
psychotic features, and mood disorders, 149
psychotic symptoms. *See* positive symptoms
psychotropic medications, 73–74
punishment, 35, 35n
purging, 344
pyromania, 320


## R


random assignment, 79
random sample, 556
rape, 236, 428–429
rapists, classification of, 431, 431t
rating scales, 122, 123t
rational-emotive therapy, 83
rational suicide, 607
rational system, 246
rationalization, 34t, 70
re-experiencing, 232
reaction formation, 34t
reactive attachment disorder, 572–577
reactivity, 124
reality principle, 33
receptors, 41
recidivism, 566
reciprocal causality, 39–40
reciprocity, 594
recovered memories, 247, 248
recticular activating system, 43
reductionism, 37
refractory period, 421
rehabilitation, 566
reinforcement, 263
rejected children, 571
rejection, 309
relapse, 149
relapse prevention, 397–398
relationships. *See* social relationships
relative risk, 392
relaxation training, 221, 292
reliability, 112
reminiscence, 607–608
remission, 149
repression, 34t
repression hypothesis, 277
research
adult transition, 591
aging, 609
alcoholism, and adoption studies, 386–387, 387t
anxiety disorders, 205–218
anxiety sensitivity, and panic attacks, 211
assessment research, 133–134
cognitive vulnerability, and depression, 159–160
common factors, identification of, 97
Danish schizophrenia project, 461–462
depression, understanding, 161
depression in women, social origins of, 156–157
dissociative disorders, 254–264
dissociative identity disorder, implicit memory in, 253
eating disorders, 350–356
family transitions, 596–600
heritability of divorce, 599–600
marriage, and mental health, 59
McMaster-Waterloo schizophrenia project, 461–462
mood disorders, 154–171
predictions of violence, accuracy of, 623–624
retrospective reports, 262, 263
schizophrenia, 458–472
sexual activity in general population, 409–410
somatoform disorders, 262–264
specific "active ingredients," identification of, 97
stress, and posttraumatic stress disorder, 240–241
treatment research, 95–96
research methods
adoption studies, 50–51
analogue studies, 170–171
animal models of psychopathology, 170–171
base rates and predictions, 624–625
burden of proof, 21
case control design, 468
case studies, uses and limitations, 22–24
clinical importance, 221
clinical research methods, 24–24t
clinical scientists, 22
comparison groups, 468
construct validity, 415
contemporary behavioural genetics research, 50
control group, 79
convenience sampling, 409
correlation coefficient, 39
correlational study, 39
cross-cultural comparisons, 316
cross-sectional study, 291
dependent variable, 79
deviation IQ, 515
dismantling studies, 96
experiment, 79
experimental group, 79
experimental method, 78, 79–80
external validity, 79
genetic linkage analysis, 495–496
heritability, 597–598
high-risk research design, 392
hypothesis, 79
hypothetical constructs, 415
independent variables, 79
internal validity, 79
longitudinal design, 291
longitudinal study, 291
multi-site studies, 95
null hypothesis, 21
operational definition, 415
placebo control group, 360
probability sampling, 409
random assignment, 79
relative risk, 392
representative sample, 555
retrospective study, 291
risk factors, 392
samples and sampling, 555–556
statistical measures, 515
statistical significance, 221
statistically significant, 79
studies used to validate clinical syndromes, 113t
treatment matching studies, 96
twin studies, 49–50, 50f
residential programs, 566–567
residential schools, 61–62
residual phase, 445
residual type of schizophrenia, 453
resilience, 578
resistance, 75
resolution phase, 421
response styles, 162
restricted expression, 309
restricting type of anorexia nervosa, 346
restriction fragment-length polymorphisms (RFLPs), 496
retrograde amnesia, 73, 487
retrospective reports, 254, 262, 263
retrospective study, 291
Rett's disorder, 536
reuptake, 41
reverse causality, 39
reverse tolerance, 376
reward pathways, 388, 388f
Rh incompatibility, 523
right cerebral hemisphere, 43
right to refuse treatment, 628
risk factors
autistic disorder, 538
cardiovascular disease (CVD), 287
completed suicide, and depression, 178

defined, 39
depression, 165f
hypertension, 287–288
mood disorders, 165f
study of, 392
substance dependence, 382–383
role changes, 588–589
role enactment, 252–253
role playing, 81, 294
role reversal, 578
Rorschach test, 128
rubella (German measles), 522
rule violations, 549–550
rules of science, 21
rumination, 345
rumination disorder, 572
ruminative style, 162

## S

sadism, 426
sadistic rapists, 431
sadness, *vs.* depression, 140, 141t
samples and sampling, 555–556
savant performance, 535
scapegoating, 596
scheduling, 420
schema, 159
schizoaffective disorder, 453
schizoid personality disorder, 304
schizophrenia
*see also* schizophrenic disorders
active phase, 445
affective disturbances, 447–448
alogia, 448
anhedonia, 447–448
antipsychotic medication, 472–475, 475t
apathy, 448
assertive community treatment (ACT), 477
avolition, 448
bizarre behaviour, 450
blunted affect, 447
catatonia, 449–450
cognitive behaviour therapy (CBT), 476
course and outcome, 445, 454–455, 454f, 455–456
cross-cultural comparisons, 457–458
delusions, 447
depot injections, 455
described, 443
disorganization, 446, 448–450
disorganized speech, 448–449
and dopamine, 42
emotional disturbances, 447–448
epidemiology, 456–458
etiology. *See* schizophrenia (etiology)
family members of patients, 444
family-oriented aftercare, 476
gender differences, 456–457, 457t
hallucinations, 446–447
inappropriate effect, 450
institutional programs, 477
and marital status, 59
negative symptoms, 446, 447–448
onset, 445
overview, 443–445
paranoid schizophrenia, 4–5
positive symptoms, 446, 447
prevalence, 458
prodromal phase, 445
psychosis, 5
psychosocial treatment, 476–477
relapse rates, 473, 473f
research, 458–472
residual phase, 445
and schizotypal personality disorder, 317, 319f
social skills training, 476
stuporous state, 450
symptoms, 443, 446–450
thinking disturbances, 448–449
token economy, 477
treatment, 472–477
schizophrenia (etiology)
adoption studies, 459
attentional dysfunction, 471
average risk, 458f–459f
biological factors, 458–465
brain areas implicated in, 463f
cognition and, 471
Continuous Performance Task (CPT) measure, 471
dopamine hypothesis, 464
expressed emotion (EE), 466–467, 467f
eye-tracking dysfunction, 471–472, 471f–472f
family attitudes, 467–469
family environment, 466
family studies, 458
functional brain imaging, 463
genetics, 458–460
heredity-environment interaction, 470f
hypothetical trajectories, 470
integration, 469–470
linkage studies, 459–460
multiple neurotransmitters, interactions of, 464–465
multiple pathways, 469–470
neurochemistry, 464–465
neuropathology, 461–464
planum temporale, 462
pregnancy and birth complications, 460
psychological factors, 466–469
schizophrenia-like personality traits, 459
schizotaxia, 469
social causation hypothesis, 465
social class, 465–466
social factors, 465–466
social selection hypothesis, 465
spectrum of schizophrenic disorders, 459
structural brain imaging, 461–463
temporal lobes, 462
threshold model, 470, 470f
twin studies, 458
viral infections, 461
vulnerability marker, 470–472
schizophrenia spectrum disorders, 303–304
schizophrenic disorders
*see also* schizophrenia
case studies, 4–5, 444, 445–446, 448–449
catatonic type, 452
classification, 450–455
disorganized schizophrenia, 445–446
disorganized type, 452
DSM-IV-TR definition, 451–452
DSM-IV-TR diagnostic criteria, 451t
DSM-IV-TR subtypes, 444, 452–453
etiology. *See* schizophrenia (etiology)
evaluation of traditional subtypes, 453
historical perspective, 450–451
paranoid type, 4–5, 444, 452
related psychotic disorders, 453–454
residual type, 453
schizophreniform disorder, 452
spectrum of, 459
symptoms and associated features, 446–450
treatment, 472–477
undifferentiated type, 453
schizophreniform disorder, 452
schizotaxia, 469
schizotypal personality disorder
case study, 315–317
clinical features, 317
comorbidity, 317
described, 304
DSM-IV-TR criteria, 318t
etiology, 317–318
historical perspective, 317
and schizophrenia, 317, 319f
treatment, 318
schizotypic signs, 469
school phobia, 570
school refusal, 570
scientific study methods. *See* research methods
seasonal affective disorder, 149, 176–177
secondary appraisal, 272
secondary gain, 263
secondary hypertension, 287
secondary prevention
cardiovascular disease, 292–293
described, 96
mental retardation, 528
secondary victimization, 236
secretin, 541
sedatives, 366, 375
selective amnesia, 249
selective mutism, 572
selective serotonin reuptake inhibitors (SSRIs), 172–223–395, 435
self, 56–57
self-concept, 56
self-control, 56, 561
self-defeating biases, 159
self-destructive impulses, 143
self-disclosure, 84
self-efficacy, 57
self-esteem, 57, 353
self-fulfilling prophesy, 58, 106
self-help groups, 95, 395–396
self-injurious behaviour, 535
self-instruction training, 82
self-monitoring, 123
self-report inventories, 127
self-stimulation, 534
self-worth, 56–57
sensate focus, 420
sensation seeking, 399
sense of self, 56–57
separation anxiety, 207, 570
separation anxiety disorder, 570
serotonin, 168–169, 169f
serotonin dysfunction, 181
serotonin hypothesis, 390
service utilization for mental health problems, 16t
severe mental retardation, 519
sex offenders, treatment for, 434–435, 435f
sex-reassignment surgery, 439
sex roles, 436
sex therapy, 420–421
sexual aggression, 431
sexual arousal, 415
sexual assault, 236, 428–429, 428t
sexual assault, and posttraumatic stress disorder (PTSD), 236
sexual aversion disorder, 412
sexual behaviour
across the lifespan, 417
anal sex, 410
condom use, 410
historical perspective, 407–408
lifetime prevalence of specific sexual activities, 410–410f
orgasmic response, 408f
sexual activity in general population, 409–410
sexual satisfaction, 409f
unconventional sexual behaviour. *See* paraphilias

sexual deviations. *See* paraphilias
sexual disorders. *See* sexual dysfunctions
sexual dysfunctions
  biological factors, 418
  biological therapies, 421
  classification, 9, 410–411, 411t
  cross-cultural comparisons, 417–418
  described, 408
  dyspareunia, 416
  epidemiology, 416–418
  erectile dysfunctions, 413, 418
  etiology, 418–419
  female orgasmic disorder, 414–415
  female sexual arousal disorder, 414
  hypoactive sexual desire disorder, 411
  inhibited sexual arousal, 414
  male erectile disorder, 413
  orgasmic disorder, 414–415
  pain during sex, 416
  premature ejaculation, 414
  prevalence, 416–417, 417f
  psychological treatments, 420–421
  psychosocial factors, 418–419
  relationship factors, 419
  sex therapy, 420–421
  sexual aversion disorder, 412
  symptoms and associated features, 408–416
  treatment, 420–421
  vaginismus, 416
sexual excitement, 405
sexual masochism, 424–426, 425
sexual orientation, and gender identity disorders, 436
sexual response cycle, 407
sexual sadism, 426
sexual satisfaction, 409f
sexual selection, 53
shared environment, 50
short-term motivational therapy, 398
short-term psychodynamic psychotherapy, 78
sick role, 263–264
single gene inheritance, 49f
single photon emission computed tomography (SPECT), 135
situational orgasmic difficulties, 414
sleep apnea, 286
sleep disorders
  breathing-related sleep disorder, 286
  circadian rhythm sleep disorder, 286
  DSM-IV-TR diagnostic category, 285
  dyssomnias, 285
  narcolepsy, 286
  nightmare disorder, 286
  parasomnias, 285, 286
  and physical well-being, 285–286
  primary hypersomnia, 285
  primary insomnia, 285
  primary sleep disorder, 285
  sleep terror disorder, 286
  sleepwalking disorder, 295
sleep terror disorder, 286
sleeping problems, 144
sleepwalking disorder, 295
smoking, 371–372
social affiliation, 273
social behaviour, and dementia, 488
social causation hypothesis, 465
social class
  and autistic disorder, 537
  and schizophrenia, 465–466
social clock, 588
social cognition, 55–56
social dysfunction, 298
social factors
  acute stress disorder (ASD), 237–238
  alcoholism, 384–385
  antisocial personality disorder (ASPD), 329–330
  anxiety disorders, 205–207
  attention-deficit/hyperactivity disorder (ADHD), 560–561
  autistic disorder, 538
  and bipolar disorders, 157–158
  cardiovascular disease (CVD), 290–291
  described, 58
  dissociative disorders, 255
  eating disorders, 350–351
  externalizing disorders, 558–560
  family transitions, 599
  gender, 60
  gender roles, 60
  internalizing disorders, 577–578
  labelling theory, 58
  marital status, 58
  marriage, 59
  mental retardation, 525–526
  mood disorders, 155–158
  paraphilias, 432–433
  posttraumatic stress disorder (PTSD), 237–238
  poverty, 60
  prejudice, 60–61
  relationships, 58–60
  schizophrenia, 465–466
  self-fulfilling prophesy, 58
  sexual dysfunctions, 419
  social causation hypothesis, 465
  social relationships, 58–60
  social roles, 58
  social selection hypothesis, 465
  social support, 60
  societal values, 61–62
  somatoform disorders, 264
  stressful life events, 155–157, 157f
  suicide, 181–182
  unipolar disorders, 155–157, 157f
social influence, 92, 96
social institutions, 96
social interaction, impaired, 531–533
social interventions
  couples therapy, 93
  family therapy, 93–94
  group therapy, 94–95
social motivation, 300–301
social phobia, 198–199, 200, 212f, 214
social problem solving, 82
Social Readjustment Rating Scale (SRRS), 271, 272t
social relationships
  changes, 588–589
  children, and troubled peer relationships, 570–571
  and depression, 160–162
  and eating disorders, 351
  and mental health, 59–60
  and paraphilias, 433
  and psychopathology, 58–60
  sexual dysfunction, 419
social roles, 58
social selection hypothesis, 465
social self, 353
social skills, 516
social skills training (SST), 81–82, 476
social support
  described, 60
  and posttraumatic stress disorder, 238
  psychotherapy as, 91–92
  stress and, 280
social systems, assessment of, 130
social work, 16
socialization, 56, 558
societal values, 61–62
socioeconomic status, and somatoform disorder, 261
sole custody, 631
somatic nervous system, 46
somatic symptoms, 144
somatic treatments, 1920s and 1930s, 21t, 41
somatization, 576
somatization disorder, 257, 258, 258t
somatoform disorders
  biological factors, 262
  body dysmorphic disorder, 259
  classification, 257–260
  comorbidity, 261
  conversion disorder, 257, 257f
  and culture, 261, 261f
  described, 256
  diagnosis by exclusion, pitfalls of, 262
  epidemiology, 260–261
  etiology, 262–264
  *vs.* factitious disorder, 260
  gender differences, 261
  hypochondriasis, 258–259
  *vs.* malingering, 260
  multisomaform disorder, 260
  pain disorder, 259
  prevalence, 260
  and primary care physicians, 264
  psychological factors, 262–264
  *vs.* psychosomatic illnesses, 256n
  research, 262–264
  retrospective reports, 262, 263
  social factors, 264
  and socioeconomic status, 261
  somatization disorder, 257, 258, 258t
  symptoms and associated features, 256–257
  treatment, 264–265
  unnecessary medical treatment, 257
specific phobia, 198
speech and hearing problems, 574
spiritual/religious tradition, 72
"splitters," 200
splitting of mental associations, 451
spontaneous remission, 86
standard deviation, 515
standard scores, 515
standards of beauty, 348–349
state anxiety, 281
state-dependent learning, 254
statistical significance, 221
statistically significant, 79
statistics, 515
stereotypic movement disorder, 572
sterilization, involuntary, 526–527
stigma, 106
stigmatophilia, 424
stimulants, 372–373
stonewalling, 598
strategic loyalties, 94
stress
  as appraisal of life events, 272
  and cardiovascular disease (CVD), 286, 288–290
  cardiovascular reactivity to stress, 288–289
  classification, 280–282
  coping. *See* coping
  critical incident stress (CIS), 241–242
  defensive deniers, 277
  definitions of, 271–272
  described, 38
  direct effects, 279f
  disclosure of trauma, and immunity, 278
  DSM-IV-TR categories, 282, 282t
  and energy, 276
  fight or flight response, 273
  general adaptation syndrome (GAS), 276, 276f

and health behaviour, 279–280
and heart attack, 270–271
historical perspective, 280
hypothalamic-pituitary-adrenal axis, 166f
illness and chronic stress, 276
illness as cause, 282
immune system responses, 274–276
indirect effects, 279f
job strain, 289
as life event, 271–272, 272t, 273t
multidimensional interaction model, 281
overview, 269–271
and posttraumatic stress disorder (PTSD), 240–241
psychophysiological responses, 274
responses to stress, 273–280
Social Readjustment Rating Scale (SRRS), 271, 272t
and social support, 280
tend and befriend, 273
traumatic stress, 230
Type A behaviour pattern, 289–290
stress hormone, 274
stress management, 292
stressful life events
agoraphobia, 206
anxiety disorders, 205–206
and genetic risk of depression, 164–165f
job strain, 289
and unipolar disorders, 155–157, 157f
stroke, 45–46
structural family therapy, 356
structured interview for DSM-IV Personality (SIDP-IV), 120t
structured interviews, 119–121, 120t
stuporous state, 450
sublimation, 34t
substance abuse
*see also* drug of abuse; substance use disorders
common elements, 366
described, 366
DSM-IV-TR criteria, 378, 379t
maladaptive pattern, 378
polysubstance abuse, 366
recurrent pattern, 378
substance dependence
*see also* substance use disorders
Aboriginal peoples, 384
and anxiety disorders, 202–366
comorbidity, 380
concept of, 368–370
course and outcome, 380
described, 366
difficulty of defining, 368
DSM-IV-TR criteria, 378, 379t
prevalence, 381, 382, 383t
proposed subtypes, 379
psychological dependence, 368
risk factors, 382–383
tolerance, 368–369
withdrawal, 369–370
substance use disorders
*see also* substance abuse; substance dependence
classification, 378–380
cognitive behaviour therapies, 396–398
coping skills training, 397
detoxification, 394–395
and the elderly, 383
epidemiology, 380–384
etiology, 384–394
goals of treatment, 394
harm reduction model, 400
medications during remission, 395
outcome results and conclusions, 398–400
overview, 365–367
and pathological gambling, 321
problems associated with, 367
relapse prevention, 397–398
self-help groups, 395–396
short-term motivational therapy, 398
symptoms and associated features, 368
treatment, 394–400
sudden cardiac death, 287
suicidal ideation, 178
suicide
and Aboriginal peoples, 152
altruistic suicide, 178
anomic suicide, 178
assisted suicide, 607
biological factors, 181
case study, 177
classification of, 178–179
common elements of, 180
contagious suicide, 182
crisis centres, 182–183
and depression, 143, 178
egoistic suicide, 178
epidemiology of, 179
etiology, 179–182
fatalistic suicide, 178
hot lines, 182–183
internalizing disorders, 575
involuntary hospitalization, 184
medication, 184
post-partum suicide, 177
psychological factors, 179
psychotherapy, 183–184
rates in Canada, 575f
rational suicide, 607
risk assessment, 627–636
social factors, 181–182
treatment of suicidal people, 182–184
suicide cluster, 182
superego, 33
sustained attention, 552
sympathetic nervous system, 47, 274, 274f–275f
symptom alleviation, 72, 73, 75
symptoms
acute stress disorder (ASD), 230–233
amnestic disorders, 489–491
anorexia nervosa, 339–342
anxiety disorders, 191–196
autistic disorder, 530–536
bulimia nervosa, 342–345
cardiovascular disease (CVD), 286–287
cognitive disorders, 484–491
coronary heart disease (CHD), 286–287
delirium, 485
dementia, 485–489
dissociative disorders, 247
externalizing disorders, 549–552
gender identity disorders, 436
hypertension, 286–287
internalizing disorders, 568–572
mental retardation, 512–517
mood disorders, 142–145
paraphilias, 407–423
personality disorders, 300–303
pervasive developmental disorders, 530–536
posttraumatic stress disorder (PTSD), 230–233
schizophrenia, 443
schizophrenic disorders, 446–450
sexual dysfunctions, 408–416
somatoform disorders, 256–257
stress, responses to, 273–280
substance use disorders, 368
synapse, 41
synaptic transmission, 41f
syndrome, 5, 550
syphilis, 32, 522
system
causality, 37–40
levels of analysis, 37t
systematic desensitization, 78–80, 219–220
systems theory
biopsychosocial approach, 29
defined, 29
described, 30
developmental psychopathology, 40
holism, 36–37
levels of analysis, 37
reductionism, 37
roots of, 36
systolic blood pressure, 287

**T**

T cells, 274
tangentiality, 449
*Tarasoff* case, 636–637
tardive dyskinesia (TD), 474
task-oriented coping, 281
Tay-Sachs disease, 522
telephone scatologia, 424
temperal lobe, 45
temperament, 54, 301–329, 557
temporal disintegration, 376
tend and befriend, 273
tension-reduction hypothesis, 391
termination of parental rights, 634
tertiary prevention
cardiovascular disease, 293–294
described, 96–97
mental retardation, 528–529
Thematic Apperception Test (TAT), 129
theoretically based classification, 104–105
theory of mind, 531–532
therapeutic alliance, 85
therapeutic neutrality, 75
therapist-client relationship, 84
thinking disturbances, 448–449
third-variable possibility, 39
thought blocking, 448
thought broadcasting, 451
thought disorder, 448
thought suppression, 213
time-out, 559
tobacco, 371–372
token economy, 81, 477
tolerance, 368–369
Tourette's disorder, 572
toxins, 522–523
toxoplasmosis, 522
trait anxiety, 281
tranquilizers, 375
transference, 76
transference relationship, 323
transition to adult life. *See* adult transition
transition to later life. *See* aging
transitive reminiscence, 608
transsexualism, 22, 436, 437
*see also* gender identity disorders
transvestic fetishism, 423–424, 436
transvestic fetishism with gender dysphoria, 424
transvestite, 423–424
trauma
biological effects of exposure, 239
of child abuse, 254, 255t
disclosure of, 278
dissociative symptoms, onset of, 247
emergency treatment, 241–242
epidemiology, 235–237
heritability coefficients, 238t
known cause of ASD and PTSD, 241
recovered memories, 247, 248
traumatic stress, 230
treatment manual, 87

treatment matching studies, 96
treatment (specific disorders)
- acute stress disorder (ASD), 241–243
- during adult transition, 592
- during aging, 609–610
- alcoholism, 394–400
- Alzheimer's disease, 505
- anorexia nervosa, 356
- antisocial personality disorder (ASPD), 331
- anxiety disorders, 218–224
- autistic disorder, 540–543
- bipolar mood disorder, 174–176
- borderline personality disorder (BPD), 323–324
- bulimia nervosa, 359–361, 361f
- cardiovascular disease (CVD), 292
- cognitive disorders, 505–508
- dependent personality disorder (DPD), 333
- dissociative disorders, 256
- externalizing disorders, 562–567
- during family transitions, 600–602
- gender identity disorders, 439
- internalizing disorders, 579
- mental retardation, 526–529
- mood disorders, 171–177
- paraphilias, 433–435
- posttraumatic stress disorder (PTSD), 241–243
- schizophrenia, 472–478
- schizotypal personality disorder, 318
- seasonal affective disorder, 176–177
- sexual dysfunctions, 419–421
- somatoform disorders, 264–265
- substance use disorders, 394–400
- suicidal behaviour, 182–184
- unipolar mood disorder, 171–174

treatments
- *see also* psychotherapy; treatment (specific disorders)
- aversion therapy, 80
- Beck's cognitive therapy, 82–83
- biological therapies, 69–70, 72–75
- choice of treatment, determination of, 98
- client-centred therapy, 84
- cognitive behaviour therapies, 70–71, 78–83
- cognitive techniques, 82
- comparison of, 70t
- contingency management, 81
- couples therapy, 93
- eclectic approach, 67–68
- ego analysis, 77
- electroconvulsive therapy, 23, 72–73
- exposure therapies, 80
- failure to receive treatment, 17
- family therapy, 93–94
- flooding, 80
- and the four paradigms, 68–71
- Gestalt therapy, 84–85
- group therapy, 94–95
- humanist therapies, 71, 83–85
- improvement without treatment, 86–87
- overview, 67–68
- psychoanalysis, 75–77
- psychodynamic psychotherapy, 77–78
- psychodynamic therapies, 70, 75–78
- psychosurgery, 73
- rational-emotive therapy, 83
- research and practice, 95–96
- social interventions, 92–97
- social skills training, 81–82
- somatic treatments, 1920s and 1930s, 21t
- systematic desensitization, 78–80
- in vivo desensitization, 80

trephining, 71
Trials of Hypertension Prevention (TOHP), 293
trichotillomania, 320
tricyclics (TCAs), 174, 224
tuberous sclerosis, 521
Turner syndrome, 521
twentieth-century paradigms, 31–36
twin studies
- alcoholism, 386
- anxiety disorders, 214–215, 215t
- attention-deficit/hyperactivity disorder (ADHD), 557
- bulimia nervosa, 355
- concordance rate, 49
- described, 49–50
- dissociative disorders, 255
- dizygotic (DZ) twins, 49
- genes, and mental disorders, 50
- heritability of divorce, 599
- implications of different findings, 50t
- logic of, 50
- monozygotic (MZ) twins, 49
- mood disorders, 164
- nonshared environment, 50
- posttraumatic stress disorder (PTSD), 238–239, 238t
- schizophrenia, 458
- shared environment, 50

two-factor theory, 239
Type A behaviour pattern, 289–290, 294
Type B behaviour pattern, 289

## U

ultrasound, 527
unconditional positive regard, 84
unconditioned response, 34
unconditioned stimulus, 34
unconscious mental processes, 245–247
undifferentiated type of schizophrenia, 453
unfit to stand trial, 615
unilateral ECT, 72
unipolar mood disorder
- *see also* mood disorders
- antidepressant medications, 172–174, 173t
- classification, 146–147
- cognitive therapy, 171–172
- course and outcome, 149, 149f
- described, 140
- dysthymia, 146
- electroconvulsive therapy, 176
- interpersonal therapy, 172
- major depressive disorder, 146, 147t
- medication, efficacy of, 174
- monoamine oxidase inhibitors (MAOs), 174
- psychotherapy, efficacy of, 174
- selective serotonin reuptake inhibitors (SSRIs), 172–173
- and stressful life events, 155–157
- treatment, 171–174
- tricyclics (TCAs), 174

untreated mental disorders, 68f
urophilia, 424

## V

vaginismus, 416
validity
- of assessment procedure, 118
- of classification systems, 112–114
- construct validity, 415
- retrospective reports, 254, 263
- Rorschach test, 128

variability, measures of, 515
variance, 515
vascular dementia, 496–497, 500, 500f
ventricles, 44
verbal communication changes, and dementia, 487
vestibulectomy, 421
vindictive rapists, 431
Vineland Social Maturity Scale, 516, 517t
violence
- Historical/Clinical/Risk Management Scheme (HCR-20), 626, 626t
- and mental illness, 623t
- predictions of, 623–627, 626t

viral infections
- and dementia, 503–504
- and schizophrenia, 460–461

voices commenting, 451
voyeurism, 426
vulnerability marker, 470–472

## W

weight set points, 354
withdrawal, 369–370
women
- battered woman syndrome, 618–619
- culture, and female sexuality, 419
- and depression, 156–157
- dissatisfaction with appearance, 338f
- and fight or flight response, 273
- sexual assault, and posttraumatic stress disorder (PTSD), 236
- tend and befriend, 273

World Health Organization, 13, 105, 457
worry, 192

## X

XYY syndrome, 521

## Y

Yale-Brown Obsessive-Compulsive Scale, 122, 123t
the Yoruba, 15
young-old, 608
Yu, Edmond, 614–615

## Z

zoophilia, 424

# Credits

## Photographs/Cartoons

**Page xxiv**, portraits of Thomas F. Oltmanns and Robert E. Emery illustrated by Van Howell/based on photos courtesy of Thomas F. Oltmanns and Robert E. Emery. Portrait of Steven Taylor illustrated by Andrew Brightup/based on photo courtesy of Steven Taylor.

**Chapter 1: Page 2,** Jan Collier Represents; **p. 6,** Mary Ellen Mark; **p. 7,** AP/Wide World Photos; **p. 8,** AP/Wide World Photos; **p. 11,** Earl Dotter; **p. 14,** Dan Habib; **p. 17,** Stone/Getty Images; **p. 19 (top),** courtesy of the Homewood Health Centre; **p. 19 (bottom),** portrait illustrated by Van Howell/based on photo from Bettmann/CORBIS; **p. 22,** Walter Curtin/Library and Archives Canada/PA-137052.

**Chapter 2: Page 28,** Jan Collier Represents; **p. 30,** CP Photo/Shaney Komulainen; **p. 32,** portrait illustrated by Van Howell/based on photo from Who/Photo; **p. 33,** Dr. David Chase/CNRI/Phototake NYC; **p. 35,** portrait illustrated by Van Howell/based on photo from Boris of Boston; **p. 37,** Peter Hvizdak/The Image Works; **p. 38,** Peter Marlow/Magnum Photos; **p. 42,** CALVIN AND HOBBES © 1993 Watterson. Distributed by UNIVERSAL PRESS SYNDICATE. All rights reserved. Reprinted with permission; **p. 43,** portrait illustrated by Deborah Crowle/based on photo of Donald Hebb courtesy of the McGill University Archives. PN000387; **p. 46,** CNRI/Phototake, NYC; **p. 51,** Aaron Haupt/Stock Boston; **p. 53,** AP/Wide World Photos; **p. 55,** portrait illustrated by Van Howell/based on photo courtesy of Albert Bandura; **p. 55,** Erich Lessing/Art Resource, NY; **p. 61,** Library and Archives Canada/PA-185530.

**Chapter 3: Page 66,** Jan Collier Represents; **p. 70,** © The New Yorker Collection, 1996 Leo Cullum from cartoonbank.com. All rights reserved. Reprinted with permission; **p. 71,** Loren McIntyre/Woodfin Camp & Associates; **p. 73,** Gary Retherford/Photo Researchers, Inc.; **p. 76,** © The New Yorker Collection, 2000 Gahan Wilson from cartoonbank.com. All rights reserved. Reprinted with permission; **p. 80,** portrait illustrated by Van Howell/based on photo courtesy of Joseph Wolpe; **p. 81,** University of Washington HIT Lab/Mary Levin; **p. 82,** portrait illustrated by Deborah Crowle/based on photo courtesy of Donald Meichenbaum; **p. 83,** AP/World Wide Photos; **p. 84,** AP/Wide World Photos; **p. 89,** AP/Wide World Photos; **p. 94,** Bruce Ayres/Stone/Getty Images; **p. 95,** portrait illustrated by Deborah Crowle/based on photo courtesy of Zindel A. Segal; **p. 96,** portrait illustrated by Deborah Crowle/based on photo courtesy of Leslie S. Greenberg.

**Chapter 4: Page 100,** Jan Collier Represents; **p. 104 (top),** AP/Wide World Photos; **p. 104 (bottom),** Getty Images; **p. 107,** portrait illustrated by Van Howell/based on photo from the archives of the American Psychiatric Association, Washington, DC, © 1994; **p. 110,** AP/World Wide Photos; **p. 117,** Helen King/CORBIS; **p. 122,** Jeff Greenberg/Index Stock Imagery; **p. 125,** portrait illustrated by Van Howell/based on photo courtesy of G.B Peterson; **p. 128,** The Far Side® by Gary Larson © 1996 FarWorks, Inc. All rights reserved. Reprinted with permission; **p. 129,** Ken Karp/Pearson Education/PH College; **p. 134,** Will & Deni McIntyre/Photo Researchers, Inc.; **p. 135,** Lewis R. Baxter, Jr., M.D.

**Chapter 5: Page 138,** Jan Collier Represents; **p. 143,** Steve Prezant/CORBIS; **p. 147,** Les Stone/The Image Works; **p. 151,** portrait illustrated by Andrew Brightup/based on photo courtesy of Roger Bland; **p. 153,** Michael Schwarz/The Image Works; **p. 156,** portrait illustrated by Van Howell/based on photo from Simon & Schuster/PH College; **p. 158,** AP/Wide World Photos; **p. 160,** AP/Wide World Photos; **p. 162,** portrait illustrated by Van Howell/based on photo courtesy of Peter Lewinsohn; **p. 170,** Prof. Jay M. Weiss; **p. 171,** portrait illustrated by Van Howell/based on photo courtesy of Aaron Beck; **p. 172,** © The New Yorker Collection, 2001 Barbara Smaller from cartoonbank.com. All rights reserved. Reprinted with permission; **p. 176,** James D. Wilson/Woodfin Camp & Associates; **p. 182,** Henry McGee/Globe Photos; **p. 183,** Todd Plitt.

**Chapter 6: Page 188,** Jan Collier Represents; **p. 191,** AP/Wide World Photos; **p. 193,** The Far Side® by Gary Larson © 1990 FarWorks, Inc. All rights reserved. Reprinted with permission; **p. 194,** Schneps/Image Bank/Getty Images; **p. 198,** Frederick Ayer/Photo Researchers, Inc.; **p. 203,** Drew Crawford/The Image Works; **p. 209,** CP Photo/Kitchener-Waterloo Record/Peter Lee; **p. 212,** portrait illustrated by Deborah Crowle/based on photo courtesy of Michel Dugas; **p. 217,** National Library of Medicine; **p. 220 (top),** portrait illustrated by Deborah Crowle/based on photo courtesy of David A. Clark; **p. 220 (bottom),** AP/Wide World Photos; **p. 223,** portrait illustrated by Deborah Crowle/based on photo courtesy of Richard P. Swinson.

**Chapter 7: Page 228,** Jan Collier Represents; **p. 230,** Stan Honda/CORBIS; **p. 232 (top),** CP Photo/Hamilton Spectator/Scott Gardner; **p. 232 (bottom),** R. Gurdebeke/The Windsor Star; **p. 238,** Rhoda Sidney; **p. 245 (top),** portrait illustrated by Van Howell/based on photo from Bettmann/CORBIS; **p. 245 (bottom),** National Library of Medicine/Mark Marten/Photo Researchers, Inc.; **p. 246,** AP/Wide World Photos; **p. 249,** CP Photo/Mike Ridewood; **p. 251,** Lois Bernstein/Liaison/Getty Images; **p. 252,** portrait illustrated by Andrew Brightup/based on photo courtesy of Nicholas P. Spanos; **p. 260,** Robbie Marantz/The Image Bank.

**Chapter 8: Page 268,** Jan Collier Represents; **p. 241 (top),** portrait illustrated by Van Howell/based on photo from David W. Hamilton/The Image Bank; **p. 241 (bottom),** EyeWire Collection/Getty Images; **p. 275,** Albert Bonniers Forlag AB; **p. 276,** portrait illustrated by Van Howell/based on photo from Elizabeth Crews/The Image Works; **p. 277,** CALVIN AND HOBBES © 1992 Watterson. Distributed by UNIVERSAL PRESS SYNDICATE. All rights reserved. Reprinted with permission; **p. 280,** AP/Wide World Photos; **p. 284,** portrait illustrated by Andrew Brightup/based on photo courtesy of the Dr. Peter AIDS Foundation. Used with permission of Shirley Young; **p. 286,** Zigy Kaluzny/Stone/Getty Images; **p. 288,** RNT Productions/CORBIS; **p. 289,** Gerd Ludwig/Woodfin Camp & Associates; **p. 292,** Newsmakers/Getty Images.

**Chapter 9: Page 296,** Jan Collier Represents; **p. 298,** CP Photo/Larry MacDougal; **p. 301,** Emmanuel Dunand/AFP/CORBIS; **p. 306,** © The New Yorker Collection, 2002 David Sipress from cartoonbank.com. All rights reserved. Reprinted with permission; **p. 309,** portrait illustrated by Andrew Brightup/based on photo courtesy of W. John Livesley; **p. 312 (top & bottom),** Everett Collection; **p. 317,** John Henley/CORBIS; **p. 321,** © Robert Tinker; **p. 323 (top),** portrait illustrated by Deborah Crowle/based on photo courtesy of Dr. Joel Paris; **p. 323 (bottom),** Mary Ellen Mark; **p. 326,** portrait illustrated by Van Howell/based on photo courtesy of Robert Hare; **p. 328,** The Toronto Sun; **p. 330,** Sergei Karpukhin/TimePix.

**Chapter 10: Page 336,** Jan Collier Represents; **p. 337,** Daniel Acker/Bloomberg News/Landov; **p. 340 (top),** portrait illustrated by Andrew Brightup/based on photo courtesy of Paul E. Garfinkel; **p. 340 (bottom),** Express Newspapers/Liaison/Getty Images; **p. 341 (top),** AP/Wide World Photos; **p. 341 (bottom),** Wallace Kirkland/TimePix; **p. 344,** Martin Keene/TophamPA/The Image Works; **p. 349,** Pierre Vauthey/CORBIS/Sygma; **p. 351,** Lean Auguste Dominique Ingres, *Turkish Bath (Bagno Torco)*, Louvre, Paris, France, Scala/Art Resource, NY; **p. 355,** Oscar Burriel/Science Photo Library; **p. 356,** Richard T. Nowitz/Photo Researchers, Inc.

**Chapter 11: Page 364,** Jan Collier Represents; **p. 365,** CP Photo/Bill Kostroun; **p. 368,** © The New Yorker Collection, 1994 Jack Ziegler from cartoonbank.com. All rights reserved. Reprinted with permission; **p. 372,** AP/Wide World Photos; **p. 375,** Stephen Ferry/Liaison/Getty Images; **p. 377,** AP/Wide World Photos; **p. 380,** portrait illustrated by Deborah Crowle/based on photo courtesy of Sherry H. Stewart; **p. 382,** Sean Murphy/Stone/Getty Images; **p. 385,** © Bill Aron/Photo Edit; **p. 390,** Gabor Geissler/Image Bank/Getty Images; **p. 391,** portrait illustrated by Deborah Crowle/based on photo courtesy of Robert Pihl; **p. 393,** AP/Wide World Photos; **p. 396,** CORBIS/Sygma; **p. 398,** portrait illustrated by Steve Mannion/based on photo courtesy of Alan Marlatt.

**Chapter 12: Page 404,** Jan Collier Represents; **p. 406,** Bill Bachmann/The Image Works; **p. 414 (top),** Esbin-Anderson/The Image Works; **p. 414 (bottom),** portrait illustrated by Andrew Brightup/based on photo courtesy of Ray Blanchard; **p. 416,** portrait illustrated by Deborah Crowle/based on photo courtesy of Yitzchak Binik; **p. 417,** Farmhouse Productions/Image Bank/Getty Images; **p. 421,** © The New Yorker Collection, 1999 Robert Mankoff from cartoonbank.com. All rights reserved. Reprinted with permission; **p. 424,** Brian Lanteime; **p. 425,** Catherine Karnow/Woodfin Camp & Associates; **p. 427,** P. Irish/The Toronto Star; **p. 433,** Alan Schein Photography/CORBIS; **p. 436 (top),** portrait illustrated by Andrew Brightup/based on photo courtesy of Ray Blanchard; **p. 436 (bottom, left and right),** © Bettmann/CORBIS.

**Chapter 13: Page 442,** Jan Collier Represents; **p. 445,** National Library of Medicine; **p. 446,** Mary Ellen Mark; **p. 450,** courtesy of the New York Academy of Medicine Library/from Dementia Praecox and Paraphrenia by Emil Kraepelin/published by E.S. Livingstone, Edinburgh, 1919; **p. 451,** portrait illustrated by Van Howell; **p. 462,** Dr. E. Fuller Torry and Dr. Weinberger/National Institute of Mental Health; **p. 469,** portrait illustrated by Andrew Brightup/based on photo courtesy of Richard W.J. Neufeld; **p. 472,** William G. Iacono; **p. 473,** portrait illustrated by Andrew Brightup/based on photo courtesy of the Department of Psychiatry, McGill University; **p. 475,** © Ray Stubblebine/Reuters/CORBIS.

**Chapter 14: Page 480,** Jan Collier Represents; **p. 482,** AP/Wide World Photos; **p. 486,** Photofest; **p. 491,** Paul Hoff, Psychiatric Hospital, Technical University of Aachen, Aachen, Germany; **p. 497 (top),** AP/Wide World Photos; **p. 497 (bottom),** Lysia Forno/Science Photo Library; **p. 501,** AP/World Wide Photos; **p. 504,** Tim Beddow/Science Photo Library.

**Chapter 15: Page 510,** Jan Collier Represents; **p. 512,** Bob D'amico/ABC/Everett Collection; **p. 517,** Elaine Rebman/Photo Researchers, Inc.; **p. 520,** AP/Wide World Photos; **p. 527 (top and bottom),** Dr. Stephen Warren/Used with permission from Warren & Nelson (*JAMA*, 1/26/94, 271; 536-542) © 1994, American Medical Association; **p. 523,** © John Griffin/The Image Works; **p. 527,** Yoav Levy/Phototake NYC; **p. 529,** AP/Wide World Photos; **p. 532,** Michael Schwarz/Liaison/Getty Images; **p. 534,** George Goodwin; **p. 535,** Dr. Lorna Selfe, Principal Educational Psychologist, Herefordshire, UK. From "Nadia: A Case of Extraordinary Drawing Ability in an Autistic Child," Academic Press; **p. 536,** portrait illustrated by Van Howell/based on photo from The Alan Mason Chesney Medical Archives of the Johns Hopkins Medical Institution; **p. 542,** portrait illustrated by Van Howell/based on a photo courtesy of O. Ivar Lovaas.

**Chapter 16: Page 546,** Jan Collier Represents; **p. 547,** © Michael Newman/Photo Edit; **p. 550,** CALVIN AND HOBBES © 1980 Watterson. Distributed by UNIVERSAL PRESS SYNDICATE. All rights reserved. Reprinted with permission; **p. 551,** portrait illustrated by Deborah Crowle/based on photo courtesy of Virginia I. Douglas; **p. 558,** © Vittoriano Rastelli/CORBIS; **p. 563,** portrait illustrated by Deborah Crowle/based on photo courtesy of Russell Schachar; **p. 565,** Cheryl Himmelstein Photography; **p. 569,** Sybil Shackman; **p. 570,** CALVIN AND HOBBES © 1989 Watterson. Distributed by UNIVERSAL PRESS SYNDICATE. All rights reserved. Reprinted with permission; **p. 571,** Tom McCarthy/Index Stock Imagery; **p. 574,** A. Tannenbaum/CORBIS/Sygma; **p. 577 (top),** portrait illustrated by Andrew Brightup/based on photo courtesy of David R. Offord, with permission from the Offord Centre for Child Studies; **p. 577 (bottom),** Portrait illustrated by Van Howell/based on a photo courtesy of Mary Ainsworth.

**Chapter 17: Page 582,** Jan Collier Represents; **p. 584 (left),** Grant le Duc; **p. 584 (middle),** Simon Cherpitel/Magnum Photos; **p. 584 (right),** Roger Dollarhide; **p. 585,** portrait illustrated by Van Howell/based on a photo courtesy of Jon Erikson; **p. 589,** © CORBIS/Sygma; **p. 590,** © The New Yorker Collection, 1999 Barbara Smaller for cartoonbank.com. All rights reserved. Reprinted with permission; **p. 591,** Al Harvey; **p. 594,** © The New Yorker Collection, 1995 Robert Weber for cartoonbank.com. All rights reserved. Reprinted with permission; **p. 595,** Arthur Grace/CORBIS/Sygma; **p. 598,** © Lon C. Diehl/Photo Edit; **p. 600,** portrait illustrated by Van Howell; **p. 604 (top),** Jon L. Barkan/Index Stock Imagery; **p. 604 (bottom),** Bob Daemmrich/The Image Works; **p. 606,** © Michael S. Yamashita/CORBIS; **p. 607,** Detroit News/Gary Porter/Liaison/Getty Images.

**Chapter 18: Page 612,** Jan Collier Represents; **p. 614,** CP Photo/Toronto Star/Dick Loek; **p. 617,** CP Photo/Ottawa Sun/Derek Ruttan; **p. 625,** portrait illustrated by Andrew Brightup/based on photo courtesy of Christopher Webster; **p. 627,** portrait illustrated by Deborah Crowle/based on photo courtesy of Stephen Porter; **p. 629 (left),** Jerry Cooke/Photo Researchers, Inc.; **p. 629 (right),** Magnum Photos; **p. 635,** © The New Yorker Collection, 1997 Frank Cotham from cartoonbank.com. All rights reserved. Reprinted with permission; **p. 636,** AP/Wide World Photos; **p. 637,** portrait illustrated by Andrew Brightup/based on photo courtesy of James Ogloff.

The University of Lethbridge

School of Health Sciences